Shawn Rosenthal
(718) 261-0157

CREDITORS' RIGHTS, DEBTORS' PROTECTION AND BANKRUPTCY THIRD EDITION

Lawrence P. King

Charles Seligson Professor of Law
New York University School of Law

Michael L. Cook

Adjunct Professor of Law
New York University School of Law

1996

MATTHEW BENDER

QUESTIONS ABOUT THIS PUBLICATION?

For questions about the **Editorial Content** appearing in these volumes or reprint permission, please call:

Ellen Siegel, J.D. .... (800) 252-9257 (ext. 8574)
Outside the United States and Canada please call .... (212) 967-7707

For assistance with replacement pages, shipments, billing or other customer service matters, please call:

Customer Services Department at .... (800) 533-1646
Outside the United States and Canada, please call .... (518) 487-3000
Fax number .... (518) 487-3584

For information on other Matthew Bender publications, please call
Your account manager or .... (800) 223-1940
Outside the United States and Canada, please call .... (518) 487-3000

Library of Congress Cataloging-in-Publication Data

King, Lawrence P., 1929–
    Creditors' rights, debtors' protection, and bankruptcy/Lawrence P. King, Michael L. Cook. — 3rd ed.
        p.   cm. — (Casebook series)
    "Times Mirror books."
    Includes index.
    ISBN 0-8205-2707-6
    1. Debtor and Creditor—United States—Cases. 2. Bankruptcy—United States—Cases. I. Cook, Michael L., 1944– II. Title. III. Series: Casebook series (New York, N.Y.)
KF1501.A7K56 1996
346.73'077—dc20
[347.30677]
                                   96-29155
                                      CIP

MATTHEW◆BENDER

MATTHEW BENDER & CO., INC.
Editorial Offices
11 Penn Plaza, New York, NY 10001-2006 (212) 967-7707
2101 Webster St., Oakland, CA 94612-3027 (510) 446-7100

(Matthew Bender & Co., Inc.)   (Pub.094)

DEDICATION OF THIRD EDITION

We dedicate this to our families.

Lawrence P. King
Michael L. Cook

PREFACE TO THIRD EDITION

The federal courts and Congress have helped to make this revised edition necessary. Since our last revision in 1989, the Supreme Court has handed down at least thirty opinions on issues ranging from bank setoffs, preferences, fraudulent transfers and bankruptcy court injunctions to the federal tax lien. The Bankruptcy Reform Act of 1994 also became effective on October 22, 1994, making important substantive changes in the Bankruptcy Code. A National Bankruptcy Review Commission is now working on still more positive legislation. As we write this preface, Congress is considering important technical amendments to the Bankruptcy Code. Moreover, virtually every weekly issue of the case reporters contains at least one more important debtor-creditor appellate opinion. All of this high-level judicial and legislative activity has been taking place while the lower courts were disposing of thousands of disputes and while the Supreme Court's Advisory Committee on Bankruptcy Rules was regularly amending the Federal Rules of Bankruptcy Procedure.

Much of the change in the past seven years has been positive. More change is in the offing, and will make this edition obsolete soon enough. Students quickly grasp from these recent developments, therefore, that debtor-creditor law is a vital, essential part of our legal system and our economy. The business downturn that coincidentally occurred shortly after the publication of the last edition of this book showed the increasing relevance of these materials to commercial law generally and to every other part of the law school curriculum, including corporate, environmental, tax, real estate and intellectual property law.

A distinguished scholar could note in a student text forty years ago that the Supreme Court 'made few contributions to bankruptcy in recent years,' and that 'the live issues relate to the interstices between the leading cases.' MacLachlan, *Bankruptcy,* at x (1956). For law students today, however, the setting is much brighter. They can look forward to a wealth of intellectual stimulation from these updated materials. They will thus learn from one appellate court that '[l]aw can be stranger than fiction in the Preference Zone.' *In re Powerine Oil Co.,* 49 F. 3d 969, 971 (9th Cir. 1995) (2-1) (Kozinski, J.). And from the seventh circuit, they will hear that '[e]ven after the passage of 11 U.S.C. § 330 (a)(1), bankruptcy is not intended to be a feast for lawyers.' *In re Taxman Clothing, Inc.,* 49 F. 3d 310, 316 (7th Cir. 1995) (Posner, Ch. J.).

The lively atmosphere at New York University School of Law, coupled with our long working experience with the nation's most effective practitioners, should help make this revised edition a useful tool for students and lawyers alike. Our combined sixty years of teaching also helped us select and shape these materials. If nothing else, we have learned some answers, but know there are still many more challenging questions.

Lawrence P. King

Michael L. Cook

June, 1996

TABLE OF CONTENTS

Chapter 1

Introduction to Creditors' Rights and Debtors' Protection

Chapter 2

Non-Judicial Collection Efforts

PAGE

Chapter 4

Attachment and Garnishment

PAGE

Chapter 5

Claims of the Federal Government

Chapter 6

Fraudulent Transfers

PAGE

Chapter 7

Exemptions

Chapter 12

Jurisdiction and Venue of Cases and Proceedings

PAGE

Chapter 17
The Debtor's Benefits

CHAPTER 1

INTRODUCTION TO CREDITORS' RIGHTS AND DEBTORS' PROTECTION

The materials in the first part of this book deal with the relationship between the debtor and its individual creditors. The second part of this book focuses on the creditors' collective remedy of bankruptcy, in which all creditors share equally.

The primary focus in Chapters 1–9 is on the individual creditor's ability to enforce a monetary claim against its debtor. As used in these materials, "debt" means liability on a claim. In turn, "claim" means a creditor's right to payment. "Creditor" means an individual or other entity that has a claim against the debtor. When we use "creditor," however, we will be referring not only to the secured and the unsecured creditor, but also to those who may be entitled to priority under applicable state or federal law.

§ 1.01 Overview of the Subject Matter

These materials necessarily deal with problem cases. When a debtor satisfies a claim against him that has been reduced to judgment, lawyers need not become involved to any significant extent. Most of the debtors in these materials, however, are either unwilling or unable to satisfy the claims asserted against them. Sometimes, the debtor has no liquid assets to satisfy the money judgment; in other cases, the debtor is recalcitrant, and simply refuses to pay; and in still others, the debtor may be willing to pay, but another creditor may have already seized assets that otherwise would have been available to satisfy the judgment.

The subject matter of these materials is concrete. Although the lawyer may have had to develop a complex, novel legal theory to establish his claim, the judgment enforcement procedure within his jurisdiction is uniform, regardless of the legal theory underlying the claim. The lawyer must have a firm understanding of the procedure in his own jurisdiction because there is no procedural code that is uniform among the states governing the enforcement of judgments. Whatever the procedure, however, the practical objective is to obtain assets to satisfy the creditor's claim.

§ 1.02 Enforcement of Money Judgments

Commercial lawyers are ordinarily not interested in imprisoning the judgment debtor or in seizing members of the debtor's family. Debt–slavery and debtors'

(Matthew Bender & Co., Inc.)   (Pub.094)

prisons were abolished long ago, in any event. Nevertheless, our judicial system contains other coercive procedures for the enforcement of money judgments, such as seizure of the debtor's property (known as "levy"), followed by a prompt judicial sale.

We shall examine here how the creditor may enforce its claim without going to court. The nonjudicial remedies range from demand letters to confessions of judgment and setoff.

If a judicial proceeding is necessary, we then consider how a creditor can satisfy the claim quickly and efficiently after obtaining a judgment. In Chapter 3 dealing with the enforcement of money judgments, we discuss the judgment creditor's problems in dealing with other competing judgment creditors, and consider the most effective ways to enforce the judgment. The materials also focus on what kinds of property are subject to judgment enforcement procedures and how to insulate that property from subsequent transfer by the debtor, voluntarily or involuntarily.

§ 1.03   Attachment

The provisional remedy of attachment has received considerable attention by the courts over the past few years. Because a creditor may be able to impair its debtor's use of property before obtaining a judgment, the courts have imposed a number of constitutional limitations, many of which are still not clearly defined. The materials consider not only the creditor's problems, but also the rights of the debtor in dealing with the drastic remedy of attachment.

§ 1.04   The United States as a Creditor

More often than not, the debtor owes substantial money to the United States. To protect the public revenues, Congress long ago enacted a special tax lien and priority legislation. The materials distinguish between the lien and priority remedy, while suggesting practical reasons for the government's choice of one remedy over the other. At the same time, counsel for the nongovernmental creditor and for the debtor must understand the rights of their clients in competing against the federal government for the debtor's assets. Finally, the materials suggest strategy for the insolvent debtor in dealing with the federal government.

§ 1.05   Fraudulent Transfers

Creditors often find that the debtor has no assets whatsoever. After conducting an investigation, the creditor may discover that the debtor transferred all of the property to a beloved family member for natural love and affection. In other cases, creditors discover that the debtor has sold the property to a good faith purchaser at a fair price, but has dissipated the sale proceeds. Chapter 6 on fraudulent transfers discusses how a creditor may recover fraudulently transferred property and some of the pitfalls in fraudulent transfer litigation. Always relevant in this chapter is a discussion of how to counsel the debtor who is contemplating a fraudulent transfer, but who does not recognize the problem. Although bankruptcy is not covered in this part of the book, the careful commercial lawyer must counsel the client as if bankruptcy were a definite possibility. In particular, the individual debtor who fraudulently transfers property with actual intent to hinder, delay or defraud creditors within one year of bankruptcy may lose the ability to get a discharge, *i.e.*, a release from all prebankruptcy debts, and may be subject to criminal sanctions if bankruptcy ensues. *In re Kaiser*, 722 F.2d 1574 (2d Cir. 1983) (individual debtor denied discharge under 11 U.S.C. § 727(a)(2) for prebankruptcy transfer and concealment); *Flushing Savings Bank v. Parr (In re Parr)*, 5 C.B.C.2d 1039, 13 B.R. 1010 (E.D.N.Y. 1981) (postbankruptcy criminal investigation ordered by district court to determine liability for prebankruptcy fraudulent transfers).

§ 1.06   Exemptions

Both debtors and creditors must understand what property is exempt from the claims of debtors, and under what circumstances. The materials not only discuss this subject, but also consider circumstances under which a debtor may be deemed to have waived the right to claim an exemption. The materials also discuss the relationship between state exemption laws, judgment enforcement procedures, and the law of fraudulent transfers. In particular, the conversion of nonexempt property (*e.g.*, cash) into exempt property (*e.g.*, an insurance policy) is examined in detail.

§ 1.07   The Lien Concept

Generally, an unsecured creditor has no interest in the property of its debtor. The debtor, therefore, may easily dispose of property and is subject only to the law of fraudulent transfers. Prior to the existence of an enforcement problem, therefore, the prudent commercial lawyer will try to secure a client's claim with a lien.

What is a lien? We shall see that it means an interest in the debtor's property to secure payment of a debt. Having lien rights in the debtor's property enables the creditor to proceed against that property to enforce the claim.

We shall see three general types of liens—judicial, consensual, and statutory. The emphasis here, however, will be on judicial liens, which are typically obtained by judgment, levy, or other legal or equitable proceedings. Consensual liens arise by agreement of the parties and include the real property mortgage, the personal property pledge or security interest under Article 9 of the Uniform Commercial Code. Statutory liens are created by statute, and include tax liens, vendors' liens (in Louisiana), and mechanics' liens.

Liens also arose at common law as a result of the creditor's possession of the debtor's property. Most of these liens, such as the artisan's lien and the innkeeper's lien, have been incorporated into the statutes of many states. Finally, as a matter of decisional law, many states permit courts to impose equitable liens upon a debtor's property to prevent an injustice.

§ 1.08 Bulk Transfers

Article 6 of the Uniform Commercial Code, dealing with bulk transfers, is covered separately in Chapter 8. The bulk sales law is intended to protect creditors against two common types of commercial fraud that are probably already covered by the fraudulent transfer law. These materials cover not only the special notice procedure to trade creditors, but also the practical consequences of a creditor's failure to act quickly to block the proposed transfer. If nothing else, the materials confirm that very little protection can be given by any statute after trade creditors get notice of a merchant's proposed sale of the stock in trade. Once the creditor has notice, the next step is to apply whatever procedural remedies may exist under state law to stop the sale, segregate the sale proceeds, or otherwise police the transaction.

§ 1.09 Insolvency

The debtor in these materials is typically insolvent, either in the bankruptcy or in the equitable sense. The Bankruptcy Code, 11 U.S.C. § 101(31), defines "insolvent" to mean, with respect to an individual or a corporation, that the "sum of such entity's debts is greater than all of such entity's property, at a fair valuation." In other words, the debtor's liabilities must exceed the fair value of its assets for it to be insolvent.

A debtor may be solvent in the bankruptcy sense, but equitably insolvent. Under the equity definition of "insolvent," the debtor is simply unable to pay its debts as they mature. Throughout these materials, the precise extent of the debtor's insolvency may be critical in determining the relative rights and priorities among creditors, as well as the amount of the creditor's distribution. For example, the priority status of the United States may very well turn on whether the debtor is insolvent in the bankruptcy sense; if so, unsecured creditors may get nothing until the United States has been paid in full.

§ 1.10 Collective Action

The financially distressed business debtor may attempt to settle with creditors out of court. The process, usually referred to as a "common law settlement," composition, or debt restructuring, is effectuated without the aid of the court. As a practical matter, the consent of virtually all creditors is necessary because the debtor cannot prevent nonassenting creditors from suing.

Alternatively, the debtor may seek reorganization relief under chapter 11 of the Bankruptcy Code. Chapter 11 provides a judicial procedure to give the debtor (individual, partnership or corporation) a reasonable chance to formulate a repayment plan with court protection from suits. The Supreme Court noted that the "primary goal of Chapter 11 is to enable the debtor to restructure [its] business so as to be able to continue operating." *NLRB v. Bildisco & Bildisco*, 104 S. Ct. 1188, 79 L. Ed. 2d 482 (1984).

The ultimate objective of chapter 11 reorganization is the consummation of a reorganization plan providing for the satisfaction of creditors' claims. The plan can include a third–party acquisition of the debtor's assets, a scale–down of debt, a moratorium on repayment, an exchange of equity for debt, or any combination of these. Essential to the reorganization process are negotiations among the debtor, creditors and possibly shareholders. The bankruptcy court becomes involved in determining whether the negotiated plan, once accepted by the requisite majority of creditors and shareholders (two–thirds in amount and 51% in number for creditors and two–thirds in amount for shareholders), meets the statutory requirements of the Bankruptcy Code. One major conceptual difference between the common law settlement and chapter 11 is the debtor's ability to bind a nonassenting minority of creditors to the reorganization plan. This power gives chapter 11 a substantial practical advantage over comparable state law collection procedures.

The financially distressed debtor who does not desire to continue in business may assign its property for the benefit of creditors under state law, or may file a petition for liquidation under chapter 7 of the Bankruptcy Code. In an assignment for the benefit of creditors, an assignee selected by the debtor will reduce the debtor's assets to cash and distribute the proceeds on a pro rata basis to creditors in accordance with applicable state law, but the debtor will not be discharged from its debts. The federal bankruptcy liquidation procedure is similar, but only the individual debtor may obtain a discharge from his or her prebankruptcy debts. Assignments for the benefit of creditors are more common for corporate debtors when liquidation is the primary objective, because this procedure is usually less expensive and a formal discharge is not needed. A more detailed consideration of bankruptcy liquidation is contained in the second part of this book (Chapters 10–17).

CHAPTER 2

NON–JUDICIAL COLLECTION EFFORTS

§ 2.01   Introduction

Creditors are generally skeptical about the efficacy of our judicial process in the collection of debts. The expense, delay,* and uncertainty inherent in the United States judicial system make creditors think twice before going to court to collect a debt. To many creditors, therefore, litigation is a last resort.

What can an aggrieved, unsecured creditor do without going to court? For a bank creditor, the answer may be simple: "set off" any funds in the borrower's general checking account. For the typical supplier of goods to an insolvent retailer, however, the setoff remedy does not exist. After the supplier's invoice remains unpaid, the range of non–judicial remedies is relatively limited: telephone calls, letters, personal meetings, or possibly reclamation under § 2–702 of the Uniform Commercial Code. Federal and state law restrict these limited remedies, a fact to be remembered by the frustrated creditor. Consider whether the restrictions described in the following cases are effective. Do they protect the debtor, or do they merely delay payment of an outstanding debt? Are judicial or legislative restrictions more effective to protect the creditor? Do consumer debtors need more protection than business debtors?

The creditor's desire to avoid litigation may lead him to the "judgment by confession" remedy. By confessing judgment, the debtor waives the right to trial in advance. What constitutional and other restrictions exist on this drastic remedy?

§ 2.02   Debt Collection Practices

[A]   Debt Collection Efforts by a Creditor

Creditors usually make every effort to collect debts without recourse to legal proceedings. The legitimate interests to be protected on both sides raise the conflict between the creditor's right to coerce, to some degree, a recalcitrant debtor, that is, the creditor's right to obtain payment of a validly contracted–for obligation, and the right of a debtor to be free from unreasonable coercion or harassment tactics. How the word "unreasonable" is defined is unanswerable in the abstract.

---

* For an egregious example of how a debtor can pervert the judicial system to delay payment of a debt, *see Overmyer v. Fidelity & Deposit Co.*, 554 F.2d 539 (2d Cir. 1977) (reprinted *infra*).

(Matthew Bender & Co., Inc.)   (Pub.094)

WEST v. COSTEN

United States District Court, Western District of Virginia
558 F. Supp. 564 (1983)

OPINION and INTERLOCUTORY SUMMARY JUDGMENT

TURK, Chief Judge.

Plaintiffs bring this class action alleging that the defendants, William C. Costen (Costen), Multi–Service Factors, Inc. (MSF), Deborah J. Kirksey (Kirksey), Janet Lee (Lee), and Virginia M. Price (Price), have violated the Fair Debt Collection Practices Act (FDCPA or the Act), 15 U.S.C. § 1692 *et seq.* The court has jurisdiction under 15 U.S.C. § 1692k(d) and 28 U.S.C. § 1331. The action is before the court on the plaintiffs' motion for partial summary judgment on the issues of liability and on the defendants' motion for summary judgment. *See* Fed.R.Civ.P. 56(c).

1. The FDCPA

In 1977 Congress enacted the FDCPA in response to national concern over "the use of abusive, deceptive and unfair debt collection practices by many debt collectors." 15 U.S.C. § 1692(a). The purpose of the FDCPA is "to protect consumers from a host of unfair, harassing, and deceptive debt collection practices without imposing unnecessary restrictions on ethical debt collectors." S.Rep. No. 382, 95th Cong., 1st Sess. 1–2, *reprinted in* 1977 U.S.Code Cong. & Ad.News 1695, 1696.

The FDCPA sets forth a nonexclusive list of unlawful debt collection practices. Although it does provide for public enforcement by the Federal Trade Commission (FTC), *see* 15 U.S.C. § 1692*l*, it is "primarily self–enforcing," S.Rep. No. 382, *supra* at 5, 1977 U.S.Code Cong. & Ad.News at 1699, through private causes of action. Individual consumers may recover actual damages and a civil penalty up to $1,000 for violations of the Act. 15 U.S.C. § 1692k(a). In the case of a class action, each named plaintiff may recover the above amounts and all other class members may recover up to the lesser of 1% of the collector's net worth or $500,000. *Id.* Attorney fees may also be awarded if the consumer proves a violation of the FDCPA. *Id.*

. . . .

3. Factual Background

The plaintiffs are all natural persons who were living in or near Roanoke at the time of their dealings with the defendants. Except for Spangler, the plaintiffs either owed, or at one time owed, the debts which the defendants attempted to collect for various creditors. Plaintiff–intervenor Dent denies owing the debt on which collection was attempted from her and her son. The defendants' collection attempts which are the subject of the case *sub judice* all occurred between September, 1978 and January, 1980.

MSF was a Pennsylvania corporation which was licensed to do business in Virginia. Costen was the president of MSF. His job was to obtain new accounts from merchants and retailers. . . . As part of his compensation, Costen received ten percent of the amount that MSF earned from the accounts that he personally sold. . . . Jeffrey P. Johnson was the vice president and secretary of MSF. Karen Mayberry was MSF's treasurer. These same individuals also served as directors of the corporation.

MSF's individual collection agents were paid on a commission basis only; they received no salary. . . . Robert Shisler, MSF's office manager, was responsible for recruiting and training new collection agents, as well as for setting and computing their commissions. . . . MSF apparently had no formal training for its "commissioned collection agents," however. . . .

Instead, they learned their collection methods on an informal basis from other individual collectors. . . .

But MSF's collection agents were told that they must comply with the FDCPA, . . . and FTC rules concerning debt collection practices were posted on the office walls where they worked. . . .

Most of the debts that MSF attempted to collect were dishonored checks. After MSF obtained an account, the creditor would deliver the bad checks to the corporation. A work card was then prepared from each check. . . . A carbon copy of the work card was kept in a master file and the hard copy was distributed to the individual collectors. . . . However, prior to the individual collectors taking any action themselves, a secretary would send the debtors a letter advising them that they had a check outstanding, who it was to, and the amount. . . . If the debtor did not respond to the initial letter within two weeks, the individual collectors would then attempt collections. . . .

The individual collectors would first mail printed forms demanding payment by a specified time. Then, if the forms did not work, they would make telephone calls to the debtors. MSF's collection agents sometimes made personal visits to the debtor's residence. All collection efforts were to be noted on the hard copy of the work card. If a check was paid, it would be returned to the client, along with the amount of the check less MSF's commission, and the work card destroyed. . . . If the check could not be collected, it would be returned to the creditor and the work card destroyed. . . .

MSF would receive between thirty and fifty percent of the amount of the check collected for its client. Costen dep. 75–76. The person who sold the account, usually Costen, would receive ten percent of MSF's share, . . . and the individual collector would receive twenty percent. Furthermore, as a standard practice, MSF always attempted to collect a $15 service charge on each bad check, regardless of the amount of the check. . . .

If the $15 service charge was collected in full, the individual collector received $7; the person who garnered the account (usually Costen) received $.75; the office manager received $1; and the balance would go to MSF for general operating expenses.

. . . .

4. The Parties' Contentions

The named plaintiffs allege that they have suffered extreme emotional distress, embarrassment, and humiliation as the results of the defendants' collection efforts. They contend that the defendants violated the FDCPA by: (1) communicating with third parties concerning the collection of debts in violation of 15 U.S.C. § 1692c(b); (2) threatening that criminal prosecution was pending or that warrants were to be issued when such was not intended or could not be done legally in violation of 15 U.S.C. § 1692e(4) and (5); (3) failing to comply with the notice and validation of debt procedures required by 15 U.S.C. § 1692g(a); (4) collecting service charges not expressly authorized by the agreement creating the debt or permitted by law in violation of 15 U.S.C. § 1692f(1); and (5) misrepresenting the amount of the debt owed and the legality of receiving service charges as compensation for collecting debts in violation of 15 U.S.C. § 1692e(2)(A) and (B).

As relief, West seeks actual damages of $1,000 and statutory damages of $1,000 from Kirksey, MSF, and Costen. Walker seeks $2,000 in actual and statutory damages from Lee, MSF, and Costen, as well as damages equal to the service charges she paid to defendants. Jackson and Preston each seek $2,000 in actual and statutory damages from Price, MSF, and Costen. In addition, Jackson seeks damages equal to the service charges she paid to defendants. Dawson and Spangler each seek $500 in actual damages and $1,000 in statutory damages from MSF and Costen. Dent likewise seeks $2,000 in actual and statutory damages from MSF and Costen.

All members of the class seek $500,000 damages from MSF and Costen for an alleged pattern of violations of the *supra* provisions. The subclass alleges that MSF and Costen have systematically violated their rights under 15 U.S.C. § 1692f(1) by collecting service charges not expressly authorized by the agreement creating the debt or permitted by law. The subclass seeks damages from MSF and Costen equal to the service charges paid to MSF. In addition, all plaintiffs request judgment against all defendants jointly and severally for attorney's fees and costs.

In opposition to plaintiffs' motion for partial summary judgment, all the defendants assert that there are genuine factual issues which preclude an interlocutory summary judgment on the claims of third party contacts, threats of criminal prosecution and failure to give notice and validation of debts. In addition, the defendants move for summary judgment on the issue of liability for alleged unauthorized service charges on the grounds that such charges are not prohibited by Virginia law. Finally, Costen moves for summary judgment in his favor on the grounds that he is not a debt collector within the meaning of the FDCPA and that the facts of this case do not legally justify piercing the corporate veil to hold him individually liable.

5. Class Certification

Assuming that the prerequisites of Fed.R.Civ.P. 23(a) are met, a class action may be maintained under Fed.R.Civ.P. 23(b)(3) if questions of law and fact common to the members of the class predominate over questions affecting individual class members, and the class action is superior to other means of litigation in terms of fairness and efficiency. *Abed v. A.H. Robins Company,* 693 F.2d 847, 855 (9th Cir. 1982). The court's order entered March 6, 1981, certified this action, as to MSF and Costen only, as a class action pursuant to Fed.R.Civ.P. 23(b)(3). The action was certified as a class action with regard to all of the plaintiffs' claims. However, in working through the motions now before the court, the court has concluded that some of the plaintiffs' claims will require the separate adjudication of each individual class member's allegations in order to determine MSF's liability to the class. Specifically, the court now finds that the third party contact and threat of arrest claims involve more individual issues than common ones. That individual issues of liability predominate over common ones is illustrated by the disposition *infra* of these claims as asserted by the named plaintiffs; partial summary judgment is granted in favor of some named plaintiffs and denied as to others. Thus, with respect to these claims, no single set of operative facts applies to each potential class member so that MSF's liability, if any, can be established as to all class members for a pattern of illegal collection practices. Instead, MSF's liability to the class members for third party contacts and threats of arrest cannot be proved unless each individual class member proves the necessary operative facts. For example, liability for threats of arrest may depend on whether each class member's creditor actually intended to have the class member arrested. Similarly, liability for third party contacts can be found only if MSF's collection agents spoke with third parties about each class member's alleged debt rather than location information. By comparison, MSF can be held liable to all class members under section 1692(a) if the undisputed facts show that MSF routinely failed to send the required written notice. Thus, because individual rather than common issues predominate with regard to the third party contact and threat of arrest claims, "the economy and efficiency of class action treatment are lost and the need for judicial supervision and the risk of confusion are magnified." 7A C. Wright & A. Miller, Federal Practice and Procedure: Civil § 1778 at 55–56 (1972). Accordingly, the court decertifies the class as to these claims.

Nevertheless, even though common questions do not predominate relative to the third party contact and threat of arrest claims, this action can proceed on an individual basis with respect to these claims. In addition, the plaintiffs' other claims can be determined on a representative basis. *See* Fed.R.Civ.P. 23(c)(4)(A). Therefore, this action will proceed as a class action as to the claims of failure to give notice and unlawful service charge practices only. The remaining claims will be treated as individual claims by the named plaintiffs only.

6. Principles of Liability

Liability under the FDCPA is possible only if a defendant is a "debt collector" within the meaning of the Act. Subject to numerous exceptions not relevant here, the FDCPA defines a "debt collector" as "any person who uses any instrumentality of interstate commerce or the mails in any business the principal purpose of which is the collection of any debts, or who regularly collects or attempts to collect, *directly or indirectly,* debts owed or due or asserted to be owed or due another." 15 U.S.C. § 1692a(6) (emphasis added). MSF is clearly a "debt collector" within the meaning of the Act because it is a "person" who uses the telephones and mails in the business of collecting debts owed or due or asserted to be owed or due another. As a corporation can act only through its agents, MSF may be held liable for the violations of its collection agents.[2]

Kirksey, Lee, and Price are also "debt collectors" under the FDCPA because they regularly collected or attempted to collect directly debts owed or due or asserted to be owed or due another. Thus, these individual debt collectors can also be held liable for violating the provisions of the FDCPA.

. . . .

8. Third Party Contacts

Like other sections of the FDCPA, its prohibition against certain third party contacts by debt collectors is designed to protect a consumer's[4] reputation and privacy, as well as to prevent loss of jobs resulting from a debt collector's communication with a consumer's employer concerning the collection of a debt. *See* S.Rep. No. 382, *supra* at 4, 1977 U.S.Code Cong. & Ad.News at 1699; 15 U.S.C. § 1692a. Section 1692c(b) provides:

> Except as provided in section 804,[5] without the prior consent of the consumer given directly to the debt collector, or the express permission of a court of competent jurisdiction, or as reasonably necessary to effectuate a post judgment

---

[2] Regardless of the Act's expansive definition of a "debt collector," MSF also can be held liable for the intentional acts of its agents under the theory of vicarious liability. *See Broadus v. Standard Drug Co.,* 211 Va. 645, 179 S.E.2d 497, 503–04 (1971). Although the employment agreement between MSF and the individual collectors refers to the latter as "independent contractors," the key consideration in determining the existence of a master–servant relationship is the alleged master's power of control of the alleged servant's actions. *Stover v. Ratliff,* 221 Va. 509, 272 S.E.2d 40, 42 (1980). Analyzed in this manner, Kirksey, Lee, Price, and its other individual collectors were agents of MSF for purposes of *respondeat superior* despite the designation of their status as "independent contractors." That MSF exercised control over the individual collectors is shown by an intra–office memorandum dated December 19, 1979, from Manager Shisler to all MSF personnel which directs that no reference may be made to pending criminal warrants and that any violation of this directive will be grounds for immediate termination. Defendants' answer to request for production of documents ex. 3.

[4] Except as provided in 15 U.S.C. § 1692c(d), the term "consumer" is used in the FDCPA to mean any natural person obligated or allegedly obligated to pay any debt. 15 U.S.C. § 1692a(3).

[5] Section 804 of the FDCPA, 15 U.S.C. § 1692b, places strict limits on the debt collector's acquisition of "location information" (*i.e.,* address, telephone number, place of employment) regarding the consumer from whom the debt collection is being attempted. In seeking location information from any person other than the consumer, the debt collector must identify himself, state only that he is confirming or correcting location information, and identify his employer only if expressly requested. Among other things, the debt collector is prohibited from stating that the consumer owes any debt; communicating by post card or by any envelope that would indicate to the reader the nature of the debt collector's business or that the debt collector is attempting to collect a debt; and communicating with a third person more than once unless requested to do so by such person or to correct or complete previously obtained information.

remedy, a debt collector may not communicate, in connection with the collection of any debt, with any person other than the consumer, his attorney, a consumer reporting agency if otherwise permitted by law, the creditor, the attorney of the creditor, or the attorney of the debt collector.

(footnote added). For the purpose of this section only, the FDCPA defines the term "consumer" to include "the consumer's spouse, parent (if the consumer is a minor), guardian, executor, or administrator." 15 U.S.C. § 1692c(d). Thus, partial summary judgment may be granted against a debt collector for third party contacts if the undisputed facts show that the debt collector, without the consumer's consent or court permission, communicated with third parties, (not including the consumer's spouse, attorney, or parents if the consumer was a minor), about the debt.

West alleges that on July 2, 1979, Kirksey came to her house and, in the presence of a third party, threatened to have an arrest warrant issued unless West made payments on her debts. West later admitted, however, that another woman, not Kirksey, talked with her about her debts in the presence of a third party, Pat Cundiff. . . . In addition, Kirksey did call Cundiff more than once in attempting to contact West. . . . But the record is unclear concerning Kirksey's reasons for contacting Cundiff more than once; thus, the court is unable to conclude that Kirksey violated section 1692c(b) by failing to comply with section 1692b(3). . . . Moreover, Kirksey testified that she would seek location information only when she talked with someone other than the consumer; she would not discuss the debt. . . . Consequently, partial summary judgment is denied as to the liability of Kirksey and MSF to West for third party contacts.

Concerning Walker's third party contact claim, on November 11, 1978, Lee spoke with Walker's grandparents and uncle about Walker's debt. . . .

There is no evidence in the record to dispute this. Consequently, partial summary judgment is granted in favor of Walker as to the liability of Lee and MSF for unlawful third party contacts.

Jackson and Preston both allege that Price spoke to their families about their debts and made threats of criminal prosecution. Jackson stated that on December 4, 1978, Price told Jackson's sister about the debts, and that on "several occasions," Price attempted to persuade members of Jackson's family to make payments by telling them that Jackson would be imprisoned unless the payments were made. . . . Preston testified that Price told Preston's wife that an arrest warrant would be issued if he did not pay his debts. . . . Preston was not aware of any communication between Price and anyone other than Preston's wife about the debts, however.

. . . .

Price testified that she did not recall talking with Jackson's mother about anything except trying to locate Jackson. . . . She admitted, however, that she may have talked with a consumer's parents about the debt if they brought it up first. . . . In light of this testimony and the specific facts in Jackson's affidavit and deposition, the court finds that it is undisputed that Price, without Jackson's consent, spoke with third parties about Jackson's debt. Accordingly, partial summary judgment is granted in favor of Jackson and against Price and MSF for unlawful third party contacts.

However, it is undisputed that the only person other than Preston with whom Price spoke about Preston's debts was Preston's wife. Under section 1692c(d), the consumer's spouse is not a third party for the purpose of section 1692c(b). Accordingly, plaintiffs' motion for partial summary judgment is denied as to Jackson's third party contact claim, and summary judgment is granted in favor of Price and MSF as to Preston's third party contact claim.

As to Dawson's third party contact claim, Dawson's sworn statement that a MSF collection agent named Childress left a payment demand notice with Dawson's teenage daughter and spoke to her about the debt, . . . is undisputed. Accordingly, Dawson is granted partial summary judgment as to the liability of MSF for unlawful third party contacts.

Turning now to Spangler's third party contact claim against MSF, the facts contained in Spangler's affidavit and deposition show that no one asserted that she was obligated to pay any debt or attempted to collect any debt from her. Rather, MFS contacted Spangler in attempting to collect on her son's debts. Spangler's son had used her address on his checks and MSF attempted to locate him there. Spangler, therefore, is not a "consumer" within the meaning of the FDCPA. *See* 15 U.S.C. § 1692a(3). Thus, the question arises whether Spangler is entitled to recover for violation of section 1692c(b). The civil liability provision of the Act provides that "any debt collector who fails to comply with any provision of this title with respect to *any person* is liable to such person. . . ." 15 U.S.C. § 1692k(a) (emphasis added). This section would suggest that Spangler is entitled to recover for a violation of section 1692c(b). On the other hand, the language of section 1692c applies to consumers only. By comparison, other sections of the FDCPA seem to protect all persons, even if they are not "consumers" within the meaning of Act. *See e.g.*, 15 U.S.C. § 1692d ("A debt collector may not engage in any conduct the natural consequence of which is to harass, oppress, or abuse *any person* in connection with the collection of a debt.") (emphasis added). Moreover, the primary purpose of section 1692c is to protect the *consumer's* privacy and employment. So it would be incongruous to permit a person other than the consumer to recover for a violation of this section. Therefore, the court holds that Spangler is not entitled to recover under section 1692c(b) for MSF's communications with her in connection with the collection of her son's debts. Accordingly, summary judgment is granted in favor of MSF as to Spangler's third party contact claim.

9. Threats of Arrest

Section 1692e(4) and (5) provide:

A debt collector may not use any false, deceptive, or misleading representation or means in connection with the collection of any debt. Without limiting the general application of the foregoing, the following conduct is a violation of this section:

. . . .

(4) The representation or implication that nonpayment of any debt will result in the arrest or imprisonment of any person . . . unless such action is lawful and the debt collector intends to take such action.

(5) The threat to take any action that cannot legally be taken or that is not intended to be taken.

Thus, a debt collector's threat to have a consumer arrested unless a debt is paid would violate section 1692e(5) if the debt collector could not lawfully do so or did not intend to take such action. Either of these violations would violate section 1692e(4) as well. And a debt collector's representation or implication that nonpayment of a debt will result in the creditor having the consumer arrested or imprisoned would also violate section 1692e(5) if the creditor did not intend to do so or could not legally take such action. Therefore, in the case *sub judice,* partial summary judgment will be granted as to liability for violation of section 1692e(4) and (5) when there is no genuine issue of material fact as to any of these elements.

On June 18, 1979, West received a payment demand notice from MSF which was signed by Kirksey and on which was written the notation "criminal warrant pending." . . . Furthermore, according to West, when she inquired at MSF about the debts, Kirksey told her that Kirksey would have a warrant issued for her arrest unless she paid weekly amounts towards her debts. . . . In late June or early July, 1979, West received another notice from MSF which stated that she should call Kirksey "immediately to prevent issuance of warrant on your worthless check." . . . Finally, West stated that Kirksey came to her home on July 2, 1979, and threatened to issue a warrant for her arrest unless she made the payments. . . .

Kirksey does not dispute that she would call consumers and tell them that there were warrants outstanding on their dishonored checks. . . . She admits that she wrote "criminal warrant pending" on the demand notice sent to West. . . . But Kirksey also testified that she told consumers that their *creditors* would have them arrested if they did not pay their debts. . . . Contrary to West's contentions, a reasonable inference may be drawn from this evidence that Kirksey did not tell West that she would have an arrest warrant issued herself unless West paid the alleged debts. So, even assuming that a debt collector cannot lawfully seek an arrest warrant against a consumer for writing a bad check, the uncertainty as to whether Kirksey threatened to personally obtain a warrant against West precludes partial summary judgment against Kirksey for violation of section 1692e(5). Furthermore, plaintiffs' motion for partial summary judgment as to Kirksey's liability under section 1692e(4) must likewise be denied. Although Kirksey's representations implied that a creditor would have West arrested unless she paid her dishonored checks, such action by a creditor is lawful and the evidence conflicts as to whether West's creditors intended to take such action. West was never arrested for the dishonored checks that Kirksey attempted to collect. Yet Kirksey knew that Kroger, one of West's creditors, had a warrant outstanding against West because she was told this by a Kroger employee. . . . Although Kirksey attempted to collect bad checks written by West to merchants other than Kroger, a reasonable inference may be drawn from the record that Kirksey believed that Kroger intended to have West arrested unless West paid her debt. Thus, it is not perfectly clear that Kirksey's handwritten notations violated section 1692e(4). Accordingly, partial summary judgment is denied as to Kirksey's liability to West for threats of arrest.

The facts concerning Walker's claim against Lee are undisputed. On November 18, 1978, Lee told Walker's grandparents and uncle that Walker would be arrested if the debt was not paid. . . . Although Walker paid one debt, on November 20, 1978, Lee called her again and threatened criminal prosecution unless she paid another debt by November 22. . . . Lee also threatened to have a warrant issued for Walker's arrest if Walker did not pay the debt by December 4, 1978. . . . Walker was never arrested for passing bad checks, however.

. . . .

Lee has failed to offer any evidence to dispute Walker's testimony. Thus, it is undisputed that Lee threatened to personally have Walker arrested unless the debts were paid. Walker was never arrested for passing bad checks and Lee has not presented any evidence that she intended to have Walker arrested. Nor is there any evidence that a creditor intended to have Walker arrested unless she paid her debts. Because there is no genuine issue that Lee threatened Walker with arrest when neither Lee nor a creditor intended to take such action, partial summary judgment is granted in favor of Walker as to Lee's liability to her under section 1692e(4) and (5).

Both Jackson and Preston allege that Price threatened them with arrest if they failed to pay their debts. According to Jackson, Price repeatedly telephoned her from December 1978 to March 1979, and threatened to have warrants issued for her arrest unless she made monthly payments on her debts. . . . Price testified, however, that she never threatened Jackson with arrest or imprisonment unless Jackson paid the dishonored checks. . . . Rather, she probably told Jackson that the "various companies that she wrote these checks to would issue warrants" if Jackson did not pay her debts. . . . In fact, Price's prediction proved accurate. After MSF returned Jackson's uncollected checks to the creditors, Jackson's creditors issued criminal warrants against her. . . .

Thus, the documentary materials before the court present a factual dispute concerning whether Price threatened to personally have Jackson arrested for failing to pay her checks. Moreover, it is undisputed that Jackson's creditors intended to, and actually did, have her arrested for passing bad checks. Accordingly, partial summary judgment is denied on the issue of Price's liability to Jackson for threats of arrest.

Turning to Preston's claim against Price for threats of arrest, on June 23, 1979, Price called Preston about some dishonored checks and said that she had a warrant pending for his arrest which she would issue if he did not pay part of the amount by the next day. . . . Although Preston made partial payments on the checks, he continued to receive oral threats from Price that she would issue a warrant for his arrest if he did not pay the remaining balance. . . . In addition, Price told him that his failure to pay his checks could result in his arrest. . . . Preston also received notices signed by Price with the notations "warrant pending" and "warrant pending on bad check" written on them. . . . There is no evidence that Preston was ever arrested for writing bad checks.

Price testified that she did not recall telling Preston what might happen to him if he did not pay the checks. . . . Price's failure of memory is insufficient to dispute Preston's statements that Price threatened him with arrest, however. Moreover, even assuming that Price never orally threatened Preston with arrest, . . . Price acknowledged that she wrote the notations on the forms sent to Preston. "Warrant pending" was "just the terminology that [Price had] heard used in the business. . . ." And it is clear that Price did not intend to take such action because she did not even know the meaning of the term "warrant." . . . As to whether a creditor intended to have Preston arrested, Price thought that whoever Preston wrote the check to would probably issue the warrant. . . . But unlike Kirksey, Price has presented no evidence that she had personally learned of a creditor's intent to issue a warrant against Preston. Therefore, partial summary judgment is granted in favor of Preston as to Price's liability to him under section 1692e(4) and (5).

Concerning Dawson's claim under section 1692e(4) and (5), the record reveals some evidence which contradicts Dawson's assertion that a MSF collection agent named Childress threatened to personally have a warrant issued against him if he did not pay for his dishonored checks. When asked whether there were any threats made against him if he did not pay his debts, Dawson replied that "they said there was a warrant out for my arrest." . . .

This testimony creates a factual question as to whether Childress threatened to personally have Dawson arrested. Moreover, Dawson further testified that, according to the Roanoke City Police Department, there was a warrant pending for his arrest at that time. . . . Accordingly, plaintiffs' motion for partial summary judgment is denied as to Dawson's threat of arrest claim.

Turning last to Spangler's threat of arrest claim, the documents before the court reveal that on June 11, 1979, she received a notice demanding that her son pay $50 within 24 hours and stating that bad check warrants were pending. . . .

Spangler called MSF and spoke with a collection agent named Messer, who informed her that she had a warrant against her son. . . . The court is of the opinion that Spangler may be entitled to recover for a violation of section 1692e because that section is not specifically limited to protecting the rights of consumers. Nevertheless, plaintiffs' motion for partial summary judgment is denied as to Spangler's threat of arrest claim because the record is unclear as to whether her son was ever actually arrested for writing bad checks.

. . . .

In light of the court's rulings above, partial summary judgment is granted against MSF in favor of Walker and Preston for violations of section 1692e(4) and (5). Partial summary judgment against MSF is denied as to the threat of arrest claims of West, Jackson, Dawson, and Spangler.

10. Validation of Debts

Among other things, 15 U.S.C. § 1692g(a) requires a debt collector to give a consumer written notice, either in the initial communication or within five days thereafter, of the amount of the debt, the name of the creditor to whom the debt is owed, and

> a statement that if the consumer notifies the debt collector in writing within the thirty–day period [after receipt of the notice] that the debt, or any portion

thereof, is disputed, the debt collector will obtain verification of the debt or a copy of a judgment against the consumer and a copy of such verification or judgment will be mailed to the consumer by the debt collector. . . .

If the consumer disputes the debt or requests validation in writing, the debt collector must cease collection efforts until he verifies the debt and mails the verification to the consumer. 15 U.S.C. § 1692g(b).

The named plaintiffs have presented evidence that they never received any written notice of their rights to verify or to dispute the validity of the debts. . . .

The defendants did include as Exhibit 2 to their answers to request for production of documents what appears to be a typewritten version of the notice required by section 1692g(a). But no named plaintiff ever received such a writing. Indeed, at their depositions, neither Kirksey nor Price were able to recall any forms supplied or used by MSF other than the types received by the plaintiffs. . . . Although a secretary sent the initial letter from MSF to the consumers, there is no evidence that the initial communications contained anything in addition to notice that a check was outstanding, who it was to, and its amount. . . . However, this evidence does give rise to a reasonable inference that MSF's secretary, rather than its collection agents, was responsible for providing consumers with the required written notice. This being the case, the court cannot grant partial summary judgment against Price, Lee, and Kirksey for failing to send written notices to the named plaintiffs. If previously met by another MSF employee, the notification requirements under section 1692g(a) would not have to be satisfied a second time by the individual collectors in connection with their collection efforts with respect to the same debts.

Nevertheless, it is undisputed that some MSF employee failed to send the named plaintiffs the required notice. By its terms, however, section 1692g(a) requires only that a debt collector send a *consumer* the written notice. Thus, while Spangler's son may be entitled to recover under section 1692g(a), Spangler cannot in that she is not a consumer under the FDCPA. Therefore, the named plaintiffs other than Spangler and Dent are granted partial summary judgment against MSF for violations of section 1692g(a).

In addition, no evidence has been presented to the court that even suggests that MSF ever sent the required notice to anyone from whom it attempted to collect a debt. Defendants have produced forms that contain the required notice. But there is no evidence whatsoever that these forms were mailed to consumers either at the initial communication or within five days thereafter. On the other hand, there is ample evidence in the attachments to the affidavits of the named plaintiffs, plaintiffs' responses to defendants' request for production of documents, and the exhibits introduced at the class certification and preliminary injunction hearing that MSF regularly disregarded the requirement of written notice. Accordingly, partial summary judgment is granted in favor of the class members on the issue of MSF's liability for a pattern of violations of section 1692g(a).

11. Service Charges

The evidence shows without question that MSF regularly collected, or attempted to collect, a $15 service charge on each bad check, regardless of the amount of the check. The plaintiffs contend that this practice violated the FDCPA by collecting an amount that was not expressly authorized by the agreements creating the debts or permitted by law, and by misrepresenting the amounts of the debts and the legality of the compensation which the defendants could receive.

A.   Collection of Amounts in Addition to Principal Obligations

Section 1692f(1) provides that a debt collector may not use any unfair or uncon-scionable means to collect or attempt to collect any debt, such as:

> The collection of any amount (including any interest, fee, charge, or expense incidental to the principal obligation) unless such amount is expressly autho-rized by the agreement creating the debt *or* permitted by law.

(emphasis added). The court is without doubt that a service charge such as that imposed by MSF is a "fee, charge, or expense incidental to the principal obligation . . . " *Id.* Because there is no factual dispute relative to MSF practice of collecting or attempting to collect the service charges, resolution of the cross–motions for summary judgment depends on whether that practice violates section 1692f(1) as a matter of law.

The lawfulness of a service charge under section 1692f(1) depends on whether the charge is "expressly authorized by the agreement creating the debt or permitted by law." Turning to the first test, the court expressly found after evidence and argument on the preliminary injunction in this case that "this charge is not expressly authorized by the agreement creating the underlying debt." Order entered January 17, 1980, p. 3. Although this finding was for the purpose of injunctive relief only, because the defendants have made no contrary representation, the court finds for the purpose of damages relief that the service charges collected by MSF were not expressly authorized by the agreements creating the underlying debts.[7]

Thus, MSF's collection of service charges is lawful under section 1692f(1) only if the charges are "permitted by law." Plaintiffs argue that because no Virginia or

---

[7] A debt collector might argue that he was collecting a charge "expressly authorized by the agreement creating the debt" in the following situation. The debt collector enters into an agreement with a retail grocery store to provide collection service on its past–due checks. As part of the agreement the debt collector will receive $15 for each check collected. In turn, the grocery is to post a sign notifying its customers that their checks are now being collected by the particular debt collector and that there will be a $15 service charge for all returned checks. The debt collector then attempts to collect the amount of the dishonored check plus the $15 service charge. Pursuant to the agreement between the grocery and debt collector, once the check is collected, the grocery would receive the amount of the check and the debt collector would keep the $15 service charge. Assuming that state law permitted collection fees to be added–on to the amount of the debt itself, whether the service charge had been properly provided for by the posting of a sign notifying the creditor's customers of its agreement with the debt collector would be determined under state contract law. Regardless, there is no evidence in the case *sub judice* that MSF entered into any such agreement with its clients. Indeed, the evidence before the court is to the contrary. MSF's collections agreement provides that the creditor shall pay to MSF "as the sole compensation under this agreement —% of the collections effected by [MSF] upon accounts referred to it by [the creditor]."

federal statute or other law authorizes the practice, the charges cannot be said to be "permitted by law." The defendants counter this thrust by "the fact that [the practice] is not prohibited by Virginia law." . . . In other words, the defendants argue that the very absence of any statutory authority concerning service charges justifies the practice because such charges are at least not prohibited by law. As defendants correctly point out, resolution of this issue depends on the interpretation of the phrase "permitted by law." In turn, interpretation of this phrase can only be done in context with the entire provision.

Looking to the plain language of 1692f(1), the court interprets the section to permit the collection of a fee in addition to the principal obligation if such fee is expressly authorized by the agreement creating the debt or is otherwise permitted by state law. Thus, the agreement creating the debt need not expressly authorize the fee if state law affirmatively permits a collection fee even if not specified in the agreement. However, the agreement must expressly authorize the fee if state law permits such a fee only if specified in the agreement. And no such fee may be collected even if provided for in the agreement if state law prohibits a collection fee in addition to the principal obligation because a contract can never impose charges that are prohibited by state law.

But Virginia law neither expressly permits nor expressly prohibits a third party debt collector from collecting add–on fees. Thus, if valid under state contract law, an agreement relative to such fees would be permitted because it would not be expressly prohibited by state law. But when, as here, the agreements creating the debts did not expressly authorize the fee, the question is whether Virginia's silence on this specific issue constitutes legal permission to collect the fee. The court holds that it does not. In the context of this case, the court interprets section 1692f(1) to mean that if state law does not expressly permit or prohibit a debt collector from collecting a service charge in addition to the amount of a dishonored check, then such charge is lawful only if the agreement creating the debt expressly authorizes it. Simply stated, "permitted by law" is different from "not prohibited by law." Permission requires an affirmative authorization, not just indulgent silence. So the fact that Virginia does not expressly prohibit such charges does not mean that state law permits them in the absence of an agreement providing for such; rather, it means the contrary. Therefore, the court holds that the service charges collected by Multi–Service were not "permitted by law" as that phrase is used in the FDCPA.

It is undisputed that Lee collected a service charge from Walker and that Price collected a service charge from Preston . . . Nor is there any question that MSF collected a service charge from Jackson.

. . . .

Accordingly, partial summary judgment is granted against MSF in favor of Walker, Preston, Jackson, and the members of the subclass for liability under section 1692f(1). In addition, partial summary judgment is granted against Lee in favor of Walker, and against Price in favor of Preston for violations of section 1692f(1).

B. Misrepresentation of the Debts and the Legality of Charges

Plaintiffs also assert that MSF's practice of attempting to collect service charges on each bad check violates section 1692e(2)(A) and (B). This section provides

> A debt collector may not use any false, deceptive, or misleading representation or means in connection with the collection of any debt [such as the] false representation of—
>
> (A) the character, amount, or legal status of any debt; or
>
> (B) any services rendered or compensation which may be lawfully received by any debt collector for the collection of a debt.

15 U.S.C. § 1692e(2)(A) and (B).

On June 18, 1979, West received a notice from MSF signed by Kirksey, which demanded total payment of $234.80 on six bad checks. . . . The notice did not advise West that MSF had added–on a service charge on each of the bad checks; it just listed the total amount of the checks as $238.80. . . .

Indeed, West was never told that MSF was adding service charges on to the checks which it attempted to collect from her. . . . Kirksey has presented no evidence to dispute these facts. Thus, at the very least, it is perfectly clear that Kirksey misrepresented the amount of West's debts. Accordingly, partial summary judgment is granted in favor of West against Kirksey and MSF for violation of section 1692e(2)(A).

Furthermore, when MSF finally did provide West with verification of the debts, the verification claimed that she owed a $20 service charge for each check. And there is no dispute that the service charges were a primary source of compensation for individual collectors and a substantial source of income for MSF. As discussed above, there was no legal basis for imposing the service charges. Therefore, the service charges were compensation which cannot be "lawfully received." Accordingly, partial summary judgment is also granted in favor of West against Kirksey and MSF for violating section 1692e(2)(B) by misrepresenting the compensation which may be lawfully received for the collection of a debt.

Turning to Walker's claims, partial summary judgment must be denied as to the liability of Lee and MSF under section 1692e(2)(A). There is some evidence that Lee told Walker that MSF was charging her a service charge and that Walker knew the amounts of the checks which Lee was collecting . . . Thus, it cannot be said that there is no genuine issue of material fact relative to whether the defendants misrepresented the amount, character, or legal status of the debts allegedly owed by Walker. Nevertheless, partial summary judgment is granted in favor of Walker against Lee and MSF for violation of section 1692e(2)(B) because it is undisputed that Lee misrepresented the compensation which she and MSF could lawfully receive.

Concerning the claims of Jackson and Preston, the record indicates that Jackson never received any written materials from MSF. Moreover, Jackson stated that when Price spoke to Jackson's sister on December 4, 1978, Price told her that Jackson had to make monthly payments for dishonored checks and service charges. . . . Because this evidence presents a factual dispute relative to whether Price or any other MSF employee failed to disclose that service charges were being added–on to the amount of the checks, partial summary judgment is denied as to the liability of Price and MSF to Jackson under section 1692e(2)(A). But there is no evidence to contradict that Price misrepresented the compensation which she and MSF could lawfully receive; therefore, partial summary judgment is granted in favor of Jackson against Price and MSF for violation of section 1692e(2)(B).

Unlike Jackson, Preston did receive printed forms from MSF which were signed by Price. These forms failed to disclose that a service charge had been added into the total amount of the alleged debt. Preston affidavit, exs. A, and D–E. Price and MSF have failed to contradict this evidence in any manner. However, there is no evidence that Price ever represented to Preston that she could lawfully collect the service charge as compensation. Accordingly, partial summary judgment is granted in favor of Preston against Price and MSF for violation of section 1692e(2)(A), and denied as to the liability of Price and MSF to Preston under section 1692e(2)(B).

With respect to Dawson's claims against MSF under section 1692e(2)(A) and (B), MSF has failed to establish any factual question as to the accuracy of Dawson's evidence. In June 1979, a MSF collection agent named Childress demanded payment from Dawson of $365 for ten dishonored checks. . . . However, it was not until after Dawson inquired at MSF about the checks that she learned that this amount included a $15 service charge on each check. . . . Accordingly, partial summary judgment is also granted in favor of Dawson against MSF for violations of section 1692e(2)(A) and (B).

The notice that Spangler received from MSF demanded that her son pay $50 within 24 hours. . . . Spangler asked for and received copies of two dishonored checks written by her son. The total amount of these two checks was $20. When Spangler inquired at MSF about the discrepancy, Messer told her that there was a $15 service charge imposed on each check. . . . There is nothing in the documentary materials before the court to dispute this evidence. Although Spangler is not a consumer under the Act, section 1692e(2)(A) and (B) does not protect only consumers; rather, it is designed to discourage certain debt collection practices. Thus, the court is of the opinion that Spangler is able to recover for a violation of section 1692e(2)(A) and (B). Therefore, because there is no genuine issue of material fact that MSF misrepresented the amount of her son's debt and the legality of its compensation from service charges, partial summary judgment is granted in favor of Spangler against MSF for violation of section 1692e(2)(A) and (B).

As discussed above, factual questions exist as to whether some of the named plaintiffs were not told service charges had been added to the debts or told that MSF could lawfully collect such charges. Thus, it cannot be said that there is no genuine issue of material fact as to whether MSF violated the rights of each class member under section 1692e(2)(A) and (B). Accordingly, partial summary judgment is denied as to the liability of MSF to the class members under section 1692e(2)(A) and (B).

12. Piercing the Corporate Veil

Costen has moved for summary judgment in his favor on the grounds that the undisputed facts show that he is not a debt collector within the meaning of the FDCPA. The court does not agree. For the purpose of the FDCPA, a "debt collector" is "any person who . . . regularly collects or attempts to collect, directly or *indirectly,* debts owed or due or asserted to be owed or due another." 15 U.S.C. § 1692a(6) (emphasis added). Costen never personally attempted to collect any debts as would MSF's collection agents. . . . Thus, it cannot be said that he regularly attempted to collect directly debts asserted to be owed another.

Nevertheless, Costen indirectly collected debts in that he obtained new collection accounts for MSF from merchants and retailers. . . . Indeed, although other people also obtained new accounts for MSF, it seems highly unlikely that MSF could have maintained a collection business without Costen's services because Costen sold more accounts than anyone else. . . . Costen's collection indirectly of debts is shown further by the fact that he received a commission on the amounts that MSF earned from the accounts that he personally obtained. Therefore, the court holds that Costen is a "debt collector" under the FDCPA and, accordingly, denies Costen's motion for summary judgment on the ground that he is not a debt collector.

Although Costen is a "debt collector" for the purpose of the court's subject matter jurisdiction over him pursuant to the FDCPA, there is no allegation or evidence that he personally violated any provisions of the Act and, unlike MSF, he cannot be held vicariously liable for the statutory violations of MSF's collection agents. An officer of a corporation cannot be held personally liable for the wrongful conduct of the corporation's employees, absent personal involvement with the conduct.

But not only was Costen MSF's President, he was also its dominant shareholder.

. . . .

[T]he undisputed facts of this case justify disregarding MSF's corporate form and imposing individual liability upon Costen for MSF's violations of the FDCPA.

. . . .

Perhaps the most important reason to disregard MSF's corporate form and impose personal liability on Costen is that it would be unfair to the plaintiffs and contrary to the purpose of the FDCPA to uphold MSF's corporate facade. Although some issues still remain for trial, upon undisputed facts MSF is liable to the plaintiffs for some blatantly illegal collection practices. Yet MSF is no longer doing business, and it thus seems likely that its assets, if any remain, will be totally inadequate to meet plaintiffs' damages. True, some of the plaintiffs may be able to recover from defendants Kirksey, Lee, and Price. But other named plaintiffs as well as the class and subclass members will recover nothing if their sole remedy lies against MSF only.

Costen apparently did not personally collect any debts. Nevertheless, he reaped substantial monetary gains from MSF's collections. Moreover, the undisputed facts compel the conclusion that Costen knew or should have known of MSF's violations of the FDCPA. He was at all times MSF's president and maintained his office on the corporate premises. . . . Thus, to give effect to the corporate vehicle here would be to shield the real owner of MSF from the liabilities which should accompany his rewards from MSF's collection practices.

Furthermore, the FDCPA's purpose "to eliminate abusive debt collection practices by debt collectors," 15 U.S.C. § 1692a, would be frustrated if MSF's corporate facade was an effective shield against persons seeking their private remedies under the Act. To uphold the corporate facade here would illustrate that a corporate collection agency, by operating with a minimum of assets and a fast cash flow, can be effectively judgment proof and yet be a thriving source of income for its owner. On the other hand, to disregard MSF's corporate form and impose liability on Costen would be consistent with the Act's expansive definition of a "debt collector" as any person "who regularly collects or attempts to collect, *directly or indirectly,* debts owed . . . or due another." 15 U.S.C. § 1692a(6) (emphasis added).

Thus, the court concludes that Costen has misused the corporate form and that justice requires that MSF's corporate form be disregarded and liability imposed upon Costen. Therefore, the plaintiffs' motion for partial summary judgment is granted as to issue of Costen's liability under the FDCPA. Accordingly, Costen is liable to the plaintiffs to the same extent as MSF is liable to the plaintiffs.

. . . .

Accordingly, the claims for which partial summary judgment have been denied and the issues of damages remain for trial.

IT IS SO ORDERED.

NOTES AND QUESTIONS

(1) Generally, the FDCPA applies only to independent debt collectors. *See Taylor v. Checkrite, Ltd.,* 627 F.Supp. 415 (S.D. Ohio 1986) (franchisor of check collection company liable for franchisee's debt collection practices when franchisor controlled franchisee's conduct, thereby rendering franchisee its agent). It exempts, among others, original creditors who collect debts "in the name of the creditor." FDCPA § 803, 15 U.S.C. § 1692a(6). *See Perry v. Stewart Title Co.,* 756 F.2d 1197, 1208 (5th Cir.) *rehearing granted in part,* 761 F.2d 237 (1985) (neither mortgage servicing company nor its assignee were debt collectors when servicing company sold loan to assignee two months before borrower defaulted and when servicing company had continued to service the loan for its assignee). *Kizer v. Finance America Credit Corp.,* 454 F. Supp. 937 (N.D. Miss. 1978) (in–house employees of finance company to whom retail installment contract had been assigned prior to any default are not "debt collectors" as defined in 15 U.S.C. § 1692a(6)), *but see In re Aldens, Inc.,* 98 F.T.C. 790 (1981) (utilizing Section 5 of the Federal Trade Commission Act, 15 U.S.C. § 45(a)(1) (1976), the Federal Trade Commission entered into consent agreement with a creditor who, though collecting under its own name, engaged in conduct which would have violated the FDCPA.).

A former exemption for attorneys acting on behalf of clients was deleted by a 1986 amendment to 15 U.S.C. § 1692a. Act of July 9, 1986, Pub. L. No. 99–361, 100 Stat. 768. Thus, attorneys "are subject to the same requirements as collection agencies under the [FDCPA]." *U.S. v. Central Adjustment Bureau, Inc.*, 667 F.Supp. 370, 381 N. 16 (N.D. Tex. 1986). *Accord, Heintz v. Jenkins* 115 S. Ct. 1489 (1995), *infra.*

(2) In communicating with any person other than the consumer for the purpose of acquiring "location information" about the consumer, *i.e.*, place of abode, telephone number, and place of employment, the debt collector cannot, among other things, (a) state that the debtor owes a debt; (b) communicate with the person more than once, unless requested by the person or unless the debt collector "reasonably believes" that the earlier response was incomplete or erroneous, or that the person now has correct or complete information; and (c) communicate with person other than the debtor's attorney after the debt collector knows that the debtor is represented by an attorney. FDCPA § 804, 15 U.S.C. § 1692b. *Bieber v. Associated Collection Services, Inc.*, 631 F.Supp. 1410, 1417 (D. Kan. 1986) (after debt collector learned that debtors were represented by an attorney, one additional question to debtor concerning whether debtors were planning to file for bankruptcy did not violate FDCPA). Moreover, the debt collector may not communicate in connection with the collection of the debt with any person other than the consumer, his attorney, the creditor, the attorney of the creditor, a consumer reporting agency, or the attorney of the debt collector, without the prior consent of the debtor, or court permission. FDCPA § 805(b), 15 U.S.C. § 1692c(b). *See Harvey v. United Adjusters*, 509 F. Supp. 1218 (D. Or. 1981). Does a third party who is contacted by the debt collector in violation of FDCPA § 805(b), 15 U.S.C. § 1692c(b), have a claim against the debt collector? *See West, supra.*

(3) The debt collector may not communicate with the consumer (i) "at any unusual time or place or a time or place known or which should be known to be inconvenient to the consumer," *U.S. Central Adjustment Bureau, Inc., supra*, 667 F.Supp. at 375 (telephone calls before 8:00 a.m. and after 9:00 p.m. prohibited), (ii) if the consumer is represented by an attorney, or (iii) at the consumer's place of employment "if the debt collector knows or has reason to know that the consumer's employer prohibits the consumer from receiving such communication." FDCPA § 805(a), 15 U.S.C. § 1692c(a); *Kleczy v. First Fed. Credit Control, Inc.*, 21 Ohio App.3d 56, 486 N.E. 2d 204 (Ct. App. 1984) (FDCPA violated when reasonable consumer would be embarrassed by collection letter sent to him at place of employment). The debt collector cannot communicate further with the consumer, if the consumer notifies the debt collector in writing that the consumer refuses to pay the debt, or wishes the debt collector to cease further communication. FDCPA § 805(c), 15 U.S.C. § 1692c(c). For the purpose of FDCPA § 805, 15 U.S.C. § 1692c, "consumer" includes the consumer's spouse, parent (if the consumer is a minor), guardian, executor or administrator. FDCPA § 805(d), 15 U.S.C. § 1692c(d).

(4) FDCPA § 806, 15 U.S.C. § 1692d, provides that a debt collector "may not engage in any conduct the natural consequence of which is to harass, oppress, or abuse any person in connection with the collection of debt." Though FDCPA § 806

lists six proscribed types of conduct, the courts, "where appropriate, [can] proscribe other improper conduct which is not specifically addressed." 1977 U.S. Code Cong. & Ad. News 1695, 1698. Is the use of an alias by a debt collector in telephone communications "conduct the natural consequences of which is to harass, oppress, or abuse" the debtor? Inquiries about jewelry, in particular, wedding rings? Discussions about garnishment? Statements that the debtor "should not have children if she could not afford them?" A letter to the debtor implying that she "removes her head" when she receives letters from the debt collector and "lacks the common sense to handle her financial matters properly?" A letter that threatens "to make an investigation in your neighborhood and to personally call on your employer?" *See Bingham v. Collection Bureau, Inc.*, 505 F. Supp. 864 (D.N.D. 1981); *Harvey v. United Adjusters*, 509 F. Supp. 1218 (D. Or. 1981); *Rutyna v. Collection Accounts Terminal, Inc.*, 478 F. Supp. 980 (N.D. Ill. 1979).

(5) FDCPA § 807, 15 U.S.C. § 1692e, provides that a "debt collector may not use any false, deceptive, or misleading representation or means in connection with the collection of any debt." FDCPA § 807 lists sixteen examples of the types of conduct prohibited by the FDCPA. In determining whether a violation of FDCPA § 807 exists, "the court will look to whether a reasonable consumer would be deceived or misled by particular language." *Blackwell v. Professional Business Services.*, 526 F. Supp. 535, 538 (N.D. Ga. 1981). *Contra Jeter v. Credit Bureau, Inc.*, 760 F.2d 1168, 1175 (11th Cir. 1985) (rejecting "reasonable consumer" test to determine whether a consumer would be deceived by particular language, and instead adopting the "least sophisticated consumer" test); *U.S. v. Central Adjustment Bureau, Inc., supra*, 667 F. Supp. at 375 ("the test is not whether a 'reasonable consumer' would be deceived . . . because the [FDCPA] is intended to protect 'unsophisticated consumers' "); *Bingham v. Collection Bureau, Inc.*, 505 F. Supp. 864, 871 (D.N.D. 1980) (The "proper standard is whether it is more likely so than not so that debtors on the low side of reasonable capacity who read a given notice or hear a given statement read into the message oppressiveness, falsehood or threat.").

(6) FDCPA § 808, 15 U.S.C. § 1692f, provides that a debt collector "may not use unfair or unconscionable means to collect or attempt to collect any debt." The eight types of prohibited conduct include (i) the collection of any amount unless such amount is expressly authorized by the agreement creating the debt or permitted by law, and (ii) use of debt collector's name on any envelope if such name indicates that its business is debt collection. *See, e.g., Rutyna v. Collection Accounts Terminal, Inc.*, 478 F. Supp. 980 (N.D. Ill. 1979) (use of return address indicating that sender was in debt collection business violated FDCPA § 808); *Wegmans Food Markets, Inc. v. Scrimpsher (In re Scrimpsher)*, 17 B.R. 999 (Bankr. N.D.N.Y. 1982) (failure to include return address in notice violated FDCPA § 808, although sending envelope contained non–violative return address).

(7) Within five days after initial communication with consumer, a debt collector must send a written notice containing, among other things, (i) the amount of the debt, (ii) the name of the creditor, (iii) a statement that if the consumer notifies the debt collector in writing within thirty days that the debt is disputed, the debt collector

will obtain verification of the debt and send a copy to the consumer. FDCPA § 809(a), 15 U.S.C. § 1692g(a). *See Ost v. Collection Bureau, Inc.,* 493 F. Supp. 701 (D.N.D. 1980). The debt collector must cease collection efforts until a copy of the verification is sent to the consumer. FDCPA § 809(b), 15 U.S.C. § 1692g(b).

The debt collector's notice must also contain a statement that, unless the consumer disputes the debt within thirty days of its receipt, the debt collector can assume that the debt is valid. The consumer, however, is not required to dispute the debt in writing. *See Harvey v. United Adjusters,* 509 F. Supp. 1218, 1221 (D. Or. 1981). The notice must contain a statement that the consumer can dispute a portion of the debt. FDCPA § 809(a)(3),(4), 15 U.S.C. § 1692g(a)(3),(4). *See Baker v. G.C. Services Corp.,* 677 F.2d 775, 777–78 (9th Cir. 1982). The failure to dispute a debt may not be construed by any court as an admission of liability by the consumer. FDCPA § 809(c), 1692g(c). FDCPA § 809 does not mandate a particular format, type size, or location for the required information and statements. *Blackwell v. Professional Business Services of Georgia, Inc.,* 526 F. Supp. 535, 538 (N.D. Ga. 1981) (information required under FDCPA § 809 was on back of notice, with no reference to it on the front, and was in a smaller print than the body of the notice); *but see Ost v. Collection Bureau, Inc.,* 493 F. Supp. 701, 703 (D.N.D. 1980) (A form of notice similar to that in *Blackwell* was found to be "a deliberate policy on the part of the collector to evade the spirit of the notice statute, and mislead the debtor into disregarding the notice.").

(8) A debt collector must bring a legal action on the debt only in the jurisdiction in which the contract was signed or in which the consumer resides at the commencement of the action. In real property situations, the action can only be commenced in the jurisdiction in which the real property is located. FDCPA § 811, 15 U.S.C. § 1692i.

(9) FDCPA § 813, 15 U.S.C. § 1692k, provides that "any debt collector who fails to comply with any provision of this subchapter with respect to any person" is liable for (i) any actual damage sustained, and (ii) such additional damages as the court may allow, but not exceeding $1,000. In case of a class action, the named plaintiffs can recover additional damages as the court may allow, but not exceeding $1,000, and all class members can recover additional damages as the court may allow, not to exceed the lesser of $500,000 or 1 percent of the net worth of the debt collector. FDCPA § 813(a)(2)(B), 15 U.S.C. § 1692k(a)(2)(B). The debt collector is also liable for costs, together with attorney's fees, as determined by the court. FDCPA § 813(a)(3), 15 U.S.C. § 1692k(a)(3); *Mares v. Credit Bureau of Raton,* 801 F.2d 1197, 1206 (10th Cir. 1986) (co–counsel representing consumer not entitled to attorney's fees when "record disclos[ed] no material contribution by [him] which varied the course of the case set long before by [lead counsel]"). Conversely, counsel representing the prevailing debt collector/defendant may not be awarded attorney's fees unless the defendant shows bad faith and harassment by the consumer. 15 U.S.C. 1692k(a)(3); *Perry v. Steward Title Co., supra,* 756 F.2d at 1211. A plaintiff need not show actual damages for a court to award statutory damages. *Baker v. G.C. Services Corp.,* 677 F.2d 775 (9th Cir. 1982); *Harvey v. United Adjusters,* 509 F. Supp. 1218 (D. Or. 1981). Is the amount of statutory damages sufficient? Does the

FDCPA offer an effective deterrent to debt collection abuses? A consumer can also recover for intentional infliction of mental distress for violations of the FDCPA, *Kleczy v. First Fed. Credit Control Co., supra*, 486 N.E.2d at 207. Compare *Carrigan v. Central Adjustment Bureau, Inc.*, 502 F. Supp. 468 (N.D. Ga. 1980) (such damages must be recoverable under applicable state law). Injunctive relief is not available to a consumer aggrieved by a debt collector's failure to comply with the requirements of the FDCPA. *Duran v. Credit Bureau of Yuma, Inc.*, 93 F.R.D. 607 (D. Ariz. 1982). *See Sibley v. Fulton Dekalb Collection Service*, 677 F.2d 830, 831 (11th Cir. 1982) ("[E]quitable relief is not available to an individual under the civil liability section of the [FDCPA].").

(10) A debt collector is not liable for any violations of the FDCPA if the debt collector shows by a preponderance of evidence that the violation was not intentional and resulted from a bona fide error. FDCPA § 813(c), 15 U.S.C. § 1692k(c). *See Baker v. G.C. Services Corp.*, 677 F.2d 775, 779 (9th Cir. 1982) (reliance on advice of counsel or a mistake about the law is insufficient by itself to raise the bona fide error defense); *Bingham v. Collection Bureau, Inc.*, 505 F. Supp. 864, 874 (D.N.D. 1981) (violation not intentional, but defendant failed to show that it resulted from bona fide errors).

(11) An action to enforce liability under FDCPA may be brought in any appropriate United States district court without regard to the amount in controversy, or in any other court of competent jurisdiction. FDCPA § 813(d), 15 U.S.C. § 1692k(d). Claim for damages under the FDCPA is not compulsory counterclaim in state action to collect the debt. *Peterson v. United Accounts, Inc.*, 638 F.2d 1134 (8th Cir. 1981).

(12) How would the *Hawley* case have been decided if the action was brought under the FDCPA?

(13) If the creditors in *Davis, supra*, and *Bast, supra*, were debt collectors, would their conduct be violative of the FDCPA? Is it unfair that certain conduct by a creditor is not actionable, while the same conduct by a debt collector is?

(14) Some states have enacted laws regulating debt collection practices by both creditors and independent debt collectors. Some continue to exclude original creditors. *Compare* Fla. Stat. c. 559 §§ 559.55–559.75 (1975); Calif. Fair Debt Collection Practices Act, c. 907 § 1788.2(c); N.D. Cent. Code § 13–05–C *with* Vt. Stat. Ann. tit. 9 § 2453(c); N.Y. Gen. Bus. c.20 art. 29–H § 600. The FDCPA does not annul, alter, affect, or exempt any person subject to its provisions from complying with state law with respect to debt collection practices, except to the extent that state law is inconsistent. FDCPA § 816, 15 U.S.C. § 1692n.

―――――――――

Kramer, Q & A ON THE FAIR DEBT COLLECTION PRACTICES ACT*

Commercial Law Bulletin
pp. 21–23 (July/August 1987)

Editor's Comment: . . . One caveat. It is important to observe that these answers have been provided by staff members of the Federal Trade Commission. While the FTC can comment on the provisions of the Act, only courts can formally interpret the Act.

** **Question:** Does the 30 day notice required by Section 809 of the Act prevent the attorney from filing suit during the 30 days?

Answer: No, according to unofficial discussions with representatives of the FTC, and an unofficial letter from that office dated November 1, 1986.

Question: If a collection agency has given the 30 day notice required by Section 809 of the Act, and then sends the claim to an attorney for legal steps, does the attorney again have to give the notice if he "communicates" with the debtor?

Answer: Yes, according to informal comments by a member of the FTC staff on January 30, 1987.

Question: If the original creditor is the same as the current creditor, does the attorney have to include in the 30 day notice required by Section 809(5) of the Act, the notification about providing the name and address of the current creditor?

Answer: No, according to the Proposed Official Staff Commentary of the FTC dated March 6, 1986.

Question: If the attorney files suit and obtains judgment within the 30 days after providing the consumer with the notice under Section 809, if the consumer then indicates a dispute and requests a verification, does it have any effect on the judgment?

Answer: No, according to an FTC staff interpretation letter dated November 17, 1986.

Question: Does Section 809 or any other provision of the Act *require* an attorney to communicate with a consumer before filing suit?

Answer: No, according to an FTC staff interpretation letter dated November 17, 1986.

Question: If the attorney routinely files suit within 30 days after receiving claims, is it appropriate to indicate this fact to the debtor at the time the 30 day notice is given as provided by Section 809?

Answer: An FTC staff interpretation letter dated November 17, 1986, states that if its is the attorney's practice "when a demand letter does not result in payment to file a complaint within the thirty day dispute period, it would avoid confusion to so advise the consumer when providing a Section 809 notice."

** Denotes one of the most frequently asked questions.

**Question: If the attorney has taken a judgment, without ever "communicating" with the consumer other than through court process, must a Section 809 notice be given if a communication takes place after the entry of a final judgment?

Answer: Yes, an FTC staff interpretation letter dated September 12, 1986, states that "to the extent that you 'communicate' with a consumer, either before or after institution of a lawsuit, by demand letter or otherwise, in an effort to collect or solicit payment of the debt or any portion thereof, you are required to comply with Section 809 of the Act."

**Question: If a consumer goes to an adjoining state to make a merchandise purchase or have medical treatments, is the attorney precluded from filing the lawsuit in the judicial district where the event occurred, even though the state law might permit the "long arm" action—keeping in mind that the creditor "pro se" could file such a "long arm" action under the provisions of the state where the transaction occurred?

Answer: Yes, the FTC Proposed Commentary dated March 7, 1986, states "where services were provided pursuant to an oral agreement, the debt collector may sue only where the consumer resides."

Question: May an attorney who might otherwise be considered a debt collector be exempt from the Act, if, as an employee or officer of the creditor, the attorney collects debts in the creditor's name?

Answer: Yes, according to an unofficial staff interpretation by the FTC dated October 20, 1986.

Question: If the first "communication" with the consumer is a letter to his or her attorney, must it include the notice required under Section 809?

Answer: No, according to an unofficial comment by FTC staff member on January 20, 1987.

Question: If the law firm simply files suit upon receipt of an account from a creditor or a debt collection agency, and does not engage in any traditional debt collection activity, do the requirements of the FDCPA, including Section 809, have applicability?

Answer: No, according to an informal staff opinion dated December 10, 1986.

Question: If an attorney gives the notice required by Section 809(a), may he still demand that payment be made in 10 days?

Answer: Yes, according to an informal staff opinion dated December 10, 1986. The opinion states that "in our view, Section 809 does not imply a 30 day 'waiting period' within which a collector must refrain from further collection efforts."

Question: If the consumer disputes a debt within the 30 day period provided in Section 809, can the attorney continue court proceedings, take a default judgment, or resort to garnishment or other methods of enforcing the judgment during the 30 day period?

Answer: Yes, according to an informal staff opinion letter dated December 10, 1986, where the letter states "Section 809(b) of the Act requires a collector to cease collection efforts pending verification of a disputed debt . . . notice of dispute does not require an attorney to stop court proceedings, postpone obtaining a default judgment, or refrain from enforcing a judgment . . . " but the attorney cannot continue "traditional collection activities" such as letters or calls.

Question: If a law firm is trying to develop information for a mortgage foreclosure, and needs information about the title owners and occupants of the property, is it permissible to contact third parties, such as title searchers and occupancy investigators, to determine the appropriate defendants?

Answer: A staff advisory opinion of the FTC dated January 5, 1987, comments, "In certain mortgage foreclosure actions, it is our understanding that in some states a tenant or other occupant at the mortgaged property may also be deemed a party in interest. In this context, the information that you would be seeking appears to encompass more than 'location information' as defined in Section 803(7) of the Act. Section 805(b) expressly provides that 'communications' for the purpose of obtaining 'location information' are excepted from the general ban on third party contacts." If the debt collector does not convey information regarding the debt, and does not reveal the existence of the debt, "a request to a third party for information about a consumer's assets does not fall within the definition of a 'communication'. . . . Thus . . . such requests are not the kind of communication that Section 805(b) prohibits. Similarly, we (FTC staff) do not believe that the term 'communication' encompasses a situation in which a debt collector merely seeks information about property interests that others may have in a debtor's assets."

Question: Does Section 805(b) prohibit an attorney or his or her agents from contacting third parties to obtain tenant occupancy information to ascertain their names and addresses so they can be named as defendants in litigation; and to obtain military affidavit information so as to comply with federal and state laws?

Answer: A staff advisory opinion of the FTC dated January 5, 1987, indicates apparently "No," if the attorney or agent "does not reveal the existence of the debt to third party." Contacts with third parties for the purpose of obtaining military affidavit information so as to comply with federal and state law presents an analogous situation.

**Question: Is it improper for the attorney to relay information to the collection agency which previously handled the claim?

Answer: No. A staff opinion dated January 6, 1987, points out that "The principal purpose of Section 805 is to restrict the publication of information concerning a debt to uninvolved parties, as this could injure the debtor's reputation or invade his privacy."

Question: Does Section 805(b) prohibit an attorney, after the filing of a lawsuit, from contacting a witness whose testimony is needed to establish the existence of the debt?

Answer: An FTC staff opinion letter dated January 8, 1987, states, "Even when an attorney is the debt collector and therefore is subject to the Act's requirements, Section 805(b) does not prohibit the attorney from interviewing witnesses in connection with litigation that may ensue as a result of filing suit . . . the Act was designed to regulate activities traditionally engaged in by debt collection agencies and not the practice of law."

Question: If the *creditor* provided a notice which contained all of the elements of a Section 809 notice, would the attorney also have to give notice, if there is a "communication" by the attorney?

Answer: Yes, according to a staff opinion of the FTC dated January 9, 1987. It states: "Even if the creditor may have provided some type of notice as part of its in-house collection process, a debt collector (including an attorney) must still provide the notice within 5 days after the initial collection communication."

Question: If a claim is in the form of a judgment, is a copy of the judgment sufficient "verification of the debt" as required by Section 809(b) of the Act?

Answer: Yes, according to an informal staff opinion letter dated December 10, 1986.

**Question: The Postal Service Administrative Support Manual (A.S.M.) permits an attorney to obtain the address of a Post Office boxholder in order to learn the address of a defendant for service of legal process. Is such a contact a violation of Sections 805(b) and 804 of the FDCPA?

Answer: No. "The A.S.M. requirement, by its terms, is limited to situations where the person seeking the information is engaged in an attempt to serve legal process. Assuming that the person requesting the information about the boxholder truthfully certifies that the purpose is to obtain the name and address in order to serve legal process, the FDCPA's provisions regarding communications with third parties are inapplicable to situations covered by the A.S.M. provision." So states an FTC staff interpretation letter dated April 21, 1987.

**Question: Is the publication of non–judicial foreclosure information relating to a debt a violation of the FDCPA if the content is required by state statute?

Answer: No. An informal staff opinion of the FTC dated May 8, 1987, states: "In our view mere compliance with the statutory requirements of a non–judicial foreclosure statute is not the type of traditional debt collection activity that Congress intended to regulate." Yet the letter points out, "The only provision of the Act that in any way addresses traditional legal activities is Section 811. This section prohibits debt collectors from bringing suits (except to enforce a security interest in real property) in a judicial district other than where the consumer signed the contract or resides at the time the action is commenced."

Question: Does the FDCPA apply to an attorney representing an insurance company that has paid its insured for injuries arising from an automobile accident and then attempts to recover the amount paid from the uninsured motorist who was responsible for the accident?

Answer: No, according to an informal FTC staff opinion dated May 22, 1987, which points out "tort claims are not 'transactions' as that term is contemplated in the definition of a 'debt,' set out in Section 803(5) of the Act. This is true no matter who is attempting to collect on those claims or the nature of the torts involved."

Question: If a non–profit governmental corporation gives a student loan, is such a loan a "debt" covered by the FDCPA?

Answer: Yes, according to an informal staff opinion of the FTC dated June 5, 1987.

A Reader Writes Us

The following letter from attorney Dennis H. Sober was received by the Editor in response to an item which appeared in a special section of the May/June 1987 Bulletin on the Fair Debt Collection Practices Act. We wish to share his comments with you.

In reference to the article, "Special Notice Required On Demand Letters To 'Consumers'," which appeared on page 16 of the May/June 1987 *Commercial Law Bulletin*, I am of the opinion that it is necessary to write you to clarify what I consider to be an omission in that information.

I think it's unwise for any attorney to assume that the notice given as a potential sample fully complies with the Fair Debt Collection Practices Act. The notice in particular fails to include the disclosures required in Section 807(11) of the Act. That section particularly requires that all communications made to collect a debt inform the consumer that the debt collector is attempting to collect a debt and that any information obtained would be used for that purpose. The failure to include this notice is a violation of Section 807. I believe it is appropriate to . . . incorporate that requirement into the final form of the disclosure notice each chooses to use.

Dennis H. Sober
Baltimore, Maryland

BENTLEY v. GREAT LAKES COLLECTION BUREAU

United States Court of Appeals, Second Circuit
6 F.3d 60 (1993)

MINER, Circuit Judge.

Plaintiff–appellant Diane Bentley appeals from a summary judgment entered in the United States District Court for the District Court of Connecticut (Covello, J.) dismissing her complaint in an action brought against defendant–appellee Great Lakes Collection Bureau, Inc. ("Great Lakes"). In the complaint, Bentley alleged that two collection letters sent to her by Great Lakes violated the Fair Debt Collection Practices Act, 15 U.S.C. §§ 1692–1692o (1988 & Supp. 1993) (the "FDCPA"). The district court found that Great Lakes did not violate the FDCPA even though some of the statements contained in the letters were not entirely accurate. For the reasons that follow, we reverse.

Background

Great Lakes is a debt collection agency that was retained by Citicorp Retail Services, Inc. ("CRSI") to provide debt collection services. The contract entered into by CRSI and Great Lakes provided that Great Lakes "must have CRSI's prior written authorization to bring legal action to affect [sic] collection of any Referred Account." The service contract further provided that Great Lakes "shall at no time state or imply in any communication to a Referred Account that CRSI will sue the debtor without [prior] written authorization" from CRSI. This action arises out of two attempts by Great Lakes to collect an outstanding debt of $483.43 owed to CRSI by Bentley.

Great Lakes sent Bentley two computer–generated collection letters "dunning letters") dated November 30, 1990 and December 18, 1990. The November 30 dunning letter included the following language:

> YOUR CREDITOR IS NOW TAKING THE NECESSARY STEPS TO RECOVER THE OUTSTANDING AMOUNT OF $483.43. THEY HAVE INSTRUCTED US TO PROCEED WITH WHATEVER LEGAL MEANS IS NECESSARY TO ENFORCE COLLECTION.

> ENCLOSE YOUR PAYMENT IN THE ENVELOPE PROVIDED AND MAKE YOUR CHECK OR MONEY ORDER PAYABLE TO GREAT LAKES BUREAU, INC.

> THIS IS AN ATTEMPT TO COLLECT A DEBT AND ANY INFORMA-TION OBTAINED WILL BE USED FOR THAT PURPOSE.

Great Lakes' computer is programmed to generate this form of letter whenever the agency receives a new account.

The December 18 letter, a follow–up form letter, stated in relevant part:

THIS OFFICE HAS BEEN UNABLE TO CONTACT YOU BY TELEPHONE, THEREFORE YOUR DELINQUENT ACCOUNT HAS BEEN REFERRED TO MY DESK WHERE A DECISION MUST BE MADE AS TO WHAT DIRECTION MUST BE TAKEN TO ENFORCE COLLECTION.

> WERE OUR CLIENT TO RETAIN LEGAL COUNSEL IN YOUR AREA, AND IT WAS DETERMINED THAT SUIT SHOULD BE FILED AGAINST YOU, IT COULD RESULT IN A JUDGMENT. SUCH JUDGMENT MIGHT, DEPENDING UPON THE LAW IN YOUR STATE, INCLUDE NOT ONLY THE AMOUNT OF YOUR INDEBTEDNESS, BUT THE AMOUNT OF ANY STATUTORY COSTS, LEGAL INTEREST, AND WHERE APPLICABLE, REASONABLE ATTOR-NEY'S FEES.

> AGAIN, DEPENDING UPON THE LAW IN YOUR STATE, IF SUCH JUDG-MENT WERE NOT THEREUPON SATISFIED, IT MIGHT BE COLLECTED BY ATTACHMENT OF AN EXECUTION UPON YOUR REAL AND PERSONAL PROPERTY. GARNISHMENT MAY ALSO BE AN AVAILABLE REMEDY TO SATISFY AN UNSATISFIED JUDGMENT, IF APPLICABLE IN THE STATE IN WHICH YOU RESIDE.

WE THEREFORE SUGGEST YOU CALL OUR OFFICE IMMEDIATELY TOLL FREE AT 1–800–874–7080 TO DISCUSS PAYMENT ARRANGEMENTS OR MAIL PAYMENT IN FULL IN THE ENCLOSED ENVELOPE.

NO LEGAL ACTION HAS BEEN OR IS NOW BEING TAKEN AGAINST YOU.

In fact, CRSI had not authorized Great Lakes "to proceed with whatever legal means is necessary to enforce collection" as represented in the first letter; and Great Lakes had made no effort to telephone Bentley prior to December 18, had not referred her account to anyone's desk and was not about to make any decisions regarding her account as represented in the second letter. According to information disclosed during discovery, Great Lakes: does not make the decision whether to initiate legal proceedings in matters involving CRSI; never recommends legal proceedings unless its advice is solicited from its clients; does not employ attorneys admitted to practice in the state of Connecticut; has no procedure by which to refer accounts to attorneys in Connecticut or in other states to commence litigation; and is not informed when any of its clients ultimately sues a debtor. Moreover, even in cases where its advice is solicited, Great Lakes recommends legal proceedings to its clients only for approximately one percent of the collection accounts referred to it.

Discussion

The FDCPA prohibits the use of "any false, deceptive, or misleading representation or means in connection with the collection of any debt." 15 U.S.C. § 1692e (1988). We apply an objective test based on the understanding of the "least sophisticated consumer" in determining whether a collection letter violates section 1692e. *Clomon v. Jackson*, 988 F.2d 1314, 1318 (2d Cir. 1993). The sixteen subsections of section 1692e provide a nonexhaustive list of practices that fall within the statute's ban. These practices include "[t]he threat to take any action that cannot legally be taken or that is not intended to be taken." 15 U.S.C. § 1692e(5). A debt collection practice may violate the FDCPA even if it does not fall within any of the subsections, *Clomon*, 988 F.2d at 1318, and a single violation of section 1692e is sufficient to establish civil liability under the FDCPA, *see* 15 U.S.C. § 1692k.

Here, the two dunning letters contained several admittedly false statements. First, the November 30 dunning letter falsely stated that CRSI had given Great Lakes the authority to initiate legal proceedings against Bentley. It implied that the commencement of legal proceedings was imminent when, in fact, this was not the case. The district court concluded that these statements "were not misleading or deceptive within the meaning of [the FDCPA]," because "accepting the plaintiff's [arguments] would cast serious question on what, if anything, a creditor could say in its attempt to collect a lawful debt." But, although the court felt that the language was not violative of the statute, the FDCPA specifically prohibits the threat to take any action "that is not intended to be taken," *see id.* § 1692e(5), and the "least sophisticated consumer" would interpret this language to mean that legal action was authorized, likely and imminent. Therefore, these statements are "false, deceptive, [and] misleading" within the meaning of the FDCPA. *See Trans World Accounts, Inc. v. FTC*, 594 F.2d 212, 216 (9th Cir. 1979).

Second, the December 18 dunning letter falsely stated that Great Lakes had attempted to contact Bentley prior to December 18 and that Bentley's account had been referred to someone's desk, where a decision would be made regarding her account. The reference to the status of Bentley's account is deceptive, implying "personal attention" to her account, when, in fact, no such "desk" existed. The letter therefore violates the FDCPA's strict prohibition against deceptive practices. The district court found that these inaccuracies in the December 18 letter were non–actionable violations of the FDCPA. We disagree. The FDCPA is a strict liability statute, *see Clomon*, 988 F.2d at 1320, and the degree of a defendant's culpability may only be considered in computing damages, *see* 15 U.S.C. § 1692k(b).

Moreover, the later letter's references to the various proceedings supplementary to judgment available to enforce collection (e.g., garnishment) also violated section 1692e(5)'s prohibition of threats to take action "that [are] not intended to be taken." *See id.* § 1692e(5). These references to legal remedies, when read in conjunction with the first paragraph of that letter, which advised that the account was being reviewed by Great Lakes to determine "what direction must be taken to enforce collection," would mislead the least sophisticated consumer. The quoted language conveys to the consumer that Great Lakes was authorized to make the decision to institute the legal action that could lead to the supplementary proceedings described. In the context of the letter, the threat of a lawsuit instigated by Great Lakes is strengthened by the statement: "No legal action has been or is now being taken against you." (emphasis added). In fact, CRSI retained the authority to decide whether legal proceedings of any kind would be instituted, and the likelihood of such proceedings on a claim for $483.43 was almost nonexistent.

Conclusion

The judgment of the district court is reversed and the case remanded for further proceedings consistent with the foregoing.

HEINTZ v. JENKINS

Supreme Court of the United States
115 S.Ct. 1489 (1995)

BREYER, Justice.

The issue before us is whether the term "debt collector" in the Fair Debt Collection Practices Act, 91 Stat. 874, 15 U.S.C. §§ 1692–1692o (1988 ed. and Supp. V), applies to a lawyer who "regularly," through litigation, tries to collect consumer debts. The Court of Appeals for the Seventh Circuit held that it does. We agree with the Seventh Circuit and we affirm its judgment.

The Fair Debt Collection Practices Act prohibits "debt collector[s]" from making false or misleading representations and from engaging in various abusive and unfair practices. The Act says, for example, that a "debt collector" may not use violence, obscenity, or repeated annoying phone calls, 15 U.S.C. § 1692d; may not falsely represent "the character, amount, or legal status of any debt," § 1692e(2)(A); and may not use various "unfair or unconscionable means to collect or attempt to collect" a consumer debt, § 1692f. Among other things, the Act sets out rules that a debt collector must follow for "acquiring location information" about the debtor, § 1692b; communicating about the debtor (and the debt) with third parties, § 1692c(b); and bringing "[l]egal actions," § 1692i. The Act imposes upon "debt collector[s]" who violate its provisions (specifically described) "[c]ivil liability" to those whom they, e.g., harass, mislead, or treat unfairly. § 1692k. The Act also authorizes the Federal Trade Commission to enforce its provisions. § 16921(a). The Act's definition of the term "debt collector" includes a person "who regularly collects or attempts to collect, directly or indirectly, debts owed [to] . . . another." § 1692a(6). And, it limits "debt" to consumer debt, i.e., debts "arising out of . . . transaction[s]" that "are primarily for personal, family, or household purposes." § 1692a(5).

The plaintiff in this case, Darlene Jenkins, borrowed money from the Gainer Bank in order to buy a car. She defaulted on her loan. The bank's law firm then sued Jenkins in state court to recover the balance due. As part of an effort to settle the suit, a lawyer with that law firm, George Heintz, wrote to Jenkins' lawyer. His letter, in listing the amount she owed under the loan agreement, included $4,173 owed for insurance, bought by the bank because she had not kept the car insured as she had promised to do.

Jenkins then brought this Fair Debt Collection Practices Act suit against Heintz and his firm. She claimed that Heintz's letter violated the Act's prohibitions against trying to collect an amount not "authorized by the agreement creating the debt," § 1692f(1), and against making a "false representation of . . . the . . . amount . . . of any debt." § 1692e(2)(A). The loan agreement, she conceded, required her to keep the car insured "against loss or damage" and permitted the bank to buy such insurance to protect the car should she fail to do so. App. to Pet. for Cert. 17. But, she said, the $4,137 substitute policy was not the kind of policy the loan agreement had in mind, for it insured the bank not only against "loss or damage" but also against her failure to repay the bank's car loan. Hence, Heintz's "representation" about the "amount" of her "debt" was "false"; amounted to an effort to collect an "amount" not "authorized" by the loan agreement; and thus violated the Act.

Pursuant to Rule 12(b)(6) of the Federal Rules of Civil Procedure, the District Court dismissed Jenkins's Fair Debt Collection lawsuit for failure to state a claim. The court held the Act does not apply to lawyers engaging in litigation. However, the Court of Appeals for the Seventh Circuit reversed the District Court's judgment, interpreting the Act to apply to litigating lawyers. *Jenkins v. Heintz*, 25 F.3d 536 (1994). The Seventh Circuit's view in this respect conflicts with that of the Sixth Circuit. *See Green v. Hocking*, 9 F.3d 18 (1993) (per curiam). We granted *certiorari* to resolve this conflict. 513 U.S. __, 115 S.Ct. 416, 130 L.Ed.2d 332 (1994). And, as we have said, we conclude that the Seventh Circuit is correct. The Act does apply to lawyers engaged in litigation.

There are two rather strong reasons for believing that the Act applies to the litigating activities of lawyers. First, the Act defines the "debt collector[s]" to whom it applies as including those who "regularly collec[t] or attemp[t] to collect, directly or indirectly, [consumer] debts owed or due or asserted to be owed or due another." § 1692a(6). In ordinary English, a lawyer who regularly tries to obtain payment of consumer debts through legal proceedings is a lawyer who regularly "attempts" to "collect" those consumer debts. *See, e.g.*, Black's Law Dictionary 263 (6th ed. 1990) ("To collect a debt or claim is to obtain payment or liquidation of it, either by personal solicitation or legal proceedings").

Second, in 1977, Congress enacted an earlier version of this statute, which contained an express exemption for lawyers. That exemption said that the term "debt collector" did not include "any attorney–at–law collecting a debt as an attorney on behalf of and in the name of a client." Pub.L. 95–109, § 803(6)(F), 91 Stat. 874, 875. In 1986, however, Congress repealed this exemption in its entirety, Pub.L. 99–361, 100 Stat. 768, without creating a narrower, litigation–related, exemption to fill the void. Without more, then, one would think that Congress intended that lawyers be subject to the Act whenever they meet the general "debt collector" definition.

Heintz argues that we should nonetheless read the statute as containing an implied exemption for those debt–collecting activities of lawyers that consist of litigating (including, he assumes, settlement efforts). He relies primarily on three arguments.

First, Heintz argues that many of the Act's requirements, if applied directly to litigating activities, will create harmfully anomalous results that Congress simply could not have intended. We address this argument in light of the fact that, when Congress first wrote the Act's substantive provisions, it had for the most part exempted litigating attorneys from the Act's coverage; that, when Congress later repealed the attorney exemption, it did not revisit the wording of these substantive provisions; and that, for these reasons, some awkwardness is understandable. Particularly when read in this light, we find Heintz's argument unconvincing.

Many of Heintz's "anomalies" are not particularly anomalous. For example, the Sixth Circuit pointed to § 1692e(5), which forbids a "debt collector" to make any "threat to take action that cannot legally be taken." The court reasoned that, were the Act to apply to litigating activities, this provision automatically would make liable any litigating lawyer who brought, and then lost, a claim against a debtor. *Green, supra*, at 21. But, the Act says explicitly that a "debt collector" may not be held liable if he "shows by a preponderance of evidence that the violation was not intentional and resulted from a *bona fide* error notwithstanding the maintenance of procedures reasonably adapted to avoid any such error." § 1692k(c). Thus, even if we were to assume that the suggested reading of § 1692e(5) is correct, we would not find the result so absurd as to warrant implying an exemption for litigating lawyers. In any event, the assumption would seem unnecessary, for we do not see how the fact that a lawsuit turns out ultimately to be unsuccessful could, by itself, make the bringing of it an "action that cannot legally be taken."

The remaining significant "anomalies" similarly depend for their persuasive force upon readings that courts seem unlikely to endorse. For example, Heintz's strongest "anomaly" argument focuses upon the Act's provisions governing "[c]ommunication in connection with debt collection." § 1692c. One of those provisions requires a "debt collector" not to "communicate further" with a consumer who "notifies" the "debt collector" that he or she "refuses to pay" or wishes the debt collector to "cease further communication." § 1692c(c). In light of this provision, asks Heintz, how can an attorney file a lawsuit against (and thereby communicate with) a nonconsenting consumer or file a motion for summary judgment against that consumer?

We agree with Heintz that it would be odd if the Act empowered a debt–owing consumer to stop the "communications" inherent in an ordinary lawsuit and thereby cause an ordinary debt–collecting lawsuit to grind to a halt. But, it is not necessary to read § 1692c(c) in that way—if only because that provision has exceptions that permit communications "to notify the consumer that the debt collector or creditor may invoke" or "intends to invoke" a "specified remedy" (of a kind "ordinarily invoked by [the] debt collector or creditor"). §§ 1692(c)(2), (3). Courts can read these exceptions, plausibly, to imply that they authorize the actual invocation of the remedy that the collector "intends to invoke." The language permits such a reading, for an ordinary court–related document does, in fact, "notify" its recipient that the creditor may "invoke" a judicial remedy. Moreover, the interpretation is consistent with the statute's apparent objective of preserving creditors' judicial remedies. We need not authoritatively interpret the Act's conduct–regulating provisions now, however. Rather, we rest our conclusions upon the fact that it is easier to read § 1692c(c) as containing some such additional, implicit, exception than to believe that Congress intended, silently and implicitly, to create a far broader exception, for all litigating attorneys, from the Act itself.

Second, Heintz points to a statement of Congressman Frank Annunzio, one of the sponsors of the 1986 amendment that removed from the Act the language creating a blanket exemption for lawyers. Representative Annunzio stated that, despite the exemption's removal, the Act still would not apply to lawyers' litigating activities. Representative Annunzio said that the Act

> "regulates debt collection, not the practice of law. Congress repealed the attorney exemption to the act, not because of attorney[s'] conduct in the courtroom, but because of their conduct in the backroom. Only collection activities, not legal activities, are covered by the act . . .. The act applies to attorneys when they are collecting debts, not when they are performing tasks of a legal nature . . .. The act only regulates the conduct of debt collectors, it does not prevent creditors, through their attorneys, from pursuing any legal remedies available to them." 132 Cong.Rec. 30842 (1986).

This statement, however, does not persuade us.

For one thing, the plain language of the Act itself says nothing about retaining the exemption in respect to litigation. The line the statement seeks to draw between "legal" activities and "debt collection" activities was not necessarily apparent to those who debated the legislation, for litigating, at first blush, seems simply one way of collecting a debt. For another thing, when Congress considered the Act, other Congressmen expressed fear that repeal would limit lawyers' "ability to contact third parties in order to facilitate settlements" and "could very easily interfere with a client's right to pursue judicial remedies." H.R.Rep. No. 99–405, p. 11 (1985) (dissenting views of Rep. Hiler). They proposed alternative language designed to keep litigation activities outside the Act's scope, but that language was not enacted. *Ibid.* Further, Congressman Annunzio made his statement not during the legislative process, but after the statute became law. It therefore is not a statement upon which other legislators might have relied in voting for or against the Act, but it simply represents the views of one informed person on an issue about which others may (or may not) have thought differently.

Finally, Heintz points to a "Commentary" on the Act by the Federal Trade Commission's staff. It says:

> "Attorneys or law firms that engage in traditional debt collection activities (sending dunning letters, making collection calls to consumers) are covered by the [Act], but those whose practice is limited to legal activities are not covered." Federal Trade Commission—Statements of General Policy or Interpretation Staff Commentary on the Fair Debt Collection Practices Act, 53 Fed.Reg. 50097, 50100 (1988) (footnote omitted).

We cannot give conclusive weight to this statement. The Commentary of which this statement is a part says that it "is not binding on the Commission or the public." *Id.* at 50101. More importantly, we find nothing either in the Act or elsewhere indicating that Congress intended to authorize the FTC to create this exception from the Act's coverage—an exception that, for the reasons we have set forth above, falls outside the range of reasonable interpretations of the Act's express language, *See, e.g., Brown v. Gardner*, 513 U.S. __, __, 115 S.Ct. 552, 555, 130 L.Ed.2d 462 (1994) (slip op., at __-__); *see also Fox v. Citicorp Credit Servs., Inc.*, 15 F.3d 1507, 1513 (CA9 1994) (FTC staff's statement conflicts with Act's plain language and is therefore not entitled to deference); *Scott v. Jones*, 964 F.2d 314, 317 (CA4 1992) (same).

For these reasons, we agree with the Seventh Circuit that the Act applies to attorneys who "regularly" engage in consumer–debt–collection activity, even when that activity consists of litigation. Its judgment is therefore *Affirmed.*

[B] Peaceful Repossession on Default

Section 9–503 of the Uniform Commercial Code provides that "[u]nless otherwise agreed a secured party has on default the right to take possession of the collateral. In taking possession a secured party may proceed without judicial process if this can be done without breach of the peace or may proceed by action."

WILLIAMS v. FORD MOTOR CREDIT CO.

United States Court of Appeals, Eighth Circuit
674 F.2d 717 (1982)

BENSON, Chief Judge.

In this diversity action brought by Cathy A. Williams to recover damages for conversion arising out of an alleged wrongful repossession of an automobile, Williams appeals from a judgment notwithstanding the verdict entered on motion of defendant Ford Motor Credit Company (FMCC).

. . . .

In July, 1975, David Williams, husband of plaintiff Cathy Williams, purchased a Ford Mustang from an Oklahoma Ford dealer. Although David Williams executed the sales contract, security agreement, and loan papers, title to the car was in the name of both David and Cathy Williams. The car was financed through the Ford dealer, who in turn assigned the paper to FMCC. Cathy and David Williams were divorced in 1977. The divorce court granted Cathy title to the automobile and required David to continue to make payments to FMCC for eighteen months. David defaulted on the payments and signed a voluntary repossession authorization for FMCC. Cathy Williams was informed of the delinquency and responded that she was trying to get her former husband David to make the payments. There is no evidence of any agreement between her and FMCC. Pursuant to an agreement with FMCC, S & S was directed to repossess the automobile.

On December 1, 1977, at approximately 4:30 a.m., Cathy Williams was awakened by a noise outside her house trailer in Van Buren, Arkansas. She saw that a wrecker truck with two men in it had hooked up to the Ford Mustang and started to tow it away. She went outside and hollered at them. The truck stopped. She then told them that the car was hers and asked them what they were doing. One of the men, later identified as Don Sappington, president of S & S Recovery, Inc., informed her that he was repossessing the vehicle on behalf of FMCC. Williams explained that she had been attempting to bring the past due payments up to date and informed Sappington that the car contained personal items which did not even belong to her. Sappington got out of the truck, retrieved the items from the car, and handed them to her. Without further complaint from Williams, Sappington returned to the truck and drove off, car in tow. At trial, Williams testified that Sappington was polite throughout their encounter and did not make any threats toward her or do anything which caused her to fear any physical harm. The automobile had been parked in an unenclosed driveway which plaintiff shared with a neighbor. The neighbor was awakened by the wrecker backing into the driveway, but did not come out. After the wrecker drove off, Williams returned to her house trailer and called the police, reporting her car as stolen. Later, Williams commenced this action.

The case was tried to a jury which awarded her $5,000.00 in damages. FMCC moved for judgment notwithstanding the verdict . . .

The district court entered judgment notwithstanding the verdict for FMCC, and this appeal followed.

Article 9 of the Uniform Commercial Code (UCC), which Arkansas has adopted and codified as Ark.Stat.Ann. § 85–9–503 (Supp.1981), provides in pertinent part:

> Unless otherwise agreed, a secured party has on default the right to take possession of the collateral. In taking possession, a secured party may proceed without judicial process if this can be done without breach of the peace. . . .

In *Ford Motor Credit Co. v. Herring*, 27 U.C.C.Rep. 1448, 267 Ark. 201, 589 S.W.2d 584, 586 (1979), which involved an alleged conversion arising out of a repossession, the Supreme Court of Arkansas cited Section 85–9–503 and referred to its previous holdings as follows:

> In pre–code cases, we have sustained a finding of conversion only where force, or threats of force, or risk of invoking violence, accompanied the repossession. *Manhattan Credit Co., Inc. v. Brewer*, 232 Ark. 976, 341 S.W.2d 765 (1961); *Kensinger Acceptance Corp. v. Davis*, 223 Ark. 942, 269 S.W.2d 792 (1954).

The thrust of Williams' argument on appeal is that the repossession was accomplished by the risk of invoking violence. The district judge who presided at the trial commented on her theory in his memorandum opinion:

> Mrs. Williams herself admitted that the men who repossessed her automobile were very polite and complied with her requests. The evidence does not reveal that they performed any act which was oppressive, threatening or tended to cause physical violence. Unlike the situation presented in *Manhattan Credit Co. v. Brewer, supra*, it was not shown that Mrs. Williams would have been forced to resort to physical violence to stop the men from leaving with her automobile.

In the pre–Code case *Manhattan Credit Co. v. Brewer*, 232 Ark. 976, 341 S.W.2d 765 (1961), the court held that a breach of peace occurred when the debtor and her husband confronted the creditor's agent during the act of repossession and clearly objected to the repossession, 341 S.W.2d at 767–68. In *Manhattan*, the court examined holdings of earlier cases in which repossessions were deemed to have been accomplished without any breach of the peace, *id.* In particular, the Supreme Court of Arkansas discussed the case of *Rutledge v. Universal C.I.T. Credit Corp.*, 218 Ark. 510, 237 S.W.2d 469 (1951). In *Rutledge*, the court found no breach of the peace when the repossessor acquired keys to the automobile, confronted the debtor and his wife, informed them he was going to take the car, and immediately proceeded to do so. As the *Rutledge* court explained and the *Manhattan* court reiterated, a breach of the peace did not occur when the "Appellant [debtor–possessor] did not give his permission but he did not object." *Manhattan, supra*, 341 S.W.2d at 767–68; *Rutledge, supra*, 237 S.W.2d at 470.

We have read the transcript of the trial. There is no material dispute in the evidence, and the district court has correctly summarized it. Cathy Williams did not raise an objection to the taking, and the repossession was accomplished without any incident which might tend to provoke violence. *See also Teeter Motor Co., Inc. v. First Nat'l Bank*, 20 U.C.C.Rep. 1119, 260 Ark. 764, 543 S.W.2d 938 (1976).

Appellees deserve something less than commendation for the taking during the night time sleeping hours, but it is clear that viewing the facts in the light most favorable to Williams, the taking was a legal repossession under the laws of the State of Arkansas. The evidence does not support the verdict of the jury. FMCC is entitled to judgment notwithstanding the verdict.

The judgment notwithstanding the verdict is affirmed.

[Dissenting opinion deleted]

BOUDREAU v. BORG–WARNER ACCEPTANCE CORP.

United States Court of Appeals, Ninth Circuit
616 F.2d 1077 (1980)

SNEED, Circuit Judge:

This is a diversity case. The appellant, a secured creditor of the appellees, appeals from a directed verdict for conversion and a jury award of $14,271.34 compensatory damages and $65,000 punitive damages. The issues on appeal are: (1) Did the district court err in its interpretation of the Security Agreement under which it conditioned the creditor's possessory rights upon the debtor's failure to accede to a demand for delivery? and (2) Does appellant's security interest in the appellees' "inventory" extend to inventory other than that acquired under the floorplan financing arrangement? We hold that the Security Agreement created a security interest in the debtor's entire inventory and that the right to self–help repossession accrued upon the debtor's failure to pay for floorplanned merchandise which had been sold. We reverse and remand.

Jurisdiction is conferred by 28 U.S.C. § 1291 (1976).

I.

FACTUAL BACKGROUND

Pursuant to a plan to expand his television repair business to include retail sales, appellee Tom Boudreau entered into a wholesale floorplan financing arrangement with appellant Borg–Warner Acceptance Corporation (BWAC). BWAC extended Boudreau credit to acquire new merchandise in exchange for a security interest in Boudreau's "inventory." The Security Agreement provided that Boudreau must repay BWAC upon the sale of financed merchandise.

On February 8, 1971, during a routine inventory of Boudreau's store, a BWAC representative determined that several financed items had been sold out of trust and submitted an inventory worksheet to Boudreau showing $810.07 due BWAC. On the following day Boudreau's shop was burglarized and many financed items were stolen. Although Boudreau reported the theft to the police and to his insurance company, which had issued a policy that named BWAC as a loss payee, he did not inform BWAC of the burglary.

On February 22, 1971, Kravitz, another BWAC representative, conducted a follow–up inventory of financed merchandise in Boudreau's store. In Boudreau's absence, Kravitz loaded floorplanned and non–floorplanned inventory and certain non–inventory items into a U–Haul. During the course of the removal, Boudreau's employee contacted Boudreau's attorney, Strickland, who informed Kravitz that some of the missing financed items were covered by theft insurance and requested that Kravitz wait for Boudreau to return before departing. Boudreau arrived and after some discussion between Kravitz and him, the inventory worksheet was adjusted slightly in Boudreau's favor. However, the parties were unable to reach a satisfactory agreement and Kravitz left with all of the items originally loaded in the U–Haul.

In response to a demand by Strickland, Kravitz subsequently returned some of the non–inventory property (*i.e.*, electronic testing equipment and tools). Boudreau refused to sign a release for the remaining items taken away and in due course commenced this action in the district court. Its jurisdiction rested on 28 U.S.C. § 1332 (1976).

The district court held that although a monetary default activated BWAC's right to accelerate the debt, the right to self–help repossession accrued only upon Boudreau's refusal to deliver the property on demand. On the basis of this interpretation of "default," and a finding that BWAC failed to issue such a demand prior to removing the items from Boudreau's store, the court directed a verdict for the plaintiff. The defendant BWAC presently appeals from the directed verdict and a jury award of $14,271.34 compensatory damages and $65,000 punitive damages.

II.

THE MEANING OF "DEFAULT"

Appellant contends that a "default," which triggers its possessory rights, occurred when Boudreau failed to meet his monetary obligations. We agree. The narrow definition of "default" adopted by the district court violates the primary rule of contract interpretation which rule requires an examination of the intent of the parties. *Cavanagh v. Schaefer*, 112 Ariz. 600, 545 P.2d 416 (1976). The specific incorporation of the Uniform Commercial Code in Paragraph 10 suggests that the parties intended to create an unconditional right of self–help repossession. Furthermore, the explicit description of "default" in the first sentence of paragraph 10 indicates that this meaning should attach to any subsequent reference to "default." *Brady v. Black Mountain Investment Co.*, 105 Ariz. 87, 459 P.2d 712 (1969). The so–called plain and ordinary meaning rule of contract interpretation also supports appellant's position. Support is also provided by *Whisenhunt v. Allen Parker Co.*, 119 Ga.App. 813, 168 S.E.2d 827, 830 (1969), in which "default" in a secured transaction context was given "its generally accepted meaning of failing to perform *or pay*" (emphasis added). It is true that the court in *Klingbiel v. Commercial Credit Corporation*, 439 F.2d 1303 (10th Cir. 1971), in adopting a definition of default, distinguished the creditor's rights of acceleration of the debtor's obligation to pay from that of repossession of the collateral. However, although a refusal to accede to a delivery demand was recognized as a species of "default," the court clearly considere d monetary "default" sufficient to activate the creditor's possessory rights.

. . . .

III.

THE DEFINITION OF "INVENTORY"

Having found that Boudreau was in "default" we now must determine the scope of BWAC's security interest.

. . . .

We conclude . . . that paragraph 4 represents the parties' explicit intention to subject Boudreau's entire inventory to BWAC's security interest. It unequivocally refers to all "inventory." It should be given its plain meaning. *See* Ariz.Rev.Stat. § 44–3109(4) (1967); *Community Bank v. Jones*, 278 Or. 647, 566 P.2d 470 (1977). Furthermore, paragraph 4 directly addresses the creation of BWAC's security interest. The dispositive force of this portion of a security agreement has been recognized. *See Mitchell v. Shepherd Mall State Bank*, 324 F.Supp. 1029 (W.D.Okl.1971), *affirmed*, 458 F.2d 700 (10th Cir. 1972); *In re Little Brick Shirthouse, Inc.*, 347 F.Supp. 827 (N.D.Ill.1972). Both decisions recognize that the provision which creates the security interest should be looked to exclusively to determine the type of property subject to that interest.

Accordingly, we hold that paragraph 4's delineation of BWAC's security interest is not qualified by other references to "inventory" which appear to be limited to floorplanned merchandise. . . . Under paragraph 4, BWAC acquired a security interest in all of Boudreau's "inventory," as defined by the Arizona version of the Uniform Commercial Code. Ariz.Rev.Stat. § 44–3109(4) (1967). It follows that all of Boudreau's "inventory" was subject to BWAC's paragraph 10 right to self–help repossession.

The district court's directed verdict for conversion of non–floorplanned inventory is reversed. The case is remanded for a determination of BWAC's liability for conversion of non–inventory property.

Reversed and Remanded.

TURNER v. IMPALA MOTORS

United States Court of Appeals, Sixth Circuit
503 F.2d 607 (1974)

PECK, Circuit Judge.

Tennessee Code Annotated (T.C.A.) § 47–9–503 is the State of Tennessee's statutory implementation of the Uniform Commercial Code's § 9–503 which authorizes a secured creditor to peacefully repossess collateral. The provision is generally known as the self–help repossession provision. This case presents the issue as to whether peaceful repossession under the Tennessee statute is action under the color of state law within the meaning of 42 U.S.C. § 1983 and state action within the meaning of the due process clause of the Fourteenth Amendment. Upon motion of the defendant–appellee, the District Court dismissed the suit for failure to state a cause of action and this appeal followed. District Judge Garrity has characterized this issue as "one of the liveliest on the current judicial scene." *Boland v. Essex County Bank*, 361 F.Supp. 917 (D.Mass. 1973).

In terms of private repossession, the facts before us offer a classic example. Plaintiff–appellant Turner purchased a 1965 Buick LaSabre in June of 1972 from the defendant–appellee Impala on a conditional sales contract. Turner executed a promissory note specifying a payment schedule of twenty–five dollars per week for twelve weeks, with the remaining balance to be paid at the rate of twenty dollars per week.

The record does not indicate the circumstances of the default but the actual payments were erratic from the beginning. The contract included a provision that "in default of payment of this note, or any part of it, said payee [Impala] may take possession of said property in any manner they [sic] may elect, and dispose of same without recourse to law. . . ."

Almost seven months after the purchase, Turner apparently defaulted on his note and without notice the auto was repossessed from a curbside on a public street. The incident occurred in the early afternoon of a weekday after Turner parked his auto in front of his mother's house. Turner had left his five–year–old son in the auto and the keys to the auto in his pocket, but the agent of Impala was not deterred. The young child was removed therefrom and the auto sped away. The record indicates that there was no hearing to determine either contractual obligations or the rights to possession.

Turner contends that the Tennessee statute is unconstitutional and that it authorizes a deprivation of property without due process. He principally relies on *Fuentes v. Shevin*, 407 U.S. 67, 92 S. Ct. 1983, 32 L. Ed. 2d 556 (1972), which held that notice and a hearing are required before the execution of a prejudgment writ of replevin. According to the appellant, the Tennessee statute allows a creditor to circumvent the requirements of notice and hearing and yet replevy his property. He contends that although the case ostensibly involves private conduct, the presence of state action is indicated by the fact that the state has intervened, authorized and encouraged repossession by secured creditors by conferring upon them special powers and exemptions from legal requirements placed on all others. Appellant also argues that the Tennessee statute, similar to the replevin statutes in *Fuentes*, deprives the debtor of his rights to notice and an opportunity to be heard. The waiver provision contained in the contract does not, appellant contends, necessarily exclude the requirements of notice and a judicial hearing on the issue of the waiver prior to the repossession. The waiver provision allows the creditor to take possession upon default.

Before we consider the constitutional dimensions of the matter before us, we must first examine the key question of jurisdictional requisites. The concept of state action as required by the Fourteenth Amendment has been found to be virtually synonymous with the "under color of state law" requirement of § 1983. *United States v.*

Price, 383 U.S. 787, 794–795 n. 7, 86 S. Ct. 1152, 16 L. Ed. 2d 267 (1966); *Palmer v. Columbia Gas of Ohio, Inc.*, 479 F.2d 153, 161 (6th Cir. 1973). *But cf., Adickes v. S. H. Kress & Co.*, 398 U.S. 144, 211, 90 S. Ct. 1598, 26 L. Ed. 2d 142 (1970) (Brennan, J., concurring and dissenting). Appellant would have us hold that the self–help repossession which took place upon the default on a private contract providing for such repossession is an act under color of state law and thus constitutes state action within the scope of the Fourteenth Amendment. If the repossession did not constitute state action but rather only an individual invasion of individual rights, the alleged wrong cannot be remedied under the auspices of the Fourteenth Amendment. *Civil Rights Cases*, 109 U.S. 3, 11, 3 S. Ct. 18, 27 L.Ed. 835 (1883). The presence of state action allows the invocation of the basic procedural safeguards announced in *Sniadach v. Family Finance Corp., infra [395 U.S. 337]*, and *Fuentes v. Shevin, supra.*

Instances of private conduct have been found to involve sufficient state action but each such conclusion should be the product of "sifting facts and weighing circumstances. . . ." *Burton v. Wilmington Parking Authority*, 365 U.S. 715, 722, 81 S. Ct. 856, 6 L. Ed. 2d 45 (1961). However, a mere finding that state action is present is insufficient. The state action must rise to the level of significant involvement. *Moose Lodge No. 107 v. Irvis*, 407 U.S. 163, 173, 92 S. Ct. 1965, 32 L. Ed. 2d 627 (1971).

The constitutional attacks on creditors' tactics such as peaceful repossession or formal legal processes gained support with Mr. Justice Douglas' majority opinion in *Sniadach v. Family Finance Corp.*, 395 U.S. 337, 89 S. Ct. 1820, 23 L. Ed. 2d 349 (1969). In that case a garnishment action had been instituted in a state court whose rules allowed the service of summons and complaint upon the alleged debtor's employer. The effect was to freeze the alleged debtor's wages until the merits of the case had been decided. The debtor was not required to be notified at the time of service upon the employer and there was no opportunity for the debtor to obtain a hearing or judicial scrutiny of the creditors' claims. The debtor was restricted to either showing that the suit was brought in bad faith or posting a bond in the amount of the garnishment. With Mr. Justice Black dissenting, the Supreme Court held that the Court Clerk's ex parte issuance of a summons pursuant to the state statute constituted state action and that the prejudgment wage garnishment without prior notice and opportunity for a hearing deprived the debtor of property without due process of law in violation of the Fourteenth Amendment.

Subsequently, the Supreme Court in *Fuentes v. Shevin*, 407 U.S. 67, 92 S. Ct. 1983, 32 L. Ed. 2d 556 (1972), speaking through Mr. Justice Stewart, held that certain state statutes providing for the summary seizure of personal property by means of a prejudgment replevin procedure involving the sheriff's execution of a writ issued by a court clerk violated the due process clause of the Fourteenth Amendment insofar as it denied a debtor the right to notice and the opportunity for a hearing prior to the loss of any possessory interest in that personal property.

However, in the recent case of *Mitchell v. W. T. Grant Co.*, 416 U.S. 600, 94 S. Ct. 1895, 40 L. Ed. 2d 406 (1974), it would appear that *Fuentes* has been effectively overruled. *See* concurring opinion of Powell, J., *id.* at 623, 94 S. Ct. 1895, and the dissenting opinion of Stewart, J., *id.* at 629, 94 S. Ct. 1895. In *Mitchell,* judicial sequestration procedures in Louisiana, similar to the replevin statutes struck down in *Fuentes,* allowed a creditor to obtain, on an ex parte basis from a judicial authority, a writ of sequestration upon submission of an affidavit and posting of a security bond. Thereupon a public official, without providing notice and a hearing to the debtor, seized the property. Distinguishing judicial control over the process from the court clerk's control in *Fuentes,* the Supreme Court found the procedure was not invalid.

Prior to *Mitchell,* the challenge to the Commercial Code's self–help repossession provisions generated considerable litigation. However, the only federal appellate courts to have met the issue to date have failed to find significant state action present. *Gibbs v. Titelman,* 502 F.2d 1107 (3rd Cir., filed August 1, 1974); *James v. Pinnix,* 495 F.2d 206 (5th Cir., 1974); *Nowlin v. Professional Auto Sales, Inc.,* 496 F.2d 16 (8th Cir. 1974), citing *Bichel Optical Laboratories, Inc. v. Marquette National Bank,* 487 F.2d 906 (8th Cir. 1973); *Shirley v. State National Bank of Connecticut,* 493 F.2d 739 (2d Cir., 1974); *Adams v. Southern California First National Bank,* 492 F.2d 324 (9th Cir. 1973), *rev'g sub nom. Adams v. Egley,* 338 F.Supp. 614 (S.D. Cal.1972), *petition for cert. filed,* 42 U.S.L.W. 3707 (U.S. June 25, 1974).

It is the district court's opinion in *Adams* that remains the most frequently cited case finding the requisite state action. In that case, the court relied upon *Reitman v. Mulkey,* 387 U.S. 369, 87 S. Ct. 1627, 18 L. Ed. 2d 830 (1967), wherein the Supreme Court found that state action existed when private housing discrimination was authorized by a provision of the California constitution. Even though the California constitution did not require discrimination in the sale and rental of housing, the Court stated that the provision in question would "significantly encourage and involve the State in private discriminations" contrary to the Fourteenth Amendment. *Id.* at 381, 87 S. Ct. 1627. Similarly, the District Court in *Adams* held that the California enactments of the U.C.C. encouraged and involved the state in private repossession and sale, as demonstrated by their incorporation in the security agreement. Appellants here have mounted that same challenge.

On appeal, the Ninth Circuit held that there was not sufficient involvement by the State of California to constitute state action. *Adams, supra,* 492 F.2d at 329. The Court distinguished *Reitman* as being a racial discrimination case having limited application to the self–help repossession cases and relied on the finding that the California statute merely codified the existing common law. The court also rejected the contention that the repossession was effectively a public function.

We are likewise persuaded that *Reitman* cannot be relied upon to justify a finding of state action here. Our opinion in *Palmer* notwithstanding, 479 F.2d 153 (6th Cir. 1973), we view *Reitman* as dealing with a state attempt to accomplish indirectly what ·it was prohibited from doing directly. We cannot ignore the fact that the context of onerous racial discrimination in which the case was set demanded special scrutiny. The injustices of racial discrimination cast a different shadow than that of the case now before us. *See Oller v. Bank of America,* 342 F.Supp. 21, 23 (N.D. Cal.1972).

Our opinion in *Palmer* likewise responded to a different circumstance. There we considered the policies of a company with monopolistic character whose business was to provide a necessity of life and whose activities and operations were pervasively and significantly regulated by governmental and quasi–governmental regulations and statutes. We therefore concluded that the state thereby achieved a position of joint participation with the company. *Id.*, 479 F.2d at 165. *See also Burton v. Wilmington Parking Authority, supra*, 365 U.S. at 726, 81 S. Ct. 856.

Appellant makes the principal point that the private activity before us should be viewed as encouraged by the statute and therefore a finding of state action is justified. While acknowledging that the point has a measure of merit, we do not find it persuasive.

It is clear that in this case the state did not exert any control or compulsion over the creditor's decision to repossess. The private activity was not commanded by the simply permissive statute. While mere existence of the statute might seem to suggest encouragement, we conclude that the effect of the statute is only to reduce a creditor's risk in making repossessions. As a practical matter, a creditor's decision is more likely to be principally influenced by the economics of the situation than by the presence of a permissive statute.

We fail to see where the creditor has sought to invoke any state machinery to its aid. Rather, the creditor has simply relied upon the terms of its security agreement pursuant to the private right of contract. Compare *Shelley v. Kraemer*, 334 U.S. 1, 68 S. Ct. 836, 92 L.Ed. 1161 (1948). Assuming that the statute was non–existent, the remedy of self–help repossession could still be utilized based on its common law heritage [11] and the private right to contract. We fail to see how the creditor is attempting to enforce any right in reliance upon a constitutional or statutory provision as in *Reitman* or is even asserting any state–created right. Rather, we see a creditor privately effectuating a right which was created in advance by contract between the parties. At best, the right is one that is merely codified, but not created, in the statute.

Appellant also argues that the statute authorizes an individual to perform the governmental function of seizing private property. As stated previously, the statute merely codified and did not create any right or state power. Were we to rely upon the mere fact of codification, we would in part be making available to a complex matrix of human behavior, as regulated by statutes, the scope of federal remedies. We decline to establish that precedent, particularly under the circumstance of a statute that is permissive in nature.

The decision of the district court is affirmed.

---

[11] The common law of Tennessee allowed repossession of personal property under conditional sales contracts without resort to legal process when the purchaser had agreed to repossession as a contractual matter. *Morrison v. Galyon Motor Co.*, 16 Tenn.App. 394, 64 S.W.2d 851 (1932).

NOTES AND QUESTIONS

(1) What objectives does U.C.C. § 9–503 address? In what ways does it benefit the creditor *and* the debtor? *See Griffith v. Valley of the Sun Recovery & Adjustment Bureau, Inc.*, 126 Ariz. 227, 613 P.2d 1283 (Ariz. Ct. App. 1980); *Morris v. First National Bank & Trust Co.*, 21 Ohio St.2d 25, 254 N.E.2d 683 (1970). Should U.C.C. § 9–503 be limited to non–consumer transactions?

(2) When the repossession results in a breach of the peace, the debtor, as in *Williams*, can bring an action for conversion and attempt to recover damages. What facts must be shown to prove a wrongful repossession because of a breach of the peace? Would the result in *Williams* have been different if the debtor physically tried to stop the repossessing agent? What if the debtor continued her complaint in a loud voice? What if the neighbors came out and supported the debtor's complaint? What if they merely watched? What if the car was parked in an enclosed driveway? How would you counsel a creditor and his agents in repossessing collateral under U.C.C. § 9–503?

(3) U.C.C. § 9–503 also provides that "[w]ithout removal a secured party may render equipment unusable, and may dispose of collateral on the debtor's premises under Section 9–504." *See Elliot v. Villa Park Trust & Savings Bank*, 63 Ill. App.3d 714, 380 N.E.2d 507 (Ill. App. Ct. 1978).

(4) In *Boudreau*, the court held that a default was sufficient to activate the creditor's possessory rights. What determines when a default has occurred?

(5) What can a creditor do after repossessing the collateral? *See* U.C.C. § 9–504.

(6) In *Turner*, the court, construing Tennessee's enactment of U.C.C. § 9–503, noted that Tennessee common law allowed repossession of personal property without resort to judicial process where the purchaser had agreed to repossession as a contractual matter. Would the court have found "state action" or "color of law," if the state common law did not recognize a contractual repossession right? *See Gary v. Darnell*, 505 F.2d 741 (6th Cir. 1974) (construing Kentucky's U.C.C. § 9–503). Under what circumstances will a court find state action in a U.C.C. § 9–503 context?

———————

McLaughlin & Cohen, SELF–HELP REPOSSESSION*

N.Y.L.J., p. 1 (March 9, 1988)

This article deals with two issues concerning the constitutionality of self–help repossession. Part I addresses the treatment of self–help repossession under New York State constitutional law; Part II addresses federal constitutional issues arising from self–help repossession by government agencies.

———————

Introduction

"Not that the story need be long, but it will take a long while to make it short," Henry David Thoreau once observed. While Thoreau certainly did not have self–help repossession in mind, his aphorism certainly is applicable to the courts' attempts to grapple with the constitutionality of that secured creditors' right.

One of the most important rights of a secured party is the right to take possession of the collateral after default without first giving the debtor notice and an opportunity to be heard.[1] This right of self–help repossession enables the secured party to obtain possession of the collateral quickly and inexpensively at a time when continued possession by the debtor could pose serious risks for the secured party. Conversely, of course, the secured party's right to self–help repossession creates risks for the debtor. A mistaken or malicious secured party can seriously disrupt a debtor's existence by taking possession in the absence of default — a situation which could be prevented if the debtor were notified and given an opportunity to be heard prior to the repossession.

Given the potential for harm to debtors from self–help repossessions, it is not surprising that debtors have frequently gone outside the confines of the UCC to block this significant power of secured parties. Most memorably, in the wake of the Supreme Court's decision in *Fuentes v. Shevin*,[2] debtors across the country sought to invalidate UCC § 9–503 as a deprivation of property without due process of law violating the 14th Amendment to the U.S. Constitution.

The sticking point in these challenges was that the 14th Amendment protects only against deprivations of property by the *state*; a private, secured creditor would, therefore, not seem to be covered by this prohibition. Debtors, however, sought to use the state–action doctrine to argue that the actions of the secured parties ought to be treated as state action. The debtors argued both that the state was inextricably involved with self–help repossessions by statutorily authorizing them and that such repossessions represented a governmental function.

These challenges were mostly unsuccessful, and when the Supreme Court decided in *Flagg Brothers v. Brooks*[3] that exercise of analogous self–help provisions of UCC § 7–210 did not constitute state action for the purposes of the 14th Amendment, a consensus developed that the use of UCC § 9–503 self–help rights was similarly invulnerable to federal constitutional attack.

As a result of *Flagg Brothers* and the lower court cases applying it to UCC § 9–503, attention has largely shifted away from federal constitutional challenges to self–help repossession. Recent cases, however, have addressed two issues worthy of continued examination. First is the constitutionality of self–help repossession under state constitutional law. *Flagg Brothers*, at most, established that self–help repossession could survive a challenge that it violates the Due Process clause of the

---

[1] UCC § 9–503 states that upon default, a secured party has the right to take possession of the collateral without judicial process if that can be done without a breach of peace. Unless otherwise noted, all references are to the 1978 official text of the UCC.

[2] 407 U.S. 67 (1972).

[3] 436 U.S. 149 (1978).

U.S. Constitution; it is necessarily silent as to the effect of *state* constitutional guarantees. Second are the issues raised when the secured party is the government. *Flagg Brothers* and its progeny dealt only with private, secured parties. Do the constitutional rules change when the secured party is the government or a quasi–governmental entity?

Part I — State Constitutional Law

While the Supreme Court decision in *Flagg Brothers* established that, as a matter of *federal* constitutional law, statutory schemes authorizing self–help creditors' remedies do not constitute state action, that decision does not necessarily resolve the matter for purposes of *state* constitutional law. Indeed, as a series of New York decisions demonstrates, the *Flagg Brothers* doctrine has not been followed in New York State constitutional jurisprudence.

Only a few months after the Supreme Court decision in *Flagg Brothers*, the New York Court of Appeals, in *Sharrock v. Dell Buick–Cadillac, Inc.*,[4] considered the constitutionality of provisions of the New York Lien Law permitting a garageman to conduct an ex parte sale of a bailed vehicle. Acknowledging the *Flagg Brothers* decision, the Court of Appeals noted that "the mere fact that an activity might not constitute state action for purposes of the Federal Constitution does not perforce necessitate that the same conclusion be reached when that conduct is claimed to be violative of the State Constitution. Indeed, on innumerable occasions this court has given our State Constitution an independent construction, affording the rights and liberties of citizens of this state even more protection than may be secured under the United States Constitution."[5]

The Court of Appeals then examined the Due Process clause of the New York Constitution — "[n]o person shall be deprived of life, liberty or property without due process of law"[6] — observing that language requiring state action as "conspicuously absent."[7] To the court, this absence does not eliminate the requirement of state involvement in the activity in question, but, rather, allows a "more flexible" approach.[8]

With this flexibility in mind, the court evaluated the state's involvement in the non–judicial foreclosure of garageperson's liens. Of particular importance to the court was the fact that although the garageman's lien existed at common law, only the statute gave the lienor the ability to enforce the lien by means of an ex parte sale. Based on this, the court indicated that the challenged statutory provision "has endowed private individuals with the same authority as has been traditionally vested with the sheriff."[9] It followed that enforcement of the garageman's lien constituted meaningful state participation.

---

[4] 45 NY 2d 152 (1978).

[5] 45 NY 2d at 159 (citations omitted).

[6] N.Y. Const., Art. I, § 6.

[7] 45 NY 2d at 160.

[8] *Id.*

[9] 45 NY 2d at 162.

No Due Process

Having decided that enforcement of the garageman's lien constituted state action for purposes of the New York State Constitution, the Court of Appeals examined whether enforcement of the lien deprived the owner of property without due process of law. Not surprisingly, the court easily concluded that the statute did not provide due process. Accordingly, the court held that the ex parte enforcement of the lien violated the Due Process clause of the New York State Constitution.

Three years after *Sharrock*, the Court of Appeals reaffirmed and extended that decision in *Svendsen v. Smith's Moving and Trucking Co.*[10] At issue in *Svendsen* was the constitutionality of UCC § 7–210 (the very section upheld as a matter of federal constitutional law in *Flagg Brothers*) insofar as it authorizes the ex parte sale of bailed goods without affording the owner the opportunity for a hearing.

Relying almost entirely on *Sharrock*, the Appellate Division, Second Department, held that the section of the UCC violated the New York Constitution.[11] As that court noted, both the New York Lien Law and UCC § 7–210 "permit the enforcement of a valid possessory lien by an ex parte non–judicial sale of the debtor's property without affording the debtor an opportunity to be heard. By these provisions, New York State has expended creditor's rights beyond the common law. . . . "[12] The Court of Appeals, in a short memorandum decision citing only to *Sharrock*, affirmed the Appellate Division's order.

Sharrock and *Svendsen* sent a strong private ex parte lien enforcement in New York.[13] This lesson was not lost on debtors' attorneys, who relied on *Sharrock* and *Svendsen* to attack ex parte repossession under UCC § 9–503 and similar statutes. Despite the seeming breadth of *Sharrock* and *Svendsen*, however, these challenges to the constitutionality of UCC § 9–503 have been largely unsuccessful.

In *Crouse v. First Trust Union Bank*,[14] the Supreme Court of Cattaraugus County relied on *Sharrock* to hold UCC §§ 9–503 and 9–504 unconstitutional under the New York State Constitution. The Appellate Division, Fourth Department, in a memorandum opinion, reversed the lower court opinion.

According to the Appellate Division, there was an important distinction between the New York Lien Law provision invalidated in *Sharrock* (and also, presumably, although not mentioned by the court, UCC § 7–210 invalidated in *Svendsen*) and the rights given to secured parties in Article 9. The invalidated statute in *Sharrock*, noted the court, gave the lienors rights beyond those existing at common law. In the court's view, however, § 9–503 "does nothing more than merely acknowledge previous lawful conduct,"[15] because, at common law, "a chattel mortgagee had the

---

[10] 54 NY 2d 865 (1981).

[11] 431 NYS 2d 94, 95 (App. Div., 2d Dep't, 1980), *aff'd* 54 NY 2d 865 (1981).

[12] 431 NYS 2d at 95 (citations omitted).

[13] The message was received by the Legislature, which amended UCC § 7–210, and added a new UCC § 7–211, in 1982 to provide for due process.

[14] 448 NYS 2d 329 (App. Div., 4th Dep't, 1982).

[15] 448 NYS 2d at 330.

right, upon default, to take possession of the chattel and thenceforth treat it as his own and to sell it if he chose."[16]

Ruling Extended

The following year, the Fourth Department reaffirmed and extended its holding in *Crouse*. In *Gallets v. General Motors Acceptance Corp.*,[17] the Appellate Division, relying exclusively on *Crouse*, upheld the constitutionality of the Motor Vehicle Installment Sales Act[18] insofar as it allows the seizing and sale of automobiles financed under a retail installment–sales contract without any prior notice or hearing.

Finally, in December 1987, the Fourth Department spoke once again about the constitutionality of UCC § 9–503. In *Jefferds v. Ellis*, the Supreme Court of Cattaraugus County (the same court reversed in *Crouse*) held that ex parte repossession pursuant to a "lease" that was actually, in substance, an Article 9 security interest violated the Due Process clause of the New York State Constitution.[19] The court distinguished *Crouse* on the ground that, while ex parte repossession under the security device in that case (essentially a chattel mortgage) was generally available under the common law, ex parte repossession in the case of a lease or conditional sale was available only if the contract so provided — which the contract in question did not. Accordingly, the right to repossess came solely from UCC § 9–503 and, therefore, represented state action.

The Appellate Division reversed.[20] In that court's view, the "lease" was essentially identical to the motor vehicle installment sales contract at issue in *Gallets*. Moreover, the court believed that repossession in conditional sales contracts was authorized at common law, even in the absence of express contractual provisions. Finally, the court indicated that is saw no reason to distinguish among Article 9 security devices as to the constitutionality of self–help repossession.

Crouse, Gallets, and *Jefferds* clearly establish the constitutionality of UCC § 9–503 in the Fourth Department. Yet, neither the other departments nor the Court of Appeals has spoken on the issue. While it does not appear likely that the other courts would differ with the Fourth Department, the *Sharrock* and *Svendsen* holdings could provide the basis to do so.

Part II — Government as Secured Party

As noted earlier, it has been the consensus since *Flagg Brothers* that the existence of UCC § 9–503 does not, of itself, constitute state action invoking federal constitutional guarantees. What happens, though, when the secured creditor utilizing UCC § 9–503 for self–help repossession is a government agency?

This difficult question was raised in the case of *Arcoren v. Peters*, which culminated recently with an en banc decision by the Eighth Circuit.[21] Arcoren had

---

16 *Id.*

17 465 NYS 2d 319 (App. Div., 4th Dep't, 1983).

18 N.Y. Personal Property Law, §§ 301–15.

19 486 NYS 2d 649 (Sup. 1985), rev'd 522 NYS 2d 398 (App. Div., 4th Cir. 1987).

20 522 NYS 2d 398 (App. Div., 4th Cir. 1987).

21 829 F.2d 671 (8th Cir. 1987).

received two loans from the Farmers Home Administration (FHA), a federal government agency. Part of the proceeds of those loans was used to purchase cattle, in which Arcoren granted the FHA a security interest. In March 1980, the FHA decided to repossess and sell Arcoren's cattle, based on allegations provided by Arcoren's uncle and a neighbor. No attempt was made to verify these allegations with Arcoren. The FHA repossessed the cattle on March 27, 1980, and sold the cattle the next day. Arcoren first learned of the repossession and sale on April 1, when he received a copy of the bill of sale from a livestock auction company.

To make matters worse, the FHA sent Arcoren a notice of acceleration on April 28, 1980. The notice form stated that Arcoren would be given the "opportunity to have a meeting before this foreclosure takes place." [22] Arcoren pursued an administrative appeal but was unsuccessful. He then sought relief in the federal courts, embarking on a journey that has produced five decisions to date.

The procedural history of this litigation is tortuous, but must be examined in order to understand the unusual framing of the substantive issues. Initially, Arcoren brought a *Bivens*–type action [23] in federal district court, alleging violation of his federal due–process right to notice and hearing before repossession of his cattle. Although the district court assumed arguendo that Arcoren had a due–process right to notice and hearing, it dismissed Arcoren's claim on the ground that the FHA administrative–appeals process afforded Arcoren the process he was due and that the existence of the appeals process obviated a *Bivens*–type action. [24]

Ruling Reversed

The U.S. Court of Appeals for the Eighth Circuit, however, reversed the district court decision, holding that the existence of the appeals process did not prevent Arcoren from bringing a *Bivens*–type action and remanded the case for further proceedings. [25] The Eighth Circuit did not, in that opinion, pass on the merits of Arcoren's claim that he had a due–process right to a hearing. [26]

On remand in the district court, the FHA officials argued, and won, on a different theory. [27] The theory was that under *Harlow v. Fitzgerald* [28] the officials possessed a qualified immunity. Under this theory, so long as there existed in 1980 (the time of repossession of the cattle) no clearly established statutory or constitutional right to notice or hearing prior to the repossession, the officials would be shielded from liability. According to the court, such right, if it exists at all, was not clearly established in 1980. According to the court, "[a]lthough the law was apparently headed in the direction of requiring notice and a hearing prior to FHA repossession of

---

22 *Arcoren v. Farmers Home Administration,* 770 F.2d 137 (8th Cir. 1985).

23 *See Bivens v. Six Unknown Named Agents,* 403 U.S. 388 (1971) (cause of action against federal government for breach of constitutional right).

24 *Arcoren v. Schooler,* Civ. 83–3017 (D.S.D. 1984), citing (on the *Bivens* point) *Bush v. Lucas,* 462 U.S. 367 (1963).

25 *Arcoren v. Farmers Home Administration,* 770 F.2d 137 (8th Cir. 1985).

26 *Id.* at 141.

27 *Arcoren v. Peters,* 627 F. Supp. 1512 (D.S.D. 1986).

28 457 U.S. 800 (1982).

collateral, it cannot be said that the law was 'clearly established' on that point in 1980."[29] Accordingly, the district court granted summary judgment for the defendants, dismissing the suit on the basis of qualified immunity.

The case was then appealed once again to the Eighth Circuit, which once again reversed the district court.[30] The Eighth Circuit, in a split decision, held that a clearly established due–process right did exist in 1980. The court somewhat curiously sidestepped the key "state action" (actually federal action here) issue, noting (in an unacknowledged echo of *Sharrock*) that the Fifth Amendment Due Process clause, unlike that of the 14th Amendment, is in passive voice; according to the court, this means that the Fifth Amendment does not require "state action."[31]

Most recently, however, the Court of Appeals for the Eighth Circuit, sitting en banc, reversed the panel opinion and affirmed the district court's dismissal.[32] While the court's opinion states that "the only issue before us on this appeal is the propriety of the ruling on qualified immunity,"[33] the opinion nonetheless contains important statements about the underlying substantive issue.

As the en banc court saw the case, whether Arcoren had a clearly established constitutional right to prior notice and hearing "turns in large part on whether *Fuentes v. Shevin* is directly applicable . . . "[34] The court noted that had Arcoren's lender been private, it clearly would have been entitled to repossess without notice or hearing.[35] The key question, of course, is whether the FHA's status as a government agency means that it cannot constitutionally rely on the self–help provisions of UCC § 9–503.

Government Agency

According to the court, the proposition is not clearly established that "the FHA had additional responsibilities under the Fifth Amendment and could not operate in the same manner as a [private] commercial lender."[36] In support of this conclusion, the court first cited *United States v. Kimbell Foods, Inc.*[37] for the proposition that there was, at least in 1980, strong authority that when FHA acted as a lender it acted in a commercial rather than a sovereign capacity.

The Eighth Circuit (en banc) then cited to cases concerning the Government National Mortgage Association (GNMA) and the Federal National Mortgage Association (FNMA)[38] to further support the proposition that the FHA does not

---

[29] 627 F. Supp. at 1519.

[30] *Arcoren v. Peters*, 811 F.2d 392 (8th Cir. 1987).

[31] *Id*. at 394.

[32] *Arcoren v. Peters*, 829 F.2d 671 (8th Cir. 1987).

[33] *Id*. at 673.

[34] *Id*. at 673–74.

[35] *Id*. at 674, citing *Bichel Optical Laboratories, Inc. v. Marquette National Bank*, 487 F.2d 906 (8th Cir. 1973).

[36] *Id*. at 674.

[37] 440 U.S. 715 (1979).

[38] *Warren v. Government Nat'l Mortgage Assoc.*, 611 F.2d 1229 (8th Cir.), *cert. denied*, 449 U.S. 847 (1980); *Roberts v. Cameron–Brown Co.*, 556 F.2d 356 (5th Cir. 1977); *Northrip v. Federal Nat'l Mortgage Assoc.*, 527 F.2d 23 (6th Cir. 1975).

run afoul of the Fifth Amendment when it is merely exercising rights granted pursuant to contract.

Two judges dissented from this en banc opinion. The major dissent, by Circuit Judge Heaney, disagreed strongly with the majority opinion. According to Judge Heaney, there is no question that Arcoren had a property interest in his cattle protected by the Fifth Amendment.[39] Moreover, he observed, it is settled law that due process requires, at a minimum, notice and a right to be heard; clearly such process was not extended to Arcoren before depriving him of his cattle.[40]

Therefore, as Judge Heaney recognized, the only issue left is whether the FHA was required to provide due process to Arcoren in connection with repossessing his cattle. Judge Heaney flatly rejected the majority's contention that the action of the FHA officials was exempt from the Fifth Amendment requirement of due process because they were acting not as a sovereign but, rather pursuant to a security agreement. According to Judge Heaney, "[r]equirements imposed upon federal officials by the United States Constitution do not fall by the wayside merely because they are acting pursuant to a state statute of which private creditors may make use."[41]

Accordingly, Judge Heaney found that it has always been clear that the Constitution prohibits government officials from depriving individuals of property without affording them due process. Thus, the FHA officials' conduct violated Arcoren's clearly established constitutional rights and they should be liable.[42]

As the multiple opinions and strong difference of views in the Eighth Circuit's en banc opinion indicate, the issue raised by the *Arcoren* case is not easy to resolve. Regardless of one's opinion as to the correct result in the case, however, the case is quite important. As the volume of government lending increases, so does the importance of the issues.

§ 2.03   Judgment by Confession

Judgments by confession, or cognovit judgments, facilitate a creditor's collection efforts because the debtor typically permits the entry of a judgment even before any default. Thus, the creditor has, in effect, a judgment lien on the debtor's property,

---

[39] 829 F.2d at 678 (*Heaney, J.*, dissenting).

[40] *Id.*

[41] *Id.* at 679. In addition, Judge Heaney noted the irony of the FHA officials' assertion of qualified immunity as government officials simultaneously with the claim of exemption from constitutional requirements because their actions were sufficiently private in nature. He noted that the majority's acceptance of this argument gave the officials a "chameleon–like quality, . . . sufficiently governmental to merit qualified immunity and sufficiently private to be exempt from constitutional requirements." Thus, they "enjoy the privileges of both private and governmental lenders, while being exempt from the responsibilities of both." *Id.* at 680–81.

[42] Chief Judge Lay wrote a brief dissent, joining Judge Heaney's opinion and adding the interesting observation that the government had not even argued that the FHA officials were not acting in their sovereign capacity. *Id.* at 678.

personal jurisdiction over an out–of–state debtor, and the debtor's waiver of procedural defects or rights to appeal.

―――――――――

D.H. OVERMYER CO. v. FRICK CO.

United States Supreme Court
405 U.S. 174, 92 S. Ct. 775, 31 L. Ed. 2d 124 (1972)

Mr. Justice BLACKMUN delivered the opinion of the Court.

This case presents the issue of the constitutionality, under the Due Process Clause of the Fourteenth Amendment, of the cognovit note authorized by Ohio Rev. Code § 2323.13

The cognovit is the ancient legal device by which the debtor consents in advance to the holder's obtaining a judgment without notice or hearing, and possibly even with the appearance, on the debtor's behalf, of an attorney designated by the holder. It was known at least as far back as Blackstone's time. 3 W. Blackstone, Commentaries 397. In a case applying Ohio law, it was said that the purpose of the cognovit is "to permit the note holder to obtain judgment without a trial of possible defenses which the signers of the notes might assert." *Hadden v. Rumsey Products, Inc.*, 196 F.2d 92, 96 (CA2 1952). And long ago the cognovit method was described by the Chief Justice of New Jersey as "the loosest way of binding a man's property that ever was devised in any civilized country." *Alderman v. Diament*, 7 N. J. L. 197, 198 (1824). Mr. Dickens noted it with obvious disfavor. Pickwick Papers, c. 47. The cognovit has been the subject of comment, much of it critical.

Statutory treatment varies widely. Some States specifically authorize the cognovit. Others disallow it. Some go so far as to make its employment a misdemeanor. The majority, however, regulate its use and many prohibit the device in small loans and consumer sales.

In Ohio the cognovit has long been recognized by both statute and court decision. 1 Chase's Statutes, c. 243, § 34 (1810); *Osborn v. Hawley*, 19 Ohio 130 (1850); *Marsden v. Soper*, 11 Ohio St. 503 (1860); *Watson v. Paine*, 25 Ohio St. 340 (1874); *Clements v. Hull*, 35 Ohio St. 141 (1878). The State's courts, however, give the instrument a strict and limited construction. *See Peoples Banking Co. v. Brumfield Hay & Grain Co.*, 172 Ohio St. 545, 548, 179 N. E. 2d 53, 55 (1961).

This Court apparently has decided only two cases concerning cognovit notes, and both have come here in a full faith and credit context. *National Exchange Bank v. Wiley*, 195 U.S. 257 (1904); *Grover & Baker Sewing Machine Co. v. Radcliffe*, 137 U.S. 287 (1890). *See American Surety Co. v. Baldwin*, 287 U.S. 156 (1932).

I

The argument that a provision of this kind is offensive to current notions of Fourteenth Amendment due process is, at first glance, an appealing one. However, here, as in nearly every case, facts are important. We state them chronologically:

1. Petitioners D. H. Overmyer Co., Inc., of Ohio, and D. H. Overmyer Co., Inc., of Kentucky, are segments of a warehousing enterprise that counsel at one point in the litigation described as having built "in three years . . . 180 warehouses in thirty states." The corporate structure is complex. Because the identity and individuality of the respective corporate entities are not relevant here, we refer to the enterprise in the aggregate as "Overmyer."

2. In 1966 a corporation, which then was or at a later date became an Overmyer affiliate, executed a contract with the respondent Frick Co. for the manufacture and installation by Frick, at a cost of $223,000, of an automatic refrigeration system in a warehouse under construction in Toledo, Ohio.

3. Overmyer fell behind in the progress payments due from it under the contract. By the end of September 1966 approximately $120,000 was overdue. Because of this delinquency, Frick stopped its work on October 10. Frick indicated to Overmyer, however, by letter on that date, its willingness to accept an offer from Overmyer to pay $35,000 in cash "provided the balance can be evidenced by interest–bearing judgment notes."

4. On November 3 Frick filed three mechanic's liens against the Toledo property for a total of $194,031, the amount of the contract price allegedly unpaid at that time.

5. The parties continued to negotiate. In January 1967 Frick, in accommodation, agreed to complete the work upon an immediate cash payment of 10% ($19,403.10) and payment of the balance of $174,627.90 in 12 equal monthly installments with 6½% interest per annum. On February 17 Overmyer made the 10% payment and executed an installment note calling for 12 monthly payments of $15,498.23 each beginning March 1, 1967. This note contained no confession–of–judgment provision. It recited that it did not operate as a waiver of the mechanic's liens, but it also stated that Frick would forgo enforcement of those lien rights so long as there was no default under the note.

6. Frick resumed its work, completed it, and sent Overmyer a notice of completion. On March 17 Overmyer's vice president acknowledged in writing that the system had been "completed in a satisfactory manner" and that it was "accepted as per the contract conditions."

7. Subsequently, Overmyer requested additional time to make the installment payments. It also asked that Frick release the mechanic's liens against the Toledo property. Negotiations between the parties at that time finally resulted in an agreement in June 1967 that (a) Overmyer would execute a new note for the then–outstanding balance of $130,997 and calling for payment of the amount in 21 equal monthly installments of $6,891.85 each, beginning June 1, 1967, and ending in February 1969, two years after Frick's completion of the work (as contrasted with the $15,498.23 monthly installments ending February 1968 specified by the first note); (b) the interest rate would be 6% rather than 6½%; (c) Frick would release the three mechanic's liens; (d) Overmyer would execute second mortgages, with Frick as mortgagee, on property in Tampa and Louisville; and (e) Overmyer's new note would contain a confession–of–judgment clause. The new note, signed in Ohio by the two petitioners here, was delivered to Frick some months later by letter dated

October 2, 1967, accompanied by five checks for the June through October payments. This letter was from Overmyer's general counsel to Frick's counsel. The second mortgages were executed and recorded, and the mechanic's liens were released. The note contained the following judgment clause:

> The undersigned hereby authorize any attorney designated by the Holder hereof to appear in any court of record in the State of Ohio, and waive this issuance and service of process, and confess a judgment against the undersigned in favor of the Holder of this Note, for the principal of this Note plus interest if the undersigned defaults in any payment of principal and interest and if said default shall continue for the period of fifteen (15) days.

8. On June 1, 1968, Overmyer ceased making the monthly payments under the new note and, asserting a breach by Frick of the original contract, proceeded to institute a diversity action against Frick in the United States District Court for the Southern District of New York. Overmyer sought damages in excess of $170,000 and a stay of all proceedings by Frick under the note. On July 5 Judge Frankel vacated an ex parte stay he had theretofore granted. On August 7 Judge Mansfield denied Overmyer's motion for reinstatement of the stay. He concluded, "Plaintiff has failed to show any likelihood that it will prevail upon the merits. On the contrary, extensive documentary evidence furnished by defendant indicates that the plaintiff's action lacks merit."

9. On July 12, without prior notice to Overmyer, Frick caused judgment to be entered against Overmyer (specifically against the two petitioners here) in the Common Pleas Court of Lucas County, Ohio. The judgment amount was the balance then remaining on the note, namely, $62,370, plus interest from May 1, 1968, and costs. This judgment was effected through the appearance of an Ohio attorney on behalf of the defendants (petitioners here) in that Ohio action. His appearance was "by virtue of the warrant of attorney" in the second note. The lawyer waived the issuance and service of process and confessed the judgment. This attorney was not known to Overmyer, had not been retained by Overmyer, and had not communicated with the petitioners prior to the entry of the judgment.

10. As required by Ohio Rev. Code § 2323.13 (C), the clerk of the state court, on July 16, mailed notices of the entry of the judgment on the cognovit note to Overmyer at addresses in New York, Ohio, and Kentucky.

11. On July 22 Overmyer, by counsel, filed in the Ohio court motions to stay execution and for a new trial. The latter motion referred to "[i]rregularity in the proceedings of the prevailing party and of the court. . . ." On August 6, Overmyer filed a motion to vacate judgment and tendered an answer and counterclaim alleging breach of contract by Frick, and damages. A hearing was held. Both sides submitted affidavits. Those submitted by Overmyer asserted lack of notice before judgment and alleged a breach of contract by Frick. A copy of Judge Mansfield's findings, conclusions, and opinion was placed in the record. On November 16 the court overruled each motion.

12. Overmyer appealed to the Court of Appeals for Lucas County, Ohio, specifically asserting deprivation of due process violative of the Ohio and Federal Constitutions. That court affirmed with a brief journal entry.

13. The Supreme Court of Ohio "sua sponte dismisse[d] the appeal for the reason that no substantial constitutional question exists herein."

We granted certiorari 401 U.S. 992 (1971).

II

This chronology clearly reveals that Overmyer's situation, of which it now complains, is one brought about largely by its own misfortune and failure or inability to pay. The initial agreement between Overmyer and Frick was a routine construction subcontract. Frick agreed to do the work and Overmyer agreed to pay a designated amount for that work by progress payments at specified times. This contract was not accompanied by any promissory note.

Overmyer then became delinquent in its payments. Frick naturally refrained from further work. This impasse was resolved by the February 1967 post–contract arrangement, pursuant to which Overmyer made an immediate partial payment in cash and issued its installment note for the balance. Although Frick had suggested a confession–of–judgment clause, the note as executed and delivered contained no provision of that kind.

Frick completed its work and Overmyer accepted the work as satisfactory. Thereafter Overmyer again asked for relief. At this time counsel for each side participated in the negotiations. The first note was replaced by the second. The latter contained the confession–of–judgment provision Overmyer now finds so offensive. However, in exchange for that provision and for its execution of the second mortgages, Overmyer received benefit and consideration in the form of (a) Frick's release of the three mechanic's liens, (b) reduction in the amount of the monthly payment, (c) further time in which the total amount was to be paid, and (d) reduction of a half point in the interest rate.

Were we concerned here only with the validity of the June 1967 agreement under principles of contract law, that issue would be readily resolved. Obviously and undeniably, Overmyer's execution and delivery of the second note were for an adequate consideration and were the product of negotiations carried on by corporate parties with the advice of competent counsel.

More than mere contract law, however, is involved here.

III

Petitioner Overmyer first asserts that the Ohio judgment is invalid because there was no personal service upon it, no voluntary appearance by it in Ohio, and no genuine appearance by an attorney on its behalf. Thus, it is said, there was no personal jurisdiction over Overmyer in the Ohio proceeding. The petitioner invokes *Pennoyer v. Neff*, 95 U.S. 714, 732 (1878), and other cases decided here and by the Ohio courts enunciating accepted and long–established principles for *in personam* jurisdiction. *McDonald v. Mabee*, 243 U.S. 90, 91 (1917); *Vanderbilt v. Vanderbilt*, 354 U.S. 416, 418 (1957); *Sears v. Weimer*, 143 Ohio St. 312, 55 N. E. 2d 413 (1944); *Railroad Co. v. Goodman*, 57 Ohio St. 641, 50 N. E. 1132 (1897); *Cleveland Leader Printing Co. v. Green*, 52 Ohio St. 487, 491, 40 N. E. 201, 203 (1895).

It is further said that whether a defendant's appearance is voluntary is to be determined at the time of the court proceeding, not at a much earlier date when an agreement was signed; that an unauthorized appearance by an attorney on a defendant's behalf cannot confer jurisdiction; and that the lawyer who appeared in Ohio was not Overmyer's attorney in any sense of the word, but was only an agent of Frick.

The argument then proceeds to constitutional grounds. It is said that due process requires reasonable notice and an opportunity to be heard, citing *Boddie v. Connecticut*, 401 U.S. 371, 378 (1971). It is acknowledged, however, that the question here is in a context of "contract waiver, before suit has been filed, before any dispute has arisen" and "whereby a party gives up in advance his constitutional right to defend any suit by the other, to notice and an opportunity to be heard, no matter what defenses he may have, and to be represented by counsel of his own choice." In other words, Overmyer's position here specifically is that it is "unconstitutional to waive in advance the right to present a defense in an action on the note." It is conceded that in Ohio a court has the power to open the judgment upon a proper showing. *Bellows v. Bowlus*, 83 Ohio App. 90, 93, 82 N. E. 2d 429, 432 (1948). But it is claimed that such a move is discretionary and ordinarily will not be disturbed on appeal, and that it may not prevent execution before the debtor has notice, *Griffin v. Griffin*, 327 U.S. 220, 231–232 (1946). *Goldberg v. Kelly*, 397 U.S. 254 (1970), and *Sniadach v. Family Finance Corp.*, 395 U.S. 337 (1969), are cited.

The due process rights to notice and hearing prior to a civil judgment are subject to waiver. In *National Equipment Rental, Ltd. v. Szukhent*, 375 U.S. 311 (1964), the Court observed:

> [I]t is settled . . . that parties to a contract may agree in advance to submit to the jurisdiction of a given court, to permit notice to be served by the opposing party, or even to waive notice altogether.

Id., at 315–316. And in *Boddie v. Connecticut, supra*, the Court acknowledged that "the hearing required by due process is subject to waiver." 401 U.S., at 378–379.

This, of course, parallels the recognition of waiver in the criminal context where personal liberty, rather than a property right, is involved. *Illinois v. Allen*, 397 U.S. 337, 342–343 (1970) (right to be present at trial); *Miranda v. Arizona*, 384 U.S. 436, 444 (1966) (rights to counsel and against compulsory self–incrimination); *Fay v. Noia*, 372 U.S. 391, 439 (1963) (habeas corpus); *Rogers v. United States*, 340 U.S. 367, 371 (1951) (right against compulsory self–incrimination).

Even if, for present purposes, we assume that the standard for waiver in a corporate–property–right case of this kind is the same standard applicable to waiver in a criminal proceeding, that is, that it be voluntary, knowing, and intelligently made, *Brady v. United States*, 397 U.S. 742, 748 (1970); *Miranda v. Arizona*, 384 U.S., at 444, or "an intentional relinquishment or abandonment of a known right or privilege," *Johnson v. Zerbst*, 304 U.S. 458, 464 (1938); *Fay v. Noia*, 372 U.S., at 439, and even if, as the Court has said in the civil area, "[w]e do not presume acquiescence in the loss of fundamental rights," *Ohio Bell Tel. Co. v. Public Utilities Comm'n*, 301 U.S. 292, 307 (1937), that standard was fully satisfied here.

Overmyer is a corporation. Its corporate structure is complicated. Its activities are widespread. As its counsel in the Ohio post–judgment proceeding stated, it has built many warehouses in many States and has been party to "tens of thousands of contracts with many contractors." This is not a case of unequal bargaining power or overreaching. The Overmyer–Frick agreement, from the start, was not a contract of adhesion. There was no refusal on Frick's part to deal with Overmyer unless Overmyer agreed to a cognovit. The initial contract between the two corporations contained no confession–of–judgment clause. When, later, the first installment note from Overmyer came into being, it, too, contained no provision of that kind. It was only after Frick's work was completed and accepted by Overmyer, and when Overmyer again became delinquent in its payments on the matured claim and asked for further relief, that the second note containing the clause was executed.

Overmyer does not contend here that it or its counsel was not aware of the significance of the note and of the cognovit provision. Indeed, it could not do so in the light of the facts. Frick had suggested the provision in October 1966, but the first note, readjusting the progress payments, was executed without it. It appeared in the second note delivered by Overmyer's own counsel in return for substantial benefits and consideration to Overmyer. Particularly important, it would seem, was the release of Frick's mechanic's liens, but there were, in addition, the monetary relief as to amount, time, and interest rate.

Overmyer may not have been able to predict with accuracy just how or when Frick would proceed under the confession clause if further default by Overmyer occurred, as it did, but this inability does not in itself militate against effective waiver. *See Brady v. United States*, 397 U.S., at 757; *McMann v. Richardson*, 397 U.S. 759, 772–773 (1970).

We therefore hold that Overmyer, in its execution and delivery to Frick of the second installment note containing the cognovit provision, voluntarily, intelligently, and knowingly waived the rights it otherwise possessed to prejudgment notice and hearing, and that it did so with full awareness of the legal consequences.

Insurance Co. v. Morse, 20 Wall. 445 (1874), affords no comfort to the petitioners. That case concerned the constitutional validity of a state statute that required a foreign insurance company, desiring to qualify in the State, to agree not to remove any suit against it to a federal court. The Court quite naturally struck down the statute, for it thwarted the authority vested by Congress in the federal courts and violated the Privileges and Immunities Clause.

Myers v. Jenkins, 63 Ohio St. 101, 120, 57 N. E. 1089, 1093 (1900), involving an insurance contract that called for adjustment of claims through the company alone and without resort to the courts, is similarly unhelpful.

IV

Some concluding comments are in order:

1. Our holding necessarily means that a cognovit clause is not, *per se*, violative of Fourteenth Amendment due process. Overmyer could prevail here only if the clause were constitutionally invalid. The facts of this case, as we observed above,

are important, and those facts amply demonstrate that a cognovit provision may well serve a proper and useful purpose in the commercial world and at the same time not be vulnerable to constitutional attack.

2. Our holding, of course, is not controlling precedent for other facts of other cases. For example, where the contract is one of adhesion, where there is great disparity in bargaining power, and where the debtor receives nothing for the cognovit provision, other legal consequences may ensue.

3. Overmyer, merely because of its execution of the cognovit note, is not rendered defenseless. It concedes that in Ohio the judgment court may vacate its judgment upon a showing of a valid defense and, indeed, Overmyer had a post–judgment hearing in the Ohio court. If there were defenses such as prior payment or mistaken identity, those defenses could be asserted. And there is nothing we see that prevented Overmyer from pursuing its breach–of–contract claim against Frick in a proper forum. Here, again, that is precisely what Overmyer has attempted to do, thus far unsuccessfully, in the Southern District of New York.

The judgment is

Affirmed.

[Concurring opinion deleted]

NOTES AND QUESTIONS

(1) What is the difference between a default judgment, a consent judgment and a judgment by confession?

(2) What are the "proper and useful purposes in the commercial world" for a judgment by confession, alluded to by the Supreme Court in *Overmyer*?

(3) What factors did the Supreme Court weigh in *Overmyer* in concluding that the judgment by confession in that case was not violative of due process?

(4) Should judgments by confession be limited to commercial debtors? *See* 16 C.F.R. § 444.2(a)(1) (effective March 1, 1985) (retail installment sellers and lenders subject to the FTC cannot include judgments by confession in consumer credit agreements).

FIORE v. OAKWOOD PLAZA SHOPPING CENTER, INC.

New York Court of Appeals
78 N.Y.2d 572, 585 N.E.2d 364, 578 N.Y.S.2d 115 (1991)

KAYE, Judge.

Judgments by confession, recognized both as "the loosest way of binding a man's property that ever was devised in any civilized country" (*Alderman v. Diament,* 7 N.J.L. 197, 198) and as devices that "serve a proper and useful purpose in the commercial world" (*Overmyer Co. v. Frick Co.,* 405 U.S. 174, 188, 92 S.Ct. 775, 783, 31 L.Ed.2d 124), in this State have been strictly limited by the Legislature (*see,* CPLR 3218). The present case calls upon us to determine whether a Pennsylvania cognovit judgment, obtained under that State's laws, should be given full faith and credit here (*see,* U.S. Const., art. IV, § 1); 28 U.S.C. § 1738). Given the procedures followed in Pennsylvania, we agree with the trial court and the Appellate Division that the Pennsylvania judgment may be enforced against defendant–appellants in New York.

I.

In July 1986, plaintiffs contracted to sell a 14.8 acre parcel located in Patton Township, Centre County, Pennsylvania, to State College Development Company, predecessor in interest to defendant Oakwood Plaza Shopping Center. Defendants Joseph Aronow and Anthony Galioto are principals in Oakwood. Under the agreement, the purchase price was to be determined by the number of square feet approved by the local authorities for use as retail sales space. Initially, the full purchase price was to be paid at closing—to occur no later than March 1987.

At defendants' request, a rider was later executed that changed the payment terms: $600,000 to be paid at closing, the remainder secured by a purchase–money mortgage and note. Closing took place on December 23, 1986, at which time plaintiffs delivered the deed to the parcel and defendants paid $700,000 toward the purchase price. Oakwood executed a $1.1 million purchase–money mortgage. Additionally, Oakwood, as well as Aronow and Galioto individually, executed a "bond and warrant" obligating them to pay $1.1 million with interest at 9% per annum. The bond contained a "warrant of attorney" through which defendants authorized plaintiffs' attorney to confess judgment against them in the amount of $1.1 million.

Defendants failed to make the required payments. On September 9, 1988, in the Pennsylvania Court of Common Pleas, plaintiffs filed a complaint in confession of judgment as well as a praecipe to enter judgment against defendants (Pa.Rules Civ.Pro., rule 2951). On the same day, the prothonotary entered final judgment against defendants in the amount of $1,216,145 and sent them a notice of entry of final judgment and a copy of the complaint. A second judgment—in the amount of $1,287,713—was obtained against defendant Oakwood on the purchase–money mortgage after Oakwood failed to appear and defend the action.

In November 1988, plaintiffs served a demand for discovery in aid of execution upon defendants. After defendants failed to respond, plaintiffs filed a motion in the

Pennsylvania Court of Common Pleas to compel discovery and impose sanctions which the court, in January 1989, granted.

Defendants, in May 1989, filed a petition to open or strike the judgment (Pa.Rules Civ.Pro., rule 2959). The Court of Common Pleas, after a hearing, denied the petition, concluding that the petition was both untimely and raised no meritorious defense. Three months later, in September 1989, defendants filed an untimely appeal of that decision which was later withdrawn. In October 1989, the Pennsylvania court, after a hearing, held defendants in criminal contempt for failure to comply with the court's order directing them to respond to plaintiffs' discovery requests. Substantial monetary penalties were imposed.

Frustrated in their enforcement efforts in Pennsylvania, plaintiffs commenced the present New York action in January 1989 by summons and notice of motion for summary judgment in lieu of complaint (*see*, CPLR 3213). The action, originally framed as one "upon an instrument for the payment of money only" (based on the bond and warrant), was later converted into an action upon the two Pennsylvania judgments. Defendants filed a cross motion to dismiss for legal insufficiency (CPLR 3211[a][7]).

Supreme Court granted plaintiffs' motion for summary judgment, concluding that the Pennsylvania court had personal jurisdiction over defendants, that due process requirements had been satisfied, and that the judgments were valid and conclusive in the forum State. As a result, the court concluded, the Pennsylvania judgments were entitled to full faith and credit. Finally, the court denied defendants' cross motion, holding that it was precluded from looking beyond the jurisdictional aspects of the Pennsylvania proceedings.

The Appellate Division affirmed, agreeing that the Pennsylvania cognovit judgment on the bond and warrant should be accorded full faith and credit. The court concluded that under the circumstances "where the parties were engaged in an arm's length business transaction, were represented by counsel, and the defendant was on actual notice of the entry of the judgment and, in fact, sought to challenge same prior to execution, it cannot be said that the cognovit judgment amounted to a deprivation of property rights without due process." (164 A.D.2d 737, 742, 565 N.Y.S.2d 799.)

On this appeal, defendants again attempt to argue the merits of the Pennsylvania judgment. In addition, defendants argue that cognovit judgments as a matter of law are not entitled to full faith and credit in this State, citing this Court's decision in *Atlas Credit Corp. v. Ezrine*, 25 N.Y.2d 219, 303 N.Y.S.2d 382, 250 N.E.2d 474. Plaintiffs respond that United States Supreme Court decisions rendered after Atlas have made clear that cognovit judgments are not *per se* unconstitutional. Rather, plaintiffs assert, a case–by–case analysis is required to determine whether defendants voluntarily, knowingly and intelligently waived their rights to notice and an opportunity to be heard. The facts clearly demonstrate that such a valid waiver was effected, according to plaintiffs, and therefore the Pennsylvania judgment should be afforded full faith and credit. Agreeing with plaintiffs' arguments, we now affirm the Appellate Division order.

II.

As a matter of full faith and credit, review by the courts of this State is limited to determining whether the rendering court had jurisdiction, an inquiry which includes due process considerations (*Parker v. Hoefer*, 2 N.Y.2d 612, 162 N.Y.S.2d 13, 142 N.E.2d 194, *cert. denied*, 355 U.S. 833, 78 S.Ct. 51, 2 L.Ed.2d 45 *see also, Augusta Lbr. & Supply v. Sabbeth Corp.*, 101 A.D.2d 846, 475 N.Y.S.2d 878; 4 Weinstein–Korn–Miller, N.Y.Civ.Prac. P. 3213.04). Thus, inquiry into the merits of the underlying dispute is foreclosed; the facts have bearing only in the limited context of our jurisdictional review (*Parker v. Hoefer, supra*, 2 N.Y.2d at 616–617, 162 N.Y.S.2d 13, 142 N.E.2d 194). Moreover, although this is a confessed judgment, defendants have been offered, and have availed themselves of, a full and fair opportunity to argue the merits in the Pennsylvania courts.

The cognovit is a contractual provision, employed as a security device, whereby the obligor consents in advance to the creditor's obtaining a judgment without notice or hearing (*see, Overmyer Co. v. Frick Co.*, 405 U.S., at 176, 92 S.Ct., at 777–78, *supra*). In the present case, the cognovit contained a "warrant of attorney," a provision that empowers any attorney to enter the obligor's appearance in any court of record and to waive—on the obligor's behalf—process and consent to the entry of judgment (*Atlas Credit Corp. v. Ezrine*, 25 N.Y.2d, at 225, 303 N.Y.S.2d 382, 250 N.E.2d 474, *supra*).

In *Atlas*, this Court held that the Pennsylvania cognovit judgment in issue was not entitled to full faith and credit. First, we concluded that the cognovit "judgment" was a judgment in name only, having none of the "minimums of judicial process" usually associated with that term. For that reason alone, the cognovit judgment was not entitled to full faith and credit (25 N.Y.2d, at 229–230, 303 N.Y.S.2d 382, 250 N.E.2d 474, *supra*). Second, as recognition of the judgment was not constitutionally mandated, we determined that enforcing the cognovit judgment would be repugnant to New York policy (25 N.Y.2d, at 230, 303 N.Y.S.2d 382, 250 N.E.2d 474). Finally, we held that even assuming the cognovit could qualify as a judgment for full faith and credit purposes, the Pennsylvania judgment was not enforceable in this State because cognovit judgments that provide for entry of a judgment by confession anywhere in the world without notice are *per se* unconstitutional (25 N.Y.2d, at 231–232, 303 N.Y.S.2d 382, 250 N.E.2d 474).

In *Atlas*, this Court noted that United States Supreme Court precedent considering cognovit judgments stood only for the proposition that the terms of a warrant of attorney should be strictly construed (25 N.Y.2d, at 227, 303 N.Y.S.2d 382, 250 N.E.2d 474, *supra*). The Supreme Court had not yet spoken on the constitutionality of such judgments. Several years after *Atlas*—in the companion cases *Overmyer Co. v. Frick Co.*, 405 U.S. 174, 92 S.Ct. 775, *supra* and *Swarb v. Lennox*, 405 U.S. 191, 92 S.Ct. 767, 31 L.Ed.2d 138—the United States Supreme Court did have the opportunity to consider whether cognovit judgments were per se unconstitutional.

In *Overmyer*, the Court ruled that Ohio's cognovit procedure was not *per se* unconstitutional (405 U.S., at 187, 92 S.Ct., at 783, *supra*). Instead, the Court directed attention to the effectiveness of the obligor's waiver of due process rights, a necessarily fact–specific inquiry, concluding from the facts that the obligor there had effectively waived those rights (*id.*). First, the Court assumed that the proper standard for determining the effectiveness of the waiver was the same as in criminal proceedings, "that is, that it be voluntary, knowing, and intelligently made" (405 U.S., at 185, 92 S.Ct., at 782). The Court emphasized that the obligors were sophisticated corporations, represented by counsel, involved in an arm's length commercial transaction. Furthermore, the cognovit clause was contained in a contract modification that had been effected after the obligor defaulted on its obligations and for which it received consideration. Thus, the Court concluded, the obligor in *Overmyer* had effectively waived its right to notice and a hearing.

Finally, the Court in *Overmyer* observed that the obligor was not—by execution of the cognovit clause—rendered defenseless (405 U.S., at 188, 92 S.Ct., at 783–84, *supra*). Rather, under Ohio law the obligor could seek to vacate the judgment—indeed, the obligor had in fact had a postjudgment hearing in an Ohio court. The concurrence emphasized the availability of postjudgment hearing as an avenue of relief for an obligor with a legitimate defense (405 U.S., at 189–190, 92 S.Ct., at 784–85 [Douglas, J., concurring]).[1]

In *Swarb*, the Supreme Court considered a constitutional challenge to the Pennsylvania cognovit judgment scheme, and rejected plaintiffs' argument that the procedure was invalid on its face. The Court, citing *Overmyer*, reiterated that "under appropriate circumstances, a cognovit debtor may be held effectively and legally to have waived those rights he would possess if the document he signed had contained no cognovit provision." (405 U.S., at 200, 92 S.Ct., at 772, *supra*.)

We therefore consider the impact of *Overmyer* and *Swarb* on our earlier holding in *Atlas* that Pennsylvania cognovit judgments are not entitled to full faith and credit.

It is evident that the conclusion reached in *Atlas* concerning the *per se* unconstitutionality of the Pennsylvania cognovit scheme is itself no longer valid in light of the subsequent Supreme Court decisions (*see, Money Mgt. v. Vetere*, 107 Misc.2d 861, 863–864, 436 N.Y.S.2d 158; *In re PCH Assocs.*, 122 B.R. 181, 194–195 [S.D.N.Y.] [questioning the continued validity of the *Atlas* analysis in light of *Overmyer* and *Swarb*]; *see also, Siegel*, N.Y. Prac. § 300, at 430–431 [Prac.2d ed.] [same]). Cognovit judgments entered in other jurisdictions cannot automatically be denied full faith and credit; rather, enforceability must depend on the facts of each case. More particularly, it must be determined that the judgment debtor made a voluntary, knowing and intelligent waiver of the right to notice and an opportunity to be heard.

In that *Overmyer* and *Swarb* did not raise full faith and credit issues, it is arguable that the determination in *Atlas* that cognovit judgments are not judgments in the ordinary sense of the word would bar enforcement of such judgments in this State.

---

[1] Justice Douglas contrasted the Ohio postjudgment procedure with the Pennsylvania procedure involved in *Swarb v. Lennox*, 405 U.S. 191, 92 S.Ct. 767, which he found imposed a stiffer—and "undue" burden of persuasion on the debtor (405 U.S., at 190, n., 92 S.Ct., at 784, n., *supra*). The Pennsylvania procedure was subsequently amended, and now places the same burden of persuasion on the debtor as was found in the Ohio scheme—sufficient evidence to raise a jury question (*see*, Pa.Rules Civ.Pro., rule 2959[e]).

Even assuming the continued validity of this line of reasoning, however, we note that the Pennsylvania cognovit judgment scheme has been amended in several areas relevant to the concerns expressed in *Atlas* (*see*, Pa.Rules Civ.Pro., rule 2951 *et seq.*). The main concern in *Atlas* was that the Pennsylvania cognovit procedure provided little in the way of judicial intervention, resembling more a "purely personal act." (25 N.Y.2d, at 230, 303 N.Y.S.2d 382, 250 N.E.2d 474, *supra*.) In addition to amending the procedure for opening the cognovit judgment to reduce the burden on the petitioning judgment debtor—thereby facilitating access to a judicial determination of the merits of the underlying claim—the Pennsylvania statute now provides that notice of entry be mailed by the court clerk rather than the plaintiff's attorney (Pa.Rules Civ.Pro., rule 236). Judgments rendered pursuant to this procedure are therefore "judgments" for full faith and credit purposes.

Defendants make one additional threshold argument concerning the validity of the Pennsylvania judgment, claiming that in the "predispute" context a hearing must be held to determine waiver prior to the entry of judgment in the forum State (*see, Isbell v. County of Sonoma*, 21 Cal.3d 61, 145 Cal.Rptr. 368, 577 P.2d 188, *cert. denied*, 439 U.S. 996, 99 S.Ct. 597, 58 L.Ed.2d 669). The distinction, according to defendants, rests on the indicia of reliability present when the cognovit judgment is entered into following the development of a full–blown controversy. This argument is without merit.

Rather than an artificial dichotomy based on the timing of the "dispute"—one that finds no support whatever—the need for a hearing should be determined on a case–by–case basis. A hearing at some stage would clearly be warranted where the record is insufficient to support a waiver determination (*see, In re PCH Assocs.*, 122 B.R. at 193–194, *supra*). We cannot agree with defendants, however, that as a matter of law there must in every instance be a prejudgment hearing to determine whether the debtor waived its right to notice and a prejudgment hearing.[2] Thus, there is no *per se* constitutional barrier to enforcement of Pennsylvania cognovit judgments.

III.

We are left then with the Supreme Court's conclusion that "due process rights to notice and hearing prior to a civil judgment are subject to waiver." (*Overmyer Co. v. Frick Co.*, 405 U.S., at 185, 92 S.Ct., at 782, *supra*.) All that remains is to apply the waiver analysis in the present case to determine whether defendants voluntarily, knowingly and intelligently waived those rights. We conclude that they did waive those rights as a matter of law.

Defendants were sophisticated parties involved in an arm's length commercial transaction—the transfer of a parcel of land for development as a shopping mall (*see, In re FRG, Inc. v. Manley*, 919 F.2d 850, 857 [3d Cir.]). The purchase price of the

---

[2] The California Supreme Court in *Isbell* was concerned with an entirely different procedure. That court—in concluding that a hearing prior to entry of judgment was required—contrasted the California scheme to the Ohio scheme involved in *Overmyer* by emphasizing that California provided for no notice of entry of judgment and severely restricted the grounds for postjudgment attack (145 Cal.Rptr. 368, 375, 577 P.2d 188, 195). As noted, the Pennsylvania scheme is identical to the Ohio scheme in these respects.

land alone was well in excess of $1 million, indicating the magnitude of the project. Furthermore, the parties were represented by counsel in negotiating the terms of the agreement. Defendant Aronow claims not to have had counsel—a fact disputed by plaintiffs—but Aronow himself is an attorney.

Defendants also claim that they received no consideration for the cognovit provision, citing the Supreme Court's observation in *Overmyer* that the creditors in that case had made specific concessions in order to obtain the confession of judgment clause. In fact, the present case resembles *Overmyer* in this respect: defendants sought modification of the payment terms—from a lump sum due at closing to a two–year payment schedule—and in return for this modification executed the bond and warrant. Clearly, that security device was given in exchange for the extended payment schedule.

Finally, defendants argue that, unlike the obligors in *Overmyer*, they were unaware of the cognovit clause, which they claim was "buried" in the bond and warrant. In *Overmyer*, the Supreme Court noted that the obligor did not contend that it was unaware of the cognovit provision and that "[i]ndeed, it could not do so in the light of the facts." (405 U.S., at 186, 92 S.Ct., at 783, *supra*.) The facts before us likewise belie defendants' assertion that they were unaware of the cognovit provision. The bond and warrant is a three–page document, with the cognovit clause the only provision on the last page, several lines above defendants' signatures. The bald assertion that these sophisticated defendants, entering upon a significant transaction, did not read the document cannot excuse their legal obligation or overcome the substantial evidence of waiver (*see, Metzger v. Aetna Ins. Co.*, 227 N.Y. 411, 416, 125 N.E. 814).

As the Supreme Court noted, "where the contract is one of adhesion, where there is great disparity in bargaining power, and where the debtor receives nothing for the cognovit provision, other legal consequences may ensue." (*Overmyer Co. v. Frick Co.*, 405 U.S., at 188, 92 S.Ct. at 783, *supra*.) By contrast, the contract here was not one of adhesion, but rather represented a bargain struck between sophisticated commercial parties. It is clear that defendants made a voluntary, knowing and intelligent waiver of their right to notice and an opportunity to be heard, and should be held to the consequences of their conduct.

Accordingly, the order of the Appellate Division should be affirmed, with costs.

WACHTLER, C.J., and SIMONS, ALEXANDER, TITONE, HANCOCK and BELLACOSA, JJ., concur.

Order affirmed, with costs.

————————————

Pitulla, TAKING NOTE*

You are representing a client in a divorce case. She does not have the income to pay all your fees as the case proceeds, but the marital estate is substantial. To secure your fee, may you obtain a confession of judgment from your client?

The practice of preparing a confession–of–judgment note for a client to sign for fees bypasses procedural due process requirements and presents opportunities for overreaching that avoid judicial scrutiny. In a very recent case, a lawyer was suspended for three years for various fee practices, including charging excessive fees, improperly obtaining and filing confessions of judgment against clients, and improperly attempting to limit his liability to a client for his possible malpractice. *Matter of Jacobs,* 594 N.Y.S.2d 794 (1993).

Other courts and regulatory bodies that have considered the use of a confession of judgment by an attorney to collect fees for legal services have condemned the practice as unethical. "[T]he practice creates a situation in which the client's ignorance of legal matters makes it unlikely that he will understand the character and effect of the instrument." *Hulland v. State Bar of California,* 503 P.2d. 608 (1972).

The confession, of course, can be used to attach a lien to the client's property for unadjudicated and unliquidated claims, and can violate Model Rule 1.8(j) prohibiting certain proprietary interests in the subject matter of the representation.

Cognovit notes or clauses are disfavored procedures, illegal in many states and highly restricted where allowed. See, for example, *Isbell v. County of Sonoma,* 577 P.2d 188, *cert. den* 439 U.S. 996 (1978). A client is certainly entitled to more than the minimum protection afforded all consumers. The use of a confession–of–judgement note to collect a fee impedes the court's right to determine the merits of a fee claim and gives the lawyer an unfair advantage over the client. See Section 53(e) of the Restatement of the Law Governing Lawyers, Tentative Draft No. 4 (4/10/91). It is extraordinary for a lawyer to ask a client to sign away her constitutional rights in his favor.

Every jurisdiction sets a high standard for the protection of clients in transactions with their lawyers. This concept is embodied in Model Rule 1.8(a), which prohibits a lawyer from acquiring a pecuniary interest adverse to a client unless the terms of the interest are fair and fully disclosed in writing to the client, the client is given an opportunity to seek the advice of independent counsel, and the client consents in writing.

Improperly obtaining a release from a client while the representation is ongoing also violates Rule 1.8(b), and if the judgment note exceeds the amount owed, as was true in the *Jacobs* case, Rule 1.5 prohibiting unreasonable fees is also violated.

The situation where a lawyer prepares a cognovit note in his favor can have especially pernicious effects. "The effort to collect unearned fees becomes highly oppressive and detrimental to the client when the attorney arms his demands with

---

* From: *Taking Note: Securing Fees By Confession of Judgement* by Joanne Pitulla. Reprinted by permission of the A.B.A. Journal, October 1993.

the force and weight of a judgment obtained on a confession of judgment, and thus prevents his client from contesting the reasonableness of the fees before judgment enters against her." *Hulland.*

Because of many complaints about abusive fee practices in divorce cases, last year the chief judge of the state of New York appointed a Committee to Examine Lawyer Conduct in Matrimonial Actions. The committee, composed of several judges, lawyers and government officials, held hearings and took extensive testimony from clients, lawyers, judges, officials and ethics experts.

Need Retainer Agreement

On May 4, 1993, the committee issued a lengthy Report with several strong recommendations. Recommendation No. 4 reads: "No attorney shall take a security interest, obtain a confession of judgment or otherwise obtain a lien from a client, without prior notice to the client in a signed retainer agreement and approval from the court after notice to the adversary. Mortgages placed on the marital residence shall be nonforeclosable against the spouse consenting to the mortgage."

The relationship between lawyer and client is confidential and fiduciary, and the client is dependent on the lawyer's advice, loyalty and good faith. The committee, therefore, recommended that a prospective client be provided with a retainer agreement, which should, at a minimum, contain this information:

"You are under no legal obligation to sign a confession of judgement or promissory note, or to agree to a lien or mortgage on your home to cover legal fees. Your attorney's written retainer agreement must specify whether, and under what circumstances, such security may be requested. In no event may such security interest be obtained by your attorney without prior court approval and notice to your adversary. An attorney's security interest in the marital residence shall be nonforeclosable against you."

§ 2.04 Setoff

A bank generally has the legal right to set off the amount it owes to its customer, *i.e.*, deposit accounts, against the amount owed to it by its customer, *i.e.*, loan or other obligations in default. The right can be traced to Roman law. *See* Comment, *Automatic Extinction of Cross–Demands: Compensation from Rome to California,* 53 Calif. L. Rev. 224 (1965).

ALLIED SHEET METAL FABRICATORS, INC. v.
PEOPLES NATIONAL BANK

Washington Court of Appeals
10 Wash. App. 530, 518 P.2d 734 cert. denied, 419 U.S. 967 (1974)

SWANSON, Chief Judge.

Allied Sheet Metal Fabricators, Inc. ("Allied") appeals from a summary judgment in favor of defendant Peoples National Bank of Washington ("Peoples") dismissing Allied's $2,000,000 claim for damages allegedly caused by Peoples' action in terminating its credit relationship with Allied.

The affidavits considered by the trial court disclosed these undisputed facts: In a series of loans commencing in 1968, Peoples financed Allied's sheet metal fabricating plant under the terms of security agreements wherein Allied pledged accounts receivable and other collateral to secure the loans. Although at the outset the financing was done on the basis of term loans, after July 1, 1969, all loans, including those here in question, were made on the basis of demand promissory notes. After loaning Allied an additional $100,000 evidenced by two $50,000 demand notes executed October 8 and 9, 1970, respectively, Peoples decided on October 15, 1970, to take immediate steps to collect Allied's total accrued debt in excess of $420,000. Peoples acted by applying Allied's checking account deposits in the bank to the debt without prior notice to Allied with the result that checks outstanding issued by Allied totaling $38,593.12 were dishonored. On October 16, 1970, Peoples notified Allied of the action it had taken and demanded payment of the entire loan balance which, after the offset of Allied's checking accounts in the amount of approximately $106,000 amounted to about $314,000.

The affidavit of Allied's president in effect claims bad faith on the part of the bank and states that the bank knew at the time the last two loans were negotiated on October 8 and 9, 1970, that the proceeds of such loans were "earmarked for the payment of specific liabilities and the general operation of the company, . . ." The affidavit of the bank's senior vice–president, Joshua Green, III, stated in substance that Allied's entire indebtedness to the bank was based upon demand promissory notes, and that Allied's financial position was such that the bank had to exercise its rights to safeguard payment of the loan balance. Thereafter, credit was given to Allied by Peoples to enable it to find other acceptable means of financing its operation, and on January 20, 1971, the balance of the indebtedness owing Peoples was paid. On the following day, Allied commenced suit against Peoples for $100,000 in damages, and later amended its complaint to claim $2,000,000.

. . . .

[T]he trial court concluded that there was no genuine issue as to any material fact and granted summary judgment of dismissal. This appeal follows.

Allied's argument is essentially that Peoples breached its contract with Allied (1) by claiming the entire balance of Allied's indebtedness due without a declaration of default pursuant to the terms of the security agreement, and (2) by failing to make any demand for payment prior to the setoff of Allied's debt against its bank accounts.

Therefore, Allied contends Peoples had no right to apply the bank accounts to Allied's debt and alleges that such misappropriation of the checking account funds resulted in the wrongful dishonor of Allied's checks to suppliers, creditors and employees and caused the damages claimed.

We are of the opinion that Allied's assertion of breach of contract is based on a misconception of what constituted the agreement between the parties. Allied apparently believes that the general written security agreement between the parties constituted a contract guaranteeing continued financing which could not be terminated without a formal declaration of default pursuant to that agreement even though the loans in question were all based on demand promissory notes. We are persuaded that the trial court, based upon the undisputed facts, correctly interpreted the nature of the agreement between the parties, and that agreement is expressed on the face of the demand notes. In short, the provisions of the security agreement are irrelevant and simply not applicable to the actions of Peoples challenged by Allied, because such actions were based on the uncontroverted terms of the demand notes. In this connection, contrary to appellant's contention, the mere fact that Peoples had provided financing to Allied continuously since 1968 effected no change in the terms of the demand notes and did not alter the rights of the parties thereby created. Allied failed to set forth any facts which indicate a commitment by Peoples for continued financing or extension of credit and therefore the demand notes, which indicate the contrary, are controlling.

Further, it is apparent that Allied's affidavits create no issue of fact, for they only show that Allied was a borrower from Peoples and that its loans were evidenced by demand promissory notes. The additional facts stated in Allied's affidavit that its obligations were secured by collateral pursuant to security agreements, that money had been loaned over a period of years, and that the bank notified debtors of Allied's accounts receivable to pay directly to Peoples bank, are nondeterminative of any issue in the case. We conclude that Peoples met its burden of showing that no genuine issue as to any material fact exists.

It is elementary that a demand note is payable immediately on the date of its execution. The general rule is well stated in 11 Am.Jur.2d, Bills & Notes § 286 (1963):

> An instrument is payable immediately if no time is fixed and no contingency specified upon which payment is to be made. A demand note is payable immediately on the date of its execution—that is, it is due upon delivery thereof; and, unless a statute declares otherwise, or a contrary intention appears expressly or impliedly upon the face of the instrument, a right of action against the maker of a demand note arises immediately upon delivery and no express demand is required to mature the note or as a prerequisite to such right of action, commencement of a suit being sufficient demand for enforcement purposes.

(Footnotes omitted.) RCW 62A.3–122(1) states in part:

> A cause of action against a maker or an acceptor accrues

. . . .

(b) in the case of a demand instrument upon its date or, if no date is stated, on the date of issue.

See also Northwestern Nat'l Bank v. Pearson, 102 Wash. 570, 173 P. 730 (1918). A second principle fundamental to banking practice which deserves emphasis is that the relationship of a depositor to the bank is that of creditor to a debtor, the bank being the debtor. This basic rule of banking law is explained in 10 Am.Jur.2d, Banks § 339 (1963):

> Although money on deposit in a bank is commonly considered to be the property of the depositor, the relationship in fact between him and the bank is that of debtor and creditor; the amount on deposit represents merely an indebtedness by the bank to the depositor. It is therefore a fundamental rule of banking law that in the case of a general deposit of money in a bank, the moment the money is deposited it actually becomes the property of the bank, and the bank and the depositor assume the legal relation of debtor and creditor.

(Footnotes omitted.) *See Carlson v. Kies,* 75 Wash. 171, 134 P. 808 (1913). *See also State ex rel. Graham v. Olympia,* 80 Wash.2d 672, 497 P.2d 924 (1972).

In the case at bar, although the bank occupied the position of debtor regarding Allied's various checking accounts, it was of course Allied's creditor as to loans. In view of this debtor–creditor relationship between the parties, we hold Peoples had the right to setoff its indebtedness—the amount Peoples owed Allied arising out of Allied's checking account deposits—against Allied's indebtedness—the amount Allied owed Peoples because of Peoples' loans to Allied.

> It is a general rule that when a depositor is indebted to a bank, and the debts are mutual—that is, between the same parties and in the same right—the bank may apply the deposit, or such portion thereof as may be necessary, to the payment of the debt due it by the depositor. . . .

10 Am.Jur.2d, Banks § 666 (1963). *See also Walton Lbr. Co. v. State Bank,* 140 Wash. 133, 248 P. 82 (1926); *Commercial Bank & Trust Co. v. Minshull,* 137 Wash. 224, 242 P. 29 (1926); *Connor v. First Nat'l Bank,* 113 Wash. 662, 194 P. 562 (1921); *Bank of California v. Starrett,* 110 Wash. 231, 188 P. 410 (1920); *Hanson v. Northern Bank & Trust Co.,* 98 Wash. 124, 167 P. 97 (1917).

Allied argues, however, that the foregoing general rule permitting a setoff in the case of a demand note does not apply until after the bank exhausts its primary collateral security, and Peoples failed to do this. In this regard, Allied relies primarily upon an early California case, *McKean v. German–American Sav. Bank,* 118 Cal. 334, 50 P. 656 (1897); however, *McKean* states a minority view, and we decline to follow it. The position adopted by the majority of modern jurisdictions is well expressed in *Olsen v. Valley Nat'l Bank,* 91 Ill.App.2d 365, 371, 234 N.E.2d 547, 550 (1968), as follows:

> A bank should not be deprived of its right of set–off simply because it has the foresight to obtain collateral in exchange for obligations owed to it. The majority rule, including Illinois, is founded on the rationale that a creditor is able to pursue any one of a number of remedies against a debtor until the debt

is satisfied. The minority rule is based upon the rule or statute that there is but one action for the recovery of a debt which is secured by collateral.

Although there appears to be no Washington authority directly in point, we are persuaded that the better reasoned view is expressed in *Olsen* which recognizes the multiple remedies of a creditor, and therefore we apply that rule to the case at bar. *See Peoples Nat'l Bank v. Peterson,* 7 Wash.App. 196, 498 P.2d 884 (1972), *aff'd,* 82 Wash.2d 822, 514 P.2d 159 (1973).

Allied also challenges Peoples' right of setoff on the basis of a generally recognized exception to that right which prohibits such setoff in the case of special purpose accounts. Allied argues that this exception applies here because Peoples exercised its right of setoff against Allied's payroll account which Allied contends is a special purpose account. *See Spiroplos v. Scandinavian–American Bank,* 116 Wash. 491, 199 P. 997 (1921).

Assuming arguendo that Allied's payroll account was a special account, Allied's argument may have presented an issue of fact; however, the affidavit of the bank's senior vice–president, Joshua Green, III, states that the payroll account was not offset but rather was placed on a control basis and that all payroll checks were, in fact, paid, with the exception of one, and that this check was paid upon representment. Further, although an affidavit of one of Allied's employees indicates that a payroll check presented on October 16 was dishonored, he does not deny that it was paid upon representment. We conclude that under such circumstances, there is no issue of fact, and any damage would be de minimis.

Allied's final contention is that even if the bank was authorized notwithstanding the terms of the security agreement to do what it did, *i.e.,* offset Allied's checking account balance against its debt to the bank without prior notice or hearing, the bank's actions nevertheless constituted an unlawful taking of property in violation of the due process provisions of the Fourteenth Amendment to the United States Constitution and article 1, § 3 of the Washington State Constitution. We reject this contention for these reasons: First, appellant premises its argument attacking the bank's actions on the erroneous assumption that the bank's authority for taking the steps it did rested, if at all, upon the terms of the security agreement. As we have previously indicated, the controlling authority for the bank's actions is not the security agreement but the contract formed by the demand notes and the rights created by the debtor–creditor relationship of the parties.

Secondly, Allied fails, by either argument or citation of authority, to support its assertion that the bank's actions in these circumstances amount to a deprivation or a taking of a significant property interest. Inasmuch as Allied's deposits to its checking account became the bank's property upon deposit and Allied was merely the bank's creditor as to such deposits, the question arises whether the bank's actions properly may be characterized as a seizure or taking of Allied's property. In any event, we need not decide this question in the absence of a showing by Allied that there was significant state involvement in the alleged taking, which is a necessary prerequisite to the implementation of due process protections. It has been consistently recognized in the cases dealing with the "state action" question that the conduct of private individuals, no matter how wrongful, does not fall within the ambit of the constitutional prohibition unless the government is involved to some significant extent in the private conduct which violates due process rights. *Moose Lodge No. 107 v. Irvis*, 407 U.S. 163, 92 S. Ct. 1965, 32 L. Ed. 2d 627 (1972); *Burton v. Wilmington Parking Authority*, 365 U.S. 715, 81 S. Ct. 856, 6 L. Ed. 2d 45 (1961).

Allied argues that state action may be found if private acts, which would be unconstitutional if done by a public body, are judicially enforced. In support of its argument, Allied directs us to *Shelley v. Kraemer*, 334 U.S. 1, 68 S. Ct. 836, 92 L.Ed. 1161 (1948), which dealt with judicial enforcement of a racially discriminative covenant, and *Reitman v. Mulkey*, 387 U.S. 369, 87 S. Ct. 1627, 18 L. Ed. 2d 830 (1967), where the state was found to be sufficiently involved to support a challenge to the constitutionality of a proposition approved by the electorate of the state of California aimed at repealing fair housing laws.

Allied's reliance on the cited cases which involved racial discrimination is misplaced in the context of the question presented here as to whether state action may be found in nonjudicial self–help between private parties. *See Oller v. Bank of America*, 342 F.Supp. 21 (N.D.Cal.1972). In the case at bar, the judiciary is not being asked to enforce what the bank has done, nor to grant affirmative relief. We have here a private transaction between a borrower and a lending institution, and the actions complained of were taken without seeking state help and without any involvement of state officials. As the court observed in *Oller*, which involved self–help repossession pursuant to a private contract, at 23:

> The Bank is not a governmental or even quasi–governmental agency; no government official acts with the Bank in the matter of repossession; the act of repossession is not compelled; the authority to repossess is based on a contractual right which had been judicially approved prior to the adoption of the statutes in question.
>
> What we have here is a private act taken by a private organization to protect its security interest in personal property that is subject to a conditional sales contract. The courts have been almost uniform in refusing to color such transactions as "State actions". [Citation omitted.]

We note that appellant places principal reliance in its brief upon *Adams v. Egley*, 338 F.Supp. 614 (S.D.Cal.1972), decided prior to *Oller*, in which the court found sufficient state action in a bank's repossession of property, pursuant to a private contract, on the basis of the fact that certain provisions of the Uniform Commercial Code had been incorporated into the contract; however, subsequent to the oral argument in this case, *Adams* was reversed on appeal. *See Adams v. Southern California First Nat'l Bank*, 492 F.2d 324 (9 Cir. 1973), petition for rehearing en banc pending.

Therefore, assuming without deciding that Allied was deprived of a significant property interest by the bank's action of setoff, we nevertheless find no significant state involvement and therefore we cannot sustain Allied's position on the basis of the federal and state constitutional prohibitions against the taking of property without due process of law.

Judgment affirmed.

FARRIS and JAMES, JJ., concur.

NOTES AND QUESTIONS

(1) Is a customer's consent required before the bank can exercise its right to set off? *See Biby v. Union National Bank*, 162 N.W.2d 370 (N.D. 1968) (although state law required depositor's prior consent, signature card agreement incorporating by reference the bank's rules and regulations deemed consent).

(2) A bank's unilateral setoff has survived constitutional scrutiny. *See Kruger v. Wells Fargo Bank*, 11 Cal.3d 352 521 P.2d 441, 113 Cal.Rptr.449 (Cal. 1974); Annot., 65 A.L.R.3d 1284 (1975).

(3) The bank's right of setoff can only be triggered if the customer's debt is due and owing. In what way was the plaintiff's debt in *Allied* due and owing? What determines whether a debt is in default?

(4) The bank's right of setoff can only be exercised if the debts are mutual. The plaintiff in *Allied* asserted that the bank set off deposits in a special payroll account. Could a bank set off deposits in an attorney's escrow account against a debt owed to the bank by the attorney personally? What about joint accounts where only one person is indebted to the bank? What about an account that includes identifiable cash proceeds from a perfected security interest in inventory? *See generally* Clark, *Bank Exercise of Setoff: Avoiding the Pitfalls*, 98 Bank. L.J. 196 (1981).

(5) Section 362(a)(7) of the Bankruptcy Code, 11 U.S.C. § 362(a)(7), automatically stays the exercise of the right of setoff once a petition for relief under the Bankruptcy Code is filed. Section 553 of the Bankruptcy Code, 11 U.S.C. § 553, preserves the creditor's right of setoff and provides some limitations to a setoff exercised within 90 days of the filing of a petition under the Bankruptcy Code. A bank's claim that is subject to setoff is deemed a secured claim. Section 506(a) to the Bankruptcy Code, 11 U.S.C. § 506(a). *See Citizens Bank of Maryland v. Strumpf*, —U.S.— 1995 WL633458 (1995)(bank's temporary withholding of payment to protect setoff rights does not violate automatic stay; intent to effect a permanent taking necessary for setoff).

(6) Federal and state laws include some limitations on the right of setoff. *See, e.g.*, Section 169 of the Fair Credit Billing Act of 1974, 15 U.S.C. § 1666h (no setoff against deposit accounts for debts arising out of bank's credit card plan).

CHAPTER **3**

ENFORCEMENT OF MONEY JUDGMENTS

§ 3.01 Introduction

This chapter will discuss the problems, some substantive, some procedural, inherent in the judgment creditor's enforcement of a claim against the debtor. Thus far, the course of study in law school has centered around substantive rights and obligations between the parties to a dispute, with the appellate decisions and statutory law being used to determine whether one party owes another an enforceable obligation. This chapter picks up after a final judicial determination results in the award of a money judgment. Enforcement of the non–money judgment is generally simple, and often the judgment is self–executing (*e.g.*, divorce). Money judgments, however, may require a number of different enforcement devices and substantial ingenuity by the judgment creditor's counsel.

The successful party is interested only in getting paid once the money judgment becomes final. In most instances, the judgment is satisfied voluntarily, although unwillingly perhaps, but no further legal problem arises. Suppose, on the other hand, the unsuccessful litigant is unwilling or unable to satisfy the judgment by use of his liquid assets. What recourse does the judgment creditor have?

§ 3.02 The Judgment Creditor's Objectives

[A] Property Available to Satisfy the Judgment

The judgment creditor must first understand what property of the debtor may be applied toward satisfaction of the judgment. This is always a matter of state law and generally includes all property in which the debtor has a property interest. Problems arise, however, when the judgment debtor holds only legal title for a third party (*e.g.*, a trust beneficiary), when the debtor's property is subject to a prior consensual lien, or when the debtor's property is held subject to a contractual restriction (*e.g.*, escrow). In these cases, the judgment creditor generally gets no greater rights than the judgment debtor. Each state also has its own "exemption" law that insulates certain types of property from the claims of creditors. The problems relating to exemption laws are covered in Chapter 7, *infra*. Finding unencumbered or "free" non–exempt assets, therefore, is always the creditor's first objective.

[B] Locating Assets

Once the judgment creditor understands what property can be reached, the next objective is to locate that property. Again, the post–judgment discovery available varies from state to state, but is generally similar to pre–trial discovery procedure (*e.g.*, subpoenas, depositions). Because the creditor has already obtained a judgment, most states will give the judgment creditor much more leeway in enforcing these devices, not only against the debtor, but also against third parties who may have possession of the judgment debtor's assets. How to use the various post–judgment discovery devices is an important tactical consideration for the judgment creditor. For example, deposing the judgment debtor's accountants may be much more effective than deposing the debtor. The accountants may have more documentary information, and will probably have maintained it in a more organized manner than the debtor. Most important, accountants have much less incentive to obstruct the examination.

[C] Keeping Assets in Place

Preventing transfer of the judgment debtor's assets is another key objective. Most states permit the judgment creditor to restrain the debtor's transfer of cash, real estate, and personal property. Again, the particular form of the restraint turns on local law, with which the judgment creditor's counsel must be thoroughly familiar. As will be shown in this chapter, competing judgment creditors may already be proceeding against the very assets sought to be frozen, and the judgment creditor may be too late. At the very least, a firm grasp of the applicable procedure may enable the judgment creditor to share in a distribution of the previously encumbered assets.

[D] Realizing on Assets

The most important objective of the judgment creditor is to realize upon the debtor's property. Counsel for the judgment creditor must understand how to reach possessory interests of the judgment debtor when title is lacking, and how to obtain turnover of property when possession is lacking. Equally important is the ability of the judgment creditor to reach such intangibles as accounts receivable, which can generate the cash to satisfy the judgment. The judgment creditor must not only be able to reach tangible property such as automobiles, jewelry and real estate, but also concealed property in the hands of family members, friends, and affiliated corporations. In many cases the individual debtor's only asset is his or her earning power. Because most states have restrictions on the ability of a judgment creditor to realize upon a debtor's income, the judgment creditor's counsel must become familiar with these procedures to be in a position to force satisfaction of the judgment quickly and effectively.

§ 3.03 Tactics

Once the judgment creditor has defined goals—locating, restraining the disposition of, and reaching the debtor's assets—counsel may turn to a variety of procedural devices. There usually is no need to use every device, and no one particular device should necessarily be used first. Which device is used and in what order are tactical considerations for the judgment creditor and counsel.

§ 3.04 Protection of the Debtor and Third Parties

Most jurisdictions provide judgment debtors with protection from abusive judgment enforcement tactics. For example, the judgment creditor who tries to reach property that does not belong to the debtor can be stopped quickly. The judgment creditor who tries to harass the judgment debtor's family members can also be stopped in appropriate circumstances. And, as we shall see in this chapter, when a judgment creditor threatens to destroy the debtor's sole source of income, the court may use its discretionary power to stay the creditor temporarily on certain conditions. *See, e.g., Moskin v. Midland Bank & Trust Co.*, 96 Misc. 2d 600 (Sup. Ct., N.Y. Co. 1978). Typically, the court may require the judgment debtor to make periodic payments to the judgment creditor as a condition to the stay of enforcement. In this way, the judgment creditor gets paid, and the judgment debtor can continue earning a living and paying other creditors.

§ 3.05 Priority Problems

This chapter also deals with the priority problem that arises when two or more judgment creditors are competing for the same assets. Because of the variety of judgment enforcement devices, the savvy lawyer representing the judgment creditor must know which device is more likely to preserve the client's priority. In one case, for example, a seemingly diligent judgment creditor obtained a restraining order, only to find that a less diligent creditor with an execution levy had priority. *See City of New York v. Panzirer*, 23 A.D.2d 158, 259 N.Y.S.2d 284 (App. Div. 1st Dep't 1965)(*infra*).

More often than not, the debtor's assets have been previously encumbered by a consensual lien, such as a mortgage or security interest. Assuming the prior lien is valid, the judgment creditor may be frustrated in enforcing the judgment. Can the property still be realized on, with the later execution creditor marshalling the sale proceeds and applying them first to the prior consensual lien? The materials will discuss the different state law approaches to this frequently asked question. But what if the prior security interest is "unperfected?" Section 9–301(b) of the Uniform Commercial Code provides that "an unperfected security interest is subordinate to the rights of . . . a person who becomes a lien creditor before the security interest is perfected. . . ." "Lien creditor," of course, is defined in U.C.C. § 9–301(d)(3) to include a judicial lien creditor. And when the United States is also a creditor, the executing judgment creditor has a host of new problems, which are discussed in Chapter 5, *infra*.

§ 3.06 The Spectre of Bankruptcy

The ultimate limitation on the judgment creditor's remedies is bankruptcy. Typically, when too many judgment creditors pursue the debtor, or even when there is just one aggressive creditor with a large judgment, the debtor will seek relief under the Bankruptcy Code. Filing a bankruptcy petition operates as an automatic stay of all judgment enforcement devices. *See* 11 U.S.C. § 362(a). Occasionally, bankruptcy is just what the judgment creditor may want, because of the broad discovery, the investigative and avoiding powers of the trustee, and other cost–saving devices. When a debtor has twelve or more creditors, three petitioning creditors are necessary to file an involuntary bankruptcy petition against the debtor. 11 U.S.C. § 303(b). Many judgment creditors find that other creditors are reluctant to join in the filing of an involuntary petition. Therefore, an aggressive pursuit of the debtor's assets by means of the available judgment enforcement devices may very well force the debtor voluntarily into bankruptcy, if the judgment creditor is not paid first. Although bankruptcy often results in the creditor's being paid, it may also result in the creditor's ending up with less than might have been realized before with a little patience. This very topic (*i.e.*, recovery outside of bankruptcy compared to a bankruptcy distribution) is usually the subject of negotiations between the judgment debtor and judgment creditor, resulting in an agreement providing for satisfaction of the judgment over a period of time. In sum, because of the possibility of bankruptcy, counsel for the judgment creditor must not only be pragmatic, but also flexible.

§ 3.07 Necessity of Having a Lien

The creditor with a mere judgment generally has no right to satisfy the claim out of the debtor's assets. Something more than a bare obligation, even though reduced to a judgment of liability, is necessary to give the creditor that right. That something more is a lien.

A lien is not, in the full sense, an interest in property as property interests are usually conceived. It gives the lienholder a right to enforce an obligation out of property subject to the lien. There are three categories of liens with the same essential underlying purpose. The three categories—consensual, judicial and statutory—are dependent upon the methods of their creation rather than the consequences that flow from them.

[A] Consensual Liens

Consensual liens are created by and dependent upon an agreement between the parties. The real estate mortgage regulated by state statute and the personal property security interest regulated by Article 9 of the Uniform Commercial Code are examples. Although these statutes may limit the consensual lien, with provisions governing matters such as perfection, priority and enforcement, the agreement or contract is the first and foremost essential feature of this lien.

[B] Judicial Liens

Judicial liens arise out of judicial proceedings. Examples are the judgment lien, attachment lien, and garnishment lien. Again, procedural statutes of a regulatory nature exist, but a judicial proceeding—pending or imminent—is the essential element. For a judgment creditor, getting the lien is all–important, because it not only establishes rights in the debtor's property, but also enables the creditor to proceed against that property to satisfy the judgment. As discussed in these materials, when the lien arises and when it attaches are of crucial importance. Many states, for example, have rules providing that a judicial lien on the debtor's personal property arises when the judgment creditor delivers a writ of execution to the sheriff so long as the sheriff levies on the property promptly.

[C] Statutory Liens

The statutory lien is created by statute, usually for the benefit of some recognized economic class. Examples include mechanics' liens, materialmen's liens, warehousemen's liens, landlord's liens, garagemen's liens, and tax liens. These liens are not dependent upon any agreement between the parties, nor is the statutory lien dependent upon any judicial proceeding pending or to be instituted.

Rarely is it necessary to distinguish among the three types of liens. In bankruptcy, however, the classification may well become important, and the details will be covered in the second part of this book. Outside of a case under the Bankruptcy Code, all three types of liens are used, absent the debtor's voluntary payment, as a means to enforce payment of a claim from property belonging to the debtor.

The judicial lien and the federal tax lien will be discussed in these materials. Secured transactions under Article 9 of the Uniform Commercial Code and real property mortgages are generally beyond the scope of this course, but will be referred to on occasion. How judicial and tax liens are created, and various issues of priority in different circumstances, are issues encompassed within the following problem. Try to resolve these issues after reading the materials dealing with federal tax liens in Chapter 5, *infra*.

GENERAL REFERENCES

6 Weinstein–Korn–Miller, New York Civil Practice, Article 52 (1983 rev. ed.).

Kennedy, *The Relative Priority of the Federal Government: The Pernicious Career of the Inchoate and General Lien*, 63 Yale L.J. 905 (1954).

Murray, *Execution Lien Creditors Versus Bona Fide Purchasers, Lenders and Other Execution Lien Creditors: Charles II and the Uniform Commercial Code*, 85 Com. L.J. 485 (1980).

Riesenfeld, *Collection of Money Judgments in American Law*, 42 Iowa L. Rev. 155 (1957).

Sherwin, How To Collect A Money Judgment (1975 rev. ed.) (Attorneys' Aid Publications).

DISCUSSION PROBLEM

Joe Debtor owned real property in New York County valued at $15,000, an automobile having a book value of $2,500, and cash in a bank savings account amounting to $10,000. Both the car and the bank account were also located in New York County. Suits were filed against Debtor in January, February and March of 1978 for debts owing to the various claimants, and these suits resulted in the following judgments against Debtor:

Creditor *A*: judgment for $20,000 on July 15, 1978;

Creditor *B*: judgment for $20,000 on August 1, 1978;

Creditor *C*: judgment for $20,000 on September 1, 1978.

In each case, the creditor docketed the judgment in New York County on the date the judgment was rendered.

In October of 1978, Creditor *B* issued a writ of execution and delivered it to the proper sheriff on the 10th. On the 12th of that month, Creditor *C* issued a writ of execution to the city marshall, the proper officer because *C*'s judgment was obtained in the Civil Court. Creditor *A* properly delivered her writ of execution to the same sheriff as *B*'s, on the 13th. On the 14th, when the sheriff attempted to levy on the car, he found possession thereof had been taken by the marshall on the 12th. The sheriff accordingly returned the writs to *A* and *B* unsatisfied, with the notation, "no property found." The car was sold by the marshall for $1,500, and the proceeds were credited against *C*'s judgment.

In November of 1978, Debtor inherited an additional parcel of realty located in New York County. This event came to *A*'s attention, and she immediately caused a writ of execution to issue and levy was made thereon. *B* and *C* join in the judicial sale of that real property, claiming a share of the proceeds or that their liens remain attached to the property if it is sold by the sheriff. The property is valued at $12,000.

When *B* started his suit, he was able to obtain an order of attachment because Debtor could not be found for service. Under that order, *B* caused the sheriff to attach Debtor's bank account. On April 1, 1978, the United States Government, through the Internal Revenue Service, filed notice of tax lien in New York County in the amount of $25,000 under an assessment made in November, 1977 for taxes owing for the years 1974 and 1975.

All parties, property or proceeds are before the court in one proceeding. The parties ask the court to adjudicate proper distribution to the extent possible so as to satisfy the respective debts.

What should the court do and why?

§ 3.08   Judgment Liens

After obtaining a judgment, the judgment creditor must take the appropriate legal steps so that judgment can be enforced against a recalcitrant debtor. In most states, the first step in judgment enforcement is to docket the judgment, thereby creating a "judgment lien."

JACKSON v. SEARS, ROEBUCK AND CO.

Arizona Supreme Court
83 Ariz. 20, 315 P.2d 871 (1957)

STRUCKMEYER, Justice.

Appellee, as plaintiff in the court below, sued Clarence O. Jackson, appellant herein, on the balance due on an account. Trial was duly had before the Court sitting without a jury and on the 18th day of May, 1955, the trial judge wrote a letter to the Clerk of Court of Maricopa County stating in part as follows: "You will please let the record show that judgment be entered for the plaintiff . . . from date. . . ." This letter was received by the Clerk on the following day, but no order was entered on the civil docket until May 31, 1955. The notation in the civil docket provides:

> May 31, 1955 Judgment entered from minutes of May 19, 1955—Div. 2—"It is Ordered that plaintiff have Judgment against the defendant for the sum of $625.59 with interest at the rate of 6% per annum from date each party to bear their own costs."

Five days prior to the above entry of judgment, that is, on May 26, 1955, appellee caused an execution to issue against real property owned by appellant, and subsequently the sheriff of Maricopa County levied upon and sold it to appellee for the amount of the judgment, together with interest and costs. It is appellant's position that on the 26th day of May, 1955 there was no valid judgment upon which execution could issue; that accordingly, all subsequent proceedings, including execution, sale, and delivery of sheriff's deed were void and a nullity.

It is the general rule that an execution issued without a judgment to support it is void, no authority is conferred upon the officer to whom it is directed, and even if a judgment is subsequently obtained, it will not have a retroactive effect so as to validate the execution. *Evans v. City of American Falls*, 52 Idaho 7, 11 P. 2d 363, 368; *Bovard v. Bovard*, 233 Mo. App. 1019, 128 S.W.2d 274. The foregoing general rule must be distinguished from those situations where the matters are merely irregularities which can, or have been, removed. There the execution is voidable and if the matter causing the irregularity has been removed, a motion to quash will be denied and the execution and levy thereunder will stand. *Mosher v. Ganz*, 42 Ariz. 314, 25 P.2d 555. There is by no means a unanimity of opinion as to whether this present case presents a curable irregularity.

At the common law, an execution might issue as soon as the final judgment was signed, before its entry of record, nor was the docketing of the judgment deemed essential to execution. *Stevens v. Manson*, 87 Me. 436, 32 Atl. 1002. Most of the early cases held that the execution, if issued after pronouncement or rendition of judgment, could not be voided by a showing that the judgment had not, in fact, been entered at the time of issuance. *Los Angeles Bank v. Raynor*, 61 Cal. 145; *Weigley v. Matson*, 125 Ill. 64, 16 N.E. 881. . . .

In recent cases, it has been held that a judgment is operative from the date of its rendition, and that the failure of the clerk to perform the ministerial act of entering the judgment of record does not delay its operation, *State v. Haney, Mo.*, 277 S.W.2d 632; *Cinebar Coal & Coke Co. v. Robinson*, 1 Wash.2d 620, 97 P.2d 128; and a judgment after its entry relates back to the time of its pronouncement. *Wickiser v. Powers*, 324 Ill.App. 130, 57 N.E.2d 522. In some states, by virtue of statute, execution may issue after judgment has been rendered; *e.g. Ex Parte Lewis*, 335 Mich. 640, 56 N.W.2d 211. At the present time, both the clear weight of authority and statutory trend do not require a formal entry after pronouncement or rendition of judgment in order for a valid execution to issue. 21 Am.Jur., Executions, section 21, p. 26.

However, in this state, both by statute and rule of procedure, the formal entry by the clerk is an indispensable prerequisite to valid execution. Rule 79(a), Rules of Civil Procedure, 16 A.R.S., requires the clerk of the court to keep a book known as the "civil docket" in which shall be entered all judgments. Rule 58(a) provides that the notation in the civil docket constitutes entry of judgment and the judgment *"is not effective before such entry."* These rules of civil procedure have been several times construed, the most recent being *Harbel Oil Co. v. Steele*, 81 Ariz. 104, 301 P.2d 757, 758, reversing 80 Ariz. 368, 298 P.2d 789. There we said, "For our purpose here it is immaterial when the order or judgment was announced or ordered—it was not effective until it was entered in the docket."

Not only is a judgment ineffective until entry thereof in the civil docket, but the legislature has provided that "the party in whose favor a judgment is given may, at any time within five years *after entry of the judgment,* have a writ of execution issued for its enforcement." A.R.S. § 12–1551, subd. A. The time of entry is the day when the clerk makes the notation in the civil docket. By the specific language of the statute, execution may not issue prior to such entry. Where the statute requires that a judgment be entered before execution, there can be no valid or lawful execution without such an entry. *Tanner v. Wilson*, 184 Ga. 628, 192 S.E. 425. Since the execution was issued five days prior to the entry of judgment, it was issued without authority of law and was a legal nullity. The subsequent acts and matters dependent thereon, including levy, sale, and the sheriff's deed are void.

Without the determination of further questions raised which need not be discussed in the light of our conclusions here, the judgment of the court below is reversed with directions that the execution be quashed and all proceedings had thereunder be vacated and set aside.

UDALL, C. J., and WINDES, PHELPS and JOHNSON, JJ., concur.

NOTES AND QUESTIONS

(1) This case illustrates the importance of thoroughly examining the local laws concerning the enforcement of judgments before proceeding to execute upon a judgment.

(2) In New York, the first step towards enforcing a judgment is to have the judgment entered by the clerk. N.Y. Civ. Prac. R. § 5017(a). In addition, a "judgment–roll," consisting of "the summons, pleadings, admissions, each judgment and each order involving the merits or necessarily affecting the final judgment," must also be simultaneously filed. On filing the judgment–roll, the clerk automatically "dockets" the judgment, which in turn creates a lien.

N.Y. Civ. Proc. R. § 5017.

(a) *Docketing by clerk; docketing elsewhere by transcript.* Immediately after filing the judgment–roll the clerk shall docket a money judgment, and at the request of any party specifying the particular adverse party or parties against whom docketing shall be made, the clerk shall so docket a judgment affecting the title to real property, provided, however, that where the clerk maintains a section and block index, a judgment affecting the title to, or the possession, use or enjoyment of, real property may be entered in such index in lieu thereof. . . .

(b) *Docketing of judgment of court of United States.* A transcript of the judgment of a court of the United States rendered or filed within the state may be filed in the office of the clerk of any county and upon such filing the clerk shall docket the judgment in the same manner and with the same effect as a judgment entered in the supreme court within the county.

(c) *Form of docketing.* A judgment is docketed by making an entry in the proper docket book as follows:

1. under the surname of the judgment debtor first named in the judgment, the entry shall consist of:

(i) the name and last known address of each judgment debtor and his trade or profession if stated in the judgment;

(ii) the name and last known address of the judgment creditor;

(iii) the sum recovered or directed to be paid in figures;

(iv) the date and time the judgment–roll was filed;

(v) the date and time of docketing;

(vi) the court and county in which judgment was entered; and

(vii) the name and office address of the attorney for the judgment creditor.

Under N.Y. Civ. Prac. R. § 5018, if a judgment affects the title to real property the judgment can be entered in the real property section and block index, if such an index is maintained. This should alert any potential real estate purchaser to the judgment creditor's lien on the title.

California similarly provides for the creation of a judgment lien by filing the appropriate notice after entry of the money judgment. Cal. Civ. Proc. Code §§ 697.310 and 697.510.

(3) While a judgment lien can protect the creditor against certain bona fide purchasers, it does not compel the debtor to pay the money judgment. In fact, the judgment lien itself has a limited lifespan. In New York the statute of limitations on a money judgment is twenty years. N.Y. Civ. Prac. R. § 211(b). In California, it is ten years on real property and five years on personal property. Cal. Civ. Proc. Code §§ 697.310(a) and 697.510(b).

(4) Note also the procedure for enforcing federal court judgments rendered "within the state." Why does New York have this procedure? *See* Fed. R. Civ. P. 69; *Knapp v. McFarland*, 462 F.2d 935 (2d Cir. 1972) (*infra*). What about federal judgments rendered outside the state? How, for example, does the out–of–state judgment creditor with a federal judgment execute on assets in another forum?

§ 3.09   Finding the Assets of the Judgment Debtor

The judgment creditor often has little or no idea what the debtor's assets are or where they may be located. Most states assist the creditor in identifying and locating assets with so–called "supplementary proceedings."

Not all of the debtor's property can be reached to enforce a money judgment, but the categories of property that can be reached are usually quite broad. In New York, the type of property available to the judgment creditor is defined by N.Y. Civ. Prac. R. § 5201:

(a) *Debt against which a money judgment may be enforced.* A money judgment may be enforced against any debt, which is past due or which is yet to become due, certainly or upon demand of the judgment debtor, whether it was incurred within or without the state, to or from a resident or non–resident, unless it is exempt from application to the satisfaction of the judgment. A debt may consist of a cause of action which could be assigned or transferred accruing within or without the state.

(b) *Property against which a money judgment may be enforced.* A money judgment may be enforced against any property which could be assigned or transferred, whether it consists of a present or future right or interest and whether or not it is vested, unless it is exempt from application to the satisfaction of the judgment.

The general rule in New York that the judgment can be enforced against *any* assignable property is contained in § 5201(b), although § 5201(a) apparently allows pursuit only of non–contingent debts. *See ABKCO Industries, Inc. v. Apple Films, Inc.,* 39 N.Y.2d 670 (1976). (Court permitted pre–judgment attachment of the licensor's right to receive 80% of the licensee's net profits for promoting the Beatles' film "Let It Be." Although, at the time of attachment, little or no revenue had been collected by the licensee, the court held that the licensor's interest was intangible personal property and was of economic significance.).

California does not permit execution against a pending cause of action, although most other types of the debtor's property are subject to levy. Cal. Civ. Proc. Code §§ 695.010, 695.030 and 699.710.

Certain property of the debtor is exempt from levy. These exemption statutes vary greatly from state to state. The general idea is to leave individual debtors with shirts on their backs and roofs over their heads. These statutes are rarely revised and thus tend to be antiquated; even when they are revised they often reflect the values and needs of another era. For example, the Massachusetts exemption statute provides that "[t]wo cows, twelve sheep, two swine and four tons of hay" are exempt. Mass. Gen. Laws Ann. ch. 235, § 34. The New York statute exempts many specific items including the family bible, family pictures and school books, the family pew, and family pets and their food (up to $450 for both). N.Y. Civ. Prac. R. § 5205. Most states also have a homestead exemption allowing a debtor to retain some equity in a primary residence. N.Y. Civ. Prac. R. § 5206; Cal. Civ. Proc. Code § 704.720 *et seq.* The subject of exemptions is covered in Chapter 7, *infra.*

The methods of finding a debtor's assets parallel the mechanisms of ordinary discovery. The creditor may (1) issue a subpoena and depose the debtor or any other person; (2) subpoena documents; or (3) have the debtor respond to written interrogatories. *See* N.Y. Civ. Prac. R. §§ 5223 and 5224; Cal. Civ. Proc. Code §§ 708.020, 708.110, 708.120 and 708.130.

§ 3.10 Preventing Transfer of the Judgment Debtor's Assets

The judgment creditor can prevent the transfer of the debtor's assets by several means. For example, if the judgment lien against real property is recorded, a subsequent transferee would take title subject to the lien. A second technique is to have the sheriff levy on the debtor's property, as discussed below, and physically remove the property from the debtor's control. A third device is to obtain a restraining notice which freezes the debtor's property by enjoining the sale, assignment or transfer until the judgment is satisfied. *See e.g.*, N.Y. Civ. Prac. R. § 5222. The restraining notice is often served simultaneously with information subpoenas so as to freeze assets while the creditor tries to determine precisely what assets belong to the debtor. The restraining notice may be served on the debtor or on any party holding the debtor's property. It remains in effect until the judgment is satisfied or expires. *Id.*

§ 3.11 Enforcing the Judgment

[A] Levy and Execution

HICKS v. BAILEY

Kentucky Court of Appeals
272 S.W.2d 32 (1954)

CLAY, Commissioner.

This suit was brought by appellant to quiet her title to a one–half undivided interest in the minerals underlying a tract of land. The basis of appellant's claim is a sheriff's deed executed in 1935 pursuant to an execution on a judgment against appellee. It is appellee's contention that this deed was and is void, and the Chancellor so adjudged.

While many questions are argued by the parties, the principal question seems to be whether or not a valid levy was made on this property by the sheriff. The record shows an execution was issued by the clerk of the Knott Circuit Court on January 5, 1934, returnable on March 15, 1934. The return on this execution is as follows:

> Executed by levying on property of W. T. Bailey, same being sold and execution collected in full.

> This Aug. 27, 1934.

This return is unique at least in two respects. The apparent return date is more than five months after the execution was returnable. The return does not show a levy upon anything identifiable.

If the sheriff's sale was valid, it must have been made pursuant to a valid levy. The sheriff had no power to make the levy after the return date on the execution, and this would make the sale void. *Deskins v. Coleman*, 286 Ky. 624, 151 S.W.2d 751.

Assuming, however, that the execution was still effective at the time the sheriff attempted to make the levy, it is obvious that because of the lack of any sort of description there was no levy on any particular property of the execution defendant. In ascertaining what passes under a sheriff's deed, we must look to the description of the property appearing in the return on the execution. *Taylor & Crate v. Asher*, 223 Ky. 574, 4 S.W.2d 385. Since no property was levied upon, it follows that the sheriff was without authority to either sell or convey this particular tract.

It is true that the deed itself contains recitations pertaining to the issuance of the execution, the levy, advertisement and sale. However, these recitations do not appear in a court record and are mere conclusions insufficient to establish that the real estate in controversy was actually levied upon by the sheriff in any one of the three modes required. *See Anderson v. Kerr*, 1951, Ky., 240 S.W.2d 91.

Appellant raises other questions which it appears unnecessary to discuss. It appearing that no valid levy was ever made on this property, the sheriff was without authority to sell it and the deed was void. The Chancellor properly adjudicated the rights of the parties.

The judgment is affirmed.

NOTES AND QUESTIONS

(1) How detailed must a writ of execution be? Must specific real property be described by metes and bounds, or is a street address sufficient? *See* N.Y. Civ. Prac. R. § 5230; Cal. Civ. Proc. Code §§ 693.010 and 699.520.

(2) The statute generally provides that a writ of execution expires within a specified limited period if the sheriff has not successfully levied against the property. *See* N.Y. Civ. Prac. R. § 5230(c) (60 days); Cal. Civ. Proc. Code § 699.560 (180 days). What if the sheriff cannot act within the time that the initial levy is in force? What happens to the judgment lien if the sheriff never successfully executes on the writ?

IN RE CONTINENTAL MIDWAY CORP.

United States District Court, District of Maryland
185 F. Supp. 867 (1960)

CHESNUT, District Judge.

This petition to review an order of the Referee has required a close consideration of the Maryland law and practice with regard to determining whether the judgment creditor in this case, who claims priority in payment, validly acquired a lien on personal property of the judgment debtor as against the Trustee in Bankruptcy. The order of the Referee determined that the creditor did not effectively obtain a lien and therefore was not entitled to priority in payment over general creditors. The controlling facts of the case as contained in the certificate of the Referee, and not here substantially challenged by counsel for the judgment creditor, are as follows:

1. The Chenille Manufacturing Company, Inc., obtained in due course a judgment against the Continental Midway Corporation (now the bankrupt) for $1,490.01 with interest and costs in the Court of Common Pleas of Baltimore City on July 19, 1956.

2. On July 26, 1956 counsel for the creditor issued a fi. fa. on the judgment and had it delivered to the sheriff for service. The next return day in the court was the first Monday of August 1956, and at that time the sheriff made a return of nulla bona on the writ.

3. On August 14, 1956 counsel for the judgment creditor delivered a second fi. fa. to the sheriff which again was returned nulla bona on the next return day, the first Monday of September 1956.

4. Again on September 11, 1956 counsel for the judgment creditor delivered a third fi. fa. to the sheriff, the return day for which was the first Monday in October 1956, and it also was returned nulla bona.

5. On November 23, 1956 the Circuit Court of Baltimore (an equity court) appointed receivers for the debtor corporation who promptly took possession of the assets. The involuntary petition in bankruptcy in this case was filed December 13, 1956. Subsequently the Trustee, having taken possession of certain personal property of the bankrupt, sold the property consisting of office furniture, fixtures and equipment located at 1500 N. Chester Street, Baltimore, Maryland, for the net sum of $1,330.

6. On January 30, 1957 the creditor filed its claim as an unsecured creditor (that is, stating that it held no security for its claim) in the amount of $1,519.96, representing the amount of the judgment plus interest and costs. On July 26, 1957 the creditor filed a petition alleging in substance that he was entitled to priority in payment by reason of a lien on the personal property above referred to which had been sold by the Trustee. And with respect to the fi. fa. issued September 11, 1956, it appears from correspondence filed in the case that the creditor requested or demanded that the sheriff levy on certain furniture and equipment in the premises 1500 N. Chester Street, alleged to be the property of the debtor. But the sheriff refused to do so saying that his deputy was informed when he started to make such a levy that the property did not belong to the debtor, and the sheriff then declined to make the levy unless the creditor would take "supplemental proceedings" in court or furnish the sheriff with an indemnity bond. This not being done the sheriff in due course returned this third writ of fi. fa. nulla bona. The Referee in his certificate stated that by virtue of testimony produced before him after the bankruptcy intervened, he found as a fact that as of September 11, 1956 there was office equipment and furniture in the premises 1500 N. Chester Street belonging to the debtor which could have been levied on by the sheriff. The Referee held hearings on the creditor's petition on September 19, 1957, August 6, 1959, which was adjourned until November 13, 1959, and finally on January 15, 1960, concluded the matter by the order of that date denying priority.

The principal contention of counsel for the creditor is that upon the delivery to the sheriff of the fi. fa. order issued July 26, 1956 the creditor thereby became entitled to a lien on all the personal property of the debtor and that the lien so acquired continued up to and including the taking of possession of the debtor's personal property above mentioned by the Trustee in Bankruptcy, and that therefore the creditor is entitled to priority in payment of at least the net sum realized by the Trustee on the sale of the office furniture and equipment. I understood counsel for the creditor to place his principal dependence upon the fi. fa. of July 26, 1956 because under section 67 of the Bankruptcy Act (11 U.S.C.A. § 107) Liens and Fraudulent Transfers, a lien obtained within four months before bankruptcy and when the debtor is insolvent would itself fall for that reason. On this basis the effect of the fi. fas. issued in August and September would be invalidated if, as counsel seem to concede, the debtor could be shown to have been insolvent at that time. However, as the Referee made no finding as to insolvency of the debtor on the

possible invalidity of a lien obtained within four months prior to the bankruptcy, I think it necessary to include a consideration of not only the first fi. fa. issued July 26, 1956 and the return thereof, but also the returns made to the second and third fi. fas. in August and September respectively.

The contention of counsel for the Trustee is that even assuming that the issuance of a fi. fa. from the Clerk of the Court and the delivery of the same to the sheriff under Maryland laws constitutes a lien on personal property of the debtor thereafter levied and scheduled by the sheriff in due course of return, nevertheless as there was no actual levy in this case on any of the furniture of the debtor and no schedule made or returned, and more particularly because the return to the first and each of the subsequent fi. fas. made by the sheriff was nulla bona, therefore any inchoate lien which might have arisen on the issuance of the fi. fa. was terminated and dissolved upon an official return of nulla bona; and that the lien could only have been revived by another fi. fa. on which the sheriff made a return of goods levied and scheduled and as no such return was ever made by him but there was a return of nulla bona in due course of time on all three writs and as the judgment creditor made thereafter no effort to subject the debtor's property to a lien until after the intervention of bankruptcy, the creditor has no proper basis for claiming priority in payment as a claim secured by a lien.

In a succinctly worded opinion the Referee decided that the creditor in this case has not established a lien and therefore denied priority in payment. I agree with the conclusion of the Referee, but think it will be worth while to develop the law applicable to the decision in more detail.

We must first turn to the Bankruptcy Act itself. It is not disputed that the Trustee in Bankruptcy succeeds in title to the assets of the bankrupt only to the extent that they have not been previously voluntarily or involuntarily by operation of law, subjected to valid claims of third persons. Section 67 (11 U.S.C.A. § 107) provides that liens obtained against the property of the bankrupt within four months prior to the bankruptcy are invalidated if obtained when the debtor was insolvent. The section does not expressly deal with liens obtained more than four months prior to the bankruptcy but it has been held by the Supreme Court in *Straton v. New*, 1931, 283 U.S. 318, 51 S. Ct. 465,75 L.Ed. 1060 that it is the clear implication of the law that such latter liens are valid and enforceable and that the determination of their validity is dependent upon the laws of the State where the property is situated. There is no dispute on this point in this case. It therefore follows that the question as to the validity of the liens here claimed by the creditor must be determined by the applicable and controlling Maryland law and practice.

In beginning the examination of the latter question it must first be borne in mind that Maryland is a so–called "common law" State. That is, by the first Constitution of the State in 1776 the law of England was adopted, insofar as was compatible with our institutions. And a similar declaration has been made in subsequent Constitutions, including the latest of 1867, whereby it is provided in Art. 5 of the Declaration of Rights, shortly stated, that the English law as it prevailed in 1776 continues to be the Maryland law subject, however, to the statutes of this State thereafter enacted subject to Maryland constitutional provisions. This is, of course, well known but possibly it is not always sufficiently borne in mind in particular cases.

With respect to the effect of judgments against a debtor, it had long ago been provided by a Maryland statute that the judgment itself constituted a lien on real property including certain leaseholds. Code 1957, Art. 26, §§ 20 and 21. *See also* Maryland Rules, Rule 620. But I am not aware that it has ever been thought or held that a judgment constituted ex propria vigora a lien of any kind on tangible personal property. By the early English law this could be done only by issuing from the court where the judgment was obtained a writ of fieri facias (shortly, popularly called a fi. fa.). This was an early English writ and was in effect an order to the sheriff of the court to enforce a judgment against the debtor by levy, seizure and sale of his personal property to the extent needed to satisfy the judgment. I understand that in practice the sheriff, after receiving the writ, proceeded thereunder to seize the goods of the debtor and to schedule them and report to the court what he had done. This report, it is said, should have been made in time to allow the parties in interest to file objections thereto; but in practice, at least in Maryland, it has been customary for the sheriff to make his return to the court of what he has done at the next succeeding return day of the court which, in Baltimore City, has generally been the first Monday of the succeeding month. And if the sheriff is unable to locate and seize and schedule the goods of the debtor, he made a return of nulla bona. When such a latter return is made the function of the writ has been completely discharged. But the creditor thereafter can obtain another fi. fa. order to the sheriff for other proceedings thereon and possibly more successful.

The earliest legislation on this subject is to be found in the 16th section of the English Statute of Frauds enacted by Parliament in the 29th year of the reign of Charles II in 1676. That well–known Act is, of course, in force in Maryland, except where later modified by statute or judicial decision. *See* Alexander's British Statutes, p. 511. Prior thereto the date of the attachment of the lien under the fi. fa. was the date of the issuance of the writ by the clerk; but the effect of the statute was to change the date of the time of the receipt of the writ by the sheriff who was thereby required to note the date of his receipt of the writ on the writ itself. And I understand that it has always been the uniform practice in Maryland for sheriffs receiving a writ of fi. fa. to endorse thereon the time of its receipt; and in Baltimore City, I am told that the sheriff endorses not only the day but also the hour of the day when it was received.

By many early decisions it is said that the date of the attachment of the lien under a fi. fa. begins when the sheriff receives the writ; but there are decisions to the effect that it is an implied condition that the creditor has the obligation to see that the writ should be promptly complied with by the sheriff and if there is undue delay the lien in favor of the particular judgment creditor may be lost by more active diligence on the part of some other creditor issuing a fi. fa. and securing an earlier levy and scheduling of goods seized by the sheriff. *See Myers Co. v. Annapolis Banking & Trust Co.*, 1936, 170 Md. 198, 183 A. 543. But where the creditor obtaining the writ of fi. fa. is properly diligent in having it executed by the sheriff, there are numerous Maryland cases which state in effect that the lien thereby secured dates from the receipt of the writ by the sheriff. *Selby v. Magruder*, 1825, 6 Har. & J., Md., 454; *Coombs v. Jordan*, 1831, 3 Bland, Md., 284; *Cunningham v. Offutt*, 6 Fed.Cas. page 977, No 3,484 (opinion by Judge of the Circuit Court of the District of Columbia in 1838); *Prentiss Tool & Supply Co. v. Whitman & Barnes Mfg. Co.,* 1898, 88 Md. 240, 41 A. 49. *See also Martin G. Imbach, Inc., v. Deegan,* 1955, 208 Md. 115, 117 A.2d 864, and opinion by Chief Judge Thomsen of this Court in *United States v. Levin,* D.C.Md.1955, 128 F. Supp. 465, and a review of the Maryland cases on the subject in an article by Judge Allan W. Rhynhart of the Peoples Court of Baltimore, 14 Md.Law Rev. 203.

More importantly, however, in the instant case the sheriff never successfully executed any of the three successive writs of fi. fa. but in due course thereafter made the return of nulla bona in each case. The fullest discussion that I have found in any Maryland case dealing with such a situation is that given by Chancellor Bland in the case of *Coombs v. Jordan,* 1831, 3 Bland, Md., 284, at page 325 where in his general discussion with regard to the beginning and ending of a lien sought to be obtained by a judgment creditor under a fi. fa. he said: "And, upon six similar principles, as a judgment does not, of itself, give rise to any lien upon personal property; and as the lien upon it can only commence, according to the statute of frauds, from the day of the actual delivery of a *fieri facias* into the hands of the sheriff, so it continues no longer, by virtue thereof, upon such property than it may be levied upon by such writ of *fieri facias*; that is, until its return day; after which, if it can be so continued at all, it can only be by the immediate renewal of such execution, or the instant delivery of another *fieri facias* to the sheriff."[1]

Counsel for the creditor seeks to support his contention by reliance almost wholly on the case of *Selby v. Magruder, supra.* The question in that case was presented to the court on a case stated, which, on first reading, seems very complex and involved, but on close reading and analysis and elimination of immaterial details can be simply stated. The final issue was a contest of priority between two separate judgment creditors each of whom had issued a fi. fa. to the sheriff. In March 1820 in the Circuit Court for Montgomery County, Creditor No. 1 issued a fi. fa. to the sheriff returnable the next November Term to realize on a judgment for large sums of money in amount over $1,000. The sheriff levied on all goods of the debtor which he could find and scheduled them as to value in the amount of $958.87½ and noted on the return that the remainder of goods of the debtor on which he had been instructed to levy could not be found because they had been secreted. In the meantime in the June Term 1820 the debtor, then apparently a resident of the District of Columbia, suffered a judgment against him in the Circuit Court for Washington County in the District of Columbia in consequence of which he apparently applied for the benefit of an insolvency or bankruptcy act of Congress applicable to the District of Columbia and was discharged from debts thereunder, and on the same day executed a deed of trust for the benefit of all his creditors to one Magruder, and this deed was promptly recorded in Montgomery County, Maryland. On November 14, 1820, judgment Creditor No. 2 issued a fi. fa. to the sheriff to recover on a judgment in his favor in Montgomery County under which on January 1, 1821

---

[1] Theodoric Bland, the Maryland Chancellor, had been a Judge of this United States District Court for Maryland from 1819 to 1824 when he resigned to become Chancellor of Maryland, a judicial office which existed in the State from 1776 until it was abolished by the Constitution of 1851.

the sheriff seized the property of the debtor which he had previously returned as secreted by the debtor. In the meantime on December 2, 1820, Creditor No. 1 issued a second fi. fa. to the sheriff under which the latter also on January 1, 1821 levied on the property of the debtor which he had previously returned as having been secreted. Subsequent to January 1, 1821 and before the sheriff had taken any further action toward selling any of the goods of the debtor under either of the fi. fas. Magruder, the Trustee, replevied the debtor's goods from the sheriff (Selby), and by consent of the parties the goods were sold by the Trustee and the proceeds substituted for the goods. The question presented to the court was whether judgment creditor No. 1 or No. 2 should receive the proceeds of sale in satisfaction of his judgment. On these particular facts peculiar to that case, the holding of the Maryland Court was that creditor No. 1 was entitled to the proceeds of sale because the sheriff had been prevented, not by his fault or lack of diligence, but by the fraudulent action of the debtor in secreting the residue of his property over and above that which had been in fact levied on by the sheriff under the first fi. fa. I think it quite apparent that the case was decided on its own particular facts which are materially different from those in the instant case where at no time were any goods actually seized or scheduled by the sheriff, but in each case the fi. fa. was returned in due course nulla bona. And I note that in later decisions the Maryland Court held that where the sheriff had not made a levy before the return day he could not properly do so thereafter. *Gaither v. Martin*, 1852, 3 Md. 146; *Busey et al. v. Tuck et al.*, 1877, 47 Md. 171. I find nothing in the *Selby* case or in any other English or American decision brou ght to my attention, to warrant the conclusion that the inchoate lien arising in favor of a judgment creditor and affecting a judgment debtor's personal property has the effect in law of continuing after the sheriff has fully performed his duties under the writ and made a return of nulla bona, not successfully challenged by appropriate action in the case by the judgment creditor.

In Freeman on Executions, 3d ed. Vol. 2, p. 1021, s. 202 (1900) will be found a full discussion of how long a lien obtained by the issuance of a fi. fa. to the sheriff will continue. The author states that it does not continue after the writ has been in due course returned by the sheriff as, of course, is the case where the writ is returned nulla bona. In support of the author's conclusion he cites a case of *Maul v. Scott*, C.C.Dist. of Columbia, 1822, Fed.Cas., No. 9306, 2 Cranch, C.C. 367 where the Court held that any lien arising upon the receipt of the writ by the sheriff is extinguished upon the return of nulla bona by the sheriff. *See also* 33 C.J.S. Executions § 123, page 289 *et seq.*, where the law is quite fully discussed as to the nature of a writ obtained by a judgment creditor on the issuance of an execution and the duration thereof. The general effect is stated to be that, in the absence of local legislation to the contrary, the writ obtained by the issuance of a fi. fa. is simply a writ to secure satisfaction of the judgment upon actual execution by the sheriff, and that when this is done by levy and seizure putting the property in the actual possession and control of the sheriff, the property can subsequently be realized upon by sale; and conversely where no levy or seizure has been made and the writ is returned by the sheriff without finding the property, as for instance a return of nulla bona, the lien does not thereafter continue unless subsequently revived by another writ; but if the sheriff does seize the goods the date of the lien thereon relates back to the time of the delivery of the writ to the sheriff. The discussion indicates quite clearly that any lien said to have been obtained at the time of the receipt of the writ by the sheriff is inchoate only until it becomes consummate by the seizure. In the instant case counsel for the Trustee contends that as there was no seizure under any of the three writs of fi. fa. issued in this case, there never became a consummated lien of any kind. I am inclined to think this view is sound and that when the Maryland cases speak of a lien arising upon delivery of the writ to the sheriff, what is meant is that the lien then arising is inchoate only and does not become consummate until the sheriff makes his seizure and files the schedule with his return.

I appreciate that it would seem on the facts stated by the Referee, counsel for the creditor though clearly diligent in his effort to secure a lien by the repetitive fi. fas. thinks that he has been unfairly frustrated in his efforts either by the failure of the sheriff to have been more effective in executing the writ or by fraud or misrepresentation on the part of some one thought by counsel to have been acting for the debtor, in informing the sheriff when he was attempting to levy on the goods that there were no goods on the premises belonging to the debtor. But I know of no principle of law which could be applied here as against the Trustee in Bankruptcy to justify the finding of the existence of a lien on merely equitable grounds when there had been no actual execution by the sheriff of any of the three orders of fi. fa. and when indeed in the instant case the sheriff had made a return to the Court showing that he had found no goods of the defendant on which to levy and schedule, and therefore in each case made the return of nulla bona.

Counsel for the creditor makes a complaint against the sheriff and says that he would have asserted a claim against him if there had not been so much delay in the bankruptcy proceedings before the order of the Referee now reviewed. But, of course, that collateral matter cannot be considered here by the Court.

The duties of the sheriff with regard to the return of writs delivered to him are stated in the Md. Code of 1957, Art. 87, §§ 5, 10, 11, 12 and 14. In this case the sheriff duly made returns on each of the three fi. fas. handed to him; and the creditor at no time challenged the return of nulla bona so made by the sheriff. Counsel have not been able to call to my attention any Maryland statute changing the English law and practice as it was in 1776 affecting the duties of the sheriff in respect to writs of fi. fa. and I have not been able to find any. Counsel for the creditor calls attention to the correspondence with the sheriff regarding the writ of fi. fa. issued September 11, 1956 in which the creditor urged the sheriff to levy on certain alleged personal property of the debtor and asked the sheriff to confer with counsel for the debtor in support of the creditor's assertion, to which the sheriff replied that he could not accept that suggestion and requested that the creditor furnish him a bond of indemnity against foreseeable liability in making a mistaken seizure, or take supplementary proceedings in court to establish the ownership of the goods as those of the debtor. The creditor did not comply with either request. I have always understood that the Sheriff had the right to insist upon a bond from the creditor where there was reasonable doubt as to the ownership of the goods, and it was so held in *Robey v. State*, Use of Mallery, 1901, 94 Md. 61, 50 A. 411 in an opinion by Chief Judge McSherry after an extended review of the English and American authorities on the point.

I therefore conclude that the Referee correctly decided the case and his opinion is affirmed.

NOTES AND QUESTIONS

(1) The common law writ of *fieri facias*, discussed in this case, ordered the sheriff to satisfy the creditor's judgment by seizure and sale of the debtor's goods and chattels. For a discussion of the common law writs, *see* Riesenfeld, *Collection of Money Judgments in American Law—A Historical Inventory and a Prospectus*, 42 Iowa L. Rev. 155 (1957).

(2) The sheriff in *Continental Midway, supra*, returned the writ *"nulla bona"* which translates literally from the Latin as "no goods," *i.e.*, the sheriff did not find any property against which the judgment could be enforced. This is a common occurrence, unfortunately, for judgment creditors. What can a creditor's lawyer do to protect the client's rights *before* the judgment is entered? *See* Chapters 4 (Attachment and Garnishment) and 6 (Fraudulent Transfers). Even if the debtor fraudulently transfers assets while suit is pending, the creditor may later sue to avoid the transfer or proceed directly against the transferred assets under the fraudulent transfer laws. *See* Unif. Fraudulent Conveyance Act §§ 9, 10, 7A U.L.A. 304, 358. What types of transfers may still be made during the pendency of a suit without risk of fraudulent transfer attack? *Id.*

KEETON v. HUSTLER MAGAZINE, INC.

United States Court of Appeals, Second Circuit
815 F.2d 857 (1987)

GEORGE C. PRATT, Circuit Judge:

Seeking to avoid the Pyrrhic victory of an unsatisfied libel judgment, appellee Kathy Keeton has tried to enforce her New Hampshire federal judgment in New York State. New York's judgment enforcement techniques are complemented by procedures designed to facilitate the registration of foreign, or out–of–state, judgments, for New York will, with specified exceptions, simply recognize a foreign judgment as its own, rather than require a separate action on the judgment.

Here, appellants challenge Keeton's attempt to register and enforce in New York her judgment for $2,000,000 plus interest rendered in the United States District Court for the District of New Hampshire against Larry Flynt and Hustler Magazine, Inc. (collectively "Hustler"). Hustler removed Keeton's enforcement proceedings from New York Supreme Court, New York County, to the United States District Court for the Southern District of New York, Edmund L. Palmieri, *Judge*, which denied Hustler's motions to enjoin enforcement of and to set aside judgment entered by Keeton in state supreme court. We affirm.

BACKGROUND

Alleging that she had been defamed by certain portrayals in Hustler magazine, Keeton sued Hustler for libel. Following her well–publicized victory on jurisdictional grounds in the Supreme Court, *see Keeton v. Hustler Magazine, Inc.*, 465 U.S. 770, 104 S. Ct. 1473, 79 L. Ed. 2d 790 (1984), the case went to trial, and on August 8, 1986, judgment on the jury's verdict of $2,000,000, plus interest, was entered for Keeton in the United States District Court for the District of New Hampshire. After its post–trial motions for judgment notwithstanding the verdict and for a new trial were denied, Hustler appealed to the United States Court of Appeals for the First Circuit. The district court denied Hustler's motion to stay execution of the judgment pending appeal unless Hustler posted a $2,000,000 supersedeas bond, but Hustler did not then, and has not to date, posted such a bond. In addition, Hustler's motion to the first circuit for a stay of execution pending appeal has twice been denied.

On October 3, 1986, Keeton filed her New Hampshire federal judgment in Supreme Court, New York County, pursuant to Article 54 of New York's Civil Practice Law and Rules, which is New York's embodiment of the Uniform Enforcement of Foreign Judgments Act, *see* N.Y. Civ. Prac. Law §§ 5401–5408 (McKinney 1978). Hustler removed Keeton's Article 54 proceeding from state supreme court to the United States District Court for the Southern District of New York, where its requests to enjoin enforcement of and to set aside the judgment, as well as for an interim stay of execution of the judgment, were denied. Additionally, the district court denied Hustler's motion to quash various subpoenas and restraining notices that had been served on the Hustler defendants. The district court concluded that Hustler's motions culminated a series of dilatory tactics taken to frustrate satisfaction of Keeton's judgment. This appeal followed.

On appeal, Hustler contends that Keeton may not register and enforce her judgment in New York while its appeal is pending in the first circuit, and that the federal registration scheme preempts any application of Article 54 to Keeton's federal judgment. Finding no merit to Hustler's arguments, we affirm.

DISCUSSION

I. *The Registration Provisions.*

Article 54 defines a foreign judgment as "any judgment, decree, or order of a court of the United States or of any other court which is entitled to full faith and credit in this state, except one obtained by default in appearance, or by confession of judgment." N.Y. Civ. Prac. Law § 5401 (McKinney 1978). Article 54 permits a qualifying foreign judgment to be filed in any county clerk's office, and directs that:

> [t]he clerk shall treat the foreign judgment in the same manner as a judgment of the supreme court of this state. A judgment so filed has the same effect and is subject to the same procedures, defenses and proceedings for reopening,

vacating, or staying as a judgment of the supreme court of this state and may be enforced or satisfied in like manner.

Id. § 5402(b); *see id.* § 5402(a).

Hustler urges that Keeton may not invoke Article 54 because to do so would contravene clear federal policy. Specifically, Hustler contends that 28 U.S.C. § 1963, which governs registration of judgments of one federal district court in another federal district, when combined with section 5018(b) of the New York Civil Practice Law and Rules, provides the exclusive means for registering and enforcing Keeton's New Hampshire federal judgment in New York. Section 1963 provides, in pertinent part:

> A judgment in an action for the recovery of money or property now or hereafter entered in any district court *which has become final by appeal* or expiration of time for appeal may be registered in any other district by filing therein a certified copy of such judgment. A judgment so registered shall have the same effect as a judgment of the district court of the district where registered and may be enforced in like manner.

28 U.S.C. § 1963 (emphasis added). Because registration pursuant to these provisions is available only when the judgment has become final by appeal, or the time for an appeal has passed, Keeton, according to Hustler, may not avail herself of any registration process unless and until Hustler's appeal to the first circuit is resolved in Keeton's favor. Hustler concludes that Article 54 simply is not available for the direct registration of foreign federal judgments in New York state court, and that to hold otherwise would run counter to the federal policy of allowing registration of only those judgments that have been made final by appeal.

Moreover, even should Keeton's judgment become final by appeal, allowing her then to comply with section 1963, Hustler asserts that only section 5018(b) of the New York Civil Practice Law and Rules, and not Article 54, would govern the registration of the judgment in New York state court. In short, Hustler argues that the only enforcement by registration technique available to Keeton is a two–step procedure: she must first register her New Hampshire federal judgment in a New York federal district pursuant to section 1963 and, then, employ section 5018(b) to docket the registered federal judgment in a county clerk's office, thereby converting it to a judgment of the supreme court of that county. Section 5018(b), entitled "[d]ocketing of judgment of court of United States," directs that:

> A transcript of the judgment of a court of the United States rendered or filed within the state may be filed in the office of the clerk of any county and upon such filing the clerk shall docket the judgment in the same manner and with the same effect as a judgment entered in the supreme court within the county.

N.Y. Civ. Prac. Law § 5018(b) (McKinney Supp. 1987).

As authority for its theory on the unavailability of Article 54 for enforcement in New York of federal court judgments, Hustler cites this court's opinion in *Knapp v. McFarland*, 462 F.2d 935 (2d Cir. 1972). *Knapp* also involved a contest over the propriety of a judgment creditor's attempt to register a federal judgment in New York state court. There, however, the underlying judgment, rendered in the United

States District Court for the Southern District of New York, had been issued in the same state in which execution was sought and, thus, the judgment creditor proceeded under a combination of 28 U.S.C. § 1962 and N.Y. Civ. Prac. Law § 5018(b). Section 1962 allows that "[e]very judgment rendered by a district court within a State shall be a lien on the property located in such State in the same manner, to the same extent and under the same conditions as a judgment of general jurisdiction in such State". 28 U.S.C. § 1962. The *Knapp* panel held that the judgment creditor properly filed its Southern District of New York judgment in Supreme Court, New York County under section 5018(b) and, therefore, under section 1962 that judgment served as a lien against the judgment debtor's property located in New York. 462 F.2d at 938.

After resolving that issue, however, the court addressed the argument that the judgment creditor also was required to comply with the separate standards of Article 54. Rejecting that position, the *Knapp* panel wrote "[a] glance at the legislative history of the statutes under consideration makes it clear that Art. 54 was intended to apply only to money judgments rendered by sister states of the United States and not to such judgments of federal district courts, whether in New York or elsewhere." *Id.* at 939. Because the sequential application of section 1963 and section 5018(b) provided a means for enforcing out–of–state federal judgments in New York, the *Knapp* panel concluded that Article 54 was intended to apply only to the judgments of other states. "The purpose of Art. 54 . . . was not to provide for enforcement by registration of federal judgments in New York, which was already authorized by CPLR § 5018(b), but for judgments of sister states." *Id.* at 940.

The quoted language from *Knapp* lends strength to Hustler's theory of the correlation of section 1963, section 5018(b), and Article 54. Nevertheless, since the judgment at issue there was rendered in a New York federal district court, *Knapp*'s comment about the effect of Article 54 on judgments of district courts "elsewhere" was dictum. *Id.* at 939.

As dictum, and because it contradicts both the plain language of Article 54 and its legislative history, the decision in *Knapp* has been criticized by commentators on Article 54. For instance, Professor David Siegel, after describing the procedure offered by section 1963 and section 5018(b) noted: "The continued availability of this easy procedure, though it involves two filings rather than one, will make Article 54 less needful for out–of–state federal judgments. *But Article 54 is an alternative even for a federal judgment.*" N.Y. Civ. Prac. Law § 5402, commentary at 508 (McKinney 1978) (emphasis added). Indeed, while recognizing that *Knapp* had suggested that Article 54 does not apply to federal judgments, Professor Siegel wrote that "under CPLR 5401 it clearly does". D. Siegel, New York Practice 577 (4th printing 1983).

With the issue of whether Article 54 is available to register an out–of–state federal judgment in New York state court properly before us on this appeal, we conclude that the dictum in *Knapp* is incorrect, and, therefore, that Keeton properly invoked Article 54 to register her New Hampshire federal judgment in Supreme Court, New York County.

As Professor Siegel indicated, the plain language of section 5401, describing a foreign judgment as "any judgment, decree, or order of a court of the United States", demands that out–of–state federal judgments be included; there can be little question that a judgment of the United States District Court for the District of New Hampshire is a "judgment . . . of a court of the United States".

Moreover, the legislative history of Article 54 supports this plain reading of that provision. In its Sixth Report to the Judicial Conference, the Committee to Advise and Consult on the CPLR recommended adoption of the 1964 version of the Uniform Enforcement of Foreign Judgments Act. The committee opined that "[t]he 1964 Act is simple and straightforward. Its basic philosophy is that a debtor who has had a full scale trial in a sister state or *federal court* need not be given a second full scale trial on the judgment in another state." Sixth Report to the Judicial Conference by the Committee to Advise and Consult on the CPLR, *reprinted in* [1969] McKinney's Session Laws 2273, 2287 (emphasis added) [hereinafter cited as *1969 CPLR Report*]. Likewise, when the matter was again submitted to the legislature the following year, the judicial conference noted that:

> The terms "foreign judgment" and "American judgment" as used in this discussion to describe the scope of this bill are identical in meaning; they include judgments of courts in states of the United States *and courts* in the *Federal jurisdiction.*

Eighth Report of the Judicial Conference on the CPLR, *reprinted in* [1970] McKinney's Session Laws 2777, 2785 (emphasis added) [hereinafter cited as *1970 CPLR Report*].

Simultaneously with its recommendation of Article 54 to the legislature, the judicial conference recommended amendment of two related sections of the Civil Practice Law and Rules, namely, sections 6201 and 3213. Those amendments were designed to make New York procedures generally more fully competent to process out–of–state judgments. The suggested amendment to section 6201 made the remedy of attachment available to "a plaintiff suing on a sister state, *federal district court* or foreign country judgment", *1969 CPLR Report* at 2288 (emphasis added), and the proposed change in section 3213 was designed to make the remedy of summary judgment in lieu of complaint available to "a judgment creditor who holds a foreign judgment (sister state, *district court* or foreign country)", *id.* at 2289 (emphasis added). Thus, the judicial conference submitted to the legislature, and the legislature adopted, a package of three bills designed to facilitate enforcement in New York of out–of–state judgments, and in support of all three bills it stated that federal court judgments were intended to be included.

The drafters of Article 54 were fully aware that an alternative federal registration scheme already existed:

> Proposed Article 54 is designed to provide for American judgments . . . which are sought to be enforced in New York, the simpler, speedier and less expensive method of enforcement which is now available in the Federal system for the enforcement of judgments of United States district courts.

1970 CPLR Report at 2786. Although the drafters' stated intention was to emulate the federal scheme, there is no basis in their report, in the legislative history of

Article 54 or in any New York statute or case law for Hustler's position that New York intended to require the filing of a foreign federal judgment in a New York federal court as a prerequisite to registration of the judgment in accordance with Article 54.

In short, Article 54 was meant to be available for enforcement of out–of–state federal judgments and sister–state judgments, and this clear intention should not be overridden simply because the same result could also be achieved by the two–step procedure offered by section 1963 and section 5018(b).

II.   *Preemption.*

Hustler urges that, even if Article 54 is construed to allow this result, it is nevertheless preempted by the important federal policy embodied in section 1963 that registration should be permitted only to those judgments made final by appeal. In Hustler's view, a state may not choose to allow registration of an out–of–state federal judgment while an appeal of that judgment is pending. We disagree.

We note, preliminarily, that Hustler points to no express language of preemption. Thus, congress's intent to preempt state law in the area of registration of federal judgments, if any, must be inferred. Such an inference would be appropriate if section 1963 were sufficiently comprehensive to suggest that congress left no room for state legislation, or if the federal interest in finality by appeal were so dominant that congress must have meant to preclude state legislation. *See Hillsborough County, Florida v. Automated Medical Laboratories, Inc.*, 471 U.S. 707, 105 S. Ct. 2371, 2375, 85 L. Ed. 2d 714 (1985). Even if preemption is not demonstrated, state law, of course, may not conflict with federal law. *See id.*

The policy of finality by appeal embraced in section 1963 is not part of a comprehensive scheme. One phrase contained in a three–sentence statute is hardly comprehensive legislation, but even if it were, the Supreme Court has noted a reluctance to infer preemption from mere comprehensiveness of regulation. *See id.* 105 S. Ct. at 2377.

Hustler's suggestion that an inference of preemption is compelled by some dominant federal interest in enforcing only those judgments that are made final by appeal is similarly unavailing. Specifically, Hustler claims that states have no interest in giving more recognition to a federal judgment than would a federal court. Nevertheless, the notion that the federal interest in finality by appeal is, in fact, dominant founders in light of congress's failure to include such a requirement in section 1962. That provision, governing the use of a federal judgment as a lien in the rendering state, unlike section 1963, does not pertain only to judgments made final by appeal. Thus, congress did not think it sufficiently important to have a federal judgment be finalized by appeal before it operated as a lien on property. Finally section 1963 on its face, shows a federal interest only in keeping federal courts from registering non–final federal judgments, and expresses no view on state practice. Consequently, we conclude that the federal government's interest in finality by appeal is not so dominant as to preclude all state legislation.

Hustler finally maintains that the direct registration of an out–of–state federal judgment under Article 54 is invalid because it directly conflicts with the finality by appeal prerequisite of section 1963. Section 1963, however, applies only to inter–district registration of federal judgments, a matter of federal practice with which Article 54 does not, indeed could not, deal. Article 54 authorizes for New York state the use of the state's enforcement powers for some out–of–state judgments. While Article 54 may permit enforcement of Keeton's judgment at an earlier stage than would section 1963, it does not thereby conflict with that section. At worst it may permit, as does section 1962, collection based on a judgment that may later be reversed. Nevertheless, that possibility and its remedy have long been contemplated in the law. *See, e.g., Northwestern Fuel Co. v. Brock*, 139 U.S. 216, 219–21, 11 S. Ct 523, 524–25, 35 L. Ed. 151 (1891). In short, New York has chosen to accord more immediate effect to out–of–state federal judgments than the federal government itself; although it permits a different result, that choice does not conflict with section 1963.

We note that Article 54 does not *require* that a federal judgment pending appeal be immediately enforced. Section 5404 provides two bases for staying enforcement:

> (a) Based upon security in foreign jurisdiction. If the judgment debtor shows the supreme court that an appeal from the foreign judgment is pending or will be taken, or that a stay of execution has been granted, the court shall stay enforcement of the foreign judgment until the appeal is concluded, the time for appeal expires, or the stay of execution expires or is vacated, upon proof that the judgment debtor has furnished the security for the satisfaction of the judgment required by the state in which it was rendered.

> (b) Based upon other grounds. If the judgment debtor shows the supreme court any ground upon which enforcement of a judgment of the supreme court of this state would be stayed, the court shall stay enforcement of the foreign judgment for an appropriate period, upon requiring the same security for satisfaction of the judgment which is required in this state.

N.Y. Civ. Prac. Law § 5404 (McKinney 1978).

As we have noted, Hustler was twice denied a stay of execution pending appeal by the first circuit. Beyond that, Hustler was not entitled to a stay under section 5404(a), because it refused to file a supersedeas bond in the New Hampshire district court, and, Judge Palmieri's determination that Hustler's conduct was simply another dilatory tactic, combined with Hustler's unwillingness to post a bond, ruled out a discretionary stay under section 5404(b).

The order of the district court denying Hustler's motions to enjoin enforcement of Keeton's judgment and to quash the subpoenas and restraining notices on the Hustler defendants is affirmed.

NOTES

(1) The judgment creditor may have a jurisdictional problem because the judgment must be enforceable in the state where the debtor's property lies. A sister

state's judgment or a federal court judgment is not automatically enforceable elsewhere. The process of enforcing another state's judgment is simplified in the twenty–five states that have adopted the Uniform Enforcement of Foreign Judgments Act, 13 U.L.A. 176, 189 (1980) (1964 Revised Act and 1948 Act). The 1964 Revised Act provides in § 2 that:

> A copy of any foreign judgment authenticated in accordance with the act of Congress or the statutes of this state may be filed in the office of the Clerk of any [District Court of any city or county] of this state. The Clerk shall treat the foreign judgment in the same manner as a judgment of the [District Court of any city or county] of this state. A judgment so filed has the same effect and is subject to the same procedures, defenses and proceedings for reopening, vacating, or staying as a judgment of a [District Court of any city or county] of this state and may be enforced or satisfied in like manner.

"Foreign judgment" is defined in § 1 of the 1964 Revised Act to mean "any judgment, decree, or order of a court of the United States or of any other court which is entitled to full faith and credit in this state."

Since, as discussed in *Keeton, supra,* to be enforceable in New York a United States district court judgment has to be filed in a county clerk's office in New York, the New York version of the Uniform Enforcement of Foreign Judgments Act provides that a sister state's judgment should simply be filed in a county clerk's office directly. N.Y. Civ. Prac. R. § 5402. The New York statute differs also in excluding judgments by default or confession of judgment from the definition of "foreign judgment." N.Y. Civ. Prac. R. § 5201.

(2) 28 U.S.C. § 1962 prohibits discrimination against a district court judgment by providing that:

> Every judgment rendered by a district court within a State shall be a lien on the property located in such State in the same manner, to the same extent and under the same conditions as a judgment of a court of general jurisdiction in such State, and shall cease to be a lien in the same manner and time.

Any federal district court's judgment may be transferred to another district, and then enforced as if it had originated in that district by virtue of 28 U.S.C. § 1963, which provides for "registration" and enforcement:

> A judgment in an action for the recovery of money or property now or hereafter entered in any district court which has become final by appeal or expiration of time for appeal may be registered in any other district by filing therein a certified copy of such judgment. A judgment so registered shall have the same effect as a judgment of the district court of the district where registered and may be enforced in like manner.

(3) The sheriff usually receives a fee from the judgment creditor for attempting to levy. If the sheriff successfully levies on the judgment debtor's property, the sheriff is entitled to an additional payment called "poundage." *See* N.Y. Civ. Prac. R. § 8012(b).

(4) In *Finberg v. Sullivan,* 634 F.2d 50 (3d Cir. 1980), the bank account of an elderly widow in Pennsylvania was attached by a lien creditor. The Pennsylvania

post–judgment garnishment statute did to provide for notice and a hearing prior to the attachment. All the funds in the account were, however, the proceeds of Social Security checks and were property exempt from attachment under both federal law and state law. The United States Court of Appeals for the Third Circuit faced the constitutional due process issues presented, *i.e.*, notice and hearing, and held the statute unconstitutional.

To eliminate the constitutional questions concerning notice, states have adopted measures to protect a debtor's interest in exempt property. One such measure requires the creditor to notify the debtor of his or her rights by serving the debtor with a list of the available exemptions. N.Y. Civ. Prac. R. §§ 5222(e), 5232(c) and 5234(a); Cal. Civ. Proc. Code § 699.540(c); Pa. R.C.P. No. 3252, 42 Pa. Cons. Stat.

(5) Most states provide for certain types of post–judgment garnishment of wages. In New York, a judgment creditor can obtain an execution against 10% of the debtor's earnings if the debtor earns more than $85 per week. N.Y. Civ. Prac. R. § 5231. California exempts the portion of the debtor's earnings necessary for the support of the debtor and the debtor's family without specifying a particular percentage. Cal. Civ. Proc. Code § 706.051.

(6) It is possible in New York for a judgment creditor to reach a greater portion of the debtor's income by proving that the debtor does not require the full amount of the protected 90% of earnings. N.Y. Civ. Prac. R. § 5226 provides that:

> Upon motion of the judgment creditor, upon notice to the judgment debtor, where it is shown that the judgment debtor is receiving or will receive money from any source, or is attempting to impede the judgment creditor by rendering services without adequate compensation, the court shall order that the judgment debtor make specified installment payments to the judgment creditor. . . . In fixing the amount of the payments, the court shall take into consideration the reasonable requirements of the judgment debtor and his dependents, any payments required to be made by him or deducted from the money he would otherwise receive in satisfaction of other judgments and wage assignments, the amount due on the judgment, and the amount being or to be received, or, if the judgment debtor is attempting to impede the judgment creditor by rendering services without adequate compensation, the reasonable value of the services rendered.

A wage turnover order can be a very useful device, particularly when the debtor has no other free assets. In one instance, while seven creditors with wage executions under N.Y. Civ. Prac. R. § 5231 waited in line for their 10% of earnings, an eighth judgment creditor convinced the court that the debtor could afford to pay him $25 per week in addition to the 10% of earnings being paid to another creditor. *Schwartz v. Goldberg*, 58 Misc. 2d 308, 295 N.Y.S.2d 245 (S. Ct. Bronx Co. 1968). *But see* the discussions of turnover orders and of priorities, *infra*.

(7) In the Consumer Credit Protection Act, Congress prohibited the garnishment of earnings above the following limits:

Maximum allowable garnishment

(a) Except as provided in subsection (b) of this section . . . , the maximum part of the aggregate disposable earnings of an individual for any workweek which is subjected to garnishment may not exceed

(1) 25 per centum of his disposable earnings for that week, or

(2) the amount by which his disposable earnings for that week exceed thirty times the Federal minimum hourly wage prescribed by section 206(a)(1) of Title 29 in effect at the time the earnings are payable,

whichever is less. In the case of earnings for any pay period other than a week, the Secretary of Labor shall by regulation prescribe a multiple of the Federal minimum hourly wage equivalent in effect to that set forth in paragraph (2).

Exceptions

(b)(1) The restrictions of subsection (a) of this section do not apply in the case of

(A) any order for the support of any person issued by a court of competent jurisdiction or in accordance with an administrative procedure, which is established by State law, which affords substantial due process, and which is subject to judicial review.

(B) any order of any court of the United States having jurisdiction over cases under chapter 13 of Title 11.

(C) any debt due for any State or Federal tax.

(2) The maximum part of the aggregate disposable earnings of an individual for any workweek which is subject to garnishment to enforce any order for the support of any person shall not exceed—

(A) where such individual is supporting his spouse or dependent child (other than a spouse or child with respect to whose support such order is used), 50 per centum of such individual's disposable earnings for that week; and

(B) where such individual is not supporting such a spouse or dependent child described in clause (A), 60 per centum of such individual's disposable earnings for that week;

except that, with respect to the disposable earnings of any individual for any workweek, the 50 per centum specified in clause (A) shall be deemed to be 55 per centum and the 60 per centum specified in clause (B) shall be deemed to be 65 per centum, if and to the extent that such earnings are subject to garnishment to enforce a support order with respect to a period which is prior to the twelve–week period which ends with the beginning of such workweek.

Execution or enforcement of garnishment order
or process prohibited

(c) No court of the United States or any State, and no State (or officer or agency thereof), may make, execute, or enforce any order or process in violation of this section.

15 U.S.C. § 1673. Note that the amount that is subject to garnishment is based on "disposable earnings," which is defined as compensation for personal services after the deduction of amounts legally required to be withheld. 15 U.S.C. § 1672(a) and (b). This section preempts state statutes, except to the extent that the state statute sets a lower maximum amount subject to garnishment. *See Evans v. Evans*, 429 F. Supp. 580 (W.D. Okla. 1976). State law continues to govern the priorities between and among wage garnishment orders.

[B] Alternative Devices for Enforcing Money Judgments

Instead of obtaining an execution and having a sheriff levy on property, a judgment creditor may proceed by a general "turnover" order:

> (a) *Property in the possession of judgment debtor.* Upon motion of the judgment creditor, upon notice to the judgment debtor, where it is shown that the judgment debtor is in possession or custody of money or other personal property in which he has an interest, the court shall order that the judgment debtor pay the money, or so much of it as is sufficient to satisfy the judgment, to the judgment creditor and, if the amount to be so paid is insufficient to satisfy the judgment, to deliver any other personal property, or so much of it as is of sufficient value to satisfy the judgment, to a designated sheriff. . . .

N.Y. Civ. Prac. R. § 5225(a).

There is a disadvantage in pursuing a turnover order. The judgment creditor may not obtain a priority against a competing judgment creditor until the turnover order is signed. Because the order cannot be signed until after the motion is heard, the delay could be considerable. Subsequent judgment creditors who proceed by writs of execution may become senior to the creditor waiting for the turnover order. *See, e.g., City of New York v. Panzirer*, 23 A.D.2d 158, 259 N.Y.S.2d 284 (1st Dep't 1965) (*infra*).

§ 3.12 Competing with Other Creditors: Priority Problems

[A] After Acquired Property

HULBERT v. HULBERT

New York Court of Appeals
216 N.Y. 430, 111 N.E. 70 (1916)

SEABURY, J. This [is] a proceeding in an action of partition for the distribution of the proceeds of a sale of real property. On March 7th, 1904, St. Paul's Church of the village of Waterloo, N. Y., docketed a judgment for $906.84 against Fred Hulbert. On April 21st, 1904, judgments for $2,830.57 and $2,351.71 respectively were docketed against said Hulbert by the defendant Story now deceased. All of these judgments were filed and docketed in the office of the clerk of Seneca county. At the time these judgments were docketed Hulbert was without property. In 1910, on the death of his father, Hulbert inherited an undivided one–third interest in the real estate which it was sought to partition in this action. On November 24th, 1913, pursuant to leave granted by the court, the St. Paul's Church issued an execution on its judgment against the property of said Hulbert. On February 6th, 1914, the sheriff of Seneca county sold Hulbert's undivided interest in said real estate to one Bacon who is a defendant herein, for the sum of $1,437.10 and issued to him a sheriff's certificate of sale which he now holds. The present action for partition or sale was not commenced until after the execution of the St. Paul's Church had been placed in the hands of the sheriff. The interest of the defendant Hulbert in said premises was sold in the partition action March 28th, 1914, for $1,753.36, which sum has been paid into the court subject to its further order. The proceeds of this sale are insufficient to pay all of the judgment liens in full. The appellants, who are executors of the estate of Story, claim that these proceeds should be applied *pro rata* on all of the liens. The respondent Bacon claims, and he has been accorded by the court below, a preference for his lien and the payment thereof has been ordered to be made in full. It is clear that Bacon acquired no rights as against the owner of the Story judgments, by virtue of the sale of the property to him and the delivery by the sheriff of a sheriff's certificate of sale, unless the fact that the execution issued by the St. Paul's Church and the act of the sheriff in advertising the property for sale served to give to the lien of the St. Paul's Church a preference over the liens of the Story judgments. It is necessary, therefore, to inquire what the status of the judgment liens was and whether the act of the St. Paul's Church in issuing an execution upon its lien and the act of the sheriff in advertising the property for sale gave to that lien a preference over the others. Pursuant to the settled rule, which is not questioned by either party upon this appeal, the three judgments referred to became liens on the after-acquired property of the judgment debtor at the time of its acquisition by the debtor. (*Matter of Hazard Estate*, 73 Hun, 22; *affd.* on opinion below, 141 N. Y. 586.) The liens of these three judgments, therefore, attached simultaneously to the interest of Hulbert upon his acquiring title to that interest on the death of his father. It was held below that the judgment of the St. Paul's Church acquired priority by reason of the execution issued thereon and the act of the sheriff in advertising the property for sale. The theory upon which the ruling was made was that the act of the St. Paul's Church in issuing the execution was such an exhibition of diligence as to entitle that judgment creditor to a preference over the liens owned by the other judgment creditors. The only authorities relied upon by the learned Appellate Division to sustain this view were the cases of *Adams v. Dyer* (8 Johns. 347, 350) and *Waterman v. Haskin* (11 Johns. 228). In *Adams v. Dyer* (*supra*) there is a short *per curiam* opinion which says: "Perhaps, the mere act of delivery of the execution to the sheriff, did not gain a preference *as to the lands*, but by the act of the sheriffs in making advertisement of the lands for sale, the first execution was begun to be executed. Here was an act by which priority, in some respects, was gained. There was priority as to the time of sale, and that priority could not be defeated by the second execution." The case of *Waterman v. Haskin* (*supra*) announces the same conclusion relying solely upon the authority of *Adams v. Dyer* (*supra*). . . .

At common law when a judgment has been rendered for a debt the sheriff was directed to cause the sum needed to be made (*fieri facias*) out of the goods and chattels of the defendant or levied (*livari facias*) out of his goods and the fruits of his land, but the land itself was not subject to be taken in satisfaction of the debt. "Our common law," say Pollock & Maitland in their History of English Law, "will not seize his land and sell it or deliver it to the creditor; seignorial claims and family claims have prevented men from treating land as an available asset for the payment of debts." (Vol. 2 [2d ed.], p. 596.) In 1285, by virtue of the statute of Westminster 2 (13 Edw. I), c. 18, the *election* was given to a creditor who sued for such debt or damages to have a writ to the sheriff "for levying the debt of the lands and chattels, or that the sheriff deliver to him all the chattels of the debtor (except his oxen and beasts of the plough) and a moiety of his land until the debt be levied." The writ of *elegit* was founded upon this statute. It was subject to certain restrictions and operated differently even as to chattels from a *fieri facias*. (2 Tidd's Prac. 939.) These restrictions need not now be commented upon, as our purpose will be served by tracing the procedure that was pursued under it in reference to the lands of the debtor. If the debtor had no land the sheriff need not take or return an inquisition. If there were lands it was necessary that the inquisition should be taken and returned, describing the land with convenient certainty, and after it is taken the sheriff delivers a moiety to the plaintiff by metes and bounds. (2 Tidd's Prac. 940.) It was formerly usual for the sheriff to deliver *actual* possession of a moiety of the lands, but at the time Mr. Tidd wrote his practice of the King's Bench (1807) the sheriff was only required to deliver legal possession, and in order to obtain actual possession the plaintiff must proceed by ejectment. The writ of *elegit*, however, has been said to be "almost unknown in the United States." (Freeman on Executions, § 370.) There are, however, instances of its use in Virginia, Alabama, North Carolina and Delaware. (Freeman on Executions, § 370.) Although authorized in New York, in practice it is doubtful if it was ever adopted. In commenting upon it Chancellor LANSING said: "Whether the *elegit* was ever introduced in practice, is doubtful, as the small value of the income of real estates, afforded little inducement to resort to it, as a means of satisfying a debt due upon a judgment." (*Catlin v. Jackson, supra,* at p. 547.)

Prior to 1732 no judicial sale of land could be made in New York under any common–law process. Such a sale was expressly prohibited by the so–called "Charter of Libertyes & Priviledges" which was enacted by the colonial legislature October 30th, 1683. (Laws of the Colony of New York, 1664–1719, vol. 1, p. 111.) By a subsequent statute passed soon afterwards by the same legislature a levy "by extent on the defendant's lands or against the defts goods and chattels & for want thereof his person" was authorized. (Nov. 2nd, 1683, chap. 12, Laws of the Colony of New York, 1664–1719, vol. 1, p. 134.) While these colonial statutes seem to have sanctioned the *elegit*, it is probable, as already remarked, that in practice that writ was not used. The act of 5 Geo. II, c. 7, which was applicable to the "Plantations and Colonies in America," provided that after September 29th, 1732, the lands of the debtor "shall be liable to and chargeable with all just debts, etc." This statute was intended to enable British subjects in England to sell real estates on execution in the colonies in order to satisfy the debts due to them. It received a liberal construction which extended it to all judgments. (*Catlin v. Jackson*, 8 John. R. 520, at p. 547.) Under this statute the *fieri facias* was the appropriate writ under which the lands could be sold, but in several essentials the effect of the execution was necessarily different from a *fieri facias* levied upon personal property only. (*Catlin v. Jackson, supra*, at p. 547; *Hanson v. Barnes' Lessee*, 3 Gill & John. Rep. [Md.] 359, 367.)

By the act of 1774 (Laws of the Colony of New York, 1769–1775, vol. 5, p. 637) provision was made for docketing the judgment in the name of the person against whom the judgment was entered, and it was declared that a judgment "not Docketed and entered in the Books" should not affect lands as to purchasers or mortgagees, or have any preference against heirs, executors or administrators. In 1787 (Laws of New York, 1785–1788, vol. 2, ch. 56, p. 467) and in 1801 (Laws of 1801, ch. 105) these provisions were substantially re–enacted. These statutes provided that the land of the debtor should be subject to sale in the same manner as his personal property, and made provision for the docketing of the judgment, and provided that a judgment not docketed should not affect lands as to purchasers or mortgagees. Whether the legal effect of these statutes was to make the judgment itself a lien upon the real estate of the debtor it is not necessary to determine. In *Koning v. Bayard* (14 Fed. Cas. No. 7924), decided in 1829, it was held that such was their legal effect. The first statute to specifically declare that "the said judgment shall be a *lien* on such lands, etc.," was the Revised Laws of 1813 (Vol. 1, ch. 50, p. 501). By that statute it was enacted "That all and singular the lands, tenements, and real estates, of any person against whom any judgment shall have been obtained in any court of record, for any debt, damages, costs or other sum of money, shall be subject to be sold upon execution to be issued upon such judgment, *and the said judgment shall be a lien on such lands, tenements, and real estates:* Provided, etc." This statute also provided that a judgment not docketed should not affect any lands and tenements *as to purchasers and mortgagees.* This statute has been several times re–enacted, amended and amplified (2 R. S. part 3, ch. VI, title 4, art. 2, sections 11 and 12, and Laws of 1840, ch. 386), and the substance of it is expressed in the present provisions of the Code of Civil Procedure relating to this subject. (*See* sections 1250 and 1251 of the Code of Civil Procedure.)

By virtue of the statutory changes which have been made in relation to this subject a judgment upon being filed and docketed becomes a lien upon the real estate of the debtor. It is no longer necessary that an execution should be issued upon the judgment in order to cause the judgment to become a lien upon real estate. . . .

The statute has now removed any doubt that may have existed on the subject and declared that the lien attaches as to land from the filing of the judgment. Under these circumstances the ruling in *Adams v. Dyer* (*supra*) and *Waterman v. Haskin* (*supra*) should not be so applied as to make the unnecessary act of issuing an execution the ground for according, as between creditors of equal rank, to one creditor a priority over another. To so apply these decisions is to fail to give effect to the existing statutory provisions on this subject.

Whatever the legal effect of the early statutes may have been, it is perfectly clear that since 1813 the judgment itself is a lien upon the real property of the debtor. The legal effect of this statutory rule is that from the moment a judgment is duly filed and docketed legal rights in the real estate of the debtor attach. In the case now under consideration the liens of the three judgments attached simultaneously to the property of Hulbert upon his acquisition of the interest derived from his father. By virtue of the statute they were at that time equal liens entitled to share *pro rata* in the proceeds of the debtor's property. Such being the case, how can it be held that the issuing of the execution and the advertising by the sheriff—acts which would be an idle ceremony—should give a preference to the creditor? Once a lien is acquired it is a right which cannot be lost by the performance of an unnecessary act by another creditor. With as much reason could it be held that as between two mortgagees holding mortgages of equal rank, the one who showed the greatest diligence in commencing an action of foreclosure should acquire a preference over the other. Under the terms of the statute the judgments of the appellants became liens on the real property of Hulbert of equal rank with the lien of the judgment of the St. Paul's Church. The lien of these judgments of the appellants, having attached, did not forfeit their position of equality and become subordinate to a lien of equal rank, merely because its owner did not do a useless thing. In *Rankin v. Scott* (25 U.S. 177, 179) Chief Justice MARSHALL said: "The principle is believed to be universal, that a prior lien gives a prior claim, which is entitled to prior satisfaction, out of the subject it binds, unless the lien be intrinsically defective, or be displaced by some act of the party holding it, which shall postpone him in a court of law or equity to a subsequent claimant. The single circumstance of not proceeding on it until a subsequent lien has been obtained and carried into execution, has never been considered as such an act." The diligence of a junior judgment creditor could not affect the lien of a senior judgment creditor, and if it could not affect the lien of a senior judgment creditor, it cannot affect the lien of equal rank. The principle that equity favors the diligent has no application where one creditor displays his diligence in the doing of useless and unnecessary things. The liens of the three judgments attached when Hulbert acquired the property. The issuing of an execution upon one of the judgments could not affect the relative rank of the liens as between themselves. It is urged that, although this reasoning was adopted in *Rockhill v. Hanna* (4 McLean, 554), where the court refused to follow *Adams v. Dyer* (*supra*) and *Waterman v. Haskin* (*supra*), that case was not followed in the United States Supreme Court. In *Rockhill v. Hanna* (56 U.S. 189, 196) the United States Supreme Court considered the question presented in *Rockhill v. Hanna* (4 McLean, 554) and intimated an opinion in accord with the rule declared in *Adams v. Dyer* (*supra*) and *Waterman v. Haskin* (*supra*), but the decision of the court was not placed on that ground, the court saying: "But we do not think it necessary to rest the decision of this case, merely on the question of diligence, or to decide whether this doctrine has been finally established as the law of Indiana. The plaintiff's lien does not, by the statement of this case, stand on an equality as to date with that of the other judgments. By electing to take the body of his debtor in execution he has postponed his lien, because the arrest operated in law as an extinguishment of his judgment."

Under the circumstances disclosed, and in view of the fact that *Adams v. Dyer* (*supra*) and *Waterman v. Haskin* (*supra*) declare a rule contrary to our existing statute, we feel compelled to hold that these decisions are no longer controlling upon us and that we should give effect to the rule declared in the statute.

The order appealed from should be modified by directing that the fund now deposited in court should be distributed *pro rata* between the three judgments, and as so modified the order should be affirmed, without costs to either party.

BARTLETT, C.J., dissenting (Dissent Omitted).

NOTES AND QUESTIONS

(1) As in *Hulbert v. Hulbert*, there are often many judgment creditors claiming an interest in the debtor's property. After the property has been sold, the proceeds must be distributed. It is at this time that the priorities between and among creditors become crucial. N.Y. Civ. Prac. R. § 5234 sets priorities as follows:

(a) Distribution of proceeds of personal property. After deduction for and payment of fees, expenses and any taxes levied upon sale, delivery, transfer or payment, the proceeds of personal property or debt acquired by a receiver or a sheriff or other officer authorized to enforce the judgment shall be distributed to the judgment creditor and any excess shall be paid over to the judgment debtor. No distribution of proceeds shall be made until fifteen days after service of the execution except upon order of the court.

(b) Priority among execution creditors. Where two or more executions or orders of attachment are issued against the same judgment debtor and delivered to the same enforcement officer, they shall be satisfied out of the proceeds of personal property or debt levied upon by the officer in the order in which they were delivered. Where two or more executions or orders of attachment are issued against the same judgment debtor and delivered to different enforcement officers, and personal property or debt is levied upon within the jurisdiction of all of the officers, the proceeds shall be first applied in satisfaction of the execution or order of attachment delivered to the officer who levied, and thereafter shall be applied in satisfaction of the executions or orders of attachment delivered to those of the other officers who, before the proceeds are distributed, make a demand upon the officer who levied, in the order of such demands. An execution or order of attachment returned by an officer before a levy or delivered to him after the proceeds of the levy have been distributed shall not be satisfied out of those proceeds.

(c) Priority of other judgment creditors. Where personal property or debt has been ordered delivered, transferred or paid, or a receiver thereof has been appointed by order, or a receivership has been extended thereto by order, and the order is filed before the property or debt is levied upon, the rights of the judgment creditor who secured the order are superior to those of the judgment creditor entitled to the proceeds of the levy. Where two or more such orders affecting the same interest in personal property or debt are filed, the proceeds of the property or debt shall be applied in the order of filing. Where delivery, transfer, or payment to the judgment creditor, a receiver, or a sheriff or other officer is not completed within sixty days after an order is filed, the judgment creditor who secured the order is divested of priority, unless otherwise specified in the order or in an extension order filed within the sixty days.

The California statute addresses a judgment creditor's priority problems with respect to personal property subject to a security interest or subject to the lien of another judgment lienholder. *See* Cal. Civ. Proc. Code §§ 697.590 and 697.600. Who would have priority if, during the course of payments on an installment lien on real property, another judgment lienholder comes along demanding a lump sum payment? *See* Cal. Civ. Proc. Code § 697.380.

(2) A judgment lien creditor does not prime bona fide purchasers of the debtor's personal property without notice. In New York, the statute protects such bona fide purchasers by not permitting the judgment lien creditor to prevail over:

1. a transferee who acquired the debt or property for fair consideration before it was levied upon; or

2. a transferee who acquired a debt or personal property not capable of delivery for fair consideration after it was levied upon without knowledge of the levy.

N.Y. Civ. Prac. R. § 5202(a)(1) and (2). Similarly, the California statute protects the buyer in ordinary course of business against a judgment creditor's lien. Cal. Civ. Proc. Code § 697.610. In contrast, a judgment lien creditor pursuing New York *real* property would prime subsequent transferees, presumably because the judgment lien is docketed and thus publicly recorded. With such sales, however, the following transfers prime the executing judgment lien creditor:

1. a transfer or the payment of the proceeds of a judicial sale, which shall include an execution sale, in satisfaction either of a judgment *previously* so docketed or of a judgment where a notice of levy pursuant to an execution thereon was *previously* so filed; or

2. a transfer in satisfaction of a mortgage given to secure the payment of the purchase price of the judgment debtor's interest in the property; or

3. a transfer to a purchaser for value at a judicial sale, which shall include an execution sale . . .

N.Y. Civ. Prac. R. § 5203(a) (emphasis added). Why is it unnecessary to give all bona fide purchasers of real property priority over the judgment creditor? As can be seen from the New York statute, prior judgment lien creditors cannot (and, indeed, should not) be primed by a later executing creditor; nor should prior purchase money mortgagees.

The good faith purchaser at a judicial sale referred to in N.Y. Civ. Prac. R. § 5203(a)(3), *supra*, takes the real property free of all liens, even those senior to the one being levied upon. Why? The senior creditor's rights are eventually taken into account when the net proceeds are distributed according to the creditors' respective priorities.

[B]   Priorities Between Execution and Non–Execution Creditors

CITY OF NEW YORK v. PANZIRER

New York Supreme Court, Appellate Division
23 A.D.2d 158, 259 N.Y.S.2d 284 (1st Dept. 1965)

BREITEL, J. The issue is whether a judgment creditor who has served a third–party information subpoena and restraining notice in judgment enforcement proceedings (but has not yet obtained a turnover order) is entitled to priority over a judgment creditor who subsequently procures a levy under an execution. The determination of the issue depends upon the applicability and effect of CPLR 5234 (subd. [c]). The dispute is between the City of New York, which served the information subpoena and restraining notice under CPLR 5222 and 5224, and thereafter instituted a turnover proceeding pursuant to CPLR 5227, and the Manufacturers Hanover Trust Company, which obtained the subsequent execution levy. The third party or garnishee holds an escrow fund otherwise belonging to the judgment debtor Mamet in the amount of $923 pursuant to a written agreement for the sale of the judgment debtor's business.

The city's judgment ($1,129.51) was obtained for sales and business taxes owed by the judgment debtor Mamet; the bank judgment ($1,308.49) was obtained for the balance due from Mamet arising from an indebtedness to the bank. The third–party escrowee was the judgment debtor's lawyer in the sale of the judgment debtor's business. The bank entered its judgment August 10, 1963. The city entered its warrant or judgment October 21, 1963. The escrowee, Mr. Panzirer, was served by the city with the information subpoena and restraining notice on November 19, 1963. The city instituted the present special proceeding for a turnover order on January 22, 1964. Thereafter and not until February 5, 1964 did the bank issue its execution and obtain a levy by service upon the escrowee–garnishee.

In short, the bank recovered the earlier judgment but was slow in pursuing its remedies against the escrowee–garnishee, although it had previously received $77 from him and therefore knew of the existence of the escrow fund. The city, on the other hand, had obtained its judgment later but moved expeditiously to recover the sum held in escrow. It chose the slower information subpoena procedure rather than that of execution levy, presumably because without the information thus obtained it could not be certain that an execution would be effective. The result, however, was that it had not obtained a delivery or turnover order before the bank had levied under its execution.

Special Term held that because of the city's diligence, and in reliance on precedents which antedate CPLR, the city was entitled to priority. It overruled the bank's contention that CPLR had established a definite priority among judgment creditors (including levying execution creditors and those resorting to enforcement proceedings in the nature of the former supplementary proceedings under the Civil Practice Act) in which only delivery and turnover orders and receiverships would rank with executions levied in determining the order of priority.

The legislative history of CPLR 5234 (subd. [c]), an entirely new provision in the practice statutes, establishes that the order of priority among judgments is to be determined strictly in accordance with the chronological service of execution levies and the filing of orders for turnover or receiverships, as the case may be. The mere service of restraining notices under CPLR 5222 in connection with subpoenas issued pursuant to CPLR 5224 does not invoke standing in the ranking of priorities. In consequence, the judgment directing turnover to the city of the moneys held by the escrowee–garnishee should be reversed and judgment entered directing turnover of such sum to the intervenor bank, pursuant to the levy made upon the escrowee–garnishee.

Under the Civil Practice Act there was no express provision for priority as between executions levied and orders for the delivery of personal property. . . . This occasioned great confusion, and the courts created varying rules. . . . It had been determined, however, that a restraining provision in a third–party subpoena in supplementary proceedings issued pursuant to section 781 of the Civil Practice Act was equivalent to an equitable lien available in the old equity practice. The subpoena service was therefore held entitled to priority over a subsequent execution levy (*Matter of Wickwire Spencer Steel Co. v. Kemkit Scientific Corp.*, 292 N. Y. 139, 142).

There is no doubt that, in the development of the several drafts of what was to become the CPLR, effort was made to rationalize the priority order among the several classes of judgment creditors. While the precise proposals first suggested in the Third Report [N.Y. Legis. Doc. 1959, No. 17, 3rd Prelim. Report of the Advisory Comm. on Prac. and Proc., pp. 731–795] (*supra*) were not adopted, the final drafts were still designed to achieve the goal of a relatively simple, almost mechanical, statutory basis for determining priorities. . . .

In both the Fifth and Sixth Reports . . . it was stated with respect to the draft provision: "This provision is new. It is intended to clarify present law. It indicates that priority is not gained merely by serving a subpoena on a garnishee, but is only gained when property is ordered delivered or paid or transferred to a receiver, and only as to that particular property. The last sentence is needed to prevent a creditor who secures such an order from sitting on its rights to the detriment of another creditor." (Fifth Preliminary Report, p. 637; Sixth Report, p. 504.)

The Fifth and Sixth Report draft provisions are identical with the present subdivision (c) of CPLR 5234 which reads as follows: "Priority of other judgment creditors. Where personal property or debt has been ordered delivered, transferred or paid, or a receiver thereof has been appointed by order, or a receivership has been extended thereto by order, *and the order is filed before the property or debt is levied upon, the rights of the judgment creditor who secured the order are superior to those of the judgment creditor entitled to the proceeds of the levy*. Where two or more such orders affecting the same interest in personal property or debt are filed, the proceeds of the property or debt shall be applied in the order of filing. Where delivery, transfer, or payment to the judgment creditor, a receiver, or a sheriff or other officer is not completed within sixty days after an order is filed, the judgment creditor who secured the order is divested of priority, unless otherwise specified in the order or in an extension order filed within the sixty days." (Emphasis supplied.)

While there is no express reference to the restraining notices authorized by CPLR 5222, it is clear enough from the language of the subdivision, and especially in the light of its legislative history, that the subdivision was intended to encompass the range of priorities, to make the ranking of priority statutory, and to eliminate both decisional variations and difficult factual tests based upon the measure of diligence exerted by members of the different classes of judgment creditors. Reference to the many decisions and commentary materials cited in the study annexed to the Third Report makes this goal evident. The only discordant note is the reference in the quoted draftsman's explanation (*supra*) that the draft is "intended to clarify present law". This suggests less than a marked change in the law, but the sentence following unequivocally describes the change in the law. On any view, the goal of having the priorities among judgments in the statute without decisional exceptions and variations should not be disregarded.

The result, then, is that in order for a judgment to attain status in the ranking of priorities there must either be a levy, an order directing delivery of property, or the appointment of a receiver. Any other measures taken by the judgment creditor, no matter how diligent, on an absolute or comparative basis, do not suffice to qualify for priority. In given situations, as in this case, the effect may be that a less diligent creditor may prevail over a more diligent one, but the values of certainty and ease of determination of priorities are better achieved. Moreover, once the practice is settled, the judgment creditor, except in the rarest of situations where he lacks information, will be able to establish his priority, and disputes about priority will be relatively easily resolved. Total lack of information will be rare, for the judgment creditor must have known enough to serve the information subpoena and restraining notice on the third person.

These conclusions do not deprive restraining notices of all usefulness, as the city argues. The restraining notices serve the purpose of preventing the third person or garnishee from surrendering the debtor's assets pending obtaining of a turnover order. It simply means that the restraining notices are no longer effectual to affect priorities, as was the case under the decisional precedents under the Civil Practice Act.

These conclusions are in consonance with those reached in a number of cases at nisi prius (*Matter of Fisher & Co. v. Bar Spa. Automatic Mach. Co.*, 43 Misc 2d 821; *Meadow Brook Nat. Bank v. Federal Ins. Co.*, N. Y. L. J., Sept. 1, 1964, p. 10, col. 5; *Matter of H & H Poultry Co. v. Lafayette Nat. Bank*, 45 Misc 2d 480; *Matter of Graze v. Bankers Trust Co.*, 45 Misc 2d 610). The commentators are also in agreement with the foregoing conclusions (6 Weinstein–Korn–Miller, N. Y. Civ. Prac., par. 5234.18; Practice Commentary by Professor David D. Siegel, *loc. cit. supra*; *see, also*, Supplementary Practice Commentary by Professor David D. Siegel [McKinney's Cons. Laws of N. Y., Book 7B, CPLR 5234, pp. 23–24, 1964 Supp.]).

Since the bank's judgment is in excess of the amount levied upon there is a deficiency still due the bank on its judgment and there can be no surplus available to the city under its turnover application.

Accordingly, the judgment directing payment to the City of New York should be reversed, on the law, without costs or disbursements to any party, and judgment directed providing for the payment of such sum to intervenor–appellant in accordance with the levy of the execution caused to be issued by it.

BOTEIN, P. J., RABIN, EAGER and STEUER, JJ., concur.

Order and judgment unanimously reversed, on the law, without costs or disbursements to any party, and judgment directed providing for the payment of such sum to intervenor–appellant in accordance with the levy of the execution caused to be issued by it. Settle order on notice.

NOTE

This case illustrates a potential drawback inherent in post–judgment discovery and why it should be conducted simultaneously with execution, if at all possible. In some states, including New York, a creditor's priority dates back to the date of delivery of the order or writ of execution if the sheriff successfully levied against the debtor's property. *See* N.Y. Civ. Prac. R. § 5234; Del. Code Ann., tit. 10, § 5081. In other states, the creditor's priority dates from the successful levy. *See* N.C. Gen. Stat. § 1–313; R.I. Gen. Laws § 9–26–31; Ind. Code § 34–1–34–9.

CLARKSON CO. v. SHAHEEN

United States Court of Appeals, Second Circuit
716 F.2d 126 (1983)

LUMBARD, Circuit Judge:

This appeal arises out of enforcement proceedings brought by the Clarkson Company Ltd., to collect on its judgment against John Shaheen, Shaheen Natural Resources (SNR) and others. On June 4, 1982, Judge Owen of the Southern District of New York granted Clarkson's claim to stock owned by SNR priority over the competing claims of four other judgment creditors, Global Forwarding, Inc., Skidmore & Mason, Inc., Bona Vista Food Services, Ltd., and United Airlines (the state judgment creditors). The state judgment creditors appeal, challenging Clarkson's priority on the ground that it never perfected a levy against the securities in question. We affirm. Several months before the state judgment creditors attempted to levy on the stock, the district court took custody of the certificates for the benefit of Clarkson. We hold that no subsequent levy against SNR's interests in the stock could give the state judgment creditors priority over Clarkson's claim.

I.

The Clarkson Company Ltd. filed the underlying lawsuit in this matter in March of 1976 as trustee in the bankruptcy of the Newfoundland Refining Company, Ltd.

(NRC), a company controlled by John Shaheen. Clarkson sought to recover money that NRC had advanced or loaned to Shaheen, Shaheen Natural Resources, Inc., which Shaheen controlled, and others. On July 22, 1980, the district court entered judgment for Clarkson against the defendants for approximately $50 million; the judgment was affirmed in relevant part on appeal to this court. *Clarkson v. Shaheen,* 660 F.2d 506 (2d Cir.1981), *cert. denied,* 455 U.S. 990, 102 S. Ct. 1614, 71 L. Ed. 2d 850 (1982). Clarkson immediately began its attempt to collect on the debt.

On July 1, 1980 after the jury had returned a verdict for Clarkson, the district court restrained the defendants from transferring assets. Nevertheless, on July 31, 1980, only nine days after the district court entered judgment on the jury's verdict, SNR transferred 185,000 shares of MacMillan Ring–Free Oil Co., Inc., to Ian Outerbridge, a Canadian attorney. The shares in MacMillan, a Delaware corporation that was controlled by Shaheen and had its principal place of business in New York, represented the bulk of SNR's principal asset. Thus, unbeknownst to Clarkson, when it levied against SNR in September, 1980 the MacMillan stock certificates were no longer in SNR's actual possession. When SNR failed to turn over the stock, Clarkson attempted to perfect its levy by commencing a "turn–over" proceeding in the district court to compel SNR's compliance with the execution levy. New York Civ.Prac.Law §§ 5225 & 5232(a) (McKinney 1978).

Clarkson did not learn of the transfer to Outerbridge until December 5, 1980. It moved immediately for relief, and in a hearing that day the court ordered MacMillan and its transfer agents not to transfer or assist in the transfer of the stock then in Outerbridge's possession. Three days later, after further consideration and a second hearing, the court ordered Outerbridge to retain the stock and to preserve any dividends or proceeds.

The following month, Clarkson began a second § 5225 turn–over proceeding to recover the MacMillan stock, this time naming Outerbridge as an additional respondent. Outerbridge voluntarily submitted himself to the jurisdiction of the court, but contested the turn–over proceeding on the ground that he had received the stocks in good faith for services rendered. The district court directed Outerbridge to bring the certificates within the jurisdiction of the Southern District. And on March 13, 1981, as the district court later described it, "the Court ordered the Spengler Carlson firm to take custody of those shares from its client Outerbridge and to hold them as 'trustee' for the Court, which the firm did. From that moment until the present, the shares have been in the *custody* of this Court." 76 Civ. 1373, slip op. at 7 (January 26, 1982) (emphasis in original).

On October 27, 1981, the district court found that the MacMillan stock transfer was a fraudulent conveyance in violation of the court's July 1, 1980 restraining order. The court specifically found that neither Shaheen nor Outerbridge acted in good faith and that the transfer was not for fair consideration. The court ordered Spengler Carlson to turn the stock over to Clarkson.[1]

Spengler Carlson refused to do so on the ground that it was subject to contradictory commands. Several other judgment creditors had begun to take an interest in

---

[1] Appeal from the orders of October 27, 1981, November 2, 1981 and January 26, 1982, which set aside the transfer to Outerbridge, was dismissed upon settlement by the parties.

the stock. They sought to enforce outstanding judgments totaling about $100,000, obtained against SNR in New York courts[2] between 1976 and 1978. In July and September of 1981, several months after Spengler Carlson had taken the stock as trustee for the district court, the state judgment creditors had levied against the stock in the firm's possession and had commenced a § 5225 turn–over proceeding against the firm in New York state court. Spengler Carlson argued that the state judgment creditors' levies made it impossible to comply with the district court's order to turn the stock over to Clarkson.

On November 2, 1981, on Clarkson's motion, the district court enjoined the state court turn–over proceedings and ordered Spengler Carlson to turn the stock over either to Clarkson or to the district court. Spengler Carlson then applied to this court for a stay of the order. However, on November 3, we denied the application, and the firm complied with our order to turn the stock over immediately to the district court.[3]

On February 3, 1982, pursuant to a January 26, 1982 decision of Judge Owen, Clarkson began proceedings under Civ.Prac.Law §§ 5225 and 5239 (McKinney 1978) to determine its priority over the state judgment creditors. In an opinion filed on June 4, 1982, the district court held that Clarkson's rights in the MacMillan shares were prior and superior to those of the state judgment creditors. This appeal followed.

II.

The district court found that Clarkson's April 2, 1981 levy against Spengler Carlson and its earlier January 28, 1981 turn–over proceeding against Outerbridge satisfied New York's statutory requirement for perfecting a levy. The state judgment creditors disagree; they argue that a levy must precede the commencement of a turn–over proceeding and that both actions must be taken against the same party. Since Clarkson failed to comply with either requirement, the argument goes, Clarkson never perfected its levy. The state judgment creditors then argue that they are entitled to priority over Clarkson because they perfected their interest in the stock by levying and proceeding against Spengler Carlson in September 1981. Thus they would claim the fruits of Clarkson's labor in tracking Shaheen's assets.

We find it unnecessary to address the argument concerning the proper order of the levy and the turn–over proceedings. We affirm on the ground that once the shares came into the custody of the court for Clarkson's benefit, no subsequent activity could give third parties a superior claim.

---

[2] Bona Vista Food Services, Ltd., recovered its judgment against SNR in the Federal District Court for the Southern District of New York; nevertheless, the four judgment creditors, including Bona Vista, who oppose Clarkson's claim refer to themselves as the "state judgment creditors."

[3] Since the office of the clerk for the Southern District of New York was closed on November 3, we appointed the deputy clerk of the Second Circuit to receive the securities as surrogate for the district court, with instructions to deliver them to the custody of the clerk of the district court the following morning.

The state judgment creditors argue at the outset that the district court's directions to Spengler Carlson constituted a mere restraining order, enjoining the firm from transferring the stock. As noted above, however, the district court specifically found that Spengler Carlson had taken the stock as trustee for the court. Indeed, the court made its view of the order clear on several occasions, stating, for instance, during a November 1981 colloquy with the parties,

> At the time that Outerbridge was directed to put the shares in this jurisdiction, I wanted them to be in the possession of the court. . . . I in effect said to Mr. Sear [of Spengler Carlson] that he was to take them and hold them for me. . . . Mr. Sear and [the firm were] to hold those in lieu of my having them personally in my possession . . . based upon the confidence that I reposed in him personally.

The court found to the same effect when it enjoined the state court proceedings concerning the stock certificates which were then in the "custody" of the court. 76 Civ. 1373, slip op. at 7 (quoted *supra*). *See also* 525 F.Supp. 625, slip op. at 629 (S.D.N.Y. 1981).

Spengler Carlson took the shares in *custodia legis* as an officer of the court. Any attempt to levy on Spengler Carlson after this time and to restrain the firm's compliance with the district court's orders would be an attempt "to interfere with the officer's possession [and] would amount to an invasion of the jurisdiction of the court itself." 1 A.L.R.3d Funds Deposited in Court as Subject of Garnishment § 2, at 939 (1965). Plaintiff cites no authority for such an invasion here.

We note that New York apparently does not follow the general rule that property in *custodia legis* is wholly immune from attachment. *Compare Wehle v. Conner*, 83 N.Y. 231 (1880) (sustaining the right of a judgment debtor to attach funds held by sheriff for judgment creditor where the debtor claimed that obligations of the creditor offset the judgment that the debtor owed the creditor) with 6 Am.Jur.2d Attachment and Garnishment § 196, at 702 (1963) ("in the absence of express statutory authority . . . , the general rule is that property or funds in custodia legis are not subject to either attachment or garnishment.") Nevertheless, the right under New York law to attach property in the custody of the court is limited. The moving party may attach only such interests as the debtor retained in the property after it passed into the court's custody. Thus, in *Dunlop v. Patterson Fire Insurance Co.*, the New York Court of Appeals allowed the defendant's creditor to attach the defendant's funds, which had been placed in court to secure the plaintiff's judgment; however, the court held that the defendant retained only a reversionary interest in the fund, contingent upon his either prevailing at trial or suffering a judgment against him for less than the amount of the fund. 74 N.Y. 145, 148–49 (1878). Only the debtor's contingent, reversionary interest was subject to attachment. *Id.* at 148–49. *Accord, Saper v. West*, 263 F.2d 422, 427 (2d Cir.) (creditor could not attach fund held in custody of court since debtor retained only a reversionary interest in the fund contingent upon the "highly remote possibility that the trial court's judgment would be reversed on appeal"), *cert. denied*, 360 U.S. 916, 79 S. Ct. 1433, 3 L. Ed. 2d 1532 (1959); *see also Mid–Jersey National Bank v. Fidelity Mortgage Investors*, 518 F.2d 640, 644 (3d Cir.1975) (citing *Saper v. West* with approval and holding that only the defendant's "contingent reversionary interest" in funds held in trust by court for benefit of plaintiff could be subject to jurisdiction of another court during the pendency of the 'trust'). The New York Court of Appeals followed *Dunlop* in *Matter of Leikind,* holding that a creditor could attach a defendant's interest in funds held in *custodia legis* for the purposes of obtaining *in rem* jurisdiction. 22 N.Y.2d 346, 353, 292 N.Y.S.2d 681, 239 N.E.2d 550 (1968). The court also held that the creditor could attach the fund to satisfy his judgment to an extent not inconsistent with the purpose for which the fund was created. *Id.*

Here, the court took custody of the stock for the benefit of Clarkson, creating a trust for the purpose of securing Clarkson's claim to enforcement of its judgment. At that point, the only interest SNR retained in the stock was the right to receive any amount not necessary to satisfy Clarkson's claim. Since the MacMillan shares are allegedly worth less than $1 million, and since Clarkson has allegedly collected only a small fraction of its $50 million judgment, SNR's contingent, reversionary interest appears to have terminated. In any event, the state judgment creditor's attachment of SNR's reversionary interest did not give them priority over Clarkson's claim to enforcement of its judgment against SNR.

Affirmed.

§ 3.13   Protection of Judgment Debtors

MOSKIN v. MIDLAND BANK & TRUST CO.

New York Supreme Court, New York County
96 Misc. 2d 600, 409 N.Y.S.2d 327 (1978)

EDWARD J. GREENFIELD, J.

Petitioner was a general partner in A.C. Kluger & Co., a brokerage firm which ceased to do business in November of 1972. Although it appears that an independent liquidator was appointed to collect the partnership assets and distribute them to the partnership's creditors, many of the partnership's debts remain unpaid and there are at least three outstanding judgments.

Each of the respondents herein, other than the Sheriff, are judgment creditors of the partnership who have issued executions directing the Sheriff to sell petitioner's seat on the New York Stock Exchange. Petitioner, through counsel, had been able to work out informal arrangements with respondents Rubin and GTE who had delivered executions to the Sheriff in November of 1976 and August of 1977, respectively, as a result of which scheduled sales were adjourned.

Thereafter, in October of 1977, respondent, Marine Midland Bank, delivered an execution to the Sheriff directing the sale of petitioner's seat. Upon receipt of this execution, the Sheriff notified GTE and Rubin, who revived their executions. The sale of petitioner's seat, which was scheduled for March 29, 1978, has been stayed by this court, pending resolution of the instant application in which petitioner seeks: (1) to vacate the executions on the ground that his seat is not the proper subject of an execution; (2) a determination that Marine Midland's judgment is unenforceable and (3) an order pursuant to CPLR 5240 denying respondents the right to execute on petitioner's seat on the Exchange.

There is no merit to petitioner's contention that his seat is not subject to a levy. The fact that any purchaser of the seat could not take a place on the floor of the Exchange unless he met the requirements imposed by and received the necessary approval of the Exchange, does not preclude a sale. However, insofar as petitioner seeks relief pursuant to CPLR 5240, which permits the court to modify, vacate or regulate enforcement procedures, petitioner has made a sufficient showing to justify a continued stay of any sale, subject to certain conditions. CPLR 5240 was designed to prevent "unreasonable annoyance, expense, embarrassment, disadvantage, or other prejudice to any person or the courts." (Third Preliminary Report of Advisory Committee on Practice and Procedure, p 314.) In an analogous situation, the court, in *Holmes v. W.T. Grant, Inc.* (71 Misc 2d 486), stayed execution on a Sheriff's sale of the home of welfare recipients, on condition that they pay the judgment creditor $20 per month. As noted therein, the exercise of the discretionary power granted by CPLR 5240 requires "harmonizing the judgment debtor's interest in avoiding irreparable . . . harm . . . with the legitimate interest of a creditor in securing payment of a valid debt." (*Id.*, p 487.) Petitioner alleges that his seat forms the sole source of his livelihood, out of which he must support himself, pay alimony and child support and pay off any judgments. Petitioner has previously made payments on the judgments secured by respondents Rubin and GTE, but apparently as a result of decrease in his income has been unable to meet these payments. As the seat forms the sole source of moneys for his own support and payments by him for the support of his ex–wife and children, the loss of his seat on the Exchange might have a more deleterious effect than the sale of defendant's home in the *Holmes* case referred to above. Respondent's speculation that petitioner might make more money if he worked for a brokerage firm rather than being self–employed is pure speculation and is not supported by any facts in the papers before the court. On the other hand, if the court stays the sale of petitioner's seat, the judgment creditors will continue to have a lien to protect their interests until the judgment is paid. A balancing of the equities clearly justifies the court in staying the sale on condition that the petitioner make periodic payments on the outstanding judgments, until the judgments are satisfied by petitioner and/or the other partners of A. C. Kluger.

As petitioner does not dispute the validity of the judgments obtained by respondents Rubin and GTE, the court will grant the petition to the extent of staying their respective executions and the Sheriff's sale of petitioner's seat pursuant thereto on condition that monthly payments on account of the judgments are paid by petitioner. The judgment to be settled hereon shall set forth suggestions as to the amount of such payments and affidavits may be submitted.

With respect to the execution delivered to the Sheriff by Marine Midland, petitioner contends that the execution is invalid on the grounds that the partnership was never properly served in the underlying action and on the further ground that the action is based on a note entered into subsequent to the dissolution of the partnership and is accordingly not enforceable. Midland obtained its judgment in

January of 1977. Service of the summons was made on one Ruth Johnson, who defendant denies was a partner of A. C. Kluger. Petitioner unequivocally states that Ms. Johnson was not a general partner. Although Marine Midland contends that it has documentation setting forth the identity of all 11 former partners, it does not state that Ms. Johnson is listed as a partner in this documentation, which has not been submitted to the court. Midland attempts to becloud the issue by refraining from stating in its papers that Ms. Johnson was a partner and merely alleges that "She obviously represented herself to the process server as such". This statement is insufficient to raise an issue as to whether she was a partner, and is sheer conjecture. Moreover, the court takes judicial notice of the fact that Ruth Johnson is not listed as a partner in the Spring 1973 Edition of Security Dealers of North America, published by Standard & Poors. Accordingly, Marine Midland's judgment against the partnership is hereby vacated on the grounds of lack of jurisdiction (*see* CPLR 5015, subd [a], par 4).

Accordingly, the petition is granted to the extent of (1) vacating the judgment and execution of Marine Midland and (2) staying execution on and the Sheriff's sale of petitioner's seat on the New York Stock Exchange by or pursuant to executions issued by respondents Rubin and GTE on condition that petitioner make monthly payments to these respondents until the judgment is satisfied in the amount set forth in the judgment to be settled hereon. If petitioner defaults in making these payments, respondents Rubin and GTE may move for leave to resume their executions. The judgment shall further provide that in the event the Sheriff schedules a sale pursuant to an execution delivered to the Sheriff by any other judgment creditor, the executions shall revive, without prejudice to petitioner to move pursuant to CPLR 5240 to stay any such sale.

NOTE

See discussion of exemptions in Chapter 7, *infra*.

§ 3.14   Protection for Judgment Creditors

OVERMYER v. FIDELITY AND DEPOSIT CO. OF MARYLAND

United States Court of Appeals, Second Circuit
554 F.2d 539 (1977)

MULLIGAN, Circuit Judge:

This appeal reveals a crass misuse of both the state and federal judicial systems to avoid the payment of a judgment. In 1973 Eliot Realty, Inc. successfully brought an action against Overmyer Distribution Services, Inc. (Overmyer Inc.) in a Justice Court in Dallas, Texas to recover possession of real property. Overmyer Inc.

appealed to the Dallas County Court obtaining from Fidelity and Deposit Company of Maryland (Fidelity), the appellee in this action, an appeal bond. Shirley and Daniel H. Overmyer, the appellants here, executed a general agreement of indemnity contracting to indemnify Fidelity for all losses, costs, damages and attorneys' fees it might sustain by reason of issuing the appeal bond. The County Court on October 12, 1973 not only affirmed the judgment of the Justice Court but further awarded Eliot Realty, Inc. money damages in the sum of $28,092.25, plus interest and costs, the value of the continued occupancy of the premises during the appeal. The court also directed that execution of the judgment be had against Overmyer Inc. and Fidelity as surety. Overmyer Inc. filed a notice of appeal but allegedly the company's counsel withdrew, leaving it unable to perfect the appeal. On December 7, 1973 Fidelity entered into a settlement agreement with Eliot Realty, Inc. by which Fidelity paid the sum of $25,535.85 to discharge its liability on the bond and to satisfy the judgment of the Texas court.

Fidelity then commenced an action in the New York State Supreme Court, County of New York, seeking to recover the amount of the judgment plus counsel fees. The defendants in that action were Overmyer Inc. and Daniel H. and Shirley Overmyer. Defendants' motion to dismiss the complaint was denied and Fidelity's cross–motion for summary judgment was granted in an order of Justice Nathaniel T. Helman on November 14, 1974. The Overmyers had questioned the good faith of Fidelity in settling the judgment. However, in an opinion in October, 1974 Justice Helman pointed out:

> There is no affidavit by any of the defendants. Their counsel may raise questions, whether of fact or of law in Texas but his own clients are the best source of the answers. No question exists as to plaintiff's obligation when it is named as a judgment debtor and execution is granted against it. This is not a case where it was solely the surety. In any event, defendants contracted to indemnify upon payment, whether plaintiff was liable or not. Defendants have no defense against their contract obligation, and their attorney cannot create one by "surmise, conjecture and suspicion" (*Shapiro v. Health Insurance Plan of Greater New York,* 7 N.Y.2d 56, 194 N.Y.S.2d 509, 163 N.E.2d 333).

Overmyer appealed from the judgment entered in November 1974 to the Appellate Division, First Department which unanimously affirmed the judgment on May 20, 1975. Overmyer then moved in the Appellate Division for a stay of enforcement of the judgment. The motion was denied as was another motion to reargue the motion for a stay. Overmyer then applied for leave to appeal to the New York Court of Appeals in both the Appellate Division and the Court of Appeals. Both motions were denied. Overmyer than applied to the United States Supreme Court for an extension of time to petition for a writ of certiorari. This was also denied.

During these appellate maneuverings the Overmyer defendants were also active in the State Supreme Court. On February 21, 1975 they moved by order to show cause to vacate the judgment pursuant to N.Y.C.P.L.R. § 5015(a)(2) upon the grounds of newly discovered evidence. Justice Markowitz denied the motion on April 11, 1975 finding the purported grounds to be without merit.

After the entry of the judgment in November a subpoena to examine Daniel H. Overmyer to determine his financial status was served upon him returnable on January 17, 1975. At his request the return date was postponed until March 17, 1975 at which time Overmyer failed to appear. Fidelity, the judgment creditor, then brought a motion on notice to punish Daniel Overmyer for contempt. On May 6, 1975 Overmyer, who had received notice of this motion, appeared by his attorneys and opposed the motion. Justice George Postel granted the motion and found Overmyer in contempt of court unless he appeared for examination on June 12, 1975. Characteristically, he failed to appear and on September 30, 1975 after notice Justice Postel signed an order finding Overmyer in contempt of court and imposed a fine of $260. The court directed that the contempt order would be purged and the fine remitted if Daniel Overmyer appeared for examination on October 29, 1975. Although Overmyer paid the fine in installments he did not appear for the October 29, 1975 examination. On June 4, 1976 after his counsel had filed papers in opposition the court once again found Overmyer in contempt directing the sheriff of any county to compel him to appear at the courthouse for examination under oath. Upon the eve of the directed apprehension Overmyer obtained a stay of the enforcement of the judgment and an order directing Fidelity to show cause why Overmyer should not be granted leave to reargue the prior motion to vacate the judgment on the grounds of newly discovered evidence. This "newly discovered evidence" was that Fidelity had influenced Overmyer Inc.'s attorneys in the Texas action to act against the Overmyer defendants' interest. With respect to this evidence Justice Tyler concluded:

> [U]pon a full presentation of defendants' "proof", it is the view of this Court that there is absolutely no basis for a stay insofar as the newly–discovered evidence is supposed to support it. All that the defendants have presented is a series of allegations that do not lead this Court to the conclusion that the instant motion should be granted. In point of fact, after reviewing the "proof" adduced by the defendants, it is the belief of this Court that the instant motion is merely another ploy utilized by Overmyer in an attempt to avoid the full force and effect of a judgment entered in the Court as well as the several orders emanating thereafter.

Unpublished opinion in *Fidelity and Deposit Company of Maryland v. Daniel H. Overmyer et al.,* Index No. 5920/74 (Sup. Ct. N.Y. County, June 23, 1976) at 5. After hearing argument on both sides, Justice Tyler denied the motion to reargue, vacated the stay and once again directed that Overmyer appear for examination. The sheriff of any county was authorized to apprehend Daniel Overmyer and compel his attendance for examination at the courthouse on June 29, 1976.

In the same opinion of June 23, 1976 Justice Tyler commented:

> This court finds the litany of evasion and noncompliance in which the defendant judgment debtor has engaged to be absolutely incredible. The utter disrespect which Overmyer has shown, not just for the prior order of this court, but for the entire system of jurisprudence by which this court and this society operates is reprehensible.

The efforts of the Overmyers to delay or defeat the day of judgment however did not end. On June 29, 1976 Daniel and Shirley Overmyer brought an action in the Southern District of New York seeking injunctive relief and damages against Fidelity, the State of New York, Justice Tyler, Thomas J. Delaney, the Sheriff of Westchester County and Edward A. Pichler, the Sheriff of New York County. Plaintiffs requested the convening of a three–judge court to consider their constitutional claims which were that the New York statutes relating to civil contempt, N.Y. Judiciary Law §§ 756, 757, 765, 767, and 769–775, were invalid because they violated the Fourth, Fifth, Eighth and Fourteenth Amendments of the United States Constitution. The complaint requested that permanent and preliminary injunctive relief be granted against the defendants to prevent enforcement of the contempt statutes. Pending the convening of the three–judge court a temporary restraining order was requested to be issued for the same purpose. Plaintiffs' complaint also contained a pendent claim against Fidelity based on its alleged influence over Overmyer Inc.'s lawyers in the Texas action. Damages of $100,000 were requested.[1]

The action came before the Hon. Milton Pollack, United States District Judge for the Southern District of New York. In an opinion and order of October 18th, 1976 the trial court denied plaintiffs' motion for a preliminary injunction[2] and granted Fidelity's motion to dismiss the complaint.[3] This appeal followed.

We need not tarry long with the constitutional issues raised by the appellants. In the court below they relied upon *Vail v. Quinlan*, 406 F.Supp. 951 (S.D.N.Y. 1976), the decision of a three–judge court finding the New York State contempt law unconstitutional. Judge Pollack found *Vail* to be inapposite since that case involved ex parte contempt findings resulting in imprisonment against pro se debtors. In the *Overmyer* case all of the motions were noticed and the plaintiffs were represented by counsel on all occasions. Moreover, the order here which Overmyer sought to enjoin was pursuant to N.Y.C.P.L.R. § 2308(a) directing the sheriff to bring Overmyer to be examined under oath; he was never threatened with incarceration. No attack was levied against this section but rather against §§ 756, 757, 765, 767

---

[1] The pendent damage claim against Fidelity was based upon allegations of its fraud and bad faith in settling the Texas action. It is significant that aside from the conclusory allegations of the complaint, the plaintiffs, as in the motion before Justice Tyler in which they attempted to vacate on the grounds of newly discovered evidence, have submitted no affidavits to support the charge of fraudulent behavior by Fidelity. On its face the accusation is incomprehensible. Why would Fidelity pay a substantial settlement for the privilege of pursuing the Overmyers to recover its damages from them?

[2] By stipulation and order of September 7, 1976 it was provided that the State of New York and Justice Tyler be granted up to 20 days after the Supreme Court's decision in *Juidice v. Vail, infra,* to answer and so are not parties to this appeal. Defendant Pichler never appeared.

[3] In denying the motion for a preliminary injunction Judge Pollack aptly characterized the specious nature of the Overmyers' federal action: "The complaint herein by conclusory allegations raises a sham issue in the light of the evidence submitted on the application for temporary and injunctive relief. . . . Plaintiffs do not satisfy the criteria for injunctive relief on the actual matter involved, *viz.,* probability of success on the merits by raising a semantic semblance to an irrelevant constitutional question. . . ." *Overmyer v. Fidelity and Deposit Co.,* 76 Civ. 2876 (MP) (S.D.N.Y. Oct. 18, 1976) at 8.

and 769–775 of the Judiciary Law which would have come into play if the New York court had decided to imprison Overmyer for contempt. In any event, *Vail v. Quinlan, supra,* was reversed by the Supreme Court, sub nom. *Juidice v. Vail,—* U.S.—, 97 S. Ct. 1211, 51 L. Ed. 2d 376 (1977) which held that the district court should have abstained under the doctrine of *Younger v. Harris,* 401 U.S. 37, 91 S. Ct. 746, 27 L. Ed. 2d 669 (1971). The Court found "[t]he contempt power lies at the core of the administration of a State's judicial system". — U.S. at —, 97 S. Ct. at 1217. Therefore, the Court concluded that granting injunctive relief would constitute an improper interference with the state system prohibited by *Younger.* The Court held that for a federal court to abstain it was only necessary for the plaintiffs to have had the opportunity to raise the federal issue before the state court; it was not necessary that a hearing be held if they failed to employ available procedures. Overmyer had ample opportunity to raise his federal claims before the state court. Thus, even if his constitutional claims had any merit, we could not consider them. Since there is no basis for diversity jurisdiction, diversity not having been alleged, the pendent claim was properly dismissed.

Appellants admit, as they must, that their constitutional argument is foreclosed here in light of *Juidice v. Vail, supra.* However they argue that this court should "correct" Judge Pollack's opinion since his holding that the constitutional issues had been decided against them in the state court barred their adjudication in the federal court. *Thistlethwaite v. City of New York,* 497 F.2d 339 (2d Cir.), *cert. denied,* 419 U.S. 1093, 95 S. Ct. 686, 42 L. Ed. 2d 686 (1974). There is no need for this court to take such action. If the appellants are correct in their position that the federal constitutional questions were never litigated in the state courts, surely the state courts are competent to make that determination without reference to or limitation by the federal opinion appealed from.

28 U.S.C. § 1912 and Federal Rule of Appellate Procedure 38 authorize this court upon a determination that an appeal is frivolous to award just damages and single or double costs to the appellee. *Teledyne Industries, Inc. v. Podell,* 546 F.2d 495 (2d Cir. 1976). The history of this litigation in the state courts and its continuation in the federal court, even before the Supreme Court had demolished the only semblance of support plaintiffs could muster, serves to illustrate that this appeal was and is frivolous. This court has been utilized, as were earlier the state and district courts, as a device to frustrate the collection of a judgment of a state court. We assess the appellants double costs and in addition $2000 in attorneys' fees.[4] The mandate shall issue forthwith and shall not be stayed by the filing of a petition for rehearing.

---

[4] It has not escaped our attention that appellants were assisted by counsel before both the district court and this court in bringing this sham suit and appeal. We have warned counsel in immigration matters about abusing the process in this court to gain delays in deportation. *Hibbert v. I.N.S.,* 554 F.2d 17, at 19 n.l. (2d Cir. 1977); *Acevedo v. I.N.S.,* 538 F.2d 918 (2d Cir. 1976). The use of this court solely as a dilatory tactic to avoid paying a judgment is a serious breach of professional ethics. *Cf. Hibbert v. I.N.S., supra,* at 19 n.l; *In re Bithoney,* 486 F.2d 319 (1st Cir. 1973). *See also* Edelstein, *The Ethics of Dilatory Motion Practice: Time for Change,* 44 Fordham L.Rev. 1069 (1976). We remind the Bar that under Fed.R. Civ.P. 11 the signature of an attorney on a pleading "constitutes a certificate by him . . . that it is not interposed for delay." We will not countenance attempts to pervert the federal judicial process into a Dickensian court where lawsuits never end.

CHAPTER 4

ATTACHMENT AND GARNISHMENT

§ 4.01   Introduction

Attachment is the pre–judgment provisional remedy that enables a plaintiff to seize, or have an enforcement officer seize, property of the defendant for purposes of obtaining jurisdiction and/or securing an eventual judgment. Attachment procedure varies widely from state to state, but is generally available only when the plaintiff is seeking a money judgment. An attorney considering attachment of a defendant's property in a particular jurisdiction must determine how the law of that jurisdiction treats each of the issues discussed below.

In addition, as will be discussed in § 4.03, *infra*, counsel must come to terms with the wholesale constitutional assault launched against attachment and other creditors' summary remedies begun in 1969 with *Sniadach v. Family Finance Corp.*, 395 U.S. 357 (1969) (absent notice and hearing, Wisconsin pre–judgment wage garnishment procedure violated the 14th Amendment requirement of due process). Although the property seizure under an attachment order is often more constructive than actual, the effect of the order is real: the defendant may not freely use, sell or encumber the property. The plaintiff thus gets a contingent lien on the defendant's property, dependent only on whether he later prevails on the underlying claim.

The defendant may not have in his possession the property to be attached. *Garnishment* is the attachment of the defendant's property held by a third person. A person who owes money to the defendant (including a bank or the defendant's employer), or who has possession or custody of the defendant's property, is known as a "garnishee." When personal property is being attached, the garnishee is often an important participant.

[A]   Actions In Which Attachment Is Proper

Courts distinguish between foreign attachment (to obtain jurisdiction) and domestic attachment (to secure a subsequent money judgment).

[1]   Foreign Attachment

Foreign attachment is the attachment of the in–state property of a nonresident defendant for purposes of (a) establishing personal jurisdiction over the defendant, and (b) eventually realizing on the property in the event of a judgment in favor of the plaintiff. *See Jonnet v. Dollar Savings Bank*, 530 F.2d 1123 (3d Cir. 1976). This

(Matthew Bender & Co., Inc.)   (Pub.094)

form of personal jurisdiction, known as "quasi in rem" jurisdiction,* was approved by the Supreme Court in *Pennoyer v. Neff*, 95 U.S. 714 (1878) (notice by publication to nonresident defendant improper unless the court first takes control of defendant's in–state property). In today's terms, *Pennoyer* means that the plaintiff must obtain the attachment order and have the sheriff levy on the property before a court has quasi in rem jurisdiction. After reading *Shaffer v. Heitner*, 433 U.S. 186 (1977), *infra*, consider whether quasi in rem jurisdiction has been drastically curtailed, if not abrogated.

The use of foreign attachment to obtain quasi in rem jurisdiction is permitted in all states. If the defendant fails to appear, a default judgment is entered for the plaintiff, to be satisfied, to the extent possible, from the proceeds of the sale of the attached property (*e.g.*, bank account, real estate, or other goods). A judgment obtained in a quasi in rem action, however, is not entitled to either res judicata or collateral estoppel effect. *See Minichiello v. Rosenberg*, 410 F.2d 106, 110–12 (2d Cir. 1968). If the plaintiff's judgment exceeds the value of the attached property, the plaintiff must initiate a new action on the merits to recover the deficiency.

If the defendant enters the jurisdiction to defend the action on the merits, in almost all states the defendant is deemed to have made a *general appearance* and to have subjected him/herself to the full in personam jurisdiction of the court. The court may, in its discretion, preserve or vacate the attachment. A prevailing plaintiff may execute on the attached property and in addition will have a valid judgment against the defendant, enforceable anywhere, for the full amount of the claim.

In most jurisdictions, therefore, the nonresident defendant in a quasi in rem action must decide whether (a) to default, lose the attached property, and retain the right to defend the actions on the merits in a subsequent proceeding, or (b) to make a general appearance and thereby be exposed to the full in personam jurisdiction of the court. Some states, however, permit the nonresident defendant to make a *limited appearance*. The defendant may enter the state and litigate the action on the merits, for the limited purpose of defending his or her interest in the attached property, and any judgment against the defendant will be limited to the value of the attached property. *See, e.g., Miller Bros. Co. v. State*, 201 Md. 535, 95 A.2d 286 (Md. 1953); *Osborn v. White Eagle Oil Co.*, 355 P.2d 1041 (Okla. 1960).

[2] Domestic Attachment

Domestic attachment is the attachment of the property of a resident defendant. The purpose of the attachment is not to obtain jurisdiction, but solely to create a lien on the attached property that will secure payment of any judgment that the plaintiff may ultimately recover. State laws governing the availability of domestic attachment vary enormously. Some states completely forbid the pre–judgment attachment or garnishment of a resident defendant's property. Mich. Comp. Laws

---

* A judgment *in personam* imposes a personal liability or obligation on one person in favor of another. A judgment *in rem* affects the interests of all persons in designated property. A *judgment quasi in rem* affects the interests of particular persons in designated property. *Shaffer v. Heitner*, 433 U.S. 186, 199 n.17 (1977), citing *Hanson v. Denckla*, 357 U.S. 235, 245 n.12 (1958).

§§ 600.4001 and 600.4011 (1968 & Supp. 1983–84). California permits attachment of a resident defendant's property in contract and quasi–contract actions. Cal. Civ. Proc. Code § 483.010 (West 1979 & Supp. 1984). New York and certain other states permit attachment of a debtor's property in all actions for a money judgment, provided that certain special circumstances exist. N.Y. Civ. Prac. Law § 6201 (McKinney 1980).

[B]   Special Circumstances Requirements

As noted above, New York and certain other states require that a plaintiff seeking to attach the defendant's property must show at least one of the following special circumstances: (1) the defendant is a non resident (*i.e.*, attachment is sought to establish quasi in rem jurisdiction); (2) the defendant is hiding; (3) the defendant is concealing or attempting to dispose of its assets; or (4) the plaintiff is suing on an unpaid judgment that is entitled to full faith and credit. *Id.*; Note, 8 A.L.R.2d 578 (1949).

These requirements reflect the legislative belief that attachment is a harsh remedy, and normally should not be suffered by a defendant who has not yet had a chance to defend the underlying action on the merits. Therefore, the plaintiff's right of attachment is limited to those situations where it is necessary to obtain jurisdiction; where wrongful conduct by the debtor may make it difficult for the plaintiff to obtain an enforceable judgment; or where the plaintiff has already prevailed on the merits, and is suing to enforce a judgment. Some states require that the attaching plaintiff first show, with evidentiary detail, a reasonable probability of prevailing on the merits of the underlying claim. *See, e.g.*, N.Y. Civ. Prac. Law 6212(a) (McKinney 1980); *Zenith Bathing Pavilion, Inc. v. Fair Oaks S.S. Corp.*, 240 N.Y. 307, 312 (N.Y. 1925) ("What is sufficient for a pleading may be insufficient for attachment"); *see also* Cal. Civ. Proc. Code § 512.010 (West 1979).

[C]   When Attachment Is Available

The plaintiff may seek an order of attachment at any time before final judgment. In some jurisdictions, including New York, the plaintiff may seek an order of attachment even before commencing the underlying action, providing he or she commences the action within a specified time. (In New York, the plaintiff must serve the summons within sixty days. N.Y. Civ. Prac. Law § 6213 (McKinney 1980)).

[D]   Procedural Requirements

The plaintiff files a motion for an order of attachment, an affidavit indicating that all statutory requirements have been satisfied and that any required special circumstances exist, a bond (or "undertaking") to guarantee the payment of the defendant's damages in the event the attachment proves wrongful, and a proposed order (or "writ") of attachment. Plaintiffs prefer to make the motion ex parte, *i.e.* without notice, out of apprehension that notice will enable the defendant to remove property from the jurisdiction. As a result of the *Sniadach* line of cases in the Supreme Court, *infra*, prior notice to the defendant is safer, but ex parte motions are probably permitted if the plaintiff establishes the probable validity of his claim in a meaningful way and the defendant is a non–resident, *Lebowitz v. Forbes Leasing & Finance Co.*, 456 F.2d 979 (3d Cir. 1972), or is about to remove or dissipate the assets. *Harrison v. Morris*, 370 F. Supp. 142 (D.S.C. 1974).

Even in emergency cases, due process requires an immediate post–attachment hearing. In New York, a plaintiff who obtains an ex parte order of attachment must move on notice to confirm the order, and if the confirmation hearing is not held within five days, the attachment has no further effect, N.Y. Civ. Prac. Law § 6211(b) (McKinney 1979), and the plaintiff may be liable for all damages suffered by the defendant.

The order of attachment is directed to the sheriff or other enforcement officer. It may order the sheriff to serve the order on the defendant (or garnishee), in which case the defendant is expected to surrender the attached property to the sheriff, or it may authorize the sheriff to seize ("levy") or otherwise exercise control over the attached property. The order may specify certain property or may simply order the sheriff to levy upon the defendant's property in an amount equal to the dollar amount of the claim in the plaintiff's complaint.

In some states, if the defendant refuses to surrender the attached property to the sheriff, the plaintiff must move for a "turnover" order, directing the defendant to do so. Failure to comply with a turnover order will subject the defendant to penalties for contempt.

[E] Effect of Attachment

The plaintiff who properly causes the defendant's property to be attached obtains a contingent "attachment lien" on the attached property. If the plaintiff prevails, his/her interest will be superior to any lien or other interest in the property arising after the attachment lien.

The attachment lien typically comes into existence when a copy of the attachment order is served on the defendant (or garnishee), or, much less frequently, when the sheriff levies on the property by actual seizure. In New York, the attachment lien on personal property arises when the order is delivered to the sheriff, provided that the sheriff effects the levy timely. N.Y. Civ. Prac. Law § 6226 (McKinney 1980).

New York permits an attachment levy on real property by the sheriff's merely filing a notice of attachment with the county clerk where the property is located. *Id.* § 6216.

[F] Rights and Remedies of the Defendant

A defendant whose property has been attached has several options:

[1] Demand for the Papers

The defendant or garnishee is usually entitled to review immediately the attachment papers. In New York, if the defendant serves a "demand for the papers" upon plaintiff's counsel, the papers must be delivered within one day. N.Y. Civ. Prac. Law § 6212(d) (McKinney 1980). Local practice may delay seizure of the attached property pending delivery of the papers.

[2] Bond

The defendant may usually obtain the release of the attached or garnished property by posting a bond. There are two general types of bond, either of which may or may not be available in any given jurisdiction. A "discharging bond" guarantees that the defendant will pay any judgment awarded the plaintiff in the underlying action. A "delivery bond" guarantees that the defendant will produce the attached property for application to the plaintiff's judgment if the plaintiff prevails. Posting either bond causes the attached property to be returned to the defendant, but only the discharging bond vacates the plaintiff's attachment lien.

[3] Motion to Vacate

The defendant may move to vacate the order of attachment on any of the following grounds: (a) the plaintiff's motion papers or bond are defective; (b) the attached property is legally exempt; (c) the plaintiff's claim is not one for which attachment is proper; (d) the value of the attached property exceeds the amount sought in the plaintiff's complaint; and (e) the attached property does not belong to the defendant.

[4] Attachment Discretionary

Attachment is a remedy that generally lies within the trial court's discretion. Even when a plaintiff has established the availability of the remedy, the court may still deny attachment when the defendant is served within the state and the plaintiff fails to show a danger that any subsequent judgment will not be satisfied. *See e.g., Elliott v. Great Atlantic & Pacific Tea Co.*, 11 Misc. 2d 133, 171 N.Y.S.2d 217 (N.Y.C. City Ct. 1957), *aff'd without opinion*, 11 Misc. 2d 136, 179 N.Y.S.2d 127 (App. Term 1st Dept. 1958).

[5] Cause of Action for Wrongful Attachment

If the defendant ultimately prevails on the underlying action, the defendant may be statutorily entitled to damages resulting from "wrongful attachment." Unless the attachment itself was not lawful, in which case damages may also be authorized, this remedy is usually available only when the defendant prevails *in toto. See, e.g.*, N.Y. Civ. Proc. Law § 6212 (McKinney 1980). For example, if the plaintiff's complaint seeks damages of $100,000, and the plaintiff attaches property of the defendant in that amount, and the plaintiff is ultimately awarded only $10,000, the defendant is not entitled to damages for wrongful attachment.

In some states, the defendant is entitled to receive such damages as part of its costs at the end of trial. *Id.* In other states, however, if the defendant wishes to recover more than the amount of the plaintiff's bond, it may have to initiate a new action based on a common law theory of liability, *e.g.*, abuse of process. Cal. Civ. Proc. Code §§ 490.010, 490.020, 490.060 (West 1979 & Supp. 1984). *See White Lighting Co. v. Wolfson*, 68 Cal. 2d 236, 438 P.2d 345 (Cal. 1968) (creditor attached property worth almost $20,000 to secure claim of $850).

[G] Lis Pendens

Lis pendens is a pre–judgment attachment–like remedy applicable only in actions involving title to, or the right to possession of, real property. The plaintiff in such an action may file a lis pendens, or notice of pendency, with the recording clerk in the county or area in which the property is located. The lis pendens itself merely states that an action has been commenced affecting title to the land in question. A purchaser of the real property will take subject to the lis pendens, *i.e.*, subject to the outcome of the litigation. *See generally* 2 Moore's Federal Practice, ¶ 3.05 at 3–25 (2d rev. ed. 1983).

Requirements for lis pendens vary from state to state, and may not be the same as the requirements for attachment. *See* New York Civ. Proc. Law § 6501 (McKinney 1980) (special circumstances required for attachment are not required for notice of pendency). In some states, a lis pendens may be filed without a court order.

[H]   Attachment in Federal Court

Fed. R. Civ. P. 64 provides:

> At the commencement of and during the course of an action, all remedies providing for seizure of person or property for the purpose of securing satisfaction of a judgment ultimately to be entered in the action are available under the circumstances and in the manner provided by the law of the state in which the district court is held, existing at the time the remedy is sought, subject to the following qualifications: (1) Any existing statute of the United States governs to the extent to which it is applicable; (2) The action in which any of the foregoing remedies is used shall be commenced and prosecuted or, if removed from a state court, shall be prosecuted after removal, pursuant to these rules. The remedies thus available include arrest, attachment, garnishment, replevin, sequestration, and other corresponding or equivalent remedies, however designated and regardless of whether by state procedure the remedy is ancillary to an action or must be obtained by an independent action.

Under 28 U.S.C. § 1450, an attachment order in a state court action is preserved if the action is removed to federal court. *See also Rorick v. Devon Syndicate, Ltd.,* 307 U.S. 299 (1939); 7 Moore's Federal Practice ¶ 64.09 at 64–40 (2d rev. ed. 1983). Other federal statutes include special garnishment and attachment rules to be followed in cases involving such federal questions as admiralty. *See e.g.*, 28 U.S.C. § 2464 (release of vessel seized by marshall under "warrant of arrest").

The right of a nonresident defendant in a diversity case to make a "limited appearance" is governed by state law. *U.S. Industries v. Gregg*, 58 F.R.D. 469, 474–76 (D. Del. 1973).

NOTES AND QUESTIONS

(1) The attachment of the property of a nonresident defendant, obtained for the purpose of establishing quasi in rem jurisdiction, may, in the court's discretion, be preserved even after the defendant makes a general appearance and defends the action on the merits. *Property Research Financial Corp. v. Superior Court*, 23 Cal.

App. 3d 413, 100 Cal. Rptr. 233 (1972); *Lebowitz v. Forbes Leasing & Fin. Co.*, 456 F.2d 979 (3d Cir. 1972). Is this fair to the nonresident defendant? Note that attachment might not be available in an action alleging the same claim against a resident defendant. What factors should a court consider in determining whether to lift an attachment? *See ITC Entertainment, Ltd. v. Nelson Film Partners*, 714 F.2d 217 (2d Cir. 1983).

(2) The sheriff may levy on tangible personal property by taking it into his or her possession. A subsequent purchaser of the property from the defendant is held to be on constructive or inquiry notice of the plaintiff's attachment lien by the defendant's inability to deliver possession.

How does the sheriff levy on property that cannot be "seized"? *See, e.g., Brunswick Corp. v. Haerter*, 182 N.W.2d 852, 857 (N.D. 1971), in which a "warrant of seizure" on bowling lanes and automatic pinsetters was executed by removing a part from each pinsetter, rendering the lanes and equipment unusable. Would such action put a bona fide purchaser on notice that the equipment had been attached?

In *Brunswick Corp., supra*, the defendant, Haerter, claimed that the plaintiff and the sheriff were liable for conversion. He argued that the sheriff's failure to remove the disabled equipment not only deprived him of the use of his building as a bowling alley, but also prevented him from renting it out for other use. How would you rule?

(3) States that permit the attachment of a nonresident's property for jurisdictional purposes generally also authorize the attachment of the assets of a foreign corporation not licensed to do business in the state. Should the attachment be lifted if the corporation thereafter obtains a license? *See Brastex Corporation v. Allen International, Inc.*, 702 F.2d 326 (2d Cir. 1982).

(4) Evaluate the rights of a defendant whose property has been attached, in a case in which attachment is permitted by statute. One commentator has noted that, in practice, defendants rarely post a bond to obtain the release of the attached property. One reason is that the surety company usually requires collateral equal in value to the attached assets. Comment, *Abuse of Process and Attachment: Towards a Balance of Power*, 30 UCLA L. Rev. 1218, 1233 (1983). Consider the enormous leverage attachment gives to the plaintiff in settlement negotiations when the defendant requires the property to operate his or her business but is unable to post a bond.

Furthermore, the right to damages for wrongful attachment may be difficult to enforce. As noted above, in some states, unless the defendant initiates a new, plenary action, the defendant's recovery is limited to the amount of the plaintiff's bond, which may or may not bear any relation to the defendant's actual damages.

(5) Should there be a federal law of attachment for federal question cases? Does it make sense that an antitrust plaintiff in federal district court in Connecticut can cause the defendant's property to be attached, whereas an antitrust plaintiff in federal district court in Michigan cannot?

§ 4.02 What Is Subject to Attachment?

[A] Introduction

In general, state statutes provide that a plaintiff may attach any property of the defendant that a judgment creditor could reach to satisfy a judgment. *See*, *e.g.*, N.Y. Civ. Prac. § 6202. Thus, property exempt from execution under state or federal law may not be attached.

Most statutes, in addition, permit the attachment (or "garnishment") of debts owed to the debtor by a third party (the "garnishee"). The garnishment of wages is the most common example, although its use has been restricted in recent years following the Supreme Court's *Sniadach* decision, reproduced *infra*. Debts other than wages, however, may be attached.

The attachment of debts suggests numerous questions: What happens if the garnishee denies its obligation to the defendant? May contingent or unliquidated debts be attached? What due process considerations or other questions arise if the garnishee is a resident and the defendant a nonresident of the forum state? Consider these questions while reading the following cases.

HARRIS v. BALK

United States Supreme Court
198 U.S. 215 25 S. Ct. 625, 49 L. Ed. 1023 (1905)

. . . .

The facts are as follows: The plaintiff in error, Harris, . . . was indebted to the defendant in error, Balk, . . . in the sum of $180, for money borrowed from Balk by Harris during the year 1896. . . . During the year above mentioned one Jacob Epstein, a resident of Baltimore, in the state of Maryland, asserted that Balk was indebted to him in the sum of over $300. In August, 1896, Harris visited Baltimore for the purpose of purchasing merchandise, and while he was in that city temporarily on August 6, 1896, Epstein caused to be issued out of a proper court in Baltimore a foreign or nonresident writ of attachment against Balk, attaching the debt due Balk from Harris, which writ the sheriff at Baltimore laid in the hands of Harris, with a summons to appear in the court at a day named. With that attachment, a writ of summons and a short declaration against Balk (as provided by the Maryland statute) were also delivered to the sheriff, and by him set up at the courthouse door, as required by the law of Maryland. Before the return day of the attachment writ Harris left Baltimore, and returned to his home in North Carolina. He did not contest the garnishee process, which was issued to garnish the debt which Harris owed Balk. After his return Harris made an affidavit on August 11, 1896, that he owed Balk $180, and stated that the amount had been attached by Epstein, of Baltimore, and by his counsel in the Maryland proceeding Harris consented therein to an order of condemnation against him as such garnishee for $180, the amount of his debt to Balk. Judgment was thereafter entered against the garnishee, and in favor of the plaintiff, Epstein, for $180. After the entry of the garnishee judgment, condemning the $180 in the hands of the garnishee, Harris paid the amount of the judgment to one Warren, an attorney of Epstein, residing in North Carolina. On August 11, 1896, Balk commenced an action against Harris before a justice of the peace in North Carolina, to recover the $180 which he averred Harris owed him. The plaintiff in error, by way of answer to the suit, pleaded in bar the recovery of the Maryland judgment and his payment thereof, and contended that it was conclusive against the defendant in error in this action, because that judgment was a valid judgment in Maryland, and was therefore entitled to full faith and credit in the courts of North Carolina. This contention was not allowed by the trial court, and judgment was accordingly entered against Harris for the amount of his indebtedness to Balk, and that judgment was affirmed by the supreme court of North Carolina. The ground of such judgment was that the Maryland court obtained no jurisdiction to attach or garnish the debt due from Harris to Balk, because Harris was but temporarily in the state, and the situs of the debt was in North Carolina.

. . . .

Mr. Justice PECKHAM, after making the foregoing statement, delivered the opinion of the court:

The state court of North Carolina has refused to give any effect in this action to the Maryland judgment; and the Federal question is whether it did not thereby refuse the full faith and credit to such judgment which is required by the Federal Constitution. If the Maryland court had jurisdiction to award it, the judgment is valid and entitled to the same full faith and credit in North Carolina that it has in Maryland as a valid domestic judgment.

The defendant in error contends that the Maryland court obtained no jurisdiction to award the judgment of condemnation, because the garnishee, although at the time in the state of Maryland, and personally served with process therein, was a nonresident of that state, only casually or temporarily within its boundaries; that the situs of the debt due from Harris, the garnishee, to the defendant in error herein, was in North Carolina, and did not accompany Harris to Maryland; that, consequently, Harris, though within the state of Maryland, had not possession of any property of Balk, and the Maryland state court therefore obtained no jurisdiction over any property of Balk in the attachment proceedings, and the consent of Harris to the entry of the judgment was immaterial. The plaintiff in error, on the contrary, insists that, though the garnishee were but temporarily in Maryland, yet the laws of that state provide for an attachment of this nature if the debtor, the garnishee, is found in the state, and the court obtains jurisdiction over him by the service of process therein; that the judgment, condemning the debt from Harris to Balk, was a valid judgment, provided Balk could himself have sued Harris for the debt in Maryland. This, it is asserted, he could have done, and the judgment was therefore entitled to full faith and credit in the courts of North Carolina. . . .

. . . .

Attachment is the creature of the local law; that is, unless there is a law of the state providing for and permitting the attachment, it cannot be levied there. If there be a law of the state providing for the attachment of the debt, then, if the garnishee be found in that state, and process be personally served upon him therein, we think the court thereby acquires jurisdiction over him, and can garnish the debt due from him to the debtor of the plaintiff, and condemn it, provided the garnishee could himself be sued by his creditor in that state. We do not see how the question of jurisdiction *vel non* can properly be made to depend upon the so–called original situs of the debt, or upon the character of the stay of the garnishee, whether temporary or permanent, in the state where the attachment is issued. Power over the person of the garnishee confers jurisdiction on the courts of the state where the writ issues. . . . If, while temporarily there, his creditor might sue him there and recover the debt, then he is liable to process of garnishment, no matter where the situs of the debt was originally. We do not see the materiality of the expression "situs of the debt," when used in connection with attachment proceedings. If by situs is meant the place of the creation of the debt, that fact is immaterial. If it be meant that the obligation to pay the debt can only be enforced at the situs thus fixed, we think it plainly untrue. The obligation of the debtor to pay his debt clings to and accompanies him wherever he goes. He is as much bound to pay his debt in a foreign state when therein sued upon his obligation by his creditor, as he was in the state where the debt was contracted. We speak of ordinary debts, such as the one in this case. It would be no defense to such suit for the debtor to plead that he was only in the foreign state casually or temporarily. His obligation to pay would be the same whether he was there in that way or with an intention to remain. It is nothing but the obligation to pay which is garnished or attached. This obligation can be enforced by the courts of the foreign state after personal service of process therein, just as well as by the courts of the domicil of the debtor. If the debtor leave the foreign state without appearing, a judgment by default may be entered, upon which execution may issue, or the judgment may be sued upon in any other state where the debtor might be found. In such case the situs is unimportant. It is not a question of possession in the foreign state, for possession cannot be taken of a debt or of the obligation to pay it, as tangible property might be taken possession of. Notice to the debtor (garnishee) of the commencement of the suit, and notice not to pay to his creditor, is all that can be given, whether the garnishee be a mere casual and temporary comer, or a resident of the state where the attachment is laid. His obligation to pay to his creditor is thereby arrested, and a lien created upon the debt itself. . . . We can see no reason why the attachment could not be thus laid, provided the creditor of the garnishee could himself sue in that state, and its laws permitted the attachment.

There can be no doubt that Balk, as a citizen of the state of North Carolina, had the right to sue Harris in Maryland to recover the debt which Harris owed him. Being a citizen of North Carolina, he was entitled to all the privileges and immunities of citizens of the several states, one of which is the right to institute actions in the courts of another state. The law of Maryland provides for the attachment of credits in a case like this. . . . Where money or credits are attached, the inchoate lien attaches to the fund or credits when the attachment is laid in the hands of the garnishee, and the judgment condemning the amount in his hands becomes a personal judgment against him. . . . [The] Maryland Code provides also that this judgment of condemnation against the garnishee, or payment by him of such judgment, is pleadable in bar to an action brought against him by the defendant in the attachment suit for or concerning the property or credits so condemned.

It thus appears that Balk could have sued Harris in Maryland to recover his debt, notwithstanding the temporary character of Harris' stay there; it also appears that the municipal law of Maryland permits the debtor of the principal debtor to be garnished, and therefore if the court of the state where the garnishee is found obtains jurisdiction over him, through the service of process upon him within the state, then the judgment entered is a valid judgment.

. . . .

It seems to us, therefore, that the judgment against Harris in Maryland, condemning the $180 which he owed to Balk, was a valid judgment, because the court had jurisdiction over the garnishee by personal service of process within the state of Maryland.

It ought to be and it is the object of courts to prevent the payment of any debt twice over. Thus, if Harris, owing a debt to Balk, paid it under a valid judgment against him, to Epstein, he certainly ought not to be compelled to pay it a second time, but should have the right to plead his payment under the Maryland judgment. It is objected, however, that the payment by Harris to Epstein was not under legal compulsion. Harris in truth owed the debt to Balk, which was attached by Epstein. He had, therefore, as we have seen, no defense to set up against the attachment of the debt. Jurisdiction over him personally had been obtained by the Maryland court. As he was absolutely without defense, there was no reason why he should not consent to a judgment impounding the debt, which judgment the plaintiff was legally entitled to, and which he could not prevent. There was no merely voluntary payment within the meaning of that phrase as applicable here.

But most rights may be lost by negligence, and if the garnishee were guilty of negligence in the attachment proceeding, to the damage of Balk, he ought not to be permitted to set up the judgment as a defense. Thus it is recognized as the duty of the garnishee to give notice to his own creditor, if he would protect himself, so that the creditor may have the opportunity to defend himself against the claim of the person suing out the attachment. . . . While the want of notification by the garnishee to his own creditor may have no effect upon the validity of the judgment against the garnishee (the proper publication being made by the plaintiff), we think it has and ought to have an effect upon the right of the garnishee to avail himself of the prior judgment and his payment thereunder. This notification by the garnishee is for the purpose of making sure that his creditor shall have an opportunity to defend the claim made against him in the attachment suit. Fair dealing requires this at the hands of the garnishee. In this case, while neither the defendant nor the garnishee appeared, the court, while condemning the credits attached, could not, by the terms of the Maryland statute, issue the writ of execution unless the plaintiff gave bond or sufficient security before the court awarding the execution, to make restitution of the money paid if the defendant should, at any time within a year and a day, appear in the action and show that the plaintiff's claim, or some part thereof, was not due to the plaintiff. The defendant in error, Balk, had notice of this attachment, certainly within a few days after the issuing thereof and the entry of judgment thereon, because he sued the plaintiff in error to recover his debt within a few days after his (Harris') return to North Carolina, in which suit the judgment in Maryland was set up by Harris as a plea in bar to Balk's claim. Balk, therefore, had an opportunity for a year and a day after the entry of the judgment to litigate the question of his liability in the Maryland court, and to show that he did not owe the debt, or some part of it, as was claimed by Epstein. He, however, took no proceedings to that end, so far as the record shows, and the reason may be supposed to be that he could not successfully defend the claim, because he admitted in this case that he did, at the time of the attachment proceeding, owe Epstein some $344.

Generally, though, the failure on the part of the garnishee to give proper notice to his creditor of the levying of the attachment would be such a neglect of duty on the part of the garnishee which he owed to his creditor as would prevent his availing himself of the judgment in the attachment suit as a bar to the suit of his creditor against himself, which might therefore result in his being called upon to pay the debt twice.

. . . .

Reversed.

Mr. Justice HARLAN and Mr. Justice DAY dissented.

NOTES AND QUESTIONS

(1) *Harris v. Balk* was an appeal from a state court decision. As the Court noted, whether a debt may be attached is a question of state law. What federal question provided the basis of the Court's jurisdiction?

(2) *Garnishment.* As discussed *supra*, garnishment is the attachment of property of the defendant in the possession of a third party. In some states attachment is called "trustee process." Other states do not distinguish between attachment and garnishment, calling both "attachment."

Garnishment procedure parallels attachment procedure in most respects. The order of garnishment directs the sheriff to levy on property of the defendant held by the garnishee. If the defendant's "property" is an obligation owed the defendant by the garnishee, like the debt owed by Harris to Balk, the garnishee is directed not to pay the obligation until the underlying action has been adjudicated. The garnishee can seek to have the order set aside on the grounds that the attached property does not belong to the debtor, or that the garnishee owes no debt to the defendant. Can the garnishee raise as a counter–or cross–claim a debt owed by the plaintiff to the garnishee? to the defendant? *See* N.Y. Civ. Proc. Law § 6414(b) (McKinney 1980).

(3) According to the Court in *Harris v. Balk*, what is the situs of a debt? What notice was Balk to get regarding Epstein's garnishment of Harris in Maryland? Does

the reasoning of the Court sanction the mere presence of a garnishee as a sufficient basis for jurisdiction?

(4) Suppose that the Supreme Court had decided that Maryland lacked jurisdiction over Harris' obligation to pay his debt to Balk, either because the situs of the debt was North Carolina, or (as is likely today) because the temporary presence of Harris in Maryland did not constitute sufficient contact between Balk and Maryland to support jurisdiction. In that case, the Maryland judgment would have not been binding in North Carolina, and Harris, having already paid Epstein, would have to pay Balk. Do the Court's final paragraphs suggest a solution to this problem? Is it an adequate one?

(5) Can a contingent contractual right to receive money, which may never become due, be attached? *See ABKCO Industries, Inc. v. Apple Films, Inc.*, 39 N.Y.2d 670, 385 N.Y.S.2d 511 (1976).

SUPREME MERCHANDISE CO. v. CHEMICAL BANK

New York Court of Appeals
70 N.Y.2d 344, 520 N.Y.S.2d 734 514 N.E.2d 1358 (1987)

KAYE, J.

A beneficiary's interest in an executory negotiable letter of credit supporting an international sale of goods is not property of the beneficiary for purposes of attachment by a party in unrelated litigation.

In connection with a sale of disposable lighters by Iwahori Kinzoku Co. (Kinzoku), a Japanese company, to Supreme Importers and D. M. Sales Corp. of New York City, on March 1, 1984, Chemical Bank issued an irrevocable letter of credit, expiring March 30, 1984, in the amount of $111,840, identifying Kinzoku as the beneficiary. The document provided that drafts drawn against it could be negotiated by any bank, which could then present the drafts together with the conforming documents to Chemical for acceptance and payment.

In an action for a money judgment against Kinzoku wholly unrelated to the letter of credit or the sale underlying it, petitioner served Chemical with an order attaching all debts and property of Kinzoku. Upon a search of its records, Chemical found no accounts in the name of Kinzoku, and so advised both the Sheriff and petitioner's counsel. Chemical thereafter discovered the letter of credit, informed petitioner, and in late May was served with a second order of attachment. Both orders of attachment were confirmed by Special Term.

Meanwhile, on April 12, 1984, Fuji Bank Ltd. (Fuji) in Japan negotiated a draft in the sum of $55,000 for Kinzoku, notwithstanding certain discrepancies between the documents presented and the documents required by the letter of credit, and paid Kinzoku. When it made payment, according to Fuji, it had no knowledge of the attachment or dispute between Kinzoku and petitioner. Fuji the following week presented Chemical with the draft and documents; Chemical obtained a waiver of the discrepancies from the account party and, on April 27, accepted the draft, thereby engaging to make payment within a 30–day period. Chemical paid Fuji $55,000 on May 29, 1984.

On April 5, 1984, Dai–ichi Kangyo Bank Ltd. (Dai–ichi) presented Chemical with a second draft it had negotiated for Kinzoku in Japan, in the sum of $56,840 together with relevant documentation. Dai–ichi had before that time paid the full draft to its customer and claims it had no knowledge of the attachment or dispute with petitioner. Again the documents contained discrepancies from the terms of the letter of credit which were waived by the account party. On April 17, Chemical accepted the draft, thereby engaging to pay it within a 30–day period. Actual payment was not made until after service of the second attachment order. Prior to the two presentments, Chemical apparently had no knowledge of the interest of the negotiating banks.

Appellant commenced this proceeding against Chemical pursuant to CPLR 6314(d) to compel the delivery of funds representing the letter of credit, alleging that both attachment orders were applicable to the proceeds of the letter of credit. Chemical responded that the second order of attachment had been served too late because it had already accepted both drafts, and that the first order was ineffective because attachment cannot reach the proceeds of executory letters of credit.

Special Term, addressing only the first order of attachment, concluded that the beneficiary's interest constituted attachable property and granted the petition to the extent of directing Chemical to deliver to the Sheriff the amount of the drafts plus interest. The Appellate Division reversed, holding as to the second order of attachment, that there was nothing attachable at the time it was served because Chemical had by then accepted the drafts and thereby become unconditionally obligated to pay them upon maturity. With respect to the first order of attachment, however, the court ruled that CPLR 5201(b) and 6202 could not be read "as authorizing creditors to reach a debtor's contingent interest as property where the effort to do so will often preclude the maturing of that interest, is likely on a repetitive basis to impair the rights of third parties, and is certain to raise a disquieting doubt as to the capacity of letters of credit to discharge their critically important function in international transactions." (117 A.D.2d 424, 431.) The Appellate Division granted leave to appeal to this court (126 A.D.2d 994). We now affirm.

As to the second order of attachment, we agree with the court below that the issue has already been decisively determined against petitioner. In *First Commercial Bank v. Gotham Originals* (64 N.Y.2d 287), we recognized that an issuing bank's obligation to pay in a commercial letter of credit transaction is fixed upon presentation of drafts and the documents specified in the letter of credit. Once the issuer accepts the drafts it becomes "directly, primarily and unconditionally obligated to the holder" and any order subsequently served on the issuer seeking to enjoin payment is too late (*id.*, at 297). Here, Chemical accepted the drafts under the credit, and the negotiating banks held the acceptances, before service of the second order of attachment. There having been nothing to attach at the time of service of the attachment order (CPLR 6214[b]), Chemical plainly did not violate that order when it made payment to the negotiating banks rather than directing the funds to the Sheriff.

The issues with respect to effectiveness of the first order of attachment, however, cannot be so readily resolved. The first order was served before Fuji or Dai–ichi negotiated the drafts for value and presented them to Chemical for payment. The letter of credit was therefore executory at the time the attachment order was served upon Chemical. If an order of attachment can reach a beneficiary's interest in an executory letter of credit, Chemical would have violated that order when it accepted the drafts and paid the negotiating banks rather than turning over the proceeds to the Sheriff.

While letters of credit have for centuries been in wide use, this issue has not arisen often in the case law. It has been the subject of two Federal court decisions—*Matter of Diakan Love v. Al–Haddad Bros. Enters.* (584 F. Supp. 782) and *Sisalcords Do Brazil v. Fiacao Brasileira De Sisal* (450 F.2d 419, *cert. denied* 406 U.S. 919), both denying attachment—but has not previously been passed on by this court.

CPLR 6214(d) provides that a levy by service of an order of attachment on a person other than defendant "is effective only if, at the time of service, such person owes a debt to the defendant or such person is in the possession or custody of property in which such person knows or has reason to believe the defendant has an interest". The core issue here is whether Kinzoku's interest in the letter of credit constituted a "debt" or "property" within the purview of the statute.

"Any debt or property against which a money judgment may be enforced as provided in section 5201 is subject to attachment." (CPLR 6202.) The statute requires that a "debt" for this purpose be a fixed obligation (CPLR 5201[a]). If a debt, Kinzoku's interest was plainly contingent and would not be subject to attachment under CPLR 5201(a); indeed, petitioner does not contend that the interest was attachable as a debt. Petitioner focuses on the further provision that "[a] money judgment may be enforced against any property which could be assigned or transferred, whether it consists of a present or future right or interest and whether or not it is vested." (CPLR 5201[b].) The word "property" is undefined. To say—as petitioner does—that Kinzoku's interest in the letter was assignable and is therefore attachable property begs the question whether the interest is "property" in the first instance. We therefore turn to the case law construing the statutory term "property."

In *ABKCO Indus. v. Apple Films* (39 N.Y.2d 670, 673), this court considered whether a contract right to net profits from future promotion of the Beatles film "Let It Be" was "property" within CPLR 5201(b), so as to support an attachment for purposes of securing jurisdiction. We rejected the argument that the debtor's contract right was too contingent because it might have no value, and held that the interest was "property" notwithstanding the uncertainties affecting its actual ultimate value. The "fact of value or lack of it", we concluded, "has no legal effect on the validity of the attachment". (39 N.Y.2d, *supra*, at 675.) Dispositive instead is whether such an interest has potential economic value to the creditor. The right to receive profits from the Beatles film was deemed worthy of pursuit by the creditor, was assignable, and hence was attachable.

(Matthew Bender & Co., Inc.)   (Pub.094)

Petitioner urges that because Kinzoku's interest could be assigned, *ABKCO* dictates the invariable conclusion that it is attachable property. We disagree. Such a mechanical application of *ABKCO* to all questions concerning attachable interests not only would swallow up CPLR 5201(a) in its entirety but also would require us to blind ourselves in every instance to the nature of the interest involved. We determine, therefore, that the mere assignability of Kinzoku's interest does not warrant the conclusion that it is "property" for purposes of CPLR 5201(b), and that in the circumstances the interest is not subject to attachment.

A guiding principle in our analysis is that, while CPLR 5201 is obviously intended to have broad reach, still the Legislature expressly put beyond the grasp of the statute the general category of contingent debts, "to preclude a levy against contingent obligations not certain to ripen into something real". (Siegel, N.Y. Prac. § 323, at 389; *see also,* Siegel, Practice Commentaries, McKinney's Cons Laws of N.Y., Book 7B, CPLR C5201:5, at 53–54.)

There is a different, and in a relevant sense even greater, contingency in the beneficiary's interest here than in *ABKCO*. A letter of credit "is an executory contract that conditions performance of the issuer's obligation (payment) upon performance by the beneficiary (delivery of specified documents)." (Harfield, Letters of Credit, at 79 [ALI–ABA Uniform Commercial Code Practice Handbook 1979] [Letters of Credit].) In the absence of compliance with the terms and conditions of a letter of credit, the issuing bank owes nothing to the beneficiary. Whereas the debtor's interest in *ABKCO* was contingent solely as to value, which depended on events beyond its own control, Kinzoku's interest is dependent upon its own future performance. Before payment would be due, Kinzoku would have to perform by timely shipment of the goods, compliance with the terms of the credit, and presentation of conforming documents. Given that a beneficiary of a letter of credit retains the option to defeat the interest and render it worthless, we are mindful that allowing attachments in this instance—unlike *ABKCO*—could serve as a disincentive to a beneficiary's performance of the underlying contract as well as the terms of the letter of credit. While this contingency is particularly pertinent in a situation where the beneficiary is a seller of goods thousands of miles from New York, we nevertheless agree with the court below that even claims that depend on further action by the debtor may constitute "property" and that this distinction from *ABKCO* is not alone dispositive (*see,* 117 A.D.2d 424, 431, *supra*).

The more profound difference from *ABKCO*, however, lies in the fact that what is at issue here is Kinzoku's interest in a negotiable letter of credit, an instrument extensively used in domestic and international trade, which because of its unique character typically implicates others than the immediate parties to the underlying transaction. The transaction before us, for example, involves not only Kinzoku and its buyer, but also the issuing bank and two negotiating banks—none of whom had any part in the dispute between petitioner and Kinzoku, yet whose interests could be affected by permitting attachment of Kinzoku's interest in the letter of credit.

We are persuaded that, for policy reasons, the rationale of *ABKCO* does not extend this far, and that Kinzoku's interest for present purposes must be considered a contingent, nonattachable "debt" under CPLR 5201(a) rather than attachable "property" under CPLR 5201(b). Letters of credit* have been recognized "as an essential lubricant that permits the wheels of international trade to turn" (*Matter of Diakan Love v. Al–Haddad Bros. Enters.*, 584 F. Supp. 782, 785, *supra*); as "indispensable to international trade" (Dolan, Letters of Credit ¶ 3.05); and as "an invaluable tool that can be employed to facilitate an unlimited variety of transactions." (Harfield, Letters of Credit, at 5.) "[T]he Board of Governors of the Federal Reserve System has stated that unavailability of letter of credit facilities would 'place U.S. businesses at an unnecessary competitive disadvantage in foreign markets.' " (Harfield, Letters of Credit, at 79, n.11.) While long known in commercial law, letters of credit have during the past decades gained acceptance in facilitating financial as well as mercantile transactions. Their peculiar value lies in the fact that by superimposing the financial strength and integrity of one party (typically a bank) on that of another (typically a seller) they add the virtual certainty that upon presentation of conforming documents payment will be made (*see*, Kozolchyk, Commercial Letters of Credit in the Americas § 18.04, at 394; Harfield, Bank Credits and Acceptances, at 19 [5th ed.]). "Letters of credit provide a quick, economic and predictable means of financing transactions for parties not willing to deal on open accounts by permitting the seller to rely not only on the credit of the buyer but also on that of the issuing bank." (*First Commercial Bank v. Gotham Originals*, 64 N.Y.2d 287, 297–98, *supra*.)

This peculiar utility derives from two of the fundamental principles pertaining to letters of credit. *First*, a letter of credit contract must be strictly construed and performed in accordance with its terms. This principle of strict construction may be illustrated by the oft–quoted statement from *Equitable Trust Co. v. Dawson Partners* (27 Lloyd's List L. Rep. 49): "There is no room for documents which are almost the same, or which will do just as well." *Second*, the credit engagement is independent of the underlying contract. (*See, First Commercial Bank v. Gotham Originals*, 64 N.Y.2d 287, 294, *supra; Laudisi v. American Exch. Natl. Bank*, 239 N.Y. 234, 243; White & Summers, Uniform Commercial Code § 18–2, at 711–13 [2d ed.]; Harfield, Letters of Credit, at 76; Dolan, Letters of Credit ¶ 6.08, at 6–40.) "Banks issuing letters of credit deal in documents and not in goods and are not responsible for any breach of warranty or nonconformity of the goods involved in the underlying sales contract". (*United Bank v. Cambridge Sporting Goods Corp.*, 41 N.Y.2d 254, 259.) Thus, adherence to the terms of the credit as set forth in the letter of credit carries with it the virtual certainty that payment will be made.

The certainty and predictability of letters of credit—and conversely, the lack of uncertainty or unpredictability—are of course important to the immediate parties, but they have an added dimension in that they induce the confidence of others, who may accept assignments or transfers or negotiate drafts for value, that so long as the terms and conditions are fulfilled the obligation to make payment will be scrupulously honored by the issuer. (*See, Matter of Diakan Love v. Al–Haddad Bros. Enters.*, 584 F. Supp. 782, 785, *supra*.) The Uniform Commercial Code itself

---

* In view of the versatility of letters of credit (*see*, White & Summers, Uniform Commercial Code § 18–1, at 709 [2d ed.]), it bears emphasis that our disposition is limited by the facts before us.

specifies only limited circumstances when an issuer is permitted to refuse to honor a draft accompanied by facially conforming documents and a customer permitted to seek an injunction. (UCC 5–144[2][b]; *United Bank v. Cambridge Sporting Goods Corp.*, 41 N.Y.2d 254, 259, *supra.*) Similarly, there are few reported instances where customers have attempted to obtain analogous relief by way of attachment, and these have been viewed by commentators as threatening the foundation and utility of letters of credit by violating the independence principle (*see*, White & Summers, Uniform Commercial Code § 18–10, at 752–53 [2d ed.]; Justice, *Letters of Credit: Expectations and Frustrations—Part 2*, 94 Banking L.J. 493, 495; *see also*, Howard, *Application of Compulsory Joinder, Intervention, Impleader and Attachment to Letter of Credit Litigation*, 52 Fordham L. Rev. 957, 993).

We recognize that these situations are materially different from the case before us, but there is at least one common consideration. If an issuer's payment is blocked by an attachment order of a plaintiff seeking to establish jurisdiction for its own unrelated dispute with the seller—thereby often embroiling the parties in a contest as to priority among creditors—it is at the cost of diminution of confidence in the certainty and integrity of letters of credit in this jurisdiction. We fully endorse the conclusion of the court below that if this attachment were upheld in the circumstances presented "it would follow in many situations that an order of attachment secured by a creditor in an effort to reach the debtor's contingent interest would (1) cause the debtor not to take action necessary to the maturing of the claim, (2) disrupt separate contractual obligations involving unrelated parties, and (3) impair the capacity of letters of credit to discharge their important and intended functions." (117 A.D.2d 424, 431, *supra.*) ⊛

Based on the nature of Kinzoku's interest coupled with the policy considerations involved in negotiable letters of credit concerned with international sales transactions, we conclude that for the purposes of attachment this interest is not "property" within the meaning of CPLR 5201(b).

Accordingly, the order of the Appellate Division should be affirmed, with costs.

Chief Judge WACHTLER, and Judges SIMONS, ALEXANDER, TITONE, HANCOCK, JR., and BELLACOSA concur.

Order affirmed, with costs.

SHAFFER v. HEITNER

United States Supreme Court
433 U.S. 186, 97 S. Ct. 2569, 53 L. Ed. 2d 683 (1977)

Mr. Justice MARSHALL delivered the opinion of the Court.

The controversy in this case concerns the constitutionality of a Delaware statute that allows a court of that State to take jurisdiction of a lawsuit by sequestering any property of the defendant that happens to be located in Delaware. Appellants contend that the sequestration statute as applied in this case violates the Due Process Clause of the Fourteenth Amendment both because it permits the state courts to exercise jurisdiction despite the absence of sufficient contacts among the defendants, the litigation, and the State of Delaware and because it authorizes the deprivation of defendants' property without providing adequate procedural safeguards. We find it necessary to consider only the first of these contentions.

I

Appellee Heitner, a nonresident of Delaware, is the owner of one share of stock in the Greyhound Corp., a business incorporated under the laws of Delaware with its principal place of business in Phoenix, Ariz. On May 22, 1974, he filed a shareholder's derivative suit in the Court of Chancery for New Castle County, Del., in which he named as defendants Greyhound, its wholly owned subsidiary Greyhound Lines, Inc.,[1] and 28 present or former officers or directors of one or both of the corporations. In essence, Heitner alleged that the individual defendants had violated their duties to Greyhound by causing it and its subsidiary to engage in actions that resulted in the corporations being held liable for substantial damages in a private antitrust suit and a large fine in a criminal contempt action. The activities which led to these penalties took place in Oregon.

Simultaneously with his complaint, Heitner filed a motion for an order of sequestration of the Delaware property of the individual defendants pursuant to Del. Code Ann., Tit. 10, § 366 (1975).[4] This motion was accompanied by a supporting

---

[1] Greyhound Lines, Inc., is incorporated in California and has its principal place of business in Phoenix, Ariz.

[4] Section 366 provides:

(a) If it appears in any complaint filed in the Court of Chancery that the defendant or any one or more of the defendants is a nonresident of the State, the Court may make an order directing such nonresident defendant or defendants to appear by a day certain to be designated. Such order shall be served on such nonresident defendant or defendants by mail or otherwise, if practicable, and shall be published in such manner as the Court directs, not less than once a week for 3 consecutive weeks. The Court may compel the appearance of the defendant by the seizure of all or any part of his property, which property may be sold under the order of the Court to pay the demand of the plaintiff, if the defendant does not appear, or otherwise defaults. Any defendant whose property shall have been so seized and who shall have entered a general appearance in the cause may, upon notice to the plaintiff, petition the Court for an order releasing such property or any part thereof from the seizure. The Court shall release such property unless the plaintiff shall satisfy the Court that because of other circumstances there is a reasonable possibility that such release may render it substantially less likely that plaintiff will obtain satisfaction of any judgment secured. If such petition shall not be granted, or if no such petition shall be filed, such property shall remain subject to seizure and may be sold to satisfy any judgment entered in the cause. The Court may at any time release such property or any part thereof upon the giving of sufficient security.

(b) The Court may make all necessary rules respecting the form of process, the manner of issuance and return thereof, the release of such property from seizure and for the sale of the property so seized, and may require the plaintiff to give approved security to abide any order of the Court respecting the property.

affidavit of counsel which stated that the individual defendants were nonresidents of Delaware. The affidavit identified the property to be sequestered as

> common stock, 3% Second Cumulative Preferenced Stock and stock unit credits of the Defendant Greyhound Corporation, a Delaware corporation, as well as all options and all warrants to purchase said stock issued to said individual Defendants and all contractural [*sic*] obligations, all rights, debts or credits due or accrued to or for the benefit of any of the said Defendants under any type of written agreement, contract or other legal instrument of any kind whatever between any of the individual Defendants and said corporation.

The requested sequestration order was signed the day the motion was filed.[5] Pursuant to that order, the sequestrator[6] "seized" approximately 82,000 shares of Greyhound common stock belonging to 19 of the defendants, and options belonging to another 2 defendants. These seizures were accomplished by placing "stop transfer" orders or their equivalents on the books of the Greyhound Corp. So far as the record shows, none of the certificates representing the seized property was physically present in Delaware. The stock was considered to be in Delaware, and so subject to seizure, by virtue of Del. Code Ann., Tit. 8, § 169 (1975), which makes Delaware the situs of ownership of all stock in Delaware corporations.

All 28 defendants were notified of the initiation of the suit by certified mail directed to their last known addresses and by publication in a New Castle County newspaper. The 21 defendants whose property was seized (hereafter referred to as appellants) responded by entering a special appearance for the purpose of moving to quash service of process and to vacate the sequestration order. They contended that the ex parte sequestration procedure did not accord them due process of law and that the property seized was not capable of attachment in Delaware. In addition, appellants asserted that under the rule of *International Shoe Co. v. Washington*, 326 U.S. 310 (1945), they did not have sufficient contacts with Delaware to sustain the jurisdiction of that State's courts.

The Court of Chancery rejected these arguments in a letter opinion which emphasized the purpose of the Delaware sequestration procedure:

> The primary purpose of "sequestration" as authorized by 10 *Del. C.* § 366 is not to secure possession of property pending a trial between resident debtors

---

(c) Any transfer or assignment of the property so seized after the seizure thereof shall be void and after the sale of the property is made and confirmed, the purchaser shall be entitled to and have all the right, title and interest of the defendant in and to the property so seized and sold and such sale and confirmation shall transfer to the purchaser all the right, title and interest of the defendant in and to the property as fully as if the defendant had transferred the same to the purchaser in accordance with law.

[5] As a condition of the sequestration order, both the plaintiff and the sequestrator were required to file bonds of $1,000 to assure their compliance with the orders of the court. App. 24. . . .

[6] The sequestrator is appointed by the court to effect the sequestration. His duties appear to consist of serving the sequestration order on the named corporation, receiving from that corporation a list of the property which the order affects, and filing that list with the court. For performing those services in this case, the sequestrator received a fee of $100 under the original sequestration order and $100 under the alias order.

and creditors on the issue of who has the right to retain it. On the contrary, as here employed, "sequestration" is a process used to compel the personal appearance of a nonresident defendant to answer and defend a suit brought against him in a court of equity. *Sands v. Lefcourt Realty Corp.*, Del. Supr., 117 A.2d 365 (1955). It is accomplished by the appointment of a sequestrator by this Court to seize and hold property of the nonresident located in this State subject to further Court order. If the defendant enters a general appearance, the sequestered property is routinely released, unless the plaintiff makes special application to continue its seizure, in which event the plaintiff has the burden of proof and persuasion.

App. 75–76. This limitation on the purpose and length of time for which sequestered property is held, the court concluded, rendered inapplicable the due process requirements enunciated in *Sniadach v. Family Finance Corp.*, 395 U.S. 337 (1969); *Fuentes v. Shevin*, 407 U.S. 67 (1972); and *Mitchell v. W.T. Grant Co.*, 416 U.S. 600 (1974). App. 75–76, 80, 83–85. The court also found no state–law or federal constitutional barrier to the sequestrator's reliance on Del. Code Ann., Tit. 8, § 169 (1975). . . . Finally, the court held that the statutory Delaware situs of the stock provided a sufficient basis for the exercise of *quasi in rem* jurisdiction by a Delaware court. . . .

On appeal, the Delaware Supreme Court affirmed the judgment of the Court of Chancery. *Greyhound Corp. v. Heitner*, 361 A.2d 225 (1976). . . .

. . . .

We noted probable jurisdiction. 429 U.S. 813.[12] We reverse.

II

The Delaware courts rejected appellants' jurisdictional challenge by noting that this suit was brought as a *quasi in rem* proceeding. Since *quasi in rem* jurisdiction is traditionally based on attachment or seizure of property present in the jurisdiction, not on contacts between the defendant and the State, the courts considered appellants' claimed lack of contacts with Delaware to be unimportant. This categorical analysis assumes the continued soundness of the conceptual structure founded on the century–old case of *Pennoyer v. Neff*, 95 U.S. 714 (1878).

[The Court's discussion of *Pennoyer v. Neff* is omitted.]

. . . .

From our perspective, the importance of *Pennoyer* is not its result, but the fact that its principles and corollaries derived from them became the basic elements of the constitutional doctrine governing state–court jurisdiction. *See, e.g.*, Hazard, *A General Theory of State–Court Jurisdiction*, 1965 Sup. Ct. Rev. 241 (hereafter

---

12 Under Delaware law, defendants whose property has been sequestered must enter a general appearance, thus subjecting themselves to *in personam* liability, before they can defend on the merits. *See Greyhound Corp. v. Heitner*, 361 A.2d 225, 235–236 (1976). Thus, if the judgment below were considered not to be an appealable final judgment, 28 U.S.C. § 1257(2), appellants would have the choice of suffering a default judgment or entering a general appearance and defending on the merits. . . .

Hazard). As we have noted, under *Pennoyer* state authority to adjudicate was based on the jurisdiction's power over either persons or property. This fundamental concept is embodied in the very vocabulary which we use to describe judgments. If a court's jurisdiction is based on its authority over the defendant's person, the action and judgment are denominated "*in personam*" and can impose a personal obligation on the defendant in favor of the plaintiff. If jurisdiction is based on the court's power over property within its territory, the action is called "*in rem*" or "*quasi in rem*." The effect of a judgment in such a case is limited to the property that supports jurisdiction and does not impose a personal liability on the property owner, since he is not before the court.[17] In *Pennoyer's* terms, the owner is affected only "indirectly" by an *in rem* judgment adverse to his interest in the property subject to the court's disposition.

By concluding that "[t]he authority of every tribunal is necessarily restricted by the territorial limits of the State in which it is established," 95 U.S., at 720, *Pennoyer* sharply limited the availability of *in personam* jurisdiction over defendants not resident in the forum State. If a nonresident defendant could not be found in a State, he could not be sued there. On the other hand, since the State in which property was located was considered to have exclusive sovereignty over that property, *in rem* actions could proceed regardless of the owner's location. Indeed, since a State's process could not reach beyond its borders, this Court held after *Pennoyer* that due process did not require any effort to give a property owner personal notice that his property was involved in an *in rem* proceeding. *See, e.g., Ballard v. Hunter*, 204 U.S. 241 (1907). . . .

The *Pennoyer* rules generally favored nonresident defendants by making them harder to sue. This advantage was reduced, however, by the ability of a resident plaintiff to satisfy a claim against a nonresident defendant by bringing into court any property of the defendant located in the plaintiff's State. *See, e.g.*, Zammit, *Quasi–In–Rem Jurisdiction: Outmoded and Unconstitutional?*, 49 St. John's L. Rev. 668, 670 (1975). For example, in the well–known case of *Harris v. Balk*, 198 U.S. 215 (1905), Epstein, a resident of Maryland, had a claim against Balk, a resident of North Carolina. Harris, another North Carolina resident, owed money to Balk. When Harris happened to visit Maryland, Epstein garnished his debt to Balk. Harris did not contest the debt to Balk and paid it to Epstein's North Carolina attorney. When Balk later sued Harris in North Carolina, this Court held that the Full Faith and Credit Clause, U.S. Const., Art. IV, § 1, required that Harris' payment to Epstein be treated as a discharge of his debt to Balk. This Court reasoned that the debt Harris owed Balk was an intangible form of property belonging to Balk, and

---

[17] "A judgment *in rem* affects the interests of all persons in designated property. A judgment *quasi in rem* affects the interests of particular persons in designated property. The latter is of two types. In one the plaintiff is seeking to secure a pre–existing claim in the subject property and to extinguish or establish the nonexistence of similar interests of particular persons. In the other the plaintiff seeks to apply what he concedes to be the property of the defendant to the satisfaction of a claim against him. Restatement, Judgments, 5–9." *Hanson v. Denckla*, 357 U.S. 235, 246 n.12 (1958).

As did the Court in *Hanson*, we will for convenience generally use the term "*in rem*" in place of "*in rem* and *quasi in rem*."

that the location of that property traveled with the debtor. By obtaining personal jurisdiction over Harris, Epstein had "arrested" his debt to Balk, 198 U.S., at 223, and brought it into the Maryland court. Under the structure established by *Pennoyer*, Epstein was then entitled to proceed against that debt to vindicate his claim against Balk, even though Balk himself was not subject to the jurisdiction of a Maryland tribunal. . . .[18]

Pennoyer itself recognized that its rigid categories, even as blurred by the kind of action typified by *Harris*, could not accommodate some necessary litigation. Accordingly, Mr. Justice Field's opinion carefully noted that cases involving the personal status of the plaintiff, such as divorce actions, could be adjudicated in the plaintiff's home State even though the defendant could not be served within that State. 95 U.S., at 733–735. Similarly, the opinion approved the practice of considering a foreign corporation doing business in a State to have consented to being sued in that State. *Id.*, at 735–736; *see Lafayette Ins. Co. v. French*, 18 How. 404 (1856). This basis for *in personam* jurisdiction over foreign corporations was later supplemented by the doctrine that a corporation doing business in a State could be deemed "present" in the State, and so subject to service of process under the rule of *Pennoyer. See, e.g., International Harvester Co. v. Kentucky*, 234 U.S. 579 (1914); *Philadelphia & Reading R. Co. v. McKibbin*, 243 U.S. 264 (1917). *See generally* Note, *Developments in the Law, State–Court Jurisdiction*, 73 Harv. L. Rev. 909, 919–923 (1960) (hereafter Developments).

[Justice Marshall next discussed the extension of *in personam* jurisdiction in cases such as *Hess v. Pawloski*, 274 U.S. 352 (1927) and *International Shoe Co. v. Washington*, 326 U.S. 310 (1945). He continued:]

Thus, the relationship among the defendant, the forum, and the litigation, rather than the mutually exclusive sovereignty of the States on which the rules of *Pennoyer* rest, became the central concern of the inquiry into personal jurisdiction. The immediate effect of this departure from *Pennoyer*'s conceptual apparatus was to increase the

---

[18] The Court in *Harris* limited its holding to States in which the principal defendant (Balk) could have sued the garnishee (Harris) if he had obtained personal jurisdiction over the garnishee in that State. 198 U.S., at 222–223, 226. The Court explained:

> The importance of the fact of the right of the original creditor to sue his debtor in the foreign State, as affecting the right of the creditor of that creditor to sue the debtor or garnishee, lies in the nature of the attachment proceeding. The plaintiff, in such proceeding in the foreign State is able to sue out the attachment and attach the debt due from the garnishee to his (the garnishee's) creditor, because of the fact that the plaintiff is really in such proceeding a representative of the creditor of the garnishee, and therefore if such creditor himself had the right to commence suit to recover the debt in the foreign State his representative has the same right, as representing him, and may garnish or attach the debt, provided the municipal law of the State where the attachment was sued out permits it.

Id., at 226. The problem with this reasoning is that unless the plaintiff has obtained a judgment establishing his claim against the principal defendant, *see, e.g., Baltimore & O. R. Co. v. Hostetter*, 240 U.S. 620 (1916), his right to "represent" the principal defendant in an action against the garnishee is at issue. *See* Beale, *The Exercise of Jurisdiction in Rem to Compel Payment of a Debt*, 27 Harv. L. Rev. 107, 118–120 (1913).

ability of the State courts to obtain personal jurisdiction over nonresident defendants. . . .

No equally dramatic change has occurred in the law governing jurisdiction *in rem*. There have, however, been intimations that the collapse of the *in personam* wing of *Pennoyer* has not left that decision unweakened as a foundation for *in rem* jurisdiction. Well–reasoned lower court opinions have questioned the proposition that the presence of property in a State gives that State jurisdiction to adjudicate rights to the property regardless of the relationship of the underlying dispute and the property owner to the forum. . . . The overwhelming majority of commentators have also rejected *Pennoyer*'s premise that a proceeding "against" property is not a proceeding against the owners of that property. Accordingly, they urge that the "traditional notions of fair play and substantial justice" that govern a State's power to adjudicate *in personam* should also govern its power to adjudicate personal rights to property located in the State. *See, e.g.,* Von Mehren & Trautman, *Jurisdiction to Adjudicate: A Suggested Analysis*, 79 Harv. L. Rev. 1121 (1966) (hereafter Von Mehren & Trautman); Traynor, *Is This Conflict Really Necessary?*, 37 Texas L. Rev. 657 (1959) (hereafter Traynor); . . .

Although this Court has not addressed this argument directly, we have held that property cannot be subjected to a court's judgment unless reasonable and appropriate efforts have been made to give the property owners actual notice of the action. *Schroeder v. City of New York*, 371 U.S. 208 (1962); *Walker v. City of Hutchinson*, 352 U.S. 112 (1956); *Mullane v. Central Hanover Bank & Trust Co.*, 339 U.S. 306 (1950). This conclusion recognizes, contrary to *Pennoyer*, that an adverse judgment *in rem* directly affects the property owner by divesting him of his rights in the property before the court. . . .

. . . .

III

The case for applying to jurisdiction *in rem* the same test of "fair play and substantial justice" as governs assertions of jurisdiction *in personam* is simple and straightforward. It is premised on recognition that "[t]he phrase, 'judicial jurisdiction over a thing,' is a customary elliptical way of referring to jurisdiction over the interests of persons in a thing." Restatement (Second) of Conflict of Laws § 56, Introductory Note (1971) (hereafter Restatement).[22] This recognition leads to the conclusion that in order to justify an exercise of jurisdiction *in rem*, the basis for jurisdiction must be sufficient to justify exercising "jurisdiction over the interests of persons in a thing."[23] The standard for determining whether an exercise of

---

[22] "All proceedings, like all rights, are really against persons. Whether they are proceedings or rights *in rem* depends on the number of persons affected." *Tyler v. Court of Registration*, 175 Mass. 71, 76, 55 N. E. 812, 814 (Holmes, C. J.), appeal dismissed, 179 U.S. 405 (1900).

[23] It is true that the potential liability of a defendant in an *in rem* action is limited by the value of the property, but that limitation does not affect the argument. The fairness of subjecting a defendant to state–court jurisdiction does not depend on the size of the claim being litigated. *Cf. Fuentes v. Shevin*, 407 U.S., at 88–90; n.32, *infra*.

jurisdiction over the interests of persons is consistent with the Due Process Clause is the minimum–contacts standard elucidated in *International Shoe.*

This argument, of course, does not ignore the fact that the presence of property in a State may bear on the existence of jurisdiction by providing contacts among the forum State, the defendant, and the litigation. For example, when claims to the property itself are the source of the underlying controversy between the plaintiff and the defendant, it would be unusual for the State where the property is located not to have jurisdiction. In such cases, the defendant's claim to property located in the State would normally indicate that he expected to benefit from the State's protection of his interest. The State's strong interests in assuring the marketability of property within its borders and in providing a procedure for peaceful resolution of disputes about the possession of that property would also support jurisdiction, as would the likelihood that important records and witnesses will be found in the State.[28] The presence of property may also favor jurisdiction in cases, such as suits for injury suffered on the land of an absentee owner, where the defendant's ownership of the property is conceded but the cause of action is otherwise related to rights and duties growing out of that ownership.

It appears, therefore, that jurisdiction over many types of actions which now are or might be brought *in rem* would not be affected by a holding that any assertion of state–court jurisdiction must satisfy the *International Shoe* standard. For the type of *quasi in rem* action typified by *Harris v. Balk* and the present case, however, accepting the proposed analysis would result in significant change. These are cases where the property which now serves as the basis for state–court jurisdiction is completely unrelated to the plaintiff's cause of action. Thus, although the presence of the defendant's property in a State might suggest the existence of other ties among the defendant, the State, and the litigation, the presence of the property alone would not support the State's jurisdiction. If those other ties did not exist, cases over which the State is now thought to have jurisdiction could not be brought in that forum.

. . . .

The primary rationale for treating the presence of property as a sufficient basis for jurisdiction to adjudicate claims over which the State would not have jurisdiction if *International Shoe* applied is that a wrongdoer

> should not be able to avoid payment of his obligations by the expedient of removing his assets to a place where he is not subject to an in personam suit. Restatement § 66, Comment a. . . .

This justification, however, does not explain why jurisdiction should be recognized without regard to whether the property is present in the State because of an effort to avoid the owner's obligations. Nor does it support jurisdiction to adjudicate the underlying claim. At most, it suggests that a State in which property is located should have jurisdiction to attach that property, by use of proper procedures,[34] as

---

28 We do not suggest that these illustrations include all the factors that may affect the decision, nor that the factors we have mentioned are necessarily decisive.

34 *See North Georgia Finishing, Inc. v. Di–Chem, Inc.,* 419 U.S. 601 (1975); *Mitchell v. W. T. Grant Co.,* 416 U.S. 600 (1974); *Fuentes v. Shevin,* 407 U.S. 67 (1972); *Sniadach v. Family Finance Corp.,* 395 U.S. 337 (1969).

security for a judgment being sought in a forum where the litigation can be maintained consistently with *International Shoe*. . . . Moreover, we know of nothing to justify the assumption that a debtor can avoid paying his obligations by removing his property to a State in which his creditor cannot obtain personal jurisdiction over him. The Full Faith and Credit Clause, after all, makes the valid *in personam* judgment of one State enforceable in all other States.[36]

It might also be suggested that allowing *in rem* jurisdiction avoids the uncertainty inherent in the *International Shoe* standard and assures a plaintiff of a forum.[37] We believe, however, that the fairness standard of *International Shoe* can be easily applied in the vast majority of cases. Moreover, when the existence of jurisdiction in a particular forum under *International Shoe* is unclear, the cost of simplifying the litigation by avoiding the jurisdictional question may be the sacrifice of "fair play and substantial justice." That cost is too high.

We are left, then, to consider the significance of the long history of jurisdiction based solely on the presence of property in a State. Although the theory that territorial power is both essential to and sufficient for jurisdiction has been undermined, we have never held that the presence of property in a State does not automatically confer jurisdiction over the owner's interest in that property. This history must be considered as supporting the proposition that jurisdiction based solely on the presence of property satisfies the demands of due process, *cf. Ownbey v. Morgan*, 256 U.S. 94, 111 (1921), but it is not decisive. "[T]raditional notions of fair play and substantial justice" can be as readily offended by the perpetuation of ancient forms that are no longer justified as by the adoption of new procedures that are inconsistent with the basic values of our constitutional heritage. *Cf. Sniadach v. Family Finance Corp.*, 395 U.S., at 340 . . . The fiction that an assertion of jurisdiction over property is anything but an assertion of jurisdiction over the owner of the property supports an ancient form without substantial modern justification. Its continued acceptance would serve only to allow state–court jurisdiction that is fundamentally unfair to the defendant.

We therefore conclude that all assertions of state–court jurisdiction must be evaluated according to the standards set forth in *International Shoe* and its progeny.[39]

IV

The Delaware courts based their assertion of jurisdiction in this case solely on the statutory presence of appellants' property in Delaware. Yet that property is not

---

[36] Once it has been determined by a court of competent jurisdiction that the defendant is a debtor of the plaintiff, there would seem to be no unfairness in allowing an action to realize on that debt in a State where the defendant has property, whether or not that State would have jurisdiction to determine the existence of the debt as an original matter. *Cf.* n.18, *supra*.

[37] This case does not raise, and we therefore do not consider, the question whether the presence of a defendant's property in a State is a sufficient basis for jurisdiction when no other forum is available to the plaintiff.

[39] It would not be fruitful for us to re–examine the facts of cases decided on the rationales of *Pennoyer* and *Harris* to determine whether jurisdiction might have been sustained under the standard we adopt today. To the extent that prior decisions are inconsistent with this standard, they are overruled.

the subject matter of this litigation, nor is the underlying cause of action related to the property. Appellants' holdings in Greyhound do not, therefore, provide contacts with Delaware sufficient to support the jurisdiction of that State's courts over appellants. If it exists, that jurisdiction must have some other foundation.

Appellee Heitner did not allege and does not now claim that appellants have ever set foot in Delaware. Nor does he identify any act related to his cause of action as having taken place in Delaware. Nevertheless, he contends that appellants' positions as directors and officers of a corporation chartered in Delaware provide sufficient "contacts, ties, or relations," *International Shoe Co. v. Washington*, 326 U.S., at 319, with that State to give its courts jurisdiction over appellants in this stockholder's derivative action. This argument is based primarily on what Heitner asserts to be the strong interest of Delaware in supervising the management of a Delaware corporation. That interest is said to derive from the role of Delaware law in establishing the corporation and defining the obligations owed to it by its officers and directors. In order to protect this interest, appellee concludes, Delaware's courts must have jurisdiction over corporate fiduciaries such as appellants.

This argument is undercut by the failure of the Delaware Legislature to assert the state interest appellee finds so compelling. Delaware law bases jurisdiction, not on appellants' status as corporate fiduciaries, but rather on the presence of their property in the State. Although the sequestration procedure used here may be most frequently used in derivative suits against officers and directors, . . . the authorizing statute evinces no specific concern with such actions. Sequestration can be used in any suit against a nonresident, and reaches corporate fiduciaries only if they happen to own interests in a Delaware corporation, or other property in the State. But as Heitner's failure to secure jurisdiction over seven of the defendants named in his complaint demonstrates, there is no necessary relationship between holding a position as a corporate fiduciary and owning stock or other interests in the corporation. If Delaware perceived its interest in securing jurisdiction over corporate fiduciaries to be as great as Heitner suggests, we would expect it to have enacted a statute more clearly designed to protect that interest.

Moreover, even if Heitner's assessment of the importance of Delaware's interest is accepted, his argument fails to demonstrate that Delaware is a fair forum for this litigation. The interest appellee has identified may support the application of Delaware law to resolve any controversy over appellants' actions in their capacities as officers and directors.[44] But we have rejected the argument that if a State's law can properly be applied to a dispute, its courts necessarily have jurisdiction over the parties to that dispute. . . .

Appellee . . . suggests that Delaware law provides substantial benefits to corporate officers and directors, and that these benefits were at least in part the

---

[44] In general, the law of the State of incorporation is held to govern the liabilities of officers or directors to the corporation and its stockholders. *See* Restatement § 309. *But see* Cal. Corp. Code § 2115 (West Supp. 1977). The rationale for the general rule appears to be based more on the need for a uniform and certain standard to govern the internal affairs of a corporation than on the perceived interest of the State of incorporation. *Cf. Koster v. Lumbermens Mutual Casualty Co.*, 330 U.S. 518, 527–528 (1947).

incentive for appellants to assume their positions. It is, he says, "only fair and just" to require appellants, in return for these benefits, to respond in the State of Delaware when they are accused of misusing their power. . . .

But like Heitner's first argument, this line of reasoning establishes only that it is appropriate for Delaware law to govern the obligations of appellants to Greyhound and its stockholders. It does not demonstrate that appellants have "purposefully avail[ed themselves] of the privilege of conducting activities within the forum State," *Hanson v. Denckla*, [327 U.S. 235, at 253 (1958)] in a way that would justify bringing them before a Delaware tribunal. Appellants have simply had nothing to do with the State of Delaware. Moreover, appellants had no reason to expect to be haled before a Delaware court. Delaware, unlike some States, has not enacted a statute that treats acceptance of a directorship as consent to jurisdiction in the State. . . . Appellants, who were not required to acquire interests in Greyhound in order to hold their positions, did not by acquiring those interests surrender their right to be brought to judgment only in States with which they had had "minimum contacts."

The Due Process Clause

> does not contemplate that a state may make binding a judgment . . . against an individual or corporate defendant with which the state has no contacts, ties, or relations.

International Shoe Co. v. Washington, 326 U.S., at 319. Delaware's assertion of jurisdiction over appellants in this case is inconsistent with that constitutional limitation on state power. The judgment of the Delaware Supreme Court must, therefore, be reversed.

It is so ordered.

[The concurring opinions of Justices Powell and Stevens and the concurring and dissenting opinion of Justice Brennan are omitted. Justice Rehnquist took no part in the consideration of this case.]

NOTES AND QUESTIONS

(1) In his concurring and dissenting opinion, Justice Brennan agreed that "the minimum–contacts analysis developed in *International Shoe* . . . represents a far more sensible construction for the exercise of state court jurisdiction than the patchwork of legal and factual fictions that has been generated from the decision in *Pennoyer v. Neff.* . . ." 433 U.S. at 219 [Justice Brennan dissenting]. In Justice Brennan's view, however, "as a general rule a state forum has jurisdiction to adjudicate a shareholder derivative action centering on the conduct and the policies of the directors and officers of a corporation chartered by that State." *Id.* at 222. (Note, however, that under the Delaware statute in *Shaffer*, the underlying claim against the defendant shareholders need not necessarily involve their corporation at all.)

(2) *Shaffer v. Heitner* requires that "all assertions of state court jurisdiction must be evaluated according to the standards set forth in *International Shoe* and its progeny." Does *quasi in rem* jurisdiction now retain any validity or function? Are less contacts necessary to establish the required "minimum contacts" for long–arm in personam if the plaintiff has attached the nonresident's in–state property? *See Intermeat, Inc. v. American Poultry, Inc.*, 575 F.2d 1017, 1023 (2d Cir. 1978). Does *Shaffer v. Heitner* suggest that a plaintiff may obtain a writ of attachment of the defendant's property in State A to secure an anticipated judgment in litigation pending in State B? *See generally*, Silverman, *Shaffer v. Heitner: The End of an Era*, 53 N.Y.U. L. Rev. 33, 71–79 (1978).

(3) The *Intermeat* case, *supra*, suggests that *Harris v. Balk* may still live on. There, the Second Circuit held that *Shaffer* had not totally disapproved of *Harris*, and found that there were enough additional contacts between an out–of–state defendant and New York State to satisfy *Shaffer's* minimum contacts test (*e.g.*, contract "conceived" in New York; contract had arbitration clause calling for arbitration in New York; and defendant resold large quantities of meat in New York). In short, the court held that a debt may be garnished in New York whenever the garnishee is doing business within the state and whenever the defendant has sufficient additional contacts with the state. Is *Intermeat* still valid after *Rush v. Savchuk*, 444 U.S. 320 (1980) (excerpted *infra*)? Bear in mind that *Shaffer* required jurisdiction to be based on the court's evaluation of the "relationship among the defendant, the forum, and the litigation." 433 U.S. at 204. Moreover, if the debt owed by the garnishee in *Intermeat* may be attached in New York because the nonresident defendant has substantial connection with New York (but is not subject to general *in personam* jurisdiction), may the debt also be attached simultaneously in another state where the garnishee is found and where the defendant also has substantial connections? Does due process require that the plaintiff's cause of action be related to the garnished debt? What other practical problems can you foresee with this analysis?

[B]   The Rise and Fall of the *Seider–Roth* Doctrine

SEIDER v. ROTH

New York Court of Appeals
17 N.Y.2d 111, 269 N.Y.S.2d 99, 216 N.E.2d 312 (1966)

DESMOND, Chief Judge.

This appeal . . . brings us a question new to this court—in a personal injury action against a nonresident defendant, is defendant's liability insurer's contractual obligation to defend and indemnify defendant a "debt" owing to defendant and as such subject to attachment under CPLR 6202? Both courts below answered that question in the affirmative. We think that is the correct answer.

The two plaintiffs, husband and wife, residents of New York, were injured in an automobile accident on a highway in Vermont, allegedly through the negligence of defendant Lemiux who lives in Quebec (the other defendant, Roth, was the driver of a third car involved in the collision). The order of attachment directed the Sheriff to levy upon the contractual obligation of Hartford Accident and Indemnity Company to defend and indemnify defendant Lemiux under a policy of automobile liability issued by Hartford to Lemiux. Hartford is an insurer doing business in New York State and the attachment papers were served on it in New York State. The Hartford–Lemiux liability policy was issued in Canada. Lemiux was personally served in Quebec.

Defendant Lemiux moved to vacate the attachment and the service of the summons and complaint on Lemiux. Special Term denied the motion on the ground that he was bound by the Second Department decision in *Fishman v. Sanders*, 18 A.D.2d 689, 235 N.Y.S.2d 861, where a similar contractual obligation of a liability insurer was held to be attachable. *Fishman v. Sanders* came to this court but we did not pass on the particular question (15 N.Y.2d 298, 258 N.Y.S.2d 380, 206 N.E.2d 326). On defendant's appeal in the present case, the same Appellate Division affirmed with one Justice dissenting alone. The majority noted that defendant–appellant was arguing for vacatur on the ground that the purported attachment was an attempt to levy "upon an obligation which is limited, conditional and dependent upon several contingencies, and is neither absolutely payable at present nor in the future." The court said, however, that the attachment had actually been made upon the insurer's existing contractual obligation under the policy. The dissenting Justice said that the insurer's obligation is not subject to attachment because it is not an indebtedness which is absolutely payable, and that nothing is or will be owing under the policy until plaintiffs recover a judgment, etc.

The controlling statutes are CPLR 5201 and 6202. . . . The whole question, therefore, is whether Hartford's contractual obligation to defendant is a debt or cause of action such as may be attached. The Hartford policy is in customary form. It requires Hartford, among other things, to defend Lemiux in any automobile negligence action and, if judgment be rendered against Lemiux, to indemnify him therefor. Thus, as soon as the accident occurred there was imposed on Hartford a contractual obligation which should be considered a "debt" within the meaning of CPLR 5201 and 6202. In fact, the policy casts on the insurer several obligations which accrue as soon as the insurer gets notice of an accident, and whether or not a suit is ever brought. For instance, under the "Insuring Agreements" and under "Additional Agreements" "No. 2," the insurer agrees upon receipt of notice of loss or damage to investigate and if expedient to negotiate or settle with the claimant. Furthermore, under "Section B" the insurer agrees to pay necessary medical and similar expenses of the insured and any other injured person.

. . . .

It is said that by affirmance here we would be setting up a "direct action" against the insurer. That is true to the extent only that affirmance will put jurisdiction in New York State and require the insurer to defend here, not because a debt owing by it to the defendant has been attached but because by its policy it has agreed to defend in any place where jurisdiction is obtained against its insured. Jurisdiction is properly acquired by this attachment since the policy obligation is a debt owed to the defendant by the insurer, the latter being regarded as a resident of this State. . . .

. . . .

The order appealed from should be affirmed, with costs, and the certified question answered in the affirmative.

. BURKE, Judge (dissenting).

This attachment, levied upon an automobile liability policy issued in Canada to a Canadian motorist in a case where the accident occurred in Vermont, ought to be vacated as there was nothing in this State to which the levy could apply. The so-called "debt" which is supposed to be subject to attachment is a mere promise made to the nonresident insured by the foreign insurance carrier to *defend and indemnify* the Canadian resident *if a suit is commenced* and *if damages are awarded* against the insured. Such a promise is contingent in nature. It is exactly this type of contingent undertaking which does not fall within the definition of attachable debt contained in CPLR 5201 (subd. [a]), *i.e.*, one which "is past due or which is yet to become due, certainly or upon demand of the judgment debtor." The bare undertaking to defend and indemnify is not an obligation "past due" and it is not certain to become due until jurisdiction over the insured is *properly* obtained. In New York "It is well settled that an indebtedness is not attachable unless it is absolutely payable at present, or in the future and not dependable upon *any* contingency." (*Herrmann & Grace v. City of New York*, 130 App.Div. 531, 535, 114 N.Y.S. 1107, 1110, *affd. on opn. of Appellate Division* 199 N.Y. 600, 93 N.E. 376; italics supplied.)

Faced with this long-established rule the plaintiffs indulge in circular ratiocination. The jurisdiction, they assert, is based upon a promise which evidently does not mature until there is jurisdiction. The existence of the policy is used as a sufficient basis for jurisdiction to start the very action necessary to activate the insurer's obligation under the policy. In other words, the promise to defend the insured is assumed to furnish the jurisdiction for a civil suit which must be validly commenced before the obligation to defend can possibly accrue. "This is a bootstrap situation." (Professor D. D. Siegel, Supplementary Commentary to CPLR 5201, McKinney's Cons.Laws of N.Y., Book 7B, 1965 Pamphlet, pp. 10–13.) It is indisputable that prior to the commencement of the suit the insurer owed no "debt" to the insured.

. . . .

The argument is made that several debts do accrue as soon as the insurer receives a notice of an accident. The first alleged obligation—the agreement "to investigate and if expedient to negotiate or settle with the claimant"—cannot be construed to impose a duty on the carrier which would amount to a "debt" under CPLR 5201 (subd. [a]). It is not an absolute commitment but one left solely within the discretion of the carrier as it necessarily must be because of the enormous number of notices of accident filed. The second alleged obligation under Insuring Agreement B, dealing with medical payments, has no relation to the third–party liability agreement under which these plaintiffs claim. The medical payment insuring agreement, like the collision insuring agreement, is a separate agreement and runs only in favor of the insured and the passengers in his car. It is also contingent upon submission of acceptable written proof, oftentimes required to be under oath, together with executed authorizations from each injured person to scrutinize his medical reports and permission for a personal physical examination of each person. Apart from the undeniable fact that this section of the policy has no relevance to the gravamen of plaintiffs' cause of action, the obligation to the insured is a conditional type, not absolute as specified by the statute and thus not attachable for jurisdictional purposes.

Not only does the text of CPLR and the contingent nature of an automobile liability policy dictatea vacatur of the warrant of attachment but, where the grounds to obtain jurisdiction are tenuous, public policy should restrain us from approving, under the guise of "in rem" jurisdiction over a nonresident motorist, "a direct action" against a foreign insurer licensed to do business in this State on a policy issued in Montreal to a resident of Quebec, Canada, for damages resulting from a Vermont accident.

The order appealed from should be reversed and the certified question answered in the negative.

FULD, VAN VOORHIS and KEATING, JJ., concur with Chief Judge DESMOND.

BURKE, J., dissents in an opinion in which SCILEPPI and BERGAN, JJ., concur.

Order affirmed, etc.

NOTES AND QUESTIONS

(1) Why did Judge Burke say that the assertion of *Seider*–type jurisdiction created a "bootstrap situation?"

(2) In *Simpson v. Loehman*, 21 N.Y.2d 305, 287 N.Y.S.2d 633, 234 N.E.2d 669 (1967), *motion for reargument den.*, 21 N.Y.2d 990, 290 N.Y.S.2d 914, 238 N.E.2d 319, the plaintiff, a New York resident, was injured when cut by the propeller of the defendant's boat. The defendant was a Connecticut resident and the accident occurred in Connecticut waters. The plaintiff obtained jurisdiction in New York by attaching the defendant's liability policy, issued by an insurer doing business in New York. The defendant argued that the plaintiff's attachment of the policy to obtain jurisdiction in New York violated, *inter alia*, the due process clause of the United States Constitution.

In upholding the attachment (Judge BURKE again dissenting), the New York Court of Appeals rejected the defendant's due process argument with a brief reference to *Harris v. Balk.* The Court then noted:

> The historical limitations on both in personam and in rem jurisdiction, with their rigid tests, are giving way to a more realistic and reasonable evaluation of the respective rights of plaintiffs, defendants, and the State in terms of fairness. . . . Such an evaluation requires a practical appraisal of the situation of the various parties rather than an emphasis upon somewhat magical and

medieval concepts of presence and power. Viewed realistically, the insurer in a case such as the present is in full control of the litigation; it selects the defendant's attorneys; it decides if and when to settle; and it makes all procedural decisions in connection with the litigation. . . . Moreover, where the plaintiff is a resident of the forum state and the insurer is present in and regulated by it, the State has a substantial and continuing relation with the controversy. For jurisdictional purposes, in assessing fairness under the due process clause and in determining the public policy of New York, such factors loom large.

21 N.Y.2d at 311.

(3) In denying reargument in *Simpson*, the Court of Appeals stated that in a *Seider*–type action, the plaintiff's recovery would be limited to the face value of the policy even if the defendant appeared and defended the action on the merits. 21 N.Y.2d at 990. This statement, which one commentator called "miraculous" (Siegal, Practice Commentaries, N.Y. Civ. Prac. Law § 5201 at p. 15 (McKinney Supp. 1968)), created on behalf of nonresident defendants the right to make a "limited appearance" in *Seider*–type actions.

(4) Note that the *Seider–Roth* doctrine raises at least two distinct issues: (a) does the insurer's obligation to indemnify and defend the defendant constitute such "property" of the defendant as may be subject to attachment under local law?; and (b) if so, does the resulting exercise of *quasi in rem* jurisdiction by the court over the defendant violate due process? Will both issues necessarily be present in every case? Which issue was emphasized in *Seider*?

(5) In both *Seider* and *Simpson*, the New York Court of Appeals analogized between *Seider*–type actions and actions under a "direct action" statute. Where enacted, direct action statutes permit a tort victim to sue the alleged tortfeasor's insurer directly and, if successful, to recover up to the policy limit. In *Watson v. Employer's Liability Insurance Corp.*, 348 U.S. 66 (1954), the Supreme Court upheld as constitutional the Louisiana direct action statute, which permitted nonresident tort victims to sue the tortfeasor's insurer in Louisiana's courts if the tort occurred in Louisiana.

(6) *Minichiello v. Rosenberg*, 410 F.2d 106 (2d Cir. 1968), was the first case to consider fully the due process attack on the *Seider–Roth* Doctrine. Citing the reasoning of the New York Court of Appeals in *Simpson v. Loehmann*, the Second Circuit agreed that the *Seider*–type action was essentially a "judicially created direct action statute." The court stressed New York's interest in seeing that its residents received compensation for their injuries, and concluded that "we thus believe that, all things considered, the Supreme Court would sustain the validity of a state statute permitting direct actions against insurers doing business in the state in favor of residents as well as on behalf of persons injured within it. . . . The state's interest in protecting its residents [injured outside the state] is as great as in the case of non–residents injured within the state." 410 F.2d at 110.

The *Minichiello* court imposed three conditions on the application of *Seider–Roth* which, it implied, were constitutionally required. First, the doctrine was only to be applied in the state where the plaintiff resided or where the injury occurred. In other words, nonresidents of New York could not commence lawsuits in New York by attaching the insurance policies of nonresident defendants if the accident occurred outside New York. Second, the defendant must be permitted to make a limited appearance. Third, no *res judicata* or collateral estoppel effect was to be given to the judgment. If the plaintiff sought recovery beyond the policy limit, he/she would have to bring a new action in a state where *in personam* jurisdiction over the defendant was available. 410 F.2d 110–12.

(7) Most courts, however, refused to follow *Seider v. Roth. See, e.g., Javorek v. Superior Court of Monterey County*, 131 Cal. Rptr. 768, 522 P.2d 728 (1976) (discussing due process issue, but concluding that the insurer's contingent obligations are not subject to attachment under California law).

(8) How would you distinguish between a *Seider*–type action and a direct action against the defendant's insurer? Isn't the insurer the real party in interest, as *Simpson* and *Minichiello* suggested? If the three conditions set out in *Minichiello v. Rosenberg* are satisfied, why should the insured object to jurisdiction at the plaintiff's residence? What interest would the insured have in the outcome of the lawsuit?

(9) *Seider v. Roth, Simpson v. Loehmann*, and *Minichiello v. Rosenberg, supra*, all preceded the Supreme Court's decision in *Shaffer v. Heitner, supra*. In *Shaffer*, the Court stated that "all assertions of state court jurisdiction are to be evaluated according to the standards of *International Shoe*," and *Shaffer* was widely viewed as overruling *Harris v. Balk*. Substantial controversy developed as to the viability of the *Seider–Roth* doctrine after *Shaffer v. Heitner. See, e.g.*, Silverman, *Shaffer v. Heitner: End of an Era*, 53 N.Y.U. L. Rev. 33, 90–99 (1978); Note, *The Constitutionality of Seider v. Roth after Shaffer v. Heitner*, 78 Colum. L. Rev. 409 (1978); *O'Connor v. Lee–Hy Paving Corp.*, 579 F.2d 194, 199 (1978) ("The fall of *Harris v. Balk* [in *Shaffer*] . . . does not necessarily topple *Seider*").

(10) The debate ended with the Supreme Court's decision in *Rush v. Savchuk*, 444 U.S. 320 (1980) (excerpted *infra*).

RUSH v. SAVCHUK

United States Supreme Court
444 U.S. 320, 100 S. Ct. 571, 62 L. Ed. 2d. 516 (1980)

[In January, 1972, Savchuk was injured in an automobile accident in Elkhart, Indiana, while travelling as a passenger in Rush's car. At the time of the accident, Savchuk and Rush were both Indiana residents. In June, 1983, Savchuk moved to Minnesota. Rush's insurer, State Farm Mutual Automobile Insurance Company, did business in Minnesota. In May, 1974, Savchuk commenced an action against Rush in the Minnesota state courts, garnishing State Farm's contractual obligation to defend and indemnify Rush. Savchuk personally served Rush in Indiana. The Minnesota Supreme Court upheld the garnishment against constitutional attack.]

Mr. Justice MARSHALL delivered the opinion of the Court.

. . . .

III

In *Shaffer v. Heitner* we held that "all assertions of state–court jurisdiction must be evaluated according to the standards set forth in *International Shoe* and its progeny." 433 U.S., at 212. That is, a State may exercise jurisdiction over an absent defendant only if the defendant has "certain minimum contacts with [the forum] such that the maintenance of the suit does not offend 'traditional notions of fair play and substantial justice.' " *International Shoe Co. v. Washington,* 326 U.S. 310, 316 (1945). In determining whether a particular exercise of state–court jurisdiction is consistent with due process, the inquiry must focus on "the relationship among the defendant, the forum, and the litigation." *Shaffer v. Heitner, supra,* at 204.

It is conceded that Rush has never had any contacts with Minnesota, and that the auto accident that is the subject of this action occurred in Indiana and also had no connection to Minnesota. The only affiliating circumstance offered to show a relationship among Rush, Minnesota, and this lawsuit is that Rush's insurance company does business in the State. *Seider* constructed an ingenious jurisdictional theory to permit a State to command a defendant to appear in its courts on the basis of this factor alone. State Farms contractual obligation to defend and indemnify Rush in connection with liability claims is treated as a debt owed by State Farm to Rush. The legal fiction that assigns a situs to a debt, for garnishment purposes, wherever the debtor is found is combined with the legal fiction that a corporation is "present," for jurisdictional purposes, wherever it does business to yield the conclusion that the obligation to defend and indemnify is located in the forum for purposes of the garnishment statute. The fictional presence of the policy obligation is deemed to give the State the power to determine the policy–holder's liability for the out–of–state accident.[14]

We held in *Shaffer* that the mere presence of property in a State does not establish a sufficient relationship between the owner of the property and the State to support the exercise of jurisdiction over an unrelated cause of action. The ownership of property in the State is a contact between the defendant and the forum, and it may suggest the presence of other ties. 433 U.S., at 209. Jurisdiction is lacking, however, unless there are sufficient contacts to satisfy the fairness standard of *International Shoe.*

Here, the fact that the defendant's insurer does business in the forum State suggests no further contacts between the defendant and the forum, and the record supplies no evidence of any. State Farm's decision to do business in Minnesota was

---

[14] The conclusion that State Farm's obligation under the insurance policy was garnishable property is a matter of state law and therefore is not before us. Assuming that it was garnishable property, the question is what significance that fact has to the relationship among the defendant, the forum, and the litigation.

completely adventitious as far as Rush was concerned. He had no control over that decision, and it is unlikely that he would have expected that by buying insurance in Indiana he had subjected himself to suit in any State to which a potential future plaintiff might decide to move. In short, it cannot be said that the *defendant* engaged in any purposeful activity related to the forum that would make the exercise of jurisdiction fair, just, or reasonable, *see Kulko v. California Superior Court*, 436 U.S. 84, 93–94 (1978); *Hanson* v. *Denckla*, 357 U.S. 235, 253 (1958), merely because his insurer does business there.

Nor are there significant contacts between the litigation and the forum. The Minnesota Supreme Court was of the view that the insurance policy was so important to the litigation that it provided contacts sufficient to satisfy due process. The insurance policy is not the subject matter of the case, however, nor is it related to the operative facts of the negligence action. The contractual arrangements between the defendant and the insurer pertain only to the conduct, not the substance, of the litigation, and accordingly do not affect the court's jurisdiction unless they demonstrate ties between the defendant and the forum.

In fact, the fictitious presence of the insurer's obligation in Minnesota does not, without more, provide a basis for concluding that there is *any* contact in the *International Shoe* sense between Minnesota and the insured. To say that "a debt follows the debtor" is simply to say that intangible property has no actual situs, and a debt may be sued on wherever there is jurisdiction over the debtor. State Farm is "found," in the sense of doing business, in all 50 States and the District of Columbia. Under appellee's theory, the "debt" owed to Rush would be "present" in each of those jurisdictions simultaneously. It is apparent that such a "contact" can have no jurisdictional significance.

An alternative approach for finding minimum contacts in *Seider*–type cases . . . is to attribute the insurer's forum contacts to the defendant by treating the attachment procedure as the functional equivalent of a direct action against the insurer. This approach views *Seider* jurisdiction as fair both to the insurer, whose forum contacts would support *in personam* jurisdiction even for an unrelated cause of action, and to the "nominal defendant." Because liability is limited to the policy amount, the defendant incurs no personal liability, and the judgment is satisfied from the policy proceeds which are not available to the insured for any purpose other than paying accident claims, the insured is said to have such a slight stake in the litigation as a practical matter that it is not unfair to make him a "nominal defendant" in order to obtain jurisdiction over the insurance company.

Seider actions are not equivalent to direct actions, however. The State's ability to exert its power over the "nominal defendant" is analytically prerequisite to the insurer's entry into the case as a garnishee. If the Constitution forbids the assertion of jurisdiction over the insured based on the policy, then there is no conceptual basis for bringing the "garnishee" into the action. Because the party with forum contacts can only be reached through the out–of–state party, the question of jurisdiction over the nonresident cannot be ignored.[19] Moreover, the assumption that the defendant has no real stake in the litigation is far from self-evident.[20]

. . . .

The justifications offered in support of *Seider* jurisdiction share a common characteristic: they shift the focus of the inquiry from the relationship among the defendant, the forum, and the litigation to that among the plaintiff, the forum, the insurer, and the litigation. The insurer's contacts with the forum are attributed to the defendant because the policy was taken out in anticipation of such litigation. The State's interests in providing a forum for its residents and in regulating the activities of insurance companies are substituted for its contacts with the defendant and the cause of action. This subtle shift in focus from the defendant to the plaintiff is most evident in the decisions limiting *Seider* jurisdiction to actions by forum residents on the ground that permitting nonresidents to avail themselves of the procedure would be unconstitutional. In other words, the plaintiff's contacts with the forum are decisive in determining whether the defendant's due process rights are violated.

Such an approach is forbidden by *International Shoe* and its progeny. If a defendant has certain judicially cognizable ties with a State, a variety of factors relating to the particular cause of action may be relevant to the determination whether the exercise of jurisdiction would comport with "traditional notions of fair play and substantial justice." *See McGee v. International Life Ins. Co.*, 355 U.S. 220 (1957); *cf. Kulko v. California Superior Court*, 436 U.S., at 98–101. Here, however, the defendant has *no* contacts with the forum, and the Due Process Clause "does not contemplate that a state may make binding a judgment . . . against an individual or corporate defendant with which the state has no contacts, ties, or relations." *International Shoe Co. v. Washington*, 326 U.S., at 319. The judgment of the Minnesota Supreme Court is, therefore,

Reversed.

[The dissenting opinions of Justices Brennan and Stevens are omitted.]

---

19 *Compare* the direct action statute upheld in *Watson v. Employers Liability Assurance Corp.*, 348 U.S. 66 (1954), which was applicable only if the accident or injury occurred in the State or the insured was domiciled there and which permitted the plaintiff to sue the insurer alone, without naming the insured as a defendant. *Id.*, at 68, n. 4.

20 A party does not extinguish his legal interest in a dispute by insuring himself against having to pay an eventual judgment out of his own pocket. Moreover, the purpose of insurance is simply to make the defendant whole for the economic costs of the lawsuit; but noneconomic factors may also be important to the defendant. Professional malpractice actions, for example, question the defendant's integrity and competence and may affect his professional standing. *Cf. Donawitz v. Danek*, 42 N. Y. 2d 138, 366 N. E. 2d 253 (1977) (medical malpractice action premised on *Seider* jurisdiction dismissed because plaintiff was a nonresident). Further, one can easily conceive of cases in which the defendant might have a substantial economic stake in *Seider* litigation—if, for example, multiple plaintiffs sued in different States for an aggregate amount in excess of the policy limits, or if a successful claim would affect the policyholder's insurability. For these reasons, the defendant's interest in the adjudication of his liability cannot reasonably be characterized as *de minimis*.

NOTES AND QUESTIONS

(1) After *Rush*, may a plaintiff attach the obligation of an insurer to defend and indemnify a defendant over whom long–arm jurisdiction is obtainable? Note that in footnote 14, the Court stated that the attachability of such "property" is a question of state law.

(2) Although "*Seider* actions are not equivalent to direct action," isn't the interest of the insured, which the Court stressed in footnote 20, the same in both instances? Although such an occurrence would be unusual, it is certainly possible for an accident to occur in a state in which in personam jurisdiction over the alleged tortfeasor cannot be obtained. *See, e.g., World–Wide Volkswagen v. Woodson*, 444 U.S. 286 (1980). In such a case, would a local statute permitting a direct action against the tortfeasor's insurer in the accident state be constitutional?

§ 4.03 Constitutional Issues in Domestic Attachment

SNIADACH v. FAMILY FINANCE CORP.

United States Supreme Court
395 U.S. 337, 89 S. Ct. 1820, 23 L. Ed. 2d 349 (1969)

Mr. Justice DOUGLAS delivered the opinion of the Court.

Respondents instituted a garnishment action against petitioner as defendant and Miller Harris Instrument Co., her employer, as garnishee. The complaint alleged a claim of $420 on a promissory note. The garnishee filed its answer stating it had wages of $63.18 under its control earned by petitioner and unpaid, and that it would pay one–half to petitioner as a subsistence allowance[1] and hold the other half subject to the order of the court.

Petitioner moved that the garnishment proceedings be dismissed for failure to satisfy the due process requirements of the Fourteenth Amendment. The Wisconsin Supreme Court sustained the lower state court in approving the procedure. 37 Wis. 2d 163, 154 N. W. 2d 259. The case is here on a petition for a writ of certiorari. . . .

The Wisconsin statute gives a plaintiff 10 days in which to serve the summons and complaint on the defendant after service on the garnishee.[2] In this case petitioner

---

[1] Wis. Stat. § 267.18(2)(a) provides:

When wages or salary are the subject of garnishment action, the garnishee shall pay over to the principal defendant on the date when such wages or salary would normally be payable a subsistence allowance, out of the wages or salary then owing, in the sum of $25 in the case of an individual without dependents or $40 in the case of an individual with dependents; but in no event in excess of 50 per cent of the wages or salary owing. Said subsistence allowance shall be applied to the first wages or salary earned in the period subject to said garnishment action.

[2] Wis. Stat. § 267.07 (1).

was served the same day as the garnishee. She nonetheless claims that the Wisconsin garnishment procedure violates that due process required by the Fourteenth Amendment, in that notice and an opportunity to be heard are not given before the *in rem* seizure of the wages. What happens in Wisconsin is that the clerk of the court issues the summons at the request of the creditor's lawyer; and it is the latter who by serving the garnishee sets in motion the machinery whereby the wages are frozen.[3] They may, it is true, be unfrozen if the trial of the main suit is ever had and the wage earner wins on the merits. But in the interim the wage earner is deprived of his enjoyment of earned wages without any opportunity to be heard and to tender any defense he may have, whether it be fraud or otherwise.

Such summary procedure may well meet the requirements of due process in extraordinary situations. *Cf. Fahey v. Mallonee*, 332 U.S. 245, 253–254; *Ewing v. Mytinger & Casselberry, Inc.*, 339 U.S. 594, 598–600; *Ownbey v. Morgan*, 256 U.S. 94, 110–112; *Coffin Bros. v. Bennett*, 227 U.S. 29, 31. But in the present case no situation requiring special protection to a state or creditor interest is presented by the facts; nor is the Wisconsin statute narrowly drawn to meet any such unusual condition. Petitioner was a resident of this Wisconsin community and *in personam* jurisdiction was readily obtainable.

The question is not whether the Wisconsin law is a wise law or unwise law. Our concern is not what philosophy Wisconsin should or should not embrace. . . . We do not sit as a super–legislative body. In this case the sole question is whether there has been a taking of property without that procedural due process that is required by the Fourteenth Amendment. We have dealt over and over again with the question of what constitutes "the right to be heard" (*Schroeder v. New York*, 371 U.S. 208, 212) within the meaning of procedural due process. *See Mullane v. Central Hanover Trust Co.*, 339 U.S. 306, 314. In the latter case we said that the right to be heard "has little reality or worth unless one is informed that the matter is pending and can choose for himself whether to appear or default, acquiesce or contest." . . . In the context of this case the question is whether the interim freezing of the wages without a chance to be heard violates procedural due process.

A procedural rule that may satisfy due process for attachments in general, . . . does not necessarily satisfy procedural due process in every case. The fact that a procedure would pass muster under a feudal regime does not mean it gives necessary protection to all property in its modern forms. We deal here with wages—a specialized type of property presenting distinct problems in our economic system. We turn then to the nature of that property and problems of procedural due process.

A prejudgment garnishment of the Wisconsin type is a taking which may impose tremendous hardship on wage earners with families to support. Until a recent Act of Congress [the Consumer Credit Protection Act][4] § 304 [15 U.S.C. § 1674] of which forbids discharge of employees on the ground that their wages have been garnished, garnishment often meant the loss of a job. Over and beyond that was the great drain on family income. As stated by Congressman Reuss:[5]

---

[3] Wis. Stat. § 267.04 (1).

[4] 82 Stat. 146, Act of May 29, 1968.

[5] 114 Cong. Rec. 1832.

> The idea of wage garnishment in advance of judgment, of trustee process, of wage attachment, or whatever it is called is a most inhuman doctrine. It compels the wage earner, trying to keep his family together, to be driven below the poverty level.

Recent investigations of the problem have disclosed the grave injustices made possible by prejudgment garnishment whereby the sole opportunity to be heard comes after the taking. Congressman Sullivan, Chairman of the House Subcommittee on Consumer Affairs who held extensive hearings on this and related problems stated:

> What we know from our study of this problem is that in a vast number of cases the debt is a fraudulent one, saddled on a poor ignorant person who is trapped in an easy credit nightmare, in which he is charged double for something he could not pay for even if the proper price was called for, and then hounded into giving up his pound of flesh, and being fired besides.

114 Cong. Rec. 1832.

The leverage of the creditor on the wage earner is enormous. The creditor tenders not only the original debt but the "collection fees" incurred by his attorneys in the garnishment proceedings:

> The debtor whose wages are tied up by a writ of garnishment, and who is usually in need of money, is in no position to resist demands for collection fees. If the debt is small, the debtor will be under considerable pressure to pay the debt and collection charges in order to get his wages back. If the debt is large, he will often sign a new contract of "payment schedule" which incorporates these additional charges.

Apart from those collateral consequences, it appears that in Wisconsin the statutory exemption granted the wage earner is "generally insufficient to support the debtor for any one week."

The result is that a prejudgment garnishment of the Wisconsin type may as a practical matter drive a wage–earning family to the wall.[9] Where the taking of one's property is so obvious, it needs no extended argument to conclude that absent notice and a prior hearing (*cf. Coe v. Armour Fertilizer Works*, 237 U.S. 413, 423) this prejudgment garnishment procedure violates the fundamental principles of due process.

Reversed.

. . . .

[Concurring opinion of Justice Harlan and dissenting opinion of Justice Black deleted.]

---

[9] "For a poor man—and whoever heard of the wage of the affluent being attached?—to lose part of his salary often means his family will go without the essentials. No man sits by while his family goes hungry or without heat. He either files for consumer bankruptcy and tries to begin again, or just quits his job and goes on relief. Where is the equity, the common sense, in such a process?" Congressman Gonzales, 114 Cong. Rec. 1833. For the impact of garnishment on personal bankruptcies *see* H. R. Rep. No. 1040, 90th Cong., 1st Sess., 20–21.

NOTES AND QUESTIONS

(1) State statutes relating to wage garnishment were widely revised after *Sniadach*. Some states abolished pre–judgment wage garnishment altogether. *See, e.g.*, Cal. Code Civ. P. § 690.6(a). In New York, a maximum of 10% of a week's wages is subject to garnishment.

(2) The Federal Consumer Credit Protection Act (FCCPA), 15 U.S.C. § 1671 *et seq.*, places a limit on wage garnishment. Under the FCCPA, creditors may garnish a maximum of 25% of a debtor's weekly "disposable earnings" (*i.e.*, gross income less "deductions required by law"), or the amount by which the debtor's disposable earnings exceed thirty times the minimum hourly wage, whichever is less. The FCCPA explicitly authorizes the states to enact stricter limits on wage garnishment, and prohibits an employer from firing an employee because of any one garnishment.

(3) Does *Sniadach* require prior notice and hearing before every case of pre–judgment garnishment? Does it require the same procedure with regard to other instances of pre–judgment attachment of a debtor's property? Does the central importance of wages in the life of the debtor and his/her family require a special rule for wage garnishment?

FUENTES v. SHEVIN

United States Supreme Court
407 U.S. 67, 92 S. Ct. 1983, 32 L. Ed. 2d 556, reh'g denied
409 U.S. 902, 93 S. Ct. 177, 34 L. Ed. 2d 165 (1972)

Mr. Justice STEWART delivered the opinion of the Court.

We here review the decisions of two three–judge federal District Courts that upheld the constitutionality of Florida and Pennsylvania laws authorizing the summary seizure of goods or chattels in a person's possession under a writ of replevin. Both statutes provide for the issuance of writs ordering state agents to seize a person's possessions, simply upon the ex parte application of any other person who claims a right to them and posts a security bond. Neither statute provides for notice to be given to the possessor of the property, and neither statute gives the possessor an opportunity to challenge the seizure at any kind of prior hearing. The question is whether these statutory procedures violate the Fourteenth Amendment's guarantee that no State shall deprive any person of property without due process of law.

I

The appellant in No. 5039, Margarita Fuentes, is a resident of Florida. She purchased a gas stove and service policy from the Firestone Tire and Rubber Co. (Firestone) under a conditional sales contract calling for monthly payments over a period of time. A few months later, she purchased a stereophonic phonograph from the same company under the same sort of contract. The total cost of the stove and stereo was about $500, plus an additional financing charge of over $100. Under the contracts, Firestone retained title to the merchandise, but Mrs. Fuentes was entitled to possession unless and until she should default on her installment payments.

For more than a year, Mrs Fuentes made her installment payments. But then, with only about $200 remaining to be paid, a dispute developed between her and Firestone over the servicing of the stove. Firestone instituted an action in a small–claims court for repossession of both the stove and the stereo, claiming that Mrs. Fuentes had refused to make her remaining payments. Simultaneously with the filing of that action and before Mrs. Fuentes had even received a summons to answer its complaint, Firestone obtained a writ of replevin ordering a sheriff to seize the disputed goods at once.

In conformance with Florida procedure, Firestone had only to fill in the blanks on the appropriate form documents and submit them to the clerk of the small–claims court. The clerk signed and stamped the documents and issued a writ of replevin. Later the same day, a local deputy sheriff and an agent of Firestone went to Mrs. Fuentes' home and seized the stove and stereo.

Shortly thereafter, Mrs. Fuentes instituted the present action in federal district court, challenging the constitutionality of the Florida prejudgment replevin procedures under the Due Process Clause of the Fourteenth Amendment. She sought declaratory and injunctive relief against continued enforcement of the procedural provisions of the state statutes that authorize prejudgment replevin.

The appellants in No. 5138 filed a very similar action in a federal district court in Pennsylvania, challenging the constitutionality of that State's prejudgment replevin process. Like Mrs. Fuentes, they had had possessions seized under writs of replevin. Three of the appellants had purchased personal property—a bed, a table, and other household goods—under installment sales contracts like the one signed by Mrs. Fuentes; and the sellers of the property had obtained and executed summary writs of replevin, claiming that the appellants had fallen behind in their installment payments. The experience of the fourth appellant, Rosa Washington, had been more bizarre. She had been divorced from a local deputy sheriff and was engaged in a dispute with him over the custody of their son. Her former husband, being familiar with the routine forms used in the replevin process, had obtained a writ that ordered the seizure of the boy's clothes, furniture, and toys.

In both No. 5039 and No. 5138, three–judge District Courts were convened to consider the appellants' challenges to the constitutional validity of the Florida and Pennsylvania statutes. The courts in both cases upheld the constitutionality of the statutes. . . .

II

Under the Florida statute challenged here,[6] "[a]ny person whose goods or chattels are wrongfully detained by any other person . . . may have a writ of replevin to recover them. . . ." Fla. Stat. Ann. § 78.01 (Supp. 1972–1973). There is no requirement that the applicant make a convincing showing before the seizure that the goods are, in fact, "wrongfully detained." Rather, Florida law automatically relies on the bare assertion of the party seeking the writ that he is entitled to one and allows a court clerk to issue the writ summarily. It requires only that the applicant file a complaint, initiating a court action for repossession and reciting in conclusory fashion that he is "lawfully entitled to the possession" of the property, and that he file a security bond

---

[6] The relevant Florida statutory provisions are the following:

Fla. Stat. Ann. § 78.01 (Supp. 1972–1973):

Right to replevin.—Any person whose goods or chattels are wrongfully detained by any other person or officer may have a writ of replevin to recover them and any damages sustained by reason of the wrongful caption or detention as herein provided. Or such person may seek like relief, but with summons to defendant instead of replevy writ in which event no bond is required and the property shall be seized only after judgment, such judgment to be in like form as that provided when defendant has retaken the property on a forthcoming bond.

Fla. Stat. Ann. § 78.07 (Supp. 1972–1973):

Bond; Requisites—Before a replevy writ issues, plaintiff shall file a bond with surety payable to defendant to be approved by the clerk in at least double the value of the property to be replevied conditioned that plaintiff will prosecute his action to effect and without delay and that if defendant recovers judgment against him in the action, he will return the property, if return thereof is adjudged, and will pay defendant all sums of money recovered against plaintiff by defendant in the action.

Fla. Stat. Ann. § 78.08 (Supp. 1972–1973):

Writ; form; return.—The writ shall command the officer to whom it may be directed to replevy the goods and chattels in possession of defendant, describing them, and to summon the defendant to answer the complaint.

Fla. Stat. Ann. § 78.10 (Supp. 1972–1973):

Writ; execution on property in buildings, etc.—In executing the writ of replevin, if the property or any part thereof is secreted or concealed in any dwelling house or other building or enclosure, the officer shall publicly demand delivery thereof and if it is not delivered by the defendant or some other person, he shall cause such house, building or enclosure to be broken open and shall make replevin according to the writ; and if necessary, he shall take to his assistance the power of the county.

Fla. Stat. Ann. § 78.13 (Supp. 1972–1973):

Writ; disposition of property levied on.—The officer executing the writ shall deliver the property to plaintiff after the lapse of three (3) days from the time the property was taken unless within the three (3) days defendant gives bond with surety to be approved by the officer in double the value of the property as appraised by the officer, conditioned to have the property forthcoming to abide the result of the action, in which event the property shall be redelivered to defendant.

in at least double the value of the property to be replevied conditioned that plaintiff will prosecute his action to effect and without delay and that if defendant recovers judgment against him in the action, he will return the property, if return thereof is adjudged, and will pay defendant all sums of money recovered against plaintiff by defendant in the action.

Fla. Stat. Ann. § 78.07 (Supp. 1972–1973). On the sole basis of the complaint and bond, a writ is issued "command[ing] the officer to whom it may be directed to replevy the goods and chattels in possession of defendant . . . and to summon the defendant to answer the complaint." . . . If the goods are "in any dwelling house or other building or enclosure," the officer is required to demand their delivery; but, if they are not delivered, "he shall cause such house, building or enclosure to be broken open and shall make replevin according to the writ. . . ." . . .

Thus, at the same moment that the defendant receives the complaint seeking repossession of property through court action, the property is seized from him. He is provided no prior notice and allowed no opportunity whatever to challenge the issuance of the writ. *After* the property has been seized, he will eventually have an opportunity for a hearing, as the defendant in the trial of the court action for repossession, which the plaintiff is required to pursue. And he is also not wholly without recourse in the meantime. For under the Florida statute, the officer who seizes the property must keep it for three days, and during that period the defendant may reclaim possession of the property by posting his own security bond in double its value. But if he does not post such a bond, the property is transferred to the party who sought the writ, pending a final judgment in the underlying action for repossession. . . .

The Pennsylvania law differs, though not in its essential nature, from that of Florida. As in Florida, a private party may obtain a prejudgment writ of replevin through a summary process of ex parte application to a prothonotary. As in Florida, the party seeking the writ may simply post with his application a bond in double the value of the property to be seized. . . . There is no opportunity for a prior hearing and no prior notice to the other party. On this basis, a sheriff is required to execute the writ by seizing the specified property. Unlike the Florida statute, however, the Pennsylvania law does not require that there *ever* be opportunity for a hearing on the merits of the conflicting claims to possession of the replevied property. The party seeking the writ is not obliged to initiate a court action for repossession. Indeed, he need not even formally allege that he is lawfully entitled to the property. The most that is required is that he file an "affidavit of the value of the property to be replevied." . . . If the party who loses property through replevin seizure is to get even a post–seizure hearing, he must initiate a lawsuit himself. He may also, as under Florida law, post his own counterbond within three days after the seizure to regain possession. . . .

III

Although these prejudgment replevin statutes are descended from the common–law replevin action of six centuries ago, they bear very little resemblance to it. Replevin at common law was an action for the return of specific goods wrongfully taken or "distrained." Typically, it was used after a landlord (the "distrainor") had seized possessions from a tenant (the "distrainee") to satisfy a debt allegedly owed. If the tenant then instituted a replevin action and posted security, the landlord could be ordered to return the property at once, pending a final judgment in the underlying action. However, this prejudgment replevin of goods at common law did *not* follow from an entirely ex parte process of pleading by the distrainee. For "[t]he distrainor could always stop the action of replevin by claiming to be the owner of the goods; and as this claim was often made merely to delay the proceedings, the writ *de proprietate probanda* was devised early in the fourteenth century, which enabled the sheriff to determine summarily the question of ownership. If the question of ownership was determined against the distrainor the goods were delivered back to the distrainee [pending final judgment]." 3 W. Holdsworth, History of English Law 284 (1927).

Prejudgment replevin statutes like those of Florida and Pennsylvania are derived from this ancient possessory action in that they authorize the seizure of property before a final judgment. But the similarity ends there. As in the present cases, such statutes are most commonly used by creditors to seize goods allegedly wrongfully detained—not wrongfully taken—by debtors. At common law, if a creditor wished to invoke state power to recover goods wrongfully detained, he had to proceed through the action of debt or detinue. These actions, however, did not provide for a return of property before final judgment. And, more importantly, on the occasions when the common law did allow prejudgment seizure by state power, it provided some kind of notice and opportunity to be heard to the party then in possession of the property, and a state official made at least a summary determination of the relative rights of the disputing parties before stepping into the dispute and taking goods from one of them.

IV

For more than a century the central meaning of procedural due process has been clear: "Parties whose rights are to be affected are entitled to be heard; and in order that they may enjoy that right they must first be notified." *Baldwin v. Hale*, 1 Wall. 223, 233. . . . It is equally fundamental that the right to notice and an opportunity to be heard "must be granted at a meaningful time and in a meaningful manner." *Armstrong v. Manzo*, 380 U.S. 545, 552.

The primary question in the present cases is whether these state statutes are constitutionally defective in failing to provide for hearings "at a meaningful time." The Florida replevin process guarantees an opportunity for a hearing after the seizure of goods, and the Pennsylvania process allows a post–seizure hearing if the aggrieved party shoulders the burden of initiating one. But neither the Florida nor the Pennsylvania statute provides for notice or an opportunity to be heard *before* the seizure. The issue is whether procedural due process in the context of these cases requires an opportunity for a hearing *before* the State authorizes its agents to seize property in the possession of a person upon the application of another.

The constitutional right to be heard is a basic aspect of the duty of government to follow a fair process of decisionmaking when it acts to deprive a person of his possessions. The purpose of this requirement is not only to ensure abstract fair play to the individual. Its purpose, more particularly, is to protect his use and possession of property from arbitrary encroachment—to minimize substantively unfair or mistaken deprivations of property, a danger that is especially great when the State seizes goods simply upon the application of and for the benefit of a private party. So viewed, the prohibition against the deprivation of property without due process of law reflects the high value, embedded in our constitutional and political history, that we place on a person's right to enjoy what is his, free of governmental interference. *See Lynch v. Household Finance Corp.*, 405 U.S. 538, 552.

The requirement of notice and an opportunity to be heard raises no impenetrable barrier to the taking of a person's possessions. But the fair process of decision–making that it guarantees works, by itself, to protect against arbitrary deprivation of property. For when a person has an opportunity to speak up in his own defense, and when the State must listen to what he has to say, substantively unfair and simply mistaken deprivations of property interests can be prevented. It has long been recognized that "fairness can rarely be obtained by secret, one–sided determination of facts decisive of rights. . . . [And] no better instrument has been devised for arriving at truth than to give a person in jeopardy of serious loss notice of the case against him and opportunity to meet it." *Joint Anti–Fascist Refugee Committee v. McGrath*, 341 U.S. 123, 170–172 (Frankfurter, J., concurring).

If the right to notice and a hearing is to serve its full purpose, then, it is clear that it must be granted at a time when the deprivation can still be prevented. At a later hearing, an individual's possessions can be returned to him if they were unfairly or mistakenly taken in the first place. Damages may even be awarded to him for the wrongful deprivation. But no later hearing and no damage award can undo the fact that the arbitrary taking that was subject to the right of procedural due process has already occurred. "This Court has not . . . embraced the general proposition that a wrong may be done if it can be undone." *Stanley v. Illinois*, 405 U.S. 645, 647.

This is no new principle of constitutional law. The right to a prior hearing has long been recognized by this Court under the Fourteenth and Fifth Amendments. Although the Court has held that due process tolerates variances in the *form* of a hearing "appropriate to the nature of the case," *Mullane v. Central Hanover Tr. Co.*, 339 U.S. 306, 313, and "depending upon the importance of the interests involved and the nature of the subsequent proceedings [if any]," *Boddie v. Connecticut*, 401 U.S. 371, 378, the Court has traditionally insisted that, whatever its form, opportunity for that hearing must be provided before the deprivation at issue takes effect. . . . "That the hearing required by due process is subject to waiver, and is not fixed in form does not affect its root requirement that an individual be given an opportunity for a hearing *before* he is deprived of any significant property interest, except for extraordinary situations where some valid governmental interest is at stake that justifies postponing the hearing until after the event." *Boddie v. Connecticut, supra*, at 378–379 (emphasis in original).

The Florida and Pennsylvania prejudgment replevin statutes fly in the face of this principle. To be sure, the requirements that a party seeking a writ must first post a bond, allege conclusorily that he is entitled to specific goods, and open himself to possible liability in damages if he is wrong, serve to deter wholly unfounded applications for a writ. But those requirements are hardly a substitute for a prior hearing, for they test no more than the strength of the applicant's own belief in his rights.[13] . . .

The minimal deterrent effect of a bond requirement is, in a practical sense, no substitute for an informed evaluation by a neutral official. More specifically, as a matter of constitutional principle, it is no replacement for the right to a prior hearing that is the only truly effective safeguard against arbitrary deprivation of property. While the existence of these other, less effective, safeguards may be among the considerations that affect the form of hearing demanded by due process, they are far from enough by themselves to obviate the right to a prior hearing of some kind.

V

The right to a prior hearing, of course, attaches only to the deprivation of an interest encompassed within the Fourteenth Amendment's protection. . . . [Here] the chattels at stake were nothing more than an assortment of household goods. Nonetheless, it is clear that the appellants were deprived of possessory interests in those chattels that were within the protection of the Fourteenth Amendment.

A

A deprivation of a person's possessions under a prejudgment writ of replevin, at least in theory, may be only temporary. The Florida and Pennsylvania statutes do not require a person to wait until a post–seizure hearing and final judgment to recover what has been replevied. Within three days after the seizure, the statutes allow him to recover the goods if he, in return, surrenders other property—a payment necessary to secure a bond in double the value of the goods seized from him.[14] But it is now well settled that a temporary, nonfinal deprivation of property is nonetheless a "deprivation" in the terms of the Fourteenth Amendment. *Sniadach v. Family Finance Corp.*, 395 U.S. 337; *Bell v. Burson*, 402 U.S. 535. . . .

The present cases are no different. When officials of Florida or Pennsylvania seize one piece of property from a person's possession and then agree to return it if he surrenders another, they deprive him of property whether or not he has the funds, the knowledge, and the time needed to take advantage of the recovery provision.

---

[13] They may not even test that much. For if an applicant for the writ knows that he is dealing with an uneducated, uninformed consumer with little access to legal help and little familiarity with legal procedures, there may be a substantial possibility that a summary seizure of property—however unwarranted—may go unchallenged, and the applicant may feel that he can act with impunity.

[14] The appellants argue that this opportunity for quick recovery exists only in theory. They allege that very few people in their position are able to obtain a recovery bond, even if they know of the possibility. Appellant Fuentes says that in her case she was never told that she could recover the stove and stereo and that the deputy sheriff seizing them gave them at once to the Firestone agent, rather than holding them for three days. She further asserts that of 442 cases of prejudgment replevin in small–claims courts in Dade County, Florida, in 1969, there was not one case in which the defendant took advantage of the recovery provision.

The Fourteenth Amendment draws no bright lines around three–day, 10–day or 50–day deprivations of property. Any significant taking of property by the State is within the purview of the Due Process Clause. While the length and consequent severity of a deprivation may be another factor to weigh in determining the appropriate form of hearing, it is not decisive of the basic right to a prior hearing of some kind.

B

The appellants who signed conditional sales contracts lacked full legal title to the replevied goods. The Fourteenth Amendment's protection of "property," however, has never been interpreted to safeguard only the rights of undisputed ownership. Rather, it has been read broadly to extend protection to "any significant property interest," *Boddie v. Connecticut*, 401 U.S., at 379, including statutory entitlements. *See Bell v. Burson*, 402 U.S., at 539; *Goldberg v. Kelly*, 397 U.S., at 262.

The appellants were deprived of such an interest in the replevied goods—the interest in continued possession and use of the goods. . . . They had acquired this interest under the conditional sales contracts that entitled them to possession and use of the chattels before transfer of title. In exchange for immediate possession, the appellants had agreed to pay a major financing charge beyond the basic price of the merchandise. Moreover, by the time the goods were summarily repossessed, they had made substantial installment payments. Clearly, their possessory interest in the goods, dearly bought and protected by contract,[16] was sufficient to invoke the protection of the Due Process Clause.

Their ultimate right to continued possession was, of course, in dispute. If it were shown at a hearing that the appellants had defaulted on their contractual obligations, it might well be that the sellers of the goods would be entitled to repossession. But even assuming that the appellants had fallen behind in their installment payments, and that they had no other valid defenses, that is immaterial here. The right to be heard does not depend upon an advance showing that one will surely prevail at the hearing. . . . It is enough to invoke the procedural safeguards of the Fourteenth Amendment that a significant property interest is at stake, whatever the ultimate outcome of a hearing on the contractual right to continued possession and use of the goods.[18]

C

[The Court rejected the argument that notice and a hearing are required only prior to the deprivation of "necessities."]

---

[16] The possessory interest of Rosa Washington, an appellant in No. 5138, in her son's clothes, furniture, and toys was no less sufficient to invoke due process safeguards. Her interest was not protected by contract. Rather, it was protected by ordinary property law, there being a dispute between her and her estranged husband over which of them had a legal right not only to custody of the child but also to possession of the chattels.

[18] The issues decisive of the ultimate right to continued possession, of course, may be quite simple. The simplicity of the issues might be relevant to the formality or scheduling of a prior hearing. But it certainly cannot undercut the right to a prior hearing of some kind.

. . . The Fourteenth Amendment speaks of "property" generally. And, under our free–enterprise system, an individual's choices in the marketplace are respected, however unwise they may seem to someone else. It is not the business of a court adjudicating due process rights to make its own critical evaluation of those choices and protect only the ones that, by its own lights, are "necessary."[21]

VI

There are "extraordinary situations" that justify postponing notice and opportunity for a hearing. *Boddie v. Connecticut*, 401 U.S., at 379. These situations, however, must be truly unusual. Only in a few limited situations has this Court allowed outright seizure without opportunity for a prior hearing. First, in each case, the seizure has been directly necessary to secure an important governmental or general public interest. Second, there has been a special need for very prompt action. Third, the State has kept strict control over its monopoly of legitimate force: the person initiating the seizure has been a government official responsible for determining, under the standards of a narrowly drawn statute, that it was necessary and justified in the particular instance. Thus, the Court has allowed summary seizure of property to collect the internal revenue of the United States, to meet the needs of a national war effort, to protect against the economic disaster of a bank failure, and to protect the public from misbranded drugs and contaminated food.

The Florida and Pennsylvania prejudgment replevin statutes serve no such important governmental or general public interest. They allow summary seizure of a person's possessions when no more than private gain is directly at stake.[29] The replevin of chattels, as in the present cases, may satisfy a debt or settle a score. But state intervention in a private dispute hardly compares to state action furthering a war effort or protecting the public health.

. . . .

The statutes, moreover, abdicate effective state control over state power. Private parties, serving their own private advantage, may unilaterally invoke state power

---

[21] The relative weight of liberty or property interests is relevant, of course, to the form of notice and hearing required by due process. . . . But *some* form of notice and hearing—formal or informal—is required before deprivation of a property interest that "cannot be characterized as *de minimis.*" *Sniadach v. Family Finance Corp., supra*, at 342 (Harlan, J., concurring).

[29] By allowing repossession without an opportunity for a prior hearing, the Florida and Pennsylvania statutes may be intended specifically to reduce the costs for the private party seeking to seize goods in another party's possession. Even if the private gain at stake in repossession actions were equal to the great public interests recognized in this Court's past decisions, . . . the Court has made clear that the avoidance of the ordinary costs imposed by the opportunity for a hearing is not sufficient to override the constitutional right. . . .

In any event, the aggregate cost of an opportunity to be heard before repossession should not be exaggerated. For we deal here only with the right to an *opportunity* to be heard. Since the issues and facts decisive of rights in repossession suits may very often be quite simple, there is a likelihood that many defendants would forgo their opportunity, sensing the futility of the exercise in the particular case. And, of course, no hearing need be held unless the defendant, having received notice of his opportunity, takes advantage of it.

to replevy goods from another. No state official participates in the decision to seek a writ; no state official reviews the basis for the claim to repossession; and no state official evaluates the need for immediate seizure. There is not even a requirement that the plaintiff provide any information to the court on these matters. The State acts largely in the dark.

VII

Finally, we must consider the contention that the appellants who signed conditional sales contracts thereby waived their basic procedural due process rights. The contract signed by Mrs. Fuentes provided that "in the event of default of any payment or payments, Seller at its option may take back the merchandise. . . . " The contracts signed by the Pennsylvania appellants similarly provided that the seller "may retake" or "repossess" the merchandise in the event of a "default in any payment." These terms were parts of printed form contracts, appearing in relatively small type and unaccompanied by any explanations clarifying their meaning.

In *D. H. Overmyer Co. v. Frick Co.*, 405 U.S. 174, the Court recently outlined the considerations relevant to determination of a contractual waiver of due process rights. Applying the standards governing waiver of constitutional rights in a criminal proceeding—although not holding that such standards must necessarily apply—the Court held that, on the particular facts of that case, the contractual waiver of due process rights was "voluntarily, intelligently, and knowingly" made. *Id.*, at 187. The contract in *Overmyer* was negotiated between two corporations; the waiver provision was specifically bargained for and drafted by their lawyers in the process of these negotiations. As the Court noted, it was "not a case of unequal bargaining power or overreaching. The Overmyer–Frick agreement, from the start, was not a contract of adhesion." *Id.*, at 186. Both parties were "aware of the significance" of the waiver provision. *Ibid.*

The facts of the present cases are a far cry from those of *Overmyer*. There was no bargaining over contractual terms between the parties who, in any event, were far from equal in bargaining power. The purported waiver provision was a printed part of a form sales contract and a necessary condition of the sale. The appellees made no showing whatever that the appellants were actually aware or made aware of the significance of the fine print now relied upon as a waiver of constitutional rights.

The Court in *Overmyer* observed that "where the contract is one of adhesion, where there is great disparity in bargaining power, and where the debtor receives nothing for the [waiver] provision, other legal consequences may ensue." *Id.*, at 188. Yet, as in *Overmyer*, there is no need in the present cases to canvass those consequences fully. For a waiver of constitutional rights in any context must, at the very *least*, be clear. We need not concern ourselves with the involuntariness or unintelligence of a waiver when the contractual language relied upon does not, on its face, even amount to a waiver.

The conditional sales contracts here simply provided that upon a default the seller "may take back," "may retake" or "may repossess" merchandise. The contracts included nothing about the waiver of a prior hearing. They did not indicate *how* or *through what process*—a final judgment, self–help, prejudgment replevin with a prior hearing, or prejudgment replevin without a prior hearing—the seller could take back the goods. Rather, the purported waiver provisions here are no more than a statement of the seller's right to repossession upon occurrence of certain events. The appellees do not suggest that these provisions waived the appellants' right to a full post–seizure hearing to determine whether those events had, in fact, occurred and to consider any other available defenses. By the same token, the language of the purported waiver provisions did not waive the appellants' constitutional right to a preseizure hearing of some kind.

VIII

We hold that the Florida and Pennsylvania prejudgment replevin provisions work a deprivation of property without due process of law insofar as they deny the right to a prior opportunity to be heard before chattels are taken from their possessor. Our holding, however, is a narrow one. We do not question the power of a State to seize goods before a final judgment in order to protect the security interests of creditors so long as those creditors have tested their claim to the goods through the process of a fair prior hearing. The nature and form of such prior hearings, moreover, are legitimately open to many potential variations and are a subject, at this point, for legislation—not adjudication.[33] . . .

For the foregoing reasons, the judgments of the District Courts are vacated and these cases are remanded for further proceedings consistent with this opinion.

It is so ordered.

Mr. Justice POWELL and Mr. Justice REHNQUIST did not participate in the consideration or decision of these cases.

Mr. Justice WHITE, with whom THE CHIEF JUSTICE and Mr. Justice BLACK-MUN join, dissenting.

Because the Court's opinion and judgment improvidently, in my view, call into question important aspects of the statutes of almost all the States governing secured transactions and the procedure for repossessing personal property, I must dissent for the reasons that follow.

. . . .

. . . It goes without saying that in the typical installment sale of personal property both seller and buyer have interests in the property until the purchase price is fully paid, the seller early in the transaction often having more at stake than the buyer. Nor is it disputed that the buyer's right to possession is conditioned upon his making the stipulated payments and that upon default the seller is entitled to possession. Finally, there is no question in these cases that if default is disputed by the buyer he has the opportunity for a full hearing, and that if he prevails he may have the property or its full value as damages.

---

[33] Leeway remains to develop a form of hearing that will minimize unnecessary cost and delay while preserving the fairness and effectiveness of the hearing in preventing seizures of goods where the party seeking the writ has little probability of succeeding on the merits of the dispute.

The narrow issue, as the Court notes, is whether it comports with due process to permit the seller, pending final judgment, to take possession of the property through a writ of replevin served by the sheriff without affording the buyer opportunity to insist that the seller establish at a hearing that there is reasonable basis for his claim of default. The interests of the buyer and seller are obviously antagonistic during this interim period: the buyer wants the use of the property pending final judgment; the seller's interest is to prevent further use and deterioration of his security. By the Florida and Pennsylvania laws the property is to all intents and purposes placed in custody and immobilized during this time. The buyer loses use of the property temporarily but is protected against loss; the seller is protected against deterioration of the property but must undertake by bond to make the buyer whole in the event the latter prevails.

In considering whether this resolution of conflicting interests is unconstitutional, much depends on one's perceptions of the practical considerations involved. The Court holds it constitutionally essential to afford opportunity for a probable–cause hearing prior to repossession. Its stated purpose is "to prevent unfair and mistaken deprivations of property." But in these typical situations, the buyer–debtor has either defaulted or he has not. If there is a default, it would seem not only "fair," but essential, that the creditor be allowed to repossess; and I cannot say that the likelihood of a mistaken claim of default is sufficiently real or recurring to justify a broad constitutional requirement that a creditor do more than the typical state law requires and permits him to do. Sellers are normally in the business of selling and collecting the price for their merchandise. I could be quite wrong, but it would not seem in the creditor's interest for a default occasioning repossession to occur; as a practical matter it would much better serve his interests if the transaction goes forward and is completed as planned. Dollar–and–cents considerations weigh heavily against false claims of default as well as against precipitate action that would allow no opportunity for mistakes to surface and be corrected.* Nor does it seem to me that creditors would lightly undertake the expense of instituting replevin actions and putting up bonds.

. . . Indeed, "[t]he very nature of due process negates any concept of inflexible procedures universally applicable to every imaginable situation. . . ." "[W]hat procedures due process may require under any given set of circumstances must begin with a determination of the precise nature of the government function involved as well as of the private interest that has been affected by governmental action." *Cafeteria Workers v. McElroy*, 367 U.S. 886, 895 (1961). . . . Viewing the issue before us in this light, I would not construe the Due Process Clause to require the creditors to do more than they have done in these cases to secure possession pending final hearing. Certainly, I would not ignore, as the Court does, the creditor's interest in preventing further use and deterioration of the property in which he has substantial interest. Surely under the Court's own definition, the creditor has a "property" interest as deserving of protection as that of the debtor. At least the debtor, who is

---

* . . . It was stipulated between appellant Fuentes and defendants in the District Court that Mrs. Fuentes was in default at the time the replevin action was filed and that notices to this effect were sent to her over several months prior to institution of the suit. (App. 25–26.)

very likely uninterested in a speedy resolution that could terminate his use of the property, should be required to make those payments, into court or otherwise, upon which his right to possession is conditioned.

. . . The Court's rhetoric is seductive, but in end analysis, the result it reaches will have little impact and represents no more than ideological tinkering with state law. It would appear that creditors could withstand attack under today's opinion simply by making clear in the controlling credit instruments that they may retake possession without a hearing, or, for that matter, without resort to judicial process at all. Alternatively, they need only give a few days' notice of a hearing, take possession if hearing is waived or if there is default; and if hearing is necessary merely establish probable cause for asserting that default has occurred. It is very doubtful in my mind that such a hearing would in fact result in protections for the debtor substantially different from those the present laws provide. On the contrary, the availability of credit may well be diminished or, in any event, the expense of securing it increased.

None of this seems worth the candle to me. The procedure that the Court strikes down is not some barbaric hangover from bygone days. The respective rights of the parties in secured transactions have undergone the most intensive analysis in recent years. The Uniform Commercial Code, which now so pervasively governs the subject matter with which it deals, provides in Art. 9, § 9–503, that:

> Unless otherwise agreed a secured party has on default the right to take possession of the collateral. In taking possession a secured party may proceed without judicial process if this can be done without breach of the peace or may proceed by action. . . .

Recent studies have suggested no changes in Art. 9 in this respect. See Permanent Editorial Board for the Uniform Commercial Code, Review Committee for Article 9 of the Uniform Commercial Code, Final Report, § 9–503 (April 25, 1971). I am content to rest on the judgment of those who have wrestled with these problems so long and often and upon the judgment of the legislatures that have considered and so recently adopted provisions that contemplate precisely what has happened in these cases.

NOTES AND QUESTIONS

(1) To what specific aspects of the Florida and Pennsylvania statutes did Justice Stewart object? Under what circumstances did Justice Stewart suggest that a pre–judgment seizure without a hearing would be appropriate?

(2) Justice White's dissent suggests that the Court's opinion, in its "ideological tinkering with state law," effectively outlaws the self–help provisions of UCC § 9–503. Is that suggestion accurate? What does Justice Stewart say about a creditor's use of non–judicial, self–help remedies for default?

(3) *Fuentes v. Shevin* was a 4–3 decision. The Court was back to full strength when *Mitchell v. W. T. Grant Co., infra,* was decided.

MITCHELL v. W. T. GRANT CO.

United States Supreme Court
416 U.S. 600, 94 S. Ct. 1895, 40 L. Ed. 2d 406 (1974)

[In February, 1972, W. T. Grant Co. filed suit against Lawrence Mitchell in the First City Court in New Orleans, Louisiana. Grant's complaint alleged that Mitchell had purchased from Grant a refrigerator, a range, a stereo, and a washing machine and was in default on the payments therefor in the amount of $547.17. Grant also alleged that it had a vendor's lien on the goods and that a writ of sequestration should issue to sequester the goods pending trial.

Grant's credit manager asserted by affidavit that Grant had reason to believe that Mitchell would encumber or dispose of the goods during the pendency of the proceedings.

Without notice to Mitchell, the judge of the First City Court issued a writ of sequestration ordering the Constable to take the goods into his possession, upon the submission by Grant of a bond in the amount of $1,125.

After the goods were seized, Mitchell filed a motion to dissolve the writ. The trial court rejected Mitchell's constitutional arguments and denied his motion. The Louisiana Supreme Court affirmed.]

Mr. Justice WHITE delivered the opinion of the Court.

. . . .

II

Petitioner's basic proposition is that because he had possession of and a substantial interest in the sequestered property, the Due Process Clause of the Fourteenth Amendment necessarily forbade the seizure without prior notice and opportunity for a hearing. In the circumstances presented here, we cannot agree.

Petitioner no doubt "owned" the goods he had purchased under an installment sales contract, but his title was heavily encumbered. The seller, W. T. Grant Co., also had an interest in the property, for state law provided it with a vendor's lien to secure the unpaid balance of the purchase price. Because of the lien, Mitchell's right to possession and his title were subject to defeasance in the event of default in paying the installments due from him. His interest in the property, until the purchase price was paid in full, was no greater than the surplus remaining, if any, after foreclosure and sale of the property in the event of his default and satisfaction of outstanding claims. . . . The interest of Grant, as seller of the property and holder of a vendor's lien, was measured by the unpaid balance of the purchase price. The monetary value of that interest in the property diminished as payments were made, but the value of the property as security also steadily diminished over time as it was put to its intended use by the purchaser.

Plainly enough, this is not a case where the property sequestered by the court is exclusively the property of the defendant debtor. The question is not whether a debtor's property may be seized by his creditors, *pendente lite*, where they hold no present interest in the property sought to be seized. The reality is that both seller and buyer had current, real interests in the property, and the definition of property rights is a matter of state law. Resolution of the due process question must take account not only of the interests of the buyer of the property but those of the seller as well.

With this duality in mind, we are convinced that the Louisiana sequestration procedure is not invalid, either on its face or as applied. Sequestration under the Louisiana statutes is the modern counterpart of an ancient civil law device to resolve conflicting claims to property. Historically, the two principal concerns have been that, pending resolution of the dispute, the property would deteriorate or be wasted in the hands of the possessor and that the latter might sell or otherwise dispose of the goods. A minor theme was that official intervention would forestall violent self–help and retaliation. . . .

Louisiana statutes provide for sequestration where "one claims the ownership or right to possession of property, or a mortgage, lien, or privilege thereon . . . if it is within the power of the defendant to conceal, dispose of, or waste the property or the revenues therefrom, or remove the property from the parish, during the pendency of the action." The writ, however, will not issue on the conclusory allegation of ownership or possessory rights [, but . . .] "only when the nature of the claim and the amount thereof, if any, and the grounds relied upon for the issuance of the writ clearly appear from specific facts" shown by a verified petition or affidavit. In the parish where this case arose, the clear showing required must be made to a judge,[5] and the writ will issue only upon his authorization and only after the creditor seeking the writ has filed a sufficient bond to protect the vendee against all damages in the event the sequestration is shown to have been improvident.

The writ is obtainable on the creditor's ex parte application, without notice to the debtor or opportunity for a hearing, but the statute entitles the debtor immediately to seek dissolution of the writ, which must be ordered unless the creditor "proves the grounds upon which the writ was issued," Art. 3506, the existence of the debt, lien, and delinquency, failing which the court may order return of the property and assess damages in favor of the debtor, including attorney's fees.

The debtor, with or without moving to dissolve the sequestration, may also regain possession by filing his own bond to protect the creditor against interim damage to him should he ultimately win his case and have judgment against the debtor for the unpaid balance of the purchase price which was the object of the suit and of the sequestration.

---

[5] Articles 282 and 283 of the Code provide, generally, that the court clerk may issue writs of sequestration. But Art. 281 confines the authority to the judge in Orleans Parish. . . . The validity of procedures obtaining in areas outside Orleans Parish is not at issue.

In our view, this statutory procedure effects a constitutional accommodation of the conflicting interests of the parties. We cannot accept petitioner's broad assertion that the Due Process Clause of the Fourteenth Amendment guaranteed to him the use and possession of the goods until all issues in the case were judicially resolved after full adversary proceedings had been completed. . . .

As to this claim, the seller here, with a vendor's lien to secure payment of the unpaid balance of purchase price, had the right either to be paid in accordance with its contract or to have possession of the goods for the purpose of foreclosing its lien and recovering the unpaid balance. . . . Wholly aside from whether the buyer, with possession and power over the property, will destroy or make away with the goods, the buyer in possession of consumer goods will undeniably put the property to its intended use, and the resale value of the merchandise will steadily decline as it is used over a period of time. Any installment seller anticipates as much, but he is normally protected because the buyer's installment payments keep pace with the deterioration in value of the security. Clearly, if payments cease and possession and use by the buyer continue, the seller's interest in the property as security is steadily and irretrievably eroded until the time at which the full hearing is held.

The State of Louisiana was entitled to recognize this reality and to provide somewhat more protection for the seller. This it did in Orleans Parish by authorizing the sequestration of property by a judge. . . . The buyer is permitted to regain possession by putting up his own bond to protect the seller. Absent that bond . . . the seller would be unprotected against the inevitable deterioration in the value of his security if the buyer remained in possession pending trial on the merits. The debtor, unlike the creditor [who posts a bond], does not stand ready to make the opposing party whole, if his possession, pending a prior hearing, turns out to be wrongful.

Second, there is the real risk that the buyer, with possession and power over the goods, will conceal or transfer the merchandise to the damage of the seller. This is one of the considerations weighed in the balance by the Louisiana law in permitting initial sequestration of the property. . . . [U]nder Louisiana law, the vendor's lien expires if the buyer transfers possession. It follows that if the vendor is to retain his lien, superior to the rights of other creditors of the buyer, it is imperative when default occurs that the property be sequestered in order to foreclose the possibility that the buyer will sell or otherwise convey the property to third parties against whom the vendor's lien will not survive. The danger of destruction or alienation cannot be guarded against if notice and a hearing before seizure are supplied. The notice itself may furnish a warning to the debtor acting in bad faith.

Third, there is scant support in our cases for the proposition that there must be final judicial determination of the seller's entitlement before the buyer may be even temporarily deprived of possession of the purchased goods. On the contrary, it seems apparent that the seller with his own interest in the disputed merchandise would need to establish in any event only the probability that his case will succeed to warrant the bonded sequestration of the property pending outcome of the suit. . . . The issue at this stage of the proceeding concerns possession pending trial and turns on the existence of the debt, the lien, and the delinquency. These are ordinarily uncomplicated matters that lend themselves to documentary proof; and we think it comports with due process to permit the initial seizure on sworn ex parte documents, followed by the early opportunity to put the creditor to his proof. The nature of the issues at stake minimizes the risk that the writ will be wrongfully issued by a judge. The potential damages award available, if there is a successful motion to dissolve the writ, as well as the creditor's own interest in avoiding interrupting the transaction, also contributes to minimizing this risk.

Fourth, we remain unconvinced that the impact on the debtor of deprivation of the household goods here in question overrides his inability to make the creditor whole for wrongful possession, the risk of destruction or alienation if notice and a prior hearing are supplied, and the low risk of a wrongful determination of possession through the procedures now employed.

Finally, the debtor may immediately have a full hearing on the matter of possession following the execution of the writ, thus cutting to a bare minimum the time of creditor–or court–supervised possession. The debtor in this case, who did not avail himself of this opportunity, can hardly expect that his argument on the severity of deprivation will carry much weight, and even assuming that there is real impact on the debtor from loss of these goods, pending the hearing on possession, his basic source of income is unimpaired.

The requirements of due process of law "are not technical, nor is any particular form of procedure necessary." *Inland Empire Council v. Millis*, 325 U.S. 697, 710 (1945). . . . Considering the Louisiana procedure as a whole, we are convinced that the State has reached a constitutional accommodation of the respective interests of buyer and seller.

III

Petitioner asserts that his right to a hearing before his possession is in any way disturbed is nonetheless mandated by a long line of cases in this Court, culminating in *Sniadach v. Family Finance Corp.*, 395 U.S. 337 (1969), and *Fuentes v. Shevin*, 407 U.S. 67 (1972). [The Court's discussion of pre–*Sniadach* cases is omitted.]

In *Sniadach v. Family Finance Corp.*, *supra*, it was said that *McKay* and like cases dealt with "[a] procedural rule that may satisfy due process for attachments in general" but one that would not "necessarily satisfy procedural due process in every case," nor one that "gives necessary protection to all property in its modern forms." *Sniadach* involved the prejudgment garnishment of wages—"a specialized type of property presenting distinct problems in our economic system." . . . Because "[t]he leverage of the creditor on the wage earner is enormous" and because "prejudgment garnishment of the Wisconsin type may as a practical matter drive a wage–earning family to the wall," it was held that the Due Process Clause forbade such garnishment absent notice and prior hearing. . . . In *Sniadach*, the Court also observed that garnishment was subject to abuse by creditors without valid claims, a risk minimized by the nature of the security interest here at stake and the protections to the debtor offered by Louisiana procedure . . . The suing creditor in *Sniadach* had no prior interest in the property attached, and the opinion did not purport to govern the typical ease of the installment seller who brings a suit to collect an unpaid balance and who does not seek to attach wages pending the outcome of the suit but to repossess the sold property on which he had retained a lien to secure the purchase price. This very case soon came before the Court in *Fuentes v. Shevin*, where the constitutionality of the Florida and Pennsylvania replevin statutes was at issue. Those statutes permitted the secured installment seller to repossess the goods sold, without notice or hearing and without judicial order or supervision, but with the help of the sheriff operating under a writ issued by the court clerk at the behest of the seller. Because carried out without notice or opportunity for hearing and without judicial participation, this kind of seizure was held violative of the Due Process Clause. This holding is the mainstay of petitioner's submission here. But we are convinced that *Fuentes* was decided against a factual and legal background sufficiently different from that now before us and that it does not require the invalidation of the Louisiana sequestration statute, either on its face or as applied in this case.

The Florida law under examination in *Fuentes* authorized repossession of the sold goods without judicial order, approval, or participation. A writ of replevin was employed, but it was issued by the court clerk. As the Florida law was perceived by this Court, "[t]here is no requirement that the applicant make a convincing showing before the seizure," . . . ; the law required only "the bare assertion of the party seeking the writ that he is entitled to one" as a condition to the clerk's issuance of the writ. . . . The Court also said that under the statute the defendant–buyer would "eventually" have an opportunity for a hearing, "as the defendant in the trial of the court action for repossession. . . ." . . . The Pennsylvania law was considered to be essentially the same . . . except that it did "not require that there *ever* be opportunity for a hearing on the merits . . . "

The Louisiana sequestration statute followed in this case mandates a considerably different procedure. A writ of sequestration is available to a mortgage or lien holder to forestall waste or alienation of the property, but, different from the Florida and Pennsylvania systems, bare, conclusory claims of ownership or lien will not suffice under the Louisiana statute. Article 3501 authorizes the writ "only when the nature of the claim and the amount thereof, if any, and the grounds relied upon for the issuance of the writ clearly appear from specific facts" shown by verified petition or affidavit. Moreover, in the parish where this case arose, the requisite showing must be made to a judge, and judicial authorization obtained. Mitchell was not at the unsupervised mercy of the creditor and court functionaries. The Louisiana law provides for judicial control of the process from beginning to end. . . .

The risk of wrongful use of the procedure must also be judged in the context of the issues which are to be determined at that proceeding. In Florida and Pennsylvania property was only to be replevied in accord with state policy if it had been "wrongfully detained." This broad "fault" standard is inherently subject to factual determination and adversarial input. . . . [I]n *Fuentes* this fault standard for replevin was thought ill–suited for preliminary ex parte determination. In Louisiana, on the other hand, the facts relevant to obtaining a writ of sequestration are narrowly confined. As we have indicated, documentary proof is particularly suited for questions of the existence of a vendor's lien and the issue of default. There is thus far less danger here that the seizure will be mistaken and a corresponding decrease in the utility of an adversary hearing which will be immediately available in any event.

Of course, as in *Fuentes*, consideration of the impact on the debtor remains. Under Louisiana procedure, however, the debtor, Mitchell, was not left in limbo to await a hearing that might or might not "eventually" occur, as the debtors were under the statutory schemes before the Court in *Fuentes*. Louisiana law expressly provides for an immediate hearing and dissolution of the writ "unless the plaintiff proves the grounds upon which the writ was issued." Art. 3506.

To summarize, the Louisiana system seeks to minimize the risk of error of a wrongful interim possession by the creditor. The system protects the debtor's interest in every conceivable way, except allowing him to have the property to start with, and this is done in pursuit of what we deem an acceptable arrangement *pendente lite* to put the property in the possession of the party who furnishes protection against loss or damage to the other pending trial on the merits.

The Court must be sensitive to the possible consequences, already foreseen in antiquity, of invalidating this state statute. Doing so might not increase private violence, but self–help repossession could easily lessen protections for the debtor. *See*, for example, *Adams v. Southern California First National Bank*, 492 F.2d 324 (CA9 1973).[13] Here, the initial hardship to the debtor is limited, the seller has a strong selling interest, the process proceeds under judicial supervision and management, and the prevailing party is protected against all loss. Our conclusion is that the Louisiana standards regulating the use of the writ of sequestration are constitutional.

[Appendix to Opinion of the Court deleted.]

Mr. Justice POWELL, concurring.

In sweeping language, *Fuentes v. Shevin*, 407 U.S. 67 (1972), enunciated the principle that the constitutional guarantee of procedural due process requires an adversary hearing before an individual may be temporarily deprived of any possessory interest in tangible personal property, however brief the dispossession and however slight his monetary interest in the property. The Court's decision today

---

[13] The advisability of requiring prior notice and hearing before repossession has been under study for several years. A number of possibilities have been put forward to modify summary creditor remedies, whether taken through some form of court process or effected by self–help under Art. 9 of the Uniform Commercial Code § 9–503. . . .

As revealed in the various studies and proposals, the principal question yet to be satisfactorily answered is the impact of prior notice and hearing on the price of credit, and, more particularly, of the mix of procedural requirements necessary to minimize the cost. The commentators are in the throes of debate, *see, e.g.*, Symposium, *Creditors' Rights*, 47 S. Cal. L. Rev. 1–164 (1973), and basic questions remain unanswered. *See generally* Note, *Self–Help Repossession; the Constitutional Attack, the Legislative Response, and the Economic Implications*, 62 Geo. L. J. 273 (1973).

We indicate no view whatsoever on the desirability of one or more of the proposed reforms. The uncertainty evident in the current debate suggests caution in the adoption of an inflexible constitutional rule. Our holding in this case is limited to the constitutionality of the Louisiana sequestration procedures.

withdraws significantly from the full reach of that principle, and to this extent I think it fair to say that the *Fuentes* opinion is overruled. . . .

. . . .

I

The constitutional guarantee of procedural due process applies to governmental deprivation of a legitimate "property" or "liberty" interest within the meaning of the Fifth or Fourteenth Amendment. It requires that any such deprivation be accompanied by minimum procedural safeguards, including some form of notice and a hearing. . . . In the present case, there can be no doubt that under state law both petitioner and respondent had property interests in the goods sought to be seques-tered. Petitioner, as the vendee–debtor under an installment sales contract, had both title and possession of the goods subject to his contractual obligation to continue the installment payments. Respondent, as the vendor–creditor, had a vendor's lien on the goods as security for the unpaid balance.

The determination of what due process requires in a given context depends on a consideration of both the nature of the governmental function involved and the private interests affected. . . . The governmental function in the instant case is to provide a reasonable and fair framework of rules which facilitate commercial transactions on a credit basis. The Louisiana sequestration statute is designed to protect the legitimate interests of both creditor and debtor. As to the creditor, there is the obvious risk that a defaulting debtor may conceal, destroy, or further encumber the goods and thus deprive the creditor of his security. This danger is particularly acute where, as here, the vendor's lien may be vitiated merely by transferring the goods from the debtor's possession. In addition, the debtor's continued use of the goods diminishes their resale value. In these circumstances, a requirement of notice and an adversary hearing *before* sequestration would impose a serious risk that a creditor could be deprived of his security.

Against this concern must be balanced the debtor's real interest in uninterrupted possession of the goods, especially if the sequestration proves to be unjustified. To be sure, repossession of certain items of personal property, even for a brief period, may cause significant inconvenience. But it can hardly be said that temporary depri-vation of such property would necessarily place a debtor in a "brutal need" situation. . . .

In my view, the constitutional guarantee of procedural due process is fully satisfied in cases of this kind where state law requires, as a precondition to invoking the State's aid to sequester property of a defaulting debtor, that the creditor furnish adequate security and make a specific factual showing before a neutral officer or magistrate of probable cause to believe that he is entitled to the relief requested. An opportunity for an adversary hearing must then be accorded promptly after sequestration to determine the merits of the controversy, with the burden of proof on the creditor.

The Louisiana statute *sub judice* satisfies these requirements and differs materially from the Florida and Pennsylvania statutes in *Fuentes*. Those statutes did not require an applicant for a writ of replevin to make any factually convincing showing that the property was wrongfully detained or that he was entitled to the writ. Moreover, the Florida statute provided only that a post–seizure hearing be held eventually on the merits of the competing claims, and it required the debtor to initiate that proceeding. The Pennsylvania statute made no provision for a hearing at any time.

By contrast, the Louisiana statute applicable in Orleans Parish authorizes issuance of a writ of sequestration "only when the nature of the claim and the amount thereof, if any, and the grounds relied upon . . . clearly appear from specific facts shown by the petition verified by, or by the separate affidavit of, the petitioner, his counsel or agent." La. Code Civ. Proc. Ann., Art. 3501 (1961). The Louisiana statute also provides for an immediate hearing, and the writ is dissolved "unless the [creditor] proves the grounds upon which the writ was issued."

. . . In brief, the Louisiana statute satisfies the essential prerequisites of procedural due process and represents a fairer balancing of the interests of the respective parties than the statutes in *Fuentes*. I therefore agree that the Louisiana procedure should be sustained against petitioner's challenge.

. . . .

Mr. Justice STEWART, with whom Mr. Justice DOUGLAS and Mr. Justice MARSHALL concur, dissenting.

The Louisiana sequestration procedure now before us is remarkably similar to the statutory provisions at issue in *Fuentes v. Shevin*, 407 U.S. 67 (1972). In both cases the purchaser–in–possession of the property is not afforded any prior notice of the seizure or any opportunity to rebut the allegations of the vendor before the property is summarily taken from him by agents of the State. In both cases all that is required to support the issuance of the writ and seizure of the goods is the filing of a complaint and an affidavit containing *pro forma* allegations in support of the seller's purported entitlement to the goods in question. Since the procedure in both cases is completely ex parte, the state official charged with issuing the writ can do little more than determine the formal sufficiency of the plaintiff's allegations before ordering the state agents to take the goods from the defendant's possession.

The question before the Court in *Fuentes* was what procedures are required by the Due Process Clause of the Fourteenth Amendment when a State, at the behest of a private claimant, seizes goods in the possession of another, pending judicial resolution of the claimant's assertion of superior right to possess the property. The Court's analysis of this question began with the proposition that, except in exceptional circumstances, the deprivation of a property interest encompassed within the Fourteenth Amendment's protection must be preceded by notice to the affected party and an opportunity to be heard. . . . Matters such as requirements for the posting of bond and the filing of sworn factual allegations, the length and severity of the deprivation, the relative simplicity of the issues underlying the creditor's claim to possession, and the comparative "importance" or "necessity" of the goods involved were held to be relevant to determining the form of notice and hearing to be provided, but not to the constitutional need for notice and an opportunity for a hearing of some kind.

The deprivation of property in this case is identical to that at issue in *Fuentes*, and the Court does not say otherwise. Thus, under *Fuentes*, due process of law permits Louisiana to effect this deprivation only after notice to the possessor and opportunity for a hearing. Because I would adhere to the holding of *Fuentes*, I dissent from the Court's opinion and judgment upholding Louisiana's ex parte sequestration procedure, which provides that the possessor of the property shall never have advance notice or a hearing of any kind.

As already noted, the deprivation of property in this case is identical to that in *Fuentes*. But the Court says that this is a different case for three reasons: (1) the plaintiff who seeks the seizure of the property must file an affidavit stating "specific facts" that justify the sequestration; (2) the state official who issues the writ of sequestration is a judge instead of a clerk of the court; and (3) the issues that govern the plaintiff's right to sequestration are limited to "the existence of a vendor's lien and the issue of default," and "[t]here is thus far less danger here that the seizure will be mistaken and a corresponding decrease in the utility of an adversary hearing," *ante*, at 618. The Court's opinion in *Fuentes*, however, explicitly rejected each of these factors as a ground for a difference in decision.

The first two purported distinctions relate solely to the procedure by which the creditor–vendor secures the State's aid in summarily taking goods from the purchaser's possession. But so long as the Louisiana law routinely permits an ex parte seizure without notice to the purchaser, these procedural distinctions make no constitutional difference.

The Louisiana affidavit requirement can be met by any plaintiff who fills in the blanks on the appropriate form documents and presents the completed forms to the court. Although the standardized form in this case called for somewhat more information than that required by the Florida and Pennsylvania statutes challenged in *Fuentes*, such ex parte allegations "are hardly a substitute for a prior hearing, for they test no more than the strength of the applicant's own belief in his rights. Since his private gain is at stake, the danger is all too great that his confidence in his cause will be misplaced. Lawyers and judges are familiar with the phenomenon of a party mistakenly but firmly convinced that his view of the facts and law will prevail, and therefore quite willing to risk the costs of litigation." . . .

Similarly, the fact that the official who signs the writ after the ex parte application is a judge instead of a court clerk is of no constitutional significance. . . . Whether the issuing functionary be judge or a court clerk, he can in any event do no more than ascertain the formal sufficiency of the plaintiff's allegations, after which the issuance of the summary writ becomes a simple ministerial act.

The third distinction the Court finds between this case and *Fuentes* is equally insubstantial. The Court says the issues in this case are "particularly suited" to ex parte determination, in contrast to the issues in *Fuentes*, which were "inherently subject to factual determination and adversarial input . . . " There is, however, absolutely no support for this purported distinction. In this case the Court states the factual issues as "the existence of a vendor's lien and the issue of default." . . . The issues upon which replevin depended in *Fuentes* were no different; the creditor–vendor needed only to establish his security interest and the debtor–vendee's default. As Mr. Justice WHITE acknowledged in his *Fuentes* dissent, the essential issue at any hearing would be whether "there is reasonable basis for his [the creditor–vendor's] claim of default." . . . Thus, the Court produces this final attempted distinction out of whole cloth.

Moreover, *Fuentes* held that the relative complexity of the issues in dispute is not relevant to determining whether a prior hearing is required by due process. "The issues decisive of the ultimate right to continued possession, of course, may be quite simple. The simplicity of the issues might be relevant to the formality or scheduling of a prior hearing. But it certainly cannot undercut the right to a prior hearing of some kind." . . . Similarly, the probability of success on the factual issue does not affect the right to prior notice and an opportunity to be heard. . . .

In short, this case is constitutionally indistinguishable from *Fuentes v. Shevin*, and the Court today has simply rejected the reasoning of that case and adopted instead the analysis of the *Fuentes* dissent. . . . I would reverse the judgment before us because the Louisiana sequestration procedure fails to comport with the requirements of due process of law. . . .

. . . .

Mr. Justice BRENNAN is in agreement that *Fuentes v. Shevin*, . . . requires reversal of the judgment of the Supreme Court of Louisiana.

NOTES AND QUESTIONS

(1) Note that the majority in *Mitchell* consisted of the minority in *Fuentes v. Shevin*, plus Justices Rehnquist and Powell, who did not participate in *Fuentes*. Justice White, who wrote the dissenting opinion in *Fuentes*, wrote the majority opinion in *Mitchell*. Did *Mitchell* explicitly overrule *Fuentes*?

(2) What aspects of the Louisiana procedure did Justice White emphasize in distinguishing *Fuentes*?

NORTH GEORGIA FINISHING, INC. v. DI–CHEM, INC.

United States Supreme Court
419 U.S. 601, 95 S. Ct. 719, 42 L. Ed. 2d 751 (1975)

[In August, 1971, Di–Chem, Inc. filed suit against North Georgia Finishing, Inc. in the Georgia state court seeking $51,279.17 allegedly due for goods sold and delivered. Under Georgia law, a plaintiff in a pending action could obtain a writ of garnishment of the defendant's property by (1) making an affidavit before "some officer authorized to issue an attachment, or the clerk of any court of record in which the said garnishment is being filed or in which the main case is filed, stating the amount claimed to be due in such action . . . and that he has reason to apprehend the loss of the same or some part thereof unless process of garnishment shall issue;" and (2) filing a bond in a sum twice the amount claimed to be due. Di–Chem caused a bank account of North Georgia to be garnished.

North Georgia moved to have the writ dissolved on due process grounds. The trial court denied the motion and the Georgia appellate courts affirmed.]

Mr. Justice WHITE delivered the opinion of the Court.

. . . .

The Georgia [Supreme Court] recognized that *Sniadach v. Family Finance Corp.* had invalidated a statute permitting the garnishment of wages without notice and opportunity for hearing, but considered that case to have done nothing more than to carve out an exception, in favor of wage earners, "to the general rule of legality of garnishment statutes." . . . The garnishment of other assets or properties pending the outcome of the main action, although the effect was to " 'impound [them] in the hands of the garnishee,' " . . . was apparently thought not to implicate the Due Process Clause.

This approach failed to take account of *Fuentes v. Shevin*, 407 U.S. 67 (1972), a case decided by this Court more than a year prior to the Georgia court's decision. There the Court held invalid the Florida and Pennsylvania replevin statutes which permitted a secured installment seller to repossess the goods sold, without notice or hearing and without judicial order or supervision, but with the help of the sheriff operating under a writ issued by the clerk of the court at the behest of the seller. That the debtor was deprived of only the use and possession of the property, and perhaps only temporarily, did not put the seizure beyond scrutiny under the Due Process Clause. "The Fourteenth Amendment draws no bright lines around three–day, 10–day, or 50–day deprivations of property. Any significant taking of property by the State is within the purview of the Due Process Clause." . . . Although the length or severity of a deprivation of use or possession would be another factor to weigh in determining the appropriate form of hearing, it was not deemed to be determinative of the right to a hearing of some sort. Because the official seizures had been carried out without notice and without opportunity for a hearing or other safeguard against mistaken repossession, they were held to be in violation of the Fourteenth Amendment.

The Georgia statute is vulnerable for the same reasons. Here, a bank account, surely a form of property, was impounded and, absent a bond, put totally beyond use during the pendency of the litigation on the alleged debt, all by a writ of garnishment issued by a court clerk without notice or opportunity for an early hearing and without participation by a judicial officer.

Nor is the statute saved by the more recent decision in *Mitchell v. W. T. Grant Co.*, 416 U.S. 600 (1974). That case upheld the Louisiana sequestration statute which permitted the seller–creditor holding a vendor's lien to secure a writ of sequestration and, having filed a bond, to cause the sheriff to take possession of the property at issue. The writ, however, was issuable only by a judge upon the filing of an affidavit going beyond mere conclusory allegations and clearly setting out the facts entitling the creditor to sequestration. The Louisiana law also expressly entitled the debtor to an immediate hearing after seizure and to dissolution of the writ absent proof by the creditor of the grounds on which the writ was issued.

The Georgia garnishment statute has none of the saving characteristics of the Louisiana statute. The writ of garnishment is issuable on the affidavit of the creditor or his attorney, and the latter need not have personal knowledge of the facts. . . . The affidavit, like the one filed in this case, need contain only conclusory allegations. The writ is issuable, as this one was, by the court clerk, without participation by a judge. Upon service of the writ, the debtor is deprived of the use of the property in the hands of the garnishee. Here a sizable bank account was frozen, and the only method discernible on the face of the statute to dissolve the garnishment was to file a bond to protect the plaintiff creditor. There is no provision for an early hearing at which the creditor would be required to demonstrate at least probable cause for the garnishment. Indeed, it would appear that without the filing of a bond the defendant debtor's challenge to the garnishment will not be entertained, whatever the grounds may be.

Respondent also argues that neither *Fuentes* nor *Mitchell* is apposite here because each of those cases dealt with the application of due process protections to consumers who are victims of contracts of adhesion and who might be irreparably damaged by temporary deprivation of household necessities, whereas this case deals with its application in the commercial setting to a case involving parties of equal bargaining power. . . . It is asserted in addition that the double bond posted here gives assurance to petitioner that it will be made whole in the event the garnishment turns out to be unjustified. It may be that consumers deprived of household appliances will more likely suffer irreparably than corporations deprived of bank accounts, but the probability of irreparable injury in the latter case is sufficiently great so that some procedures are necessary to guard against the risk of initial error. We are no more inclined now than we have been in the past to distinguish among different kinds of property in applying the Due Process Clause. *Fuentes v. Shevin*, 407 U.S., at 89–90.

Enough has been said, we think, to require the reversal of the judgment of the Georgia Supreme Court. The case is remanded to that court for further proceedings not inconsistent with this opinion.

So ordered.

Mr. Justice STEWART, concurring.

It is gratifying to note that my report of the demise of *Fuentes v. Shevin*, 407 U.S. 67, *see Mitchell v. W. T. Grant Co.*, 416 U.S. 600, 629–636 (dissenting opinion), seems to have been greatly exaggerated. Cf. S. Clemens, cable from Europe to the Associated Press, quoted in 2 A. Paine, Mark Twain: A Biography 1039 (1912).

[The concurring opinion of Justice Powell is omitted.]

Mr. Justice BLACKMUN, with whom Mr. Justice REHNQUIST joins, dissenting.

The Court once again—for the third time in less than three years—struggles with what it regards as the due process aspects of a State's old and long–unattacked commercial statutes designed to afford a way for relief to a creditor against a delinquent debtor. On this third occasion, the Court, it seems to me, does little more than make very general and very sparse comparisons of the present case with *Fuentes v. Shevin*, 407 U.S. 67 (1972), on the one hand, and with *Mitchell v. W. T. Grant Co.*, 416 U.S. 600 (1974), on the other; concludes that this case resembles *Fuentes* more than it does *Mitchell;* and then strikes down the Georgia statutory structure as offensive to due process. One gains the impression, particularly from the final paragraph of its opinion, that the Court is endeavoring to say as little as possible in explaining just why the Supreme Court of Georgia is being reversed. And, as a result, the corresponding commercial statutes of all other States, similar to but not exactly like those of Florida or Pennsylvania or Louisiana or Georgia, are left in questionable constitutional status, with little or no applicable standard by which to measure and determine their validity under the Fourteenth Amendment. This, it seems to me, is an undesirable state of affairs, and I dissent. I do so for a number of reasons:

1. *Sniadach v. Family Finance Corp.,* . . . was correctly regarded by the Georgia Supreme Court, as a case relating to the garnishment of *wages.* . . . *Sniadach* should be allowed to remain in its natural environment—wages—and not be expanded to arm's–length relationships between business enterprises of such financial consequence as North Georgia Finishing and Di–Chem.

2. The Court, *ante,* at 606, regards the narrow limitations of *Sniadach* as affected by *Fuentes.* . . . Indeed, perhaps *Sniadach* for a time was so expanded (somewhat surprisingly, I am sure, to the *Sniadach* Court) by the implications and overtones of *Fuentes.* But . . . *Sniadach's* expansion was surely less under *Mitchell* than it might have appeared to be under *Fuentes.*

3. I would have thought that, whatever *Fuentes* may have stood for in this area of debtor–creditor commercial relationships, with its 4–3 vote by a bobtailed Court, it was substantially cut back by *Mitchell.* Certainly, Mr. Justice STEWART, the author of *Fuentes* and the writer of the dissenting opinion in *Mitchell,* thought so:

> The deprivation of property in this case is identical to that at issue in *Fuentes,* and the Court does not say otherwise. . . .

> In short, this case is constitutionally indistinguishable from *Fuentes v. Shevin,* and the Court today has simply rejected the reasoning of that case and adopted instead the analysis of the *Fuentes* dissent. . . .

> Yet the Court today has unmistakably overruled a considered decision of this Court that is barely two years old. . . . The only perceivable change that has occurred since the *Fuentes* case is in the makeup of this Court.

Surely, Mr. Justice BRENNAN thought so when he asserted in dissent that he was "in agreement that *Fuentes* . . . requires reversal" of the Louisiana judgment. And surely, Mr. Justice POWELL thought so, substantially, when, in his concurrence, he observed:

> The Court's decision today withdraws significantly from the full reach of [the *Fuentes*] principle, and to this extent I think it fair to say that the *Fuentes* opinion is overruled. . . .

I accept the views of these dissenting and concurring Justices in *Mitchell* that *Fuentes* at least was severely limited by *Mitchell*, and I cannot regard *Fuentes* as of much influence or precedent for the present case.

4. *Fuentes*, a constitutional decision, obviously should not have been brought down and decided by a 4–3 vote when there were two vacancies on the Court at the time of argument. It particularly should not have been decided by a 4–3 vote when Justices filling the vacant seats had qualified and were on hand and available to participate on reargument.[1] Announcing the constitutional decision, with a four–Justice majority of a seven–Justice shorthanded Court, did violence to Mr. Chief Justice Marshall's wise assurance, in *Briscoe v. Commonwealth's Bank of Kentucky*, 8 Pet. 118, 122 (1834), that the practice of the Court "except in cases of absolute necessity" is not to decide a constitutional question unless there is a majority "of the whole court."

. . . .

The admonition of the Great Chief Justice, in my view, should override any natural, and perhaps understandable, eagerness to decide. Had we bowed to that wisdom when *Fuentes* was before us, and waited a brief time for reargument before a full Court, whatever its decision might have been, I venture to suggest that we would not be immersed in confusion, with *Fuentes* one way, *Mitchell* another, and now this case decided in a manner that leaves counsel and the commercial communities in other States uncertain as to whether their own established and long–accepted statutes pass constitutional muster with a wavering tribunal off in Washington, D.C. This Court surely fails in its intended purpose when confusing results of this kind are forthcoming and are imposed upon those who owe and those who lend.

5. Neither do I conclude that, because this is a garnishment case, rather than a lien or vendor–vendee case, it is automatically controlled by *Sniadach*. *Sniadach*, as has been noted, concerned and reeks of wages. North Georgia Finishing is no wage earner. It is a corporation engaged in business. It was protected (a) by the fact that the garnishment procedure may be instituted in Georgia only after the primary suit has been filed or judgment obtained by the creditor, thus placing on the creditor the obligation to initiate the proceedings and the burden of proof, and assuring a full hearing to the debtor; (b) by the respondent's statutorily required and deposited double bond; and (c) by the requirement of the respondent's affidavit of apprehension of loss. It was in a position to dissolve the garnishment by the filing of a single bond. These are transactions of a day–to–day type in the commercial world. They are not situations involving contracts of adhesion or basic unfairness, imbalance, or inequality. . . . The clerk–judge distinction, relied on by the Court, surely is of little significance so long as the court officer is not an agent of the creditor. The Georgia system, for me, affords commercial entities all the protection that is required by the Due Process Clause of the Fourteenth Amendment.

---

[1] *Fuentes* was decided June 12, 1972. Mr. Justice Powell and Mr. Justice Rehnquist had taken their respective seats as Members of the Court five months before, on January 7. *Fuentes* had been argued November 9, 1971.

6. Despite its apparent disclaimer, the Court now has embarked on a case–by–case analysis (weighted heavily in favor of *Fuentes* and with little hope under *Mitchell*) of the respective state statutes in this area. That road is a long and unrewarding one, and provides no satisfactory answers to issues of constitutional magnitude.

I would affirm the judgment of the Supreme Court of Georgia.

Mr. Chief Justice BURGER dissents for the reasons stated in numbered paragraph 5 of the opinion of Mr. Justice BLACKMUN.

NOTES AND QUESTIONS

(1) Examine the chart on the following page. Does it accurately characterize the significant factors in the *Sniadach* line of cases? What factors would you add?

(2) What minimum due process protections must a state attachment statute contain to satisfy the Supreme Court?

(3) In *Sniadach*, *Fuentes*, and *North Georgia Finishing*, the Court struck down attachment statutes in part because they did not provide for a pre–seizure or prompt post–seizure hearing. In *Sniadach* and *North Georgia Finishing*, however, the debtor obtained a hearing before the trial on the merits by moving to dismiss the garnishment proceedings or quash the writ of attachment. *Sniadach*, *supra*, 395 U.S. at 338, *North Georgia Finishing*, *supra*, 419 U.S. at 604. Isn't it, therefore, misleading to state that there may be no hearing on the attachment until the trial on the merits? Why wouldn't a prompt hearing on such a motion satisfy the due process objection? Who would have the burden of proof at such a hearing? What other considerations would be relevant?

(4) The Uniform Commercial Code contains "self–help"–type remedies for creditors with certain security interests. *See*, *e.g.*, § 9–503 (after default, secured creditor may take possession of collateral if possible without breach of the peace); § 9–504 (creditor may sell collateral after notice to debtor). Should the creditor be required to obtain a judicial hearing before or promptly after seizing collateral under § 9–503? *See Flagg Bros., Inc. v. Brooks*, 436 U.S. 149 (1978) (action by warehouseperson who, pursuant to UCC § 7–210, sells belongings of person whose warehouse account is in default does not violate 14th Amendment because there is no "state action"); *cf. Svendsen v. Smith's Moving & Trucking Co.*, 54 N.Y.2d 865 (1981) (UCC § 7–210 violates due process clause of New York State Constitution). *See also* Chapter 2, *supra*, § 2.02[C].

(5) Does it make sense that a state procedure that provides some governmental supervision over the seizure of a debtor's property be unconstitutional because the supervision is inadequate, whereas a procedure that authorizes no governmental supervision at all cannot be attacked because there is no "state action?"

CONNECTICUT v. DOEHR

— U.S. —, 111 S. Ct. 2105 (1991)

JUSTICE WHITE delivered an opinion, Parts I, II, and III of which are the opinion of the Court.*

This case requires us to determine whether a state statute that authorizesprejudgment attachment of real estate without prior notice or hearing, without ashowing of extraordinary circumstances, and without a requirement that the person seeking the attachment post a bond, satisfies the Due Process Clause of the fourteenth Amendment. We hold that, as applied to this case, it does not.

I

On March 15, 1988, Petitioner John F. DiGiovanni submitted an application to the Connecticut Superior Court for an attachment in the amount of $75,000 onrespondent Brian K. Doehr's home in Meridan, Connecticut. DiGiovanni took thisstep in conjunction with a civil action for assault and battery that he was seeking to institute against Doehr in the same court. The suit did not involve Doehr's real estate nor did DiGiovanni have any pre–existing interest either in Doehr's home or any of his other property.

Connecticut law authorizes prejudgment attachment of real estate withoutaffording prior notice or the opportunity for a prior hearing to the individualwhose property is subject to the attachment. The State's prejudgment remedystatute provides, in relevant part:

> "The court or a judge of the court may allow the prejudgment remedy to be issued by an attorney without hearing as provided in sections 52–278c and 52–278d upon verification by oath of the plaintiff or of some competent affiant, that there is probable cause to sustain the validity of the plaintiff's claims and (1) that the prejudgment remedy requested is for an attachment of real property . . . " Conn. Gen. Stat. § 52–278e (1991).[1]

---

* The Chief Justice, Justice Blackmun, Justice Kennedy, and Justice Souter join Parts I, II, and III of this opinion, and Justice Scalia joins Parts I and III.

[1] The complete text of § 52–278e reads:

"Allowance of prejudgment remedy without hearing. Notice to defendant. Subsequent hearing and order. Attachment of real property of municipal officers. (a) The court or a judge of the court may allow the prejudgment remedy to be issued by an attorney without hearing as provided in sections 52–278c and 52–278d upon verification by oath of the plaintiff or of some competent affiant, that there is probable cause to sustain the validity of the plaintiff's claim and (1) that the prejudgment remedy requested is for an attachment of real property; or (2) that there is reasonable likelihood that the defendant (A) neither resides in nor maintains an office or place of business in this state and is not otherwise subject to jurisdiction over his person by the court, or (B) has hidden or will hide himself so that process cannot be served on him or is about to remove himself or his property from this state or (D) is about to fraudulently dispose of or has fraudulently disposed of any of his property with intent to hinder, delay or defraud his creditors or (E) has fraudulently hidden or withheld money, property or effects which should be liable to the satisfaction of his debts or (F) has stated he is insolvent or has stated he is unable to pay his debts as they mature.

The statute does not require the plaintiff to post a bond to insure the payment of damages that the defendant may suffer should the attachment prove wrongfully issued or the claim prove unsuccessful.

As required, DiGiovanni submitted an affidavit in support of his application. In five one–sentence paragraphs, DiGiovanni stated that the facts set forth in his previously submitted complaint were true; that "I was willfully, wantonly and maliciously assaulted by the defendant, Brian K. Doehr"; that "said assault and battery broke my left wrist and further caused an ecchymosis to my right eye, as well as other injuries"; and that "I have further expended sums of money for medical care and treatment." The affidavit concluded with the statement, "In my opinion, the foregoing facts are sufficient to show that there is probable cause that judgment will be rendered for the plaintiff."

On the strength of these submissions the Superior Court judge, by an orderdated March 17, found "probable cause to sustain the validity of the plaintiff'sclaim" and ordered the attachment on Doehr's home "to the value of $ 75,000."The sheriff attached the property four days later, on March 21. Only after thisdid Doehr receive notice of the attachment. He also had yet to be served withthe complaint, which is ordinarily necessary for an action to commence in Connecticut. *Young v. Margiotta,* 136 Conn. 429, 433, 71 A.2d 924, 926 (1950). As the statute further required, the attachment notice informed Doehr that he had the right to a hearing: (1) to claim that no probable cause existed to sustain the claim; (2) to request that the attachment be vacated, modified, or that a bond be substituted; or (3) to claim that some portion of the property was exempt from execution. Conn. Gen. Stat. § 52–278e(b) (1991).

Rather than pursue these options, Doehr filed suit against DiGiovanni in Federal District Court, claiming that § 52–278e (a)(1) was unconstitutional under the Due Process Clause of the Fourteenth Amendment.[2] The District Court upheld the statute

---

"(b) If a prejudgment remedy is granted pursuant to this section, the plaintiff shall include in the process served on the defendant the following notice prepared by the plaintiff: YOU HAVE RIGHTS SPECIFIED IN THE CONNECTICUT GENERAL STATUTES, INCLUDING CHAPTER 903a, WHICH YOU MAY WISH TO EXERCISE CONCERNING THIS PREJUDGMENT REMEDY. THESE RIGHTS INCLUDE: (1) THE RIGHT TO A HEARING TO OBJECT TO THE PREJUDGMENT REMEDY FOR LACK OF PROBABLE CAUSE TO SUSTAIN THE CLAIM; (2) THE RIGHT TO A HEARING TO REQUEST THAT THE PREJUDGMENT REMEDY BE MODIFIED, VACATED OR DISMISSED OR THAT A BOND BE SUBSTITUTED; AND (3) THE RIGHT TO A HEARING AS TO ANY PORTION OF THE PROPERTY ATTACHED WHICH YOU CLAIM IS EXEMPT FROM EXECUTION.

"(c) The defendant appearing in such action may move to dissolve or modify the prejudgment remedy granted pursuant to this section in which event the court shall proceed to hear and determine such motion expeditiously. If the court determines at such hearing requested by the defendant that there is probable cause to sustain the validity of the plaintiff's claim, then the prejudgment remedy granted shall remain in effect. If the court determines there is no probable cause, the prejudgment remedy shall be dissolved. An order shall be issued by the court setting forth the action it has taken."

[2] Three other plaintiffs joined Doehr, challenging § 52–278e(a)(1) out of separate instances of attachment by different defendants. These other plaintiffs and defendants did not participate in the Court of Appeals and are no longer parties in this case.

and granted summary judgment in favor of DiGiovanni. *Pinsky v. Duncan,* 716 F. Supp. 58 (Conn. 1989). On appeal, a divided panel of the United States Court of Appeals for the Second Circuit reversed. *Pinsky v. Duncan,* 898 F.2d 852 (1990).[3] Judge Pratt, who wrote the opinion for the court, concluded that the Connecticut statute violated due process in permitting *ex parte* attachment absent a showing of extraordinary circumstances. "The rule to be derived from *Sniadach* and its progeny, therefore, is not that post attachment hearings are generally acceptable provided that the plaintiff files a factual affidavit and that a judicial officer supervises the process, but that a prior hearing may be postponed where exceptional circumstances justify such a delay, *and where* sufficient additional safeguards are present." *Id.,* at 855. This conclusion was deemed to be consistent with our decision in *Mitchell v. W. T. Grant Co.,* 416 U.S. 600, 40 L. Ed. 2d 406, 94 S. Ct. 1895 (1974), because the absence of a preattachment hearing was approved in that case based on the presence of extraordinary circumstances.

A further reason to invalidate the statute, the court ruled, was the highly factual nature of the issues in this case. In *Mitchell,* there were "uncomplicated matters that lent themselves to documentary proof" and "the nature of the issues at stake minimized the risk that the writ [would] be wrongfully issued by a judge." *Id.,* at 609–610. Similarly, in *Mathews v. Eldridge,* 424 U.S. 319, 343–344, 47 L. Ed. 2d 18, 96 S. Ct. 893 (1976), where an evidentiary hearing was not required prior to the termination of disability benefits, the determination of disability was "sharply focused and easily documented." Judge Pratt observed that in contrast the present case involved the fact–specific event of a fist fight and the issue of assault. He doubted that the judge could reliably determine probable cause when presented with only the plaintiff's version of the altercation. "Because the risk of a wrongful attachment is considerable under these circumstances, we conclude that dispensing with notice and opportunity for a hearing until after the attachment, without a showing of extraordinary circumstances, violates the requirements of due process." 898 F.2d at 856. Judge Pratt went on to conclude that in his view, the statute was also constitutionally infirm for its failure to require the plaintiff to post a bond for the protection of the defendant in the event the attachment was ultimately found to have been improvident.

Judge Mahoney was also of the opinion that the statutory provision for attaching real property in civil actions, without a prior hearing and in the absence of extraordinary circumstances, was unconstitutional. He disagreed with Judge Pratt's opinion that a bond was constitutionally required. Judge Newman dissented from the holding that a hearing prior to attachment was constitutionally required and, like Judge Mahoney, disagreed with Judge Pratt on the necessity for a bond.

The dissent's conclusion accorded with the views of Connecticut Supreme Court, which had previously upheld § 52–278e(b) in *Fermont Division, Dynamics Corp. of America v. Smith,* 178 Conn. 393, 423 A.2d 80 (1979). We granted certiorari to resolve the conflict of authority. 498 U.S. (1990).

---

[3] The Court of Appeals invited Connecticut to intervene pursuant to 28 U.S.C. § 2403(b) after oral argument. The State elected to intervene in the appeal, and has fully participated in the proceedings before this Court.

II

With this case we return to the question of what process must be afforded by a state statute enabling an individual to enlist the aid of the State to deprive another of his or her property by means of the prejudgment attachment or similar procedure. Our cases reflect the numerous variations this type of remedy can entail. In *Sniadach v. Family Finance Corp. of Bay View,* 395 U.S. 337, 23 L. Ed. 2d 349, 89 S. Ct. 1820 (1969), the Court struck down a Wisconsin statute that permitted a creditor to effect prejudgment garnishment of wages without notice and prior hearing to the wage earner. In *Fuentes v. Shevin,* 407 U.S. 67, 32 L. Ed. 2d 556, 92 S. Ct. 1983 (1972), the Court likewise found a Due Process violation in state replevin provisions that permitted vendors to have goods seized through an *ex parte* application to a court clerk and the posting of a bond. Conversely, the Court upheld a Louisiana *ex parte* procedure allowing a lienholder to have disputed goods sequestered in *Mitchell v. W. T. Grant Co.,* 416 U.S. 600, 40 L. Ed. 2d 406, 94 S. Ct. 1895 (1974). *Mitchell,* however, carefully noted that *Fuentes* was decided against "a factual and legal background sufficiently different . . . that it does not require the invalidation of the Louisiana sequestration statute." *Id.,* at 615. Those differences included Louisiana's provision of an immediate postdeprivation hearing along with the option of damages; the requirement that a judge rather than a clerk determine that there is a clear showing of entitlement to the writ; the necessity for a detailed affidavit; and an emphasis on the lien–holder's interest in preventing waste or alienation of the encumbered property. *Id.,* at 615–618. In *North Georgia Finishing, Inc. v. Di–Chem, Inc.,* 419 U.S. (1975), the Court again invalidated an *ex parte* garnishment statute that not only failed to provide for notice and prior hearing but that also failed to require a bond, a detailed affidavit setting out the claim, the determination of a neutral magistrate, or a prompt postdeprivation hearing. *Id.,* at 606–608.

These cases "underscore the truism that 'due process unlike some legal rules, is not a technical conception with a fixed content unrelated to time, place and circumstances.' " *Mathews v. Eldridge, supra,* at 334 (quoting *Cafeteria Workers v. McElroy,* 367 U.S. 886, 895, 6 L. Ed. 2d 1230, 81 S. Ct. 1743 (1961)). In *Mathews,* we drew upon our prejudgment remedy decisions to determine what process is due when the government itself seeks to effect a deprivation on its own initiative. *Mathews,* 424 U.S. at 334. That analysis resulted in the now familiar threefold inquiry requiring consideration of "the private interest that will be affected by the official action"; "the risk of an erroneous deprivation of such interest through the procedures used, and the probable value, if any, of additional or substitute safeguards"; and lastly "the Government's interest, including the function involved and the fiscal and administrative burdens that the additional or substitute procedural requirement would entail." *Id.,* at 335.

Here the inquiry is similar but the focus is different. Prejudgment remedy statutes ordinarily apply to disputes between private parties rather than between an individual and the government. Such enactments are designed to enable one of the parties to "make use of state procedures with the overt, significant assistance of state officials," and they undoubtedly involve state action "substantial enough to implicate the Due Process Clause." *Tulsa Professional Collection Services, Inc. v. Pope,* 485 U.S. 478,

486, 99 L. Ed. 2d 565, 108 S. Ct. 1340 (1988). Nonetheless, any burden that increasing procedural safeguards entails primarily affects not the government, but the party seeking control of the other's property. *See Fuentes v. Shevin, supra,* at 99–101 (WHITE, J., dissenting). For this type of case, therefore, the relevant inquiry requires, as in *Mathews,* first, consideration of the private interest that will be affected by the prejudgment measure; second, an examination of the risk of erroneous deprivation through the procedures under attack and the probable value of additional or alternative safeguards; and third, in contrast to *Mathews,* principal attention to the interest of the party seeking the prejudgment remedy, with, nonetheless, due regard for any ancillary interest the government may have in providing the procedure or forgoing the added burden of providing greater protections.

We now consider the *Mathews* factors in determining the adequacy of the procedures before us, first with regard to the safeguards of notice and a prior hearing, and then in relation to the protection of a bond.

III

We agree with the Court of Appeals that the property interests that attachment affects are significant. For a property owner like Doehr, attachment ordinarily clouds title; impairs the ability to sell or otherwise alienate the property; taints any credit rating; reduces the chance of obtaining a home equity loan or additional mortgage; and can even place an existing mortgage in technical default where there is an insecurity clause. Nor does Connecticut deny that any of these consequences occurs.

Instead, the State correctly points out that these effects do not amount to a complete, physical, or permanent deprivation of real property; their impact is less than the perhaps temporary total deprivation of household goods or wages. *See Sniadach, supra,* at 340; *Mitchell, supra,* at 613. But the Court has never held that only such extreme deprivations trigger due process concern. *See Buchanan v. Warley,* 245 U.S. 60, 74, 62 L. Ed. 149, 38 S. Ct. 16 (1917). To the contrary, our cases show that even the temporary or partial impairments to property rights that attachments, liens, and similar encumbrances entail are sufficient to merit due process protection. Without doubt, state procedures for creating and enforcing attachments, as with liens, "are subject to the strictures of due process." *Peralta v. Heights Medical Center, Inc.,* 485 U.S. 80, 85, 99 L. Ed. 2d 75, 108 S. Ct. 896 (1988) (citing *Mitchell, supra,* at 604; *Hodge v. Muscatine County,* 196 U.S. 276, 281, 49 L. Ed. 477, 25 S. Ct.237 (1905)).**⁴**

---

⁴ Our summary affirmance in *Spielman–Fond, Inc. v. Hanson's Inc.,* 417 U.S. 901 (1974), does not control. In *Spielman–Fond,* the District Court held that the filing of a mechanic's lien did not amount to the taking of a significant property interest. 379 F. Supp. 997, 999 (Ariz. 1973) (three–judge court) (*per curiam*). A summary disposition does not enjoy the full precedential value of a case argued on the merits and disposed of by a written opinion. *Edelman v. Jordan,* 415 U.S. 651, 671, 39 L. Ed. 2d 662, 94 S. Ct. 1347 (1974). The facts of *Spielman–Fond* presented an alternative basis for affirmance in any event. Unlike the case before us, the mechanic's lien statute in *Spielman–Fond* required the creditor to have a pre–existing interest in the property at issue. 379 F. Supp. at 997. As we explain below, a heightened plaintiff interest in certain circumstances can provide a ground for upholding procedures that are otherwise suspect. *Infra,* at 15 , 115, L Ed 2d, at 16.

We also agree with the Court of Appeals that the risk of erroneous deprivation that the State permits here is substantial. By definition, attachment statutes premise a deprivation of property on one ultimate factual contingency — the award of damages to the plaintiff which the defendant may not be able to satisfy. *See Ownbey v. Morgan,* 256 U.S. 94, 104–105, 65 L. Ed. 837, 41 S. Ct. 433 (1921); R. Thompson & J. Sebert, Remedies: Damages, Equity and Restitution § 5.01 (1983). For attachments before judgment, Connecticut mandates that this determination be made by means of a procedural inquiry that asks whether "there is probable cause to sustain the validity of the plaintiff's claim." Conn. Gen. Stat. § 52–278e(a). The statute elsewhere defines the validity of the claim in terms of the likelihood "that judgment will be rendered in the matter in favor of the plaintiff." Conn. Gen. Stat. § 52–278c(a)(2) (1991); *Ledgebrook Condominium Assn. v. Lusk Corp.* 172 Conn. 577, 584, 376 A.2d 60, 63–64 (1977). What probable cause means in this context, however, remains obscure. The State initially took the position, as did the dissent below, that the statute requires a plaintiff to show the objective likelihood of the suit's success. Brief for Petitioner 12; *Pinsky,* 898 F.2d at 861–862 (Newman, J., dissenting). DiGiovanni, citing ambiguous state cases, reads the provision as requiring no more than that a plaintiff demonstrate a subjective good faith belief that the suit will succeed. Brief for Respondent 25–26. *Ledgebrook Condominium Assn., supra,* at 584, 376 A.2d at 63–64; *Anderson v. Nedovich,* 19 Conn. App. 85, 88, 561 A.2d 948, 949 (1989). At oral argument, the State shifted its position to argue that the statute requires something akin to the plaintiff stating a claim with sufficient facts to survive a motion to dismiss.

We need not resolve this confusion since the statute presents too great a risk of erroneous deprivation under any of these interpretations. If the statute demands inquiry into the sufficiency of the complaint, or, still less, the plaintiff's good–faith belief that the complaint is sufficient, requirement of a complaint and a factual affidavit would permit a court to make these minimal determinations. But neither inquiry adequately reduces the risk of erroneous deprivation. Permitting a court to authorize attachment merely because the plaintiff believes the defendant is liable, or because the plaintiff can make out a facially valid complaint, would permit the deprivation of the defendant's property when the claim would fail to convince a jury, when it rested on factual allegations that were sufficient to state a cause of action but which the defendant would dispute, or in the case of a mere good–faith standard, even when the complaint failed to state a claim upon which relief could be granted. The potential for unwarranted attachment in these situations is self–evident and too great to satisfy the requirements of due process absent any countervailing consideration.

Even if the provision requires the plaintiff to demonstrate, and the judge to find, probable cause to believe that judgment will be rendered in favor of the plaintiff, the risk of error was substantial in this case. As the record shows, and as the State concedes, only a skeletal affidavit need be and was filed. The State urges that the reviewing judge normally reviews the complaint as well, but concedes that the complaint may also be conclusory. It is self–evident that the judge could make no realistic assessment concerning the likelihood of an action's success based upon these one–sided, self–serving, and conclusory submissions. And as the Court of

Appeals said, in a case like this involving an alleged assault, even a detailed affidavit would give only the plaintiff's version of the confrontation. Unlike determining the existence of a debt or delinquent payments, the issue does not concern "ordinarily uncomplicated matters that lend themselves to documentary proof." *Mitchell*, 416 U.S. at 609. The likelihood of error that results illustrates that "fairness can rarely be obtained by secret, one–sided determination of facts decisive of rights . . . [And] no better instrument has been devised for arriving at truth than to give a person in jeopardy of serious loss notice of the case against him and an opportunity to meet it." *Joint Anti–Fascist Refugee Committee v. McGrath*, 341 U.S. 123, 170–172, 95 L. Ed. 817, 71 S. Ct. 624 (1951) (Frankfurter, J., concurring).

What safeguards the State does afford do not adequately reduce this risk. Connecticut points out that the statute also provides an "expeditious" postattachment adversary hearing, § 52–278e(c);[5] notice for such a hearing, § 52–278e(b); judicial review of an adverse decision, § 52–278l(a); and a double damages action if the original suit is commenced without probable cause, § 52–568(a)(1). Similar considerations were present in *Mitchell* where we upheld Louisiana's sequestration statute despite the lack of predeprivation notice and hearing. But in *Mitchell*, the plaintiff had a vendor's lien to protect, the risk of error was minimal because the likelihood of recovery involved uncomplicated matters that lent themselves to documentary proof, *Mitchell, supra*, at 609–610, and plaintiff was required to put up a bond. None of these factors diminishing the need for a predeprivation hearing is present in this case. It is true that a later hearing might negate the presence of probable cause, but this would not cure the temporary deprivation that an earlier hearing might have prevented. "The Fourteenth Amendment draws no bright lines around three–day, 10–day or 50–day deprivations of property. Any significant taking of property by the State is within the purview of the Due Process Clause." *Fuentes*, 407 U.S. at 86.

Finally, we conclude that the interests in favor of an *ex parte* attachment, particularly the interests of the plaintiff, are too minimal to supply such a consideration here. Plaintiff had no existing interest in Doehr's real estate when he sought the attachment. His only interest in attaching the property was to ensure the availability of assets to satisfy his judgment if he prevailed on the merits of his action. Yet there was no allegation that Doehr was about to transfer or encumber

---

5 The parties vigorously dispute whether a defendant can in fact receive a prompt hearing. Doehr contends that the State's rules of practice prevent the filing of any motion—including a motion for the mandated postattachment hearing—until the return date on the complaint, which in this case was 30 days after service. Connecticut Practice Book § 114 (1988). Under state law at least 12 days must elapse between service on the defendant and the return date. Conn. Gen. Stat. § 52–46 (1991). The State counters that the postattachment hearing is available upon request. *See Fermont Division, Dynamics Corp. of America v. Smith*, 178 Conn. 393, 397–398, 423 A.2d 80, 83 (1979) ("Most important, the statute affords to the defendant whose property has been attached the opportunity to obtain an immediate postseizure hearing at which the prejudgment remedy will be dissolved unless the moving party proves probable cause to sustain the validity of his claim"). We assume, without deciding, that the hearing is prompt. Even on this assumption, the State's procedures fail to provide adequate safeguards against the erroneous deprivation of the property interest at stake.

his real estate or take any other action during the pendency of the action that would render his real estate unavailable to satisfy a judgment. Our cases have recognized such a properly supported claim would be an exigent circumstance permitting postponing any notice or hearing until after the attachment is effected. *See Mitchell, supra,* at 609; *Fuentes, supra,* at 90–92; *Sniadach,* 395 U.S. at 339. Absent such allegations, however, the plaintiff's interest in attaching the property does not justify the burdening of Doehr's ownership rights without a hearing to determine the likelihood of recovery.

No interest the government may have affects the analysis. The State's substantive interest in protecting any rights of the plaintiff cannot be any more weighty than those rights themselves. Here the plaintiff's interest is *de minimis.* Moreover, the State cannot seriously plead additional financial or administrative burdens involving predeprivation hearings when it already claims to provide an immediate post deprivation hearing. Conn. Gen. Stat. §§ 52–278e(b) and (c) (1991); *Fermont,* 178 Conn. at 397–398, 423 A.2d at 83.

Historical and contemporary practice support our analysis. Prejudgment attachment is a remedy unknown at common law. Instead, "it traces its origin to the Custom of London, under which a creditor might attach money or goods of the defendant either in the plaintiff's own hands or in the custody of a third person, by proceedings in the mayor's court or in the sheriff's court." *Ownbey,* 256 U.S. at 104. Generally speaking, attachment measures in both England and this country had several limitations that reduced the risk of erroneous deprivation which Connecticut permits. Although attachments ordinarily did not require prior notice or a hearing, they were usually authorized only where the defendant had taken or threatened to take some action that would place the satisfaction of the plaintiff's potential award in jeopardy. See C. Drake, Law of Suits by Attachments, §§ 40–82 (1866) (hereinafter Drake); 1 R. Shinn, Attachment and Garnishment § 86 (1896) (hereinafter Shinn). Attachments, moreover, were generally confined to claims by creditors. Drake §§ 9–10; Shinn § 12. As we and the Court of Appeals have noted, disputes between debtors and creditors more readily lend themselves to accurate *ex parte* assessments of the merits. Tort actions, like the assault and battery claim at issue here, do not. *See Mitchell, supra,* at 609–610. Finally, as we will discuss below, attachment statutes historically required that the plaintiff post a bond. Drake §§ 114–183; Shinn § 153.

Connecticut's statute appears even more suspect in light of current practice. A survey of state attachment provisions reveals that nearly every State requires either a preattachment hearing, a showing of some exigent circumstance, or both, before permitting an attachment to take place. (See appendix.) Twenty–seven States, as well as the District of Columbia, permit attachments only when some extraordinary circumstance is present. In such cases, preattachment hearings are not required but postattachment hearings are provided. Ten States permit attachment without the presence of such factors but require prewrit hearings unless one of those factors is shown. Six States limit attachments to extraordinary circumstance cases but the writ will not issue prior to a hearing unless there is a showing of some even more compelling condition.[6] Three States always require a preattachment hearing. Only Washington, Connecticut, and Rhode Island authorize attachments without a prior hearing in situations that do not involve any purportedly heightened threat to the plaintiff's interests. Even those States permit *ex parte* deprivations only in certain types of cases: Rhode Island does so only when the claim is equitable; Connecticut and Washington do so only when real estate is to be attached, and even Washington requires a bond. Conversely, the States for the most part no longer confine attachments to creditor claims. This development, however, only increases the importance of the other limitations.

We do not mean to imply that any given exigency requirement protects an attachment from constitutional attack. Nor do we suggest that the statutory measures we have surveyed are necessarily free of due process problems or other constitutional infirmities in general. We do believe, however, that the procedures of almost all the States confirm our view that the Connecticut provision before us, by failing to provide a preattachment hearing without at least requiring a showing of some exigent circumstance, clearly falls short of the demands of due process.

IV

A

Although a majority of the Court does not reach the issue, Justices MARSHALL, STEVENS, O'CONNOR, and I deem it appropriate to consider whether due process also requires the plaintiff to post a bond or other security in addition to requiring a hearing or showing of some exigency.[7]

As noted, the impairments to property rights that attachments affect merit due process protection. Several consequences can be severe, such as the default of a homeowner's mortgage. In the present context, it need only be added that we have repeatedly recognized the utility of a bond in protecting property rights affected by the mistaken award of prejudgment remedies. *Di–Chem,* 419 U.S. at 610, 611

---

6 One State, Pennsylvania, has not had an attachment statute or rule since the decision in *Jonnet v. Dollar Savings Bank of New York City,* 530 F.2d 1123 (CA3 1976).

7 Ordinarily we will not address a contention advanced by a respondent that would enlarge his or her rights under a judgment, without the respondent filing a cross–petition for certiorari. *E. g., Trans World Airlines, Inc. v. Thurston,* 469 U.S. 111, 119, n. 14, 83 L. Ed. 2d 523, 105 S. Ct. 613 (1985). Here the Court of Appeals rejected Doehr's argument that § 52–278e(a)(1) violates due process in failing to mandate a preattachment bond. Nonetheless, this case involves considerations that in the past have prompted us "to consider the question highlighted by respondent." *Berkemer v. McCarty,* 468 U.S. 420, 435–436, n. 23, 82 L. Ed. 2d 317, 104 S. Ct. 3138 (1984). First, as our cases have shown, the notice and hearing question and the bond question are intertwined and can fairly be considered facets of same general issue. Thus, "without undue strain, the position taken by respondent before this Court . . . might be characterized as an argument in support of the judgment below" insofar as a discussion of notice and a hearing cannot be divorced from consideration of a bond. *Ibid.* Second, this aspect of prejudgment attachment "plainly warrants our attention, and with regard to which the lower courts are in need of guidance." *Ibid.* Third, "and perhaps most importantly, both parties have briefed and argued the question." *Ibid.*

(Powell, J., concurring in judgment); id., at 619 (BLACKMUN, J., dissenting); *Mitchell,* 416 U.S. at 606, n. 8.

Without a bond, at the time of attachment, the danger that these property rights may be wrongfully deprived remains unacceptably high even with such safeguards as a hearing or exigency requirement. The need for a bond is especially apparent where extraordinary circumstances justify an attachment with no more than the plaintiff's *ex parte* assertion of a claim. We have already discussed how due process tolerates, and the States generally permit, the otherwise impermissible chance of erroneously depriving the defendant in such situations in light of the heightened interest of the plaintiff. Until a postattachment hearing, however, a defendant has no protection against damages sustained where no extraordinary circumstance in fact existed or the plaintiff's likelihood of recovery was nil. Such protection is what a bond can supply. Both the Court and its individual members have repeatedly found the requirement of a bond to play an essential role in reducing what would have been too great a degree of risk in precisely this type of circumstance. *Mitchell, supra,* at 610, 619; *Di–Chem, supra,* at 613 (Powell, J., concurring in judgment); *id.,* at 619 (BLACKMUN, J., dissenting); *Fuentes,* 407 U.S. at 101 (WHITE, J., dissenting).

But the need for a bond does not end here. A defendant's property rights remain at undue risk even when there has been an adversarial hearing to determine the plaintiff's likelihood of recovery. At best, a court's initial assessment of each party's case cannot produce more than an educated prediction as to who will win. This is especially true when, as here, the nature of the claim makes any accurate prediction elusive. *See Mitchell, supra,* at 609–610. In consequence, even a full hearing under a proper probable–cause standard would not prevent many defendants from having title to their homes impaired during the pendency of suits that never result in the contingency that ultimately justifies such impairment, namely, an award to the plaintiff. Attachment measures currently on the books reflect this concern. All but a handful of States require a plaintiff's bond despite also affording a hearing either before, or (for the vast majority, only under extraordinary circumstances) soon after, an attachment takes place. (See appendix.) Bonds have been a similarly common feature of other prejudgment remedy procedures that we have considered, whether or not these procedures also included a hearing. *See Ownbey,* 256 U.S. at 101–102 n. 1; *Fuentes, supra,* at 73, n. 6, 75–76, n. 7,81–82; *Mitchell, supra,* at 606, and n. 6; *Di–Chem, supra,* at 602–603, n. 1, 608.

The State stresses its double damages remedy for suits that are commenced without probable cause. Conn. Gen. Stat. § 52–568(a)(1).[8] This remedy, however, fails to make up for the lack of a bond. As an initial matter, the meaning of "probable cause" in this provision is no more clear here than it was in the attachment provision

---

[8] Section 52–568(a)(1) provides:

"Any person who commences and prosecutes any civil action or complaint against another, in his own name, or the name of others, or asserts a defense to any civil action or complaint commenced and prosecuted by another (1) without probable cause, shall pay such other person double damages, or (2) without probable cause, and with a malicious intent unjustly to vex and trouble such other person, shall pay him treble damages."

itself. Should the term mean the plaintiff's good faith or the facial adequacy of the complaint, the remedy is clearly insufficient. A defendant who was deprived where there was little or no likelihood that the plaintiff would obtain a judgment could nonetheless recover only by proving some type of fraud or malice or by showing that the plaintiff had failed to state a claim. Problems persist even if the plaintiff's ultimate failure permits recovery. At best a defendant must await a decision on the merits of the plaintiff's complaint, even assuming that a § 52–568(a)(1) action may be brought as a counterclaim. *Hydro Air of Connecticut, Inc. v. Versa Technologies, Inc.,* 99 F.R.D. 111, 113 (Conn. 1983). Settlement, under Connecticut law, precludes seeking the damages remedy, a fact that encourages the use of attachments as a tactical device to pressure an opponent to capitulate. *Blake v. Levy,* 191 Conn. 257, 464 A.2d 52 (1983). An attorney's advice that there is probable cause to commence an action constitutes a complete defense, even if the advice was unsound or erroneous. *Vandersluis v. Weil,* 176 Conn. 353, 361, 407 A.2d 982, 987 (1978). Finally, there is no guarantee that the original plaintiff will have adequate assets to satisfy an award that the defendant may win.

Nor is there any appreciable interest against a bond requirement. Section 52–278e(a)(1) does not require a plaintiff to show exigent circumstances nor any pre–existing interest in the property facing attachment. A party must show more than the mere existence of a claim before subjecting an opponent to prejudgment proceedings that carry a significant risk of erroneous deprivation. *See Mitchell,* 416 U.S. at 604–609; *Fuentes, supra,* at 90–92; *Sniadach,* 395 U.S. at 339.

B

Our foregoing discussion compels the four of us to consider whether a bond excuses the need for a hearing or other safeguards altogether. If a bond is needed to augment the protections afforded by preattachment and postattachment hearings, it arguably follows that a bond renders these safeguards unnecessary. That conclusion is unconvincing, however, for it ignores certain harms that bonds could not undo but that hearings would prevent. The law concerning attachments has rarely, if ever, required defendants to suffer an encumbered title until the case is concluded without any prior opportunity to show that the attachment was unwarranted. Our cases have repeatedly emphasized the importance of providing a prompt postdeprivation hearing at the very least. *Mitchell, supra,* at 606; *Di–Chem,* 419 U.S. at 606–607. Every State but one, moreover, expressly requires a preattachment or postattachment hearing to determine the propriety of an attachment.

The necessity for at least a prompt postattachment hearing is self–evident because the right to be compensated at the end of the case, if the plaintiff loses, for all provable injuries caused by the attachment is inadequate to redress the harm inflicted, harm that could have been avoided had an early hearing been held. An individual with an immediate need or opportunity to sell a property can neither do so, nor otherwise satisfy that need or recreate the opportunity. The same applies to a parent in need of a home equity loan for a child's education, an entrepreneur seeking to start a business on the strength of an otherwise strong credit rating, or simply a homeowner who might face the disruption of having a mortgage placed in technical default. The extent of these harms, moreover, grows with the length of the suit. Here, oral argument indicated that civil suits in Connecticut commonly take up to four to seven years for completion. (Tr. of Oral Arg. 44.) Many state attachment statutes require that the amount of a bond be anywhere from the equivalent to twice the amount the plaintiff seeks. *See, e. g.,* Utah Rule of Civ. Proc. 64C(b). These amounts bear no relation to the harm the defendant might suffer even assuming that money damages can make up for the foregoing disruptions. It should be clear, however, that such an assumption is fundamentally flawed. Reliance on a bond does not sufficiently account for the harms that flow from an erroneous attachment to excuse a State from reducing that risk by means of a timely hearing.

If a bond cannot serve to dispense with a hearing immediately after attachment, neither is it sufficient basis for not providing a preattachment hearing in the absence of exigent circumstances even if in any event a hearing would be provided a few days later. The reasons are the same: a wrongful attachment can inflict injury that will not fully be redressed by recovery on the bond after a prompt postattachment hearing determines that the attachment was invalid.

Once more, history and contemporary practice support our conclusion. Historically, attachments would not issue without a showing of extraordinary circumstances even though a plaintiff bond was almost invariably required in addition. Drake §§ 4, 114; Shinn §§ 86, 153. Likewise, all but eight States currently require the posting of a bond. Out of this 42 State majority, all but one requires a preattachment hearing, a showing of some exigency, or both, and all but one expressly require a postattachment hearing when an attachment has been issue *ex parte.* (See appendix.) This testimony underscores the point that neither a hearing nor an extraordinary circumstance limitation eliminates the need for a bond, no more than a bond allows waiver of these other protections. To reconcile the interests of the defendant and the plaintiff accurately, due process generally requires all of the above.

V

Because Connecticut's prejudgment remedy provision, Conn. Gen. Stat. § 52–278e(a)(1), violates the requirements of due process by authorizing prejudgment attachment without prior notice or a hearing, the judgment of the Court of Appeals is affirmed, and the case is remanded to that court for further proceedings consistent with this opinion.

It is so ordered.

APPENDIX
Prejudgement Attachment Statutes

	Pre-Attach Hrg Required Unless Exigent Circs	Attachment Only in Exigent Circs; No Pre-Attach Hrg Required	Pre-Attach Hrg Even in Most Exigent Circs	Bond Required	Post-Attach Hrg Required
Alabama		X		X	X
Alaska	Pre-Attachment hrg always required			X	
Arizona	X			X	X
Arkansas		X		X	X
California	X			X	X
Colorado		X		X	X
Connecticut	X	(or unless attachment of real estate)			X
Delaware		X		X	X
DC		X		X	X
Florida		X		X	X
Georgia		X		X	X
Hawaii	Pre-attachment of hrg always required.			X	X
Idaho	X			X	X
Illinois		X		X	X
Indiana		X		X	X
Iowa		X		X	X
Kansas		X		X	X
Kentucky			X	X	
Louisiana		X		X	X
Maine	X				X
Maryland		X			X
Massachusetts	X			X/O*	X
Michigan		X			X
Minnesota			X	X	X
Mississippi		X		X	X
Missouri		X		X	X
Montana		X		X	X
Nebraska		X		X	X
Nevada	X				X
New Hampshire	X				X
New Jersey	X			X/O	X
New Mexico		X		X	X
New York		X		X	X
North Carolina		X		X	X
North Dakota		X		X	X
Ohio			X	X	X
Oklahoma	X			X	X
Oregon	Pre-Attachment hrg always required.				
Pennsylvania	Rescinded in light of 530 F.2d 1123 (CA3 1976).				
Rhode Island	X	(but not if equitable claim)		X/O	
South Carolina		X		X	X
South Dakota		X		X	X
Tennessee		X		X	X**
Texas			X	X	X
Utah			X	X	X
Vermont	X				X
Virginia		X		X	X
Washington			X	X***	X
	(except for real estate on a contract claim)				
West Virginia		X		X	X
Wisconsin		X		X	X
Wyoming			X	X	X

* An "X/O" in the "Bond Required" column indicates that a bond may be required at the discretion of the court.

** The court may, under certain circumstances, quash the attachment at the defendant's request without a hearing.

*** A bond is required except in situations in which the plaintiff seeks to attach the real property of a defendant who, after diligent efforts, cannot be served.

SEPARATE OPINIONS

Chief Justice RENQUIST, with whom Justice BLACKMUN joins, concurring in part and concurring in the judgment.

I agree with the Court that the Connecticut attachment statute, "as applied in this case," *ante* p. 1, fails to satisfy the Due Process Clause of the Fourteenth Amendment. I therefore join Parts I, II and III of its opinion. Unfortunately, the remainder of the Court's opinion does not confine itself to the facts of this case, but enters upon a lengthy disquisition as to what combination of safeguards are required to satisfy Due Process in hypothetical cases not before the Court. I therefore do not join Part IV.

As the Court's opinion points out, the Connecticut statute allows attachment not merely for a creditor's claim, but for a tort claim of assault and battery; it affords no opportunity for a pre–deprivation hearing; it contains no requirement that there be "exigent circumstances," such as an effort on the part of the defendant to conceal assets; no bond is required from the plaintiff; and the property attached is one in which the plaintiff has no pre–existing interest. The Court's opinion is, in my view, ultimately correct when it bases its holding of unconstitutionality of the Connecticut statute as applied here on our cases of *Sniadach v. Family Finance Corp.*, 395 U.S. 337, 23 L. Ed. 2d 349, 89 S. Ct. 1820 (1969); *Fuentes v. Shevin*, — U.S.— (1972), *Mitchell v. W. T. Grant Co.*, 416 U.S. 600, 40 L. Ed. 2d 406, 94 S. Ct. 1895 (1974), and *North Georgia Finishing v. Di–Chem, Inc.*, 419 U.S. 601, 42 L. Ed. 2d 751, 95 S. Ct. 719 (1975). But I do not believe that the result follows so inexorably as the Court's opinion suggests. All of the cited cases dealt with personalty—bank deposits or chattels—and each involved the physical seizure of the property itself, so that the defendant was deprived of its use. These cases, which represented something of a revolution in the jurisprudence of procedural due process, placed substantial limits on the methods by which creditors could obtain a lien on the assets of a debtor prior to judgment. But in all of them the debtor was deprived of the use and possession of the property. In the present case, on the other hand, Connecticut's pre–judgment attachment on real property statute, which secures an incipient lien for the plaintiff, does not deprive the defendant of the use or possession of the property.

The Court's opinion therefore breaks new ground, and I would point out, more emphatically than the Court does, the limits of today's holding. In *Spielman–Fond, Inc. v. Hanson's, Inc.*, 379 F. Supp. 997, 999 (D. Ariz. 1973), the District Court held that the filing of a mechanics' lien did not cause the deprivation of a significant property interest of the owner. We summarily affirmed that decision. 417 U.S. 901, 41 L Ed 2d 208, 94, S Ct 2596 (1974). Other courts have read this summary affirmance to mean that the mere imposition of a lien on real property, which does not disturb the owner's use or enjoyment of the property, is not a deprivation of property calling for procedural due process safeguards. I agree with the Court, however, that upon analysis the deprivation here is a significant one, even though the owner remains in undisturbed possession. "For a property owner like Doehr, attachment ordinarily clouds title; impairs the ability to sell or otherwise alienate the property; taints any credit rating; reduces the chance of obtaining a home equity loan or additional mortgage; and can even place an existing mortgage in technical default when there is an insecurity clause." *Ante,* at 11, 115 L Ed 2d, at 14. Given the elaborate system of title records relating to real property which prevails in all of our states, a lienor need not obtain possession or use of real property belonging to a debtor in order to significantly impair its value to him.

But in *Spielman–Fond, Inc., supra,* there was, as the Court points out *ante,* at 12, n 4, 115 L Ed 2d, at 14, an alternate basis available to this Court for affirmance of that decision. Arizona recognized a pre–existing lien in favor of unpaid mechanics and materialmen who had contributed labor or supplies which were incorporated in improvements to real property. The existence of such a lien upon the very property ultimately posted or noticed distinguishes those cases from the present one, where the plaintiff had no pre–existing interest in the real property which he sought to attach. Materialman's and mechanic's lien statutes award an interest in real property to workers who have contributed their labor, and to suppliers who have furnished material, for the improvement of the real property. Since neither the labor nor the material can be reclaimed once it has become a part of the realty, this is the only method by which workmen or small businessmen who have contributed to the improvement of the property may be given a remedy against a property owner who has defaulted on his promise to pay for the labor and the materials. To require any sort of a contested court hearing or bond before the notice of lien takes effect would largely defeat the purpose of these statutes.

Petitioner in its brief relies in part on our summary affirmance in *Bartlett v. Williams,* 464 U.S. 801, 78 L. Ed. 2d 67, 104 S. Ct. 46 (1983). That case involved a *lis pendens,* in which the question presented to this Court was whether such a procedure could be valid when the only protection afforded to the owner of land affected by the *lis pendens* was a post–sequestration hearing. A notice of lis pendens is a well established traditional remedy whereby a plaintiff (usually a judgment creditor) who brings an action to enforce an interest in property to which the defendant has title gives notice of the pendency of such action to third parties; the notice causes the interest which he establishes, if successful, to relate back to the date of the filing of the *lis pendens.* The filing of such notice will have an effect upon the defendant's ability to alienate the property, or to obtain additional security on the basis of title to the property, but the effect of the *lis pendens* is simply to give notice to the world of the remedy being sought in the lawsuit itself. The *lis pendens* itself creates no additional right in the property on the part of the plaintiff, but simply allows third parties to know that a lawsuit is pending in which the plaintiff is seeking to establish such a right. Here, too, the fact that the plaintiff already claims an interest in the property which he seeks to enforce by a lawsuit distinguishes this class of cases from the Connecticut attachment employed in the present case.

Today's holding is a significant development in the law; the only cases dealing with real property cited in the Court's opinion, *Peralta v. Heights Medical Center, Inc.,* 485 U.S. 80, 85, 99 L. Ed. 2d 75, 108 S. Ct. 896 (1988), and *Hodge v. Muscatine County,* 196 U.S. 276, 281, 49 L. Ed. 477, 25 S. Ct. 237 (1905), arose out of lien foreclosure sales in which the question was whether the owner was entitled to proper notice. The change is dramatically reflected when we compare today's decision with the almost casual statement of Justice Holmes, writing for a unanimous Court in *Coffin Brothers v. Bennett,* 277 U.S. 29, 31, 72 L. Ed. 768, 48 S. Ct. 422 (1928):

> "Nothing is more common than to allow parties alleging themselves to be creditors to establish in advance by attachment a lien dependent for its effect upon the result of the suit."

The only protection accorded to the debtor in that case was the right to contest his liability in a post–deprivation proceeding.

It is both unwise and unnecessary, I believe, for the Court to proceed, as it does in Part IV, from its decision of the case before it to discuss abstract and hypothetical situations not before it. This is especially so where we are dealing with the Due Process Clause which, as the Court recognizes, unlike some legal rules, is not a technical conception with a fixed content unrelated to time, place and circumstances, *ante,* at 10, 115 L Ed 2d, at 13. And it is even more true in a case involving constitutional limits on the methods by which the states may transfer or create interests in real property; in other areas of the law, *dicta* may do little damage, but those who insure titles or write title opinions often do not enjoy the luxury of distinguishing between *dicta* and holding.

The two elements of due process with which the Court concerns itself in Part IV — the requirement of a bond, and of "exigent circumstances" — prove to be upon analysis so vague that the discussion is not only unnecessary, but not particularly useful. Unless one knows what the terms and conditions of a bond are to be, the requirement of a "bond" in the abstract means little. The amount to be secured by the bond and the conditions of the bond are left unaddressed — is there to be liability on the part of a plaintiff if he is ultimately unsuccessful in the underlying lawsuit, or is it instead to be conditioned on some sort of good faith test? The "exigent circumstances" referred to by the Court are admittedly equally vague; non–residency appears to be enough in some states, an attempt to conceal assets is required in others, an effort to flee the jurisdiction in still others. We should await concrete cases which present questions involving bonds and exigent circumstances before we attempt to decide when and if the Due Process Clause of the Fourteenth Amendment requires them as prerequisites for a lawful attachment.

JUSTICE SCALIA, concurring in part and concurring in the judgment.

Since the manner of attachment here was not a recognized procedure at common law, *cf. Pacific Mutual Life Ins. Co. v. Haslip,* 499 U.S. 1, 24, 113 L. Ed. 2d 1, 111 S. Ct. 1032 (1991) (Scalia, J., concurring in judgment), I agree that its validity under the Due Process Clause should be determined by applying the test we set forth in *Mathews v. Eldridge,* 424 U.S. 319, 47 L. Ed. 2d 18, 96 S. Ct. 893 (1976); and I agree that it fails that test. I join Parts I and III of the Court's opinion, and concur in the judgment of the Court.

Analytical Comparison: Sniadach, Fuentes, Mitchell, North Georgia Finishing and Doehr

STATE	REMEDY IN ISSUE	STATUTORY REQUIRE-MENTS	WHO ISSUES WRIT	HEARING RE-QUIRED BY STATUTE?	HOLDING
Wisconsin (Sniadach)	Pre-Judgment garnishment of wages (suit on note)	File complaint and serve gar-nishee	Clerk of court (ex parte)	None until trial on merits	Unconstitutional (8-1)
Florida (Fuentes)	Replevin (ven-dor lien)	"Bare" assertion of entitlement to writ; bond	Clerk of court (ex parte)	None until trial on merits	Unconstitutional (4-3)
Pennsylvania (Fuentes)	Replevin (ven-dor lien)	Asserted value of property in affidavit; bond	Prothonotary (clerk) (ex par-te)	Possibly none (not required to sue on merits after obtain-ing writ)	Unconstitutional (4-3)
Louisiana (Mitchell)	Sequestration (vendor lien)	Specific facts showing nature and amount of claim; bond.	Judge (ex parte)	Immediate hearing on validity of writ after seizure	Constitutional (5-4)
Georgia (North Geor-gia Finishing	Garnishment of bank ac-count (to pre-serve assets for eventual judgment).	Conclusory assertion of debt and feared loss of property; bond	Clerk of court (ex parte)	None before trial; writ dissolvable only by bond.	Unconstitutional (6-3)
Connecticut (Doehr)	Attachment	Asserted injury; opinion of prob-able cause	Judge (ex parte)	Yes; post-attach-ment.	Unconstitutional (9-0)

CHAPTER 5

CLAIMS OF THE FEDERAL GOVERNMENT

Congress has given the federal government preferential status over other creditors in certain situations. 31 U.S.C. § 3713 grants the federal government an unsecured, but absolute, priority over other creditors in nonbankruptcy insolvency cases (*e.g.*, receiverships, assignments for the benefit of creditors). The Federal Tax Lien Act, Internal Revenue Code of 1954, 26 U.S.C. § 6321 *et seq.*, also grants the United States the status of a secured creditor with a broad general lien against "all property and rights to property" of a taxpayer who neglects or refuses to pay a tax liability after assessment and demand. Although the federal priority does not give the United States a lien on the debtor's property, the federal government may, in an appropriate case, rely on its priority rather than its tax lien. As you read these materials, consider the relative advantages of one remedy over the other.

The financially distressed debtor usually has the United States as a creditor. Income taxes, employee withholding taxes, and Small Business Administration loans are often unpaid when medium–sized and smaller businesses have financial problems. During the period of greatest losses, the debtor may very well be keeping the business alive by failing to remit employee withholdings. Those agents responsible for collecting or withholding (*e.g.*, corporate officers) who use withheld tax funds are themselves personally liable under Internal Revenue Code § 6672. An evil motive need not be shown to hold the agent liable. *Monday v. United States*, 421 F.2d 1210 (7th Cir.), *cert. denied*, 400 U.S. 821 (1970). Criminal penalties may also be imposed under Internal Revenue Code § 7512 and § 7515. *See, e.g., United States v. Dreske*, 536 F.2d 188 (7th Cir. 1976). Because of these important consequences, management of a troubled business about to be liquidated must consider the relative advantages of a state law assignment for the benefit of creditors, where the United States has an absolute priority, and bankruptcy, where the United States has a sixth priority for unsecured tax claims under 11 U.S.C. § 507(a)(6). Analyze why bankruptcy might be less desirable to management. If management decides to make an assignment for the benefit of creditors, also consider whether involuntary bankruptcy is still a risk.

§ 5.01 The Federal Priority

The "federal priority" is set forth in 31 U.S.C. § 3713. As in its statutory predecessor, 31 U.S.C. § 191 (generally referred to by its Revised Statutes designation as § 3466), § 3713 grants the federal government a priority for all debts due it in nonbankruptcy insolvency cases, whether arising from taxes or otherwise.

After reading the cases in these materials, consider whether the federal priority is necessary. Should this priority be restricted? If so, to what extent? What is the attitude of the Supreme Court of the United States toward this priority? *See generally* MacLachlan, Bankruptcy, § 155 at 152–53 (1956).

---

§ 3713. Priority of Government Claims

(a) (1) A claim of the United States Government shall be paid first when—

    (A)   a person indebted to the Government is insolvent and—

        (i)   the debtor without enough property to pay all debts makes a voluntary assignment of property;

        (ii)   the property of the debtor, if absent, is attached; or

        (iii)   an act of bankruptcy is committed; or

    (B)   the estate of a deceased debtor, in the custody of the executor or administrator, is not enough to pay all debts of the debtor.

(2) This subsection does not apply to a case under title 11.

(b) A representative of a person or an estate (except a trustee acting under title 11) paying any part of a debt of the person or estate before paying a claim of the Government is liable to the extent of the payment for unpaid claims of the Government.

UNITED STATES v. EMORY

United States Supreme Court
314 U.S. 423, 62 S. Ct. 317 86 L. Ed. 315 (1941)

Mr. Justice BYRNES delivered the opinion of the Court.

This case involves the application of § 3466 of the Revised Statutes to a claim of the United States under the National Housing Act in an equity receivership proceeding in a state court.

The St. James Distillery, a corporation, executed a note to the Industrial Bank and Trust Company of St. Louis on September 23, 1935. On July 14, 1936, the Bank endorsed the note and delivered it to the Federal Housing Administration, acting on behalf of the United States, under a contract of insurance and guaranty provided for in Title I of the National Housing Act. The United States, through the Federal Housing Administration, on that date reimbursed the Bank in the amount of $5988.88, the balance due on the note. Emory, claiming wages due him, filed a petition on August 27, 1936 in the Circuit Court of Phelps County, Missouri, alleging that the St. James Distillery was hopelessly insolvent and praying that a receiver be appointed. On September 9, the Circuit Court found all the issues in Emory's favor and appointed a receiver who took possession of the corporate assets.

After deductions for the costs of the receivership, the assets available for distribution totaled $678. Against this amount the wage claims of "about twelve individuals" were filed. The separate amounts of these claims were neither stipulated nor determined by the courts below; their aggregate was "about $900." The United States, on behalf of the Federal Housing Administration, filed a claim for the $5988.88 due on the note. The wage claimants asserted priority under § 1168 of the Revised Statutes of Missouri;[1] the United States asserted priority under § 3466 of the Revised Statutes of the United States.[2]

The Circuit Court of Phelps County decided that the claim of the United States should be treated as an ordinary claim against the estate, and that the wage claims should be paid first. On appeal, the Springfield Court of Appeals held that the claim of the United States on behalf of the Federal Housing Administration was accorded preference over ordinary claims by § 3466 of the Revised Statutes of the United States. Consequently, it was of the opinion that the Circuit Court had erred in treating the claim of the United States as an ordinary claim. However, it held further that the error was of no consequence, since the Missouri statute granted priority to wage claims even over other preferred claims and no assets would remain after they had been satisfied. Rehearing was denied, and the Supreme Court of Missouri denied a petition for certiorari. We granted certiorari because of the importance of the question and because of an asserted conflict of decisions.

The applicability of § 3466 to this case is clear. The section applies in terms to cases "[1] in which a debtor, not having sufficient property to pay all his debts, makes a voluntary assignment thereof, or [2] in which the estate and effects of an absconding, concealed, or absent debtor are attached by process of law, . . . [or] [3] in which an act of bankruptcy is committed." This case falls within the third

---

[1] Mo. Rev. Stat. (1929) § 1168, so far as pertinent, provides: "Hereafter when the property of any company, corporation, firm or person shall be seized upon by any process of any court of this state, or when their business shall be . . . put into the hands of a receiver or trustee, then in all such cases the debts owing to laborers or servants, which have accrued by reason of their labor or employment, to an amount not exceeding one hundred dollars to each employee, for work or labor performed within six months next preceding the seizure or transfer of such property, . . . shall be first paid in full; and if there be not sufficient to pay them in full, then the same shall be paid to them pro rata, after paying the costs."

[2] U.S. Rev. Stat. § 3466 (U.S.C., Title 31, § 191) provides: "Whenever any person indebted to the United States is insolvent, or whenever the estate of any deceased debtor, in the hands of the executors or administrators, is insufficient to pay all the debts due from the deceased, the debts due to the United States shall be first satisfied; and the priority hereby established shall extend as well to cases in which a debtor, not having sufficient property to pay all his debts, makes a voluntary assignment thereof, or in which the estate and effects of an absconding, concealed, or absent debtor are attached by process of law, as to cases in which an act of bankruptcy is committed."

category. It is agreed that the St. James Distillery was insolvent "on or before August 1936" and that in response to a creditor's petition a receiver was appointed to liquidate the corporate assets. The appointment of a receiver under such circumstances is among the most common examples of an "act of bankruptcy." *Cf.* § 3 (a) (4) of the Bankruptcy Act, U.S.C., Title 11, § 21 (a) (4).

Just such proceedings as this, therefore, are governed by the plain command of § 3466 that "debts due to the United States shall be first satisfied." The purpose of this section is "to secure adequate public revenues to sustain the public burden" (*United States v. State Bank of North Carolina*, 6 Pet. 29, 35), and it is to be construed liberally in order to effectuate that purpose (*Bramwell v. U.S. Fidelity & Guaranty Co.*, 269 U.S. 483, 487). In view of this language, purpose, and rule of construction, the priority asserted here by the United States appears to be securely established.

The court below, however, held otherwise. In granting priority to the wage claims over that of the United States, it relied upon Missouri law. It recognized, as the authorities obliged it to recognize,[3] that the state statute could not prevail if it was in conflict with § 3466. But it decided that no such conflict arose, for the reason that § 3466 had been impliedly modified by § 64a of the Bankruptcy Act,[4] which, like the Missouri statute, requires that wage claims be satisfied before those of the United States.

The judgment below must have rested upon either of the following theories: Congress intended by § 64a of the Bankruptcy Act to subordinate claims of the United States to wage claims in non–bankruptcy proceedings generally; or that Congress intended by § 64a to modify § 3466 only so far as to grant priority over the United States to wage claimants in state non–bankruptcy proceedings when they would be entitled to such priority by otherwise applicable state law.

There is a difficulty common to both theories which we regard as insurmountable. Neither the language of § 64a nor the Congressional history of the legislation here involved supports the proposition that § 64a was intended to eliminate, either partially or wholly, the priority of claims of the United States in non–bankruptcy proceedings.

---

[3] *Field v. United States*, 9 Pet. 182, 200; *United States v. Oklahoma*, 261 U.S. 253; *Barnett v. American Surety Co.*, 77 F.2d 225; *In re Dickson's Estate*, 197 Wash. 145, 154–155, 84 P. 2d 661. *Cf. United States v. Summerlin*, 310 U.S. 414.

[4] Section 64a of the Bankruptcy Act, so far as pertinent, provides: "The debts to have priority, in advance of the payment of dividends to creditors, and to be paid in full out of bankrupt estates, and the order of payment, shall be (1) . . . [costs of preserving the estate, etc.]; (2) wages, not to exceed $600 to each claimant, which have been earned within three months before the date of the commencement of the proceeding, due to workmen, servants, clerks, or traveling or city salesmen on salary or commission basis, whole or part time, whether or not selling exclusively for the bankrupt; (3) . . . [certain expenses of creditors connected with the liquidation of the estate]; (4) taxes legally due and owing by the bankrupt to the United States or any State or any subdivision thereof . . . ; and (5) debts owing to any person, including the United States, who by the laws of the United States is entitled to priority . . . "

The provisions of § 3466 have been in force since 1797, without significant modifications. 1 Stat. 515. The first three federal bankruptcy acts[5] specifically preserved the priority of the United States over all other claimants in bankruptcy proceedings in the federal courts. Section 64 of the Bankruptcy Act of 1898,[6] however, disturbed this state of affairs. It provided an order of distribution of the assets of bankrupt estates in which certain wage claims preceded non–tax claims of the United States. While § 64 has been altered since 1898 in several particulars, the priority of wage claims over non–tax claims of the United States has continued. Consequently, we must look to the Act of 1898 for evidence that the priority accorded to wage claims by § 64 was intended to apply to more than bankruptcy proceedings in the federal courts.

We find no such evidence. The entire Act of 1898, as § 2 in particular plainly reveals, was designed to create federal courts of bankruptcy and to define their functions. Indeed, § 64 itself, in subdivision (a), refers to the "court"; § 1 provides that, as used in the Act, "court" means "the court of bankruptcy in which the proceedings are pending"; and § 1 also provides that "courts of bankruptcy," as used in the Act, mean the federal district courts and a few other federal courts. There is no internal sign that any part of § 64 was intended to apply to state courts or to non–bankruptcy proceedings in the federal courts. We have looked in vain in the committee reports and the debate upon the bill for any external hint of such an intention.

It is not strange, therefore, that both courts and commentators have assumed that the application of § 64 of the Act of 1898 was limited to federal bankruptcy proceedings, and that the priority of claims of the United States in non–bankruptcy proceedings remained unaffected. *Bramwell v. U.S. Fidelity & Guaranty Co.*, 269 U.S. 483; *Price v. United States*, 269 U.S. 492; *Stripe v. United States*, 269 U.S. 503; *United States v. Butterworth–Judson*, 269 U.S. 504; *Mellon v. Michigan Trust Co.*, 271 U.S. 236, 238–239; *Spokane County v. United States*, 279 U.S. 80; *New York v. Maclay*, 288 U.S. 290. *See* Rogge, *The Differences in Priority of the United States in Bankruptcy and in Equity Receiverships*, 43 Harv. L. Rev. 251; Blair, *The Priority of the United States in Equity Receiverships*, 39 Harv. L. Rev. 1. We are

---

[5] Act of 1800, c. 19, § 62, 2 Stat. 19; Act of 1841, c. 9, § 5, 5 Stat. 441; Act of 1867, c. 176, § 28, 14 Stat. 517.

[6] Section 64 of the Bankruptcy Act of 1898 (30 Stat. 544) provided:

(a) The court shall order the trustee to pay all taxes legally due and owing by the bankrupt to the United States, State, county, district, or municipality in advance of the payment of dividends to creditors, and upon filing the receipts of the proper public officers for such payment he shall be credited with the amount thereof . . .

(b) The debts to have priority, except as herein provided, and to be paid in full out of bankrupt estates, and the order of payment shall be (1) the actual and necessary cost of preserving the estate subsequent to filing the petition; (2) the filing fees paid by creditors in involuntary cases; (3) . . . [the costs of administration]; (4) wages due to workmen, clerks, or servants which have been earned within three months before the date of the commencement of proceedings, not to exceed three hundred dollars to each claimant; and (5) debts owing to any person who by the laws of the States or the United States is entitled to priority.

aware of but a single case in which an appellate court has specifically passed upon the contention that the priority granted to the United States in non–bankruptcy proceedings by § 3466 has been modified by § 64 of the Bankruptcy Act. And in that case, the contention was rejected. *Matter of Kupshire Coats, Inc.*, 272 N.Y. 221, 5 N.E. 2d 715.[7]

While the point was not discussed in the courts below, it is now urged that the objectives and provisions of the National Housing Act require us to hold that claims of the United States arising under it are not entitled to the priority awarded by § 3466. We are aware of no canon of statutory construction compelling us to hold that the word "first" in a 150 year old statute means "second" or "third," unless Congress later has said so or implied it unmistakably.

Certainly, there is no provision in the National Housing Act expressly relinquishing the priority of the United States with respect to claims arising under it. At best, therefore, such an intention on the part of Congress must be found in some patent inconsistency between the purposes of the Housing Act and § 3466. The plain objective of the Housing Act was to stimulate the building trades and to increase employment. In order to induce banks and other lending institutions to get the program under way, Congress promised that the United States would make good up to 20% on the losses they might incur on such loans.[8] As between the Government and the lending institutions, it was clearly intended that the United States should bear the losses resulting from defaults. But beyond this we may not go. There is nothing to show a further intention that the United States should relinquish its priority as to claims against defaulting and insolvent borrowers whose notes it takes up from the lending institution pursuant to the insurance contract. That is, the ultimate collection of bad loans was consigned to the United States rather than to the lending institutions, but the collecting power of the United States was neither abridged nor qualified.[9]

We are told, however, that the broad purposes of the Act would be thwarted if we failed to assume that Congress intended to surrender this priority. The reason advanced is that suppliers of goods and services would refuse to extend credit to those desiring to make property improvements if they knew that in the event of insolvency their claims would be subordinated to those of the United States. The fatal weakness of this contention is that the Federal Housing Administration imposes an ironclad requirement that the proceeds of insured loans be used for no purpose other than the improvements described in the application for the loan.[10] Indeed,

---

[7] A similar contention with respect to § 57j of the Bankruptcy Act was rejected in *Matter of Simpson, Inc.*, 258 App. Div. 148, 15 N.Y.S. 2d 1021.

[8] 48 Stat. 1246, c. 847, § 2.

[9] The priority granted by § 3466 is, of course, no guaranty that the United States will be saved from loss. In the instant case, for example, the assets available for distribution are so small that the United States will lose heavily even if its claim is first satisfied.

[10] "Modernization Credit Plan," Bulletin No. 1 (Aug. 10, 1934) pp. 15, 16–17, *id.* (Sept. 12, 1934 revision) p. 22; *id.* (July 15, 1935 revision) p. 19; *id.* (July 20, 1936 revision) pp. 6–7; "Property Improvement Loans Under Title I" (Feb. 4, 1938) pp. 4, 23; *id.* (July 1, 1939 revision) p. 15; *id.* (March 15, 1940 revision) p. 10.

lending institutions frequently pay the proceeds of the loan directly to the suppliers of goods and services rather than to the property owner, and the practice has met with the enthusiastic approval of the Administration.[11]

Consequently, the argument against the application of § 3466 is reduced to this: Private persons in general are reluctant to extend credit when they know that in the event of the borrower's insolvency the claims of the United States will receive priority, and this circumstance is particularly undesirable in times of economic stress. In the first place, whatever may be the merits of the contention, it should be addressed to Congress and not to this Court. In the second place, the argument proves too much. If it is sound as applied to this kind of a claim of the United States, it is equally sound as applied to all claims as to which the United States asserts priority under § 3466.

Neither *Cook County National Bank v. United States*, 107 U.S. 445, nor *United States v. Guaranty Trust Co.*, 280 U.S. 478, requires a different conclusion. In the former case, the United States was denied its § 3466 priority in connection with a claim against a national bank for the amount of certain funds of the United States deposited with it. The decision was based on two grounds. First, the National Banking Act undertook to provide a complete system for the establishment and government of banks, and it included specific provisions concerning the distribution of the assets of insolvent banks which were plainly inconsistent with the granting of priority to general claims of the United States. Second, the National Banking Act expressly authorized the Secretary of the Treasury to require national banks accepting deposits of federal funds to give satisfactory security; it was held to be fairly inferable that Congress intended the United States to look to this provision rather than to § 3466 for protection.

The claims which were denied priority in the *Guaranty Trust* case arose under Title II of the Transportation Act of 1920. That Act provided for the funding of debts to the United States which the railroads had contracted during the period of wartime control, and also provided for new loans to the railroads. In holding § 3466 inapplicable to the collection of these loans the Court emphasized that the basic purpose of the Act was to promote the general credit status of the railroads, that the railroads were required to furnish adequate security for the payment of both the old and new loans, and that the interest rate of 6% on one class of loans was "much greater than that which ordinarily accompanies even a business loan carrying such assurance of repayment as would have resulted from an application of the priority rule." 280 U.S. at 486. These factors persuaded the Court that Congress had intended to exclude these loans from the scope of § 3466.

In the instant case, none of these circumstances is present. The National Housing Act contains no reference to the liquidation of estates of insolvent borrowers, and consequently no direct inconsistency with § 3466 is possible. The purpose of Title I was not the strengthening of the *general* credit of property owners, but the stimulation of the building trades by affording assurances to lending institutions in

---

[11] "Modernization Credit Plan," Bulletin No. 1 (Sept. 12, 1934 revision) p. 29; *id.* (July 15, 1935 revision) p. 15; "Property Improvement Loans Under Title I" (Feb. 4, 1938) p. 33; *id.* (July 1, 1939 revision) p. 30; *id.* (March 15, 1940 revision) regulation No. VIII.

order to induce them to make loans for property improvements. No security was required of the borrowers, and the interest charge was low.[12] Only the plainest inconsistency would warrant our finding an implied exception to the operation of so clear a command as that of § 3466. We think such inconsistency is wholly wanting here.

Section 3466 is applicable to this proceeding, and it requires that the claim of the United States be first satisfied.

Reversed.

Mr. Justice REED, dissenting:

The purpose and provisions of the National Housing Act[1] lead me to the conclusion that § 3466 of the Revised Statutes is inapplicable to the claim of the Administrator in this case.[2]

A statute is not to be interpreted by its text alone, as though it were a specimen under laboratory control. It takes meaning from other enactments forming the whole body of law bearing upon its subject.[3] If, like § 3466, it has been upon the books for years, the precedents interpreting its meaning must be considered in connection with it, particularly when, as here, new legislation is passed which may be inconsistent with its application.[4]

---

[12] Not until 1939, four years after the note in this case was executed, did the Federal Housing Administration even require the lending institutions to pay premiums for the insurance of Title I loans. 53 Stat. 805, c. 175, § 2. The income from these premiums was to be used primarily to meet operating expenses under Title I and secondarily to meet losses resulting from defaults. In his report dated April 1, 1941, the Administrator estimated that for the fiscal year ending June 30, 1941, this income from premiums would prove sufficient to reimburse the United States for less than half its losses under Title I, and that $4,000,000 of public funds would be required to meet the balance. Report of the Federal Housing Administration for the year ending Dec. 31, 1940, p. 11.

[1] Act of June 27, 1934, c. 847, Tit. I, § 2, 48 Stat. 1246, as amended 49 Stat. 299, 49 Stat. 722, 49 Stat. 1187, 49 Stat. 1234. The statute as thereafter amended subsequently to the events of this case may be found as 12 U.S.C. § 1703 (1940).

[2] Previous decisions in other courts concededly are to the contrary. *In re Long Island Sash & Door Corp.*, 259 App. Div. 688, 20 N. Y. S. 2d 573, aff'd mem. 284 N. Y. 713, 31 N. E. 2d 48, *cert. den.* 312 U.S. 696; *In re Dickson's Estate*, 197 Wash. 145, 84 P. 2d 661. Accord, *Korman v. Federal Housing Administrator*, 113 F.2d 743 (App. D. C.); *Wagner v. McDonald*, 96 F.2d 273 (C. C. A. 8th); *In re Weil*, 39 F. Supp. 618 (M. D. Pa.); *In re Wilson*, 23 F. Supp. 236 (N. D. Tex.); *cf. Federal Reserve Bank of Dallas v. Smylie*, 134 S. W. 2d 838 (Tex. Civ. App.) (Farm Credit Administration); *see* 52 Harv. L. Rev. 320. *United States v. Summerlin*, 310 U.S. 414, held only that the claim assigned to the administrator became a claim of the United States not subject to a state statute of "non–claim." It did not pass upon the right to priority under § 3466 in the decedent's estate. *Compare Dupont de Nemours & Co. v. Davis*, 264 U.S. 456, where the Director General of the railroads was held free from limitation, with *Mellon v. Michigan Trust Co.*, 271 U.S. 236, where the Director General was denied priority under § 3466. *United States v. Marxen*, 307 U.S. 200, 203, expressly did not decide the point.

[3] *Keifer & Keifer v. R. F. C.*, 306 U.S. 381, 389.

[4] *United States v. Marxen*, 307 U.S. 200, 206; *United States v. Knott*, 298 U.S. 544, 547–48; *Mellon v. Michigan Trust Co.*, 271 U.S. 236, 240.

From past interpretation we learn that the traditional function of § 3466 is the assurance of the public revenue,[5] whatever may be the expense to the competing creditors. Their interests are subordinated to the general advantage.[6] Title I of the National Housing Act, however, is not a revenue measure—it was intended to stimulate recovery and employment in the construction industries and to enable property–owners to obtain funds for sorely needed repairs by insuring financial institutions against loss on loans for such work.[7] This was accomplished by what is, in effect, a guarantee that all losses on rehabilitation loans, up to a predetermined percentage (20% here) of the total made by the financial institution, would be borne by the United States, either by taking over loans in default or paying the deficit.[8] That loss Congress intended the Government to bear.[9] In estimating the loss, it relied upon the experience of private companies which were unaided by any such priority as § 3466.[10] Loans could not be made for a longer term than five years, and many would be for less. Stable economic improvement was hardly to be expected within that time, and yet, many of those who borrowed would die, or default, and undergo some sort of financial liquidation. The enforcement of § 3466 under those circumstances would shift the loss from the Government to competing creditors, thus hampering the efforts of private business and capital to achieve that economic recovery which was the aim of the legislation.[11]

---

[5] *Spokane County v. United States*, 279 U.S. 80, 92; *Price v. United States*, 269 U.S. 492, 500; *Bramwell v. U.S. Fidelity Co.*, 269 U.S. 483, 487.

[6] *United States v. Fisher*, 2 Cranch 358, 389.

[7] Message of the President, May 14, 1934, 78 Cong. Rec. 8739–40 (Senate), *id.* at 8773–74 (House). Concerning the doldrums of the construction industry, *see* 78 Cong. Rec. 11194, 11198, 11210, 11211; Hearings on Sen. 3603, Committee on Banking and Currency, 73d Cong., 2d Sess., May 16–24, 1934, pp. 166 ff. Concerning the need for repairs, *see* 78 Cong. Rec. 11194, 11214; Hearings on Sen. 3603, *supra*, at pp. 36, 48, 288, 290.

[8] Regulation No. 18—Modernization Credit Plan—Title I, National Housing Act, provided: "The Federal Housing Administration will reimburse any insured institution on losses up to a total aggregate amount equal to 20% of the total face amount of all qualified notes taken or current face value of notes purchased by the financial institution, during the time the insurance contract is in force, and held by it or on which it continues liable. . . ." Modernization Credit Plan, Bulletin No. 1, p. 30 (revised reissue, Dec. 10, 1934).

[9] Senator Bulkley, chairman of the subcommittee (78 Cong. Rec. 11974) stated to the Senate: "It is contemplated that there will be a loss to the Government under this title, but that probably the loss will not be very great. . . . The reason we justify this provision is that it will make possible a considerable expenditure of money on needed repairs and renovation and thereby stimulate business in trades which very much need stimulation at this time." 78 Cong. Rec. 11981, 73d Cong., 2d Sess.

[10] 78 Cong. Rec. 11195–11196, 11981, 11982, 73d Cong., 2d Sess. *See* Hearings on Sen. 3603, *supra*, at pp. 293–94.

[11] These loans were to be so–called "character" loans, in reliance on the character and stable earnings of the borrower. 78 Cong. Rec. 11194, 11195, 11981. It was expected that while many persons at the time had no stable income, the Act would temporarily promote new employment which once under way was hoped would continue long enough of its own force to culminate in permanent business recovery and repayment of the borrowed money. Hearings on Sen. 3603, *supra*, at pp. 46, 173.

(Matthew Bender & Co., Inc.)

Nothing in the hearings, the debates or the Act show definitively that Congress considered the application of § 3466 to government claims under the National Housing Act. If the two Acts alone were to be appraised, it might well be concluded that, as they are not necessarily inconsistent, both should be enforced. But the determination of Congressional purpose is not so simple as that. Upon the assumption that the applicability of § 3466 never came to the attention of Congress, we must find legislative purpose not from the language of the two Acts alone but from generalizations as to the object of the new statute and from judicial interpretations of the meaning of the old. To reach a sound conclusion as to the applicability of the priority statute and the purpose of Congress deduced merely from the state of the law at the time of the enactment of the Housing Act, we need to weigh the precedents under § 3466 quite as carefully as the Acts themselves, in order to develop the legal situation into which the Housing Act was injected. When this is done, it is apparent that, each time this Court has considered legislative purpose as to § 3466 in relation to government claims under public financial legislation affecting creditors competing with the Government, it has determined § 3466 did not apply.[12]

The National Housing Act was "one of the latest of a series of enactments, extending over more than a century, through which the Federal Government has recognized and fulfilled its obligation to provide a national system of financial institutions. . . ."[13] § 3466 is inconsistent with this purpose.[14] It is not significant that in the case of *Cook County National Bank* the debtor bank against which priority was denied was in the federal financial system, while here the debtor is a private corporation which has participated in a federal financing plan. The intrusion of a novel priority, uncertain in amount because unrecorded, into the intricate credit system of the Nation at a time of strain, would be a drag on recovery, rather than a stimulus. Suppliers of goods or services in all fields of credit activity would be moved to constrict their advances to a borrower known to have created a secret but valid lien upon his assets superior to all general creditors. The full reach of the implication of credit dislocation may be readily gauged by the fact that, at the end of 1936, 1,326,102 separate rehabilitation loans had been made under Title I for an aggregate amount of $500,220,642.[15] Possible priorities will now exist for every outstanding dollar.

The facts of this case show how government aid to a debtor may be a snare for his other creditors if the priority statute operates in this class of claims. About a dozen claimants became creditors in the aggregate amount of some nine hundred dollars for labor. Such labor claims were entitled to the preference under Missouri law common to labor claims. But for the priority of the Government's claim, they

---

[12] *Cook County Nat. Bank v. United States*, 107 U.S. 445; *United States v. Guaranty Trust Co.*, 280 U.S. 478; *cf. Sloan Shipyards v. U.S. Fleet Corp.*, 258 U.S. 549; *Mellon v. Michigan Trust Co.*, 271 U.S. 236.

[13] Validity of Certain Provisions of the National Housing Act, 38 Ops. Atty. Gen. 258, 262.

[14] *Cook County Nat. Bank v. United States*, 107 U.S. 445.

[15] Third Annual Report of the Federal Housing Administration, House Doc. No. 48, 75th Cong., 1st Sess., p. 7.

would receive all of the realization from the assets—about two–thirds of their claims. But a month before the appointment of the receiver, the Federal Housing Administration took over from a bank a note of about $6000. From a deferred position in the hands of the bank, this debt is said to have stepped into a preferred position by transfer to the government agency. As such, it absorbs all of the assets, and the laborers who trusted their employer's credit get nothing. Such a preference of creditors, brought about by the debtor, would be an act of bankruptcy.

In 1920, when the railroads needed funds but lacked credit for private borrowing, government loans were authorized by Congress, based upon such prospective earning power and security as would furnish reasonable assurance of repayment.[16] In *United States v. Guaranty Trust Co.*, 280 U.S. 478, we held that the rehabilitating functions and the security provisions of the Transportation Act of 1920 were so inconsistent with § 3466 as to preclude its application in the receivership of a debtor railroad. Even more inconsistent considerations exist in this case. Congress was confronted with widespread need of repairs on property owned by persons without the cash or credit to secure them.[17] Moreover, not only homeowners but, like the railroads, hard pressed business establishments, such as the distillery in this case, were to be assisted in securing modernization loans.[18] Instead of lending these people federal funds, Congress lent them federal credit on which to borrow private funds, with the evident purpose of keeping the program as much as possible a matter of private enterprise handled in the course of private affairs. Assurance of repayment was rested not on a combination of security and earning power but deliberately upon earning power alone.[19] Whereas, with the railroads, interest corresponding to the risk was charged, no premium was charged for the insurance of loans under Title I—with the expectation that the Government would pay the loss as its contribution to recovery.[20] The declared purpose of the United States to absorb the losses of the lenders is clearly inconsistent with the priority over other creditors given by § 3466. It seems beyond doubt, to me, that Congress did not expect a priority under Title I which the *Guaranty Trust* case certainly denied it under Title II relating to insured mortgages.[21]

---

[16] Transportation Act of 1920, § 210, 41 Stat. 468.

[17] 78 Cong. Rec. 11199, 11388, 11981, 73d Cong., 2d Sess.; Hearings on Sen. 3603, *supra*, at pp. 30, 172, 174, 179.

[18] The loan limit of Title I was soon increased to meet business needs. Amendment of May 28, 1935; 49 Stat. 299.

[19] 78 Cong. Rec. 11194, 11195, 11981, 11982, 73d Cong., 2d Sess.; Hearings on Sen. 3603, *supra*, at pp. 37, 39, 293.

[20] Senator Bulkley stated: "The lender receives 20–percent insurance automatically as an inducement to make loans of this particular character. Frankly it is contemplated that the Government will lose some money." 78 Cong. Rec. 11982, 73d Cong., 2d Sess. *See also* 78 Cong. Rec. 11195; Hearings on Sen. 3603, *supra*, at pp. 34–35.

[21] Moreover, since July 1, 1939, there is a .75% insurance charge under Title I, so that in the future, whatever the decision here, even Title I would seem to be governed by the *Guaranty Trust* case. 24 C.F.R. § 501.18 (Supp. 1939.)

Even in the mechanics of its operation, Title I repudiated the benefits of § 3466. Collection was left to the financial institution after default, so long as there was hope of partial liquidation.[22] The lender, of course, had no priority.

The judgment should be affirmed on the ground that no priority exists by virtue of § 3466.

Mr. Justice ROBERTS, Mr. Justice DOUGLAS and Mr. Justice JACKSON concur in this dissent.

NOTES AND QUESTIONS

(1) In 1967, two leading commentators wrote:

The ancient insolvency priority statute, section 3466, has remained unchanged with respect to collective insolvency proceedings other than bankruptcy. Despite the frequent review and revision of the priority rules in bankruptcy, and the recent major overhaul of the priorities of federal tax liens in individual proceedings, Congress has made no substantive amendment of the insolvency provision in nearly 170 years.

Plumb and Wright, Federal Tax Liens, 166 (1967). In 1982, Congress amended title 31, including the priority statute. The statute is now written with greater clarity, but has not changed substantively. Should Congress have made more sweeping revisions

---

[22] Modernization Credit Plan, Bulletin No. 1, *supra*, at p. 8 states:

It is to the interest of the financial institution to carry the collection process on a defaulted note as far as there is reasonable prospect of ultimate payment inasmuch as complete reimbursement for any expenses incurred is provided as specified hereinafter. This policy will tend to conserve the insurance reserve of 20% for possible later losses and also will maintain the understanding of the local community that these notes require the same prompt handling by makers as any other credit obligation. . . . it is the policy of the Federal Housing Administration to permit financial institutions every possible latitude in making collections on delinquent items. It is only after it clearly appears that further collection efforts will be fruitless that the Federal Housing Administration will insist that claim be made. Financial institutions are, therefore, given a full year after default on the note to effect collection. . . . If 10% of the amount due on the note is collected within the first year after default on the note and so long thereafter as 5% at least is collected in each six–month period, the Federal Housing Administration will not require that claim be made, but will permit the financial institution to proceed with its collection efforts. Claims may include: (1) Net unpaid principal; (2) uncollected earned interest (after maturity interest is not to be claimed at a rate exceeding 6% per annum); (3) uncollected "late charges"; (4) uncollected court costs, including fees paid for issuing, serving and filing summons; (5) attorney's fees not exceeding 15% of the amount collected on the defaulted note; (6) handling fee of $5 for each note, if judgment is secured, plus 5% of amount collected subsequent to return of unsatisfied property execution.

in the statute? *See* Plumb, *The Federal Priority In Insolvency: Proposals for Reform,* 70 Mich. L. Rev. 3 (1972).

(2) When are the priority provisions of § 3713 applied? Note that the "acts of bankruptcy"[1] set forth in § 3 of the former Bankruptcy Act of 1898 were eliminated from the Bankruptcy Code. *See* § 303(h) of the Bankruptcy Code, 11 U.S.C. § 303(h). Section 3713 specifically excludes cases under the Bankruptcy Code from its coverage. Query: Why was not the "act of bankruptcy" concept also eliminated from the federal priority when the statute was amended in 1982? Should the events set forth in § 303(h) of the Bankruptcy Code that support the filing of an involuntary bankruptcy petition (debtor "generally not paying . . . debts as [they] become due," or appointment of custodian for substantially all of debtor's property) now be considered the "acts of bankruptcy"?

(3) As set forth in *United States v. Emory, supra,* what is the purpose of the federal priority? Courts have construed the priority statute broadly to meet these ends. *See, e.g., Bramwell v. United States Fidelity Co.,* 269 U.S. 483 (1926); *United States v. Key,* 397 U.S. 322 (1970); *United States v. Coyne,* 540 F. Supp. 175 (D.D.C. 1981).

(4) In *Emory,* the Supreme Court held that the priority scheme established under § 64 of the former Bankruptcy Act (former 11 U.S.C. § 103), which granted certain wage claims priority over non–tax claims of the federal government, did not similarly limit the federal priority under former § 3466 in nonbankruptcy insolvency cases. Under § 507(a)(7) of the Bankruptcy Code (11 U.S.C. § 507(a)(7)), seventh priority continues to be granted in the distribution scheme for certain prepetition unsecured *tax* claims, but the priority scheme in bankruptcy no longer grants a priority to other, federal non–tax claims. Nonetheless, § 3713, which, therefore, does not apply in cases under the Bankruptcy Code, continues to apply broadly to *all* claims of the federal government in nonbankruptcy settings. Is the difference between the two statutes practical? Might it lead to an increased number of involuntary bankruptcy cases filed by creditors who seek to have their claims treated on a better footing with the claims of the United States?

(5) How have the courts defined the term "insolvency" for the purpose of invoking the federal priority scheme? *See United States v. Oklahoma,* 261 U.S. 253 (1923); *Massachusetts v. United States,* 333 U.S. 611 (1948); and *United States v. Press Wireless,* 187 F.2d 294 (2d Cir. 1951). Is this the bankruptcy definition of insolvency, or the equitable definition? *See* 11 U.S.C. § 101(26).

(6) Although not provided for in the statute, the costs and expenses of liquidating an insolvent debtor's estate, including reasonable and necessary attorneys' fees, will be paid prior to federal claims. *See, e.g., Abrams v. United States,* 274 F.2d 8 (8th Cir. 1960); *Hammond v. Carthage Sulphite Pulp & Paper Co.,* 34 F.2d 155 (N.D.N.Y. 1928). Why have courts created this exception to the absolute terms of the statute?

(7) Section 3713(b), as did its statutory predecessor 31 U.S.C. § 192, imposes personal liability on estate fiduciaries for debts due the federal government if

---

[1] These "acts" were generally considered prejudicial to the rights of creditors, and included a fraudulent transfer, preferential transfer, and the debtor's permitting a creditor to get a judicial lien on its property and failing to vacate the lien before sale.

insufficient funds are withheld to satisfy the government's claim. Under case law construing former § 192, a fiduciary's liability was limited to those circumstances in which it had actual knowledge or notice of the debt owed to the United States. *See Want v. C.I.R.*, 280 F.2d 777 (2d Cir. 1960); *United States v. Vibradamp Corp.*, 257 F. Supp. 931 (S.D. Cal. 1966).

UNITED STATES v. TEXAS

United States Supreme Court
314 U.S. 480, 62 S. Ct. 358, 86 L.Ed. 356 (1941)

Mr. Justice BYRNES delivered the opinion of the Court.

W. L. Nix was a manufacturer and distributor of motor fuel, doing business in Texas under the name of Texas Refinery. On November 20, 1933, M. R. Ingraham, who held a demand note secured by a chattel mortgage on certain tanks belonging to Nix, brought an action in the District Court of Gregg County, Texas. He alleged that demand had been made on the note, that it had not been paid, that Nix owned no property in Texas other than that of Texas Refinery, that the value of the mortgaged tanks was insufficient to discharge the note, that the tanks were not used "for a separate purpose" but in the "operation of the said refinery as a unit," and that Nix was insolvent. He asked that judgment be entered in his favor for the amount of the note, that the mortgage be foreclosed, and that in the meantime a receiver be placed in charge of "the whole of the property" of Texas Refinery. On the same day a receiver was appointed, and he was subsequently authorized to sell all of the refinery property.

On November 21, R. P. Ash intervened in the proceedings as the holder of an overdue note secured by a mortgage on the physical plant of the refinery not subject to the Ingraham mortgage. Both the State of Texas and the United States then intervened with the claims for state and federal gasoline taxes, which are the subject of the present dispute. Later, both the Ingraham and Ash mortgage notes were assigned to Howard Dailey.

The District Court found that Nix was insolvent on November 20, 1933, and continued to be insolvent thereafter. The sum available for distribution after sale of the refinery property by the receiver was $7466.92. The court found that, of these proceeds, $1294.80 was allocable to those assets which were subject to the mortgages held by Dailey, and it ordered that his claim to that amount be first satisfied. It determined that Nix was liable to the United States for $19,343.91 in federal gasoline taxes, and to Texas for $40,312.51 in state gasoline taxes. As between the state and federal claims, it decided that the United States was entitled to priority, and concluded that nothing would be left to apply to the Texas claim.

From this order Texas appealed to the Court of Civil Appeals for the Second District. That court certified the controlling questions to the Supreme Court of Texas.

The Supreme Court, on the authority of *State v. Wynne*, 134 Tex. 455, 133 S. W. 2d 951, a companion case decided the same day, answered the questions in such a way as to require that the claim of Texas be first satisfied, that of Dailey second, and that of the United States third. The Court of Civil Appeals thereupon so ruled, noting that the assets available would not completely satisfy even the claim of Texas and that Dailey and the United States would receive nothing. A motion by the United States for a rehearing was denied, and the Supreme Court of Texas refused to review the decision of the Court of Civil Appeals. We granted the petition of the United States for certiorari because of the important question of the fiscal relationship between state and federal governments which is involved.

No question as to the rights of Dailey, the mortgagee, is raised by this appeal. We confine ourselves, therefore, to the only question presently open to decision: the relative priority of the claims of the United States and Texas.

The United States rests its assertion of priority upon § 3466 of the Revised Statutes.[1] Despite the contention of Texas to the contrary, that section clearly applies to this proceeding. As we recently remarked in *United States v. Emory*,[2] § 3466 covers in terms the case of an insolvent debtor who has committed an act of bankruptcy, and there are few more familiar examples of an act of bankruptcy than the appointment of a receiver because of the debtor's insolvency. *Cf.* § 3 (a) (4) of the Bankruptcy Act, U.S.C., Title 11, § 21 (a) (4). Here the district court expressly found that Nix was insolvent, and it appointed a receiver. It is true that the original petition was filed by a mortgagee rather than by a general creditor. But, if any limitations upon the operation of § 3466 might otherwise have flowed from this circumstance, they were removed by the subsequent character of the proceeding. The receiver was placed in control of all of Nix's assets, rather than only those subject to the mortgage, and all of the assets were eventually liquidated. Parties other than the mortgagee, including Texas itself, intervened and were heard. We think that realities require us to treat the proceeding as a general equity receivership within the scope of § 3466.

We are thus brought to the important issue in the case. Article 7065a–7 of the Texas Civil Statutes declared that all gasoline taxes due by any distributor to the State "shall be a preferred lien, first and prior to any and all other existing liens, upon all of the property of any distributor, devoted to or used in his business as a distributor. . . ."[3] It is the State's position that under this section it held a specific

---

[1] U.S. Rev. Stat. § 3466 (U.S.C., Title 31, § 191) provides: "Whenever any person indebted to the United States is insolvent, or whenever the estate of any deceased debtor, in the hands of the executors or administrators, is insufficient to pay all the debts due from the deceased, the debts due to the United States shall be first satisfied; and the priority established shall extend as well to cases in which a debtor, not having sufficient property to pay all his debts, makes a voluntary assignment thereof, or in which the estate and effects of an absconding, concealed, or absent debtor are attached by process of law, as to cases in which an act of bankruptcy is committed."

[2] *Ante*, p. 423.

[3] The full text of the paragraph, as of Nov. 20, 1933, when the receiver was appointed read: "All taxes, fines, penalties and interest due by any distributor to the State shall be a preferred lien, first and prior to any and all other existing liens, upon all of the property of

and perfected lien upon the refinery property which entitled it to priority despite § 3466 of the Revised Statutes.

Section 3466 mentions no exception to its requirement that "the debts due to the United States shall be first satisfied." It is nevertheless true that in several early decisions this Court read an exception into the section in the case of previously executed mortgages. *Thelusson v. Smith*, 2 Wheat. 396, 426; *Conard v. Atlantic Insurance Co.*, 1 Pet. 386; *Brent v. Bank of Washington*, 10 Pet. 596, 611, 612. This doctrine seems to have been based on the theory that mortgaged property passes to the mortgagee and is no longer a part of the estate of the mortgagor. *See Conard v. Atlantic Insurance Co., supra*, at 441–442. The question of whether the priority of the United States under § 3466 would also be defeated by a specific and perfected lien upon property, whose title remained in the debtor was reserved in those cases. *Ibid.; Brent v. Bank of Washington, supra*, at 611–612. However, it was determined that a general judgment lien upon the lands of an insolvent debtor does not take precedence over claims of the United States unless execution of the judgment has proceeded far enough to take the land out of the possession of the debtor. *Thelusson v. Smith, supra*, at 425–426.

In more recent years the Court has had occasion to consider the argument that liens created in favor of States or counties by state statutes entitled them to priority over the United States under § 3466. In *Spokane County v. United States*, 279 U.S. 80, the priority of the United States was upheld. The state statutes involved provided that if a certain personal property tax was not paid, and if the personal property against which it had been assessed was no longer in the hands of the delinquent taxpayer, the amount of the unpaid tax should become a lien upon all the real and personal property of the taxpayer. They went on to prescribe the procedure by which the lien was to be enforced. The Court determined that the statutory lien did not become specific until this procedure had been followed. Since these procedural conditions had not been satisfied in the case before it, the Court refused priority to the tax claims of the county. It specifically declined to consider what "the effect of more completed procedure in the perfecting of the liens under the law of the State" would have been. 279 U.S. at 95.

The New York statute in *New York v. Maclay*, 288 U.S. 290, declared that the corporate franchise tax there involved should "be a lien and binding upon the real and personal property of the corporation . . . until the same is paid in full." 288 U.S. at 292. Although the franchise taxes in question were overdue, the State had taken no steps to perfect and liquidate its lien at the time the receiver was appointed for the insolvent corporation. Under such circumstances, the Court was of the opinion that the tax claim of the State did not deprive the claim of the United States

---

any distributor, devoted to or used in his business as a distributor, which property shall include refinery, blending plants, storage tanks, warehouses, office buildings and equipment, tank trucks or other motor vehicles, or any other property devoted to such use, and each tract of land on which such refinery, blending plant, tanks or other property is located, or which is used in carrying on such business." This section was repealed on May 1, 1941 by Article XVII, § 28 of the Acts of the 47th Legislature, and simultaneously replaced without significant change by a new Article 7065b–8.

of its priority under § 3466. It was at pains to make clear, however, that it intended by its decision to lend no support to the assumption that the doctrine of the mortgage cases, whatever its current vitality, would require the subordination of unsecured claims of the United States to a specific and perfected lien. 288 U.S. at 293–294.[4]

We think that it is equally unnecessary to test that assumption here. Prior to the appointment of the receiver on November 20, 1933, the State of Texas had made no move to assert the lien proclaimed in Article 7065a–7. And the priority which attached to the claim of the United States on that day (*United States v. Oklahoma*, 261 U.S. 253, 260) could not be divested by any subsequent proceedings in connection with the State's lien. *New York v. Maclay, supra*, at 293.

It is urged, however, that Article 7065a–7 by its own force creates a specific and perfected lien. Support for this contention is said to lie in the fact that the statutory lien purports to affect only the property of the distributor which is "devoted to or used in his business as a distributor," rather than his property in general. This is thought to make the lien sufficiently specific. Moreover, the State argues, and the Supreme Court of Texas has declared,[5] that the provisions of the Texas Civil Statutes which govern the levy, seizure and sale of the property of delinquent taxpayers generally[6] are inapplicable to the gasoline tax. We are of course bound by this authoritative construction of the statute.

With respect to this contention it may first be said that the "property devoted to or used in his business as a distributor" is neither specific nor constant. But a more important consideration is that the amount of the claim secured by the lien is unliquidated and uncertain. As we said in *New York v. Maclay*: "If the state were to . . . omit to ascertain the debt, it would never be able to sell anything, for it would not know how much to sell." 288 U.S. at 293. That the legislature of Texas recognized this is revealed by another section of the statute. Article 7065a–8 (d) declared that, in the event of default, when it might become necessary for the State "to bring suit or to intervene . . . for the establishment or collection" of its claims in judicial proceedings, the tax reports required of the distributor by other provisions of the statute[7] should be "prima facie evidence of the contents thereof," but "the incorrectness of said report or audit may be shown." Thus, it was clearly envisaged that the amount of the taxes due, for which the lien was security, should be left to determination by the courts.

As to the nature of the proper procedure for levy, seizure, and sale, it is enough to say that some procedure is essential. As we have indicated, the statutory scheme

---

[4] In *United States v. Oklahoma*, 261 U.S. 253, the question was not reached because it was found that the "insolvency" upon which the operation of § 3466 is conditioned was absent. The Court sustained the priority of the United States under § 3466 in *United States v. Knott*, 298 U.S. 544. The Florida statutes there involved required foreign surety corporations to deposit certain bonds with the State Treasurer for the protection of Florida residents. This arrangement was held to create no more than "an inchoate general lien" for the benefit of unknown persons who might become entitled to the fund, and not to limit the effect of § 3466.

[5] *State v. Wynne*, 134 Tex. 455, at 473.

[6] *See*, esp., Articles 7266, 7272, and 7275 of the Texas Civil Statutes.

[7] Article 7065a, §§ 2 (b), 2 (d), 8 (a), and 8 (b).

reveals that the legislature contemplated resort to the courts. In addition to the statutory provisions referred to above, Article 7065a–8 (e) regulates the pleadings in suits by the Attorney General to collect the tax, and Article 7065a–9 determines the venue of such suits. Consequently, while it was clearly intended by Article 7065a–7 to create a lien in favor of the State, we must conclude that of necessity it was nothing more than an inchoate and general lien. Certainly it did not of its own force divest the taxpayer of either title or possession. It could not become specific until the exact amount of the taxes due had been determined; and it could not be enforced without the assistance of the courts. Like the tax lien in *New York v. Maclay, supra,* it served "merely as a *caveat* of a more perfect lien to come." 288 U.S. at 294.

We are not now called upon to decide whether the chattel mortgages held by Dailey are entitled to priority over the claim of the United States.[8] We hold only that the tax claim of the United States is entitled to priority over the tax claim of Texas. The case is remanded to the Court of Civil Appeals for proceedings not inconsistent with this opinion.

Reversed.

Mr. Justice JACKSON took no part in the consideration or decision of this case.

BANK OF WRANGELL v. ALASKA ASIATIC LUMBER MILLS, INC.

United States District Court, District of Alaska
84 F. Supp. 1 (1949)

FOLTA, District Judge.

The question presented in this controversy concerns the rank and priority to be accorded the claims of the United States for taxes in the sum of $18,951.53, the claim of the Bank of Wrangell for the balance due on its mortgages on the real property of the insolvent debtor in the sum of $48,520, the claim of the Town of Wrangell for taxes in the sum of $4,952.10, and the mechanic's lien claim of Walter J. Stutte, based on improvements constructed on the mortgaged mill premises, in the sum of $1,683.22.

The Receiver, who was appointed on August 11, 1947, has, pursuant to the orders of this Court, reduced the assets to cash and now has available for distribution, after deducting the amount of $10,000 borrowed from the mortgagee bank for expenses of administration, approximately $32,000 for distribution among the claimants named.

No question is raised as to the validity of the liens on which these claims are based or the other liens specified. The controversy, therefore, resolves itself primarily into

---

[8] The texts of the mortgages are not contained in the record; and Dailey did not appear in this Court.

a contest between the United States and the Bank under § 3466 R.S., 31 U.S.C.A. § 191, which provides that: "Whenever any person indebted to the United States is insolvent, or whenever the estate of any deceased debtor, in the hands of the executors or administrators, is insufficient to pay all the debts due from the deceased, the debts due to the United States shall be first satisfied; and the priority established shall extend as well to cases in which a debtor, not having sufficient property to pay all his debts, makes a voluntary assignment thereof, or in which the estate and effects of an absconding, concealed, or absent debtor are attached by process of law, as to cases in which an act of bankruptcy is committed."

Incredible as it may seem, the question whether a mortgage lien is entitled to priority over the United States under this statute has not yet been decided by the Supreme Court.

In *Thelusson v. Smith*, 2 Wheat. 396, page 425, 4 L.Ed. 271, involving a contest between a judgment creditor who had made no levy under his judgment and the United States, the court in upholding the priority of the United States said: "Exceptions there must necessarily be as to the funds out of which the United States are to be satisfied, but there can be none in relation to the debts due from a debtor of the United States to individuals. The United States are to be first satisfied; but then, it must be out of the debtor's estate. If, therefore, before the right of preference has accrued to the United States, the debtor has made a bona fide conveyance of his estate to a third person, or has mortgaged the same to secure a debt, or if his property has been seized under a fi. fa., the property is divested out of the debtor, and cannot be made liable to the United States. A judgment gives to the judgment–creditor a lien on the debtor's lands, and a preference over all subsequent judgment–creditors. But the act of congress defeats this preference, in favor of the United States, in the cases specified in the 65th section of the act of 1799."

In *Conard v. Atlantic Insurance Co.*, 1 Pet. 386, page 441, 7 L.Ed. 189, in answer to the contention that the priority of the United States could be defeated only by an absolute conveyance and not by a mortgage lien, for which *Thelusson v. Smith, supra,* was cited, the court said, that its language in that case is conclusive on the point of the priority of the mortgage, and added: "It is true, that in the discussions in courts of equity, a mortgage is sometimes called a lien for debt. And so it certainly is, and something more; it is a transfer of the property itself, as security for the debt. This must be admitted to be true at law; and it is equally true in equity; for in this respect, equity follows the law. It does not consider the estate of the mortgagee as defeated and reduced to a mere lien, but it treats it as a trust estate, and according to the intention of the parties, as a qualified estate, and security. When the debt is discharged, there is a resulting trust for a mortgagor. It is, therefore, only in a loose and general sense, that it is sometimes called a lien, and then only by way of contrast to an estate absolute and indefeasible. But it has never yet been decided by this court, that the priority of the United States will divest a specific lien, attached to a thing, whether it be accompanied by possession or not."

In 9 Op.Atty.Gen. 28, it was assumed that the United States was not entitled to priority under § 3466 over a mortgage, and in *Savings & Loan Soc. v. Multnomah County*, 169 U.S. 421, 428, 18 S. Ct. 392, 395, 42 L.Ed. 803, the court said, purely by way of illustration however, that: "This court has always held that a mortgage of real estate, made in good faith by a debtor to secure a private debt, is a conveyance of such an interest in the land, as will defeat the priority given to the United States by act of congress in the distribution of the debtor's estate. *United States v. Hooe*, 3 Cranch 73, [2 L.Ed. 370]; *Thelusson v. Smith*, 2 Wheat. 396, 426, [4 L.Ed. 271]; *Conard v. Atlantic Ins. Co.*, 1 Pet. 386, 441, [7 L.Ed. 189]."

The claimants here differ as to the effect of the decision in *United States v. Guaranty Trust Co.*, 8 Cir., 33 F.2d 533. That case deals with two classes of claims, those arising under the Federal Transportation Act, 49 U.S.C.A. § 71 et seq., and those arising before that Act went into effect. It would appear that the decision holds that the priority of the United States was subordinate to the mortgage liens attaching before the other indebtedness accrued, 33 F.2d at pages 537, 539, and that the claims of the first class were governed by the provision of the Transportation Act rather than by § 3466, 33 F.2d at page 536. In affirming this decision, however, 280 U.S. 478, 50 S. Ct. 212, 74 L.Ed. 556, the Supreme Court held that claims arising under the Transportation Act were not entitled to priority. Thus, although the matter is left in some doubt, since it appears that the mortgages referred to by the Court of Appeals in Class (a) on page 536 of 33 F.2d were executed between 1888 and 1912, 33 F.2d at page 534, long before the passage of either Transportation Act, it would seem that the decision referred to is an authority for the view that the United States is not entitled to priority over mortgage liens. This decision was thus construed in *Guaranty Trust Co. v. Pacific & I. N. Ry. Co.*, D.C., 17 F.Supp. 646, and priority over the mortgage lien of bondholders was denied the United States on the authority thereof.

However, doubt is cast on the force of such decisions, as precedents for the view urged here by the Bank, by what the court said in *New York v. Maclay*, 288 U.S. 290, 294, 53 S. Ct. 323, 324, 77 L.Ed. 754: "Later cases have drawn a distinction between the liens of judgments and of mortgages. These last have been thought to have the effect of a conveyance, divesting the debtor of his title and leaving nothing but an equity to which a preference can attach. *Conard v. Atlantic Insurance Co.*, 1 Pet. 386, 7 L.Ed 189; *Brent v. Bank of Washington*, 10 Pet. 596, 611, 612, 9 L.Ed. 547; *Savings & Loan Society v. Multnomah County*, 169 U.S. 421, 428, 18 S. Ct. 392, 42 L.Ed. 803. We do not now determine whether the holding in the mortgage cases is to be applied in jurisdictions where a mortgage upon real estate is a lien and nothing more (*Trimm v. Marsh*, 54 N.Y. 599, 13 Am.St.Rep. 623), nor whether, if so applied, it imports a modification of the holding in the *Thelusson* case as to the lien of a judgment. *Cf. United States v. Canal Bank*, 3 Story 79, 81, Fed.Cas.No.14,715; *United States v. Duncan*, 4 McLean 607, 630, Fed.Cas.No.15,003. A mortgage, even though a lien, is one much more specific than a judgment or a tax, much closer to ownership. *Conard v. Atlantic Insurance Co., supra*, page 443, of 1 Pet., 7 L.Ed. 189; *In re Boyd*, 4 Sawy. 262, 264, Fed.Cas.No.1,746. Into these refinements and their consequences, there is no need to enter now."

And in *United States v. Texas*, 314 U.S. 480, 484–485–486, 62 S. Ct. 350, 352, 86 L.Ed. 356:

Section 3466 mentions no exception to its requirement that "the debts due to the United States shall be first satisfied." It is nevertheless true that in several early decisions this Court read an exception into the section in the case of previously executed mortgages. *Thelusson v. Smith*, 2 Wheat. 396, 426, 4 L.Ed. 271; *Conard v. Atlantic Insurance Co.*, 1 Pet. 386, 7 L.Ed. 189; *Brent v. Bank of Washington*, 10 Pet. 596, 611, 612, 9 L.Ed. 547. This doctrine seems to have been based on the theory that mortgaged property passes to the mortgagee and is no longer a part of the estate of the mortgagor. *See Conard v. Atlantic Insurance Co., supra*, 1 Pet. at pages 441–442, 7 L.Ed. 189. The question of whether the priority of the United States under § 3466 would also be defeated by a specific and perfected lien upon property, whose title remained in the debtor, was reserved in those cases. *Ibid.; Brent v. Bank of Washington, supra*, 10 Pet. at pages 611–612, 9 L.Ed. 547. However, it was determined that a general judgment lien upon the lands of an insolvent debtor does not take precedence over claims of the United States unless execution of the judgment has proceeded far enough to take the land out of the possession of the debtor. *Thelusson v. Smith, supra*, 2 Wheat. at pages 425–426, 4 L.Ed. 271. . . .

It was at pains to make clear, however, that it intended by its decision to lend no support to the assumption that the doctrine of the mortgage cases, whatever its current vitality, would require the subordination of unsecured claims of the United States to a specific and perfected lien. 288 U.S. at pages 293–294, 53 S. Ct. at page 324, 77 L.Ed. 754.

Again the court declined to pass upon the question whether the mortgage lien accorded top priority by Texas was entitled to such priority as against the United States because that question was not before it, 314 U.S. at page 488, 62 S. Ct. 350, 86 L.Ed. 356.

In *United States v. Waddill, Holland & Flinn*, 323 U.S. 353, at pages 355–356, 65 S. Ct. 304, at page 306, 89 L.Ed. 294, involving the priority of the United States under § 3466, R.S. over the liens of a landlord and a municipality, the court, in again calling attention to the fact that although it had in the past recognized that certain exceptions could be read into § 3466, R.S. said:

The question has not been expressly decided however, as to whether the priority of the United States might be defeated by a specific and perfected lien upon the property at the time of the insolvency or voluntary assignment, and added:

It is within this suggested exception that the landlord and the municipality seek to bring themselves. Once again, however, we do not reach a decision as to whether such an exception is permissible for we do not believe that the asserted liens of the landlord and the municipality were sufficiently specific and perfected on the date of the voluntary assignment to cast any serious doubt on the priority of the claim of the United States.

Likewise in *Illinois v. Campbell*, 329 U.S. 362, 370, 67 S. Ct. 340, 345, 91 L.Ed. 348, the court said that it had never decided "whether the priority (under § 3466) is overcome by a fully perfected and specific lien," and that "again we need not decide it, for we are of the opinion that the Illinois lien was not sufficiently specific or perfected, in the purview of controlling decisions, to defeat the government's priority."

While these dicta and the decisions cited appear to assume that a mortgage lien is specific and perfected and, therefore, entitled to priority over the United States under § 3466, yet, as has been noted, in late years, the Supreme Court has had occasion to point out that it has not decided that question or whether a lien found to be specific and perfected would be accorded such priority. These reminders by the Supreme Court would seem to warrant the inference that the position of mortgages under § 3466, R.S., regardless of what it might once have been when the title theory of mortgages prevailed, *New York v. Maclay*, 288 U.S. 290, 294, 53 S. Ct. 323, 77 L.Ed. 754, has been somewhat undermined or at least is being questioned. Indeed the criteria adopted for determining whether a lien is specific and perfected are such as to put even a mortgage to the test. These require that there be definiteness in at least three particulars as of the crucial time (the appointment of the Receiver in the case at bar), namely: (1) the identity of the lienor; (2) the amount of the lien; (3) the property to which it attaches, of or upon which there must be a levy, seizure, distraint or other statutory proceeding to divest or set it apart from the property of the debtor. *In re Lincoln Chair & Novelty Co.*, 274 N.Y. 353, 9 N.E.2d 7, 9; *Spokane County v. United States*, 279 U.S. 80, 93–94, 49 S. Ct. 321, 73 L.Ed. 621; *People of State of New York v. Maclay*, 288 U.S. 290, 293, 53 S. Ct. 323, 77 L.Ed. 754; *United States v. Texas*, 314 U.S. 480, 487–488, 62 S. Ct. 350, 86 L.Ed. 356; *United States v. Waddill, Holland & Flinn*, 323 U.S. 353, 358, 65 S. Ct. 304, 89 L.Ed. 294; *Illinois v. Campbell*, 329 U.S. 362, 372–376, 67 S. Ct. 340, 91 L.Ed. 348.

A mortgage on real property in this jurisdiction is not a conveyance, Section 56–1–11, A.C.L.A.1949, but a mere security for the debt. The debtor, therefore, is neither divested of his property nor of the possession thereof. While the lien is specific as to the identity of the lienor, default and the amount due must be established in court in the case of the ordinary mortgage, as distinguished from one expressly conferring the power to re–enter, repossess and sell. It would, therefore, seem that a mortgage lien does not differ substantially from ordinary tax liens before seizure, levy or distraint or the determination of the amount due in a proceeding in court, in the absence of which specificity and perfection would appear to be lacking, in that the amount due would not be known and there would be no appropriation of specific property for the satisfaction of the claim. Moreover, the reiterated declaration of the court that it has not yet decided whether a specific and perfected lien will be accorded priority as against the United States under § 3466 may be interpreted as a warning that when the question is squarely presented, the decision may result in a subordination of mortgage liens. Notwithstanding that possibility, however, this Court feels bound by the decisions cited and the dicta referred to, and is unwilling to depart from the traditional view of the character and nature of a mortgage lien. Accordingly, the Court holds that after the bank's loan of $10,000 for the expenses of the receivership is repaid, the claim of the Bank of Wrangell is entitled to priority out of the remainder of the proceeds realized from the sale of the real property covered by its mortgages, that, under Section 16–1–113, A.C.L.A.1949, the Town of Wrangell and, under Section 26–1–3, id., Walter J. Stutte, in that order, are entitled to priority over the Bank. However, since the Bank mortgages do not cover the personal property of the debtor, and the real and personal properties were sold as one parcel, and the tax claim of the Town of Wrangell against the personal property is neither specific nor perfected, it follows that the United States is entitled to payment out of so much of the proceeds as may be properly allocable to the personal property. Accordingly, the Receiver will be instructed to have an appraisal made of the personal property for the purpose of determining what proportion of the proceeds from the sale of the entire property should be credited to the personal property.

UNITED STATES v. SAIDMAN

United States Court of Appeals, D.C. Circuit
231 F.2d 503 (1956)

WASHINGTON, Circuit Judge.

This appeal presents these questions: whether under § 3466 of the Revised Statutes, 31 U.S.C.A. § 191, the claim of the United States for unpaid taxes is entitled to prior payment (1) over a landlord's lien for rent created by Section 45–915 of the D.C.Code, 1951, and (2) over a tax claim of the District of Columbia given priority by Section 47–2609, D.C.Code, 1951.

Lobel Enterprises, Inc. operated a grocery business in the District of Columbia on premises leased from Square Deal Market, Inc. On August 17, 1953, alleging that it was unable to pay its debts in full, Lobel assigned all of its property in trust to an assignee for the benefit of creditors. The assignee sold the assets on September 14, 1953, and, after payment of the expenses of administration, there remains in the hands of the successor trustee Saidman the amount of $1,548.81 for distribution to creditors.

On the date of the assignment Lobel was indebted to its landlord in the amount of $900 on account of two monthly rental payments of $450 each due July 1, 1953, and August 1, 1953. Lobel was also indebted on the date of the assignment to the United States for unpaid Federal taxes in the amount of $934.88, plus interest, and to the District of Columbia for unpaid sales and compensating–use taxes in the amount of $753.93, plus interest. Each of these creditors urged that its claim was entitled to prior payment from the available fund. The successor trustee filed his final account which was referred to the Auditor of the District Court. The Auditor recommended that the balance of $1,548.81 available for creditors be distributed to pay the landlord's claim of $900 in full and to pay the claim of the United States to the extent of $648.81, the amount remaining. Objections were filed to the Auditor's report by both the United States and the District of Columbia. After a hearing, the District Court ordered that the landlord's claim be paid in full, and that the District of Columbia take the remainder of the fund, or $648.81. The United States has appealed, claiming that § 3466 of the Revised Statutes gives it priority over the claims of both the landlord and the District of Columbia.

I. *Priority as between the United States and the landlord.*

§ 3466 of the Revised Statutes, 31 U.S.C.A. § 191, provides that—

> Whenever any person indebted to the United States is insolvent . . . the debts due to the United States shall be first satisfied; and the priority established shall extend as well to cases in which a debtor, not having sufficient property to pay all his debts, makes a voluntary assignment thereof. . . .

Its purpose is to secure adequate public revenue to sustain the public burdens, and it is to be construed liberally to effectuate that purpose.[1] *United States v. Emory,* 1941, 314 U.S. 423, 426, 62 S. Ct. 317, 86 L.Ed. 315. The section gives an "absolute priority" to "the payment of indebtedness owing the United States, whether secured by liens or otherwise." *United States v. City of New Britain,* 1954, 347 U.S. 81, 85, 74 S. Ct. 367, 370, 98 L.Ed. 520. Its words "are broad and sweeping and, on their face, admit of no exception to the priority of claims of the United States." *United States v. Waddill Co.,* 1945, 323 U.S. 353, 355, 65 S. Ct. 304, 306, 89 L.Ed. 294.

Notwithstanding the unqualified preference given by § 3466, persons claiming that they held a perfected and specific lien on the debtor's property have frequently contested the right of the United States to have the debts due it satisfied first. The Supreme Court has, however, never decided whether the absolute priority accorded by § 3466 would be overcome by a fully perfected and specific lien upon the property, since it has always found that the lien involved was not sufficiently specific and perfected. *United States v. State of Texas,* 1941, 314 U.S. 480, 484–486, 62 S. Ct. 350, 86 L.Ed. 356, and cases there cited; *United States v. Waddill Co., supra,* 323 U.S. at page 355, 65 S. Ct. 304; *People of State of Illinois ex rel. Gordon v. Campbell,* 329 U.S. at pages 370–371, 67 S. Ct. 340; *United States v. Gilbert Associates,* 1953, 345 U.S. 361, 365, 73 S. Ct. 701, 97 L.Ed. 1071. *United States v. Waddill Co.* indicates that for this purpose a lien is not sufficiently specific when, on the date of the assignment, the lien has not been actually asserted, and the amount of the lien or the precise property to which the lien has attached is unknown or unascertainable, 323 U.S. at pages 357–358, 65 S. Ct. 340, 89 L.Ed. 294; and that a lien is not perfected when, on the date of the assignment, the debtor has not been divested of title to, or possession of, the property involved. 323 U.S. at pages 358–359, 65 S. Ct. 340. Other cases reiterate that the priority of the United States is not destroyed where the lien–holder has not taken possession of, or acquired title to, the debtor's property subject to the lien prior to the time when § 3466 becomes effective.[2] *See Spokane County v. United States,* 1929, 279 U.S. 80, 93–94, 49 S.

---

[1] § 3466 is derived from Section 5 of the Act of March 3, 1797, c. 20, 1 Stat. 515, which was enacted as an aid in the collection of taxes. *Price v. United States,* 1926, 269 U.S. 492, 500–501, 46 S. Ct. 180, 70 L.Ed. 373. Its provisions have been in force since 1797 without significant modification. *United States v. Emory,* 314 U.S. at page 428, 62 S. Ct. 317; *People of State of Illinois ex rel. Gordon v. Campbell,* 1946, 329 U.S. 362, 370, 67 S. Ct. 340, 91 L.Ed. 348. For a review of the early history of the provision, *see United States v. Fisher,* 1805, 2 Cranch 358, 6 U.S. 358, 2 L.Ed. 304.

[2] The early cases are entirely consistent with this rule. In *Conard v. Atlantic Ins. Co.,* 1928, 1 Pet. 386, 26 U.S. 386, 7 L.Ed. 189, the debtor had assigned a cargo of tea to the insurance company to secure a loan prior to the time the priority of the United States attached to the

Ct. 321, 73 L.Ed. 621; *United States v. State of Texas*, 314 U.S. at page 488, 62 S. Ct. 350, 86 L.Ed. 356; *People of State of Illinois ex rel. Gordon v. Campbell*, 329 U.S. at page 376, 67 S. Ct. 340, 89 L.Ed. 294; *United States v. Gilbert Associates, supra*. In the last case the Supreme Court said, 345 U.S. at page 366, 73 S. Ct. at page 704:

> In claims of this type "specificity" requires that the lien be attached to certain property by reducing it to possession, on the theory that the United States has no claim against property no longer in the possession of the debtor. *Thelusson v. Smith*, 2 Wheat. 396, 4 L.Ed. 271. Until such possession, it remains a general lien. There is no ground for the contention here that the Town had perfected its lien by reducing the property to possession. . . . The taxpayer had not been divested by the Town of either title or possession. The Town, therefore, had only a general, unperfected lien.

In this case the District Court concluded as a matter of law that the landlord had a "specific lien" on specific property. No conclusion was stated that the lien was "perfected." The landlord contends, however, that its lien was both specific and perfected. Our first task is then to ascertain whether this contention is correct, under the tests laid down by the Supreme Court for our guidance.[3]

The lien of the landlord arose under Section 45–915 of the D.C.Code, 1951, which gives a landlord a

> tacit lien for his rent upon such of the tenant's personal chattels, on the premises, as are subject to execution for debt, to commence with the tenancy and continue for three months after the rent is due and until the termination of any action for such rent brought within said three months.

---

debtor's property. It was held that the tea was not covered by the priority, since title to it had been transferred to the mortgagee. It was stated as dictum in *Thelusson v. Smith*, 1817, 2 Wheat. 396, 15 U.S. 396, 4 L.Ed. 271, that if, before the right of preference has accrued to the United States, the debtor has conveyed bona fide his estate to a third person, or has mortgaged it to secure a debt, or if his property has been seized under a *fieri facias*, the property cannot be made liable to the United States because divested out of the debtor. The actual decision in the *Thelusson* case was, however, that the United States had priority over a prior judgment creditor who had a lien but who had not perfected it by levying on the property itself. *See also Brent v. Bank of Washington*, 1836, 10 Pet. 596, 35 U.S. 596, 9 L.Ed. 547, decided on the ground that the debtor did not have legal or equitable title to bank stock and thus the priority of the United States did not attach to the stock. As stated in *United States v. State of Texas*, 314 U.S. at pages 484–485, 62 S. Ct. at page 352, these cases seem to have been decided on the "theory that mortgaged property passes to the mortgagee and is no longer a part of the estate of the mortgagor."

[3] There is no contention that the United States does not have the benefit of whatever rights § 3466 may give it. The conditions necessary to bring that section into play are present. Lobel was indebted to the United States, since taxes are debts. *Price v. United States*, 1926, 269 U.S. 492, 499, 46 S. Ct. 180, 70 L.Ed. 373; *State of Illinois ex rel. Gordon v. United States*, 1946, 328 U.S. 8, 9, 66 S. Ct. 841, 90 L.Ed. 1049. It voluntarily assigned its property for the benefit of creditors, alleging that it was unable to pay its debts in full. It actually was insolvent.

The lien may be enforced under Section 45–916[4] by attachment issued on affidavit; by execution on the chattels, after judgment against the tenant, wherever they are found; and by action against any purchaser of the chattels with notice of the lien.

We said in *Moses v. Labofish*, 1942, 76 U.S.App.D.C. 401, 402, 132 F.2d 16, 17, that the lien is created by the statute and exists independently of the several means of enforcement.[5] But for present purposes this is not enough. In the *Waddill* case, the Supreme Court noted that the landlord's lien there involved had been declared by the Supreme Court of Appeals of Virginia to be a fixed and specific statutory lien on all goods found on the premises, not merely an inchoate lien, and " 'that such a lien exists independent of the right of distress or attachment, which are merely remedies for enforcing it' ". 323 U.S. at page 356, 65 S. Ct. at page 306, 89 L.Ed. 294. Yet it held that this did not determine whether the lien was "sufficiently specific and perfected to raise questions as to the applicability" of the Federal priority. 323 U.S. at pages 356–357, 65 S. Ct. at page 306. Its conclusion was that the landlord's lien was unspecific and unperfected in its actual legal effect, and was therefore inferior to the claim of the United States.

While Section 45–915 of the Code creates a lien, described as tacit, for rent for three months upon such of the personal chattels on the premises as are subject to execution for debt, the section does not state that the lien shall have priority nor does it purport to place title to, or possession of, the chattels in the landlord. The landlord may acquire title to or possession of the chattels on which the lien exists by following the first or second method prescribed by Section 45–916 for enforcing the lien, but affirmative action to accomplish this is required. The statutory provisions then do not of their own force create a specific and perfected lien in the sense long understood as essential to overturn the Federal priority.

Nor did the landlord have a specific and perfected lien in actual fact. The identity of the lienor, the landlord, and the amount of the lien, or $900, were of course known on the date of the assignment. But at that time the landlord had done nothing to indicate that it would insist upon its statutory lien. It had not filed the required affidavit and attached the tenant's property, or any part thereof; it had not obtained judgment against the tenant and levied execution on its property or any part thereof.

---

[4] Section 45–916 reads as follows:

The said lien may be enforced—

First. By attachment, to be issued upon affidavit that the rent is due and unpaid; or, if it be not due, that the defendant is about to remove or sell some part of said chattels.

Second. By judgment against the tenant and execution, to be levied on said chattels, or any of them, in whosesoever hands they may be found.

Third. By action against any purchaser of said chattels, with notice of the lien, in which action the plaintiff may have judgment for the value of the chattels purchased by the defendant not exceeding the rent in arrear.

[5] In the *Moses* case, the lien would seem actually to have been specific and perfected within the tests laid down by the Supreme Court for purposes of applying Section 3466, although that section was not there involved. The landlord had obtained judgment against the tenant, and the marshal had levied on the chattels before the tenant filed his voluntary petition in bankruptcy.

Thus, although the statute makes the lien apply generally to such personal property on the premises as is subject to execution for debt,[6] the specific part of the property required to satisfy the lien had not been segregated and the debtor had not been divested of title or possession as to any part of his property. Apart from any other factors, the failure of the landlord to acquire title or take possession prior to the assignment compels the holding, under the Supreme Court cases cited, that its lien was not perfected in the sense required to defeat priority under § 3466. The landlord here had merely "a caveat of a more perfect lien to come," *People of State of New York v. Maclay*, 1933, 288 U.S. 290, 294, 53 S. Ct. 323, 324, 77 L.Ed. 754, a lien which might have been, but was not, made perfect before the determinative date.

We must conclude that the United States is entitled to have its tax claim paid in full before the claim of the landlord becomes eligible for payment.

II. *Priority as between the United States and the District of Columbia.*

The United States bases its claim to priority on the unrestricted right to first payment of its debts accorded by § 3466, already discussed, whereas the claim of the District for priority rests on Section 47–2609 of the District of Columbia Code, 1951.[7] Section 47–2609 is found in the title relating to sales taxes and is made applicable to compensating–use taxes by Section 47–2707 of the Code. It provides that where property is assigned for the benefit of creditors, these taxes for which the debtor is liable "shall be a prior and preferred claim"; and it is the duty of any United States marshal, receiver, assignee, or any other officer to "first pay to the Collector the amount of said taxes . . . before making any payment of any moneys to any judgment creditor or other claimants of whatsoever kind or nature." Personal liability for the tax is imposed if the officer violates the terms of the section.[8]

---

6 It is agreed that the whole fund available for distribution here was derived from personal property on the premises that was subject to execution for debt.

7 This section reads:

Whenever the business or property of any person subject to tax under the terms of this chapter, shall be placed in receivership or bankruptcy, or assignment is made for the benefit of creditors, or if said property is seized under distraint for property taxes, all taxes, penalties, and interest imposed by this chapter for which said person is in any way liable shall be a prior and preferred claim. Neither the United States marshal, nor a receiver, assignee, or any other officer shall sell the property of any person subject to tax under the terms of this chapter under process or order of any court without first determining from the Collector the amount of any such taxes due and payable by said person, and if there be any such taxes due, owing, or unpaid under this chapter it shall be the duty of such officer to first pay to the Collector the amount of said taxes out of the proceeds of said sale before making any payment of any moneys to any judgment creditor or other claimants of whatsoever kind or nature. Any person charged with the administration or distribution of any such property as aforesaid who shall violate the provisions of this section shall be personally liable for any taxes accrued and unpaid which are chargeable against the person otherwise liable for tax under the terms of this section.

8 This provision is comparable to Section 3467 of the Revised Statutes, as amended, 31 U.S.C.A. § 192, which states:

In *District of Columbia v. Greenbaum*, 1955, 96 U.S.App.D.C. 168, 171, 223 F.2d 633, 636, we stated in footnote 13 of the opinion that the scope of Section 47–2609[9] will be similar to that of § 3466 of the Revised Statutes in local insolvency proceedings, as distinguished from bankruptcy proceedings under the Federal Bankruptcy Act. But that statement was not a holding that the District's priority will be equivalent to that of the United States under § 3466 in contests between the two. Although the United States was an appellee in that case, it did not urge priority for its tax claim under § 3466, the Supreme Court having already decided that in proceedings under the Bankruptcy Act the taxes due the United States take the priority accorded them by Section 64, sub. a of the Bankruptcy Act, rather than having a first priority under § 3466. *See Guarantee Title & Trust Co. v. Title Guaranty & Surety Co.*, 1912, 224 U.S. 152, 32 S. Ct. 457, 56 L.Ed. 706, and *cf. State of Missouri v. Ross*, 1936, 299 U.S. 72, 57 S. Ct. 60, 81 L.Ed. 46, and *United States v. Emory*, 1941, 314 U.S. 423, 427–429, 62 S. Ct. 317, 86 L.Ed. 315. Thus, our statement in the *Greenbaum* case, at footnote 13, related to the scope, in local insolvency proceedings, of the District's first priority for sales and use taxes in relation to creditors other than the Federal Government. *A fortiori* the District's claim would be prior to that of a landlord who has not perfected his lien, for the reasons already given in connection with our discussion of § 3466 and the landlord's lien. But the question here, as to the rights of the United States and the District under statutes giving each a first priority, was not present or decided in the *Greenbaum* case.

That question must now be decided. We are faced with the dilemma of choosing between two statutes enacted by Congress, each giving a first priority in terms absolute, each applicable here, and each imposing a personal liability on the assignee if he pays any other debt of the insolvent assignor first. Obviously, neither statute can be applied as it is written without violating the other, and we must therefore find some solution from extraneous aids.

We have searched the legislative history in vain for some indication from the Congress as to whether, in enacting the District statute, it intended to create an exception from § 3466 of the Revised Statutes with respect to the District sales and use taxes. As we noted in the Greenbaum case,[10] the section follows almost verbatim the Maryland sales tax statute, Md.Ann.Code, 1951, art. 81, § 339. In fact, sales–tax officials of Maryland were invited to sit with the subcommittee and advise it in writing the bill. 95 Cong.Rec. 6087 (1949). Obviously, the Maryland statute, even though in terms absolute, could not and did not make the state taxes prior to the claims of the United States in insolvency proceedings of the types covered by § 3466.[11] But in legislating for the District of Columbia Congress is not subject

---

Every executor, administrator, or assignee, or other person, who pays, in whole or in part, any debt due by the person or estate for whom or for which he acts before he satisfies and pays the debts due to the United States from such person or estate, shall become answerable in his own person and estate to the extent of such payments for the debts so due to the United States, or for so much thereof as may remain due and unpaid.

[9] There referred to as Section 132 of the District of Columbia Revenue Act of 1949.

[10] *See* 96 U.S.App.D.C. at pages 170–171, 223 F.2d at pages 635–636.

[11] *See*, for example, *Spokane County v. United States*, 1929, 279 U.S. 80, 49 S. Ct. 321, 73 L.Ed. 621; *United States v. State of Texas*, 1941, 314 U.S. 480, 62 S. Ct. 350, 86 L.Ed.

to the same limitations as are state legislatures, *Neild v. District of Columbia*, 1940, 71 App.D.C. 306, 309–311, 110 F.2d 246, 249–251, and we can hardly impute to it without more an intent to have the District taxes occupy a priority status equivalent only to that of state taxes.

Other factors lead us to resolve the priority dispute in favor of the District. Section 47–2609 is a more recently enacted statute awarding priority to only one kind of tax claim whereas the Federal statute prescribes a general priority for all kinds of debts. The limited nature of the District's priority given by a later statute using language just as forceful as that of § 3466[12] requires the inference that Congress intended to create an exception from the broad and general Federal priority in this one respect. *Cf. Cook County National Bank v. United States*, 1882, 107 U.S. 445, 2 S. Ct. 561, 27 L.Ed. 537; *Mellon v. Michigan Trust Co.*, 1926, 271 U.S. 236, 46 S. Ct. 511, 70 L.Ed. 924; *United States v. Guaranty Trust Co.*, 1930, 280 U.S. 478, 50 S. Ct. 212, 74 L.Ed. 556. In all of the cases just cited the Supreme Court held that later acts of Congress created an exception, as to specific debts due the United States, from the general priority accorded by § 3466, even though the act did not in terms refer to § 3466 and the legislative history was apparently silent on the matter. The repugnancy between the two priority statutes here is far clearer than the inconsistency in any of the cited cases.

We conclude that Section 47–2609 as the later, more specific, and more limited enactment creates an exception to § 3466 to the extent of the District's claim for sales and use taxes, and that the District's claim for such taxes has first priority in local insolvency proceedings over the United States. We are reinforced in this conclusion by the consideration that since Congress has the obligation to provide revenues for both the District and the Federal Government, there could have been no real incentive for subordinating the District's taxes in an insolvency proceeding.

Our decision requires that the case be remanded. It remains to consider how the available fund of $1,548.81 is to be distributed on remand. The District did not appeal from the order of the District Court. Under it the District was awarded $648.81 although, had it appealed, it would have been entitled to the full amount of its claim. We will not direct the District Court to increase the amount allowed the District. On remand the District Court may either order that the $900 previously allowed to the landlord be paid to the United States, or if it can justify so doing despite the failure to appeal, allow the District its full claim and allot the balance to the United States.

Remanded for proceedings consistent with this opinion.

BASTIAN, Circuit Judge (concurring in part and dissenting in part).

I concur in so much of Judge Washington's opinion as holds the lien of the District of Columbia to be superior to that of the United States; but believe that the landlord's

---

356; *People of State of Illinois ex rel. Gordon v. Campbell*, 1946, 329 U.S. 362, 67 S. Ct. 340, 91 L.Ed. 348; *United States v. Gilbert Associates*, 1953, 345 U.S. 361, 73 S. Ct. 701, 97 L.Ed. 1071.

[12] It may, indeed, be more forceful.

statutory lien is superior to those of both the United States and the District of Columbia.

This case involves a dispute over priority of payment out of assets in the hands of an assignee for the benefit of creditors. Claims to the fund are (1) landlord's lien for rent, (2) claim of the United States for unpaid federal income withholding taxes, 26 U.S.C.A. (Internal Revenue Code of 1939) §§ 1621–1636, and Federal Insurance Contribution Act taxes (id. §§ 1400–1432), and (3) claim of the District of Columbia for unpaid gross sales and compensating–use taxes, Title 47, District of Columbia Code, 1951, §§ 2601–2619, 2701–2711.

Lobel Enterprises, Inc., a Delaware corporation having its principal place of business in the District of Columbia, made an assignment of all of its property to Albert E. Steinem, in trust for the benefit of its creditors, pursuant to Title 28, §§ 2601–2610 of the District of Columbia Code 1951. The deed of assignment was duly filed and, on the assignee's petition, bond was fixed by the District Court. After intermediate proceedings, the matter was referred to the Auditor of the District Court, to state the final account of the assignee and to make recommendations concerning fees and allowances and distribution of the balance. Later, Harry Saidman, one of the appellees herein, was appointed trustee to succeed Albert E. Steinem, who had died. There was not enough realized from the property of the assignor to satisfy in full the preferred claims of the landlord, the United States, and the District of Columbia, to say nothing of the claims of general creditors. It therefore became necessary for the court to determine the order of priority of payment of the preferred creditors. The Auditor filed his report, embracing both the first and final account of the deceased trustee and Harry Saidman, trustee, with his recommendations. Objections to the Auditor's report and motions to sustain objections were filed by the United States and by the District of Columbia.

After considering the objections, the trial court, in its order and conclusions of law confirming the Auditor's report, held that the landlord had a specific lien on the personal chattels and is entitled to have its claim for rent paid first; that the claim of the District of Columbia for unpaid sales and use taxes is entitled to priority over the tax claim of the United States and should be paid second in order; that the tax claim of the United States is third in order of payment. The United States appeals.

The District of Columbia did not appeal, but filed a brief setting forth its position and claiming that the trial court should be affirmed insofar as the court ruled that it (the District of Columbia) is entitled to payment of its claim prior to that of the United States, but asking that this court determine that the landlord is not entitled to payment prior to payment of the claim of the District of Columbia.

There is no question concerning the validity or the amounts of the three claims involved in this appeal. The amount of the landlord's lien was fixed by the statute, at the amount due on the date of the assignment, all having accrued within the three month statutory period hereinafter referred to.

With respect to the general law of liens, I believe that priority of (statutory) liens is determined by another principle of law, namely, "the first in time is the first in right." Authorities for this are numerous and we find that Chief Justice Marshall elucidated it in *Rankin v. Scott*, 1827, 12 Wheat. 177, 25 U.S. 177, at page 179, 6 L.Ed. 592:

> The principle is believed to be universal, that a prior lien gives a prior claim, which is entitled to prior satisfaction, out of the subject it binds, unless the lien be intrinsically defective, or be displaced by some act of the party holding it, which shall postpone him, in a court of law or equity, to a subsequent claimant.[1]

In 1828 the Supreme Court, recognizing the commercial use of liens as a form of security in our financial structure, stated in *Conard v. Atlantic Insurance Co.*, 1828, 1 Pet. 386, 26 U.S. 386, at page 441, 7 L.Ed. 189:

> . . . it has never yet been decided by this court, that the priority of the United States will divest a specific lien, attached to a thing, whether it be accompanied by possession or not.

From a reading of cases concerning statutory liens, we find that where the statute is concerned, Rev.Stat. § 3466 (1875), 31 U.S.C.A. § 191, unsecured demands are subordinated,[2] consensual liens are probably preserved,[3] and perfected liens remain undetermined after years of discussion.[4]

In an early leading case, *Thelusson v. Smith*, 1817, 2 Wheat. 396, 15 U.S. 396, at page 425, 4 L.Ed. 271, the Supreme Court stated:

> The United States [debts] are to be first satisfied; but then, it must be out of the debtor's estate.

The Court added:

> If, therefore, before the right of preference has accrued to the United States, the debtor has made a *bona fide* conveyance of his estate to a third person, or has mortgaged the same to secure a debt, or if his property has been seized under a *fi. fa.*, the property is divested out of the debtor, and cannot be made liable to the United States.

In *United States v. Atlantic Municipal Corp.*, 1954, 212 F.2d 709, we find that the Fifth Circuit, in interpreting § 3466 of the Revised Statutes, and relying on

---

[1] The " 'first in time is the first in right' " rule is reiterated by the Supreme Court in *United States v. City of New Britain*, 1954, 347 U.S. 81, 85, 74 S. Ct. 367, 370, 92 L.Ed 520, cited by the majority, although in that case the Court found the lien involved not sufficiently specific and perfected—different, I think from the lien involved here.

[2] *United States v. State of Texas*, 1941, 314 U.S. 480, 62 S. Ct. 350, 86 L.Ed. 356; *United States v. Knott*, 1936, 298 U.S. 544, 56 S. Ct. 902, 80 L.Ed. 1321; *People of State of New York v. Maclay*, 1933, 288 U.S. 290, 53 S. Ct. 323, 77 L.Ed. 754; *Spokane County v. United States*, 1929, 279 U.S. 80, 49 S. Ct. 321, 73 L.Ed.621.

[3] *Brent v. Bank of Washington*, 1836, 10 Pet. 596, 35 U.S. 596, 9 L.Ed. 547; *Conard v. Atlantic Insurance Co., supra*; *United States v. Hooe*, 1805, 3 Cranch 73, 7 U.S. 73, 2 L.Ed. 370.

[4] *United States v. State of Texas, supra. See* Rogge, *The Differences in the Priority of the United States in Bankruptcy and in Equity Receiverships*, 43 Harv.L. Rev. 251 (1929); Sainer, *Correlation of Priority and Lien Rights in the Collection of Federal Taxes*, 95 U.Pa.L.Rev. 739 (1947).

United States v. City of New Britain, referred to in Note 1, *supra*, stated, 212 F.2d at page 711:

> This statute applies only as against unsecured debts, that is, debts not secured by a specific and perfected lien. It has never been, we think it will never be, applied as it is sought to be applied here, to accord payment to a debt due the United States in preference to a claim secured by a lien which is prior in time and superior in law to the lien of the United States securing the debt for which preferential payment is sought.

We find no exception to this holding, for in *United States v. Security Trust & Savings Bank*, 1950, 340 U.S. 47, 71 S. Ct. 111, 95 L.Ed. 53, and in *United States v. Gilbert Associates*, 1952, 345 U.S. 361, 73 S. Ct. 701, 97 L.Ed. 1071, it is evident that the Supreme Court was considering only the priority of inchoate and general liens over that of the claim of the United States for taxes. Again, in *People of State of Illinois ex rel. Gordon v. Campbell*, 1946, 329 U.S. 362, 67 S. Ct. 340, 91 L.Ed. 348, the Supreme Court points out that it [the Court] has never decided whether the priority, Rev.Stat. § 3466, is overcome by a fully perfected and specific lien, and goes on to say that it need not be decided in that case.

In the instant case, the landlord bases his claim to priority on a local statute giving to the landlord a lien for rent on such of the tenant's personal chattels on the premises as are subject to execution for debt. The statute (now Title 45) was adopted in 1867. This act of Congress of February 22, 1867, entitled "An Act to amend the Laws of the District of Columbia in Relation to Judicial Proceedings therein", 14 Stat. 403, contains, among other radical and important changes in the then existing law, a provision, designated as Section 12 of the Act, and which was subsequently incorporated into the Revised Statutes of the United States for the District of Columbia as Sections 677 to 679, both inclusive, of that revision, whereby the power of distraint exercised by landlords at common law to seize the goods of their tenants for rent in arrear was abolished and, in place of it, it was enacted that:

> The landlord shall have a tacit lien upon such of the tenant's personal chattels, on the premises, as are subject to execution for debt, to commence with the tenancy and continue for three months after the rent is due, and until the termination of any action for such rent brought within the said three months.

And this lien *may be enforced*:

> 1st. By attachment, to be issued upon affidavit that the rent is due and unpaid; or, if not due, that the defendant is about to remove or sell some part of said chattels; or,

> 2d. By judgment against the tenant and execution to be levied on said chattels or any of them, in whosesoever hands they may be found; or,

> 3d. By action against any purchaser of said chattels, with notice of the lien, in which action the plaintiff may have judgment for the value of the chattels purchased by the defendant, not exceeding the rent, arrear, and damages.

The District of Columbia claims priority on an Act of Congress of local application in the District of Columbia, Title 47, § 2609, District of Columbia Revenue Act of 1949, 63 Stat. 117, ch. 146. The statute provides:

> Whenever the business or property of any person subject to tax under the terms of this chapter, shall be placed in receivership or bankruptcy, or assignment is made for the benefit of creditors, or if said property is seized under distraint for property taxes, all taxes, penalties, and interest imposed by this chapter for which said person is in any way liable shall be a prior and preferred claim.

The United States predicates its claim on a general statute dating back to 1797, which has been known as Revised Statutes § 3466 and is found in 31 U.S.C.A. § 191. This statute provides:

> Whenever any person indebted to the United States is insolvent, or whenever the estate of any deceased debtor, in the hands of the executors or administrators, is insufficient to pay all the debts due from the deceased, the debts due to the United States shall be first satisfied; and the priority established shall extend as well to cases in which a debtor, not having sufficient property to pay all his debts, makes a voluntary assignment thereof, or in which the estate and effects of an absconding, concealed, or absent debtor are attached by process of law, as to cases in which an act of bankruptcy is committed.

Referring to the statutes quoted above, it is to be noted that the statute creating a lien in favor of the landlord does more than accord to him a right or priority of claim for distribution of assets. It creates a perfected lien on specific personal property. We find but one exception to this rule, cf. *Fowler v. Rapley*, 1872, 15 Wall. 328, 82 U.S. 328, 21 L.Ed. 35, that being goods sold in the ordinary course of business. With the exception of this perfected lien on specific property, the landlord has no priority under the District of Columbia law. The fact remains, however, that the landlord does have a perfected lien on specific personal chattels of the tenant found on the premises. Furthermore, there is nothing required of the landlord to perfect this lien. Section 916 of Title 45 provides for enforcement of this specific lien but, in my view, is directed only to the sale or removal of the chattels by the tenant and to the purchaser of said chattels with notice of the lien. Actually the lien is perfected and attaches when the tenant moves the chattels onto the premises. It applies to all chattels on the leased premises which are subject to execution for debt. It commences with the tenancy and, as this court has said in *Moses v. Labofish*, 1942, 76 U.S.App.D.C. 401, 132 F.2d 16, at page 17:

> The lien is created by the statute and exists independently of the several means of enforcement which the statute permits.

Shortly after the adoption of the Act of 1867, the Supreme Court, in *Webb v. Sharp*, 1871, 13 Wall. 14, 80 U.S. 14, 20 L.Ed. 478, had occasion to consider the effect of that Act and whether it was superior to a chattel mortgage subsequently placed on the property to which the lien attaches. The Court held, 13 Wall. at page 16:

> The landlord's lien is an implied or tacit lien, created by law to secure the performance of another contract, and, of the two, the landlord's is the prior lien, and cannot be displaced by the other. The landlord's lien attached to the printing–press the moment it was placed upon the demised premises, before

the mortgage was given, and as long as it remained on the premises the lien continued until each instalment of rent became due and for three months afterwards, and then ceased as to that instalment. Had the tenant made an absolute and bona fide sale of the press, the case would have been a different one. The law protects bona fide purchasers without notice of the landlord's lien. Goods sold in the ordinary course of trade undoubtedly become discharged from the lien; otherwise business could not be safely carried on. This was so decided by the Supreme Court of Iowa in giving construction to a similar law of that State [citing *Grant v. Whitwell*, 9 Iowa 152, 156]. But neither the words nor the reason of the law call for a postponement of the landlord's lien to that of a subsequent mortgage or execution creditor, so long as the goods remain on the demised premises and continue to be the property of the tenant.

Several years thereafter (1878), the then Supreme Court of the District of Columbia, in General Term, had the same statute before it in the case of *Bryan v. Sanderson*, 10 D.C. 431, 3 MacArthur 431. There it was held that when a chattel trust has been executed by a tenant upon his furniture after the same has been placed upon the leased premises, and a judgment creditor's bill, to which the landlord is made a party defendant, is filed against the tenant, and the landlord, in his answer to such bill, asserts his lien for rent in arrear and asks judgment of the same out of the funds to be realized from the sale of such furniture, the landlord has precedence over the deed of trust, notwithstanding the fact that he had taken no steps prescribed by the statute for enforcing his tacit lien. The court adopted as its own opinion the report of the Special Auditor,[5] and quoted with approval his language, as follows:

"In the second place, it is doubtless true that the lien created by the statute must be enforced, if at all, in strict compliance with its provisions. But where the disposition of the property upon which the lien exists, or of the proceeds arising from its sale, has been assumed by a court of equity, does the lien need to be enforced? It will be observed that the statutory lien differs in a material respect from its common–law prototype, the right to distrain. Under the latter, unless distraint were actually made, the landlord acquired no lien; his was an inchoate right to a lien to be perfected by distress, rather than a lien in itself. But the lien of the statute exists independently of the prescribed methods of enforcing it. Indeed, commencing with the tenancy, it exists *before* those methods have been or can be resorted to—*i.e.*, before any rent has accrued. 'A statutory lien implies security upon the thing before the warrant to seize it is levied. It ties itself to the property from the time it attaches to it, and the levy and sale of the property are only the means of enforcing it.' In other words, if the lien is given by the statute, proceedings are not necessary to fix the *status* of the property. (*Morgan v. Campbell*, 22 Wall. 381 [22 L.Ed. 796]; *see, also, Grant v. Whitwell*, 9 Iowa [152] 153; *Carpenter v. Gillespie*, 10 Iowa 592; *Doane v. Garretson*, 24 Iowa [351] 355.) These Iowa decisions are upon a statute substantially the same as the statute in force in this District."

---

[5] The Special Auditor was J. J. Darlington, Esq., for many years one of the leading members of the District of Columbia bar.

See also Fowler v. Rapley, supra; The Richmond v. Cake, 1 App.D.C. 447; *Spilman v. Geiger,* 61 App.D.C. 164, 58 F.2d 890; where the court held that the landlord's lien for rent on tenant's personal chattels on the leased premises was superior to a chattel mortgage given by the tenant after the tenancy commenced but before the commencement of the period for which the rent remained unpaid.

Certainly if, as the Supreme Court held in *Thelusson v. Smith, supra,* debts of the United States are to be settled "out of the debtor's estate"—as certainly should be the case—we can see that the debtor's estate is what is left after satisfying the liens on the property because, of course, the debtor's estate is that and that only. To hold otherwise would mean that the Government's rights under § 3466 are superior even to a first mortgage. The Supreme Court has held, *see Webb v. Sharp, supra,* that this lien is superior to a first mortgage placed on the chattels after the tenancy commenced; consequently it follows, that if the Government's lien is superior to the Landlord's lien, it is also superior to a mortgage lien. Such a ruling would mean that the debts of the United States, instead of being satisfied out of the debtor's estate, *see Thelusson v. Smith, supra,* would be satisfied out of the estate of the landlord. This should not be so. I hesitate to consider the effect on the commercial life of the country if the rule were otherwise. Certainly no one would consider loaning money as a first mortgage on real or personal property if it could be displaced by the debtor's subsequent failure to pay his withholding, federal insurance contributions, or District sales and use taxes.

It follows that since the landlord has this perfected lien on specific property he takes priority over the claims of both the United States and the District of Columbia, inasmuch as the rights of both the United States and the District of Columbia are rights of priority to be paid out of the general assets.

In attempting to answer the claim of the landlord's priority, both the United States and the District of Columbia rely on the authority of *United States v. Waddill Co.,* 1945, 323 U.S. 353, 65 S. Ct. 304, 89 L.Ed. 294. In that case the Court held that the Virginia statute clearly subordinates the claims of both the landlord and the municipality to that of the United States. The Court makes it clear that in the past it recognized that certain exceptions could be read into the statute and that the question as to whether the priority of the United States might be defeated by a specific and perfected lien upon the property at the time of the insolvency or voluntary assignment has not been expressly decided. Once again that Court reaches no decision with respect to an exception.

> . . . we do not reach a decision as to whether such an exception is permissible for we do not believe that the asserted liens of the landlord and the municipality were sufficiently specific and perfected on the date of the voluntary assignment to cast any serious doubt on the priority of the claim of the United States.

Id., 323 U.S. at pages 355, 356, 65 S. Ct. at page 306.

The Court went on to point out, in the *Waddill* case, how the lien in question was not perfected and the property involved not sufficiently specific.

> Tested by its legal effect under Virginia law, the landlord's lien in this instance appeared to serve "merely as a *caveat* of a more perfect lien to come."

People of State of New York v. Maclay, supra, 288 U.S. at page 294, 53 S. Ct. at page 324, 77 L.Ed. 754. As of the date of the voluntary assignment, it was neither specific nor perfected. It gave the landlord only a general power over unspecified property rather than an actual interest in a definitive portion or portions thereof.

Specificity was clearly lacking as to the lien on June 19, 1941, the date of the assignment. On that day it was still uncertain whether the landlord would ever assert and insist upon its statutory lien. Until that was done it was impossible to determine the particular six months' rent, or a proportion thereof, upon which the lien was based. The lien did not relate to any particular six months' rent but could attach only for the rent which might be due at or after the time when the lien was asserted. *Wades v. Figgatt*, 75 Va. 575, 582. And if it were asserted at a time when the tenancy had terminated or would terminate within six months of the date to which rent had been fully paid, the lien could only cover less than six months' rent. Conceivably the amount of rent due or to become due was uncertain on the day of the assignment. The landlord may have been mistaken as to the rental rate or as to payments previously made and the tenant may have been entitled to a set–off. *See Allen v. Hart*, 18 Gratt. 722, 59 Va. 722, 737; *Hancock v. Whitehall Tobacco Warehouse Co.*, 100 Va. 443, 447, 41 S.E. 860. Moreover, while the lien legally attached to all such property as might be on the premises when the lien was asserted or within thirty days prior to distraint, the landlord could distrain goods only to the extent necessary to satisfy the rent justly believed to be due, the tenant possessing an action for damages for excessive distraint. Va.Code, § 5783; *Fishburne v. Engledove*, 91 Va. 548, 22 S.E. 354; *Gurfein v. Howell*, 142 Va. 197, 128 S.E. 644. Thus until the extent of the lien was made known by the landlord and until some steps had been taken to distrain or attach sufficient property to satisfy the lien, it was impossible to specify the goods actually and properly subject to the lien. Some of the goods on the premises may have been subject to mortgages or liens which attached before the goods were brought on the premises, in which case the landlord's lien would be inferior. Va.Code, § 5523. And if other goods were removed after the date of the voluntary assignment but more than thirty days before the distraint, or attachment, the right of distraint and attachment as to those goods would disappear. Va.Code, § 5523; *Dime Deposit & Discount Bank [of Scranton, Pa.] v. Wescott*, 113 Va. 567, 75 S.E. 179. These factors compel the conclusion that neither the rent secured by the lien nor the property subject to the lien was sufficiently specific and ascertainable on the day of the voluntary assignment to fall within the terms of the suggested exception.

Id., 323 U.S. at pages 357, 358, 65 S. Ct. at page 306.

Thus, in *Waddill*, the Supreme Court again expressly left open the question as to whether the landlord would have a prior right had he properly asserted his lien.

In the instant case, the landlord's lien under the District of Columbia statute, and as held in *Moses v. Labofish, supra*, is a perfected lien. As indicated earlier, nothing is required of the landlord to perfect his lien—the need of distraint at common law having been abolished. It [the lien] attaches the moment the tenant moves the personal chattels on to the premises. It applies to *all* chattels on the leased premises subject to execution for debt. It is exact in its terms with respect to the time and the amount due, for the lien not only commences with the tenancy but also continues for three months after the rent is due and until the termination of any action for such rent brought within the said three months. The landlord's lien is, in my opinion, both specific and perfected.

I think that the judgment of the District Court was in all respects correct, and should be affirmed.

NOTES AND QUESTIONS

(1) What standards must be satisfied before a state statutory lien is entitled to priority over a federal government claim?

(2) For descriptions of the application of the "choate lien test," *see United States v. Bond*, 279 F.2d 837 (4th Cir.), *cert. denied*, 364 U.S. 895 (1960); *Creditors Exchange Service, Inc. v. United States*, 277 F. Supp. 885 (S.D. Tex. 1967); *In re Xelco Corp.*, 28 Wash. App. 878, 626 P.2d 1013 (1981).

(3) When are mortgage liens and statutory landlord's liens entitled to priority over an unsecured claim of the federal government? Should the criteria used to determine priority of liens asserted by states and municipalities over the federal government be the same as those used to determine the priority of private liens?

(4) What standards does the court of appeals in *United States v. Saidman, supra*, use in deciding between the two competing federal statutes?

(5) *See generally* Kennedy, *The Relative Priority of the Federal Government: The Pernicious Career of the Inchoate and General Lien*, 63 Yale L.J. 905 (1954).

LAPADULA & VILLANI, INC. v. UNITED STATES

United States District Court, Southern District of New York
563 F. Supp. 782 (1983)

OPINION & ORDER

SPRIZZO, District Judge.

Plaintiff corporations, Lapadula & Villani, Inc., Lapadula & Villani Equipment Corp. and Harlem River Rigging Corp., terminated their respective business operations and liquidated their assets.[1] The proceeds of the liquidations were

---

[1] The liquidations yielded $189,428.32, $61,914.42 and $19,613.66 respectively.

insufficient to satisfy the claims of the corporations' creditors. Plaintiffs therefore deposited the proceeds of the liquidations (the proceeds of the three liquidations are hereinafter collectively referred to as the "Fund") and commenced this interpleader action seeking a distribution of the Fund on August 10, 1977. Plaintiffs also requested the imposition of a moratorium on the accrual of interest and penalties due various taxing authorities from and after August 18, 1976 on the grounds that the taxing authorities negligently and without due cause delayed authorizing the sale of plaintiffs' assets, thereby reducing the amounts realized and causing additional interest and penalties to accrue.

Six creditors claim an interest in the Fund. They include, *inter alia*, the United States, on behalf of the Internal Revenue Service ("IRS"),[2] the Federal Deposit Insurance Corporation ("FDIC"), successor in interest to the claims of the Franklin National Bank, which seeks to recover on various security interests that it holds in certain of plaintiffs' equipment and other property; and the State of New York, which seeks to recover for various unpaid state taxes.

The IRS has moved for summary judgment contending that it is entitled to an absolute priority over all other creditors pursuant to 31 U.S.C. § 191. It also has moved to dismiss that portion of plaintiffs' complaint which seeks the imposition of a moratorium. The FDIC, in response to the IRS's motion for summary judgment, argues that it is likewise entitled to a priority under section 191.

Section 191 provides that, whenever any person indebted to the United States is insolvent and commits an act of bankruptcy, the debts due the United States shall be satisfied first. The statute was enacted to insure that adequate public revenues would be available to shoulder public burdens and to discharge public debts. *United States v. Emory*, 314 U.S. 423, 426, 62 S. Ct. 317, 319, 86 L.Ed. 315 (1941).

Plaintiff corporations are indebted to the United States by virtue of their unpaid federal taxes and are insolvent in that their assets are insufficient to satisfy their debts. *See United States v. Oklahoma*, 261 U.S. 253, 260, 43 S. Ct. 295, 297, 67 L.Ed. 638 (1923); *United States v. Press Wireless, Inc.*, 187 F.2d 294, 295–96 (2d Cir. 1951). Moreover, the parties conceded at oral argument that each of the three plaintiff corporations has committed the requisite act of bankruptcy.[3] The Court, therefore, finds that the IRS is clearly entitled to the absolute priority granted by the statute.

While the FDIC asserts that it too is entitled to an absolute priority since it is a federal agency entrusted with the implementation of the National Banking Act, the Court does not agree. The Supreme Court has held that section 191 may not be invoked by an agency which is not an integral part of the governmental mechanism. *See Sloan Shipyards Corp. v. United States Shipping Board Emergency Fleet Corp.*,

---

[2] As of January 31, 1982, the claims by the IRS against the plaintiffs for unpaid taxes amounted to $208,921.32 from Lapadula & Villani, Inc., $3,547.77 from Lapadula & Villani Equipment Corp. and $24,501.02 from Harlem River Rigging Corp. The IRS also seeks statutory interest and penalties.

[3] The acts of bankruptcy committed by the plaintiffs include failure to discharge liens lodged against them by creditors.

258 U.S. 549, 570, 42 S. Ct. 386, 389, 66 L.Ed. 762 (1922). *See also SBA v. McClellan*, 364 U.S. 446, 449, 81 S. Ct. 191, 194, 5 L. Ed. 2d 200 (1960); *USDA v. Remund*, 330 U.S. 539, 542, 67 S. Ct. 891, 892, 91 L.Ed. 1082 (1947). The FDIC's profits do not inure to the benefit of the United States and its losses are not borne by the United States. Thus, the public treasury will be unaffected by the FDIC's success or failure in recovering the debts owed to it as successor in interest to the claims of the Franklin National Bank. It follows that the FDIC is not an integral part of the governmental mechanism but is rather a separate legal entity serving essentially a proprietary rather than a sovereign function. Since the purpose of the statute would not be served by permitting the FDIC to invoke the provisions of § 191, the Court concludes that the FDIC is not entitled to an absolute priority.[4]

There remains for consideration the IRS's motion to dismiss that portion of plaintiffs' complaint which seeks the imposition of a moratorium on the accrual of interest and penalties after August 18, 1976. Plaintiffs' request for a moratorium may be viewed either as a request for a declaration with respect to federal taxes or as a demand that the collection of said taxes be restrained. In either case, the Court lacks jurisdiction to grant such relief.

The Declaratory Judgment Act, 28 U.S.C. § 2201, expressly provides that a Court may not declare the rights and other legal relations of interested parties where federal taxes are in issue,[5] *see Bob Jones University v. Simon*, 416 U.S. 725, 732–33 n. 7, 94 S. Ct. 2038, 2044 n. 7, 40 L. Ed. 2d 496 (1974); *Falik v. United States*, 343 F.2d 38, 42 (2d Cir.1965). Moreover, the Anti–Injunction Act, 26 U.S.C. § 7421, expressly prohibits suits to restrain the assessment or collection of taxes. *See Commissioner v. Shapiro*, 424 U.S. 614, 96 S. Ct. 1062, 47 L. Ed. 2d 278 (1976); *Enochs v. Williams Packing & Navigation Co.*, 370 U.S. 1, 7, 82 S. Ct. 1125, 1129, 8 L. Ed. 2d 292 (1962); *Laino v. United States*, 633 F.2d 626, 629 (2d Cir.1980). Finally, the United States has not consented to waive its sovereign immunity with respect to plaintiffs' claim for a moratorium.[6] Accordingly, the IRS's motion to dismiss this claim is granted.

Since the IRS is entitled to a priority pursuant to 31 U.S.C. § 191, and since its tax claims against Lapadula & Villani, Inc. and Harlem River Rigging Corp. exceed the proceeds of their respective liquidations, the IRS is entitled to their allocable shares of the Fund. With regard to Lapadula & Villani Equipment Corp., the IRS is entitled to $3,547.77 in back taxes, plus statutory interest and penalties accrued

---

[4] The FDIC relies upon *In re Big 'D'iscount Stores, Ltd.*, 2 B.C.D. 1073 (Bkrt-cy.Ct.Col.Div.S.C.1976), which held that the FDIC is an agency of the United States entitled to a section 191 priority. To the extent that the case supports the FDIC's position, this Court declines to follow it.

[5] The one exception to this proscription is cases brought under § 7428 of the Internal Revenue Code of 1954. This is not a case commenced pursuant to that statute.

[6] While the United States has waived its sovereign immunity with respect to interpleader suits or suits in the nature of interpleader, 28 U.S.C. § 2410(a)(5), plaintiffs' claim for a moratorium is neither an action in interpleader, nor an action in the nature of interpleader. The Second Circuit has squarely held that § 2410 cannot be used by taxpayers to circumvent the express prohibitions in IRC § 7421 and 28 U.S.C. § 2201. *Laino v. United States*, 633 F.2d at 633 n. 8; *Falik v. United States*, 343 F.2d 38, 40 (2d Cir. 1965).

to August 10, 1977.[7] Of the approximately $58,000 remaining in Lapadula & Villani Equipment Corp.'s allocable share of the Fund, the Court observes that the FDIC and New York State have agreed that the New York State Tax Commissioner shall be entitled to $24,400 prior to satisfaction of the FDIC's debt. [FDIC's] Memorandum of Law in Reply to New York State Tax Commission's Affidavit and Alex Spizz's Affirmation in Support of Attorneys' Fees at 3.

All parties are directed to advise the Court by June 15, 1983 whether there is any dispute regarding the distribution of the remaining funds attributable to Lapadula & Villani Equipment Corp.

SO ORDERED.

NOTES AND QUESTIONS

(1) Despite the broad language of former § 3466, which, like § 3713, extended a priority to all debts of the federal government, the claims of the FDIC were not accorded a priority in *Lapadula & Villani, Inc. v. United States, supra.* Why did the court restrict the application of the statute? Does the restriction make sense? *See* and *compare In re Big 'D' iscount Stores, Ltd.*, 2 B.C.D. 1073 (Bankr. D.S.C. 1976) ("[I]t is held, as a matter of law, that FDIC is an agency of the United States and its claim is entitled to the priority granted the United States under § 64a(5) of the [old] Bankruptcy Act and [former] 31 U.S.C. § 191 in the distribution of the bankruptcy estate.").

(2) Under the federal priority statute, interest on a claim of the federal government ceases to accrue at the beginning of the proceedings. *See United States v. Sullivan,* 254 F. Supp. 254 (D.R.I. 1966). What is the rationale for limiting the accrual of interest when the debtor is insolvent? Should post–bankruptcy interest on a federal government claim be accorded priority if an estate becomes solvent during the administration of the estate? *See* the result under §§ 501, 726(a)(5) and 1129(a)(7)(A)(ii) of the Bankruptcy Code, 11 U.S.C. §§ 501, 726(a)(5) and 1129(a)(7)(A)(ii).

§ 5.02   The Federal Tax Lien

Section 6321 of the Internal Revenue Code grants the federal government a far–reaching lien for taxes. The lien reaches "all property or rights to property, whether real or personal, belonging to "any person who fails to pay "any tax . . . after demand," and, under 26 U.S.C. § 6322, arises "at the time the assessment is made. . . ." The lien also covers property exempt from creditors' claims under state

---

[7] The Court observes that in insolvency proceedings governed by § 191, interest payable from the estate of the insolvent ceases to accrue on the date the petition is filed. *United States v. Sullivan*, 254 F.Supp. 254, 256 (D.R.I. 1966).

law and the taxpayer's after–acquired property. *Glass City Bank v. United States*, 326 U.S. 265, 267 (1945). Demand for payment must be made "as soon as practicable, and within 60 days after the making of an assessment" pursuant to § 6203. Internal Revenue Code § 6303, 26 U.S.C. § 6303.

[A] Assessment

Creation of the lien turns on the making of an assessment under § 6201 of the Internal Revenue Code by the Commissioner of Internal Revenue. 26 U.S.C. § 6321. When a taxpayer acknowledges liability, assessment occurs almost immediately after the tax return is received, and customarily amounts to no more than a notation of the liability on a list in the district director's office. If the taxpayer understates the liability and a deficiency is discovered through audit procedures, assessment is prohibited until 90 days (or 150 days if the notice is addressed to a taxpayer outside of the United States) after the taxpayer is mailed a formal notice of deficiency. *See* § 6213(a) of the Internal Revenue Code, 26 U.S.C. § 6213(a). If the taxpayer files a petition for redetermination of the deficiency with the Tax Court, assessment is barred until the court reaches a final decision. A "jeopardy assessment," however, can be made before completion of an audit and issuance of a notice if the Internal Revenue Service finds that the assessment or collection of a deficiency will be jeopardized by delay or if a receivership or certain cases under the Bankruptcy Code have been commenced. *See* Internal Revenue Code §§ 6861(a) and 6871(a), 26 U.S.C. §§ 6861(a) and 6871(a).

Once the lien arises after assessment and the taxpayer does not satisfy the government's claim, the lien continues until the tax liability is satisfied or becomes unenforceable under the applicable statute of limitations. The government may toll the statute of limitations by refiling its notice in the original office and in the taxpayer's current jurisdiction. *See* Internal Revenue Code § 6323(g), 26 U.S.C. § 6323(g).

[B] Filing of Lien

The tax lien does not have to be filed to be valid against the taxpayer. Section 6323(f), however, provides filing requirements (place for filing, form and content, indexing) that give the federal tax lien priority over claims of other creditors. An unfiled tax lien will not be valid against purchasers, holders of security interests, mechanic's lienors and judgment lien creditors until the government complies with § 6323(f) (mechanics of filing). Internal Revenue Code § 6323(a), 26 U.S.C. § 6323(a).

[C] Priorities

Section 6323(b) contains a so–called "super–priority" to protect the priority of certain subsequently arising interests (*e.g.*, purchasers of certain types of personal property, certain attorney's lienors, certain insurers) even though the Internal Revenue Service has previously filed notice of its tax lien. Local real estate tax liens, if they prime preexisting liens, will also prime a federal tax lien that is prior in time. *Compare* the statute (Internal Revenue Code § 6323(b)(6)) *with* the results in the two *Buffalo Savings Bank* cases, *infra*, which were decided before amendment of the statute. In some instances, however, protection is limited to persons who do not have actual notice or knowledge of the lien (*e.g.*, purchasers of securities, motor vehicles, personal property). The Internal Revenue Code also protects the priority of claims held by participants in certain commercial transactions against previously filed tax liens in which a file search would be a significant burden, . Internal Revenue Code § 6323(c), 26 U.S.C. § 6323(c).

Federal tax liens are also subordinate to certain security interests that come into existence within 45 days of the federal tax lien filing by reason of disbursements made within that time period if: (1) the security interest is in property in existence at the time of the filing; and (2) the security interest was perfected against a judgment creditor at the time of the filing. Internal Revenue Code § 6323(d), 26 U.S.C. § 6323(d). What types of security interests are covered here? *See Texas Oil & Gas Corp. v. United States*, 466 F.2d 1040 (5th Cir. 1972), *cert. denied*, 410 U.S. 929 (1973) (accounts receivable financing). Does this pose an unreasonable burden on secured lenders? Must they search the records every forty–five days to be sure no tax lien was filed? *See* U.C.C. § 9–301(4).

Liens existing *prior* in time to the federal tax lien may prime that lien. They must satisfy either requirements of the judicially created "choate" lien doctrine set out in *United States v. Vermont*, 377 U.S. 351 (1964), set out *infra*, or the requirements of 26 U.S.C. § 6323(a), which protects "purchasers, holders of security interests, mechanic's lienors, and judgment lien creditors" against an unfiled federal tax lien.

When a lien or security interest has priority over a federal tax lien, § 6323(e) of the Internal Revenue Code sets forth the extent of the priority, subject to the extent that the item has priority under local law.

[D]   Release of Lien

A taxpayer may apply to obtain release of a lien if the taxpayer (1) has paid the entire assessment or the assessment has become legally unenforceable; or (2) is able to bond the assessment acceptably. *See* Internal Revenue Code § 6325, 26 U.S.C. § 6325.

[E]   Levy

Section 6331(a) of the Internal Revenue Code permits the IRS to levy on (*i.e.*, seize) the taxpayer's property ten days after notice and demand. If the collection is in jeopardy, the IRS may levy immediately.

The following materials explore the rights given the federal government by the federal tax lien law, and also show the kind of priority problems encountered with these liens.

REFERENCES

Plumb, Federal Tax Liens (3d rev. ed. 1981) (ALI–ABA).

Seligson, Levin & Smith, Creditors' Rights, 1966 Ann. Survey Am. L. 297, 324.

Internal Revenue Code
SUBCHAPTER C: LIEN FOR TAXES

SEC. 6321. LIEN FOR TAXES.

If any person liable to pay any tax neglects or refuses to pay the same after demand, the amount (including any interest, additional amount, addition to tax, or assessable penalty, together with any costs that may accrue in addition thereto) shall be a lien in favor of the United States upon all property and rights to property, whether real or personal, belonging to such person.

SEC. 6322. PERIOD OF LIEN.

Unless another date is specifically fixed by law, the lien imposed by section 6321 shall arise at the time the assessment is made and shall continue until the liability for the amount so assessed (or a judgment against the taxpayer arising out of such liability) is satisfied or becomes unenforceable by reason of lapse of time.

SEC. 6323. VALIDITY AND PRIORITY AGAINST CERTAIN PERSONS.

(a) PURCHASERS, HOLDERS OF SECURITY INTERESTS, MECHANIC'S LIENORS, AND JUDGEMENT LIEN CREDITORS.—The lien imposed by section 6321 shall not be valid as against any purchaser, holder of a security interest, mechanic's lienor, or judgment lien creditor until notice thereof which meets the requirements of subsection (f) has been filed by the Secretary.

(b) PROTECTION FOR CERTAIN INTERESTS EVEN THOUGH NOTICE FILED.—Even though notice of a lien imposed by section 6321 has been filed, such lien shall not be valid—

    (1) SECURITIES.—With respect to a security (as defined in subsection (h)(4))—

        (A)   as against a purchaser of such security who at the time of purchase did not have actual notice or knowledge of the existence of such lien; and

        (B)   as against a holder of a security interest in such security who, at the time such interest came into existence, did not have actual notice or knowledge of the existence of such lien.

(2) MOTOR VEHICLES.—With respect to a motor vehicle (as defined in subsection (h)(3)), as against a purchaser of such motor vehicle, if—

    (A) at the time of the purchase such purchaser did not have actual notice or knowledge of the existence of such lien, and

    (B) before the purchaser obtains such notice or knowledge, he has acquired possession of such motor vehicle and has not thereafter relinquished possession of such motor vehicle to the seller or his agent.

(3) PERSONAL PROPERTY PURCHASED AT RETAIL.—With respect to tangible personal property purchased at retail, as against a purchaser in the ordinary course of the seller's trade or business, unless at the time of such purchase such purchaser intends such purchase to (or knows such purchase will) hinder, evade, or defeat the collection of any tax under this title.

(4) PERSONAL PROPERTY PURCHASED IN CASUAL SALE.—With respect to household goods, personal effects, or other tangible personal property described in section 6334(a) purchased (not for resale) in a casual sale for less than $250, as against the purchaser, but only if such purchaser does not have actual notice or knowledge (A) of the existence of such lien, or (B) that this sale is one of a series of sales.

(5) PERSONAL PROPERTY SUBJECT TO POSSESSORY LIEN.—With respect to tangible personal property subject to a lien under local law securing the reasonable price of the repair or improvement of such property, as against a holder of such a lien, if such holder is, and has been, continuously in possession of such property from the time such lien arose.

(6) REAL PROPERTY TAX AND SPECIAL ASSESSMENT LIENS.—With respect to real property, as against a holder of a lien upon such property, if such lien is entitled under local law to priority over security interests in such property which are prior in time, and such lien secures payment of—

    (A) a tax of general application levied by any taxing authority based upon the value of such property;

    (B) a special assessment imposed directly upon such property by any taxing authority, if such assessment is imposed for the purpose of defraying the cost of any public improvement; or

    (C) charges for utilities or public services furnished to such property by the United States, a State or political subdivision thereof, or an instrumentality of any one or more of the foregoing.

(7) RESIDENTIAL PROPERTY SUBJECT TO A MECHANIC'S LIEN FOR CERTAIN REPAIRS AND IMPROVEMENTS.—With respect to real property subject to a lien for repair or improvement of a personal residence (containing not more than four dwelling units) occupied by the owner of such residence, as against a mechanic's lienor, but only if the contract price on the contract with the owner is not more than $1,000.

(8) ATTORNEYS' LIENS.—With respect to a judgment or other amount in settlement of a claim or a cause of action, as against an attorney who, under local law, holds a lien upon or a contract enforceable against such judgment or amount, to the extent of his reasonable compensation for obtaining such judgment or procuring such settlement, except that this paragraph shall not apply to any judgment or amount in settlement of a claim or of a cause of action against the United States to the extent that the United States offsets such judgments or amount against any liability of the taxpayer to the United States.

(9) CERTAIN INSURANCE CONTRACTS.—With respect to a life insurance, endowment, or annuity contract, as against the organization which is the insurer under such contract, at any time—

    (A)   before such organization had actual notice or knowledge of the existence of such lien;

    (B)   after such organization had such notice or knowledge, with respect to advances required to be made automatically to maintain such contract in force under an agreement entered into before such organization had such notice or knowledge; or

    (C)   after satisfaction of a levy pursuant to section 6332(b), unless and until the Secretary delivers to such organization a notice, executed after the date of such satisfaction, of the existence of such lien.

(10) PASSBOOK LOANS.—With respect to a savings deposit, share, or other account, evidenced by a passbook, with an institution described in section 581 or 501 to the extent of any loan made by such institution without actual notice or knowledge of the existence of such lien, as against such institution if such loan is secured by such account and if such institution has been continuously in possession of such passbook from the time the loan is made.

(c) PROTECTION FOR CERTAIN COMMERCIAL TRANSACTIONS, FINANCING AGREEMENTS, ETC.—

(1) IN GENERAL.—To the extent provided in this subsection, even though notice of a lien imposed by section 6321 has been filed, such lien shall not be valid with respect to a security interest which came into existence after tax lien filing but which—

    (A)   is in qualified property covered by the terms of a written agreement entered into before tax lien filing and constituting—

    (i)   a commercial transactions financing agreement,

    (ii)   a real property construction or improvement financing agreement, or

    (iii)   an obligatory disbursement agreement, and

    (B)   is protected under local law against a judgment lien arising, as of the time of tax lien filing, out of an unsecured obligation.

(2) COMMERCIAL TRANSACTIONS FINANCING AGREEMENT.—For purposes of this subsection—

(A) DEFINITION.—The term "commercial transactions financing agreement" means an agreement (entered into by a person in the course of his trade or business)—

(i) to make loans to the taxpayer to be secured by commercial financing security acquired by the taxpayer in the ordinary course of his trade or business, or

(ii) to purchase commercial financing security (other than inventory) acquired by the taxpayer in the ordinary course of his trade or business;

but such an agreement shall be treated as coming within the term only to the extent that such loan or purchase is made before the 46th day after the date of tax lien filing or (if earlier) before the lender or purchaser had actual notice or knowledge of such tax lien filing.

(B) LIMITATION ON QUALIFIED PROPERTY.—The term "qualified property", when used with respect to a commercial transactions financing agreement, includes only commercial financing security acquired by the taxpayer before the 46th day after the date of tax lien filing.

(C) COMMERCIAL FINANCING SECURITY DEFINED.—The term "commercial financing security" means (i) paper of a kind ordinarily arising in commercial transactions, (ii) accounts receivable, (iii) mortgages on real property, and (iv) inventory.

(D) PURCHASER TREATED AS ACQUIRING SECURITY INTEREST.—A person who satisfies subparagraph (A) by reason of clause (ii) thereof shall be treated as having acquired a security interest in commercial financing security.

(3) REAL PROPERTY CONSTRUCTION OR IMPROVEMENT FINANCING AGREEMENT.—For purposes of this subsection—

(A) DEFINITION.—The term "real property construction or improvement financing agreement" means an agreement to make cash disbursements to finance—

(i) the construction or improvement of real property,

(ii) a contract to construct or improve real property, or

(iii) the raising or harvesting of a farm crop or the raising of livestock or other animals.

For purposes of clause (iii), the furnishing of goods and services shall be treated as the disbursement of cash.

(B) LIMITATION ON QUALIFIED PROPERTY.—The term "qualified property", when used with respect to a real property construction or improvement financing agreement, includes only—

(i) in the case of subparagraph (A)(i), the real property with respect to which the construction or improvement has been or is to be made,

(ii)   in the case of subparagraph (A)(ii), the proceeds of the contract described therein, and

(iii)   in the case of subparagraph (A)(iii), property subject to the lien imposed by section 6321 at the time of tax lien filing and the crop or the livestock or other animals referred to in subparagraph (A)(iii).

(4) OBLIGATORY DISBURSEMENT AGREEMENT.—For purposes of this subsection—

    (A)   DEFINITION.—The term "obligatory disbursement agreement" means an agreement (entered into by a person in the course of his trade or business) to make disbursements, but such an agreement shall be treated as coming within the term only to the extent of disbursements which are required to be made by reason of the intervention of the rights of a person other than the taxpayer.

    (B)   LIMITATION ON QUALIFIED PROPERTY.—That term "qualified property", when used with respect to an obligatory disbursement agreement, means property subject to the lien imposed by section 6321 at the time of tax lien filing and (to the extent that the acquisition is directly traceable to the disbursements referred to in subparagraph (A)) property acquired by the taxpayer after tax lien filing.

    (C)   SPECIAL RULES FOR SURETY AGREEMENTS.—Where the obligatory disbursement agreement is an agreement ensuring the performance of a contract between the taxpayer and another person—

(i)   the term "qualified property" shall be treated as also including the proceeds of the contract the performance of which was ensured, and

(ii)   if the contract the performance of which was ensured was a contract to construct or improve real property, to produce goods, or to furnish services, the term "qualified property" shall be treated as also including any tangible personal property used by the taxpayer in the performance of such ensured contract.

(d) 45–DAY PERIOD FOR MAKING DISBURSEMENTS.—Even though notice of a lien imposed by section 6321 has been filed, such lien shall not be valid with respect to a security interest which came into existence after tax lien filing by reason of disbursements made before the 46th day after the date of tax lien filing, or (if earlier) before the person making such disbursements had actual notice or knowledge of tax lien filing, but only if such security interest—

(1) is in property (A) subject, at the time of tax lien filing, to the lien imposed by section 6321, and (B) covered by the terms of a written agreement entered into before tax lien filing, and

(2) is protected under local law against a judgment lien arising, as of the time of tax lien filing, out of an unsecured obligation.

(e) PRIORITY OF INTEREST AND EXPENSES.—If the lien imposed by section 6321 is not valid as against a lien or security interest, the priority of such lien or security interest shall extend to—

(1) any interest or carrying charges upon the obligation secured,

(2) the reasonable charges and expenses of an indenture trustee or agent holding the security interest for the benefit of the holder of the security interest,

(3) the reasonable expenses, including reasonable compensation for attorneys, actually incurred in collecting or enforcing the obligation secured,

(4) the reasonable costs of insuring, preserving, or repairing the property to which the lien or security interest relates,

(5) the reasonable costs of insuring payment of the obligation secured, and

(6) amounts paid to satisfy any lien on the property to which the lien or security interest relates, but only if the lien so satisfied is entitled to priority over the lien imposed by section 6321,

to the extent, that, under local law, any such item has the same priority as the lien or security interest to which it relates.

(f) PLACE FOR FILING NOTICE: FORM.—

(1) PLACE FOR FILING.—The notice referred to in subsection (a) shall be filed—

(A)   UNDER STATE LAWS.—

(i)   REAL PROPERTY.—In the case of real property, in one office within the State (or the county, or other governmental subdivision), as designated by the laws of such State, in which the property subject to the lien is situated; and

(ii)   PERSONAL PROPERTY.—In the case of personal property, whether tangible or intangible, in one office within the State (or the county, or other governmental subdivision), as designated by the laws of such State, in which the property subject to the lien is situated; or

(B)   WITH CLERK OF DISTRICT COURT.—In the office of the clerk of the United States district court for the judicial district in which the property subject to the lien is situated, whenever the State has not by law designated one office which meets the requirements of subparagraph (A); or

(C)   WITH RECORDER OF DEEDS OF THE DISTRICT OF COLUMBIA.—In the office of the Recorder of Deeds of the District of Columbia, if the property subject to the lien is situated in the District of Columbia.

(2) SITUS OF PROPERTY SUBJECT TO LIEN.—For purposes of paragraphs (1) and (4), property shall be deemed to be situated—

(A)   REAL PROPERTY.—In the case of real property, at its physical location; or

(B) PERSONAL PROPERTY.—In the case of personal property, whether tangible or intangible, at the residence of the taxpayer at the time the notice of lien is filed.

For purposes of paragraph (2)(B), the residence of a corporation or partnership shall be deemed to be the place at which the principal executive office of the business is located, and the residence of a taxpayer whose residence is without the United States shall be deemed to be in the District of Columbia.

(3) FORM.—The form and content of the notice referred to in subsection (a) shall be prescribed by the Secretary. Such notice shall be valid notwithstanding any other provision of law regarding the form or content of a notice of lien.

(4) INDEXING REQUIRED WITH RESPECT TO CERTAIN REAL PROPERTY.—In the case of real property, if—

(A) under the laws of the State in which the real property is located, a deed is not valid as against a purchaser of the property who (at the time of purchase) does not have actual notice or knowledge of the existence of such deed unless the fact of filing of such deed has been entered and recorded in a public index at the place of filing in such a manner that a reasonable inspection of the index will reveal the existence of the deed, and

(B) there is maintained (at the applicable office under paragraph (1)) an adequate system for the public indexing of Federal Tax liens,

then, the notice of lien referred to in subsection (a) shall not be treated as meeting the filing requirements under paragraph (1) unless the fact of filing is entered and recorded in the index referred to in subparagraph (B) in such a manner that a reasonable inspection of the index will reveal the existence of the lien.

(g) REFILING OF NOTICE.—For purposes of this section—

(1) GENERAL RULE.—Unless notice of lien is refiled in the manner prescribed in paragraph (2) during the required refiling period, such notice of lien shall be treated as filed on the date on which it is filed (in accordance with subsection (f)) after the expiration of such refiling period.

(2) PLACE FOR FILING.—A notice of lien refiled during the required refiling period shall be effective only—

(A) if—

(i) such notice of lien is refiled in the office in which the prior notice of lien was filed, and

(ii) in the case of real property, the fact of refiling is entered and recorded in an index to the extent required by subsection (f)(4); and

(B) in any case in which, 90 days or more prior to the date of a refiling of notice of lien under subparagraph (A), the Secretary received written information (in the manner prescribed in regulations issued by the Secretary) concerning a change in the taxpayer's residence, if a notice of such lien is also filed in accordance with subsection (f) in the State in which such residence is located.

(3) REQUIRED REFILING PERIOD.—In the case of any notice of lien, the term "required refiling period" means—

(A) the one–year period ending 30 days after the expiration of 6 years after the date of the assessment of the tax, and

(B) the one–year period ending with the expiration of 6 years after the close of the preceding required refiling period for such notice of lien.

(4) TRANSITIONAL RULE.—Notwithstanding paragraph (3), if the assessment of the tax was made before January 1, 1962, the first required refiling period shall be the calendar year 1967.

(h) DEFINITIONS.—For purposes of this section and section 6324—

(1) SECURITY INTEREST.—The term "security interest" means any interest in property acquired by contract for the purpose of securing payment or performance of an obligation or indemnifying against loss or liability. A security interest exists at any time (A) if, at such time the property is in existence and the interest has become protected under local law against a subsequent judgment lien arising out of an unsecured obligation, and (B) to the extent that, at such time, the holder has parted with money or money's worth.

(2) MECHANIC'S LIENOR.—The term "mechanic's lienor" means any person who under local law has a lien on real property (or on the proceeds of a contract relating to real property) for services, labor, or materials furnished in connection with the construction or improvement of such property. For purposes of the preceding sentence, a person has a lien on the earliest date such lien becomes valid under local law against subsequent purchasers without actual notice, but not before he begins to furnish the services, labor, or materials.

(3) MOTOR VEHICLE.—The term "motor vehicle" means a self–propelled vehicle which is registered for highway use under the laws of any State or foreign country.

(4) SECURITY.—The term "security" means any bond, debenture, note, or certificate or other evidence of indebtedness, issued by a corporation or a government or political subdivision thereof, with interest coupons or in registered form, share of stock, voting trust certificate, or any certificate of interest or participation in, certificate of deposit or receipt for, temporary or interim certificate for, or warrant or right to subscribe to or purchase, any of the foregoing; negotiable instrument; or money.

(5) TAX LIEN FILING.—The term "tax lien filing" means the filing of notice (referred to in subsection (a)) of the lien imposed by section 6321.

(6) PURCHASER.—The term "purchaser" means a person who, for adequate and full consideration in money or money's worth, acquires an interest (other than a lien or security interest) in property which is valid under local law against

subsequent purchasers without actual notice. In applying the preceding sentence for purposes of subsection (a) of this section, and for purposes of section 6324—

    (A) a lease of property,

    (B) a written executory contract to purchase or lease property,

    (C) an option to purchase or lease property or any interest therein, or

    (D) an option to renew or extend a lease of property,

which is not a lien or security interest shall be treated as a interest in property.

(i) SPECIAL RULES.—

    (1) ACTUAL NOTICE OR KNOWLEDGE.—For purposes of this subchapter, an organization shall be deemed for purposes of a particular transaction to have actual notice or knowledge of any fact from the time such fact is brought to the attention of the individual conducting such transaction, and in any event from the time such fact would have been brought to such individual's attention if the organization had exercised due diligence. An organization exercises due diligence if it maintains reasonable routines for communicating significant information to the person conducting the transaction and there is reasonable compliance with the routines. Due diligence does not require an individual acting for the organization to communicate information unless such communication is part of his regular duties or unless he has reason to know of the transaction and that the transaction would be materially affected by the information.

    (2) SUBROGATION.—Where, under local law, one person is subrogated to the rights of another with respect to a lien or interest, such person shall be subrogated to such rights for purposes of any lien imposed by section 6321 or 6324.

[F]　Property to Which the Federal Tax Lien Attaches

AQUILINO v. UNITED STATES

United States Supreme Court
363 U.S. 509, 80 S. Ct. 1277, 4 L. Ed. 2d. 1365 (1960)

Mr. Chief Justice WARREN delivered the opinion of the Court.

In this case we are asked to determine which of two competing claimants—the Federal Government by virtue of its tax lien, or certain petitioning subcontractors by virtue of their rights under Section 36–a of the New York Lien Law—is entitled to a sum of money owed under a general construction contract which was performed by the taxpayer.

The taxpayer, Fleetwood Paving Corporation, is a general contractor, which in July or August 1952, agreed to remodel a restaurant belonging to one Ada Bottone, herein referred to as the owner. The petitioners in August and September of that year entered into a subcontract with the taxpayer to supply labor and materials for the remodeling job. Shortly thereafter, the petitioners performed their obligations under the subcontract, but were not fully compensated by the contractor–taxpayer. Therefore, on November 3, 1952, and on November 10, 1952, they filed notices of their mechanic's liens on the owner's realty in the office of the Clerk of Westchester County. In June 1953, they instituted actions in the New York Supreme Court to foreclose those liens.

By order of court, the owner was permitted to deposit with the Clerk of the court the $2,200 which she still owed under the original construction contract, and she was thereafter dismissed as a defendant in the action. The Government, having previously levied upon the owner's alleged indebtedness to the taxpayer, was permitted by the court to enter the case as a party defendant.

The Government asserted precedence over the claims of petitioners because of the following facts: The Director of Internal Revenue in December 1951 and March 1952 received assessment lists containing assessments against the taxpayer for unpaid federal withholding and social security taxes. On October 31, 1952, the Director filed a notice of federal tax liens in the office of the Clerk of the City of Mount Vernon, New York, which is the city wherein the taxpayer maintained its principal place of business. The Government claimed priority for its tax lien under Sections 3670 and 3671 of the Internal Revenue Code of 1939.[1] The petitioners contended that since the contractor–taxpayer owed them more than $2,200 for labor and materials supplied to the job, under the New York Lien Law, Section 36–a,[2]

---

[1] Section 3670:

> If any person liable to pay any tax neglects or refuses to pay the same after demand, the amount (including any interest, penalty, additional amount, or addition to such tax, together with any costs that may accrue in addition thereto) shall be a lien in favor of the United States upon all property and rights to property, whether real or personal, belonging to such person.

Section 3671:

> Unless another date is specifically fixed by law, the lien shall arise at the time the assessment list was received by the collector and shall continue until the liability for such amount is satisfied or becomes unenforceable by reason of lapse of time.

These provisions also appear in the 1954 Code. Int. Rev. Code of 1954, §§ 6321, 6322.

[2] McKinney's N. Y. Laws, Lien Law (1958 Supp.), § 36–a, provides as follows:

> The funds received by a contractor from an owner for the improvement of real property are hereby declared to constitute trust funds in the hands of such contractor to be applied first to the payment of claims of subcontractors, architects, engineers, surveyors, laborers and materialmen arising out of the improvement, and to the payment of premiums on surety bond or bonds filed and premiums on insurance accruing during the making of the improvement and any contractor and any officer, director or agent of any contractor who applies or consents to the application of such funds for any other purpose and fails to pay the claims hereinbefore mentioned is guilty of larceny and punishable as provided in section thirteen hundred and two of the penal law. Such trust

he had no property interest in the $2,200 which the owner still owed under the original remodeling contract.

The New York Supreme Court, Special Term, 140 N. Y. S. 2d 355, granted petitioner's motion for summary judgment. The ground for the decision was that the Government's tax lien was ineffective since it had not been filed in the office designated by New York law for the filing of liens against realty. On appeal, the Appellate Division affirmed, but on the ground that there was no debt due from the owner to the taxpayer to which the Government's lien could attach, 2 App. Div. 2d 747, 153 N. Y. S. 2d 268. The court reasoned that the fund deposited by the owner was a substitute for her realty to which the mechanic's liens had attached; and that since the Government had no lien on the owner's property, it could have no lien on the fund substituted for that property. On appeal, the New York Court of Appeals held that the tax lien had taken effect prior to the petitioners' claims. It therefore reversed the lower New York courts, and ruled that the motion of the United States for summary judgment, rather than that of petitioners, should have been granted by the Supreme Court, Special Term. 3 N. Y. 2d 511, 146 N. E. 2d 774. We granted certiorari, 359 U.S. 904.

The threshold question in this case, as in all cases where the Federal Government asserts its tax lien, is whether and to what extent the taxpayer had "property" or "rights to property" to which the tax lien could attach. In answering that question, both federal and state courts must look to state law, for it has long been the rule that "in the application of a federal revenue act, state law controls in determining the nature of the legal interest which the taxpayer had in the property . . . sought to be reached by the statute."[3] *Morgan v. Commissioner*, 309 U.S. 78, 82. Thus, as we held only two Terms ago, Section 3670 "creates no property rights but merely attaches consequences, federally defined, to rights created under state law. . . ." *United States v. Bess*, 357 U.S. 51, 55.[4] However, once the tax lien has attached

---

may be enforced by civil action maintained as provided in article three–a of this chapter by any person entitled to share in the fund, whether or not he shall have filed, or had the right to file, a notice of lien or shall have recovered a judgment for a claim arising out of the improvement. For the purpose of a civil action only, the trust funds shall include the right of action upon an obligation for moneys due or to become due to a contractor, as well as moneys actually received by him.

Section 36–a was repealed on September 1, 1949. N. Y. Laws 1959, c. 696, § 14. The subject matter covered by § 36–a is now included in McKinney's N. Y. Laws, Lien Law (1959 Supp.), §§ 70, 71.

[3] It is suggested that the definition of the taxpayer's property interests should be governed by federal law, although supplying the content of this nebulous body of federal law would apparently be left for future decisions. We think that this approach is unsound because it ignores the long–established role that the States have played in creating property interests and places upon the courts the task of attempting to ascertain a taxpayer's property rights under an undefined rule of federal law. It would indeed be anomalous to say that the taxpayer's "property and rights to property" included property in which, under the relevant state law, he had no property interest at all.

[4] It is said that because of the unique circumstances which existed in *Bess*, that case does not control here. However, aside from the fact that *Bess* involved proceeds payable under

to the taxpayer's state–created interests, we enter the province of federal law, which we have consistently held determines the priority of competing liens asserted against the taxpayer's "property" or "rights to property."[5] *United States v. Vorreiter,* 355 U.S. 15, reversing 134 Colo. 543, 307 P.2d 475; *United States v. White Bear Brewing Co.,* 350 U.S. 1010, reversing 227 F. 2d 359; *United States v. Colotta,* 350 U.S. 808, reversing 224 Miss. 33, 79 So. 2d 474; *United States v. Scovil,* 348 U.S. 218; *United States v. Liverpool & London & Globe Ins. Co.,* 348 U.S. 215; *United States v. Acri,* 348 U.S. 211; *United States v. City of New Britain,* 347 U.S. 81; *United States v. Gilbert Associates,* 345 U.S. 361; *United States v. Security Trust & Sav. Bank,* 340 U.S. 47; *Illinois v. Campbell,* 329 U.S. 362; *United States v. Waddill, Holland & Flinn, Inc.,* 323 U.S. 353. The application of state law in ascertaining the taxpayer's property rights and of federal law in reconciling the claims of competing lienors is based both upon logic and sound legal principles. This approach strikes a proper balance between the legitimate and traditional interest which the State has in creating and defining the property interest of its citizens, and the necessity for a uniform administration of the federal revenue statutes.

Petitioners contend that the New York Court of Appeals did not make its determination in the light of these settled principles. Relying upon the express language of Section 36–a of the Lien Law and upon a number of lower New York court decisions interpreting that statute, petitioners conclude that the money actually received by the contractor–taxpayer and his right to collect amounts still due under the construction contract constitute a direct trust for the benefit of subcontractors, and that the only property rights which the contractor–taxpayer has in the trust are bare legal title to any money actually received and a beneficial interest in so much of the trust proceeds as remain after the claims of subcontractors have been settled. The Government, on the other hand, claims that Section 36–a merely gives the subcontractors an ordinary lien, and that the contractor–taxpayer's property rights encompass the entire indebtedness of the owner under the construction contract.

---

an insurance policy, whereas this case involves proceeds payable under a construction contract, it is apparent that the relevant circumstances of the two cases are essentially identical. In both cases the Government was attempting to assert its tax lien against what it thought to be the "property and rights to property" of the taxpayer. In both cases an adverse party claimed the right to the property in question on the theory that the taxpayer had never acquired a state–created property interest to which the Government's tax lien could attach. Finally, in both cases, the Government attempted to characterize the problem as one involving a conflict between competing claimants to be settled solely by the application of federal law.

Bess held that state law determines the property interests of a taxpayer in the cash surrender value of an insurance policy, as well as in the proceeds payable upon death. The same considerations which led to our conclusion in *Bess* require that we look to state law in determining the general contractor's property interests in this case.

[5] It is suggested that the rule announced by *Bess* and applied in this case is inconsistent with the mandate that federal law governs the relative priority of federal tax liens and state–created liens. However, we fail to perceive wherein lies the inconsistency. It is one thing to say that a taxpayer's property rights have been and should be created by state law. It is quite another thing to declare that in the interest of efficient tax administration one must look to federal law to resolve the conflict between competing claimants of the taxpayer's state–created property interests.

This conflict should not be resolved by this Court, but by the highest court of the State of New York. We cannot say from the opinion of the Court of Appeals that it has been satisfactorily resolved.[6] We find no discussion in the court's opinion to indicate the nature of the property rights possessed by the taxpayer under state law. Nor is the application to be made of federal law clearly defined. We believe that it is in the interests of all concerned to have these questions decided by the state courts of New York. We therefore vacate the judgment of the Court of Appeals, and remand the case to that court so that it may ascertain the property interests of the taxpayer under state law and then dispose of the case according to established principles of law.

Vacated and remanded.

Mr. Justice HARLAN, dissenting in Nos. 1 and 23.[*]

I am unable to subscribe to the reasoning which underlies the Court's disposition of these cases. By holding that they both turn on whether the taxpayer had "property" under state law to which the Government's lien could attach, the Court has sanctioned a result consistently prohibited by us in a line of cases dealing with the priority of federal tax liens.[1]

In both cases, the delinquent taxpayer is a defaulting general contractor whose subcontractors remain unpaid. The Government's lien is asserted against the chose in action which the general contractor allegedly holds against the owner of the real estate on which the improvements were made, in respect of amounts due from the owner under the construction contract. If the subcontractors had sought to enforce their claims by imposing a lien on that chose in action, there is no question that the Government's lien would prevail. Under the decisions of this Court cited in note 1, *supra*, a federal tax lien asserted against a taxpayer's property under §§ 3670 and 3671 of the Internal Revenue Code of 1939[2] prevails over all other claims against

---

[6] Subsequent to the Court of Appeals' decision in the instant case, and after this Court's decision in *United States v. Bess*, 357 U.S. 51, the New York Court of Appeals decided the case of *In re City of New York*, 5 N. Y. 2d 300, 157 N. E. 2d 587, pending on petition for a writ of certiorari *sub nom. United States v. Coblentz*. No. 259, this Term [*post*, p. 841]. The *Coblentz* case is not authority for the disposition of the instant case. The latter involves a determination of property rights under § 36–a of the New York Lien Law, whereas the *Coblentz* case was concerned with the taxpayer's property interests under an assignment contract, § 475 of the New York Judiciary Law, and § B15–37.0 of the New York City Administrative Code.

[*] [No. 23 is *United States v. Durham Lumber Co. et al., post*, p. 522.]

[1] *United States v. Security Trust & Savings Bank*, 340 U.S. 47 (1950); *United States v. City of New Britain*, 347 U.S. 81 (1954); *United States v. Acri*, 348 U.S. 211 (1955); *United States v. Liverpool & London & Globe Ins. Co., Ltd.*, 348 U.S. 215 (1955); *United States v. Scovil*, 348 U.S. 218 (1955); *United States v. Colotta*, 350 U.S. 808 (1955); *United States v. White Bear Brewing Co.*, 350 U.S. 1010 (1956); *United States v. Vorreiter*, 355 U.S. 15 (1957); *United States v. Ball Construction Co., Inc.*, 355 U.S. 587 (1958); *United States v. Hulley*, 358 U.S. 66 (1958).

[2] The text of these sections, applicable in the *Aquilino* case, are set forth in note 1 of the Court's opinion in No. 1, *ante*, p. 511. The comparable provisions of the Internal Revenue Code of 1954, §§ 6321 and 6322, applicable in the *Durham Lumber* case, are printed in notes 1 and 2 of the Court's opinion in No. 23, *post*, p. 524.

such property except (1) those which attach and become "choate" before the federal lien attaches, and (2) those specifically protected by § 3672 (a).[3] It is conceded that the interest of the subcontractors in the present cases are not protected by § 3672 (a) and would not be considered choate under the applicable decisions. *See United States v. Kings County Iron Works*, 224 F. 2d 232 (C. A. 2d Cir. 1955).

The Court believes, however, that the present cases are different, because under state law, the general contractor in *Aquilino* held his claim against the owner in trust for the subcontractors to the extent of their claims, and because the subcontractors in *Durham Lumber* were given, to the extent of their claims, a direct right of action against the owner in respect of his debt to the general contractor, and that in these circumstances the rights of the subcontractors in the owner's debt are superior to those of the general contractor. It is said that, to the extent of the subcontractors' claims, the general contractor, under state law, thus had no "property" interest in the amounts due him from the owner, and that under the principles enunciated in *United States v. Bess*, 357 U.S. 51, a federal tax lien can attach only to a property interest which exists under state law.

I cannot see how it makes any difference, for purposes of the federal tax–lien statute, whether state law purports to prefer subcontractors over the general contractor and parties claiming through him by giving the subcontractors a lien on the general contractor's right of action against the owner or by giving them a prior right to collect the debt itself. In both instances, the owner is under a contractual duty to pay the general contractor and the latter is under a contractual duty to pay the subcontractors. In both instances, the subcontractors are attempting to satisfy their claims against the general contractor. And in both instances, they are seeking to satisfy themselves by claiming precisely the same thing—a prior right in the proceeds of the debt which arises by virtue of the contractual relationship between the owner and the general contractor.[4] In neither instance can the subcontractors collect more than that to which the subcontract entitles them, and in neither can the owner be required to pay more than that to which the main contract obligates him. If federal law requires that subordination of the general contractor's interest be ignored in the one instance, it does so equally in the other.

---

[3] That section, as amended, provides: "Such lien shall not be valid as against any mortgagee, pledgee, purchaser, or judgment creditor until notice thereof has been filed by the collector. . . ." 53 Stat. 882. The comparable provision of the Internal Revenue Code of 1954 is § 6323 (a).

[4] It is noteworthy that the North Carolina law involved in the *Durham Lumber* case requires the general contractor to furnish the owner with a statement of subcontractors' claims "before receiving any part of the *contract price, as it may become due*," and that it is thereafter the duty of the owner to retain an appropriate amount "from the money *then due the contractor*," N. C. Gen. Stat., 1950, § 44–8. (Emphasis added.) Although this section indicates that the general contractor has no right to collect the proceeds of the main contract until the statutory conditions are satisfied, it obviously recognizes the owner's contractual obligation as the real basis of the transaction and the source of the subcontractors' rights. The subcontractors' claims are thus not akin to liens on the owner's real estate, as this Court suggests, but are asserted solely in respect of the monetary claim held by the general contractor against the owner.

The *Bess* case does not require a contrary conclusion. That case held only that while a federal tax lien attached to the cash surrender value of a life insurance policy owned by the taxpayer, it did not attach to the proceeds paid on his death, because under state law he had no right to such proceeds during his life. There was no reason under those circumstances why state property concepts should not control. To read that case as standing for the proposition that such concepts must also be controlling in cases such as these defeats the rule that "[t]he relative priority of the lien of the United States for unpaid taxes is . . . always a federal question to be determined finally by the federal courts." *United States v. Acri*, 348 U.S. 211, 213. It is one thing to say, as the Court did in *Bess*, that the federal interest in uniform application of federal tax liens does not require, as a general rule, that state property concepts be disregarded. It is quite another to permit such concepts to control the extent of a federal lien's application in situations indistinguishable from those where the Court has in fact, rightly or wrongly, enforced a uniform federal rule. Given federal supremacy in this field, it surely cannot be that the federal courts may not appraise for themselves the true impact of state–created rights upon the priority of federal tax liens within the criteria established by this Court. *Cf. Carpenter v. Shaw*, 280 U.S. 363, 367; *City of Detroit v. Murray Corporation*, 355 U.S. 489, 492. To recognize the substantial equivalence of the situations is not to create a new rule of federal property law but to require an evenhanded application of an already established one. It seems to me that Judge Fuld of the New York Court of Appeals was quite right in holding in the *Aquilino* case that New York could not, consistently with the past decisions of our Court, defeat the otherwise superior federal lien upon the owner's debt to the general contractor by converting the debt into a trust for the benefit of the subcontractor.[5]

To read *Bess* as the Court does can only lead to confusion in the administration of the federal tax lien statute. A taxpayer's property in a debt is surely diminished by the imposition of a lien on his interest, for he has no right to collect the liened portion nor to alienate it. Yet in precisely this situation, we have held that the federal tax lien is not affected by such diminution. *United States v. Liverpool & London Globe Ins. Co.*, 348 U.S. 215. If this holding is to be preserved after today's decision, subsequent cases must turn on the elusive distinction between diminishing a greater property interest and initially conferring a lesser one.[6] The very difficulty which

---

[5] "It is, by now, exceedingly well settled that no state–created rule may defeat the paramount right of the United States to levy and collect taxes uniformly throughout the land. (*See United States v. Vorreiter*, 355 U.S. 15, revg. 134 Col. 543; *United States v. White Bear Brewing Co.*, 350 U.S. 1010, revg. 227 F. 2d 359; *United States v. Colotta, supra*, 350 U.S. 808, revg. 224 Miss. 33; *United States v. Scovil, supra*, 348 U.S. 218, 220–221; *United States v. New Britain, supra*, 347 U.S. 81, 84–87; *United States v. Kings Country Iron Works, supra*, 224 F. 2d 232, 237). That being so, it follows that the provision in this state's Lien Law, to which respondents point—that funds received by a contractor from the owner for the improvement of real property shall be deemed 'trust funds' for the payment of subcontractors (§ 36–a; § 13, subd. [7])—may not be construed to affect the rights of the government or the priority of its tax lien." 3 N. Y. 2d, at 516, 146 N. E. 2d, at 777–778.

[6] It will not do to distinguish the present type of case from the lien–priority cases on the ground that in the latter cases the taxpayer remains the owner in a very real sense and can

this Court experiences in trying to determine whether under New York law the general contractor really holds only a bare legal title in trust for the subcontractors or has full ownership of the debt subject to a lien in favor of the subcontractors demonstrates the futility of attempting to draw such distinctions for federal purposes. I venture to suggest that on remand, the Court of Appeals can with equal facility label the subcontractors' interests "property" or a "lien," the relevant incidents of the relationship being the same in either case. Why should not that court and the legislatures of other States readily respond in choosing the former alternative?

I would affirm the judgment in No. 1, and would reverse in No. 23 on the ground that North Carolina can under no circumstances accord subcontractors a right in the proceeds of the debt arising from the construction contract superior to the Government's lien without satisfying one of the two requirements laid down by federal law. If the federal standard of choateness is thought to be an undesirable restriction on the States' freedom to regulate property relationships, the cases establishing that standard should be expressly overruled and not emasculated by dubious distinctions.

Mr. Justice BLACK, while adhering to the dissenting views expressed by him in *Commissioner v. Stern*, 357 U.S. 39, 47, and *United States v. Bess*, 357 U.S. 51, 59, concurs in this opinion.

AQUILINO v. UNITED STATES

New York Court of Appeals
10 N.Y.2d 271, 219 N.Y.S.2d 254, 176 N.E.2d 826 (1961)

FULD, Judge.

This case is before us on remand from the United States Supreme Court. When it was previously here (3 N.Y.2d 511, 169 N.Y.S.2d 9), we concluded that a tax lien asserted by the United States was superior to claims advanced by subcontractors and, in consequence, held the Government entitled to a sum of money owed under a general construction contract performed by the taxpayer. The Supreme Court, believing that we had slighted State law and given undue emphasis to Federal

------

continue to enjoy the property if he discharges the debt it secures. In both instances, the taxpayer is temporarily deprived of certain incidents of ownership as a device for securing the payment of a debt, and is restored to the full enjoyment of the property only when the debt is discharged. And it is illusory to say that ownership of a debt which can be neither collected nor alienated is any more "real" than the ownership of no debt at all. Whether the diminution of the taxpayer's interest is sufficiently definite and complete to conclude the federal lien is precisely the question on which this Court has held federal law must control. It is admitted that, if the federal standard of "choateness" developed by this Court in the lien–priority cases is applied, the incidents of ownership retained by the taxpayers here must in fact be deemed greater than those retained by taxpayers in cases where state–created liens imposed on their interests have prevailed over the Government's lien.

decisions, vacated the judgment and remanded the case for further consideration (363 U.S. 509, 80 S. Ct. 1277, 1285).

Fleetwood Paving Corporation owes the United States Government a sum of money representing unpaid withholding and social security taxes. In December, 1951, and March, 1952, the local Collector of Internal Revenue received assessment lists including assessments against Fleetwood. Some time later, Fleetwood, as general contractor, agreed with one Ada Bottone to remodel a restaurant which she owned. Thereafter in the summer of 1952, Fleetwood entered into subcontracts with Home Maintenance Company and Colonial Sand and Stone Company to furnish labor and materials for the remodeling job.

On October 31, 1952, some days before the subcontractors, who had completed their work, filed their respective notices of mechanic's liens against the owner's realty, notice of the Federal tax liens was filed against Fleetwood. The owner thereupon deposited in court the sum of $2,200, which she still owed Fleetwood, and it is this fund which the competing claimants seek.

The courts below, each giving different reasons, denied the Government's claim of priority for its tax lien and granted the plaintiffs' motions for summary judgment. We reached a contrary decision; it was our opinion that the Government's lien was asserted against the indebtedness of the owner to the contractor–taxpayer and that such indebtedness constituted "property" and "rights to property," as those terms are used in the controlling Federal statute (Internal Revenue Code of 1939, U.S. Code, tit. 26, § 3670 [now numbered § 6321]).

As indicated above, the Supreme Court found our approach to the resolution of the problem unsatisfactory. In *United States v. Bess* (357 U.S. 51), the court had explicitly declared that section 3670 of the Internal Revenue Code "creates no property rights but merely attaches consequences, federally defined, to rights created under state law" (p. 55). Quoting this language, the Supreme Court sent the present case back to us so that we might "ascertain the property interests of the taxpayer under state law" and then apply Federal law to determine the priority of the competing claims (363 U.S., at pp. 515–516). More specifically, we were directed to explore the meaning and impact of former section 36–a of our Lien Law and to determine whether under its terms the contractor–taxpayer holds bare legal title to the sum due from the owner, as trustee for the subcontractors, or whether it has full ownership of the debt, subject only to a lien in favor of the subcontractors.

It is to be noted at the outset that we are called upon to construe a statute no longer on the books and deal with law as it existed between 1942 and 1959. Section 36–a of the Lien Law, enacted in 1930, was repealed in 1959, its provisions, with modifications, being transferred to a new article 3–A. (L. 1959, ch. 696, enacting Lien Law, §§ 70–79; see 1959 Report of N. Y. Law Rev. Comm., p. 185; N. Y. Legis. Doc., 1959, No. 65 [F].)

Section 36–a was one among a series of provisions of the Lien Law directed against various injurious and irresponsible practices in the construction industry. Chief among the evils sought to be eradicated was that of "pyramiding," a practice whereby owners or contractors use money advanced in the course of one project, as loans or as contract payments, to commence or complete another project. In the case of a contractor, the so–called trust fund provisions of the Lien Law prohibited diversion, to purposes unrelated to a particular improvement, of contract payments from the owner which were intended to pay the expense of that improvement, including the cost of labor and materials. (*See* 1942 Report of N. Y. Law Rev. Comm., pp. 298–306; N. Y. Legis. Doc., 1942, No. 65 [H], pp. 28–36.)

The device which the Legislature used, throughout all the versions of section 36–a, to attempt to prevent the misuse of building contract payments was that of declaring that "The funds received by a contractor from an owner for the improvement of real property . . . constitute trust funds in the hands of such contractor to be applied first to the payment of claims of subcontractors . . . laborers and materialmen arising out of the improvement". If this legislative declaration and the legislative history of the trust fund provisions were all that were before us, the conclusion that the fund at issue in this case is the *res* of a trust held by the contractor rather than his own property would be relatively free from doubt. The fact is, however, that various other provisions of the statute, as well as a number of cases decided by this and other courts, complicate our decision.

In its earliest version, section 36–a, after designating the moneys received by the contractor a "trust fund", prescribed only one means of enforcing the trust, namely, by criminal prosecution. As originally enacted in 1930, the section provided that "any contractor . . . who applies or consents to the application of such [trust] funds for any other purpose [than the payment of the claims of the statutory beneficiaries] and fails to pay the claims hereinbefore mentioned is guilty of larceny". On the basis of this language, this court, after disposing of the case on other grounds, stated in *Raymond Concrete Pile Co. v. Federation Bank & Trust Co.* (288 N. Y. 452, 462), that "The purpose of the sections [25–a and 36–a] . . . is solely penal and not to provide civil remedies." This statement, as well as others similar to it, has been heavily relied upon in a number of cases. (*See, e.g., Gramatan–Sullivan v. Koslow*, 240 F. 2d 523, 525; *Matter of Case v. Panzarella*, 27 Misc. 2d 854, *affd.* 266 App. Div. 962; *Travis v. Nansen*, 176 Misc. 44.)

However, the primary ground for decision in the *Raymond Concrete* case was that the statutory beneficiaries of the Lien Law trust were not privileged to trace payments made to the contractor–trustee into the hands of an assignee for value, absent proof that the assignee had actual notice of the existence of unpaid claims for supplies and materials (288 N. Y. at p. 459). This holding, as distinguished from the dicta in the case, clearly supports the view that a section 36–a contractor–trustee holds the funds he receives as trustee, rather than as owner, until he has paid the claims of all of the statutory beneficiaries.

In any event, though, even if we were to accept the dicta of *Raymond Concrete* as authoritative and treat the case as holding that the provisions of the Lien Law did not provide for a true trust since they did not allow for a civil remedy, the holding must be limited to sections 25–a and 36–a *as they read before 1942*. In that year, 1942, the Legislature amended section 36–a by adding the following language:

> Such trust may be enforced by civil action maintained as provided in article three–a of this chapter by any person entitled to share in the fund, whether or

not he shall have filed, or had the right to file, a notice of lien or shall have recovered a judgment for a claim arising out of the improvement. For the purpose of a civil action only, the trust funds shall include the right of action upon an obligation for moneys due or to become due to a contractor.

And a new article 3–A was added to the Lien Law, entitled "Enforcement of Trusts" (L. 1942, ch. 808), to provide, among other matters, that the trust provisions may be enforced by a "representative action brought for the benefit of all persons entitled to share in the [trust] fund" (Lien Law, § 71).

Although these 1942 amendments seem, on their face, to be designed to overcome the effect of the dicta in the *Raymond Concrete* case (288 N. Y. 452, *supra*), the fact is that they were prepared before the decision was handed down. Actually, the amendments were designed to resolve problems raised by *Wickes Boiler Co. v. Godfrey–Keeler Co.* (116 F. 2d 842) and *Amiesite Constr. Co. v. Luciano Contr. Co.* (284 N. Y. 223). (*See* 1942 Report of N. Y. Law Rev. Comm., pp. 297–298; N. Y. Legis. Doc., 1942, No. 65 [H], pp. 27–28.) In the former case, the trust benefits under the Lien Law were held to be available only to those who had perfected mechanic's liens, and, in the latter case, it was decided that a subcontractor's right to moneys owing to a contractor, but still in the hands of the State—which had contracted for the improvement—was inferior to that of the contractor's assignee.

The 1942 amendments clarified the situation. They established beyond dispute, first, that subcontractors and other statutory beneficiaries could enforce their interest "whether or not" they had filed a notice of lien and, second, that the *res* of the trust included a "right of action upon an obligation for moneys due or to become due to [the] contractor". Not only did these amendments put an end to the limitations placed upon the statutory trust fund provisions in the *Wickes Boiler Co.* case (116 F. 2d 842, *supra*) and the *Amiesite Constr. Co.* case (284 N. Y. 223, *supra*), but they overcame the dicta in the *Raymond Concrete* case (288 N. Y. 452, *supra*). (*See* 1958 Report of N. Y. Law Rev. Comm., p. 520; N. Y. Legis. Doc., 1958, No. 65[F], p. 16; *Metropolitan Cas. Ins. Co. v. Barr Wrecking Corp.*, 180 Misc. 200, 203–204, per Froessel, J.)

Even after the 1942 amendments, however, some cases continued to question whether the rights and duties of the contractor–trustee under the Lien Law trust fund provisions were comparable to those of trustee of a trust of the usual sort. Chief among such cases was *Gramatan–Sullivan v. Koslow* (240 F. 2d 523, *supra*). A contractor, indebted to the defendant, had paid him money which he had received from the owner under a contract to improve his property. The plaintiff, a subcontractor, sought to recover from the defendant the full amount of his claim against the contractor on the ground that the latter had held the fund as trustee. The Court of Appeals for the Second Circuit, although allowing recovery for claims which had matured before the defendant received the funds, refused recovery as to the subcontractor's claims which had not matured as of that time. Relying heavily on the *Raymond Concrete* case (288 N. Y. 452, *supra*), the court wrote that "no . . . more was intended [by the 1942 amendments to section 36–a] than to attach the civil sanction to the same liability to which the criminal sanction already attached" (240 F. 2d, at p. 527). Furthermore, reasoned the court, since the *Raymond Concrete* case held that it was a necessary condition of criminal liability that the contractor who diverted funds be in default in the payment of a claim and, since there could be no default as to claims which have not arisen, there could be no civil liability in favor of one whose claims had not matured at the time of the diversion (240 F. 2d, at pp. 525–526).

In other words, it was the view of the Federal court in the *Gramatan* case that the trust arose only after claims for payment had matured and it only extended, at any particular time, to the funds then necessary to satisfy mature claims then outstanding. Thus, the court not only declared that "the [section 36–a] trust is not of the usual kind", but went on to say that "it is [not a] breach of trust for the contractor . . . to use any of the payments for his own purposes" while the work was still in progress (240 F. 2d, at pp. 525–526). Although we agree that the statutory trusts set up by the Lien Law are "not of the usual kind", it is our opinion that *Gramatan* went far beyond both our statute and our cases in its description of the degree of control and interest which a statutory trustee has in the trust fund.

In the first place, it placed undue reliance on the dicta in the *Raymond Concrete* case (288 N. Y. 452, *supra*) concerning the extent of criminal liability. *Raymond Concrete* was, after all, a civil and not a criminal suit. Furthermore, the only claim there in issue had actually matured at the time of the asserted diversion of trust funds (288 N. Y. 452, 456, *supra*). Under these circumstances, what the court said about the contractor not being criminally liable for a diversion of trust funds at a time when no statutory beneficiary holds an unmatured claim was beside the point.

In the second place, the view espoused in the *Gramatan* case does not comport with either the language or the design of the legislation. The policy proclaimed by our statute is to protect those whose skill, labor and materials made possible the performance of a construction contract and who in fact, creating the improvement, actually gave rise to the owner's obligation to pay. The Legislature sought to assure that the funds received from an owner should "reach [their] ultimate destination— material and labor". (*See* 1942 Report of N. Y. Law Rev. Comm., pp. 298–300; N. Y. Legis. Doc., 1942, No. 65[H], pp. 28–30.) It is difficult to believe that the Legislature would have designated the fund concerned a "trust" and yet intended the trust to arise only when the claims of the statutory beneficiaries had matured. This would have been to provide a protection which would not protect.

The rule that the funds of an express trust may not be diverted to nontrust purposes, whether or not claims of beneficiaries are outstanding and whether or not the diversion is subsequently remedied, serves the purpose of closing the door to a violation of the trust purpose before the violation can arise. However proper the intentions of the trustee, if he is empowered to make nice calculations about how far he may use the trust for his own purposes before the need to pay beneficiaries arises, the danger exists that the beneficiaries may suffer loss as a result of miscalculation or other untoward contingencies. There is no good reason to suppose that the Legislature, by declaring payments to a contractor to be "trust funds", did not intend thereby to avoid the very same possibilities of harm to the statutory beneficiaries as was intended by the rule against diversion of the funds of an express trust.

The wording of section 36–a is, unfortunately, not as clear as it could be. The section renders a contractor guilty of larceny if he "applies or consents to the application of such funds for any other purpose [than satisfying the claims of the statutory beneficiaries] *and* fails to pay [such] claims". It was this seeming conjunction of consent to the diversion of trust funds *and* subsequent failure to pay which led the court in the *Raymond Concrete* case to interpolate that "Nothing in the section bars the contractor from using the moneys received for any purpose he may see fit provided he does not fail to pay all such claims out of other moneys which he may then have or which he may afterwards receive" (288 N. Y., at p. 459).

It must be borne in mind, however, that this statement was made by the court in discussing a hypothetical possibility of criminal responsibility and, consequently, the court was applying the rule of "strict" construction generally invoked in such cases. In the light of the subsequent 1942 amendments which created a form of civil liability, particularly in view of the Legislature's explicit declaration that these provisions "be construed liberally to secure [their] beneficial interests and purposes" (Lien Law, § 23) and its frequently repeated concern for the plight of the statutory beneficiaries, the court's reading of the statute in the *Raymond Concrete* case is no longer either supportable or permissible. The statutory words of conjunction must be read as meaning no more than that the Legislature envisages that a failure to pay claims is a strong, almost invariable, consequence of a diversion of trust funds and that the diversion is prohibited in order to avoid its almost certain consequence.

However valid, therefore, the conclusion may once have been that the section did not bar the contractor from using the moneys received for any purpose he chose, we hold that it is no longer applicable under the statute as it was amended in 1942. The only purposes for which the contractor may use the funds are trust purposes. In other words, such funds are to be "applied first" to the payment of the statutory beneficiaries. The contractor has a beneficial interest only in so much of the proceeds as remain after the claims of all beneficiaries have been settled.

The only features of this trust which make it at all exceptionable, which—to cull from the language of the *Gramatan–Sullivan* case (240 F. 2d 523, 525, *supra*)— indicate that it is "not a trust of the usual kind" are (1) that the contractor–trustee is not under the necessity of holding the fund intact until the improvement is completed, required as he is to pay the claims of the subcontractors as they mature; (2) that the contractor–trustee may, under specified conditions, assign his rights to future payments due from an owner (Lien Law, § 13, subd. [1–a]; *Arrow Iron Works v. Greene*, 260 N. Y. 330, 340); (3) that the contractor–trustee is privileged to commingle funds (Lien Law, § 36–a); and (4) that the remedy available is a class action rather than one prosecutable by an individual (Lien Law, § 71). In our judgment, none of these items gives the contractor–trustee such a beneficial interest in the fund as to constitute him its owner rather than its trustee.

As to the first item, the power given the contractor to "dip into" the trust fund in order to satisfy subcontractors' claims as they arise is no more than a necessity of his doing business and it is comparable to an express direction in the usual trust to favor one class of beneficiaries over another. As to the second item, a contractor may, it is true, assign moneys due under his contract, but he may do so, subdivision

(6) of section 13 of the Lien Law specifies, only by covenanting that "he will receive any moneys advanced . . . and will hold the right to receive such moneys as trust funds to be first applied to the payment of trust claims". This provision represents but another attempt to adjust the trust concept to the exigencies of the contracting business by allowing for interim financing. It does not, however, weaken the trust concept, since its only effect is to substitute the proceeds of the assignment for the moneys due or to become due from the owner as the trust fund to which suppliers of labor and material may look for payment. As to the contractor–trustee's power to commingle funds, the third feature remarked, the degree to which it represents a departure from normal trust principles is considerably mitigated by the elaborate provisions found in the statute for accounting for trust proceeds and expenditures (Lien Law, § 36–d). And, finally, concerning the fourth feature, although the circumstance that the civil remedy provided is a class action may somewhat diminish a beneficiary's rights, it cannot be said that it gives the trustee a property right in the fund or adds one iota to his power to control it.

Our construction of the trust fund provisions of the Lien Law is consonant with this State's legislative policy of protecting laborers and materialmen as evidenced in the original enactment of those provisions and the numerous amendments— including indeed those enacted in 1959—designed to make them more effective. It also constitutes a reaffirmation of the policy reflected by this court's recent decisions in this area. (*See, e.g., Cranford Co. v. Leopold & Co.*, 298 N. Y. 676; *United States Fid. Guar. Co. v. Triborough Bridge Auth.*, 297 N. Y. 31; *see, also*, Seligson, Creditors' Rights, 1957 Annual Survey of American Law, pp. 323–334; Seligson, Creditors' Rights, 36 N. Y. U. L. Rev. 601, 612.)

Our conclusion, then, is that, as a matter of New York law, a contractor does not have a sufficient beneficial interest in the moneys, due or to become due from the owner under the contract, to give him a property right in them, except insofar as there is a balance remaining after all subcontractors and other statutory beneficiaries have been paid. This being so, it follows that the tax lien herein asserted by the Government against the property of the contractor–taxpayer is ineffective to reach such moneys and that the plaintiff subcontractors are entitled to the court–deposited fund.

The judgment of the Appellate Division should be affirmed, with costs.

Chief Judge DESMOND and Judges DYE, FROESSEL, VAN VOORHIS, BURKE and FOSTER concur.

Judgment affirmed.

NOTES AND QUESTIONS

(1) As shown by the two decisions in *Aquilino, supra*, determining the outcome of priority contests between competing state and federally created tax liens is a two–step process. State law must first determine whether the taxpayer has "property"

or "rights to property" to which the federal lien may attach, while federal law, which governs the validity and priority of a federal lien, determines whether a preexisting state–created lien is sufficiently "choate" to prime a federal tax lien under the "first–in–time–first–in–right" rule. The procedure and its underlying rationale are explained in Judge Fuld's dissent in *Buffalo Savings Bank, infra*, which was, in effect, adopted by the United States Supreme Court in the second *Buffalo Savings Bank* opinion, *infra. See Tillery v. Parks*, 630 F.2d 775 (10th Cir. 1980); *Randall v. H. Nakashima & Co., Ltd.*, 542 F.2d 270 (5th Cir. 1976).

(2) Courts have interpreted the reach of § 6321 of the Internal Revenue Code extremely broadly. *See, e.g.: United States v. Fidelity & Deposit Co. of Maryland*, 214 F.2d 565 (5th Cir. 1954) (lien attaches to property exempt under state law); *Rice Inv. Co.v. United States*, 625 F.2d 565 (5th Cir. 1980) (lien attaches to after–acquired property); *Texas Western Financial Corp. v. McCraw Candies, Inc.*, 347 F. Supp. 445 (N.D. Tex. 1972) (lien attaches to choses in action); and *Randall v. H. Nakashima & Co., Ltd.*, 542 F.2d 270 (5th Cir. 1976) (taxpayer's contract rights under partially executory contract for equipment constituted property to which tax lien attached before taxpayer conveyed his contract rights).

(3) What was the final holding in the *Aquilino* case? For a comprehensive discussion of problems related to determining what is the taxpayer's property, *see* Plumb, Federal Tax Liens, 27–38 (3d rev. ed. 1981) (ALI–ABA); Young, *Priority of The Federal–Tax Lien*, 34 U. Chi. L. Rev. 723 (1967).

(4) Section 6334 of the Internal Revenue Code, 26 U.S.C. § 6334, limits § 6321 by creating a federal exemption from the tax lien for (1) wearing apparel and school books; (2) fuel, provisions, personal effects, furniture; (3) books and tools of a trade, business or profession; (4) unemployment benefits; (5) undelivered mail; (6) certain annuity and pension payments; (7) worker's compensation; (8) judgments for support of minor children; and (9) a minimum exemption for wages, salary and other income.

(5) Under § 6331(b) of the Internal Revenue Code, 26 U.S.C. § 6331(b), the Internal Revenue Service may levy, seize and sell property subject to a tax lien. For a discussion of the rights of the Internal Revenue Service as a secured creditor in a case under the Bankruptcy Code, *see United States v. Whiting Pools, Inc.*, 462 U.S. 198, 103 S. Ct. 2309 (1983). The following excerpt from the Court's opinion succinctly describes how the United States may enforce its tax lien:

> The enforcement provisions of the Internal Revenue Code of 1954, 26 U.S.C. §§ 6321–6326 (1976 ed. and Supp. V), do grant to the Service powers to enforce its tax liens that are greater than those possessed by private secured creditors under state law. . . . But those provisions do not transfer ownership of the property to the IRS.

> The Service's interest in seized property is its lien on that property. The Internal Revenue Code's levy and seizure provisions, 26 U.S.C. §§ 6331 and 6332, are special procedural devices available to the IRS to protect and satisfy its liens, . . . and are analogous to the remedies available to private secured creditors. . . . They are provisional remedies that do not determine the

Service's rights to the seized property, but merely bring the property into the Service's legal custody. . . . At no point does the Service's interest in the property exceed the value of the lien. . . . The IRS is obligated to return to the debtor any surplus from a sale. 26 U.S.C. § 6342(b). Ownership of the property is transferred only when the property is sold to a bona fide purchaser at a tax sale. . . . In fact, the tax sale provision itself refers to the debtor as the owner of the property after the seizure but prior to the sale. Until such a sale takes place, the property remains the debtor's and thus is subject to the turnover requirement of § 542(a).

. . . .

When property seized prior to the filing of a petition is drawn into the Chapter 11 reorganization estate, the Service's tax lien is not dissolved; nor is its status as a secured creditor destroyed. The IRS, under § 363(e), remains entitled to adequate protection for its interests, to other rights enjoyed by secured creditors, and to the specific privileges accorded tax collectors. Section 542(a) simply requires the Service to seek protection of its interest according to the congressionally established bankruptcy procedures, rather than by withholding the seized property from the debtor's efforts to reorganize.

103 U.S. at 2315–2317. (Citations and footnotes deleted). *See* Chapter 14, *infra*.

BUFFALO SAVINGS BANK v. VICTORY

New York Court of Appeals
11 N.Y.2d 31, 226 N.Y.S.2d 382, 181 N.E.2d 413 (1962)
rev'd. sub. nom. United States v. Buffalo Savings Bank, 371 U.S. 228
reh'g. den. 12 N.Y.2d 1100, 240 N.Y.S.2d 164, 190 N.E.2d 536 (1963)

BURKE, J. The issue here is whether the payment of local real estate taxes and assessments as expenses of sale, rather than the application of that amount toward the payment of a Federal lien filed against the mortgagor prior to the accrual of local taxes, disregards the alleged right of the tax lien of the United States to prior payment.

We find that the Federal tax lien is not entitled to priority over subsequently accrued local tax liens—superior to the mortgage debt—since the respective liens are not comparable charges on real property and the "mortgagee" has an absolute preference over Federal liens.

Plaintiff commenced this action in October, 1958 to foreclose its real property mortgage given by Joseph B. Victory, dated and recorded April 5, 1946. At the time of verification of the complaint there was a balance due on the bond of $1,473.75, with interest at the rate of 5% per annum from January 10, 1958. The United States was *made a party because of a tax lien it filed in the Erie County Clerk's office January 15, 1953 against the mortgagor, since deceased.* Its answer stated a balance due on the lien of $689.07, plus interest. Plaintiff did not advance any sums for payment of local real property taxes and assessments, which became liens upon the land on and after July 1, 1957.

The mortgagee moved for summary judgment providing that the premises be sold free of the United States tax lien, but *subject* to all real property taxes and assessments. This motion was granted by the Erie County Court. On appeal by the respondent, the Appellate Division reversed and remitted the case to the County Court, stating that the discretionary authority to have the property sold *subject* to all local real estate taxes "may not properly be exercised in a case such as this in which there is a problem of circular priorities" (11 A D 2d 160). Thereafter the County Court once more granted summary judgment in favor of the mortgagee providing that the premises be sold and directing that the Referee "shall, as a part of the expenses of the sale, pay out of the proceeds of said sale all real estate taxes, assessments and water rates which are liens upon the property sold, and redeem the property sold from any sales for unpaid real estate taxes, assessments or water rates which have not apparently become absolute". The judgment further foreclosed all rights, liens, and equities of redemption in the premises, except as to the one–year period of redemption granted to the United States by section 2410 of title 28 of the United States Code.

On appeal by the United States, the Appellate Division modified the judgment by providing that "the rule of priorities laid down in *United States v. New Britain* (347 U.S. 81) applies" (13 A D 2d 208), and that the local tax liens were not to be paid as expenses of the sale.

The appellant mortgagee contends that the foreclosure procedure of New York is determined by our State law and that a direction to pay local taxes and assessments as expenses of the sale was a proper direction within section 1087 of the New York Civil Practice Act. The United States contends that this court is barred from reaching a determination reversing the Appellate Division and affirming the judgment of Erie County Court. (*United States v. New Britain*, 347 U.S. 81.)

Although the United States Supreme Court in recent years has passed on the question of priority of liens and the resulting effect upon mortgagees, their decisions provide no clear command governing us here.

The case of *United States v. New Britain* (*supra*) is distinguishable from the present case.

There the Supreme Court assumed, in the posture of the case as it reached that court, that the contest was between the local government and the Federal Government over their respective rights in surplus funds.

In the usual case, as here, however, the state of facts shows that the dispute is really between the mortgagee and creditors of the mortgagor. The debts of the mortgagor obviously can only be satisfied out of such equity in the real property as the mortgagor may have. When the property is sold in foreclosure, the equity of the mortgagor is extinguished except in the event the bid provides a surplus. Any interest of the mortgagor is fully protected. The mortgagor can bid at the sale, bring surplus money proceedings and resist a deficiency judgment by adducing proof that the value of the property exceeded the bids. In New York State the local government is not paid out of the surplus as the mortgage is the subject to its liens, but the Federal Government as a creditor of the mortgagor can look only to the surplus for the satisfaction of its lien. The local government lien is not a levy against the mortgagor, but against the land and must be paid together with other costs from whatever funds the sale of the land produces before (if there were no creditors of the mortgagor) any claimed interest of the mortgagor could be asserted. Our State law has not characterized the nature and extent of the Federal tax lien, but has determined the nature and extent of the property interests of the taxpayer (admittedly a State function), which in the case of real property is conditioned upon the payment of annually recurring governmental land taxes, the payment of which may not be avoided by a foreclosure sale. Of course, the Federal Government's claim, which is based on the claimed interest of the mortgagor, can have no better standing, that is, the Federal lien is also to be paid when there is a surplus in which the mortgagor would have an interest. It would manifestly be unjust to require a mortgagee to pay a creditor of a mortgagor when it appears that the mortgagor had no equity in the real property.

In the *New Britain* suit (*supra*) the court, at the outset, held that the contestants were vying over rights to funds which were considered as surplus. Federal liens securing unpaid withholding and unemployment taxes and insurance contributions owed by the mortgagor attached to his interest in the property subsequent to two mortgages and a judgment lien, but prior to city liens for unpaid real estate and water taxes. Connecticut law provided that the statutory liens for real estate taxes and water rent took precedence over all other liens or incumbrances. Mr. Justice Minton, speaking for the court, conceding that the mortgagee had a preference, stated at pages 85–86: "It does not follow, however, that the City's liens must receive priority as a whole. We believe that priority on these statutory liens is determined by another principle of law, namely, 'the first in time is the first in right.' . . . We think that Congress had this cardinal rule in mind when it enacted § 3670, a schedule of priority not being set forth therein. Thus, the priority of each statutory lien contested here must depend on the time it attached to the property in question and became choate."

Although it may have been the clear intent of Congress that this Federal tax lien have a priority determined by the timeliness with which it attached to the interest of the mortgagor in the real property, *New Britain* does not indicate that it was the intent of Congress to upset established State procedures in foreclosure actions or curtail the absolute preference granted to mortgagees. The statement (p. 88) that "The United States is not interested in whether the State receives its taxes and water rents prior to mortgagees and judgment creditors" is far too removed, in the light of the real issue here, from the court's interpretation of congressional intent to have any relation thereto.

Not to be lost sight of in its discussion of the relative priority of the liens is the court's statement that Congress intended to assert the Federal lien "as to any funds *in excess of the amount* necessary to pay the mortgage and judgment creditors." (*United States v. New Britain*, 347 U.S. 81, 88 *supra*; italics supplied.) The Supreme

Court there recognized that the mortgagor's interest in the proceeds of the foreclosure sale, and consequently the United States lien, reaches only surplus moneys.

But such surplus funds cannot be created by the judgment, for they are the moneys paid for the land in excess of the amount decreed in the judgment. A judgment which omits an item of sale expense in order to create a surplus fund to which subsequent liens can attach violates the statute. Rights of lienors in surplus funds are to be protected, but the law of this State cannot be subverted to create a surplus where none might otherwise exist. Our State law does not prevent such lienors from bidding at a foreclosure sale in order to protect their liens; but, inasmuch as they are not forced to bid a sum which will create a surplus, it would be inequitable to force the foreclosing mortgagee to bid an inflated price creating a surplus through the scheme of "circular priorities".

In this case the respondent's claim that its lien, founded on the interest of the defaulting mortgagor in the real property, should be granted a priority over the lien on the land, concededly superior to not only the mortgagor's interests in the realty but the mortgagee's interest as well, depends on the obviously fallacious contention that the lien of the municipality upon the land is akin to the lien of the Federal Government as a creditor of the mortgagor. The plain answer is that the Federal Government is only the creditor of a debtor whose interest in the land is subordinate to the local government lien, which need not be reduced to judgment nor perfected by a filing in the County Clerk's office. As a lien for taxes for essential services supplied for the benefit of the land, it attached directly to the particular parcel of real property. The Federal lien was filed in the Clerk's office against a presumed equity in the real property held by the mortgagor. This respondent imagines a surplus, which is as yet nonexistent, against which it would press a lien arising from a debt owed to it by the mortgagor. But in a foreclosure suit the equity of the mortgagor upon which a Federal lien depends should be established according to law, not by an ipse dixit.

The real estate tax and water–rent liens are not liens which attach to the property merely because of an unconnected indebtedness of the owner of the land, as are Federal tax liens. The property itself, in its very nature as land, incurs the indebtedness. It matters not who owns the land for, even if the United States in foreclosing its lien had a Receiver appointed to sell the land, the property could not have been transferred free and clear of the local tax liens attaching while the United States was in possession (see *Borock v. City of New York*, 268 F.2d 412).

Thus, the circumstances in the present case are quite different from those assumed in *United States v. New Britain (supra)*. The question is not "the relative priority of statutory federal and municipal liens to the proceeds of a mortgage foreclosure sale of the property to which the liens attached" (*United States v. New Britain, supra*, p. 82), but whether the payment of the Federal lien filed against the mortgagor should be mandated where there is no evidence that the mortgagor has a financial interest at the time of foreclosure. Here we are faced with the true parties in interest—the mortgagee and the Federal Government. Under New York law no funds are deemed surplus until the expenses of the sale, the costs of the action and the amount of the foreclosed mortgage debt plus interest have been fully paid. (Civ. Prac. Act,

§ 1082). The procedure [1] in this State requires the officer conducting the foreclosure sale to pay out of the proceeds all taxes, assessments and water rates which are liens on the property, unless the judgment directs otherwise. These payments are expenses of the sale by statute. Therefore, the question of what, if any, financial interest the mortgagor–taxpayer had on which the Federal Government had a lien can only be determined under the State law after the foreclosure sale.

The procedure adopted by the Appellate Division does not follow New York State procedure. Up to the present time the expenses of sale have always been determined by State, rather than Federal, law, and even the judgment in *New Britain* (*Brown v. General Laundry Serv.*, 19 Conn. Supp. 335) recognized that the expenses of sale have priority over any other claim to the moneys realized on the sale. Certainly precedent demands that we should reaffirm the principle that State procedures govern.

Moreover, the Supreme Court in a recent decision has allowed State law to control the procedure of foreclosure and payment of liens. In *United States v. Brosnan* (264 F. 2d 762, *affd.* 363 U.S. 237) Federal tax liens attached to property subject to a purchase–money mortgage, but prior to local tax liens.[2] Upon default in payment of the mortgage, the mortgagee caused a confession of judgment to be entered on the bond. A writ of *fieri facias* for the sale of the property issued to the Sheriff. The United States was not a party to this action. "The sheriff held the sale of the property on January 3, 1956; it was bid in by Brosnan and Jacob [assignees of the mortgagee] for $6,203 and, it is presumed, the discharge of the mortgage indebtedness. *The amount of the bid went to satisfy* costs of the sale, and for various outstanding local taxes." (264 F.2d, p. 764; emphasis supplied.)

More than a year later the United States brought an action to enforce its lien, but the District Court (164 F. Supp. 357) and the Court of Appeals for the 3d Circuit (264 F. 2d 762, *supra*) held that the junior lien of the Government was extinguished even though the United States had not been joined as a party. The Supreme Court affirmed the determinations below (363 U.S. 237). The opinion was replete with references to State law and procedure—something not found in *New Britain*.

The Supreme Court's attention was drawn to the fact that Pennsylvania gave its own tax liens more favorable treatment than it rendered the Federal liens at pages

---

[1] (Civ. Prac. Act, § 1087)—"Where a judgment rendered in an action to foreclose a mortgage upon real property directs a sale of the real property, the officer making the sale must pay out of the proceeds, unless the judgment otherwise directs, all taxes, assessments and water rates which are liens upon the property sold and redeem the property sold from any sales for unpaid taxes, assessments or water rates, which have not apparently become absolute. The sums necessary to make those payments and redemptions are deemed expenses of the sale within the meaning of that expression as used in any provision of this article. The provisions of this section shall not apply to any judgment in an action wherein any municipal corporation of this state is the plaintiff and the purchaser at the foreclosure sale thereunder."

[2] The Federal liens, amounting to $40,403.34 attached to the property between April 11, 1949 and November 28, 1951 (Exhibit B to complaint of United States). The local taxes paid out of the proceeds of the sale were county, township and school taxes for the period 1952–1955 in the amount of $5,756.90 (Transcript of Record, p. 22).

25 to 27 of the United States' brief: "Indeed, Pennsylvania law itself treats state tax liens more favorably than federal tax liens. A Pennsylvania statute provides that 'The lien of all taxes . . . against any real estate within this Commonwealth shall be divested by any judicial sale of such land: Provided, The amount of the purchase money shall equal the amount of the said taxes' (Purdon's Penna Statutes Annotated, Title 53, Section 7104, Appendix, *infra*, p. 36). While Pennsylvania law permits discharge of a junior lien on realty through foreclosure of a prior mortgage at a sheriff's sale, the Commonwealth's liens may be divested only to the extent permitted by statute [cases cited]. Thus, under Pennsylvania law the state's tax lien will be discharged through foreclosure only if the state's tax claim is paid in full out of the proceedings. The decision below holds, however, that the same foreclosure proceeding wipes out the federal lien even though the United States receives not a single penny toward payment of its claim."

The dissent makes it clear that the objection to Pennsylvania procedure in extinguishing the lien of the Federal Government was not that it was done according to State procedure, but that Pennsylvania procedure did not provide for notice to junior lienors (363 U.S. 261).

Although the main facet of the *Brosnan* case was a sanction of Pennsylvania's procedure, whereby the United States was not required to be a party to the action in order to extinguish its lien, the affirmance also necessarily sanctioned that State's procedure of paying local taxes out of the proceeds of the sale without the necessity of creating a surplus with which to pay liens prior to the local tax liens. (Purdon's Pennsylvania Statutes Ann., tit. 53, §§ 7103–7105.) This is a departure from the holding in the *New Britain* case, as that case is construed by the respondents. The Supreme Court in *Brosnan* also gave effect to the preference accorded to mortgagees by State and Federal law, and the decision tends toward the principal stated in the dissenting opinion of Haynsworth, J., in *United States v. Bond* (279 F.2d 837, 848, *cert. den.* 364 U.S. 895).

According to respondent's reasoning, the mortgagee, concededly not under any obligation to pay the Federal lien on the interest of the mortgagor at the time the lien was filed, becomes obligated when it bids in at the foreclosure sale simply because the mortgagee as bidder under State law must bear the cost of unpaid local taxes on the land falling due subsequent to the filing of the Federal lien. This imposition of liability is justified on the assumption that at the time of foreclosure the undetermined financial interest of the mortgagor has a value at least equal to the amount of the unpaid taxes which fell due subsequent to the filing of the Federal lien.

The circumstances present in the case of the foreclosure of a real estate tax lien by a municipality illustrate best the paradoxical result of the application of the rule respondent asserts. Under that rule the municipality which is foreclosing the tax lien for local taxes, which accrued subsequent to the filing of a tax lien filed against the equity of the property owner, shall be obligated to discharge the Federal tax lien in order to secure a clear title. But the interest of such a property owner obviously is worthless, since neither the property owner nor the public would bid on the tax lien which the municipality ultimately had to foreclose. In spite of this evidence of lack of value, the respondent would contend that the Federal lien has a priority because the nonexistent financial interest of the property owner cannot be diminished by giving priority to local taxes accrued subsequent to the filing of the Federal lien and that, therefore, the municipality must satisfy the Federal lien. In other words, the financial interest of the property owner which was nil develops value through the default of the property owner on local taxes. This *nonsequitur* had to be resorted to because respondent realizes its lien is not a lien on the land, but is only a lien on the equity of the owner. Therefore, it had to invent an equity which the owner could be said to possess at the time of the foreclosure in order to avoid the controlling State law which provides that the nature and extent of the property interests of a defaulting mortgagor can only be determined after a foreclosure sale conducted according to the State laws. The patent infirmity of this contrivance explains why the respondent has improperly invoked a canon, in a matter involving disparate liens, which is relevant only to the relationships of kindred liens, *i.e.*, "the first in time is the first in right".

Such a rule, if accepted now, would adversely affect the credit rating of all municipal bonds which are marketed on the assumption that local taxes are a first lien on the land within the municipality. It would also impair the borrowing power of municipalities because it makes the municipality liable for the personal debts a tax delinquent property owner owes to the Federal Government. Finally, it would cloud the title of properties which the municipalities have resold after acquisition through tax lien foreclosures.

The logic of the respondent appears to be as circular as the type of priority that it would have this court stamp with approval. The procedure that it proposes is novel to this State. Were local taxes not owing upon the land, the United States could not, through its own admissions, compel the creation of a surplus in which its lien would share with the judgment creditors. Is it logical that the Federal Government should be entitled to compel the mortgagee to treat the amount of real estate taxes subsequently accruing as a surplus to be applied toward payment of the Federal lien?

To accede to this attempt to foist the personal debts of the mortgagor owing to the United States on the mortgagee is to agree to the imposition of an indirect tax on savings banks who have invested billions of dollars in mortgages and on the savings of our citizens invested in mortgages which have been accorded a preference even under Federal law (U.S. Code, tit. 26, § 6323, subd. [a]). If the preference is to be whittled down, it should be done explicitly by a statute enacted by the representatives of the States in the national Congress and not by the courts.

The direction in the resettled judgment of foreclosure that the Referee should pay the real estate taxes, assessments and water rates out of the proceeds of the sale as expenses of the sale is not only in conformity with State law (Civ. Prac. Act, § 1087), but is also in keeping with the preference conferred on the mortgagee by State and Federal law protecting "all those rights which the Congress must have known the mortgagee commonly and usually possesses" (*United States v. Bond*, 279 F. 2d 837, 851, *supra*). Being the proper procedure of this State, the resettled judgment of foreclosure of October 20, 1960 should be affirmed.

The judgment of the Appellate Division, entered June 13, 1961, should be reversed and the judgment of the County Court, Erie County, entered October 20, 1960, reinstated, without costs.

FULD, J. (dissenting). By its present decision, the court is holding that a Federal tax lien filed against a mortgagor prior to the accrual of local real estate taxes and assessments—which are superior to the mortgage debt—is not entitled to priority over those subsequently accrued local liens. I cannot agree. In my view, the conclusion reached by the majority stands opposed to controlling authority. (*See United States v. New Britain*, 347 U.S. 81; *see, also, United States v. Bond*, 279 F.2d 837 [4th Cir.]; *United States v. Christensen*, 269 F.2d 624 [9th Cir.]; *Stadelman v. Hornell Woodworking Corp.*, 172 F. Supp. 156 [U.S. Dist. Ct., W. D. N. Y.]; *United States v. Lord*, 155 F. Supp. 105 [U.S. Dist. Ct., N. H.]; *Union Central Life Ins. Co. v. Peters*, 361 Mich. 283.) Nor may the impact of such authority be avoided by having the State, through legislative enactment or court decision, label local taxes and assessments "expenses of the sale", that is, of the mortgage foreclosure sale following the action brought by the mortgagee (Civ. Prac. Act, § 1087).

Once it has been determined, under State law, that the taxpayer has property or rights to property, "state law is inoperative to prevent the attachment of liens created by federal statutes in favor of the United States." (*United States v. Bess*, 357 U.S. 51, 57.) Moreover, when a Federal tax lien has attached to property of the taxpayer, as undoubtedly it had here, State law may not destroy it. (See *Commissioner v. Stern*, 357 U.S. 39.) As already indicated, calling the local taxes "expenses of the sale" does not help the local taxing authority, for it is to substance, not form, that the courts look. Local taxes do not result from the mortgage foreclosure sale; on the contrary, they pre–exist the sale. Accordingly, the State's characterization of them as "expenses of the sale"—appropriate though it may be for the State's own purposes—is thoroughly unreal in our present context and completely ineffectual to affect the priority of the Federal lien. (*Cf. United States v. Gilbert Associates*, 345 U.S. 361.)

In deciding questions concerning the relevant priorities of a Federal tax lien and other liens, it is perfectly clear that State law determines the nature and extent of the property interests of the taxpayer and that Federal law determines the priority of the competing claims themselves. (*See, e.g., Aquilino v. United States*, 363 U.S. 509, 515–516; *United States v. Brosnan*, 363 U.S. 237, 240; *United States v. Bess*, 357 U.S. 51, 55, *supra; United States v. Acri*, 348 U.S. 211, 213.) Although the court's opinion herein does not expressly reject this proposition—as to the proper role of State and Federal law in this area—its decision stands squarely opposed to it. What the court has done, under State law, is to characterize the nature and extent of the Federal lien and determine its priority in competition with local liens—a function exclusively reserved to the Federal law. (*See Aquilino v. United States*, 363 U.S. 509, *supra.*) Thus, the majority describes the Government's status in the present action as that merely of "a creditor of the mortgagor" and concludes that, since the Government's position "is based on the claimed interest of the mortgagor, [it] can have no better standing [than the mortgagor], that is, the Federal lien is also to be paid when there is a surplus [over mortgage debt plus local taxes] in which the mortgagor would have an interest" (opinion, p. 37). To employ the language of the opinion in the *Brosnan* case, this is not an authorized State determination of the " 'property and rights to property' . . . to which a government tax lien attaches," but rather an unauthorized State determination of "matters directly affecting the nature or operation of [federal tax] liens" (363 U.S. 237, 240).

Furthermore, giving priority to the after–accrued local taxes, as the majority is here doing, is directly contrary to the Supreme Court's decision in *United States v. New Britain* (347 U.S. 81, *supra*). In that case, in addition to prior mortgages and a prior judgment lien, the taxpayer's property was incumbered by a Federal tax lien and, subsequent in time to such lien, by a municipal tax lien. The Connecticut Supreme Court reasoned, as the majority does here, that, since Federal law subordinated the Federal tax lien to mortgage and judgment liens and since, under State law, these mortgage liens were subordinated to real property tax liens, the Federal tax lien had to be subordinated to the local real property tax lien. (*See Brown v. General Laundry Serv.*, 139 Conn. 363, 373.) In answer to this argument, the Supreme Court of the United States declared (347 U.S., at p. 88):

> We do not agree. The United States is not interested in whether the State receives its taxes and water rents prior to mortgagees and judgment creditors. That is a matter of state law. But as to any funds in excess of the amount necessary to pay the mortgage and judgment creditors, Congress intended to assert the federal lien.

Even more recently, in *United States v. Brosnan* (363 U.S. 237, *supra*), the Supreme Court, citing numerous decisions, "rejected" the very position taken by the majority in this case (363 U.S., at p. 241):

> This Court has repeatedly rejected the contention that because a fee owned by a taxpayer was already encumbered by a lien which enjoyed seniority under state law, the Government's lien necessarily attached subject to that lien.

The rule adopted in the *New Britain* case as the Federal rule for resolving conflicts between a Federal tax lien and local real property tax liens is the olden one that " 'the first in time is the first in right' " (347 U.S., at p. 85). As there pointed out, "When the debtor is insolvent, Congress has expressly given priority to the payment of indebtedness owing the United States, whether secured by liens or otherwise, by § 3466 of the Revised Statutes, 31 U.S.C. (1946 ed.) § 191. In that circumstance, where all the property of the debtor is involved, Congress has protected the federal revenues by imposing an absolute priority". Where, however, the court continued (p. 85), "the debtor is not insolvent, Congress has failed to expressly provide for federal priority, with certain exceptions not relevant here". (*And see* Internal Revenue Code of 1939, U.S. Code, tit. 26, § 3672; Internal Revenue Code of 1954, U.S. Code, tit. 26, § 6323) [1] And, added the court, "There is nothing in the language of § 3672 to show that Congress intended antecedent federal tax liens to rank behind any but the specific categories of interests set out therein" (p. 88), that is, mortgagees, judgment creditors, pledgees and purchasers. Accordingly, the relative

---

[1] It is appropriate to note at this point that the record before us, like the record in *New Britain* (347 U.S., at p. 85), does not indicate that the mortgagor–taxpayer was insolvent.

priority of each lien here involved "must depend upon the time [each of them] attached to the property in question and became choate" (p. 86. *See, also, United States v. Bond*, 279 F. 2d 837, *supra*; *United States v. Christensen*, 269 F. 2d 624, *supra*).

The court seeks to distinguish *New Britain* from the present case on the ground that the contest there "was between the local government and the Federal government over their respective rights in surplus funds", whereas here the "facts [show] that the dispute is really between the mortgagee and creditors of the mortgagor" (opinion, p. 36). Starting from this premise, the majority urges that, if the contest were between the Federal Government and the local taxing authorities, *New Britain* would control and the Government would prevail. But, since the dispute here is between the United States, as a creditor of the mortgagor, and the mortgagee, the latter must prevail, because (the argument proceeds) the Government can have no better standing than the mortgagor himself. And the court seeks to bolster this conclusion by claiming that "the respective liens [in this case] are not comparable charges on real property" (p. 35). In my judgment, the proffered ground for distinction is not tenable.

It is true that in *New Britain* the contest was between the city and the Federal Government but, as the facts disclosed and later developments made clear (*see Brown v. General Laundry Serv.*, 19 Conn. Supp. 335), the real parties in interest were the Federal Government and private lienors of the debtor's real estate who were entitled to priority over the Federal lien by the express terms of the Federal lien statutes. The State of Connecticut received its taxes in full at the expense of lienors whose liens were prior to those of the Federal Government. The fact that the contest in *New Britain* was between the city and the Federal Government and in this case between the mortgagee and the Government neither compels nor justifies a difference in result.

As I have already noted, it is the majority's assertion that the lien for local taxes must take precedence over the Government's lien because the respective liens are not comparable charges on real property. This is its position (pp. 36–38): On the one hand, "The local government lien is not a levy against the mortgagor, but against the land". On the other hand, the Federal Government's status is only that of "a creditor of the mortgagor", its claim merely one "based on the claimed interest of the mortgagor". And its lien, rather than being a lien which "attach[es] directly to the particular parcel of real property", as does that of the local government, "attach[es] to the property merely because of an unconnected indebtedness of the owner of the land". In other words, the Federal lien is not against the land, but "against a presumed equity in the real property held by the mortgagor."

Having made these distinctions, the court goes on to suggest that the difference in the way these liens arise assures priority to the liens of the local taxing authorities over the lien of the Federal Government. From this and the status ascribed to the Federal lien, it is the court's conclusion that "the Federal Government's claim, which is based on the claimed interest of the mortgagor, can have no better standing [than the mortgagor's claim], that is, the Federal lien is also to be paid when there is a surplus [above the mortgage debt and expenses of sale, including local taxes] in which the mortgagor would have an interest" (opinion, p. 37).

The fallacy of this argument, I venture, is that it mistakes the Federal law with respect to the status and incidence of the Federal interest. The Federal Government is no mere unsecured creditor of a delinquent taxpayer. It is, rather, the holder of "a lien . . . upon all property or rights to property, whether real or personal, belonging to such person" (Internal Revenue Code of 1954, U.S. Code, tit. 26, § 6321). Such a lien attaches to the real property owned by the taxpayer at the time the "[tax] assessment is made" (U.S. Code, tit. 26, § 6322), not to whatever equity he may have in it after a subsequent mortgage sale. In short, the Federal lien is not, as the majority insists, "against a presumed equity in the real property held by the mortgagor", but against the land itself. The rights of the Federal Government to the proceeds of the mortgage sale are not, therefore, limited to those of the mortgagor.

Let me state the matter somewhat differently. The lien of the United States arose when the assessments were made, and it attached to the mortgaged property at that time. Consequently, if the sale of the property had then been held, that lien could have been satisfied out of the proceeds of such sale after payment of proper expenses and of the amount then due on the mortgage plus interest to the date of payment. The local taxes here involved had not yet come into being and might never have become liens against the property. They might have been paid by the mortgagor or the property might have been foreclosed before they became due. Since, therefore, the liens of the local authorities had at best only a potential existence, we do not reach the question whether those liens were choate when the Federal liens attached. It comports neither with reality nor with law to give such "potential liens" priority over the pre–existing matured Federal lien by labeling them "expenses of the sale" in foreclosure proceedings.

Indeed, an argument very similar to that made by the court here, namely, that the respective charges of the Federal Government and the local taxing authorities are "not comparable charges on real property", was expressly made and rejected in the *New Britain* case (347 U.S. 81, *supra*). It had evidently been argued that the local tax liens should take precedence over the Federal tax lien because they were "specific" while the Federal lien was "general". With respect to this contention, the Supreme Court declared (p. 84):

> [T]he fact that one group of liens [the local] is specific and the other [the federal] general in and of itself is of no significance in these cases. . . . Thus, the general statutory liens of the United States are as binding as the specific statutory liens of the City. The City gains no priority by the fact that its liens are specific while the United States' liens are general.

Finally, a word must be said about the majority's characterization of the decision in *United States v. Brosnan* (363 U.S. 237, *supra*) as "a departure" from the holding in the *New Britain* case. In the first place, *Brosnan* was concerned with a question whether a Federal tax lien could be extinguished under a State procedure for foreclosure in which the Federal Government, *a junior lienor*, was not, and need not have been, a party; what was involved, therefore, was not the problem of priority at issue here. In the second place, although local taxes had been paid out of the proceeds of the mortgage sale and thus had, in effect, achieved priority, that issue was never raised on appeal, the sole issue being—to cull from the court's opinion— "whether the federal lien was effectively extinguished by state proceedings to which the United States was not, nor was required under state law to be, a party" (363 U.S., at pp. 238–239). The third and (to me) conclusive reason why *Brosnan* may not be taken to be a departure from the *New Britain* holding is that in *Brosnan* the Supreme Court actually cited *New Britain* with approval (363 U.S., at p. 241, n. 4) and restated one of the principles which it had announced; thus, it wrote in *Brosnan* (p. 241): "This Court has repeatedly rejected the contention that because a fee owned by a taxpayer was already encumbered by a lien which enjoys seniority under state law, the Government's lien necessarily attached subject to that lien". As is evident, far from supporting the majority view in the present case, the opinion in *Brosnan* stands with *New Britain* to refute it.

In sum, then, in situations of this kind, the lien of the Federal Government must be recognized as prior in right to that of the local taxing authorities. This follows from the fact that it is prior in time. But this does not mean that those local taxing authorities will not collect their taxes. The majority opinion has placed the contest in its proper setting. The dispute is between the mortgagee and the Federal Government as a creditor of the mortgagor. The local taxing authorities will be paid at the expense of the mortgagee so there will be no adverse economic impact upon the taxing authorities. The mortgagee's interest in the proceeds of the mortgage sale may, perhaps, be diminished. But the mortgagee is not left without recourse where the mortgagor is liable for payment of the debt secured by the mortgage and he is not insolvent. In such a case, the mortgagee may collect the "residue" or balance due from the mortgagor by way of a deficiency judgment (Civ. Prac. Act, §§ 1082, 1083).

I would affirm the judgment of the Appellate Division.

Chief Judge DESMOND and Judges DYE, FROESSEL and VAN VOORHIS concur with Judge BURKE; Judge FULD dissents in an opinion in which Judge FOSTER concurs.

Judgment of Appellate Division, entered June 13, 1961, reversed and judgment of the County Court, Erie County, entered October 20, 1960, reinstated, without costs.

UNITED STATES v. BUFFALO SAVINGS BANK

United States Supreme Court
371 U.S. 228, 83 S. Ct. 314,9 L. Ed. 2d. 283 (1963)
reh'g. den. sub. nom. Buffalo Savings Bank v. Victory
12 N.Y.2d 1100, 240 N.Y.S.2d 164, 190 N.E.2d 536 (1963)

PER CURIAM.

In 1946, respondent Buffalo Savings Bank made a loan secured by a real estate mortgage. The United States filed notice of a federal tax lien against the mortgagor's property in 1953. Thereafter, in 1957 and 1958, liens for unpaid real estate taxes and other local assessments attached to the property. The bank instituted foreclosure proceedings, naming the United States as a party. The trial court's decree ordered the property sold and the payment of local real estate taxes and other assessments as part of the expenses of the sale prior to the satisfaction of the tax lien of the United States. The United States appealed and the New York Supreme Court, Appellate Division, reversed, only to be reversed in turn by the New York Court of Appeals, which reinstated the trial court's judgment on the ground that the federal tax lien attached only to the mortgagor's interest in the surplus after the foreclosure sale and therefore was subordinate to the local taxes as "expenses of sale." 11 N.Y. 2d 31, 181 N.E. 2d 413.

We must reverse the judgment of the New York Court of Appeals for failure to take proper account of *United States v. New Britain*, 347 U.S. 81. That case rules this one, for there the Court quite clearly held that federal tax liens have priority over subsequently accruing liens for local real estate taxes, even though the burden of the local taxes in the event of a shortage would fall upon the mortgagee whose claim under state law is subordinate to local tax liens.

A similar argument based on the general character of the federal tax lien was made and specifically rejected in *New Britain*. Moreover, the state may not avoid the priority rules of the federal tax lien by the formalistic device of characterizing subsequently accruing local liens as expenses of sale. *Cf. United States v. Gilbert Associates, Inc.*, 345 U.S. 361. Finally, respondent's reliance on *United States v. Brosnan*, 363 U.S. 237, and *Crest Finance Co. v. United States*, 368 U.S. 347, is misplaced. *Brosnan* was concerned with foreclosure procedures, not with priorities, and in connection with the latter subject relied upon *New Britain* among other cases. *Crest* is wholly inapposite here.

The judgment is therefore reversed and the cause remanded for further proceedings not inconsistent with this opinion.

Reversed and remanded.

Mr. Justice DOUGLAS dissents.

UNITED STATES v. VERMONT

United States Supreme Court
377 U.S. 351, 84 S. Ct. 1267, 12 L. Ed. 2d. 370 (1964)

Mr. Justice STEWART delivered the opinion of the Court.

This case involves a conflict between two liens upon the property of a solvent Vermont taxpayer—a federal tax lien arising under the provisions of 26 U.S.C. §§ 6321 and 6322[1] and an antecedent state tax lien based on a Vermont law worded in terms virtually identical to the provisions of those federal statutes.

---

[1] 26 U.S.C. § 6321 provides:

If any person liable to pay any tax neglects or refuses to pay the same after demand, the amount (including any interest, additional amount, addition to tax, or assessable

On October 21, 1958, the State of Vermont made an assessment and demand on Cutting & Trimming, Inc., for withheld state income taxes of $1,628.15. The applicable Vermont statute, modeled on the comparable federal enactments, provides that if an employer required to withhold a tax fails to pay the same after demand, "the amount, including interest after such demand, together with any costs that may accrue in addition thereto, shall be a lien in favor of the state of Vermont upon all property and rights to property, whether real or personal, belonging to such employer," and that "[s]uch lien shall arise at the time the assessment and demand is made by the commissioner of taxes and shall continue until the liability for such sum, with interest and costs, is satisfied or becomes unenforceable."[2]

More than three months later, on February 9, 1959, the Commissioner of Internal Revenue made an assessment against Cutting & Trimming of $5,365.96 for taxes due under the Federal Unemployment Tax Act. Under §§ 6321 and 6322, this amount became "a lien in favor of the United States upon all property and rights to property, whether real or personal, belonging to such person," which arose "at the time the assessment is made and shall continue until the liability for the amount so assessed is satisfied or becomes unenforceable by reason of lapse of time."[3]

On May 21, 1959, the State instituted suit in a state court against Cutting & Trimming, joining as a defendant Chittenden Trust Company, a Burlington bank which, as the result of a writ served on May 25, disclosed that it had in hand sums owing to Cutting & Trimming. On October 23, 1959, judgment was entered against Cutting & Trimming and against Chittenden Trust Company.

In 1961, the United States brought the present action in the Federal District Court for Vermont to foreclose the federal lien against the property of Cutting & Trimming held by the Trust Company. Vermont's answer alleged that the state assessment of

---

penalty, together with any costs that may accrue in addition thereto) shall be a lien in favor of the United States upon all property and rights to property, whether real or personal, belonging to such person.

26 U.S.C. § 6322 provides:

Unless another date is specifically fixed by law, the lien imposed by section 6321 shall arise at the time the assessment is made and shall continue until the liability for the amount so assessed is satisfied or becomes unenforceable by reason of lapse of time.

[2] 32 V.S.A. § 5765.

[3] *See* note 1, *supra*. Notice of the federal lien was filed on June 2, 1959, pursuant to 26 U.S.C. § 6323, which provides:

(a) *Invalidity of lien without notice.* Except as otherwise provided in subsection (c), the lien imposed by section 6321 shall not be valid as against any mortgagee, pledgee, purchaser, or judgment creditor until notice thereof has been filed by the Secretary or his delegate—. . . .

No claim is made here that Vermont's lien comes within any of the four classifications to which § 6323 accords priority until notice of the federal tax lien has been filed. Consequently, we put to one side such cases as *United States v. Pioneer American Ins. Co.*, 374 U.S. 84, *United States v. Ball Construction Co.*, 355 U.S. 587, and *United States v. Scovil*, 348 U.S. 218, which are concerned with the federal standards to be applied in determining whether the security interests envisaged in that provision have in fact been created. *See also United States v. Gilbert Associates*, 345 U.S. 361, 363–365.

October 21, 1958, gave its lien priority over the federal lien. On cross–motions for judgment on the pleadings, the District Court held that the state lien had priority, and directed the Trust Company to apply the moneys which it held first to the payment of principal and interest on that lien, and to pay any balance to the United States. 206 F.Supp. 951.

The Court of Appeals affirmed, reasoning that, under this Court's decision in *United States v. New Britain*, 347 U.S. 81, "[i]t would seem that if the general federal tax lien under §§ 6321 and 6322 is thus sufficiently 'choatc' to prevail over a later specific local tax lien, a general state tax lien under an almost identically worded statute must also be 'choate' enough to prime a later and equally general federal tax lien," 317 F.2d 446, 452. Accordingly, the appellate court applied "the 'cardinal rule' laid down by Chief Justice Marshall in *Rankin & Schatzell v. Scott*, 12 Wheat. (25 U.S.) 177, 179 (1827): 'The principle is believed to be universal that a prior lien gives a prior claim, which is entitled to prior satisfaction, out of the subject it binds. . . .' " *Id.*, at 450. Because of the importance of the question in the administration of the state and federal revenue laws, we granted certiorari. 375 U.S. 940. For the reasons which follow, we affirm the judgment of the Court of Appeals.

Both parties urge that decision here is governed by *United States v. New Britain*, 347 U.S. 81. In that case, involving conflicting municipal and federal statutory liens, the Court held that "the priority of each statutory lien contested here must depend on the time it attached to the property in question and became choate." *Id.*, at 86. In determining the choateness of the liens involved, the Court "accept[ed] the [state court's] holding as to the specificity of the City's liens since they attached to specific pieces of real property for the taxes assessed and water rent due," but it went on to stress that "liens may also be perfected in the sense that there is nothing more to be done to have a choate lien—when the identity of the lienor, the property subject to the lien, and the amount of the lien are established. The federal tax liens are general and, in the sense above indicated, perfected." *Id.*, at 84. Vermont's claim for the priority of its lien over the later federal lien is based on the fact that its lien is as completely "perfected" as was the federal lien in *New Britain*. Opposing this claim, the United States urges that different standards of choateness apply to federal and state liens, even where, as here, they are based on statutes identical in every material respect. The argument, in short, is that an antecedent state lien, in order to obtain priority over a federal lien based on §§ 6321 and 6322, cannot, like the federal lien, attach to all of the taxpayer's property, but must rather, like the municipal liens in *New Britain*, attach to specifically identified portions of that property.

The requirement that a competing lien must be choate in order to take priority over a later federal tax lien stems from the decision in *United States v. Security Trust & Savings Bank*, 340 U.S. 47. There, an attachment lien which gave no right to proceed against the attached property unless judgment was obtained within three years or within an extension provided by the statute was held junior to a federal tax lien which had arisen after the date of the attachment but prior to the date of judgment on the ground that "[n]umerous contingencies might arise that would prevent the attachment lien from ever becoming perfected by a judgment awarded and recorded. Thus the attachment lien is contingent or inchoate—merely a *lis pendens* notice that a right to perfect a lien exists." *Id.*, at 50. The *Security Trust* rationale has since been applied in a case where a federal tax lien arose prior to judgment on a garnishment lien, *United States v. Liverpool & London Ins. Co.*, 348 U.S. 215,[4] and comparable defects have been held to require the according of priority to the federal lien in a series of cases involving competing mechanics' liens.[5]

In addition to setting out the specific ground of decision, however, the *Security Trust* opinion went on to state:

> In cases involving a kindred matter, *i.e.*, the federal priority under R.S. § 3466, it has never been held sufficient to defeat the federal priority merely to show a lien effective to protect the lienor against others than the Government, but contingent upon taking subsequent steps for enforcing it. . . . If the purpose of the federal tax lien statute to insure prompt and certain collection of taxes due the United States from tax delinquents is to be fulfilled, a similar rule must prevail here.

340 U.S., at 51. Relying on this statement, the United States urges us to read *Security Trust* as establishing the proposition that federal tax liens are entitled to priority, not only over "a *lis pendens* notice that a right to perfect a lien exists," but over any antecedent lien which is not sufficiently perfected to prevail against the explicit priority which R.S. § 3466 gives to claims of the United States in situations involving insolvency.[6] More particularly, it is suggested that the state liens at issue here did not meet the standards of "specificity" until Vermont attached the funds held by the Chittenden Trust Company, at which time the federal tax lien had already come into existence. This argument fails to discriminate between the standards applicable under the federal tax lien provisions and those applicable to an insolvent debtor under R.S. § 3466.

Section 3466 on its face permits no exception whatsoever from the statutory command that "[w]henever any person indebted to the United States is insolvent . . . debts due to the United States shall be first satisfied." The statute applies to all the insolvent's debts to the Government, whether or not arising from taxes, and whether or not secured by a lien. In *United States v. Gilbert Associates*, 345 U.S. 361, without questioning that the lienor was identified, the amount of the lien certain or the property subject to the lien definite, this Court accorded priority to

---

[4] *See also United States v. Acri*, 348 U.S. 211 (attachment lien).

[5] *United States v. Hulley*, 358 U.S. 66; *United States v. Vorreiter*, 355 U.S. 15; *United States v. White Bear Brewing Co.*, 350 U.S. 1010; *United States v. Colotta*, 350 U.S. 808.

[6] Revised Statutes § 3466 provides:

> Whenever any person indebted to the United States is insolvent, or whenever the estate of any deceased debtor, in the hands of the executors or administrators, is insufficient to pay all the debts due from the deceased, the debts due to the United States shall be first satisfied; and the priority hereby established shall extend as well to cases in which a debtor, not having sufficient property to pay all his debts, makes a voluntary assignment thereof, or in which the estate and effects of an absconding, concealed, or absent debtor are attached by process of law, as to cases in which an act of bankruptcy is committed.

subsequently arising claims of the United States against an insolvent debtor on the ground that:

> In claims of this type, "specificity" requires that the lien be attached to certain property by reducing it to possession, on the theory that the United States has no claim against property no longer in the possession of the debtor. . . . The taxpayer had not been divested by the Town of either title or possession. The Town, therefore, had only a general, unperfected lien.

Id., at 366.[7]

The state tax commissioner's assessment and demand in the present case clearly did not meet that standard, nor, so far as that goes, did the writ of attachment served on the Chittenden Trust Company.[8] But the *New Britain* case, 347 U.S. 81, in which "[t]he taxpayer had not been divested by the Town of either title or possession," makes quite clear that different standards apply where the United States' claim is based on a tax lien arising under §§ 6321 and 6322.[9] "When the debtor is insolvent, Congress has expressly given priority to the payment of indebtedness owing the United States, whether secured by liens or otherwise, by § 3466 of the Revised Statutes, 31 U.S.C. . . . § 191. In that circumstance, where all the property of the debtor is involved, Congress has protected the federal revenues by imposing an absolute priority [citing *United States v. Gilbert Associates*, 345 U.S. 361; *United States v. Waddill, Holland & Flinn*, 323 U.S. 353]. Where the debtor is not insolvent, Congress has failed to expressly provide for federal priority . . . although the United States is free to pursue the whole of the debtor's property wherever situated." *United States v. New Britain*, 347 U.S. 81, 85.

It is undisputed that the State's lien here meets the test laid down in *New Britain* that "the identity of the lienor, the property subject to the lien, and the amount of the lien are established." 347 U.S., at 84. Moreover, unlike those cases in which the *Security Trust* rationale was applied to subordinate liens on the ground that judgment had not been obtained prior to the time the federal lien arose,[10] it is as true of Vermont's lien here [11] as it was of the federal lien in *New Britain* that "The assessment is given the force of a judgment, and if the amount assessed is not paid when due, administrative officials may seize the debtor's property to satisfy the debt." *Bull v. United States*, 295 U.S. 247, 260.[12]

---

[7] *See also Illinois v. Campbell*, 329 U.S. 362, 375–376; *United States v. Waddill Co.*, 323 U.S. 353, 359–360.

[8] Indeed, this Court has repeatedly reserved the question whether the priority given the United States by R.S. § 3466 can be overcome even by a prior specific and perfected lien. *United States v. Gilbert Associates*, 345 U.S. 361, 365; *Illinois v. Campbell*, 329 U.S. 362, 370; *United States v. Waddill Co.*, 323 U.S. 353, 355–356; *United States v. Texas*, 314 U.S. 480, 484–486; *New York v. Maclay*, 288 U.S. 290, 294; *Spokane County v. United States*, 279 U.S. 80, 95.

[9] *See also Crest Finance Co. v. United States*, 368 U.S. 347.

[10] *See* notes 4 and 5, *supra*, and accompanying text.

[11] *See* 317 F.2d, at 448, n. 2.

[12] The municipal liens accorded priority in *New Britain* were also characterized as summarily enforceable. *See* Brief for the United States, No. 92, 1953 Term, p. 27, n. 13.

For these reasons, we hold that this antecedent state lien arising under a statute modeled after §§ 6321 and 6322 is sufficiently choate to obtain priority over the later federal lien arising under those provisions. Accordingly, the judgment of the Court of Appeals is

Affirmed.

NOTES AND QUESTIONS

(1) In *Buffalo Savings Bank, supra,* the courts dealt with a circular priority problem in which the mortgagee had priority over a subsequent federal tax lien. The New York Court of Appeals held that the federal tax lien was subordinate to subsequently arising local real estate taxes, which were deemed expenses of sale and primed the mortgagee's interest under state law, which permitted local real estate tax liens to prime competing liens even if perfected prior in time. The Supreme Court reversed. As a result, the mortgagee was left in last place in the order of payment and unsatisfied because there were insufficient funds in the estate. Subsequently, in 1966, Congress granted local real estate taxes and special assessments a priority over previously filed federal tax liens. This avoids the harsh result in the *Buffalo Savings Bank* case because the federal government has consented to being taxed in this limited instance. This change in the law stabilized secured loans on *real* property, but lenders with liens on *personal* property still have to deal with the circular priority problem illustrated in *Buffalo Savings Bank. See* Internal Revenue Code § 6323(b)(6), 26 U.S.C. § 6323(b)(6).

(2) To obtain priority over a federal tax lien, prior liens not covered by a statutory exception must continue to meet the test for "choateness" set forth in *United States v. New Britain,* 347 U.S. 81 (1954), before the federal tax lien arises. A state lienor is protected under the test if the amount of the underlying debt, the identity of the lienor, and the identity of property subject to the lien are all established at the time notice of the tax lien is filed. *Accord, General Telephone of Illinois v. Robinson,* 545 F. Supp. 788 (D. Fla. 1982); *Lanning Equipment Corp. v. United States,* 346 F. Supp. 1068 (N.D. Ohio. 1972).

(3) In *United States v. Vermont, supra,* both the federal and state tax liens were general. The lien asserted by the State of Vermont, however, was held to be sufficiently "choate" to obtain priority in payment over the subsequent federal tax lien from property of a solvent taxpayer. Have the courts developed the same standards for testing "choateness" under the federal priority statute and the federal tax lien law? How would the court have decided the controversy if the taxpayer were insolvent? *See United States v. Gilbert Associates, Inc.,* 345 U.S. 361 (1953). *See also* 31 U.S.C. § 3713, *supra, and compare* the holding of the Pennsylvania Supreme Court in *In re Estate of Berretta,* 426 A.2d 1098, 1106, 493 Pa. 441 (1981):

> [W]e would conclude that the provisions of § 6323 of the Internal Revenue Code must be read so as to limit the operation of the Federal Insolvency Statute

in tax delinquent cases. We arrive at this conclusion for the following reasons: (1) there is a plain inconsistency between the Tax Lien Act and the Federal Insolvency Statute; (2) the Tax Lien Act evidences a Congressional intent that federal priorities be limited in the tax area; (3) the Supreme Court of the United States has restricted federal priority in federal lending cases for reasons that are also applicable in tax cases (restricting the priority would not endanger the specific objectives of the federal programs and it would have adverse commercial consequences); and (4) to grant absolute federal priority would be destructive of commercial stability and would frustrate legitimate commercial expectations.

UNITED STATES v. McDERMOTT

Supreme Court of the United States
507 U.S. 447, 113 S. Ct. 1526 (1993)

SCALIA, Justice.

We granted certiorari to resolve the competing priorities of a federal tax lien and a private creditor's judgment lien as to a delinquent taxpayer's after–acquired real property.

I

On December 9, 1986 the United States assessed Mr. and Mrs. McDermott for unpaid federal taxes due for the tax years 1977 through 1981. Upon that assessment, the law created a lien in favor of the United States on all real and personal property belonging to the McDermotts, 26 U.S.C. §§ 6321 and 6322, including after–acquired property, *Glass City Bank v. United States*, 326 U.S. 265, 66 S.Ct. 108, 90 L.Ed. 56 (1945). Pursuant to 26 U.S.C. § 6323(a), however, that lien could "not be valid as against any purchaser, holder of a security interest, mechanic's lienor, or judgment lien creditor until notice thereof . . . has been filed." (Emphasis added.) The United States did not file this lien in the Salt Lake County Recorder's Office until September 9, 1987. Before that occurred, however—specifically, on July 6, 1987—Zions First National Bank, N.A., docketed with the Salt Lake County Clerk a state–court judgment it had won against the McDermotts. Under Utah law, that created a judgment lien on all of the McDermotts' real property in Salt Lake County, "owned . . . at the time or . . . thereafter acquired during the existence of said lien." Utah Code Ann. § 78–22–1 (1953).

On September 23, 1987 the McDermotts acquired title to certain real property in Salt Lake County. To facilitate later sale of that property, the parties entered into an escrow agreement whereby the United States and the Bank released their claims to the real property itself but reserved their rights to the cash proceeds of the sale, based on their priorities in the property as of September 23, 1987. Pursuant to the escrow agreement, the McDermotts brought this interpleader action in state court to establish which lien was entitled to priority; the United States removed to the United States District Court for the District of Utah.

On cross–motions for partial summary judgment, the District Court awarded priority to the Bank's judgment lien. The United States Court of Appeals for the Tenth Circuit affirmed. *McDermott v. Zions First Nat'l Bank, N.A.*, 945 F.2d 1475 (1991). We granted *certiorari*. 504 U.S. ___, 112 S.Ct. 2272, 119 L.Ed.2d 199 (1992).

II

Federal tax liens do not automatically have priority over all other liens. Absent provision to the contrary, priority for purposes of federal law is governed by the common–law principle that " 'the first in time is the first in right.' " *United States v. New Britain*, 347 U.S. 81, 85, 74 S.Ct. 367, 370, 98 L.Ed. 520 (1954); *cf. Rankin & Schatzell v. Scott*, 12 Wheat. 177, 179, 6 L.Ed. 592 (1827) (Marshall, C.J.). For purposes of applying that doctrine in the present case—in which the competing state lien (that of a judgment creditor) benefits from the provision of § 6323(a) that the federal lien shall "not be valid . . . until notice thereof . . . has been filed"—we must deem the United States' lien to have commenced no sooner than the filing of notice. As for the Bank's lien: our cases deem a competing state lien to be in existence for "first in time" purposes only when it had been "perfected" in the sense that "the identity of the lienor, the property subject to the lien, and the amount of the lien are established." *United States v. New Britain*, 347 U.S., at 84, 74 S.Ct., at 369 (emphasis added); *see also id.*, at 86, 74 S.Ct., at 370; *United States v. Pioneer American Ins. Co.*, 374 U.S. 84, 83 S.Ct. 1651, 10 L.Ed.2d 770 (1963).

The first question we must answer, then, is whether the Bank's judgment lien was perfected in this sense before the United States filed its tax lien on September 9, 1987. If so, that is the end of the matter; the Bank's lien prevails. The Court of Appeals was of the view that this question was answered (or rendered irrelevant) by our decision in *United States v. Vermont*, 377 U.S. 351, 84 S.Ct. 1267, 12 L.Ed.2d 370 (1964), which it took to "stan[d] for the proposition that a non–contingent . . . lien on all of a person's real property, perfected prior to the federal tax lien, will take priority over the federal lien, regardless of whether after–acquired property is involved."[1] 945 F.2d, at 1480. That is too expansive a reading. Our opinion in *Vermont* gives no indication that the property at issue had become subject to the state lien only by application of an after–acquired–property clause to property that the debtor acquired after the federal lien arose. To the contrary, the opinion says that the state lien met (presumably at the critical time when the federal lien arose) "the test laid down in *New Britain* that . . . 'the property subject to the lien . . . [be] established.' " 377 U.S., at 358, 84 S.Ct., at 1271 (citation omitted).[2] The

---

[1] As our later discussion will show, we think it contradictory to say that the state lien was "perfected" before the federal lien was filed, insofar as it applies to after–acquired property not acquired by the debtor until after the federal lien was filed. The Court of Appeals was evidently using the term "perfected" (as the Bank would) in a sense not requiring attachment of the lien to the property in question; our discussion of the Court of Appeals' opinion assumes that usage.

[2] The dissent cannot both grant the assumption "that the debtor in *Vermont* acquired its interest in the bank account before the federal lien arose," *post*, at 1533, n. 2, and contend

argument of the United States that we rejected in *Vermont* was the contention that a state lien is not perfected within the meaning of *New Britain* if it "attach[es] to all of the taxpayer's property," rather than "to specifically identified portions of that property." 377 U.S., at 355, 84 S.Ct., at 1269.[3] We did not consider, and the facts as recited did not implicate, the quite different argument made by the United States in the present case: that a lien in after–acquired property is not "perfected" as to property yet to be acquired.

The Bank argues that, as of July 6, 1987, the date it docketed its judgment lien, the lien was "perfected as to all real property then and thereafter owned by" the McDermotts, since "[n]othing further was required of [the Bank] to attach the non–contingent lien on after–acquired property." Brief for Respondents 21. That reflects an unusual notion of what it takes to "perfect" a lien.[4] Under the Uniform Commercial Code, for example, a security interest in after–acquired property is generally not considered perfected when the financing statement is filed, but only when the security interest has attached to particular property upon the debtor's acquisition of that property. §§ 9–203(1) and (2), 3 U.L.A. 363 (1992); § 9–303(1), 3A U.L.A. 117 (1992). And attachment to particular property was also an element of what we meant by "perfection" in *New Britain*. *See* 347 U.S., at 84, 74 S.Ct., at 369 ("when . . . the property subject to the lien . . . [is] established"); *id.*, at

that "the debtor's interest in the bank account . . . could have been uncertain or indefinite from the creditors' perspective," *id.*, at 1533, n. 2. In the same footnote, the dissent misdescribes the "critical argument that we rejected" in *Vermont*. *Ibid.* It was not that "the State's claim could not be superior unless the account had been 'specifically identified' as property subject to the State's lien," *ibid.*, but rather that the State's claim could not be superior unless it had "attach[ed] to specifically identified portions of that property," *United States v. Vermont*, 377 U.S. 351, 355, 84 S.Ct. 1267, 1269, 12 L.Ed.2d 370 (1964).

[3] The dissent claims that "the Government's 'specificity' claim rejected in *Vermont* is analytically indistinguishable from the 'attachment' argument the Court accepts today," since "[i]f specific attachment is not required for the state lien to be 'sufficiently choate,' then neither is specific acquisition." Post, at 1532–1533 (citation omitted). But the two are not comparable. Until the debtor has acquired the subject property, it is impossible to say that "the property subject to the lien [has been] . . . established," *United States v. New Britain*, 347 U.S. 81, 84, 74 S.Ct. 367, 369, 98 L.Ed. 520 (1954). Judicial attachment, on the other hand (and it is important to note that judicial attachment of the property, rather than attachment of the lien to the property, was what the Government's argument in *Vermont* involved), merely brings into the custody of a court property that is already—prior to judicial attachment—known to be subject to the lien.

[4] The dissent accepts the Bank's central argument that perfection occurred when "there was 'nothing more to be done' by the Bank 'to have a choate lien' on any real property the McDermotts might acquire." Post, at 1532 (quoting *United States v. New Britain, supra*, at 84, 74 S.Ct., at 369); *see also* post, at 1533–1534. This unusual definition of perfection has been achieved by making a small but substantively important addition to the language of *New Britain*. "[N]othing more to be done to have a choate lien" (the language of *New Britain*) becomes "nothing more to be done by the Bank to have a choate lien." Once one recognizes that the dissent's concept of a lien's "becom[ing] certain as to the property subject thereto," *see* post, at 1532, 1534, is meaningless, *see* n. 5, *infra*, it becomes apparent that the dissent, like the Bank, would simply have us substitute the concept of "best efforts" for the concept of perfection.

86, 74 S.Ct., at 370 ("the priority of each statutory lien contested here must depend on the time it attached to the property in question and became [no longer inchoate]").[5] The Bank concedes that its lien did not actually attach to the property at issue here until the McDermotts acquired rights in that property. Brief for Respondents 16, 21. Since that occurred after filing of the federal tax lien, the state lien was not first in time.[6]

But that does not complete our inquiry: Though the state lien was not first in time, the federal tax lien was not necessarily first in time either. Like the state lien, it applied to the property at issue here by virtue of a (judicially inferred) after–acquired–property provision, which means that it did not attach until the same instant the state lien attached, viz., when the McDermotts acquired the property; and, like the state lien, it did not become "perfected" until that time. We think, however, that under the language of § 6323(a) ("shall not be valid as against any . . . judgment lien creditor until notice . . . has been filed"), the filing of notice renders the federal tax lien extant for "first in time" priority purposes regardless of whether it has yet attached to identifiable property. That result is also indicated by the provision, two subsections later, which accords priority, even against filed federal tax liens, to security interests arising out of certain agreements, including "commercial transactions financing agreement[s]," entered into before filing of the tax lien. 26 U.S.C. § 6323(c)(1). That provision protects certain security interests that, like the after–acquired–property judgment lien here, will have been recorded before the filing of the tax lien, and will attach to the encumbered property after the filing of the tax lien, and simultaneously with the attachment of the tax lien (*i.e.,* upon the debtor's acquisition of the subject property). According special priority to certain state security interests in these circumstances obviously presumes that otherwise the federal tax lien would prevail—*i.e.,* that the federal tax lien is ordinarily dated, for

---

[5] The dissent refuses to acknowledge the unavoidable realities that the property subject to a lien is not "established" until one knows what specific property that is, and that a lien cannot be anything other than "inchoate" with respect to property that is not yet subject to the lien. Hence the dissent says that, upon its filing, the lien at issue here "was perfected, even as to the real property later acquired by the McDermotts, in the sense that it was definite as to the property in question, noncontingent, and summarily enforceable." Post, at 1532. But how could it have been at that time, "definite" as to this property, when the identity of this property (established by the McDermotts' later acquisition) was yet unknown? Or "noncontingent" as to this property, when the property would have remained entirely free of the judgment lien had the McDermotts not later decided to buy it? Or "summarily enforceable" against this property when the McDermotts did not own, and had never owned, it? The dissent also says that "[t]he lien was immediately enforceable through levy and execution against all the debtors' property, whenever acquired." Post, at 1532. But of course it was not "immediately enforceable" (as of its filing date, which is the relevant time) against property that the McDermotts had not yet acquired.

[6] The dissent suggests, post, at 1532, n. 1, that the Treasury Department regulation defining "judgment lien creditor," 26 CFR § 301.6323(h)–1(g) (1992), contradicts our analysis. It would, if it contained only the three requirements that the dissent describes. In fact, however, it says that to prevail the judgment lien must be perfected, and that "[a] judgment lien is not perfected until the identity of the lienor, the property subject to the lien, and the amount of the lien are established." *Ibid.*

purposes of "first in time" priority against § 6323(a) competing interests, from the time of its filing, regardless of when it attaches to the subject property.[7]

The Bank argues that "[b]y common law, the first lien of record against a debtor's property has priority over those subsequently filed unless a lien–creating statute clearly shows or declares an intention to cause the statutory lien to override." Brief for Respondents 11.[8] Such a strong, "first–to–record" presumption may be appropriate for simultaneously–perfected liens under ordinary statutes creating private liens, which ordinarily arise out of voluntary transactions. When two private lenders both exact from the same debtor security agreements with after–acquired–property clauses, the second lender knows, by reason of the earlier recording, that that category of property will be subject to another claim, and if the remaining security is inadequate he may avoid the difficulty by declining to extend credit. The Government, by contrast, cannot indulge the luxury of declining to hold the taxpayer liable for his taxes; notice of a previously filed security agreement covering after–acquired property does not enable the Government to protect itself. A strong "first–to–record" presumption is particularly out of place under the present tax–lien statute, whose general rule is that the tax collector prevails even if he has not recorded at all. 26 U.S.C. §§ 6321 and 6322; *United States v. Snyder*, 149 U.S. 210, 13 S.Ct. 846, 37 L.Ed. 705 (1893). Thus, while we would hardly proclaim the statutory meaning we have discerned in this opinion to be "clear," it is evident enough for the purpose at hand. The federal tax lien must be given priority.

The judgment of the Court of Appeals is reversed, and the case is remanded for further proceedings consistent with this opinion.

So Ordered.

Justice THOMAS, with whom Justice STEVENS and Justice O'CONNOR join, dissenting.

---

[7] The dissent contends that "there is no persuasive reason for not adopting as a matter of federal law the well–recognized common–law rule of parity and giving the Bank an equal interest in the property." Post, at 1534, n. 4. As we have explained, the persuasive reason is the existence of § 6323(c), which displays the assumption that all perfected security interests are defeated by the federal tax lien. There is no reason why this assumption should not extend to judgment liens as well. A "security interest," as defined in § 6323, is not an insignificant creditor's preference. The term includes only interests protected against subsequent judgment liens. *See* 26 U.S.C. §§ 6323(h)(1) and 6323(c)(1)(B). Moreover, the text of § 6323(a) ("The lien . . . shall not be valid as against any purchaser, holder of a security interest, mechanic's lienor, or judgment lien creditor") treats security interests and judgment liens alike. Parity may be, as the dissent says, a "well–recognized common–law rule," post, at 1534, n. 4, but we have not hitherto adopted it as the federal law of tax liens in 127 years of tax lien enforcement.

[8] The dissent notes that "[n]othing in the law of judgment liens suggests that the possibility, which existed at the time the Bank docketed its judgment, that the McDermotts would not acquire the specific property here at issue was a 'contingency' that rendered the Bank's otherwise perfected general judgment lien subordinate to intervening liens." Post, at 1533. Perhaps. But priorities here are determined, not by "the law of judgment liens" but by § 6323(a), as our case–law has interpreted it. The requirement that competing state liens be perfected is part of that jurisprudence.

I agree with the Court that under 26 U.S.C. § 6323(a) we generally look to the filing of notice of the federal tax lien to determine the federal lien's priority as against a competing state–law judgment lien. I cannot agree, however, that a federal tax lien trumps a judgment creditor's claim to after–acquired property whenever notice of the federal lien is filed before the judgment lien has "attached" to the property. Ante, at 1529. In my view, the Bank's antecedent judgment lien "ha[d] [already] acquired sufficient substance and ha[d] become so perfected," with respect to the McDermotts' after–acquired real property, "as to defeat [the] later–filed federal tax lien." *United States v. Pioneer American Ins. Co.*, 374 U.S. 84, 88, 83 S.Ct. 1651, 1655, 10 L.Ed.2d 770 (1963).

Applying the governing "first in time" rule, the Court recognizes—as it must— that if the Bank's interest in the property was "perfected in the sense that there [was] nothing more to be done to have a choate lien" before September 9, 1987 (the date the federal notice was filed), *United States v. New Britain*, 347 U.S. 81, 84, 74 S.Ct. 367, 369, 98 L.Ed. 520 (1954), "that is the end of the matter; the Bank's lien prevails," ante, at 1528. Because the Bank's identity as lienor and the amount of its judgment lien are undisputed, the choateness question here reduces to whether "the property subject to the lien" was sufficiently "established" as of that date. *New Britain, supra,* at 84, 74 S.Ct., at 369. Accord, *Pioneer American, supra,* 374 U.S., at 89, 83 S.Ct., at 1655. See 26 CFR § 301.6323(h)–1(g) (1992). The majority is quick to conclude that "establish[ment]" cannot precede attachment, and that a lien in after–acquired property therefore cannot be sufficiently perfected until the debtor has acquired rights in the property. *See* ante, at 1529–1530. That holding does not follow from, and I believe it is inconsistent with, our precedents.

We have not (before today) prescribed any rigid criteria for "establish[ing]" the property subject to a competing lien; we have required only that the lien "become certain as to . . . the property subject thereto." *New Britain, supra,* 347 U.S., at 86, 74 S.Ct., at 370 (emphasis added). Our cases indicate that "certain" means nothing more than "[d]etermined and [d]efinite," *Pioneer American, supra,* 374 U.S., at 90, 83 S.Ct., at 1656, and that the proper focus is on whether the lien is free from "contingencies" that stand in the way of its execution, *United States v. Security Trust & Savings Bank*, 340 U.S. 47, 50, 71 S.Ct. 111, 113, 95 L.Ed. 53 (1950). In *Security Trust*, for example, we refused to accord priority to a mere attachment lien that "had not ripened into a judgment," *New Britain, supra,* 347 U.S., at 86, 74 S.Ct., at 370, and was therefore "contingent upon taking subsequent steps for enforcing it," 340 U.S., at 51, 71 S.Ct., at 114. And in *United States v. Vermont*, 377 U.S. 351, 84 S.Ct. 1267, 12 L.Ed.2d 370 (1964), we recognized the complete superiority of a general tax lien held by the State of Vermont upon all property rights belonging to the debtor, even though the lien had not "attach[ed] to [the] specifically identified portions of that property" in which the Federal Government claimed a competing tax lien. *Id.* at 355, 84 S.Ct., at 1269. With or without specific attachment, *Vermont's* general lien was "sufficiently choate to obtain priority over the later federal lien," because it was "summarily enforceable" upon assessment and demand. *Id.* at 359, and n. 12, 84 S.Ct., at 1272, and n. 12.

Although the choateness of a state–law lien under § 6323(A) is a federal question, that question is answered in part by reference to state law, and we therefore give due weight to the State's " 'classification of [its] lien as specific and perfected.' " *Pioneer American, supra*, 374 U.S., at 88, n. 7, 83 S.Ct., at 1655, n. 7 (quoting *Security Trust, supra*, 340 U.S., at 49, 71 S.Ct., at 113). Here, state law establishes that upon filing, the Bank's judgment lien was perfected, even as to the real property later acquired by the McDermotts, in the sense that it was definite as to the property in question, noncontingent, and summarily enforceable. Pursuant to Utah statute, from the moment the Bank had docketed and filed its judgment with the clerk of the state court on July 6, 1987, it held an enforceable lien upon all nonexempt real property owned by the McDermotts or thereafter acquired by them during the existence of the lien. *See* Utah Code Ann. § 78–22–1 (1953). The lien was immediately enforceable through levy and execution against all the debtors' property, whenever acquired. *See Belnap v. Blain*, 575 P.2d 696, 700 (Utah 1978). *See also* Utah Rule Civ.Proc. 69. And it was "unconditional and not subject to alteration by a court on equitable grounds." *Taylor National, Inc. v. Jensen Brothers Constr. Co.*, 641 P.2d 150, 155 (Utah 1982). Thus, the Bank's lien had become certain as to the property subject thereto, whether then existing or thereafter acquired, and all competing creditors were on notice that there was "nothing more to be done" by the Bank "to have a choate lien" on any real property the McDermotts might acquire. *New Britain*, 347 U.S., at 84, 74 S.Ct., at 369. *See Vermont, supra*, 377 U.S., at 355, 84 S.Ct., at 1269.[1]

The Court brushes aside the relevance of our *Vermont* opinion with the simple observation that that case did not involve a lien in after–acquired property. Ante, at 1528–1529. This is a wooden distinction. In truth, the Government's "specificity" claim rejected in *Vermont* is analytically indistinguishable from the "attachment" argument the Court accepts today. *Vermont*'s general lien applied to all of the debtor's rights in property, with no limitation on when those rights were acquired, and remained valid until the debt was satisfied or became unenforceable. *See* 377 U.S., at 352, 84 S.Ct., at 1268. The United States claimed that its later–filed tax lien took priority over *Vermont*'s as to the debtor's interest in a particular bank account, because the State had not taken "steps to perfect its lien by attaching the bank account in question" until after the federal lien had been recorded. Brief for United States in *United States v. Vermont*, O.T.1963, No. 509, p. 12. "Thus," the Government asserted, "when the federal lien arose, the State lien did not meet one of the

---

[1] The Department of Treasury regulations defining "judgment lien creditor" for purposes of § 6323(a) set forth only three specific requirements for a choate lien (corresponding to the three "establish[ment]" criteria of *New Britain*). The judgment creditor must "obtai[n] a valid judgment" (thus establishing the lienor) for the recovery of "specifically designated property or for a certain sum of money" (thus establishing the amount of the lien), and if recording or docketing is "necessary under local law" for the lien to be effective against third parties, the judgment lien "is not perfected with respect to real property until the time of such recordation or docketing." 26 CFR § 301.6323(h)–1(g) (1992). The last requirement— recording or docketing—is the only specific requirement recognized in the regulations for establishing the real property subject to the judgment lien. The regulations in no way suggest that § 6323(a) imposes any "attachment" condition for after–acquired property. Such a condition would be, in effect, an additional recordation requirement that is not otherwise imposed by local law.

three essential elements of a choate lien: that it attach to specific property." *Ibid.* In rejecting the federal claim of priority, we found no need even to mention whether the debtor had acquired its property interest in the deposited funds before or after notice of the federal lien. If specific attachment is not required for the state lien to be "sufficiently choate," 377 U.S., at 359, 84 S.Ct., at 1272, then neither is specific acquisition.[2]

Like the majority's reasoning today, *see* ante, at 1529, the Government's argument in *Vermont* rested in part on dicta from *New Britain* suggesting that "attachment to specific property [is] a condition for choateness of a State–created lien." Brief for United States in *United States v. Vermont, supra*, at 19. *See New Britain*, 347 U.S., at 86, 74 S.Ct., at 370 ("[T]he priority of each statutory lien contested here must depend on the time it attached to the property in question and became choate"). *New Britain*, however, involved competing statutory liens that had concededly "attached to the same real estate." *Id.* at 87, 74 S.Ct., at 371. The only issue was whether the liens were otherwise sufficiently choate. Thus, like *Security Trust* (and, in fact, like all of our cases before *Vermont*), *New Britain* provided no occasion to consider the necessity of attachment to property that was not specifically identified at the time the state lien arose.

Nothing in the law of judgment liens suggests that the possibility, which existed at the time the Bank docketed its judgment, that the McDermotts would not acquire the specific property here at issue was a "contingency" that rendered the Bank's otherwise perfected general judgment lien subordinate to intervening liens. Under the relevant background rules of state law, the Bank's interest in after–acquired real property generally could not be defeated by an intervening statutory lien. In some States, the priority of judgment liens in after–acquired property is determined by the order of their docketing. 3 R. Powell, *Law of Real Property* ¶ 481[1], p. 38–36 (P. Rohan rev. 1991) (hereinafter Powell). *See, e.g., Lowe v. Reierson*, 201 Minn. 280, 287, 276 N.W. 224, 227 (1937). In others, the rule is that "[w]hen two (or more) judgments are successively perfected against a debtor and thereafter the debtor acquires a land interest[,] these liens, attaching simultaneously at the time of the land's acquisition by the debtor, are regarded as on a parity and no priority exists." 3 Powell ¶ 481[1], pp. 38–35 to 38–36. *See, e.g., Bank of Boston v. Haufler*, 20 Mass.App. 668, 674, 482 N.E.2d 542, 547 (1985); *McAllen State Bank v. Saenz*, 561 F.Supp. 636, 639 (SD Tex.1982). Thus, under state common law, the Bank would either retain its full priority in the property by virtue of its earlier filing or, at a minimum, share an equal interest with the competing lienor.[3] The fact that the

---

[2] Even assuming, as the majority does, that the debtor in *Vermont* acquired its interest in the bank account before the federal lien arose, the critical argument that we rejected in that case was the contention that the State's claim could not be superior unless the account had been "specifically identified" as property subject to the State's lien. 377 U.S., at 355, 84 S.Ct., at 1269. At the time of the federal filing, the debtor's interest in the bank account, like the McDermotts' interest in the property at issue here, could have been uncertain or indefinite from the creditors' perspective. Nevertheless, in both cases, the particular property was "known to be subject to the [state] lien," ante, at 1529, n. 3, simply because that lien, by its terms, applied without limitation to all property acquired at any time by the debtor.

[3] Article 9 of the Uniform Commercial Code is inapposite, and the Court's reliance on it misplaced. *See* ante, at 1529. The technical rules governing the perfection and priority of

prior judgment lien remains effective against third parties without further efforts by the judgment creditor is enough for purposes of § 6323(a), since the point of our choateness doctrine is to respect the validity of a competing lien where the lien has become certain as to the property subject thereto and the lienor need take no further action to secure his claim. Under this federal–law principle, the Bank's lien was sufficiently choate to be first in time.[4]

I acknowledge that our precedents do not provide the clearest answer to the question of after–acquired property. *See* ante, at 1531. But the Court's parsimonious reading of *Vermont* undercuts the congressional purpose—expressed through repeated amendments to the tax lien provisions in the century since *United States v. Snyder*, 149 U.S. 210, 13 S.Ct. 846, 37 L.Ed. 705 (1893)—of "protect[ing] third persons against harsh application of the federal tax lien," Kennedy, *The Relative Priority of the Federal Government: The Pernicious Career of the Inchoate and General Lien*, 63 Yale L.J. 905, 922 (1954). The attachment requirement erodes the "preferred status" granted to judgment creditors by § 6323(a), and renders a choate judgment lien in after–acquired property subordinate to a "secret lien for assessed taxes." *Pioneer American*, 374 U.S., at 89, 83 S.Ct., at 1655. I would adhere to a more flexible choateness principle, which would protect the priority of validly docketed judgment liens.

Accordingly, I respectfully dissent.

§ 5.03 Priority of Federal Nontax Claims Against Solvent Estate

Neither the Federal Tax Lien Act nor the federal priority provision of § 3713 establishes priorities between a federal nontax claim and claims asserted by other creditors when the debtor is solvent. In the following cases, the Supreme Court

---

the special security interests in personal property created by Article 9 have no application to traditional judgment liens in real property, *see* § 9–102, 3 U.L.A. 73 (1992), and should have no bearing on the federal doctrine of "choateness." In the context of determining the relative priority of a competing statutory judgment lien, it is Article 9's notion of perfection that is the more "unusual." Ante, at 1529.

[4] Even if the Court were correct that attachment is the determinative criterion of choateness, we would have a tie, since the federal lien "did not attach [to the after–acquired property] until the same instant the state lien attached." Ante, at 1530. That being so, there is no persuasive reason for not adopting as a matter of federal law the well–recognized common–law rule of parity and giving the Bank an equal interest in the property. *See* 3 Powell ¶ 481[1]. Section 6323(a)'s requirement that the federal lien be "filed" to be effective may determine when the lien arises for general priority purposes, but the word "filed" provides no textual basis for concluding that a tie goes to the Government, and simply declaring that it does, *see* ante, at 1530, does not make it so. The special exception in § 6323(c), which protects later–arising security interests that are based on certain preferred financing agreements, *see* ante, at 1530, does not imply that judgment creditors lose out. Indeed, § 6323(c) demonstrates that Congress has considered the question of later–arising property, and the absence of an analogous provision in § 6323(a) suggests that Congress was content to let the courts apply one of the existing background rules to determine the relative priority (or parity) of the federal lien as against competing judgment liens in after–acquired property.

determined that, in the absence of a federal priority statute, issues arising in this situation should be determined by federal law.

UNITED STATES v. KIMBELL FOODS, INC.

United States Supreme Court
440 U.S. 715, 99 S. Ct. 1448, 59 L. Ed. 2d 711 (1979)

Mr. Justice MARSHALL delivered the opinion of the Court.

We granted certiorari in these cases to determine whether contractual liens arising from certain federal loan programs take precedence over private liens, in the absence of a federal statute setting priorities.[1] To resolve this question, we must decide first whether federal or state law governs the controversies; and second, if federal law applies, whether this Court should fashion a uniform priority rule or incorporate state commercial law. We conclude that the source of law is federal, but that a national rule is unnecessary to protect the federal interests underlying the loan programs. Accordingly, we adopt state law as the appropriate federal rule for establishing the relative priority of these competing federal and private liens.

I

A

No. 77–1359 involves two contractual security interests in the personal property of O.K. Super Markets, Inc. Both interests were perfected pursuant to Texas' Uniform Commercial Code (UCC).[2] The United States' lien secures a loan guaranteed by the Small Business Administration (SBA). The private lien, which arises from security agreements that preceded the federal guarantee, secures advances respondent made after the federal guarantee.

In 1968, O.K. Super Markets borrowed $27,000 from Kimbell Foods, Inc. (Kimbell), a grocery wholesaler. Two security agreements identified the supermarket's equipment and merchandise as collateral. The agreements also contained a standard "dragnet" clause providing that this collateral would secure future advances from Kimbell to O.K. Super Markets. Kimbell properly perfected its security interests by filing financing statements with the Texas Secretary of State according to Texas law.

In February 1969, O.K. Super Markets obtained a $300,000 loan from Republic National Bank of Dallas (Republic). The bank accepted as security the same property specified in Kimbell's 1968 agreements, and filed a financing statement with the Texas Secretary of State to perfect its security interest. The SBA guaranteed 90% of this loan under the Small Business Act, which authorizes such assistance[3] but,

---

[1] 436 U.S. 903 (1978); 439 U.S. 817 (1978).

[2] Tex. Bus. & Com. Ann. § 9101 *et seq.* (1968).

[3] Section 7 (a) of the Small Business Act, 72 Stat. 387, as amended, 15 U.S.C. § 636 (a)(1), permits extension of financial assistance to small businesses when funds are "not

with one exception, does not specify priority rules to govern the SBA's security interests.[4]

O.K. Super Markets used the Republic loan proceeds to satisfy the remainder of the 1968 obligation and to discharge an indebtedness for inventory purchased from Kimbell on open account. Kimbell continued credit sales to O.K. Super Markets until the balance due reached $18,258.57 on January 15, 1971. Thereupon, Kimbell initiated state proceedings against O.K. Super Markets to recover this inventory debt.

Shortly before Kimbell filed suit, O.K. Super Markets had defaulted on the SBA–guaranteed loan. Republic assigned its security interest to the SBA in late December 1970, and recorded the assignment with Texas authorities on January 21, 1971. The United States then honored its guarantee and paid Republic $252,331.93 (90% of the outstanding indebtedness) on February 3, 1971. That same day, O.K. Super Markets, with the approval of its creditors, sold its equipment and inventory and placed the proceeds in escrow pending resolution of the competing claims to the funds. Approximately one year later, the state court entered judgment against O.K. Super Markets, and awarded Kimbell $24,445.37, representing the inventory debt, plus interest and attorney's fees.

Kimbell thereafter brought the instant action to foreclose on its lien, claiming that its security interest in the escrow fund was superior to the SBA's[5] The District Court held for the Government. On determining that federal law controlled the controversy, the court applied principles developed by this Court to afford federal statutory tax liens special priority over state and private liens where the governing statute does not specify priorities. *Kimbell Foods, Inc. v. Republic Nat. Bank of Dallas*, 401 F. Supp. 316, 321–322 (ND Tex. 1975). *See, e.g., United States v. Security Trust & Sav. Bank*, 340 U.S. 47 (1950); *United States v. Pioneer American Ins. Co.*, 374 U.S. 84 (1963).[6] Under these rules, the lien "first in time" is "first in right."[7] However, to be considered first in time, the nonfederal lien must be "choate," that is, sufficiently specific, when the federal lien arises.[8] A state–created lien is not

---

otherwise available on reasonable terms from non–Federal sources." The SBA prefers to guarantee private loans rather than to disburse funds directly. § 636 (a)(2); 13 CFR §§ 120.2 (b)(1), 122.15 (c) (1978).

[4] *See* n. 36, *infra.*

[5] Jurisdiction was premised on 28 U.S.C. § 2410.

[6] The tax liens were authorized by 26 U.S.C. § 3670 (1952 ed.), currently codified at 26 U.S.C. § 6321. This statute established the time when the tax lien arose, 26 U.S.C. § 3671 (1952 ed.), currently codified at 26 U.S.C. § 6322, and required the filing of notice for the lien to be valid against specified creditors. 26 U.S.C. § 3672 (1952 ed.), currently codified, as amended, at 26 U.S.C. § 6323 (a). But until 1966, the statute did not specify priority rules to resolve conflicts between federal tax liens and rival liens. The Federal Tax Lien Act of 1966, 80 Stat. 1125, as amended, 26 U.S.C. §§ 6323 (b), (c), (d), (e), set specific priorities to displace the doctrines that this Court had created. *See infra*, at 738.

[7] This well–accepted common–law principle for resolving lien priority disputes, *see Rankin v. Scott*, 12 Wheat. 177, 179 (1827); *United States v. New Britain*, 347 U.S. 81, 85–86 (1954), also underlies the Uniform Commercial Code's priority structure. *See* Uniform Commercial Code § 9–312 (5), 3 U.L.A. 85 (1979 pamphlet) (hereinafter Model UCC); J. White & R. Summers, Uniform Commercial Code 905 (1972).

[8] *See, e.g., United States v. Security Trust & Sav. Bank*, 340 U.S. 47 (1950); *United States v. New Britain, supra*, at 86; *United States v. Acri*, 348 U.S. 211, 213 (1955); *United States*

choate until the "identity of the lienor, the property subject to the lien, and the amount of the lien are established." *United States v. New Britain*, 347 U.S. 81, 84 (1954); *see United States v. Vermont*, 377 U.S. 351, 358 (1964). Failure to meet any one of these conditions forecloses priority over the federal lien, even if under state law the nonfederal lien was enforceable for all purposes when the federal lien arose.

Because Kimbell did not reduce its lien to judgment until February 1972, and the federal lien had been created either in 1969, when Republic filed its financing statement, or in 1971, when Republic recorded its assignment, the District Court concluded that respondent's lien was inchoate when the federal lien arose. 401 F. Supp., at 324–325. Alternatively, the court held that even under state law, the SBA lien was superior to Kimbell's claim because the future advance clauses in the 1968 agreements were not intended to secure the debts arising from O.K. Super Market's subsequent inventory purchases. *Id.*, 325–326.

The Court of Appeals reversed. *Kimbell Foods, Inc. v. Republic Nat. Bank of Dallas*, 557 F. 2d 491 (CA5 1977). It agreed that federal law governs the rights of the United States under its SBA loan program, *id.*, at 498 n. 9, 503 n. 16, and that the "first in time, first in right" priority principle should control the competing claims. *Id.*, at 502–503. However, the court refused to extend the choateness rule to situations in which the Federal Government was not an involuntary creditor of tax delinquents, but rather a voluntary commercial lender. *Id.*, at 498, 500–502. Instead, it fashioned a new federal rule for determining which lien was first in time, and concluded that "in the context of competing state security interests arising under the U.C.C.," the first to meet UCC perfection requirements achieved priority. *Id.*, at 503[9]

The Court of Appeals then considered which lien qualified as first perfected. Disagreeing with the District Court, the court determined that, under Texas law, the

---

v. R. F. Ball Construction Co., 355 U.S. 587 (1958) (*per curiam*); *United States v. Pioneer American Ins. Co.*, 374 U.S. 84 (1963); *United States v. Vermont*, 377 U.S. 351, 355 (1964); *United States v. Equitable Life Assurance Soc.*, 384 U.S. 323, 327–328 (1966).

This Court originally formulated the choate lien test to govern conflicts arising under the federal insolvency statute, Rev. Stat. § 3466, 31 U.S.C. § 191, which awards the United States priority over other creditors in collecting debts from insolvents. In theory, the statute does not defeat liens that are choate at the time of insolvency. But in practice, it has proved difficult for nonfederal lienors to satisfy the strictures of the choateness test. *See New York v. Maclay*, 288 U.S. 290 (1933); *United States v. Texas*, 314 U.S. 480 (1941); *United States v. Waddill, Holland & Flinn, Inc.*, 323 U.S. 353 (1945); *United States v. Gilbert Associates, Inc.*, 345 U.S. 361 (1953).

The Court later applied the choateness doctrine outside the insolvency context together with the first–in–time requirement to give federal tax liens special priority. *See United States v. Security Trust & Sav. Bank, supra*, at 51. For a discussion of the history of the choate lien test, *see* Kennedy, *The Relative Priority of the Federal Government: The Pernicious Career of the Inchoate and General Lien*, 63 Yale L.J. 905 (1954) (hereinafter Kennedy, *Relative Priority*).

[9] In so holding, the Court of Appeals refused to formulate a federal doctrine of general applicability, "leav[ing] for another day" questions involving the priority of other nonfederal liens, such as state tax and mechanic's liens. 557 F. 2d, at 503 n. 15.

1968 security agreements covered Kimbell's future advances, and that the liens securing those advances dated from the filing of the security agreements before the federal lien arose. *Id.*, at 494–498, 503. But the Court of Appeals did not adopt Texas law. Rather, it proceeded to decide whether the future advances should receive the same treatment under federal common law. After surveying three possible approaches,[10] the court held that Kimbell's future advances dated back to the 1968 agreements, and therefore took precedence over Republic's 1969 loan. *Id.*, at 503–505.

B

At issue in No. 77–1644 is whether a federal contractual security interest in a tractor is superior to a subsequent repairman's lien in the same property. From 1970 to 1972, Ralph Bridges obtained several loans from the Farmers Home Administration (FHA), under the Consolidated Farmers Home Administration Act of 1961.[11] Like the Small Business Act, this statute does not establish rules of priority. To secure the FHA loans, the agency obtained a security interest in Bridges' crops and farm equipment, which it perfected by filing a standard FHA financing statement with Georgia officials on February 2, 1972. Bridges subsequently took his tractor to respondent Crittenden for repairs on numerous occasions, accumulating unpaid repair bills of over $1,600. On December 21, 1973, Bridges again had respondent repair the tractor, at a cost of $543.81. When Bridges could not pay the balance of $2,151.28, respondent retained the tractor and acquired a lien therein under Georgia law. Ga. Code § 67–2003 (1978).

On May 1, 1975, after Bridges had filed for bankruptcy and had been discharged from his debts,[12] the United States instituted this action against Crittenden to obtain possession of the tractor.[13] The District Court rejected the Government's claim that the FHA's security interest was superior to respondent's, and granted summary judgment for respondent on alternative grounds. First, it held that the agency had not properly perfected its security interest because the financing statement inadequately described the collateral. Civ. Action No. 75–37–COL (MD Ga. Sept. 25, 1975). Second, it found that even if the description were sufficient, both federal and state law accorded priority to respondent's lien. *Ibid.*

---

[10] One approach afforded priority to liens intervening between execution of a security agreement covering future advances and extension of those advances. Another gave priority only to future advances made before the advancing creditor received actual notice of an intervening lien, while a third rule afforded priority regardless of actual notice. The court rejected the first option and found that Kimbell would prevail under either of the other two since it did not have notice of the SBA guarantee. *Id.*, at 503–504.

[11] The statute, now redesignated the Consolidated Farm and Rural Development Act, *see* 86 Stat. 657, authorizes federal financial assistance for farmers who are "unable to obtain sufficient credit elsewhere to finance their actual needs at reasonable rates and terms." 75 Stat. 307, as amended, 7 U.S.C. § 1922 (1976 ed., Supp. III).

[12] Bridges' bankruptcy did not affect the relative priority of the Government and respondent. The priority rights afforded the United States under § 64a of the Bankruptcy Act do not defeat valid pre-existing liens. *See* 11 U.S.C. § 104(a); 3A W. Collier, Bankruptcy § 64.02 [2] (14th ed. 1975).

[13] Jurisdiction was invoked under 28 U.S.C. § 1345.

The Court of Appeals affirmed in part and reversed in part. It first ruled that "the rights and liabilities of the parties to a suit arising from FHA loan transaction must, under the rationale of the *Clearfield Trust* doctrine, be determined with reference to federal law." 563 F. 2d 678, 680–681 (CA5 1977) (footnotes omitted). *See Clearfield Trust Co. v. United States*, 318 U.S. 363 (1943). In fashioning a federal rule for assessing the sufficiency of the FHA's financing statement, the court elected to follow the Model UCC rather than to incorporate Georgia law. 563 F. 2d, at 681–682. And, it determined that the description of the collateral was adequate under the Model UCC to perfect the FHA's security interest. *Id.*, at 682–683.

The Court of Appeals then addressed the priority question and concluded that neither state law nor the first–in–time, first–in–right and choateness doctrines were appropriate to resolve the conflicting claims. *Id.*, at 683–689. In their place, the court devised a special "federal commercial law rule," using the Model UCC and the Tax Lien Act of 1966 as guides. *Id.*, at 679, 688–690.[14] This rule would give priority to repairman's liens over the Government's previously perfected consensual security interests when the repairman continuously possesses the property from the time his lien arises. *Id.*, at 690–691.[15] Applying its rule, the Court of Appeals concluded that Crittenden's lien for only the final $543.81 repair bill took precedence over the FHA's security interest. *Id.*, at 692.[16]

---

[14] Section 9–310 of the Model UCC provides:

> When a person in the ordinary course of his business furnishes services or materials with respect to goods subject to a security interest, a lien upon goods in the possession of such person given by statute or rule of law for such materials or services takes priority over a perfected security interest unless the lien is statutory and the statute expressly provides otherwise.

Model UCC § 9–310 (1979 pamphlet). The Tax Lien Act of 1966 extends similar protection to repairmen:

> Even though notice of a [federal tax lien] has been filed, such lien shall not be valid
>
> . . . .
>
> With respect to tangible personal property subject to a lien under local law securing the reasonable price of the repair or improvement of such property, as against a holder of such a lien, if such holder is, and has been, continuously in possession of such property from the time such lien arose.

26 U.S.C. § 6323 (b) (5).

[15] The court found it unnecessary to determine whether the same result would obtain under Georgia's Commercial Code. 563 F. 2d, at 688 n. 17, 689.

[16] Other Courts of Appeals have adopted divergent approaches regarding the priority of federal security interests arising from loan programs. *Compare, e.g., Chicago Title Ins. Co. v. Sherred Village Associates*, 568 F. 2d 217 (CA1 1978), *cert. pending*, No. 77–1611; *United States v. General Douglas MacArthur Senior Village, Inc.*, 470 F. 2d 675 (CA2 1972), *cert. denied sub nom. County of Nassau v. United States*, 412 U.S. 922 (1973); *United States v. Oswald & Hess Co.*, 345 F. 2d 886 (CA3 1965); *Willow Creek Lumber Co. v. Porter County Plumbing & Heating, Inc.*, 572 F. 2d 588 (CA7 1978); *United States v. Latrobe Construction Co.*, 246 F. 2d 357 (CA8), *cert. denied*, 355 U.S. 890 (1957); *T. H. Rogers Lumber Co. v. Apel*, 468 F. 2d 14 (CA10 1972), with, *e.g., United States v. Gregory–Beaumont Equipment Co.*, 243 F. 2d 591 (CA8 1957); *United States v. California–Oregon Plywood, Inc.*, 527 F. 2d 687 (CA9 1975). *See also United States v. Union Livestock Sales Co.*, 298 F. 2d 755 (CA4

II

This Court has consistently held that federal law governs questions involving the rights of the United States arising under nationwide federal programs. As the Court explained in *Clearfield Trust Co. v. United States, supra*, at 366–367:

> When the United States disburses its funds or pays its debts, it is exercising a constitutional function or power. . . . The authority [to do so] had its origin in the Constitution and the statutes of the United States and was in no way dependent on the laws [of any State]. The duties imposed upon the United States and the rights acquired by it . . . find their roots in the same federal sources. In absence of an applicable Act of Congress it is for the federal courts to fashion the governing rule of law according to their own standards.

(Citations and footnote omitted.)

Guided by these principles, we think it clear that the priority of liens stemming from federal lending programs must be determined with reference to federal law. The SBA and FHA unquestionably perform federal functions within the meaning of *Clearfield*. Since the agencies derive their authority to effectuate loan transactions from specific Acts of Congress passed in the exercise of a "constitutional function or power," *Clearfield Trust Co. v. United States, supra*, at 366, their rights, as well, should derive from a federal source.[17] When Government activities "aris[e] from and bea[r] heavily upon a federal . . . program," the Constitution and Acts of Congress " 'require' otherwise than that state law govern of its own force." *United States v. Little Lake Misere Land Co.*, 412 U.S. 580, 592, 593 (1973).[18] In such contexts, federal interests are sufficiently implicated to warrant the protection of federal law.[19]

That the statutes authorizing these federal lending programs do not specify the appropriate rule of decision in no way limits the reach of federal law. It is precisely when Congress has not spoken " 'in an area comprising issues substantially related to an established program of government operation,' " *id.*, at 593, quoting Mishkin 800, that *Clearfield* directs federal courts to fill the interstices of federal legislation

---

1962); *United States v. Kramel*, 234 F. 2d 577 (CA8 1956); *United States v. Chappell Livestock Auction, Inc.*, 523 F. 2d 840 (CA8 1975); *Bumb v. United States*, 276 F. 2d 729 (CA9 1960).

[17] *See United States v. Standard Oil Co.*, 332 U.S. 301, 305–306 (1947); *United States v. Seckinger*, 397 U.S. 203, 209–210 (1970); Friendly, *In Praise of Erie—And of the New Federal Common Law*, 39 N.Y.U.L. Rev. 383, 410 (1964); *see also Sola Electric Co. v. Jefferson Electric Co.*, 317 U.S. 173, 176 (1942); *Board of County Comm'rs v. United States*, 308 U.S. 343, 349–350 (1939).

[18] *See United States v. Security Trust & Sav. Bank*, 340 U.S., at 49; *cf. United States v. Yazell*, 382 U.S. 341, 356 (1966).

[19] *See United States v. Standard Oil Co., supra*, at 305–307; Mishkin, *The Variousness of "Federal Law": Competence and Discretion in the Choice of National and State Rules for Decision*, 105 U. Pa. L. Rev. 797, 800, and n. 15 (1957) (hereinafter Mishkin); Comment, *Adopting State Law as the Federal Rule of Decision: A Proposed Test*, 43 U. Chi. L. Rev. 823, 825 (1976); *see also Bank of America Nat. Trust & Sav. Assn. v. Parnell*, 352 U.S. 29, 33–34 (1956); *Miree v. DeKalb County*, 433 U.S. 25, 29, 31–32 (1977).

"according to their own standards." *Clearfield Trust Co. v. United States*, 318 U.S., at 367.[20]

Federal law therefore controls the Government's priority rights. The more difficult task, to which we turn, is giving content to this federal rule.

III

Controversies directly affecting the operations of federal programs, although governed by federal law, do not inevitably require resort to uniform federal rules. *See Clearfield Trust Co. v. United States, supra*, at 367; *United States v. Little Lake Misere Land Co., supra*, at 594–595. Whether to adopt state law or to fashion a nationwide federal rule is a matter of judicial policy "dependent upon a variety of considerations always relevant to the nature of the specific governmental interests and to the effects upon them of applying state law." *United States v. Standard Oil Co.*, 332 U.S. 301, 310 (1947).[21]

Undoubtedly, federal programs that "by their nature are and must be uniform in character throughout the Nation" necessitate formulation of controlling federal rules. *United States v. Yazell*, 382 U.S. 341, 354 (1966); *see Clearfield Trust Co. v. United States, supra*, at 367; *United States v. Standard Oil Co., supra*, at 311; *Illinois v. Milwaukee*, 406 U.S. 91, 105 n. 6 (1972). Conversely, when there is little need for a nationally uniform body of law, state law may be incorporated as the federal rule of decision.[22] Apart from considerations of uniformity, we must also determine whether application of state law would frustrate specific objectives of the federal programs. If so, we must fashion special rules solicitous of those federal interests.[23]

---

[20] *See Board of County Comm'rs v. United States, supra*, at 349–350; *National Metropolitan Bank v. United States*, 323 U.S. 454, 456 (1945); *Holmberg v. Armbrecht*, 327 U.S. 392, 395 (1946); *Moor v. County of Alameda*, 411 U.S. 693, 701–702, and n. 12 (1973).

[21] As explained by one commentator:

> Whether state law is to be incorporated as a matter of federal common law . . . involves the . . . problem of the relationship of a particular issue to a going federal program. The question of judicial incorporation can only arise in an area which is sufficiently close to a national operation to establish competence in the federal courts to choose the governing law, and yet not so close as clearly to require the application of a single nationwide rule of substance.

Mishkin 805.

[22] *Miree v. DeKalb County, supra*, at 28–29; *see RFC v. Beaver County*, 328 U.S. 204, 209–210 (1946); *United States v. Brosnan*, 363 U.S. 237, 241–242 (1960); *United States v. Yazell, supra*, at 356–357; *Auto Workers v. Hoosier Cardinal Corp.*, 383 U.S. 696, 701–703 (1966).

[23] *See United States v. Allegheny County*, 322 U.S. 174, 183 (1944); *RFC v. Beaver County, supra*, at 209–210; *Auto Workers v. Hoosier Cardinal Corp., supra*, at 706–707; *Wallis v. Pan American Petroleum Corp.*, 384 U.S. 63, 68 (1966); *United States v. Little Lake Misere Land Co.*, 412 U.S. 580, 595–597 (1973); *Johnson v. Railway Express Agency, Inc.*, 421 U.S. 454, 465–466 (1975); *Miree v. DeKalb County, supra*, at 31–32; *Robertson v. Wegmann*, 436 U.S. 584, 590–593 (1978); *see also De Sylva v. Ballentine*, 351 U.S. 570, 581 (1956).

Finally, our choice–of–law inquiry must consider the extent to which application of a federal rule would disrupt commercial relationships predicated on state law.[24]

The Government argues that effective administration of its lending programs requires uniform federal rules of priority. It contends further that resort to any rules other than first in time, first in right and choateness would conflict with protectionist fiscal policies underlying the programs. We are unpersuaded that, in the circumstances presented here, nationwide standards favoring claims of the United States are necessary to ease program administration or to safeguard the Federal Treasury from defaulting debtors. Because the state commercial codes "furnish convenient solutions in no way inconsistent with adequate protection of the federal interest[s]," *United States v. Standard Oil Co.*, *supra*, at 309, we decline to override intricate state laws of general applicability on which private creditors base their daily commercial transactions.

A

Incorporating state law to determine the rights of the United States as against private creditors would in no way hinder administration of the SBA and FHA loan programs. In *United States v. Yazell*, *supra*, this Court rejected the argument, similar to the Government's here, that a need for uniformity precluded application of state coverture rules to an SBA loan contract. Because SBA operations were "specifically and in great detail adapted to state law," 382 U.S., at 357, the federal interest in supplanting "important and carefully evolved state arrangements designed to serve multiple purposes" was minimal. *Id.*, at 353. Our conclusion that compliance with state law would produce no hardship on the agency was also based on the SBA's practice of "individually negotiat[ing] in painfully particularized detail" each loan transaction. *Id.*, at 345–346. These observations apply with equal force here and compel us again to reject generalized pleas for uniformity as substitutes for concrete evidence that adopting state law would adversely affect administration of the federal programs.

Although the SBA Financial Assistance Manual on which this Court relied in *Yazell* is no longer "replete with admonitions to follow state law carefully," *id.*, at 357 n. 35, SBA employees are still instructed to, and indeed do, follow state law.[25] In fact, a fair reading of the SBA Financial Assistance Manual, SOP 50–10 (SBA Manual), indicates that the agency assumes its security interests are controlled to

---

[24] *See United States v. Brosnan*, *supra*, at 241–242; *United States v. Yazell*, *supra*, at 352–353; *Wallis v. Pan American Petroleum Corp.*, *supra*, at 68; *United States v. Little Lake Misere Land Co.*, *supra*, at 599–603.

[25] The applicable regulations recognize that "[i]n order to implement and facilitate th[e] Federal loan programs," SBA offices should comply with state law, in particular, with state procedural requirements for obtaining enforceable security interests. 13 CFR § 101.1(d)(3) (1978). And the SBA routinely follows such rules, Tr. of Oral Arg. in No. 77–1359, p. 43, as it did here by requiring Republic to file a financing statement and a notice of assignment. That the SBA conforms its transactions to state law is also reflected in the security agreement between Republic and O.K. Super Markets, approved by the SBA, which provided that the contract would be construed according to Texas law and bound the parties' assigns to this provision. App. in No. 77–1359, p. 68.

a large extent by the commercial law of each State.[26] Similarly, FHA regulations expressly incorporate state law. They mandate compliance with state procedures for perfecting and maintaining valid security interests, and highlight those rules that differ from State to State. *E.g.*, 7 CFR §§ 1921.104(c)(1), 1921.105, 1921.106, 1921.107, 1921.108, 1921.111, 1930.5, 1930.8, 1930.9, 1930.14, 1930.17, 1930.27 (1978).[27] To ensure that employees are aware of new developments, the FHA also issues "State supplements" to "reflect any State statutory changes in its version of the UCC." § 1921.111(c); *see, e.g.*, §§ 1802.80, 1904.108(d), 1930.46(d)(3). Contrary to the Government's claim that the FHA complies only with state procedural rules, Reply Brief for United States in No. 77–1644, p. 7, the agency's reliance on state law extends to substantive requirements as well. Indeed, applicable regulations suggest that state rules determine the priority of FHA liens when federal statutes or agency regulations are not controlling. 7 CFR §§ 1872.2(c), 1921.111(b), 1930.43, 1930.44, 1930.46(d)(1), (3) (1978); see also § 1955.15(d).

Thus, the agencies' own operating practices belie their assertion that a federal rule of priority is needed to avoid the administrative burdens created by disparate state commercial rules.[28] The programs already conform to each State's commercial

---

[26] For example, the Manual stresses that the borrower's inventory should be used as collateral only after careful consideration of the protection afforded under state law:

> Uniform Commercial Code—Factor's Lien Laws. Most states have adopted the Uniform Commercial Code or Factor's Lien Laws. Under such laws it is possible to obtain a general lien covering all existing and to–be–acquired inventory. Generally, these statutes also provide that the lien may follow the accounts receivable or proceeds resulting from the sale of the inventory. . . . The loan specialist should inquire as to any prior liens against either inventories or receivables. The lien obtained under the Code (or Factor's Lien Laws) covering accounts receivable or other proceeds resulting from the sale of the inventory is not generally invalidated by the fact that the borrower thereafter deals with the accounts receivable or proceeds as his own. . . . However, a careful study should be made of borrower's credit circumstances to determine the measures of control and supervision to be imposed. . . . Although the collateral may not require close supervision from inception, the security agreement should contain provisions that borrower shall . . . comply with such other servicing practices as are deemed necessary by counsel to safeguard the collateral.

> Accounts receivable resulting from the sale of inventories assigned to SBA prior to adoption of the Code in code states shall be serviced in accordance with applicable local law existing prior to the date of adoption of the Code. This is not necessary however, if in the opinion of counsel, servicing can be performed in a manner permitted under the Code without adversely affecting SBA's interest.

SBA Manual ¶ 29(a)(4)(b) (1977). See also n. 25, *supra.*

[27] After publication of the 1978 Code of Federal Regulations, the FHA began reorganizing its regulations to provide separate rules for each loan program. Most provisions of 7 CFR cited throughout this opinion have been recodified with modifications not relevant here. *See, e.g.*, 43 Fed. Reg. 5504, 7978, 23986, 55882–55895, 56643–56647, 59078 (1978); 44 Fed. Reg. 1701, 4431–4458, 6354, 10979–10980 (1979). For convenience, we refer to the 1978 version of the FHA regulations contained in 7 CFR.

[28] The differences between the rules, moreover, are insignificant in comparison with the similarities. All States except Louisiana have enacted Art. 9 of the UCC with minor variations.

standards. By using local lending offices and employees who are familiar with the law of their respective localities,[29] the agencies function effectively without uniform procedures and legal rules.

Nevertheless, the Government maintains that requiring the agencies to assess security arrangements under local law would dictate close scrutiny of each transaction and thereby impede expeditious processing of loans. We disagree. Choosing responsible debtors necessarily requires individualized selection procedures, which the agencies have already implemented in considerable detail. Each applicant's financial condition is evaluated under rigorous standards in a lengthy process.[30] Agency employees negotiate personally with borrowers, investigate property offered as collateral for encumbrances, and obtain local legal advice on the adequacy of proposed security arrangements.[31] In addition, they adapt the terms of every loan to the parties' needs and capabilities.[32] Because each application currently receives individual scrutiny, the agencies can readily adjust loan transactions to reflect state priority rules, just as they consider other factual and legal matters before disbursing Government funds. As we noted in *United States v. Yazell*, 382 U.S., at 348, these lending programs are distinguishable from "nationwide act[s] of the Federal Government, emanating in a single form from a single source." (Footnote omitted.) Since there is no indication that variant state priority schemes would burden current methods of loan processing, we conclude that considerations of administrative convenience do not warrant adoption of a uniform federal law.

B

The Government argues that applying state law to these lending programs would undermine its ability to recover funds disbursed and therefore would conflict with

---

See Model UCC 1–2 (1979 pamphlet). As Judge Friendly observed in *United States v. Wagematic Corp.*, 360 F.2d 674, 676 (CA2 1966):

> When the states have gone so far in achieving the desirable goal of a uniform law governing commercial transactions, it would be a distinct disservice to insist on a different one for the segment of commerce, important but still small in relation to the total, consisting of transactions with the United States.

[29] *See* 13 CFR §§ 101.3, 101.7(a) (1978); 7 CFR §§ 1800.1–1800.4 (1978).

[30] *See* 13 CFR §§ 120.2(c), (d), as amended, 43 Fed. Reg. 3702 (1978); 13 CFR §§ 122.15, 122.16 (1978); SBA Manual ¶¶ 10, 11, 16–40; 7 CFR §§ 1801.2–1801.4, 1904.108, 1904.127, 1904.175, 1980.175 (1978).

[31] *See United States v. Yazell*, 382 U.S., at 344–346; 13 CFR §§ 101.2–1, 101.7(a), 122.16 (1978); SBA Manual ¶¶ 16–17, 21(c), 23(a)–(f), 29(a)(8), 30(*l*), 31(b)(6); 7 CFR §§ 1801.1–1801.4, 1801.11, 1921.107, 1930.5 (1978).

[32] The Court of Appeals in No. 77–1644 believed that a uniform federal law was necessary to determine the sufficiency of the FHA's financing statement in part because the agency uses standard forms with preprinted descriptions of collateral commonly taken as security. 563 F.2d, at 682. However, the form also has a blank space for listing specific property. *See* App. in No. 77–1644, p. 12 (Form FHA 440–25). And the FHA regulations advise that individual descriptions be made, specifically when "major items of equipment" are involved. 7 CFR §§ 1921.105(e)(1), (2) (1978). Since the standard FHA forms leave spaces for recording the details of each loan, the agency can take account of local law without altering these materials. *See, e.g.*, App. in No. 77–1644, p. 8 (Form FHA 440–4).

program objectives. In the Government's view, it is difficult "to identify a material distinction between a dollar received from the collection of taxes and a dollar returned to the Treasury on repayment of a federal loan." Brief for United States in No. 77–1359, p. 22. Therefore, the agencies conclude, just as "the purpose of the federal tax lien statute to insure prompt and certain collection of taxes"[33] justified our imposition of the first–in–time and choateness doctrines in the tax lien context, the federal interest in recovering on loans compels similar legal protection of the agencies' consensual liens. However, we believe significant differences between federal tax liens and consensual liens counsel against unreflective extension of rules that immunize the United States from the commercial law governing all other voluntary secured creditors. These differences persuade us that deference to customary commercial practices would not frustrate the objectives of the lending programs.

That collection of taxes is vital to the functioning, indeed existence, of government cannot be denied. *McCulloch v. Maryland*, 4 Wheat. 316, 425, 428, 431 (1819); *Springer v. United States*, 102 U.S. 586, 594 (1881). Congress recognized as much over 100 years ago when it authorized creation of federal tax liens. Act of July 13, 1866, ch. 184, § 9, 14 Stat. 107, recodified as amended in 26 U.S.C. §§ 6321–6323. The importance of securing adequate revenues to discharge national obligations justifies the extraordinary priority accorded federal tax liens through the choateness and first–in–time doctrines. By contrast, when the United States operates as a moneylending institution under carefully circumscribed programs, its interest in recouping the limited sums advanced is of a different order. Thus, there is less need here than in the tax lien area to invoke protective measures against defaulting debtors in a manner disruptive of existing credit markets.

To equate tax liens with these consensual liens also misperceives the principal congressional concerns underlying the respective statutes. The overriding purpose of the tax lien statute obviously is to ensure prompt revenue collection. The same cannot be said of the SBA and FHA lending programs.[34] They are a form of social welfare legislation, primarily designed to assist farmers and businesses that cannot obtain funds from private lenders on reasonable terms.[35] We believe that had Congress intended the private commercial sector, rather than taxpayers in general, to bear the risks of default entailed by these public welfare programs, it would have established a priority scheme displacing state law. Far from doing so, both Congress and the agencies have expressly recognized the priority of certain private liens over

---

[33] *United States v. Security Trust & Sav. Bank*, 340 U.S. , at 51.

[34] Congress did not delineate specific priority rules in either the tax lien statute prior to 1966, the insolvency statute, or the statutes authorizing these lending programs. *See* nn. 6 and 8, *supra*. Accordingly, the Government urges that we establish identical priority rules for all three situations. This argument overlooks the evident distinction between lending programs for needy farmers and businesses and statutes created to guarantee receipt of debts due the United States. We, of course, express no view on the proper priority rules to govern federal consensual liens in the context of statutes other than those at issue here.

[35] *See* nn. 3 and 11, *supra*; 15 U.S.C. § 631 (1976 ed. and Supp. III) (declaration of policy); 7 U.S.C. § 1921 (congressional findings); 43 Fed. Reg. 55883 (1978) (to be codified in 7 CFR § 1941.2); S. Rep. No. 566, 87th Cong., 1st Sess., 1, 64 (1961); Hearings on H.R. 4384 before the House Committee on Agriculture, 78th Cong., 2d Sess., 43–45 (1944).

the agencies' security interests,[36] thereby indicating that the extraordinary safe-guards applied in the tax lien area are unnecessary to maintain the lending programs.

The Government's ability to safeguard its interests in commercial dealings further reveals that the rules developed in the tax lien area are unnecessary here, and that state priority rules would not conflict with federal lending objectives.[37] The United States is an involuntary creditor of delinquent taxpayers, unable to control the factors that make tax collection likely. In contrast, when the United States acts as a lender or guarantor, it does so voluntarily, with detailed knowledge of the borrower's financial status. The agencies evaluate the risks associated with each loan, examine the interests of other creditors, choose the security believed necessary to assure repayment, and set the terms of every agreement.[38] By carefully selecting loan recipients and tailoring each transaction with state law in mind, the agencies are fully capable of establishing terms that will secure repayment.[39]

---

[36] A 1958 amendment to the Small Business Act subordinates SBA liens to state and local property tax liens when the tax liens would be superior to nonfederal security interests under state law. 72 Stat. 396, 15 U.S.C. § 646. The FHA has established by regulation that purchase–money security interests take priority over previously arising FHA liens. 7 CFR § 1921.106 (1978); see § 1930.44. In appropriate circumstances, the FHA also subordinates its liens to interests that are junior under state law. 7 U.S.C. § 1981(d) (1976 ed. and Supp. III); see, e.g., 7 CFR § 1930.30 (1978).

[37] We reject the Government's suggestion that the choateness and first–in–time doctrines are needed to prevent States from "undercutting" the agencies' liens by creating "arbitrary" rules. Brief for United States in No. 77–1359, pp. 24–25. Adopting state law as an appropriate federal rule does not preclude federal courts from excepting local laws that prejudice federal interests. See, e.g., RFC v. Beaver County, 328 U.S., at 210; De Sylva v. Ballentine, 351 U.S., at 581; United States v. Little Lake Misere Land Co., 412 U.S., at 596. The issue here, however, involves commercial rules of general applicability, based on codes that are remarkably uniform throughout the Nation. See n. 28, supra.

[38] See nn. 30, 31, supra.

[39] The facts presented here demonstrate the ease with which the agencies could have protected themselves. O. K. Super Markets informed the SBA of Kimbell's security interests in the inventory. Had the agency followed its guidelines and checked local records, it would have discovered the 1968 security agreements Kimbell filed with its financing statements. See SBA Manual ¶¶ 29(a)(3), (4), (8), 31(b)(6). Thus, the agency should have known that the agreements secured future advances. The SBA was also informed in the loan guarantee application that O. K. Super Markets intended to discharge the debts it owed Kimbell from the Republic loan proceeds. See App. in No. 77–1359, p. 72. Additionally, as a result of negotiations with O. K. Super Markets' creditors, the SBA was aware that Kimbell would not guarantee any portion of the Republic loan because it wanted its account paid in full before advancing further credit. Id., at 62–63. In these circumstances, the SBA easily could have persuaded Kimbell either to subordinate its liens covering future advances or to terminate the 1968 security arrangements once the obligations were satisfied. This procedure, moreover, would have comported with agency practices. The SBA Manual allows employees to impose conditions on third parties when "advisable," and to note such agreements on the appropriate forms. Id., ¶ 30(e).

With respect to the FHA loan, the agency could have followed the practices of private lenders in protecting themselves from subsequent liens that take priority under state law. For example, the FHA might have secured its loan with property not subject to repairman's liens or demanded more substantial collateral.

The Government nonetheless argues that its opportunity to evaluate the credit worthiness of loan applicants provides minimal safety. Because the SBA and FHA make loans only when private lenders will not, the United States believes that its security interests demand greater protection than ordinary commercial arrangements. We find this argument unconvincing. The lending agencies do not indiscriminately distribute public funds and hope that reimbursement will follow. SBA loans must be "of such sound value or so secured as reasonably to assure repayment." 15 U.S.C. § 636(a)(7); *see* 13 CFR § 120.2(c)(1) (1978). The FHA operates under a similar restriction. 7 CFR § 1833.35 (1978). Both agencies have promulgated exhaustive instructions to ensure that loan recipients are financially reliable and to prevent improvident loans.[40] The Government therefore is in substantially the same position as private lenders, and the special status it seeks is unnecessary to safeguard the public fisc. Moreover, Congress' admonitions to extend loans judiciously supports the view that it did not intend to confer special privileges on agencies that enter the commercial field. Accordingly, we agree with the Court of Appeals in No. 77–1359 that "[a]s a quasi–commercial lender, [the Government] does not require . . . the special priority which it compels as sovereign" in its tax–collecting capacity. 557 F.2d, at 500.

The Federal Tax Lien Act of 1966, 80 Stat. 1125, as amended, 26 U.S.C. § 6323, provides further evidence that treating the United States like any other lender would not undermine federal interests. These amendments modified the Federal Government's preferred position under the choateness and first–in–time doctrines, and recognized the priority of many state claims over federal tax liens.[41] In enacting this legislation, Congress sought to "improv[e] the status of private secured creditors" and prevent impairment of commercial financing transactions by "moderniz[ing] . . . the relationship of Federal tax liens to the interests of other creditors." S. Rep. No. 1708, 89th Cong., 2d Sess., 1–2 (1966); *see also* H. R. Rep. No. 1884, 89th Cong., 2d Sess., 35 (1966). This rationale has even greater force when the Government acts as a moneylender. We do not suggest that Congress' actions in the tax lien area control our choice of law in the commercial lien context. But in fashioning federal principles to govern areas left open by Congress, our function is to effectuate congressional policy. *E.g.*, *RFC v. Beaver County*, 328 U.S. 204, 209–210 (1946). To ignore Congress' disapproval of unrestricted federal priority in an area as important to the Nation's stability as taxation would be inconsistent with this function. Thus, without a showing that application of state laws would impair federal operations, we decline to extend to new contexts extraordinary safeguards largely rejected by Congress.

---

[40] *E.g.*, 13 CFR § 120.2, as amended, 43 Fed. Reg. 3702 (1978); 13 CFR §§ 122.2, 122.3 (1978); SBA Manual ¶¶ 5–7; nn. 30, 31, *supra*.

[41] *See* nn. 6 and 8, *supra*. Of particular relevance here, the Act added mechanic's liens to the list of private interests already protected against unrecorded tax liens. 26 U.S.C. § 6323(a). Holders of consensual security interests also receive priority over unrecorded tax liens. *Ibid.* Moreover, the Act gives priority to many types of nonfederal liens even when the Government has filed notice of the tax lien. § 6323(b). Included in this group are repairman's liens in personal property, § 6323(b)(5), *see* n. 14, *supra*, and in limited situations, liens securing future advances. § 6323(c).

C

In structuring financial transactions, businessmen depend on state commercial law to provide the stability essential for reliable evaluation of the risks involved. *Cf. National Bank v. Whitney*, 103 U.S. 99, 102 (1881). However, subjecting federal contractual liens to the doctrines developed in the tax lien area could undermine that stability. Creditors who justifiably rely on state law to obtain superior liens would have their expectations thwarted whenever a federal contractual security interest suddenly appeared and took precedence.[42]

Because the ultimate consequences of altering settled commercial practices are so difficult to foresee,[43] we hesitate to create new uncertainties, in the absence of careful legislative deliberation. Of course, formulating special rules to govern the priority of the federal consensual liens in issue here would be justified if necessary to vindicate important national interests. But neither the Government nor the Court of Appeals advanced any concrete reasons for rejecting well–established commercial rules which have proven workable over time. Thus, the prudent course is to adopt the readymade body of state law as the federal rule of decision until Congress strikes a different accommodation.[44]

---

[42] The cases under consideration illustrate the substantial new risks that creditors would encounter. Neither the financing statement filed by Republic nor its security agreement mentioned the SBA. App. in No. 77–1359, pp. 67–69. To give the federal lien priority in this situation would undercut the reliability of the notice filing system, which plays a crucial role in commercial dealings. Subsequent creditors such as Crittenden and prior creditors such as Kimbell would have no trustworthy means of discovering the undisclosed security interest. Even those creditors aware of a federal agency's lien would have to adjust their lending arrangements to protect against the stringent choateness requirements. In recognition of these burdens, commentators have criticized the doctrine for frustrating private creditors' expectations as well as generating inconsistencies in application. *See, e.g.,* 2 G. Gilmore, Security Interests in Personal Property 1052–1073 (1965); Plumb, *Federal Liens and Priorities—Agenda for the Next Decade*, 77 Yale L.J. 228 (1967); Kennedy, *From Spokane County to Vermont: The Campaign of the Federal Government Against the Inchoate Lien*, 50 Iowa L. Rev. 724 (1965); Kennedy, *Relative Priority*; Comment, *The Relative Priority of Small Business Administration Liens: An Unreasonable Extension of Federal Preference?*, 64 Mich. L. Rev. 1107 (1966).

Considerable uncertainty would also result from the approach used in the opinions below. Developing priority rules on a case–by–case basis, depending on the types of competing private liens involved, leaves creditors without the definite body of law they require in structuring sound business transactions.

[43] For example, the decision below in No. 77–1359 noted that priority rules favoring the Government could inhibit private lenders' extension of credit to the very people for whom Congress created these programs. 557 F.2d, at 500. *See* MacLachlan, *Improving the Law of Federal Liens and Priorities*, 1 B.C. Ind. and Com. L. Rev. 73, 74–76 (1959).

[44] *See RFC v. Beaver County*, 328 U.S., at 209–210; *United States v. Brosnan*, 363 U.S., at 242; *United States v. Yazell*, 382 U.S., at 352, and nn. 26–27; *Wallis v. Pan American Petroleum Corp.*, 384 U.S., at 68.

IV

Accordingly, we hold that, absent a congressional directive, the relative priority of private liens and consensual liens arising from these Government lending programs is to be determined under nondiscriminatory state laws. In No. 77–1359, the Court of Appeals found that Texas law gave preference to Kimbell's lien. We therefore affirm the judgment in that case. Although the issue was contested, the Court of Appeals in No. 77–1644 did not decide whether and to what extent Georgia treats repairman's liens as superior to previously perfected consensual liens. Nor did the court assess the sufficiency of the FHA's financing statement under Georgia law. Because "[t]he federal judges who deal regularly with questions of state law in their respective districts and circuits are in a better position than we to determine how local courts would dispose of [such] issues," *Butner v. United States, ante,* at 58 (footnote omitted), we vacate the judgment in No. 77–1644 and remand for resolution of these issues.

So ordered.

CHAPTER 6

FRAUDULENT TRANSFERS

§ 6.01 Introduction

Relatively modern statutes, such as the Uniform Fraudulent Transfer Act, the Uniform Fraudulent Conveyance Act and the Bankruptcy Code (*see* text of these statutes, *infra*), define at least four operative kinds of fraudulent transfers. At common law, however, the fraudulent conveyance was "roughly defined as an infringement of the creditor's right to realize upon the available assets of his debtor." Glenn, The Law of Fraudulent Conveyances § 1 (1931). Regardless of how defined, one writer noted that fraudulent transfer law "imposes a substantive prohibition: the debtor may not dispose of his property with the intent or the effect of placing it beyond the reach of his creditors." Countryman, Cases and Materials on Debtor and Creditor, 127 (1974).

Despite relatively clear statutory definitions and neatly stated legal maxims, the attorney's difficulty is in ascertaining the facts. In some cases, it may be relatively easy to counsel an uninformed client who is about to hinder his creditors by conveying his assets to a relative without consideration during the pendency of litigation. On the other hand, the fraudulent transfer doctrine may often be a major consideration in structuring sophisticated corporate transactions. Many business entities—corporations, partnerships and individuals— are insolvent. Consequently, clients may want counseling as to whether a transfer can be set aside by a creditor or by a trustee in bankruptcy of an insolvent seller.

§ 6.02 The Elements of a Fraudulent Transfer

In ascertaining whether a fraudulent transfer exists, consider what property, if any, was fraudulently conveyed. By whom? To whom? In some of the instances, a "fraudulent transfer" will not stand up and identify itself. Even a transfer by a solvent debtor may be invalidated if the creditor or trustee in bankruptcy can show actual intent to hinder, delay, or defraud creditors. *See Eisenberg v. Flaten (In re Allied Development Corp.), infra.* Similarly, a transfer by a solvent business entity may be avoided if the entity was left with unreasonably small capital to conduct its business after the transfer, and received less than fair consideration. *See New York Credit Men's Adjustment Bureau v. Adler,* 2 B.R. 752, 756 (S.D.N.Y. 1980). The important thing to grasp is that a fraudulent transfer may take many forms. The debtor may form a one–man corporation (*see Shapiro v. Wilgus, infra*); arrange for

(Matthew Bender & Co., Inc.)   (Pub.094)

a friend to purchase his property at an execution sale for a price substantially below its true value (*see Lefkowitz v. Finkelstein Trading Corp.*, 14 F. Supp. 898 (S.D.N.Y. 1936)); or agree to rescind a profitable contract (*see Wilson v. Holub*, 202 Iowa 549, 210 N.W. 593 (1926)).

The precursor to the modern fraudulent transfer statutes was the Statute of Elizabeth, 13 Eliz. c.5 (1571), which applied to conveyances made with intent "to delay, hinder or defraud creditors and others of their just and lawful actions, suits, debts. . . ." The Statute of Elizabeth still constitutes the inherited common law of many jurisdictions. Glenn, Fraudulent Conveyances and Preferences § 62b (rev. ed. 1940). Eighteen states, including California, Texas and Florida, have adopted the Uniform Fraudulent Transfer Act ("UFTA"), first approved by the National Conference of Commissioners on Uniform State Laws in 1984 as a replacement for the Uniform Fraudulent Conveyance Act ("UFCA"). The UFCA, first promulgated in 1919, is still in effect in sixteen states, including New York and New Jersey. As you read the cases in this chapter, consider whether the UFTA changed prior law, and if so, to what extent. Also, consider how the differences between certain key definitions in the UFTA and the fraudulent transfer provisions of the Bankruptcy Code may affect a court's ultimate determination of whether a fraudulent transfer has been effected. *See generally*, Kennedy, *The Uniform Fraudulent Transfer Act*, 18 U.C.C.L.J. 195 (1986); Baird & Jackson, *Fraudulent Conveyance Law and Its Proper Domain*, 38 Vand. L. Rev. 829 (1985); Cook & Mendales, *The Uniform Fraudulent Transfer Act: An Introductory Critique*, 62 Am. Bankr. L.J. 87 (1988); Cook, Axelrod & Frankel, *The Judicially Created "Innocent Shareholder" Defense to Constructive Fraudulent Transfer Liability in Failed Leveraged Buyouts*, 43 So. Car. L. Rev. 777 (1992).

[A] Fair Consideration

"Fair consideration" is defined in the UFCA to include good faith as well as fair equivalence. The Bankruptcy Code and UFTA eliminate the requirement of good faith, and instead use only the phrase "reasonably equivalent value."

[B] Insolvency

The UFCA sets forth a hybrid test for insolvency that compares the present fair market value of the debtor's assets with the amount the debtor will need to pay his probable liability on debts as they mature. The Bankruptcy Code and UFTA, by contrast, provide a simple "balance sheet" test for insolvency. *Schick Oil & Gas, Inc. v. EDIC (In re Schick Oil & Gas, Inc.)*, 35 B.R. 282, 285 (Bankr. W.D. Okla. 1983). Under UFTA § 2, a debtor is insolvent if the sum of its debts is greater than that of its assets "at a fair valuation" (an undefined term). Moreover, UFTA § 2(b) contains a rebuttable presumption that a debtor who is generally not paying its debts as they become due is insolvent. The plaintiff creditor need only show, in most cases, that the debtor has generally stopped paying its debts as they become due, placing the burden of proving solvency on the debtor.

[C]   Transfer

The Bankruptcy Code's definition of "transfer" (11 U.S.C. § 101(51)) is arguably broader than the UFCA'S definition of "conveyance." The UFTA definition, for all intents and purposes, is identical to that of the Bankruptcy Code. *See* UFTA § 1(12). Is a guaranty a transfer under these statutes? What about an assignment of accounts receivable? An order of attachment properly obtained according to state law?

The UFCA (§ 3) differentiates between fair consideration needed for an absolute transfer and that needed for a security transfer. Do the Bankruptcy Code and UFTA also make this distinction? *See* 11 U.S.C. § 548 and UFTA § 1(12).

[D]   Relevance of Transferor's Intent

The actual fraud provisions of the UFTA (§ 4(a)(1)), the UFCA (§ 7) and the Bankruptcy Code (11 U.S.C. § 548(a)(1)) require a subjective inquiry into the transferor's intent. The constructive fraud provisions (UFTA § 4(a)(2); UFCA §§ 4, 5, and 6; 11 U.S.C. § 548(a)(2)) require a more objective analysis. Do UFTA § 4(a)(2)(ii), UFCA § 6 and 11 U.S.C. § 548(a)(2)(B)(iii) establish a standard that requires both subjective and objective examination? *See* Note, *Good Faith and Fraudulent Conveyances*, 97 Harv. L. Rev. 495, 499 n.18 (1983) (opining that the "intent" in UFCA § 6 is "quite different" from that in UFCA § 7).

§ 6.03   Standing to Sue

Which creditors have standing to commence a fraudulent transfer action under the various provisions of the UFTA and the UFCA? Note that under the Bankruptcy Code, only the trustee may bring the action as a general rule. *See American National Bank v. Mortgageamerica Corp. (In re Mortgageamerica Corp.)*, 714 F.2d 1266, 1273 (5th Cir. 1983); *Exchange National Bank of Chicago v. Van Brock (In re Lang)*, 2 C.B.C. 2d 829, 833 (Bankr. S.D.N.Y 1980); *but cf. In re Automated Business Systems, Inc.*, 642 F.2d 200 (6th Cir. 1981); *Committee of Unsecured Creditors v. Monsour Medical Center (In re Monsour Medical Center)*, 2 C.B.C. 2d 1363, 1367 (Bankr. W.D. Pa. 1980).

§ 6.04   Necessary Parties

Finally, who are the necessary parties to a fraudulent transfer action? The transferor? The transferee? *Compare Hamilton National Bank v. Halsted*, 9 N.Y.S. 852 (App. Div. 1st Dep't 1890), *modified*, 134 N.Y. 520 (1892) (both tranferor and transferee necessary) and *General Motors Acceptance Corp. v. Key*, No. IP 80–427–C, *slip op* (S.D. Ind. Jan. 28, 1981) *with In re Waters*, 8 B.R. 163 (Bankr. N.D. Ga. 1981) (debtor not indispensable); *Murray v. Murray*, 358 So.2d 723, 725 (Miss. 1978); *Allan v. Moline Plow Co.*, 14 F.2d 912, 915 (8th Cir. 1926); *and Etchegoyen v. Hamill (In re Farmer's Market)*, 22 B.R. 71, 75 (Bankr. 9th Cir. 1982). *See also* Fed. R. Bankr. P. 7019.

§ 6.05 Statutes, Cases, Notes and Questions

[A] Statutes

UNIFORM FRAUDULENT TRANSFERS ACT

1984 ACT

. . . .

PREFATORY NOTE

The Uniform Fraudulent Conveyance Act was promulgated by the Conference of Commissioners on Uniform State Laws in 1918. The Act has been adopted in 25 jurisdictions, including the Virgin Islands. It has also been adopted in the sections of the Bankruptcy Act of 1938 and the Bankruptcy Reform Act of 1978 that deal with fraudulent transfers and obligations.

The Uniform Act was a codification of the "better" decisions applying the Statute of 13 Elizabeth. *See* Analysis of H.R. 12339, 74th Cong., 2d Sess. 213 (1936). The English statute was enacted in some form in many states, but, whether or not so enacted, the voidability of fraudulent transfer was part of the law of every American jurisdiction. Since the intent to hinder, delay, or defraud creditors is seldom susceptible of direct proof, courts have relied on badges of fraud. The weight given these badges varied greatly from jurisdiction, and the Conference sought to minimize or eliminate the diversity by providing that proof of certain fact combinations would conclusively establish fraud. In the absence of evidence of the existence of such facts, proof of a fraudulent transfer was to depend on the evidence of actual intent. An important reform effected by the Uniform Act was the elimination of any requirement that a creditor has obtained a judgment or execution returned unsatisfied before bringing an action to avoid a transfer as fraudulent. *See American Surety Co. v. Conner*, 251 N.Y. 1, 166 N.E. 783, 67 A.L.R. 244 (1929) (per C.J. Cardozo).

The Conference was persuaded in 1979 to appoint a committee to undertake a study of the Uniform Act with a view to preparing the draft of a revision. The Conference was influenced by the following considerations:

(1) The Bankruptcy Reform Act of 1978 has made numerous changes in the section of that Act dealing with fraudulent transfers and obligations, thereby substantially reducing the correspondence of the provisions of the federal bankruptcy law on fraudulent transfers with the Uniform Act.

(2) The Committee on Corporate Laws of the Section of Corporations, Banking & Business Law of the American Bar Association, engaged in revising the Model Corporation Act, suggested that the Conference review provisions of the Uniform Act with a view to determining whether the Acts are consistent in respect to the treatment of dividend distributions.

(3) The Uniform Commercial Code, enacted at least in part by all 50 states, had substantially modified related rules of law regulating transfers of

personal property, notably by facilitating the making and perfection of security transfers against attack by unsecured creditors.

(4) Debtors and trustees in a number of cases have avoided foreclosure of security interests by invoking the fraudulent transfer section of the Bankruptcy Reform Act.

(5) The Model Rules of Professional Conduct adopted by the House of Delegates of the American Bar Association on August 2, 1983, forbid a lawyer to counsel or to assist a client in conduct that the lawyer knows is fraudulent.

. . . .

The Committee determined to rename the Act the Uniform Fraudulent Transfer Act in recognition of its applicability to transfers of personal property as well as real property, "conveyance" having a connotation restricting it to a transfer of personal property. As noted in Comment (2) accompanying § 1(2) and Comment (8) accompanying § 4, however, this Act, like the original Uniform Act, does not purport to cover the whole law of voidable transfers and obligations. The limited scope of the original Act did not impair its effectiveness in achieving uniformity in the areas covered. *See* McLaughlin, *Application of the Uniform Fraudulent Conveyance Act*, 46 Harv.L.Rev. 404, 405 (1933).

The basic structure and approach of the Uniform Fraudulent Conveyance Act are preserved in the Uniform Fraudulent Transfer Act. There are two sections in the new Act delineating what transfers and obligations are fraudulent. Section 4(a) is an adaptation of three sections of the U.F.C.A.; § 5(a) is an adaptation of another section of the U.F.C.A.; and § 5(b) is new. One section of the U.F.C.A. (§ 8) is not carried forward into the new Act because deemed to be redundant in part and in part susceptible of inequitable application. Both Acts declare a transfer made or an obligation incurred with actual intent to hinder, delay, or defraud creditors to be fraudulent. Both Acts render a transfer made or obligation incurred without adequate consideration to be constructively fraudulent — *i.e.*, without regard to the actual intent of the parties — under one of the following conditions:

(1) the debtor was left by the transfer or obligation with unreasonably small assets for a transaction or the business in which he was engaged;

(2) the debtor intended to incur, or believed that he would incur, more debts than he would be able to pay; or

(3) the debtor was insolvent at the time or as a result of the transfer or obligation.

As under the original Uniform Fraudulent Conveyance Act a transfer or obligation that is constructively fraudulent because insolvency concurs with or follows failure to receive adequate consideration is voidable only by a creditor in existence at the time the transfer occurs or the obligation is incurred. Either an existing or subsequent creditor may avoid a transfer or obligation for inadequate consideration when accompanied by the financial condition specified in § 4(a)(2)(i) or the mental state specified in § 4(a)(2)(ii).

Reasonably equivalent value is required in order to constitute adequate consideration under the revised Act. The revision follows the Bankruptcy Code in eliminating good faith on the part of the transferee or obligee as an issue in the determination of whether adequate consideration is given by a transferee or obligee. The new Act, like the Bankruptcy Act, allows the transferee or obligee to show good faith in defense after a creditor establishes that a fraudulent transfer has been made or a fraudulent obligation has been incurred. Thus a showing by a defendant that a reasonable equivalent has been given in good faith for a transfer or obligation is a complete defense although the debtor is shown to have intended to hinder, delay, or defraud creditors.

A good faith transferee or obligee who has given less than a reasonable equivalent is nevertheless allowed a reduction in a liability to the extent of the value given. The new Act, like the Bankruptcy Code, eliminates the provision of the Uniform Fraudulent Conveyance Act that enables a creditor to attack a security transfer on the ground that the value of the property transferred is disproportionate to the debt secured. The premise of the new Act is that the value of the interest transferred for security is measured by and thus corresponds exactly to the debt secured. Foreclosure of a debtor's interest by a regularly conducted, noncollusive sale on default under a mortgage or other security agreement may not be avoided under the Act as a transfer for less than a reasonably equivalent value.

The definition of insolvency under the Act is adapted from the definition of the term in the Bankruptcy Code. Insolvency is presumed from proof of a failure generally to pay debts as they become due.

The new Act adds a new category of fraudulent transfer, namely, a preferential transfer by an insolvent insider to a creditor who had reasonable cause to believe the debtor to be insolvent. An insider is defined in much the same way as in the Bankruptcy Code and includes a relative, also defined as in the Bankruptcy Code, a director or officer of a corporate debtor, a partner, or a person in control of a debtor. This provision is available only to an existing creditor. Its premise is that an insolvent debtor is obliged to pay debts to creditors not related to him before paying those who are insiders.

The new Act omits any provision directed particularly at transfers or obligations of insolvent partnership debtors. Under § 8 of the Uniform Fraudulent Conveyance Act any transfer made or obligation incurred by an insolvent partnership to a partner is fraudulent without regard to intent or adequacy of consideration. So categorical a condemnation of a partnership transaction with a partner may unfairly prejudice the interests of a partner's separate creditors. The new Act also omits as redundant a provision in the original Act that makes fraudulent a transfer made or obligation incurred by an insolvent partnership for less than a fair consideration to the partnership.

Section 7 lists the remedies available to creditors under the new Act. It eliminates as unnecessary and confusing a differentiation made in the original Act between the remedies available to holders of matured claims and those holding unmatured claims. Since promulgation of the Uniform Fraudulent Conveyance Act the Supreme Court has imposed restrictions on the availability and use of prejudgment remedies.

As a result many states have amended their statutes and rules applicable to such remedies, and it is frequently unclear whether a state's procedures include a prejudgment remedy against a fraudulent transfer or obligation. A bracketed paragraph is included in Section 7 for adoption by those states that elect to make such a remedy available.

Section 8 prescribes the measure of liability of a transferee or obligee under the Act and enumerates defenses. Defenses against avoidance of a preferential transfer to an insider under § 5(b) include an adaptation of defenses available under § 547(c)(2) and (4) of the Bankruptcy Code when such a transfer is sought to be avoided as a preference by the trustee in bankruptcy. In addition a preferential transfer may be justified when shown to be made pursuant to a good faith effort to stave off forced liquidation and rehabilitate the debtor. Section 8 also precludes avoidance, as a constructively fraudulent transfer, of the termination of a lease on default or the enforcement of a security interest in compliance with Article 9 of the Uniform Commercial Code.

The new Act includes a new section specifying when a transfer is made or an obligation is incurred. The section specifying the time when a transfer occurs is adapted from Section 548(d) of the Bankruptcy Code. Its premise is that if the law prescribes a mode for making the transfer a matter of public record or notice, it is not deemed to be made for any purpose under the Act until it has become such a matter of record or notice.

The new Act also includes a statute of limitations that bars the right rather than the remedy on expiration of the statutory periods prescribed. The law governing limitations on actions to avoid fraudulent transfers among the states is unclear and full of diversity. The Act recognizes that laches and estoppel may operate to preclude a particular creditor from pursuing a remedy against a fraudulent transfer or obligation even though the statutory period of limitations has not run.

UNIFORM FRAUDULENT TRANSFER ACT

§ 1.   Definitions

As used in this [Act]:

(1) "Affiliate" means:

(i) a person who directly or indirectly owns, controls, or holds with power to vote, 20 percent or more of the outstanding voting securities of the debtor, other than a person who holds the securities,

(A) as a fiduciary or agent without sole discretionary power to vote the securities; or

(B) solely to secure a debt, if the person has not exercised the power to vote;

(ii) a corporation 20 percent or more of whose outstanding voting securities are directly or indirectly owned, controlled, or held with power to vote, by the debtor or a person who directly or indirectly owns, controls, or holds, with power to vote, 20 percent or more of the outstanding voting securities of the debtor, other than a person who holds the securities,

(A) as a fiduciary or agent without sole power to vote the securities; or

(B) solely to secure a debt, if the person has not in fact exercised the power to vote;

(iii) a person whose business is operated by the debtor under a lease or other agreement, or a person substantially all of whose assets are controlled by the debtor; or

(iv) a person who operates the debtor's business under a lease or other agreement or controls substantially all of the debtor's assets.

(2) "Asset" means property of a debtor, but the term does not include:

(i) property to the extent it is encumbered by a valid lien;

(ii) property to the extent it is generally exempt under nonbankruptcy law; or

(iii) an interest in property held in tenancy by the entireties to the extent it is not subject to process by a creditor holding a claim against only one tenant.

(3) "Claim" means a right to payment, whether or not the right is reduced to judgment, liquidated, unliquidated, fixed, contingent, matured, unmatured, disputed, undisputed, legal, equitable, secured, or unsecured.

(4) "Creditor" means a person who has a claim.

(5) "Debt" means liability on a claim.

(6) "Debtor" means a person who is liable on a claim.

(7) "Insider" includes:

(i) if the debtor is an individual,

(A) a relative of the debtor or of a general partner of the debtor;

(B) a partnership in which the debtor is a general partner;

(C) a general partner in a partnership described in clause (B); or

(D) a corporation of which the debtor is a director, officer, or person in control;

(ii) if the debtor is a corporation,

(A) a director of the debtor;

(B) an officer of the debtor;

(C) a person in control of the debtor;

(D) a partnership in which the debtor is a general partner;

(E) a general partner in a partnership described in clause (D); or

(F) a relative of a general partner, director, officer, or person in control of the debtor;

(iii) if the debtor is a partnership,

(A) a general partner in the debtor;

(B) a relative of the general partner in, a general partner of, or a person in control of the debtor;

(C) another partnership in which the debtor is a general partner;

(D) a general partner in a partnership described in clause (C); or

(E) a person in control of the debtor;

(iv) an affiliate, or an insider of an affiliate as if the affiliate were the debtor; and

(v) a managing agent of the debtor.

(8) "Lien" means a charge against or an interest in property to secure payment of a debt or performance of an obligation, and includes a security interest created by agreement, a judicial lien obtained by legal or equitable process or proceedings, a common–law lien, or a statutory lien.

(9) "Person" means an individual, partnership, corporation, association, organization, government or governmental subdivision or agency, business trust, estate, trust, or any other legal or commercial entity.

(10) "Property" means anything that may be the subject of ownership.

(11) "Relative" means an individual related by consanguinity within the third degree as determined by the common law, a spouse, or an individual related to a spouse within the third degree as so determined, and includes an individual in an adoptive relationship within the third degree.

(12) "Transfer" means every mode, direct or indirect, absolute or conditional, voluntary or involuntary, of disposing of or parting with an asset or an interest in an asset, and includes payment of money, release, lease, and creation of a lien or other encumbrance.

(13) "Valid lien" means a lien that is effective against the holder of a judicial lien subsequently obtained by legal or equitable process or proceedings.

§ 2. Insolvency

(a) A debtor is insolvent if the sum of the debtor's debts is greater than all of the debtor's assets at a fair valuation.

(b) A debtor who is generally not paying his [or her] debts as they become due is presumed to be insolvent.

(c) A partnership is insolvent under subsection (a) if the sum of the partnership's debts is greater than the aggregate, at a fair valuation, of all of the partnership's assets and the sum of the excess of the value of each general partner's nonpartnership assets over the partner's nonpartnership debts.

(d) Assets under this section do not include property that has been transferred, concealed, or removed with intent to hinder, delay, or defraud creditors or that has been transferred in a manner making the transfer voidable under this [Act].

(e) Debts under this section do not include an obligation to the extent it is secured by a valid lien on property of the debtor not included as an asset.

§ 3. Value

(a) Value is given for a transfer or an obligation if, in exchange for the transfer or obligation, property is transferred or an antecedent debt is secured or satisfied, but value does not include an unperformed promise made otherwise than in the ordinary course of the promisor's business to furnish support to the debtor or another person.

(b) For the purposes of Sections 4(a)(2) and 5, a person gives a reasonably equivalent value if the person acquires an interest of the debtor in an asset pursuant to a regularly conducted, noncollusive foreclosure sale or execution of a power of sale for the acquisition or disposition of the interest of the debtor upon default under a mortgage, deed of trust, or security agreement.

(c) A transfer is made for present value if the exchange between the debtor and the transferee is intended by them to be contemporaneous and is in fact substantially contemporaneous.

§ 4. Transfers Fraudulent as to Present and Future Creditors

(a) A transfer made or obligation incurred by a debtor is fraudulent as to a creditor, whether the creditor's claim arose before or after the transfer was made or the obligation was incurred, if the debtor made the transfer or incurred the obligation:

(1) with actual intent to hinder, delay, or defraud any creditor of the debtor; or

(2) without receiving a reasonably equivalent value in exchange for the transfer or obligation, and the debtor:

(i) was engaged or was about to engage in a business or a transaction for which the remaining assets of the debtor were unreasonably small in relation to the business or transaction; or

(ii) intended to incur, or believed or reasonably should have believed that he [or she] would incur, debts beyond his [or her] ability to pay as they became due.

(b) In determining actual intent under subsection (a)(1), consideration may be given, among other factors, to whether:

(1) the transfer or obligation was to an insider;

(2) the debtor retained possession or control of the property transferred after the transfer;

(3) the transfer or obligation was disclosed or concealed;

(4) before the transfer was made or obligation was incurred, the debtor had been sued or threatened with suit;

(5) the transfer was of substantially all the debtor's assets;

(6) the debtor absconded;

(7) the debtor removed or concealed assets;

(8) the value of the consideration received by the debtor was reasonably equivalent to the value of the asset transferred or the amount of the obligation incurred;

(9) the debtor was insolvent or became insolvent shortly after the transfer was made or the obligation was incurred;

(10) the transfer occurred shortly before or shortly after a substantial debt was incurred; and

(11) the debtor transferred the essential assets of the business to a lienor who transferred the assets to an insider of the debtor.

§ 5.   Transfers Fraudulent as to Present Creditors

(a) A transfer made or obligation incurred by a debtor is fraudulent as to a creditor whose claim arose before the transfer was made or the obligation was incurred if the debtor made the transfer or incurred the obligation without receiving a reasonably equivalent value in exchange for the transfer or obligation and the debtor was insolvent at that time or the debtor became insolvent as a result of the transfer or obligation.

(b) A transfer made by a debtor is fraudulent as to a creditor whose claim arose before the transfer was made if the transfer was made to an insider for an antecedent debt, the debtor was insolvent at that time, and the insider had reasonable cause to believe that the debtor was insolvent.

§ 6.   When Transfer is Made or Obligation is Incurred

For the purposes of this [Act]:

(1) a transfer is made:

(i) with respect to an asset that is real property other than a fixture, but including the interest of a seller or purchaser under a contract for the sale of the asset, when the transfer is so far perfected that a good–faith purchaser of the asset from the debtor against whom applicable law permits the transfer to be perfected cannot acquire an interest in the asset that is superior to the interest of the transferee; and

(ii) with respect to an asset that is not real property or that is a fixture, when the transfer is so far perfected that a creditor on a simple contract cannot acquire a judicial lien otherwise than under this [Act] that is superior to the interest of the transferee;

(2) if applicable law permits the transfer to be perfected as provided in paragraph (1) and the transfer is not so perfected before the commencement of an action for relief under this [Act], the transfer is deemed made immediately before the commencement of the action;

(3) if applicable law does not permit the transfer to be perfected as provided in paragraph (1), the transfer is made when it becomes effective between the debtor and the transferee;

(4) a transfer is not made until the debtor has acquired rights in the asset transferred;

(5) an obligation is incurred:

(i) if oral, when it becomes effective between the parties; or

(ii) if evidenced by a writing, when the writing executed by the obligor is delivered to or for the benefit of the obligee.

§ 7. Remedies of Creditors

(a) In an action for relief against a transfer or obligation under this [Act], a creditor, subject to the limitations in Section 8, may obtain:

(1) avoidance of the transfer or obligation to the extent necessary to satisfy the creditor's claim;

[(2) an attachment or other provisional remedy against the asset transferred or other property of the transferee in accordance with the procedure prescribed by [ ];]

(3) subject to applicable principles of equity and in accordance with applicable rules of civil procedure,

(i) an injunction against further disposition by the debtor or a transferee, or both, of the asset transferred or of other property;

(ii) appointment of a receiver to take charge of the asset transferred or of other property of the transferee; or

(iii) any other relief the circumstances may require.

(b) If a creditor has obtained a judgment on a claim against the debtor, the creditor, if the court so orders, may levy execution on the asset transferred or its proceeds.

§ 8. Defenses, Liability, and Protection of Transferee

(a) A transfer or obligation is not voidable under Section 4(a)(1) against a person who took in good faith and for a reasonably equivalent value or against any subsequent transferee or obligee.

(b) Except as otherwise provided in this section, to the extent a transfer is voidable in an action by a creditor under Section 7(a)(1), the creditor may recover judgment for the value of the asset transferred, as adjusted under subsection (c), or the amount necessary to satisfy the creditor's claim, whichever is less. The judgment may be entered against:

(1) the first transferee of the asset or the person for whose benefit the transfer was made; or

(2) any subsequent transferee other than a good faith transferee who took for value or from any subsequent transferee.

(c) If the judgment under subsection (b) is based upon the value of the asset transferred, the judgment must be for an amount equal to the value of the asset at the time of the transfer, subject to adjustment as the equities may require.

(d) Notwithstanding voidability of a transfer or an obligation under this [Act], a good–faith transferee or obligee is entitled, to the extent of the value given the debtor for the transfer or obligation, to

(1) a lien on or a right to retain any interest in the asset transferred;

(2) enforcement of any obligation incurred; or

(3) a reduction in the amount of the liability on the judgment.

(e) A transfer is not voidable under Section 4(a)(2) or Section 5 if the transfer results from:

(1) termination of a lease upon default by the debtor when the termination is pursuant to the lease and applicable law; or

(2) enforcement of a security interest in compliance with Article 9 of the Uniform Commercial Code.

(f) A transfer is not voidable under Section 5(b):

(1) to the extent the insider gave new value to or for the benefit of the debtor after the transfer was made unless the new value was secured by a valid lien;

(2) if made in the ordinary course of business or financial affairs of the debtor and the insider; or

(3) if made pursuant to a good–faith effort to rehabilitate the debtor and the transfer secured present value given for that purpose as well as an antecedent debt of the debtor.

§ 9.   Extinguishment of [Claim for Relief] [Cause of Action]

A [claim for relief] [cause of action] with respect to a fraudulent transfer or obligation under this [Act] is extinguished unless action is brought:

(a) under Section 4(a)(1), within 4 years after the transfer was made or the obligation was incurred or, if later, within one year after the transfer or obligation was or could reasonably have been discovered by the claimant;

(b) under Section 4(a)(2) or 5(a), within 4 years after the transfer was made or the obligation was incurred; or

(c) under Section 5(b), within one year after the transfer was made or the obligation was incurred.

§ 10. Supplementary Provisions

Unless displaced by the provisions of this [Act], the principles of law and equity, including the law merchant and the law relating to principal and agent, estoppel, laches, fraud, misrepresentation, duress, coercion, mistake, insolvency, or other validating or invalidating cause, supplement its provisions.

§ 11. Uniformity of Application and Construction

This [Act] shall be applied and construed to effectuate its general purpose to make uniform the law with respect to the subject of this [Act] among states enacting it.

§ 12. Short Title

This [Act] may be cited as the Uniform Fraudulent Transfer Act.

§ 13. Repeal

The following acts and all other acts and parts of acts inconsistent herewith are hereby repealed:

UNIFORM FRAUDULENT CONVEYANCE ACT

7A U.L.A. 164 (1978)

§ 1. Definition of Terms

In this act "Assets" of a debtor means property not exempt from liability for his debts. To the extent that any property is liable for any debts of the debtor, such property shall be included in his assets.

"Conveyance" includes every payment of money, assignment, release, transfer, lease, mortgage or pledge of tangible or intangible property, and also the creation of any lien or incumbrance.

"Creditor" is a person having any claim, whether matured or unmatured, liquidated or unliquidated, absolute, fixed or contingent.

"Debt" includes any legal liability, whether matured or unmatured, liquidated or unliquidated, absolute, fixed or contingent.

§ 2. Insolvency

(1) A person is insolvent when the present fair salable value of his assets is less than the amount that will be required to pay his probable liability on his existing debts as they become absolute and matured.

(2) In determining whether a partnership is insolvent there shall be added to the partnership property the present fair salable value of the separate assets of each general partner in excess of the amount probably sufficient to meet the claims of

his separate creditors, and also the amount of any unpaid subscription to the partnership of each limited partner, provided the present fair salable value of the assets of such limited partner is probably sufficient to pay his debts, including such unpaid subscription.

§ 3. Fair Consideration

Fair consideration is given for property, or obligation,

(a) When in exchange for such property, or obligation, as a fair equivalent therefor, and in good faith, property is conveyed or an antecedent debt is satisfied, or

(b) When such property, or obligation is received in good faith to secure a present advance or antecedent debt in amount not disproportionately small as compared with the value of the property, or obligation obtained.

§ 4. Conveyances by Insolvent

Every conveyance made and every obligation incurred by a person who is or will be thereby rendered insolvent is fraudulent as to creditors without regard to his actual intent if the conveyance is made or the obligation is incurred without a fair consideration.

§ 5. Conveyances by Persons in Business

Every conveyance made without fair consideration when the person making it is engaged or is about to engage in a business or transaction for which the property remaining in his hands after the conveyance is an unreasonably small capital, is fraudulent as to creditors and as to other persons who become creditors during the continuance of such business or transaction without regard to his actual intent.

§ 6. Conveyances by a Person About to Incur Debts

Every conveyance made and every obligation incurred without fair consideration when the person making the conveyance or entering into the obligation intends or believes that he will incur debts beyond his ability to pay as they mature, is fraudulent as to both present and future creditors.

§ 7. Conveyance Made With Intent to Defraud

Every conveyance made and every obligation incurred with actual intent, as distinguished from intent presumed in law, to hinder, delay, or defraud either present or future creditors, is fraudulent as to both present and future creditors.

§ 8. Conveyance of Partnership Property

Every conveyance of partnership property and every partnership obligation incurred when the partnership is or will be thereby rendered insolvent, is fraudulent as to partnership creditors, if the conveyance is made or obligation is incurred,

(a) To a partner, whether with or without a promise by him to pay partnership debts, or

(b) To a person not a partner without fair consideration to the partnership as distinguished from consideration to the individual partners.

§ 9. Rights of Creditors Whose Claims Have Matured

(1) Where a conveyance or obligation is fraudulent as to a creditor, such creditor, when his claim has matured, may, as against any person except a purchaser for fair consideration without knowledge of the fraud at the time of the purchase, or one who has derived title immediately or mediately from such a purchaser,

(a) Have the conveyance set aside or obligation annulled to the extent necessary to satisfy his claim, or

(b) Disregard the conveyance and attach or levy execution upon the property conveyed.

(2) A purchaser who without actual fraudulent intent has given less than a fair consideration for the conveyance or obligation, may retain the property or obligation as security for repayment.

§ 10. Rights of Creditors Whose Claims Have Not Matured

Where a conveyance made or obligation incurred is fraudulent as to a creditor whose claim has not matured he may proceed in a court of competent jurisdiction against any person against whom he could have proceeded had his claim matured, and the court may,

(a) Restrain the defendant from disposing of his property,

(b) Appoint a receiver to take charge of the property,

(c) Set aside the conveyance or annul the obligation, or

(d) Make any order which the circumstances of the case may require.

§ 11. Cases Not Provided For in Act

In any case not provided for in this Act the rules of law and equity including the law merchant, and in particular the rules relating to the law of principal and agent, and the effect of fraud, misrepresentation, duress or coercion, mistake, bankruptcy or other invalidating cause shall govern.

§ 12. Construction of Act

This act shall be so interpreted and construed as to effectuate its general purpose to make uniform the law of those states which enact it.

§ 13. Name of Act

This act may be cited as the Uniform Fraudulent Conveyance Act.

§ 14. Inconsistent Legislation Repealed

Sections _____ are hereby repealed, and all acts or parts of acts inconsistent with this Act are hereby repealed.

BANKRUPTCY CODE §§ 548, 101

11 U.S.C. § 548

Fraudulent transfers and obligations

(a) The trustee may avoid any transfer of an interest of the debtor in property, or any obligation incurred by the debtor, that was made or incurred on or within one year before the date of the filing of the petition, if the debtor voluntarily or in voluntarily—

(1) made such transfer or incurred such obligation with actual intent to hinder, delay, or defraud any entity to which the debtor was or became, on or after the date that such transfer was made or such obligation was incurred, indebted; or

(2) (A) received less than a reasonably equivalent value in exchange for such transfer or obligation; and

(B)(i) was insolvent on the date that such transfer was made or such obligation was incurred, or became insolvent as a result of such transfer or obligation;

(ii) was engaged in business or a transaction, or was about to engage in business or a transaction, for which any property remaining with the debtor was an unreasonably small capital; or

(iii) intended to incur, or believed that the debtor would incur, debts that would be beyond the debtor's ability to pay as such debts matured.

(b) The trustee of a partnership debtor may avoid any transfer of an interest of the debtor in property, or any obligation incurred by the debtor, that was made or incurred on or within one year before the date of the filing of the petition, to a general partner in the debtor, if the debtor was insolvent on the date such transfer was made or such obligation was incurred, or became insolvent as a result of such transfer or obligation.

(c) Except to the extent that a transfer or obligation voidable under this section is voidable under section 544, 545, or 547 of this title, a transferee or obligee of such a transfer or obligation that takes for value and in good faith has a lien or may retain any interest transferred, may retain any lien transferred, or may enforce any obligation incurred, as the case may be, to the extent that such transferee or obligee gave value to the debtor in exchange for such transfer or obligation.

(d)(1) For the purposes of this section, a transfer is made when such transfer is so perfected that a bona fide purchaser from the debtor against whom applicable law permits such transfer to be perfected cannot acquire an interest in the property transferred that is superior to the interest in such property of the transferee, but if such transfer is not so perfected before the commencement of the case, such transfer is made immediately before the date of the filing of the petition.

(2) In this section—

(A) "Value" means property, or satisfaction or securing of a present or antecedent debt of the debtor, but does not include an unperformed promise to furnish support to the debtor or to a relative of the debtor; and

(B) a commodity broker, forward contract merchant, stockbroker, financial institution or securities clearing agency that receives a margin payment, as defined in section 741(5) or 761(15) of this title, or settlement payment, as defined in section 741(8) of this title, takes for value to the extent of such payment; and

(C) a repo participant that receives a margin payment, as defined in section 741(5) or (15) of this title, or settlement payment, as defined in section 741(8) of this title, in connection with a repurchase agreement, takes for value to the extent of such payment.

---

11 U.S.C. § 101(32)

"Insolvent" means—

(A) with reference to an entity other than a partnership, financial condition such that the sum of such entity's debts is greater than all of such entity's property, at a fair valuation, exclusive of—

  (i)   property transferred, concealed, or removed with intent to hinder, delay, or defraud such entity's creditors; and

  (ii) property that may be exempted from property of the estate under section 522 of this title; and

(B) with reference to a partnership, financial condition such that the sum of such partnership's debts is greater than the aggregate of, at a fair valuation—

  (i)   all of such partnership's property, exclusive of property of the kind specified in subparagraph (A)(i) of this paragraph; and

  (ii) the sum of the excess of the value of each general partner's nonpartnership property, exclusive of property of the kind specified in subparagraph (A) of this paragraph, over such partner's nonpartnership debts;

11 U.S.C. § 101(54)

"[T]ransfer" means every mode, direct or indirect, absolute or conditional, voluntary or involuntary, of disposing of or parting with property or with an interest in property, including retention of title as a security interest and foreclosure of the debtor's equity of redemption;

———————————

FRAUDULENT TRANSFERS:
STATUTORY CROSS–REFERENCE*

Operative Voidable Transfers	UFTA	UPCA	Bankruptcy Code (11 U.S.C.)
1. Transfer with actual intent to hinder, delay, or defraud creditors.	§4(a)(1) {Defense: §8(a)} (good faith buyer for equivalent value)	§7	§548(a)(1)
2. Transfer by insolvent debtor.	§5(a) {Defense: §8(e)} (§8(e)(1) (lease termination); and §8(e)(2) (enforcement of Article 9 security interest))	§4	§548(a)(2)(A)-(B)(i)
3. Transfer by business debtor with unreasonably small capital.	§4(a)(2)(i) {Defense: §8(e)}	§5	§548(a)(2)(A)-(B)(ii)
4. Transfer by debtor about to incur debts.	§4(a)(2)(ii) {Defense: §8(e)}	§6	§548(a)(2)(A)-(B)(iii)
5. Insider transfers.	§5(b) {Defense: §8(e); §8(f)(1) (subsequent new value); §8(f)(2) (ordinary course of business); §8(f)(3) (good faith rehabilitation)}	—	—
Statute of Limitations	§9 {later of 4 years or 1 year after transfer should have been discovered: actual intent (§9(a)); 4 years: constructive intent (§9(b)); and one year: insider transfer (§9(c)).}	—	§546(a)(1) (2 years from later of order for relief, or 1 year from election/appointment of first trustee if that occurs within first two years of case, unless case closed or dismissed.)

Key Definitions

Term	UPTA	UPCA	Bankruptcy Code (11 U.S.C.)
"Claim"	§1(3)	—	§101(5)
"Creditor"	§1(4)	§1,¶3	§101(10)
"Debt"	§1(5)	§1,¶4	§101(12)
"Insider"	§1(7)	—	§101(31)
"Transfer"	§1(12)	§1,¶2 (defines "conveyance")	§101(54)
"Insolvency"	§2	§2	§101(32) (defines "insolvent")
"Value"	§3	§3 (defines "fair consideration")	§548(d)(2)(A)

---

* Updated and reprinted from Cook & Mendales, *The Uniform Fraudulent Transfer Act: An Introductory Critique*, 62 Am. Bankr. L.J. 87, 96 (1988). Copyright © 1988 by American Bankruptcy Law Journal. Reprinted by permission.

[B]   Cases, Notes and Questions

TWYNE'S CASE

Star Chamber
3 Coke 80b, 76 Eng. Rep. 809 (1601)

. . . Pierce was indebted to Twyne in four hundred pounds, and was indebted also to C. in two hundred pounds. C. brought an action of debt against Pierce, and pending the writ, Pierce being possessed of goods and chattels of the value of three hundred pounds, in secret made a general deed of gift of all his goods and chattels real and personal whatsoever to Twyne, in satisfaction of his debt; notwithstanding that Pierce continued in possession of the said goods, and some of them he sold; and he shore the sheep, and marked them with his own mark: and afterwards C. had judgment against Pierce, and had a *fieri facias* directed to the Sheriff of Southampton, who by force of the said writ came to make execution of the said goods; but divers persons, by the command of the said Twyne, did with force resist the said sheriff, claiming them to be the goods of the said Twyne by force of the said gift; and openly declared by the commandment of Twyne, that is was a good gift, and made on a good and lawful consideration. And whether this gift on the whole matter, was fraudulent and of no effect by the said Act of 13 Eliz. or not, was the question. And it was resolved by . . . the whole Court of Star Chamber, that this gift was fraudulent, within the statute of 13 Eliz. And in this case divers points were resolved:

1st. That this gift had the signs and marks of fraud, because the gift is general, without exception of his apparel, or any thing of necessity . . .

2nd. The donor continued in possession, and used them as his own; and by reason thereof he traded and trafficked with others, and defrauded and deceived them.

3rd. It was made in secret . . .

4th. It was made pending the writ.

5th. Here was a trust between the parties, for the donor possessed all, and used them as his proper goods and fraud is always apparelled and clad with a trust, and a trust is the cover of fraud.

6th. The deed contains, that the gift was made honestly, truly, and *bona fide* . . .

Secondly, it was resolved, that notwithstanding here was a true debt due to Twyne, and a good consideration of the gift, yet it was not within the proviso of the said Act of 13 Eliz. by which it is provided, that the said Act shall not extend to any estate or interest in lands, &c. goods or chattels made on a good consideration and *bona fide*; for although it is on a true and good consideration, yet it is not *bona fide*, for no gift shall be deemed to be *bona fide* within the said proviso which is accompanied with any trust; as if a man be indebted to five several persons, in the several sums of twenty pounds, and hath goods of the value of twenty pounds, and makes a gift of all his goods to one of them in satisfaction of his debt, but there is trust between them, that the donee shall deal favourably with him in regard of his poor estate, either to permit the donor, or some other for him, or for his benefit, to use or have possession of them, and is contented that he shall pay him his debt when he is able; this shall not be called *bona fide* within the said proviso; for the proviso saith on a good consideration, and *bona fide*; so a good consideration doth not suffice, if be not also *bona fide*: and therefore, reader, when any gift shall be to you in satisfaction of a debt, by one who is indebted to others also; 1st, Let it be made in a public manner, and before the neighbours, and not in private, for secrecy is a mark of fraud. 2nd, Let the goods and chattels be appraised by good people to the very value, and take a gift in particular in satisfaction of your debt. 3rd, Immediatcly after the gift, take the possession of them; for continuance of the possession in the donor, is a sign of trust. And know, reader, that the said words of the proviso, on a good consideration, and *bona fide*, do not extend to every gift made *bona fide*; and therefore there are two manners of gifts on a good consideration, . . . consideration of nature or blood, and a valuable consideration. As to the first, in the case before put; if he who is indebted to five several persons, to each party in twenty pounds, in consideration of natural affection, gives all his goods to his son, or cousin, in that case, forasmuch as others should lose their debts, &c. which are things of value, the intent of the Act was, that the consideration in such case should be valuable; for equity requires, that such gift, which defeats others, should be made on as high and good consideration as the things which are thereby defeated are; and it is to be presumed, that the father, if he had not been indebted to others, would not have dispossessed himself of all his goods, and subjected himself to his cradle; and therefore it shall be intended, that it was made to defeat his creditors: and if consideration of nature or blood should be a good consideration within this proviso, the statute would serve for little or nothing, and no creditor would be sure of his debt. And as to gifts made *bona fide*, it is to be known, that every gift made *bona fide*, either is on a trust between the parties, or without any trust: every gift made on trust is out of this proviso; for that which is betwixt the donor and donee, called a trust *per nomen speciosum*, is in truth, as to all the creditors, a fraud, for they are thereby defeated and defrauded of their true and due debts. And every trust is either expressed, or implied: an express trust is, when in the gift, or upon the gift, the trust by word or writing is expressed: a trust implied is, when a man makes a gift without any consideration, or on a consideration of nature, or blood only. . . .

And when a man, being greatly indebted to sundry persons, makes a gift to his son, or any of his blood, without consideration, but only of nature, the law intends a trust betwixt them, . . . that the donee, would, in consideration of such gift being voluntarily and freely made to him, and also in consideration of nature, relieve his father, or cousin, and not see him want who had made such gift to him, . . . : so note, valuable consideration is a good consideration within this proviso; and a gift made *bona fide* is a gift made without any trust either expressed or implied: by which it appears, that as a gift made on a good consideration, if it be not also *bona fide*, is not within the proviso; so a gift made *bona fide*, if it be not on a good consideration, is not within the proviso; but it ought to be on a good consideration, and also *bona fide*. . . .

And because fraud and deceit abound in these days more than in former times, it was resolved in this case by the whole Court, that all statutes made against fraud should be liberally and beneficially expounded to suppress the fraud. Note, reader, according to their opinions, divers resolutions have been made. . . .

[A]lthough the preamble [to one of the fraud statutes] speaks only of creditors; yet it is provided by the body of the Act generally, that all gifts of goods and chattels made or to be made on trust to the use of the donor, shall be void and no effect, but that is to be intended as to all strangers who are to have prejudice by such gift, but between the parties themselves it stands good: but the stat. 13 Eliz. c. 5. extends to it, for thereby it is enacted and declared, that all feoffments, gifts, grants, &c. "to delay, hinder or defraud creditors, and others, of their just and lawful actions, suits, debts, accounts, damages, penalties, forfeitures, heriots, mortuaries and reliefs," shall be void, &c. So that this Act doth not extend only to creditors, but to all others who had cause of action, or suit, or any penalty, or forfeiture, &c.

. . . .

. . . [W]here a man had conveyed his land to the use of himself for life, and afterwards to the use of divers others of his blood, with future power of revocation, . . . and afterwards, and before the power of revocation began, he, for valuable consideration, bargained and sold the land to another and his heirs: this bargain and sale is within the remedy of the said statute. For although the statute saith, "the said first conveyance not by him revoked, according to the power by him reserved," which seems by the literal sense to be intended of a present power of revocation, for no revocation can be made by force of a future power until it comes in *cssc:* yet it was held that the intent of the Act was, that such voluntary conveyance which was originally subject to a power of revocation, be it in *praesenti* or in *futuro*, should not stand against a purchaser *bona fide* for a valuable consideration; and if other construction should be made, the said Act would serve for little or no purpose, and it would be no difficult matter to evade it: so if A. had reserved to himself a power of revocation with the assent of B. and afterwards A. bargained and sold the land to another, this bargain and sale is *good*, and within the remedy of the said Act; for otherwise the good provision of the Act, by a small addition, and evil invention, would be defeated. . . .

. . . .

2nd, It was resolved, that if a man hath power of revocation, and afterwards, to the intent to defraud a purchaser, he levies a fine, or makes a feoffment, or other conveyance to a stranger, by which he extinguishes his power, and afterwards bargains and sells the land to another for a valuable consideration, the bargainee shall enjoy the land, for as to him, the fine, feoffment, or other conveyances, by which the condition was extinct, was void by the said Act; and so the first clause, by which all fraudulent and covinous conveyances are made void as to purchasers, extend to the last clause of the Act, . . . when he who makes the bargain and sale had power of revocation. And it was said, that the statute of 27 El. hath made voluntary estates made with power of revocation, as to purchasers, in equal degree with conveyances made by fraud and covin to defraud purchasers.

. . . [T]his Act is made against all fraud and deceit, and doth not help any purchaser, who doth not come to the land for a good consideration lawfully and without fraud or deceit; and such conveyance made on trust is void as to him who purchases the land for a valuable consideration *bona fide*, without deceit or cunning.

And by the judgment of the whole Court Twyne was convicted of fraud, and he and all the others of a riot.

NOTES AND QUESTIONS

(1) The Star Chamber enumerated a number of "signs and marks of fraud" in connection with Pierce's transfer of all of his real and personal property to Twyne. What are they? These so–called "badges of fraud" are still employed today as circumstantial evidence of a debtor's actual intent to hinder, delay, or defraud his creditors. *See* Cook, *Fraudulent Transfer Liability Under the Bankruptcy Code*, 17 Hous. L. Rev. 263, 270–71 (1980).

(2) Proving actual intent to hinder, delay, or defraud creditors through direct evidence may be difficult; accordingly, "the finding of the requisite intent may be predicated upon the concurrence of facts which, while not direct evidence of actual intent, lead to the irresistible conclusion that the transferor's conduct was motivated by such intent." 4 Collier, Bankruptcy, ¶ 548.05[5], at 548–33 (15th rev. ed. 1983); *Loftis v. Minar (In re Montanino)*, 4 C.B.C. 2d 362, 369 (Bankr. D.N.J. 1981).

(3) What standard of proof is required in actual intent cases? *See Glenmore Distilleries Co. v. Seideman*, 267 F. Supp. 915, 919 (E.D.N.Y. 1967) ("mere suspicion does not suffice"); *Tyler v. Capitol Chemical Industries, Inc. (In re Metro Paper, Inc.)*, 8 B.C.D. 1027, 1029 (Bankr. D.D.C. 1982) (actual intent to defraud must be proved by clear and convincing evidence).

(4) The Star Chamber suggests that to avoid the appearance of fraud, the debtor and his transferee should obtain an independent appraisal of the value of the property transferred—a practical tip that is as useful now as it was four centuries ago. What other practical advice does the court offer?

SHAPIRO v. WILGUS

United States Supreme Court
287 U.S. 348, 53 S. Ct. 142, 77 L. Ed. 355 (1932)

CARDOZO, J. . . .

. . . . Herbert P. Robinson was engaged in business in Philadelphia as a dealer in lumber. He was unable to pay his debts as they matured, but he believed that he would be able to pay them in full if his creditors were lenient. Indeed, he looked for a surplus of $100,000 if the business went on under the fostering care of a receiver. Most of the creditors were willing to give him time. Two creditors, including the petitioner, were unwilling, and threatened immediate suit. Thus pressed, the debtor cast about for a device whereby the business might go on and the importunate be held at bay. He had to reckon with obstructions erected by the local law. The law of Pennsylvania does not permit the appointment of a receiver for a business conducted by an individual as distinguished from one conducted by a corporation or a partnership. . . . To make such remedies available there was need to take the title out of Robinson and put it somewhere else. The act responded to the need. On January 9, 1931, the debtor brought about the formation of a Delaware corporation, the Miller Robinson Company. On the same day he made a conveyance to this company of all his property, real and personal, receiving in return substantially all the shares of stock and a covenant by the grantee to assume the payment of the debts. Three days later, on January 12, 1931, in conjunction with a simple contract creditor, he brought suit against the Delaware corporation in the federal court, invoking the jurisdiction of that court on the ground of diversity of citizenship. The bill of complaint alleged that creditors were pressing for immediate payment; that one had entered suit and was about to proceed to judgment; that the levy of attachments and executions would ruin the good will and dissipate the assets; and that the business, if protected from the suits of creditors and continued without disturbance could be made to pay the debts and yield a surplus of $100,000 for the benefit of stockholders. To accomplish these ends there was a prayer for the appointment of receivers with an accompanying injunction. The corporation filed an answer admitting all the averments of the bill and joining in the prayer. A decree, entered the same day, appointed receivers as prayed for in the complaint, and enjoined attachments and executions unless permitted by the court. Four days thereafter, on January 16, 1931, the petitioner began suit against Robinson in the Court of Common Pleas, and on February 4, 1931, recovered a judgment against his debtor for $1,007.65 upon a cause of action for money loaned. On February 26, 1931, he submitted a petition to the United States District Court in which he charged that the conveyance from Robinson to the corporation and the ensuing receivership were parts of a single scheme to hinder and delay creditors in their lawful suits and remedies, and he prayed that he be permitted to issue a writ of *fieri facias* against the chattels in the possession of the receivers and to sell them so far as necessary for the satisfaction of his judgment. The petition was denied, and the denial affirmed upon appeal.

The conveyance and the receivership are fraudulent in law as against non–assenting creditors. They have the unity of a common plan, each stage of the transaction drawing color and significance from the quality of the other; but, for convenience, they will be considered in order of time as if they stood apart. The sole purpose of the conveyance was to divest the debtor of his title and put it in such a form and place that levies would be averted. The petition to issue execution and the answer by the receivers leave the purpose hardly doubtful. Whatever fragment of doubt might otherwise be left is dispelled by the admissions of counsel on the argument before us. One cannot read the opinion of the Court of Appeals without seeing very clearly that like admissions must have been made upon the argument there. After a recital of the facts the court stated in substance that the aim of the debtor was to prevent the disruption of the business at the suit of hostile creditors and to cause the assets to be nursed for the benefit of all concerned. Perceiving that aim and indeed even declaring it, the court did not condemn it, but found it fair and lawful. In this approval of a purpose which has been condemned in Anglo–American law since the Statute of Elizabeth there is a misconception of the privileges and liberties vouchsafed to an embarrassed debtor. A conveyance is illegal if made with an intent to defraud the creditors of the grantor, but equally it is illegal if made with an intent to hinder and delay them. Many an embarrassed debtor holds the genuine belief that if suits can be staved off for a season, he will weather a financial storm, and pay his debts in full. The belief, even though well founded does not clothe him with a privilege to build up obstructions that will hold his creditors at bay. This is true in Pennsylvania under the Uniform Fraudulent Conveyance Act. . . . It is true under the Statute of Elizabeth . . . which, in any case not covered by the later act, is still the governing rule. Tested by either act, this conveyance may not stand. . . .

The conveyance to the corporation being voidable because fraudulent in law, the receivership must share its fate. It was part and parcel of a scheme whereby the form of a judicial remedy was to supply a protective cover for a fraudulent design. The design would have been ineffective if the debtor had been suffered to keep the business for himself. It did not gain validity when he transferred the business to another with a capacity for obstruction believed to be greater than his own. The end and aim of this receivership was not to administer the assets of a corporation legitimately conceived for a normal business purpose and functioning or designed to function according to normal business methods. What was in view was very different. A corporation created three days before the suit for the very purpose of being sued was to be interposed between its author and the creditors pursuing him, with a restraining order of the court to give check to the pursuers. We do not need to determine what remedies are available for the conservation of the assets when a corporation has been brought into existence to serve legitimate and normal ends. Ordinarily a creditor who seeks the appointment of receivers must reduce his claim to judgment and exhaust his remedy at law. . . . True indeed it is that receivers have at times been appointed even by federal courts at the suit of simple contract creditors if the defendant was willing to waive the irregularity and to consent to the decree. . . . We have given warning more than once, however, that the remedy in such circumstances is not to be granted loosely, but is to be watched with jealous eyes. . . . Never is such a remedy available when it is a mere weapon of coercion, a means for the frustration of the public policy of the state or the locality. It is one thing for a creditor with claims against a corporation that is legitimately his debtor to invoke the aid of equity to conserve the common fund for the benefit of himself and of the creditors at large. Whatever hindrance and delay of suitors is involved in such a remedy may then be incidental and subsidiary. It is another thing for a debtor, cooperating with friendly creditors, to bring the corporation into being with the hindrance and delay of suitors the very aim of its existence. The power to intervene before the legal remedy is exhausted is misused when it is exercised in aid of such a purpose. Only exemplary motives and scrupulous good faith will wake it into action.

The receivership decree assailed upon this record does not answer to the test. We have no thought in so holding to impute to counsel for the debtor or even to his client a willingness to participate in conduct known to be fraudulent. The candor with which the plan has been unfolded goes far to satisfy us, without more that they acted in the genuine belief that what they planned was fair and lawful. Genuine the belief was, but mistaken it was also. Conduct and purpose have a quality imprinted on them by the law.

There remains a question of procedure. . . . The petitioner was entitled to an order in the alternative either for the payment of his judgment out of the assets in the hands of the receivers or in default thereof for leave to issue execution. The refusal to grant relief in one or other of these forms is a departure from the bounds of any legitimate discretion which is not without redress.

The decree is reversed and the cause remanded to the District Court for further proceedings in conformity with this opinion.

FLUSHING SAVINGS BANK v. PARR

New York Supreme Court, Appellate Division
81 A.D.2d 655, 438 N.Y.S.2d 374 (2d Dept. 1981), appeal dismissed
54 N.Y.2d 770, 443 N.Y.S.2d 61 426 N.E.2d 752 (1981)

This appeal arises out of the litigation that ensued as a result of the financial collapse of the Parr Meadows Race Track. Plaintiff, as lead lender for a consortium of financial institutions, financed the construction of the racetrack in August, 1976 in the amount of $14,000,000. The building loan was personally guaranteed by defendants Ronald and Alfred Parr, the principals of defendant Parr Meadows Racing Association, Inc., the mortgagor. The association defaulted on the loan on July 1, 1977 and filed a petition for reorganization with the Bankruptcy Court in October, 1977. Plaintiff, unable to foreclose on the mortgage since the racetrack was part of the bankruptcy estate, obtained a judgment against the Parrs on their personal guaranties. This judgment was never satisfied.

On June 12, 1979 the association's bankruptcy petition was dismissed. In order to preserve the racetrack from foreclosure for all its unsecured creditors, Ronald Parr, who had filed a bankruptcy petition on June 12, 1979, conveyed the property from the association to himself. In addition, between 1973 and 1979, the Parrs had made various other conveyances from themselves to their relatives and controlled corporations.

Plaintiff, thereafter, commenced the instant action, *inter alia*, to declare all the conveyances made between 1973 and 1979 to be fraudulent conveyances and to set them aside. . . . With respect to the association's conveyance of the racetrack to Ronald Parr, plaintiff sought only a declaration that it was fraudulent. During the pendency of this action, the association filed a new petition for reorganization with the Bankruptcy Court. Shortly thereafter, Ronald Parr's individual bankruptcy proceeding was conditionally dismissed and he attempted to reconvey the racetrack back to the association. This reconveyance was barred by a Federal injunction. . . .

The matter is before this court after Special Term denied defendants' motion for summary judgment dismissing the complaint and plaintiff's cross motion for summary judgment on its second cause of action. The cross motion should have been granted.

Plaintiff's second cause of action alleges that the association's conveyance of the racetrack to Ronald Parr was a fraudulent conveyance, in that it was made with the actual intent to hinder and delay the plaintiff from foreclosing on the mortgage. . . .

The record on appeal clearly shows that the conveyance was for the purpose of avoiding foreclosure by the plaintiff by keeping the subject property within a bankruptcy estate. Such activity necessarily hindered and delayed plaintiff. The question before us then, is whether proof of an actual intent to hinder or delay, without actual intent to defraud, is a fraudulent conveyance pursuant to section 276 of the [New York] Debtor and Creditor Law.

A reading of section 276 leads to the conclusion that by the use of the disjunctive, "hinder" and "delay" exist independently of an intent to defraud. Although some courts have interpreted section 276 to require fraudulent intent . . . , we hold that "[a] conveyance is illegal if made with an intent to defraud the creditors of a grantor, but equally it is illegal if made with an intent to hinder and delay them" [citing *Shapiro v. Wilgus*] . . .

A deliberate attempt to stave off creditors by putting property in such a form and place that creditors cannot reach it, even when the purpose of that action is not to defraud them of ultimate payment but only to obtain enough time to restore the debtor's affairs, comes within the meaning of "hinder" and "delay". . . .

[Judgment of the lower court is reversed on the law.]

NOTES AND QUESTIONS

(1) The Supreme Court's clear message in *Shapiro v. Wilgus* is that if a debtor transfers his property to hinder or even merely delay his creditors, the transfer will be deemed actually fraudulent, despite the debtor's honest intentions. Actual intent to defraud is not necessary. *Accord Consove v. Cohen (In re Roco Corp.)*, 701 F.2d 978, 984 (1st Cir. 1983); *Klein v. Rossi*, 251 F. Supp. 1, 2 (E.D.N.Y. 1966); *but cf. Stratton v. Sioux Falls Paint and Glass (In re Stratton)*, 23 B.R. 284 (D.S.D. 1982). Why do you think this apparently radical principle has survived unchanged in Anglo–American jurisprudence?

(2) Justice Cardozo twice refers to the formation of the one–man corporation, the transfer of all the debtor's assets to the new entity, and the subsequent suit for an equity receivership, as a "scheme." In general, you should examine closely *all* of the debtor's actions in connection with a suspected fraudulent transfer, and not simply the transfer itself, to determine whether the debtor's overriding purpose in effecting the transactions was fraudulent.

(3) The petitioner's remedy in *Shapiro* was recovery of his judgment from the debtor's assets in the hands of the receiver. The UFCA (§ 9) and the Bankruptcy Code (11 U.S.C. § 550) both codify this principle: the creditor (or trustee) may avoid the transfer and recover the property or its equivalent from a transferee that, like the one–man corporation in *Shapiro*, did not receive the debtor's property in good faith. *See Southern Industries, Inc. v. Jeremias*, 66 A.D.2d 178, 183, 411 N.Y.S.2d 945, 949 (2d Dep't 1978), *infra*; *Consove v. Cohen (In re Roco Corp.)*, 21 B.R. 429, 436, 9 B.C.D. 233 (Bankr. 1st Cir. 1982), *aff'd*, 701 F.2d 978 (1st Cir. 1983); *Dean v. Davis*, 242 U.S. 438, 445 (1917); *Reaves v. National Bank (In re Reaves)*, 8 B.R. 177, (Bankr. D.S.D. 1981).

UNITED STATES v. WEST

United States District Court, District of Delaware
299 F. Supp. 661 (1969)

LATCHUM, District Judge.

On August 15, 1963, the Small Business Administration (SBA) loaned J. E. West, Inc., a Delaware corporation, $12,000.00, secured by a corporate judgment note, a mortgage on 4.89 acres of real estate located in Broad Creek Hundred, Sussex County, Delaware and a chattel mortgage. The corporate indebtedness was further secured by a guaranty agreement, dated August 15, 1963, signed by John Emory West and his wife, Mary Catherine West, in their individual capacities. On December 31, 1964, while the SBA loan was still outstanding. John Emory West and Mary Catherine West conveyed certain properties, known as 553 East Fourth Street and 534 Cooper Street, Laurel, Delaware, which they owned as individuals, to their son, David L. West. After J. E. West, Inc. defaulted on the loan, the United States, on June 29, 1966, entered a judgment by confession in this court on the corporate note against J. E. West, Inc. On June 30, 1966 the United States also entered in this proceeding a judgment by confession in the amount of $7,261.22 against John Emory West and Mary Catherine West on the guaranty agreement.

On September 1, 1966, David L. West conveyed the two properties received from his parents to his brother, Douglas H. West. Nearly two years later, on May 24, 1968, the United States caused a writ of *fieri facias* to be issued in these proceedings directing the United States Marshal to seize and attach the properties at 553 East Fourth Street and 534 Cooper Street, Laurel, Delaware. Thereafter, on December 4, 1968, the United States caused a writ of *venditioni exponas* to be issued, directing the Marshal to sell the seized properties at public sale to satisfy the judgment against Mr. and Mrs. West. Pursuant to the writ, the Marshal advertised the properties to be sold at public sale on January 22, 1969.

Prior to the sale, on January 20, 1969, Douglas West, as the record owner of the properties involved, intervened and petitioned the court for a stay of the sale. The court entered an order on January 23, 1969 temporarily staying the sale and ordering a hearing to be held on January 31, 1969 on the issue raised by the petition of Douglas West, *i.e.* the fraudulency of the conveyance by John Emory West and Mary Catherine West to David L. West. Although the hearing was ordered in conjunction with the stay order, it was intended and acknowledged by the parties to be an evidentiary hearing at which the government would prove the fraudulency of the conveyance in order to have the transaction set aside. Thus, this opinion will determine whether or not the government is entitled as a creditor of Mr. and Mrs. West to have the conveyance to David L. West set aside as fraudulent, though title is now in Douglas H. West, and proceed with its plans to sell the properties upon execution process.

Initially, it is clear that, in the absence of any applicable federal statute, the Delaware statutory and case law is controlling. . . . The government argues . . . that the conveyance in question is fraudulent under 6 Del.C. § 1304, a verbatim adoption of section 4 of the Uniform Fraudulent Conveyance Act. . . . In order to rule that the conveyance was fraudulent this court must find (1) that it was made without fair consideration and (2) that the debtor was insolvent or was rendered insolvent by the conveyance. The actual intent of the parties to the conveyance is of no consequence since this section establishes "an external test of constructive or legal fraud . . . ", . . . as contrasted with the subjective "actual intent . . . to defraud". . . .

In opposition to the government's effort to have the 1964 conveyance set aside as fraudulent the intervenor has argued . . . that since the three–year statute of limitations has expired as to any legal remedy to which the government might be entitled . . . this court must bar the government's equitable action to set aside the conveyance on the theory that "equity follows the law." . . . However, "[i]t is well settled that the United States is not bound by state statutes of limitation or subject to the defense of laches in enforcing its [sovereign or governmental] rights." . . . In this case the government is in the position of a creditor which is striving to protect "public money" previously obtained by a corporation through an SBA loan on which the debtors are guarantors. It is, thus, "acting in its governmental capacity" and cannot be barred by the applicable statute of limitations or laches. . . .

In an action to set aside a fraudulent conveyance the burden is on the creditor to prove that the conveyance was fraudulent. . . . However, it is the law in Delaware and elsewhere that

> where a transaction alleged to be fraudulent takes place between persons of near blood relationship, it will be more closely scrutinized than if it were between strangers, because where such intimacy of relationship exists fraud is easily practiced and effectively concealed.

. . . While the Delaware cases which have articulated this requirement of a careful examination of family transactions specifically involved allegations of actual fraud . . . in the absence of any indication in the decided cases to the contrary, it can be assumed that the Delaware courts would adhere to this same policy in considering [constructively fraudulent] conveyances and that this would be reflected in the burden of proof . . .

In the opinion of this court Delaware would certainly require the defendant (intervenor) to show the solvency of the debtor at the time of the conveyance to avoid a finding of fraudulency once the creditor has established that the conveyance was to a close relative and was unsupported by fair consideration. . . . A reasonable basis for such a presumption and shifting of the burden of going forward with the evidence is recognition by the courts of "the notorious tendency of the spouses [and other close relatives] to aid each other in enjoying secretly reserved property interests and to be generous to each other before they are just to creditors." . . .

In any event the government, as the creditor in this case, has established on the basis of the record that the conveyance in question was not for a fair consideration. . . . The deed between John Emory and Mary Catherine West and David L. West recites a consideration of "one dollar . . . and other valuable and lawful considerations," but Mrs. West testified at the hearing that she and her husband did not request or receive *any* consideration from their son, David, in return for the properties conveyed. The intervenor argues [,] . . . however, that "natural love and affection" formed the basis for the conveyance and that this is "good consideration" for an executed contract. . . . Since "the question of fair consideration as it pertains to an alleged fraudulent conveyance must be determined from the standpoint of creditors . . ." , it is clear that no "fair equivalent" is exchanged when the conveyance is simply for natural love and affection. The creditor's interest will not be protected since the debtor's property has departed without any fair equivalent taking its place. The cases have uniformly held that such a conveyance is purely voluntary. . . .

Since the creditor in this case has satisfactorily proven the absence of fair consideration in the questioned family transaction, a *prima facie* case of constructive fraud . . . has been established and the only question remaining for the court to decide is whether or not the intervenor has presented sufficient evidence to rebut the presumption that the debtors, who are jointly and severally liable on the guaranty, were insolvent at the time of the conveyance or were rendered insolvent by that transaction. . . .

. . . The court has before it three primary sources of information on this matter: (1) the testimony adduced at the two evidentiary hearings, (2) a financial statement filed by Mr. and Mrs. West with the SBA dated December 31, 1964, and (3) the statement of all property of the bankrupt contained in a Debtor's Petition of Mr. and Mrs. West dated October 3, 1968 and filed with this court in a bankruptcy proceeding. From all of this the court is simply unable to draw any rational conclusion about the solvency or insolvency of either of the debtors at the time in question.

There are a number of inconsistencies between certain financial data contained in testimony at the hearings and that contained in the financial statement or the bankruptcy petition. Mary Catherine West testified to the ownership of a number of parcels of real estate with improvements at the time in question, but the exact nature of this ownership was not made clear, *i.e.* whether they were solely or jointly owned. She offered laymen's appraisals of the value of these properties, but her estimations were supported by the testimony of an experienced real estate broker in only two instances. The testimony concerning the liabilities existing against these properties was sometimes definitive and precise but it was also sometimes speculative and unreliable. Mrs. West's testimony about the existence of debts which were unrelated to her real estate interest was vague and uncertain. In sum, the testimonial and documentary evidence concerning the financial status of Mary Catherine West at the time in question is so replete with inconsistency, uncertainty, and unreliability as to leave the court with no alternative, short of bald conjecture, but to rule that the intervenor has failed to rebut the presumption of insolvency arising . . . from the government's proof of a conveyance by a debtor to a close relative for less than fair consideration by "clear and satisfactory evidence" or even by evidence merely "tending" to show solvency of the debtor at the time of the conveyance.

Even more significant in this regard is the fact that the record contains virtually no information about the financial status of John Emory West. Mr. West testified at the first hearing, but he did not relate any significant information to the court as to his solvency at the end of 1964. He did not appear at the second hearing and Mrs. West acknowledged that she was unable to testify to the extent of her husband's indebtedness, if any, at the time in question. She did state that he was engaged in a house moving business with Jack Ridgeway at that time and that they owned some equipment related to that business, but it was their son, Douglas, who took the stand to give more specific details about the business. Douglas testified that the business involved several trucks and a station wagon, but he did not know whether the vehicles belonged to the corporation or were owned individually. He stated that the business also required wood timbers worth between $80 and $130, an undisclosed number of steel beams estimated to cost $150 each, and several dollies costing $100 to $150 each. Aside from this rather general, imprecise information about the business assets, Douglas was unable to apprise the court of the nature or extent of his father's interest in the property or his indebtedness, if any, in either his personal or his business affairs.

The government has clearly established a *prima facie* case of [constructive] fraud . . . and the intervenor has not rebutted the presumption that Mr. and Mrs. West were insolvent at the time of the conveyance or were rendered insolvent by it. . . .

Since the intervenor, Douglas West, is a purchaser of the property in question from the fraudulent grantee, David West, he is subject to having the conveyance set aside and to any other remedies which would normally be available to the defrauded creditor just as though the property was still in the possession of the fraudulent grantee, unless he is a bona fide purchaser for valuable consideration without notice of the fraud. . . . It is incumbent upon the intervenor to satisfy the court that he was a bona fide purchaser for value without either actual or constructive notice of the fraud. . . .

The deed between David West and Douglas West for the properties in question, dated September 1, 1966, recites consideration in the amount of $2,000.00. One of the properties was listed on the 1964 financial statement as having a market value of $8,500.00 subject to a mortgage with $5000 outstanding. Mrs. West testified at the second hearing that another parcel was worth $3,500. However, Douglas West testified at the first hearing that he paid David only $100 for the three properties.

While adequacy of consideration is not normally questioned since a purchaser need only give valuable consideration to qualify for bona fide purchaser status, . . . it is the general rule that a person who purchases property for grossly inadequate consideration is not a bona fide purchaser. . . . Consideration of $100 for three pieces of real estate, which were apparently valued at over $10,000 less than two years beforehand is certainly grossly inadequate. For this reason alone the defendant has failed to establish himself as a bona fide purchaser from the fraudulent grantee. But, furthermore, Douglas West has not shown that there was nothing about the transaction with his brother to put him on notice of the fraudulent nature of the earlier conveyance from his parents as to raise a duty to inquire as to that fact. . . . From the nature of the relationships of the parties and from the amounts of consideration, both stated and actual, involved in the two conveyances, Douglas West was certainly put on notice and incurred a duty to inquire into the propriety of the conveyance from his parents to his brother, David, with regard to the rights of his parents' creditors.

Douglas West has not satisfied this court that he was a bona fide purchaser for value from David West without notice of the fraudulent nature of the conveyance by which David obtained the properties. Therefore, Douglas stands in the shoes of the actual fraudulent grantee and is properly subject to having the conveyance set aside by the government.

Finding the evidence in the record as stated above, and in view of the strict rules of evidence which are applied to family transactions under section 4 of the Uniform Fraudulent Conveyance Act, . . . I conclude that a constructively fraudulent conveyance occurred which must be set aside in favor of the plaintiff. . . .

NOTES AND QUESTIONS

(1) In *Twyne's Case, supra,* the Star Chamber noted that "natural affection" was not good consideration for a debtor's transfer of property. In *West,* the court finds that a debtor's transfer to a relative or family member creates a presumption of fraud that warrants shifting the burden of proof of fair consideration from the creditor to the debtor. Do you think the court is correct in shifting the presumption as to the debtor's insolvency as well? *See Walker v. Treadwell (In re Treadwell),* 699 F.2d 1050 (11th Cir. 1983); *Marine Midland Bank v. Stein,* 105 Misc. 2d 768, 433 N.Y.S.2d 325 (N.Y. Sup. Ct. 1980); *In re Colandrea,* 17 B.R. 568 (Bankr. D. Md. 1982); *see also Waldschmidt v. Shelton (In re Shelton),* 33 B.R. 377 (M.D. Tenn. 1983) (post–petition reconveyance, by debtor's parents to debtor, of property that debtor had allegedly fraudulently transferred, pre–petition, to parents for no consideration, did not "cure" earlier transfer; trustee's action to avoid earlier transfer should proceed to trial).

(2) In some cases, the family member may be the aggrieved creditor rather than the one acting in collusion with the debtors. *See, e.g., Spear v. Spear,* 101 Misc.

2d 341, 421 N.Y.S.2d 277 (N.Y. Sup. Ct. 1979) (debtor's execution of confession of judgment in favor of creditor–girlfriend constituted fraudulent transfer voidable by former wife who was bona fide creditor of debtor); *cf. Gray v. Snyder*, 704 F.2d 709 (4th Cir. 1983) (court remanded case for determination of whether value of former wife's release of debtor–husband's support obligations was reasonably equivalent to value of husband's transfer to wife of his half–interest in their residence).

(3) Why did the court in *West, supra*, find the debtors' testimony and documentary evidence as to their solvency unpersuasive? As a practical matter, how could the debtors have presented their case differently (and more successfully)? *See generally Thomas Farm Systems, Inc. v. Drive–Kore, Inc. (In re Thomas Farms Systems, Inc.)*, 18 B.R. 541, 543 (Bankr. E.D. Pa. 1982).

(4) The effect of any fraudulent transfer is depletion of the debtor's estate to the detriment of its creditors. As the court in *West* aptly summarized, "The creditor's interest will not be protected since the debtor's property has departed without any fair equivalent taking its place." In general, you should analyze a fraudulent transfer by determining its effect on the debtor's estate: "[t]he touchstone . . . is the unjust diminution of the estate of the debtor that otherwise would be available to the creditor." Glenn, *The Law of Fraudulent Conveyances*, § 195 (1931). *See also Meister v. Jamison (In re Jamison)*, 6 C.B.C.2d 1264, 1256 (Bankr. D. Conn. 1982) ("[A]nalysis of [a] . . . fraudulent transfer must be directed at what the debtor surrendered and what the debtor received irrespective of what any third party may have gained or lost."); *Newfield v. Ettlinger*, 22 Misc. 2d 769, 194 N.Y.S. 2d 670 (Sup. Ct. 1959) (no fraudulent transfer if debtor's estate is not diminished), *appeal dismissed conditionally*, 10 A.D. 2d 947, 205 N.Y.S.2d 908 (N.Y. App. Div. 1st Dept 1960).

MARINE MIDLAND BANK v. MURKOFF

Supreme Court, Appellate Division
120 A.D.2d 122 (2d Dep't 1986)
appeal dismissed, 69 N.Y.2d 875, 507 N.E.2d 322 (1987)

LAZER, J.

In these two appeals the appellant is a judgment creditor who succeeded in setting aside the judgment debtor's conveyance of his interest in his jointly owned home to his wife. Dissatisfied with constructive fraud as the sole ground for the relief granted and having failed in a subsequent effort to expand the ground to include actual intent to defraud, the judgment creditor seeks the additional relief from us. It also argues that its remedies against the property and the wife of the judgment debtor should be broadened. We conclude that the plaintiff did establish its claim of an actual intent to defraud and thus is entitled to counsel fees, but the remainder of the relief it seeks is inappropriate.

I

The action has its genesis in the financial troubles of Rocket Stores, Inc., in which the defendants, Norman and Abby Murkoff, who are husband and wife, and Richard Shafran, who is Abby's brother, held a controlling interest. During the period from 1974 to 1977, Norman Murkoff guaranteed three notes that Rocket Stores made to the plaintiff, but on July 7, 1977, Rocket Stores filed a petition in bankruptcy and subsequently defaulted on the notes. Within a few weeks, the plaintiff brought three separate actions against Norman Murkoff based on the guarantees and obtained three judgments totaling $78,921.97.

While these actions were pending, Norman Murkoff conveyed to Abby his interest in the home they owned as tenants by the entirety. The plaintiff then commenced this action to set aside the conveyance, alleging that it was fraudulent under Debtor and Creditor Law article 10. By the terms of Debtor and Creditor Law article 10, a conveyance is deemed fraudulent as to creditors not only where it is made with actual intent "to hinder, delay or defraud" creditors (Debtor and Creditor Law § 276), but also where the fraud is constructive, i.e., the conveyance is made without fair consideration by a person (1) who is insolvent or will thereby be rendered insolvent (Debtor and Creditor Law § 273), or (2) against whom an action is pending or a judgment has been docketed for money damages (Debtor and Creditor Law § 273-a), or (3) who is engaged in a business for which his capital is unreasonably small (Debtor and Creditor Law § 274), or (4) who believes he will incur debts beyond his ability to pay (Debtor and Creditor Law § 275).

The complaint contained four causes of action, each alleging that the conveyance was fraudulent under a different section of the Debtor and Creditor Law. The primary defense was that the conveyance had been made in good faith because of Norman Murkoff's ill health and his long-standing promise to Abby's father to convey his interest to her once the mortgage had been satisfied.

The plaintiff obtained summary judgment on its cause of action under Debtor and Creditor Law § 273 (conveyance by a person who is or will thereby be rendered insolvent) and § 273-a (conveyance by a person against whom an action is pending), neither of which requires proof of an actual intent to defraud. A judgment was entered on March 28, 1984, directing the clerk to record the money judgments the plaintiff had previously obtained as liens against the real property of Abby Murkoff "to the extent of Norman B. Murkoff's prior interest therein". The two remaining causes of action were severed and a second judgment was ultimately entered on September 17, 1984, after trial, dismissing the plaintiff's claim under Debtor and Creditor Law § 274 (conveyance by person with unreasonably small capital) for failure of proof. The claim under Debtor and Creditor Law § 276 was dismissed on the ground that the plaintiff had not met its burden of proving actual intent to hinder, delay or defraud creditors. The appeal from the summary judgment is on the ground that the relief afforded was too narrow; the appeal from the judgment after trial relates solely to the cause of action based on actual fraud (Debtor and Creditor Law § 276).

The significance of these appeals to the plaintiff is twofold. To recover attorneys' fees under Debtor and Creditor Law § 276-a, actual intent to hinder, delay or defraud must be established (Debtor and Creditor Law § 276–a; *see, Farm Stores v. School Feeding Corp.*, 102 AD2d 249, 256, 257, *affd* 64 NY2d 1065 *on opn at App. Div., Schmitt v. Morgan*, 98 AD2d 934, 936, *appeal dismissed* 62 NY2d 914; *Southern Indus. v. Jeremias*, 66 AD2d 178, 185–186). Therefore, unless the plaintiff can obtain a judgment based on actual intent to defraud, attorneys' fees are unavailable. Even more important is the fact that while the plaintiff has been awarded a lien against Norman's interest in the entirety despite the conveyance to Abby, that interest remains subject to Abby's right of survivorship (*see, Hiles v. Fisher*, 144 NY 306) and is thus of limited value. According to the plaintiff, where a tenancy by the entirety is involved, the creditor's relief should exceed mere maintenance of a lien even if nothing more than constructive fraud has been established, but certainly if actual intent to defraud has been proved against both spouses. The remedies the plaintiff seeks are (1) termination of the tenancy by the entirety and its transformation into a tenancy in common, (2) a money judgment against Abby Murkoff in the amount of the judgment against Norman, up to one half the value of the property, and (3) the imposition of a constructive trust on the interest Norman transferred, compelling Abby to hold that interest for the benefit of the plaintiff and pay to it one half of the rental income from the property.

II

The burden of proof to establish actual fraud under Debtor and Creditor Law § 276 is upon the creditor who seeks to have the conveyance set aside (*Brody v. Pecoraro*, 250 NY 56), and the standard for such proof is clear and convincing evidence (*Lowendahl v. Baltimore & Ohio R. R. Co.*, 247 App Div 144, *affd* 272 NY 360, *rearg denied* 273 NY 584; *Cooper v. Maurer*, 37 NYS2d 992; *see also*, 24 NY Jur, Fraudulent Conveyances, § 12, at 407).

Debtor and Creditor Law § 276 clearly distinguishes constructive fraud from actual intent to defraud, for it states: "Every conveyance made and every obligation incurred with actual intent, as distinguished from intent presumed in law, to hinder, delay, or defraud either present or future creditors, is fraudulent as to both present and future creditors." Despite the statutory distinction, the plaintiff asserts that facts constituting proof sufficient to establish intent presumed in law, such as the mere conveyance of property at less than full consideration by a debtor in peril, establish as well a rebuttable presumption of actual intent to defraud. By this theory, proof of constructive fraud constitutes clear and convincing evidence of intentional fraud sufficient to thrust upon the defendant the obligation to come forward with evidence that will defeat the plaintiff's case. Although our ultimate finding sustains the plaintiff's claim of actual intent to defraud, it is important for us to dispose of the presumption contention which continues to becloud debtor and creditor jurisprudence (*see, Scola v. Morgan*, 66 AD2d 228; *Torr v. Torr*, 18 AD2d 722; *Burch v. Jeruss*, 281 App Div 991; *Campbell v. Brown*, 268 App Div 324, *appeal dismissed* 294 NY 702; *Cody v. Hovey*, 256 App Div 1038; *Sabatino v. Cannizzaro*, 243 App Div 20; *Gates & Co. v. B. N. Bldrs.*, 238 App Div 163). The authorities the plaintiff cites in support of the presumption theory (*see, Ga Nun v. Palmer*, 216 NY 603; *Smith v. Reid*, 134 NY 568) are no longer controlling under the scheme effectuated by the State's fraudulent conveyance act, and we therefore reject the notion that such a presumption of intentional fraud exists.

When the Uniform Fraudulent Conveyance Act was drafted, the rebuttable presumption of fraud concept had a widespread following in the States (*see, e.g., Miles v. Monroe*, 96 Ark 531, 132 SW 643; *Kennard v. Curran*, 239 Ill 122, 87 NE 913; *Flood v Bollmeier*, 165 Iowa 88, 144 NW 579; *Underleak v. Scott*, 117 Minn 136, 134 NW 731; *Parker v. Fenwick*, 147 NC 525, 61 SE 378). In drafting the Uniform Fraudulent Conveyance Act which later became New York's Debtor and Creditor Law article 10, the National Conference of Commissioners on Uniform State Laws sought to eliminate the confusion in existing laws which stemmed, in part, from judicial attempts to stretch the original English fraudulent conveyance statute, the Statute of Elizabeth (13 Eliz, ch 5) and its offspring (*see, e.g.,* New York's 1829 statute [2 Rev Stat of NY, part II, ch VII, tit III (1st ed)]), which permitted relief only on a showing of actual intent to defraud, to apply to situations where no such actual intent could be proven (*see, Prefatory Note, Uniform Fraudulent Conveyance Act*, 7A, ULA 427, 428).

To eliminate the undesirable reasoning underlying the judicially created presumptions while at the same time recognizing that a remedy was often required when the creditor was wronged without judicially provable intent to defraud, the draftsmen of the uniform act eliminated the presumption as a basis for finding a conveyance fraudulent (*see,* Prefatory Note, *op. cit.,* 1918 Proceedings of 28th Ann Meeting of Natl Conf of Commrs on Uniform State Laws, at 353). Since the authors of the legislation were the National Commissioners on Uniform State Laws and the legislation was enacted by New York's Legislature without change, the commissioners' notes are a clear indication of legislative intent (*see, Matter of Fisher v. New York State Employees' Retirement Sys.*, 279 App Div 315, affd 304 NY 899) to displace and eradicate the State's common–law presumption of intent to defraud flowing from certain acts and to provide relief based on those acts on the rationale of constructive fraud. That being so, it is apparent to us that the presumption has ceased to exist.

III

Having dispensed with the outmoded presumption, we must still decide whether on this record the plaintiff's evidence requires us to overturn the trial court's determination that intent to defraud had not been established by clear and convincing evidence. The elimination of the presumption does not mean that the facts which formerly gave rise to it are irrelevant to the claim of actual intent to defraud. To the contrary, fraudulent intent, by its very nature, is rarely susceptible to direct proof and must be established by inference from the circumstances surrounding the allegedly fraudulent act (*see, Stewart v. Lyman*, 62 App Div 182, 186; *United Parcel Serv. v. Norris Corp.*, 102 Misc 2d 231; *Matter of Gafco, Inc. v. H.D.S. Mercantile Corp.*, 47 Misc 2d 661). The circumstances established by the evidence suffice to prove the defendants' actual intent to defraud.

The conveyance was made shortly after Rocket Stores had filed for bankruptcy and shortly after the plaintiff had commenced actions to enforce Norman's guarantee of Rocket's obligations. A transfer from husband to wife is ordinarily scrutinized carefully (*see, In re Rosenfield's Will*, 213 NYS2d 1009, *affd* 18 AD2d 718), but the familial relationship is not all that is involved here. In addition to being Norman's wife, Abby Murkoff was Rocket's part–time bookkeeper for some five years prior to the bankruptcy, and its full–time bookkeeper thereafter. The knowledge of Rocket's financial dealings obtained by Abby in the course of her duties necessarily belies the defendants' claim that she was unaware of Norman's personal guarantee of the corporate notes, and the timing of the conveyance in these circumstances is a clear indication of the defendants' joint purpose.

The conclusion that the defendants acted with intent to defraud is buttressed by their conduct after the conveyance. While it may not be terribly significant that Norman and not Abby dealt with the tenants of the house which was the subject of Norman's conveyance, it is notable that the rent collected each month was deposited in a bank account in Norman's name, from which the expenses of the house were paid. Retention of control of the property after a conveyance is regarded as an indication that the conveyance was fraudulent (*see, Scola v. Morgan*, 66 AD2d 228, *supra; Southern Indus. v. Jeremias*, 66 AD2d 178, *supra; Takacs v. Kapela*, 264 App Div 871; *Bement v. Dean*, 246 App Div 670).

The defendants' explanation also adds to the strength of the plaintiff's case. The story that the conveyance was the result of Norman's 1959 promise to Abby's father to give his interest to her after the mortgage was paid and his subsequent concerns for his own health is beyond belief. Although the mortgage had apparently been satisfied in March of 1977, the conveyance was not made until some 5 1/2 months later, when Norman was a defendant in three actions seeking substantial damages. Such fortuitous timing makes it difficult to accept the contention that the conveyance was intended to carry out an alleged promise to Abby's father. With respect to Norman's illness, the credibility defect is even sharper. The alleged motive for the transfer, to ensure Abby's succession to the property upon Norman's death, amounts to no motive at all, since such succession is an inherent aspect of Abby's interest as a tenant by the entirety. Moreover, Norman had been working full time since his 1975 illness. Since the transfer was not made while he was actually sick, the conveyance two years later and after he had recovered does not support the proffered explanation.

The circumstances surrounding the conveyance establish clearly and convincingly the defendants' "actual intent . . . to hinder, delay, or defraud" plaintiff. The Supreme Court, Dutchess County, thus erred in dismissing Marine Midland's fourth cause of action after trial and judgment pursuant to Debtor and Creditor Law § 276 should be granted on that cause of action and the matter remitted for an assessment of attorneys' fees pursuant to Debtor and Creditor Law § 276–a.

IV

We turn then to the matter of other remedies. Contending that the judgment permitting a levy on Norman's interest and the Debtor and Creditor Law's other remedies are inadequate (*see*, Debtor and Creditor Law § 278), the plaintiff seeks termination of the original tenancy by the entirety and its transformation into a tenancy in common, a declaration that Abby holds the property as a constructive trustee, entitling plaintiff to the rents and profits which have accrued since the conveyance, and a money judgment against Abby Murkoff.

In support of its claim that the tenancy by the entirety should be terminated, the plaintiff first contends that what has been granted—the right to levy upon the interest of one tenant by the entirety—is a dubious entitlement at best and equity should grant a more effective remedy. Second, with Abby Murkoff's participation in the fraud proved, equity should intervene to prevent her from profiting from her own wrongdoing by retaining the property free of the plaintiff's interest if she outlives her husband. Neither contention is persuasive.

Even before the Legislature's adoption of the Uniform Fraudulent Conveyance Act, it was established that the relief to which a defrauded creditor was entitled in an action to set aside a fraudulent conveyance was limited to that which could have been obtained had there been no conveyance (*Hamilton Natl. Bank v. Halsted*, 134 NY 520). *Hamilton Natl. Bank* involved the fraudulent transfer of certain shares of stock, which had subsequently been sold by the assignee, himself a participant in the fraud. Prior to the fraudulent conveyance the shares had been encumbered by a valid lien which preexisted any interest on the part of the creditor and which was subsequently satisfied upon the sale by the assignee. The issue was whether the defrauded creditor was entitled to judgment for the full value of the shares or for their value as encumbered. The Court of Appeals rejected the creditor's argument that the assignee should be punished for his fraud, reasoning that the creditor's equitable interest—the only basis upon which it could follow the shares into the assignee's hands—extended only to property which was available prior to the conveyance to satisfy its claim. Such a rule is consistent with the act, the remedy provisions of which allow the creditor only to reach the property as if there had been no conveyance (Debtor and Creditor Law § 278), or, if its claim has not yet been established, to protect the property for its benefit (Debtor and Creditor Law § 279).

Terminating the tenancy by the entirety would clearly violate the rule in *Hamilton Natl. Bank (supra)*. Like the securities there, Norman's interest in the property prior to the conveyance was "encumbered" by Abby's right of survivorship, and had plaintiff attempted to satisfy its judgment against Norman by levy at that time, his interest would have been sold subject to Abby's right (*see, Hiles v. Fisher*, 144 NY 306, *supra; First Fed. Sav. & Loan Assn. v. Lewis*, 14 AD2d 150, 154). Transforming the tenancy by the entirety into a tenancy in common obviously would extinguish the right of survivorship (*see, Stelz v. Shreck*, 128 NY 263; *Hohenrath v. Wallach*, 37 AD2d 248, *appeal dismissed*, 30 NY2d 674), giving the plaintiff the ability to assert its judgment against an undivided one-half interest in the property.

Although *Hamilton Natl. Bank (supra)* is old, we see no indication in modern jurisprudence that a creditor's rights should be expanded by the fashioning of punitive remedies not previously available. To begin with, the remedies explicitly provided in the fraudulent conveyance act (*see*, Debtor and Creditor Law §§ 278, 279) go no further than *Hamilton Natl. Bank* permits and have not been enlarged in the more than 60 years since the statute was enacted. Further, the recent trend in the Legislature has been to expand the rights not of creditors, but of debtors, by regulating the terms and manner of entry into contracts (*see*, General Obligations Law § 5–702 [plain language] [originally enacted by L 1977, ch 747 as § 5–701 (b), (c), renum by L 1978, ch 199 as § 5–702]) and collection practices (*see*, CPLR 5222 [d], [e] [notice of service of restraining notice on third party] [added by L 1982, ch 882]; General Business Law art 29–H [prohibition of unfair debt collection practices] [added by L 1973, ch 753]; CPLR 305, 503 [f]; 513 [venue and notice rules for consumer credit actions] [as amended by L 1973, ch 238]; CPLR art 62 [requirements for provisional remedy of attachment] [added by L 1962, ch 308]), and by expanding the list of property exempt from execution (*see*, CPLR 5206 [a] [4] [added by L 1980, ch 717]; CPLR 5205 [h] [added by L 1980, ch 116]; CPLR 5205 [g] [added by L 1978, ch 17]; CPLR 5205 [a] [5] [amended by L 1976, ch 697]) and dischargeable in bankruptcy (Debtor and Creditor Law art 10–A [added by L 1982, ch 540]). Indeed, the only recent legislation significantly expanding the rights of creditors has been addressed to the special problem of enforcing matrimonial judgments (CPLR 5241, 5242 [added by L 1985, ch 809]).

Punishment is not a proper basis for granting relief in a fraudulent conveyance action. No matter how "scandalous" the conduct, punishment is a matter for other tribunals (*Hamilton Natl. Bank v. Halsted*, 134 NY 520, 522, *supra*) and, indeed, certain fraudulent conveyances come within the purview of the Penal Law (*see*, Penal Law art 185). In a more modern context, the Court of Appeals has held that punitive damages are not properly awarded in a fraudulent conveyance action, reasoning that the act of removing property from the reach of a creditor is not misconduct so " 'gross and wanton' " as to justify such an award (*see, James v. Powell*, 19 NY2d 249, 260; *see also, Borkowski v. Borkowski*, 39 NY2d 982; *but see, Keen v. Keen*, 113 AD2d 964, *lv dismissed*, 67 NY2d 646). This is consistent with the uniform act, the purpose of which is "to enable a creditor to obtain his due despite efforts on the part of a debtor to elude payment" (*Hearn 45th St. Corp. v. Jano*, 283 NY 139, 142). The remedies it provides (*see*, Debtor and Creditor Law §§ 278, 279) are clearly geared toward reestablishing the status quo *ante*, rather than punishing the debtor. Depriving Abby of her survivorship interest is plainly punitive and it is not a permissible remedy.

Clarkson Co. v. Shaheen (533 F Supp 905), on which the plaintiff relies, disregarded this nonpunitive principle. In *Clarkson*, the survivorship interest of the debtor's wife in tenancy by the entirety property was terminated in order to prevent her from benefiting by her participation in the fraud. *Clarkson* reached its legal conclusion as to New York law on the basis of *Van Alstyne v. Tuffy* (103 Misc 455), which held that the heirs of a man who murdered his wife and then committed suicide could not inherit the property the victim and murderer held as tenants by the entirety. *Van Alstyne* is simply another in the long line of cases which preclude a murderer or his heirs from succeeding to the property of the victim (*see, Riggs v. Palmer*, 115 NY 506; *Bierbrauer v. Moran*, 244 App Div 87; *Matter of Sengillo*, 206 Misc 751; *Matter of Sparks*, 172 Misc 642; *Matter of Santourian*, 125 Misc 668). The *Van Alstyne* principle is that "where the natural and direct consequence of a criminal act is to vest property in the criminal, whether he be a thief or a murderer, the thought of his being allowed to enjoy it is too abhorrent for the courts of this state, or of the United States, to countenance . . . [a]nd equity will restrain in such case though contract, testament or statute be thereby nullified" (*Van Alstyne v. Tuffy, supra*, at p. 459). That principle, however, is inapplicable to the law of fraudulent conveyances.

We also reject the plaintiff's claims to a money judgment against Abby Murkoff. A money judgment against the grantee is sometimes an available form of relief (*see, Brown v. Kimmel*, 68 AD2d 896; *see also, Halsey v. Winant*, 233 App Div 103, *revd on other grounds* 258 NY 512), but because the defrauded creditor is not entitled to an enhancement of position beyond what it was before the fraud, such a judgment may be granted only where the grantee has disposed of the wrongfully conveyed property or depreciated it (*Wasey v. Holbrook*, 141 App Div 336, *affd* 206 NY 708; *Mallouk v. American Exch. Natl. Bank*, 157 App Div 711, *affd* 216 NY 670) or has tortiously interfered with it (*James v. Powell*, 25 AD2d 1, *appeal dismissed* 17 NY2d 812). Since the judgment appealed from gives the plaintiff the same rights it had prior to the conveyance, the lien of the judgment against Norman Murkoff remains as valid and enforceable as it was before the conveyance. A money judgment against Abby has no basis in statute or in case law.

Nor is the plaintiff entitled to the imposition of a constructive trust for its benefit on the property which was fraudulently conveyed. Apart from the fact that such a remedy has no explicit mention in the Debtor and Creditor Law, the cases that have employed the term "constructive trustee" in connection with a fraudulent conveyance (*see, Julien J. Studley, Inc. v. Lefrak*, 48 NY2d 954, 956; *Matter of Lack v. Kreiner*, 91 AD2d 813, 814; *Laco X–Ray Sys. v. Fingerhut*, 88 AD2d 425, 431, *appeal dismissed* 58 NY2d 606) have described transferees where the transfer was in derogation of the duty corporate directors and officers owe to creditors deriving from the principle that the corporate assets constitute a trust fund for the benefit of creditors (*see, Julian J. Studley, Inc. v. Lefrak*, 66 AD2d 213, *affd* 48 NY2d 954, 956, *supra*, "essentially for reasons stated in the opinion of the Appellate Division"). Reliance on these authorities therefore is inappropriate outside the corporate context. Moreover, even in those cases, constructive trusts were not employed as remedies.

The creditor's remedy in a fraudulent conveyance action is limited to reaching the property which would have been available to satisfy the judgment had there been no conveyance; the limited remedies explicitly permitted under the statute confirm this interpretation. The imposition of a constructive trust upon the transferee would provide the plaintiff with an equitable interest in the property which could not have been achieved solely by entering the judgment, even in the absence of a conveyance. Norman's interest in the property may be reached by levy despite the fact that it stands in Abby's name and the plaintiff may also resort to remedies provided by the CPLR for the collection of judgments (*see*, CPLR art 52). Current public policy provides no basis for the creation of new common–law remedies against evasive debtors.

Accordingly, the judgment entered upon the plaintiff's summary judgment motion should be affirmed insofar as appealed from, but the judgment dismissing the cause of action based on intentional fraud should be reversed insofar as appealed from and the matter remitted to the Supreme Court, Dutchess County, for an assessment of attorneys' fees.

MOLLEN, P. J., WEINSTEIN and RUBIN, JJ., concur.

TROLL v. CHASE NATIONAL BANK

United States Court of Appeals, Second Circuit
257 F.2d 825 (1958)

LUMBARD, J.

. . . .

The plaintiff is a receiver appointed by the . . . Court . . . in an action brought by the Attorney General . . . for the liquidation of the Eastern Insurance Company. . . . [T]he receiver was expressly authorized . . . by the . . . Court to bring this action. . . .

. . . [T]he plaintiff seeks to recover certain bonds which Eastern put up as collateral for two loans extended by the Chase bank. Two theories of recovery are advanced by the plaintiff, (1) that the bank converted the bonds, and (2) that the pledge constituted a voidable fraudulent conveyance under New York Debtor and Creditor Law. . . .

On January 10, 1951, Eastern, which had not previously done business with Chase, opened a deposit account with Chase with an initial deposit of $290,308.34. Copies of corporate resolutions in the usual form designating the officers authorized to make withdrawals and loans on Eastern's behalf were filed with Chase on January 12, 1951. Thereafter the bank received for Eastern, United States Treasury Bonds in face amount of $275,000 against payment out of the insurance company's account. The bonds were held in a "safekeeping" or custodian account.

In . . . March 1951, . . . Eastern . . . applied for a loan of $490,000 and as security proffered $500,000 face amount New York City Housing Authority 2% Bonds (due from 1998 to 2001) and the $275,000 face amount United States Treasury Bonds previously deposited in the custodian account. The loan application was approved and Eastern then delivered to Chase a duly executed demand note for $490,000 together with authorizing corporate resolutions. Chase paid the $490,000 to a stockbroker for the $500,000 New York City Housing Authority Bonds which Chase then retained.

On May 24, 1951 Eastern borrowed an additional $50,000 from Chase and executed a new demand note for $540,000 the total then owed.

Following this, on July 16, 1951, Eastern borrowed an additional $100,000 from Chase and executed a separate demand note and deposited with Chase on July 26 additional collateral of $100,000 Port Authority Bonds and $100,000 New York City Housing Authority 2 ¼% Bonds, due in 1996. This collateral by the terms of the note was to stand as security for the payment of " . . . this note and of all other liabilities" of Eastern. The term "liabilities" was thereafter defined as including "any and all indebtedness, notes . . . and liabilities of any kind . . . now or hereafter existing . . . and whether heretofore or hereafter incurred."

On July 26, 1951 Eastern instructed Chase to sell the $100,000 Port Authority Bonds and apply the proceeds in payment of the July 16, 1951 note for $100,000. This was done and the loan was paid in full. Chase continued to hold the remaining collateral, the $100,000 Housing Authority Bonds, as security for the May 24 loan, which at the time of trial remained unpaid to the extent of $412,123.91. The application of the $100,000 Housing Authority Bonds to the collateral pledged for repayment of the May note was pursuant to the express contract provision noted above and the definition of security in the May and July notes. The term "security" was therein defined to include any property owned by Eastern "which [has] been or at any time shall be delivered to or otherwise come into the possession . . . of the Bank."

Although in the district court the plaintiff attempted to secure the return both of the Treasury Bonds and the New York City Housing Authority Bonds, he has limited his claim on appeal to the question of the legality of Chase's retention of the $100,000 Housing Authority Bonds as collateral.

. . . [T]he plaintiff advances the ingenious argument that Eastern was insolvent when the bank retained the $100,000 Housing Authority Bonds as collateral for the May note after the July note was paid and that in so doing Chase unlawfully converted the bonds because the general property rights to them had passed to the creditors of insolvent Eastern under the New York "Trust Fund Doctrine." We cannot agree that there was an illegal conversion under such a doctrine or any other theory.

While the exact meaning and limits of the New York "trust fund" doctrine are unclear, the doctrine has never been applied against a good faith purchaser for value. . . . The theory that the assets of a corporation constitute a "trust fund" for its creditors on insolvency has been used in actions brought against directors of the insolvent corporation . . . and third parties who took a conveyance from an insolvent corporation with knowledge of the insolvency. . . .

It is clear, however, that the trust fund doctrine has no application to a transferee who takes in good faith and for value. . . .

The crucial issues therefore, determinative of both of the theories of recovery advanced by the plaintiff, are whether Chase was acting in good faith and whether value was given by the bank.

It is clear that Chase had no actual knowledge of any insolvency on the part of Eastern. Chase was acting under an express contract right in holding the security deposited for the payment of Eastern's indebtedness. . . .

Nor did the facts put Chase on notice of Eastern's insolvency. We conclude that the finding of the district court that the facts did not disclose any "warning flag to put [Chase] on notice . . . [or] to cause a prudent and reliable lending institution to withhold extending credit" is clearly correct and indeed is the only permissible inference which could have been drawn from the facts.

There is no principle of law or logic which would require a commercial bank to investigate the books of a borrower who fully secures a loan. Absent circumstances which would place a bank on notice that a prospective borrower may in fact be insolvent, it would be an absurd restriction on the extension of credit and the banking business to expect a commercial bank to conduct such a preliminary examination of a borrower where the loan is to be amply secured.1

And even had the bank made such an investigation, no showing has been made that it would have discovered any insolvency. . . .

We come, therefore, to the question of consideration. On July 16, 1951, the date on which the Housing Authority Bonds were delivered to the Chase bank by Eastern, it is clear that the additional loan of $100,000 was sufficient consideration for the deposit of the additional securities. The deposit of these securities was governed by the terms of the note and thus the securities were also collateral for the earlier loan which was still unpaid. It is immaterial that Chase did not perform until July 26 the mechanics of making entries that the bonds were collateral for the earlier note as well as the new note as Chase had the right to do so at all times.

We have a further question whether under the law of New York the debt of $540,000 was "disproportionately small as compared with the value" of the pledged bonds. . . . Here the transaction whereby Chase transferred the collateral from one note to the other may be construed as receiving property as security for an antecedent debt. The question then is whether the debt was "disproportionately small as compared with the value of the property."

The value of the securities pledged to repay the loan was not disproportionately large as compared with the amount of the loan. At the time Chase retained the $100,000 Housing Authority Bonds as collateral for the unpaid May note, Eastern owed $540,000 to Chase. At this time the face value of all the bonds held as collateral was $875,000, but the market value on July 26, 1951 was only $776,500 due to a drop in bond prices. The record shows that the market value of the $500,000 Housing Authority Bonds purchased in March of 1951 dropped from 98 to around 75 six months later in September. Obviously the value of the property pledged was not disproportionate to the debt.

. . . .

The record amply supports the conclusion of the district judge that Chase did not unlawfully convert the bonds. It is also clear that there was fair consideration for the pledge of the bonds. . . . [I]t is unnecessary for us to pass on the alleged errors pertaining to the reception of evidence.

The judgment of the district court is affirmed.

NOTES AND QUESTIONS

(1) For a more recent discussion of the "corporate trust fund" theory, *see American National Bank v. Mortgageamerica Corp. (In re Mortgageamerica Corp.)*, 714 F.2d 1266 (5th Cir. 1983).

(2) Does the court in *Troll, supra*, adequately explain why the value of the bonds pledged to repay the loan was not disproportionately large as compared to the amount of the loan? Is it possible to establish a rigid standard for determining the proportionate values of property in a security exchange? What guidelines should be followed? *See, e.g., Rubin v. Manufacturers Hanover Trust Co.*, 661 F.2d 979, 991–94 (2d Cir. 1981); *Zellerbach Paper Co. v. Valley National Bank*, 13 Ariz. App. 431, 477 P.2d 550 (1970).

(3) The court stated that the bank's transfer of collateral from one note to another could be "construed as receiving property as security for an antecedent debt." In general, value given on account of an antecedent debt may constitute fair consideration for fraudulent transfer purposes. *See, e.g., Strongin v. International Acceptance Bank*, 70 F.2d 248, 252 (2d Cir.), *cert. denied*, 293 U.S. 575 (1934); *Inland Security Co. v. Estate of Kirshner*, 382 F. Supp. 338, 347 (W.D. Mo. 1974); *Beldock v. Faberge, Inc. (In re S & W Exporters*, Inc.), 16 B.R. 941, 945 (Bankr. S.D.N.Y. 1982).

(4) An important factor in the court's decision in *Troll* was its finding that the bank had acted in good faith. The court also found that, given the facts presented, the bank had no obligation to investigate the debtor's financial status. Are these two positions compatible? *Cf. Chorost v. Grand Rapids Factory Showrooms, Inc.*, 77 F. Supp. 276, 281 (D.N.J. 1948), *aff'd*, 172 F.2d 327 (3d Cir. 1949) (discussing transferee liability). Under what circumstances should good faith of a transferee be dependent upon the transferee's good faith inquiry into the debtor's solvency or financial condition? *See Burroughs v. Fields*, 546 F.2d 215, 218 (7th Cir. 1976) (transferee was corporate officer and director); *O'Connell v. Hoban (In re Famous State Fair Meat Products, Inc.)*, 19 B.R. 48, 50–51 (Bankr. E.D. Pa. 1982). *See also* Note, *Good Faith and Fraudulent Conveyances*, 97 Harv. L. Rev. 495 (1983) (criticizing courts that examine good faith of transferee as part of fair consideration analysis).

CENTRAL NATIONAL BANK v. COLEMAN
(In re B–F Building Corp.)

United States Court of Appeals, Sixth Circuit
312 F.2d 691 (1963)

O'SULLIVAN, J.

This appeal involves the petition of appellant, Central National Bank of Cleveland, for an order directing payment of $10,000.00 to it from funds in the hands of the trustee of the B–F Building Corporation, a bankrupt. Such funds were proceeds from the sale of real estate owned by the bankrupt. The bank claims that it is entitled to such funds by virtue of an assignment of $10,000.00 of such funds made as collateral security for a note given by B–F Building Corporation to such bank on February 14, 1958. . . . The referee and the District Court denied the petition, finding that the giving and taking of the aforesaid note, secured by such assignment, constituted a fraudulent transfer. . . .

The bankrupt, B–F[,] . . . was the owner of certain real property which it leased to the Baird–Foerst Corporation. Baird–Foerst, which is also bankrupt, was a distributor of General Electric appliances. W. J. Baird was president of, and held controlling interests in, both corporations.

In October, 1957, B–F, owning the premises then occupied by Baird–Foerst, purchased a new site on a land contract. The purchase price was $275,000.00 with a $20,000.00 down payment. Monthly installment payments of $2,151.95 on the balance were to commence February 1, 1958. Two checks of $10,000.00 were issued by B–F to make the down payment. The first, dated October 18, 1957, was returned several times because of insufficient funds, but was finally paid on October 22, 1957. On November 4, 1957, Baird–Foerst borrowed $10,000 from appellant bank and gave the bank its ninety–one day unsecured demand promissory note. November 5, 1957, Baird–Foerst gave its check for $10,000.00 to B–F and on November 6, B–F paid $10,000.00 to complete the down payment on the land contract. B–F paid nothing further on this contract, defaulting on the first installment date, February 1, 1958.

In the days preceding February 14, 1958, General Electric, Baird–Foerst's chief creditor, had moved into the affairs of that corporation. At that time, Baird–Foerst and its landlord, B–F, were both "in trouble." Some hasty plans were thereupon made by the appellant bank and W.J. Baird. On February 14, 1958, the B–F Building Corporation gave the appellant bank its demand cognovit note for $10,000.00. W. J. Baird endorsed it. This note, prepared by the bank, was dated November 4, 1957, although admittedly executed on February 14, 1958. The note recited that it was secured by the "proceeds from the sale of the property belonging to the corporation known as 5801 State Road, Parma, Ohio."

A contemporaneous letter of assignment directed an escrow agent to pay to the bank $10,000.00 out of escrow funds held in connection with the uncompleted sale of B–F's aforesaid real estate. B–F received no money from the bank, but the Baird–Foerst note of November 4 was returned to Baird–Foerst. Subsequently, a Notice of Assignment of Accounts Receivable was prepared by one of the bank's attorneys and was executed by B–F on February 24, 1958. This instrument was dated February 14, 1958, and was filed with the county recorder on February 24, 1958. Judgment was taken on the B–F note on February 25, 1958. Baird–Foerst filed a voluntary petition in bankruptcy on February 21, 1958. Involuntary proceedings against B–F were begun on March 17, 1958.

The District Judge held that "the transactions which are the subject of these proceedings were fraudulent [transfers] under . . . the Bankruptcy Act." . . . [The lower court found] that the execution of the note on February 14, 1958, was fraudulent because the transaction was supported by "no consideration ["] . . . and was made at a time when B–F was insolvent. B–F's insolvency as of February 14, 1958, is clear. There was testimony by an accountant that on that date the fair salable value of B–F's property was less than its debts. . . . The debts considered by this witness did not take into account a claim of the General Electric Company against

B–F in excess of $800,000.00. Such claim, upon a guaranty given by B–F, was sustained by this court. . . .

The bank advances two arguments in support of its contention that the transfer was supported by fair consideration: first, that the February 14, 1958, note was given in exchange for the satisfaction of an antecedent debt (of Baird–Foerst); and second, that the transaction on February 14 amounted to a novation between the bank, Baird–Foerst and B–F. It is true that the satisfaction of an antecedent debt may be considered as fair consideration to support a transfer made by a debtor. . . . In the usual case, however, the payment of another's debt is held to be a transfer without fair consideration. . . .

In the case before us, the most that the evidence shows is that an antecedent debt of Baird–Foerst was satisfied. While under certain circumstances such a transaction might be considered as fair consideration, for instance, if the payment was part of a good faith novation agreement, . . . we are satisfied on the record here that the referee was justified in finding that it was not. The only thing the bank gave for B–F's demand note, its full face amount secured by assignment of the escrow cash, was an unsecured and probably worthless note of Baird–Foerst. The absence of "good faith", one of the essential elements in the definition of fair consideration, is manifest on the record.

The question of whether consideration is fair is one of fact and one to which considerable weight is given to the findings made by the trier of the facts. . . . We will not set aside a referee's findings, affirmed by a District Judge, in the absence of a clear showing of mistake. . . .

. . . .

Judgment affirmed.

BARR & CREELMAN MILL & PLUMBING SUPPLY CO. v. ZOLLER
(*In re Dolomite 3 Corp.*)

United States Court of Appeals, Second Circuit
109 F.2d 924 (1940)

CLARK, J.

Dolomite Marine Corporation and its wholly owned subsidiary, Dolomite 3 Corporation, have filed separate petitions for reorganization. . . . Barr & Creelman Mill & Plumbing Supply Co., . . . has asked for the allowance of a claim secured by lien in the sum of $11,469.68 against Dolomite 3 Corporation for materials ordered by the parent corporation, but used in the construction of a vessel owned by the subsidiary debtor. It has filed notice . . . of a lien on the vessel in this amount and would admittedly be entitled to it except for a credit claimed by Dolomite 3's trustee and allowed below in the amount of $6,000 as funds illegally paid to the claimant before the incurring of the present indebtedness. This appeal by the claimant raises solely the question of the validity of the credit.

The credit is based upon the fact that appellant received and cashed three checks, totaling $6,000, drawn by Dolomite 3 Corporation in favor of appellant as payee. These checks were given from six to ten months before the reorganization proceedings were begun, at a time when Dolomite 3 admittedly owed nothing to appellant, and were used to satisfy appellant's then existing claim against Dolomite Marine Corporation, the parent of Dolomite 3. Each check showed on its face that it was the check of Dolomite 3; the first one given (as well as another small check not in issue) bore the notation, "For Account of Dolomite Marine Corp.," and they were all signed by the "Asst. Secy." of Dolomite 3, who held a like office and signed checks on the same bank for Dolomite Marine Corporation.

The District Court held that under the circumstances the claimant was charged with a duty of ascertaining the true situation between the corporations and must now credit the amount of these payments against the claim. We think, however, that the trustee of Dolomite 3 has failed to support his burden of proving the three checks to be illegal transfers which he as trustee could set aside under any applicable provision of the Bankruptcy Act. . . .

Dolomite Marine, the parent, is a ship–building company. It undertook the construction of vessels through separate subsidiary corporations created especially for the purpose. Dolomite 3 is one of these subsidiaries. It has identical directors and officers, and shares the offices of its parent. Its assets at all times consisted of the unfinished vessel and whatever cash and materials were on hand. Its liabilities—in addition to notes to a bank financing the construction under an agreement to which Dolomite Marine and Petroleum Heat & Power Co. were also parties—included obligations to Dolomite Marine in an intercompany account for expenses incurred by Dolomite Marine on its behalf. . . .

. . . [W]e are not convinced of the unlawfulness of the payments. Appellant had sold materials to Dolomite Marine, which Dolomite Marine used in constructing the ship owned by Dolomite 3. Appellant looked to Dolomite Marine as its debtor, but Dolomite Marine was in turn a creditor of Dolomite 3. It would have been proper for Dolomite 3 to satisfy part of its debt to Dolomite Marine by writing these checks in favor of Dolomite Marine's creditor, the appellant. The meager record does not afford means of determining whether such a novation actually occurred. Accordingly we should remand the case for a finding on this question of fact, were we not of the view that the trustee must lose in any event.

. . . The [t]ransfers [are not] fraudulent under . . . the [Bankruptcy Act], because although they were made within a year of the reorganization proceedings the trustee failed to show that Dolomite 3 either (a) was rendered insolvent, or (b) was left with unreasonably small capital, or (c) intended to incur or believed it would incur debts beyond its ability to pay, or (d) had any actual intent to defraud. . . . [W]e have to consider only a single "other reason" under New York law, namely, that the payments were ultra vires. For there was no fraudulent conveyance under the Uniform Fraudulent Conveyance Act, . . . under the [Bankruptcy Act], . . .

The trustee's power to recapture the payments as ultra vires cannot be derived from the power of the corporation to do so. Dolomite 3 was made to issue the checks by its sole stockholder, Dolomite Marine. The will of Dolomite Marine was the will of Dolomite 3, and both corporations must be deemed to have ratified the transaction. The trustee is therefore limited to the rights of creditors. Creditors, of course, are not prejudiced by the corporation's acts of ratification. . . . But, so far as we have been able to discover, a creditor's power to upset an executed ultra vires transaction seems to be dependent in New York upon his ability to establish a right of action under the so–called "trust fund doctrine." We must, therefore, consider whether the trustee has brought his case within the uncertain limits of that much debated theory as understood and applied in New York.

The well–publicized criticisms of the trust fund doctrine are appreciated in New York, for the Court of Appeals has said recently [that] "this 'trust fund doctrine' has been the subject of much adverse commentary and has often been repudiated as a fiction unsound in principle and vexing in business practice. . . . We do not stop now to canvass the limits of such a theory. It is enough that the facts of the present case—so we hold—do not call for application of the doctrine." . . .

The idea, as we are repeatedly told, is that the capital stock of a corporation is a trust fund for the benefit of the corporation's creditors, not to be impaired by diversion for the direct or indirect benefit of the stockholders. Certain aspects of the rule have been codified, and a New York corporation's power to declare dividends and reduce stated capital is regulated. . . . But there seems to be some part of the doctrine remaining as state common law and applicable to other asset withdrawals which impair capital. Under this law the trustee may perhaps be held to fail here, because he has shown neither insolvency of the debtor nor impairment of its capital at the time of or by the payments, or because the rule cannot be invoked against a payee of a corporate check under circumstances such as those here disclosed. As we shall point out, our decision might possibly rest on one of the first grounds; in any event we think it can rest on the last ground.

Generally it is stated as a part of the trust fund rule that creditors may attack only those impairments of capital which render the corporation insolvent. . . . But the contrary has been held by [a] New York . . . Court in . . . a case where insolvency did not occur until six years after some of the transfers there ruled invalid were made. . . .

Again it is not clear how far in New York the trustee must go in proving capital impaired. Impairment of capital has been defined as the reduction of assets below the capital stock of the company. . . . The assets of Dolomite 3 were upwards of $175,000; its capital stock was $1,000. If the word "assets" be literally interpreted, a withdrawal of $6,000 did not come even close to impairing capital. But we think it more probable that "assets" must be interpreted as the excess of total assets over total debts, for otherwise a prohibition of capital impairment would be meaning- less. . . . Here the corporation never showed a surplus; its assets were never more than its liabilities, plus its capital stock. On this basis a diversion of $6,000 in assets, without reducing liabilities accordingly, would constitute an impairment of capital.

But the third ground is firmer. Though in New York unlawful payments may be recovered from directors, they apparently may not be from stockholders who receive them without notice. . . . Such payments may or may not be recovered from third parties, depending on circumstances. . . .

The figures above quoted are relevant only as bearing on whether the payee should have been deemed on notice. If the recipient of the check would be apt to discover nothing disturbing upon investigation, New York will not invoke the trust fund rule against him. "The rule of responsibility of the payee of corporate paper is strict and sometimes harsh and is not to be extended. . . . We think that rule should not be stretched so as to apply it to the facts of this case upon the basis of the figurative expression that the capital of a corporation is held in trust for its creditors." . . . Here the evidence does not persuade us that the circumstances were such as to arouse the appellant's suspicions. Dolomite 3 and Dolomite Marine had close inter–company accounts; appellant had grounds to believe that the payments would be adjusted on the books of parent and subsidiary in some lawful manner. . . . [W]e need say no more than that the facts of the present case do not call for application of the doctrine.

. . . The judgment is therefore reversed. . . .

SWAN, J (concurring in result).

. . . To justify the set–off the debtor's trustee must prove that . . . $6,000 of the money of Dolomite 3 Corporation was misappropriated to pay debts of Dolomite Marine Corporation. There was no misappropriation if Dolomite 3 was indebted to Dolomite Marine and received credit on that debt for its payments to the appellant. The trustee made no proof that such was not the fact. There is much in the record to suggest that it may have been. . . .

NOTES AND QUESTIONS

(1) The court in *B–F Building Corp.* states a basic principle of fraudulent transfer law: transfers made solely for the benefit of third parties lack fair consideration. *See also Rubin v. Manufacturers Hanover Trust Co.*, 661 F.2d 979, 991 (2d Cir. 1981); *Klein v. Tabatchnick*, 610 F.2d 1043, 1047 (2d Cir. 1979); *Gough v. Titus (In re Christian & Porter Aluminum Co.)*, 584 F.2d 326, 337 (9th Cir. 1978). What is the *Barr & Creelman* court's corollary to that rule? *See* Rubin, *supra*, at 991–92 ("[A]lthough 'transfers *solely* for the benefit of third parties do not furnish fair consideration' . . . the transaction's benefit to the debtor 'need not be direct; it may come indirectly through benefit to a third person. . . .' If the consideration given to the third person has ultimately landed in the debtor's hands, or if the giving of the consideration to the third person otherwise confers an economic benefit upon the debtor, then the debtor's net worth has been preserved . . . provided, of course, that the value of the benefit received by the debtor approximates the value of the property or obligation he has given up.") (citations omitted). How important to the *Barr & Creelman* court was the fact that Dolomite 3 was a wholly–owned subsidiary

of Dolomite Marine, with identical officers and directors? *Cf. Mayo v. Pioneer Bank & Trust Co.*, 270 F.2d 823, 830 (5th Cir. 1959), *cert. denied*, 362 U.S. 962 (1960) (no fraudulent transfer when there was "such a degree of identity and commingling of affairs" between transferor and transferee that the two could not be considered separate legal entities); *In re Nelsen*, 24 B.R. 701 (Bankr. D. Or. 1982).

(2) Related corporate entities often pay or guaranty payment of each other's debts. What potential fraudulent transfer problems are created by "upstream" (subsidiary–to–parent) or "cross–stream" (subsidiary–to–sibling–subsidiary) guaranties? *See generally Rubin v. Manufacturers Hanover Trust Co., supra*; Rosenberg, *Intercorporate Guaranties and the Law of Fraudulent Conveyances: Lender Beware*, 125 U. Pa. L. Rev. 235 (1976); Coquillette, *Guaranty of and Security for the Debt of a Parent Corporation by a Subsidiary Corporation*, 30 Case W. Res. L. Rev. 433 (1980); R.E. Cherin, H.L. Ash, & J.H. Burlingame, *Enforceability of Guarantees and Other Credit Support Provided Among Members of a Corporate Group: A Bibliography*, 34 Bus. Law. 2029 (1979); *Tuller v. Nantahala Park Co.*, 276 S.C. 667, 281 S.E.2d 474 (1981).

(3) A somewhat similar problem arises in a so–called "leveraged acquisition," where inter–corporate guaranties and stock or asset pledges may constitute part of a transaction that prefers the target company's shareholders over its creditors, and leaves the target either insolvent or undercapitalized. *See generally Wells Fargo Bank v. Desert View Building Supplies, Inc.*, 475 F. Supp. 693 (D. Nev. 1978), *aff'd*, 633 F.2d 225 (9th Cir. 1980); *United States v. Gleneagles Investment Co.*, 565 F. Supp. 556 (M.D. Pa. 1983), *aff'd sub nom.*, *United States v. Tabor Court Realty Corp.*, 803 F.2d 1288 (3d Cir. 1986), *cert. denied sub nom.*, *McClellan Realty Co. v. United States*, 107 S.Ct. 3229 (1987) (*infra*); *In re Atlas Foundry Co.*, 155 F. Supp. 615 (D.N.J. 1957); *but cf. In re Greenbrook Carpet Co.*, 722 F.2d 659 (11th Cir. 1984); Carlson, *Leveraged Buyouts in Bankruptcy*, 20 Ga. L. Rev. 73 (1985); Baird & Jackson, *Fraudulent Conveyance Law and Its Proper Domain*, 38 Vand. L. Rev. 829, 854 (1985); Murdoch, Sartin & Zadek, *Fraudulent Conveyances and Leveraged Buyouts I Leveraged Buyouts and Fraudulent Transfers: Life After Gleneagles*, 43 Bus. Law 1 (Nov. 1987); Kirby, McGuinness & Kandel, *Fraudulent Conveyance Concerns In Leveraged Buyout Lending*, 43 Bus. Law 27 (Nov. 1987); Carl, *Fraudulent Transfer Attacks on Guaranties in Bankruptcy*, 60 Am. Bankr. L.J. 109 (1986); Note, *Fraudulent Conveyance Law and Leveraged Buyouts*, 87 Colum. L. Rev. 1491 (1987).

KUPETZ v. WOLF

United States Court of Appeals, Ninth Circuit
845 F.2d 842 (1988)

SNEED, Circuit Judge:

The district court, by way of a summary judgment and directed verdict, determined that the bankrupt made neither fraudulent conveyances under various California fraudulent conveyance statutes and section 548 of the Bankruptcy Code nor improper corporate distributions under California law. 77 B.R. 754. The Trustee in bankruptcy appeals these determinations. We affirm.

I.

FACTS AND PROCEEDINGS BELOW

Wolf & Vine, a mannequin manufacturing company, is the debtor in proceedings before the United States Bankruptcy Court for the Central District of California. Prior to July 31, 1979, Wolf & Vine had been owned 50% by Morris Wolf and 50% by the Marmon Group, Inc. (Marmon). Wolf announced his intention to retire and dispose of his share in the business. Marmon, being obligated under an earlier agreement to purchase the business, began looking for a suitable purchaser of the entire business. After reviewing several potential buyers they decided that David Adashek, an individual backed by Continental Illinois National Bank (the Bank), was suitable.

On July 31, 1979, a series of transactions took place that essentially left Adashek in full control of the company. These transactions amounted to what is known as a leveraged buyout (LBO). There was no evidence in the proceedings below that either Marmon or Wolf knew how the purchase of their stock was to be financed.

The separate transactions were as follows:

(1) Adashek formed Little Red Riding Hood (Riding Hood), a Wisconsin corporation having $100.00 in capital;

(2) Riding Hood purchased all the shares of Wolf & Vine from Wolf and Marmon for $3 million, $1.1 million paid immediately and $1.9 million to be paid in installments over the next two years;

(3) Riding Hood financed the transaction with a $1.1 million loan from the Bank and the Bank issued letters of credit in favor of the sellers for the remaining amount;

(4) Riding Hood merged into Wolf & Vine, which, as the survivor corporation, assumed the obligation of Riding Hood to the sellers, Wolf and Marmon; and

(5) Wolf & Vine pledged its assets to the Bank to secure the $1.1 million loan and the letters of credit. Thus, Adashek effectively pledged the assets of Wolf & Vine to finance his acquisition of that corporation.

All would be well if only Wolf & Vine could service its debt. Adashek, presumably aware of this fact, proceeded to make significant changes in the way the company was run. Apparently Wolf, who had been retained as president, disagreed with some of the changes and several months later resigned. For a time Wolf & Vine made payments to Mr. Wolf and Marmon pursuant to the purchase agreement. For example, in July 1980, Wolf was paid $401,235.75 and Marmon was paid $142,427.32. A year later, however, in July 1981, although Wolf and Marmon were each paid $798,750, the payment of Wolf was made by the Bank under the letter of credit.[1] During this time Wolf & Vine failed to perform as well as Adashek had anticipated and in December 1981 it filed for bankruptcy under Chapter 11. It later changed its petition to a Chapter 7 liquidation proceeding.

In May 1983, the Trustee filed a complaint in the district court alleging that the manner in which the sale was financed constituted fraudulent conveyances to Wolf and Marmon under state law and bankruptcy law, improper distributions to shareholders, breaches of fiduciary duty, and civil conspiracy. The Trustee argues that Wolf and Marmon were the beneficiaries of fraudulent conveyances in the form of payments of the purchase price that left the company's creditors without a chance of collecting the amounts owed to them. The Trustee's claims against Adashek and the Bank were settled leaving only Wolf and Marmon as defendants.

On a summary judgment motion by Wolf and Marmon, the district court decided that there was no creditor whose claim was in existence on the date of the sale, July 31, 1979. For this reason the court granted the defendants' motion for summary judgment on three claims now on appeal. First, it entered judgment against the Trustee's claim that the selling shareholders had received fraudulent conveyances under section four of the Uniform Fraudulent Conveyance Act (UFCA), Cal. Civ. Code § 3439.04 (West 1970), which prohibits transfers lacking fair consideration when the transferee is left insolvent. Second, it rejected the Trustee's claim that the payments to the selling shareholders violated California corporate statutes prohibiting distributions to shareholders when the corporation is as a result not left with enough retained earnings. Cal. Corp. Code § 500 (West 1977 & Supp. 1988). Third, it granted summary judgment on the claim that the selling shareholders received distributions prohibited because the company was not left with enough money to meet its liabilities as they matured. Cal. Corp. Code § 501 (West 1977).

The case proceeded to a jury trial. After the Trustee presented his case, the district court directed a verdict in favor of the selling shareholders on the remaining claims, including two now on appeal. First, a verdict was directed on the claim that the selling shareholders received fraudulent conveyances under section five of the UFCA, Cal. Civ. Code § 3439.05 (West 1970), prohibiting transfers without fair consideration when the transferee has or is thereby left with unreasonably small capital. Second, a verdict was directed on a claim that the July 1981 payments to the selling shareholders were fraudulent transfers under Bankruptcy Code section 548(a)(2)(A) and (B)(ii). The Trustee now appeals both the summary judgment decisions and the directed verdict on the claims listed above.

. . . .

---

[1] Apparently, there is some confusion about whether the 1981 payment to Marmon was also under a letter of credit.

IV.

DISCUSSION

A. *Trustee's Claims*

The Trustee makes three primary claims on appeal, two based on state law and one on federal law. First, he argues that the payments to the selling shareholders are subject to attack under the state fraudulent conveyance law. Section 544(b) of the Bankruptcy Code permits the Trustee to stand in the shoes of a creditor to assert any state law claims that a creditor may have.[2] Second, the Trustee argues that the 1981 payments were fraudulent transfers under Bankruptcy Code section 548. That section in part prohibits transfers by the debtor made without fair consideration when the debtor is left insolvent or with unreasonably small capital. Inasmuch as the purpose of California fraudulent conveyance law in no way differs from that of Bankruptcy Code § 548,[3] the discussion applicable to the first disposes of claims under the latter as well. Third, it is contended by the Trustee that the payments to the selling shareholders were improper distributions under Cal. Corp. Code §§ 500 and 501, which prohibit payments made when the corporation does not have enough retained earnings, or is unable to meet its liabilities, at the time of, or as a result of, the transaction. For reasons discussed below, we find that none of these claims has merit.

B. *The LBO as a Fraudulent Conveyance*

1. *Background*

LBOs pose difficult issues when the purchased corporation becomes bankrupt. An LBO is a purchase transaction based on pledging the assets of the purchased entity to secure the purchase price. Typically, a small group of investors and managers combine to purchase the outstanding shares of a company by creating a large debt by either issuing high–yield "junk bonds" or obtaining a loan from a financial institution. Almost no equity capital is invested. The debt, to repeat, is secured by pledging the assets of the acquired company as security.

Existing unsecured creditors are vulnerable in an LBO. From their perspective, a pledge of the company's assets as collateral to finance the purchase of the company reduces the assets to which they can look for repayment. As some of the acquired companies have failed, creditors have begun to assert that LBOs are fraudulent as to creditors.[4] In this case, the Trustee's attack is, at bottom, such an assertion.

---

[2] The trustee may avoid any transfer of an interest of the debtor in property or any obligation incurred by the debtor that is voidable under applicable law by a creditor holding an unsecured claim that is allowable under section 502 of this title or that is not allowable only under section 502(e) of this title.

11 U.S.C. § 544(b) (1982).

[3] *See Coder v. Arts*, 213 U.S. 223, 241–244 (1909); 4 L. King, *Collier on Bankruptcy* ¶ 548.01[1] (15th ed. 1988).

[4] Business lawyers and academic commentators have taken note of the potential liability to creditors of selling shareholders and lending institutions in LBO transactions. *See* Baird

The present law of fraudulent conveyances has its roots in the Statute of 13 Elizabeth passed by Parliament in 1571. The statute was directed at a practice by which debtors sold their property to friends or relatives for a nominal sum, thus defeating creditors' attempts to satisfy their claims against the debtor. Once the creditor had given up its claim against the debtor, the debtor would reclaim the property that purportedly had been transferred.

The basic thrust of that early statute was to prohibit transfers that hinder, delay, or defraud creditors. Such transfers were prevented by making the collusive transferee liable to the creditor in the amount of the transfer. For four centuries, the primary difficulty has been how to decide which transfers in fact hinder, delay, or defraud creditors. Because intent to defraud is difficult to prove, courts rely on "badges of fraud." Thus, certain indicia of fraud may lead to the conclusion that the debtor had fraudulent intent. The most common of these, now found in the UFCA and in Bankruptcy Code section 548, is to assume fraudulent intent when an *insolvent debtor makes a transfer and gets nothing or very little in return.*

In an LBO, the lender, by taking a security interest in the company's assets, reduces the assets available to creditors in the event of failure of the business.[5] The form of the LBO, while not unimportant, does not alter this reality.[6] Thus, where the parties in an LBO fully intend to hinder the general creditors and benefit the selling shareholders the conveyance is fraudulent under UFCA § 7.[7] The per se rules of the UFCA also may apply. A transfer made by an insolvent debtor who does not receive *fair* consideration is a fraudulent conveyance.[8] And if a transaction

& Jackson, *Fraudulent Conveyance Law and Its Proper Domain*, 38 Vand. L. Rev. 829, 851 (1985); Murdoch, Sartin, & Zadek, *Leveraged Buyouts and Fraudulent Transfers: Life After Gleneagles*, 43 Bus. Law. 1 (1987); Kirby, McGuinnes, & Kandel, *Fraudulent Conveyance Concerns in Leveraged Buyout Lending*, 43 Bus. Law. 27 (1987); Note, *Fraudulent Conveyance Law and Leveraged Buyouts*, 87 Colum. L. Rev. 1491 (1987).

[5] Professors Baird and Jackson point out in *Fraudulent Conveyance Law and its Proper Domain*, 38 Vand.L. Rev. 829 (1985) that "[e]ven under the narrowest view of fraudulent conveyance law, the leveraged buyout may be a fraudulent conveyance."

[6] *See United States v. Tabor Court Realty Corp.*, 803 F.2d 1288, 1302 (3d Cir. 1986), *cert. denied*, — U.S. — , 107 S. Ct. 3229, 97 L. Ed. 2d 735 (1987). As Baird and Jackson note, courts "typically have had no difficulty construing such a segmented transaction as one deal. Courts will now allow the labels that interested parties place on their own transactions to control the rights of third parties." Baird & Jackson, *supra*, at 851.

[7] Every conveyance made and every obligation incurred with actual intent, as distinguished from intent presumed in law, to hinder, delay, or defraud either present or future creditors, is fraudulent as to both present and future creditors.
Cal. Civ. Code § 3439.07 (West 1970). In this opinion, references to the UFCA are to be taken as reference to the California version of the UFCA.

In 1986, the California legislature replaced the UFCA with the Uniform Fraudulent Transfer Act (UFTA). Cal. Civ. Code §§ 3439–3439.12 (West Supp. 1988). The UFTA applies only to transfers made on or after January 1, 1987 and thus has no relevance to this case.

[8] Every conveyance made and every obligation incurred by a person who is or will be thereby incurred by a person who is or will be thereby rendered insolvent is fraudulent as to creditors without regard to his actual intent if the conveyance is made or the obligation is incurred without a fair consideration.
Cal. Civ. Code § 3439.04 (West 1970).

leaves the firm with unreasonably small capital the transaction may be attacked.[9]

2. *Existing Case Law*

The few courts[10] that have looked at the reach of fraudulent conveyance law in the context of LBOs have based their decisions, implicitly at least, on whether there was evidence of intentional fraud. Thus, those transactions in which all was "above board" to begin with have been "ratified" by the courts even though the creditors may have suffered in the end. In *Credit Managers Ass'n v. Federal Co.*, 629 F. Supp. 175 (C.D. Cal. 1985), the court dealt with an attack on an LBO transaction on the basis of theories the same as those of the Trustee in this case: fraudulent conveyance, improper distribution, and equitable subordination. The court, after noting the possibility that fraudulent conveyance law could vitiate all LBOs, refused to employ this approach and declined to overturn the LBO.

---

[9] Every conveyance made without fair consideration when the person making it is engaged or is about to engage in a business or transaction for which the property remaining in his hands after the conveyance is an unreasonably small capital, is fraudulent as to creditors and as to other persons who become creditors during the continuance of such business or transaction without regard to his actual intent.

Cal. Civ. Code § 3439.05 (West 1970).

[10] Academics have recently joined the fray. Professors Baird and Jackson believe that fraudulent conveyance law should not be applied to LBOs. Baird & Jackson, *supra* note 3. They argue that LBOs are often economically efficient and may therefore benefit creditors. Thus, LBOs must not be penalized by a law designed to prevent "genuinely" fraudulent conveyances. From their perspective, the problem with applying fraudulent conveyance law to these transactions is that it gives creditors the ability to "whipsaw" the debtor, taking advantage of the successful LBO and suing under fraudulent conveyance theories if it is unsuccessful. Baird and Jackson also assume that creditors can protect themselves from dangers posed by LBOs by adjusting the terms on which they grant credit. In conclusion, Baird & Jackson find that "the inability of creditors to contract around the fraudulent conveyance remedy when it is in their interest may suggest that fraudulent conveyance law should be applied in bankruptcy to a narrow range of cases in which there is little chance that creditors would find the transfer in their interest." *Id.* at 854. Presumably these cases would be those in which actual intent to defraud is present.

In *United States v. Tabor Court Realty Co.*, 803 F.2d 1288 (3d Cir. 1986), *cert. denied,* — U.S. —, 107 S. Ct. 3229, 97 L. Ed. 2d 735 (1987), the court noted that Baird and Jackson's "analysis is limited to transactions in which 'the transferee parted with value when he entered into the transaction and [the] transaction was entered in the ordinary course.' " *Id.* at 1297 (quoting Baird & Jackson, *supra*, at 855). In several footnotes the court more directly criticized Baird & Jackson's premise that creditors could protect themselves from LBOs through contract provisions, noting that they fail to consider that some creditors, such as tax and judgment creditors, are involuntary creditors. *Id.* at 1297 n.2. That, in fact, was the particular situation that court confronted. These involuntary creditors, such as tax claimants and tort judgment holders, have had no chance to agree to restrict LBO transactions. Another commentator has pointed out that realities of the marketplace make it likely that the creditors with the economic power to force a debtor to forego an LBO, or restrict the conditions under which one may take place, are more likely to take a security interest than they are to contract for restrictive conditions. This leaves only small trade creditors, with little relative economic power, at the mercy of a decision to undergo a buyout. Note, *Fraudulent Conveyance Law and Leveraged Buyouts*, 87 Colum. L. Rev. 1491, 1512 (1987).

In contrast, when the LBO was intentionally designed to defraud the creditors, the courts have had little difficulty in finding the transaction fraudulent. In *United States v. Gleneagles Inv. Co.*, 565 F. Supp. 556 (M.D. Pa. 1983), for example, the court found violations of both the intentional and constructive fraud sections of the UFCA. This decision was upheld by the Third Circuit in *United States v. Tabor Court Realty Corp.*, 803 F.2d 1288 (3d Cir. 1986), *cert. denied*, — U.S. —, 107 S. Ct. 3229, 97 L. Ed. 2d 735 (1987), which relied substantially on the suspicious circumstances surrounding the transaction that evidenced actual intent to defraud. *Tabor*, 803 F.2d at 1297.

3. *Analysis of the Wolf & Vine LBO*

We decline to use the law of fraudulent conveyance to force the selling shareholders in this case to give up the payments they have received. We are so moved by a combination of factors. First, there is no evidence of any intention on the part of the selling shareholders to defraud the corporation's creditors. Second, the selling shareholders did not know that Adashek intended to finance the purchases through an LBO. Third, the Trustee represents no creditors whose claims against the estate arose before July 31, 1979, and who did not have full opportunity to evaluate the effect of the LBO on Wolf & Vine's creditworthiness. Fourth, the form of the transactions employed by the LBO reflects a sale by Wolf and Marmon to an entity other than Wolf & Vine. Each of these factors requires amplification.

a. *Intent to defraud*

Turning to intent to defraud, there is no evidence that the selling shareholders intended to defraud the Wolf & Vine creditors. Indeed, the Trustee has dropped any such claim on appeal and our review of the trial transcript indicates this was proper. Although lack of fraudulent intent does not bar a fraudulent conveyance claim under a constructive intent provision of the law, we hesitate to utilize constructive intent to frustrate the purposes intended to be served by what appears to us to be a legitimate LBO. Nor do we think it appropriate to utilize constructive intent to brand most, if not all, LBOs as illegitimate. We cannot believe that virtually all LBOs are designed to "hinder, delay, or defraud creditors."

b. *Knowledge of leveraging*

The legitimacy of the LBO in this case is reinforced not only by the absence of an intent to defraud Wolf & Vine creditors, but also by the fact that Wolf did not know that his buyout would be leveraged. There was, in fact, uncontradicted evidence that Wolf did not know that Adashek had pledged Wolf & Vine assets to make the acquisition until the bankruptcy petition was filed more than two years after the sale of the Wolf stock. Reporter's Transcript (R.T.) II–156–60, 180–84. Whether Marmon knew about the method of acquisition is not clear from the record.

The Trustee makes much of the fact that the selling shareholders did not thoroughly investigate Adashek and his proposed business plan for acquiring and running the company.[11] The suggestion is that the ignorance of Wolf and possibly

---

[11] We note, however, that the Trustee never presented any evidence that a more thorough investigation would have turned up facts that would have put the selling shareholders on guard.

Marmon was the result of indifference. We are sensitive to the issue and in some circumstances would find it of controlling importance.[12] Here Marmon and Wolf appear to have been fairly careful in selecting a purchaser for the company. Clearly there was a screening of prospective purchasers. Several purchasers were rejected outright as not being financially sound enough to make the acquisition. R.T. II–155–56. Of greater importance is the fact that Wolf and Marmon knew that Adashek was backed by the Continental Illinois Bank which had agreed to issue a letter of credit to back the transaction. R.T. III–18. Admittedly, the LBO's legitimacy is not strengthened by the fact that neither Wolf nor Marmon asked Adashek for a financial statement, acquisition plan or business plan.[13] R.T. II–54; II–162–63. But they were aware that Adashek's net worth was in excess of $5 million, that he was a successful investor, and that Continental was willing to back his purchase by the issuance of irrevocable letters of credit. We conclude the selling shareholders neither knew nor had reason to know that Adashek planned a leveraged acquisition of Wolf & Vine.

c. Absence of July 31, 1979 creditors

Our comfort with that conclusion is enhanced by the absence of presently existing creditors with claims that arose prior to the LBO. The Trustee, however, argues that there is such a claim. He contends that the National Industrial Group Pension Plan (NIGPP) has a claim that arose prior to July 31, 1979. A division of Wolf & Vine was a participant in this plan. Wolf & Vine withdrew from the plan on November 1, 1981 and it thereby incurred withdrawal liability[14] of $200,000. This withdrawal liability arose by virtue of the Multiemployer Pension Plan Amendments Act of 1980 (MPPAA), 29 U.S.C. § 1381 et seq. (1982). The MPPAA was not enacted until September 26, 1980, over a year after the sale of Wolf & Vine. Nonetheless, the Trustee argues that NIGPP, through the MPPAA, had a contingent claim prior to the sale date, July 31, 1979 because, prior to that date, Congress was actively considering passage of the bill that ultimately became the MPPAA.[15] The Trustee

---

[12] In some circumstances, of course, controlling shareholders of a corporation are obligated to make certain that the business' creditors are not harmed by transactions in which the business enters. *See, e.g., Pepper v. Litton*, 308 U.S. 295, 306–07, 60 S. Ct. 238, 245–46, 84 L. Ed. 281 (1939); *Brown v. Presbyterian Ministers Fund*, 484 F.2d 998, 1005 (3d Cir. 1973).

[13] We note that from Wolf's perspective there was little point in investigating further because Marmon had long before agreed to buy him out. As far as he understood matters he was merely expediting the transaction by selling directly to Adashek instead of to Marmon and having Marmon resell to Adashek.

[14] Withdrawal liability is imposed on employers that withdraw from the plan so that the plan will be partially reimbursed for the amount by which the plan is unfunded for benefits that are projected to accrue to that employer's employees.

[15] The MPPAA was created to deal with the problems encountered by the Pension Benefits Guaranty Corporation (PBGC), a federally chartered corporation designed to guarantee benefits to employees whose plans had terminated. Its discretionary authority to force employers to pay the corporation for their unfunded pension benefits upon withdrawal was about to become mandatory. Congress was alarmed at the prospect of the PBGC being bankrupted by having to pick up the bill for financially troubled plans. Congress addressed

cites no authority for this proposition and we reject it. To make substantive results turn on when Congress commenced to consider a provision rather than when it was enacted would be to forsake the stability of a rock for treachery of quicksand.

Thus, all existing creditors had the opportunity to gain the knowledge of Wolf & Vine's financial status and its heavy debt structure prior to extending credit to it.[16] Creditors easily could have asked for financial information before extending credit. Moreover, the transaction was well–publicized within the industry. To ask

---

the problem in two ways. First, it continually rolled back the date at which the PBGC became mandatorily obligated to pick up the liability for terminated plans. Second, it began to devise legislation that would force employers to pay their share of the PBGC's unfunded liability upon withdrawal by the employer. Proposals included a retroactive date in order to prevent employers from withdrawing during the time that the proposal was being considered by Congress. At one time the retroactive date was February 27, 1979. The bill was apparently under consideration during most of 1979 and 1980. When it was finally enacted, the retroactive date had been changed to April 29, 1980.

16 The relevant statutes dictate, in most cases, that a transfer cannot be set aside as a fraudulent conveyance unless the creditor had a claim in existence at the time of the purported fraudulent conveyance. Under section five of the UFCA, Cal. Civ. Code § 3439.05, however, a conveyance made without fair consideration that leaves the transferor with unreasonably small capital is fraudulent, despite lack of fraudulent intent, "as to creditors *and as to other persons who become creditors during the continuance of such business or transaction.*" (emphasis added.) Thus, it would appear that even a post–purchase transaction creditor, such as those present in this case, may attack a transaction if the other grounds of § 3439.05 are met. The California courts do not seem to have doubted the plain language of the statute that later–arising creditors may attack conveyances that meet the other requirements of the statute. (At least one California court, however, has stated that only a person that was a creditor at the time of the transaction has standing to sue under section five. *Pope v. National Aero Finance Co.*, 236 Cal. App. 2d 722, 728, 46 Cal. Rptr. 233, 237 (1965) (referring to § 3439.04, .05, .06) (citing *TWM Homes, Inc. v. Atherwood Realty & Inv. Co.*, 214 Cal. App. 2d 826, 843, 29 Cal. Rptr. 887, 896 (1963) (referring only to § 3439.04)).) But like Judge Rafeedie in *Credit Managers*, we believe this grant of standing to sue must be modified in light of an LBO in which there was no actual intent to defraud. Judge Rafeedie put it well:

> [W]hen the California legislature passed [the predecessor statute to § 3439.05] in 1939, it clearly did not intend to cover leveraged buyouts which are very public events. The legislature was addressing instead transactions that have the earmarks of fraud. . . . If there is no limit on when a creditor can sue to set aside a transfer, fraudulent conveyance law becomes an insurance policy for creditors. . . . Credit could liberally be extended to such companies regardless of their assets or cash flow with the knowledge that the buyout could always be attacked later if the company folded.

Credit Managers, 629 F. Supp. at 181. Because fraudulent conveyance statutes were designed to protect creditors from *secret* transactions by debtors, the same rules should not apply when the transaction is made public. Future creditors may not complain when they knew or could easily have found out about the transaction. This certainly appears to be the case in this particular LBO. The transaction was well–publicized and the Trustee has not claimed or presented evidence that any of the future creditors were not aware of Wolf & Vine's financial dealings. In the context of this well–publicized LBO, this court will not permit later–arising creditors to attack an LBO purchase transaction as a fraudulent conveyance under section five of the UFCA.

Wolf to underwrite the creditors' losses, due partially at least to their failure to inquire adequately, would not be just.

d. *The form of the LBO*

As already mentioned, we are influenced by the formal structure of this LBO. The sale was complete as of July 31, 1979. Payments were spread over a three–year period. A large portion of the purchase price was paid on July 31, 1979, and the remainder was secured by an *irrevocable* letter of credit. Thus, the transaction bore the indicia of a "straight" sale rather than the marks of a serial redemption by Wolf & Vine of its own stock. The Trustee's case would be stronger had the "selling" shareholders known, or should have known, that their stock was being paid for by an asset depleting transfer by Wolf & Vine. This case, however, does not present such facts. In this case the creditors of Wolf & Vine were placed at risk by Adashek's failure to manage the business properly. Wolf and Marmon should not be considered Adashek's guarantor.

There is no evidence that Wolf and Marmon did not act in good faith throughout the transaction. They sold their shares for a fair price to another company that, though very thinly capitalized, was backed by the substantial personal assets of a wealthy purchaser and his relationship with a major bank. While we should not be understood as insulating all LBOs from fraudulent conveyance laws, we do affirm the district court's decision on the state fraudulent conveyance law claim and the § 548 bankruptcy claim in this case.

C. *Improper Corporate Distributions*

We now address the Trustee's argument that the payments to Wolf and Marmon were improper distributions under Cal. Corp. Code §§ 500 and 501. We begin by repeating that the Trustee has no standing to attack the 1979 payments because no creditor exists holding a claim that arose before the 1979 payments. The Trustee also may not attack payments made by the Bank under letters of credit. The Trustee's contention that he has standing to attack the July 1980 payments and perhaps the July 1981 payment to Marmon is more substantial. To establish that the 1980–81 payments constituted improper distributions, the Trustee must show that at the time the payments were made, the corporation did not have enough retained earnings or was unable to meet its liabilities at the time of, or as a result of, the payments.

The district court dismissed these claims by summary judgment. It reached this conclusion by relating each installment payment back to the date of the initial transaction in 1979. Quite correctly, the Trustee points out that distributions to shareholders, however, must be scrutinized at the time they are made and not at the time the parties contracted that they would be made in the future. Cal. Corp. Code § 166 (West 1977 & Supp. 1988); 1 Ballantine & Sterling, California Corporation Laws § 143.03[4][c], at 8–66 (4th ed. 1987).[17]

---

[17] For example, in *McConnell v. Estate of Butler*, 402 F.2d 362 (9th Cir. 1968), the corporation had enough money under the California earned surplus requirement to make the full distribution at the time the agreement to convert shares to debentures was made. However, by the time the debenture holders wanted to collect, the earned surplus requirement could

Under the district court's relation of all payments back to 1979 it focused its attention on the financial condition of the company at that time. It found that the capital left in the company was not "unreasonably small," one of the elements of improper corporate distribution. Summary judgment against the Trustee followed thereafter. In reaching this result the court observed that it was:

> not persuaded that [the expert's] testimony, or any other evidence at trial, established a *prima facie* case that Wolf & Vine was left with an unreasonably small capital as a result of Adashek's financing his transaction as a leveraged buyout. In any event, there was certainly no evidence that the sale from Marmon and Wolf to Little Red Riding Hood left Wolf & Vine with unreasonably small capital.

Excerpt of Record (E.R.) tab 249, at 20–21.

We have some difficulty in sustaining the district court's summary judgment because of certain questions we have concerning the manner in which it reached its decisions.[18] We are convinced, however, that the district court reached the correct result. As already indicated, we do not view the 1980–81 payments as a distribution by Wolf & Vine to its former shareholders, Wolf and Marmon. They received the installment payments to which they were entitled under the sales agreement with Riding Hood. These payments, if distributions at all within the meaning of Cal. Corp. Code §§ 500 and 501, were distributions by Wolf & Vine to its then existing shareholder, Adashek, for whose benefit the distributions were made. In substance, no distributions to Wolf and Marmon were made. Adashek was the beneficiary of these distributions. What was said in Part B of this opinion concerning the appropriateness of creditors of Wolf & Vine, whose claims accrued subsequent to

---

no longer be met. The court, interpreting the predecessor statute to Cal. Corp. Code §§ 501 and 502, decided that the corporation had to be solvent and have sufficient surplus at the time the payment was made, not just when the deal was struck. *Id.* at 366; *see Robinson v. Wangemann*, 75 F.2d 756, 757–58 (5th Cir. 1935).

[18] The district court concluded, presumably as a result of the cross–examination of the expert witness, that the expert "made a number of assumptions which undermine the appropriateness of his findings," that he "used questionable methods in appraising the solvency of Wolf & Vine after the sale," that he failed "to research the business . . . , discuss the company with former employees or others in the industry, or learn about the mannequin industry," and that he "was told to value the company as if it were liquidated and each asset was sold apart from all other assets and not to value it as a going concern." E.R. tab 249, at 19–20. Under cross–examination, the plaintiff's expert witness demonstrated he knew little about the mannequin industry in general and nothing about the valuation of assets. Our review of the trial transcript, R.T. III–151 to IV, pt. 1, at 61, supports the district court's view that the testimony of the Trustee's expert witness was hardly persuasive. Nonetheless, the district court did not ask, as it should have, whether the evidence permitted only one reasonable conclusion as to the verdict. *Peterson v. Kennedy*, 771 F.2d 1244, 1256 (9th Cir. 1985), *cert. denied*, 475 U.S. 1122, 106 S. Ct. 1642, 90 L. Ed. 2d 187 (1986). Instead, the district court appeared to focus on whether the Trustee has proved a "prima facie" case of unreasonably small capital. The district court apparently confused its analysis of whether the burden of proof on the issue of unreasonably small capital should have shifted to the plaintiffs, with the standard for rendering a directed verdict.

the sale by Wolf and Marmon, looking to former shareholders for relief from the consequences of the subsequent failure of Wolf & Vine is equally applicable at this point. Were the proceeding arising from the bankruptcy of Adashek it would be pertinent to inquire whether Wolf and Marmon received a preference as a result of the 1980–81 payments. That, however, is not the issue before us.

We, therefore, conclude that Cal. Corp. Code §§ 500 and 501 are inapplicable to the 1980–81 payments to Wolf and Marmon.

AFFIRMED.

UNITED STATES v. TABOR COURT REALTY CORP.

United States Court of Appeals, Third Circuit
803 F.2d 1288 (1986)
cert. denied sub nom. McClellan Realty Co. v. United States
483 US 1005, 107 S. Ct. 3229, 97 L. Ed. 2d 735

ALDISERT, Chief Judge.

We have consolidated appeals from litigation involving one of America's largest anthracite coal producers that emanate from a district court bench trial that extended over 120 days and recorded close to 20,000 pages of transcript. Ultimately, we have to decide whether the court erred in entering judgment in favor of the United States in reducing to judgment certain federal corporate tax assessments made against the coal producers, in determining the priority of the government liens, and in permitting foreclosure on the liens. To reach these questions, however, we must examine a very intricate leveraged buy–out and decide whether mortgages given in the transaction were fraudulent conveyances within the meaning of the constructive and intentional fraud sections of the Pennsylvania Uniform Fraudulent Conveyances Act (UFCA), 39 Pa. Stat. §§ 354–357, and if so, whether a later assignment of the mortgages was void as against creditors.

The district court made 481 findings of facts and issued three separate published opinions: *United States v. Gleneagles Investment Co.*, 565 F. Supp. 556 (M.D. Pa. 1983) (*Gleneagles I*); 571 F. Supp. 935 (1983) (*Gleneagles II*); and 584 F. Supp. 671 (1984) (*Gleneagles III*). We are told that this case represents the first significant application of the UFCA to leveraged buyout financing.

We will address seven issues presented by the appellants and an amicus curiae, the National Commercial Finance Association, and by the United States and a trustee in bankruptcy as cross appellants:

* whether the court erred in applying the UFCA to a leveraged buy–out;

* whether the court erred in denying the mortgage assignee, McClellan Realty, a "lien superior to all other creditors";

* whether the court erred in "collapsing" two separate loans for the leveraged buy–out into one transaction;

* whether the court erred in holding that the mortgages placed by the borrowers on November 26, 1973 were invalid under the UFCA;

* whether the court erred in holding that the mortgages placed by the guarantors were invalid for lack of fair consideration;

* in the government's cross–appeal, whether the court erred in determining that the mortgage assignee, McClellan Realty, was entitled to an equitable lien for municipal taxes paid; and

* in the government's and trustee–in–bankruptcy's cross–appeal, whether the court erred in placing the mortgage assignee, McClellan Realty, on the creditor list rather than removing it entirely.

We will summarize a very complex factual situation and then discuss these issues seriatim.

I.

These appeals arise from an action by the United States to reduce to judgment delinquent federal income taxes, interest, and penalties assessed and accrued against Raymond Colliery Co., Inc. and its subsidiaries (the Raymond Group) for the fiscal years of June 30, 1966 through June 30, 1973 and to reduce to judgment similarly assessed taxes owed by Great American Coal Co., Inc. and its subsidiaries for the fiscal year ending June 30, 1975.

The government sought to collect these tax claims from surface and coal lands owned by the Raymond Group as well as from lands formerly owned by it but which, as a result of allegedly illegal and fraudulent county tax sales, were later owned by Gleneagles Investment Co., Inc. In addition, the government sought to assert the priority of its liens over liens held by others. The district court held in favor of the government on most of its claims and concluded the litigation by promulgating an order of priority of liens on Raymond Group lands.

Raymond Colliery, incorporated in 1962, was owned by two families, the Gillens and the Clevelands. It owned over 30,000 acres of land in Lackawanna and Luzerne counties in Pennsylvania and was one of the largest anthracite coal producers in the country. In 1966, Glen Alden Corporation sold its subsidiary, Blue Coal Corporation, to Raymond for $6 million. Raymond paid $500,000 in cash and the remainder of the purchase price with a note secured by a mortgage on Blue Coal's land. Lurking in the background of the financial problems present here are two important components of the current industrial scene: first, the depressed economy attending anthracite mining in Lackawanna and Luzerne Counties, the heartland of this industry; and second, the Pennsylvania Department of Environmental Resources' 1967 order directing Blue Coal to reduce the amount of pollutants it discharged into public waterways in the course of its deep mining operations, necessitating a fundamental change from deep mining to strip or surface mining.

Very serious problems surfaced in 1971 when Raymond's chief stockholders — the Gillens and Clevelands — started to have disagreements over the poor performance of the coal producing companies. The stockholders decided to solve the problem by seeking a buyer for the group. On February 2, 1972, the shareholders granted James Durkin, Raymond's president, an option to purchase Raymond for $8.5 million. The stockholders later renewed Durkin's option at a reduced price of $7.2 million.

Durkin had trouble in raising the necessary financing to exercise his option. He sought help from the Central States Pension Fund of the International Brotherhood of Teamsters and also from the Mellon Bank of Pittsburgh. Mellon concluded that Blue Coal was a bad financial risk. Moreover, both Mellon and Central States held extensive discussions with Durkin's counsel concerning the legality of encumbering Raymond's assets for the purpose of obtaining the loan, a loan which was not to be used to repay creditors but rather to buy out Raymond's stockholders.

After other unsuccessful attempts to obtain financing for the purchase, Durkin incorporated a holding company, Great American, and assigned to it his option to purchase Raymond's stock. Although the litigation in the district court was far–reaching, most of the central issues have their genesis in 1973 when the Raymond Group was sold to Durkin in a leveraged buy–out through the vehicle of Great American.

A leveraged buy–out is not a legal term of art. It is a shorthand expression describing a business practice wherein a company is sold to a small number of investors, typically including members of the company's management, under financial arrangements in which there is a minimum amount of equity and a maximum amount of debt. The financing typically provides for a substantial return of investment capital by means of mortgages or high risk bonds, popularly known as "junk bonds." The predicate transaction here fits the popular notion of a leveraged buy–out. Shareholders of the Raymond Group sold the corporation to a small group of investors headed by Raymond's president; these investors borrowed substantially all of the purchase price at an extremely high rate of interest secured by mortgages on the assets of the selling company and its subsidiaries and those of additional entities that guaranteed repayment.

To effectuate the buy–out, Great American obtained a loan commitment from Institutional Investors Trust on July 24, 1973, in the amount of $8,530,000. The 1973 interrelationship among the many creditors of the Raymond Group, and the sale to Great American — a seemingly empty corporation which was able to perform the buy–out only on the strength of a massive loan from IIT — forms the backdrop for the relevancy of the Pennsylvania Uniform Fraudulent Conveyance Act, one of the critical legal questions presented for our decision.

Durkin obtained the financing through one of his two partners in Great American.[1] The loan from IIT was structured so as to divide the Raymond Group into borrowing companies and guarantor companies. The loan was secured by mortgages on the assets of the borrowing companies, but was also guaranteed by mortgages

---

[1] Durkin owned 40% of Great American. Hyman Green owned 10%, and James R. Hoffa, Jr. owned the remaining 50%. Durkin and Green concealed Hoffa's ownership interest in Great American from IIT. Hoffa apparently came into the picture when Durkin attempted to borrow money from the Central States Pension Fund of the International Brotherhood of Teamsters to finance the purchase.

on the assets of the guarantor companies. We must decide whether the borrowers' mortgages were invalid under the UFCA and whether there was consideration for the guarantors' mortgages.

The IIT loan was closed on November 26, 1973. The borrowing companies in the Raymond Group received $7 million in direct proceeds from IIT. The remaining $1.53 million was placed in escrow as a reserve account for the payment of accruing interest. The loans were to be repaid by December 31, 1976, at an interest rate of five points over the prime rate but in no event less than 12.5 percent. In exchange, each of the borrowing companies — Raymond Colliery, Blue Coal, Glen Nan, and Olyphant Associates — created a first lien in favor of IIT on all of their tangible and intangible assets; each of the guarantor companies — all other companies in the Raymond Group — created a second lien in favor of IIT on all of their tangible and intangible assets. The loan agreement also contained a clause which provided IIT with a priority lien on the proceeds from Raymond's sales of its surplus lands. Finally, the agreement provided that violations of any of the loan covenants would permit IIT to accelerate the loan and to collect immediately the full balance due from any or all of the borrowers or guarantors.

The exchange of money and notes did not stop with IIT's advances to the borrowing companies. Upon receipt of the IIT loan proceeds, the borrowing companies immediately transferred a total of $4,085,000 to Great American. In return, Great American issued to each borrowing company an unsecured promissory note with the same interest terms as those of the IIT loan agreement. In addition to the proceeds of the IIT loan, Great American borrowed other funds to acquire the purchase price for Raymond's stock.

When the financial dust settled after the closing on November 26, 1973, this was the situation at Raymond: Great American paid $6.7 million to purchase Raymond's stock, the shareholders receiving $6.2 million in cash and a $500,000 note; at least $4.8 million of this amount was obtained by mortgaging Raymond's assets.

Notwithstanding the cozy accommodations for the selling stockholders, the financial environment of the Raymond Group at the time of the sale was somewhat precarious. At the time of the closing, Raymond had multi–million dollar liabilities for federal income taxes, trade accounts, pension fund contributions, strip mining and back–filling obligations, and municipal real estate taxes. The district court calculated that the Raymond Group's existing debts amounted to at least $20 million on November 26, 1983. 565 F. Supp. at 578.

Under Durkin's control after the buy–out, Raymond's condition further deteriorated. Following the closing the Raymond Group lacked the funds to pay its routine operating expenses, including those for materials, supplies, telephone, and other utilities. It was also unable to pay its delinquent and current real estate taxes. Within two months of the closing, the deep mining operations of Blue Coal were shut down; within six months of the closing, the Raymond Group ceased all strip mining operations. Consequently, the Raymond Group could not fulfill its existing coal contracts and became liable for damages for breach of contract. The plaintiffs in the breach of contract actions exercised their right of set–off against accounts they owed the Raymond Group. Within seven months of the closing, the Commonwealth of

Pennsylvania and the Anthracite Health & Welfare Fund sued the Raymond Group for its failures to fulfill back–filling requirements in the strip mining operations and to pay contributions to the Health & Welfare Fund. This litigation resulted in injunctions against the Raymond Group companies which prevented them from moving or selling their equipment until their obligations were satisfied. Moreover, Lackawanna and Luzerne counties announced their intent to sell the Raymond Group properties for unpaid real estate taxes. Finally, on September 15, 1976, IIT notified the borrowing and guarantor Raymond companies that their mortgage notes were in default. On September 29, 1976, IIT confessed judgments against the borrowing companies for the balance due on the loan and began to solicit a buyer for the Raymond Group mortgages.

New *dramatis personae* came on stage and orchestrated additional financial dealings which led to the purchase of the IIT mortgages. These dealings form the backdrop for additional legal issues to be decided here. Pagnotti Enterprises, another large anthracite producer, was the prime candidate to purchase the mortgages from IIT. In December 1976, James J. Tedesco, on behalf of Pagnotti, commenced negotiations for the purchase. Tedesco signed an agreement on December 15, 1976. Pursuant to the mortgage sale contract — and prior to the closing of the sale and assignment of the mortgages — IIT and Pagnotti each placed $600,000 in an escrow account to be applied to the payment of delinquent real estate taxes on properties listed for the county tax sales or to be used as funds for bidding on the properties at the tax sales.

IIT and Pagnotti agreed that bidding on the properties at the Lackawanna and Luzerne county tax sales would be undertaken by nominee corporations. Pursuant to their agreement, more new business entities then entered the picture. Tabor Court Realty was formed to bid on Raymond's properties at the Lackawanna County tax sale; similarly, McClellan Realty was formed to bid on Blue Coal's lands in Luzerne County. Pagnotti prepaid the delinquent taxes that predated IIT's mortgages to Lackawanna County. On December 17, 1976, Tabor Court Realty obtained Raymond's Lackawanna lands for a bid of $385,000; yet by this date an involuntary petition in bankruptcy had been filed against Blue Coal, a chief Raymond subsidiary, by its creditors. A similar proceeding was instituted against another subsidiary, Glen Nan. Based on the failure of Tabor Court to pay other delinquent taxes, on December 16, 1980, Lackawanna County held a second tax sale of Raymond's lands. At that sale, Joseph Solfanelli, acting on behalf of Gleneagles Investment, bid and acquired Raymond's lands for $535,290.39. These transactions did not stand up. At trial, the parties stipulated that both county tax sales were invalid and that Raymond's lands purportedly sold to Tabor Court and Gleneagles remained assets owned by Raymond.

On January 26, 1977, the sale and assignment of the IIT mortgages took place. Pagnotti paid approximately $4.5 million for the IIT mortgages; at that time, the mortgage balance was $5,817,475.69. Pagnotti thereafter assigned the mortgage to McClellan, thus making McClellan a key figure in this litigation. On December 12, 1977, Hyman Green, one of Durkin's co–shareholders in Raymond, was told that McClellan intended to sell, at a private sale, many of Raymond's assets encumbered as collateral on the IIT mortgages. McClellan did just that — it foreclosed. On February 28, 1978, in a private sale, Loree Associates purchased the assets from McClellan for $50,000. This sale was not advertised nor were the assets offered to any other parties. Additionally, the sale was not recorded on the books of either Loree Associates or McClellan until May 1983, six months after the start of the litigation below. Nor was this the only private sale. On October 6, 1978, McClellan foreclosed on the stock of Raymond and sold it at a private sale for $1 to Joseph Solfanelli, as trustee for Pagnotti. Again, the sale was not advertised nor was anyone other than Green informed of the sale. No appraisals were obtained for either the stock or the collateral purportedly sold by McClellan at these sales.

This, then, constitutes a summary of the adjudicative facts that undergird the litigation below and the appeals before us.

II.

The instant action was commenced by the United States on December 12, 1980 to reduce to judgment certain corporate federal tax assessments made against the Raymond Group and Great American. The government sought to assert the priority of its tax liens and to foreclose against the property that Raymond had owned at the time of the assessments as well as against properties currently owned by Raymond. The United States argued that the IIT mortgages executed in November 1973 should be set aside under the Uniform Fraudulent Conveyance Act and further that the purported assignment of these mortgages to Pagnotti should be voided because at the inception Pagnotti had purchased the mortgages with knowledge that they had been fraudulently conveyed.

As heretofore stated, after a bench trial, the district court issued three separate published opinions. In *Gleneagles I*, 565 F. Supp. 556 (1983), the court concluded, *inter alia*, that the mortgages given by the Raymond Group to IIT on November 26, 1973 were fraudulent conveyances within the meaning of the constructive and intentional fraud sections of the Pennsylvania Uniform Fraudulent Conveyances Act, 39 Pa. Stat. §§ 354–357. In *Gleneagles II*, 571 F. Supp. 935 (1983), the court further held that the mortgages to McClellan Realty were void as against the other Raymond Group creditors. In its third opinion, 584 F. Supp. 671 (1984), the court set out the priority of the creditors. The court granted McClellan and Tabor Court an equitable lien ahead of the creditors for the Pennsylvania municipal taxes they paid in Raymond's behalf prior to the 1976 Lackawanna County tax sale of Raymond's properties. However, the court placed McClellan, as assignee of the IIT mortgages, near the bottom of the list of creditors. The trustee in bankruptcy of Blue Coal and Glen Nan argues that McClellan's rights were totally invalidated and that McClellan has no standing whatsoever as a creditor.

The Raymond Group — four coal mining companies that executed the mortgages (Raymond Colliery, Blue Coal, Glen Nan, and Olyphant Associates) as well as interrelated associated companies that had placed guarantee mortgages and subsidiaries of such associated companies — has appealed. As heretofore stated, all these mortgages, subsequently invalidated by the district court, had been granted to IIT on November 26, 1973 and assigned by IIT to appellant McClellan. For the purpose of this appeal, we shall refer to the Raymond Group as "appellants", or "McClellan".

Jurisdiction was proper in the trial court, 28 U.S.C. §§ 1340, 1345. We are satisfied that jurisdiction on appeal is proper based on 28 U.S.C. § 1291. Although one or two parties have questioned the timeliness of McClellan's appeal based on a contention that partially defective service of McClellan's motion for a new district court trial failed to toll the running of the 60–day period for filing appeals under Rule 4(a)(1) of the Federal Rules of Appellate Procedure, we are satisfied that this was not fatal. *See Thompson v. INS*, 375 U.S. 384, 84 S. Ct. 397, 11 L. Ed. 2d 404 (1964).

III.

McClellan initially challenges the district court's application of the Pennsylvania Uniform Fraudulent Conveyances Act (UFCA), 39 Pa. Stat. §§ 351–363, to the leveraged buy–out loan made by IIT to the mortgagors, and to the acquisition of the mortgages from IIT by McClellan. The district court determined that IIT lacked good faith in the transaction because it knew, or should have known, that the money it lent the mortgagors was used, in part, to finance the purchase of stock from the mortgagors' shareholders, and that as a consequence of the loan, IIT and its assignees obtained a secured position in the mortgagors' property to the detriment of creditors. Because this issue involves the interpretation and application of legal precepts, review is plenary. *Universal Minerals, Inc. v. C.A. Hughes & Co.*, 669 F.2d 98, 102 (3d Cir. 1981).

In applying section 353(a) of the UFCA, the district court stated:

> The initial question . . . is whether the transferee, IIT, transferred its loan proceeds in good faith. . . . IIT knew or strongly suspected that the imposition of the loan obligations secured by the mortgages and guarantee mortgages would probably render insolvent both the Raymond Group and each individual member thereof. In addition, IIT was fully aware that no individual member of the Raymond Group would receive fair consideration within the meaning of the Act in exchange for the loan obligations to IIT. Thus, we conclude that IIT does not meet the standard of good faith under Section 353(a) of the Act. *See e.g., Cohen v. Sutherland*, 257 F.2d [737] at 742 [(2d Cir. 1958)] (transferee's knowledge that the transferor is insolvent defeats assertion of good faith); *Epstein v. Goldstein*, 107 F.2d 755, 757 (2d Cir. 1939) (transferee's knowledge that no consideration was received by transferor relevant to the issue of good faith).

565 F. Supp. at 574.

McClellan argues that "the only reasonable and proper application of the good faith criteria as it applies to the lender in structuring a loan is one which looks to the lender's *motives* as opposed to his *knowledge*." Br. for appellants at 17. McClellan argues that good faith is satisfied when "the lender acted in an arms–length transaction without ulterior motive or collusion with the debtor to the detriment of creditors." *Id.*

Section 354 of the UFCA is a "constructive fraud" provision. It establishes that a conveyance made by a person "who is or will be thereby rendered insolvent, is fraudulent as to creditors, without regard to his actual intent, if the conveyance is made . . . without a fair consideration." 39 Pa. Stat. § 354. Section 353 defines fair consideration as an exchange of a "fair equivalent . . . in good faith." 39 Pa. Stat. § 353. Because section 354 excludes an examination of intent, it follows that "good faith" must be something other than intent; because section 354 also focuses on insolvency, knowledge of insolvency is a rational interpretation of the statutory language of lack of "good faith." McClellan would have us adopt "without ulterior motive or collusion with the debtor to the detriment of creditors" as the good faith standard. We are uneasy with such a standard because these words come very close to describing intent.

Surprisingly, few courts have considered this issue. In *Epstein v. Goldstein*, 107 F.2d 755, 757 (2d Cir. 1939), the court held that because a transferee had no knowledge of the transferor's insolvency, it could not justify a finding of bad faith, implying that a showing of such knowledge would support a finding of bad faith. In *Sparkman and McClean Co. v. Derber*, 4 Wash. App. 341, 481 P.2d 585 (1971), the court considered a mortgage given to an attorney by a corporation on the verge of bankruptcy to secure payment for his services. The trial court found that the transaction had violated section 3 of the UFCA (here, section 353) because it had been made in bad faith. On appeal the Washington Court of Appeals stated that "prior cases . . . have not precisely differentiated the good faith requirement . . . of fair consideration [in UFCA section 3] from the actual intent to defraud requirement of [UFCA section 7]." *Id.* at 346, 481 P.2d at 589. The court then set forth a number of factors to be considered in determining good faith: 1) honest belief in the propriety of the activities in question; 2) no intent to take unconscionable advantage of others; and 3) no intent to, or knowledge of the fact that the activities in question will, hinder, delay, or defraud others. *Id.* at 348, 481 P.2d at 591. Where "any one of these factors is absent, lack of good faith is established and the conveyance fails." *Id. See also Wells Fargo Bank v. Desert View Bldg. Supplies, Inc.*, 475 F. Supp. 693, 696–97 (D. Nev. 1978) (lender lacked good faith when exchanging its securities for preexisting loans in context of an impending bankruptcy), *aff'd mem.*, 633 F.2d 225 (9th Cir. 1980).

We have decided that the district court reached the right conclusion here for the right reasons. It determined that IIT did not act in good faith because it was aware, first, that the exchange would render Raymond insolvent, and second, that no member of the Raymond Group would receive fair consideration. We believe that this determination is consistent with the statute and case law.

McClellan and amicus curiae also argue that as a general rule the UFCA should not be applied to leveraged buy–outs. They contend that the UFCA, which was passed in 1924, was never meant to apply to a complicated transaction such as a leveraged buy–out. The Act's broad language, however, extends to any "conveyance" which is defined as "every payment of money . . . and also the creation of any lien or incumbrance." 39 Pa. Stat. § 351. This broad sweep does not justify exclusion of a particular transaction such as a leveraged buy–out simply because it is innovative or complicated. If the UFCA is not to be applied to leveraged buy–outs, it should be for the state legislatures, not the courts, to decide.

In addition, although appellants' and amicus curiae's arguments against general application of the Act to leveraged buy–outs are not without some force, the application of fraudulent conveyance law to certain leveraged buyouts is not clearly bad public policy.[2] In any event, the circumstances of this case justify application. Even the policy arguments offered against the application of fraudulent conveyance law to leveraged buy–outs assume facts that are not present in this case. For example, in their analysis of fraudulent conveyance law, Professors Baird and Jackson assert that their analysis should be applied to leveraged buy–outs only where aspects of the transaction are not hidden from creditors and the transaction does not possess other suspicious attributes. *See* Baird and Jackson, *Fraudulent Conveyance Law and Its Proper Domain*, 38 Vand. L. Rev. 829, 843 (1985). In fact, Baird and Jackson conclude their article by noting that their analysis is limited to transactions in which "the transferee parted with value when he entered into the transaction and that transaction was entered in the ordinary course." *Id.* at 855 (footnote omitted). In the instant case, however, the severe economic circumstances in which the Raymond Group found itself, the obligation, without benefit, incurred by the Raymond Group, and the small number of shareholders benefited by the transaction suggest that the transaction was not entered in the ordinary course, that fair consideration was not exchanged, and that the transaction was anything but unsuspicious. The policy arguments set forth in opposition to the application of fraudulent conveyance law to leveraged buy–outs do not justify the exemption of transactions such as this.[3]

IV.

McClellan next argues that under section 359(2) of the UFCA, it is entitled to a lien superior to all other creditors on Raymond's property. Br. for appellants at 27. Once again, review of this issue is plenary. *Universal Minerals*, 669 F.2d at 102.

---

[2] A major premise of the policy arguments opposing application of fraudulent conveyance law to leveraged buy–outs is that such transactions often benefit creditors and that the application of fraudulent conveyance law to buy–outs will deter them in the future. *See* Baird and Jackson, *Fraudulent Conveyance Law and Its Proper Domain*, 38 Vand. L. Rev. 829, 855 (1985). An equally important premise is that creditors can protect themselves from undesirable leveraged buy–outs by altering the terms of their credit contracts. *Id.* at 835. This second premise ignores, however, cases such as this one in which the major creditors (in this instance the United States and certain Pennsylvania municipalities) are involuntary and do not become creditors by virtue of a contract. The second premise also ignores the possibility that the creditors attacking the leveraged buy–out (such as many of the creditors in this case) became creditors before leveraged buy–outs became a common financing technique and thus may not have anticipated such leveraged transactions so as to have been able to adequately protect themselves by contract. These possibilities suggest that Baird and Jackson's broad proscription against application of fraudulent conveyance law to leveraged buy–outs may not be unambiguously correct.

[3] It should also be noted that another basic premise of the Baird and Jackson analysis is that as a general matter fraudulent conveyance law should be applied only to those transactions to which a rational creditor would surely object. Baird and Jackson, at 834. Although a rational creditor might under certain circumstances consent to a risky but potentially beneficial leveraged buy–out of a nearly insolvent debtor, no reasonable creditor would consent to the intentionally fraudulent conveyance the district court correctly found this transaction to be. Thus, the application of fraudulent conveyance law to the instant transaction appears consistent even with Baird and Jackson's analysis.

A.

Section 359 establishes a two–tier system to protect certain purchasers from the effects of the UFCA. Section 359(1) permits a purchaser who has paid "fair consideration without knowledge of the fraud at the time of the purchase" to maintain the conveyance as valid against a creditor. 39 Pa. Stat. § 359(1). Section 359(2) of the Act specifies that a "purchaser who, without actual fraudulent intent, has given less than a fair consideration for the conveyance or obligation may retain the property or obligation as security for repayment." 39 Pa. Stat. § 359(2).

In *Gleneagles II*, the district court found that Pagnotti, who purchased the IIT mortgages for $4,047,786 and transferred them to McClellan Realty, was not entitled to protection under section 359(1). The court determined that although Pagnotti had given a "fair equivalent" for the IIT mortgages, it did not do so without knowledge of the fraud at the time of the purchase. 571 F. Supp. at 952.

In *Gleneagles III*, the district court concluded that McClellan, Pagnotti's assignee, was not entitled to the partial protection of section 359(2). The court stated that although it had found in *Gleneagles II* that Pagnotti had not acted in good faith in acquiring the IIT mortgages, this was not equivalent to a finding that Pagnotti had given "less than fair consideration." 584 F. Supp. at 682. The court, however, also implied that notwithstanding its finding that Pagnotti had not acted with "actual fraudulent intent," it had not "purchased the IIT mortgages in good faith." *Id.* The court ruled that good faith is at least required to merit protection under section 359(2). The court therefore found that Pagnotti was not entitled to such protection. *Id.*

McClellan faults this reasoning with an argument that, at least facially, seems persuasive. It argues that the district court's finding that Pagnotti acted with knowledge of the fraud means that Pagnotti acted without good faith and therefore paid "less than fair consideration" as defined by section 353 of the Act. Therefore, McClellan reasons, absent a finding of "actual fraudulent intent," it is entitled to protection under section 359(2).

Admittedly, section 359(2) is inartfully drafted and a literal reading of the section could conceivably command this result. We believe, however, that the public policy behind the UFCA compels a different interpretation. The Act protects both *purchasers* and *third parties*. We see a distinction here. The Act protects those *purchasers*, who, without actual fraudulent intent and without a lack of good faith, have paid less than a fair equivalent for the property received. Conversely, the Act does not protect purchases having a fraudulent intent or a lack of good faith. We are not satisfied that the UFCA affords third parties greater protection than purchasers. The purposes of the Act would be nullified if third parties who in bad faith paid less than a fair equivalent could take the property in a better position than an original purchaser who at the outset had engaged in a fraudulent transfer. *See e.g., Dealers Discount Corp. v. Vantar Properties, Inc.*, 45 Misc. 2d 49, 50, 256 N.Y.S.2d 257, 259 (1964).

We are most uneasy with an interpretation that would deny rights to the purchaser, Pagnotti, but confer them on its assignee, McClellan. Such a literal reading of the statute's language would require us to ignore the statute's purpose. We are reminded of Judge Roger J. Traynor's advice, "We need literate, not literal judges."

B.

Moreover, we find support in analogizing to the federal bankruptcy laws. Section 548(c) of the Bankruptcy Code — the successor to section 67(d)(6) of the Bankruptcy Act — provides that a transferee or obligee of a fraudulent transfer or obligation who takes for value and in good faith may retain the interest transferred or the obligation incurred. 11 U.S.C. § 548(c).[4] This section of the Bankruptcy Code thus closely tracks section 359(2) of the UFCA. Indeed, bankruptcy's leading commentator explains that: "The major similarity between the Bankruptcy Code and the UFCA is reflected in the portion of subsection [548(c)] that permits the good faith transferee or obligee to retain his lien." 4 Collier on Bankruptcy ¶ 548.07, at 548–65 (15th ed. 1986). McClellan acknowledges that "[t]he fraudulent conveyance provisions of the Code are modeled on the UFCA, and uniform interpretation of the two statutes [is] essential to promote commerce nationally. *Cohen v. Sutherland*, 257 F.2d 737, 741 (2d Cir. 1958). . . ." Br. for appellants at 29.

In two cases similar to the one at bar, courts have denied protection to lenders under section 67(d) of the Bankruptcy Act because, although their conduct was not intentionally fraudulent, the lenders exhibited a lack of good faith. *In re Allied Development Corp.*, 435 F.2d 372, 376 (7th Cir. 1970); *In re Venie*, 80 F. Supp. 250, 256 (W.D. Mo. 1948). The same principles should apply here to deny protection to Pagnotti where the record supports the district court's findings that Pagnotti lacked good faith. *See The Uniform Fraudulent Conveyance Act in Pennsylvania*, 5 U. Pitt. L. Rev. 161, 186 (1939) (Section 359(2) language "without actual fraudulent intent" should mean without knowledge).

C.

McClellan next challenges the district court's finding that as Pagnotti's assignee, it too, lacked good faith, and therefore was disqualified from protection under the Act. McClellan states that "[t]he District Court never suggests, much less finds, that McClellan's dealings with IIT concerning its purchase of the mortgages were anything but at arms–length." Br. for appellants at 25. The district court's determination that McClellan lacked good faith is a factual finding reviewed on the clearly erroneous standard. *Krasnov v. Dinan*, 465 F.2d 1298, 1299–1300 (3d Cir. 1972).

Although McClellan attempts to distance itself from Pagnotti, the party that purchased the mortgages from IIT and assigned them to McClellan, it cannot do this successfully. A well–recognized rule provides that an assignee gets only those rights held by its assignor and no more. The district court clearly held that Pagnotti did not obtain the mortgages in good faith. *Gleneagles II*, 571 F. Supp. at 952. The court supported its findings with facts from the record. *See id.* at 952–56. Because McClellan's rights as an assignee are no greater than Pagnotti's and because

---

[4] "Fair consideration" is defined under Section 353 of the Bankruptcy Code as an exchange of fair equivalents in good faith.

McClellan does not show how the district court's finding of Pagnotti's lack of good faith was clearly erroneous, McClellan is charged with the same quality of faith.[5]

D.

McClellan also presents two arguments that relate to the amount of recovery by the creditors. It argues first that it is entitled to credit for $6.1 million that Raymond shareholders Gillen and Cleveland paid to the creditors and the Commonwealth in settlement of prior actions against those shareholders. The district court found that:

> The Creditors have claimed in this litigation that the Gillen and Cleveland Defendants are liable for sales of Raymond Group assets made after November 26, 1973 to satisfy the Raymond Group's debt to IIT and others. There is no basis for this Court to apply the $6,100,000 paid by the Gillens and Clevelands to particular injuries suffered by the Creditors as the result of the fraudulent conveyances. Moreover, the settlement agreements provided that the monies paid were also in settlement of other lawsuits by the Creditors and the Commonwealth against the Gillens and Clevelands. There is no basis on the present record for a conclusion by this Court that the $6,100,000 paid by the Gillens and Clevelands pursuant to the settlement agreements was intended solely to compensate the Creditors and the Commonwealth for damages flowing from the Gillens' and Clevelands' acceptance of the IIT loan proceeds on November 26, 1973.

Gleneagles III, 584 F. Supp. at 682.

We agree. The settlement agreement terms are very specific. The United States agreed to release the "Cleveland Group" from all claims. The agreement defined the Cleveland Group as: "Robert W. Cleveland and Sons, Inc., William T. Kirchoff, Jay W. Cleveland and the Estate of Royal E. Cleveland, as well as any members of either the Robert W. or Royal E. Cleveland families against whom claims by the creditors might be asserted." App. at 480. None of these individuals or entities are currently parties to this action. Any effort by the remaining defendants to come within, or to benefit from, the settlement agreement is clearly not justified by the terms thereof. *See* app. at 479–84.

---

[5] McClellan also argues that under section 359(3), no duty was imposed on it, or its assignor, Pagnotti, to make an inquiry into the circumstances of the sale. Section 359(3) provides that:

> (3) Knowledge that a conveyance has been made as a gift or for nominal consideration shall not by itself be deemed to be knowledge that the conveyance was a fraud on any creditor of the grantor, or impose any duty on the person purchasing the property from the grantee to make inquiry as to whether such conveyance was or was not a fraud on any such creditor.

39 Pa. Cons. Stat. § 359(3). However, Pagnotti's knowledge went far beyond mere knowledge "that a conveyance has been made as a gift or for nominal consideration." *See Gleneagles II*, 571 F. Supp. at 952–58.

E.

McClellan next contends that the district court erred in not crediting McClellan for that portion of the IIT loan that was not passed through to Raymond's shareholders: although "the District Court acknowledged that $2,915,000, or approximately 42 percent, of the IIT loan proceeds originally went for the benefit of . . . creditors, IIT and McClellan received no credit therefor in regard to the partial validity of their liens." Br. for appellants at 28. McClellan argues that the district court determined that "[t]he wrong committed upon the creditors . . . [was] the diversion of some 58 percent of the loan proceeds from the IIT loan to [Raymond's] shareholders." *Id.* at 29. It concludes that to invalidate the entire mortgage would be to provide Raymond's creditors with a "double recovery." *Id.* at 28. We understand the dissent to agree with McClellan's analysis when noting that " 'creditors have causes of action in fraudulent conveyance law only to the extent they have been damaged.' " Dissenting typescript at 1307 (citations omitted).

McClellan and, by implication, the dissent mischaracterize the district court's findings and conclusions regarding the fraudulent nature of the IIT loans. The district court did not determine that the loan transaction was only partially — or, to use McClellan's formulation, 58% — fraudulent. Nor did the district court conclude that Raymond's creditors had been wronged by only a portion of the transaction. Instead, the district court stated that:

> McClellan Realty's argument rests on the incorrect assumption that some portions of the IIT mortgages are valid as against the Creditors. In *Gleneagles I*, 565 F. Supp. at 580, 586, this Court found that IIT and Durkin engaged in an intentionally fraudulent transaction on November 26, 1973. The IIT mortgages are therefore invalid in their entirety as to creditors.

Gleneagles III, 584 F. Supp. at 683. In essence, the district court ruled that the *aggregate* transaction was fraudulent, notwithstanding the fact that a portion of the loan proceeds was allegedly used to pay existing creditors.

This determination is bolstered by the fact that most of the $2,915,000 allegedly paid to the benefit of Raymond's creditors went to only one creditor — Chemical Bank. In *Gleneagles I*, the district court found that $2,186,247 of the IIT loan proceeds were paid to Chemical Bank in satisfaction of the mortgage that Raymond had taken to purchase Blue Coal (a Raymond subsidiary). *See* 565 F. Supp. at 570, 571 (findings 132(k) and 140). The purpose of this payment is of critical significance:

> The Gillens and the Clevelands [Raymond's shareholders] required satisfaction of the Chemical Bank mortgage as a condition of sale of their Raymond Colliery stock at least in part because Royal Cleveland had personally guaranteed repayment of that loan.

Id. at 571 (finding 141). McClellan does not challenge this finding on appeal. Thus, of the $2.9 million allegedly paid to benefit Raymond's creditors, $2.2 million were actually intended to benefit Raymond's shareholders and to satisfy a condition for the sale. The remaining amounts allegedly paid to benefit Raymond's creditors were applied to the closing costs of the transaction. *See id.* at 570 (finding 133).

On this record, the district court's characterization of the transaction as a whole as fraudulent cannot reasonably be disputed. The court's consequent determination that the "IIT mortgages are . . . invalid in their entirety as to creditors" is supported by precedent. *See Newman v. First National Bank*, 76 F.2d 347, 350–51 (3d Cir. 1935).[6]

Moreover, as the district court correctly noted, it sits in equity when fashioning relief under the UFCA. *Gleneagles III*, 584 F. Supp. at 682. Consequently, our review of the district court's action is severely limited. *Evans v. Buchanan*, 555 F.2d 373, 378 (3d Cir. 1977), *cert. denied*, 434 U.S. 880, 98 S. Ct. 235, 54 L. Ed. 2d 306 (1977).

The district court determined that "[t]he Creditors . . . would not be placed in the same or similar position which they held with respect to the Raymond Group in 1973 merely by replacing the $4,085,000 of IIT loan proceeds that were misused on November 26, 1973." *Gleneagles III*, 584 F. Supp. at 681. We agree with the district court and are persuaded that this court's decision in *Newman* controls. In *Newman* we held that where a creditor was prevented from recovering on its judgment as a result of a fraudulent scheme between the debtor and another creditor, a judgment obtained by the defrauding creditor was totally void. We stated that "[i]f we extract from the fraudulent actors every advantage which they derived from their fraud and restore the creditor to the position which lawfully belonged to it at the time the fraud was perpetrated and give it all rights which, but for the fraud, it had under the law, we feel that equity would adequately be done." *Id.* at 350. Here, the district court found that only by voiding the entire amount could the creditors be placed in the same position they held before the November 26, 1973 misuse of the loans. To the extent that this determination was based on facts, we do not view them as clearly erroneous; to the extent the conclusion was based on law, we find no error. Consequently, we do not believe that the district court's equitable remedy was "arbitrary, fanciful, or unreasonable," or the product of "improper standards, criteria, or procedures." *Evans*, 555 F.2d at 378.

For the above reasons, therefore, we will not disturb the district court's determination that McClellan is not entitled to a "lien superior to all other creditors" as the assignee of all or part of the IIT mortgages.[7]

---

[6] On broadly analogous facts, the *Newman* court found that a defendant bank's fraudulent conduct rendered its judgment against a debtor "wholly void":

> Therefore, the whole of it should be set aside. Setting aside only the more vicious part (the $3,500 sham loan) is not enough. *It was the act of the Bank in obtaining the judgment by fraud not the amount of the judgment that defeated the [creditor] recovering on its judgment.*

Newman v. First National Bank, 76 F.2d 347, 350–51 (3d Cir. 1935) (emphasis added).

[7] Moreover, even if we were to adopt the analysis of McClellan and the dissent and accept the argument that the IIT mortgages should not be invalidated to the extent that the loan proceeds benefitted Raymond's creditors, we would not conclude that only $4,085,000 of the mortgages should be set aside. McClellan and the dissent apportion the IIT loan proceeds into three categories: $4,085,000 conveyed to Raymond shareholders; $1,530,000 retained by IIT as interest reserve; and $2,915,000 used to pay existing creditors. McClellan and the

V.

McClellan, joined by the amicus, next argues that the district court erred "by collapsing two separate loans into one transaction." Br. for appellants at 30. The loan arrangement was a two–part process: the loan proceeds went from IIT to the borrowing Raymond Group companies, which immediately turned the funds over to Great American, which used the funds for the buy–out. McClellan contends that the district court erred by not passing on the fairness of the transaction between IIT and the Raymond Group mortgagors. Review of this issue is plenary. *Universal Minerals*, 669 F.2d at 102.

Contrary to McClellan's contentions, the district court did examine this element of the transaction, stating: "[W]e find that the obligations incurred by the Raymond Group and its individual members to IIT were not supported by fair consideration. The mortgages and guarantee mortgages to secure these obligations were *also* not supported by fair consideration." *Gleneagles I*, 565 F. Supp. at 577 (emphasis supplied).

Admittedly, in the course of its determination that the IIT–Raymond Group transaction was without fair consideration under section 353(a), the court looked beyond the exchange of funds between IIT and the Raymond Group. But there was reason for this. The two exchanges were part of one integrated transaction. As the court concluded: "[t]he $4,085,000 in IIT loan proceeds which were lent immediately by the borrowing companies to Great American were merely passed through the borrowers to Great American and ultimately to the selling stockholders and cannot be deemed consideration received by the borrowing companies." *Id.* at 575.

The district court's factual findings support its treatment of the IIT–Raymond Group–Great American transaction as a single transaction. For example, Durkin, president of Great American, solicited financing from IIT for the purchase. *Id.* at 566 (finding 70). The loan negotiations included representatives of all three parties. *Id.* at 567 (findings 83–87). The first closing was aborted by IIT's counsel because of, *inter alia*, concern about "unknown individuals" involved with Great American. *Id.* at 567–68 (finding 89(a)). The $7 million loaned by IIT to the borrowing companies was "immediately placed in an escrow account"; "simultaneously" with the receipt of the IIT proceeds, the borrowing companies loaned Great American the

---

dissent concede at least for the purposes of argument that $4,085,000 was fraudulently conveyed; they contend that the other amounts benefitted Raymond's creditors. To the extent that the $1,530,000 interest reserve was applied to that portion of the loan that passed to Raymond's shareholders, however, it did not benefit Raymond's creditors. Thus, even under McClellan's and the dissent's analysis, *some* portion (*e.g.*, 58%) of the IIT mortgages used to fund the $1,530,000 million interest reserve should be invalidated. In addition, McClellan and the dissent ignore the implications of the fact that most of the $2,915,000 allegedly paid to the benefit of Raymond's creditors went to Chemical Bank. *See infra*, at 1302.

Finally, it must be remembered that IIT recovered over $4.5 million of its loans through repayments from the Raymond Group companies. *Gleneagles III*, 584 F. Supp. at 683. We agree with the district court that, "even assuming that a valid portion of the IIT mortgages originally existed, that portion was extinguished by the payments on the debt in excess of that portion made by the mortgagors before the assignment of the IIT mortgages." *Id.*

cash for the buy–out and received in return "an unsecured note promising to repay the loans to the borrowing companies on the same terms and at the same interest rate as pertained to the loans to the borrowing companies from IIT." *Id.* at 570 (findings 127–29).

Appellant cannot seriously challenge these findings of fact. We are satisfied with the district court's conclusion that the funds "merely passed through the borrowers to Great American." This necessitates our agreement with the district court's conclusion that, for purposes of determining IIT's knowledge of the use of the proceeds under section 353(a), there was one integral transaction.[8]

VI.

McClellan next faults the district court's determination that the Raymond Group was rendered insolvent by "the IIT transaction and the instantaneous payment to the selling stockholders of a substantial portion of the IIT loan in exchange for their stock." *Gleneagles I*, 565 F. Supp. at 580. McClellan disputes the method of computation used by the district court. The question of insolvency is a mixed question of law and fact. Our review of the legal portions of the issue is plenary, while review of the factual portion is according to the clearly erroneous standard. *Universal Minerals*, 669 F.2d at 102.

A.

Section 352 of the UFCA defines insolvency as "when the present, fair, salable value of [a person's] assets is less than the amount that will be required to pay his probable liability on his existing debts as they become absolute and matured." 39 Pa. Stat. § 352(1). As heretofore stated, the district court calculated the Raymond Group's existing debts as "at least $20,000,000 on November 26, 1973." *Gleneagles I*, 565 F. Supp. at 578. The court then compared Raymond's debt to the "present, fair, salable value" of its assets and found the Group insolvent. *Id.* at 578–80. In doing so, the court relied on *Larrimer v. Feeney*, where the Pennsylvania Supreme Court stated:

> A reasonable construction of the . . . statutory definition of insolvency indicates that it not only encompasses insolvency in the bankruptcy sense *i.e.* a deficit net worth, but also includes a condition wherein a debtor has insufficient presently salable assets to pay existing debts as they mature. If a debtor has a deficit net worth, then the present salable value of his assets must be less than the amount required to pay the liability on his debts as they mature. A debtor may have substantial paper net worth including assets which have a small salable value, but which if held to a subsequent date could have a much higher salable value. Nevertheless, *if the present salable value of [his] assets*

---

8 Admittedly, McClellan's and amicus' arguments could have some validity where the lender is unaware of the use to which loans proceeds are to be put. That is not the case here. IIT was intimately involved with the formulation of the agreement whereby the proceeds of its loan were funnelled into the hands of the purchasers of the stock of a corporation that was near insolvency. Try as they might to distance themselves from the transaction now, they cannot rewrite history.

[is] less than the amount required to pay existing debts as they mature the debtor is insolvent.

411 Pa. 604, 608, 192 A.2d 351, 353 (1963) (emphasis supplied, citation omitted). Guided by this teaching, the court found that: (1) the Raymond Group's coal production, which had been unprofitable since 1969, "could not produce a sufficient cash flow to pay the company's obligations in a timely manner"; (2) the sale of the Raymond Group's surplus lands, which had provided a substantial cash flow, was "abruptly cut off" by the terms of the IIT agreement; and (3) sale of its equipment could not generate adequate cash to meet Raymond's existing debts as they matured. *Gleneagles I*, 565 F. Supp. at 579–80. These determinations are the factual components of the insolvency finding; McClellan contends that at least one of the findings is clearly erroneous.

B.

McClellan challenges the second of these determinations, arguing that under Montana and New York law, "[p]roper application of § 352(1) requires the valuation of an asset at its *present value*, provided it can be liquidated within a reasonably immediate period of time — not its value if liquidated immediately." Br. for appellants at 37 (citing *Duncan v. Landis*, 106 F. 839 (3d Cir. 1901); *In re Crystal Ice & Fuel Co.*, 283 F. 1007 (D. Mont. 1922); *Tumarkin v. Gallay*, 127 F. Supp. 94 (S.D.N.Y. 1954)). McClellan argues that the court's characterization of "Raymond Group's vast lands, culm banks, and coal reserves [as] . . . highly illiquid assets which could not be sold except over an extended period of time," 565 F. Supp. at 579, was clearly erroneous. However, the court did not disregard the potential of these lands. It applied the *Larrimer* criteria of Pennsylvania, not those of Montana or New York. It held that sale of these lands would have been insufficient to meet Raymond's debts as they matured:

> [The] cash flow [from land sales] was abruptly cut off by the IIT agreement which provided that, for the land sales which occurred in 1974 and 1975, IIT would receive a total of $1,832,500 of the first $2,500,000 of land sale proceeds received by the Raymond Group. The remaining proceeds of $667,500 would be placed by IIT in a "funded reserve" and would be used to pay the Raymond Group's creditors. However, if the lands were taxed as ordinary income to the Raymond Group, which was exceedingly likely and in fact came to pass, each land sale would result in a cash loss to the Raymond Group as the amount of federal taxes due would exceed the funds allocated to the "funded reserve" from that sale. Moreover, no cash would be available for creditors other than IIT, the Ford Motor Credit Co. and Thrift Credit from the sale of surplus lands. Thus, the cash that could be generated by the operation of the Raymond Group's business was grossly insufficient to meet its obligations.

Id. We conclude that McClellan has not demonstrated that this finding was clearly erroneous. We are satisfied that the district court followed the guidance of Pennsylvania courts in analyzing the Raymond Group's insolvency. Its application of the law was not in error, nor were its factual determinations clearly erroneous.

VII.

McClellan next argues that the district court erred in holding that the mortgages were invalid under section 357 of the UFCA, 39 Pa. Stat. § 357. Review of this issue is plenary. *Universal Minerals*, 669 F.2d at 102.

As distinguished from the "constructive fraud" sections of the UFCA discussed *supra*, section 357 invalidates conveyances made with an intent to defraud creditors: "Every conveyance made and every obligation incurred with actual intent, as distinguished from intent presumed in law, to hinder, delay, or defraud either present or future creditors, is fraudulent as to both present and future creditors." 39 Pa. Const. Stat. § 357. Under Pennsylvania law, an intent to hinder, delay, or defraud creditors may be inferred from transfers in which consideration is lacking and where the transferor and transferee have knowledge of the claims or creditors and know that the creditors cannot be paid. *Godina v. Oswald*, 206 Pa. Super. 51, 55, 211 A.2d 91, 93 (1965). Direct evidence is not necessary to prove "actual intent." *Continental Bank v. Marcus*, 242 Pa. Super. 371, 377, 363 A.2d 1318, 1321 (1976). In Pennsylvania, the existence of actual intent is a question of fact, *Golder v. Bogash*, 325 Pa. 449, 452, 188 A. 837, 838 (1937); therefore, the court's determination is reviewed on the clearly erroneous standard. *Krasnov v. Dinan*, 465 F.2d 1298, 1299–1300 (3d Cir. 1972).

A.

The evidence recited by the district court supports its finding of an intent to hinder creditors. McClellan does not challenge the sufficiency of this evidence, but rather its application, arguing that from this evidence the court inferred intent, and that inferences and presumptions are proscribed by section 357. The argument was rejected by the Pennsylvania courts in *Godina v. Oswald*, 206 Pa. Super. 51, 211 A.2d 91 (1965). There, the court ruled that " '[s]ince fraud is usually denied, it must be inferred from all facts and circumstances surrounding the conveyance, including subsequent conduct.' " *Id.* at 55, 211 A.2d at 93 (quoting *Sheffit v. Koff*, 175 Pa. Super. 37, 41, 100 A.2d 393, 395 (1953)). This is precisely what the district court did here. *See Gleneagles I*, 565 F. Supp. at 580–83.

B.

Appellant also objects to the district court's statement that "[i]f the parties could have foreseen the effect on creditors resulting from the assumption of the IIT obligation by the Raymond Group . . . the parties must be deemed to have intended the same." 565 F. Supp. at 581. McClellan argues that the court erred in applying the concept of foreseeability, an issue only relevant to negligence. This presents a slightly more troublesome question, because we believe that one of the cases cited by the district court does not support the challenged statement. *See Chorost v. Grand Rapids Factory Show Rooms, Inc.*, 172 F.2d 327, 329 (3d Cir. 1949) (actual fraud may be found on the basis of circumstantial evidence notwithstanding willful ignorance of defrauding parties). We do find support, however, in *In re Process–Manz Press, Inc.*, 236 F. Supp. 333 (N.D. Ill. 1964), also cited by the district court. That case does not address foreseeability, but relies on the proposition that a party is deemed to have intended the natural consequences of his acts. *Id.* at 347. We are satisfied that this principle supports the district court's conclusion.[9]

C.

We conclude that the court's finding on intent was not clearly erroneous.

VIII.

Finally, McClellan challenges the district court's invalidation of the guarantee mortgages. The district court invalidated these mortgages because the guarantors did not receive fair consideration. 565 F. Supp. at 577.

McClellan, relying on *Telefast, Inc. v. VU–TV, Inc.* 591 F. Supp. 1368 (D. N.J. 1984), argues that the guarantors were so closely associated with the borrower companies that they received sufficient indirect consideration from the benefits to the borrowing companies. In *Telefast*, however, the existence of fair consideration was undisputed. *See id.* at 1370. The court held that the cross–collateral guarantor company also benefitted from the fair consideration provided to the borrowers. *Id.* at 1378–79. The consideration in the underlying transaction here, however, was determined to be deficient. Any indirect benefit to guarantor companies deriving from that consideration would, *a fortiori*, also be deficient. The district court did not err in so holding.

IX.

We now turn to the cross appeals.

A.

The government argues that the district court erred in finding that Pagnotti, who had paid real estate taxes prior to the Lackawanna and Luzerne County tax sales, is entitled to an equitable lien for the municipal taxes that it paid. During the litigation the parties stipulated that the purported county tax sales were invalid, and that ownership based on the tax sales was invalid. The district court reasoned that:

> Raymond Colliery's Commonwealth and pre–1974 real estate taxes were first liens on the lands of Raymond Colliery and were paid by L. Robert Lieb when the Pagnotti Defendants were neither owners of the land nor owners of the IIT mortgages. Because of this Court's conclusion in *Gleneagles II* that the 1976 tax sale was invalid, the 1976 Tabor Court bid on the lands of Raymond Colliery was tantamount to a payment of Raymond Colliery's real estate taxes and likewise was also a payment made before the Pagnotti Defendants owned the lands of Raymond Colliery or the IIT mortgages. These tax payments discharged liens on the lands of Raymond Colliery which were ahead of those claimed by the United States. Equitably, the Pagnotti Defendants should now receive a lien position reflecting these tax payments ahead of the lien position accorded the United States. Likewise, because the above tax payments by the

---

[9] Furthermore, even if the error were not harmless, it would not effect the outcome because the court's conclusion that the transfer violated the constructive fraud provision of section 354 was correct. A section 357 violation is cumulative only.

Pagnotti Defendants discharged liens ahead of the liens claimed in this litigation by the various counties and other municipalities, the Pagnotti Defendants should receive liens reflecting the tax payments ahead of those lienors.

. . . [T]he April 1977 payment to the City of Scranton should be treated in the same manner as the 1976 tax sale bid.

Gleneagles III, 584 F. Supp. at 685.

When fashioning equitable relief, such as here, a court acts with broad discretion. *Lacks v. Fahmi*, 623 F.2d 254, 256 (2d Cir. 1980). We therefore review the district court's decision to grant an equitable lien for abuse of discretion, which "exists only when the judicial action is arbitrary, fanciful, or unreasonable, or when improper standards, criteria, or procedures are used." *Evans v. Buchanan*, 555 F.2d 373, 378 (3d Cir. 1977), *cert. denied*, 434 U.S. 880, 98 S. Ct. 235, 54 L. Ed. 2d 160 (1977).

In *Newman v. First National Bank*, 76 F.2d 347 (3d Cir. 1935), we held that even a grantee guilty of international fraud was entitled to be paid, prior to other creditors, from the sale proceeds of the subject property for the amount of taxes the grantee had paid as owner of the subject property. *Id.* at 351. The district court found that the taxes for which payments were made, both prior to and at the 1976 tax sale, constituted prior liens for taxes or the upset price (past due taxes) owing against the parcels of land which were the subject of the 1976 tax sale. *Gleneagles II*, 571 F. Supp. at 947–49 (findings 166, 188, 190). These findings are not challenged. Based on *Newman*, the district court did not act in an "arbitrary, fanciful, or unreasonable" manner in granting McClellan an equitable lien for the taxes it paid on Raymond property, prior to the liens of other creditors.

B.

The United States and cross–appellant trustee in bankruptcy for two major Raymond Group companies, Blue Coal Corporation and Glen Nan, complain that the court erred by awarding McClellan a place on the creditors' list as assignee of the IIT mortgages, albeit number 16 in a list of 17 liens. The court determined that this priority lien reflected $17,319,326.58, the amount claimed by McClellan to be due on the direct mortgages assigned by IIT to it, including principal and interest. *Gleneagles III*, 584 F. Supp. at 688. *See also id.* at 678 (finding 462). Cross appellants argue that under section 9–504 of the Pennsylvania Uniform Commercial Code, the IIT mortgages should be invalidated in their entirety and that McClellan is entitled to no recognition in the order of liens. Review of this issue is plenary. *Universal Minerals, Inc.*, 669 F.2d at 102.

The Uniform Commercial Code confers upon a secured party the right, upon default, to dispose of collateral by sale or lease, subject to the requirement that "every aspect of the disposition including the method, manner, time, place and terms must be commercially reasonable." 13 Pa. Con. Stat. § 9504. When a private sale of repossessed collateral has been made, and the debtor raises the question of the commercial reasonableness of that sale, the great weight of authority holds that the burden of proof is shifted to the secured party seeking a deficiency judgment to show that, under the totality of circumstances, the disposition of collateral was commercially reasonable. *United States v. Willis*, 593 F.2d 247, 258 (6th Cir. 1979); *see* cases collected in 59 A.L.R.3d, 378–80 (1974) (reasonableness of disposition of collateral); 69 Am. Jur. 2d *Secured Transactions* § 623, pp. 530–31 (1973). Here the district court found that the McClellan's foreclosure sales of Raymond's assets were commercially unreasonable. *Gleneagles III*, 584 F. Supp. at 690 (conclusion 37).

When there has been a commercially unreasonable disposition of collateral, the effect of that disposition upon a creditor's entitlement to recovery of remaining debt must be considered. Pennsylvania courts have held that "failure to establish commercial reasonableness of the resale price creates a presumption that the value of the collateral equaled the indebtedness secured, thereby extinguishing the indebtedness unless the secured party rebuts the presumption." *Savoy v. Beneficial Consumer Discount Co.*, 503 Pa. 74, 78, 468 A.2d 465, 467 (1983).

Cross appellants argue, and McClellan does not dispute, that McClellan failed to produce any evidence regarding the value of the property sold in its foreclosure sales of Raymond's assets to rebut the *Savoy* presumption. It will be remembered that at a private sale McClellan sold certain Raymond assets to Loree Associates for $50,000 and all of the Raymond's stock to Joseph Solfanelli, as trustee for Pagnotti, for $1. *Gleneagles III*, 584 F. Supp. at 676 (findings 429–30). McClellan responds that the UCC is not intended to have a punitive effect and that consequently "[t]he rebuttable presumption rule is inapplicable here for it is not appropriate or fair to impose such a drastic, punitive measure upon McClellan." Reply Br. for appellants at 24.

We nevertheless believe that *Savoy* controls. There the creditor had failed to rebut the presumption, absent evidence of the value of the collateral, that the value of the collateral sold equals the indebtedness. The *Savoy* trial court took judicial notice of the market value of the collateral, but on appeal the Pennsylvania Supreme Court adopted a strict interpretation of the statute and invalidated the creditor's lien *in toto*: "[Creditor's] entitlement to a deficiency judgment has been extinguished by its failure to rebut the presumption as to the value of the collateral." 503 Pa. at 79–80, 468 A.2d at 468. Because the district court found McClellan's sale of the Raymond collateral commercially unreasonable, *Savoy* requires that we reverse the district court's decision in *Gleneagles III* to the extent that it recognizes McClellan's status as a creditor as against the trustee in bankruptcy. To the extent that the district court recognized a mortgage lien, *see* 584 F. Supp. at 688, as distinguished from an equitable lien representing county tax payment, the district court erred in failing to invalidate the mortgage lien completely.

X.

We have carefully considered all the contentions of appellants and cross appellants. The judgment of the district court will be affirmed in all respects, except we will vacate that portion of § 4 of the final order and judgment, app. at 173, relating to the McClellan mortgage lien set forth as Number 16 in priority, *see* 584 F. Supp. at 688, and remand these proceedings with a direction that an order be entered declaring void the assigned IIT mortgages and other security instruments of McClellan as against the trustee in bankruptcy and further declaring that as to the trustee, McClellan possesses no rights as a creditor with respect to the putative assignment of the IIT mortgages.

A. LEON HIGGINBOTHAM, JR., Circuit Judge, concurring in part and dissenting in part.

I concur in the majority's judgment that Pennsylvania's fraudulent conveyance laws may be applied to a leveraged buyout where, as here, a few shareholders seek to use it as a device to benefit themselves and take advantage of the creditors of a clearly faltering corporation. Since I find that the purposes underlying Pennsylvania's fraudulent conveyance law dictate that only a portion of the disputed transfer of funds be set aside, however, I must dissent from that part of the majority's opinion which declares the IIT mortgage loans wholly void.

The basic objective of fraudulent conveyance law is to preserve estates and to prevent them from being wrongfully drained of assets. *See Melamed v. Lake County National Bank*, 727 F.2d 1399, 1401 (6th Cir. 1984). Fraudulent conveyance law is not intended to add to estates for the unjustified benefit of creditors. In fact, "creditors have causes of action in fraudulent conveyance law only to the extent they have been damaged." *A/S Kreditt–Finans v. Cia Venetico–De Navegacion*, 560 F. Supp. 705, 711 (E.D. Pa. 1983), *aff'd*, 729 F.2d 1446 (3d Cir. 1984). IIT made four separate loans totalling $8,530,000. Of this, $4,085,000 was passed through Raymond Group companies to shareholders and $1,530,000 was retained by IIT as an interest reserve as part of the invalid transaction. However, $2,915,000 was used to pay existing debts (including an existing mortgage loan owned by Chemical Bank). To the extent that the IIT funds were used to pay existing creditors, the assets available to creditors generally were not diminished and the Raymond Group's estate was not improperly depleted. I would therefore hold that only the transfer of the $4,085,000 between IIT and the Raymond Group's shareholders and the creation of the $1,530,000 interest reserve for IIT should be set aside.

MELLON BANK, N.A., Appellant

v.

METRO COMMUNICATIONS, INC.

v.

The COMMITTEE OF UNSECURED CREDITORS

United States Court of Appeals, Third Circuit
945 F.2d 635 (1991)

ROSENN, Circuit Judge.

This appeal, arising in the context of a failed leveraged buyout, had its roots in the congenial climate of mergers and acquisitions that beguiled corporate America during the decade of the nineteen–eighties. The appeal raised important questions regarding a bankruptcy trustee's avoidance powers under 11 U.S.C. §§ 547(b) and

548(a)(2) of the bankruptcy code. The debtor is Metro Communications (Metro), the corporation acquired in the leveraged buyout. Mellon Bank, N.A. (Mellon or Bank) financed the acquisition; Mellon lent the acquiror 1.85 million dollars to purchase all of the capital stock of the target corporation, Metro. Metro guaranteed and secured the acquisition loan with substantially all of its assets. Simultaneously with the leveraged buyout, Mellon extended a 2.3 million dollar credit line to Metro. At a later date, Mellon extended another 2.25 million dollars to Metro in the form of letters of credit. These loans were also collateralized by the security interest in substantially all of Metro's assets. Within a year of the leveraged buyout, Metro filed a bankruptcy petition under chapter 11.

The bankruptcy court held that Metro's guaranty of the acquisition loan and the execution of a security interest in connection therewith constituted a fraudulent conveyance under 11 U.S.C. § 548(a)(2). We reverse.

I.

Metro Communications, also known as Metrosports, the debtor, had been in the business of television and radio sports syndication for about ten years prior to its bankruptcy. Metro, incorporated in Maryland in 1972, originally had its headquarters in Rockville, Maryland. Its business included acquiring the rights to broadcast sporting events, contracting with radio and television stations for such broadcasts, and selling rights to advertise during the broadcasts.

In April of 1984, Metro's stockholders sold all of their capital stock to Total Communications, Inc. (TCI), a wholly owned subsidiary of Total Communication Systems Co. (TCS). The principals of TCI created it solely for the purpose of acquiring the stock of Metro and becoming its sole shareholder. TCS, in turn, is the wholly owned subsidiary of Mass Communication and Management, Ltd. (MCM). These affiliated corporations were in the business of syndicating and producing television programs of college athletic events. TCS owned and operated mobile television production studios used in the broadcasting of athletic events nationally.

TCI acquired Metro for the purpose of creating a synergy of complementary services; Metro, as the buyer and seller of broadcasting rights, contracted regularly with companies, such as TCS, to produce and broadcast the athletic events. The two companies, TCS and Metro, developed a joint marketing concept known as TCS/Metro, and issued press releases and other promotional materials which stressed that the companies were working as a joint venture, joining their strengths and "working as a team."

To finance the purchase of the Metro stock, TCI borrowed $1,850,000 from Mellon on April 6, 1984. On the same day, Mellon loaned Metro $2,300,000 for use as working capital under a line of credit agreement. Pursuant to guaranty and suretyship agreements dated April 6, 1984, TCI guaranteed the repayment of the loan to Metro, Metro guaranteed the repayment of the loan to TCI, and TCS and MCM jointly guaranteed the repayment of both loans.

In addition to the guarantees, Metro entered into an agreement dated April 16, 1984, with Mellon Bank wherein Metro conveyed to the Bank a security interest in substantially all of Metro's property, including its general intangibles and accounts receivable. The security agreement provided that the collateral secured "all . . . indebtedness, obligations and liabilities of [Metro] to the Bank, now or hereafter existing, including but not limited to those arising under the Guaranty, and those arising under the Metrosports Loan Agreement."

On September 7, 1984, Metro and Mellon entered into a Letter of Credit Agreement to finance Metro's purchase of broadcast rights for the PAC–10 Conference football season. The Letter of Credit Agreement provided that Mellon's reimbursement rights were secured under the April 6, 1984 security agreement between Mellon and Metro and guaranteed by TCI, TCS, and MCM. Between December 18, 1984 and January 2, 1985, Mellon disbursed the full $2,250,000 face amount of the letters of credit in response to the PAC–10's drawing requests. The following chart summarizes the loans received and guaranties made by Metro:

TRANSACTION	DATE	AMOUNT
Guaranty of Acquisition Loan	4/6/84	$1,850,000
Working Capital Line of Credit	4/6/84	$2,300,000
PAC–10 Letter of Credit	12/18/84	$2,250,000

The Bank perfected its security interests in the collateral pledged by Metro by filing UCC–1 financing statements in the Maryland State Department of Assessment and Taxation on April 9, 1984 and the Clerk's Office of the Circuit Court of Montgomery County, Maryland, on April 17, 1984. The Bank filed additional UCC–1 financing statements in the appropriate offices in Pennsylvania on February 1 to and including February 5, 1985.

On March 12, 1985, PAC–10 filed a complaint against Metro, TCS, and various related entities in the United States District Court for the Northern District of California, alleging breaches of various agreements covering the broadcasting of PAC–10 basketball and football games. Simultaneously with the filing of the complaint, PAC–10 obtained an ex parte order which permitted pre–judgment attachment of Metro's assets. Pursuant to the order, PAC–10 attached certain outstanding accounts receivable of Metro. Three days later, on March 15, 1985, Metro filed a petition for reorganization under Chapter 11 of the Bankruptcy Code.

On January 30, 1986, the Bank filed an adversary proceeding against Metro and PAC–10 to determine the validity, priority, and extent of the Bank's security interest and to ascertain the parties' respective rights in an escrow account which PAC–10 had attempted to attach. The Official Unsecured Creditor's Committee ("the Committee") intervened, claiming that the Bank had received preferential transfers pursuant to 11 U.S.C. § 547(b) and that a fraudulent conveyance had occurred pursuant to 11 U.S.C. § 548(a)(2).

PAC–10, Metro and the Bank have agreed to a settlement of their disputes over the escrow account and have presented their settlement to the bankruptcy court for approval. The bankruptcy court has stated that it will defer ruling on the proposed settlement until this appeal is resolved.

Prior Court Proceedings

After a two–day bench trial, the bankruptcy court on February 10, 1989, filed an opinion and order holding that Metro's guaranty of the acquisition loan and the grant of the security interest was a fraudulent conveyance under 11 U.S.C. § 548(a)(2). *In re Metro Communications, Inc.*, 95 B.R. 921 (Bankr.W.D.Pa.1989). The court ordered the Bank and Metro to file an accounting, showing all amounts subject to disgorgement. In October of 1988, after the bench trial but before the bankruptcy court filed its decision, Mellon assigned all its claims against Metro to Grant Street National Bank (GSNB), which is now in liquidation. On February 17, 1989, counsel for Mellon and GSNB (together, the Banks) filed a motion to amend the February 10, 1989 order under Rule 59(e) of the Federal Rules of Civil Procedure. That motion, filed on behalf of GSNB as successor in interest to Mellon, sought to exclude from the scope of the bankruptcy court's order payments made by Metro to Mellon with respect to loans made directly to Metro from Mellon more than 90 days prior to Metro's bankruptcy filing.

On February 27, 1989, GSNB filed its Notice of Unconditional Assignment of Claim to it by Mellon Bank. The bankruptcy court issued a second order on April 4, 1989, permitting GSNB to intervene in the adversary proceeding as an additional plaintiff and amending its February 10, 1989 order in accordance with the relief requested. On April 10, 1989, the Banks filed their notice of appeal in the district court.

In a third order, dated May 15, 1989, the bankruptcy court expressly directed the entry of a final judgment on its prior order of February 10, 1989, as amended April 4, 1989, and certified it under Fed.R.Civ.P. 54(b) for appeal to the district court, stating that certification was in the interest of fostering a speedy, economical and orderly resolution of the appeal. The Banks filed a supplementary joint notice of appeal within 10 days after the docketing of this May 15 order.

On February 12, 1991, the district court entered an order affirming the bankruptcy court's rulings in all respects except for the award of pre–judgment interest. Mellon and GSNB each appealed to this court; we consolidated the appeals.

II.

C. *Fraudulent Transfer Under Section 548(a)(2)*

The bankruptcy court held that Metro's guaranty and the security interest collateralizing the guaranty of the 1.85 million dollar loan to TCI which was used to buy out Metro's shareholders constituted a fraudulent conveyance under 11 U.S.C. § 548(a)(2). It is unclear whether the bankruptcy court meant this to be an alternative holding to its voiding of Mellon's security interest under section 547. At any rate, we must reach this question in light of our decision that the security interest did not constitute a voidable preference.

The present law of fraudulent conveyances has ancient roots. Section 548 is derived from the Statute of 13 Elizabeth passed by Parliament in 1571. The statute was aimed at a practice by which overburdened debtors placed their assets in friendly hands thereby frustrating creditors' attempts to satisfy their claims against the debtor. After the creditors had abandoned the effort to recover on their claims, the debtor would obtain a reconveyance of the property that had been transferred. Such transactions operated as a fraud against the debtor's creditors because the debtor's estate was depleted without exchanging property of similar value from which the creditor's claims could be satisfied.

The current embodiment of the law of fraudulent conveyances, section 548(a) provides, in full, that:

the trustee may avoid any transfer of an interest of the debtor in property, that was made or incurred on or within one year before the date of filing of the petition, if the debtor voluntarily or involuntarily—

(1) made such transfer or incurred such obligation with actual intent to hinder, delay, or defraud any entity to which the debtor was or became, on or after the date that such transfer was made or such obligation was incurred, indebted; or

(2)(A) received less than a reasonably equivalent value in exchange for such transfer or obligation; and

(b)(i) was insolvent on the date that such transfer or such obligation was incurred, or became insolvent as a result of such transfer or obligation;

(ii) was engaged in business or a transaction, or was about to engage in business or a transaction, for which any property remaining with the debtor was an unreasonably small capital; or

(iii) intended to incur, or believed that the debtor would incur, debts that would be beyond the debtor's ability to pay as such debts matured.

Subsection (a)(1) deals with actual fraud; the trustee is required to prove actual intent to defraud the debtor's creditors. Subsection (a)(2) addresses constructive fraud; the fraud on the creditors will be presumed if certain objective criteria are met. In this case, the Committee has made no allegations of intentional fraud. There is no evidence of any intention on the part of the parties to hinder or delay creditors or to commit any fraud. The bankruptcy court here held that Metro engaged in constructive fraud within the terms of section 548(a)(2).

At first glance, it seems difficult to reconcile the original purpose of the fraudulent conveyance laws with what has become a common, arms–length transaction—the leveraged buyout, or in business parlance, the LBO. Where there exists no intentional fraud, setting aside the security interest of a lender who has indisputably given reasonably equivalent value, cash for a promise to repay a loan, appears to be a patent anomaly. As one commentator has stated, "[a] firm that incurs obligations in the course of a buyout does not seem at all like the Elizabethan deadbeat who sells his sheep to his brother for a pittance." Baird & Jackson, *Fraudulent Conveyance Law and Its Proper Domain*, 38 Vand.L.Rev. 829, 852 (1985). Nonetheless, a thorough understanding of the typical LBO transaction reveals that there is a potential for abuse of the debtor's creditors, particularly those who are unsecured, when a company is purchased through an LBO.

Although the formal structure of LBOs may differ, the substance of LBOs follow a general pattern. A leveraged buyout refers to the acquisition of a company ("target corporation") in which a substantial portion of the purchase price paid for the stock of a target corporation is borrowed and where the loan is secured by the target corporation's assets. Commonly, the acquiror invests little or no equity. Thus, a fundamental feature of leveraged buyouts is that equity is exchanged for debt.

TCI's acquisition of the target Metro followed the typical pattern: Mellon extended a loan of 1.85 million dollars to TCI for the purchase of Metro; Metro guaranteed the loan and secured it with its assets, thus significantly adding to its debt structure. TCS and MCM, the parent and grandparent corporations of TCI also guaranteed the acquisition loan.

The effect of an LBO is that a corporation's shareholders are replaced by secured creditors. Put simply, stockholders' equity is supplanted by corporate debt. The level of risk facing the newly structured corporation rises significantly due to the increased debt to equity ratio. This added risk is borne primarily by the unsecured creditors, those who will most likely not be paid in the event of bankruptcy. The lender, which normally assumes a senior, secured position vis–a–vis other creditors, is at risk only to the extent that the loan is under–collateralized. An LBO may be attractive to the buyer, seller, and lender because the structure of the transaction could allow all parties to the buyout to shift most of the risk of loss to other creditors of the corporation if the provisions of section 548(a)(2) were not applied.

The selling shareholders receive direct benefit in the LBO transaction as they are cashed out, usually at a price above the price the shares were trading shortly before the acquisition is announced. The new purchaser also benefits from the transaction by thereby achieving ownership of the corporation. The lender is attracted by the higher interest rates and fees usually associated with LBOs. The target corporation, however, receives no direct benefit to offset the greater risk of now operating as a highly leveraged corporation. As legal scholars have noted, the target firm may not at all reflect the Elizabethan deadbeat, but may in fact wind up as the sacrificial lamb. Wahl & Wahl, *Fraudulent Conveyance Law and Leveraged Buyouts*, 16 William Mitchell L.Rev. 343, 353 (1990).

The reasonableness of the remedy provided by section 548(a)(2) has been questioned. *See, e.g.*, Carlson, *Leveraged Buyouts in Bankruptcy*, 20 Georgia L.Rev. 73 (1985) (lenders should have good faith defense of section 548(c) despite the fraudulent conveyance laws are intended to protect the debtor's creditors, a lender cannot hide behind the position, although sympathetic, that it has parted with reasonable value. The purpose of the laws is estate preservation; thus, the question whether the debtor received reasonable value must be determined from the standpoint of the creditors. *But cf., In re Greenbrook Carpet Co., Inc.*, 722 F.2d 659, 661 (11th Cir. 1984) (court held that although bank knew that corporation would immediately re–lend proceeds of the loan to principal shareholders to purchase a company in return for unsecured note, the issue under section 548 was "whether the bank received more consideration that it was due"); *Kupetz v. Wolf*, 845 F.2d 842, 847 (9th Cir. 1988) (court refused to apply section 548(a)(2) to force selling shareholders to disgorge the payments they received where there was not indication of actual intent to defraud and no knowledge of the LBO structure used to purchase their shares).

Moreover, the statutory language provides no exception for the leveraged buyout transaction. Section 548 applies to "any transfer of an interest of the debtor in property." The definitional section of the Act states that transfer means "every mode, direct or indirect, absolute or conditional, voluntary or involuntary, of disposing of or parting with property or with an interest in property." 11 U.S.C. § 101(54). This definitional language is sufficiently broad to encompass a leveraged buyout transaction that falls within its terms. We therefore turn to the analysis of the particular requirements of section 548.

Reasonably Equivalent Value

Section 548(a)(2)(A) requires the trustee to show that the debtor received "less than a reasonably equivalent value." Because Metro did not receive the proceeds of the acquisition loan, it did not receive any direct benefits from extending the guaranty and security interest collaterizing that guaranty. However, in evaluating whether reasonably equivalent value has been given the debtor under section 548, indirect benefits may also be evaluated. If the consideration Metro received from the transaction, even though indirect, approximates the value it gave TCI, this can satisfy the terms of the statute. *See Rubin v. Manufacturers Hanover Trust Co.*, 661 F.2d 979, 991 (2d Cir. 1981) (although transfers solely for the benefit of third parties do not furnish fair consideration, the transaction's benefit to the debtor need not be direct and may come through a third party). These indirect economic benefits must be measured and then compared to the obligations that the bankrupt incurred. Here, as well as in determining insolvency under section 548(a)(2)(B)(i), it is appropriate to take into account intangible assets not carried on the debtor's balance sheet, including, inter alia, good will. *See Mutual Life Ins. Co. v. Menin*, 115 F.2d 975, 977 (2d Cir. 1940), *cert. denied*, 313 U.S. 578, 61 S.Ct. 1096, 85 L.Ed. 1536 (1941) (debtor's good will is property asset which may be sold in bankruptcy proceedings); *see also In re Da–Sota Elevator Co.*, 939 F.2d 654, 656 (8th Cir. 1991). The touchstone is whether the transaction conferred realizable commercial value on the debtor reasonably equivalent to the realizable commercial value of the assets transferred. Thus, when the debtor is a going concern and its realizable going concern value after the transaction is equal to or exceeds its going concern value before the transaction, reasonably equivalent value has been received.

The bankruptcy court rejected Mellon's argument that one of the indirect benefits that Metro received as a result of the LBO was the ability to borrow working capital from Mellon. The court reasoned that the 2.3 million dollar credit line extended contemporaneously with the 1.85 million dollar loan to TCI amounted to a liability because "all that Debtor really received was the opportunity to incur an additional $2.3 million of debt." The court concluded that because of accruing interest, Metro received "substantially less than a reasonably equivalent value in exchange." 95 B.R. at 934. This analysis is flawed. The ability to borrow money has considerable value in the commercial world. To quantify that value, however, is difficult. Quantification depends upon the business opportunities the additional credit makes available to the borrowing corporation and on other imponderables in the operation or expansion of its business.

The bankruptcy court also did not account for the value created by the LBO itself. The Banks cite what appears to be legitimate and reasonable expectation that the affiliation of these two corporations, TCS and Metro, would produce a strong synergy. Through the LBO, Metro established a permanent relationship with a production company with highly sophisticated equipment and an experienced and reputable production and technical staff. The complementary nature of the two corporations' businesses would appear to create a stronger and more profitable combination. What was unpredicted, however, was the Supreme Court's decision in *National Collegiate Athletic Assoc. v. Board of Regents of the University of Oklahoma*, 468 U.S. 85, 104 S.Ct. 2948, 82 L.Ed.2d 70 (1984), which Mellon points to as the reason for Metro's dramatic and unforseen decline. Mellon alleges that the Court's holding that certain NCAA restrictions imposed on the broadcasting of college football games of member NCAA institutions violated antitrust laws had the unexpected result of increasing competition and severely decreasing revenues from advertising. The problem universal to all LBOs—transactions characterized by their high debt relative to equity interest—is that they are less able to weather temporary financial storms because debt demands are less flexible than equity interest.

Thus, the indirect benefits to Metro of this guaranty were the ability to obtain substantial credit due to its new association with the TCS corporate group and the synergy expected to result from the combination of these corporations.[1] The value, however, of the synergy obtained in the corporations' affiliation and the value of obtaining the credit are difficult to quantify in dollars without the aid of expert witnesses. Regrettably, no such testimony was forthcoming in this case.

The value of consideration received must be compared to the value given by the debtor to determine whether the debtor received less than reasonably equivalent value. The bankruptcy court correctly found that the contingent nature of the debt was illusory because TCI had no assets of any kind except the debtor. The parties do not dispute that TCI was merely a shell corporation formed for the sole purpose

---

[1] John L. Phillips, a consultant in the telecommunications industry and a certified public accountant formerly employed by Price, Waterhouse & Co., who actively assisted with the management of Total Communications, Inc., explained the benefits to be derived by the companies involved in the LBO. Speaking specifically about the benefits to be derived by Metro, he testified:

The benefits to Metro again were quite clear. Metro had a history of having to negotiate for facilities . . . and by having a facility like Total Communications Systems . . . it had a reputation of being—of having state of the art quality production equipment and it also had a reputation of having better than average production—quality production people. So this would add to Metrosports in terms of being able to in some cases upgrade the quality of its production work associated with its programming and in other cases establishing a consistency of quality because of being able to use in many respects the same people. This is very valuable to any syndicator or someone who owns rights, programming rights. It's very valuable in terms of being able to go to advertisers, okay, and to stations and be able to say, I'm going to be able to deliver you a consistency of quality of production. The other aspect of benefit to Metrosports, you don't have to be a genius to see, it received working capital.

Q. Through the loans from Mellon Bank?

A. Right. Which, of course, proved to be needed.

of acquiring Metro. All parties, including the lender, assumed that Metro would be servicing the debt.

However, the court ignored the value of guarantees made by TCS and MCM. In valuing the cost of Metro's guaranty, the right of contribution from co–guarantors need to be balanced against the amount of debt for which Metro is liable. Carl, *Fraudulent Transfer Attacks on Guaranties in Bankruptcy*, 60 Amer.Bank.L.J. 109, 114 (1986) ("If there are multiple guarantors for the same obligation, the right of contribution entitles a paying guarantor to have its co–guarantors pay it their proportionate share of the principal debt it paid.") Thus, the value of the guaranty, 1.85 million dollars, must be reduced to the extent contribution was available at the time of the loan from Metro's co–guarantors.

No evidence, however, has been offered regarding the value of these rights to contribution. We do know that the assets of the guaranteeing corporations were sufficiently valuable to justify an immediate additional loan by Mellon to TCS of 2.3 million dollars and letters of credit for an additional 2.25 million dollars. These loans enabled Metro, as demonstrated by its balance sheet of June 30, 1984, immediately to achieve a very sharp rise in its broadcasting rights amounting to a grant total of $26,240,705. Although the ability to obtain credit is the lifeblood of the commercial world and governmental operational survival, and the synergistic strength expected from the merger here, no doubt had value, the Committee introduced no evidence to support its burden of showing that Metro received less than reasonably equivalent value in exchange for its guaranty and security interest. The Committee acted on the blind assumption that they had no value and the bankruptcy court agreed.

Insolvency or Undercapitalization

Under section 548, not only must the Committee prove that the debtor did not receive reasonably equivalent value, the Committee must also prove that the debtor was "insolvent on the date that such transfer was made or such obligation was incurred, or became insolvent as a result of such transfer." 11 U.S.C. § 548(a)(2)(B)(i). The bankruptcy court swiftly concluded that Metro was rendered insolvent by the LBO, stating that clear logic showed that "the very transactions themselves caused a serious case of insolvency." 95 B.R. at 934.

The bankruptcy code defines insolvency as a "financial condition such that the sum of such entity's debts is greater than all of such entity's property, at a fair valuation." 11 U.S.C. § 101(31)(A). This test is frequently described as the "balance sheet test." The debtor's asserts and liabilities are tallied at fair valuation to determine whether the corporation's debts exceed its assets. Under section 548, insolvency is to be measured at the time the debtor transferred value or incurred an obligation. In present case, Metro's solvency must be measured on April 6, 1984, the date on which Metro guaranteed the acquisition loan.

The bankruptcy court reasoned that the LBO rendered Metro insolvent because it assumed that the 1.85 million paid to the former shareholders of Metro reflected the fair market value of Metro and that Metro's pledge of its stock and assets in equal amount necessarily rendered it insolvent. The court stated:

Debtor's former shareholders were paid $1.85 million in exchange for their shares of stock. If, as is often stated, fair market value is the sum a willing buyer will pay a willing seller in an arm's–length transaction, then Debtor's stock had a fair valuation of $1.85 million. Debtor pledged its stock and all of its remaining unencumbered assets as collateral for said $1.85 loan guaranty. For all intents and purposes, Debtor was now liable for payment of the principal and interest on the loan, the proceeds of which it did not receive and the funding for which it did not have. A clearer case of insolvency would be difficult to construct.

In re Metro, 95 B.R. at 934. Thus, the court concluded in one short paragraph that the transaction rendered Metro insolvent. Not only is the bankruptcy court surprisingly cavalier in fashioning what amounts to a *per se* rule that LBO loans collateralized with the target's assets are fraudulent, the court's analysis is flawed by several fundamental errors.

First, even assuming that Metro's fair market value was 1.85 million dollars, the guaranties of TCS and MCM should have been counted as reducing Metro's liability to something below 1.85 million dollars. Second, the court erred in stating that Metro "pledged its stock and all of its remaining unencumbered assets." Metro, of course, cannot, and did not, pledge its own stock as the corporation's stock was held by another entity—TCI. The bankruptcy court thus, in essence, double counted when it stated that Metro pledged stock as well as assets. For these reasons, as well as reasons we discuss below, the bankruptcy court's superficial analysis fails to show that the guaranty of the acquisition loan rendered Metro insolvent.

The record is sparse with respect to the financial condition of Metro at the time of the two loans on April 6, 1984, of 1.85 million dollars to accomplish the stock purchase and 2.3 million dollars for working capital. James Canavan, assistant vice–president of Mellon, testified that the loans would not have been made without the guaranty and surety agreements of TCM and TCS. Although we do not have a financial statement of Metro for April 6, 1984, Metro's corporate income tax return with accompanying balance sheet for the period ending April 16, 1984, shows the total assets of the company and liabilities without the Mellon loans of April 6, 1984. The income tax return, prepared on a cash basis, does not report accounts receivable or accounts payable and, therefore, is incomplete. Nonetheless, it does reflect that the corporation had a net worth of $133,873 at the time and was not insolvent. Thus, it appears that the purchaser of the capital stock of Metro paid primarily for goodwill.[2] In the absence of any evidence as to the value of the accounts receivable

---

[2] Goodwill is the difference between the value of the consideration given and the fair market value of the Company's identifiable net assets. E.R. Brownslee, K. Ferrs, M.C. Haskins, Corporate Financing Reporting, 144 (1990).

Although the purchaser obtained little value in tangible assets, TCI secured much more in solid expectations of the Company's future potential after the infusion of needed working capital and the benefits of the synergism effectuated by the permanent combination of three operating companies, MCM, TCS, and Metro. As for Mellon, apparently it looked for collateralization of its loans to its security interest in Metro's potential profits after the synergistic effects of the combination of the corporations and the infusion of new working capital and, most importantly, to the guaranty and surety agreements of MCM and TCS, not to the security interest in Metro's limited assets.

and the sum owing on the accounts payable, and no proof of the value of Metro's rights to contribution, one cannot determine on this record whether the guaranty of the 1.85 million dollar loan and the accompanying security interest rendered the corporation insolvent.

When we examine the balance sheet of June 30, 1984, prepared on an accrual basis, after the ingestion of 2.3 million dollars working capital and the expansion of the company's broadcasting rights, we find accounts receivable of $1,828.016 and accounts payable of $762,745. The corporations' assets have now shot up to an aggregate $28,370,697 consisting primarily of broadcasting rights, and its liabilities amounted to $27,684,167, comprised principally of obligations under its broadcast rights and bank loans of $3,500,000. The net worth of the company shows improvement—now $343,265—despite the liability of the bank loans and demonstrates that the Mellon loans did not render Metro insolvent, even without considering the value of the guarantees of TCS and MCM, but improved its financial condition.

We conclude that the Committee failed to satisfy its burden of proving that Metro was insolvent on the date of the transfer or became insolvent as a result of the transfer. As the Committee did not raise the issue of unreasonably small capital or the debtor's intent to incur debts beyond its ability to pay, we need not discuss these issues. Thus, we hold that the guaranty and security interest securing the acquisition loan did not constitute a fraudulent conveyance as provided by section 548 of the bankruptcy code.

III.

We also hold that the Committee failed to satisfy its burden of proof in showing that Metro failed to receive reasonably equivalent value when it executed the guaranty and security interest of the acquisition loan and that the loan rendered it insolvent under section 548(a)(2). Accordingly, the order of the district court will be reversed insofar as it affirms the order of the bankruptcy court of February 10, 1989, as amended, and the case will be remanded to the district court with instructions to reverse the foregoing order of the bankruptcy court. Costs taxed to the appellees.

SELIGSON v. NEW YORK PRODUCE EXCHANGE

United States District Court, Southern District of New York
394 F. Supp. 125 (1975)

CARTER, D. J.

Defendants New York Produce Exchange ("Exchange") and New York Produce Exchange Clearing Association ("Association") renew their motions for summary judgment with respect to the third count of the amended complaint ("complaint"). . . .

. . . Plaintiff is the trustee in bankruptcy of Ira Haupt & Co. ("Haupt"), which was the principal commodities broker for Allied Crude Vegetable Oil Refining Corporation ("Allied") for purposes of Allied's cottonseed oil futures trading on the Exchange during the latter part of 1963.

The Exchange is a self–regulated contract market on which commodities futures are traded. A broker generally purchases futures through the Association, initially by paying to the Association a fixed percentage of the purchase price as "original margin." Thereafter, in the event of a price decline, the purchaser may be required by the Association to provide such additional "variation margin" as is necessary to protect the Association from the effects of such price decline.

A futures contract is "cleared" through the Association when the Association "accepts" it, thereby gaining the rights and assuming the obligations of both parties to the contract.

During the latter part of 1963, Haupt and other brokers acting on behalf of Allied acquired a substantial "long" position in cottonseed oil futures. By November 14, 1963, Allied was the purchaser in approximately 90% of the futures contracts traded on the Exchange. On that day, the Board of Managers of the Exchange learned of the magnitude of Allied's holdings from the Commodity Exchange Authority, and at a meeting held that day, the Board appointed a Control Committee to determine the precise extent of Allied's position.

From November 14–November 19, 1963, the market for cottonseed oil futures declined sharply. In its extraordinary long position, Allied was highly vulnerable to the price decline. During this period, the Association repeatedly called upon Haupt to furnish variation margin and Haupt in turn requested reimbursement from Allied. By November 19, 1963, Allied was unable to meet Haupt's margin calls, and that day it filed a petition under Chapter XI of the Bankruptcy Act.

Later in the day on November 19, representatives of Haupt informed a joint meeting of the Executive Committee of the Exchange and the Board of Directors of the Association that it would be unable to meet its margin obligations if the market continued to drop.

After consultation with members of the Board of Managers of the Exchange, the Executive Committee of the Exchange recommended to the Board of Managers that trading in cottonseed oil futures be suspended until further notice and that settlement prices be fixed. On November 20, the Exchange did not open, and the Board of Managers formally adopted the Executive Committee's recommendations of the previous day.

On or about November 22, 1963, Haupt discovered that warehouse receipts, which Allied had given it as collateral for Allied's indebtedness, were worthless. The receipts were forged, and the vegetable oils purportedly represented by the receipts were non–existent. On March 23, 1964, an involuntary petition in bankruptcy was filed against Haupt.

. . . [T]he plaintiff trustee . . . seeks to set aside Haupt's payments of over $12 million in variation margin to the Association from November 14 to November 20 . . . [as] fraudulent transfers. . . . It is alleged that the variation margin was transferred without fair consideration at a time when Haupt was insolvent, and that both the Association and the Exchange were fraudulent transferees. . . .

. . . .

With respect to the *Association* alone, the court denied its original motion for summary judgment . . . on the ground that the record was inadequate to permit a determination of . . . whether Haupt was "insolvent" . . . at the time of the margin payments, from November 14–19, or whether it was rendered insolvent by those payments . . . [,]

. . . whether "fair consideration," . . . was given in exchange for Haupt's transfer of $12 million to the Association. . . . [and]

. . . whether . . . the court should find that the Association was *not* the transferee of the payments [because] . . . the Association was a known agent which had received money paid to it by mistake and had innocently and in good faith paid the money over to its members, its principals. . . .

With respect to the *Exchange's* motion for summary judgment . . . the court's previous opinion first found that there was no dispute that the Exchange was neither the transferee nor the transferee's grantee of the variation margin. The court therefore concluded that "liability if it exists must be premised on the principle . . . , that the act of a clearing house is, in certain circumstances, deemed to be the act of the contract market with which it is affiliated." . . .

(1) *Haupt's Insolvency between November 14 and 19, 1963*

. . . Between November 14 and 19, Haupt paid to the Association variation margin in the amount of over $12 million. Allied never reimbursed Haupt for these payments. The payments of commodity margin to the Association and the Chicago Board of Trade were the only significant changes in Haupt's financial condition from November 14–20. Haupt's accounts receivable from Allied for this and Allied's other indebtedness were secured by warehouse receipts. After the payments of variation margin, Allied's total indebtedness to Haupt was approximately $31.8 million. The warehouse receipts given to Haupt as collateral were spurious, and Haupt discovered that fact on or about November 22, 1963.

On November 25, 1963, Haupt had a deficit of approximately $25.25 million in its net worth account reflecting the application of a reserve of approximately $31.8 million for the indebtedness of Allied, then in bankruptcy.

With respect to Allied, it is undisputed that by its own admission, it had a capital deficiency as of July 31, 1963, of $34 million. . . . Allied held an extraordinary long position in cottonseed futures prior to and during the period, November 14–19. During that period, there was a substantial decline in the price of such futures.

. . . [A] senior Haupt employee, Jack E. Stevens, . . . was informed on November 15, 1963, that Allied was experiencing financial difficulties, and that Allied officers would meet the following day to attempt to work out these difficulties. On November 16, he was informed that the officers of Allied had met but that they had failed to arrive at any solution to Allied's problems. On November

18 and 19, Stevens was informed of the failure of Allied to meet outstanding margin calls of November 14, 15 and 18. Also on November 18 and 19, several Haupt employees reported to Stevens concerning the financial predicament of Allied, the deteriorating condition in the commodity market, and the status of the allied account. . . .

In addition, Stevens was repeatedly warned from September, 1963, through November 19, 1963, by officials of the Exchange and the Association and by numerous other persons of the magnitude of Haupt's financial exposure and of the need for establishing the legitimacy of Allied's position. . . . Stevens was also aware of Allied's withdrawal from Haupt of excess variation margin generated by the rising market through November 14. . . . Stevens did not inform the partners of Haupt of the relevant facts or of the significance of the information. . . .

In opposing the Association's motion for summary judgment, the trustee first claims that there is a genuine issue as to the ultimate fact of Haupt's insolvency during the period, November 14–19. The trustee directs the court's attention to the finding by Judge Palmieri that as of November 20, 1963, Haupt was "hopelessly insolvent," primarily as a result of its transactions with Allied. . . . Judge Palmieri's determination was based on the definition of "insolvency" in the Bankruptcy Act, . . . [which is] substantially equivalent [to that of the N.Y. Debtor and Creditor].

Plaintiff contends that the court may infer from [the] finding of insolvency as of November 20, that Haupt was also insolvent during the period, November 14–19. . . . [T]he referee may "draw his own inferences from the wretched financial condition of the bankrupt at the time of adjudication and infer bankruptcy as of [a] prior date." . . . There must, however, be a showing that there was "continuity or no change of position" in the bankrupt's financial condition between the earlier and later dates. . . .

. . . [I]t is substantially undisputed that between November 14 and November 20, there was no significant change in Haupt's financial condition except the margin payments to the Association and the Chicago Board of Trade. These can be accounted for, and the amounts involved may be precisely calculated. I therefore hold that the trustee may rely, at least in part, on the finding that Haupt was insolvent as of November 20, to establish that it was also insolvent during the period, November 14–19, or that it was rendered insolvent by the payments of variation margin during that period. At a minimum, the trustee has raised a genuine issue of material fact as to whether Haupt was insolvent from November 14–19.

There is also a genuine issue of material fact as to the "present fair salable value," as of November 14–19, of the Allied receivables representing both Allied's indebtedness to Haupt prior to November 14, and its indebtedness as a result of Haupt's payments of variation margin from November 14 through November 19. The proper valuation of the receivables is crucial to a determination of Haupt's solvency or insolvency during the six–day period in question.

In support of its claim that Haupt was solvent, the Association contends that the Allied receivables should have been valued at their face value of approximately $31.8 million, and that Haupt therefore had a net worth of over $6 million throughout this period. The Association argues that Allied was a large, "going enterprise", and that as a result, "there [was] no basis for questioning [the] worth and sufficiency [of the receivables] as of the times when Haupt made margin payments to the Association." . . .

In addition, the Association cites an "accounting authority" for the proposition that Haupt's balance sheet showed its financial condition "at a particular moment of time." As of the "moment" under consideration, November 14–19, the receivables were properly carried at their face value of $31.8 million. According to the Association, the fact that on November 25, the receivables were written off as worthless has no bearing whatever on Haupt's solvency as of the period six to eleven days earlier.

With respect to the warehouse receipts held as collateral, the Association argues similarly that because Haupt had no reason to suspect that they were forgeries as of November 14–19, they should properly be valued at full value for that period. The fact that on November 22, 1963, Haupt discovered them to be forgeries is, according to the Association, irrelevant.

In reply, plaintiff argues that the crucial fact is the *actual* value of the Allied receivables as of November 14–19, *not* merely the *stated* value or the value erroneously attributed to them by Haupt during that period on the basis of misinformation supplied by Allied. In support of this position, plaintiff argues that the court may infer the value of the receivables as of November 14–19, from evidence of their value on November 25, 1963.

In *Hassan v. Middlesex County National Bank*, . . . the trustee sought to establish that the bankrupt was insolvent as of October 23–25, 1961. The only evidence of the value of certain assets was a closing inventory taken some three months later, on January 23, 1962. The Court of Appeals for the First Circuit held that the value of the assets as of October 23–25, 1961, could be calculated by taking the January 23, 1962, figures and working backward through the entries in the ledger to reflect sales and purchases in the interim. The court emphasized, however, that the trustee must establish that there were no substantial changes in the assets of the corporation between the two dates. . . .

"Retrojection" was also permitted by the Fifth Circuit in *Haynes & Hubbard, Inc. v. Stewart*, . . . where the trustee determined the value of certain mortgaged property as of a date prior to bankruptcy on the basis of its value subsequent to the filing of the petition.

In the present case, it is undisputed that on November 22 and 25, 1963, the Allied warehouse receipts and receivables respectively were worthless. . . . I hold that the trustee may rely wholly or in part on the worthlessness of the Allied warehouse receipts and receivables on November 22 and 25, 1963, to establish their value as of November 14–19. The trustee has therefore raised a genuine issue of material fact as to the value of these assets during the period in question.

The court will consider Allied's undoubted insolvency on November 19 and thereafter in determining its financial condition and hence the value of its obligations during the earlier period, November 14–19.

Moreover, in establishing that the Allied receivables were either worthless or worth a fraction of their face value, the trustee may also rely, at least in part, on the fact that Haupt has recovered nothing on its claim in bankruptcy against Allied. This fact is not, however, determinative. . . .

In disputing the Association's contention that as of November 14–19, the receivables should be valued at face value, the trustee relies not only on the value of the receivables *subsequent* to November 19, but on evidence of Allied's financial condition *prior to* and *during* the period in question.

In *Irving Trust Co. v. Jacob Weckstein & Sons, Inc.,* . . . a voidable preference action, the court accepted an accountant's valuation of certain notes held by the bankrupt at 30% of their face value as of the date of transfer. The court held that the discount was justified, *inter alia*, because a receiver had been appointed for the account debtor one month before the valuation date; because conditions in the account debtor's industry were unfavorable; and because recoveries from insolvencies in the account debtor's business had rarely exceeded 30–40%. . . . In valuing accounts receivable, other cases have laid emphasis on the degree of risk and uncertainty facing the account debtor on the valuation date. . . .

. . . The trustee in the present case has presented evidence of Allied's financial condition and of conditions in the market prior to and during the period, November 14–19. . . . [T]he evidence here indicates that the Allied receivables should be valued at substantially less than face value. First, as noted, Allied had a capital deficiency of $34 million as of July 31, 1963, and its petition under Chapter XI admitted insolvency as of that date. Second, throughout November, 1963, and during the five–day period, November 14–19, Haupt was in a precarious financial position because of its extraordinary, speculative long position. . . . The ability of Allied to pay its obligations was dependent on a rise in prices. Such a rise was most unlikely because the prices were already inflated by Allied's massive speculative purchases and would probably decline sharply when Allied ceased to purchase. In any event, this evidence would seem sufficient in and of itself to raise a genuine issue of material fact as to the value of Allied's receivables as of November 14–19.

As noted, the Association contends that it is significant that Haupt believed that the Allied receivables were entitled to full value and that the warehouse receipts were genuine. Haupt carried the receivables at full value on its books, and the Association contends that this was proper accounting practice since Haupt was not aware of any reason that the receivables should be discounted. Without accepting the Association's apparent contention that an insolvent company which is defrauded into believing that it is solvent should be deemed solvent, the court concludes that the trustee has raised a genuine issue as to Haupt's knowledge of Allied's true financial condition. . . . The nature and extent of the knowledge of Stevens and other Haupt employees of facts bearing on the value of the Allied receivables must be examined more fully at trial.

. . . .

(2) Fair Consideration

The Association argues that it gave "fair consideration" for the transfers, . . . and that therefore it was not a fraudulent transferee even if Haupt was insolvent at the time of the transfers. . . .

It appears to be undisputed that the Association provided certain services and things of benefit to Haupt. *First,* the Association accepted, cleared and guaranteed contracts for Haupt upon Haupt's commitment to pay such variation margin as might be required in the future under Association rules. *Second,* in exchange for payments of variation margin, the Association refrained from liquidating Haupt's account. Moreover, the variation margin payments were credited to Haupt, diminishing Haupt's potential liability in the event of liquidation of its account. *Third,* just as Haupt had an obligation to pay variation margin to the Association when it was in a net debit position, it had the *right* to *receive* payments of variation margin from the Association when it was in a net credit position.

Finally, the Association contends that when Haupt had cleared contracts prior to the six–day period in question, it had incurred an obligation to the Association; this antecedent debt was consideration for the subsequent payment by Haupt of over $12 million in variation margin.

In opposition, the trustee first contends that there is a genuine issue as to whether any of these forms of consideration was given in good faith and hence as to whether any of these considerations constituted "fair consideration". . . .

. . . [T]he Court of Appeals for this circuit [has] held that to constitute "fair consideration" for purposes of [the fraudulent transfer provisions of the Bankruptcy Act], consideration must be given in good faith. The court stated that the requirements of "fair consideration" under [the New York Debtor and Creditor Law] are the same . . . [T]he Court of Appeals indicated that if the transferee had knowledge of the unfavorable financial condition of the transferor at the time of the transfer, it could not meet the good faith requirement. . . .

. . . [T]he Association was at least aware of Haupt's and Allied's precarious position in the market. The Association has made no showing of good faith. The court believes that the Association's awareness of Haupt's position in the market may support an inference that it was aware of Haupt's financial condition. The trustee has therefore raised a genuine issue of material fact as to the Association's good faith.

The Association contends that the issue of good faith was foreclosed by the court's finding in its original opinion that certain facts were "insufficient to give rise to an inference of bad faith regulation." . . . That finding was, however, confined exclusively to the issue of good faith *regulation,* and has no application whatever to the question of whether the Association *gave consideration* in good faith.

. . . [T]he consideration must be such that the bankrupt's estate is not depleted as a result of the transfer.

Assuming that the consideration provided by the Association would support a simple contract, there remains a substantial question whether such considerations as the promise of the Association to clear Haupt's contracts or its forbearance to liquidate Haupt's position in any way offset the depletion of the estate caused by the transfer of $12 million in margin.

In the same vein, the trustee contends that the value of certain of the consideration was dependent on Haupt's continued operation as a broker–dealer, and that in view of Haupt's collapse, such consideration was of no value in arresting the depletion of the estate. . . .

. . . . [T]he court believes that in light of Haupt's collapse, it is most unlikely that Haupt's contingent right to receive such payments served in any way to preserve Haupt's estate.

. . . . [A]ntecedent indebtedness may constitute "fair consideration." . . . [H]owever, the Association has not cited any authority for the proposition that under Association rules, Haupt owed an antecedent obligation.

Moreover, even assuming that there was an antecedent debt, the Association has made no showing that it acted in good faith in giving the initial consideration which gave rise to that antecedent obligation. . . .

In summary, there remain several genuine issues of material fact with respect to the requirement of fair consideration, and the Association has not shown that as a matter of law it gave such fair consideration for Haupt's transfers of variation margin.

(3) *The Association as Transferee of the Margin Payments*

On this motion, the Association renews its contention that it may not properly be deemed the transferee of the margin payments . . . [because] a known agent who receives money paid to him by mistake is protected from liability if innocently and in good faith he has paid money over to his principal before receipt of a notice of the payor's mistake. . . .

. . . The Association collects variation margin from members in a net debit position, and makes payments of excess variation margin to members in a net credit position. Each day, after the daily settlement, the total amount of the variation margin drafts paid by the Association to members in a net credit position is equal to the total amount of the variation margin checks received by it from members in a net debit position. During the period, November 14–19, the Association followed its usual practices with respect to the $12 million in variation margin which it received from Haupt which was then in a net debit position.

. . . .

It is most doubtful that the Association has presented facts sufficient to support a finding of an agency relationship. . . . The Association's sole contention in this regard is that it was a mere "conduit" for the transmittal of margins from debit to credit members. The use of this figure of speech is hardly a substitute for a showing of facts as to the precise nature of the relationship between the Association and its credit members.

. . . .

In the instant case, the Association has presented no evidence whatever tending to show that Haupt's obligation to pay variation margins was owed directly to the credit members, the alleged principals, rather than to the Association, the alleged agent. Indeed, Association By–Law . . . suggests the contrary. It refers to "margin calls or any other obligation *to the Association*" . . . , indicating that the obligation to pay variation margin is owed to the *Association, not* to the credit members. In fact, the By–Laws suggest that the Association collects variation margin on its own account, and that it remains the Association's property until the Association decides to pay its own obligations to net credit members. . . .

There has been no showing whatever of facts tending to establish that the other characteristics of an agency relationship were present. For example, the Association has not shown that in collecting margin payments it was subject to the control of net credit members or that it had consented to act in a fiduciary capacity for the benefit of credit members. . . .

The Association has also failed to present evidence that Haupt made the margin payments by *mistake* . . .

Finally, as noted, the Association's undisputed awareness of Haupt's and Allied's market position raises a serious issue as to the Association's good faith in accepting the variation margin payments. . . .

. . . [T]he Association's motion for summary judgment as to the third count of the amended complaint is in all respects denied.

(4) *Liability of the Exchange*

The trustee seeks to hold the Exchange accountable for the action of the Association in receiving alleged fraudulent transfers . . . [because] in certain circumstances, the acts of a clearing house may be attributed to the exchange with which it is affiliated.

. . . . [T]he undisputed facts show that the Exchange did not exercise [absolute power and] control over the Association, and I therefore conclude that the Association's acts should not be attributed to the Exchange.

. . . .

NOTES AND QUESTIONS

(1) Because proof by direct evidence of the debtor's insolvency on the critical date of the allegedly fraudulent transfer may be difficult, "insolvency frequently must be determined by proof of . . . factors from which insolvency may be inferred." *Constructora Maza, Inc. v. Banco de Ponce*, 616 F.2d 573, 577 (1st Cir. 1980). In order to re–create a picture of the debtor's financial condition at the time of the transfer, it may be necessary to work backwards from that date, to show factors

from which the debtor's insolvency may be presumed. As noted by the court in *Seligson*, this accounting process is known as "retrojection." *See also Misty Management Corp. v. Lockwood*, 539 F.2d 1205, 1213 (9th Cir. 1976); *New York Credit Men's Adjustment Bureau v. Adler*, 2 B.R. 752 (S.D.N.Y. 1980); *Kanasky v. Randolph (In re R. Purbeck & Associates Ltd.)*, 27 B.R. 953 (Bankr. D. Conn. 1983). Section 2(b) of the UFTA makes it easier for a creditor to prove insolvency: it contains a rebuttable presumption of insolvency when a debtor has generally stopped paying its debts as they become due.

(2) For a discussion of how certain assets should be valued for the insolvency equation, *see Consove v. Cohen (In re Roco Corp.)*, 701 F.2d 978 (1st Cir. 1983) (fixed assets); *Constructora Maza, Inc. v. Banco de Ponce*, 616 F.2d 573 (1st Cir. 1980) (accounts receivable); *Darby v. Shawnee Southwest, Inc.*, 399 F. Supp. 587, 591–92 (W.D. Okla. 1975) (inventory); *In re Emerald Hills Country Club, Inc.*, 32 B.R. 408, 414–15 (Bankr. S.D. Fla. 1983) (real property); *Hemphill v. T & F Land Co. (In re Hemphill)*, 18 B.R. 38, 46–47 (Bankr. S.D. Iowa 1982) (same).

(3) Calculation of a debtor's liabilities must include the value of contingent and unliquidated liabilities as well as absolute, matured obligations. UFCA §§ 1, 2; 11 U.S.C. §§ 101(4), 101(11), 101(31); UFTA §§ 1(3); 1(4); 1(5). Contingent assets and liabilities need not be considered at face value, but should be discounted by the probability that the contingency will materialize. *See In re Xonics Photochemical, Inc.*, 841 F.2d 198 (7th Cir. 1988). How can the value of contingent, unmatured, or unliquidated liabilities be established? *See Tri–Continental Leasing Corp. v. Zimmerman*, 485 F. Supp. 495, 499–500 (N.D. Cal. 1980). In *Seligson, supra*, the court noted, for example, that the debtor's contingent right to receive variation margin payments was probably worthless unless the debtor continued its business as a broker–dealer. Must contingent assets be calculated as well? *See Hemphill, supra* (value of contingent subrogation or contribution rights must be included as assets). Exempt property must be excluded from the debtor's assets when using the Bankruptcy Code's balance sheet test of insolvency. *In re Coleman*, 21 B.R. 832, 9 B.C.D. 364 (Bankr. S.D. Tex. 1982).

BULLARD v. ALUMINUM CO. OF AMERICA

United States Court of Appeals, Seventh Circuit
468 F.2d 11 (1972)

CAMPBELL, D. J.

The defendant Aluminum Company of America (Alcoa) appeals from an order of the district court which granted the motion of the plaintiff, trustee in bankruptcy of the estate of Kritzer Radiant Coils Inc. (Kritzer Radiant), for summary judgment. The district court held that a transfer of $23,370.60 from the bankrupt to Alcoa was a "fraudulent transfer" under . . . of the Bankruptcy Act. . . . Alcoa raises three contentions on appeal: (1) that the transfer was not fraudulent inasmuch as there was no evidence that Alcoa participated in a scheme to defeat the other creditors of Kritzer Radiant or that the transaction involving the transfer of monies was lacking in good faith; (2) that summary judgment was improperly entered since the pleadings and affidavits raised genuine issues of material fact concerning the intentions and motives of Alcoa; and (3) that the district court erred in failing to hold Alcoa had a right under the Bankruptcy Act to retain the $23,370.60 as security for repayment of the actual consideration given by Alcoa.

The facts as gleaned from the pleadings, affidavits and from defendant's answers to plaintiff's interrogatories show that on December 1st, 1965, the date of the transfer in question, the bankrupt, Kritzer Radiant, was indebted to Alcoa in the amount of $46,741.20. As of that time 85% of the outstanding capital stock of Kritzer Radiant was owned by Bastian Morely Company, Inc. (Bastian Morely) and the remaining 15% of the stock was held by Henry Kritzer, Sr. Henry Kritzer at that time also owned 15% of the outstanding common stock of Bastian Morely and was a director of that Company. The $46,741.20 debt of Kritzer Radiant, which had been personally guaranteed by Henry Kritzer, had been reduced to a judgment against Kritzer individually and in favor of Alcoa in the Circuit Court of Lake County, Illinois. For a period of time prior to December 1st, 1965, both Kritzer Radiant and Bastian Morely had dealt with Alcoa as a supplier of materials used in manufacturing their products. Bastian Morely was also indebted to Alcoa as of that date in the amount of $11,319.78.

On the critical date of December 1, 1965 an agreement was entered into by and between Kritzer Radiant. Henry Kritzer, Bastian Morely and Alcoa. Pursuant to this agreement, Kritzer Radiant paid to Alcoa $23,370.60 in full satisfaction of the antecedent debt owed Alcoa in the amount of $46,741.20. Additionally, Alcoa released Henry Kritzer from the judgment it had recovered against him in the state court. Finally, Bastian satisfied its debt to Alcoa in the amount of $11,319.78, and ordered from Alcoa additional materials for payment upon receipt. On the date the settlement agreement was executed, Kritzer Radiant was insolvent and there existed creditors of Kritzer Radiant with outstanding claims against it.

. . . .

As the district court indicated in its memorandum opinion, essentially four elements must be present for a transfer to be fraudulent under the Bankruptcy Act:

1. The transfer must occur within one year of the initiation of the bankruptcy proceedings;

2. Creditors of the debtor must exist at the time of the transfer;

3. The debtor must be insolvent at the time of the transfer; and

4. There must be a failure of consideration for the transfer.

The bankruptcy petition here was filed on November 22nd, 1966, clearly within one year of the date of the transfer in question. Creditors of Kritzer Radiant were in existence when the transfer was made. Also there is no serious dispute regarding the insolvency of Kritzer Radiant on the date of the transfer. Alcoa then possessed a financial statement of Kritzer Radiant which reflected a negative net worth. Also, some three weeks prior to the execution of the settlement agreement the defendant wrote its attorneys suggesting that certain precautions be undertaken " . . . should either Bastian Morely or Kritzer Radiant Coils go into bankruptcy within four months of the transaction." While it is true that the defendant denied the allegation of insolvency in its answer, we agree with the district court that since Alcoa did not challenge plaintiff's assertion by counter–affidavit nor make any attempt to demonstrate the inaccessibility of information on this question, the issue of insolvency did not present a fact issue precluding the entry of summary judgment.

Thus, the question becomes, under the undisputed facts as set forth above, whether the transfer from Kritzer Radiant to Alcoa was for "fair consideration." Where the transfer is made to extinguish an antecedent debt, the Bankruptcy Act provides that the consideration given must represent a "fair equivalent" for the antecedent debt and must be given in "good faith." . . . As the defendant itself recognizes, a transfer lacking in good faith is fraudulent within the meaning of the Bankruptcy Act even though fair equivalent may have been present. And the question of good faith depends under the circumstances on whether the "transaction carries the earmarks of an arms–length bargain." . . .

Considering all the facts that attended this transaction we agree with the district court that the transfer was fraudulent within the meaning of § 67d(2)(a)of the Bankruptcy Act. We find most significant the relationship of the parties to the settlement agreement and the respective allocation of its benefits. Henry Kritzer, the President of the bankrupt as well as a director and stockholder of Bastian Morely, was released entirely and without any consideration on his part from a legally enforceable state court judgment against him. Moreover, Bastian Morely, the principal stockholder of the bankrupt, was permitted to retain its supplier and, for a consideration, extinguished its own antecedent debt to Alcoa. Finally, Alcoa acquired an advantage over the other creditors of the bankrupt at a time when Alcoa was certainly aware of the precarious financial position of Kritzer Radiant. Thus the primary and important benefits of this transaction ran to parties other than the bankrupt. Since transfers made to benefit third parties are not considered as made for "fair" consideration . . . , we agree that on these facts, which are not disputed by the defendant, the transfer here was a fraudulent one within . . . 67d(2)(a) of the Bankruptcy Act.

Alcoa next contends that summary judgment was improper here since there was a fact question raised by the pleadings and affidavits as to the motives and intentions of Alcoa with respect to this transaction. In this regard Alcoa maintains that the transfer here could not have been fraudulent unless Alcoa participated in a scheme to defeat the other creditors of Kritzer Radiant or unless Alcoa acted on bad faith in valuing the properties exchanged. We have been unable to find any support, either statutory or in case law, for this argument. Indeed the Act itself is to the contrary. A transfer made without "fair consideration", such as the one involved here, represents but one of the several types of fraudulent transfers defined in the Act. . . . [U]nder the section of the Act on which the Trustee proceeded in this case, the motives and intentions of Alcoa are simply immaterial.

Lastly, Alcoa contends that under the Bankruptcy Act, it may retain the transferred funds as security for payment of its antecedent debt. Under our long–standing rule that issues not presented to the district court cannot be raised for the first time on appeal, we need not consider this question.

For the reasons given the judgment of the district court is hereby affirmed.

NOTES AND QUESTIONS

(1) The *Bullard* court correctly states the general rule that transfers for the benefit of third parties lack fair consideration. Does the court correctly apply this principle? *See B–F Building Corp.* and *Barr & Creelman, supra,* and the notes following those cases.

(2) To what extent was Kritzer Radiant's estate diminished by its settlement with Alcoa? How would you assess the benefit received by the debtor's estate on account of the settlement? The court "found most significant the relation of the parties to the settlement agreement and the respective allocation of its benefits." Although the court may have analyzed the *allocation* of those benefits, do you think it properly *quantified* the actual benefit received by the debtor?

(3) The court notes that "Alcoa acquired an advantage over the other creditors of the bankrupt at a time when Alcoa was certainly aware of the precarious financial condition of Kritzer Radiant." Is that fact relevant to a determination of whether Alcoa received a fraudulent transfer? *See Nicklaus v. Peoples Bank & Trust Co.,* 369 F.2d 683 (8th Cir. 1966) (noting distinctions between fraudulent transfers and preferences).

(4) As the *Bullard* court points out, the relevant date for determining the debtor's insolvency is the date of the transfer. Moreover, if the debtor is rendered insolvent by the transfer, *i.e.,* becomes insolvent after and because of the transfer, the transfer will also be deemed constructively fraudulent, assuming that the other statutory requirements are satisfied. *See, e.g., Palestroni v. Jacobs,* 18 N.J. Super. 438, 87 A.2d 356 (N.J. Super. Ct. App. Div. 1952). The only measuring date for determining fair consideration, however, is the actual date of the transfer: subsequent appreciation or depreciation of the value of the consideration is irrelevant. *Day v. Central Fidelity Bank, N.A. (In re Appomattox Agri–Service, Inc.),* 6 B.C.D. 1239, 1241 (Bankr. W.D. Va. 1980); *Greene v. Newman (In re Newman),* 15 B.R. 658 (S.D.N.Y. 1981).

(5) Determining when the transfer occurred—a necessary step for evaluating insolvency and fair consideration—is not always easy. Under § 548(d)(1) of the Bankruptcy Code, a fraudulent transfer is deemed made when it becomes valid against a subsequent bona fide purchaser pursuant to applicable state law. Section 6 of the UFTA is similar: if the transfer must be made a matter of public record to be effective as against third persons, it is not deemed made under the UFTA until it has become recorded. The UFCA contains no comparable provision defining the time of the transfer; the controlling date is the *actual* date of the transfer. If a debtor's real property, which is subject to a mortgage, is subsequently sold at a foreclosure

sale, may the sale be avoided as a fraudulent transfer? This issue has generated considerable debate. The Fifth Circuit has held that a mortgagee's non–judicial foreclosure sale, conducted within the statutory one–year reachback period, was a fraudulent transfer. *Abramson v. Lakewood Bank & Trust Co.*, 647 F.2d 547 (5th Cir. 1981) (2–1), *cert. denied*, 454 U.S. 1164 (1982); *Durrett v. Washington National Insurance Co.*, 621 F.2d 201 (5th Cir. 1980). The panels in those two cases inexplicably ignored the Fifth Circuit's prior holding in *Gordon v. Eaton Corp. (In re Wilco Forest Machinery, Inc.)*, 491 F.2d 1041, 1047 (5th Cir. 1974) ("the transfer . . . occurred when the filing requirements were met, . . . over a year prior to . . . bankruptcy. Therefore, it was too remote in time to constitute a fraudulent transfer. . . ."). The Ninth Circuit, by contrast, has rejected the reasoning of *Durrett*, noting that the effect of the Fifth Circuit's holding "would significantly chill participation at foreclosure sales." *Madrid v. Lawyers Title Insurance Corp. (In re Madrid)*, 725 F.2d 1197, 1202 (9th Cir. 1984). The *Madrid* court held that the transfer of the debtor's interest in her real property occurred at the time the deed of trust (similar to a mortgage) was recorded under state law, not at the time of the subsequent foreclosure sale. *Accord Alsop v. State (In re Alsop)*, 5 C.B.C.2d 797 (Bankr. D. Alaska 1981), *aff'd*, 22 B.R. 1017, 9 B.C.D. 993 (D. Alaska 1982); *Wickham v. United American Bank (In re Thompson)*, 18 B.R. 67 (Bankr. E.D. Tenn. 1982). Other courts, like the Bankruptcy Appellate Panel in *Madrid*, have held that the transfer occurred at the time of the regularly conducted, non–collusive foreclosure sale, but that the transfer was not fraudulent because the percentage of the property's market value received constituted fair consideration. *Lawyers Title Insurance Corp. v. Madrid (In re Madrid)*, 6 C.B.C.2d 1133 (Bankr. 9th Cir. 1982) (64–67% of property's fair market value received at sale). UFTA § 5(b) adopts this view. *See* Official Comment accompanying UFTA § 5(b) (premise of the subsection is that "a sale of the collateral by the secured party as the normal consequence of default . . . [is] the safest way of establishing the fair value of the collateral. . ."), citing 2 G. Gilmore, *Security Interests in Personal Property 1227* (1965). Finally, some courts and commentators have argued that "the transfer in question is not the creation of the original lien when the deed of trust was given and recorded, but the termination of the debtor's equity at the time of the foreclosure sale." Treister, Recent Bankruptcy Decisions (Part 1), ALI–ABA Course Materials J., Vol. 7 No. 1, at 52 (1982); *accord Rosner v. Worcester (In re Worcester)*, 28 B.R. 910, 914 (Bankr. C.D. Cal. 1983). *See generally* Alden, Gross, and Borowitz, Real Property Foreclosure as a Fraudulent Conveyance: Proposals for Solving the Durrett Problem, 38 Bus. Law 1605 (1983); Zinman, Houle, and Weiss, Fraudulent Transfers According to Alden, Gross and Borowitz: A Tale of Two Circuits, 39 Bus. Law. 977 (1984).

SOUTHERN INDUSTRIES, INC. v. JEREMIAS

New York Supreme Court, Appellate Division (2d Dept.)
66 A.D.2d 178, 411 N.Y.S.2d 945 (1978)

DAMIANI, J.

The principal issue in this case is whether a transfer of substantially all of the assets of an insolvent corporation to a director thereof in return for the satisfaction of an antecedent debt is barred by the fraudulent conveyance provisions of the Debtor and Creditor Law. We hold the transfer invalid.

Ernest Jeremias was an officer, director and major stockholder of a publicly held corporation named Mazel Knitting Mills, Inc. Jeremias had loaned the corporation substantially in excess of $200,000 and this debt was reflected in the corporate books. The petitioner, Southern Industries, Inc., was a supplier of yarn to Mazel Knitting Mills on an open account.

There came a time when Mazel Knitting Mills ceased to do business and, in August, 1976, a meeting of shareholders was called to deal with its troubled financial condition. At the meeting it was resolved that the corporation, through its board of directors, should sell all of its machinery, equipment, furniture and inventory and use the proceeds to satisfy creditors to the extent possible. On August 9, 1976, pursuant to this resolution, Jeremias, acting as president of Mazel Knitting Mills, sold all its furniture, fixtures, equipment, inventory and certain of its machinery to himself in consideration of the cancellation of $150,000 of the antecedent debt owed to him by the corporation.

Southern Industries was Mazel Knitting Mills' other major creditor. After the corporation ceased doing business, the account of Southern Industries remained unpaid and, in October, 1976, it commenced an action against Mazel Knitting Mills. On December 2, 1976, judgment was entered in favor of Southern Industries and against Mazel in the sum of $31,062.89. Early in January, 1977, an execution on that judgment was issued to the Sheriff of Kings County and thereafter he entered Mazel's place of business and levied upon the entire contents of the premises. The Sheriff scheduled a sale for February 18, 1977.

On February 2, 1977, prior to the date fixed for the Sheriff's sale, a public auction was held at the instance of Jeremias, who contended that he, and not the corporation, was the owner of the property. The proceeds of the auction were in excess of $60,000.

After serving restraining notices, Southern Industries commenced this special proceeding . . . against Jeremias and the auctioneers to compel them to satisfy its judgment from the proceeds of the auction. Upon consent of all the parties, the proceeding was dismissed as to the auctioneers upon condition that they deposit $35,000 of the proceeds with the Treasurer of Nassau County. After a hearing, Special Term awarded judgment to petitioner directing that its judgment against Mazel Knitting Mills be satisfied from the funds on deposit with the County Treasurer, together with interest, costs and disbursements, but denying petitioner's application for a counsel fee and Sheriff's poundage. Jeremias has appealed from so much of the judgment as is adverse to him and the petitioner has appealed from so much thereof as denies it a counsel fee and the Sheriff's poundage.

New York has adopted the provisions of the Uniform Fraudulent Conveyance Act. . . . Section 276 of . . . [that] Law provides that every conveyance made with the *actual intent* to hinder, delay or defraud creditors is fraudulent and void. In this connection the actual intent to defraud consists of deception intentionally practiced to frustrate the legal rights of another. . . . A prime example of this type of fraud is where a debtor transfers his property to another while retaining the use thereof so as to continue in business free from the claims of creditors. The actual intent to defraud was not proven in this case. Mazel Knitting Mills did not transfer its property to Jeremias in order to put that property out of the reach of creditors while it still continued in business.

Section 273 of the Debtor and Creditor Law covers constructive, as opposed to actual, fraud. Constructive fraud may be defined as a breach of a duty which, irrespective of moral guilt and intent, the law declares fraudulent because of its tendency to deceive, to violate a confidence or to injure public or private interests which the law deems worthy of special protection. . . . [W]ithout regard to the actual intent to defraud, every conveyance made by a person who is or will thereby be rendered insolvent is fraudulent as to creditors if made without "fair consideration." It appears that Mazel Knitting Mills was insolvent at the time of the transfer. It owed Jeremias in excess of $200,000 and another $30,000 to the petitioner, but its assets, consisting of furniture, fixtures, equipment, inventory and machinery, brought only $60,000 at a subsequent auction sale. In any event, there is no doubt that the transfer of substantially all of its assets to Jeremias left nothing with which to pay the debt it owed to petitioner. Since at the time of the transfer Mazel Knitting Mills was, or was rendered, insolvent, that transfer must be set aside if it was made without fair consideration.

. . . .

Special Term held that the cancellation of an antecedent debt owed to a major stockholder of a corporation was *not* a fair equivalent for the property transferred to his ownership. . . . [T]he amount realized at the forced sale of previously transferred property does not necessarily reflect the ordinary market value of such property . . . However, it is not contended on this appeal that the cancellation of a valid $150,000 antecedent debt in exchange for property which brought only $60,000, did not constitute a fair equivalent of valuable consideration. The proof in this case establishes that there was an exchange of equivalent value; but in addition thereto, the law requires that the transfer must be made in "good faith".

. . . .

A major case dealing with the interpretation of the phrase "good faith" as used in the act is *Sparkman & McLean Co. v. Derber*, . . . where it was held that a person seeking to set aside a conveyance upon the basis of lack of good faith must prove that one or more of the following factors is lacking: (1) an honest belief in the propriety of the activities in question; (2) no intent to take unconscionable advantage of others; and (3) no intent to, or knowledge of the fact that the activities in question will hinder, delay, or defraud others. The term "good faith" does not merely mean the opposite of the phrase "actual intent to defraud". That is to say, an absence of fraudulent intent does not mean that the transaction was necessarily entered into in good faith. The lack of good faith imports a failure to deal honestly, fairly and openly.

Measured by these standards, the instant transfer must be deemed void for lack of good faith because it was consummated with the intent to obtain an unconscionable advantage for one, who is an officer, director and major stockholder of the corporation over the rights of other general creditors. Former New York law expressly forbade the granting of a preference to the creditors of an insolvent corporation and it prohibited a corporation which had refused to pay its obligations, when due, from transferring any of its property to an officer, director or stockholder for the payment of an antecedent debt or for any consideration other than full value paid in cash (former Stock Corporation Law, § 15). The purpose of section 15 of the former Stock Corporation Law was explained . . . as follows:

> The evil to be obviated by that section was the giving of a preference by an insolvent corporation to its officers, directors and stockholders who should become aware of the insolvency before that fact could become known to the general public. It was feared that in such a case they would be likely to devote the property of the corporation to the payment of their own debts and thereby leave nothing for the other creditors who did not know of its condition. The transfer of any of its property to any officer, director or stockholder, directly or indirectly, for the payment of any debt or upon any other consideration than the full value of the property, paid in cash, was prohibited, because such a transfer by an insolvent corporation would permit the transferee to receive the property of the corporation for his debt and thereby obtain a preference over the other creditors. . . .

Section 15 of the former Stock Corporation Law was . . . not incorporated into the new [Business Corporation] law upon the ground that it had become "superfluous" because the matter was "adequately covered" in the Uniform Fraudulent Conveyance provisions of the Debtor and Creditor Law and in the Bankruptcy Act. . . . Jeremias contends that because the express statutory prohibition of the former law was repealed, it was perfectly lawful for Mazel Knitting Mills to grant a preference in the payment of a debt owed to him, as one of its stockholders, officers and directors, over the debts owed to other general creditors of the corporation. We disagree.

The courts of many jurisdictions have held that the preferential satisfaction of debts owed by insolvent corporations to their directors, over debts due to other general creditors, is barred by the common law. . . .

Whether it be upon the theory that directors of insolvent corporations are trustees for the benefit of all creditors, or upon the theory that it would be inequitable to allow directors to use inside information and their controlling voice in corporate affairs to benefit themselves over the claims of others, the common law forbids preferences to directors of insolvent corporations as being contrary to principles of fair, honest and open dealing . . . Accordingly, the transfer in this case is void because, although made for a fair consideration, it was not made in good faith.

Jeremias argues that in the event we find the transfer invalid, the proceeds of the auction sale should be distributed to the parties based upon the relative proportion that the debt owed to each of them bears to all the corporate debts. The ordinary rule of distribution of the assets of an insolvent corporation is equality among creditors of the same class. Upon insolvency, assets must be equally distributed among creditors without preference or priority. However, whenever judicial preference has been established by superior legal diligence, that preference is always preserved in the distribution of assets by the court. Thus, a creditor who is diligent enough to make a levy by execution or attachment upon an insolvent's property prior to the commencement of insolvency proceedings acquires a lien which is not divested by those subsequent proceedings . . . The parties concede that the Sheriff levied upon the corporate property. The petitioner in this case "won the race". It is no longer a general creditor but, rather, as a levying judgment creditor, it is entitled to the satisfaction of its judgment from the proceeds of the auction sale presently on deposit.

The petitioner has cross–appealed from so much of the judgment as denied it a counsel fee and an award of Sheriff's poundage. . . . Special Term was correct in denying an award of a counsel fee. As stated above, the transfer in question was made without an actual intent to defraud and is invalid only under the constructive fraud provisions of . . . the Debtor and Creditor Law. Where the prevailing party fails to prove that the transfer was made with the actual intent to defraud, the provision for an award of counsel fee is inoperative . . .

The law provides that where a conveyance is fraudulent as to a creditor, such creditor may, as against any person other than a bona fide purchaser, disregard the conveyance and levy execution upon the property conveyed . . . Petitioner contends therefore that the issue of execution to the Sheriff and his subsequent levy upon the property was valid, entitling it to an award of the Sheriff's poundage.

Poundage is a fee awarded to the Sheriff in the nature of a percentage commission upon moneys recovered pursuant to a levy or execution of attachment . . . The defendant against whom the execution is levied must respond to the Sheriff for his poundage . . . In this case the Sheriff did not take the property in question into his possession, but apparently levied by serving a copy of the execution upon the judgment debtor. Although a Sheriff's sale was scheduled, it did not take place because prior to the date set therefor the assets were sold at a public auction conducted on behalf of Jeremias. Petitioner then commenced this special proceeding . . . to compel the private auctioneer and Jeremias to satisfy its judgment from the auction proceeds. Thus, the Sheriff never conducted an auction and never collected any moneys on account of petitioner's judgment against Mazel Knitting Mills. With certain exceptions, the statute authorizes the Sheriff to receive poundage only on amounts actually collected . . . Where no actual collection on the execution is made, the Sheriff is entitled to poundage only where the parties settle, the execution is vacated or set aside, or the person that issued the process interferes with the collection of the money. . . . .

NOTES AND QUESTIONS

(1) The court in *Southern Industries, supra,* explains that the provisions of the repealed New York Stock Corporation Law, which would have proscribed the actions taken by the debtor's officer, director, and major stockholder, were considered "superfluous" in the new Business Corporation Law because the legal effect of the transactions was "adequately covered" by New York's adoption of the UFCA. Transactions that are valid under basic principles of corporate law, however, may frequently be subject to fraudulent transfer attack. For example, consideration sufficient to support an ordinary contract—*i.e.,* "good consideration"—will not necessarily be "fair" consideration for fraudulent transfer purposes. *Cohen v. Sutherland,* 257 F.2d 737, 742 (2d Cir. 1958). What other examples can you think of ? *See generally* Clark, *The Duties of the Corporate Debtor to its Creditors,* 90 Harv. L. Rev. 505 (1977).

(2) At what stage does "failure to deal honestly, fairly and openly," which is the way the *Southern Industries* court summarizes its standards for lack of good faith (and, therefore, lack of fair consideration in the *constructively* fraudulent transfer context), reach the level of bad faith that would warrant a finding of actual intent to hinder, delay, or defraud creditors? Can you formulate more precise standards than the ones offered by the court? Remember that under the new Bankruptcy Code and the UFTA, "reasonably equivalent value" replaces the former Bankruptcy Act's "fair consideration," and *eliminates* the requirement of good faith. *See* Levin, *An Introduction to the Trustee's Avoiding Powers,* 53 Am. Bankr. L.J. 173, 181 (1979).

(3) Southern Industries levied upon the debtor's property in the hands of the debtor's transferee prior to seeking avoidance of the fraudulent transfer. Could it have done so if it had not been a judgment creditor? *See* UFTA §§ 1(3) and (4), 7(A); UFCA § 9(1)(b); *Montana Association of Credit Management v. Hergert,* 181 Mont. 442, 593 P.2d 1059 (1979). If another judgment creditor had levied upon the debtor's property before Southern Industries did, what result would have ensued? What action could Southern Industries have taken if its claim against the debtor had not yet matured? *See* UFTA § 7(A); UFCA § 10; *Getty Refining & Marketing Co. v. Park Oil, Inc.,* 385 A.2d 147, 148–49 (Del. Ch. 1978). How can a creditor whose claim has not matured show that it is in fact a creditor? *See Pittsburgh Iron Works Co. v. Moon Motor Lodge,* 413 Pa. 224, 196 A.2d 335 (1964); UFTA § 1(3) and (4). Must the standards for the issuance of a preliminary injunction be met in order to obtain relief under UFTA § 7 and UFCA § 10? *See Oksner v. Superior Court of the County of Los Angeles,* 229 Cal. App. 2d 672, 40 Cal. Rptr. 621 (Cal. Dist. Ct. App. 1964); *Empire Boxboard Corp. v. Active Paper Box Co.,* 115 N.Y.S.2d 14 (N.Y. Sup. Ct. 1952); and Official Comment (3) accompanying UFTA § 7.

ORR v. KINDERHILL CORPORATION

United States Court of Appeals, Second Circuit
991 F.2d 31 (1993)

McLAUGHLIN, Circuit Judge.

Plaintiff Ashley S. Orr, the receiver of American Partners, Inc., is a judgment creditor of defendant Kinderhill Corporation. While Orr's damage action against Kinderhill was pending, Kinderhill deeded certain real property to its wholly–owned subsidiary, defendant Kinderhill Investment Company ("KIC"), for nominal consideration. After the transfer, but before the deeds were recorded, Kinderhill distributed the stock in KIC to Kinderhill stockholders. Key Bank of Eastern New York, with knowledge of these transactions, later lent money to KIC and took back mortgages on the real property as security.

After he obtained a judgment against Kinderhill, Orr sued in the District Court for the Northern District of New York (Con. G. Cholakis, Judge) to set aside as a fraudulent conveyance Kinderhill's transfer of the property to KIC and KIC's subsequent transfer to Key Bank of a security interest in the real property. The district court granted partial summary judgment to Orr and set aside the transfer of real property, holding: (1) that a six–year limitations period applies to actions under New York Debtor & Creditor Law § 273–a; and (2) that the transfer was not supported by fair consideration and was therefore fraudulent. The district court also granted partial summary judgment to Key Bank on Orr's claim under Debtor & Creditor Law § 273, holding that it was time–barred. Because the transfer of real property and the distribution of stock were an integrated transaction not supported by fair consideration, we now affirm.

Background

Twenty years ago when limited partnerships were popular as tax shelters, Thomas A. Martin founded Kinderhill. It was to serve as managing general partner in various limited partnerships engaged in thoroughbred breeding and racing. Martin has been the company's president and principal shareholder. Since 1979, Key Bank has been Kinderhill's primary lender.

American Partners, a California corporation, had been a co–general partner with Kinderhill in several limited partnerships. In August 1984, American Partners went into receivership and Orr, as its receiver, sued Kinderhill and Martin in the United States District Court for the Southern District of California (the "California Action") for over one million dollars in managements fees that American Partners claimed it was owed.

In December 1985, while the California Action was pending against it, Kinderhill decided to restructure, apparently for tax reasons. Its Board of Directors approved a plan to create a wholly–owned subsidiary (KIC) to which Kinderhill would then transfer the ten tracts of land (totalling 700 acres) it owned in Columbia County, New York (the "New York Property"). To complete the deal, Kinderhill would distribute all its shares in KIC to its own shareholders.

On New Years Eve, 1985, Kinderhill deeded nine of the ten New York tracts to KIC for nominal consideration (one to ten dollars). Nine months later, Kinderhill conveyed the tenth tract to KIC, also for nominal consideration. KIC assumed several outstanding mortgages on the New York Property totalling $780,000, although the land was worth between $3.45 and $4.4 million. KIC did not record the deeds until November 6, 1986 (seven tracts), November 11, 1986 (two tracts), and January 20, 1987 (one tract).

In September 1986, after Kinderhill had deeded the New York Property to KIC, but before the deeds were recorded, Kinderhill approved a plan, effective October 1, 1986, for the distribution of all KIC shares to Kinderhill shareholders. Upon the distribution, KIC and Kinderhill no longer had a formal corporate relationship, although Martin continued to control and operate both companies.

By 1986, Kinderhill had begun to experience financial difficulty as a result of a recession in the thoroughbred industry that was exacerbated by adverse changes in the tax laws. Key Bank watched all this from afar. It had identified the company's cash flow problems as early as 1985, and, indeed, had placed its Kinderhill loans on watch status in March 1986. For the fiscal year ended September 30, 1986, Kinderhill lost $612,825, and had a negative cash flow over twice that amount.

In early 1987, Martin came back to Key Bank for financing, requesting that it provide a $2.5 million revolving line of credit to KIC, secured by the New York Property. Key Bank ordered a title report which disclosed the transfers of the property from Kinderhill to KIC and the nominal consideration paid by KIC. Key Bank also received Kinderhill's audited financial statements for fiscal year 1986, which disclosed that "[t]he Court [adjudicating the California Action] has indicated that it has decided to grant judgement [sic] to the plaintiff in an amount approximating $1,250,000 . . . .." Key Bank approved the loan and, on March 13, 1987, KIC gave Key Bank a $2.5 million mortgage on the New York Property to secure advances under the line of credit.

On June 17, 1987, Orr obtained a judgment in the California Action against Kinderhill individually for $159,338, and against Kinderhill and Martin, jointly and severally, for $1,071,489, plus prejudgment interest. The Ninth Circuit subsequently affirmed that judgment, but Orr has been able to collect only $42,000 from Kinderhill and Martin.

In March 1991, Orr brought the present action against Kinderhill, KIC, Key Bank, Martin, his wife, and the trustee of a trust established by Martin, seeking to set aside several transfers of property (including Kinderhill's transfers of the New York Property to KIC) as fraudulent under Debtor & Creditor Law §§ 273 and 273–a. After some discovery, both Orr and Key Bank moved for summary judgment on the claims relating to the validity of Key Bank's mortgages. Key Bank asserted several affirmative defenses, including a claim that Orr's action was barred by the applicable statutes of limitations.

In an opinion and order dated August 26, 1991, Judge Cholakis denied the summary judgment motions. He held that the six–year limitations period of N.Y.Civ.Prac.L. & R. ("CPLR") § 213(1) applied to fraudulent conveyance actions under both sections 273 and 273–a. First, there being no evidence that Key Bank was amenable to suit in California, he rejected Key Bank's claim that California's four–year limitations period applied to the section 273 claim under New York's borrowing statute, CPLR § 202. *See Stafford v. International Harvester Co.*, 668 F.2d 142, 152 (2d Cir. 1981) "New York's borrowing statute does not require the application of the statute of limitations of a jurisdiction if the cause of action could never have been brought in that jurisdiction."). Second, he held that Orr's section 273–a claim was controlled by CPLR § 213(1)'s six–year limitations period, not CPLR § 214(2)'s three–year period governing causes of action created by statute. On the other hand, he denied plaintiff Orr's motion for summary judgment because there were questions of fact regarding whether KIC gave fair consideration for the New York Property.

After further discovery and additional submissions to the court, both parties renewed their motions for summary judgment. In an opinion and order dated March 30, 1992, Judge Cholakis granted summary judgment to plaintiff Orr on his 273–a claim, concluding that KIC had not given "fair consideration" for the New York Property. The district court granted defendant Key Bank summary judgment on Orr's section 273 claim, thereby reversing itself on the statute–of–limitations issue. Judge Cholakis held that, because Key Bank had now demonstrated that it was amenable to jurisdiction in California, the action could have been brought there and, therefore, New York's borrowing statute did apply. Because Orr's section 273 claim was untimely under the California limitations period of four years, the court concluded that Key Bank was entitled to summary judgment.

Judge Cholakis entered a partial summary judgment reflecting his opinion and he certified an interlocutory appeal under Fed.R.Civ.P. 54(b). On appeal, Key Bank challenges Judge Cholakis's award of summary judgment to Orr on his section 273–a claim; and Orr cross–appeals Judge Cholakis's award of summary judgment to Key Bank on the section 273 claim.

Discussion

Statute of Limitations

Key Bank argues that Orr's claim under Debtor & Creditor Law § 273–a was barred by CPLR § 214(2), which imposes a three–year statute of limitations on "an action to recover upon a liability, penalty or forfeiture created or imposed by statute." We agree with the district court, however, that the three–year period governing liability created by a statute does not apply to an action by a judgment creditor to set aside a fraudulent conveyance.

CPLR § 214(2) "does not apply to liabilities existing at common law which have been recognized or implemented by statute." *State v. Danny's Franchise Sys., Inc.*, 131 A.D.2d 746, 746, 517 N.Y.S.2d 157, 158 (2d Dept. 1987), *appeal dismissed*, 70 N.Y.2d 940, 524 N.Y.S.2d 672, 519 N.E.2d 618 (1988). Rather, section 214(2) applies only when a statute creates a new liability that did not exist at common law and would not exist but for the statute. *See Aetna Life & Casualty Co. v. Nelson*, 67 N.Y.2d 169, 174, 501 N.Y.S.2d 313, 315, 492 N.E.2d 386, 388 (1986); *Danny's*

Franchise Sys., 131 A.D.2d at 746, 517 N.Y.S.2d at 158. Moreover, " 'the statute must be essential to the cause of action' [and] . . . the statutory liability must truly be new." Practice Commentaries, CPLR § 214:2, at 521 (quoting *Bryden v. Wilson Memorial Hosp.*, 136 A.D.2d 843, 523 N.Y.S.2d 686 (3d Dept.1988)). That the statute merely enlarges the common–law scheme of liability or grants additional remedies is insufficient to bring it within CPLR § 214(2). *State v. Cortelle Corp.*, 38 N.Y.2d 83, 86–87, 378 N.Y.S.2d 654, 656–57, 341 N.E.2d 223, 224–25 (1975); *Danny's Franchise Sys.*, 131 A.D.2d at 747, 517 N.Y.S.2d at 159; *State v. Bronxville Glen I Assocs.*, 181 A.D.2d 516, 581 N.Y.S.2d 189, 190 (1st Dept.1992).

Section 273–a provides:

Every conveyance made without fair consideration when the person making it is a defendant in an action for money damages or a judgment in such an action has been docketed against him, is fraudulent as to the plaintiff in that action without regard to the actual intent of the defendant if, after final judgment for the plaintiff, the defendant fails to satisfy the judgment.

N.Y. Debtor & Creditor Law § 273–a.

When Debtor & Credit Law § 273–a was enacted in 1961, the liability it imposed was not novel. Fraudulent conveyance actions were common in New York long before 1961. *See, e.g., Buttles v. Smith*, 281 N.Y. 226, 22 N.E.2d 350 (1939); *Farmers' Loan & Trust Co. v. Meyer*, 222 A.D. 123, 225 N.Y.S. 561 (1st Dept.1927); *West Shore Furniture Co. v. Murphy*, 141 N.Y.S. 835 (Sup.Ct.Ulster County 1913). Indeed, nearly four hundred years ago, the infamous Star Chamber declared fraudulent a conveyance by a debtor of all his goods and chattels to one creditor during the pendency of another creditor's action. *Twyne's Case*, 76 Eng.Rep. 809 (Star Chamber 1601); *see also Hadlock v. Eric*, 23 F.Supp. 692, 693 (S.D.N.Y.1938) ("section 273 of the Debtor and Creditor Law does not itself create new liabilities but was a codification of and the embodiment of existing presumptions established by a long line of decisions of the courts of the State of New York"). Section 273–a simply fleshed out the meaning of a fraudulent conveyance by stigmatizing certain conveyances made during litigation. Thus, CPLR § 214(2) does not apply to actions under Debtor & Creditor Law § 273–a.

We agree with the district court that actions under section 273–a are governed by the six–year limitations period of CPLR § 213(1). *See Martin v. Martin*, 29 A.D.2d 864, 865, 288 N.Y.S.2d 374, 376 (2d Dept.1968), *aff'd in relevant part, modified on other grounds*, 23 N.Y.2d 858, 298 N.Y.S.2d 68, 245 N.E.2d 801 (1969); *RCA Corp. v. Tucker*, 696 F.Supp. 845, 857 n. 9 (E.D.N.Y.1988). An action to set aside a fraudulent conveyance under section 273–a is an action for constructive fraud. *See Republic Ins. Co. v. Levy*, 69 Misc.2d 453, 454, 329 N.Y.S.2d 918, 922 (Sup.Ct.Rockland Cty.1972). Compare Debtor & Creditor Law §§ 276 (governing actual fraud) & 276–a (authorizing award of attorneys' fees for proof of actual fraud have long been subject to the catch–all limitations period of CPLR § 213(1), *see Dolmetta v. Uintah Nat'l Corp.*, 712 F.2d 15, 18 (2d Cir. 1983); *Dybowski v. Dyboswka*, 146 A.D.2d 604, 605, 536 N.Y.S.2d 838, 839 (2d Dept.1989), and its predecessor, Civ.Prac.Act § 53. *See Hearn 45 St. Corp. v. Jano*, 283 N.Y. 139, 144,

27 N.E.2d 814, 817 (1940); *Buttles*, 281 N.Y. at 236, 22 N.E.2d at 353; *McCabe v. Gelfand*, 58 Misc.2d 497, 499, 295 N.Y.S.2d 583, 585 (Sup.Ct.Kings County 1968). *See generally* Samuel M. Hesson, *The Statute of Limitations in Actions to Set Aside Fraudulent Conveyances and in Actions Against Directors by Creditors of Corporations*, 32 Cornell L.Q. 222, 224–27 (1946); Note, Statutory Limitation for Fraud Actions, 13 St.John's L.Rev. 114, 115–19 (1938).

Fair Consideration

Key Bank also argues that the district court erred by holding that Kinderhill's conveyance of the New York Property to KIC was not supported by fair consideration. In the eyes of Key Bank, the transfer to KIC instantly inflated the value of KIC shares held by Kinderhill, thereby providing the requisite fair consideration. We need not address this argument, however, because we will not turn a blind eye to the reality that the transfer of the New York Property and the spin–off of KIC shares constituted a single, integrated transaction. This transactions, viewed in its entirety, was not supported by fair consideration.

In equity, "substance will not give way to form, [and] technical considerations will not prevent substantial justice from being done." *Pepper v. Litton*, 308 U.s. 295, 305, 60 S.Ct. 238, 244, 84 L.Ed. 281 (1939); *see also Dean v. Davis*, 242 U.S. 438, 443, 37 S.Ct. 130, 131, 61 L.Ed. 419 (1917); *Warren v. Union Bank of Rochester*, 157 N.Y. 259, 270–71, 51 N.E. 1036, 1039 (1898). Thus, an allegedly fraudulent conveyance must be evaluated in context; "[w]here a transfer is only a step in a general plan, the plan 'must be viewed as a whole with all its composite implications.' " *Pereira v. Checkmate Communications Co. (In re Checkmate Stereo & Elec., Ltd.)*, 9 B.R. 585, 612 (Bankr.E.D.N.Y.1981) (quoting *Buffum v. Peter Barceloux Co.*, 289 U.S. 227, 232, 53 S.Ct. 539, 541, 77 L.Ed. 1140 (1933)), *aff'd*, 21 B.R. 402 (E.D.N.Y.1982); *accord Yoder v. T.E.L. Leasing, Inc. (In re Suburban Motor Freight, Inc.)*, 124 B.R. 984, 998 (Bankr.S.D.Ohio 1990); *Gafco, Inc. v. H.D.S. Mercantile Corp.*, 47 Misc.2d 661, 664–65, 263 N.Y.S.2d 109, 114 (N.Y.Civ.Ct.1965); *Gruenebaum v. Lissauer*, 185 Misc. 718, 728, 57 N.Y.S.2d 137, 145 (Sup.Ct.N.Y.County 1945), *aff'd*, 270 A.D. 836, 61 N.Y.S.2d 372 (1st Dept.1946).

The record is clear that Kinderhill's conveyance of the New York Property to KIC and Kinderhill's subsequent distribution of KIC shares were elements of a single restructuring plan adopted by Kinderhill's board of directors in December 1985. Key Bank acknowledged as much, both in contemporaneous internal lending documents and at oral argument. So viewed, the restructuring was not supported by fair consideration for, in effect, it was a gratuitous transfer of the New York Property by Kinderhill.

We recently analyzed a similar transaction in the tax context. *See Salomon Inc. v. United States*, 976 F.2d 837 (2d Cir. 1992). As part of a corporate restructuring, *Salomon* transferred certain assets to a newly formed subsidiary and then spun–off the subsidiary to its shareholders. We rejected *Salomon*'s invitation to analyze the two-steps of the transaction separately for tax purposes: "[i]n substance, if not in form, the direct and the circuitous transaction are the same. Each achieves a rapid transfer of . . . property outside the [corporate] group. To distinguish between them would deny economic reality." *Id.* at 842 (citations omitted) (taxpayer required to pay back tax benefits associated with assets transferred out of corporate group); *see also Shapiro v. Wilgus*, 287 U.S. 348, 353–54, 53 S.Ct. 142, 143–44, 77 L.Ed. 355 (1932); *Gruenebaum*, 185 Misc. at 728, 57 N.Y.S.2d at 145.

We reach the same conclusion here. The net effect of Kinderhill's restructuring was the transfer of the New York Property without any corresponding benefit to Kinderhill. Thus, as the bank knew prior to the mortgages, *see* Debtor & Creditor Law § 278(1), the transaction was not supported by fair consideration, and, accordingly, the district court properly set it aside as a fraudulent conveyance under Debtor & Creditor Law § 273–a. *See* 1 Garrard Glenn, *Fraudulent Conveyances and Preferences* § 195, at 348 (rev. ed. 1940) ("real test of a fraudulent conveyance . . . is the unjust diminution of the debtor's estate"); *see, e.g., United Towing Co. v. Phillips*, 242 F.2d 627, 631–32 (5th Cir.), *cert. denied*, 355 U.S. 861, 78 S.Ct. 93, 2 L.Ed.2d 68 (1957); *Republic Ins. Co. v. Levy*, 69 Misc.2d at 450–51, 329 N.Y.S.2d at 918–20; *In re Campbell's Estate*, 164 Misc. 632, 299 N.Y.S. 442 (Sur.Ct.N.Y.County 1937); *cf. Salomon v. Kaiser (In re Kaiser)*, 722 F.2d 1574, 1582–83 (2d Cir. 1983) (transferring assets beyond creditors' reach without consideration received in exchange is fraudulent).

Conclusion

In sum, we hold that the district court correctly applied a six–year limitations period to Orr's claim under Debtor & Creditor Law § 273–a. Because Kinderhill's transfer of the New York Property and subsequent distribution of KIC shares were an integrated transaction, not supported by fair consideration, we affirm the district court's award of summary judgment to Orr on his claim under Debtor & Creditor Law § 273–a. In view of our affirmance on the appeal, the cross–appeal, which seeks no additional relief, is moot.

HBE LEASING CORPORATION v. FRANK

United States Court of Appeals, Second Circuit
48 F.3d 623 (1995)

NEWMAN, Chief Judge.

This appeal concerns the application of fraudulent conveyance law to multi–party transactions involving an insolvent judgment debtor. In one set of transactions, the debtor exchanged mortgages for funds and immediately transferred the funds to a third party. In another set of transactions, the debtor paid the attorney's fees of its co–defendants in a civil action. The primary question in both circumstances is whether the debtor received fair consideration for its property.

Clemence Frank ("Clemence") appeals from an order of the District Court for the Southern District of New York (Gerard L. Goettel, Judge) voiding two mortgages that she held in real property owned by judgment debtor H.H. Frank Enterprises, Inc. ("Enterprises"). The appellees, judgment creditors of Enterprises who were petitioners in the District Court ("Petitioners"), cross–appeal from the District Court's insofar as it dismissed their claims against a group of attorneys who allegedly received fraudulent conveyances from Enterprises ("the Attorneys"). We affirm the avoidance of one of Clemence's mortgages on the ground that she knew or should have known that it was part of a single transaction from which Enterprises received no benefit. However, we reverse the avoidance of her other mortgage and remand for further proceedings, because Enterprises may have used the proceeds from that mortgage for legitimate corporate purposes. On the cross–appeal, we reverse and remand the dismissal of Petitioners' claims against the Attorneys, because although the District Court properly found that Enterprises received fair consideration for these payments, it failed to consider Petitioners' alternative theory that the payments were made with actual fraudulent intent.

Background

Petitioners in this proceeding to set aside fraudulent conveyances represent a group of leasing companies and their assigns who were prevailing plaintiffs in a civil RICO action were: eight individuals, including Hiram H. Frank and Hiram J. Frank, who are the husband and son, respectively, of appellant Clemence Frank; three corporations, including Enterprises, in which Hiram J. Frank owns a majority interest; and H.H. Frank Enterprises, Inc. Pension Plan ("the Pension Plan"). After a jury trial, the District Court entered judgment for the plaintiffs for trebled RICO damages of $19,670,142 plus interest, for which the defendants are jointly and severally liable; for common law fraud damages against various defendants totaling $6,556,714; and for punitive damages totaling $5,000,000. That judgment was affirmed on a prior appeal. *HBE Leasing Corp. v. Frank*, 22 F.3d 41 (2d Cir. 1994).

With the judgment largely unsatisfied, Petitioners commenced this supplementary proceeding in aid of judgment, pursuant to Fed.R.Civ.P. 69(a) and N.Y.C.P.L.R. § 5225(b) (McKinney 1978), to void certain transfers from Enterprises to Clemence and to the Attorneys as fraudulent conveyances under New York law. Neither Clemence nor the Attorneys were defendants in the underlying RICO action.[1]

The contested transfers to Clemence consist of two mortgages on real property owned by Enterprises. These mortgages secured notes for $250,000 and $100,000, respectively, which Clemence received from Enterprises when she advanced those same amounts to the corporation. At the time of these mortgage transactions in 1992, Enterprises was a defendant in the RICO action, but no judgment had yet been entered. Clemence was not at that time an officer, director, or shareholder of Enterprises, although she had been a director until at least mid–1990. Petitioners do not deny that Clemence advanced a total of $350,000 at the time the mortgages were created, nor do they dispute in this action that the money she advanced derived

---

[1] Petitioners also instituted a separate diversity proceeding in the District Court to void other alleged fraudulent conveyances by the judgment debtors, including other transfers to Clemence and some of the Attorneys. *See HBE Leasing Corp. v. Frank*, 851 F.Supp. 571 (S.D.N.Y.1994).

from her own separate funds. Rather, their claim that the mortgages represented fraudulent conveyances stems from the fact that shortly after Enterprises received the $250,000 loan from Clemence, Enterprises disbursed these funds to her son, Hiram J. Frank, purportedly as repayment for loans he had earlier made to Enterprises. Similarly, shortly after Enterprises received the $100,000 loan from Clemence, the corporation disbursed approximately $60,000 of these monies to the Attorneys.

The total of the contested conveyances to the Attorneys comprised Enterprises' payment of $775,722 in fees for legal services allegedly rendered not to Enterprises itself, but to its co–defendants for what Enterprises contends was part of a unified legal defense in the RICO action. This sum does not include an additional $344,000 in fees that Enterprises paid to its own attorneys or $741,000 that the Pension Plan paid to various attorneys.

In an opinion, the District Court accepted three separate grounds for voiding Clemence Frank's mortgages. *HBE Leasing Corp. v. Frank*, 837 F.Supp. 57 (S.D.N.Y.1993). First, relying on the "Deep Rock" doctrine of equitable subordination, *see Taylor v. Standard Gas & Electric Co.*, 306 U.S. 307, 59 S.Ct. 543, 83 L.Ed. 669 (1939) ("Deep Rock"), it found that Clemence was an "insider" whose loans represented capital contributions to Enterprises, regardless of whether the proceeds were used for legitimate corporate purposes, and that the mortgages should therefore be equitably subordinated to the claims of Petitioners. *HBE Leasing*, 837 F.Supp. at 60–61. Second, the Court found that Clemence had received the mortgages as part of a single transaction in which the mortgage proceeds were improperly transferred to her son, Hiram J. Frank. Because Enterprises itself received no benefit from the completed transaction, the District Court found the transfer of the mortgages to Clemence to be fraudulent, regardless of whether she knew of the entire transaction. *Id.* at 61. Third, the Court found that Clemence had not taken the mortgages in good faith. *Id.* at 62.

The District Court also found that Enterprises' payments to the Attorneys were not fraudulent transfers, because Enterprises realized a benefit from the Attorneys' representation of its co–defendants as part of a joint defense in the RICO action. *Id.* at 63. The Court also reasoned that it would place too great a burden on trial lawyers if they had to inquire into the financial resources of their clients before they accepted payment of legal fees. *Id.* at 63–64.

Finally, in an unpublished order the District Court determined that further discovery and a hearing would be necessary to resolve a separate claim against Clemence relating to a transfer from her husband, Hiram H. Frank. Accordingly, the District Court severed this claim for further proceedings.

Discussion

A. *Appellate Jurisdiction*

We must initially consider the question of our appellate jurisdiction, which arises because this supplementary proceeding involves multiple claims, not all of which have been adjudicated.[2] On November 2, 1993, the District Court entered its order and opinion adjudicating Petitioners' claims pertaining to Clemence's mortgages and Enterprises' payments to the Attorneys. Subsequently, on December 17, 1993, the District Judge denied a motion by Clemence to stay the November 2 order as it related to her mortgages. The Judge reasoned that a stay would needlessly delay the sale of valuable properties, and that if Clemence succeeded in having the order overturned on appeal, any deficiency in the sale proceeds could be satisfied by the Petitioners, who were all solvent. Finally, on January 13, 1994, the District Court entered a document called a "judgment" (signed on December 15, 1993), which purported to dispose of the two previously decided claims, and which severed for further proceedings a third claim relating to a transfer to Clemence from her husband, Hiram H. Frank. Neither this "judgment" nor any order contained an express determination that there was no just reason for delay. The judgment, however, ordered Clemence "to execute and file all documents necessary and appropriate to vacate and remove any mortgage lien she may have asserted against the property of HH Frank Enterprises, Inc. as to the aforesaid mortgages."

The parties contend that we have jurisdiction over this appeal pursuant to 28 U.S.C. § 1291 (1988), which grants us jurisdiction when the District Court has entered a final judgment. Rule 54(b) of the Federal Rules of Civil Procedure sets out the requirements for the entry of a partial final judgment in multi–claim or multi–party actions. A final judgment may be entered as to some—but fewer than all—claims or parties "only upon an express determination that there is no just reason for delay and upon an express direction for the entry of judgment." Fed.R.Civ.P. 54(b). The Rule makes clear that if the District Court does not both direct entry of judgment and expressly determine that there is no just reason for delay, then its order or decision is not final, whether or not it is labeled a "judgment."[3]

Once separate claims or claims against separate parties have been fully adjudicated, Rule 54(b) commits the decision to enter a judgment to the discretion of the District Court. *See Curtiss–Wright Corp. v. General Electric Co.*, 446 U.S. 1, 8, 100 S.Ct. 1460, 1464–65, 64 L.Ed.2d 1 (1980); *Ginett v. Computer Task Group, Inc.*, 962 F.2d 1085, 1092 (2d Cir. 1992). But the exercise of this discretion must follow the procedures set out by the Rule, and the requirement of an express determination that there is no just reason for delay has not been taken lightly by this Circuit. We have found an abuse of discretion where entry of judgment has been accompanied by a mere repetition of the statutory language that "there is no just reason for delay," without any reasoned explanation for such determination. *See, e.g., Harriscom*

---

[2] A Rule 69(a) proceeding in aid of judgment is treated as a separate action for purposes of determining whether the District Court's decision is "final." *See King v. Ionization International, Inc.*, 825 F.2d 1180, 1184 (7th Cir. 1987); 7 James W. Moore et al., *Federal Practice* ¶ 69.05[2] (2d ed.); *see also Fox v. Capital Co.*, 299 U.S. 105, 57 S.Ct. 57, 81 L.Ed. 67 (1936).

[3] In the absence of such determination and direction, any order or other form of decision, however designated, which adjudicates fewer than all the claims or the rights and liabilities of fewer than all the parties shall not terminate the action as to any of the claims or parties . . .. Fed.R.Civ.P. 54(b).

Svenska AB v. Harris Corp., 947 F.2d 627, 629–30 (2d Cir. 1991); *Cullen v. Margiotta*, 618 F.2d 226, 228 (2d Cir. 1980). A fortiori, the entry of a "judgment" unaccompanied even by the statutory formula is not a sufficient basis for our jurisdiction. *In re Chateaugay Corp.*, 928 F.2d 63, 64 (2d Cir. 1991).

In the instant case, the District Court did not expressly determine that there was no just reason for delay in entering judgment. Contrary to the contention of the parties, the explanation given by the District Court for denying Clemence's motion for a stay does not supply the missing express determination, because there is simply no evidence that the District Court intended its ruling on the stay to constitute a Rule 54(b) certification. The requirement of an express determination cannot be met if the District Court does not make clear that such determination is for the purpose of certifying a final judgment (e.g., by labeling its order a "Rule 54(b) Certification"). Because there was no Rule 54(b) certification, the District Court's order remains interlocutory.[4]

However, an immediate appeal may be taken from an interlocutory order granting an injunction. *See* 28 U.S.C. § 1291(a)(1) (1988). An order has the practical effect of granting injunctive relief within the meaning of section 1291(a)(1) if it is " 'directed to a party, enforceable by contempt, and designed to accord or protect some or all of the substantive relief sought by a complaint,' " *Abish v. Northwestern National Insurance Co.*, 924 F.2d 448, 453 (2d Cir. 1991) (quoting *Korea Shipping Corp. v. New York Shipping Ass'n*, 811 F.2d 124, 126 (2d Cir. 1987)), and if the appealing party demonstrates " ' "serious, perhaps irreparable, consequences," ' " *id.* (quoting *Korea Shipping*, 811 F.2d at 126 (quoting *Carson v. American Brands, Inc.*, 450 U.S. 79, 84, 101 S.Ct. 993, 996, 67 L.Ed.2d 59 (1981))).[5]

---

[4] Clemence and Petitioners contend that even without a Rule 54(b) certification, the order voiding Clemence's mortgages is final under the doctrine of *Forgay v. Conrad*, 47 U.S. (6 How.) 201, 204, 12 L.Ed. 404 (1848). Under the *Forgay* doctrine, "an order is treated as final if it directs the immediate delivery of property and subjects the losing party to irreparable harm if appellate review is delayed." *In re Martin–Trigona (Schlehan v. Olympic Worldwide Communications, Inc.)*, 763 F.2d 135, 138 (2d Cir. 1985). Our cases cast considerable doubt on whether *Forgay* is still applicable in a multi–claim or multi–party action in the absence of a Rule 54(b) certification. *See In re Chateaugay Corp.*, 922 F.2d 86, 91 (2d Cir. 1990), *cert. denied*, 502 U.S. 1093, 112 S.Ct. 1167, 117 L.Ed.2d 413 (1992); *Martin–Trigona*, 763 F.2d at 139; *Zwack v. Kraus Brothers & Co.*, 237 F.2d 255, 262 (2d Cir. 1956). *But see* 15A Charles A. Wright et al., *Federal Practice and Procedure* § 3910, at 327 (1992) (arguing that immediate appeal should be available under *Forgay* doctrine where Rule 54(b) has been deliberately ignored); *cf.* 6 Moore, *supra*, ¶ 54.32, at 54–186 (stating that inapplicability of *Forgay* hardship rule in multi–claim case is "anomalous"). In this case it is unnecessary to consider the continued vitality of the *Forgay* doctrine in the multi–claim context, because an interlocutory appeal is available to Clemence pursuant to 28 U.S.C. § 1292(a)(1), on the ground that the District Court's order grants an injunction. *Cf.* 9 Moore, *supra*, ¶ 110.11, at 100–11 (suggesting that orders appealable under *Forgay* are more properly treated as injunctions).

[5] Our cases have not made clear whether a showing of serious consequences is always required for an interlocutory appeal pursuant to section 1292(a)(1). *See Volvo North America Corp. v. Men's International Professional Tennis Council*, 839 F.2d 69, 75 (2d Cir.), *cert. denied*, 487 U.S. 1219, 108 S.Ct. 2872, 101 L.Ed.2d 908 (1988). Because the threat of irreparable injury is present here, we need not decide this issue.

The District Court's order granted injunctive relief against Clemence insofar as it directed her to remove any liens she may have asserted on the property that is subject to her mortgages. Unlike the provisional remedies of attachment and replevin, which do not constitute injunctions for the purpose of section 1292(a)(1), *see* 16 Charles A. Wright et al., *Federal Practice and Procedure* § 3922, at 43 (1977), the District Court's order is directed to a party, and it is presumably enforceable, if necessary, by contempt. The order is also plainly designed to accord the substantive relief sought by Petitioners. Finally, it threatens Clemence with irreparable harm, because it contemplates the immediate delivery and sale of the mortgaged property but does not require a bond or other security from Petitioners. In these respects, the order is far more than a simple adjudication of liability or a declaration of property rights, and it is accordingly subject to interlocutory appeal under section 1292(a)(1).[6]

Although the District Court's injunctive order is interlocutory, in the sense that another claim remains to be adjudicated, the District Court has fully adjudicated Petitioners' claim for injunctive relief, and the merits relating to Clemence's mortgages are therefore before us in precisely the same manner as they would be on appeal from a final judgment. *See* 16 Wright, *supra*, § 3921, at 21–22. We also find that this is an appropriate case in which to exercise our discretion to assert pendent appellate jurisdiction over Petitioners' cross–appeal, *see, e.g., Golino v. City of New Haven*, 950 F.2d 864, 868–69 (2d Cir. 1991), *cert. denied*, __ U.S. __, 112 S.Ct. 3032, 120 L.Ed.2d 902 (1992); *San Filippo v. United States Trust Co. of New York*, 737 F.2d 246, 255 (2d Cir. 1984), *cert. denied*, 470 U.S. 1035, 105 S.Ct. 1408, 84 L.Ed.2d 797 (1985), because determining whether Clemence's second mortgage represents a fraudulent conveyance depends in part on the merits of Petitioners' claim against the Attorneys.

B. *Standard of Review*

In a special proceeding under New York C.P.L.R. § 5225(b),[7] applicable in the District Court via Fed.R.Civ.P. 69(a), a court may grant summary relief where there

---

[6] We note also that the order is effectively an injunction against suit in another court, because it requires Clemence to remove mortgage liens that she had sought to enforce through a receivership in state court. "An order that prohibits a party from pursuing litigation in another court is unquestionably an injunction for purposes of interlocutory appeal . . . ." 16 Wright, *supra*, § 3923, at 48; *accord FDIC v. Geldermann, Inc.*, 975 F.2d 695, 967 (10th Cir. 1992); *Phillips v. Chas. Schreiner Bank*, 894 F.2d 127, 130 (5th Cir. 1990); *Klein v. Adams & Peck*, 436 F.2d 337, 339 (2d Cir. 1971). *But see Hershey Foods Corp. v. Hershey Creamery Co.*, 945 F.2d 1272, 1278–79 (3d Cir. 1991) (order staying proceedings in another court is not injunction within meaning of section 1292(a)(1) if it does not relate to ultimate relief sought).

[7] C.P.L.R. § 5225(b) authorizes a special proceeding by judgment creditors against third parties to recover money or personal property in which a judgment debtor has an interest; it does not explicitly relate to interests in real property. Nevertheless, all of the parties appear to have assumed that section 5225(b) provides the procedural basis for this proceeding. In any event, since diversity jurisdiction exists, the District Court had jurisdiction to entertain what would otherwise have been a plenary action based on New York substantive law, and no aspect of our disposition turns on the technical availability of section 5225(b).

are no questions of fact, but "it must conduct a trial on disputed issues of fact on adverse claims in a turnover matter," *General Motors Acceptance Corp. v. Norstar Bank of Hudson Valley*, 156 A.D.2d 876, 549 N.Y.S.2d 862, 863 (1989); *see also Port of New York Authority v. 62 Cortlandt Street Realty Co.*, 18 N.Y.2d 250, 273 N.Y.S.2d 337, 340, 219 N.E.2d 797, 799 (1966) (summary judgment standard applies to special proceedings), *cert. denied*, 385 U.S. 1006, 87 S.Ct. 712, 17 L.Ed.2d 544 (1987). The District Court implicitly treated the parties' submissions as motions for summary judgment: finding that no material facts were in dispute, it entered judgment without a trial on the basis of the affidavits and appended exhibits. We therefore review its decision de novo.

C. *Substantive Fraudulent Conveyance Law*

Petitioners contend that the transfers to Clemence Frank and the Attorneys were fraudulent under the New York Uniform Fraudulent Conveyance Act ("UFCA"), N.Y.Debt. & Cred.Law ("DCL") §§ 270–281 (McKinney 1990). The UFCA identifies several situations involving "constructive fraud," in which a transfer made without fair consideration constitutes a fraudulent conveyance, regardless of the intent of the transferor. One situation involving constructive fraud is identified by DCL § 273–a:

Every conveyance made without fair consideration when the person making it is a defendant in an action for money damages or a judgment in such an action has been docketed against him, is fraudulent as to the plaintiff in that action without regard to the actual intent of the defendant if, after final judgment for the plaintiff, the defendant fails to satisfy the judgment.

In this case, Enterprises made the contested transfers after it became a defendant in Petitioners' RICO action, and Enterprises has now failed to satisfy the final judgment in that action. Thus, the transfers are fraudulent under section 273–a unless they were made for "fair consideration," which is defined by DCL § 272:

Fair consideration is given for property, or obligation,

a. When in exchange for such property, or obligation, as a fair equivalent therefor, and in good faith, property is conveyed or an antecedent debt is satisfied, or

b. When such property, or obligation is received in good faith to secure a present advance or antecedent debt in amount not disproportionately small as compared with the value of the property, or obligation obtained.

Even where fair consideration is given in exchange for the debtor's property, a transfer may be fraudulent under the UFCA if it is marked by "actual fraud," that is, if it is made "with actual intent, as distinguished from intent presumed in law, to hinder, delay, or defraud either present or future creditors," DCL § 276.

1. Clemence Frank's Mortgages

Clemence received her mortgages from Enterprises as security for contemporaneous advances to the corporation of $350,000 of her own funds. On the surface, then, Clemence appears to have given fair consideration for the mortgages, because they secured present advances of the same value. *See* DCL § 272(b). Nevertheless, the

District Court ruled on three somewhat related grounds that the mortgages should be voided under the constructive fraud provisions of DCL § 273-a. We consider each of these grounds in turn, and then apply the resulting legal principles to the mortgage transactions.

a. *Equitable subordination.* Of the three grounds, it will be convenient to consider first the District Court's view that the mortgages could be voided under the doctrine of equitable subordination, without regard to the ultimate fate of the funds Clemence advanced. This conclusion was based on a finding that Clemence was an "insider" of Enterprises whose cash advances were deemed to be capital contributions rather than loans. The doctrine of equitable subordination, however, simply does not apply to state–law fraudulent conveyance claims. Equitable subordination is distinctly a power of federal bankruptcy courts, as courts of equity, to subordinate the claims of one creditor to those of others. *See generally* Scott M. Browning, *Note, No Fault Equitable Subordination,* 34 Wm. & Mary L.Rev. 487 (1993); Helen D. Chaitman, *The Equitable Subordination of Bank Claims,* 39 Bus.Law. 1561 (1984). This broad equitable power to disallow and reorder claims, first announced in bankruptcy case law, *see* Deep Rock, *supra*; *Pepper v. Litton,* 308 U.S. 295, 60 S.Ct. 238, 84 L.Ed. 281 (1939), and now codified in the Bankruptcy Code at 11 U.S.C. § 510(c) (1988), derives from the Bankruptcy Court's role as administrator of the debtor's estate for the equal benefit of all creditors, *see, e.g., Pepper,* 308 U.S. at 303–05, 60 S.Ct. at 243–45.

Unlike the Bankruptcy Code, the UFCA is a set of legal rather than equitable doctrines, whose purpose is not to provide equal distribution of a debtor's estate among creditors, but to aid specific creditors who have been defrauded by the transfer of a debtor's property. *See Boston Trading Group, Inc. v. Burnazos,* 835 F.2d 1504, 1508 (1st Cir. 1987).[8] Thus, the UFCA does not bestow a broad power to reorder creditor claims or to invalidate transfers that were made for fair consideration, at least where no actual intent to hinder, delay, or defraud creditors has been shown. As the definition of "fair consideration" in DCL § 272 makes clear, even the preferential repayment of pre–existing debts to some creditors does not constitute a fraudulent conveyance, whether or not it prejudices other creditors, because "[t]he basic object of fraudulent conveyance law is to see that the debtor uses his limited assets to satisfy some of his creditors; it normally does not try to choose among them." *Boston Trading,* 835 F.2d at 1509; *see also Atlanta Shipping Corp. v. Chemical Bank,* 818 F.2d 240, 249 (2d Cir. 1987); *Ronga v. Chiusano,* 97 A.D.2d 753, 468 N.Y.S.2d 174, 175 (1983); 1 Garrard Glenn, *Fraudulent Convey-ances and Preferences* § 289, at 488–90 (1940).

New York courts have carved out one exception to the rule that preferential payments of pre–existing obligations are not fraudulent conveyances: preferences to a debtor corporation's shareholders, officers, or directors are deemed not to be transfers for fair consideration. *See Farm Stores, Inc. v. School Feeding Corp.,* 102

---

[8] In order to promote a uniform national interpretation of the UFCA, both this Circuit and the courts of New York have encouraged recourse to the case law of other jurisdictions. *See Atlanta Shipping Corp. v. Chemical Bank,* 818 F.2d 240, 249 (2d Cir. 1987); *Southern Industries, Inc. v. Jeremias,* 66 A.D.2d 178, 411 N.Y.S.2d 945, 949 (1978).

A.D.2d 249, 477 N.Y.S.2d 374, 378 (1984), *aff'd*, 64 N.Y.2d 1065, 489 N.Y.S.2d 877, 479 N.E.2d 222 (1985); *Southern Industries, Inc. v. Jeremias*, 66 A.D.2d 178, 411 N.Y.S.2d 945, 949 (1978). This exception is indirectly relevant to Clemence's mortgages, because Enterprises used the proceeds from one of them to pay off antecedent debts to its principal shareholder, Hiram J. Frank, under *Farm Stores*, these preferential payments to a controlling shareholder would be fraudulent conveyances. But the *Farm Stores* preference exception cannot be applied directly to Clemence's mortgages, regardless of whether she was a corporate insider, because each of her mortgages secured a contemporaneous advance of funds, not a pre-existing debt. Unlike the preferential payment of pre-existing debts, the transfer of a debtor's property to secure a present advance of commensurate value does not ordinarily prejudice other creditors, because the debtor receives new value in exchange for the property conveyed.

In sum, Clemence Frank's mortgages may not be directly invalidated either under the doctrine of equitable subordination or as preferences to a corporate insider. If analyzed without regard to the ultimate fate of the funds she advanced, these mortgages could not be found to be fraudulently conveyed. They might be fraudulent, however, if analyzed as part of a larger transaction. This view underlies the District Court's second basis for voiding the mortgages, to which we now turn.

b. *"Collapsing" the transactions.* It is well established that multilateral transactions may under appropriate circumstances be "collapsed" and treated as phases of a single transaction for analysis under the UFCA. *See, e.g., Orr v. Kinderhill Corp.*, 991 F.2d 31, 35–36 (2d Cir. 1993). This approach finds its most frequent application to lenders who have financed leveraged buyouts of companies that subsequently become insolvent. *See United States v. Gleneagles Investment Co.*, 565 F.Supp. 556 (M.D.Pa.1983) (Pennsylvania UFCA), *aff'd sub nom. United States v. Tabor Court Realty Corp.*, 803 F.2d 1288 (3d Cir. 1986), *cert. denied*, 483 U.S. 1005, 107 S.Ct. 3229, 97 L.Ed.2d 735 (1987); *Crowthers McCall Pattern, Inc. v. Lewis*, 129 B.R. 992, 998 (S.D.N.Y.1991) (New York UFCA); *Wieboldt Stores, Inc. v. Schottenstein*, 94 B.R. 488, 500–04 (N.D.Ill.1988) (Illinois UFCA); *In re Best Products Co.*, 168 B.R. 35, 56–57 (Bankr.S.D.N.Y.1994) (New York UFCA). The paradigmatic scheme is similar to that alleged here: one transferee gives fair value to the debtor in exchange for the debtor's property, and the debtor then gratuitously transfers the proceeds of the first exchange to a second transferee. The first transferee thereby receives the debtor's property, and the second transferee receives the consideration, while the debtor retains nothing.

Under these circumstances, the initial transfer of the debtor's property to the first transferee is constructively fraudulent if two conditions are satisfied. First, in accordance with the foregoing paradigm, the consideration received from the first transferee must be reconveyed by the debtor for less than fair consideration or with an actual intent to defraud creditors. If, instead, the debtor retains the proceeds from the first exchange, reconveys them for fair consideration, or uses them for some other legitimate purpose, including the preferential repayment of pre-existing debts, and if the debtor does not make the subsequent transfer with actual fraudulent intent, then the entire transaction, even if "collapsed," cannot be a fraudulent conveyance, because it does not adversely affect the debtor's ability to meet its overall obligations. *See Atlanta Shipping*, 818 F.2d at 249; *see also* 1 Glenn, *supra*, § 275, at 471 ("[W]here a transfer for value . . . is put forward as a fraudulent conveyance, the test is whether, as a result of the transaction, the debtor's estate was unfairly diminished.").

Second, and contrary to the approach taken by the District Court, the transferee in the leg of the transaction sought to be voided must have actual or constructive knowledge of the entire scheme that renders her exchange with the debtor fraudulent. *See Kupetz v. Wolf*, 845 F.2d 842, 847–49 (9th Cir. 1988); *Atlanta Shipping Corp.*, 818 F.2d at 249; *Tabor Court*, 803 F.2d at 1296; *Crowthers McCall*, 129 B.R. at 998; *Wieboldt Stores*, 94 B.R. at 502–03. The case law has been aptly summarized in the following terms:

In deciding whether to collapse the transaction and impose liability on particular defendants, the courts have looked frequently to the knowledge of the defendants of the structure of the entire transaction and to whether its components were part of a single scheme.

In re Best Products, 168 B.R. at 56–57 (quoting *In re Best Products Co.*, 157 B.R. 222, 229 (Bankr.S.D.N.Y. (1993)). The existence of a knowledge requirement reflects the UFCA's policy of protecting innocent creditors or purchasers for value who have received the debtor's property without awareness of any fraudulent scheme. Thus, an appropriate creditor may void or disregard a fraudulent conveyance to any person "except a purchaser for fair consideration without knowledge of the fraud at the time of the purchase." DCL § 278(1); *see also FDIC v. Malin*, 802 F.2d 12, 19 (2d Cir. 1986); *Farm Stores*, 477 N.Y.S.2d at 379.

However, the transferee need not have actual knowledge of the scheme that renders the conveyance fraudulent. Constructive knowledge of fraudulent schemes will be attributed to transferees who were aware of circumstances that should have led them to inquire further into the circumstances of the transaction, but who failed to make such inquiry. *See, e.g. Tabor Court*, 803 F.2d at 1295 (lenders "knew, or should have known" that monies would not be retained by debtor). There is some ambiguity as to the precise test for constructive knowledge in this context. While some cases have stated that purchasers who do not make appropriate inquiries are charged with "the knowledge that ordinary diligence would have elicited." *United States v. Orozco–Prada*, 636 F.Supp. 1537, 1543 (S.D.N.Y.1986), *aff'd*, 847 F.2d 836 (2d Cir. 1988); *see also Morse v. Howard Park Corp.*, 50 Misc.2d 834, 272 N.Y.S.2d 16, 22 (Sup.Ct.1966), other appear to have required a more active avoidance of the truth, *see Schmitt v. Morgan*, 98 A.D.2d 934, 471 N.Y.S.2d 365, 367 (1983) (test is whether subsequent purchaser who did not make serious inquiry "was shielding himself from knowledge that a fraudulent conveyance had occurred"); 1 Glenn, *supra*, § 304, at 532 (transferee may be charged with knowledge only when there is "conscious turning way from the subject").[9]

---

[9] We note that the burden of proving knowledge is on the party seeking to void the transaction. *See Gelbard v. Esses*, 96 A.D.2d 573, 465 N.Y.S.2d 264, 268 (1983). In fact, even the burden of production shifts to the transferee only if the creditor asserts that the transferee paid inadequate consideration and evidence concerning such consideration is within

c. *Lack of good faith.* The District Court bolstered its view that the mortgage transactions could be collapsed by deeming Clemence not to have acted in good faith. Petitioners attempt to assert lack of good faith as a ground for voiding the mortgages independent of the role that mental state plays in the analysis whereby the transactions are collapsed. This use of bad faith as an independent ground cannot be sustained. Though some New York cases have broadly construed the reference to "good faith" in DCL § 272's definition of "fair consideration," *see, e.g., Southern Industries,* 411 N.Y.S.2d at 949 (voiding preferences to corporate insiders), other authorities have cautioned against an expansive reading of the UFCA's reference to good faith, *see, e.g., Boston Trading Group,* 835 F.2d at 1512–13. We believe that where, as here, a transferee has given equivalent value in exchange for the debtor's property, the statutory requirement of "good faith" is satisfied if the transferee acted without either actual or constructive knowledge of any fraudulent scheme. *See Atlanta Shipping,* 818 F.2d at 249; 1 Glenn, *supra,* § 295, at 512 (UFCA requirement of "good faith" refers solely to "whether the grantee knew, or should have known, that he was not trading normally, but that . . . the purpose of the trade, so far as the debtor was concerned, was the defrauding of his creditors").

d. *Application of legal principles.* In the application of this framework to Clemence Frank's mortgages, the initial question is whether Enterprises received fair consideration from the entire multilateral transaction surrounding each mortgage. With regard to the first mortgage, the $250,000 that Clemence advanced to Enterprises was immediately passed on to the company's majority shareholder, Hiram J. Frank, as a preference to a corporate insider. Because this preferential payment in the second stage of the transaction was a fraudulent conveyance under the holding of *Farm Stores, supra,* the net result was that Clemence received a mortgage from Enterprises while Hiram J. Frank received money from Clemence. Thus, at the end of the day Enterprises itself received nothing in exchange for the first mortgage.[10]

---

control of the transferee. *Id.; ACLI Government Securities Inc. v. Rhoades,* 653 F.Supp. 1388, 1391 (S.D.N.Y.1987), *aff'd,* 842 F.2d 1287 (2d Cir. 1988). Because there is no dispute about the nature of the consideration provided by Clemence, she has satisfied any burden of production she may have had. *See United States v. McCombs,* 30 F.3d 310, 323–26 (2d Cir. 1994).

[10] Clemence nonetheless argues that Petitioners were not prejudiced by this collapsed transaction, because Hiram J. Frank used the funds he received to remove a lien from another piece of property that can now be levied upon by Petitioners. In other words, the $250,000 is still available to Petitioners, even though it is in Hiram J. Frank's rather than Enterprises' possession. Though a transfer may not be challenged as fraudulent unless it prejudices the complaining creditor, *see, e.g., Citizens & Southern National Bank v. Auer,* 640 F.2d 837, 838 (6th Cir. 1981) (Tennessee UFCA), prejudice is not eliminated in this case by the fact that Hiram J. Frank, to whom the mortgage proceeds were transferred, is jointly liable with Enterprises to the Petitioners.

A creditor is prejudiced, sufficiently to void a fraudulent transfer, when an asset in the hands of its debtor is converted into funds that find their way to another debtor of the creditor. The availability of an alternative collection opportunity does not eliminate prejudice in this context. Of course, the opportunity to void Clemence's mortgage and to collect from Hiram J. Frank would not permit any recovery in excess of Petitioners' judgment; no such excess recovery is alleged, and the judgment remains unsatisfied.

With regard to the second mortgage, approximately $60,000 of the money that Clemence advanced went to the Attorneys to pay for legal services, while the remaining $40,000 was used for other corporate purposes. If both of these payments were legitimate corporate expenditures, then the second mortgage and the subsequent payments would not be fraudulent transfers even when viewed as a single scheme. Although the District Court found that the payments to the Attorneys were legitimate corporate expenditures, it voided the second mortgage in its entirety. This was error in two respects. First, since Petitioners have not even alleged facts that would render improper the portion of the proceeds not paid to the Attorneys, the transaction is not fraudulent, at least as it pertains to this much of the second mortgage. Second, we must remand the District Court's order as it pertains to the portion of the mortgage proceeds used to pay the Attorneys, because, as we conclude below, there is a genuine factual dispute as to whether these payments to the Attorneys were fraudulent transfers.

The second stage of the inquiry as to whether the transactions may be collapsed concerns Clemence's knowledge. Clemence was a director of Enterprises at least until the middle of 1990, if not longer. While she was a director, the corporation was frequently used by Hiram J. Frank as a conduit for various payments for family and other noncorporate purposes, and Clemence's fiduciary role charged her with constructive knowledge of these basic aspects of the company's financial affairs, *see Hanson Trust PLC v. ML SCM Acquisition Inc.*, 781 F.2d 264, 274–75 (2d Cir. 1986). In addition, Clemence concedes that she knew that Enterprises was a defendant in a RICO fraud action. She also concedes that she knew that her son, Hiram J. Frank, had made "large loans" to Enterprises, which put her on notice that he might cause the company to make preferential payments to himself with the proceeds from the mortgages. This information should have been sufficient to alert Clemence to the danger that Enterprises might improperly funnel to third parties the money she was advancing, and she should have made reasonably diligent inquiries into the use of the mortgage proceeds. Under the circumstances, her failure to inquire represented a conscious turning away from the subject. Thus, with regard to both mortgages, the undisputed facts are sufficient to charge Clemence with constructive knowledge of schemes in which her cash advances were expended by Enterprises for improper purposes.

2. Payments to the Attorneys

Petitioners also contend that Enterprises fraudulently conveyed $775,722 in legal fees to the Attorneys, approximately $60,000 of which derived from the proceeds of Clemence's second mortgage. The contested fees represented payment for legal services that the Attorneys rendered as counsel for Enterprises' co–defendants in the RICO action. Petitioners argue that the Attorneys' legal services were not "fair consideration" within the meaning of DCL § 272 because they were not provided directly to Enterprises itself. The Attorneys respond that their services were "fair consideration" for Enterprises' payments because Enterprises benefitted from the unified defense of which these services were a part.

The District Court agreed with the Attorneys. It found that it was to the advantage of each defendant in the RICO action to present a unified defense and to have all co–defendants adequately represented, because all of the defendants were threatened with joint and several liability. The District Court reasoned:

One can question the wisdom of retaining some of the attorneys, a number of whom were prominent, expensive New York City criminal lawyers. However, the selection of the proper counsel is always a matter of individual choice. The plaintiffs have never disputed that bona fide legal services were rendered by the attorneys to one or more of the defendants or that their disbursements were not actually incurred.

Having presided at the very lengthy trial and considered the numerous motions, we conclude . . . that in a conspiracy case such as this, Enterprises did receive a benefit from the funds it laid out on behalf of the other parties, albeit it paid far too high a price for that benefit. Nor do we believe that there was anything unethical in this approach in light of the common interest of all of the defendants and their right to have a joint defense if it was to their benefit.

HBE Leasing, 837 F.Supp. at 63 (footnotes omitted). The District Court therefore concluded that the benefit Enterprises received from the Attorneys' services represented fair consideration for Enterprises' payments, and it accordingly dismissed Petitioners' claim against the Attorneys.

In determining whether Enterprises received fair consideration, the District Court correctly disregarded the form of this transaction and looked instead to its substance. Under DCL § 272, "fair consideration" means a fair equivalent that the debtor receives in exchange for its property or obligation. Thus, when a debtor transfers its property but the transferee gives the consideration to a third party, the debtor ordinarily will not have received fair consideration in exchange for its property. However, under the well established doctrine of *Rubin v. Manufacturers Hanover Trust Co.*, 661 F.2d 979 (2d Cir. 1981), the fact that the consideration initially goes to third parties may be disregarded to the extent that the debtor indirectly receives a benefit from the entire transaction. *See id.* at 991–92; *see also In re Fairchild Aircraft Corp.*, 6 F.3d 1119, 1127 (5th Cir. 1993); *In re Jeffrey Bigelow Design Group, Inc.*, 956 F.2d 479, 485 (4th Cir. 1992); *Mellon Bank, N.A. v. Metro Communications, Inc.*, 945 F.2d 635, 646–47 (3d Cir. 1991), *cert. denied*, 503 U.S. 937, 112 S.Ct. 1476, 117 L.Ed.2d 620 (1992); *In re W.T. Grant Co.*, 699 F.2d 599, 609 (2d Cir.), *cert. denied*, 464 U.S. 822, 104 S.Ct. 89, 78 L.Ed.2d 97 (1983). While *Rubin* has most often been applied in cases decided under the fraudulent conveyance provisions of federal bankruptcy law, its approach to indirect benefits is equally applicable under the parallel provisions of the UFCA. *See Telefast, Inc. v. VU–TV, Inc.*, 591 F.Supp. 1368, 1379–81 (D.N.J.1984) (New Jersey UFCA); *In re Chomakos*, 170 B.R. 585, 590 (Bankr.E.D.Mich.1993) (Michigan UFCA).

Petitioners contend that the District Court's finding that Enterprises indirectly received "a benefit" from the Attorneys' services does not satisfy *Rubin*'s test for fair consideration. Under the UFCA and the parallel provisions of federal bankruptcy law, "fair consideration" is defined quantitatively as "a fair equivalent" or an "amount not disproportionately small as compared with the value of the property, or obligation obtained [from the debtor]." DCL § 272; *see also* 11 U.S.C. § 548(a)(2)(A) (1988). Thus, to determine whether a debtor indirectly received fair consideration under the *Rubin* doctrine, the fact–finder must first attempt to measure the economic benefit that the debtor indirectly received from the entire transaction, and then compare that benefit to the value of the property the debtor transferred. *Rubin*, 661 F.2d at 993. The mere fact that the debtor received a benefit is therefore insufficient to find fair consideration. *Id.*

Despite the considerable force of Petitioners' argument, we believe that the quantitative analysis normally required by *Rubin* is inappropriate in this case where multiple co–defendants were threatened with joint and several liability, they mounted a common defense, and one defendant paid the legal fees of the others. As the District Court correctly noted, individual defendants may choose to pay as much to their attorneys for their defense as they consider worthwhile, as long as the payments fall within a fair range of reasonable compensation for *bona fide* legal services or are reimbursement for legitimate expenses incurred during the defense.[11] The same should be true of the defendants in this case who were threatened with joint and several liability and conducted a common defense to protect their common interests. The existence of some adverse interests among the co–defendants might reasonably have required each defendant to have individual counsel, but to the extent that the several defense attorneys conducted a joint defense, they effectively advanced the interests of all defendants simultaneously. *See United States v. Schwimmer*, 892 F.2d 237, 243–44 (2d Cir. 1989) (recognizing joint defense privilege), *cert. denied*, 502 U.S. 810, 112 S.Ct. 55, 116 L.Ed.2d 31 (1991). Thus, the services that each defense attorney performed in the course of conducting a joint defense provided a benefit to each defendant. *Rubin*'s quantitative approach, requiring some measurement of the value of the benefit to each defendant, is not applicable under these circumstances because the full value of the joint defense inured to the benefit of all defendants, and there is no point in trying to quantify the incremental value added by the joint defense beyond the value of individual representation. These joint services represented "fair consideration" for the payment of reasonable compensation, regardless of which defendant paid the bill. We need not decide whether some inquiry concerning apportionment would be warranted in a case where the defenses of all the defendants did not overlap to the extent that occurred in this case.

Because Petitioners do not dispute that Enterprises' payment of the Attorneys' fees represented a reasonable rate of compensation for *bona fide* legal services rendered to defendants with substantially overlapping defenses, the District Court correctly concluded that Enterprises received fair consideration in exchange for its payments. However, the District Court failed to consider an alternative theory of liability offered by Petitioners: that Enterprises paid the Attorneys' fees with actual intent to defraud its creditors. Under DCL § 276, a transfer made with actual intent to hinder, delay, or defraud present or future creditors is fraudulent as to such creditors, regardless of whether the debtor receives fair consideration for its property. *See United States v. McCombs*, 30 F.3d 310, 327–28 (2d Cir. 1994); *ACLI Government Securities, Inc. v. Rhoades*, 653 F.Supp. 1388, 1395 n. 32 (S.D.N.Y.1987), *aff'd*, 842 F.2d 1287 (2d Cir. 1988). Actual fraudulent intent must

---

[11] This conclusion follows directly from the definition of "fair consideration" in DCL § 272: the legal services rendered by defense counsel represent a "fair equivalent" that the defendant receives in exchange for the legal fees he or she pays.

be proven by clear and convincing evidence, but it may be inferred from the circumstances surrounding the transaction, including the relationship among the parties and the secrecy, haste, or unusualness of the transaction. *See McCombs*, 30 F.3d at 328. However, a transfer motivated by actual fraudulent intent may not be voided if a transferee who paid fair consideration did not have actual or constructive knowledge of such intent. *Dunham v. Tabb*, 27 Wash.App. 862, 621 P.2d 179, 182 (1980); DCL § 278.

The record establishes the existence of genuine factual disputes pertaining both to Enterprises' intent in paying the Attorneys' fees and the Attorneys' knowledge of that intent. Enterprises paid the legal fees of its co–defendants at the direction of its controlling shareholder, Hiram J. Frank, who was thereby relieved of the burden of paying for his own defense. Even though Enterprises received fair consideration in exchange for its payments, this arrangement effectively transferred substantial assets from the corporation to Hiram J. Frank and the other co–defendants. Because a fact–finder might reasonably conclude that the purpose behind this arrangement was to hinder, delay, or defraud Enterprises' future judgment creditors, the District Court should not have dismissed Petitioners' claims against the Attorneys at this stage in the proceedings. We therefore reverse and remand for further proceedings on this issue.[12]

The result of this inquiry will also determine Clemence Frank's liability on her second mortgage. As discussed above, this mortgage represented a voidable fraudulent transfer of Enterprises' property only to the extent that the subsequent transfer of $60,000 of the mortgage proceeds to the Attorneys was itself a fraudulent conveyance.[13] At most, however, these interlocking transactions resulted in a single fraudulent transfer of Enterprises' property. If the Petitioners establish on remand that the transfer to the Attorneys was fraudulent, they may recover this property from Clemence or (if it is shown that the Attorneys had actual or constructive knowledge of the fraudulent scheme) from the Attorneys. *See United States v. Red Stripe, Inc.*, 792 F.Supp. 1338, 1344 (E.D.N.Y.1992); DCL § 278(1)(a). But an unjustified double recovery would result if Petitioners could void both the relevant portion of Clemence's second mortgage and the transfer of the proceeds to the Attorneys. *Cf. In re Checkmate Stereo & Electronics, Ltd.*, 9 B.R. 585, 622 (Bankr.E.D.N.Y.1981) (allowing only single recovery by imposing joint and several liability on multiple transferees under New York UFCA and Bankruptcy Code), *aff'd*, 21 B.R. 402 (E.D.N.Y.1982); Robert J. White, *Leveraged Buyouts & Fraudulent Conveyance*

---

[12] Other material factual disputes raised by the parties may be considered on remand. However, after reviewing the record de novo, we conclude that there is no basis for the Attorneys' argument that Petitioners' claims are barred by the doctrines of waiver, laches, or equitable estoppel; the Petitioners are therefore entitled to summary judgment on these defenses.

[13] We ruled above that, under the facts of this case, Clemence's relationship to the affairs of Enterprises created a duty of inquiry as to its uses of her funds, and that her lack of inquiry charges her with constructive knowledge of how those funds were in fact expended. Therefore, whether the $60,000 portion of her second mortgage can be voided depends, on remand, only on establishment of the actual fraudulent intent of Enterprises with respect to the payments to the Attorneys.

Law Under the Bankruptcy Code, 1991 Ann.Surv.Am.L. 357, 410–11 (1992) (bankruptcy trustee may recover only once from multiple transferees in multilateral fraudulent conveyance). Thus, if Petitioners elect to void the relevant portion of the mortgage, any judgment against the Attorneys must be reduced by an equivalent amount. This election of remedies does not affect Petitioners' rights vis–a–vis Clemence's other mortgage or the other payments to the Attorneys.

Conclusion

We affirm the order of the District Court as it pertains to Clemence Frank's mortgage securing her $250,000 note. We reverse the order as it pertains to Clemence Frank's other mortgage, securing her $100,000 note, and insofar as it dismisses Petitioners' claims against the Attorneys, and remand for further proceedings consistent with this opinion. No costs.

HBE LEASING CORPORATION v. FRANK

United States Court of Appeal, Second Circuit
61 F.3d 1054 (1995)

PARKER, Circuit Judge:

Facing a $21 million judgment, Hiram J. Frank ("Frank") conveyed the bulk of his considerable property to his lawyers, his fiancee, and his mother. Whether New York fraudulent conveyance law permits the judgment creditor to set aside these conveyances is the issue raised in these appeals from a final judgment of the United States District Court for the Southern District of New York (Brieant, Judge).

In the course of defending a multi–million dollar civil RICO and common law action brought against Frank and certain related people and entities.[1] Frank conveyed away virtually all of the defendants' assets. Three of the five successful plaintiffs in the RICO action (collectively denominated "HBE"), now judgment creditors facing a recalcitrant Frank and having recovered only a tiny portion of the judgment, challenged these conveyances as fraudulent under the New York Uniform Fraudulent Conveyance Act, N.Y. Debt. & Cred. Law ("DCL") §§ 270–281 (McKinney 1990), in three separate proceedings. First, HBE challenged one set of conveyances in proceedings supplementary to the RICO judgment. In that case,

---

[1] The RICO judgment was entered on November 10, 1992 and subsequently affirmed by this Court. *HBE Leasing Corp. v. Frank*, 22 F.3d 41 (2d Cir. 1994) ("HBE II"). *HBE Leasing Corp.* and other leasing companies had entered into agreements with Frank whereby the leasing companies would purchase and lease back what they thought were new egg–harvesting machines to Frank, who operated large chicken farms. The leasing companies eventually discovered, after Frank stopped making lease payments, "that no actual equipment was ever purchased or installed, and that the entire leasing arrangement was a sham concocted" by Frank. *Id.* at 43. Judgment against all defendants amounted to almost $25 million.

Judge Gerard L. Goettel, who had presided over the RICO trial, set aside certain transfers and upheld others, as explained below. *HBE Leasing Corp. v. Frank*, 837 F.Supp. 57 (S.D.N.Y. 1993) ("HBE I"). On appeal, this Court affirmed in part and reversed in part. *HBE Leasing Corp. v. Frank*, 48 F.3d 623 (2d Cir. 1995) ("HBE IV"). Second, in this independent action, HBE challenged another set of conveyances, to Frank's fiancee, mother and lawyers. These conveyances are the subject of Judge Charles L. Brieant's summary judgment rulings in the decision now on appeal. *HBE Leasing Corp. v. Frank*, 851 F.Supp. 571 (S.D.N.Y. 1994), *modified*, No. 93 Civ. 1597 (S.D.N.Y. May 24, 1994) ("HBE III"). Third, HBE challenged the transfer of a note in a separate action brought in the Southern District of Florida.

Frank's disposition of his assets during the RICO litigation may be summarized as follows:

1. Frank encumbered real estate owned by H.H. Frank Enterprises, Inc. ("Enterprises"), one of the RICO defendants controlled by Frank, by conveying two mortgages valued at $350,000 to his mother, Clemence Frank, who was not a defendant in the RICO action. In *HBE I*, Judge Goettel voided these transfers. This Court in *HBE IV* affirmed the avoidance of one of the mortgages and reversed and remanded as to the second mortgage. 48 F.3d at 629.

2. During the RICO litigation, Frank paid numerous defense attorneys from Enterprises's coffers. $775,000 of these payments were challenged as fraudulent in *HBE I*. Although Judge Goettel declined to set aside these payments, that ruling was reversed and remanded in *HBE IV*. *Id.*

3. Frank cashed over $200,000 in bonds from which he purchased an exempt Florida residence. This transfer of assets has not been challenged.

4. Frank made several transfers in October 1990 to his then–fiancee, Susan Murphy Frank ("Murphy"): a $383,000 Liberty, New York, residence, $864,000 in bonds (to be held in trust by Wallace Berkowitz), a $56,000 yacht, and an $11,000 engagement ring.[2] In the present action, HBE moved for summary judgment to void these transfers as fraudulent. Judge Brieant granted the motion, voiding all the transfers to Murphy and awarding judgment to HBE in the amount of the assets' combined value. Murphy and Berkowitz appeal.

5. In July 1991 Frank transferred $1,010,200 in bonds to attorneys Carl P. Goldstein and Richard A. Stoloff and their firm, Goldstein & Stoloff, Esqs. (hereafter collectively "Goldstein"). That transfer has not been challenged.

6. On November 5, 1992 (immediately after the jury verdict in the RICO case), Frank transferred to Goldstein a $227,000 bond (North Broward Bond), a $144,000 mortgage (Chern Mortgage) and a $278,000 note (Fox Run Note).[3] HBE moved for summary judgment to void the three conveyances as fraudulent. In *HBE III*, Judge Brieant granted the motion in part, voiding the transfer of the North Broward Bond and entering judgment against Goldstein for the value of the bond plus interest,

---

[2] Any disputes or discrepancies as to the monetary value of these or other assets involved in this case are not relevant to the issues on appeal. Listed here are rounded numbers derived from the May 24, 1994 Final Judgment in *HBE III*.

[3] These values are taken from Goldstein's brief on appeal.

for a total of $258,000. The district court's order does not address the Chern Mortgage and Fox Run Note; however, because the court entered final judgment, HBE's claims as to the mortgage and note were effectively dismissed. Goldstein appeals with respect to the bond; HBE cross–appeal with respect to the mortgage and note.

7. Frank transferred a note valued at $201,000 to his Florida attorneys in November 1992. That conveyance was challenged in the Southern District of Florida and voided by Judge Kenneth Ryskamp on June 16, 1994.

8. In August 1991 and October 1992, Frank transferred bonds worth $482,000 to Clemence Frank. In *HBE III*, Judge Brieant granted Clemence Frank's motion for summary judgment and dismissed HBE's claims against her. HBE cross–appeals as to that ruling.

For the reasons set forth below, we hold that (1) the transfers to Murphy are voidable and we therefore affirm that portion of the district court's judgment; (2) the transfers of the North Broward Bond and Fox Run Note are voidable and we therefore affirm as to the bond and reverse and remand as to the note; (3) there exist genuine issues of material fact as to the transfer of the Chern Mortgage and we therefore reverse and remand on that issue; and (4) there exist genuine issues of material fact as to the transfer of the bonds to Clemence Frank and we therefore reverse that portion of the court's judgment and remand for further proceedings.

The Statutes

This diversity case arises under the New York Uniform Fraudulent Conveyance Act. Several provisions of that act are at issue. First, DCL § 276 forbids a transfer made with actual intent to defraud creditors:

Every conveyance made and every obligation incurred with actual intent, as distinguished from intent presumed in law, to hinder, delay, or defraud either present or future creditors, is fraudulent as to both present and future creditors.

The district court voided the North Broward Bond and the Murphy transfers not under DCL § 276, however, but under DCL § 273–a, which permits a creditor to attack certain transfers regardless of the transferor's state of mind:

Every conveyance made without fair consideration when the person making it is a defendant in an action for money damages or a judgment in such an action has been docketed against him, is fraudulent as to the plaintiff in that action without regard to the actual intent of the defendant if, after final judgment for the plaintiff, the defendant fails to satisfy the judgment.

DCL § 273–a "fleshed out the [common law] meaning of a fraudulent conveyance by stigmatizing certain conveyances made during litigation." *Orr v. Kinderhill Corp.*, 991 F.2d 31, 35 (2d Cir. 1993).

No one disputes that Frank was a defendant in an action for money damages who did not satisfy the judgment and who made certain conveyances while the action was in progress. The dispute is whether the conveyances were made with, or without, "fair consideration." The term "fair consideration" is defined in DCL § 272:

Fair consideration is given for property, or obligation,

a. When in exchange for such property, or obligation, as a fair equivalent therefor, and in good faith, property is conveyed or an antecedent debt is satisfied, or

b. When such property, or obligation is received in good faith to secure a present advance or antecedent debt in amount not disproportionately small as compared with the value of the property, or obligation obtained.

The meaning of DCL § 272 is primarily at issue in these appeals.

Finally, DCL §§ 278 and 279 set out remedies for creditors challenging fraudulent conveyances. Section 279 pertains to creditors whose claims have not matured. Section 278 pertains to creditors, like HBE, whose claims have matured, and provides:

1. Where a conveyance or obligation is fraudulent as to a creditor, such creditor, when his claim has matured, may, as against any person except a purchaser for fair consideration without knowledge of the fraud at the time of the purchase, or one who has derived title immediately or mediately from such a purchaser.

    a.   Have the conveyance set aside or obligation annulled to the extent necessary to satisfy his claim, or

    b.   Disregard the conveyance and attach or levy execution upon the property conveyed.

2. A purchaser who without actual fraudulent intent has given less than a fair consideration for the conveyance or obligation, may retain the property or obligation as security for repayment.

With that framework in mind, we turn to the issues raised on appeal.

The Conveyances To Murphy

Frank conveyed the bond and residence to Murphy pursuant to a prenuptial agreement dated October 18, 1990, more than two years after the RICO suit was filed and some two years prior to judgment. Frank and Murphy were married a few days later. The district court noted that although prenuptial agreements are usually effective under New York law "as between the parties to them, . . . such transfer do not in and of themselves meet the criteria of § 272 of the Debtor & Creditor Law so as to be non–fraudulent and binding on third party creditors." *HBE III*, 851 F.Supp. at 573. "[P]romises of future benefits," the district court stated, "cannot be a substitute for present 'property' under § 272(a)." *Id.* at 574. The court accordingly held as a matter of law that the transfers to Murphy were fraudulent under DCL § 273–a.

The district court also found that Frank's gifts of the ring and the boat, which were conveyed independently of the prenuptial agreement, were fraudulent conveyances. Murphy does not appeal the judgment as to the boat, and although the expresses moral outrage that the court could find the gift of an engagement ring to be susceptible to avoidance as a fraudulent conveyance, she does not raise any intelligible legal arguments on this score; certainly her promise to marry Frank does not constitute "property" conveyed in exchange for the ring.

Rather, the gravamen of Murphy's appeal[4] is her claim that she gave fair consideration for the property she received pursuant to the prenuptial agreement, by giving up, in the same agreement, her statutory marital rights. She argues that her agreement to forsake marital rights itself was a conveyance of property in good faith and in fair exchange for the residence and bonds, and thus constituted "fair consideration" under DCL § 272(a).

Section 272(a) says that fair consideration is given for property when "in exchange for such property, . . . as fair equivalent therefor, and in good faith, property is conveyed or an antecedent debt is satisfied." The test is profitably analyzed as follows: (1) Murphy, as the recipient of the debtor's property (the residence and the bonds), must either (a) convey property in exchange or (b) discharge an antecedent debt in exchange; and (2) such exchange must be a "fair equivalent" of the property received; and (3) such exchange must be "in good faith."[5]

Judge Brieant did not make findings or discuss the second and third elements— fair equivalent value and good faith. Rather, he considered only the first element and ruled against Murphy as a matter of law; she did not convey property or discharge an antecedent debt in exchange for the residence and bonds. Murphy does not contend there was an antecedent debt; her claim is that she conveyed property. She is incorrect. What she did was to make an executory promise; she gave up certain contingent rights that otherwise might accrue to her benefit in the future, if she married Frank and if she later divorced him or he predeceased her. A promise of this sort is not a conveyance of property.

The term "conveyance" is defined in DCL § 270 as "every payment of money, assignment, release, transfer, lease, mortgage or pledge of tangible or intangible property, and also the creation of any lien or incumbrance." Murphy argues that she pledged intangible property—by definition, a conveyance. But in fact she did not; at most what she promised in exchange for the residence and bonds was to give up contingent, inchoate interests in property. *Cf. Federal Deposit Ins. Co. v. Malin*, 802 F.2d 12, 17 (2d Cir. 1986) (separation agreement in which husband agreed to transfer residence to wife was a "conveyance" and not a mere "executory contract to convey real property" where wife's rights came immediately into existence upon signing agreement, and transfer was not contingent on parties' obtaining divorce).

The conveyances to Murphy, if not reachable by creditors under the Fraudulent Conveyance Act, would shelter Frank's assets from parties he wronged. He could empty his estate with impunity when sued by his victims, transfer his property to his fiancee and receive nothing but inchoate interests in return—nothing from which HBE could recover its judgment—and yet enjoy the benefits of the property now nominally owned by his wife. That is the sort of injustice fraudulent conveyance law is designed to prevent. *See Orr v. Kinderhill Corp.*, 991 F.2d at 36 (quoting

---

[4] For convenience, we omit reference to Wallace Berkowitz, who joins Murphy's appeal insofar as it concerns the bonds which he holds as trustee on Murphy's behalf.

[5] The "good faith" in § 272 is the good faith of the transferee—in this case, Murphy (and Goldstein and Clemence Frank). By contrast, to prove actual fraud under § 276, a creditor must show intent to defraud on the part of the transferor.

1 G. Glenn, *Fraudulent Conveyances and Preferences* § 195, at 348 (rev. ed. 1940))
(" 'real test of a fraudulent conveyance . . . is the unjust diminution of the debtor's
estate' ").

Murphy relies heavily upon *FDIC v. Malin*, but the decision does not help her.
The issue there (as well as in the state court decisions cited by Murphy) was whether
a judgment creditor of the husband could set aside as fraudulent the husband's
conveyance of a residence to his wife in a separation agreement while suit was
pending against him. This Court held that the wife was protected from the creditor
by virtue of DCL § 278, which provides that a creditor may have a fraudulent
conveyance set aside except as to "a purchaser for fair consideration without
knowledge of the fraud at the time of the purchase." *Id.* at 16. That provision itself
is not at issue in the present case (Murphy did not disclaim knowledge of the pending
RICO suit at the time if the transfers), but the *Malin* decision is relevant because
the court—after determining that the conveyance of the house was effected by the
separation agreement, prior to the date of the creditor's judgment lien, and that the
wife had no knowledge of the fraud at the time of the conveyance—had to decide
whether the wife took the residence "for fair consideration," as defined in § 272.

The *Malin* Court held that the three elements of § 272 identified above were
established. First, and most important here, the residence was exchanged in
satisfaction of an antecedent debt. "In the domestic relations context, it is well settled
in New York that a husband's obligation to support his wife is an antecedent debt
sufficient to satisfy the definition of fair consideration." *Id.* at 18.

Applying the definition of fair consideration established by section 272 and as
refined by New York precedent, we likewise conclude that the conveyance at issue
here was entered into for fair consideration. At the time the separation agreement
was executed, Leonard Malin was under an affirmative obligation to provide support
to his wife. Additionally, he had antecedent liability for maintenance and child
support. In satisfaction of his antecedent debts, Leonard Malin conveyed real estate
and other property to his wife.

Id. at 19 (citations omitted). When the prenuptial agreement in this case was
signed, by contrast, Frank had no affirmative duty to provide support to Susan
Murphy and no antecedent debts owed to her. In exchange for the residence and
bonds, Murphy neither conveyed property nor, unlike Phyllis Malin, did she release
antecedent debts. That is the fundamental difference between the Malins' agreement
and the Frank–Murphy agreement, as concerns the rights of creditors.

The Court in *Malin* went on to hold that the wife had acted in good faith as she
had no knowledge of her husband's indebtedness, and that the consideration she gave
was of equivalent value. *Id.* at 19–20. In reference to the latter point, the Court noted
that a "separation agreement works the relinquishment of rights and remedies
otherwise conferred by law" and that the Malins' agreement had the earmark of a
"bargained for" contract. *Id.* at 20. Murphy latches onto this language, arguing that
because her prenuptial agreement with Frank has the same characteristics (a
contentious point), conveyances made pursuant to it cannot be challenged by
creditors as fraudulent. But the *Malin* Court made these observations only to show
fair equivalent value; the other elements of § 272 must also be satisfied to avoid

a finding of presumptive fraud under § 273–a. As shown above, Murphy has failed as a matter of law to establish the first element—that she conveyed property or discharged an antecedent debt in exchange for the residence and bonds.

Murphy also relies upon *Miele v. United States*, 637 F.Supp. 998 (S.D. Fla. 1986), which supports her appeal insofar as it held that a waiver of marital rights in a prenuptial agreement constituted valuable consideration in exchange for a parcel of real property, thereby defeating the government's effort to set aside as fraudulent the conveyance of the property. *Id.* at 1000. But the court in *Miele* was not construing a provision similar to § 272 of New York Debtor & Creditor Law, which defines "fair consideration" in specific terms. Rather, the court denied relief to the government because it failed to show that the property had been conveyed to the fiancee with fraudulent intent. And one indication of the lack of fraudulent intent, the court noted, was that the fiancee had relinquished "some valid marital rights" in exchange for the property. *Id.*

We do not hold that a prenuptial agreement may never be supported by consideration. Indeed, we need not and do not decide whether the Murphy–Frank prenuptial agreement is supported by consideration as concerns the rights of Murphy and Frank to enforce that agreement. Nor do we hold that all prenuptial agreements are per se constructively fraudulent as to creditors. We hold only that the contingent property interests relinquished by Murphy in her prenuptial agreement with Frank did not constitute "fair consideration," as defined in DCL § 272, adequate to save Frank's transfers to Murphy from being set aside as fraudulent conveyances under DCL § 273–a. The district court's award of summary judgment and order with respect to the challenged conveyances to Murphy are accordingly affirmed.

The Conveyances To Goldstein

It is conceded that the North Broward Bond, Chern Mortgage and Fox Run Note were transferred to Goldstein prior to judgment in the RICO case, in large part to secure the payment of future legal fees and expenses. In exchange Goldstein promised to render extensive legal services, over an extended period of time and in several courts, for an agreed flat fee of $350,000. That promise does not constitute "fair consideration" under the statute.

DCL § 272(b) provides that fair consideration is given for property when the property "is received in good faith to secure a present advance or antecedent debt in amount not disproportionately small" (emphasis added). Goldstein strives hard to label its promised services a "present" advance, but the facts are just not there. In its main brief on appeal (at 6), Goldstein avers: "The legal work to be performed was fixed and definite and required the Defendant attorneys to prosecute this appeal from a lengthy and prolonged three month trial,[6] engage specific counsel to perform legal work on the appeal, and to represent Defendants Hiram J. Frank, H.H. Frank Enterprises, Inc. and Hiram H. Frank in proceedings supplementary to Judgment [in both Florida and New York]." In reality, the work contemplated was neither "fixed" nor "definite," but was rather of considerably uncertain scope and duration (the

---

6 The context indicates that by "this appeal" Goldstein is actually referring to the appeal from the RICO verdict.

present appeals being an illustration). *See Clarkson Company Ltd. v. Shaheen*, 525 F.Supp. 625, 630 (S.D.N.Y. 1981) (transfer of shares to lawyer to secure future services that were "open–ended, indefinite, of highly uncertain duration" was fraudulent conveyance under New York law); *see also Hay v. Duskin*, 9 Ariz.App. 599, 604–605, 455 P.2d 281, 286–87 (1969) (under Arizona's counterpart statute, fixed and definite future attorney's services, to be commenced immediately, may constitute fair consideration, where there is good faith and proportionality of value); *see generally Annot.*, 45 A.L.R.2d 500 (1956). Where to draw the line between permissible present advances and promises of indefinite services may be difficult in close cases, but this does not appear to us to be a close case. The extended legal work envisioned by Frank and Goldstein certainly did not constitute a "present advance" for purposes of DCL § 272(b). Again, there is no need to reach, and the district court did not reach, the factual issues of good faith and equivalent value.

Goldstein also argues on appeal that the transfers were expressly allowed in a restraining order signed by Judge Goettel on November 9, 1992, which enjoined all defendants in the RICO action from transferring any property except as ordered by the court, and except for "reasonable living expenses and attorneys fees." Goldstein misread Judge Goettel's order as "permitt[ing] the defendants to transfer their property in order to pay past and future attorneys' fees." Goldstein Reply Brief at 1. The order authorized Frank to pay reasonable attorney's fees; it did not authorize him to make fraudulent conveyances to his attorneys.

The district court correctly held that Goldstein's argument "runs counter to the text of New York Debtor and Creditor Law § 272 . . . which requires that property be exchanged for fair consideration which is present." *HBE III*, 851 F.Supp. at 574. As the court also aptly observed, "[w]hile ability to pay legal expenses is often essential to protection of a citizen's rights, a blanket authorization for transfers at the expense of creditors for unevaluated future legal services would put the Bar in a position of being subject to frequent suspicion of unjust involvement in schemes of the very kind shown at trial in the prior [RICO] case." *Id.*

Goldstein further asserts, however, that he was also owed fees—$75,010—for services performed through October 30, 1992, that is, prior to the conveyances at issue. If true, to that extent, the property conveyed to Goldstein would satisfy the "antecedent debt" prongs of DCL § 272(a) and (b). Nonetheless, fair consideration is still lacking as a matter of law with respect to the $227,000 bond and $278,000 note, because the conceded values of those two securities each far exceeds the allegedly outstanding legal fees. Thus, under § 272(a), the value of antecedent debt satisfied ($75,010) is not a "fair equivalent" of the bond or note conveyed to Goldstein; under § 272(b), the value of antecedent debt secured is "disproportionately small as compared with the value of the property." *See Clarkson Company*, 525 F.Supp. at 629–30 (value of stock pledged to debtor's attorney was grossly disproportionate to antecedent debt). We therefore conclude as a matter of law that fair consideration was not given for two of the three challenged conveyances to Goldstein—the North Broward Bond and the Fox Run Note—and these are subject to being set aside as constructively fraudulent.

The circumstances relating to the Chern Mortgage are somewhat different. That mortgage, which secured a debt of approximately $144,000 at the time of its transfer to Goldstein, apparently encumbers a chicken farm that is no longer in operation. We believe that genuine questions of fact exist as to whether the present value of the Chern Mortgage is a "fair equivalent" of the $75,010 under § 272(a), or whether the $75,010 is "disproportionately small as compared with" the present value of the mortgage under § 272(b). *See United States v. McCombs*, 30 F.3d 310, 326 (2d Cir. 1994) (sufficiency of consideration under DCL § 272 depends on facts and circumstances of each particular case). HBE is therefore not entitled to summary judgment as to the Chern Mortgage.

Judge Brieant granted summary judgment to HBE as to the North Broward Bond only, voiding the transfer and awarding judgment against Goldstein in the amount of the bond plus interest. That order is affirmed over Goldstein's appeal. Without explanation, however, Judge Brieant did not void the Chern Mortgage and the Fox Run Note. Aside from the matter of the alleged $75,010 in prior legal fees, we see no basis in this record for differentiating among the three conveyances.

Accordingly, for the reasons set forth above, we reverse the district court decision insofar as it dismissed HBE's claims as to the Chern Mortgage and the Fox Run Note. HBE is entitled to summary judgment on the Fox Run Note claim, and we remand for an appropriate disposition, including the calculation of interest. As to the Chern Mortgage, we remand for the district court to make factual findings on the following questions, if necessary: whether the $75,010 were indeed earned as claimed, prior to the judgment in the RICO action; whether that amount is reasonable under Judge Goettel's restraining order; whether the present value of the Chern Mortgage represents a "fair equivalent" of the $75,010 under DCL § 272(a); or whether the $75,010 is "disproportionately small" under DCL § 272(b); whether Goldstein acted "in good faith" under either part of DCL § 272; and, finally, whether Frank transferred the mortgage with the "actual intent" to hinder, delay or defraud HBE under DCL § 276. If Goldstein prevails on all of these matter, the Chern Mortgage should not be set aside.

The Conveyances To Clemence Frank

The district court granted summary judgment to Clemence Frank, denying HBE any relief with respect to the bonds transferred to her in August 1991 and October 1992. *HBE III*, 851 F.Supp. at 575. This ruling is challenged in HBE's cross–appeal.

The district court concluded that HBE failed to come forward with sufficient evidence to establish the existence of a genuine issue of material fact with respect to its claims against Clemence Frank. *See* Fed.R.Civ.P. 56(c); *Celotex Corp. v. Catrett*, 477 U.S. 317, 106 S.Ct. 2548, 91 L.Ed.2d 265 (1986). We disagree. HBE presented evidence supporting its claims that the conveyances of bonds to Clemence Frank were constructively fraudulent under DCL § 273–a and actually fraudulent under DCL § 276—for example, that Clemence Frank paid in exchange significantly less cash ($355,000) than the value of the bonds ($482,000), that said cash cycled through Frank's accounts and ended up benefiting Clemence Frank herself (i.e., illusory consideration) or was reconveyed by Frank for less than fair consideration or with fraudulent intent, and that Clemence Frank knew about the pending RICO judgment. These are material facts in dispute. *See HBE IV*, 48 F.3d at 635 (multiple transactions may be collapsed and treated as phases of single transaction where (1) consideration received in exchange for initial transfer of debtor's property is reconveyed by debtor for less than fair consideration or with fraudulent intent, and (2) transferee of initial conveyance has actual or constructive knowledge of scheme); *Orr v. Kinderhill Corp.*, 991 F.2d at 35 (court "will not turn a blind eye to the reality" that challenged conveyance and subsequent transfers "constituted a single, integrated transaction").

Accordingly, we hold that the district court erred in granting summary judgment to Clemence Frank, and the matter is remanded for further proceedings, consistent both with this opinion and the opinion of this Court in *HBE IV*, 48 F.3d 623.

Conclusion

We affirm the judgment of the district court as to the claims involving Susan Murphy Frank and Wallace Berkowitz, affirm as to the claim involving the North Broward Bond, reverse and remand as to the claims involving the Chern Mortgage and the Fox Run Note, and reverse and remand as to the claims involving Clemence Frank.

Costs to be taxed equally against defendants Murphy, Goldstein and Clemence Frank.

EISENBERG v. FLATEN
(*In re Allied Development Corp.*)

United States Court of Appeals, Seventh Circuit
435 F.2d 372 (1970)

CASTLE, C.J.

Respondents–appellants, Donald S. Eisenberg, American Exchange Bank, and Commercial State Bank, prosecute this appeal from the judgment order of the District Court denying their petitions for review of an order of the referee in bankruptcy finding liens asserted by the appellants to be null and void. The liens are based on a second mortgage on a lumber–yard property, an asset of the bankrupt, Allied Development Corporation.

Allied was engaged in the business of development, sale and management of real estate. Its assets included real estate encumbered by mortgages held by a close affiliate engaged in the insurance business. Some of the corporate officers of each of the corporations were corporate officers of the other. Prior to the date of the second mortgage here in question, August 27, 1964, the Insurance Department of the State of Wisconsin directed that these mortgages be repaid immediately. Allied sought financial assistance from respondent–appellant Donald S. Eisenberg, a partner in the law firm which represented Allied, to accomplish the repayments to the insurance company. Eisenberg made a loan of $90,000.00 to Allied. He received as security the August 27, 1964 junior mortgage on the lumber–yard owned by Allied. He did not record the mortgage until September 22, 1964, some three weeks later. On January 19, 1965 Allied filed a petition for relief under Chapter XI of the Bankruptcy Act . . . On June 3, 1965, Eisenberg assigned the mortgage to the American Exchange Bank and the Commercial State Bank, respondents–appellants, as additional security for repayment of pre–existing loans made to him aggregating $57,340.00 plus interest. The Chapter XI arrangement proceeding failed, and on July 21, 1966 Allied was adjudicated a bankrupt. The trustee in bankruptcy filed a petition asserting the invalidity of the August 27, 1964 second mortgage and requesting that the parties be ordered to show cause why the fund remaining from the sale of the property ($68,055.44) should not be declared free of any lien of said mortgage and be deposited with the general funds of the bankrupt's estate.

Among other grounds, the trustee's petition alleged invalidity of the mortgage under § 67(d)(2)(d) of the Bankruptcy Act [actual intent to hinder delay or defraud creditors]. Following a hearing on the petition, the referee filed an opinion containing his findings of fact and conclusions of law. He concluded that as to both Eisenberg and the two banks the mortgage and the assignment thereof were made with actual intent to hinder, delay or defraud creditors. On review the District Court in affirming the order entered by the referee pointed to an alternative basis for concluding that the mortgage was invalid as to the banks, i.e., that the banks were not bona fide lienors and, therefore, were not entitled to the protection afforded by the concluding proviso of § 67(d)(6).[4]

The record discloses that when Eisenberg made the loan of $90,000.00 to Allied it was agreed that the second mortgage he took as security would not be recorded. Eisenberg, in his testimony characterized the date of the mortgage, August 27, 1964, as that "fateful day" when the Wisconsin authorities were ready "to lower the boom" on . . . Allied's affiliate, which had been directed to secure repayment of the loans for which Allied's property stood as security. Eisenberg further testified that on that date "there were several judgments that were intercepted at the courthouse steps and people talked out of filing them"; that "we didn't want any mortgages, liens or judgments or anything else to be of record to in any way taint the credit of Allied"; that "Allied was in a cash liquid bad position and I did not record it [the second mortgage] because . . . I didn't want the Chamber of Commerce report to pick up the fact that Allied had granted a mortgage for $90,000.00 and I felt no problem at all in not recording it."

The record further discloses that Allied and its related corporations, Madison American Guaranty Insurance Company and Brooks and Woodington, Inc., were then engaging in a check–kiting practice, and Friday, September 18, 1964 the Wisconsin Banking Commission informed the appellant banks, in which Allied and

---

[4] § 67(d)(6) provides: "A transfer made or an obligation incurred by a debtor adjudged bankrupt under this title, which is fraudulent under this subdivision against creditors of such debtor having claims provable under this title, shall be null and void against the trustee, except as to a bona fide purchaser, lienor, or obligee for a present fair equivalent value: . . . *And provided further*, That such purchaser, lienor, or obligee, who without actual fraudulent intent has given a consideration less than fair, as defined in this subdivision, for such transfer, lien, or obligation, may retain the property, lien, or obligation as security for repayment."

Brooks and Woodington, Inc. had their accounts, that on the following Monday they would be permitted to credit those accounts only with deposited sums which represented cash or its equivalent. This augmented the crisis Allied was experiencing with respect to cash liquidity and over the week–end it sold some two and one–half to three million dollars worth of its properties. On September 22, 1964 Eisenberg recorded the mortgage he had been withholding from record because "at that point the situation did not look too good".

The appellants predicate the existence of error requiring reversal as to all of them on a contention that the record fails to support the finding and conclusion that the agreement to withhold the mortgage from record, and the failure to record it for three weeks, was with actual intent to hinder, delay or defraud creditors of Allied. We disagree as to the asserted insufficiency of the evidence in this respect. Eisenberg's testimony concerning the reason for not recording the mortgage is in our opinion most convincing that such action was precisely directed to the very purpose of hindering or delaying existing creditors and misleading future creditors. His testimony was to the effect that at the very time the mortgage was given, but its existence being withheld from public knowledge, Allied's existing creditors were being persuaded not to take judgments against Allied. And, it is reasonable to infer that Allied's purpose in keeping mention of the mortgage out of the Chamber of Commerce report had its impact on future creditors. Allied and Eisenberg were anxious that nothing of record "in any way taint the credit of Allied", and there is evidence that Allied obtained at least several thousands of dollars in new credit during the period the $90,000.00 mortgage, due to failure to record it, was not reflected by sources normally relied upon for credit information.

Certainly, the finding and conclusion with respect to the existence of actual intent is not "clearly erroneous" insofar as it rests on factual considerations. Nor is it the product of the application of incorrect legal criteria. In this latter connection we find inapposite appellants' argument that failure to record a mortgage for a three week period does not, of itself, establish "actual intent" to hinder, delay or defraud creditors. Here the failure to record does not stand in isolation. It was not only deliberate—the product of agreement—but it was accompanied by admitted purpose which establishes the "actual" intent requisite to invalidate an obligation . . . the Bankruptcy Act. . . . The record in this case establishes actual intent. There is that concurrence of facts which leads to the irresistible conclusion that the withholding of the mortgage from record was calculated to mislead creditors. On the record before us it would tax credulity to say that in keeping the mortgage off the record Allied and Eisenberg had no purpose to hinder, delay or defraud creditors. On this phase of the appeal we conclude that the record amply supports the denial of Eisenberg's claim to a lien against the proceeds from the sale of the property.

The appellant banks advance a separate and independent contention upon which they predicate the existence of an additional error requiring reversal of the rejection of their claims to liens. In this respect the banks contend that even though the record is viewed as supporting the holding that Allied and Eisenberg actually intended to hinder, delay or defraud creditors by withholding the recording of the mortgage, and the lien of the mortgage is therefore void as against the trustee in bankruptcy insofar as a claim of lien on the part of Eisenberg is concerned, nevertheless, the record presents no basis in fact or law warranting a conclusion that the banks were guilty of actual fraudulent intent in taking the assignment of the mortgage. Consequently, they urge they are entitled to assert the mortgage lien against the trustee under the provisions of § 67(d) (6) of the Bankruptcy Act to the extent of repayment of the $57,340.00 plus interest which Eisenberg owes to them—the pre–existing loans with respect to which Eisenberg assigned the mortgage to the banks as additional security.

The referee made a factual finding, undisturbed by the District Court on review, that neither of the banks knew of the delay in the recording of the mortgage when some nine months after its execution the banks took the assignment from Eisenberg as additional collateral for his pre–existing loans. The record does disclose, however, that at the time of the assignment the banks knew Allied had initiated a Ch. XI arrangement proceeding; had filed claims therein; were aware of financial irregularities of Allied; and were aware of the check kiting and of the action taken by the Wisconsin Banking Commission with respect thereto. The record reflects that all of the negotiating for additional collateral between the banks and Eisenberg was done by William Hobbins, president of the American Exchange Bank, on behalf of both banks; that on May 18, 1965 Hobbins wrote Eisenberg that he was "not interested in any security based upon mortgages originating with Allied Development Corporation"; and Hobbins testified that his reason for making such statement was "I had my belly full of Allied Development Corporation and their other activities". In the face of this background the banks accepted the assignment on the mortgage without a title search, did not get an opinion on the title, and made no investigation of the facts or circumstances surrounding the issuance of the mortgage. An examination of title would have disclosed the delay in recording.

Actual fraudulent intent "requires a conscious realization by the lienor that the lien will work a fraud on the debtor's creditors". *In re Peoria Braumeister Co.*, . . . We agree with the banks that under the particular factual circumstances here involved the standard enunciated in *Braumeister* has not been met. But we agree with the District Court that the record convincingly establishes lack of good faith on the part of the banks in taking the assignment, and that, consequently, absence of *bona fide* status precludes them from invoking the concluding proviso of § 67(d) (6).

Despite their knowledge that Allied was already the subject of custody of the bankruptcy court in a Ch. XI proceeding; their familiarity with the previous irregular conduct of Allied with respect to financial transactions; and their previous express rejection of collateral in the form of any security originating with Allied, the banks accepted the assignment of the Allied mortgage given to Eisenberg without bothering to make any inquiry into the circumstances of its issuance. In this connection Hobbins testified the banks took the assignment because "it was the best and only thing we could get". While the banks' lack of knowledge of or participation in the withholding of the mortgage from record relieves the banks of actual intent to hinder, delay or defraud Allied's creditors by such failure to record the mortgage, nevertheless, the circumstances surrounding the banks' acceptance of the assignment demonstrates lack of good faith on the part of the banks.

And, we are not persuaded by the banks' argument that good faith on the part of the purchaser or lienor is not a prerequisite to the application of the concluding proviso of § 67(d) (6)—that the absence of actual fraudulent intent suffices to protect them. The proviso refers to " . . . such purchaser, lienor, or obligee" and the antecedent of "such" is "a bona fide purchaser, lienor, or obligee". *See* note 4, *supra*.

Nor, in view of the context in which it appears, do we regard the comment in *Braumeister* . . . to the effect that a grantee who is "guilty of constructive fraud is entitled to protection to the extent of the consideration he paid" as dictating a construction of the proviso which dispenses with the requirement of good faith. *Braumeister* involved a situation where a lender took a note from the bankrupt in the amount of $3,000 but only advanced $2,500 cash. Good faith of the lender was found. In reaching the conclusion that the lender was entitled to the protection of the mortgage lien to the extent of the amount actually advanced, this Court said . . .:

> We arrive at this conclusion by virtue of Section 67 sub. d(6) of the Bankruptcy Act . . . which provides that a bona fide lienor who, without actual fraudulent intent, has given a consideration less than fair for such lien, may retain the lien as security for repayment.

The comment later in the opinion . . . with respect to protection afforded to a grantee or lienor "guilty of constructive fraud" is but a recognition that constructive fraud, *i.e.*, fraudulent intent presumed in law, is not necessarily inconsistent with the existence of good faith on the part of the grantee or lienor. It is not a holding that good faith is not a prerequisite to the application of the proviso.

We conclude that the lack of good faith on the part of the banks precludes the banks from successfully invoking the protection accorded a bona fide lienor under the concluding proviso of § 67(d) (6).

The judgment order appealed from is affirmed . . .

NOTES AND QUESTIONS

(1) The bankruptcy court in *Allied Development* found that both the transfer of the debtor's mortgage to Eisenberg, and the subsequent assignment of that mortgage to the two banks, were made with actual intent to hinder, delay, or defraud the debtor's creditors. How did the district and circuit courts modify the lower court's analysis of the assignment to the banks?

(2) Why doesn't the Seventh Circuit discuss fair consideration with respect to the initial transfer?

(3) How significant to the court's decision is the debtor's having obtained "several thousands of dollars in new credit during the [three–week] period" while the mortgage remained unrecorded? How might the court's reasoning have changed if no credit had been extended until after the lenders were aware of the mortgage?

(4) Do you think the record adequately supports a finding that the banks lacked good faith sufficient to afford them the protection of Bankruptcy Act § 67(d)(6)? *Cf. Hassett v. McColley (In re O.P.M. Leasing Services)*, 28 B.R. 740 (Bankr. S.D.N.Y. 1983).

(5) For a discussion of liability of subsequent transferees under the Bankruptcy Code, *see Davis v. Cook Construction Co. (In re SLF News Distributors, Inc.)*, 649 F.2d 613 (8th Cir. 1981); *Kuhn v. Nance (In re Nance)*, 26 B.R. 105 (Bankr. S.D. Ohio 1982); *but cf. Burtrum v. Laughlin (In re Laughlin)*, 18 B.R. 778 (Bankr. W.D. Mo. 1982). *See generally* Note, *Good Faith and Fraudulent Conveyances*, 97 Harv. L. Rev. 495 (1983).

CHAPTER 7

EXEMPTIONS

§ 7.01 Introduction

The large and diverse body of state exemption laws places certain types of debtors' property beyond the reach of creditors. This conglomeration of state laws has the reputation of being remarkably diverse, inconsistent, unfair and obsolete. The laws variously exempt property from private creditors and from the powers of a bankruptcy trustee. Rooted in the prisons of Olde England, the slow creep towards debtor forgiveness and the promotion of rehabilitation have been characterized by fits and starts through the history of exemption statutes. Some laws currently in effect date from early this century. They closely approximate today's lifestyles by exempting such modern necessities as swarms of bees, lettered gravestones, squirrels that are not for sale, "comfortable beds," 100 chickens for personal or family use, and a musket or two. Some states are very lenient, and offer a safe harbor from creditors limited only by the assets and creativity of the debtor. Other states seem inexplicably stern in allowing debtors to retain little property. One court expressed the exasperation that any analysis of these exemption statutes will engender:

> While I have spent considerable time searching for precedence [sic], I am satisfied that it was more or less time wasted, as the exemption laws in the different states are so dissimilar.

In re Bray, 8 F. Supp. 761 (D.N.H. 1934).

The goals of a policy that protects certain parts of a debtor's property are salutary. Avoidance of pauperism and the consequent burden on society, the "preservation" of family, and the promotion of debtor self–help and rehabilitation have finally gained greater importance than punishing a debtor.

The origins of exemption laws vary from state to state and from region to region. Of the original 13 states, New England most clearly reflects the strict parsimonious approach adapted from Great Britain. Moving west, there is a general liberalizing trend peaking in Texas and California. This trend has been variously explained as a result of the "frontier spirit," a regional attempt to attract settlers, or as a vestige of early Spanish influence, where debt was not viewed as harshly as in Great Britain.

Exemption laws are organized (or disorganized) in many ways. They are thus found scattered about the legal landscape. This fact, plus the elective nature of the federal bankruptcy exemption statute, makes reference to several sets of statutes necessary and any attempt at generalization foolhardy. Compounded by some liberal constructions of the more antiquated of the statutes, analysis of what could be a straightforward subject requires covering several bases.

Exemption statutes are of several general types. They may exempt specific property with no limit as to value, such as an immunity for all social security benefits. They may exempt property to the extent "needed for support" or as "necessary," raising tough definitional questions with regard to items such as alimony, trust income, and life insurance. Other classes of property are limited to a total sum certain, such as $20,000 for a homestead, or to a total amount allowable per item, such as home furnishings or jewelry.

§ 7.02 Sources of Exemption Laws

There are three basic sources for exemption laws. Federal law provides a general exemption statute at 11 U.S.C. § 522 (1982 & Supp. IV 1986) that is available only to natural persons seeking relief under the Bankruptcy Code. Debtors may elect either section 522 or the applicable exemptions under laws of the debtor's domicile, 11 U.S.C. § 522(b), but some states, pursuant to an "opt–out" provision in section 522(b)(1), may require the debtor's exclusive use of the state–law exemption. *See, e.g.*, N.Y. Debtor & Creditor Law § 284 (McKinney Supp. 1988); Cal. Civ. Proc. Code § 703.130 (West 1987); Ind. Code § 34–2–28 (1986); Okla. Stat. tit. 31 § 1(B) (Supp. 1987–1988); *see generally* 7 Collier on Bankruptcy (15th rev. ed. 1988). When available, the federal exemption law must be elected in total, not paragraph by paragraph. *See generally* Schuchman & Rorer, *Personal Bankruptcy Data for Opt–Out Hearings and Other Purposes*, 56 Am. Bankr. L.J. 1 (1982).

Federal law also provides "exemptions" in other statutes. With regard to federal tax liens, 26 U.S.C. § 6334 (1982 & Supp. IV 1986) is the exclusive source of exemption law. Federal law also extends protection in one form or another to social security benefits, 42 U.S.C. § 407 (1982 & Supp. IV 1986); veterans' benefits, 38 U.S.C. § 3101 (1982 & Supp. IV 1986); civil service retirement benefits, 5 U.S.C. § 8346 (1982); savings deposits of servicemen, 10 U.S.C. § 1035(d) (1982); longshoremen's benefits, 33 U.S.C. § 916 (1982); seamen's wages, 46 U.S.C. §§ 11108, 11109 (1982 & Supp. III 1985); railroad employee benefits, 45 U.S.C. § 352(e) (1982 & Supp. III 1985); and finally, a specified percentage of disposable earnings in the Consumers Credit Protection Act, 15 U.S.C. § 1673 (1982 & Supp. IV 1986) (no more than 25% of aggregate disposable earnings for any work–week or other pay period).

State constitutions may also provide for some form of exemption, notably for a debtor's homestead. *See, e.g.*, Tex. Const. art. XVI, § 50 (1973); Kan. Const. art. XV, § 9; Colo. Const. art. XVIII, § 1. Many different types of state statutes also include explicit or de facto exemption laws. For example, a complete survey of New York State's exemption statutes would require reference to that state's insurance, labor, banking, wage, estate power & trust, debtor–creditor and civil practice laws. At this level, exemption law becomes a morass.

In recognition of the potential for confusion and the unfairness caused by a lack of uniformity, the Commission on Uniform Laws promulgated the Uniform

Exemptions Act, 13 U.L.A. 207 (1976), excerpted below. To date, however, the UEA has only been adopted in Alaska. *See* Alaska Stat. §§ 09.38.010 to 09.38.510 (1982).

There has recently been significant amendment and a general modernization of many of the state exemption laws, at least in terms of enlarging the monetary ceilings. Many inequities and loopholes still remain, however.

Federal law does not preempt the law of exemptions except with regard to federal tax liens. "[I]n case of execution upon judgments in civil actions the United States are [sic] subject to the same exemptions as apply to private persons by the law of the State in which the property levied on is found. . . ." *Fink v. O'Neil*, 106 U.S. 272, 284–85 (1882). *See Holden v. Stratton*, 198 U.S. 202 (1905). This is most evident from the elective and "opt–out" nature of the federal bankruptcy exemption. Are other federal "exemptions" subject to state limitation? Could the federal government limit a state constitutional homestead exemption? Could lenient state exemption laws, especially regarding the ability to transfer exemption rights, run afoul of the constitutional right to contract? *See generally* Countryman, *For a New Exemption Policy in Bankruptcy*, 14 Rutgers L. Rev. 678 (1960); Vukowich, *Debtors' Exemption Rights*, 62 Geo. L.J. 779 (1946); Plumb, *The Recommendations of the Commission on the Bankruptcy Laws—Exempt and Immune Property*, 61 Va. L. Rev. 1 (1975).

[A]   Excerpts from the Uniform Exemptions Act, 13 U.L.A. (1976)

Section 2. [Adjustment of Dollar Amounts]

(a) The dollar amounts in the Act change, as provided in this section, according to and to the extent of changes in the Consumer Price Index for Urban Wage Earners and Clerical Workers: U.S. City Average, All Items, 1967 = 100, compiled by the Bureau of Labor Statistics, United States Department of Labor, and hereafter referred to as the Index. The Index for December of the year preceding the year in which this Act becomes effective is the Reference Base Index.

(b) The dollar amounts change on July 1 of each even–numbered year if the percentage of change, calculated to the nearest whole percentage point, between the Index for December of the preceding year and the Reference Base Index, is 10 percent or more, but:

(1) the portion of the percentage change in the Index in excess of a multiple of 10 percent is disregarded and the dollar amounts change only in multiples of 10 percent of the amounts appearing in this Act on the date of enactment; and

(2) the dollar amounts do not change if the amounts required by this section are those currently in effect as a result of earlier application of this section.

(c) If the Index is revised, the percentage of change is calculated on the basis of the revised Index. If a revision of the Index changes the Reference Base Index, a revised Reference Base Index is determined by multiplying the Reference Base Index applicable by the rebasing factor furnished by the Bureau of Labor Statistics. If the Index is superseded, the Index referred to in this section is the one represented by the Bureau of Labor Statistics as reflecting most accurately changes in the purchasing power of the dollar for consumers.

(d) The [appropriate state official] shall adopt a rule announcing:

(1) on or before April 30 of each year in which dollar amounts are to change, the changes in dollar amounts required by subsection (b); and

(2) promptly after the changes occur, changes in the Index required by subsection (c) including, if applicable, the numerical equivalent of the Reference Base Index under a revised Reference Base Index and the designation or title or any index superseding the Index.

Section 4. [Homestead Exemption]

(a) An individual is entitled to an exemption as a homestead of his interest in property in this State used as a home by him or his dependents, but the value of the homestead exemption may not exceed $10,000.

(b) If property owned jointly, by the entirety, in common, or as community property is used by one or more individual owners or their dependents as a home, each owner is entitled to a homestead exemption of his interest in the property as provided in subsection (a). The aggregate value of multiple homestead exemptions allowable with respect to a single living unit may not exceed $20,000. If there are multiple owners of property exempt as a homestead, the value of the exemption of each individual owner may not exceed his aliquot portion of $20,000.

(c) A homestead exemption may be claimed in real or personal property, or both, without regard to the nature of the individual's interest in the property. It may be claimed in an interest in a cooperative that owns property used as a home by the individual or his dependents. . . .

Section 5. [Property Exempt without Limitation]

An individual is entitled to exemption of the following property:

(1) a burial plot for the individual and his family;

(2) health aids reasonably necessary to enable the individual or a dependent to work or to sustain health;

(3) benefits the individual has received or is entitled to receive under federal social security or state unemployment compensation, or under federal, state, or local public assistance legislation;

(4) benefits paid or payable for medical, surgical, or hospital care to the extent they are or will be used to pay for the care;

(5) veteran's benefits; and

(6) an award under a crime victim's reparations act.

Section 6. [Property Exempt to Extent Reasonably Necessary for Support]

(a) An individual is entitled to exemption of the following property to the extent reasonably necessary for the support of him and his dependents:

(1) benefits paid or payable by reason of disability, illness, or unemployment;

(2) money or property received and rights to receive money or property for alimony, support, or separate maintenance;

(3) proceeds of insurance, a judgment, or a settlement, or other rights accruing as a result of bodily injury of the individual or of the wrongful death or bodily injury of another individual of whom the individual was or is a dependent;

(4) proceeds or benefits paid or payable on the death of an insured, if the individual was the spouse or a dependent of the insured; and

(5) assets held, payments made, and amounts payable under a stock bonus, pension, profit–sharing, annuity, or similar plan or contract, providing benefits by reason of age, illness, disability, or length of service.

(b) The phrase "property to the extent reasonably necessary for the support of him and his dependents" means property required to meet the present and anticipated needs of the individual and his dependents, as determined by the court after consideration of the individual's responsibilities and all the present and anticipated property and income of the individual, including that which is exempt.

(c) This section does not affect property exempt under Section 5.

Section 7. [Exemption of Unmatured Life Insurance Contracts]

Except as provided in this section, an individual is entitled to exemption of unmatured life insurance contracts owned by him. If the contracts have accrued dividends, interest, and loan values aggregating more than $5,000 available to the individual, a creditor may obtain a court order requiring the individual debtor to pay the creditor, and authorizing the creditor on the debtor's behalf to obtain payment of, the amount of the accrued dividends, interest, and loan values in excess of $5,000 or the amount of the creditor's claim, whichever is less.

Section 8. [Exemptions of Personal Property Subject to Value Limitations]

(a) An individual is entitled to exemption of the following property to the extent of a value not exceeding $500 in any item of property:

(1) furnishings and appliances reasonably necessary for one household;

(2) if reasonably held for the personal use of the individual or a dependent, wearing apparel, animals, books, and musical instruments; and

(3) family portraits and heirlooms of particular sentimental value to the individual.

(b) An individual is entitled to exemption of jewelry, not exceeding $500 in aggregate value, if held for the personal use of the individual or a dependent.

(c) An individual is entitled to exemption, not exceeding $1,000 in aggregate value, of implements, professional books, and tools of the trade; and to an exemption of one motor vehicle to the extent of a value not exceeding $1500.

(d) In addition to any exemption provided by this Act or other law, an individual is entitled to exemption of cash and other liquid assets to the extent of a value not exceeding (1) $500 if the individual claims a homestead exemption (Section 4), or

(2) $1500 if the individual does not claim a homestead exemption. The term "liquid assets" includes deposits, securities, notes, drafts, unpaid earnings not otherwise exempt, accrued vacation pay, refunds, prepayments, and other receivables.

Section 9. [Tracing Exempt Property]

(a) If property, or a part thereof, that could have been claimed as an exempt homestead under Section 4, a burial plot under Section 5(1), a health aid under Section 5(2), or personal property subject to a value limitation under paragraph (1) or (2) of subsection (a) or subsection (c) of Section 8, has been sold or taken by condemnation, or has been lost, damaged, or destroyed and the owner has been indemnified therefor, the individual is entitled to an exemption of proceeds that are traceable for 18 months after the proceeds are received. The exemption of proceeds under this subsection does not entitle the individual to claim an aggregate exemption in excess of the value limitation otherwise allowable under Section 4 or 8.

(b) Money or other property exempt under paragraph (3), (4), (5), or (6) of Section 5, or exempt to the extent reasonably necessary for support under Section 6, remains exempt after its receipt by, and while it is in the possession of, the individual or in any other form into which it is traceable, for example, in a bank or savings account.

(c) Money or other property and proceeds exempt under this Act are traceable under this section by application of the principle of first–in first–out, last–in first–out, or any other reasonable basis for tracing selected by the individual.

Section 10. [Claim Enforceable against Exempt Property]

(a) Notwithstanding other provisions of this Act:

(1) a creditor may make a levy against exempt property of any kind to enforce a claim for:

(i) alimony, support, or maintenance;

(ii) unpaid earnings of up to one month's compensation or the full–time equivalent of one month's compensation for personal services of an employee; or

(iii) state or local taxes; and

(2) a creditor may make a levy against exempt property to enforce a claim for:

(i) the purchase price of the property or a loan made for the express purpose of enabling an individual to purchase the property and used for that purpose;

(ii) labor or materials furnished to make, repair, improve, preserve, store, or transport the property; and

(iii) a special assessment imposed to defray costs of a public improvement benefiting the property.

(b) Except as provided in Section 11, limiting the enforcement of certain security interests, this Act does not affect any statutory lien or security interest in exempt property.

(c) A creditor having a claim enforceable under subsection (a) against exempt property, before, at the time of, or a reasonable time after making a levy on property of an individual, shall serve on the individual a notice of the levy and of the basis for the creditor's right to make a levy on exempt property.

Section 11. [Limitation on Enforcement of Certain Security Interests in Exempt Property]

Unless the individual, after written notice to him of his rights under this section, voluntarily surrenders to the secured creditor possession of the collateral, a creditor may not, by taking possession or otherwise, enforce a nonpossessory, nonpurchase–money security interest in the following property to the extent the individual is entitled to exemption thereof under this Act:

(1) health aids reasonably necessary to enable the individual or dependent to work or to sustain health;

(2) furnishings and appliances reasonably necessary for one household;

(3) wearing apparel, animals, books, and musical instruments reasonably held for the personal use of the individual or dependent;

(4) family portraits and heirlooms of particular sentimental value;

(5) jewelry held for the personal use of the individual or dependent; and

(6) implements, professional books, and tools of the trade.

Section 12. [Waiver of Exemptions]

A waiver of exemptions executed in favor of an unsecured creditor before a levy on an individual's property is unenforceable, but an enforceable security interest may be given in exempt property except as limited in Section 11.

[B] Typical State Exemption Laws

OKLAHOMA STATUTES ANNOTATED (1988)

Title 31
Homestead and Exemptions

§ 1. Property exempt from attachment, execution or other forced sale—Bankruptcy proceedings

A. Except as otherwise provided in this title and notwithstanding subsection B of this section, the following property shall be reserved to every person residing in the state, exempt from attachment or execution and every other species of forced sale for the payment of debts, except as herein provided.

1. The home of such person, provided that such home is the principal residence of such person.

2. A manufactured home, provided that such manufactured home is the principal residence of such person.

3. All household and kitchen furniture held primarily for the personal, family or household use of such person or a dependent of such person.

4. Any lot or lots in a cemetery held for the purpose of sepulcher.

5. All implements of husbandry used upon the homestead.

6. Tools, apparatus and books used in any trade or profession of such person or a dependent of such person.

7. All books, portraits and pictures, and wearing apparel, that are held primarily for the personal, family or household use of such person or a dependent of such person.

8. The person's interest, not to exceed Four Thousand Dollars ($4,000.00) in aggregate value, in wearing apparel that is held primarily for the personal, family or household use of such person or a dependent of such person;

9. All professionally prescribed health aids for such person or a dependent of such person.

10. Five milk cows and their calves under six (6) months old, that are held primarily for the personal, family or household use of such person or a dependent of such person.

11. One hundred chickens, that are held primarily for the personal, family or household use of such person or a dependent of such person.

12. Two horses and two bridles and two saddles, that are held primarily for the personal, family or household use of such person or a dependent of such person.

13. Such person's interest, not to exceed One Thousand Five Hundred Dollars ($1,500.00) in value, in one motor vehicle.

14. One gun, that is held primarily for the personal, family or household use of such person or a dependent of such person.

15. Ten hogs, that are held primarily for the personal, family or household use of such person or a dependent of such person.

16. Twenty head of sheep, that are held primarily for the personal, family or household use of such person or a dependent of such person.

17. All provisions and forage on hand, or growing for home consumption, and for the use of exempt stock for one (1) year.

18. Seventy–five percent (75%) of all current wages or earnings for personal or professional services earned during the last ninety (90) days, except as provided in Title 12 of the Oklahoma Statutes in garnishment proceedings for collection of child support.

19. Such person's right to receive alimony, support, separate maintenance or child support payments to the extent reasonably necessary for the support of such person and any dependent of such person.

20. Subject to the Uniform Fraudulent Transfer Act, Section 112 *et seq.* of Title 24 of the Oklahoma Statutes, any interest in a retirement plan or arrangement qualified for tax exemption purposes under present or future Acts of Congress; provided, such interest shall be exempt only to the extent that contributions by or on behalf of a participant were not subject to federal income taxation to such

participant at the time of such contributions, plus earnings and other additions thereon; provided further, any transfer or rollover contribution between retirement plans or arrangements which avoids current federal income taxation shall not be deemed a transfer which is fraudulent as to a creditor under the Uniform Fraudulent Transfer Act. "Retirement plan or arrangement qualified for tax exemption purposes" shall include without limitation, trusts, custodial accounts, insurance, annuity contracts and other properties and rights constituting a part thereof. By way of example and not by limitation, retirement plans or arrangements qualified for tax exemption purposes permitted under present Acts of Congress include defined contribution plans and defined benefit plans as defined under the Internal Revenue Code ("IRC"), individual retirement accounts, individual retirement annuities, simplified employee pension plans, Keogh plans, IRC Section 403(a) annuity plans, IRC Section 403(b) annuities, and eligible state deferred compensation plans governed under IRC Section 457. This provision shall be in addition to and not a limitation of any other provision of the Oklahoma Statutes which grants an exemption from attachment or execution and every other species of forced sale for the payment of debts. This provision shall be effective for retirement plans and arrangements in existence on, or created after the effective date of this act; and

21. Such person's interest in a claim for personal bodily injury, death or workers' compensation claim, for a net amount not in excess of Fifty Thousand Dollars ($50,000.00), but not including any claim for exemplary or punitive damages.

B. No natural person residing in this state may exempt from the property of the estate in any bankruptcy proceeding the property specified in subsection (d) of Section 522 of the Bankruptcy Reform Act of 1978 (Public Law 95–598), except as may otherwise be expressly permitted under this title or other statutes of this state.

C. In no event shall any property under paragraph 5 or 6 or subsection A of this section, the total value of which exceeds Five Thousand Dollars ($5,000.00), of any person residing in this state be deemed exempt.

NEW HAMPSHIRE REVISED STATUTES (1987)

511:2 Exemptions. The following goods and property are exempted from attachment and execution:

I. The wearing apparel necessary for the use of the debtor and his family.

II. Comfortable beds, bedsteads and bedding necessary for the debtor, his wife and children.

III. Household furniture to the value of $2,000.

IV. One cook stove, one heating stove and one refrigerator and necessary utensils belonging to the same.

V. One sewing machine, kept for use by the debtor or his family.

VI. Provisions and fuel to the value of $400.

VII. The uniform, arms and equipments of every officer and private in the militia.

VIII. The Bibles, school books and library of any debtor, used by him or his family, to the value of $800.

IX. Tools of his occupation to the value of $1,200.

X. One hog and one pig, and the pork of the same when slaughtered.

XI. Six sheep and the fleeces of the same.

XII. One cow; a yoke of oxen or a horse, when required for farming or teaming purposes or other actual use; and hay not exceeding 4 tons.

XIII. Domestic fowls not exceeding $300 in value.

XIV. The debtors' interest in one pew in any meetinghouse in which he or his family usually worship.

XV. The debtor's interest in one lot or right of burial in any cemetery.

XVI. One automobile to the value of $1,000.

XVII. Jewelry owned by the debtor or his family to the value of $500.

VERMONT STATUTES ANNOTATED (1973)

§ 2740. Goods and chattels; exemptions from attachment and execution

The goods or chattels of a debtor may be taken and sold on execution, except the following articles, which shall be exempt from attachment and execution, unless turned out to the officer to be taken on the attachment or execution, by the debtor; such suitable apparel, bedding, tools, arms and articles of household furniture, as may be necessary for sustaining life; one sewing machine kept for use; one cow not exceeding in value $100.00; the best swine or the meat of one swine; sheep not exceeding in number ten, nor in value $100.00, and one year's product of such sheep in wool, yarn or cloth; forage sufficient for keeping not exceeding ten sheep, one cow and two oxen or horses, as the debtor may select, through one winter; ten cords of fire wood or five tons of coal; twenty bushels of potatoes; the pistols, side arms and equipment of a soldier in the service of the United States, and kept by him or his heirs as mementoes of his service; growing crops; ten bushels of grain; one barrel of flour; three swarms of bees and their hives with their produce in honey; two hundred pounds of sugar; lettered gravestones; the Bibles and other books used in a family; one pew or slip in a meetinghouse or place of religious worship; live poultry not exceeding in value $10.00; the professional books and instruments of physicians and dentists to the value of $200.00; the professional books of clergymen and attorneys at law, to the value of $200.00; one tool chest kept for use by a mechanic; one yoke of oxen or steers, as the debtor may select; two horses kept and used for team work, and such as the debtor may select in lieu of oxen or steers, but not exceeding in value the sum of $300.00; one two–horse wagon with whiffletrees and neck yoke or one one–horse wagon used for teaming, or one ox–cart, as the debtor may choose; one sled or one set of traverse sleds, either for oxen or horses, as the debtor may select; two harnesses, two halters, two chains, one plow, and one ox yoke, which, with the oxen or steers or horses which the debtor may select for team work, shall not exceed in value $350.00; but personal property shall not be exempt from attachment on an action brought to recover payment for the purchase price thereof, or for material or labor expended on the same.

NEW YORK CIVIL PRACTICE LAW AND RULES (1987)

§ 5205. Personal property exempt from application to the satisfaction of money judgments.

(a) Exemption for personal property. The following personal property when owned by any person is exempt from application to the satisfaction of a money judgment except where the judgment is for the purchase price of the exempt property or was recovered by a domestic, laboring person or mechanic for work performed by that person in such capacity:

1. all stoves kept for use in the judgment debtor's dwelling house and necessary fuel therefor for sixty days; one sewing machine with its appurtenances;

2. the family bible, family pictures, and school books used by the judgment debtor or in the family; and other books, not exceeding fifty dollars in value, kept and used as part of the family or judgment debtor's library;

3. a seat or pew occupied by the judgment debtor or the family in a place of public worship;

4. domestic animals with the necessary food for those animals for sixty days, provided that the total value of such animals and food does not exceed four hundred fifty dollars; all necessary food actually provided for the use of the judgment debtor or his family for sixty days;

5. all wearing apparel, household furniture, one mechanical, gas or electric refrigerator, one radio receiver, one television set, crockery, tableware and cooking utensils necessary for the judgment debtor and the family;

6. a wedding ring; a watch not exceeding thirty–five dollars in value; and

7. necessary working tools and implements, including those of a mechanic, farm machinery, team, professional instruments, furniture and library, not exceeding six hundred dollars in value, together with the necessary food for the team for sixty days, provided, however, that the articles specified in this paragraph are necessary to the carrying on of the judgment debtor's profession or calling.

(b) Exemption of cause of action and damages for taking or injuring exempt personal property. A cause of action, to recover damages for taking or injuring personal property exempt from application to the satisfaction of a money judgment, is exempt from application to the satisfaction of a money judgment. A money judgment and its proceeds arising out of such a cause of action is exempt, for one year after the collection thereof, from application to the satisfaction of a money judgment.

(c) Trust exemption. 1. Except as provided in paragraphs three and four of this subdivision, any property while held in trust for a judgment debtor, where the trust has been created by, or the fund so held in trust has proceeded from, a person other than the judgment debtor, is exempt from application to the satisfaction of a money judgment.

2. For purposes of this subdivision, any trust, custodial account, annuity or insurance contract established as part of either a Keogh (HR–10) plan or a retirement plan established by a corporation, which is qualified under section 401 of the United States Internal Revenue Code of 1986, as amended, shall be considered a trust which has been created by or which has proceeded from a person other than the judgment debtor, even though such judgment debtor is (i) a self–employed individual, (ii) a partner of the entity sponsoring the Keogh (HR–10) plan, or (iii) a shareholder of the corporation sponsoring the retirement plan.

3. This subdivision shall not impair any rights an individual has under a qualified domestic relations order as that term is defined in section 414(p) of the United States Internal Revenue Code of 1986, as amended.

4. Additions to an asset described in paragraph two of this subdivision shall not be exempt from application to the satisfaction of a money judgment if (i) made after the date that is ninety days before the interposition of the claim on which such judgment was entered, or (ii) deemed to be fraudulent conveyances under article ten of the debtor and creditor law.

(d) Income exemptions. The following personal property is exempt from application to the satisfaction of a money judgment, except such part as a court determines to be unnecessary for the reasonable requirements of the judgment debtor and his dependents:

1. ninety per cent of the income or other payments from a trust the principal of which is exempt under subdivision (c);

2. ninety per cent of the earnings of the judgment debtor for his personal services rendered within sixty days before, and at any time after, an income execution is delivered to the sheriff or a motion is made to secure the application of the judgment debtor's earnings to the satisfaction of the judgment; and

3. payments pursuant to an award in a matrimonial action, for the support of a wife, where the wife is the judgment debtor, or for the support of a child, where the child is the judgment debtor; where the award was made by a court of the state, determination of the extent to which it is unnecessary shall be made by that court.

(e) Exemptions to members of armed forces. The pay and bounty of a non–commissioned officer, musician or private in the armed forces of the United States or the state of New York; a land warrant, pension or other reward granted by the United States, or by a state, for services in the armed forces; a sword, horse, medal, emblem or device of any kind presented as a testimonial for services rendered in the armed forces of the United States or a state; and the uniform, arms and equipments which were used by a person in the service, are exempt from application to the satisfaction of a money judgment; provided, however, that the provisions of this subdivision shall not apply to the satisfaction of any order or money judgment for the support of a person's child, spouse, or former spouse.

(f) Exemption for unpaid milk proceeds. Ninety per cent of any money or debt due or to become due to the judgment debtor for the sale of milk produced on a farm operated by him and delivered for his account to a milk dealer licensed pursuant to article twenty–one of the agriculture and markets law is exempt from application to the satisfaction of a money judgment.

(g) Security deposit exemption. Money deposited as security for the rental of real property to be used as the residence of the judgment debtor or the judgment debtor's family; and money deposited as security with a gas, electric, water, steam, telegraph or telephone corporation, or a municipality rendering equivalent utility services, for services to judgment debtor's residence or the residence of judgment debtor's family, are exempt from application to the satisfaction of a money judgment.

(h) The following personal property is exempt from application to the satisfaction of money judgment, except such part as a court determines to be unnecessary for the reasonable requirements of the judgment debtor and his dependents:

1. any and all medical and dental accessions to the human body and all personal property or equipment that is necessary or proper to maintain or assist in sustaining or maintaining one or more major life activities or is utilized to provide mobility for a person with a permanent disability; and

2. any guide dog or hearing dog, as those terms are defined in section one hundred eight of the agriculture and markets law, or any animal trained to aid or assist a person with a permanent disability and actually being so used by such person, together with any and all food or feed for any such dog or other animal.

§ 5206. Real property exempt from application to the satisfaction of money judgments.

(a) Exemption of homestead. Property of one of the following types, not exceeding ten thousand dollars in value above liens and encumbrances, owned and occupied as a principal residence, is exempt from application to the satisfaction of a money judgment, unless the judgment was recovered wholly for the purchase price thereof:

1. a lot of land with a dwelling thereon,

2. shares of stock in a cooperative apartment corporation, or

    3.   units of a condominium apartment,

    4.   a mobile home.

But no exempt homestead shall be exempt from taxation or from sale for non–payment of taxes or assessments.

(b) Homestead exemption after owner's death. The homestead exemption continues after the death of the person in whose favor the property was exempted for the benefit of the surviving spouse and surviving children until the majority of the youngest surviving child and until the death of the surviving spouse.

(c) Suspension of occupation as affecting homestead. The homestead exemption ceases if the property ceases to be occupied as a residence by a person for whose benefit it may so continue, except where the suspension of occupation is for a period not exceeding one year, and occurs in consequence of injury to, or destruction of, the dwelling house upon the premises.

(d) Exemption of homestead exceeding ten thousand dollars in value. The exemption of a homestead is not void because the value of the property exceeds ten thousand dollars but the lien of a judgment attaches to the surplus.

(e) Sale of homestead exceeding ten thousand dollars in value. A judgment creditor may commence a special proceeding in the county in which the homestead is located against the judgment debtor for the sale, by a sheriff or receiver, of a homestead exceeding ten thousand dollars in value. The court may direct that the notice of petition be served upon any other person. The court, if it directs such a sale, shall so marshall the proceeds of the sale that the right and interest of each person in the proceeds shall correspond as nearly as may be to his right and interest in the property sold. Money, not exceeding ten thousand dollars, paid to a judgment debtor, as representing his interest in the proceeds, is exempt for one year after the payment, unless, before the expiration of the year, he acquires an exempt homestead, in which case, the exemption ceases with respect to so much of the money as was not expended for the purchase of that property; and the exemption of the property so acquired extends to every debt against which the property sold was exempt. Where the exemption of property sold as prescribed in this subdivision has been continued after the judgment debtor's death, or where he dies after the sale and before payment to him of his proportion of the proceeds of the sale, the court may direct that portion of the proceeds which represents his interest be invested for the benefit of the person or persons entitled to the benefit of the exemption, or be otherwise disposed of as justice requires.

(f) Exemption of burying ground. Land, set apart as a family or private burying ground, is exempt from application to the satisfaction of a money judgment, upon the following conditions only:

    1.   a portion of it must have been actually used for that purpose;

    2.   it must not exceed in extent one–fourth of an acre; and

    3.   it must not contain any building or structure, except one or more vaults or other places of deposit for the dead, or mortuary monuments.

(Matthew Bender & Co., Inc.)

§ 7.03 Homestead Exemption

One of the oldest and most firmly entrenched exemptions provides for the family homestead. State constitutions and statutes have made certain that no creditor will throw any Texan off his ranch, or leave any child homeless in California. Similar provisions do the same in most of the states.

Homestead exemptions almost always have some monetary limit, ranging from as high as $50,000 (Mass. Gen. Laws Ann. ch. 188, § 1 (West 1979)), to a mere $3,500 (Mich. Comp. Laws § 700.286 (1979)). Regardless of amount, it was the homestead exemption that originally maintained the traditional values represented in the following cases.

PRINCE v. HAKE

Wisconsin Supreme Court
75 Wis. 638, 44 N.W. 825 (1890)

LYON, J. (*after stating the facts as above.*) The complaint shows that the lots which the sheriff was about to sell by virtue of the execution constituted the homestead of Mahoney, the plaintiff's intestate, and the answer alleges no fact which destroys the homestead right. The demurrer to the answer should therefore have been sustained. Although it is alleged in the answer that Mahoney kept a house of prostitution upon the lots, and in the building claimed as his homestead, and sold liquors illegally on the same lots, still he owned the property and occupied it as his home. This exempted the property from sale on execution for his debt, no matter to what other uses he put it, or that he used it for criminal purposes, or committed crime upon it. The statute (Rev. St. § 29–3) exempts from seizure or sale, on execution, a certain quantity of land owned and occupied by any resident of the state as a homestead. This exemption is unqualified. No exception is made against an occupant who conducts an unlawful business, or commits crime upon such premises, and the courts have no authority to interpolate such an exception therein. The law provides the punishment which may be inflicted upon a person convicted of the crimes with which Mahoney is charged, but the forfeiture of his homestead right is no part of such punishment. . . .

. . . In the present case the right to the exemption does not depend upon the business in which Mahoney was engaged, but upon his ownership and occupancy of the premises as his home. Surely the vilest of criminals out of prison may have a home. In *Walsch v. Call*, had the debtor been a licensed dealer in liquors, and had his right to an exemption out of his stock in trade been challenged because he permitted gambling in his saloon, or gambled therein himself, we should have a case in principle like the present case. In the circumstances supposed, we cannot doubt the court would sustain the debtor's right to the exemption there claimed . . .

HARLAN v. SCHULZE

California Court of Appeals
7 Cal. App. 287, 94 P. 379 (1908)

CHIPMAN, P. J. . . .

The answer then sets forth that plaintiff claims title through a deed dated December 2, 1905, from said Josephine Quick and William Quick, her husband; avers that Josephine Quick, on October 5, 1901, filed "a pretended declaration of homestead, which declaration is claimed by plaintiff to be a valid homestead declaration"; that plaintiff took said deed with notice of said deed to said Manning: that at the time said pretended homestead was filed "the house upon said premises was not suitable for the dwelling of a family, and was not a dwelling, but was a place of business, to wit, a house of prostitution . . ."

All the findings of fact adverse to plaintiff are challenged for insufficiency of facts to support them. The undisputed evidence was that at the time the homestead was declared the fee–simple title to the lot was in Josephine Quick; that she and her husband first rented the property, and were living on it when her husband bought it and the deed was made to Mrs. Quick; that she was then the wife of William Quick, and that they both resided at that time on the premises; that the husband worked away from his home at times for different persons in the neighborhood, but made the premises his home and had no other; that the family consisted of Quick and his wife. . . .

The ideal home which respondent describes is greatly to be desired, but does the law make it a prerequisite to claiming the benefit of a homestead? So far as is disclosed by the homestead act no personal qualifications touching the moral character of the claimant are prescribed. Nor does the statute undertake to exclude the vicious, the criminal, or the immoral from the protection given by it, or to deprive them from the shelter intended thus to be thrown around the family, however unworthy. The right to declare a homestead on one's home is in no wise dependent upon right living. If we may inquire into one species of immorality, why not into all? And where can a just line of discrimination be drawn? There may be irreconcilable differences between husband and wife. They may be committing acts of cruelty towards each other at times unbearable. The marriage vow may be recklessly violated by one or the other. The children may be surrounded by an atmosphere destructive of moral health or growth, and daily witnesses of revolting conduct by their parents, and yet we see nothing in the law that would prohibit such a family from protecting itself by a valid homestead. The homestead is as much for the benefit of the husband (and children where there are any) as for the wife, and there is not the slightest evidence in this case that the husband was a party or had knowledge of the conduct of his wife and the uses made of their home in his absence. Judge Baldwin said in Lies v. De Diablar, 12 Cal. 328: "The adultery or abandonment by the wife did not divest the property of the character of homestead. . . . We do not see that the statute has made the crime of adultery, or abandonment, or desertion by the wife of the husband, or of the family, a cause of defeating or impairing her right." . . .

The remaining question is, were the premises used primarily as a place in which to carry on the business of prostitution within the rule laid down in the cases cited by respondent? . . .

    . . . .

It would be strange indeed if the occupants of a house could not use part of it for family revenue, no matter how favorable the opportunity might be to do so, without forfeiting the home itself. In *Estate of Levy* the court, referring to cases cited, said: "These cases are all authority for the proposition that, if the building is the actual bona fide residence of a party, he may legally select it and the land on which it is situated as homestead, even though, incidentally, a part thereof, no matter how large, may be used by him for other purposes than the family residence. . . . In no case has it been decided that where a portion of a building is dedicated to residence purposes, and is actually occupied by the claimant as the home of himself and his family, and such occupation is not merely incidental to the carrying on of some business in other parts of the building, the building and the land on which it is situated cannot be legally selected as a homestead."

The undisputed testimony was that Mrs. Quick lived upon the homestead premises, and that it was the only house or residence she and her husband then had. The defendant testified that this was her home, and the court found that she resided there. There is not a particle of evidence that the primary object of the family in purchasing and occupying the place was to establish and carry on the business of prostitution; that the residence was incidental to the business. On the contrary, whatever of this kind of business was carried on in the house was incident to the residence of the family. Unless we can say that this incidental use destroyed the right to claim a homestead because of its immorality, we cannot say that the homestead was void. That the personal character of the claimant, or her personal conduct, however immoral, in conducting her home, can be inquired into, and alone made the test of her right to a homestead, we do not believe. If she can declare a homestead, though she earns a living in part and incidentally by the art of millinery, or renting rooms, or other legitimate occupation, there is no law that would deprive her of this right because she violated the seventh commandment. The cases all hold that the statute is remedial, and should be given a liberal construction.

    . . . .

NOTES

State Homestead Provisions.

Kans. Const. art. 15, § 9.

Homestead exemption. A homestead to the extent of one hundred and sixty acres of farming land, or of one acre within the limits of an incorporated town or city, occupied as a residence by the family of the owner, together with all the improvements on the same, shall be exempted from forced sale under any process of law, and shall not be alienated without the joint consent of husband and wife, when that relation exists; but no property shall be exempt from sale for taxes, or for the payment of obligations contracted for the purchase of said premises, or for the erection of improvements thereon: *Provided*, The provisions of this section shall not apply to any process of law obtained by virtue of a lien given by the consent of both husband and wife: *And provided further*, That the legislature by an appropriate act or acts, clearly framed to avoid abuses, may provide that when it is shown the husband or wife while occupying a homestead is adjudged to be insane, the duly appointed guardian of the insane spouse may be authorized to join with the sane spouse in executing a mortgage upon the homestead, renewing or refinancing an encumbrance thereon which is likely to cause its loss, or in executing a lease thereon authorizing the lessee to explore and produce therefrom oil, gas, coal, lead, zinc, or other minerals.

Tex. Const. art. XVI, § 50
(amended 1973)

The homestead of a family, or of a single adult person, shall be, and is hereby protected from forced sale, for the payment of all debts except for the purchase money thereof, or a part of such purchase money, the taxes due thereon, or for work and material used in constructing improvements thereon, and in this last case only when the work and material are contracted for in writing, with the consent of both spouses, in the case of a family homestead, given in the same manner as is required in making a sale and conveyance of the homestead; nor may the owner or claimant of the property claimed as homestead, if married, sell or abandon the homestead without the consent of the other spouse, given in such manner as may be prescribed by law. No mortgage, trust deed, or other lien on the homestead shall ever be valid, except for the purchase money therefor, or improvements made thereon, as hereinbefore provided, whether such mortgage, or trust deed, or other lien, shall have been created by the owner alone, or together with his or her spouse, in case the owner is married. All pretended sales of the homestead involving any condition of defeasance shall be void. . . .

Tex. Rev. Civ. Stat. Ann. art. 3833 (Vernon 1983).

Homestead

(a) If it is used for the purposes of a home, or as a place to exercise the calling or business to provide for a family or a single, adult person, not a constituent of a family, shall consist of:

(1) for a family, not more than two hundred acres, which may be in one or more parcels, with the improvements thereon, if not in a city, town, or village; or

(2) for a single, adult person, not a constituent of a family, not more than one hundred acres, which may be in one or more parcels, with the improvements thereon, if not in a city, town, or village; or

(3) for a family or a single, adult person, not a constituent of a family, a lot or lots amounting to not more than one acre of land, together with any improvements thereon, if in a city, town or village.

(b) Temporary renting of the homestead shall not change its homestead character when no other homestead has been acquired.

(c) The exemption provided to homesteads under this article apply to all homesteads in this state regardless of the dates they were created.

(2) The cases are generally in accord that a homestead need not be solely residential, but may have some business element as well. *See, e.g., Prince v. Hake, supra*; and *Harlan v. Schulze, supra.*

(3) When laws set an upper limit in value for an exemption, the method of valuation becomes important. Reference must be made to the laws of the particular jurisdiction to determine the valuation standard. For homesteads, the general rule is to look to the debtor's equity in the property. *See* 11 U.S.C. § 522(d)(1) (1982); Wash. Rev. Code § 6.15.010 (West Supp. 1988). For other property, the tendency has been to look to fair market value as of the time of filing for bankruptcy rather than to negotiated price, value at time of claim for exemption or levy, or the price paid for the property. 11 U.S.C. § 522(a)(2) (1982 & Supp. IV 1986); Minn. Stat. § 550, 37, subd.21 (1988); S.D. Comp. Laws Ann. § 21–19–23 (1987). *But cf. In re Setley*, 11 B.R. 106 (Bankr. D. Minn. 1981), where the court looked to the debtors' equity in an automobile, rather than its market value.

O'BRIEN v. JOHNSON

Supreme Court, Minnesota
275 Minn. 305, 148 N.W.2d 357 (1967)

OTIS, Justice.

Plaintiff O'Brien has brought this action against defendants Johnson to secure an adjudication that property she owns in the city of Brainerd is her homestead and as such exempt from the claims of defendants who are judgment creditors. Defendants have counterclaimed, praying for a determination that their judgments are liens on plaintiff's property and seeking the right to levy execution on it. Defendants appeal from a judgment declaring the property to be the homestead of the plaintiff and exempt from execution.

On October 3, 1955, Mrs. Johnson sustained personal injuries while a guest on premises owned by Mrs. O'Brien and her husband, Cornelius O'Brien. On October 22, 1955, the Johnsons sued the O'Briens for damages. During the next 2 months the O'Briens conveyed to their children real estate they owned in Brainerd, including the subject of this litigation (for convenience called the Juel Block), as well as real estate in Ironton, Deerwood, and Baxter. They retained, as their homestead, property referred to as "the Stiles Addition."

The Johnsons' tort actions resulted in verdicts on January 16, 1958, amounting to $96,300, of which only $11,021.35 has been paid in satisfaction of their claims.

A motion for judgment n. o. v. or a new trial was denied on February 9, 1959, and on March 5 the court ordered judgments in favor of the Johnsons, subject to a 10–day stay. On March 10 the O'Briens appealed from the order and the court further stayed the entry of judgment on bonds of $250 each. The following day the O'Brien children reconveyed the Juel Block to Cornelius O'Brien and Sadie O'Brien as joint tenants, and on March 14 the elder O'Briens occupied an apartment in the Juel Block as their residence. Meanwhile, on March 13 they had contracted to sell the homestead they formerly occupied in the Stiles Addition. . . .

The defendants assert that the conveyances from the elder O'Briens to their children were in fraud of creditors; that the O'Briens were not entitled to a double exemption in both the Juel Block and the proceeds of the sale of the Stiles Addition; that the stay of judgment and failure to require a supersedeas bond in the tort action constituted prejudicial error; that Mrs. O'Brien is estopped from asserting any homestead rights in the Juel Block; that the property is subject to a constructive trust or equitable lien; and that the notice of lis pendens which they filed on February 27, 1956, is tantamount to an attachment.

The trial court found, among other things, that the conveyances from the elder O'Briens to their children were made with the grantees' knowledge that the grantors intended to defraud defendants; that the Juel Block had a market value of $80,000; that the O'Briens occupied it as their homestead on March 14, 1959; and that except for the availability of other property previously referred to, having little value, the establishment of the Juel Block as plaintiff's homestead rendered her insolvent. The court concluded that Mrs. O'Brien was entitled to retain the Juel Block free from the claims asserted by the Johnsons.

1. Much of defendants' argument is devoted to the sequence of events which frustrated their imposing liens on the Juel Block. While it is true that in spite of the diligent and persistent efforts of counsel to satisfy the just claims of his clients the O'Briens succeeded in establishing their homestead during the period when the stay of judgment without an adequate bond prevented the liens from attaching, nevertheless we find no fraud in their availing themselves of the order which the trial court had jurisdiction to grant as a routine discretionary matter.

In our opinion the failure to provide a supersedeas bond and the assurances by counsel that the O'Briens had ample security are circumstances which could not result in prejudice to the Johnsons since they did not occur until after the O'Briens had occupied the Juel Block.

2. The defendants have argued with justification that the transfer of the Juel Block from Cornelius O'Brien to his children was an attempt to defraud creditors. However, it does not follow that the ultimate vesting of title in Mr. and Mrs. O'Brien,

Sr., was also fraudulent. The reconveyance from the children to their parents rendered that issue moot since it accomplished the very end which the defendants sought. In any event, the Johnsons were not prejudiced by the transfers since they would have had no greater rights against the elder O'Briens had title remained in their names. No liens could have attached to the Juel Block under any circumstances until the Johnsons' right to enter judgment ripened on March 5, 1959. The basic question then is whether judgment debtors can lawfully surrender an existing homestead and establish a new one in property which they then own and which has substantially greater value, with intent thereby to put their assets out of the reach of creditors and render themselves insolvent.

Under Minn. Const. art. 1, § 12, "[a] reasonable amount of property shall be exempt from seizure or sale for the payment of any debt or liability. The amount of such exemption shall be determined by law." Minn. St. c. 510 as it applies to this case provides that a house occupied by a debtor as his dwelling and the land on which it is situated, up to one–third of an acre, constitute his homestead and that of his family, exempt from seizure or sale for any of his debts.

It has long been the law of this state that a judgment debtor may assert an exemption for the express purpose of evading his creditors. This we have held is not fraud, regardless of the debtor's motive. The rule was applied and followed as early as *Jacoby v. Parkland Distilling Co.*, 41 Minn. 227, 43 N.W. 52, where the debtor's wife sought a judgment declaring the claims of creditors not to be a lien on their homestead. The court rejected evidence offered by creditors to prove that the property in question was occupied in contemplation of insolvency and with intent to defraud them. Speaking through Mr. Justice Mitchell, this court held that "by moving into a house which he already owns, [the debtor] takes nothing from his creditors which the law secures to them, or in which they have any vested right. . . . [F]raud can never be predicated on an act which the law permits." 41 Minn. 229, 43 N.W. 52.

Defendants rely on *Kangas v. Robie*, (8 Cir.) 264 F. 92, where the Federal court distinguished the Jacoby case. In *Kangas* the debtor secreted assets received from the sale of goods furnished by his creditors and with the proceeds purchased a homestead. The court found that the debtor was guilty of fraud which, it held, distinguished the case from *Jacoby*, since there the debtor already owned the property and did not acquire a homestead with assets realized from his willful failure to pay his just obligations.

Defendants cite two other cases as controlling: *Small v. Anderson*, 139 Minn. 292, 166 N.W. 340, and *Nash v. Bengtson*, 179 Minn. 7, 228 N.W. 177. Both cases, however, involve transfers of title in fraud of creditors, whereas in the instant case, as we have previously indicated, no prejudice resulted and whatever transfers occurred resulted in reconveyances restoring substantially the status quo. We therefore conclude that under well–established principles the O'Briens had a right to sell their existing homestead, occupy instead the more valuable Juel Block, and thereafter enjoy an exemption in it, notwithstanding their purpose was to prevent the Johnsons' judgments from attaching as liens.

3. Because the Juel Block is commercial property consisting of stores and apartments and has a value in excess of $100,000, yielding a gross income of $1,600 a month (which is also exempt), the defendants urge us to follow the rule adopted in *Anderson v. Shannon*, 146 Kan. 704, 73 P.2d 5, 114 A.L.R. 200. There the Kansas court refused to recognize a homestead exemption in a commercial building used primarily for a theater, a result we would find manifestly proper and reasonable but for our statute. In the *Jacoby* case Mr. Justice Mitchell said (41 Minn. 231, 43 N.W. 53):

> . . . Unfortunately our statute fixes no limit as to value upon a homestead exemption. It must be confessed that such a law may be greatly abused, and permit great moral frauds; but this is a question for the legislature, and not for the courts.

For over one hundred years we have deplored the injustices which have arisen from the application of our statutory exemptions. The purpose of the constitutional exemption as we see it is to render the family home secure, not to permit a debtor who already enjoys that protection to escape his just obligations by seeking refuge in valuable income–producing property of which his homestead is but a small part. Nevertheless, the law is so well settled that however distasteful it may be, we feel reluctantly compelled to apply it.

4. Defendants protest what they assert is a double exemption resulting from the O'Briens' occupying the Juel Block as their homestead at a time when the proceeds of the Stiles Addition sale, amounting to $13,000, were also exempt. Under the provisions of Minn. St. 510.07, "[t]he owner may sell and convey the homestead without subjecting it, or the proceeds of such sale for the period of one year after sale, to any judgment or debt from which it was exempt in his hands."

In *Donaldson v. Lamprey*, 29 Minn. 18, 22, 11 N.W. 119, 121, we held that to permit a plurality of exemptions was "a fraud upon the spirit of the statute." Undoubtedly § 510.07 was intended to conserve the proceeds realized from the sale of a homestead in order to make them available for the purchase or improvement of another dwelling. However, no such limitation is contained in the statute and we are not at liberty to read one in. Where, as here, property already owned by the debtor is occupied as his homestead following the sale of a previous homestead, it strikes us that the statute perverts the purpose of the constitution when it permits concurrent and simultaneous exemptions in both the new homestead and the proceeds of the old, if the proceeds are diverted to wholly extraneous purposes and are not made available to creditors. We recognize that when both § 510.01 and § 510.07 are given effect they may operate as "a vehicle for fraud and rank injustice." We therefore echo what our predecessors have said and urge appropriate legislation to correct the problem, but hold that under existing law defendants are entitled to no relief.

Other errors assigned by defendants do not, in our opinion, merit further discussion.

Affirmed.

SWAYNE v. CHASE

Texas Supreme Court
88 Tex. 218, 30 S.W. 1049 (1895)

BROWN, J. Plaintiffs in error were husband and wife, and occupied and owned a homestead in the city of Ft. Worth, upon which was their residence, and which they insured in various insurance companies to the amount of $60,000. The property was destroyed by fire. One of the policies on Chase's house was issued by the Phoenix Insurance Company. Chase was indebted to John F. Swayne in the sum of $22,000, upon which judgment had been rendered. Swayne sued out a writ of garnishment against the Phoenix Insurance Company, which answered, setting up the facts, admitting the indebtedness to Chase upon the policy and stating that it was for insurance upon his homestead. Chase and wife intervened, claiming that money due upon the policy was exempt, because it was the proceeds of a policy of insurance upon their homestead. Swayne replied to the plea of intervention that Chase, being indebted in the sum of $300,000, and being insolvent and in contemplation of his insolvency, with the intent to defraud his creditors, and especially the plaintiff, invested in the improvements upon his homestead (that which was insured, and for which the money was claimed from the insurance company) the sum of $125,000, with the purpose of withdrawing and abstracting from his assets an unnecessary and unreasonable amount, thereby placing the same beyond the reach of his creditors, especially the plaintiff; that Chase had procured policies of insurance upon his residence from various insurance companies to the aggregate amount of $60,000; and that, after paying plaintiff's debt, there would remain $35,000 or $40,000,—a sum more than sufficient to erect a dwelling in the place of the one destroyed, the sum of $5,000 being alleged to be a reasonable amount for that purpose. To this supplemental petition the district court sustained a demurrer, and upon trial gave judgment for the interveners. The court of civil appeals reversed the judgment of the district court, holding that all of the insurance money over and above a reasonable sum for rebuilding the residence should be subjected to the payment of the debts of the interveners.

The following questions arise upon the presentation of this case: (1) Was the investment made in the house for which the insurance is claimed, deprived of the exemption under the constitution by the alleged fraud of the plaintiff in error E. E. Chase? (2) If the property itself was exempt from forced sale under the constitution, is the insurance money derived from the policy thereon likewise exempt under the constitution? (3) Can the court limit the amount of the insurance money to which the plaintiffs in error are entitled as being exempt to what may be considered a reasonable sum to be invested in another residence?

The first question is definitely settled against the contention of the defendant in error. . . .

The allegations of the supplemental petition amount, in substance, to a charge that Chase, being largely indebted, insolvent, and the head of a family, invested in his homestead improvements a large amount of his funds, with the intent to defraud his creditors by placing the same beyond the reach of the law. The proposition in effect is that an insolvent debtor cannot invest his money or property in a homestead by which it will be protected from the payment of his debts. The object of the constitutional provision is to protect the homes of insolvent debtors from forced sale, and, if the contention of plaintiff be correct, only such as become insolvent after the investment is made can be protected. While it is true that the amount alleged to have been invested in the homestead by Chase is large, the constitution places no limit on the value of such improvements which are permitted to be made. The amount invested does not change the principle involved, for, if it be a fraud to invest a large amount for such purposes and under such circumstances it is equally a fraud to so invest for like purposes a smaller amount. There might be a state of facts under which such investment would not be protected, as in the case of *Shepherd v. White*, 11 Tex. 346, where the property purchased as a homestead was paid for by another, so that a resulting trust existed, or if the property invested had been acquired by fraud, so that the title thereto did not pass by the sale. But the allegations in the supplemental petition present no such case. The demurrer was properly sustained to the supplemental petition.

The second question has likewise been decided in favor of the plaintiffs in error in the case of *Cameron v. Fay*, 55 Tex. 58, in which it was held that the money due from an insurance company upon a policy of insurance issued upon the homestead is not subject to garnishment at the suit of a creditor. That decision is vigorously attacked and severely criticized, but, whatever may be said of it, an examination of the authorities will show that it is abundantly supported by the decisions of the ablest courts in the Union, and opposed by but few. . . .

If the policy were considered strictly a personal contract, and did not attach to the realty, then the proceeds must in such case be assets in the hands of the administrator. . . . What does the insurance money represent to the payee of the policy? No one is permitted to insure property in which he has no interest, and, in case the title is terminated, the policy becomes void, because there is no interest to support it. The validity of a policy of insurance is made to depend upon the correctness of answers as to the value, title, locality, and other conditions, and the amount to be paid is regulated by and based upon the value of the property insured. The purpose of taking out the insurance is to enable the owner to restore the thing insured in case of loss, or to reimburse him for the loss of it. The house in this case was the subject of the insurance. The agreed proportion of its value was the measure of damages to be paid upon its loss. The policy was dependent upon its existence, and payable upon its destruction. The proceeds stand to the owner in the place of the property lost. It is the value of the house paid by the insurance company, not because it acquires the property, but because it agreed to pay so much for the house if destroyed by fire. . . .

Can the courts limit the amount of the money derived from an insurance policy upon the homestead improvements that may be protected from the debts of the owner to a sum reasonably sufficient to build a house for the family to live in, and subject the remainder to the payment of debts? . . .

We must, as before stated, apply to the money arising from the policy of insurance the same rule that the constitution applies to the improvements, which is that there is no limitation upon their value, and the courts of this state have no power to say that only a reasonable portion of such a fund shall be exempt. It is all exempt when derived from a policy on the homestead improvements. It is said that the amount involved is a large sum for an insolvent debtor to be permitted to withhold from his creditors for the purpose of building a residence for his family. The amount invested in the house, according to the allegations, was larger, and yet the constitution of the state exempted the house. If there be injustice in the matter, it arises out of the constitutional provision exempting the house of such value, for there is no wrong done in protecting from the debt of defendant in error the money arising out of the destruction of that to which he had no right. Whatever judges of courts may think of the policy of exempting homestead improvements of great value from the payment of the debts of the owner, the policy of the state is too unmistakably settled by the specific changes made from time to time in the constitution for any court to assume to give a new policy to the state upon this question. The people of Texas made the constitution, and they have a right to change it if it is found to work harshly and unjustly, but the courts have no choice but to enforce and obey its mandates.

The court of civil appeals erred in reversing the judgment of the district court, and remanding this cause, for which error the judgment of the court of civil appeals is reversed, and the judgment of the district court is affirmed.

NOTES AND QUESTIONS

(1) Generally, a debtor need only occupy a residence for the property to qualify as a homestead, but some states require some sort of declaration. *See, e.g.*, Colo. Rev. Stat. § 13–55–107 (1974); Mass. Gen. Laws Ann. ch. 188 § 2 (West 1977); Va. Code § 34–6 (1984); *White v. Stump*, 266 U.S. 310 (1924); Haskins, *Homestead Exemptions*, 63 Harv. L. Rev. 1289 (1950). *But cf. Myers v. Matley*, 130 F.2d 775 (9th Cir. 1942), *aff'd*, 318 U.S. 622 (1943). What should such a statement look like? Could the declaration be used as possible evidence of other than good faith? Some exemption laws subject a homestead to debts incurred before declaration as a homestead. *See, e.g.*, Iowa Code § 561.21 (1952); Ky. Rev. Stat. § 427.060 (Supp. 1988); Mo. Ann. Stat. § 513.510 (Vernon 1950); Vt. Stat. Ann. tit. 27, § 107 (Supp. 1987). Note, *Creation of the Homestead & its Requirements*, 26 Calif. L. Rev. 241 (1938).

(2) Homestead exemptions traditionally required the property to be real estate. Today, the statutes will often include mobile or motor homes and interests in cooperative or condominium apartments. *See, e.g.*, 11 U.S.C. § 522(d)(1) (1982); N.Y. Civ. Prac. Law § 5206 (McKinney 1988); *In re Bell*, 181 F. Supp. 387 (D. Or. 1960) (a houseboat is exempt as a motor home); *In re Foley*, 97 F. Supp. 843 (D. Neb. 1951) (trailer house may be exempt as dwelling house).

(3) The following excerpt shows how courts liberally construe the homestead exemption and their reasoning:

Appellee Robert Howard Gamble purchased approximately six acres of land in Duval County and had the deed executed in favor of his wife, Mildred Franklin Gamble, a free dealer. The husband subsequently constructed a home on the property and made other expenditures in the way of upkeep, insurance and taxes. In August, 1941, appellant filed its bill of complaint in the Circuit Court, praying that said property be levied upon and sold to pay a certain judgment secured by it against Robert Howard Gamble. Gamble and his wife filed separate answers, in which the wife claimed the property as her separate property, while Gamble claimed it as his homestead, entitled to exemption from plaintiff's judgment under the Constitution. . . .

It is settled law in Florida that Section 1, Article X, of the Constitution, relating to the homestead, should be liberally construed in the interest of the home, and that a homestead exemption extends to any right or interest the head of a family may hold in land. *Pasco v. Harley*, 73 Fla. 819, 75 So. 30; *Hill v. First National Bank*, 73 Fla. 1092, 75 So. 614; *Milton v. Milton*, 63 Fla. 533, 58 So. 718. There is no question that Gamble was the head of a family and that his contributions to his wife's separate property gave him an equitable interest on the basis of which he could claim his homestead exemption. It was not essential that he hold the legal title to the land.

This court has also held that a one–half interest, the right of possession, or any beneficial interest in land gave the claimant a right to exempt it as his homestead. *Morgan v. Bailey*, 90 Fla. 47, 105 So. 143; *Hill v. First National Bank*, 73 Fla. 1092, 75 So. 614; *Coleman v. Williams*, 146 Fla. 45, 200 So. 207. It is only necessary that the homestead status attaches prior to the attachment of the creditors' lien.

Bessemer Properties v. Gamble, 158 Fla. 38, 38–39, 27 So. 2d 832, 832–33 (1946).

(4) Another common prerequisite for the homestead exemption is "ownership" of the property. Clearly, the debtor need not be the holder in fee, but how significant an interest must be to qualify is disputed. *See* Annot., 89 A.L.R. 511 (1934). Generally, both legal and equitable titles are protectable. *Storey v. Storey*, 275 Mich. 675, 267 N.W. 763 (1936). Remainders or future interests are generally insufficient unless coupled with possession or a non–permissive right of possession. *See* Annot., 74 A.L.R.2d 1355 (1960). Leasehold interests have been held to be sufficient, Annot., 89 A.L.R. 555 (1934), as have life estates. *Arighi v. Rule & Sons*, 41 Cal. App. 2d 852, 107 P.2d 970 (3d Dist. 1940); *Ehlers v. Campbell*, 159 Neb. 328, 66 N.W.2d 585 (1954). Most states allow homestead status to an undivided interest or to one held in joint tenancy, tenancy in common, or as community property. *See* Annot., 89 A.L.R. 511 (1934); Annot., 74 A.L.R.2d 1355 (1960). For a twist involving community property, *see Schoenfeld v. Norberg*, 11 Cal. App. 3d 755, 90 Cal. Rptr. 47 (1st Dist. 1970).

(5) Profits or rents derived from a homestead are generally held to be exempt. *See, e.g.*, S.C. Const. art. III § 28; Mo. Ann. Stat. § 513.475(1) (Vernon Supp. 1988); Va. Code § 34–18 (1984).

(6) Many statutes require the debtor to be head of a household or a family in order to claim the homestead exemption. *See, e.g.,* N.D. Cent. Code § 28–22–01 *et seq.* (Supp. 1987). Is it legitimate to discriminate against unmarried debtors? What about a wife/husband who is a debtor under the Bankruptcy Code, but whose spouse heads the household? A divorced person? Note that the federal exemption applies to individuals in their own right.

(7) The head of household requirement is an antiquated basis for the homestead exemption. Has the shift towards urban living been adequately recognized? How about the trend toward rental of primary residence? Can you think of any way to limit abuses of the exemption? Remember the problem of federal legislation in conflict with state constitutional provisions. What happens when the homestead's value exceeds some antiquated measure? What should happen?

(8) In *Swayne v. Chase, supra,* the court held that the proceeds of insurance on a homestead were also exempt from creditors' claims, a rule adopted by most states to provide a place in which the family may later live. *See, e.g., Houghton v. Lee,* 50 Cal. 101 (1875); *Bernheim v. Davitt,* 9 Ky. L. Rptr. 229, 5 S.W. 193 (1887); *Holmes v. Marshall,* 145 Cal. 777, 79 P. 534 (1905); *Gardenhire v. Glasser,* 26 Ariz. 503, 226 P. 911 (1924); *Goldburg Co. v. Salyer,* 188 Va. 573, 50 S.E.2d 272 (1948); Annot., 63 A.L.R. 1286 (1930); Annot., 96 A.L.R. 410 (1935); Note, *Exemption of Income from Property Purchased with Exempt Insurance Proceeds,* 47 Yale L.J. 1408 (1938); Note, *Debtor's Estates—Right of Debtor to Claim Homestead Exemption in Insurance Proceeds from Non–Exempt Property Destroyed by Fire,* 6 Wash. & Lee L. Rev. 202 (1949).

§ 7.04   Personal Property

Another of the cornerstones of the federal bankruptcy exemption is coverage for personal property such as household furnishings, apparel, and tools of the debtor's trade. Although some states exempt unlimited amounts of personal property, *see* Okla. Stat. tit. 31 § 1.A. (1977), most statutes limit the exemption to specific numbers of an item, up to a certain value, or require the item to be in some way "necessary."

IN RE MULLEN

United States District Court, District of Maine
140 F. 206 (1905)

HALE, District Judge. This case comes before me on the certificate of John F. Sprague, Esq., one of the referees of this court. The certificate shows that the trustee in bankruptcy filed a petition praying for authority to sell a portion of the bankrupt's estate at private sale, and among the articles so specified were one canoe and one rifle. It appears that at the hearing before the referee counsel for the bankrupt objected to the sale of the canoe and rifle, claiming that they are exempt from attachment and seizure on execution by virtue of the statutes of Maine. Whereupon the referee made an order exempting the canoe, but refusing to exempt the rifle. Section 6 of the bankruptcy act (Act July 1, 1898, c. 541, 30 Stat. 548 [U.S.Comp. St. 1901, p. 3424]), relative to exemptions of bankrupts, provides that the act shall not affect the allowance to bankrupts of the exemptions which are prescribed by the state laws in force at the time of the filing of the petition. Section 64, par. 6, c. 83, of the revised statutes of the state of Maine, provides for the exemption of "the tools necessary for his [the debtor's] trade or occupation . . . not exceeding fifty dollars in value." In applying exemption laws of the several states, the federal courts in bankruptcy cases adopt the construction announced by the highest court of the state the statute of which is involved. . . .

The Supreme Court of Maine, in construing the statute regarding the registration of guides, in *State v. Snowman*, 94 Me. 112, 46 Atl. 818, 50 L. R. A. 544, 80 Am. St. Rep. 380, has said:

> It is well known that most sportsmen who frequent remote streams and lakes, and traverse the trackless forests, which cover large portions of the state, do so under the guidance and direction of guides. Guides may be regarded as instrumentalities in fishing and hunting. Guides should possess such skill, experience, sagacity, and probity that not only the safety of the sportsman but the welfare of the state can be properly intrusted to them. They should be under such restrictions that it shall be for their interest to discountenance violation of the fish and game laws. The Legislature has deemed it wise to create such a body of men, who shall pursue such vocation under the supervision of the commissioners of inland fisheries and game, and shall assist the commissioners in protecting and preserving the property of the state.

It may be assumed that the bankrupt in this case belonged to the body of men thus described by the court of Maine, and therefore that he was one of the "instrumentalities in fishing and hunting" referred to by the court. I think the referee is correct in holding that:

> The canoe is necessary for the guide in performing his work while acting for fishing parties, and his service in guiding hunters is of such a nature that without it he could not take them over the vast stretches of water in the wilderness of northern Maine, and effect satisfactory results in his business.

I confirm the holding of the referee that the canoe is a tool or instrument of use and service, which should be exempt under the statute of Maine and under the bankruptcy act. I do not find that a canoe is enumerated in the bankrupt's schedules, but I assume that the referee has before him an amended schedule or some other evidence formally bringing to his attention the fact that the canoe is a part of the estate, and is of a value not exceeding $50. It must be observed here that the schedules ought to contain a careful enumeration of everything in the estate, whether or not any exemption is claimed in reference to any article enumerated.

I also sustain the ruling of the referee holding that the rifle cannot be exempt as being an implement necessary in the business of guiding. While the court of Maine has held that the "safety of the sportsman" is intrusted to the guide, I do not think it is the intention of the court to hold that it is a part of the duty of the guide to protect the sportsman by means of a rifle from the attacks of wild beasts or from other physical force in the wilderness. I therefore fully sustain the referee in his finding in the premises, and confirm his order that the trustee amend his report on exempted property by adding thereto one canoe, valued as described in said schedule. I assume, as I have said, that such value does not exceed $50.

INDEPENDENCE BANK v. HELLER

California Court of Appeals
275 Cal. App. 2d 84, 79 Cal. Rptr. 868 (1969)

SHINN, J.—Independence Bank recovered a judgment of $80,889.93 against John Heller and Paul W. Heller upon a promissory note for money loaned; execution was issued and levied upon the furniture of Paul W. Heller contained in his apartment. Heller filed a claim of exemption of all the property; upon demand of the bank a hearing was had, evidence was introduced and an order was made and entered; the order provided that certain of the property was subject to execution, that the remainder was exempt from execution and the marshal was ordered to return the exempt property to Heller; the bank appeals.

Heller claimed the property was exempt as necessary household furniture under section 690.2 of the Code of Civil Procedure which exempts: "Necessary household, table, and kitchen furniture belonging to the judgment debtor, including one refrigerator, washing machine, sewing machine, stove, stovepipes and furniture; wearing apparel, beds, bedding and bedsteads, hanging pictures, oil paintings and drawings drawn or painted by any member of the family, and family portraits and their necessary frames, provisions and fuel actually provided for individual or family use, sufficient for three months, and three cows and their suckling calves, four hogs and their suckling pigs, and food for such cows and hogs for one month; also one radio, one television receiver, one piano, one shotgun and one rifle."

The greater part of the property had been purchased by Heller, some of it was held by him on consignment by dealers and the remainder had come to Heller as a bequest from his mother. The apartment consists of an entry hall, living room, dining room, two bedrooms, a kitchen and a hallway; the furniture was available for use by Heller and was occasionally used. . . .

The facts, which were undisputed, created a unique problem for the trial court. Among the reported cases in this or other jurisdictions we have found no helpful precedent. We have discovered no case in which a man who was unable to pay his debts was ensconced in a luxuriously furnished home and relying upon exemption laws in resisting the efforts of his creditors to collect their debts. We have not been able to find a case in which execution was levied upon furniture sufficient to furnish a moderately sized house. Most all the cases that considered claims of exemption involved the seizure of no more than a few articles of furniture or wearing apparel.

The court held that 5 statues and 13 pictures (suitable for hanging) were subject to execution and that all other articles were exempt. Included in the exempted articles were pieces of wooden furniture sufficient for all the rooms in the apartment, 2 sets of china, plates, dishes, wine glasses, highball glasses, juice glasses, cordial glasses, beer mugs, water goblets, service plates, salad plates, soup dishes, sauce dishes, cups and saucers, vases, platters, trays, bowls, knives, forks, ash trays and miscellaneous pieces of the same general order. All the wooden pieces were of heavy construction, many of them elaborately carved; most of the tables were marble–topped. All the articles were of good quality; none was of extraordinary value.

It is not questioned by appellant that the property held to be exempt was household and table furniture within the purview of section 690.2. The contentions are that none of the articles taken under the writ was necessary for Heller's use and that errors were committed in the hearing. . . .

In view of the presumed good faith of Heller and the court's application of the law to the implied findings upon the factual issue and because the exemption laws should be liberally construed we have concluded that the order should be affirmed.

Heller testified he is the son of wealthy parents, was reared and had lived in an atmosphere of affluence and elegance which he has maintained in the furnishing of his apartment. This signifies that he is possessed of a desire to live in the midst of the finery to which he had become accustomed. He also testified he is an interior decorator and that it is necessary to have his apartment furnished in a style that will impress prospective clients with his professional ability. There was no significant evidence of his use of the property for exhibition, and it is not contended that it was necessary for that purpose.

It is well settled that in deciding whether furniture or wearing apparel is necessary and should be exempted from execution the court will consider the station in life of the owner and the manner of comfortable living to which he has become accustomed. . . .

The rule fits into section 690.2 which protects the ownership of some possessions because of their artistic and cultural value as well as the things that are necessary for physical use. It is of common knowledge that people who take pride in their homes frequently furnish them with things that are beautiful and elegant as well as useful such as several sets of china of different patterns, a variety of crystal glasses of different styles and tables and chairs in excess of the number that are indispensable.

The word "necessary" as used in the statute should not be given the meaning of indispensable. By its terms section 690.2 forbids the interpretation that the exemption is limited to the things the owner cannot do without. Hanging pictures, drawings, paintings, a piano, a radio, a television receiver, a shotgun and a rifle are not exempted *in addition* to household furniture; they are included *as* household furniture, not because they are suitable for physical use but because they contribute to the pleasure and comfort of the owner and perhaps to his pride of ownership. In the eyes of the law they are not less necessary than a chair or a rug. Sections of the code other than section 690.2 exempt a great variety of possessions only if their use is essential in the owner's work but the Legislature has made it clear there is no such limitation with respect to household furniture.

It was proper for the court to consider and give due weight to the testimony of Heller that he had furnished his apartment in a manner to which he had been long accustomed. The statute could have been applied so as to exempt only one set of china, a dozen drinking glasses, a dozen plates and cups and saucers, one of every article of tableware and similar articles to declare as non–exempt all the remaining pieces. In other words the judge could have selected piece by piece those articles which would meet the minimum requirements of an adequately furnished home and held all the pieces that remained over to be subject to execution. This decision of what is necessary household furniture would have ignored the rule under which the courts give consideration to the custom and practice generally followed by many householders of adding to the bare essentials additional articles which they consider necessary to their pleasure, convenience and comfort. We believe such a limitation of the right of exemption would have unduly restricted the right and that the court correctly declined to do so.

It is the universal rule that exemption statutes are to be liberally construed in favor of the debtor. . . .

The statutes do not extend the right of exemption to things that are purely ornamental and do not serve some useful purpose but the applicable statutory law of California is that hanging pictures and the means for providing music serve a useful purpose if only by reason of their aesthetic value. . . .

In determining the question of exemption the court gave liberal construction to the term "necessary household furniture," as it was required to do. We believe the court's decision of the factual issue was reasonable and that the order should not be disturbed.

The order is affirmed.

IN RE DeMARTINI

United States District Court, Southern District of New York
414 F. Supp. 69 (1976)

BRIEANT, District Judge. This appeal from an order of Hon. John J. Galgay, Bankruptcy Judge, made March 3, 1976, presents a purely legal question: Is a used color television set exempt property of a householder bankrupt pursuant to § 5205(a), New York CPLR, applicable here by 11 U.S.C. § 24? The learned Bankruptcy Judge held that it was exempt as "necessary household furniture."

Believing this to be an unduly expansive construction of the New York statute, upon which this exemption depends for its vitality, we reverse. . . .

By no construction will a $600.00 color television set pass as "necessary" furniture, in a statute so drawn as to limit the exemption for books to $50.00 and watches (truly necessary) to $35.00. This statute has been amended once in 1954, and re–enacted in 1962, both events occurring after television became commonplace. The statute was amended in 1954 to add "one radio receiver," the appliance most nearly comparable to television. That this addition was deemed necessary is some suggestion that the New York legislature realized that a radio, and *a fortiori* a color television, was not already exempt as necessary household furniture. The familiar rule "expressio unius exclusio alterius est" applies, and would be applied in New York. Since the statute does not exempt television sets, they are not exempt. Further, one house of the legislature appears to have passed in two separate sessions, an amendment to exempt television sets, here again recognizing that there is a legislative need for such reform.

That such a reform would be a good one, we do not doubt; but it had best be left to the state legislative power, which may want to limit the value of the set, as it has done with exempt books and watches. . . .

WIKLE v. WESTHEM
(*In re Westhem*)

United States Court of Appeals, Ninth Circuit
642 F.2d 1139 (1981)

SNEED, Circuit Judge:

This case raises the question whether under the circumstances of this case a diamond ring having a fair market value of more than $3000 and described as "one emerald cut diamond of approximately four (4) carats in weight with two side diamonds" is exempt property pursuant to 11 U.S.C. § 24 (now 11 U.S.C. § 522(b)) and Cal.Civ.Proc. Code § 690.1. The bankruptcy judge held it was not, but on appeal from this decision the district court reversed and held that it was. *In re Westhem*, 459 F. Supp. 556 (C.D. Cal.1978). We affirm the district court.

As the district court pointed out, the facts are not substantially disputed. Emily Westhem's original engagement ring had belonged to Andrew Westhem's grandmother. A number of years ago it was stolen and the insurance proceeds were used to purchase the ring here in question. In this manner the ring which we hold to be exempt is linked to a former ring of great sentimental value. Emily Westhem also wears a wedding band which the trustee in bankruptcy has not put in issue.

The present section 690.1 of the California Code of Civil Procedure exempts "[n]ecessary household furnishings and appliances and wearing apparel, ordinarily and reasonably necessary to, and personally used by, the debtor and his resident family." This provision has been given a liberal construction. *Los Angeles Finance Co. v. Flores*, 110 Cal.App.2d Supp. 850, 243 P.2d 139 (1952). The most comprehensive analysis of the "wearing apparel" exemption appears in *In re Estate of*

Millington, 63 Cal. App. 498, 218 P. 1022 (1923). The *Estate of Millington* court recognized that, while no general rule could be drawn, "wearing apparel may include something more than mere clothing." *Id.* at 504, 218 P. at 1024. However, that court pointed out, and in its holding confirmed, that "expensive diamonds worn as mere ornaments" were not exempt. *Id.* at 504, 218 P. at 1024–25. A further gloss on the wearing apparel exemption was provided by *Los Angeles Finance Co. v. Flores, supra,* where it was said:

> The determination of whether or not a certain article is exempted in the hands of a debtor . . . involves a determination of whether or not under all the circumstances *that article* is necessary to be worn by *that debtor.* . . .

110 Cal.App.2d Supp. at 856, 243 P.2d at 143 (emphasis in original).

These principles require that we affirm the district court. It is not uncommon for an article that replaces another, to which great sentimental value had attached, to acquire a considerable portion of that value itself. An engagement ring also is not just another "expensive ornament."

We restrict our holding to the facts of this case. It is not intended to state a general rule and should not be interpreted as making "expensive diamonds worn as mere ornaments" exempt property.

Affirmed.

NOTES

(1) Courts usually are stricter in defining a "tool of the trade" than a "necessary" item of personal property. *See, e.g., In re Turnbull,* 106 F. 667 (D. Mass. 1901) (denying a watch as wearing apparel or tool of plumber); *In re Coller,* 111 F. 503 (D. Mass. 1901) (reluctantly exempting a watch of a cabinet maker who had timekeeping duties, but making him exchange his watch worth $25 for one worth $10); *In re Nixon,* 34 F.2d 667 (N.D. Okla. 1929) (exempting attorney's books and bookcases from general creditors but not from priority wage claimants); *Holt v. Flournoy,* 24 So. 2d 171 (La. Ct. App. 1945) (denying auto as tool of trade when used to commute under a Louisiana statute); *Rietz v. Butler,* 322 F. Supp. 1029 (N.D. Ga. 1971) (denying exemption for a 6–string guitar as tool of trade under a Georgia law). *See generally* Note, *Implements of the Debtor's Trade,* 35 Mich. L. Rev. 1013 (1937); Note, *Automobile as a Tool or Instrument of Trade,* 20 Tul. L. Rev. 628 (1946).

(2) Along the same lines, in *Coleman v. Lake Air Bank (In re Coleman),* 5 B.R. 76, 2 C.B.C. 2d 608, 6 B.C.D. 669 (Bankr. M.D. Tenn. 1980), a case decided under 11 U.S.C. § 522 (1982 & Supp. IV 1986), the judge held that "the phrases 'household furnishings' and 'household goods' . . . should be given a liberal construction to include *any* personal property normally used by debtors or their dependents in or about their residence. These phrases include home entertainment items, such as a stereo system, regardless of how elaborate." (citation omitted, emphasis added).

In *Beard v. Dial Plan (In re Beard)*, 5 B.R. 429, 2 C.B.C. 2d 895, 6 B.C.D. 786 (Bankr. S.D. Iowa 1980), the court exempted a stereo, cameras and a video recorder holding "[h]ousehold goods extend to property that even though not necessary or even useful are adjuncts of a family's enjoyment and convenience." In *Brake v. Graham*, 214 Ala. 10, 106 So. 188 (1925), mounted deer horns were exempted as household goods and framed photos as furniture.

(3) In case you were thinking it was safe to generalize, at least with regard to personal property exemptions, *see General Finance Corp. v. Ruppe (In re Ruppe)*, 3 B.R. 60, 1 C.B.C.2d 479, 5 B.C.D. 1404 (Bankr. D. Colo. 1980), where the court denied exemptions for movie cameras and projectors on the basis of their clearly recreational nature; *McPherson v. Associates Financial Services (In re McPherson)*, 18 B.R. 240 (Bankr. D.N.M. 1982), allowing gun cabinets as furnishings under 11 U.S.C. § 522 (1982 & Supp. IV 1986), but denying exemption to the guns as household goods. *Accord In re Cole*, 15 B.R. 322 (Bankr. W.D. Mo. 1981). In *In re Libby*, 103 F. 776 (D. Vt. 1900), an apparently schizophrenic court denied exemption to a race–horse as a "work horse," but allowed a pig, though the debtor had freshly slaughtered swine on the hook.

IN RE RICHARDS

United States District Court, Southern District of Texas
64 F. Supp. 923 (1946)

KENNERLY, District Judge.

This is a petition by the bankrupt, Charles Eugene Richards, a married man and head of a family, to review an order of a Referee in Bankruptcy holding that a diamond ring belonging to the bankrupt is not exempt under the Exemption Laws of Texas, Title 57, Vernon's Civil Statutes of Texas.

The facts are substantially these:

(a) The bankrupt, a resident of Houston, Texas, in this District and Division, and an employee of a furniture company, filed his petition in bankruptcy November 6, 1945, was on that date adjudged a bankrupt, and the case referred to a Referee. He did not list the ring in question in his original petition and schedules.

(b) At the first meeting of creditor, the bankrupt was present, and was examined. He was wearing the ring on his finger, and the Referee directed him to deliver it to the Trustee. He did, and it has since been in possession of the Trustee.

(c) Thereafter the bankrupt was permitted to amend, and amended, his schedules, and listed the ring and also showed an indebtedness to J. Marion West, secured by a chattel mortgage on the ring and a 1939 Tudor DeLuxe Ford.

(d) The Trustee, in reporting and setting aside the exemptions of the bankrupt, refused to include therein the ring as exempt, and the bankrupt filed his exceptions to the Trustee's report. After a hearing, the Referee found and held the ring not to be exempt.

(e) The bankrupt acquired the ring about 1929, and has since constantly worn it on his finger. Three or four years ago, the stone originally in the ring was exchanged by bankrupt for a more valuable stone, which is now in the ring. The Referee finds the ring cost $750, and that its present value is $1500. The ring was acquired by the bankrupt after he had incurred the indebtedness to Murray B. Jones, which is the principal indebtedness of the estate. This indebtedness to Jones is evidenced by a judgment in favor of Jones against the bankrupt, dated October 21, 1929.

1. Prior to the Act of the Texas Legislature of May 6, 1935, it is doubtful if there was a Texas Statute under which a ring such as is this could lawfully be set aside to a bankrupt as exempt. By such Act, Article 3832, Vernon's Civil Statutes of Texas was amended by providing for the exemption to families of *"All wearing apparel."* Bankrupt claims the ring is wearing apparel within the meaning of such Act.

But citing *Lyon & Matthews Co. v. Praetorians*, Tex.Civ.App., 142 S.W. 29, *Edwards v. Kearzey*, 96 U.S. 595, 24 L.Ed. 793, *The Queen*, D.C., 93 F. 834, 835, and other similar cases, the Trustee and creditors take the position that since the bankrupt's debt to Creditor Jones was contracted before bankrupt acquired the ring, and before the passage of the Act of 1935, the question of the exemption of the ring must be decided in accordance with the law as it was at the time the debt was contracted and/or bankrupt acquired the ring. That position, however, is not meritorious. The Bankrupt Act provides that exemptions shall be allowed and must be set aside in accordance with *the laws in force at the time of the filing* of the petition in bankruptcy. This, a Court of Bankruptcy, has limited jurisdiction. It may only gather in and administer such assets of a bankrupt as are permitted by the Bankruptcy Act. Any property exempt to the bankrupt at the time of the filing of his petition must be set aside to him. If the ring is set aside to the bankrupt as exempt, it is not necessary to here discuss or decide what rights, if any, under the principles of law discussed in the cited decisions, Creditor Jones may thereafter have and assert in other forums against the Bankrupt and/or the ring.

2. No Texas Court has as yet construed the Act of 1935, exempting to families *"all wearing apparel,"* and, as stated, the Trustee and creditors insist that even though bankrupt constantly wore the ring on his finger for a number of years, it is not "wearing apparel" and, therefore, not exempt to him.

Exemption Statutes have ever been favored Legislation in Texas. As early as 1839, the Congress of the Republic of Texas passed an Act, exempting from execution, etc., to heads of families certain personal property. All the Constitutions, except the Constitution of the Republic, have permitted or required the law–making body to provide for such exemptions. The wording of the present Constitution (1876) is shown in the margin. By the Act of August 15, 1870 there was exempted to every family, all household and kitchen furniture, all implements of husbandry, all tools and apparatus belonging to any trade or profession, all books belonging to private or public libraries, certain livestock, etc. There was exempted to every citizen not a head of a family, one horse, bridle and saddle, all wearing apparel, all tools, apparatus and books belonging to his private library, etc. This Act became Articles

3832 and 3835 in the Texas Revised Statutes of 1925 (Vernon's Annotated Texas Civil Statutes). There was no change in these exemptions material to this discussion until the Act of May 6, 1935, when Article 3832 was amended, and there was exempted to families *"All wearing apparel,"* etc. The emergency clause quoted in the margin shows the reasons for the passage of this Act and this Amendment.

3. Since no Texas Court has so far construed the Act of 1935, exempting to families "all wearing apparel," it will I think be found helpful to look to the decisions of the Texas Courts construing exemptions generally.

Since the days of the Republic, Laws allowing exemptions have been most liberally construed. *Cobbs v. Coleman*, 14 Tex. 594; *Rodgers v. Ferguson*, 32 Tex. 533; *Helm v. Pridgen*, Tex.Civ.App., 1 White & W. Civ. Cas.Ct.App.§§ 643, 644; *Betz v. Maier*, 12 Tex.Civ.App. 219, 33 S.W. 710; *Rock Island Plow Co. v. Alten*, Tex.Civ.App., 111 S.W. 973; *Parker v. Sweet*, 60 Tex.Civ.App. 10, 127 S.W. 881: *Patterson v. English*, Tex.Civ.App., 142 S.W. 18: *Cities Service Oil Co. v. North River Ins. Co.*, 130 Tex. 186, 107 S.W.2d 994; *In re Hawthorne*, D.C., 45 F.Supp. 374; *J. M. Radford Grocery Co. v. McKean*, Tex.Civ.App., 41 S.W.2d 639; *Pickens v. Pickens*, Tex.Civ.App., 52 S.W.2d 1087, *set aside on other grounds* 125 Tex. 410, 83 S.W.2d 951; *Cities Service Oil Co. v. North River Ins. Co.*, Tex.Civ.App., 82 S.W.2d 184, *reversed on other grounds* 130 Tex. 186, 107 S.W.2d 994; *Illich v. Household Furniture Co.*, Tex.Civ.App., 103 S.W.2d 873; *Moore v. Neyland*, Tex.Civ.App., 180 S.W.2d 658; *Gaddy v. First Nat. Bank of Beaumont*, Tex.Civ.App., 283 S.W. 277, *certified questions answered* 115 Tex. 393, 283 S.W. 472.

The opinion in the case of *Cities Service Oil Co. v. Insurance Co.*, Tex.Civ.App., 82 S.W.2d 184, 186, which arose prior to the passage of the Act of May 6, 1935, is so enlightening as to the history of the holdings of the Texas Courts on the subject of Exemptions, that I quote therefrom:

> Why the lawmaking bodies of Texas specifically mentioned "all wearing apparel" belonging to "persons who are not constituents of a family," and made no such mention when providing for exemptions "to every family," does not disturb us, in the light of the humane and wholesome decisions handed down by the appellate courts of Texas.

> These courts have held that a dray is a "wagon," in *Cone v. Lewis*, 64 Tex. 331, 53 Am.Rep. 767; a diamond ring is "wearing apparel," in *First Nat. Bank v. Robinson*, Tex.Civ.App., 124 S.W. 177; an automobile is a "carriage," in *Parker v. Sweet*, 60 Tex.Civ.App. 10, 127 S.W. 881; a piano is "household furniture," in *Alsup v. Jordan*, 69 Tex. 300, 6 S.W. 831, 5 Am.St.Rep. 53; that with the exempted horse there is included a "bridle and saddle," "shoes" upon the horse's feet, and a "rope" about his neck, as well as "martingales," in *Cobbs v. Coleman, supra*, and *Dearborn v. Phillips*, 21 Tex. 449. And these decisions rest in part upon the fact that they are necessary for the beneficial enjoyment of the property exempted by actual designation.

> An unbroken colt is held to be a "horse," in *Hall v. Miller*, 21 Tex.Civ.App. 336, 51 S.W. 36; and the lowly mule, so useful and so seldom ornamental, the butt of the jester, who spoke contemptuously of him as being "without pride

of ancestry or hope of posterity," is held to be a "horse," in *Allison v. Brookshire*, 38 Tex. 199. And Mr. Justice Willson, in the case of *Robinson v. Robertson*, reported in 2 Willson Civ. Cas.Ct.App. § 253, page 193 declares the uncouth jackass, at whose feet lies the responsibility for the useful mule's existence, to be a "horse."

The remedial character and meritorious purposes of the exemption statutes have moved appellate courts to deal with them most considerately, and Mr. Justice Willson points to the fact that "the rule is well supported and is constantly growing in favor, that exemption laws, being remedial, beneficial and humane in their character, must be liberally construed."

The Supreme Court, in the *Cobbs* case, *supra*, speaking through Mr. Justice Hemphill, declared that "the law would not permit the horse to be so stripped as to be almost valueless, nor suffer the spirit of the freeman, who owns him, to be exposed to unnecessary humiliation," and with such pronouncement we heartily agree.

If the law is thuswise so jealous of the pride and feelings of its freemen as that it will not permit a creditor to strip from the freeman's horse, the bridle, saddle, rope halter, and even the martingales, with which the animal is accoutered, how much more readily should the law, with jealous earnestness, say to the freeman: "No creditor shall strip from the sacred body of the wife of your bosom, from the tender form of the precious child she bore you, or from your own frame, the clothing you have purchased with your earnings to hide your nakedness and that of your beloved dependents. This unnecessary humiliation shall never be visited upon you, with the consent of the law."

4. It will also be found helpful to examine the decisions of Texas Courts construing Statutes similar to the Act of 1935.

In *Alsup & Thompson v. Jordan*, 69 Tex. 302, 6 S.W. 831, 833, 5 Am.St.Rep. 53, the provision for the exemption of "all household and kitchen furniture," found in the Act of 1870 (Article 3832, Texas Statutes), was construed. The particular question was whether a piano was exempt to a family. It was there held to be the purpose of the Legislature to exempt all household furniture, regardless of its value and regardless of whether it is *necessary, convenient,* or *ornamental.* I quote the language of Justice Stayton:

It is evident that the value of the piano entered into the verdict, and it is urged that the charge of the court in regard to its exemption was erroneous, and that, as matter of law, it was properly subject to forced sale. The statute provides as follows: "The following property shall be reserved to every family, exempt from attachment or execution, and every other species of forced sale for the payment of debts: . . . all household and kitchen furniture." Rev.St. art. 2335 [Vernon's Ann. Civ.St. art. 3832]. The general definition of "household," when used as a qualifying word, is pertaining or belonging to the house or family, and it is so evidently used in the statute under consideration, the purpose of which is to exempt articles belonging to a family. And in such a connection the word "furniture" is one of *very broad signification* and, according to lexicographers, embraces a supply of *necessary, convenient,* or *ornamental* articles with which a residence is equipped. The statute declares that "the ordinary signification shall be applied to words, except words of art or words connected with a particular trade or subject–matter, when they have the signification attached to them by experts in such art or trade, or with reference to such subject–matter." Rev.St., art. 3138 [Vernon's Ann.Civ.St. art. 10].

Here, it is claimed that the ring was part of Bankrupt's wearing apparel. It is clear that if, strictly speaking, it was not "necessary" to his wearing apparel, it was "convenient" and/or "ornamental."

The case of *First National Bank of Eagle Lake v. Robinson,* Tex.Civ.App., 124 S.W. 177, 179, arose under the law exempting "all wearing apparel" to single men (Article 3835). The matter under investigation was whether or not one Canaday, apparently a single man and owner of a diamond ring, was insolvent on a certain date. Canaday wore the ring on his finger as part of his apparel, and the Court uses this language:

> As to Canaday having a diamond ring which he wore, we fail to appreciate the reasoning which would subject it to execution. *If worn by the owner, it was a constituent part of his attire, and in our judgment is within what the Legislature meant to include by the term "wearing apparel."* Rings are customarily worn, and under appellee's theory of the exemption a sheriff with an execution could remove the pendants from a lady's ears, or a badge from the veteran's coat.

The Trustee and creditors strongly attack this case, but it appears to me to have been correctly decided, and is very persuasive here. It is cited with approval in *Cities Service Oil Co. v. Insurance Co., supra.*

Other interesting and helpful cases are *Patterson v. English,* Tex.Civ.App., 142 S. W. 18, 19; *In re Evans & Co.,* D.C., 158 F. 153; *In re Smith,* D.C., 96 F. 832; *Cobbs v. Coleman,* 14 Tex. 594, 597; *Rodgers v. Ferguson,* 32 Tex. 533.

5. I have examined other cases cited.

All that was decided in *Rivas v. Noble,* 5 Cir., 241 F. 673, was that there was no statute of Florida exempting a diamond ring worn on the finger of a bankrupt, and therefore, the Bankrupt Court could not set it aside to him as exempt. At the time *Langever v. Stitt,* 5 Cir., 237 F. 83, was decided, it is probable there was no law in force in Texas exempting to the head of a family wearing apparel or a diamond ring, etc. The same may be said of Judge Hutcheson's opinion as District Judge in the unreported case of Ramon Otto, Jr., Bankrupt. The following cited cases seem to throw no special light on the question: *McNabb v. Terminal Bldg. Corp. of Dallas,* Tex.Civ.App., 93 S.W.2d 189; *Bow v. Hodges,* Tex. Civ. App., 101 S.W.2d 1043; *Dodge v. Knight,* Tex.Sup., 16 S.W. 626; *Vought v. Kanne,* 8 Cir., 10 F.2d 747; *In re Miller,* 8 Cir., 74 F.2d 86; *Ralph v. Cox,* 1 Cir., 1 F.2d. 435; *In re Gemmell,* D.C., 155 F. 551; *In re Blanchard,* D.C., 161 F. 793; *In re Sachs,* 3 Cir., 96 F.2d 823; *In re Deacon;* D.C., 27 F.Supp. 296.

My conclusion is that the ring in question is exempt to the Bankrupt, Charles Eugene Richards, and that the Referee was in error in declining to set it aside to him. It follows that an Order should enter reversing the Order entered by the Referee, and declaring the ring to be exempt, and directing the Trustee to deliver it to the Bankrupt.

Let such an order be prepared and presented.

IN RE GEMMELL

United States District Court, Western District of Pennsylvania
155 F. Supp. 551 (1907)

EWING. District Judge. On January 9, 1907, the trustee of the estate of said bankrupt presented his petition to the court, praying for an attachment of said bankrupt for his neglect and refusal, after notice by the trustee, to surrender a diamond ring alleged to belong to his estate, and thereupon the petition was referred to S. R. Longenecker to take testimony and make report, with the form of decree he recommended.

From the report of the referee, who recommends that an attachment issue against the said bankrupt, and from the testimony taken on the hearing had before him, it appears that at the time the petition in bankruptcy was filed and subsequent thereto the bankrupt was the owner of a diamond ring, the value of which was variously estimated at from $400 to $1,000, which ring he did not include in his schedules, but which at the time of his examination before the referee he agreed to deliver up in case it was not exempt under the wearing apparel provision of the exemption law of this state. The bankrupt filed exceptions to the referee's finding and the decree he recommends, and the whole contest here is as to whether or not said ring is properly included within the provisions of the exemption law of Pennsylvania of 1849 as wearing apparel.

This ring was worn and owned by the bankrupt himself, not by his wife, nor any other member of his family; and, if there be anything about a gentleman's attire more unnecessary and less worthy to be included within the phrase "wearing apparel" than a diamond ring, I do not know what it can be. Watches of moderate value have been held to be included among "wearing apparel," and in one instance even a diamond stud of the value of $250, but that only after it had been conclusively shown that the owner had worn it for a number of years to fasten his shirt bosom together and apparently had nothing to take its place. The financial condition of this bankrupt for a considerable time prior to this proceeding was not such as to warrant him in indulging in such extravagances.

He made no claim for exemption, "except petitioner's personal effects, wearing apparel, and such items belonging to the person as are exempt by the laws of the state of Pennsylvania, relating either to himself or members of his family." Pursuant to this claim no list of exempt property was ever made or requested, and no enumeration thereof asked, by the bankrupt. It might be, if this were an heirloom or a ring of comparatively little value, that it would be allowed as "wearing apparel"; but to permit persons in straitened financial circumstances to invest large sums of money in articles of value only for mere personal adornment at the expense of their creditors would be rank injustice. The bankrupt himself values this ring at from $750 upwards, and states that on several occasions he had made presents to his wife of diamonds for which he had paid from $100 to $200 at a time, and yet his creditors have been during all this deprived of payment largely because of such expenditures by him. In Dox's Appeal, 30 Pa. Super. Ct. 393, it was decided that a diamond ring could not properly be classed as wearing apparel under a bequest in a will, and, if not wearing apparel under these circumstances, I do not think a ring of this value could properly be classed as wearing apparel under the exemption law.

The exceptions to the report of the referee are therefore overruled and dismissed, and it is now directed that the bankrupt deliver up to the trustee, within 10 days after notice of this order, the said diamond ring, or pay him the fair value thereof.

NOTES

(1) Jewelry and ornamental apparel are the subject of great disagreement between jurisdictions. *In re Smith*, 96 F. 832 (W.D. Tex. 1899), held a diamond shirt stud to be exempt wearing apparel. One suggested rule of thumb for predicting exempt status allowed exemption when jewelry was bought for ornamental apparel, and denied it when there was merely an investment purpose. *Sherrill v. Leech (In re Leech)*, 171 F. 622 (6th Cir. 1909).

(2) Disclaiming any need to inquire "as to extravagance or bad taste of a debtor's wearing apparel in any consideration relating to its necessity," the Western District of Virginia approved an exemption for a $2,500 mink stole. *In re Perry*, 6 B.R. 263 (Bankr. W.D. Va. 1980). In a disagreement over more pressing questions a Wisconsin court exempted a Mason's ceremonial uniform, even though worn infrequently, *In re Jones*, 97 F. 773 (E.D. Wis. 1899), while the less generous Vermont court held only the Mason's hat exempt, because of its multiple uses, vesting the trustee with title to the sword and belt. *In re Everleth*, 129 F. 620 (D. Vt. 1904).

(3) Even the most compassionate court will draw a line when exemptions claimed exceed the imaginable needs of the debtor. *See Burdette v. Jackson*, 179 F. 229 (4th Cir. 1910), where the court refused to exempt cemetery plots far beyond the conceivable needs of the debtor and his family. *See generally* Annot., 41 A.L.R.3d 609 (1972).

(4) The law is far more severe when the federal government is the creditor asserting its tax lien, which is *not* affected by any state exemption laws. *See* Plumb, Federal Tax Liens, 19 (3d rev. ed. 1972) and cases cited therein. Expensive apparel, such as furs, are *not* deemed necessary under 26 U.S.C. § 6334(a)(1) (1982 & Supp. 1986).

PHILLIPS v. C. PALOMO & SONS

United States Court of Appeals, Fifth Circuit
270 F.2d 791 (1959)

WISDOM, Circuit Judge.

This appeal concerns exemptions under the law of Texas: When a partnership in bankruptcy owns four truck–trailers, is one truck–trailer exempt to each of four partners under an exemption statute allowing "every family" two horses and a wagon? We are compelled to answer, "Yes".

Canuto Palomo and his three sons, Esteban, Domingo, and Louis Palomo, organized a partnership, C. Palomo & Sons, in November, 1954, to engage in the wholesale fruit, vegetable, and produce business. Canuto furnished the entire capital, which was divided among the partners in the following proportions:

Canuto Palomo	50%	$13,420.74
Domingo Palomo	20%	5,367.84
Louis Palomo	20%	5,367.84
Esteban Palomo	10%	2,684.05

In May, 1958, the Palomos and the partnership filed voluntary petitions in bankruptcy. The partnership scheduled debts of $111,559.78 and assets of $80,475.38, including four truck–trailers and other property claimed as exempt amounting to $41,500. At the time of the bankruptcy, the partnership books showed that Canuto Palomo had a credit balance of $7,797.42, but that his three sons had overdrawn their capital accounts and were each indebted to the partnership in the amount of about $3,000.

Within one week before the bankruptcy, and at a time when the partnership was insolvent, the partners, on advice of counsel, agreed to set aside for their individual use certain truck–trailers bought in the name of the partnership. There was no actual transfer of title certificates, but each partner took actual possession of one truck–trailer. The Palomos contend that each partner, as the head of a family, is entitled to the exemption of a truck–trailer, although the truck–trailers were partnership property.

The trustee in bankruptcy recommended that the exemptions not be allowed. After a hearing, the referee found "that the claiming of said property as exempt was an afterthought on the part of the bankrupts, and was done for the purpose of hindering, delaying and defrauding the partnership creditors". The referee found that "if, as partners, the individual bankrupts owned any interest in the property claimed as exempt", it was only an undivided interest to the extent of the individual partner's interest in the partnership; for example, "Esteban Palomo owned only a 10% interest in the truck and trailer claimed by him as exempt". Nevertheless, the referee overruled the trustee's objections and granted the exemptions, "following the opinion of Judge Allred *In re Thompson*, 103 F.Supp. 942". The district court for the Southern District of Texas approved and adopted the referee's findings. The trustee now appeals from the judgment of the district court.

Section 6 of the Bankruptcy Act provides that the Act "shall not affect the allowance to bankrupts of exemptions which are prescribed . . . by the State laws . . .". 11 U.S.C.A. § 24. Accordingly, we are bound by Texas exemption laws and we must follow the construction Texas courts place on such laws. *Meritz v. Palmer*, 5 Cir., 1959, 266 F.2d 265; *Peyton v. Farmers National Bank of Hillsboro, Texas*, 5 Cir., 1919, 261 F. 326; *Duncan v. Ferguson McKinney Dry Goods Co.*, 5 Cir., 1907, 150 F. 269.

Unlike states having a traditional common law background and an inherited prejudice against exemptions, "it has ever been the settled policy in Texas to make liberal exemptions of property . . . not designed to confer exclusive privileges, nor to favor any particular class of persons; they are general laws embracing the whole community". 18 Tex.Jur., Exemptions, Sec. 3, 801. In an early leading case the Texas Supreme Court observed that the policy of "liberality has been extended from time to time, until today Texas, in this particular surpasses all the other states of the American Union"; the "wonderful improvement and progress of the past few years attest the wisdom of that policy." *Green v. Raymond*, 1880, 58 Tex. 80. This Court recently reviewed the jurisprudence in Texas relating to exemptions. *Meritz v. Palmer*, 5 Cir., 1959, 266 F.2d 265. Judge Hutcheson, for the Court, citing *Green v. Raymond* and numerous other Texas decisions, reemphasized that the courts have consistently recognized that the "genius and spirit of the Texas exemption laws" require their liberal construction.

In most jurisdictions an individual partner is not entitled to an exemption or a homestead out of the partnership property. The rule is otherwise in Texas. 18 Tex.Jur., Exemptions, Sec. 12, p. 814; 4 A.L.R. 300, 328, 335.

In the case of *In re Pagel Electric & Ice Co.*, D.C.S.D.Tex.1926, 14 F.2d 974, 975, Charles, Frank, and Louis Pagel, bankrupts, claimed as exempt ten lots in the town of Schulenburg. They also claimed an electric light plant, ice plant, and plumbing plant, including all machinery situated on the land, and all wire, poles, tools, apparatus, and equipment necessary and used in the operation of the plants. The referee found that the Pagels used the location to operate their business as the heads of families and that they were also machinists and mechanics. Judge Hutcheson, then sitting as district judge, adopted the opinion and order of the referee holding:

> [T]he fact that the personal property claimed by the bankrupts as exempt to them may have consisted in part of property which they owned as partners, or as joint owners, would not affect their right to claim such as exemptions, but that such property was exempt to them under the provisions of article 3785 title 55 of the Revised Civil Statutes of 1911. This rule is supported by the case of *St. Louis Type Foundry Co. v. International Live Stock Printing & Publishing Co.*, 74 Tex. 651, 12 S.W. 842, 15 Am.St.Rep. 870, as also by the case of *Willis v. Morris*, 66 Tex. 628, 1 S.W. 799, 59 Am.Rep. 634, wherein the Supreme Court held that the tools of their trade were exempt to partners, and the fact that they employed mechanics using large and expensive machinery did not

deprive them of the homestead exemption to the place of their business and the necessary machinery annexed to the freehold. . . . [T]he fact that they [the partners] owned the property jointly, or as partners, did not deprive them of the right to claim and hold said property exempt as their business homestead. The right of partners, or joint owners, to claim their homestead being jointly owned, or partnership property, is well established in Texas. The rule in Texas is laid down and distinguished in 4 American Law Reports 335–339, and the doctrine is announced and sustained in the case of *Swearingen and Garrett v. Bennett*, 65 Tex. 267. It is also upheld in the case of *Gordon v. McCall*, 20 Tex.Civ.App. 283, 48 S.W. 1111. The exemptions of homesteads taken out of jointly owned, or partnership property, have been held in the cases of *Williams v. Meyer*, (Tex.Civ.App.) 64 S.W. 66 and *Allen v. Meyer*, (Tex.Civ.App.) 65 S.W. 645; also the cases of *Willis v. Morris*, 66 Tex. 628, 1 S.W. 799; *Clements v. Lacy*, 51 Tex. 151.

In *St. Louis Type Foundry v. International Livestock Journal Print & Publishing Co.*, 1889, 74 Tex. 651, 12 S.W. 842, a case often cited, the question was whether, the press, type, and material belonging to a partnership was exempt to the individual partners under the Texas statute allowing as exemptions to persons not constituents of a family "all tools, apparatus, and books belonging to any trade or profession". The court stated:

> It often happens, says Mr. Freeman, "that property designated as exempt by statute belongs to two or more persons, either as co–tenants or co–partners." The question, then, arises whether this property must be treated as exempt to the same extent as if held in severalty. The answers are irreconcilable, and the opposing opinions are both supported by very respectable authorities. . . . [C]o–tenants and co–partners have been placed on the same footing in a majority of the states, and both have been given the full benefit of the exemption laws. This position, even where the words of the statute do not clearly indicate an intent to deal with undivided interests, is made tenable by the general rule that these statutes must be liberally construed, so as to promote the policy on which they are based, and accomplish the purposes to which they are directed.

[74 Tex. 651, 12 S.W. 843.] Continuing, the court held:

> One of the principal purposes of the statute is to protect whatever interest or title would be subject to seizure under execution or attachment. The partnership interest is liable to the levy of such writs, and is therefore entitled to the protection which the statute affords. We think that "all tools, apparatus, and books belonging to any trade or profession" although they may constitute partnership property, are entitled to the exemption.

In the *St. Louis Type Foundry* case the parties were not constituents of a family. Here each is the head of a family. Article 3832 of the Texas Revised Statutes, exempting certain property "to every family" is broader however, than Article 3835 exempting property to persons who are not constituents of a family.

In re Thompson D.C.S.D.Tex.1952, 103 F.Supp. 942, 944, is virtually on all fours with the instant case. In that case a partnership, composed of a father–in–law having a 50% interest and two sons–in–law each having a 25% interest, owned seven trucks. Judge Allred held:

> No Texas case affirmatively holds that each partner would be entitled to a separate truck; but, by analogy to *In re Pagel Electric & Ice Co.*, and, in view of the unusual liberality of construction generally applied to exemptions by the Texas courts, I hold that each bankrupt, as the head of a family, was entitled to the exemption of one truck. It could hardly be doubted that if the partnership had owned land or lots and each of the bankrupts lived upon or made use of respective portions of it, each could claim his separate homestead; they would not be entitled to just one homestead between them. The statutory exemption is to every family, not just the family of one partner.

We feel under the same compulsion as Judge Allred. In view of the unusual liberality of construction applied to exemptions by Texas courts and in view of the *Pagel* case and *St. Louis Type Foundry* case, we hold that each Palomo partner was entitled to a truck and trailer combination as exempt property.

We realize that Esteban Palomo, for example, who had only $2,684.05 in the partnership when it was formed and who owed the partnership $3,000 when the bankruptcy petition was filed emerges with a Mack Truck Tractor valued at $9,500 and a Freuhauf Reefer Van Trailer valued at $3,500. But we must take the law as we find it.

We realize also that during the existence of a partnership, in Texas, as in all states, no partner has any exclusive right to any specific item but has only an undivided interest in all of the property to the extent of his partnership interest. Now, however, Esteban Palomo, who had only a 10% interest, has full ownership of a truck and trailer worth $13,000; Domingo, who has 25% interest, has a truck and trailer worth $16,000; Louis who had the same interest as Domingo is given a truck and trailer worth $6,500; and Canuto, who had a 50% interest ends up with truck and trailer worth $3,500. It may seem a strange result that allows a partner to draw from his firm a larger share of assets than he is entitled to under the partnership agreement. But the underprivileged partners are not complaining and the equities existing between one partner and another give their creditors no additional rights. An exemption does not depend upon the extent of a partner's indebtedness nor whether a particular partner has drawn from the partnership more than his proper share. Texas law gives each partner two horses and a wagon, not a fractional undivided interest in two horses and a wagon.

Since the trucks were exempt, their transfer from the partnership to the individual partners cannot be characterized, in law, as a transfer for the purpose of hindering, delaying and defrauding creditors. Article 67, sub. d of the Bankruptcy Act specifically excludes exempt property, and the trustee does not take title to exempt property. A conveyance of exempt property therefore cannot be a fraud on creditors. *Kilgo v. United Distributors*, 5 Cir., 1955, 223 F.2d 167. Similarly, under Texas law, it "is well settled that a conveyance of exempt property may not be attacked on the ground that it was made in fraud of creditors". *Chandler v. Welborn*, Tex. 1956, 294 S.W.2d 801, 805.

The judgement is

Affirmed.

YOUNG v. WRIGHT

Idaho Supreme Court
77 Idaho 244, 290 P.2d 1086 (1955)

SMITH, Justice.

Respondent brought this action to recover damages from appellants on account of appellants' attachment, in a separate action, and resultant detention for a time, of respondent's 1948 Mac L.S.F.W. truck, admitted to be a motor vehicle, *i.e.*, a motor driven truck. Respondent alleges that the reasonable worth of the truck is $7,000 and that he earns approximately $75 a day, four days a week, from use of the truck.

Appellants filed general demurrers to respondent's complaint. The trial court overruled the demurrers, whereupon appellants refused to plead further. The trial court thereupon made findings of fact and conclusions of law, and entered judgement in favor of respondent against appellants from which appellants perfected this appeal.

Appellants by their assignments of error present the question:—whether the motor driven truck was exempt from attachment and execution under the provisions of I.C. § 11–205, subd. 6, which exempts property from execution, as follows:

> Two (2) oxen, two (2) horses, or two (2) mules and their harness; and one (1) cart, wagon, dray or truck, by the use of which a cartman, drayman, truck-man, huckster, peddler, hackman, teamster or other laborer habitually earns a living; and one horse with vehicles and harness or other equipment used by a physician, surgeon or minister of the gospel in making his professional visits, with food for such oxen, horses or mules for six (6) months.

In concise terms, the legislature thereby exempted two draft animals, their harness, *and* one vehicle, with food for the animals for six months. Noteworthy however, the legislature did not exempt any vehicular fuel or value equivalent.

The language of such exemption statute has remained unchanged in all the particulars under consideration here, since its enactment during the year 1881 as C.C.P. 1881, sec. 440, subd. 6, at a time prior to the advent of motor vehicles.

Respondent points to the motor vehicle codes of this state which show that the legislature since and including the year 1913 has recognized the motor truck; that therefore "truck" as used in I.C., sec., 11–205, subd. 6, should be construed to include the motor truck.

Motor vehicles were first recognized by the legislature during the year 1913. The legislature then defined motor vehicles, with certain exceptions, as including all vehicles propelled by any power *other than muscular power*. Idaho Sess.Laws 1913, c. 179, sec. 13; C.S. sec. 1589. Subsequent legislation retained the same definition of motor vehicles, with exceptions, used upon public highways, I.C. § 49–201.

A motor driven truck is not a "truck" which the legislation refers to, to be propelled by *the muscular power* of any of the draft animals mentioned in such exemption statute. The legislature has not yet declared a motor vehicle as is involved in this action to be exempt from attachment or execution; nor any motor vehicle to be so exempt except as its value shall not exceed $200. I.C. § 11–205, subds. 3 and 4.

> For the courts to add to the statute any articles not enumerated would in effect
> be judicial legislation. . . .

Statutory enactments should be read and construed in the light of conditions of affairs and circumstances existing at the time of their adoption. . . .

IN RE JOHNSON

Bankruptcy Court, Western District of Kentucky
14 B.R. 14 (1981)

MERRITT S. DEITZ, Jr., Bankruptcy Judge.

Is a bus a bus, or is it a car?

Reluctantly we conclude that it is a car.

Bankruptcy petitioner, Theodore Roosevelt Johnson, Sr., has claimed as exempt his 1969 Dodge bus. The bus has a seating capacity of 60 passengers. Upon it are occasionally transported members of Johnson's church congregation.

The trustee vehemently objects. He points to the state exemption statute, KRS 427.010, which in pertinent part permits the exemption of "one motor vehicle and its necessary accessories, including one spare tire, not exceeding $2,500 in value . . . .".

The trustee patiently explains that the legislature intended the term "motor vehicle" to be synonymous with "automobile".

Enacted in 1980, the statute excluded earlier statutory limits upon the *uses* to which a motor vehicle might be put, so we must cast altogether aside the trustee's concern with the voluminous seating capacity of the behemoth. The record is silent on the size of the petitioner's family and their transportation needs.

Is a Moped a motor vehicle? What would the licensing arm of the state Department of Transportation say to the contention that a bus is not a motor vehicle? What would Gertrude Stein have to say about what a motor vehicle is?

Such rhetorical questions having been considered, we are bold to say that a bus is a motor vehicle.

In our dialectic, during this era of motorized evolution, we are inclined to regard the "bus" and the "automobile" as species of the genus, "motor vehicle".

This Bankruptcy Court is answerable to an appellate forum of literal bent. That is good, for it gives us guidance and certainty in ascribing to the legislature the ability to express its intent in clear, simple, precise English.

As this trustee will recall, District Judge Thomas Ballantine, in reviewing a decision of this court, recently held that a statutory 15–day limitation upon the recording of chattel mortgages imposed a recording limitation *not* of indeterminate length, as was contended, but a limitation of *15 days.*

Guided by that clarity of perception, we find with conviction that a motor vehicle is a motor vehicle, and not necessarily an automobile. We expressly reserve, until it is properly presented, any consideration of the reverse proposition that an automobile is neither a bus nor a motor vehicle.

Abundantly confident that this opinion will find its way alongside *Marbury v. Madison* and *McCulloch v. Maryland* in the lasting library of legal logic, it is hereby

ORDERED that Theodore Roosevelt Johnson, Sr. is entitled to the claimed exemption, and the trustee shall comport his activities accordingly in administration of the estate.

NOTES

(1) Expansive definitions and redefinitions in the law of exemptions have not been limited to the term "necessary." Often, items currently in common usage were invented or popularized after the passage or revision of a state's exemption statute. This has been especially true with motor vehicles, as the foregoing cases show. With varying degrees of success, debtors have sought to exempt their autos and/or trucks as carriages, drays, buggies, carts, teams, trucks, or yokes and harnesses. In one case, an exemption was denied for a tractor–trailer because it did not fit "within any reasonable interpretation of the language 'team . . . with harness, yoke, one wagon truck, cart or dray.' " *In re Rash*, 81 F. Supp. 389, 393 (W.D. Wash. 1948). *Accord Poznanovic v. Maki*, 209 Minn. 379, 296 N.W. 415 (1941). Nor would the Washington Supreme Court view a logging truck as "work cattle," limiting the law to "bovines" and allowing expansion by the legislature alone. *Grimm v. Naugle*, 34 Wash. 2d 75, 208 P.2d 123 (1949); *accord In re Green*, 19 F. Supp. 925 (S.D.N.Y. 1937). *See* Annot., 28 A.L.R. 68 (1924). More recently, one court would not hold a motor vehicle to be "household goods" under 11 U.S.C. § 552(d)(3) (1982 & Supp. IV 1986). *In re Martinez*, 22 B.R. 7 (Bankr. D.N.M. 1982). Elsewhere, however, a garden tractor and mower were held exempt as household goods. *In re Jones*, 5 B.R. 655, 6 B.C.D. 848 (Bankr. M.D.N.C. 1980).

(2) Courts have been more sympathetic to arguments that motor vehicles gain exemption as tools of the trade. In *Kelly v. Degelau*, 244 Iowa 873, 58 N.W.2d 374

(1953), an auto used to commute 2½ miles a day was exempt because it was "used habitually to earn a living." An auto used extensively in farming operations was held exempt as a "wagon, cart or dray" in *Printz v. Shepard*, 128 Kan. 210, 211, 276 P. 811 (1929). In *Lames v. Armstrong*, 162 Iowa 327, 144 N.W. 1 (1913), an insurance agent's car was exempt as a replacement for the "horse and buggy" of the statutory language.

Assumptions can be traps, however, as shown by *In re McClellan's Estate*, 187 Iowa 866, 174 N.W. 691 (1919). There, an auto formerly used in the debtor's business, and presumably exempt, was lost to creditors because the debtor had retired and could not have used it as a tool of the trade. As well, in *Jones v. Scott*, 167 So. 117 (La. Ct. App. 1936), a district judge's claim of exemption for an auto as an instrument necessary for the exercise of his trade was denied.

(3) *See Roberts v. Parker*, 117 Iowa 389, 90 N.W. 744 (1902), for a lengthy discussion of whether a bicycle can be an exempt vehicle.

(4) *See generally* Annot., 37 A.L.R.2d 714 (1954); Note, *Automobile as Vehicle Within Meaning of Execution Exemption Statute*, 17 Iowa L. Rev. 265 (1932).

EDWARDS v. HENRY

Michigan Court of Appeals
97 Mich. App. 173, 293 N.W.2d 756 (1980)

PER CURIAM.

The defendant was evicted from the apartment she rented from the plaintiff, leaving the rent in arrears in the amount of $177.10. The plaintiff brought an action in small claims court for the rent and other damages and received a default judgment of $193.30, including costs. The plaintiff immediately sought garnishment of the defendant's checking account in the Michigan National Bank. Pursuant to the writ of garnishment, the bank removed the $103.96 in the defendant's checking account to an escrow account, and eventually delivered that amount to the district court.

The defendant's income at the time was derived from ADC benefits and wages of $72 per week from her part time job. Acting upon the defendant's motion for post–judgment relief, the district court determined that the defendant's ADC benefits were exempt from garnishment despite their being commingled with wages in the checking account, citing *Pease v. North American Finance Corp.*, 69 Mich. App. 165, 244 N.W.2d 400 (1976). Applying a formula based on the relative amounts of the defendant's benefits and wages, the court ordered $43.96 of the garnished account returned to the defendant and the remaining $60 paid to the plaintiff in partial satisfaction of the judgment. The remainder of the judgment was settled by a large voluntary payment from the defendant and a court ordered plan for discharging the balance in installments.

The district court rejected the defendant's claim that subchapter II of the Consumer Credit Protection Act (CCPA), 15 U.S.C. §§ 1671–1677, exempted from garnishment that portion of her account monies attributable to her wages. On direct appeal to the circuit court, the orders of the district court were affirmed. She appeals by leave granted. The plaintiff has filed no responsive brief.

The CCPA provides, in pertinent part:

(a) The Congress finds:

(1) The unrestricted garnishment of compensation due for personal services encourages the making of predatory extensions of credit. Such extensions of credit divert money into excessive credit payments and thereby hinder the production and flow of goods in interstate commerce.

(2) The application of garnishment as a creditors' remedy frequently results in loss of employment by the debtor, and the resulting disruption of employment, production, and consumption constitutes a substantial burden on interstate commerce.

(3) The great disparities among the laws of the several States relating to garnishment have, in effect, destroyed the uniformity of the bankruptcy laws and frustrated the purposes thereof in many areas of the country.

(b) On the basis of the findings stated in subsection (a) of this section, the Congress determines that the provisions of this subchapter are necessary and proper for the purpose of carrying into execution the powers of the Congress to regulate commerce and to establish uniform bankruptcy laws.

15 U.S.C. § 1671.

For the purposes of the subchapter:

(a) The term "earnings" means compensation paid or payable for personal services, whether denominated as wages, salary, commission, bonus, or otherwise, and includes periodic payments pursuant to a pension or retirement program.

(b) The term "disposable earnings" means that part of the earnings of any individual remaining after the deduction from those earnings of any amounts required by law to be withheld.

(c) The term "garnishment" means any legal or equitable procedure through which the earnings of any individual are required to be withheld for payment of any debt.

15 U.S.C. § 1672.

(a) Except as provided in subsection (b) of this section and in section 1675 of this title, the maximum part of the aggregate disposable earnings of an individual for any workweek which is subjected to garnishment may not exceed

(1) 25 per centum of his disposable earnings for that week, or

(2) The amount by which his disposable earnings for that week exceed thirty times the Federal minimum hourly wage prescribed by section

206(a)(1) of Title 29 in effect at the time earnings are payable, whichever is less. In the case of earnings for any pay period other than a week, the Secretary of Labor shall by regulation prescribe a multiple of the Federal minimum hourly wage equivalent in effect to that set forth in paragraph (2).

15 U.S.C. § 1673.

The question on appeal is whether subchapter II of the CCPA shelters from garnishment that portion of a worker's checking account funds attributable to her wages and falling within the statute's maximum.

The defendant urges us to follow the lead of a Utah county court and answer the question in the affirmative. We find, however, that the report cases available to us are much more persuasive and do not favor the defendant's position. Three of these cases are particularly notable, each making a slightly different point against extension of the statute's reach to the "wages" filling an earner's account.

John O. Melby & Company Bank v. Anderson, 88 Wis.2d 252, 254, 276 N.W.2d 274 (1979), examined the findings and statements of purpose set forth in 15 U.S.C. § 1671 and concluded that the Congress had focused in subchapter II on abuse of the wage garnishment remedy by the consumer credit industry and the injuries that befall debtors whose employees are compelled to withhold wages. The *Anderson* Court also commented that the statute's reference to the "workweek" and "pay period" as bases for computing the maximum allowable garnishment served to illustrate the Congressional intent to affect only the passing of wages from employer to employee.

Our question was also answered in the negative by *Dunlop v. First National Bank of Arizona*, 399 F.Supp. 855 (D.Ariz.1975). The District Court in that case pointed out that the provisions considered here were only part of a larger single enactment, which in subchapters I and III, 15 U.S.C. §§ 1601–1665 and 15 U.S.C. §§ 1681–1681t, "specifically address[es] . . . problem areas within which financial institutions have a role to play". That Court continued, "Where Congress has specifically used a term . . . in certain places within the statute . . . and excluded it in another . . . the court should not read that term into the excluded section". 399 F.Supp. at 856.

The *Dunlop* Court pointed out that the "administrative red tape" involved in following portions of weekly paychecks into bank accounts would be "staggering". 399 F.Supp. at 856, fn. 7. This concern was more directly before the Court in *Usery v. First National Bank of Arizona*, 586 F.2d 107 (CA 9, 1978), in which the Secretary of Labor, seeking to enforce subchapter II under the authority granted him by 15 U.S.C. § 1676, sought to compel a bank to calculate the portion of wage earners' accounts attributable to protected wages before honoring garnishment orders. The Court made virtually the same analysis of the CCPA that was set out in *Anderson* and *Dunlop*. In considering the only textual support claimed by the defendant here, the Court said:

> The definition of earnings as compensation "paid or payable" in section 302(a) is not inconsistent with this view, and is quite consistent with an interpretation that confines the duty to apply the exemption exclusively to the

employer or those in the position of the employer. The term "paid" as applied to the employer will cover those amounts which have been accrued on the employer's books, and thus are "paid" in the accounting sense, even though such funds have not yet been transmitted to the employee. This construction is an adequate explanation for the use of the terms "paid or payable." Moreover, we find it unreasonable to use the single word "paid" as the basis for the sweeping extension of the Act advocated by the Department. 586 F.2d at 110. To the Secretary's claim that his interpretation of the statute that he was charged to enforce was entitled to deference, the *Usery* Court responded, "[T]he agency's interpretation departs so widely from the statutory mandate that it is explicable more easily as an organic reflex to extend its own jurisdiction than as a reasoned interpretation of the statute".

586 F.2d at 111.

The defendant points out that statutory restrictions on garnishment of money paid or payable as veterans' or Social Security benefits have been held to protect those funds on deposit citing *Philpott v. Essex County Welfare Board*, 409 U.S. 413, 93 S.Ct. 590, 34 L.Ed.2d 608 (1973), and *Porter v. Aetna Casualty & Surety Co.*, 370 U.S. 159, 82 S.Ct. 1231, 8 L.Ed.2d 407 (1962). It is her claim that the CCPA should be interpreted so as to afford an equal degree of protection to funds earned in private employment.

This argument was rejected in each of the three cases we have considered in this opinion. The *Usery* Court pointed out that the statute protecting veterans' benefits expressly provides shelter "either before or after receipt by the beneficiary". 38 U.S.C. § 3101a. It went on to comment that 42 U.S.C. § 407, at issue in *Philpott*, protects Social Security payments from "execution, levy, attachment, garnishment, or other legal process", while the CCPA refers only to garnishment of wages. 586 F.2d at 111.

We believe that there exists a significant difference between the purposes underlying the protection of government benefits and that upon which the CCPA is based. Recipients of government benefits are by definition deemed to be entitled to them by need or merit. In a sense, the government has an interest in the money it distributes even after it has passed into the hands of the recipient. Veterans' benefits are also exempt from state and Federal taxation. In that connection, the Supreme Court of the United States has said:

> These payments are intended primarily for the maintenance and support of the veteran. To that end neither he nor his guardian is obliged to keep the moneys on his person or under his roof. As the immunity from taxation is continued after the payments are received, the usual methods of receipt must be deemed available so that the amounts paid by the Government may be properly safeguarded and used as the needs of the veteran may require.

Lawrence v. Shaw, 300 U.S. 245, 250, 57 S.Ct. 443, 81 L.Ed. 623 (1937).

In conclusion, we note that where there exists no split of authority in the Federal courts concerning the interpretation of a Federal statute, state courts should be very cautious in differing with the prevailing view in that system, if they do not feel themselves precluded altogether from doing so. The CCPA has never, to our knowledge, been afforded by a Federal court the reach the defendant would ask to give it. For this reason and for the reasons set forth above, we affirm the lower court.

NOTES AND QUESTIONS

(1) Note that garnishment does not affect earnings once paid to the debtor. For protection against the bankruptcy trustee's powers, a further ground for exemption is necessary after payment by the employer. *See generally*, Bruun, *Wage Garnishment in California: A Study and Recommendations*, 53 Calif. L. Rev. 1214 (1965); Abrahams & Feldman, *The Exemption of Wages from Garnishment: Some Comparisons and Comments*, 3 DePaul L. Rev. 153 (1954).

(2) As a general rule, future earnings, income, or other additions to the debtor's pocket are not part of the debtor's bankruptcy estate. 11 U.S.C. § 541(a)–(b)(1982 & Supp. IV 1986). *See, e.g., In re Haynes*, 679 F.2d 718 (7th Cir.), *cert. denied*, 459 U.S. 970 (1982) (military retirement pay held to be postbankruptcy compensation for services, and not available to prebankruptcy creditors). Amounts due for previously performed services are included in the estate. Note that although statutes may exempt a minimum percentage of personal service income, there is rarely a ceiling. Can you justify a debtor's retaining 75% of a $500,000 annual salary?

(3) Many federal assistance programs incorporate an exemption for their benefits. Absent such a provision, the debtor's public assistance payments can be reached by a creditor unless state law provides otherwise. *See, e.g.*, Minn. Stat. § 550.37, Subd. 14 (1988) (exempting AFDC, supplementary social security and medical payments).

(4) Workers' compensation is generally held to be exempt. Annot., 31 A.L.R.3d 532 (1970). Private disability insurance will not fall under a life insurance exemption, and needs a particular state law for benefits to be beyond the reach of creditors. *See Atlantic Life Insurance Co. v. Ring*, 167 Va. 121, 187 S.E. 449 (1936); *In re Jennings Estate*, 212 Tenn. 107, 368 S.W.2d 289 (1963).

(5) Unemployment benefits are generally exempt either by federal or state statute. *See, e.g.*, 45 U.S.C. § 352(e) (1982 & Supp. 1985) (railroad unemployment benefits); Md. Ann. Code art. 95A, § 16(c) (1985); N.Y. Labor Law § 595 (McKinney 1977).

(6) Alimony and child support are not generally exempt to payor or recipient. *But cf.* 11 U.S.C. § 522(d)(10)(D) (1982 & Supp. IV 1986); N.Y. Civ. Prac. Law § 5205 (McKinney 1978 & Supp. 1988). What about post–divorce decree debts incurred in reliance on alimony payments: are the payments subject to creditors' levy?

(7) Several states exempt cash on deposit in credit unions or savings and loan associations from creditors' claims. Apparently, a simple transfer of funds to a qualifying account can put the allowed amount beyond the reach of claimants. *See,*

e.g., Cal. Fin. Code § 14864 (West 1982) ($1,500 in credit union exempt); N.Y. Banking Law § 407 (McKinney 1971) ($600 in savings & loan exempt); N.Y. Banking Law § 461 (McKinney 1971 & Supp. 1988) ($600 in credit union exempt); Vt. Stat. Ann. tit. 8 § 1869 (1969) ($1,000 in savings & loan exempt).

PORTER v. AETNA CASUALTY & SURETY CO.

United States Supreme Court
370 U.S. 159, 82 S. Ct. 1231, 8 L. Ed. 2d 407 (1962)

Mr. Justice CLARK delivered the opinion of the Court.

This case raises the question of whether benefits paid by the United States Veterans' Administration retain their exempt status under 38 U.S.C. § 3101 (a) after being deposited in an account in a federal savings and loan association. Petitioner, an incompetent Air Force veteran, had suffered a judgment at the hands of respondent. The latter in an effort to satisfy its judgment attached a checking account and two accounts in local federal savings and loan associations, all of which had been established by petitioner's Committee with funds received from the Veterans' Administration as disability compensation due the petitioner. The District Court, on motion, held all three of the accounts exempt under the statute. 185 F. Supp. 302. Respondent appealed as to the savings and loan association accounts, and the Court of Appeals for the District of Columbia reversed in a divided opinion. 111 U.S. App. D. C. 267, 296 F. 2d 389. Certiorari was granted in view of the importance of the question in the administration of the Act. 368 U.S. 937. We agree with the District Court that the funds involved here are exempt under the statute; therefore we reverse the judgment below.

Since 1873 it has been the policy of the Congress to exempt veterans' benefits from creditor actions as well as from taxation. In 1933 in *Trotter v. Tennessee*, 290 U.S. 354, the Court had occasion to pass upon the exemptive provision of the World War Veterans' Act of 1924, 43 Stat. 607, 613. It held that the exemption spent its force when the benefit funds "lost the quality of moneys" and were converted into "permanent investments." This distinction was adopted by the Congress when the Act was amended in 1935, 49 Stat. 607, 609, to provide, *inter alia*, that such payments shall be exempt "either before or after receipt by the beneficiary" but that the exemption shall not "extend to any property purchased in part or wholly out of such payments." Thereafter in *Lawrence v. Shaw*, 300 U.S. 245 (1937), the Court held that bank credits derived from veterans' benefits were within the exemption, the test being whether as so deposited the benefits remained subject to demand and use as the needs of the veteran for support and maintenance required. It was noted that the allowance of interest on such deposits would not destroy the exemption. Two years later the Court held that negotiable notes and United States bonds purchased with veterans' benefits and "held as investments" had no federal statutory immunity. *Carrier v. Bryant*, 306 U.S. 545 (1939). The Act was again amended in

1958, but no significant changes were made in the exemption provision. As so written it is here at issue.

It appears that the practices and procedures vary as to withdrawal of funds from federal savings and loan associations. Under the law the depositor is a shareholder rather that a creditor, and his deposits are subject to withdrawal only after a 30–day demand. However, the District Court found that a withdrawal from the accounts here involved could be made "as quickly as a withdrawal from a checking account. . . ." In addition, the integrity of the deposits was assured by federal supervision of the associations plus federal insurance of the accounts. Under such conditions the funds were subject to immediate and certain access and thus plainly had "the quality of moneys." As to whether the deposits were "permanent investments," we note they were not of a speculative character nor were they time deposits at interest. Moreover, it affirmatively appears that at times petitioner drew moneys from the savings and loan fund for his support and maintenance requirements and that no other funds whatever are now available to him, his disability payments having been cut off. It therefore appears clear to us that the savings and loan deposits here, rather than being investments, are the only funds presently available to meet petitioner's needs.

Since legislation of this type should be liberally construed, *see Trotter v. Tennessee, supra,* at 356, to protect funds granted by the Congress for the maintenance and support of the beneficiaries thereof, *Lawrence v. Shaw, supra,* at 250, we feel that deposits such as are involved here should remain inviolate. The Congress, we believe intended that veterans in the safekeeping of their benefits should be able to utilize those normal modes adopted by the community for the purpose—provided the benefit funds, regardless of the technicalities of title and other formalities, are readily available as needed for support and maintenance, actually retain the qualities of moneys, and have not been converted into permanent investments.

Reversed.

NOTE

Although the great majority of cases hold that exempt payments or proceeds from exempt property will retain that exemption, conflicts have arisen over how long the exemptions persist. Lines are drawn using a specific time period, or for a specific use. *See e.g., Rutter v. Shumway,* 16 Colo. 95, 26 P. 321 (1891); *Gaddy v. First National Bank,* 115 Tex. 393, 283 S.W. 472 (1926); *Krueger v. Wells Fargo Bank,* 11 Cal. 3d 352, 521 P.2d 441, 113 Cal. Rptr. 449 (1974) (re deposit of unemployment and disability benefits); Cohen, *Exemption of Property Purchased with Exempt Funds,* 27 Va. L. Rev. 573 (1941); Note, *Exemption of Income from Property Purchased with Exempt Insurance Proceeds,* 47 Yale L.J. 1408 (1938); Annot., 67 A.L.R. 1203 (1930); *contra Stebbins v. Peeler,* 29 Vt. 289 (1857); *Nichols, Shepard & Co. v. Goodheart,* 5 Ill. App. 574 (1880).

ROSS v. SIMSER

Minnesota Supreme Court
193 Minn. 407, 258 N.W. 582 (1935)

STONE, Justice

Action on a promissory note wherein a verdict was directed for plaintiff. Defendant appeals from the order denying her alternative motion for judgment notwithstanding the verdict or a new trial.

First & Farmers' National Bank of Blue Earth and First National Bank of St. Paul were garnished. The latter disclosed that it had in its possession two bonds belonging to defendant. Defendant's motion for discharge of the garnishees was denied and judgment entered against them for delivery of the bonds as property of plaintiff so that they might be applied by execution sale upon plaintiff's claim. From that judgment defendant also appeals. . . .

2. The bonds impounded by the garnishment, two in number, each for $1,000, had been purchased by defendant with the proceeds of an insurance policy on her husband's life wherein she was the beneficiary. By statute, Mason's Minn. St. 1927, § 9447 (14), money received by, or payable to, a surviving wife or child from insurance upon the life of a deceased husband or father, not exceeding $10,000, is exempt from attachment or sale under a judgment. The claim for defendant is that the bonds, having been purchased with her insurance money, are also exempt; that is, that the exemption extends beyond the insurance money to anything purchased therewith. That claim we cannot allow simply because we must take the statute as we find it and are not at liberty to add to it by a process which, if indulged in, would be an amendment and, in effect judicial legislation.

In Iowa, where the statute exempts "the avails" of such insurance, the rule is that property purchased with the proceeds of insurance enjoys the same exemption. *Cook v. Allee*, 119 Iowa, 226, 93 N. W. 93; *Booth v. Martin*, 158 Iowa 434, 139 N. W. 888. Putting aside the effect of statutory differences, the rule is pretty well settled the other way. 25 C. J. 82; 11 R.C.L. 530. In *Merrell Drug Co. v. Dixon*, 131 Ky. 212, 115 S.W. 179, 24 L.R.A. (N.S.) 1018, it was held that the exemption of proceeds of insurance did not extend to property purchased therewith. To the same effect is *Pefly v. Reynolds*, 115 Kan. 105, 222 P. 121. In similar fashion, there was refusal to extend an exemption of the proceeds of a workman's compensation award to furniture purchased therewith in *Martin v. Lamb*, Wayne Circuit Judge, 228 Mich. 396, 200 N. W. 160. Under our homestead law, which is to be interpreted liberally but not "strained," we held that, before the amendment of what is now section 8342 of Mason's Minn. St. 1927, by section 3458, Revised Laws 1905, the proceeds of a homestead were not exempt. *Fred v. Bramen*, 97 Minn. 484, 107 N. W. 159, 114 Am. St. Rep. 740. In *Stephenson v. Lohn*, 115 Minn. 166, 131 N. W. 1018, 1019, the rule was applied (to the proceeds of an Indian allotment) "that, in the absence of a statute to the contrary, where property exempt from execution is voluntarily sold for money, or other property not exempt, the proceeds of the sale are not exempt."

It is held that, if proceeds of insurance are deposited in a bank to the credit of the beneficiary, the exemption attaches to the deposit. The reason is that the beneficiary–depositor retains control of the money with the same right and opportunity to use it as such as though the deposit had not been made. Payment of insurance is usually by the check or draft of the insurer which is but the evidence of so much credit. The exemption, of course, attaches to that credit, which does not change its character, and, obviously, should not lose its exemption, simply because, by its transfer to a bank, the latter, rather than the insurer, becomes the debtor. *See Merrell Drug Co. v. Dixon*, 131 Ky. 212, 115 S. W. 179, 24 L.R.A. (N.S.) 1018; *Holmes v. Marshall*, 145 Cal. 777, 79 P. 534, 69 L.R.A. 67, 104 Am. St. Rep. 86, 2 Ann. Cas. 88; and annotation in 67 A.L.R. 1203. But that is neither this case nor parallel to it. Here the insurance money, instead of being deposited to the credit of the beneficiary, was used by her in the purchase of property. Were we to hold otherwise than we do, no limit could be set. Whatever was purchased, whatever the form of investment and subsequent change therein, and no matter to what use the property was put or what the enhancement in its value, the exemption would still attach.

Both the order and judgment under review are affirmed.

REYNOLDS v. HAINES

Iowa Supreme Court
83 Iowa 342, 49 N.W. 851 (1891)

BECK, C.J. 1. The plaintiffs caused process of garnishment to be issued against the Capitol Insurance Company upon a judgment against defendant, claiming that the insurance company is a debtor of defendant upon a policy issued to him upon which there had been a loss of the property insured. A motion to dismiss the proceeding was sustained, upon the grounds, which were not disputed, that the property insured was exempt from execution, being books, instruments, etc., used by defendant, who was a physician and surgeon, in the practice of his profession.

2. The question presented for decision by the record is this: Are the avails of insurance upon personal property which is exempt under the statute from debts of the assured also exempt? The statute (Code. § 3072) declares that, "if the debtor is a resident of this state, and is the head of a family, he may hold exempt from execution" certain personal property, which includes the books, instruments, etc., of a physician, the property covered by the policy of insurance in this case. There is no provision as to the exemption or liability of the proceeds or avails of such property when disposed of by sale or otherwise.

3. The purpose of the statute is to secure to the debtor who is the head of the family—a physician and surgeon in this case—the instruments, books, and other

articles which enable him to practice his profession. Its purpose is to secure the necessaries of life—food, raiment, and shelter—to families who are dependent upon heads thereof, by securing to them the instruments and means by the use of which they are enabled to support their families. The exemption is plainly for the benefit of families of debtors, for those having no family can claim no exemption. The statute must be liberally construed, to carry out its purpose and spirit. *Bevan v. Hayden*, 13 Iowa, 122; *Davis v. Humphrey*, 22 Iowa, 139; *Kaiser v. Seaton*, 62 Iowa, 463, 17 N. W. Rep. 664. The debtor in the case before us was authorized, under the statute, to hold the property in question exempt from debts, if it were used for the purpose of his profession. It is plain that the use for which the property was kept determined the question of its exemption. The books, instruments, etc., of the physician and surgeon may be kept subject to the authority to change them, by sale or otherwise, in order to procure those of better character or improved construction. It is plain that the physician may sell his books, and replace them by better ones. Such sale is a proper use of his books and instruments in his profession. Another proper use of his books and instruments is their preservation from injury and destruction. He may insure them,to protect himself and family from loss from fire. The fact that they were insured would not make them subject to his debts. If they are destroyed by fire, the indemnity secured by insurance stands in the place of the books. It is intended to preserve the physician's library by securing means for its restoration after it is lost by fire. Surely that indemnity which is the indebtedness of the insurance company, or the money paid by it, stands in the place of the library, and ought to be, as it is, exempt from execution. The money due on the policy stands in the place of the property destroyed, and this must be true whether the money takes the place of the property by contract, or is acquired *in invitum* by proceedings against the owner.

It is plain that a trespasser, by appropriating the property and converting it to his own use, cannot make it subject to the payment of the owner's debts by holding the value of the property the measure of the debtor's damages for the trespass, subject to garnishment by the creditors. If he could do this, it would be a convenient method to defeat the exemptions of the statute. As we before remarked, the object of the statute is to secure to the family the benefit of certain property. These benefits cannot be enjoyed unless the debtor have the unrestricted use and control of the property, free from liability for debts as long as it is owned and used by him. When it is used for other purposes than the support of the family, it becomes liable for debts. But the change of the property into money will not indicate an immediate abandonment of the claim of exemption to the money on the ground of a purpose to invest it in like or other exempt property. Until an opportunity exists to make such investment, which is not a change of articles of exempt property, the debtor ought not to be presumed to abandon his claim. The debtor, as we have seen, has the authority to change the articles of exempt property by sale and purchase, exchange, or otherwise. He cannot be presumed to have abandoned his right to this authority until he has had an opportunity to exercise it. The creditor cannot complain of its exercise. He is defeated of no right thereby. The property is held free of his debt, and he is not prejudiced by the change to the other like property.

These doctrines and conclusions find support in the following decisions of this court: *Kaiser v. Seaton*, 62 Iowa, 463, 17 N. W. Rep. 664; *Mudge v. Lanning*, 68 Iowa, 641, 27 N. W. Rep. 793. *See, also,* cases cited in *Kaiser v. Seaton, supra,* and the following: *Evans v. Harvester Works*, 63 Iowa, 204, 18 N. W. Rep. 881; *Brainard v. Simmons*, 67 Iowa, 646, 25 N. W. Rep. 844; *Leavitt v. Metcalf*, 2 Vt. 342; *Mulliken v. Winter*, 2 Duv. 256, *Tillotson v. Walcott*, 48 N. Y. 188.

Counsel for plaintiffs cite *Wooster v. Page*, 54 N. H. 125. It is not in harmony with our conclusions. We think that the reasoning upon which it is based is not sound. Other cases cited by the same counsel are not in conflict with our conclusions. They are to the effect that sales of exempt property, with no purpose to reinvest the avail in other like property, or to exchange the articles of exempted property, or are cases involving the exemption of pension money, and some other cases involving like questions, none of which are in conflict with our conclusions in this case. We reach the conclusion that the judgment of the district court ought to be affirmed.

STATE v. AVCO FINANCIAL SERVICE INC.

New York Court of Appeals
50 N.Y. 2d 383, 406 N.E. 2d 1075, 429 N.Y.S. 2d 181 (1980)

FUCHSBERG, J.

The Attorney–General, acting on a consumer complaint, instituted this special proceeding under subdivision 12 of section 63 of the Executive Law to enjoin respondent Avco's use of a security clause in a loan agreement form. The petition alleged that the clause was illegal and void as against public policy on the theory that it constituted an impermissible waiver of the personal property exemption afforded a judgment debtor under CPLR 5205 (subd [s]). Special Term summarily declared the clause invalid for this reason. Although the Appellate Division, over a single dissent, affirmed the order and judgment, it did so on the ground that the provision was unconscionable (70 AD2d 859). We now reverse, holding that it is not illegal and that the determination of unconscionability was improperly made without any opportunity for an evidentiary presentation as to the commercial and bargaining context in which the clause appears.

The clause at issue is one regularly inserted by Avco, a finance company, in its loan agreements. Its terms unmistakably provide: "This loan is secured by . . . all household goods, furniture, appliances, and consumer goods of every kind and description owned at the time of the loan secured hereby, or at the time of any refinance or renewal thereof, or cash advanced under the loan agreement secured hereby, and located about the premises at the Debtor's residence (unless otherwise stated) or at any other location to which the goods may be moved."

It is not denied that this language must be understood to create a security interest in items of personal property which include the ones made exempt from the reach of a judgment creditor by CPLR 5205 (subd [a]). From its inception, this statute—along with its venerable antecedents—has embodied the humanitarian policy that the law should not permit the enforcement of judgments to such a point that debtors and their families are left in a state of abject deprivation (*see Stewart v. Brown*, 37 NY 350, 351; *Griffin v. Sutherland*, 14 Barb 456, 459).

It is well recognized, however, that simply because the law exempts such property from levy and sale upon execution by a judgment creditor does not mean that the exemption statute was intended to serve the far more paternalistic function of restricting the freedom of debtors to dispose of these possessions as they wish (*see Montford v. Grohman*, 36 NC App 733; *Mutual Loan & Thrift Corp. v. Corn*, 182 Tenn 554; *Swan v. Bournes*, 47 Iowa 501, 503; 1 Jones, Chattel Mortgages and Conditional Sales [6th ed], § 114). No statute precludes exempt property from being sold; nor is there any which expressly interdicts the less drastic step of encumbering such property. So, for example, while contractual waivers of a debtor's statutory exemptions are usually held to be void (*see Caravaggio v. Retirement Bd. of Teachers' Retirement System*, 36 NY2d 348, 357–358; *Kneettle v. Newcomb*, 22 NY 249), the law has not forbidden a debtor to execute a mortgage upon the property so protected and thus create a lien which may be foreclosed despite the property's exempt status (*see* Banking Law, § 356 [governing security interests in household furniture]; Uniform Commercial Code, § 9–102, subd [1], *Matter of Brooklyn Loan Corp. v. Gross*, 259 App Div 165, 166; *Emerson v. Knapp*, 129 App Div 827; 6 Weinstein–Korn–Miller, NY Civ Prac, par 5205.7). The clause here permits no more and, hence, cannot be said to contravene the exemption statute.

The Attorney–General nevertheless argues that the clause should be invalidated under the doctrine of unconscionability. The contention, as accepted by the majority of the Appellate Division, is that "the inequality of bargaining position and the granting to the creditor of enforcement rights greater than those which the law confers upon a judgment creditor armed with execution, lead inevitably to the conclusion that the absence of choice on the part of the debtor left him with no recourse but to grant to his creditor rights which in good conscience, the law should not enforce" (70 AD2d 859, 860). The clause is also alleged to be unconscionable in that its broad terms create security interests even in items not sold or financed by Avco and function mainly as an *in terrorem* device to spur repayment.

In this connection, we note initially that the statute under which this proceeding was brought (Executive Law, § 63, subd 12) lists "unconscionable contractual provisions" as a type of "fraudulent" conduct against which the Attorney–General is authorized to move. Furthermore, an application for injunctive or other relief under this provision is one which may properly look to the exercise of a sound judicial discretion (*State of New York v. Princess Prestige Co.*, 42 NY2d 104, 108). But the petition here provided no opportunity for the operation of such discretion on the issue of unconscionability since it alleged only that the clause per se was "illegal" and "void as against public policy and contrary to law", theories which, as we have seen, are not consonant with established law. Indeed, the only ground presented to nisi prius was that the clause violated CPLR 5205 (subd [a]); the petitioner never raised an unconscionability argument until it arrived at the Appellate Division.

As a general proposition, unconscionability, a flexible doctrine with roots in equity (*see Chesterfield v. Janssen*, Ves Sen 125, 155–156; 28 Eng Rep 82, 100 [Ch 1750]; *Hume v. United States*, 132 US 406, 411), requires some showing of "an absence of meaningful choice on the part of one of the parties together with contract terms which are unreasonably favorable to the other party" (*Williams v. Walker–Thomas Furniture Co.*, 350 F2d 445, 449). The concept, at least as defined in the Uniform Commercial Code—which both parties seem to agree governs the transactions at issue here—is not aimed at "disturbance of allocation of risks because of superior bargaining power" but, instead, at "the prevention of oppression and unfair surprise" (McKinney's Cons Laws of NY, Book 62½, Uniform Commercial Code, § 2–302, Official Comment 1). To that extent at least it hailed a further retreat of *caveat emptor*.

By its nature, a test so broadly stated is not a simple one, nor can it be mechanically applied (*see* White and Summers, Handbook on the Uniform Commercial Code [2d ed], p 151). So, no doubt precisely because the legal concept of unconscionability is intended to be sensitive to the realities and nuances of the bargaining process, the Uniform Commercial Code goes on to provide: "When it is claimed or appears to the court that the contract or any clause thereof may be unconscionable the parties shall be afforded a reasonable opportunity to present evidence as to its commercial setting, purpose and effect to aid the court in making the determination" (Uniform Commercial Code, § 2–302, subd 2).

That such evidence may be crucial is made plain too by the drafters' own explication of unconscionability as "whether . . . the clauses involved are so one–sided as to be unconscionable under the circumstances existing at the time of the making of the contract" (McKinney's Cons Laws of NY, Book 62½, Uniform Commercial Code, § 2–302, Official Comment 1; *see Wilson Trading Corp. v. David Ferguson, Ltd.*, 23 NY2d 398, 403–404). And, in the light of this dependency upon the particular circumstances surrounding a transaction, courts and commentators have consistently construed subdivision 2 of section 2–302 to mandate at least the opportunity for an evidentiary hearing (*Matter of People v. Long Is. Home*, 32 AD2d 618 [proceeding under Executive Law, § 63, subd 12]; *Sinkoff Beverage Co. v. Schlitz Brewing Co.*, 51 Misc 2d 446, 448; *Fleischmann Distilling Corp. v. Distillers Co.*, 395 F Supp 221, 233, n 18; *see* Ellinghaus, *In Defense of Unconscionability*, 78 Yale LJ 757, 812, n 257; 1 Anderson's Uniform Commercial Code, § 2–302:5).

But as indicated, here a case on unconscionability was not presented to Special Term either in form or substance. Nor was that issue available when raised on appeal for the first time (*see, e.g., City of New York v. State of New York*, 39 NY2d 951, 953). Specifically, at no point did the Attorney–General by affidavits from borrowers or otherwise make any factual showing as to such matters as, for instance, deception of borrowers as to the clause's content or existence (*cf. Jefferson Credit Corp. v. Marcano*, 60 Misc 2d 138; *Matter of State of New York v. ITM Corp.*, 52 Misc 2d 39), or the presence of language difficulties or illiteracy affecting its execution, or any other reasons that would have made it unlikely that consent was freely and knowingly given (*see Frostifresh Corp. v. Reynoso*, 52 Misc. 2d 26), all within the embrace of what is sometimes referred to as "procedural unconscionability" (*see* White and Summers, Handbook of the Uniform Commercial Code [2d ed], § 4–3, at p 150). Nor, for that matter, in light of the limited scope of its petition, was there occasion to delve into, much less attempt to prove, the now belated assertion of so–called "substantive unconscionability" (*see, generally*, Leff, *Unconscionability and the Code—The Emperor's New Clause*, 115 U of Pa L Rev 485, 487; *cf. Jones v. Star Credit Corp.*, 59 Misc 2d 189 [Wachtler, J.]).

Accordingly, the order of the Appellate Division should be reversed and the petition should be dismissed, without costs, with leave to the petitioner to commence a new proceeding, if it be so advised.

Chief Judge COOKE and Judges JASEN, JONES, WACHTLER and MEYER concur; Judge GABRIELLI taking no part.

Order reversed, etc.

BENEFICIAL CONSUMER DISCOUNT CO. v. HAMLIN

Pennsylvania Supreme Court
263 Pa. Super. 393, 398 A.2d 193 (1977)

PRICE, Judge.

This matter came before the court below on appellees' preliminary objection to appellant's complaint in replevin. From an order sustaining appellees' objection alleging lack of subject matter jurisdiction, appellant brings this appeal. For the reasons detailed below, we reverse and remand to the lower court.

The facts giving rise to this appeal are as follows. On March 27, 1975, appellant, Beneficial Consumer Discount Company, extended a loan to appellees. In return for the loan, appellees executed a personal note payable to appellant in the amount of $912.00 and a security agreement granting appellant a security interest in their household furnishings. The loan to appellees was not a purchase–money transaction, and the money was not used by them to purchase the household furnishings. The security agreement provided that appellees were to retain possession of the furnishings unless and until they defaulted in repaying the loan. At some unspecified time, conceded by all to be within the time requirement for such transactions, appellant filed a financing statement in the Prothonotary's Office of Allegheny County recording its security interest in the furnishings. Again at some unspecified time, appellees became delinquent in the repayment of the loan.

On January 23, 1976, appellees filed voluntary petitions in bankruptcy in the United States District Court for the Western District of Pennsylvania (BK 76–73, BK 76–74). In schedule A–2 of their petitions, they listed appellant as one of their creditors and noted their indebtedness to appellant in the amount of $760.87. In additional schedules, appellees listed their assets as consisting entirely of their household furnishings, valued at $380.00, which had been pledged to appellant as security for the loan. In accordance with section 6 of the Bankruptcy Act (11 U.S.C. § 24), which permits bankrupts to claim property exempt from bankruptcy proceedings as prescribed by the law of their domicile, *see* Act of April 9, 1849, P.L. 533, § 1, 12 P.S. § 2161 (1967), appellees each claimed exemptions of $190.00 for a total of $380.00, thus claiming their household furnishings as exempt from the bankruptcy proceedings.

Pursuant to section 58 of the Bankruptcy Act (11 U.S.C. § 94), a notice of the first meeting of creditors was mailed to appellant on January 30, 1976. Appellant, however, failed to enter an appearance to present its claim. On April 19, 1976, the bankruptcy judge entered an order discharging appellees' debt to appellant and awarding their household furnishings as their exemption. Appellant did not file objections to the discharge, nor to the grant of exemptions. *See* Bankruptcy Act, section 14b (11 U.S.C. § 32(b)).

Prior to the discharge, appellant made demand upon appellees to relinquish their household furnishings in accordance with the security agreement. Upon appellees' refusal, appellant commenced an action in replevin on April 2, 1976, in the Court of Common Pleas of Allegheny County to enforce its security interest. . . .

In spite of the foregoing analysis, the supreme court failed to apply a consistent rule to secured interests in pledged personal property when it decided the case of *Hawley v. Hampton*, 160 Pa. 18, 28 A.471 (1894). While the court in *Gangwere's* ruled that a mortgage interest arising from a pledge of real property was not within the purview of the statute because the enforcement of that interest resulted in an in rem judgment, the court in *Hawley* held that a creditor's interest arising from a similar pledge of personal property was likewise not within the statute, because such a pledge of personal property entailed an implied waiver of the exemption statute. *Id.* at 20, 28 A.2d at 472 (adopting the opinion of the lower court). The court had held as early as 1854 that the debtor's interest arising from the exemption statute was an interest personal to the debtor and could be waived by him. *See Case v. Dunmore*, 23 Pa. 93 (1854). *Hawley* merely extended this principle to find an implied waiver in any pledge of personal property.

Throughout the subsequent years, it was the practice of creditors to include a waiver–of–exemption clause in all loan agreements. *See* Graubert, *Waiver of Debtors' Exemptions in Pennsylvania*, 48 Dick.L.Rev. 130, 132, 138 (1944). Consequently, although there developed an extensive body of law relating to the interpretation of these waiver clauses, *see* Pendleton, *Debtors' Exemption in Pennsylvania*, pp. 88–93 (1886), the continued validity of the implied waiver principle went unchallenged.

In 1973 this court took the first step towards alleviating the imbalance that often exists in consumer loan transactions and ruled that "no waiver may be found unless it is also found that the debtor has voluntarily relinquished a right he knows he has." *Transnational Consumer Discount Co. v. Kefauver*, 224 Pa.Super. 475, 478, 307 A.2d 303, 304 (1973). Indeed, the wisdom of the rule permitting debtors to voluntarily waive the benefits of the exemption statute had been questioned within years of its formulation. Although in 1854 the supreme court ruled that a debtor may expressly waive the exemption, *Case v. Dunmore, supra*, eleven years later, the court stated:

> That he may waive this option under the Act of 1849 . . . has been expressly declared in many cases, in some, however, with regrets expressed that we did not set out with a different construction and hold the privilege or option indefeasible. If it were *res integra*; if, with the experience and observation we have had, we were now for the first to pass upon the question whether debtors could waive their rights under the Act of 1849 or widows theirs under the Act of 14th April 1851, we would be very likely to deny it altogether, and to stick to the statutes as they are written.

Firmstone v. Mack, 49 Pa. 387, 393 (1865). With this explanation, the court refused to extend the waiver doctrine to permit laborers to waive the statutory exemption provision applicable to their wages. *See* Act of April 15, 1845, P.L. 459, § 5, 42 P.S. § 886 (1966). . . .

In *Mayhugh v. Coon*, the supreme court overruled the wavier doctrine that was recognized as early as 1865 as inconsistent with the policy and language of the exemption statute. In making its decision, however, the court did not restrict its holding to the express waiver rule enunciated in *Case v. Dunmore*. Instead, the court included all waivers, even those arising by implication. "We therefore hold that the provisions of the Act of April 9, 1849, *supra*, may not be waived either expressly or by implication." 460 Pa. at 138, 331 A.2d at 457 (footnote omitted).

In applying this holding to the rationale enunciated in *Hawley*, we are constrained to conclude that the implied waiver previously found in the pledge of personal property is inconsistent with the *Mayhugh* pronouncement. Accordingly, we interpret *Mayhugh* to prohibit appellant from enforcing its security interest in appellees' personal property, pledged as security for a debt, when that personal property has been set aside as appellees' exemption.

This conclusion is further mandated when the implied waiver doctrine is analyzed with respect to the policy and purposes of the exemption statute. In reviewing the legislative intent in enacting the statute, the supreme court in *Mayhugh* reasoned:

> The legislature was obviously concerned with the situation of the debtor and not . . . with the protection of the creditor. This series of enactments reflected a realization that justice to a creditor may well result in oppression to a debtor. Furthermore, it represented an application [*sic*, appreciation?] that stripping the poor and distressed of all of their worldly possessions in an effort to satisfy an obligation, albeit just, was not in the public interest where the result was to create a condition rendering the debtor and his dependents public charges. . . . [I]t is clear that there was an appreciation that the freedom from imprisonment would be meaningless if the debtor could, nevertheless, be stripped of all belongings and deprived of all means of regaining a modicum of economic stability. The policy and object of the legislation in conferring the exemption benefits was to afford the debtor, and his family, the prime necessities of life, and to furnish the insolvent a nucleus with which to begin life anew.

460 Pa. at 134, 331 A.2d at 455.

Applying this policy to the instant case, we are confronted with a situation in which the $380.00 worth of household furnishings awarded to appellees as their exemption represents their only assets "with which to begin life anew." To deprive them of even this meager allowance through a tenuous construction of an implied waiver of the exemption statute is directly contrary to the holding of the supreme court in *Mayhugh v. Coon, supra.*

In ruling that a debtor may not expressly or impliedly waive the benefits of the exemption statute by pledging his personal property as security for a loan, we are not unmindful of the practical implications of our decision. Although it may be argued that to prohibit appellant from enforcing its security interest in the pledged collateral may countenance an injustice and discourage other creditors from extending aid to distress debtors, the supreme court in *Mayhugh* answered these arguments in this manner:

> The court in *Case [v. Dunmore,]* was concerned with "a poor man . . . unjustly kept out of money due to him" 23 Pa. at 95. While this may have had some validity during the middle of the 19th century it is clearly inapplicable to the sophisticated lending institutions of this day. Unlike in former years where the debtor and creditor may have been on a relatively equal basis, such is clearly not the case in our current society nor can it be seriously argued that today's credit industry would be critically jeopardized or curtailed because the creditor was required in all cases to respect the exemptions. The fact that the majority of the states of this nation have embraced the principle that this exemption cannot be waived refutes any argument that such a position would adversely affect the financial sector.

460 Pa. at 137, 331 A.2d at 456 (footnote omitted).

Accordingly, we reverse the order of the court below sustaining appellees' preliminary objection raising the issue of subject matter jurisdiction and remand for proceedings consistent with this opinion.

NOTES AND QUESTIONS

(1) As with all others, exemption rules are made to be broken, either by exception or circumvention. Some exceptions to the rule are universal, such as the preeminence of federal tax liens. *See* 15 U.S.C. § 1673(b)(1)(C) (1982 & Supp. IV 1986); 26 U.S.C. §§ 6634(a) and (c) (1982 and Supp. IV 1986). Many, such as those recognizing the validity of a contractual waiver, vary greatly and require particular attention to the laws of the jurisdiction. A waiver of certain exempt property rights may be void *ab initio* as against public policy. Alternatively, such a waiver may be void because of undue influence, unconscionability or duress, depending on the fact situation. Finally, such a waiver may be perfectly acceptable in the correct circumstances, such as a purchase–money mortgage on a homestead.

(2) Some states are less reluctant to allow adults to waive their rights.

Ga. Code § 44–13–40 (1933)

Any debtor may, except as to wearing apparel and $300.00 worth of household and kitchen furniture and provisions, waive or renounce his right to the benefit of the exemption provided for by the Constitution and laws of this state by a waiver, either general or specific, in writing simply stating that he does so waive or renounce such right, which waiver may be stated in the contract of indebtedness or may be made contemporaneously therewith or may be subsequent to the execution of the contract of indebtedness in a separate paper. (Ga. L. 1878–79, p. 99, § 6; Code 1882, § 2039a; Civil Code 1895, § 2863; Civil Code 1910, § 3413; Code 1933, § 51–1101).

The policy behind this section is to permit a hard pressed debtor to use his exemption to obtain credit which in his extremity, may save him. *Mims v. Dixie Finance Corp.*, 426 F. Supp. 627 (N.D. Ga. 1976).

For an attempt to protect the consumer, and also to make credit somehow available, *see* Minn. Stat. Ann. § 550.37, Subd. 19 (1983).

(3) Note that the public policy behind these protections can be subverted by a positive assignment of rights to property rather than a waiver of a defense. Does this open as much room for abuse in a consumer credit situation as a waiver? How difficult is it to change merely the boilerplate?

(4) 11 U.S.C. § 522(e) (1982 & Supp. IV 1986) (the Bankruptcy Code) declares waiver of federal exemptions unenforceable. Cases in agreement that exemption protection cannot be waived prospectively or by executory contract include *Iowa Mutual Insurance Co. v. Parr*, 189 Kan. 475, 370 P.2d 400 (1962); *Resolute Insurance Co. v. Pennington*, 423 Pa. 472, 224 A.2d 757 (1966); *Celco, Inc. of America v. Davis Van Lines, Inc.*, 226 Kan. 366, 598 P.2d 188 (1979). The states are well divided on the waiver question and reference to the applicable statute is particularly appropriate here. *See, e.g.,* Wash. Rev. Code Ann. § 6.15.050 (West Supp. 1988) (allowing waiver); W. Va. Code § 38–9–6 (1974) (voiding it); Annot., 94 A.L.R.2d 967 (1964).

(5) Exemptions can be lost by dishonesty, fraud or fraudulent conveyance. *See, e.g., Hyman v. Stern*, 43 F.2d 666 (4th Cir. 1930).

(6) They can be lost by failure to claim them in a timely manner. *See, e.g.,* Colo. Rev. Stat. § 38–41–202 (1982); Wash. Rev. Code § 6.15.050 (West Supp. 1988).

(7) Legislatively favored creditors can "pierce" an exemption. Examples of such creditors are recipients of alimony and child support (11 U.S.C. § 523(a)(5) (1982 & Supp. IV 1986)), certain tort creditors, federal tax claimants, holders of purchase money security interests used to induce loans post–declaration of bankruptcy, mechanics or materialmen holding liens on exempt property, creditors who loaned for "necessities" after the declaration of bankruptcy, and lien creditors not extinguished by the proceedings. *See* 11 U.S.C. § 522(f) (1982); Uniform Exemption Act § 10, 13 U.L.A. 232 (1976).

(8) Note that an individual debtor may always voluntarily discharge a lien on otherwise exempt property by paying the lienor the value of the exempt property. 11 U.S.C. § 722 (1982).

§ 7.05 Life Insurance

NEW YORK INSURANCE LAW § 3212

(McKinney (1988) (Amended))

§ 3212. Exemption of proceeds and avails of certain insurance and annuity contracts

(a) In this section:

(1) The term "proceeds and avails", in reference to policies of life insurance, includes death benefits, cash surrender and loan values, premiums waived, and dividends, whether used in reduction of premiums or in whatever manner used or applied, except where the debtor has, after issuance of the policy, elected to receive the dividends in cash.

(2) An annuity contract includes any obligation to pay certain sums at stated times, during life or lives, or for a specified term or terms, issued for a valuable consideration, regardless of whether such sums are payable to one or more persons, jointly or otherwise, but does not include payments under a life insurance policy at stated times during life or lives, or for a specified term or terms.

(3) The term "creditor" includes every claimant under a legal obligation contracted or incurred after December thirty–first, nineteen hundred thirty–nine.

(4) The term "execution" includes execution by garnishee process and every action, proceeding or process whereby assets of a debtor may be subjected to the claims of creditors.

(b)(1) If a policy of insurance has been or shall be effected by any person on his own life in favor of a third person beneficiary, or made payable otherwise to a third person, such third person shall be entitled to the proceeds and avails of such policy as against the creditors, personal representatives, trustees in bankruptcy and receivers in state and federal courts of the person effecting the insurance.

(2) If a policy of insurance has been or shall be effected upon the life of another person in favor of the person effecting the same or made payable otherwise to such person, the latter shall be entitled to the proceeds and avails of such policy as against the creditors, personal representatives, trustees in bankruptcy and receivers in state and federal courts of the person insured. If the person effecting such insurance shall be the spouse of the insured, he or she shall be entitled to the proceeds and avails of such policy as against his or her own creditors, trustees in bankruptcy and receivers in state and federal courts.

(3) If a policy of insurance has been or shall be effected by any person on the life of another person in favor of a third person beneficiary, or made payable

otherwise to a third person, such third person shall be entitled to the proceeds and avails of such policy as against the creditors, personal representatives, trustees in bankruptcy and receivers in state and federal courts of the person insured and of the person effecting the insurance.

(4)(A) The person insured pursuant to paragraph one of this subsection or the person effecting the insurance other than the spouse of the insured pursuant to paragraph two hereof, and the person effecting the insurance pursuant to paragraph three hereof, or the executor or administrator of any such persons, or a person entitled to the proceeds or avails of such policy in trust for such persons shall not be deemed a third person beneficiary, assignee or payee.

(B) A policy shall be deemed payable to a third person beneficiary if and to the extent that a facility–of–payment clause or similar clause in the policy permits the insurer to discharge its obligation after the death of the person insured by paying the death benefits to a third person.

(5) This section shall be applicable whether or not the right is reserved in any such policy to change the designated beneficiary and whether or not the policy is made payable to the person whose life is insured if the beneficiary, assignee or payee shall predecease such person; and no person shall be compelled to exercise any rights, powers, options or privileges under such policy.

(c)(1) No money or other benefits payable or allowable under any policy of insurance against disability arising from accidental injury or bodily infirmity or ailment of the person insured, shall be liable to execution for the purpose of satisfying any debt or liability of the insured, whether incurred before or after the commencement of the disability, except as provided in subsection (e) hereof.

(2) With respect to debts or liabilities incurred for necessaries furnished the insured after the commencement of disability, the exemption shall not include any income payment benefits payable as a result of any disability of the insured, and with respect to all other debts or liabilities incurred after the commencement of disability of the insured, the exemption of income payment benefits payable as a result of any disability of the insured shall not at any time exceed payment at a rate of four hundred dollars per month for the period of such disability.

(3) When a policy provides for lump sum payment because of a dismemberment or other specific loss of insured, such payment shall be exempt from execution of insured's creditors.

(4) This subsection shall not affect the assignability of any benefit otherwise assignable.

(d)(1) The benefits, rights, privileges and options which, under any annuity contract are due or prospectively due the annuitant, who paid the consideration for the annuity contract, shall not be subject to execution.

(2) The annuitant shall not be compelled to exercise any such rights, powers or options contained in the annuity contract, nor shall creditors be allowed to interfere with or terminate the contract, except as provided in subsection (e) hereof and except that the court may order the annuitant to pay to a judgment creditor or apply on the

judgment in installments, a portion of such benefits that appears just and proper to the court, with due regard for the reasonable requirements of the judgment debtor and his family, if dependent upon him, as well as any payments required to be made by the annuitant to other creditors under prior court orders.

(3) The benefits, rights, privileges or options accruing under such contract to a beneficiary or assignee shall not be transferable nor subject to commutation. If the benefits are payable periodically or at stated times, the same exemptions and exceptions contained herein for the annuitant shall apply with respect to such beneficiary or assignee.

(e)(1) Every assignment or change of beneficiary or other transfer is valid, except in cases of transfer with actual intent to hinder, delay or defraud creditors, as defined by article ten of the debtor and creditor law. In such cases creditors shall have all the remedies provided by such article ten.

(2)(A) Subject to the statute of limitations, the amount of premiums or other consideration paid with actual intent to defraud creditors as provided in article ten of the debtor and creditor law, together with interest on such amount, shall enure to the benefit of creditors from the proceeds of the policy or contract; but the insurer issuing such policy or contract shall be discharged of liability thereunder by making payments in accordance with its terms, or in accordance with any assignment, change of beneficiary or other transfer, unless before any such payment such insurer shall have received written notices, by or on behalf of any such creditor, of a claim to recover any benefits on the ground of a transfer or payment made with intent to defraud such creditor.

(B) The notice shall specify the amount claimed or sufficient facts to enable the insurer to ascertain such amount, the insurance or annuity contract, the person insured or annuitant, and the transfers or payments sought to be avoided on the ground of fraud.

(3)(A) Notwithstanding any inconsistent provision of this section or other law, any right of subrogation to benefits to which a local social services district, the department of social services, or the commissioner of health or his designee, shall be entitled shall be valid and enforceable to the extent benefits are available under any individual accident and health insurance, group or blanket accident and health insurance, or noncancellable disability insurance policy, or any subscriber contract made by a corporation subject to the provisions of article forty–three of this chapter, except that no such right of subrogation shall be enforceable if such benefits may be claimed by the department of social services, an appropriate social services official or the commissioner of health or his Designee, by agreement or other established procedure, directly from an insurance carrier.

(B) The right of subrogation does not attach to insurance benefits paid or provided under any health insurance policy prior to the receipt by the carrier issuing such insurance of written notice from the department of social services, a local social services district, or the commissioner of health or his designee, of the exercise of subrogation rights.

(C) No right of subrogation to insurance benefits available under any health insurance policy shall be enforceable unless written notice of the exercise of such subrogation right is received by the carrier within two years from the date services for which benefits are provided under the policy or contract are rendered.

(4) No terms of any policy or contract which directly or indirectly prevent or prohibit the assignment of rights under any policy or contract prevent a local social services district, the department of social services, or the commissioner of health or his designee, from claiming benefits to which it shall be subrogated. The right of subrogation attaches to any benefits paid or provided under any policy, plan or contract upon receipt of written notice of the exercise of such subrogation rights.

(f) This section shall likewise apply to group insurance policies or annuity contracts, to the certificates or contracts of fraternal benefit societies, and to the policies or contracts of cooperative life and accident insurance companies.

IN RE MESSINGER

United States Court of Appeals, Second Circuit
29 F.2d 158, cert denied sub nom Reilly v. Messinger
279 U.S. 855 (1928)

AUGUSTUS N. HAND, Circuit Judge. The bankrupt listed among his assets two insurance policies, payable to his wife as beneficiary, in each of which he had reserved the right to change the beneficiary. After the trustee in bankruptcy had qualified, he demanded that the policies be turned over to him by the bankrupt, who accordingly surrendered them. Thereafter the bankrupt applied to the referee for an order directing the trustee to return the policies on the ground that the trustee, because of the provisions of section 55a of the Insurance Law of the state of New York (Consol. Laws, c. 28), had no interest in them. The referee directed the return of the policies, his order was thereafter confirmed by the District Court, and from the order of confirmation the trustee has taken this appeal.

The question raised by this appeal is whether the life insurance policies made payable to the bankrupt's wife, but in which he had reserved the right to change the beneficiary, became exempt from the claims of his creditors under the provisions of section 55a of the state Insurance Law.

Section 6 of the Bankruptcy Act (11 USCA § 24) provides that:

This act shall not affect the allowance to bankrupts of the exemptions which are prescribed by the state laws in force at the time of the filing of the petition in the state wherein they have had their domicile for the six months or the greater portion thereof immediately preceding the filing of the petition.

Section 55a of the Insurance Law provides:

If a policy of insurance, whether heretofore or hereafter issued, is effected by any person on his own life or on another life, in favor of a person other than himself, or, except in cases of transfer with intent to defraud creditors, if a policy of life insurance is assigned or in any way made payable to any such person, the lawful beneficiary or assignee thereof, other than the insured or the person so effecting such insurance, or his executors or administrators, shall be entitled to its proceeds and avails against the creditors and representatives of the insured and of the person effecting the same, whether or not the right to change the beneficiary is reserved or permitted, and whether or not the policy is made payable to the person whose life is insured if the beneficiary or assignee shall predecease such person: Provided, that, subject to the statute of limitations, the amount of any premiums for said insurance paid with intent to defraud creditors, with interest thereon, shall enure to their benefit from the proceeds of the policy; but the company issuing the policy shall be discharged of all liability thereon by payment of its proceeds in accordance with its terms, unless before such payment the company shall have written notice, by or in behalf of a creditor, of a claim to recover for transfer made or premiums paid with intent to defraud creditors, with specification of the amount claimed.

Section 70a of the Bankruptcy Act (11 USCA § 110[a]) determines the disposition of life insurance policies, so far as they may not come within the exemptions under state laws which are permitted by section 6, *supra*. The pertinent clauses of section 70a are as follows:

The trustee of the estate of a bankrupt, upon his appointment and qualification . . . shall . . . be vested by operation of law with the title of the bankrupt, as of the date he was adjudged a bankrupt, except in so far as it is to property which is exempt, to all . . . (3) powers which he might have exercised for his own benefit, but not those which he might have exercised for some other person; . . . (5) property which prior to the filing of the petition he could by any means have transferred or which might have been levied upon and sold under judicial process against him: Provided, that when any bankrupt shall have any insurance policy which has a cash surrender value payable to himself, his estate, or personal representatives, he may, within thirty days after the cash surrender value has been ascertained and stated to the trustee by the company issuing the same, pay or secure to the trustee the sum so ascertained and stated, and continue to hold, own, and carry such policy free from the claims of the creditors participating in the distribution of his estate under the bankruptcy proceedings, otherwise the policy shall pass to the trustee as assets. . . .

The Supreme Court construed section 70a in *Cohen v. Samuels*, 245 U.S. 50, 38 S. Ct. 36, 62 L. Ed. 143, before section 55a of the Insurance Law was adopted, and at a time when there was no state statute which could be thought to exempt the proceeds of insurance policies from the claims of creditors. In that case, as here, the policies were payable to certain beneficiaries, and the bankrupt reserved the right to change the beneficiaries. In spite of the fact that the policies were not payable to the bankrupt, the Supreme Court held that the cash surrender value was an asset which passed to the trustee under section 70a, *supra*, because the insured had power, by reason of the reservation in the policies, to make them payable to himself. To the same effect was *Cohn v. Malone*, 248 U.S. 450, 39 S. Ct. 141, 63 L. Ed. 352, and our own decision in *Matter of Greenberg*, 271 F. 258.

Does section 55a of the Insurance Law allow an exemption to the bankrupt within the provisions of section 6 of the Bankruptcy Act? Only in such event can the Insurance Law apply, for the Bankruptcy Act must govern as between it and a state law, and the cash surrender value would pass to the trustee under section 70a, unless it is "property which is exempt."

There can be no doubt that, within the terms of section 6, the state law could have exempted the reserved power of the bankrupt from the claims of his creditors even to the extent of allowing him to exercise it in his own interest, for, as the Supreme Court said in *Holden v. Stratton*, 198 U.S. at page 212, 25 S. Ct. 659, 49 L. Ed. 1018, it is "couched in unlimited terms, and is accompanied with no qualification whatever."

In *Holden v. Stratton* a statute of the state of Washington provided "that the proceeds or avails of all life insurance shall be exempt from all liability for any debt." It was held that this statute exempted the cash surrender value of policies payable to the wife of the bankrupt, if she survived him, in which the power to change the beneficiary was reserved, and was valid under section 6 of the Bankruptcy Act. But in the present case the language of the Insurance Law does not in terms grant an exemption to the avails of the policy in the hands of the bankrupt, for it only provides that the "beneficiary . . . other than the insured . . . shall be entitled to [the] proceeds and avails against the creditors and representatives of the insured, . . . whether or not the right to change the beneficiary is reserved or permitted, and whether or not the policy is made payable to the person whose life is insured if the beneficiary . . . shall predecease such person."

The statute does not exempt the bankrupt if he exercises his reserved power to change the beneficiary for his personal advantage, and, indeed, precludes an exemption in such case by saying that the "beneficiary . . . *other than the insured*" shall be entitled to the proceeds and avails. But it plainly does attempt to exempt the "proceeds and avails," so far as beneficiaries, other than the bankrupt, may have an interest in the policy. It does not protect the insured against his creditors, and only seeks to prevent them from affecting the rights of the beneficiaries other than himself. While the insured may still change the beneficiary, and appoint to himself under the reserved power, by reason of the New York Insurance Law, he cannot be compelled to do this, as he would have been prior to the enactment of section 55a, because, to do so, would deprive the beneficiaries of their interest. Thus there is an allowance of an exemption to the bankrupt to the extent of the right of the trustee to compel him to exercise the reserved power. While the benefit inures directly to the beneficiary, and not to the bankrupt, yet it is an exemption of the bankrupt himself to the extent indicated. . . .

The only Circuit Court of Appeals which may perhaps be thought to have differed with the foregoing conclusions is the Fifth, in *Morgan v. McCaffrey*, 286 F. 922. There a statute of Florida was considered, which seems sweeping in its exemptions, but the court, in construing its meaning limited its effect to the exemption of rights coming into being after the death of the insured. While the language of the act resembles that dealt with by the Supreme Court in *Holden v. Stratton*, 198 U.S. 202, 25 L. Ed. 656, 49 L. Ed. 1018, the latter case is not referred to. But, in any event,

Morgan v. McCaffrey, supra, can have no bearing on the situation before this court, because the statute as there construed limited the exemption to cases where the death of the insured had occurred. . . .

In view of the foregoing considerations, the order of the District Court is modified, so as to provide that the trustee in bankruptcy shall be entitled to the cash surrender value of the policies to the extent of the proved claims of creditors, if any, which existed on March 31, 1927, and also so as to provide that, if the bankrupt shall at any time exercise his power to change the beneficiary for his personal advantage, the cash surrender value shall constitute unadministered assets of the bankrupt estate. As thus modified, the decree is affirmed.

HOME SECURITY LIFE INSURANCE CO. v. McDONALD

North Carolina Supreme Court
277 N.C. 275, 177 S.E.2d 291 (1970)

BOBBITT, Chief Justice.

The Bankruptcy Act § 70(a), 11 U.S.C.A. § 110(a), in part provides: "The trustee of the estate of a bankrupt . . . upon his . . . appointment and qualification, shall . . . be vested by operation of law with the title of the bankrupt as of the date of the filing of the petition . . . , *except insofar as it is to property which is held to be exempt,* to all of the following kinds of property . . . (3) powers which he might have exercised for his own benefit but not those which he might have exercised solely for some other person . . . (5) property, including rights of action, which prior to the filing of the petition he could by any means have transferred or which might have been levied upon and sold under judicial process against him, or otherwise seized, impounded, or sequestered: . . . *And provided further,* That when any bankrupt, who is a natural person, shall have any insurance policy which has a cash surrender value payable to himself, his estate, or personal representatives, he may, within thirty days after the cash surrender value has been ascertained and stated to the trustee by the company issuing the same, pay or secure to the trustee the sum so ascertained and stated, and continue to hold, own, and carry such policy free from the claims of the creditors participating in the distribution of his estate under the bankruptcy proceedings, otherwise the policy shall pass to the trustee as assets;. . . ." (Our italics.)

The Bankruptcy Act § 6, 11 U.S.C.A. § 24, in part provides: "This title (Bankruptcy) shall not affect the allowance to bankrupts *of the exemptions which are prescribed . . . by the State laws in force at the time of the filing of the petition. . . ."* (Our italics.)

On the basis of these statutory provisions, it is well established that the cash surrender value of the policies under consideration is an asset of the bankrupt estate, *Cohen v. Samuels,* 245 U.S. 50, 38 S.Ct. 36, 62 L.Ed. 143 (1917), and *Cohn v.*

Malone, 248 U.S. 450, 39 S.Ct. 141, 63 L.Ed. 352 (1919), *unless* included within the exemption laws of the State of North Carolina, *Smalley v. Laugenour,* 196 U.S. 93, 97, 25 S.Ct. 216, 217, 49 L.Ed. 400, 402 (1905), and *Holden v. Stratton,* 198 U.S. 202, 25 S.Ct. 656, 49 L.Ed. 1018 (1905).

The Washington statute, Laws 1895, c. 125, under consideration in *Holden v. Stratton, supra,* provided "that *the proceeds or avails* of all life insurance shall be exempt from all liability for any debt." (Our italics.)

Ordinarily, the beneficiary named in a life insurance policy has a vested interest therein which cannot be destroyed without his (her) consent in the absence of conditions or stipulations to the contrary. *Wilson v. Williams,* 215 N.C. 407, 2 S.E. 2d 19 (1939), and cases cited. Unless he reserves the right to change the beneficiary, the insured cannot, without the consent of the beneficiary, obtain the cash surrender value. In such case, the right to the cash surrender value does not pass to the trustee in bankruptcy under subparagraphs (3) and (5) of § 70(a) of the Bankruptcy Act. *Massachusetts Mut. Life Ins. Co. v. Switow,* 30 F.Supp. 809 (W.D. Ky.1940). Thus, without reference to the North Carolina statutory and constitutional provisions discussed below, the cash surrender value of a policy in which the insured has not reserved the right to change the beneficiary is not an asset of the bankrupt estate. . . .

It is noted that *Holden v. Stratton, supra,* recognized expressly, and that *Whiting v. Squires, supra,* recognized impliedly, the right of a State, if its constitution so provided or permitted, to exempt "the proceeds or avails," including the cash surrender value, of a life insurance policy in which the wife is the named beneficiary and in which the insured (bankrupt) reserved the right to change the beneficiary . . .

On March 23, 1931, the General Assembly enacted Chapter 179, Session Laws of 1931, entitled "An Act Determining the Rights of Creditors and Beneficiaries under Policies of Life Insurance." This statute, now codified as G.S. § 58-206, provides: "If a policy of insurance is effected by any person on his own life or on another life in favor of a person other than himself, or, except in cases of transfer with intent to defraud creditors, if a policy of life insurance is assigned or in any way made payable to any such person, *the lawful beneficiary or assignee thereof,* other than the insured or the person so effecting such insurance or the executor or administrator of such insured or of the person effecting such insurance, *shall be entitled to its proceeds and avails* against creditors and representatives of the insured and of the person effecting same, *whether or not the right to change the beneficiary is reserved or permitted, and whether or not the policy is made payable to the person whose life is insured if the beneficiary or assignee shall predecease such person:* Provided, that subject to the statute of limitations, the amount of any premiums for said insurance paid with the intent to defraud creditors, with interest thereon, shall inure to their benefit from the proceeds of the policy; but the company issuing the policy shall be discharged of all liability thereon by payment of its proceeds in accordance with its terms unless, before such payment, the company shall have written notice by or in behalf of the creditor, of a claim to recover for transfer made or premiums paid with intent to defraud creditors, with specifications of the amount claimed." (Our italics.) . . .

The 1931 statute (G.S. § 58–206) was taken practically verbatim from the 1927 New York statute construed in *In re Messinger*, 29 F.2d 158 (2d Cir. 1928), *cert. den.*, *Reilly v. Messinger*, 279 U.S. 855, 49 S.Ct. 351, 73 L.Ed. 996 (1929). In deciding the question presented in that case, a bankruptcy proceeding, it was held that the cash surrender value of a policy of life insurance is exempt from the claims of the trustee in bankruptcy of the insured even though the right to change the beneficiary is reserved.

In *Smith v. Metropolitan Life Ins. Co.*, 43 F.2d 74 (3d Cir. 1930), it was decided, in accord with the construction placed upon New Jersey exemption statutes by cited decisions of the Court of Chancery of New Jersey, that the trustee in bankruptcy was not entitled to the cash surrender value of a life insurance policy in which the wife was the named beneficiary notwithstanding the insured (bankrupt) had reserved the right to change the beneficiary. The New Jersey statutory provisions considered are similar to those in G.S. § 58–206 except that the clause in G.S. § 58–206, "whether or not the right to change the beneficiary is reserved or permitted," did not appear in the New Jersey statutes. . . .

Decisions in accord with *In re Messinger, supra*, and *Smith v. Metropolitan Life Ins. Co., supra*, based on statutes similar to G.S. § 58–206 in that they exempt the "proceeds" or "avails" of life insurance policies, include the following: *In re Beckman*, 50 F.Supp. 339 (N.D.Ala.1943); *In re White*, 185 F.Supp. 609 (N.D.W.Va. 1960); *Klebanoff v. Mutual Life Insurance Co.*, 246 F.Supp. 935 (D.Conn.1965); *In re Summers*, 253 F.Supp. 113, 116 (N.D.Ind.1966), and cases there cited; *In re Lamb*, 272 F.Supp. 393, 396 (E.D.La.1967).

As stated in *In re White, supra*, 185 F.Supp. at 613: "Since the leading case of Holden v. Stratton, supra, there have been a host of cases construing statutes of various states and unanimously holding that the words 'proceeds' or 'proceeds and avails' when used in life insurance exemption statutes comprehend the protection of cash surrender values and other values built up during the life of the policies as well as the death benefits."

Although we are presently concerned only with policies in which the wife of the insured (bankrupt) is the named beneficiary, the protection afforded by G.S. § 58–206 is not limited to any particular class of beneficiaries. It relates to a policy on the life of the insured payable to any third party beneficiary. Under an Alabama statute substantially the same as G.S. § 58–206, it was held that the trustee in bankruptcy was not entitled to the cash surrender value of a policy in which the beneficiaries were the uncle and an aunt by marriage of the insured (bankrupt). *In re Beckman*, 50 F.Supp. 339 (N.D.Ala.1943). Too, under the 1927 New York statute considered in *In re Messinger*, supra, where the mother and sister of the insured (bankrupt) were the beneficiaries of policies assigned within four months of bankruptcy to a creditor of the insured, the cash surrender value ("avails") realized by the creditor assignee was held exempt from the claims of the trustee in bankruptcy. . . .

Unquestionably, under G.S. § 58–206, considered alone, the "proceeds and avails," including the cash surrender value, of a policy in which the wife is named as beneficiary, are exempt from the claims of the trustee in bankruptcy, "whether or not the right to change the beneficiary is reserved or permitted." . . .

For the reasons stated, the judgment of the court below is affirmed.

Affirmed.

WILSON v. MUTUAL BENEFICIAL LIFE INSURANCE CO.

South Carolina Supreme Court
182 S.C. 131, 188 S.E. 803 (1936)

BAKER, Justice.

This action was commenced by Robert E. Wilson, trustee in bankruptcy of Raymond Fretwell, bankrupt, against the Mutual Benefit Life Insurance Company of Newark, N. J., Raymond Fretwell, and Lila Brownlee Fretwell on April 16, 1932, for the purpose of recovering the cash surrender value of two insurance policies issued by the Mutual Benefit Life Insurance Company, on the life of the bankrupt, Raymond Fretwell, and interest from the date of the adjudication in bankruptcy of Raymond Fretwell. For brevity, the Mutual Benefit Life Insurance Company will hereinafter be referred to as the "Company."

On January 4, 1908, the Company issued to the said Raymond Fretwell an insurance policy, insuring the life of Raymond Fretwell in the sum of $3,000, made payable to the executors, administrators, or assigns of the insured, with the right to change the beneficiary reserved to the insured. . . .

On July 10, 1920, the company issued another policy to Raymond Fretwell, insuring his life in the sum of $2,000, made payable to his wife, the codefendant Lila Brownlee Fretwell, provided she survived the insured, otherwise to the executors, administrators, or assigns of the insured. The right to change the beneficiary was reserved by the insured.

Section 7985 of the Code of Laws for South Carolina 1932 provides as follows: "A policy of insurance upon the life of any person which has already been or may hereafter be taken out in which it is expressed to be for the benefit of any married woman, or of herself and her children, or of herself and children of her husband, whether procured by herself or her husband, shall enure to the use and benefits of the person or persons for whose use and benefit it is expressed to be taken out; and the sum or net amount of the insurance becoming due and payable by the terms of the policy shall be payable to the person or persons aforesaid, free and discharged from the claims of the representatives of the husband, or of any of his creditors, or any party or parties claiming by, through or under him or them or either of them; Provided, however, That if the premium paid in any one year out of the property or funds of the husband shall exceed the sum of five hundred dollars, the exemption from the claims of the creditors of the husband shall not apply to so much of said premium so paid as shall be in excess of five hundred dollars, but such excess, with the interest thereon, or so much thereof as may be necessary, shall enure to the benefit of such creditors if the same be necessary for their payment."

The Legislature has not by the slightest inference referred to the cash surrender value of an insurance policy, but it has expressly provided that the *insurance becoming due and payable* under the terms of the policy shall be payable to the parties named therein free and discharged of all claims of the insured's creditors or his personal representatives. We think that it was the intent of the Legislature to provide for an insured's widow and his or their children by securing to them *at the time of his death*, the benefits of the proceeds of insurance policies in force coming within the category provided by said section, and therefore, the statute does not apply to the facts of this case.

. . . .

NOTES

(1) "[A]lmost all states exempt the cash surrender value of policies reserving the power to change the beneficiary if that power has not been exercised for the benefit of the bankrupt. . . ." *Pearl v. Goldberg*, 300 F.2d 610, 611–612 (2d Cir. 1962). *Accord Schwartz v. Coen*, 131 F.2d 879 (2d Cir. 1942); *Cannon v. Lincoln National Life Insurance Co.*, 208 Wis. 452, 243 N.W. 320 (1932).

(2) The great number of life insurance instruments has given rise to questions about exemption for variations that resemble a current asset rather than an insurance policy. Term and straight insurance are clearly exempt, and group life insurance is often exempt as well. *See, e.g.*, Wash. Rev. Code § 48.18.420 (1984); N.Y. Ins. Law § 166(6) (McKinney 1966); Mass. Gen. Laws Ann. ch. 175 § 135 (West 1987).

One important criterion is whether the policy is vested, or whether the insured has retained the right to change the beneficiary. Although endowment policies often resemble a time deposit, there has been a tendency to hold them as exempt due to their life insurance feature. *See Slurszberg v. Prudential Insurance Co. of America*, 15 N.J. Misc. 423, 192 A. 451 (1936); *Fox v. Swartz*, 235 Minn. 337, 51 N.W.2d 80 (1952); *cf. In re Bray*, 8 F. Supp. 761 (D.N.H. 1934). *See generally* Annot., 30 A.L.R.2d 751 (1953); Riesenfeld, *Life Insurance and Creditors' Rights in the United States*, 4 U.C.L.A. L. Rev. 583 (1957). Accident and disability insurance policies cannot be treated as life insurance and need a separate exemption of their own. *See, e.g.*, Mont. Code Ann. § 33–15–513 (1987).

(3) Annuities also need a separate exemption, either explicitly or by judicial interpretation. *See In re Power*, 115 F.2d 69 (7th Cir. 1940); *In re Walsh*, 19 F. Supp. 567 (D. Minn. 1937). N.Y. Ins. Law § 3212(e), *supra*, provides that benefits due or prospectively due an annuitant who paid consideration for the annuity contract are exempt from execution; the annuitant may not be compelled to exercise any power in the contract; and that creditors may not interfere with or terminate the annuity contract. There are exceptions for (a) transfers with actual intent to hinder,

delay or defraud creditors, and (b) when the court orders the annuitant to pay to a judgment creditor such portion of the benefits as appears just and proper. The Revised Code of Washington has a very similar exemption for annuities with two important and different limitations. Firstly, the total exemption that any one person can claim under all annuities to be paid him is $250 per month. Above this level, annuity payments are subject to garnishment as if they were wages. Also, a court may order the annuitant to pay to judgment creditors any portion of the excess over $250 as "may appear just and proper, after due regard for the reasonable requirements of the judgment debtor and his family." Wash. Rev. Code Ann. § 48.18.430(b), (c) (1984). Secondly, any payments or premiums made "with intent to defraud creditors" are not exempted. Wash. Rev. Code Ann. § 48.18.430(a), *supra. See generally* Mass. Gen. Laws Ann. ch. 175 §§ 119A, 132C (West 1987); Mont. Code Ann. § 33–15–514 (1987); Annot., 169 A.L.R. 1360 (1947).

(4) In *In re Driscoll*, 142 F. Supp. 300 (S.D. Cal. 1956), a debtor completely paid off his insurance policy two weeks before filing a bankruptcy petition. The court allowed an exemption for the entire policy, finding neither fraud nor bad faith.

(5) On insurance and exemptions, *see generally* Annot., 63 A.L.R. 1286 (1929); Annot., 68 A.L.R. 1215 (1930); 103 A.L.R. 239 (1936); Fraenkel, *Creditors' Rights in Life Insurance*, 4 Fordham L. Rev. 39 (1935); Note, *Creditors' Rights in Insurance Policies During the Life of the Insured*, 84 U. Pa. L. Rev. 236 (1935); Cohen, *Exemption of Property Purchased with Exempt Funds*, 27 Va. L. Rev. 573 (1941); Faris, *Exemption of Insurance and Other Property in the Virginias and Carolinas*, 17 Wash. & Lee L. Rev. 19 (1960).

NOTE ON CONVERSION OF NON–EXEMPT PROPERTY TO EXEMPT PROPERTY

Exempt property is, by definition, not available to creditors. Accordingly, a transfer of exempt property cannot be voidable under the fraudulent transfer laws. *See, e.g., Phillips v. C. Palomo & Sons*, 270 F.2d 791 (5th Cir. 1959).

What happens when, during the pendency of suit or on the eve of bankruptcy, a debtor converts non–exempt property (*e.g.*, cash) into exempt property (*e.g.*, insurance policies exempt under state law). *Bank of Pennsylvania v. Adlman*, (*In re Adlman*), 541 F.2d 999 (2d Cir. 1976), is a good case in point. There, the court confirmed the general rule that the debtor's exchange, on the eve of bankruptcy, of non–exempt property for exempt property, is not, *per se*, a fraudulent transfer, absent extrinsic evidence of fraud. The housewife debtor in *Adlman* had guaranteed her husband's debts. The husband's financial condition deteriorated in 1973 and, on October 12, 1973, the wife sold the family home, to which she held title exclusively, to her husband's relatives for the sum of $125,000, subject to a first mortgage. The debtor realized approximately $60,000 from the sale.

The debtor also owned insurance policies on the lives of her husband and her father, and was the beneficiary under these policies. Under the New York Insurance

Law, these policies are exempt from the claims of creditors. Shortly before and simultaneously with the actual transfer of her house, the debtor drew checks on her checking account to pay approximately $52,000 on a loan outstanding against her insurance policies, and to pay $7,600 in premiums on these policies. Less than six months later, the debtor and her husband filed bankruptcy petitions. She claimed the life insurance policies, with a face value of $275,000, as exempt.

An objecting creditor argued, among other things, that the debtor in *Adlman* had sold her house, repaid the loans on her life insurance policies, and prepaid the insurance premiums with actual intent to hinder, delay or defraud creditors; and that the debtor had engaged in these transactions for the purpose of removing non–exempt assets from the reach of her creditors. The bankruptcy court agreed, but made no finding of extrinsic facts to support the conclusion that there was an *actual* intent to defraud creditors, apparently reasoning that merely by placing non–exempt funds into an exempt category constituted sufficient evidence of such intent. In reversing, the Second Circuit held that the bankruptcy judge was in error: "Absent convincing evidence of extrinsic fraud, it was incorrect as a matter of law for the Bankruptcy Judge to conclude that [the debtor] had actual intent to defraud her creditors." 541 F.2d at 1005.

What type of "extrinsic evidence" is needed to show actual fraud? In one case, the debtor bought merchandise on credit immediately prior to bankruptcy, and used the sale proceeds of the merchandise to buy exempt homestead property, rather than pay his suppliers. The Eighth Circuit denied the debtor's claim to a homestead exemption on those facts in *Kangas v. Robie*, 264 F. 92 (8th Cir. 1920). *See also Wudrick v. Clements*, 451 F.2d 988, 990 (9th Cir. 1971) ("A different case would be presented if on the eve of bankruptcy a debt were created with no intention of repaying the creditor, either by purchasing goods on credit or borrowing money without security."); *Hanson v. First Nat'l. Bank in Brookings*, 848 F.2d 866, 869 (8th Cir. 1988) (debtors' prebankruptcy sale of non–exempt assets to family members for fair market value and use of proceeds to buy exempt life insurance policies and to prepay homestead real estate mortgage, after obtaining legal advice, *held* not fraudulent because of lack of extrinsic evidence showing requisite intent); *Norwest Bank Nebraska, N.A. v. Tveten*, 848 F.2d 871 (8th Cir. 1988) (2–1) (physician debtor's discharge denied when he claimed exempt status for $700,000 worth of property and additional exemption for proceeds of life insurance policies; debtor's avowed purpose found to be placing assets beyond creditors' reach); *EFA Acceptance Corp. v. Cadarette (In re Cadarette)*, 601 F.2d 648, 650 (2d Cir. 1979) (discharge denied when debtor, whose business was on verge of collapse, transferred title to expensive car, boat and trailer, for no consideration, to fiancee within three weeks of bankruptcy; debtor–transferor continued to pay service charges on car and use car after transfer). Note, "Purchase of Homestead as Fraud on Creditors" 161 A.L.R. 1287 (1946); *Turnbaugh v. Santos*, 146 F.2d 168 (9th Cir. 1944) (debtor's insolvency at time of transfer held immaterial, and homestead exemption allowed), cited with approval in *In re Dudley*, 72 F. Supp. 943 (S.D. Cal. 1947), *aff'd sub nom. Goggin v. Dudley*, 166 F.2d 1023 (9th Cir. 1948).

Can it not be argued that exemption laws are legalized frauds on creditors? Or is there a public policy permitting debtors to keep certain essential property despite the frustration of their creditor's claims? *See Legislative History of Bankruptcy Reform Act of 1978*, H.R. Rep. No. 95–595, 95th Cong., 1st Sess. 360–1 (1977) ("As under current law, the debtor will be permitted to convert non–exempted property into exempt property before filing a bankruptcy petition. *See Hearings*, pt. 3, at 1355–58. The practice is not fraudulent as to creditors, and permits the debtor to make full use of the exemptions to which he is entitled under the law."). As the *Adlman* case shows, the debtor will usually not lose an exemption merely because he or she takes advantage of state exemption laws when financial troubles are already far advanced. To deprive the debtor of an exemption, the unpaid creditor will need a persuasive set of facts, or as the Second Circuit held in *Adlman, supra,* "extrinsic evidence" to support a finding of actual intent to hinder, delay or defraud creditors.

Statutes governing insurance exemptions have created a large body of case law and commentary. Although the statutes tend to preserve to creditors the right to recover premiums paid in fraud of creditors, the defrauded creditors still have a hard time proving actual fraud. *See generally*, McLaughlin, *Application of the Uniform Fraudulent Conveyance*, 46 Harv. L. Rev. 404, 417 (1933); Cohen, *Execution Process and Life Insurance*, 39 Colum. L. Rev. 139 (1939); Cohen, *Creditors' Rights to Insurance Proceeds*, 40 Colum. L. Rev. 975 (1940). In *Doethlaff v. Penn Mutual Life Insurance Co.*, 117 F.2d 582 (6th Cir.), *cert. denied sub nom. Gardner v. Doethlaff*, 313 U.S. 579 (1941), the court held that the payment of life insurance premiums by an insolvent debtor did not constitute a fraud on creditors. Similarly, in *Schwartz v. Seldon*, 153 F.2d 334, 336 (2d Cir. 1945), the court upheld the exemption of a life insurance policy on the assumption that the debtor himself had paid off loans on the policy while insolvent, reasoning that "the policy would not lose its exempt character unless the payment constituted a transfer made with 'actual intent' to defraud creditors. . . ."

§ 7.06   Immune Assets

Assets in which the debtor has an interest, but over which he or she has no control, are often immune from claims of creditors or the trustee in bankruptcy. They include those in which the debtor's interest is so remote (*i.e.*, contingent) as to be inalienable, and funds held in trust for the debtor that are inalienable, either by statute or by the governing document.

MORRISSEY v. NATIONAL MARITIME UNION

United States District Court, Southern District of New York
357 F. Supp. 659 (1975)

The Amalgamated Bank of New York ("the Bank") moves for an order pursuant to Rule 69, Fed. R. Civ. P., instructing the Bank with regard to two Writs of Execution and Levies served upon it and discharging the Bank from all liability which might arise after its compliance with the Court's mandate. The Bank is directed to remit to the United States Marshal sums on deposit in the name of Charles Snow ("Snow") and Charles and Dorothy Snow and the monthly payments of trust income currently paid Joseph Curran ("Curran") pursuant to the National Maritime Union Officers' Pension Fund.

Plaintiff James M. Morrissey obtained a judgment against Snow and Curran, among others, in this Court on July 15, 1975. On July 30, 1975, the Bank was served with Writs of Execution and Levies upon the goods and chattels of the judgment debtors.

The Bank holds a savings account in the name of Charles Snow or Dorothy Snow with a balance of $4,345.69 and a checking account in the name of Charles Snow containing $20.11. Snow claims that the funds in the savings account belong to his wife.

In addition, the Bank is trustee of the trust fund of the National Maritime Union Officers' Pension Fund and in that capacity remits a monthly payment of $4,641.03 to Curran, which Curran asserts is exempt from execution.

The applicable portion of Rule 69, Fed. R. Civ. P., under which the Bank moves, reads:

> Process to enforce a judgment for the payment of money shall be a writ of execution, unless the court directs otherwise. The procedure on execution, in proceedings supplementary to and in aid of a judgment, and in proceedings on and in aid of execution shall be in accordance with the practice and procedure of the state in which the district court is held, existing at the time the remedy is sought, except that any statute of the United States governs to the extent that it is applicable.

Thus, the Court must look to New York law to determine the appropriate practices and procedures governing execution of the judgment. N.Y.C.P.L.R. § 5205(d) and (e) (McKinney 1963) states:

> (d) Trust exemption. Any property while held in trust for a judgment debtor, where the trust has been created by, or the fund so held in trust has proceeded from, a person other than the judgment debtor, is exempt from application to the satisfaction of a money judgment.

> (e) Income exemptions. The following personal property is exempt from application to the satisfaction of a money judgment, except such part as a court determines to be unnecessary for the reasonable requirements of the judgment debtor and his dependents:

> 1. ninety per cent of the income or other payments from a trust the principal of which is exempt under subdivision (d);

> 2. ninety per cent of the earnings of the judgment debtor for his personal services rendered within sixty days before, and at any time after, an income execution is delivered to the sheriff or a motion is made to secure the application of the judgment debtor's earnings to the satisfaction of the judgment; and

> 3. payments pursuant to an award in a matrimonial action, for the support of a wife, where the wife is the judgment debtor, or for the support of a child, where the child is the judgment debtor; where

the award was made by a court of the state, determination of the extent to which it is unnecessary shall be made by that court.

The Court must determine whether and to what extent the assets of Curran and Snow held by the Bank are reachable by the judgment creditor Morrissey.

C.P.L.R. § 5205(d) appears to insulate the trust principal from invasion by the judgment creditor. Under subsection (e), however, at least 10% of the income from a trust can be reached. The remaining 90% is exempt if necessary for "the reasonable requirements of the judgment debtor and his dependents." The question of necessity is to be determined by the Court.

As stated in *In re Dolard*, 275 F. Supp. 1001, 1005 (C.D. Cal. 1967):

> I must construe § 5205 as more than an exemption statute and as having the effect of prohibiting levy upon 90% of income from a New York trust unless there is finding that some portion of the 90% is not necessary for the beneficiary and his dependents.

The judgment creditor is obliged to show some facts to aid the Court in its decision, but, "the burden of showing 'necessity' rests upon the judgment debtor." *Dickens v. Director of Finance*, 45 Misc. 2d 882, 883, 258 N.Y.S.2d 211, 212 (Sup. Ct. N.Y. Co. 1965). *See also, In re Dolard, supra* at 1006; 6 J. Weinstein, H. Korn, A. Miller, New York Civil Practice § 5205.24 (1974).

Curran has failed to sustain his burden of showing that the sums the judgment creditor seeks to reach are necessary for himself or his dependents. Therefore, 100% of the trust income is reachable.

The income exemption of C.P.L.R. § 5205(e)(2) applies to "ninety per cent of the earnings of the judgment debtor for his personal services rendered within sixty days before and at any time after, an income execution. . . ." The applicability of the exemption to Snow's bank account hinges upon whether or not the funds on deposit represent earnings for personal services rendered within sixty days prior to income execution. The affidavit of Snow's attorney urges that they are and cites as authority *Power v. Loonam*, 49 Misc. 2d 127, 266 N.Y.S.2d 865 (Sup. Ct. Nassau Co. 1966). In that case, however, the judgment debtor's wife swore that the account contained her husband's salary earned for their living expenses while the couple's attorney stated that the salary check was deposited on the date of the service of the creditor's restraining order. Even with these facts present, the court commented:

> It is unfortunate that there was a paucity of proof presented in this case. Nevertheless, on the facts before it, the court finds that the fund does represent earnings of the husband and, accordingly, the restraining notice should be vacated at least as to the amount which is exempt under statute. [citation omitted] 49 Misc. 2d at 129, 266 N.Y.S.2d at 867.

Here, the Court is presented with no more than the conclusory statements of Snow's attorney. In the absence of adequate proof that the funds in the Snows' joint account consist of earnings for personal services rendered within 60 days of the execution, the 90% exemption does not apply.

New York Banking Law § 675 (McKinney 1971) provides that:

(a) When a deposit of cash, securities, or other property has been made or shall hereafter be made in or with any banking organization or foreign banking corporation transacting business in this state, or shares shall have been already issued or shall be hereafter issued, in any savings and loan association or credit union transacting business in this state, in the name of such depositor or shareholder and another person, and in form to be paid or delivered to either, or the survivor of them, such deposit or shares and any additions thereto made, by either of such persons, after the making thereof, shall become the property of such persons as joint tenants and the same, together with all additions and accruals thereon, shall be held for the exclusive use of the persons so named, and may be paid or delivered to either during the lifetime of both or to the survivor after the death of one of them.

As the Appellate Division, 2d Department observed in *Lambert v. Lambert*, 42 App. Div. 2d 903, 347 N.Y.S.2d463, 464–65 (2d Dep't 1973):

When a husband opens a joint bank account in the names of himself and his wife, with a right of survivorship, it is presumed that he intends a joint tenancy with his wife and that she thereby receives a present gift of a moiety or one half of the value of the property on deposit (*Matter of Granwell*, 20 N.Y.2d 91; *Matter of Bricker [Krimer] v. Krimer*, 13 N.Y.2d 22, 27–28; Banking Law, § 675). The presumption that a joint tenancy was intended, however, is merely a rebuttable presumption as to funds withdrawn prior to the death of the depositor (*Matter of Bricker [Krimer] v. Krimer, supra*, p. 27; *Matter of Porianda*, 256 N.Y. 423; *Pendley v. Pendley*, 163 Misc. 571, 574). "For the depositors themselves, the form [of the account] is not conclusive in any contest during their joint lives as to the title to the moneys, nor conclusive after the death of either as to moneys then withdrawn" (*Moskowitz v. Marrow*, 251 N.Y. 380, 396–397).

The matter of Mrs. Snow's right of survivorship in the joint account is irrelevant; at issue is a judgment creditor's power to reach jointly held funds deposited in the names of his debtor and another.

The majority of states permit a creditor to reach some portion of funds on deposit in a joint account. *See* Annot. 11 ALR 3d 1465 (1967). New York is no exception. *Denton v. Grumbach*, 2 App. Div. 2d 420, 157 N.Y.S.2d 91 (3d Dep't 1956). The burden is on the depositors to indicate the proportionate interests represented by the account. *Olshan v. East New York Savings Bank*, 28 F. Supp. 727 (E.D.N.Y. 1939); *Denton v. Grumbach, supra*.

[I]f personal property, including bank accounts, is taken in the names of a husband and wife, and it is established that the husband's sole money was used, then, in the absence of proof of a different intent declared at the time of the execution, the wife merely has a right to succeed by survivorship and during the husband's life, he retains complete ownership, control and right of disposition and the wife has no interest therein enforceable against him.

Glass v. Glass, 35 Misc. 2d 665, 666–667, 231 N.Y.S.2d 327, 330 (Sup. Ct. Queens Co. 1962).

The source of the Snow's account is solely Snow himself. Merely by placing his assets in an account which also bears his wife's name and from which he may withdraw at will, Snow may not be permitted to insulate himself from a judgment creditor. The entire amount on deposit in the Snow's joint account is to be paid to the United States Marshal.

As regards the Bank's desire to be discharged from liability in the event it pays money under its control to the Marshal, N.Y.C.P.L.R. § 5209 (McKinney 1963) provides:

> A person who, pursuant to an execution or order, pays or delivers, to the judgment creditor or a sheriff or receiver, money or other personal property in which a judgment debtor has or will have an interest, or so pays a debt he owes the judgment debtor, is discharged from his obligation to the judgment debtor to the extent of the payment or delivery.

Interpleader is available to protect the Bank from liability to interested third parties.

On the applicable law and the facts as presented, the Court directs that the Amalgamated Bank of New York remit to the United States Marshal for the Southern District of New York all trust income payable to Joseph Curran pursuant to the National Maritime Union Officers' Pension Fund and all sums on deposit in the name of Charles Snow and Charles and Dorothy Snow in accordance with the Writs of Execution and Levies served on the Bank on July 30, 1975.

It is so ordered.

ADAMS v. DUGAN

Oklahoma Supreme Court
196 Okla. 156, 163 P.2d 227 (1945)

WELCH, Justice.

This action was brought to enjoin the sale of land under execution. The trial court sustained demurrer to plaintiff's petition. The petition alleged that plaintiff is the qualified and acting executor of the estate of Walter Barr Steedman, deceased, and is also the testamentary trustee of the real property under a trust thereof established by the will of such decedent. A copy of the will to which reference was made was attached to the petition.

. . . .

It is obvious from the terms of the will that the legal title to the land is vested in plaintiff, Mack B. Adams, and that there is thereby created an active trust. 60 O.S.A. § 144, and *Hill v. Hill*, 49 Okl. 424, 152 P. 1122. The trustee is given full power of sale. That holds true as to any portion of the real estate remaining even though the widow might elect to take under the statutes of descent and distribution.

The will does not provide that George Steedman shall receive any part or portion of the specific real estate described in the return of levy. The levy is sought to be made upon the real estate. The will vests title thereto in plaintiff Adams as trustee. George Steedman can never own an interest in that specific property except, first, the same is not sold by the trustee, and, second, that said George Steedman be living at the end of the trust period. In view of those contingencies it is little more than mere speculation to assume or anticipate that he will ever receive any part or interest in the specific realty. As to George Steedman's present interest in this land it is but little more if any than a mere contingent expectancy. At best then, George Steedman can be classed only as a contingent remainderman.

The great weight of authority is to the effect that such contingent interest is not subject to levy and sale under execution.

In discussing the rule in 23 C.J., pages 335 and 336, the notes to the text state one of the sound reasons for the rule as follows: "The reason given is that such a policy would encourage gambling and speculation and that the purchasers at such sales would not put a high estimate on the possibility of the defendant in execution afterward acquiring any interest in the land and that the danger of sacrifice is a strong reason for not subjecting contingent interests to sale under execution. *Plumlee v. Bounds*, 118 Ark. 274, 176 S.W. 140. To same effect *Kenwood Trust, etc., Bank v. Palmer*, 209 Ill.App. 370."

In 33 C.J.S., Executions, page 169, subsec. d of § 36, under executory devises, it is stated: " . . . However, such a devise subject to a condition which makes the estate wholly contingent and a mere possibility cannot be reached on execution."

The case of *Crum v. Crum*, 65 Ohio App. 431, 30 N.E.2d 448, supports the statement and is quite similar in facts to the present case. We quote paragraph 3 of the syllabus of the Crum case as follows: "Where such will contains the further provision that 'if any of my said children be not living at the time of the final distribution of my estate, then their share shall pass to their heirs who are of my blood, and if all the children of any one of my said sons be deceased at the time of the final distribution of my estate, the wife of such deceased son, should she then be living, shall inherit the one–fifth share of such said deceased son, the remaining four–fifths to revert to the residue of my estate,' the interest of the children of testator is contingent upon surviving the wife of testator and is not subject to levy and sale on execution."

A statement helpful in many respects herein is found in 33 C.J.S., Executions, page 175, a part of subsec. c of § 41, as follows: " . . . Under many of the statutes, the rule is laid down that where the legal title is vested in the trustee under a passive, simple, or dry trust, with no duty except to convey to the person ultimately entitled, the interest of the cestui que trust is subject to seizure and sale under execution; but where the land is held by the trustee under an active trust, requiring the continuance of the legal title in him to enable him to perform his duties, the equitable estate is not subject to execution. It is also the generally accepted doctrine in the United States, in construing statutes based on 29 Car. II, that in order to subject the equitable estate of a cestui que trust to execution at law, the trust must be clear and simple, and for the benefit of the debtor alone, and that equitable interests held jointly with another person are not subject to sale under execution."

In *Home Bank of Lexington v. Fox*, 113 S.C. 378, 102 S.E. 643, this syllabus rule is stated: "Execution cannot be levied on a contingent interest of the debtor under a testamentary trust." *See also San Diego Trust, etc., v. Heustis*, 121 Cal.App. 675, 10 P.2d 158; *B. F. Goodrich Co. v. Thrash*, 15 Wash.2d 624, 131 P.2d 734.

We are in accord with the statement in 33 C.J.S., Executions, page 167, § 36, to the effect that the general rule is that all possible interests in land, contingent or otherwise, which are real and substantial are subject to seizure and sale on execution and that generally if the interest is assignable it is subject to execution. Where the contingencies are such, however, as to render the interest in the specific property a mere remote possibility the difficulty in determining the value of the interest for sale upon execution gives strong practical and legal reasons for denial of the right to so levy. Especially so where sacrifice of the judgment debtor's expectancy is probably without substantial benefit to the judgment creditor.

Under the facts here the value to be placed upon the contingent interest of George Steedman in this real estate can be nothing more than speculation and the benefits to be gained by the judgment creditor are equally so. We conclude that the legal title of the trustee who must retain the same in the full performance of his active trust should not be subjected to the cloud of such an effort to sell under execution.

The judgment is reversed, and the cause remanded, with directions to overrule defendant's demurrer to plaintiff's petition, and to proceed consistent with the views herein expressed.

GIBSON, C. J., and OSBORN, BAYLESS, DAVISON, and ARNOLD, JJ., concur.

HURST, V. C. J., dissents.

JUDSON v. WITLIN
(In re Witlin)

United States Court of Appeals, Fifth Circuit
640 F.2d 661 (1981)

TUTTLE, Circuit Judge:

The bankrupt appeals from the denial by the bankruptcy judge, affirmed by the district court, of his claim that three qualified trusts under the Keogh plan are exempt from the claims of his creditors.

The parties do not dispute the facts. The bankrupt was a doctor who was self–employed who had contributed sums totalling $13,481 to his own retirement plan. Each of the plans contained a Keogh plan statutory trust which provided that the benefits of the trust might not be assigned nor alienated. This provision stated:

> The benefits provided hereunder shall not be subject to alienation, assignment, garnishment, attachment, execution or levy of any kind, and any attempts to cause such benefits to be so subjected shall not be recognized except to such extent as may be required by law.

The funds were intact, no benefits having been drawn from them by the beneficiary up to the date of bankruptcy.

The bankruptcy judge concluded that the spendthrift trust provisions would have protected an employee bankrupt if he had been employed by a person other than himself, but that since the employee was also the employer, nothing in the spendthrift trust provisions protecting the employee provided any protection for the bankrupt as settlor of the trust and that it was as employer that the trustee in bankruptcy resisted the claim that the funds should be exempt. This judgment of the bankruptcy judge was affirmed by the trial court and this appeal followed.

Appellant's argument is based primarily upon what he claims to have been the policy of Congress in setting up the Keogh retirement plans—that is, that Congress established a policy to assist professional persons and others who are self–employed to ameliorate the conditions in their senior years by having protected retirement funds available for their use.

The trustee, on the other hand, contends that the spendthrift trust created by a settlor for himself as *c'estui* or beneficiary is void as against the settlor's creditors. He points to the fact that under these plans, either the settlor or the beneficiary, they being of course the same person, could withdraw these funds and thus become subject only to a tax penalty because the plans would thus no longer be qualified under the Internal Revenue laws.

This Court has held that where no other provision is contained in a federal statute dealing with exemptions, state law governs under Section 6 of the Bankruptcy Act:

> Under the Bankruptcy Act, exemptions allowed by state law are preserved in bankruptcy for the residents of respective states. 11 U.S.C.A. § 24. State laws creating exemptions control as to the kind and amount of property which is exempt. 1 Collier, Bankruptcy, Section 6.13 at 861–63 (14 ed. 1969). In applying the exemption laws of a state the Federal Courts follow the construction placed thereon by the courts of the state. *Phillips v. C. Palomo & Sons*, 270 F.2d 791 (5th Cir. 1959).

Williams v. Wirt, 423 F.2d 761 (5th Cir. 1970).

The plans with which we are concerned created what has been recognized in Florida as a spendthrift trust:

> A spendthrift trust is one that is created with the view of providing a fund for the maintenance of another, and at the same time securing it against his own improvidence or incapacity for self protection. *Croom v. Ocala Plumbing & Electric Co.*, 62 Fla. 460, 57 So. 243. The typical spendthrift trust is one in which the life cestui's right to recover income is inalienable, either by his own act or that of his creditors, during all or a part of the life of the beneficiary. *See* Bogert, Trusts and Trustees, V.J. Sec. 222, p. 715; Griswold, Spendthrift Trusts, Sec. 1, p. 3; Scott on Trust, V. 1, Sec. 152, p. 744.

Waterbury v. Munn, 159 Fla. 754, 32 So.2d 603 at 605.

While the parties cite no Florida cases for the proposition, we are satisfied that under the common law of trusts, the law is as stated by Professor Bogert in the same work which was cited in *Waterbury:*

> If a settlor creates a trust for his own benefits and inserts a spendthrift clause, it is void as far as then existing or future creditors are concerned, and they can reach his interests under the trust. Bogert, Trusts and Trustees, 2d ed. § 223, pp. 438, 439.

There is, of course, a strong public policy that will prevent any person from placing his property in what amounts to a revocable trust for his own benefit which would be exempt from the claims of his creditors. Many states have enacted statutes which give effect to this policy. *See* fn. to text, Bogert at pp. 438–439. We find no Congressional policy that would counter the common law principle. If Congress had intended such Keogh plans to be exempt from attachment for the debts of the employer–settlor, it could easily have said so. *Cf.* 38 U.S.C. § 3101(a) which states that certain veterans' benefits "shall be exempt from the claims of creditors."

We are satisfied that the bankruptcy court correctly held these Keogh funds to be property which passed to the trustee and that they were not exempt under any provisions of the bankruptcy laws.

The judgment is AFFIRMED.

PLANNED CONSUMER MARKETING, INC. v. COATS AND CLARK, INC.

New York Court of Appeals
71 N.Y.2d 442, 522 N.E.2d 30, 527 N.Y.S.2d 185 (1988)

ALEXANDER, Judge.

The Employee Retirement Income Security Act (ERISA) (29 U.S.C. § 1001 *et seq.*) mandates that all State laws, insofar as they relate to employee benefit plans, are superseded (29 U.S.C. § 1144[a]) and that benefits provided by an employee benefit plan qualified under the act may not be assigned or alienated (29 U.S.C. § 1056[d][1]). The question presented is whether these provisions preclude a judgment creditor from proceeding in State court for a turnover of funds deposited into a qualified ERISA plan allegedly in violation of State laws prohibiting fraudulent conveyances (*see*, Debtor and Creditor Law §§ 273, 273–a, 274, 276; Business Corporation Law §§ 510, 719; EPTL 7–3.1). We conclude that ERISA does not preempt vindication of these State laws whose purpose is to inhibit the transfer of money in defraud of creditors, not to assess or regulate employee benefit plans.

I.

Planned Consumer Marketing, Inc. (PCM), was incorporated in 1972 by Edwin Lee and his brother as a joint venture. In 1973 and 1974 PCM entered into two contracts with Coats and Clark, Inc. (C & C), agreeing to promote that company's products. When C & C refused to pay the full amount due under the contracts, PCM sued for breach; C & C, alleging inadequate performance, counterclaimed for recovery of money already received. At trial, C & C prevailed on its counterclaim and judgment was entered in 1981 in the amount of $72,838.75.[1] PCM failed to satisfy the judgment, claiming to have had no employees and not to have conducted any business since 1977 or 1978. C & C subsequently discovered, however, that PCM — by Edwin Lee, its president — had deposited various sums of money into accounts at Dry Dock Savings Bank and Dollar Savings Bank (since merged) amounting to over $200,000 in the name of Planned Consumer Marketing Profit Sharing Plan (Plan). The Plan had been established in 1974, and qualified by the Internal Revenue Service as an employee benefit fund under the Employee Retirement Income Security Act of 1974 (29 U.S.C. § 1001 *et seq.*). The beneficiaries under the Plan were identified as Edwin Lee, Lee's brother and Lee's secretary; Edwin Lee and his brother were the trustees.

C & C commenced a special proceeding pursuant to CPLR article 52, seeking to have both banks turn over the funds out of which C & C might satisfy the judgment against PCM.[2] The petition contains nine causes of action alleging, among other things, that PCM created and contributed to the Plan during the period PCM was purportedly inoperative in order to defraud C & C in violation of various provisions of the Debtor and Creditor Law (§§ 510, 719) and EPTL (7–3.1), and that Edwin Lee operated PCM and the Plan for his personal benefit. PCM and Lee moved to dismiss the proceeding on the ground that Supreme Court lacks subject matter jurisdiction over the Plan insofar as ERISA preempts State laws that relate to employee benefit plans, and, in any event, precludes the alienation of assets in a trust regulated by that act.

Supreme Court denied the motion, concluding that the gist of the petition was the violation of State fraud laws, not provisions of ERISA. The Appellate Division modified by dismissing the first two causes of action as relating solely to issues regulated by ERISA,[3] striking the relief requested in the seventh and eighth causes

---

[1] With continuing accrual of postjudgment interest, the amount has surpassed $100,000.

[2] CPLR 5225(b) provides in relevant part: "Upon a special proceeding commenced by the judgment creditor, against a person in possession or custody of money . . . in which the judgment debtor has an interest, or against a person who is a transferee of money . . . from the judgment debtor, where it is shown that the judgment debtor is entitled to the possession of such property or that the judgment creditor's rights to the property are superior to those of the transferee, the court shall require such person to pay the money, or so much of it as is sufficient to satisfy the judgment". Similarly, CPLR 5227 provides for the same proceeding for recovery of a debt owed the judgment debtor (*see*, Siegel, Practice Commentaries, McKinney's Cons. Laws of N.Y., Book 7B, CPLR C5227:3, at 287).

[3] The first cause of action alleged that the Plan did not exist as a legal entity because there was no written indenture of trust. PCM produced the document, however, and that claim was dismissed as moot, or in the alternative as preempted by ERISA. The second cause of action

of action as improperly seeking to reach ERISA funds,[4] and finding ERISA did not preempt the third, fourth, fifth, sixth and ninth causes of action.[5] The court held that these claims were not preempted by ERISA because "Congress never intended that ERISA be invoked to shield the use of an employee benefit plan as an instrumentality of fraud to defeat the rights of creditors" (127 A.D.2d 355, 370, 513 N.Y.S.2d 417). The appeal is before this court by leave of the Appellate Division, certifying the following question: "Was the order of this Court, which modified the order of the Supreme Court, properly made?" For the reasons that follow, we affirm the order of the Appellate Division and answer the question certified in the affirmative.

II.

A.

After careful study of the inequities and inconsistencies plaguing private retirement pension programs, Congress enacted ERISA in 1974 to protect "the interests of participants in employee benefit plans and their beneficiaries" (29 U.S.C. § 1001[b]; *Shaw v. Delta Air Lines*, 463 U.S. 85, 90–91, 103 S.Ct. 2890, 2896–2897, 77 L.Ed.2d 490; *Sasso v. Vachris*, 66 N.Y.2d 28, 31, 494 N.Y.S.2d 856, 484 N.E.2d 1359). As described by the United States Supreme Court, ERISA is "a 'comprehensive and reticulated statute' . . . adopted . . . to ensure that 'if a worker has been promised a defined pension benefit upon retirement — and if he has fulfilled whatever conditions are required to obtain a vested benefit . . . he actually receives it' " (*Alessi v. Raybestos–Manhattan, Inc.*, 451 U.S. 504, 510, 101 S.Ct. 1895, 1899, 68 L.Ed.2d 402, quoting *Nachman Corp. v. Pension Benefit Guar. Corp.*, 446 U.S. 359, 361, 375, 100 S.Ct. 1723, 1726, 1733, 64 L.Ed.2d 354). In furtherance of these purposes, ERISA prescribes requirements for reporting and disclosure of financial information, authorizes certain methods of funding and vesting of benefits, and establishes standards of conduct and responsibility for the fiduciaries of employee benefit plans (29 U.S.C. §§ 1021–1114).

To assure uniformity in the creation and administration of these plans, Congress eliminated the potential for conflicting or inconsistent State regulation by including

---

alleged that the Plan was not a legal entity because Lee engaged in activities in contravention of the terms of the Plan, which claims, the Appellate Division held, are preempted by ERISA.

[4] The seventh and eighth causes of action allege the unlawful transfer of corporate assets in violation of Debtor and Creditor Law and Business Corporation Law, but do not allege the fraudulent transfer of assets into the Plan itself. Thus, to the extent that the wrongs alleged in these claims do not implicate the validity of transfers to the ERISA plan, the Plan's funds, the Appellate Division held, are beyond the reach of creditors under these claims (*Helmsley–Spear, Inc. v. Winter*, 74 A.D.2d 195, 426 N.Y.S.2d 778, *aff'd*. 52 N.Y.2d 984, 438 N.Y.S.2d 79, 419 N.E.2d 1078).

[5] The Appellate Division interpreted the sixth cause of action as having stated a claim pursuant to Business Corporation Law §§ 510 and 719, which provide remedies for enforcement of a director's liability exclusively to the corporation, not to the creditors of the corporation. The count was dismissed with leave to renew, however, under Business Corporation Law § 720, which authorizes an action, by a judgment creditor, to set aside unlawful conveyances. Insofar as PCM is aggrieved by the dismissal with leave to replead, we address the challenge to the subject matter jurisdiction of that cause of action as well.

a supersedure clause, stating that ERISA "shall supersede any and all State laws insofar as they may now or hereafter relate to any employee benefit plan"(29 U.S.C. § 1144[a]; *see generally*, Hutchinson & Ifshin, *Federal Preemption of State Law Under the Employee Retirement Income Security Act of 1974*, 46 U.Chi.L.Rev. 23 [1978]).[6] This preemption clause has been described as "virtually unique" in its breadth and scope (*Franchise Tax Bd. v. Laborers Vacation Trust*, 463 U.S. 1, 24, n. 26, 103 S.Ct. 2841, 2854, n. 26, 77 L.Ed.2d 420). The language, "relate to", is to be interpreted broadly (*Shaw v. Delta Air Lines*, 463 U.S. 85, 96–97, 103 S.Ct. 2890, 2899–2900, *supra*), and the statute itself defines the term "State" for purposes of preemption as "a State, any political subdivisions thereof, or any agency or instrumentality of either, which purports to regulate, *directly or indirectly*, the terms and conditions of employee benefit plans" (29 U.S.C. § 1144[c][2] [emphasis added]). Hence, ERISA "preclude[s] the States from avoiding through form the substance of preemption provision" (*Alessi v. Raybestos–Manhattan, Inc.*, 451 U.S. 504, 525, 101 S.Ct. 1895, 1907, *supra*).

Relying on these principles, and on our decision in *Retail Shoe Health Commn. v. Reminick*, 62 N.Y.2d 173, 476 N.Y.S.2d 276, 464 N.E.2d 974, *cert. denied sub nom. Reminick v. Maltz*, 471 U.S. 1022, 105 S.Ct. 2034, 85 L.Ed.2d 316, PCM and Edwin Lee, individually, challenge the finding of subject matter jurisdiction over the third, fourth, fifth, sixth and ninth causes of action, arguing that application of the State Debtor and Creditor Law, the Business Corporation Law, and EPTL to funds deposited into a trust regulated by ERISA is expressly preempted by that act.

In *Retail Shoe*, an ERISA plan brought an action in State court against its accountants for alleged negligence in failing to detect and report the misappropriation of fund assets. The accountants subsequently asserted third–party claims against the individual trustees for contribution or indemnity based on allegations that they contributed to the losses sustained by the plan due to breaches of their fiduciary duties as ERISA trustees (*Retail Shoe Health Commn. v. Reminick*, 62 N.Y.2d 173, 176, 476 N.Y.S.2d 276, 464 N.E.2d 974, *supra*). We held that State courts were foreclosed from entertaining the claims against the trustees. The gravamen of the claims over, we said, was liability due to breaches of fiduciary duties established by ERISA. "It is substantive claims of just this character that fall squarely within the scope and thus the pre–emption of ERISA" (*Retail Shoe Health Commn. v. Reminick*, 62 N.Y.2d 173, 178, 476 N.Y.S.2d 276, 464 N.E.2d 974, *supra*). Insofar as the act (29 U.S.C. § 1132) provides that the District Courts of the United States shall have exclusive jurisdiction over civil actions arising under ERISA (with certain exceptions not relevant), the claims against the individual trustees could not be entertained in State court.

The exercise of Federal supremacy, however, is not lightly presumed (*Alessi v. Raybestos–Manhattan, Inc.*, 451 U.S. 504, 522, 101 S.Ct. 1895, 1905, 68 L.Ed.2d 402, *supra*), and preemption of State laws " 'is not favored "in the absence of persuasive reasons — either that the nature of the regulated subject matter permits

---

[6] The statute provides for exceptions to the preemption mandate for State laws which regulate insurance, banking and securities, and "any generally applicable criminal law of a State" (29 U.S.C. § 1144[b]).

no other conclusion, or that the Congress has unmistakably so ordained" ' " (*Alessi v. Raybestos–Manhattan, Inc.*, 451 U.S. 504, 522, 101 S.Ct. 1895, 1905, 68 L.Ed.2d 402, *supra*, quoting *Florida Lime & Avocado Growers v. Paul*, 373 U.S. 132, 142, 83 S.Ct. 1210, 1217, 10 L.Ed.2d 248). Although Congress expressly reserved for Federal jurisdiction regulation of employee benefit plans, no court has held that ERISA precludes any State court action even where an ERISA plan is only tangentially implicated. As the Supreme Court has recognized, some State actions "may affect employee benefit plans in too tenuous, remote, or peripheral a manner to warrant a finding that the law 'relates to' the plan" (*Shaw v. Delta Air Lines*, 463 U.S. 85, 100, n. 21, 103 S.Ct. 2890, 2901, n. 21, *supra*). Only State laws that purport to regulate, directly or indirectly, the terms and conditions of employee benefit plans are preempted (*Sasso v. Vachris*, 66 N.Y.2d 28, 32, 494 N.Y.S.2d 856, 484 N.E.2d 1359). The causes of action stated here, unlike the indemnity actions in *Retail Shoe*, do not purport to relate, directly or indirectly, to the terms and conditions of employee benefit plans and are therefore not preempted by ERISA. We turn first to the three causes of action alleging violations of the Debtor and Creditor Law.

The Debtor and Creditor Law renders certain conveyances of assets void as to creditors: a conveyance made without fair consideration, rendering the transferor insolvent (Debtor and Creditor Law § 273); a conveyance made without fair consideration by a business person leaving him or her with unreasonably small capital (Debtor and Creditor Law § 274); a conveyance made by a defendant during the pendency of an action for money damages or after the docketing of such judgment is void as to the plaintiff in that action (Debtor and Creditor Law § 273–a); and a conveyance made with actual intent to defraud is fraudulent as to both present and future creditors (Debtor and Creditor Law § 276; *see generally*, 30 N.Y.Jur.2d, Creditors' Rights and Remedies, §§ 230–270). The third, fourth and fifth causes of action allege that PCM created and contributed to the Plan, with the intent to avoid creditors, at a time when PCM was a counterclaim defendant against C & C, and when PCM was insolvent and inoperative, leaving it with an unreasonably small capital — all in violation of these provisions.

The gravamen of these causes of action have no relation to the provisions established by ERISA; rather their thrust is that the Plan was used as a vehicle for Lee to shield the assets of PCM from PCM's creditors. The statutory provisions invoked by C & C seek to inhibit fraudulent conveyances and to protect creditors from debtors' efforts to elude payment. They do not purport to relate, directly or indirectly, to employee benefit plans in general, nor do they have the effect of impermissibly regulating such plans; they neither prohibit, nor permit any particular method of administering an ERISA plan or of calculating the benefits to be derived therefrom (*see, Alessi v. Raybestos–Manhattan, Inc.*, 451 U.S. 504, 524, 101 S.Ct. 1895, 1907, *supra*). Moreover, C & C does not seek to enforce rights under the Plan, nor could it as it is not one of the enumerated parties empowered to bring a civil action under ERISA (*see*, 29 U.S.C. § 1132[a]). That the conveyances at issue here were directed to an ERISA fund is incidental. Congress could not have intended by the supersedure clause that ERISA foreclose the vindication of State laws that prohibit conveyances in defraud of creditors.

The sixth cause of action claims that Edwin Lee, as director and officer of PCM, violated the Business Corporation Law by wrongfully distributing corporate assets. Business Corporation Law § 720 enables a judgment creditor of a corporation to bring an action against a director or officer "[t]o set aside an unlawful conveyance, assignment or transfer of corporate assets, where the transferee knew of its unlawfulness". Corporations are creatures of State law whose internal affairs are to be governed by State law unless Federal law expressly provides otherwise (*Burks v. Lasker*, 441 U.S. 471, 478, 99 S.Ct. 1831, 1837, 60 L.Ed.2d 404; *Santa Fe Indus. v. Green*, 430 U.S. 462, 479, 97 S.Ct. 1292, 1304, 51 L.Ed.2d 480, quoting *Cort v. Ask*, 422 U.S. 66, 84, 95 S.Ct. 2080, 2091, 45 L.Ed.2d 26). Thus, in *Sasso v. Vachris*, 66 N.Y.2d 28, 494 N.Y.S.2d 856, 484 N.E.2d 1359, *supra*, we held that Business Corporation Law § 630, which provides an enforcement mechanism for employees to recover unpaid wages, salaries and contributions to employee benefit funds directly from the 10 largest shareholders of a closely held corporation, is not preempted by ERISA. The purpose of Business Corporation Law § 630, we concluded, was remedial in nature, providing an additional enforcement mechanism by which employees could recover delinquent contributions, and did not "relate to" the terms and conditions of employee benefit plans, but to the scope of shareholder immunity.

Similarly, the purpose of Business Corporation Law § 720 is to furnish a means of redressing the wrongful disposition of corporate assets by the corporation's officers and directors (*Cornell Mfg. Co. v. Mushlin*, 70 A.D.2d 123, 131, 420 N.Y.S.2d 231). Such a cause of action does not purport to relate to the management of an ERISA trust, or to the trustee's fiduciary obligations. The cause of action implicates the Plan tangentially — only insofar as it was the ERISA plan allegedly used as a device to effectuate a fraudulent scheme. The rights sought to be vindicated do not arise under ERISA. C & C does not challenge Lee in his capacity as trustee of an ERISA fund but as an officer of a corporation who has mismanaged that corporation's funds in such a way as to avoid the corporation's obligations to its creditors. We conclude that such a State cause of action under the Business Corporation Law, vindicating fraud and corporate mismanagement, is not preempted by ERISA (*see, Cornell Mfg. Co. v. Mushlin*, 70 A.D.2d 123, 129–130, 420 N.Y.S.2d 231, *supra* [State cause of action for corporate misconduct involving excessive contributions to ERISA fund under Business Corporation Law § 720 not preempted]; *Goben v. Barry*, 237 Kan. 822, 703 P.2d 1378 [ERISA plan established in violation of State law of corporate fiduciary duty at a time when assets placed therein were subject to court action based upon breach of that duty may be garnished pursuant to judgment rendered in action]; *Smith v. Crowder Jr. Co.*, 280 Pa. Super. 626, 421 A.2d 1107 [ERISA does not preempt State cause of action against officer or director for wrongfully contributing corporate assets to ERISA trust for personal benefit]; *cf., Deiches v. Carpenters' Health & Welfare Fund*, 572 F.Supp. 766 (D.C.N.J.1983) [ERISA does not preempt application of State insolvency and reorganization preference statute]).

With regard to the ninth cause of action — arising under EPTL 7–3.1 — we conclude, as above, that Lee's interest in the ERISA account may be reached by C & C upon proof that Lee created the trust for his own benefit to defraud creditors.

EPTL 7–3.1(a) provides that a "disposition in trust for the use of the creator is void as against the existing or subsequent creditors of the creator." If C & C establishes sufficient evidence of circumstances such as would warrant piercing the PCM corporate veil, C & C may reach Lee's interest in the Plan because it would have been created by Lee himself for his own benefit and, by definition, would be subject to the 'spendthrift trust' rule enunciated in EPTL 7–3.1.

Moreover, it is worth noting that, following the Appellate Division decision in this case, the Legislature amended EPTL 7–3.1 to provide for an exception from the "spendthrift trust" rule for certain retirement plans even though created for the benefit of the creator — *i.e.*, by a self–employed individual, or by a partner of the entity or a shareholder of the corporation sponsoring the retirement plan (L.1987, ch. 108, § 2, eff. June 8, 1987, added subd. [b]). The purpose of the amendment is to afford to employee benefit plans created by nonincorporated entities the same protection granted in *Helmsley–Spear, Inc. v. Winter*, 74 A.D.2d 195, 426 N.Y.S.2d 778, *affd.* 52 N.Y.2d 984, 438 N.Y.S.2d 79, 419 N.E.2d 1078, *supra*, to ERISA plans created by corporate employers (*see*, Governor's Bill Jacket, L.1987, ch. 108). The amendment, however, specifically provides that conveyances to such plans "shall not be exempt from application to the satisfaction of a money judgment if (i) made after the date that is ninety days before the interposition of the claim on which such judgment was entered, or *(ii) deemed to be fraudulent conveyances under article 10 of the debtor and creditor law*" (EPTL 7–3.1 [b] [2], as amended [emphasis added]). To hold that EPTL 7–3.1 (a) is preempted here by ERISA would create the anomalous result that judgment creditors could, under the amended provision, reach assets fraudulently conveyed to retirement plans that otherwise fit the definition of a "spendthrift trust", but could not reach assets fraudulently conveyed into an ERISA plan. Finally, we need not address the concern that the preemption provision in section 1144 of ERISA may bar rescission by a State court of an employer's contributions to an employee benefit trust, no matter how fraudulent the conveyance, where the integrity of the plan's funding would be jeopardized and innocent participants in the plan would be thereby injured (*see*, *Smith v. Crowder Jr. Co.*, 280 Pa. Super. 626, 421 A.2d 1107, 1114, *supra*), insofar as here, C & C seeks to reach only Lee's interest in the Plan, and those funds may not be shielded merely because they have been deposited in an ERISA trust.

B.

Alternatively, PCM and Lee argue that to the extent State laws dealing with fraudulent conveyances, corporate wrongdoing and the creation of spendthrift trusts authorize a judgment creditor to reach assets in an ERISA trust, their application here impermissibly conflicts with the antialienation clause of ERISA, and is therefore preempted. In support of this argument, they cite *Helmsley–Spear, Inc. v. Winter*, 74 A.D.2d 195, 426 N.Y.S.2d 778, *affd.* 52 N.Y.2d 984, 986, 438 N.Y.S.2d 79, 419 N.E.2d 1078, *supra*, and *Ellis Natl. Bank v. Irving Trust Co.*, 786 F.2d 466 (2d Cir.), both of which rejected a "fraud" exception to the antialienation provision of ERISA.[7]

---

[7] The Federal circuits appear to be split with respect to ERISA's antialienation provision and the garnishment or attachment of an employee's ERISA funds (*compare*, *United Metal*

ERISA requires that each pension plan provide that benefits may be assigned or alienated (29 U.S.C. § 1056[d][1]), and the Internal Revenue Service has promulgated regulations pursuant to ERISA to the effect that "benefits provided under the plan may not be . . . assigned . . . alienated or subject to attachment, garnishment, levy, execution or other legal or equitable process" (Fed Treas Reg [26 CFR] § 1.401 [a]–13 [b] [1] [1980]). In *Helmsley–Spear*, the employer sought to attach the assets, including those in an ERISA fund, of an employee convicted of having stolen checks from his employer. The Appellate Division held, and we agreed, that under those circumstances, vested benefits from an ERISA trust are exempt from attachment by creditors (*Helmsley–Spear, Inc. v. Winter*, 74 A.D.2d 195, 198, 426 N.Y.S.2d 778, *supra*). Similarly in *Ellis* (*supra*), the Second Circuit held that the antialienation provision of ERISA prohibits an employer from reclaiming certain funds contributed to an ERISA trust even though those funds represent moneys ultimately derived from fraudulent practices against the employer for which the employee was convicted. Both cases involved an employer's attempt to reach assets of an employee in satisfaction of a judgment based on wrongdoing wholly unrelated to the creation and disposition of funds into an ERISA account. The fraud occurred separately from and independently of the employee's ERISA interests, and there was no attempt to abuse the Federal shield of ERISA assets in order to violate State fraud laws.

Here, however, the very creation and enhancement of the trust is alleged to have been in defraud of creditors. Although the legislative history of this provision is sparse (*see, Ellis Natl. Bank v. Irving Trust Co.*, 786 F.2d 466, 470, *supra*, citing *Northwest Airlines v. Roemer*, 603 F.Supp. 7, 9–10 (D.C.Minn.1984); and H.Conf.Rep. No. 93–1280, 93d Cong., 2d Sess, reprinted in 1974 U.S.Code Cong. & Ad.News 4639, 5061), suggested purposes of the antialienation clause include the protection of the spendthrift employee from " 'his own financial improvidence in dealing with third parties' . . . and the prohibition of involuntary levies by third party creditors on vested plan benefits" (*Ellis Natl. Bank v. Irving Trust Co.*, 786 F.2d 466, 470, *supra*, quoting *American Tel. & Tel. Co. v. Merry*, 592 F.2d 118, 124 [2d Cir. 1979]). The antialienation provision, however, has never been held to be absolute, and indeed several courts have recognized, for example, an exception for family support orders (*see, e.g., American Tel. & Tel. Co. v. Merry*, 592 F.2d 118, *supra*; the exception has since been codified *see*, 29 U.S.C. § 1056[d][3], added 1984, Pub.L. 98–397). These purposes neither expressly nor impliedly conflict with the prevention of debtor fraud — a field traditionally within the power of the States

---

Prods. v. National Bank, 811 F.2d 297 [6th Cir.1987], *appeal pending* — U.S. —, 107 S.Ct. 3260, 97 L.Ed.2d 760 [no implied exception to antialienation provision allowing employer to garnish employee's ERISA pension when employee commits fraud against employer]; and *Ellis Natl. Bank v. Irving Trust Co.*, 786 F.2d 466 [2d Cir. 1986] [no criminal misconduct exception to ERISA's antialienation provision], with *Crawford v. La Boucherie Bernard*, 815 F.2d 117 [D.C. Cir. 1987], *cert. denied sub nom. Goldstein v. Crawford*, — U.S. —, 108 S.Ct. 328, 98 L.Ed.2d 355 [traditional trust remedies for wrongful depletion of assets not preempted by antialienation provision of ERISA]; and *St. Paul Fire & Mar. Ins. v. Cox*, 752 F.2d 550 [11th Cir.1985] [garnishment undertaken to satisfy liabilities arising from criminal misconduct toward employer constitutes exception to antialienation provision of ERISA]).

to police. We conclude, therefore, that the application of State laws voiding conveyances made in defraud of creditors does not impermissibly conflict with the
identified purposes of the antialienation provision in ERISA.

Accordingly, the order of the Appellate Division should be affirmed, with costs.

TRUST, ETC. UNDER KEOGH PLAN OR RETIREMENT PLAN —
PROTECTION FROM MONEY JUDGMENTS OR CREDITORS

CHAPTER 108

Approved and effective June 8, 1987

AN ACT to amend the civil practice law and rules, in relation to personal property
exempt from application to the satisfaction of money judgments and the estates,
powers and trusts law, in relation to when dispositions in trust for the creator are
void as against creditors

*The People of the State of New York, represented in Senate and Assembly, do
enact as follows:*

§ 1. Subdivision (c) of section five thousand two hundred five of the civil practice
law and rules, as relettered by chapter one hundred twenty–nine of the laws of
nineteen hundred seventy–six, is amended to read as follows:

(c) Trust exemption. 1. Except as provided in paragraphs three and four of this
subdivision, any property while held in trust for a judgment debtor, where the trust
has been created by, or the fund so held in trust has proceeded from, a person other
than the judgment debtor, is exempt from application to the satisfaction of a money
judgment.

2. For purposes of this subdivision, any trust, custodial account, annuity or
insurance contract established as part of either a Keogh (HR–10) plan or a retirement
plan established by a corporation, which is qualified under section 401 of the United
States Internal Revenue Code of 1986[1] as amended, shall be considered a trust
which has been created by or which has proceeded from a person other than the
judgment debtor, even though such judgment debtor is (i) a self–employed individual, (ii) a partner of the entity sponsoring the Keogh (HR–10) plan, or (iii) a
shareholder of the corporation sponsoring the retirement plan.

3. This subdivision shall not impair any rights an individual has under a qualified
domestic relations order as that term is defined in section 414(p) of the United States
Internal Revenue Code of 1986,[2] as amended.

4. Additions to an asset described in paragraph two of this subdivision shall not
be exempt from application to the satisfaction of a money judgment if (i) made after

---

[1] U.S.C.A. § 401.
[2] U.S.C.A. § 414(p).

the date that is ninety days before the interposition of the claim on which such judgment was entered, or (ii) deemed to be fraudulent conveyances under article ten of the debtor and creditor law.[3]

§ 2. Section 7–3.1 of the estates, powers and trusts law is amended to read as follows:

§ 7–3.1 Disposition in trust for creator void as against creditors

(a) A disposition in trust for the use of the creator is void as against the existing or subsequent creditors of the creator.

(b)(1) For purposes of paragraph (a) of this section, a trust, custodial account, annuity or insurance contract established as part of either a Keogh (HR–10) plan or a retirement plan established by a corporation, which is qualified under section 401 of the United States Internal Revenue Code of 1986,[4] as amended, shall not be considered a disposition in trust for the use of the creator, even though the creator is (i) a self–employed individual, (ii) a partner of the entity sponsoring the Keogh (HR–10) plan, or (iii) a shareholder of the corporation sponsoring the retirement plan; provided, however, that nothing in this section shall impair any rights an individual has under a qualified domestic relations order as that term is defined in section 414(p) of the United States Internal Revenue Code of 1986,[5] as amended.

(2) Additions to an asset described in subparagraph one of this paragraph shall not be exempt from application to the satisfaction of a money judgment if (i) made after the date that is ninety days before the interposition of the claim on which such judgment was entered, or (ii) deemed to be fraudulent conveyances under article ten of the debtor and creditor law.[6]

§ 3. This act shall take effect immediately.

NEW YORK ESTATES, POWERS AND TRUSTS LAW (1979)

N.Y. Est. Powers & Trusts Law § 7–1.5. (McKinney 1979) When trust interest inalienable; exception

(a) The interest of the beneficiary of any trust may be assigned or otherwise transferred, except that:

(1) The right of a beneficiary of an express trust to receive the income from property and apply it to the use of or pay it to any person may not be transferred by assignment or otherwise unless a power to transfer such right, or any part thereof, is conferred upon such beneficiary by the instrument creating or declaring the trust.

------

[3] Debtor and Creditor Law § 270 et seq.
[4] 26 U.S.C.A. § 401.
[5] 26 U.S.C.A. 414(p).
[6] Debtor and Creditor Law § 270 et seq.

(2) The proceeds of a life insurance policy which, under a trust or other agreement, are upon the death of the insured left with the insurance company may not be (A) transferred, (B) subject to commutation or encumbrance or (C) subject to legal process except in an action for necessaries, if provisions to such effect were incorporated in such trust or other agreement.

(b) Notwithstanding subparagraph (a)(1):

(1) The beneficiary of an express trust to receive income from property and apply it to the use of or pay it to any person may, unless otherwise provided in the instrument creating or declaring such trust, transfer any amount in excess of ten thousand dollars of the annual income to which the beneficiary is entitled from such trust to the spouse, issue, ancestors, brothers, sisters, uncles, aunts, nephews or nieces of the beneficiary, or to a trustee, committee, conservator, curator, custodian, guardian of the property of a minor, or the donee of a power during minority for the benefit only of any such person bearing such relationship to the beneficiary, provided that such transfer is evidenced by a written instrument signed and acknowledged by the beneficiary and delivered to the trustee of the trust, together with an affidavit by the beneficiary that such transfer and any like transfer concurrently in effect are for all or part of the excess over ten thousand dollars of the annual income from such trust to which such beneficiary is entitled, and that he has not received and is not to receive any consideration in money or money's worth for the transfer.

(2) Any such transfer shall be effective in any year only as to income from such trust in excess of ten thousand dollars, and for this purpose all previous like transfers applicable to a given year shall be taken into account. In the event that two or more transfers are made in or for any year in a total amount exceeding the income from such trust properly transferable hereunder, transferees shall be preferred in the order in which the instruments of transfer were delivered to the trustee.

(3) A trustee shall be exonerated and fully discharged for any payment made to a transferee in reliance on the affidavit of a beneficiary described in subparagraph (1).

(4) The provisions of this paragraph do not apply to subparagraph (a)(2):

(c) A transferee of income may, if he has not received or is not to receive any consideration in money or money's worth therefor, make a further transfer of such income only to one or more of the permissible transferees referred to in subparagraph (b)(1), other than the prior transferor; provided, however, that upon the death of a transferee any income not so transferred by him shall be an asset of his estate, subject to his testamentary disposition or passing to his distributees under the statute of descent and distribution.

(d) The beneficiary of an express trust to receive the income from property and apply it to the use of or pay it to any person is not precluded by anything contained in this section from transferring or assigning any part or all of such income to or for the benefit of persons whom the beneficiary is legally obligated to support.

NOTES AND QUESTIONS

(1) Most states will not allow creditors to reach the income on a spendthrift trust. *See, e.g.*, Wash. Rev. Code § 6.32.250 (Supp. 1987). *See also* 11 U.S.C. § 541(c)(2) (1982 & Supp. IV 1986). Some jurisdictions allow claims for alimony and child support to pierce the immunity. Often limits are set on the amount of funds protected by a trust, either limited to a sum certain, *see* Va. Code § 55–19 (1986), or to some amount "necessary" for the "reasonable requirements of the debtor" standard. N.Y. Civ. Prac. Law § 5226 (McKinney 1978).

(2) If transferable by the debtor or within the reach of creditors, the corpus of a trust will also pass to the trustee in bankruptcy. If the future interest in the corpus is inalienable, however, it is also inviolate. Even a vested interest may be immune. Restatement (Second) of Trusts § 153 (1959).

(3) Two dodges used to protect the corpus of a trust have been to make vesting dependent on a condition precedent of solvency or on a condition subsequent that the cestui qui trust will not seek bankruptcy relief or become insolvent. 11 U.S.C. § 541(c)(1)(B) (1982 & Supp. IV 1986) has eliminated the use of these tactics.

(4) Trusts in which payments of income from the corpus are discretionary offer somewhat of an obstacle to creditors, as do trusts for specific purposes such as "education and support." *Cf.* N.Y. Est. Powers & Trusts Law § 7–3.4 (McKinney 1979).

(5) Self–settled spendthrift trusts do not remove assets from the reach of claimants. What about individual retirement accounts? *See* Cal. Civ. Proc. Code § 704.115 (West 1987), providing those accounts with a limited exemption.

(6) *See generally* Halbach, *Creditors' Rights in Future Interests*, 43 Minn. L. Rev. 217 (1958); Plumb, *Exempt and Immune Property*, 61 Va. L. Rev. 1, 77 (1975); Annot., 119 A.L.R. 19 (1939); Annot., 34 A.L.R.2d 1335 (1954).

CHAPTER 8

BULK TRANSFERS

§ 8.01 Introduction

A common threat of fraud to creditors in the business setting was and is a debtor's outright sale of all or much of its business assets, leaving the creditors high and dry after the debtor has absconded with the sale proceeds. These transactions, called bulk sales, are regulated by Article 6 of the Uniform Commercial Code.

Official Comment 2 to U.C.C. § 6–101 explains the frauds against which the Article was designed to provide protection:

> (a) The merchant, owing debts, who sells his stock in trade to a friend for less than it is worth, pays his creditors less than he owes them, and hopes to come back into business through the back door some time in the future.

> (b) The merchant, owing debts, who sells his stock in trade to anyone for any price, pockets the proceeds, and disappears leaving his creditors unpaid.

Following the Panic of 1893, which led many businessmen to resort to these unsavory practices, many states passed laws regulating bulk sales. By the early 1900's, many states had such laws. The non–uniformity of these laws, however, proved to be burdensome in interstate business transactions. Article 6 was drafted ostensibly to provide uniformity among the states.

Whether uniformity was in fact achieved is questionable. Although other articles of the Uniform Commercial Code provide for optional provisions, see, e.g., U.C.C. § 9–401 (with three options for the various states to choose among in determining the place for financing statements to be filed) perhaps no other article by its own terms provides for as much non–uniformity as does Article 6, with its optional provision § 6–106. Without § 6–106, Article 6 essentially provides for notice of a bulk sale to the transferor's creditors and, if the requisite notice is not given, the sale is "ineffective" against any creditor of the transferor. See U.C.C. § 6–105. Section 6–106 provides that the proceeds of the sale must be applied to the transferor's debts. Even absent this substantive non–uniformity, some states have adopted numerous non–uniform provisions that combine to make Article 6 more uniform in theory than in actuality. For the reasons discussed in the Harris and Baker article, infra, 32 states have now repealed Article 6; 4 have revised it; and only 10 states, such as New York and Deleware, have retained some form of the statute as of July 1, 1996.

The provisions of Article 6 will be considered in conjunction with the following problem.

PROBLEM

You represent *B* who is interested in purchasing *S*'s dress business. *S* manufactures women's coats and dresses and sells directly to retail outlets all over the country. The negotiations for the deal have been concluded and you now want to make sure your client's ownership of the business and all of its assets cannot be subjected to the claims of any of *S*'s creditors. As part of the sale, *S* agrees to pay all his debts and they are not being assumed by *B*.

Outline the steps you will take to protect *B*.

If, instead, you represented a creditor of *S* who received notification of the sale, and was fearful of not getting paid, what action would you suggest he take?

REFERENCES

Baker, *Bulk Transfers Act—Patch, Bury, or Renovate?* 38 Bus. Law. 1771(1983).

Bamberger, *Article 6 of the UCC: Uniformity Gone Awry*, 26 Bus. Law. 329(1970).

Dusenberg & King, *Sales & Bulk Transfers under the Uniform Commercial Code*, 3A Bender's U.C.C. Service (MB), Chapter 15 (1966).

Harris & Baker, *How the Proposed Revisions to UCC Article 6 (Bulk Transfers) Would Affect Creditors*, 92 Comm. L.J. 123 (1987) (reprinted *infra*).

Hawkland, *Proposed Revisions to U.C.C. Article 6*, 38 Bus. Law. 1729 (1983).

Hawkland, *Remedies of Bulk Transfer Creditors Where There Has Been Compliance With Article 6*, 74 Com. L.J. 257 (1969).

Hogan, *The Highways and Some of the Byways in the Sales and Bulk Sales Articles of the Uniform Commercial Code*, 48 Cornell L.Q. 1 (1962).

Larson, *Bulk Transfers: Some Interpretive Problems*, 2 Rut.–Cam. 101 (1970).

Levit, *Bulk Transfers: Stepchild of the Uniform Commercial Code?* 46 Notre Dame Law. 694 (1971).

Rapson, *U.C.C. Article 6: Should It Be Revised or "Deep–Sixed"?* 38 Bus. Law. 1753 (1983).

§ 8.02   Statutes, Cases, Notes and Questions

[A]   Statute

UNIFORM COMMERCIAL CODE: ARTICLE 6

BULK TRANSFERS

§ 6–101.   Short Title

This Article shall be known and may be cited as Uniform Commercial Code—Bulk Transfers.

§ 6–102.   "Bulk Transfers"; Transfers of Equipment; Enterprises Subject to This Article; Bulk Transfers Subject to This Article

(1) A "bulk transfer" is any transfer in bulk and not in the ordinary course of the transferor's business of a major part of the materials, supplies, merchandise or other inventory (Section 9–109) of an enterprise subject to this Article.

(2) A transfer of a substantial part of the equipment (Section 9–109) of such an enterprise is a bulk transfer if it is made in connection with a bulk transfer of inventory, but not otherwise.

(3) The enterprises subject to this Article are all those whose principal business is the sale of merchandise from stock, including those who manufacture what they sell.

(4) Except as limited by the following section all bulk transfers of goods located within this state are subject to this Article.

§ 6–103.   Transfers Excepted From This Article

The following transfers are not subject to this Article:

(1) Those made to give security for the performance of an obligation;

(2) General assignments for the benefit of all the creditors of the transferor, and subsequent transfers by the assignee thereunder;

(3) Transfers in settlement or realization of a lien or other security interests;

(4) Sales by executors, administrators, receivers, trustees in bankruptcy, or any public officer under judicial process;

(5) Sales made in the course of judicial or administrative proceedings for the dissolution or reorganization of a corporation and of which notice is sent to the creditors of the corporation pursuant to order of the court or administrative agency;

(6) Transfers to a person maintaining a known place of business in this State who becomes bound to pay the debts of the transferor in full and gives public notice of that fact, and who is solvent after becoming so bound;

(7) A transfer to a new business enterprise organized to take over and continue the business, if public notice of the transaction is given and the new enterprise

assumes the debts of the transferor and he receives nothing from the transaction except an interest in the new enterprise junior to the claims of creditors;

(8) Transfers of property which is exempt from execution.

Public notice under subsection (6) or subsection (7) may be given by publishing once a week for two consecutive weeks in a newspaper of general circulation where the transferor had its principal place of business in this state an advertisement including the names and addresses of the transferor and transferee and the effective date of the transfer. As amended 1962.

§ 6–104. Schedule of Property, List of Creditors

(1) Except as provided with respect to auction sales (Section 6–108), a bulk transfer subject to this Article is ineffective against any creditor of the transferor unless:

(a) The transferee requires the transferor to furnish a list of his existing creditors prepared as stated in this section; and

(b) The parties prepare a schedule of the property transferred sufficient to identify it; and

(c) The transferee preserves the list and schedule for six months next following the transfer and permits inspection of either or both and copying therefrom at all reasonable hours by any creditor of the transferor, or files the list and schedule in (a public office to be here identified).

(2) The list of creditors must be signed and sworn to or affirmed by the transferor or his agent. It must contain the names and business addresses of all creditors of the transferor, with the amounts when known, and also the names of all persons who are known to the transferor to assert claims against him even though such claims are disputed. If the transferor is the obligor of an outstanding issue of bonds, debentures or the like as to which there is an indenture trustee, the list of creditors need include only the name and address of the indenture trustee and the aggregate outstanding principal amount of the issue.

(3) Responsibility for the completeness and accuracy of the list of creditors rests on the transferor, and the transfer is not rendered ineffective by errors or omissions therein unless the transferee is shown to have had knowledge. As amended 1962.

§ 6–105. Notice to Creditors

In addition to the requirements of the preceding section, any bulk transfer subject to this Article except one made by auction sale (Section 6–108) is ineffective against any creditor of the transferor unless at least ten days before he takes possession of the goods or pays for them, whichever happens first, the transferee gives notice of the transfer in the manner and to the persons hereafter provided (Section 6–107).

§ 6–106. Application of the Proceeds

In addition to the requirements of the two preceding sections:

(1) Upon every bulk transfer subject to this Article for which new consideration becomes payable except those made by sale at auction it is the duty of the transferee to assure that such consideration is applied so far as necessary to pay those debts of the transferor which are either shown on the list furnished by the transferor (Section 6–104) or filed in writing in the place stated in the notice (Section 6–107) within thirty days after the mailing of such notice. This duty of the transferee runs to all the holders of such debts, and may be enforced by any of them for the benefit of all.

(2) If any of said debts are in dispute the necessary sum may be withheld from distribution until the dispute is settled or adjudicated.

(3) If the consideration payable is not enough to pay all of the said debts in full distribution shall be made pro rata.

> **Note:** *This section is bracketed to indicate division of opinion as to whether or not it is a wise provision, and to suggest that this is a point on which State enactments may differ without serious damage to the principle of uniformity.*
>
> *In any State where this section is omitted, the following parts of sections, also bracketed in the text, should also be omitted, namely:*
>
> *Section 6–107(2) (e), 6–108(3) (c), 6–109(2).*
>
> *In any State where this section is enacted, these other provisions should be also.*

Optional Subsection (4)

[(4) The transferee may within ten days after he takes possession of the goods pay the consideration into the (specify court) in the county where the transferor had its principal place of business in this state and thereafter may discharge his duty under this section by giving notice by registered or certified mail to all the persons to whom the duty runs that the consideration has been paid into that court and that they should file their claims there. On motion of any interested party, the court may order the distribution of the consideration to the persons entitled to it.] As amended 1962.

> **Note:** *Optional subsection (4) is recommended for those states which do not have a general statute providing for payment of money into court.*

§ 6–107. The Notice

(1) The notice to creditors (Section 6–105) shall state:

    (a) that a bulk transfer is about to be made; and

    (b) the names and business addresses of the transferor and transferee, and all other business names and addresses used by the transferor within three years last past so far as known to the transferee; and

    (c) whether or not all the debts of the transferor are to be paid in full as they fall due as a result of the transaction, and if so, the address to which creditors should send their bills.

(2) If the debts of the transferor are not to be paid in full as they fall due or if the transferee is in doubt on that point then the notice shall state further:

(a) the location and general description of the property to be transferred and the estimated total of the transferor's debts;

(b) the address where the schedule of property and list of creditors (Section 6–104) may be inspected;

(c) whether the transfer is to pay existing debts and if so the amount of such debts and to whom owing;

(d) whether the transfer is for new consideration and if so the amount of such consideration and the time and place of payment; [and]   ʼ

[(e) if for new consideration the time and place where creditors of the transferor are to file their claims.]

(3) The notice in any case shall be delivered personally or sent by registered or certified mail to all the persons shown on the list of creditors furnished by the transferor (Section 6–104) and to all other persons who are known to the transferee to hold or assert claims against the transferor. As amended 1962.

Note: *The words in brackets are optional. See Note under § 6–106.*

§ 6–108. Auction Sales; "Auctioneer"

(1) A bulk transfer is subject to this Article even though it is by sale at auction, but only in the manner and with the results stated in this section.

(2) The transferor shall furnish a list of his creditors and assist in the preparation of a schedule of the property to be sold, both prepared as before stated (Section 6–104).

(3) The person or persons other than the transferor who direct, control or are responsible for the auction are collectively called the "auctioneer". The auctioneer shall:

(a) receive and retain the list of creditors and prepare and retain the schedule of property for the period stated in this Article (Section 6–104);

(b) give notice of the auction personally or by registered or certified mail at least ten days before it occurs to all persons shown on the list of creditors and to all other persons who are known to him to hold or assert claims against the transferor; [and]

[(c) assure that the net proceeds of the auction are applied as provided in this Article (Section 6–106).]

(4) Failure of the auctioneer to perform any of these duties does not affect the validity of the sale or the title of the purchasers, but if the auctioneer knows that the auction constitutes a bulk transfer such failure renders the auctioneer liable to the creditors of the transferor as a class for the sums owing to them from the transferor up to but not exceeding the net proceeds of the auction. If the auctioneer consists of several persons their liability is joint and several. As amended 1962.

Note: *The words in brackets are optional. See Note under § 6–106.*

§ 6–109.   What Creditors Protected; [Credit for Payment to Particular Creditors]

(1) The creditors of the transferor mentioned in this Article are those holding claims based on transactions or events occurring before the bulk transfer, but creditors who become such after notice to creditors is given (Sections 6–105 and 6–107) are not entitled to notice.

[(2) Against the aggregate obligation imposed by the provisions of this Article concerning the application of the proceeds (Section 6–106 and subsection (3) (c) of 6–108) the transferee or auctioneer is entitled to credit for sums paid to particular creditors of the transferor, not exceeding the sums believed in good faith at the time of the payment to be properly payable to such creditors.]

Note: *The words in brackets are optional. See Note under § 6–106.*

§ 6–110.   Subsequent Transfers

When the title of a transferee to property is subject to a defect by reason of his non–compliance with the requirements of this Article, then:

(1) a purchaser of any of such property from such transferee who pays no value or who takes with notice of such non–compliance takes subject to such defect, but

(2) a purchaser for value in good faith and without such notice takes free of such defect.

§ 6–111.   Limitation of Actions and Levies

No action under this Article shall be brought nor levy made more than six months after the date on which the transferee took possession of the goods unless the transfer has been concealed. If the transfer has been concealed, actions may be brought or levies made within six months after its discovery.

Note to Article 6: *Section 6–106 is bracketed to indicate division of opinion as to whether or not it is a wise provision, and to suggest that this is a point on which State enactments may differ without serious damage to the principle of uniformity.*

In any State where Section 6–106 is not enacted, the following parts of sections, also bracketed in the text, should also be omitted, namely:

Sec. 6–107(2) (e), 6–108(3) (c), 6–109(2).

In any State where Section 6–106 is enacted, these other provisions should be also.

[B]   Cases, Notes and Questions

NOTES AND QUESTIONS

(1) In U.C.C. § 6–102(1), does a "major part" of the inventory refer to the quantity or value of the goods sold? *Compare* U.C.C. § 6–102(1) *with* Wis. Stat. § 406.102(1) (1964) (bulk transfer is transfer of a major part in value of the inventory of the enterprise). *Cf. Zenith Radio Distributing Corp. v. Mateer*, 311 Ill. App. 263, 35 N.E.2d 815 (1941). Under the California version of Article 6, a bulk transfer is a transfer of a "substantial part" of the inventory of an enterprise. Cal. Com. Code § 6102(1). "Substantial part" has been held to mean somewhere in the vicinity of 5% of the value of the merchandise. *Reed v. Anglo Scandinavian Corp.*, 298 F. Supp. 310, 313 (E.D. Cal. 1969).

(2) Refer to U.C.C. § 6–102(3). Is the principal business of a restaurant the sale of merchandise? What is the principal business of a bar? Several states, including California, Florida, Idaho, New York, and Washington, have amended U.C.C. § 6–102 to include restaurants. What is the rationale for excluding restaurants from the scope of Article 6? Do these enterprises not have valuable inventory on which their trade creditors rely? How is the "principal business" of an enterprise to be determined?

(3) The business of Zonk Out Video is renting video cassettes. Zonk Out has numerous creditors who are breathing down the neck of Herman Hip, the sole proprietor who owns it. Herman sells all his cassettes to Timid Transferee. Must Timid comply with Article 6? *See* U.C.C. § 6–102(3).

(4) If *X* transfers 25% of his inventory to *A* on Monday, 25% of his inventory to *B* on Tuesday, 25% of his inventory to *C* on Wednesday, and 25% to *D* on Thursday, must *A*, *B*, *C* & *D* comply with Article 6?

(5) What if 100% of the inventory at one of a company's three stores is transferred? Need there be compliance with Article 6? *Cf. National Bank of Royal Oak v. Frydlewicz*, 67 Mich. App. 417, 241 N.W.2d 471, 474 (1976) (bulk transfer where 100% of inventory at manufacturer's retail outlet is transferred).

(6) *XYZ* has three stores with equal inventory in three different states. *XYZ* decides to sell, in bulk, all of its inventory in State *X*. What result? *See Leach v. Burns Brick Co. (In re Albany Brick Co.)*, 12 U.C.C. Rep. Serv. 165 (Bankr. M.D. Ga. 1972).

(7) *ABC* business trades all its pizza ovens for pool tables. Is this a transfer subject to Article 6? *See Danning v. Daylin, Inc.*, 488 F.2d 185, 188–89 (9th Cir. 1973).

(8) You represent a bank that is considering giving a small businessman a loan in exchange for a security interest in all of his inventory. The bank has heard rumors, however, that the businessman plans to abscond to Jamaica with the funds. The bank isn't concerned with losing money on the security interest—it is comfortably oversecured—but rather worries about having to comply with Article 6. Need it? *Compare* Cal. Com. Code § 6102(5) (bulk mortgages subject to provisions of U.C.C.) *with* U.C.C. § 6–103(1).

(9) Is a sale by a debtor–in–possession under chapter 11 of the Bankruptcy Code exempt from compliance with Article 6? *Compare* U.C.C. § 6–103(4) *with* 11 U.S.C. § 1107.

(10) Refer to U.C.C. § 6–103(6). How would a transferee know that it remained solvent after assuming the transferor's debts? How can a transferee know with certainty what the transferor's debts are?

(11) How long must a transferor remain solvent under U.C.C. § 6–103(6)?

(12) Does a transferee comply with U.C.C. § 6–105 if he mails notice of a bulk transfer ten days before the transfer? *See Starman v. John Wolfe, Inc.*, 490 S.W.2d 377, 384 (Mo. App. 1973) (creditors must *receive* notice at least ten days before transferee takes possession of the goods).

(13) Seller and Buyer negotiate the principal terms of the sale of all of Seller's inventory to Buyer. Seller, whose business is the sale of goods from inventory, demands a substantial down payment at the time the contract is signed; the closing and the rest of the payment will occur in thirty days. Is Buyer already in noncompliance with Article 6? *See* U.C.C. § 6–105.

(14) Seller sells all its merchandise to Buyer, who grants to a bank a security interest in all the assets. There is no compliance with Article 6. Does Seller's pre–existing creditor have rights in the assets superior to the bank? *See* U.C.C. § 6–110; *Mayfield Dairy Farms, Inc. v. McKenney*, 612 S.W.2d 154, 156–157 (Tenn. 1981) (where bank officer is told seller has no unsecured creditors, bank takes in good faith and without notice, and, therefore, its security interest in the assets is superior to the rights of seller's creditor).

(15) The bulk transfer statute of limitations is six months from the date of the transfer unless the transfer has been concealed. *See* U.C.C. § 6–111. What is "concealment"? Is it merely the failure to give notice of the impending bulk transfer? *Compare Columbian Rope Co. v. Rinek Cordage Co.*, 461 A.2d 312, 313 (Pa. Super. 1983) (complete failure to notify transferor's creditors is concealment) *with Aluminum Shapes, Inc. v. K–A–Liquidating Co.*, 290 F. Supp. 356, 358 (W.D. Pa. 1968) (affirmative concealment, not mere non–disclosure or failure to give public notice, necessary to toll running of statute of limitations). *See also Murdock v. Plymouth Enterprises, Inc. (In re Curtina International, Inc.)*, 23 B.R. 969, 975 (Bankr. S.D.N.Y. 1982) (six–month statute of limitations in Article 6 tolled for trustee in bankruptcy for two years under 11 U.S.C. § 108 if an order for relief is entered before the expiration of the six month period).

ADRIAN TABIN CORP. v. CLIMAX BOUTIQUE, INC.

New York Court of Appeals
34 N.Y.2d 210, 356 N.Y.S.2d 606, 313 N.E.2d 66 (1974)

JASEN, Judge.

The plaintiff, Adrian Tabin Corporation, is a creditor of the defendant L. D. J. Dress, Inc., a New York corporation engaged in the retail sale of dresses. L. D. J. (transferor) sold its business in bulk to one Paul Warman, who in turn resold to defendant Climax Boutique, Inc. (transferee), in which he is a principal. At the closing, the transferor furnished a bill of sale, which was preserved by the transferee, containing a schedule of the property transferred, together with an affidavit averring that the business was "free and clear of any and all liens, mortgages, security interests, levies, debts, taxes or other claims" and "that the Transferor is not indebted to anyone and has no creditors." In addition, before consummation of the sale, the transferee's attorney made a lien search, which disclosed no liens, and inquired of the transferor's attorney as to creditors and was assured that there were none.

Upon learning of the sale, the plaintiff brought an action to have it declared ineffective because the transferee had failed to give notice to it as a creditor, as required by section 6–105 of the Uniform Commercial Code. The trial court voided the sale holding that the transferee had a duty to inquire carefully as to the existence of creditors, intimating that a review of the seller's books and questioning of the transferor as to the source of the merchandise was required. Lacking such an inquiry, the court held the sale was ineffective. The Appellate Division, by a divided court, reversed, holding that under the Uniform Commercial Code a transferee of a bulk sale who lacks knowledge of creditors of his transferor may rely on an affidavit of no creditors and need not make a careful inquiry. The court was further of the view that, even if the careful inquiry requirement of the former law (Personal Property Law, § 44, Consol.Laws, c. 41) were superimposed on the Uniform Commercial Code, the transferee's actions were in sufficient compliance.

We affirm and hold that the transferee of a bulk sale who has no knowledge of creditors of the transferor may rely on an affidavit of no creditors furnished by the transferor and that the Uniform Commercial Code imposes no duty of careful inquiry as existed under former law.

The language of section 6–104 is simple and unambiguous. In pertinent part, subdivision (1) provides that a bulk transfer is ineffective as against creditors of the transferor unless the transferee requires the transferor to furnish a list of creditors and the transferee preserves the list for six months and allows reasonable inspection thereof. Subdivision (3) places upon the transferor the responsibility for the accuracy and completeness of the list and provides that the transfer is not ineffective because of errors or omissions in the list unless the transferee had knowledge. "Knowledge", as carefully defined by the code draftsmen, means actual knowledge (Uniform Commercial Code, § 1–201, subd. [25]), not constructive knowledge. And as the official comment to subdivision (3) above makes clear, the sanction for the accuracy of the list of creditors is the false swearing statute of the State.

Concededly, cases interpreting the pre–Uniform Commercial Code New York Bulk Sales Act (former Personal Property Law, § 44) stand for the proposition that before a transferee may rely on an affidavit of no creditors, he must make careful inquiry and otherwise have no knowledge of such creditors of the transferor. (*Klein v. Schwartz, Sup.*, 128 N.Y.S.2d 177; *Willner Butter & Egg Corp. v. Roth*, 192 Misc. 970, 83 N.Y.S.2d 16; *Carl Ahlers, Inc. v. Dingott*, 173 Misc. 873, 18 N.Y.S.2d 434; *Marcus v. Knitzer*, 168 Misc. 9, 4 N.Y.S.2d 308; *Heilmann v. Powelson*, 101 Misc. 230, 167 N.Y.S. 662.) But on the face of section 6–104 of the Uniform Commercial Code, there is no requirement of careful inquiry.[1] Notwithstanding the commentary accompanying subdivision (3) of section 6–104 that it is declarative of precode New York law (*see* McKinney's Cons.Laws of N.Y., Book 62½, Uniform Commercial Code, § 6–104, p. 735), in our view, the judicial gloss on the former law has not been carried over. As the report of the New York Law Revision Commission more accurately states, subdivision (3) of section 6–104 is merely in "general accord" with precode law. (1955 Report of N.Y.Law Rev.Comm. [Study of the Uniform Commercial Code], p. 1747.) Although at first reading this provision may seem harsh on the transferor's creditors, a requirement of careful inquiry might, on the other hand, tend to restrain the free alienation of property. Hence, it is in this situation that the code protects the innocent transferee because "the desirability of allowing transfers to go forward outweighs the value of protecting the omitted creditor." (Hogan, *The Highways and Some of the Byways in the Sales and Bulk Sales Articles of the Uniform Commercial Code*, 48 Cornell L.Q., 1, 37.)

Although the Supreme Court of New Jersey has not yet passed upon the precise issue before us, we note two decisions from the intermediate appellate court of that State in accord with this analysis. In *Federal Ins. Co. v. Pipeco Steel Corp.*, 125 N.J.Super. 563, 312 A.2d 510, the defendant imported three shipments of steel from Japan, each of which was subject to import duty. Federal Insurance Co. furnished bonds in favor of the United States to secure payment of the same. Ultimately, Federal was compelled to pay on the bonds. Thereafter, Pipeco made a bulk transfer omitting Federal and the United States from the list of creditors furnished to the transferee. Federal then brought an action against the transferor and the transferee seeking to recover the sums paid to the United States and alleging that the bulk sale was ineffective as to it because notice of the transfer had not been given as required by the bulk sale provisions of the New Jersey Commercial Code. (N.J.S.A. 12A:6–105.) There was nothing in the record to suggest that the transferee had actual knowledge of the claim of the United States or Federal. The trial court agreed that the bulk sale was ineffective for failure to give notice and granted summary judgment for Federal. On appeal, it was urged that since Pipeco was partly engaged in importing, the transferee had *constructive* knowledge that an import duty might be owing to the United States and should have inquired into that possibility. The appellate court disagreed and reversed, stating: "The statute does not render a transfer ineffective unless the transferee is shown to have had knowledge that the list of creditors was incomplete. This statutory language does not embrace the concept

---

[1] Indeed, there was none in former section 44 of the Personal Property Law. The requirement was of judicial creation and, it has been suggested, resulted from mistaken application of precedent. (*See* Note, 52 North Carolina L.Rev. 165, 167–168.)

of constructive notice or constructive knowledge. Actual knowledge is required." (125 N.J.Super. 563, 312 A.2d 510.) (Accord *Silco Automatic Vending Co. v. Howells*, 102 N.J.Super. 243, 245 A.2d 765, *affd.* 105 N.J.Super. 511, 253 A.2d 480; Hansell, *Bulk Transfers Under Article 6 of the Iowa Uniform Commercial Code*, 19 Drake L.Rev. 275, 284; Shkolnick, *The Nebraska Uniform Commercial Code: Article 6—Bulk Transfers*, 43 Neb.L.Rev. 760, 766; White & Summers, Handbook of the Law Under the Uniform Commercial Code, § 19–3, pp. 650, 651.)

This is not to say, however, that the omitted creditor is entirely without remedy. The Uniform Fraudulent Conveyance Act (Debtor and Creditor Law, § 270 *et seq.*, Consol.Laws, c. 12) was not repealed by the enactment of the Uniform Commercial Code. Under section 276 of that law, if a transferee knowingly participates in a conveyance made with actual intent to "hinder, delay, or defraud . . . present and future creditors" of the transferor, the goods may be recovered from the transferee by the transferor's creditors *notwithstanding literal compliance with the bulk trans-fer provisions of the Uniform Commercial Code.* (*See, generally*, Hawkland, *Remedies of Bulk Transfer Creditors Where There Has Been Compliance With Article 6*, 74 Commercial L.J. 257; 1 Glenn, Fraudulent Conveyances and Prefer-ences, § 313.) Also, section 60 of the Bankruptcy Act (U.S.Code, tit. 11, § 96) proscribing preferential transfers may apply in a given context. Conceivably, a preferential transfer could occur in a bulk sale triggering the filing of a petition for involuntary bankruptcy against the transferor. Upon adjudication of the transferor as a bankrupt, the transferee could be required to turn the property over to the trustee if, at the time of the conveyance, the transferee had reasonable cause to believe the transferor was insolvent.

Optional section 6–106[2] of the official text of the Uniform Commercial Code, not yet adopted in New York and to which legislative attention is invited, provides additional protection for the omitted creditor. This section obligates the transferee to apply the proceeds of the transfer to the debts of the transferor. In practical effect, optional section 6–106 provides an additional 30 days, from the date when the notice to creditors (Uniform Commercial Code, §§ 6–105, 6–107) would ordinarily be given, for unlisted or omitted creditors to assert their claims. (*See* Hawkland, *Remedies of Bulk Transfer Creditors Where There Has Been Compliance With Article 6*, 74 Commercial L.J. 257, 262.) Adoption of this expedient provision would go far toward furnishing additional protection for the simple, unsecured creditor.

We recognize, as is so ably stated in the dissenting opinion, that strong reasons grounded in public policy and in the equities of the situation can be raised as a basis for imposing a duty of careful inquiry upon the transferee of a bulk sale. Neverthe-less, it is our view that the simple and unambiguous language of section 6–104 and

---

[2] "§ 6–106. Application of the Proceeds. In addition to the requirements of the two preceding sections: (1) Upon every bulk transfer subject to this Article for which new consideration becomes payable except those made by sale at auction it is the duty of the transferee to assure that such consideration is applied so far as necessary to pay those debts of the transferor which are either shown on the list furnished by the transferor (Section 6–104) or filed in writing in the place stated in the notice (Section 6–107) within thirty days after the mailing of such notice. This duty of the transferee runs to all the holders of such debts, and may be enforced by any of them for the benefit of all."

(Matthew Bender & Co., Inc.)

the precise and careful definition of knowledge as used in the code (§ 1–201, subd. [25]) preclude such a construction.

For the reasons stated, the order of the Appellate Division should be affirmed, with costs.

GABRIELLI, Judge (dissenting).

The question presented is whether subdivision (3) of section 6–104 of the Uniform Commercial Code has obviated the rule established by case law in New York that the buyer of a going business in a bulk sale transaction must make adequate inquiry concerning the seller's undisclosed creditors or be subject to the claims of those creditors. We conclude that such an inquiry is required to be made.

On January 9, 1970, L. D. J. Dress, Inc. sold its dress shop to one Warman, who, in turn, sold it to defendant, Climax Boutique, Inc., as a going business in a bulk sales transaction. The seller gave the defendant buyer an affidavit that it had no creditors. Plaintiff in this action, however, had sold dresses to the seller L. D. J. for which there was a balance due. The affidavit of no creditors was supplied defendant at the closing. Prior to that defendant's attorney had made a lien search which disclosed nothing, was informally told by L. D. J.'s attorney that there were no creditors (even including the landlord and utilities), and inspected L. D. J.'s check-book seeing that indeed checks had been written to certain of L. D. J.'s creditors. Defendant, through its attorney or otherwise, however, never attempted to review L. D. J.'s books; nor was the source of the merchandise included in the bulk sale ever questioned. The parties stipulated that the defendant had no knowledge of the plaintiff's claim prior to the sale.

The Trial Judge held that the affidavit of no creditors furnished by the seller was not such a list of creditors as was contemplated under the Bulk Sales Act (Uniform Commercial Code, art. 6) to save the defendant harmless from claims of the seller's creditors; and that defendant failed to make the sort of thorough inquiry which the law required. As a consequence of these findings he enjoined the sale and ordered the appointment of a receiver unless the defendants should pay the plaintiff the amount due together with costs and disbursements. (On the appeal to the Appellate Division the action was discontinued as to defendant L. D. J.)

The Appellate Division majority reversed and dismissed the complaint. After first noting the case law in New York interpreting former section 44 of the Personal Property Law, to the effect that in addition to taking the required list of creditors from the seller, the buyer was under a duty to make careful inquiry as to the possible existence of creditors, the majority held such law to be inapplicable in light of new subdivision (3) of section 6–104 of the Uniform Commercial Code, which places responsibility on the seller for the accuracy of the list and preserves the effectiveness of the sale even though there might be errors or omissions in the list, unless the buyer be shown to have had the knowledge of the list's accuracy. A literal interpretation of that section was said to obviate any duty on the buyer to make inquiry. Besides, said the majority, the inquiry that was made, *i.e.*, the lien search, the conversation and the inspection of check stubs, would have satisfied the old rule in any event. The two dissenters could not agree that the old rule regarding inquiry had been overcome by the statute and noted that the defendant should have been put on notice the affidavit of no creditors was false since it would be unlikely that a going business would have no outstanding debts.

Section 6–104 provides generally that a bulk transfer is ineffective against any creditor of the seller unless the buyer requires the seller to furnish a list of his existing creditors. Sections 6–105 and 6–107 then confer upon the buyer the duty of notifying the seller's creditors of the sale at least 10 days in advance of the sale. These provisions are as stated in the Official Comment following section 6–105 (McKinney's Cons.Laws of N.Y., Book 62½, Uniform Commercial Code, p. 738) "the heart of the Article," the whole purpose of which is (pp. 716–717) to deal with two common forms of commercial fraud, namely:

> (a) The merchant, owing debts, who sells out his stock in trade to a friend for less than it is worth, pays his creditors less than he owes them, and hopes to come back into the business through the back door some time in the future.

> (b) The merchant, owing debts, who sells out his stock in trade to any one for any price, pockets the proceeds, and disappears leaving his creditors unpaid.

With these salutary aims in mind, how do we deal with subdivision (3) of section 6–104 which seems calculated, as applied by the court below in the instant case, to defeat the whole purpose and intent of article 6? Subdivision (3) states: "Responsibility for the completeness and accuracy of the list of creditors rests on the transferor, and the transfer is not rendered ineffective by errors or omissions therein unless the transferee is shown to have had knowledge." The inclusion of this subdivision may very likely have been due to legislative oversight. The purpose of article 6 is to safeguard creditors while at the same time providing for the smooth and relatively uninterrupted flow of the sale transaction (*see* Hogan, *The Highways and Some of the Byways In the Sales and Bulk Sales Articles of the Uniform Commercial Code*, 48 Cornell Law Quarterly 1, 37; Levit, *Bulk Transfers—Stepchild of the Uniform Commercial Code*, 46 Notre Dame Lawyer?, 694, 706, 707). The model article 6 of the Uniform Commercial Code, in addition to carrying section 6–104 also carries section 6–106. As explained by former Dean William D. Hawkland (Remedies of Bulk Transfer Creditors Where There Has Been Compliance With Article 6, 74 Commercial L.J. 257) prior to the drafting of the Uniform Commercial Code many States followed the New York law which did not require the buyer to apply consideration to the debts of the seller. The idea was that the seller's creditors were adequately protected if they knew that he was about to realize funds as the result of the bulk sale. This notice was sufficient to safeguard the creditors. Other States, however, followed the Pennsylvania law, and provided that creditors were not adequately protected unless the buyer was obligated to apply the consideration for the sale to the debts of the seller. Thus, when the Uniform Commercial Code draftsmen came to article 6 they wrote in a section 6–106 adopting the Pennsylvania approach which, in effect, requires the buyer to wait 30 days before paying over the consideration during which time claims of the seller's creditors could be satisfied out of this fund. Section 6–106 was labeled "optional". Nineteen jurisdictions have accepted sections 6–106 and 31, including New York, have rejected it. In New York we consider the list and buyer's notice adequate protection to the creditor as we did before the Uniform Commercial Code was adopted. But at that time we had no provision which saved the buyer harmless upon the seller's furnishing a list. At that time the case law required the buyer to make thorough inquiry (*Klein v. Schwartz*, 128 N.Y.S.2d 177; *Willner Butter & Egg Corp. v. Roth*, 192 Misc. 970, 83 N.Y.S.2d 16; *Heilmann v. Powelson*, 101 Misc. 230, 167 N.Y.S. 662). Thus, the creditor would have be en adequately protected.

Hawkland notes a relationship between subdivision (3) of section 6–104 and section 6–106[1] and from this we can see that where the statute covering bulk sales contains both subdivision (3) of section 6–104 and section 6–106, the consequences to a creditor omitted from the list would not be as onerous as they are in New York where there is no section 6–106. At least the odds are that prior to the expiration of the 30 days' waiting period carried in section 6–106, a creditor would get wind of the sale and have time to lay claim to a portion of the proceeds. At the same time, the buyer would be spared the necessity of making the inquiry required under our case law. However, where, as in New York, there is no section 6–106, there should probably be no subdivision (3) of section 6–104 which acts to cut off the omitted creditor's rights irrevocably as of the time of the closing as interpreted by the court below, a result in complete and total derogation of the aims of article 6. As stated by yet another writer: "If the purpose of article 6 is to give creditors who extend credit on the faith of a stock of merchandise advance notice so that they can take such steps as are necessary to protect themselves against a bulk transfer, the Code and pre–existing law simply afford no adequate protection in the absence of section 6–106" (Barkin and Gilbert, *Bulk Transfers In Florida—The Creditor Protected*, 20 Univ. of Florida L.Rev. 158, 167). It appears, then, that without section 6–106, there is no salutary purpose to be served by the inclusion of subdivision (3) of section 6–104.

We are disposed to conclude that despite the inclusion of subdivision (3) of section 6–104 in the New York statute the pre–existing case law regarding the duty of the buyer to investigate the seller's creditors persists. If such a case law rule is not superimposed on subdivision (3) the whole purpose of article 6 is subverted. Thus,

---

[1] "Although creditors, by and large, have applauded section 6–106, its enactment has caused difficulties for transferees because it imposes on them the enormous responsibility of correctly applying the proceeds. . . . Although optional section 6–106(4) resolves a major difficulty in the administration of the application of proceeds rule, two troublesome problems remain. One involves the relationship between section 6–104(3) and section 6–106. Under section 6–104(3) a transferee may rely on the accuracy of the list of creditors given by the transferor unless he has knowledge that this list is inaccurate. On the other hand, section 6–106 apparently gives protection to creditors who file their claims within thirty days after the notice of transfer is mailed. These two provisions come into play where the transferor delivers to the transferee an affidavit of 'no creditors'. In that case, assuming the transferee has no knowledge of any creditor of the transferor, may the transferee safely pay the new consideration to the transferor, or must he wait thirty days to see if any creditors file? 'The prudent answer seems clear enough. He must wait thirty days. This answer makes section 6–106 unpopular with transferors who are forced to wait thirty days after the transaction is closed to get their money' [citing himself A Transactional Guide to the Uniform Commercial Code, 855–6 [1964])." (74 Commercial L.J. 257, 262).

responsibility for the accuracy of the list of creditors rests on the seller unless the buyer has actual knowledge which must be arrived at through reasonable investigation, *i.e.*, at the very least an inspection of the seller's books together with a search for liens.[2] In other words, the part of subdivision (3) which preserves the creditors' rights if the buyer has knowledge subsumes that the buyer has acted to acquire that knowledge. We are aided in this analysis by three factors. First, the New York Annotations state that subdivision (3) of section 6–104, although new to the statute, is "but declaratory of the New York law," citing those cases which imposed the investigatory duty on the buyer.[3] Second, an absurdity would be formulated into legal doctrine were it to be held that, as in this case, a buyer would not actually know (even without investigating) that a going mercantile establishment would have to have at least some current creditors. Third, as before stated, a decision to allow the seller to have the final word as to whether or not there are any creditors and if there are, their identities, would frustrate the express purpose of the article. His responsibility extends to furnishing a list. The buyer must verify that list through his own investigation so as to give him a basis for the acquisition of actual knowledge.

We emphasize that adherence to the position and concept adopted by the majority will permit a buyer to be entirely free of any liability despite even his own reckless disregard of the natural consequences of his failure or refusal to make any inquiry of the liability status of the business being purchased—all to the damage and loss of innocent creditors of the seller. Such a concept—permitting a buyer to completely ignore the realities of the business world and, further, to cavalierly brush aside any inquiry as to the status of the seller's business debts—destroys one of the prime aims of article 6, to wit, to safeguard creditors.

We would not rest our view for reversal, as we might, on the ground that an affidavit of no creditors is not a list contemplated under section 6–104. (*See* the Commentary of Donald J. Rapson, McKinney's Cons.Laws of N.Y., Book 62½, Uniform Commercial Code, § 6–101, p. 711.) To do this would be to postpone the inevitable question of the construction to be given subdivision (3) of section 6–104 when a list is furnished which turns out to be incomplete. The proper ruling is and should be that either where a list is furnished, or where an affidavit of no creditors is furnished, the buyer must investigate, and that a reckless disregard of what might be uncovered by an investigation is tantamount to knowledge within the meaning of the statute. This is not a substitute of constructive knowledge for actual knowledge, but a recognition that willful or reckless avoidance of knowledge should be and is the equivalent of knowledge.

The order of the Appellate Division should be reversed and the judgment of the trial court reinstated.

---

[2] The checking for liens and an inspection of checks written by the seller in this case did not amount to an adequate investigation.

[3] *Klein v. Schwartz*, 128 N.Y.S.2d 177; *Carl Ahlers, Inc. v. Dingott*, 173 Misc. 873, 18 N.Y.S.2d 434; *Marcus v. Knitzer*, 168 Misc. 9, 4 N.Y.S.2d 308; *Willner Butter & Egg Corp. v. Roth*, 192 Misc. 970, 83 N.Y.S.2d 16. (McKinney's Cons.Laws of N.Y., Book 62½, Uniform Commercial Code, § 6–104, p. 735.)

JONES, WACHTLER and STEVENS, JJ., concur with JASEN, J.

GABRIELLI, J., dissents and votes to reverse in a separate opinion in which BREITEL, C. J., concurs.

SAMUEL RABIN, J., taking no part.

Order affirmed.

————————

NOTES AND QUESTIONS

(1) Under *Adrian Tabin, supra,* what kind of investigation of the existence of creditors of the transferee *must* a buyer undertake to comply with Article 6?

What kind of investigation *can* a buyer reasonably undertake?

What steps does the dissent think are required for a careful inquiry of the transferee's creditors?

How can a buyer compel a seller to make his books available for inspection?

(2) Would the result in *Adrian Tabin* be different if, instead of giving the buyer an affidavit of no creditors, its agents had told the buyer it had no creditors? *See* U.C.C. § 6–104(2).

(3) How could Adrian Tabin Corporation have protected itself when it relied upon the L.D.J. inventory in extending it credit? *See* U.C.C. §§ 9–306(2), 9–307; *Martin Marietta Corp. v. New Jersey National Bank,* 612 F.2d 745, 754 (3d Cir. 1979).

(4) How could a transferee structure an asset purchase agreement to protect itself against a result following the dissenting opinion in the above case?

(5) Do you believe Adrian Tabin Corporation relied upon the L.D.J. inventory in extending it credit?

Does an individual who slips on a banana peel negligently left lying in a supermarket rely on the market's inventory for satisfaction of his claim? Does such an individual have the right to be notified of a bulk transfer? *See* U.C.C. §§ 6–105, 6–107(3).

(6) Climax Boutique, Inc. was not Adrian Tabin's transferee. Why was U.C.C. § 6–110 not dispositive in *Adrian Tabin?*

(7) What remedies do a transferor's creditors have under Article 6? *Cf.* U.C.C. § 6–111.

(8) What remedies do a transferor's creditors have outside Article 6? *See* Chapter 6 (Fraudulent Transfers).

(9) The dissent's holding in *Adrian Tabin, supra,* seems to be that a willful or reckless avoidance of knowledge is the equivalent of knowledge under section 6–104. Did the buyer here willfully or recklessly avoid knowledge?

BILL VOORHEES CO. v. R. & S. CAMPER SALES, INC.

United States Court of Appeals, Fifth Circuit
605 F.2d 888 (1979)

FAY, Circuit Judge:

This diversity action concerns the personal liability of a transferee under the Alabama enactment of article 6 of the Uniform Commercial Code, the Alabama Bulk Transfers Act, Ala. Code tit. 7, §§ 7–6–101 to –111 (1975). The district court held that a transferee who fails to give notice to creditors as required under section 7–6–105 is not personally liable to the transferor's unpaid and unnotified creditors for the value of transfer property no longer held by the transferee. From this judgment, the plaintiff–creditor appeals. We affirm.

R & S Camper Sales of Birmingham, Inc. (the Birmingham corporation) and R & S Camper Sales, Inc. (the Huntsville corporation) are separate entities. In oral argument, counsel for appellee stated that after problems arose within the original R & S corporation, the Birmingham group split off from the Huntsville corporation. The corporations share the same officers and directors, though they serve in different capacities.

Bill Voorhees Company, Inc. (Voorhees), plaintiff–appellant, sold trailers and campers to the Birmingham corporation on unsecured credit. Most of the Birmingham corporation's inventory and equipment, including that sold by Voorhees, constituted collateral under a blanket security agreement covering a debt of over $100,000 with Central Bank of Alabama. In 1976, the bank discovered that the Birmingham corporation had violated its security agreement by failing to forward proceeds to the bank after selling campers. After meeting with the bank's vice–president, the Birmingham corporation agreed to go out of business. Without giving notice to creditors or otherwise complying with article 6, the Birmingham corporation transferred all its inventory to the Huntsville corporation. Subsequently Huntsville sold all but eight units of the inventory to third parties at prices that approximated market value, deducted a ten percent commission, and directly paid off the bank's secured claim. Appellant does not contest the bank's superior right to this $100,000. The Huntsville corporation, however, also realized an additional $36,000 from the sales, which it turned over to the Birmingham corporation. The Birmingham corporation paid other creditors with the $36,000, leaving appellant Voorhees' claim unsatisfied. Voorhees sued, alleging violations of the BulkTransfers Act.[1] The district court held that the Birmingham corporation owed Voorhees

---

[1] The district court did not find a fraudulent conveyance, and appellant did not allege one occurred in its complaint. This is not a case in which a corporation is selling its stock at substantially less than its worth nor is it a situation in which the debtor has pocketed all the proceeds and disappeared. *See* U.C.C. § 6–101, comments 2–4. The defendants attempted to consign the inventory but by failing to observe the formalities they conducted a bulk sale without complying with the notice provisions.

$31,158.40, that the bulk sale did not comply with article 6, that Voorhees could levy upon approximately eight items still in the hands of the Huntsville corporation, and that Voorhees could recover property from any third–party purchasers who paid no value or who bought with notice of the noncompliance. Neither party contests these decisions. The district court also held, however, that the Huntsville corporation is not personally liable for the value of the trailers that it has already sold to good faith purchasers.

Appellant Voorhees argues that when a transferor and transferee do not comply with the notice provisions of article 6, the creditor should have recourse against the transferee personally for the value of the dissipated property, in addition to the creditor's right to levy on remaining property.

Under *Erie* our duty is to determine how the Supreme Court of Alabama would rule on transferee liability. Before turning to what little law exists on the subject, it may be helpful to outline the possible bases for such liability. Theoretically, a money judgment against a transferee when bulk transfer property has been resold might take four forms: the transferee could be liable (1) on the transferor's debt, (2) for conversion, (3) for traceable funds, or (4) for the value of the dissipated property. As to the first possibility, all agree that the transferee's noncompliance with article 6 does not impose liability for the transferor's original debt. *E.g., Get It Kwik of America v. First Alabama Bank*, Ala.App., 361 So.2d 568 (1978); *Cornelius v. J & R Motor Supply Corp.*, 468 S.W.2d 781 (Ky.App.1971). *See* J. White & R. Summers, Handbook of the Law Under the Uniform Commercial Code 655 (1972). To sue for conversion, a creditor must have a right to possession. *E.g., Charles S. Martin Distributing Co. v. Indon Industries, Inc.*, 134 Ga.App. 179, 213 S.E.2d 900 (1975), *rev'd on other grounds*, 234 Ga. 845, 218 S.E.2d 562 (1975). Voorhees was not a secured creditor and has no claim for possession, so conversion is not at issue here. The third theory can involve two types of traceable funds: the initial purchase price the transferee pays the transferor, or the receipts the transferor collects upon resale of the property to third parties. Here, for the most part, both funds are the same because the Huntsville corporation paid the Birmingham corporation only after resale to consumers. Evidently all monies paid to the Birmingham corporation have been dispensed to other creditors and are not traceable. The ten percent commission the Huntsville corporation retained is, therefore, the only fund that might be recoverable, but the record does not reflect whether these funds are actually traceable and appellant has not pursued this issue on appeal. The final theory for imposing a money judgment is, therefore, Voorhees' only possible theory for recovering a money judgment against the Huntsville corporation. The transferee would have to be held liable for the value of the property which it has resold and for which proceeds are not traceable.

Unfortunately, article 6 does not detail remedies for its breach, and the comments supply little evidence of the drafters' intentions. A noncomplying transfer is "ineffective." U.C.C. §§ 6–104, –105. The Official Comments only mention actions against the property as possible remedies: levy or appointment of a receiver to take the goods under local procedures. U.C.C. § 6–104, comment 2; § 6–111, comment 2. Actions against the transferee personally are conspicuous by their absence. The drafters' concern that the sections created a "trap for the unwary" and "unusual obligations" on even a good faith transferee might indicate a desire to limit the drastic remedies of article 6 to in rem actions against the property and proceeds.

Despite the lack of direction from the code, most of the few courts deciding whether to impose money judgments have held transferees liable for the value of dissipated or commingled bulk transfer property. *Darby v. Ewings Home Furnishings*, 278 F.Supp. 917 (W.D.Okl.1967); *Moskowitz v. Michaels Artists and Engineering Supplies, Inc.*, 29 Colo.App. 44, 477 P.2d 465 (1970); *Cornelius v. J & R Motor Supply Corp.*, 468 S.W.2d 781 (Ky.App.1971); *Starman v. John Wolfe, Inc.*, 490 S.W.2d 377 (Mo.App.1973). *See Bomanzi of Lexington, Inc. v. Tafel*, 415 S.W.2d 627, 631 (Ky.App. 1967); *National Bank of Royal Oak v. Frydlewicz*, 67 Mich.App. 417, 241 N.W.2d 471 (1976). *See generally* Commentary, *Article 6: Rights of an Aggrieved Creditor of a Bulk Transferor*, 10 B.C.Indus. & Com.L. Rev. 281 (1969); Annot., 47 A.L.R.3d 1114, 1142 (1973). In essence, the transferee is treated like a trustee who must account for the bulk property or be held accountable for the proceeds of its sale.

Some courts have decided to hold the transferee accountable because of the legislature's adoption of optional section 6–106. *E.g., Darby v. Ewings Home Furnishings*, 278 F.Supp. 917 (W.D.Okl.1967). That section directs the transferee to assure that the bulk sale proceeds are first applied to pay the transferor's debts,[2] but it does not really address this situation, in which the parties totally failed to comply with the Act. It does, however, evidence a legislative intention to treat the transferee like a trustee for some purposes. *See* U.C.C. § 6–101, comment 3.

---

[2] Optional section 6–106 reads as follows:

Application of the Proceeds

In addition to the requirements of the two preceding sections:

(1) Upon every bulk transfer subject to this Article for which new consideration becomes payable except those made by sale at auction it is the duty of the transferee to assure that such consideration is applied so far as necessary to pay those debts of the transferor which are either shown on the list furnished by the transferor (Section 6–104) or filed in writing in the place stated in the notice (Section 6–107) within thirty days after the mailing of such notice. This duty of the transferee runs to all the holders of such debts, and may be enforced by any of them for the benefit of all.

(2) If any of said debts are in dispute the necessary sum may be withheld from distribution until the dispute is settled or adjudicated.

(3) If the consideration payable is not enough to pay all of the said debts in full distribution shall be made pro rata.

Optional Subsection (4)

(4) the transferee may within ten days after he takes possession of the goods pay the consideration into the (specify court) in the county where the transferor had its principal place of business in this state and thereafter may discharge his duty under this section by giving notice by registered or certified mail to all the persons to whom the duty runs that the consideration has been paid into that court and that they should file their claims there. On motion of any interested party, the court may order the distribution of the consideration to the persons entitled to it.

Section 6–106 was not, however, adopted in Alabama. Prior to Alabama's adoption of the Uniform Commercial Code, transferees held the proceeds of bulk transfers in trust for creditors. 1911 Ala.Acts 94, 1949 Ala.Acts 447 (repealed 1966). *See Roberts v. Norrell*, 212 F.Supp. 897 (N.D.Ala.1963).[3] A transferee of a fraudulent conveyance held the property in constructive trust and was liable to creditors for the value of disposed property. *E.g., First National Bank of Birmingham v. Love*, 232 Ala. 327, 167 So. 703 (1936); *Dickinson v. National Bank of Republic*, 98 Ala. 546, 14 So. 550 (1893). This earlier law, however, was repealed with the adoption of the Uniform Commercial Code. Ala.Code tit. 7, § 7–10–103 (1975). We must look, therefore, to more recent Alabama case law on whether money judgments can be imposed on transferees.

Two Alabama court decisions have touched on the issue of money judgments against transferees, although neither expressly decided whether a transferee is liable for the value of dissipated bulk property. In *Get It Kwik of America v. First Alabama Bank*, Ala.App., 361 So.2d 568 (1978), the Alabama Court of Civil Appeals considered the three other theories of liability in deciding a bank's right to set off a transferee's bank account against the transferor's debt after a partially noncomplying bulk sale. The court held that a transferee is not liable on the debt, but can be liable to a secured creditor for conversion. Under its definition of "proceeds," it also held that a secured party did not have a security interest in the funds received from sale of the collateral by the transferee. It did not discuss liability under normal tracing rules, which might have governed recovery of the ten percent commission in this case. Whether a transferee was liable under article 6 for the value of property was not at issue in *Get It Kwik*; however, the court did mention the topic:

> The court in *Darby v. Ewings Home Furnishings*, 5 U.C.C.Rep. 198, 278 F.Supp. 917 (D.C.W.D.Okl.1967), held that § 6–106 of the U.C.C. renders a transferee personally liable to creditors of the transferor for the value of the property purchased or the amount paid if there is a failure to comply with the bulk transfer provisions.
>
> However, § 6–106 was not adopted by Alabama and thus has no applicability in the present case.

361 So.2d at 571. This statement may be evidence that the Alabama courts would not hold the Huntsville corporation liable.[4]

---

[3] The question of transferee liability also arose under the original Bulk Sales Acts. The original Acts did not expressly impose liability. The uncertainty over whether transferees became receivers of the property led legislatures to enact provisions specifically making transferees trustees. *See Settegast v. Second National Bank*, 126 Tex. 330, 87 S.W.2d 1070, 1072 (1935). Alabama also enacted a later amendment imposing trusts on transferees. 1949 Ala.Acts 447 (repealed 1966). It is unclear why the 1949 amendment was enacted, but its adoption may indicate that the Alabama legislature believes legislative authority is necessary before trusts are imposed on transferees.

[4] Analogizing to the *Darby* decision, the Georgia Court of Appeals also held that Georgia's failure to adopt optional section 6–106 was evidence of a legislative intent that transferees should not be personally liable. *American Express Company v. Bomar Shoe Company*, 125 Ga.App. 408, 187 S.E.2d 922 (1972), *aff'd on rehearing*, 127 Ga.App. 837, 195 S.E.2d 479 (1973).

The second decision is by the Supreme Court of Alabama. In *McKesson Robbins v. Bruno's Inc.*, Ala., 368 So.2d 1 (1979), the supreme court reversed, under Alabama Rule 8, the dismissal of a creditor's complaint against a transferee and another creditor. The court stated the issues as whether the complaint stated a cause of action against the transferee for participating in a scheme to hinder collection of the plaintiff's debt, and whether the creditor had "any action against the transferee" for failing to comply with article 6. On rehearing the court stressed that it was not holding that the bulk sales act had been violated, but that a complaint alleging participation " 'in a scheme, artifice or device to hinder or delay [a creditor] in the collection of a debt' is more that 'the bare bones of pleading.' " By its failure to grant summary judgment on the article 6 cause of action, the Alabama court did hold that article 6 grants a creditor some rights against a transferee. Just what those rights are, however, and whether those rights might be limited to in rem actions against property held by the creditor, was left unanswered.

We are in the difficult position, therefore, of deciding a state law question when the statute is almost silent, the court decisions are not definitive, and prior remedial law on point has been repealed. In addition, the few indications we have of what the drafters intended and what the courts would decide seem contrary to the trend of decisions in other states. Although normally other Uniform Commercial Code decisions might be given great weight in the interest of uniformity, the remedy sections of article 6 were purposefully left open for nonuniform state provisions. *See* U.C.C. § 6–111, comment 2.

In light of the lack of mention of actions against transferees in the statute, the repeal of pre–existing remedial legislation, the Alabama legislature's failure to adopt section 6–106, and the statements of the Alabama court in *Get It Kwik*, we agree with the trial court's *Erie* guess and conclude that under Alabama law transferees are not personally liable for the value of disposed bulk property to a creditor who does not receive notice of the bulk sale.

The decision of the district court is AFFIRMED.

NOTE

Personal liability of the transferee has been held to exist both in states that have adopted U.C.C. § 6–106, *see Darby v. Ewing's Home Furnishings*, 278 F. Supp. 917 (W.D. Okla. 1967), and in states that have not adopted section 6–106, *see Murdock v. Plymouth Enterprises, Inc. (In re Curtina International, Inc.)*, 23 B.R. 969, 979 (Bankr. S.D.N.Y. 1982).

The court, however, was evidently holding that a transferee was not liable on the *debt*, as opposed to liability for the *value* of property, because it went on to state that the transferee held the proceeds from resale in trust and could be garnished by the transferor's creditor. For a later decision holding that article 6 does impose obligations on the transferee for breach, see *Indon Industries, Inc. v. Charles S. Martin Distributing Co., Inc.*, 234 Ga. 845, 218 S.E.2d 562 (1975).

VERCO INDUSTRIES v. SPARTAN PLASTICS
(In re Verco Industries)

United States Court of Appeals, Ninth Circuit
704 F.2d 1134 (1983)

BOOCHEVER, Circuit Judge.

This appeal from the Bankruptcy Appellate Panel, 10 B.R. 347, presents a novel issue as to whether a debtor–in–possession which invalidated a sale for failure to comply with bulk transfer laws and retained the sale property for the benefit of the estate's creditors, may recover the balance owed on the sale free from the buyer's claim of set–off. Because the buyer is entitled to a set–off we reverse in part.

I.

Facts

The material facts are undisputed. On December 21, 1979, Verco Industries ("Verco") closed a sale to Spartan Plastics ("Spartan") of machinery, tools, and a building lease used in manufacturing practice bombs for the military. Verco tendered a bill of sale for the personal property, an assignment of its leasehold interest in the manufacturing facility, and a covenant not to compete. Spartan's consideration consisted of $125,595 cash, $85,000 worth of castings, a $36,860 prepaid sublease, assumption of approximately $20,000 of Verco's outstanding obligations, and a promissory note back to Verco for $31,545. The promissory note was increased to $37,310 following Verco's assignment of a rental deposit on the leasehold interest sold to Spartan. Spartan immediately provided all the promised consideration except for payment of the promissory note which was not due until July 1, 1980. Spartan's failure to pay the note is the subject of the present appeal.

On July 23, 1980, Verco filed for bankruptcy under Chapter 11 of the Bankruptcy Code and became a debtor–in–possession with basically the same powers as a trustee in bankruptcy. See 11 U.S.C. § 1107 (Supp. 1981). Acting pursuant to 11 U.S.C. § 544 (Supp.1981), Verco sued Spartan in bankruptcy court to invalidate the transfer of personal property called for in the sale on the grounds that it violated provisions of California's bulk transfer and fraudulent conveyance laws, Cal.Com.Code §§ 6105 & 6107 (Deering Supp.1982), and Cal.Civ.Code § 3440 (Deering 1972). Verco also sought to enforce payment of the $37,310 promissory note pursuant to 11 U.S.C. § 541 (Supp.1981), which makes a bankruptcy trustee or debtor–in–possession the successor in interest to the debtor's property.

The bankruptcy court invalidated the transfer as against Verco's creditors because Spartan had failed to satisfy the notice provisions of California's bulk transfer laws, Cal.Comm.Code §§ 6105 & 6107 and had violated Cal.Civ.Code § 3440, by failing to take possession of the property within a commercially reasonable time. The court ordered that the debtor–in–possession retain the property for the benefit of the estate under 11 U.S.C. §§ 550 & 544(b) (Supp.1981). The court also concluded that because the transfer was invalid and Verco retained possession of the property, Spartan was relieved of its obligation to pay the promissory note.

Verco appealed the promissory note ruling to the three–judge Bankruptcy Appellate Panel ("panel") for the Ninth Circuit pursuant to 28 U.S.C. § 160 (Supp.1981). The panel reversed the bankruptcy court, holding that, as a debtor–in–possession, Verco need not elect between invalidating the property transfer[1] on behalf of the creditors under 11 U.S.C. § 544(b) and recovering the full sale price on behalf of the debtors' estate under 11 U.S.C. § 541(a)(1).

Raising the issue *sua sponte*, two of the panel judges also concluded that Spartan had no right of set–off against Verco for the consideration it paid on the goods retained by Verco. The third panel member concurred in the panel's decision to allow Verco to recover on the note but differed on the last issue, arguing that Spartan was entitled to a set–off under 11 U.S.C. § 553(a) (permitting a set–off of mutual debts that arose before commencement of the case).

Spartan appeals, arguing that: (1) the promissory note was unenforceable after Verco invalidated the transfer and retained the property; or (2) it has a right of set–off for the consideration it paid on the goods retained by Verco.

II.

Recovery on the Note

The bankruptcy panel found that Verco, as debtor–in–possession, could recover the amount of the promissory note from Spartan despite the fact that it had successfully set aside the transfer of assets. It is undisputed that a debtor–in–possession has the powers of a trustee in bankruptcy, 11 U.S.C. § 1107, and ascends to the rights of creditors to set aside a non–complying bulk transfer under 11 U.S.C. § 544(b) as well as acquiring all the debtor's legal rights and remedies under 11 U.S.C. § 541(a)(1). We agree with the panel below that Verco may assert both of these rights and recover the property and the amount due on the note.

The California bulk transfers law is designed to protect the creditors of the transferor. Failure to give the notice required under section 6107 renders any bulk transfer fraudulent and void against any creditor of the transferor. Cal.Com.Code § 6105; *Danning v. Daylin, Inc.*, 488 F.2d 185, 187 (9th Cir.1973). The transfer is not void, however, as between the parties to the transaction. *Cooley v. Brennan*, 102 Cal. App.2d 952, 228 P.2d 104 (1951). The transferor may maintain an action for the purchase price of the assets despite a violation of the bulk transfer laws, *Jeffrey v. Volberg*, 159 Cal.App.2d 815, 324 P.2d 964 (1956); *Escalle v. Mark*, 43 Nev. 172, 183 P. 387 (1919), and the sale will not be set aside as to the transferor's right to recover the purchase price even if the transferor's creditors make claims on all or part of the transferred assets. *Clifton v. Dunn*, 208 Ga. 326, 66 S.E.2d 735 (1951). We think it clear that had bankruptcy not intervened, Verco's creditors would have

---

[1] Because Spartan conceded at oral argument before the bankruptcy panel that the transfer could have been invalidated for violating California's bulk transfer provisions, the panel proceeded on that ground alone without reference to Spartan's alleged violation of Cal.Civ.Code § 3440's "possession" requirement. We do the same.

been able to set aside the sale to Spartan as to them without depriving Verco of its right to payment of the promissory note. We see no reason why the intervening bankruptcy of Verco should alter this situation given that Verco assumes both of these rights upon becoming debtor–in–possession.

The cases relied upon by Spartan, *Matter of Seward Dredging Co.*, 242 F. 225, 228 (2d Cir.), *cert. denied*, 245 U.S. 651, 38 S.Ct. 11, 62 L.Ed. 531 (1917) and *J.H. Hincke Printing Co. v. Bailey*, 263 P. 719, 721, 83 Colo. 242 (1928), do not compel a different result. The courts in those cases noted the bankruptcy trustee's dual responsibility to the estate and its creditors, and implied that when the trustee has two rights to property he must opt to enforce *either* right. Those cases, however, deal with situations where the trustee has two rights to title of the same property. Therefore a choice between remedies is warranted. In the present case, there are two rights to different property: the creditor's right to the transferred assets and the estate's right to the unpaid balance of the note.[2]

III.

Set–Off

> Although we acknowledge that Verco has a valid claim for the unpaid amount of the note from Spartan, we also believe that Spartan would have a claim against conveyance. Those provisions have been eliminated, however, and the modern view is that *a transferee guilty of fraudulent behavior* may nevertheless prove a claim against a bankrupt estate, once he returns the fraudulently conveyed property to the estate. . . . A rule to the contrary would allow the estate to recover the voidable conveyance and to retain whatever consideration it had paid therefor. Such a result would clearly be inequitable.

539 F.2d at 1214 (emphasis added) (citations omitted); *see also Buffum v. Barceloux Co.*, 289 U.S. 227, 237, 53 S.Ct. 539, 543, 77 L.Ed. 1140 (1933); *Barber v. Coit*, 144 F. 381 (6th Cir.1906). *Cf.* 73 Am.Jur.2d *Subrogation* § 79, at 648 (1974) (when transfer avoided by creditors of transferor, transferee subrogated to rights of creditors whose claims were paid). Similarly, we find that to allow Verco to recover the entire purchase price without allowing Spartan a claim against the estate would result in an "inequitable" double recovery.

The bankruptcy panel's attempt to distinguish *Misty* on the ground that the debtor–transferor was the non–complying party misreads *Misty's* facts. *Misty* clearly involved "a transferee guilty of fraudulent behavior." *Id.* Verco's contention that *Misty* is an inapplicable "fraudulent conveyance case" is also unpersuasive. Both are bankruptcy cases in which the transferees' conduct led to the transfers being set aside pursuant to the same section of the Bankruptcy Act. (In *Misty*, the transfer was set aside pursuant to § 70(e) of the old Act, the predecessor to § 544(b), the

---

2 *Danning v. Daylin, Inc.*, 488 F.2d 185 (9th Cir.1973), and *Schainman v. Dean*, 24 F.2d 475 (9th Cir.1928), cited by Verco, are also inapposite to the facts of the present case. These cases uphold the right of a trustee in bankruptcy to set aside a noncomplying transfer despite the fact that the *full* purchase price had been paid. The issues of the right to recover unpaid portions of the purchase price or set–off were not involved.

provision employed in this case.) Although the rationale for invalidating the transfers in the two situations is somewhat different, the same inequitable result is involved in both instances. Accordingly, Spartan has a claim against the estate which may be set–off against Verco's recovery on the note.

We note that Spartan was not guilty of any actual fraud in connection with the transfer of assets. At most, Spartan was negligent in failing to take immediate possession of the subject property and in failing properly to circulate notice of the bulk transfer to Verco's creditors. Spartan concedes that Verco is entitled to invalidate the transfer and retain the property for the benefit of its creditors. Spartan's negligence is not relevant, however, to whether Spartan is entitled to a set–off. *See Misty*, 539 F.2d at 1214.

There is no merit to Verco's contention that Spartan is precluded from claiming a set–off for the consideration it has paid because it did not raise the issue below. The bankruptcy panel clearly addressed and decided the issue, and it became part of the record on appeal. Fed.R.App.P. 10(a). The bankruptcy panel having considered the issue, we may review it on appeal. *Yellow Truck & Coach Mfg. Co. v. Edmondson*, 155 F.2d 367, 368 (6th Cir.1946).

Section 553 of the Bankruptcy Code permits "a creditor to offset a mutual debt owing by such a creditor to the debtor that arose before the commencement of the case . . . against a claim of such a creditor that arose before the commencement of the case. . . ." The timing and mutuality elements must both be satisfied to establish a set–off under the section. 4 Collier On Bankruptcy ¶¶ 553.04, 553.05, 553.08 (15th ed. 1982).

We agree with the concurring member of the bankruptcy panel that both elements are satisfied here:

> The estate's claim is based on a note given by Spartan Plastics to Verco Industries before the commencement of the case. Any claim Spartan Plastics can establish that arises from recovery of the fraudulently conveyed property "shall be determined, and shall be allowed . . . the same as if such claim had arisen before the date of the filing of the petition." 11 U.S.C. § 502(h). Thus the timing elements of section 553 are satisfied.

> "To be mutual, the debts must be in the same right and between the same parties, standing in the same capacity." 4 Collier on Bankruptcy, 15th ed. p. 553–22. A claim that is deemed to have arisen before bankruptcy is by necessary implication deemed to have been owed to the estate's predecessor, here Verco Industries. Thus, from a pre–bankruptcy perspective, the two debts were between the same parties in their corporate capacities. . . . Spartan's debt under the note is to the estate; Spartan's claim, when fixed, will be against the estate. Mutuality is therefore satisfied.

A set–off claim would not defeat the estate's invalidation of the transfer because the claim is not allowable under 11 U.S.C. § 502(d) until after the property has been surrendered to the estate. We also agree with the concurring panel member that although the "right" to seek set–off is a legal issue, the "amount" of any set–off presents a factual question that must be determined on remand. The amount of the claim will presumably bear the same relationship to the total purchase price of $305,765 as the value of the bulk sales property bore to the total consideration tendered by Verco.

We find no support for Verco's contention that section 502(h) only serves to reinstate an existing claim where property is recovered by the trustee. As noted in *Collier*:

> the import of Section 502(h) is that where a claim is allowable as provided in that section, its status is as a claim in existence on the date of the filing of the petition regardless of when, after the petition, the trustee has taken the necessary action and recovered.

3 *Collier, supra*, ¶ 502.08, at 502–92 n. 6. We also find no support for Verco's contention that where a transferor is blameless, no claim may be proven against it.[3]

CONCLUSION

The decision of the bankruptcy panel is reversed in part, and the matter is remanded to the bankruptcy trial court to determine the amount of Spartan's set–off.[4]

NOTE

See also Murdock v. Plymouth Enterprises, Inc. (In re Curtina International, Inc.), 23 B.R. 969, 980–981 (Bankr. S.D.N.Y. 1982). There the court held that, although a non–complying bulk transferee had to turn over to the trustee the value of the goods received (which had previously been sold to others), the amount to be turned over would be reduced by any traceable proceeds from the voided bulk sale held by the trustee. In addition, the court held that the transferee was entitled to file a proof of claim for the amount it paid the estate for the voided transfer.

---

[3] In *Barber v. Coit*, 144 F. 381 (6th Cir.1906), a case vigorously argued by both parties, the court made clear that the primary consideration was not the parties' relative fault, but whether the debtor's creditors would be adequately protected. *Id*. at 383. In the present case, as in *Barber*, "the creditors [would] lose nothing they are justly entitled to by giving up the money [to Spartan], for they have the property and it would be manifestly inequitable for them to hold both property and money." *Id*.

[4] As noted in the statement of facts, $5,765 of the $37,310 at issue represents the security deposit on the lease assigned to Spartan. Verco argues that no defense exists to paying at least the $5,765 because the assignment of the rental deposit had nothing to do with the consideration owing for the invalidated transfer of personal property. Spartan responds by arguing that Verco's refusal to vacate the assigned premises resulted in rental payments being in arrears far in excess of the security deposit. Given the disputed nature of the issue and the fact that neither the bankruptcy court nor the panel ruled on whether the security deposit should be treated separately from the note, this court cannot resolve the issue. Accordingly, on remand, the bankruptcy court should resolve this question in the course of calculating the amount of Spartan's set–off right.

IN RE GRUBER INDUSTRIES

United States District Court, Eastern District of New York
345 F. Supp. 1076 (1972)

RE, Judge:

In this petition for review, petitioner, Beacon Fast Freight Co. (Beacon) urges the court to set aside an order of the Referee in Bankruptcy which enjoined Beacon from proceeding with any legal action on a default judgment that it had obtained against Gruber Brothers (Brothers) on August 12, 1970.

Brothers, on September 2, 1969, had sold and transferred all of its assets to Gruber Industries, Inc. (Industries), and, pursuant to the formal sales agreement, Industries assumed all of the liabilities of Brothers. On June 15, 1970, Industries filed a petition for an arrangement under Chapter XI, section 322 of the Bankruptcy Act, and was adjudicated a bankrupt on March 3, 1971. On September 22, 1970 Beacon attempted to satisfy its judgment against Brothers by levying on the assets of Industries. The case, therefore, presents a question of priority between Beacon, a creditor of Brothers, the transferor of the assets, and the Trustee in Bankruptcy of Industries, the transferee.

When notified of the levy by the New York City Marshal, on October 7, 1970, Industries initiated the notice to show cause which resulted in the order of the Referee enjoining Beacon from proceeding with the levy. The order, however, was without prejudice to Beacon filing a general claim in the Bankruptcy proceedings.

The pertinent facts are set forth in the decision of the Referee, and no useful purpose will be served by their repetition. Suffice it to say that Beacon, who had been doing business with Brothers, asserts that it never received notice of the transfer of the assets from Brothers to Industries. Not having been notified of the transfer, Beacon asserts further that it continued to do business with the company as Brothers. Beacon, therefore, contends that the transfer was concealed and fraudulent since it was not ascertainable by any action of Industries in its subsequent dealings with Beacon. It argues that the first time that it had notice of the transfer from Brothers to Industries was on August 5, 1970, when it was notified that it had been listed as a creditor of Industries, pursuant to the Chapter XI proceeding. Notwithstanding Beacon's contentions, the Referee found that the transfer was "publicly conducted without intent to conceal or . . . defraud."

Beacon also contends that notice of the transfer was not given pursuant to sections 6–105 and 6–107 of the New York Uniform Commercial Code. Unless there is compliance with the notice requirement, in the language of the Code, the transfer "is ineffective against any creditor of the transferor." This, of course, implies that a judgment creditor of the transferor may levy execution on the property. Furthermore, section 6–111 of the New York Uniform Commercial Code expressly provides that " . . . if the transfer has been concealed, actions may be brought or levies made within six months after its discovery." Hence, Beacon contends that since it obtained its judgment within six months of its discovery of the "concealed" transfer, it should be permitted to proceed to enforce its judgment against Brothers.

Beacon does not dispute the findings of fact made by the Referee. Rather, it asserts that the specific conclusions of law drawn from the facts are incorrect, and a proper subject for judicial review.

On the record presented the court cannot find that the Referee's findings were clearly erroneous or that the transfer was concealed or fraudulent. General Orders in Bankruptcy, Order 47. Nevertheless, even if the court were to assume that the transfer was concealed Beacon cannot prevail on this petition to review the order of the Referee.

Since the property was in *custodia legis*, it is conceded that the Referee had jurisdiction to determine the issue presented. Simply stated, therefore, the question presented, is whether the Referee was correct in his decision that the rights of the Trustee in Bankruptcy were superior to those of Beacon, a creditor of the transferor.

On the established facts there is no doubt that the Referee was correct in holding that the rights of the Trustee in Bankruptcy were superior to those of Beacon.

Although sections 6–104 and 6–105 of the New York Uniform Commercial Code provide that a transfer in violation of the code would be "ineffective" against any creditors of the transferor, this terminology has been interpreted by the Courts to mean "voidable" and not "void". This follows the meaning established from its inception in the Bulk Sales Act, section 44 of the New York Personal Property Law, McKinney's Consol.Laws, c. 41, where the term "void", which was used in that section, was construed to mean "voidable". A case in point is *City of New York v. Johnson*, 137 F.2d 163 (2d Cir. 1943) where, without complying with the Bulk Sales Act, a transfer was made to a copartner which assumed the liabilities of the transferor. The transferee was adjudicated a bankrupt. The City of New York, that had claims against the transferor, attempted to impress a lien upon the funds, in the hands of the trustee, which represented the proceeds of the sale of the property. The court dismissed the application of the City of New York, and held that the trustee had the rights of a judgment creditor pursuant to Section 70(c) of the Bankruptcy Act.

In rejecting the contention that the transfer was void, the court stated:

> We are referred to no authority and can see no reason for holding that the word "void" means more than "voidable" where the remedies given by the act are invoked, or that the consequences to bona fide purchasers from a fraudulent grantee are materially different under the Bulk Sales Act from such consequences under the Fraudulent Conveyance Act. The Bulk Sales Act gives the creditors of a transferor no rights other than equities which, like those of the creditors of a transferor under the Fraudulent Conveyance Act, can be cut off by bona fide purchasers. 137 F.2d at 165.

In holding that the rights of the trustee were superior to those of the creditors of the transferor, the court wrote:

> Under Section 70, sub. c of the Bankruptcy Act, 11 U.S.C.A. § 110, sub. c, the trustee was vested with all the rights of a judgment–creditor of the bankrupt

to which the assets of United Upholsterers (transferor) had been conveyed. Subdivision c provides that: "The trustee, as to all property in the possession or under the control of the bankrupt at the date of bankruptcy or otherwise coming into the possession of the bankruptcy court, shall be deemed vested as of the date of bankruptcy with all the rights, remedies, and powers of a creditor then holding a lien thereon by legal or equitable proceedings, whether or not such a creditor actually exists." *Id.* at 164.

There is abundance of authority for the proposition that a transfer in bulk, not in compliance with Article 6 of the Uniform Commercial Code, is merely voidable, and that the intervention of bankruptcy creates superior rights for the trustee. *In the Matter of Dee's, Inc.*, 311 F.2d 619 (3d Cir. 1962); *In re Vanity Fair Shoe Corporation*, 84 F.Supp. 533 (S.D.N.Y.1949), *aff'd sub nom. Schwartz v. A. J. Armstrong Co.*, Inc. 179 F.2d 766 (2d Cir. 1950).

A Trustee in Bankruptcy acquires title to a bankrupt's assets as of the date of the filing of the petition and, under the Bankruptcy Act, he is given the rights and status of a creditor holding a lien, whether or not such a creditor actually exists. In the case at bar, therefore, on June 15, 1970, when the section 322 petition was filed, the Trustee in Bankruptcy of Industries acquired the rights set forth in section 70c of the Bankruptcy Act. Clearly, therefore, since the bankruptcy proceedings were commenced prior to the lien acquired by Beacon, the trustee's rights to the property are superior to *those of Beacon. City of New York v. Johnson, supra; Schwartz v. A. J. Armstrong, supra; In the Matter of Dee's, Inc., supra.*

The cases cited by *Beacon*, in its memorandum in support of its petition for review, are readily distinguishable since they do not deal with the rights of a creditor of a transferor versus the Trustee in Bankruptcy of the transferee. *See e.g. E. J. Trum, Inc. v. Blanchard Parfums, Inc.*, 33 A.D.2d 689, 306 N.Y. S.2d 316 (1969); *Pittsburgh Plate Glass Co. v. Magni–Flood Corporation of America, Inc.*, Sup., 235 N.Y.S.2d 258 (1962).

It is also pertinent that, by virtue of section 67a of the Bankruptcy Act, which is expressly made applicable to a Chapter XI proceeding, any lien obtained within four months of the filing of the petition is null and void if the debtor is insolvent, or if the lien was obtained by fraud. Since Beacon asserted its claim after the filing of the section 322 petition by Industries on June 15, 1970, it cannot prevail over the rights of the trustee by virtue of his status as a lien creditor.

Finally, petitioner's contention that its rights are unaffected by the bankruptcy proceeding because it is attaching the assets of Brothers, and not those of the bankrupt, is without merit. As indicated in the cited cases, until the bulk transfer has been rendered null and void, the assets were lawfully the property of Industries and subject to the satisfaction of its debts.

For the foregoing reasons, the order of the Referee in Bankruptcy is affirmed.

NOTE

In re Gruber Industries, Inc., supra, was decided under the Bankruptcy Act, but the result should not be changed by the Bankruptcy Code. Section 544(a)(1) provides:

> (a) The trustee shall have, as of the commencement of the case, and without regard to any knowledge of the trustee or of any creditor, the rights and powers of, or may avoid any transfer of property of the debtor or any obligation incurred by the debtor that is voidable by—
>
> > (1) a creditor that extends credit to the debtor at the time of the commencement of the case, and that obtains, at such time and with respect to such credit, a judicial lien on all property on which a creditor on a simple contract could have obtained a judicial lien, whether or not such a creditor exists. . . .

Harris and Baker, HOW THE PROPOSED REVISIONS TO UCC ARTICLE 6 (BULK TRANSFERS) WOULD AFFECT CREDITORS[*]

92 Commercial Law Journal, 123 (1987)

Uniform Commercial Code Article 6 addresses a fraud that apparently was common around the turn of the century: a merchant would acquire his stock in trade on credit, then sell his entire inventory ("in bulk") and abscond with the proceeds.[1] Fraudulent conveyance law often provided no remedy for intentional fraud of this kind because it protected buyers who purchased in good faith and for adequate value.[2] In many cases, the creditors' only hope of recovery was to locate the seller and obtain judgment against him, perhaps in a distant jurisdiction. To prevent this perceived injury to creditors, pre–UCC bulk sales laws generally required buyers in bulk to notify creditors of the seller prior to a bulk sale.[3] In some states, the buyer

----

[*] Copyright © 1987 by Commercial Law Journal. Reprinted by permission. This article does not necessarily represent the views of any organization with which either of the authors is affiliated, nor do the authors necessarily endorse the policy decisions they discuss.

[1] *See* Billig, *Bulk Sale Laws: A Study in Economic Adjustment,* 77 U. Pa. L. Rev. 72, 75–78 (1928). Although both existing and revised Article 6 refer to transfers, we often refer in this article to sales, which are by far the most common bulk transfers.

[2] This protection dates at least to the Statute of Fraudulent Conveyances, 13 Eliz., ch. 5 (1571). Both the Uniform Fraudulent Conveyance Act (UFCA) and its successor, the Uniform Fraudulent Transfer Act (UFTA), afford protection to good faith transferees for adequate value. UFCA §§ 9, 10, 7A U.L.A. 577, 630 (master ed. 1985); UFTA § 8(a), 7A U.L.A. 662. A similar result obtains in bankruptcy. *See* 11 U.S.C. § 548(c) (1982 & Supp. III 1985) (good faith transferee for value has a lien on or may retain any interest transferred to the extent of value given).

[3] *See, e.g.,* Billig, *supra* note 1, at 72–74.

also was obligated to apply the proceeds of the bulk sale to payment of the seller's creditors. Failure to comply with these statutory duties resulted in the sale being avoidable by aggrieved creditors; that is, the creditors could reach the transferred property in the hands of the buyer.[4]

In many ways, Article 6 follows pre–UCC bulk sales laws. It requires buyers in bulk to send notice to the seller's creditors[5] and, in some states, to apply the sale proceeds to payment of the seller's debts.[6] A non–complying sale is "ineffective" against creditors of the seller, who may apply the transferred property to payment of their claims against the seller.[7] Article 6 reflects its turn–of–the–century roots. It covers only property that creditors of that time readily could reach: inventory and related equipment.[8] And it covers only those businesses that were perceived to present an undue risk to creditors: enterprises whose principal business is the sale of merchandise from stock, including those who manufacture what they sell.[9]

Since the early bulk sales laws were enacted, the American economy has changed dramatically. Service businesses have proliferated, and intangibles (*e.g.*, accounts receivable) have become much more valuable to creditors. Some have suggested that Article 6 has become anachronistic and should be expanded to reflect new risks faced by contemporary business creditors. Others have agreed with this characterization but draw a contrary conclusion. In their view, the widespread availability of credit reporting services, long–arm statutes, and floating liens on all kinds of business assets now enables creditors to protect themselves adequately, so that Article 6 no longer is needed.

Over the past decade, committees of the American Bar Association and of the Commercial Law League of America have addressed Article 6 with a view toward conforming it to modern credit risks and practices. Each group produced suggested revisions to the Article.[10] In 1985 the National Conference of Commissioners on Uniform State Laws ("NCCUSL"), in conjunction with the American Law Institute ("ALI"), appointed a Drafting Committee to revise Article 6. The Drafting Committee has sought the advice of a wide variety of interested organizations, among them the American Bar Association and the Commercial Law League of America. Their representatives have participated fully in the drafting process, which has been characterized by extended meetings and vigorous debate.[11]

---

[4] *See, e.g.*, 1 G. Glenn, Fraudulent Conveyances and Preferences § 314. Some statutes imposed personal liability on the non–complying buyer.

[5] *See* UCC §§ 6–105, 6–107.

[6] *See* UCC § 6–106 (bracketed in the UCC official text to indicate division of opinion as to whether it is a wise provision).

[7] *See* UCC § 6–104 and comment 2; § 6–105.

[8] *See* UCC § 6–102(1), (2).

[9] *See* UCC § 6–104(3).

[10] Hawkland, *Proposed Revisions to Article 6*, 38 Bus. Law. 1729 (1983) (recommendations of ABA Uniform Commercial Code Committee); Braunstein, *The President's Page*, 84 Com. L.J. (1979) (summary of proposals of CLLA).

[11] The other organizations represented at Drafting Committee meetings are the National Association of Credit Management, the National Auctioneers Association, the National Bankruptcy Conference, and the National Commercial Finance Association.

In its deliberations, the Drafting Committee has been sensitive to the views both of those who believe that existing Article 6 provides too little protection to creditors and of those who think the burdens Article 6 imposes outweigh any corresponding benefits it affords. The Committee has endeavored to produce a statute that adequately protects creditors while not unduly impairing good faith transactions. The Committee has not finished its work; however, it has decided upon a new approach to Article 6 that the final draft is likely to reflect. The Committee's changes would be far–reaching. If adopted by the NCCUSL and the ALI, they would affect not only the scope of the Article, but also the buyer's duties and the creditors' remedies in the event of the buyer's non–compliance.

This article discusses most of the Drafting Committee's major recommendations, with emphasis on the protections that revised Article 6 would afford to creditors.[12] Because the drafting continues apace, this article does not refer to specific statutory language reflecting those recommendations. Instead, it summarizes the recommendations with a view toward informing the public about the potential effects of revised Article 6. Readers are encouraged to express their comments, criticisms, and suggestions for improvements to the chair of the Drafting Committee, Gerald L. Bepko, Vice President, Indiana University, 355 Lansing Street, Indianapolis, Indiana 46202.

For those who wish more information, copies of the Committee's most recent draft are available upon payment of a $3.00 duplication and mailing charge from Edith O. Davies, Executive Secretary, National Conference of Commissioners on Uniform State Laws, Suite 610, 645 North Michigan Avenue, Chicago, Illinois 60611.

THE SCOPE OF REVISED ARTICLE 6

Existing Article 6 rests upon two premises: special legislation is desirable to minimize the risk that a business might use a bulk sale to perpetrate a fraud on its creditors; and the most effective deterrent to that fraud is the imposition on the buyer of a duty to notify the seller's creditors of an impending bulk sale.[13] The Drafting Committee has reconsidered those premises in the light of contemporary business practices. Its recommendations reflect the belief that although the premises remain valid to a considerable extent, the premises must be refined to reflect the debtor–creditor relationships that have developed since the enactment of the early bulk sales laws.

Which Businesses? Which Assets?

As indicated above, existing Article 6 follows the early bulk sales laws in limiting its scope to transfers of inventory and related equipment by enterprises whose principal business is the sale of merchandise from stock. The Committee believes that the bulk transfer risk is inherent in the sale of all businesses, regardless of the types of assets that are the subject of the sale and regardless of the types of activities

---

[12] For a discussion of the proposed revisions to Article 6 with a different focus, *see* Harris, *The Article 6 Drafting Committee's New Approach to Asset Acquisitions*, 42 Bus. Law. — (August, 1987), from which portions of this article derive. Those portions appear with the permission of *The Business Lawyer* and the American Bar Association.

[13] *See* UCC § 6–101 comments 2, 3, and 4.

in which the business is engaged. Thus revised Article 6 would apply to sales of all kinds of tangible and intangible business assets by all kinds of businesses. In keeping with the traditional scope of the UCC, real estate would be excluded. Because it views negotiable instruments as cash equivalents, the Committee believes that their conversion into cash does not present a bulk sales risk and would exclude them from the revised Article. In addition, sales of securities, which usually are regulated, are excluded.

Which Sales Present a Bulk Sales Risk?

Not every sale of a large portion of a business's assets is likely to present a substantial risk that a business will seriously impair its creditors' ability to collect their debts. In the Committee's view, this risk is most likely to arise when the business unexpectedly sells most of its assets and either ceases to conduct business altogether or continues to conduct a business that differs substantially from the one conducted prior to the sale. Revised Article 6 generally would cover sales of that kind. A few important aspects of this coverage are noteworthy. First, creditors ought to expect a business to conduct sales that are usual in the seller's trade or industry and those that are of a kind customarily conducted by the particular seller. Creditors have little need for advance notice of those ordinary course sales, which existing Article 6 excludes[14] and which the Committee would exclude from the revised Article. Second, when the seller retains assets having a value equal to or greater than those sold, the risk to creditors is not increased to an extent that justifies application of Article 6, and the revised Article would not apply to those sales.[15] Finally, the buyer is not a guarantor of the seller's debts. Before he suffers liability, he must have some reason to know that the transaction poses a bulk transfer risk. If, after reasonable inquiry, the buyer would have lacked notice that the seller will cease to remain in substantially the same business as the seller conducted before the sale, the revised Article 6 would exclude the sale from its coverage.[16]

Which Other Sales Are Excluded?

Existing Article 6 excludes a number of transactions that otherwise would be bulk transfers, but which usually pose no bulk sales risk. The Committee recommends that the revised Article retain these exclusions and suggests that some of them be clarified and made more useful.

Like existing Article 6, revised Article 6 would exclude transactions that are regulated by other law, including general assignments for the benefit of creditors,[17]

---

[14] "A 'bulk transfer' is any transfer in bulk and not in the ordinary course of the transferor's business. . . ." UCC § 6–102(1).

[15] Existing Article 6 covers only transfers of a "major part" of the seller's inventory. § 6–102(1). A "major part" is more than half. *See, e.g., Wikelund Wholesale Co. v. Tile World Factory Tile Warehouse*, 57 111. App. 3d 269. 271–72, 372 N.E.2d 1022, 1023 (1978); Froehle, *Livingston & Roth v. Stan Smith Enter.*, 27 Ohio App. 3d 359, 501 N.E.2d 105, 107 (1986). A transfer of a "substantial part" of the transferor's equipment is covered if it is made in connection with a bulk transfer of inventory. UCC § 6–102(2).

[16] What the buyer knows or should know is irrelevant under existing Article 6.

[17] UCC § 6–103(2).

judicial sales, and sales conducted by bankruptcy trustees.[18] Transactions that create security interests in inventory and equipment are subject to the public notice provisions of Article 9 and are excluded from existing Article 6.[19] In order to take account of the expanded scope of revised Article 6, which would include the sale of intangibles, the exclusion would be revised to contemplate sales of accounts and chattel paper that are subject to Article 9.[20]

To the extent that the debtor lacks equity in any of the assets sold, unsecured creditors are not injured by the sale. Thus revised Article 6 would not apply to sales of assets to the extent that they are encumbered with a security interest or lien. Existing Article 6 excludes transfers in settlement or realization of a lien or security interest,[21] and revised Article 6 would make it clear that the exclusion contemplates sales of collateral to the extent that the buyer assumes the secured obligation or applies the proceeds to satisfy the secured obligation. In a similar vein, revised Article 6 would not apply to sales of assets to the extent that they are generally exempt from execution.

Existing Article 6 also excludes two types of sales to successor businesses. Section 6–103(6) excludes sales to "a person maintaining a known place of business in this State who becomes bound to pay the debts of the transferor in full and gives public notice of that fact, and who is solvent after becoming so bound." Because buyers of businesses are unwilling to assume *all* debts of a seller (even those debts that are unliquidated or unknown), and because buyers of a multi–state business may wish to discontinue conducting the business in some of the states in which the seller operated, this exclusion rarely is used. The Drafting Committee believes that an exclusion of this kind should provide an incentive for buyers to assume and pay the debts of bulk sellers. To promote its use, the Committee would require only that a solvent buyer assume the fixed and liquidated debts of which he has knowledge and give public notice of that fact. For this purpose, public notice would be given by publishing in a newspaper of general circulation where the seller is located.[22]

Existing Section 6–103(7) excludes sales "to a new business enterprise organized to take over and continue the business, if public notice of the transaction is given and the new enterprise assumes the debts of the transferor and he receives nothing from the transaction except an interest in the new enterprise junior to the claims of creditors." These sales would include those that accompany the incorporation of a sole proprietorship or partnership. Revised Article 6 would keep this exclusion but eliminate the public notice requirement as unnecessary.

The Drafting Committee recommends two new exclusions that are particularly noteworthy. First, the Drafting Committee believes that the value of the assets in

---

[18] UCC § 6–103(4).

[19] UCC §§ 6–103(1), 9–111.

[20] Article 9 generally applies to sales of accounts and chattel paper. UCC § 9 102(1)(b). However, it does not apply to sales of accounts or chattel paper as part of a sale of the business out of which they arose, UCC § 9–104(f), to which revised Article 6 would apply.

[21] UCC § 6–103(3).

[22] *Cf.* UCC § 6–103 (providing for notice by publication). For purposes of revised Article 6, a seller is located at its place of business. If it has more than one place of business, it is located at its chief executive office. These rules derive from UCC § 6–103(3)(d).

some sales is so small that the cost of compliance with Article 6 cannot be justified. These small–scale sales of $10,000 or less would be excluded. Second, the Committee believes that some sales involve large enough sums that compliance is neither necessary nor cost–justified. In the experience of the Committee and its advisors, large–scale bulk transfers rarely result in injury to creditors, perhaps because the parties publicize them or perhaps because the prompt and secret disposition of the assets and removal of the proceeds is not feasible. Given the reduced risk, the costs of compliance become unjustifiable. Accordingly, the Drafting Committee recommends excluding bulk sales in which the consideration exceeds $10,000,000.

Will More Transactions Be Covered?

One can only surmise whether revised Article 6 would cover more or fewer transactions than does the current Article. The revised Article would expand the scope of existing bulk transfer laws by covering types of businesses and types of assets not currently covered. Thus, for creditors of service businesses, revised Article 6 would afford protection where none exists currently. On the other hand, the "going–out–of–business" requirement would exclude some transfers that are subject to the current Article, as would the revised exclusions and the new monetary limits.

PROTECTION TO CREDITORS

When Must Notice Be Given?

Current UCC provisions require the bulk buyer to obtain from the seller a list of his creditors and give notice to each one at least ten days before the buyer takes possession of the goods or pays for them, whichever happens first.[23] Because of the delay between sending the notice and its receipt, creditors often have less than ten days to act after learning of the impending bulk sale. Critics of existing Article 6 argue that the notice period should be extended to afford creditors ample time to react to it. On the other hand, creditors often have an interest in the successful consummation of a legitimate bulk sale, the proceeds of which can be applied to their claims against the seller. The parties to a bulk sale may be willing to complete it only if they can do so with alacrity. As the waiting period between notice and consummation of the sale is extended, the likelihood of legitimate sales being thwarted increases, often to the detriment of the seller's creditors.

In an effort to permit legitimate sales to close quickly, while protecting the seller's creditors against the risk that the seller will abscond with the sale proceeds, the Drafting Committee decided upon the following recommendations. First, the notice period would be extended from ten days to forty–five days. During this period, creditors may take any action that the law permits to collect their claims against the seller.[24] Second, recognizing that the seller's creditors are not materially injured

---

[23] UCC §§ 6–104, 6–105, 6–107.

[24] Existing Article 6 provides a remedy only against a non–complying bulk buyer. It does not speak to the creditors' remedies against their debtor, the bulk seller. Depending on local law and the circumstances surrounding the sale, creditors may refuse to continue to extend credit to the seller, acquire a pre–judgment lien on the seller's assets, or enjoin the sale. If grounds exist, an involuntary bankruptcy petition against the seller may be sustained. *See* 11 U.S.C. § 303 (1982 & Supp. III 1985). With one exception, *see infra* page 132, revised Article 6 also would leave the rights of creditors against the seller to non–UCC law.

as long as they are able to reach either the assets or their price, the Committee would permit the buyer to take control over the assets sold before the expiration of the notice period, provided that none of the sale proceeds (other than earnest money not to exceed ten percent of the sale price) are paid to the seller prior to the expiration of the period. In this way, the buyer may become the owner of the assets immediately and hold the sale price in escrow during the forty–five day notice period. Alternatively, if the assets remain within the creditors' reach during the notice period, the buyer is free to pay the price to the seller immediately.

What Kind of Notice Must the Buyer Give?

Existing Article 6 requires the buyer to give notice of the impending bulk transfer to each creditor who appears on the seller's list of creditors by delivering it personally or by sending it by registered or certified mail. In addition, the buyer must deliver or mail notice to each creditor of whom the buyer has knowledge, even if the creditor does not appear on the seller's list.[25] With a view toward easing the buyer's burden of compliance and toward reducing litigation over what the buyer knew, the Drafting Committee explored the possibility of permitting a buyer to give notice by filing in a public office instead of by sending individual notices. The Committee recommends that each state be given the choice of two alternative notice provisions. Both alternatives would permit a buyer to give notice directly to creditors, as under existing Article 6. Under one alternative, if the sale price exceeds $2,000,000, the buyer would be permitted instead to give notice by filing with the office of the Secretary of State in which the seller is located. The other alternative would permit notice by filing in all bulk sales.

Which Creditors Are Entitled to Notice?

Existing Article 6 generally does not distinguish among the seller's creditors. It requires the bulk buyer to give notice to "all persons shown on the list of creditors" furnished by the seller and to "all other persons who are known to the buyer to hold or assert claims against the seller."[26] This language arguably includes holders of unliquidated and contingent claims, as well as those to whom an individual seller owes consumer debts (*e.g.*, the holder of a security interest in the seller's home refrigerator or the holder of a mortgage on the seller's home).[27] The Drafting Committee thinks that the protected class of creditor is too broad. The Committee would require the buyer to send notice only to those who hold claims that arise out of the seller's business and that either are liquidated, fixed, and undisputed or are

---

[25] UCC § 6–107(3).

[26] *Id.*

[27] Section 6–109 distinguishes among creditors only on the basis of the time at which the transactions or events giving rise to their claims occurred. Some courts have followed comment 1 to that section, which states that "[t]he claims referred to of course include unliquidated claims." *E.g., Stone's Pharmacy, Inc. v. Pharmacy Accounting Management, Inc.*, 812 F.2d 1063, 1065–66 (8th Cir. 1987). *Contra Aluminum Shapes, Inc. v. K–A Liquidating Co.*, 290 F. Supp. 356, 358 (W.D. Pa. 1968) (§ 6–109(1) "refers to persons holding liquidated claims rather than assertions of potential liability for breach of contract") (alternate holding). The definition of "creditor" in § 1–201(12) is silent in this regard. Sections 6–104(2) and 6–106(2) refer specifically to disputed claims.

known by the seller to have been asserted against him. This class would include trade creditors, as well as those who have actually asserted their breach of warranty and tort claims. Of course, notice by filing would be available to all creditors.

What Happens to the Proceeds?

In a substantial minority of jurisdictions, existing Article 6 obligates the bulk transferee to apply the sale proceeds *pro rata* to creditors of the seller.[28] When one or more claims are unliquidated, disputed, or allegedly secured, performing this duty may prove quite difficult, and distribution of the proceeds may be delayed considerably.[29] In addition, since preferences generally are permitted under state law, the appropriateness of mandating a *pro rata* distribution is questionable. On the other hand, creditors must know what will happen to the proceeds in order to assess the riskiness of the transaction and react appropriately to notice of an impending bulk transfer. If the intended distribution of proceeds indicates a lack of appropriate concern for creditors, then the creditors should be apprised of that fact so that they can take steps to prevent the sale or tie up the proceeds. If the proceeds are to be distributed in a manner that is favorable to creditors, then advance knowledge of that fact will facilitate the transaction by obviating any need for creditor interference.

The Drafting Committee's resolution of these competing interests is to require that the buyer give creditors advance notice of how he undertakes to distribute the proceeds and to pay the proceeds in accordance with his undertaking. Under revised Article 6, the buyer and the seller would be free to agree to any disposition of proceeds that they wish: payment to a single creditor, to creditors *pro rata*, to the seller, or to any combination of persons. In some cases, the buyer may undertake to pay some or all of the seller's creditors, with the hope that they will continue to extend credit without interruption. In other cases, the buyer and seller may agree that the seller will receive the entire proceeds of the sale. In those cases, the buyer discharges his obligations to the seller's creditors by giving notice of that agreement and paying the proceeds to the seller.

Of course, the seller may wish to inform his creditors what he intends to do with the proceeds, lest the creditors assume the worst and attempt to interfere with the sale. The seller is free to do so; however, the buyer who performs his undertaking by paying the proceeds to the seller would bear no liability for the seller's failure to live up to the seller's stated intentions. Revised Article 6 would impose liability in favor of any creditor against the seller, or any agent of the seller, who intentionally applies the proceeds in a manner that deviates substantially from the seller's stated intentions. In this way, an officer or employee of a corporate seller may become personally liable to creditors who are injured by the deviation.

---

[28] Optional UCC § 6–106 has been adopted in approximately twenty jurisdictions.

[29] The courts have construed optional UCC § 6–106(1) as preserving the priority of secured parties and lienors in the proceeds of a bulk transfer and obligating the buyer to distribute accordingly the consideration he pays for the goods. *See, e.g., Huguelet v. M & M Assocs.*, 375 So. 2d 1150 (Fla. Dist. Ct. App. 1979) (Article 9 secured party); *In re Clement Bulk Sale*, 98 Dauph. 55, 71 Pa. D. & C.2d 717 (1976) (pre–transfer judicial lien creditor).

CREDITORS' REMEDIES UPON THE BUYER'S NON–COMPLIANCE

What Are the Shortcomings of the Existing Remedy?

Existing Article 6 has its roots in fraudulent conveyance law. The consequence of a non–complying transfer is that the transfer is "ineffective" against aggrieved creditors of the seller. Their remedy ordinarily is to set aside the transfer to the extent necessary to satisfy their claims, not to collect damages from the buyer.[30]

This *in rem* remedy may cause injustice if the seller enters bankruptcy before the Article 6 statute of limitations expires. Suppose, for example, the buyer neglects to send notice to one creditor who appears on the seller's list but sends notice to all the others. In that case, the seller's trustee may avoid the entire transfer and apply the recovery for the benefit of all the seller's creditors.[31] Under this rule, the aggrieved creditor is disadvantaged, because it must share the value of the property transferred with all the other creditors even though they were not aggrieved and would not have been entitled to share in the transferred property outside bankruptcy. The buyer, too, is injured. He may be compelled to return to the seller's bankruptcy estate all the property transferred even though, absent bankruptcy, only that one creditor would have been able to set aside the transfer, only to the extent necessary to satisfy its claim.

Even if all the seller's creditors have rights under Article 6, the *in rem* remedy may work injustice in the event of the seller's bankruptcy. If the trustee of the seller's estate avoids the transfer, the property no longer is available to satisfy the claims of the buyer's creditors. Through no fault of their own, the buyer's creditors may find that a substantial portion of their debtor's assets has been removed from their reach for the purpose of satisfying the seller's creditors, all but one of whom may have been afforded the protections of Article 6.[32]

How Would the New Remedy Work?

To avoid these results, the Drafting Committee would substitute for the *in rem* remedy against the transferred property a damage claim against the non–complying buyer. Once a creditor who is entitled to notice[33] establishes that the buyer failed in any respect to comply with the requirements of Article 6, the buyer would be personally liable to that creditor for the amount of its claim against the seller. A non–complying buyer would be relieved from this liability only to the extent that he can establish that his compliance with Article 6 would not have resulted in the creditor receiving more than the creditor in fact received. This change in state law remedy will affect the result in bankruptcy. Bankruptcy Code Section 544(b) permits

---

[30] *See supra* note 7.

[31] *See* 11 U.S.C. §§ 544(b), 550, 551 (1982 & Supp. III 1985); *Moore v. Bay*, 284 U.S. 4 (1931).

[32] Even in the absence of bankruptcy, the "ineffective" nature of a non–complying bulk sale gives rise to a variety of problems in resolving competing claims to the goods. Many of these problems are analyzed in Harris, *The Interaction of Articles 6 and 9 of the Uniform Commercial Code: A Study in Conveyancing, Priorities, and Code Interpretation*, 39 Vand. L. Rev. 179 (1986).

[33] *See supra* pages 130–131.

the trustee to avoid only those transfers of the debtor's (seller's) property and those obligations incurred by the debtor that a creditor holding an unsecured claim can avoid under non–bankruptcy law. Because the seller's creditors would not be able to avoid a non–complying bulk sale, the seller's bankruptcy trustee likewise would be unable to assert any rights to the assets.

Under existing Article 6, the non–complying buyer may "pay twice" for the goods that are the subject of a bulk sale. First, the buyer may pay the purchase price to the seller; then, he may lose the goods or their value to the aggrieved creditors. Trying to mimic this result, the Drafting Committee recommends that a buyer who fails to comply with revised Article 6 become liable to aggrieved creditors for no more than twice the consideration paid for the assets, regardless of the total of the creditors' claims. This maximum liability would be reduced by amounts paid to the seller and by amounts paid to the seller's creditors. The former reduction derives from existing law, under which the buyer who "pays twice" pays once to the seller and once to the seller's creditors. Unless he receives credit for amounts that are paid to the seller (and that creditors have the right to apply to payment of their claims), the buyer might face liability of three times the purchase price. The grant of credit for amounts paid to the seller's creditors recognizes that, to the extent that they receive payments, creditors as a group are not injured by the bulk sale.

This belief — that creditors are not injured by a bulk sale if the proceeds of the sale are paid to them — gave rise to the recommendation that the liability of a non–complying buyer who makes a good faith effort to comply be limited to an amount equal to that portion of the contract price that was not received by the seller's creditors. Thus if the buyer inadvertently fails to send a notice to one creditor but otherwise complies with the revised Article, and the seller applies the entire proceeds to the payment of particular debts, the creditor who received no notice and no share of the proceeds would have no Article 6 remedy.[34] This result is consistent with the fact that, although the seller is obligated to pay its debts, no unsecured creditor has a right to any particular share of the seller's assets.[35]

When Must an Aggrieved Creditor Bring Its Action?

Because bulk sales law imposes "unusual obligations on buyers," even those who act in good faith, existing Article 6 contains a short, six–month statute of limitations.[36] When a transfer has been concealed, the statute is tolled until the transfer is discovered.[37] Cases disagree about whether, and under what circumstances, deliberate non–compliance constitutes concealment.[38]

---

[34] If the seller enters bankruptcy, creditors who received the sale proceeds may be required to return the payments to the estate for the benefit of all creditors. *See* 11 U.S.C. §§ 547, 550, 551 (1982 & Supp. III 1985).

[35] This represents a modification of optional UCC § 6–109(2). That section grants credit for honest payments made to particular creditors against the buyer's obligation in optional UCC § 6–106 to distribute the sale proceeds to the seller's creditors pro rata.

[36] UCC § 6–111 and comment 1.

[37] *Id.*

[38] *See, e.g., Lang v. Graham (In re Borba)*, 736 F.2d 1317 (9th Cir. 1984) (construing California law) (tolling provision of § 6–111 refers to affirmative concealment, not to mere

The Drafting Committee would keep the six–month statute of limitations for those sales in which, despite having made a good faith effort, the buyer failed to comply with Article 6. The Committee would resolve the problem of deliberate non–compliance by extending the limitations period to one year if the buyer fails to make a good faith effort to comply but does not intentionally conceal the sale. If, however, the buyer intentionally conceals the sale, the one–year period would not begin until the sale is, or should have been, discovered.

WILL REVISED ARTICLE 6 BENEFIT CREDITORS?

As currently proposed, revised Article 6 contains much that the Drafting Committee expects will benefit creditors. It covers more types of assets sold by more types of businesses than does existing Article 6. Notice must be given not only of the fact of the sale but also of the intended distribution of the proceeds. The longer, forty–five day notice period will afford creditors more time to react to the impending sale. Aggrieved creditors may recover damages from the non–complying buyer instead of having to locate the actual assets that were sold. And in many cases the revised statute of limitations will afford creditors more time to pursue the non–complying buyer.

No one pretends that revised Article 6 is a creditor's panacea. It was not intended to be one. Just as the preceding paragraph points to provisions that increase the protection that Article 6 would give to creditors, so one easily can identify provisions that treat creditors less favorably than does existing Article 6. Those who would improve bulk sales law must determine whether revised Article 6, taken as a whole, affords sufficient protection to creditors without unduly impairing legitimate sales of business assets. The Drafting Committee has attempted to strike an appropriate balance. It awaits your reaction.

---

failure to give notice); *Columbian Rope Co. v. Rinek Cordage Co.*, 314 Pa. Super. 585, 461 A.2d 312 (1983) (when circumstances do not reveal to creditors that transfer has occurred, complete failure to give notice is concealment); *SVM Inv. v. Mexican Exporters, Inc.*, 685 S.W.2d 424, 430 (Tex. Ct. App. 1985) (concealment requires affirmative efforts at concealing the transfer and complete and total failure to comply with Article 6 notice provisions).

CHAPTER 9

COLLECTIVE INSOLVENCY REMEDIES

Creditors generally dislike the piecemeal dismemberment of the debtor described in the earlier chapters. The so–called "race of diligence" rewards only the most aggressive creditors, usually at the expense of more rational, patient and sympathetic creditors. Outside of the federal bankruptcy scheme, state law provides not only informal, non–judicial procedures, but also judicial procedures, such as assignments for the benefit of creditors and receiverships. Although the non–bankruptcy devices generally depend upon broad creditor acceptance and negotiating ability, bankruptcy always remains a distinct possibility.

§ 9.01 Out–of–Court Settlements

The insolvent business debtor usually thinks first in terms of out–of–court negotiations with creditors (often referred to as "workouts"), rather than formal court proceedings. Creditors are usually receptive because the suppliers of goods and services to the debtor do not like to lose their customers. Trade associations have been formed in many industries (*e.g.*, textile, fur) for the purpose of helping financially distressed debtors formulate repayment plans. As a practical matter, however, a substantial degree of cooperation between creditors is necessary for any workout to succeed.

Why do creditors generally favor out–of–court settlements? As previously noted, they will be able to continue to deal with the debtor as a customer. In more pragmatic terms, creditors are often able to obtain some control over the debtor's future operations, although there are recognized risks in exercising too much control. *See In re W.T. Grant Co.*, 699 F.2d 599 (2d Cir. 1983), *cert. den. Cossoff v. Rodman*, 104 S. Ct. 89 (1983); *Melamed v. Lake County Nat'l Bank*, 727 F.2d 1399, (6th Cir. 1984); *Fidelity Bank, N.A. v. United States*, 616 F.2d 1181 (10th Cir. 1980); Bartlett & Lapatin, *The Status of a Creditor as a "Controlling Person,"* 28 Mercer L. Rev. 639 (1977); Douglas–Hamilton, *Creditor Liabilities Resulting from Improper Interference with the Management of a Financially Troubled Debtor*, 31 Bus. Law. 343 (1975); Douglas–Hamilton, *When Are Creditors in Control of Debtor Companies?* 26 Practical Lawyer 61 (October 15, 1980); Fortgang, Novikoff & Feintuch, *The Dangers of Creditor Control of Debtors, (Part 1)*, 12 ALI–ABA Course Materials Journal 7 (Dec. 1987); and Fortgang, Novikoff & Feintuch, *The Dangers of Creditor Control of Debtors (Part 2)*, 12 ALI–ABA Course Materials Journal 27

(Feb. 1988). Creditors also expect a greater return in less time if they do not have to go to court.

The out–of–court settlement represents a chance to avoid an often wasteful liquidation. The going–concern value of the debtor's assets will ordinarily exceed their liquidation value by a substantial amount. Most important, when a forced liquidation ensues, not only will the creditors be hurt, but also stockholders or partners. In addition, secured lenders recognize that when such collateral as equipment is used in the debtor's business, it can help to pay off the outstanding indebtedness. If sold at foreclosure, the equipment will most likely bring only a fraction of its going–concern value. Many of the same principles apply when the secured creditor's collateral consists of inventory (particularly work in process) and accounts receivable. Collecting the debtor's receivables is much more difficult when the debtor's business is defunct.

The composition is an agreement providing for the debtor's partial payment in full satisfaction of the accepting creditors' claims. Occasionally, the creditors agree only to an extension or moratorium, which merely provides for the creditors' postponing enforcement of their claims, but receiving full payment over a period of time. Both of these techniques—composition or moratorium—may be used simultaneously, but require the agreement of the debtor and at least two creditors because of the common law contract rule that one creditor cannot be bound by an agreement to accept less than the full amount of its claim. When two or more creditors agree with the debtor, however, their mutual agreement to take less than the full amount of their debts provides the necessary consideration to make the agreement enforceable between the debtor and each accepting creditor. What happens when the creditor has a guarantor? Will the guarantor be released if the creditor consents to the composition or the moratorium? What can the creditor do to preserve its rights against the guarantor?

The out–of–court settlement depends entirely on the voluntary agreement of the affected creditors. It is ineffective as against non–assenting creditors. Nevertheless, because this procedure is relatively fast and inexpensive, it is still immensely popular in certain industries, particularly when the debtor has a small or medium–sized business with relatively few creditors (usually less than thirty).

IN RE PLAZA MUSIC CO.

United States District Court, Southern District of New York
10 F. Supp. 310 (1934), aff'd, 77 F.2d 1010 (2d Cir. 1935)

PATTERSON, District Judge.

The question is whether, on nonpayment of notes given under a common–law composition and on subsequent bankruptcy of the debtor, a creditor may prove claim for the unpaid balance of his original claim or only for the unpaid balance due under the composition.

In the summer of 1932 Plaza Music Co., Inc., was in financial difficulties. It made an offer of composition to creditors. The offer recited the debtor's hope of continuing in business and "reorganizing" with the creditors' cooperation, and put to the creditors the proposition of a 50 per cent. settlement, payable 20 per cent. in cash and 30 per cent. in notes of the debtor. Another term of the offer was that one Germain, treasurer of the debtor, would subordinate his claim of $23,914.54 for money loaned to the debtor, by converting it into a capital investment.

This offer was accepted by more than 90 per cent. of the creditors, the petitioner Paine among them. The acceptance read that, in consideration of similar consents by other creditors and of the moneys to be advanced to effect settlement, the creditor "agrees to a settlement of its claim against the Plaza Music Company . . . by the acceptance of 50% thereof, to be payable as follows: 20% in cash; 30% in six notes of 5% each. . . ." The acceptance also referred to the subordination of Germain's claim and declared that it would be effective on consents by not less than 90 per cent. of the creditors.

The 20 per cent. in cash was paid and notes for 30 per cent. were delivered. Germain's claim of $23,914.54 was wiped out. But the notes were never paid. The debtor continued in business for some time, incurring new obligations, and went into bankruptcy a year later. Paine filed proof of claim for $17,622.94, which was the amount of his original debt less what he had received in cash on the composition. The trustee in bankruptcy objected that the claim was excessive. The referee held that the claim should be reduced to $6,659.40, which represented the unpaid notes received on the composition. Paine submits that the referee erred in ordering the reduction.

A composition pursuant to the Bankruptcy Act is practically the equivalent of a discharge in bankruptcy. If notes given by the debtor as part of the composition are not paid, the original debt is not revived. The creditors' only rights are on the composition notes. This result has been reached from a consideration of the provisions of the Bankruptcy Act relative to compositions and of the policy of the act. *In re Mirkus* (C. C. A. 2) 289 F. 732; *Jacobs v. Fensterstock*, 236 N. Y. 39, 139 N. E. 772. But as the composition involved here was not one under the Bankruptcy Act, these authorities have no application.

The validity of the composition as a common–law settlement is unquestionable. Consideration for each creditor's promise to take less than the amount owed him is found not merely in the promises of the other creditors, but also in the promise of Germain to subordinate his claim. The only question is whether the later default of the debtor on the composition notes revived the original claims of the creditors.

It is a general rule in common–law compositions that the nonperformance by the debtor of his engagements under the arrangement operates to revive the original claims, giving creditors their option to enforce those claims or to pursue their rights under the composition. Sometimes the composition agreement provides in express terms that on default of the debtor the creditors shall be relegated to their pre–existing claims. *Whitney v. Whitaker*, 2 Metc. (Mass.) 268; *Pupke v. Churchill*, 91 Mo. 81, 3 S. W. 829; *Penniman v. Elliott*, 27 Barb. (N. Y.) 315. And in the ordinary case where there is no specific provision to this effect, but where the debtor merely agrees to pay a percentage and the compounding creditors agree to accept the percentage in full satisfaction, there is a presumption that the parties intend the payment rather than the new promise to be the contemplated discharge of the old claims. *Clarke v. White*, 12 Pet. 178, 9 L. Ed. 1046; *Ransom v. Geer* (C. C. N. Y.) 12 F. 607; *In re Carton* (D. C.) 148 F. 63, decided by Judge Hough; *Hadley Falls Nat. Bank v. May*, 29 Hun (N. Y.) 404, *affirmed* 99 N. Y. 671; *Chapman v. Dennison*, 77 Me. 205; *National Bank v. Porter*, 122 Mass. 308; *Cobleigh v. Pierce*, 32 Vt. 788; Restatement, Contracts §§ 417–419. This is true even where notes given on the composition bear the indorsement of a third person. *In re Clarence A. Nachman Co.* (C. C. A. 2) 6 F.(2d) 427. In such cases the failure of the debtor to pay in accordance with the composition removes the impediment to the creditors' enforcement of their original claims.

But the effect to be attached to the debtor's default under the composition depends on the intent of the parties as evidenced by the composition agreement. If the agreement is one in which the creditors take the debtor's promise, rather than later payment, in satisfaction, their pre–existing claims are extinguished forthwith and on later nonperformance of the promise the creditors have nothing but their rights under the composition. The intent to accept the promise in full satisfaction may appear either by express provision of the agreement or by fair implication from its terms. *Good v. Cheeseman*, 2 Barn. & Adol. 328; *Brown v. Farnham*, 55 Minn. 27, 56 N. W. 352; *Mullin v. Martin*, 23 Mo. App. 537; *Bartlett v. Woodworth–Mason Co.*, 69 N. H. 316, 41 A. 264; *Swartz v. Brown*, 135 App. Div. 913, 119 N. Y. S. 1024; *Washington Securities Co. v. American Nitrogen Products Co.*, 142 Wash. 624, 253 P. 1070. *See, also, Kromer v. Heim*, 75 N. Y. 574, 577, 31 Am. Rep. 491. It may be inferred where the debtor transfers his property as part of the composition (*Brown v. Farnham, supra*), or where certain creditors take a deferred position under the composition (*Washington Securities Co. v. American Nitrogen Products Co., supra*). And the intent to make the agreement an executed one will be found more readily in the case of a composition than in an ordinary accord. Williston on Contracts, § 1847.

Here the promise of the debtor to pay a percentage and the promise of the creditors to accept it in full settlement have no particular significance one way or the other. If this were the extent of the agreement, the presumption that it is the performance and not the promise that is to control the discharge of the original claims would govern the case. But an important feature of the composition was the subordination of Germain's claim to the claims of the other creditors. That subordination was and still is to the advantage of the compounding creditors. In this respect, at least, the composition was thoroughly executed. Germain cannot be restored to his original status as a creditor, because the bankrupt has past–composition creditors who would be prejudiced, and, for all that appears, some of the composition creditors are standing on their rights under the composition. The composition being a finality as to this creditor, the inference is a reasonable one that it was intended by the parties to be final as to the other creditors who assented to it. Just as Germain took stock in extinguishment of his claim, so the others took cash and notes in extinguishment of their claims. The suggestion that whatever the construction of the agreement the creditor should have the option of rescinding it on the debtor's nonperformance

(Williston on Contracts, § 1848) is inadmissible here, for the subordinating creditor cannot get back what he relinquished. The result is that the debtor's subsequent failure to pay the notes did not revive the original claims.

The case is different, I think, from a composition where indorsed notes are given in settlement, as in the *Nachman* Case, *supra*. Such a composition is executory as to the surety as well as the debtor. Moreover, the surety is not altogether committed; he is released if the creditor on the debtor's default elects to rely on his original claim.

It follows that the proving creditor was entitled to prove for only the unpaid balance of his claims under the composition. The referee's order reducing the claim to this amount was right, and will be affirmed.

NOTES AND QUESTIONS

(1) What arguments can be made by counsel for the debtor to induce creditors to go along with an out–of–court settlement? To preserve a valuable lease? To preserve a valuable government contract? To preserve substantial tax loss carry–overs? *See* Krause, *Insolvent Debtor Adjustments Under Relevant State Court Statutes as Against Proceedings Under the Act*, 12 Bus. Law 184 (1957).

(2) As noted in the *Plaza Music* case, *supra*, the consideration for the composition exists in the undertaking of two or more creditors to forebear from enforcing their claims. *White v. Kuntz*, 107 N.Y. 518, 14 N.E. 423 (1887).

(3) The court in *Plaza Music*, *supra*, found that the original claims were released by execution of the composition agreement and the delivery of notes, thereby limiting the creditor to a claim only for the unpaid balance due under the composition. In *In re Clarence A. Nachman Co.*, 6 F.2d 427 (2d Cir. 1925), cited in *Plaza Music*, the court held that the creditors could prove their original claims, reasoning that the parties had intended to revive the original claims if the debtor failed to perform its obligations under the composition. Can you reconcile the two cases? In a more recent case, the federal district court of Pennsylvania applied reasoning similar to the Second Circuit's analysis in the *Nachman* case:

> An executed composition between a debtor and his creditors settles the claims and extinguishes the debts included within it, and the rights and remedies of the parties depend thereafter on the new agreement. On the other hand, an inchoate composition merely suspends the rights of action on the original claims while it remains in force, and a breach of the composition will revive them. If the discharge of a debtor is made conditional on payment, he may sue on the original cause of action if payment is not made. . . . The cause of action for breach of an agreement between the debtor and his creditors varies according to the nature of the agreement. If that agreement does not contemplate the release of the debtor until full performance, a breach for default voids

the composition and revives the original debt. The creditor may then sue for the remaining portion of the debt.

Warner Lambert Pharmaceutical Co. v. Sylk, 348 F. Supp. 1039, 1044 (E.D. Pa. 1971) (citations deleted), *aff'd*, 475 F.2d 1398 (3d Cir. 1973). *Accord Farmers' Bank of Dardanelle v. Sellers*, 167 Ark. 152, 267 S.W. 591 (1925). *See In re Stratton Group, Ltd.*, 12 B.R. 471 (Bankr. S.D.N.Y. 1981), for comparison of result under the federal bankruptcy laws. In *Warner Lambert*, the court emphasized that the terms of the particular agreement will determine the point at which the debtor is discharged from its debts. Accordingly, careful draftsmanship is required to preserve the rights of creditors under the agreement should the debtor fail to fulfill his obligations.

(4) The out–of–court settlement may also be used in conjunction with a sale of most of the debtor's assets, with elaborate provisions for a pro rata distribution of the sale proceeds to creditors. When, if ever, does Article 6 of the Uniform Commercial Code apply? What must the parties do to comply with Article 6? Should they, in any event? *See* Harris, *The Bulk Sale as a Vehicle for Effecting Out–of–Court Settlement with Creditors*, 55 Comm. L.J. 317 (1950).

(5) Does it make any difference whether the transferee assumes the transferor's debts? Is it relevant whether the assuming transferee is solvent after such assumption? *See* U.C.C. §§ 6–103(6) and 6–103(7) (1977).

(6) *See generally* Shimm, *The Impact of State Law on Bankruptcy*, 1971 Duke L.J. 879, 881–883; Note, Wiseman, *Compositions with Creditors: Executed and Executory Secret Preferences*, 28 U. Pitt. L. Rev. 344 (1966).

§ 9.02   Assignments for the Benefit of Creditors

An assignment effects a transfer of all of the debtor's assets to an assignee who has the duty of promptly liquidating these assets and distributing the proceeds to creditors on a pro rata basis. If any surplus remains, it reverts to the debtor.

Assignments for the benefit of creditors are provided for by statute in more than forty states, which supplant or augment the common law. In other states, assignments are governed by common law. Generally, the statutes provide for the recording of the assignment document itself, filing of a list of the debtor's assets and liabilities, and the posting of a bond by the assignee. Either the debtor or the assignee must also give formal notice of the assignment to all creditors, but the assignee must later account to a designated court for the disposition of the debtor's property. The primary task of the assignee is to liquidate the debtor's assets promptly, and then make a pro rata distribution of the net cash proceeds to creditors. The assignee takes the debtor's assets, however, subject to any existing liens, claims or any other valid encumbrances. *See, e.g., Kaufman v. Sbarro of Sunrise Mall, Inc.*, 47 A.D.2d 734, 365 N.Y.S.2d 219 (1st Dep't 1975); *In re Samuel August & Co.*, 228 F.Supp. 443 (D.N.J. 1964). Under sections 9–301(1) and (3) of the Uniform Commercial Code, an assignee also will have the status of a lien creditor with the power to avoid any security interest that is unperfected under state law at the date of the assignment.

In effect, the assignee is a fiduciary responsible for the distribution of the debtor's property. *See, e.g., In re W.T. Byrns, Inc.*, 260 F. Supp. 442 (E.D. Va. 1966).

What distinguishes the assignment for the benefit of creditors from a fraudulent transfer? Does it not hinder and delay creditors from exercising their legal remedies against the debtor's property? Absent some evidence of fraud, courts have sustained the assignment because it benefits all creditors generally. *See* Shimm, *The Impact of State Law on Bankruptcy*, 1971 Duke L.J. 879, 888–892. If a creditor does not trust the assignee, may it file an involuntary petition in bankruptcy against the debtor? *See* 11 U.S.C. § 303(h). For a discussion of the remedies available to the corporate debtor *see* Greenfield, *Alternatives to Bankruptcy For the Business Debtor*, 51 L.A.B.J. 135 (1975–1976).

IN RE MAINE STATE RACEWAYS

United States District Court, District of Maine
97 F. Supp. 1016 (1951)

CLIFFORD, District Judge.

This matter comes before this Court on the petition of Robert Bosse, Ernest C. Wilkins, and Hall & Knight Hardware Company, petitioning creditors in involuntary bankruptcy, for review of two orders of the Referee in Bankruptcy, both dated March 17, 1951.

The first order complained of relates to the denial by the Referee of the motion made by petitioners for a summary judgment declaring Maine State Raceways a bankrupt.

The second order complained of relates to the granting by the Referee of the motion made by Maine State Raceways for a summary judgment declaring that the so–called Trust Mortgage, executed by Maine State Raceways on September 7, 1950, was not a general assignment for the benefit of creditors.

Maine State Raceways, a Maine corporation, will be hereinafter referred to as Raceways.

Petitioners assert that they are aggrieved by certain allegedly erroneous rulings of the Referee, contained in those orders and in the opinion which accompanied those orders. Specifically, petitioners allege that the Referee erred, (1) in his ruling that there was a substantial question of material fact involved in the issue relating to petitioners' contention that they were creditors of Raceways; and, (2) in his ruling that there was a substantial question of material fact involved in the issue relating to petitioners' contention that the Trust mortgage herein referred to was made by Raceways with the intent to hinder, delay, or defraud creditors; and, (3) in his ruling that the Trust Mortgage, as a matter of law, was not a general assignment for the benefit of creditors; and, (4) in his ruling setting the matter down for trial and limiting the evidence to be received in the trial to the issues set out by him.

All of these questions are raised with respect to the first order complained of by petitioners, that is, the order denying petitioners' motion for summary judgment. The only point raised with respect to the second order relates to the alleged error numbered (3) above, holding that the Trust Mortgage was not a general assignment for the benefit of creditors.

It has been contended by Raceways, in its briefs, that Petitioners' motion for summary judgment, as presented to the Referee, was defective in that it did not precisely state the grounds on which summary judgment was sought. On review of the Referee's orders, this Court assumes that the issues on which the Referee ruled were properly before him for decision, unless the contrary plainly appears. From a reading of the Referee's opinion, it is clear that he considered the issues raised by petitioners' motion to be whether or not Raceways, as a matter of law, had committed the first and the fourth Acts of Bankruptcy.[1] That was a reasonable construction of petitioners' motion and the supporting affidavits and exhibits. In overlooking possible technical objections to the motion and addressing himself to the heart of the controversy apparently raised by the motion, the Referee acted in the liberal spirit of the Federal Rules of Civil Procedure 28 U.S.C.A. This Court will likewise overlook any technical defects of pleading, since it can do so without prejudice to any party to the proceeding.

The order of the Referee is interlocutory, insofar as it refuses to grant summary judgment on the ground that the pleadings and affidavits present substantial questions of material fact requiring hearing on the merits. No right of petitioners has been foreclosed. After hearing, on the merits, petitioners may still prevail on those questions. If they do not prevail, they still have the right to seek review from this Court. *In re Schimmel*, D.C.E.D.Pa.1913 203 F. 181; *See In re Prindible*, 3 Cir., 1940, 115 F.2d 21, 22.

The third allegation of error relates to the ruling of the Referee that, as a matter of law, the Trust Mortgage was not a general assignment for the benefit of creditors. That ruling was a final determination of that issue. As a result of that ruling, petitioners and all other creditors are foreclosed from hereafter asserting, before the Referee, that Raceways committed the fourth Act of Bankruptcy. This issue is properly before the Court for review at this time.

The interpretation of the so–called Trust Mortgage has given this Court much concern. As the Referee correctly stated in his opinion, the Trust mortgage, was a transfer, of all the real property and the tangible personal property of Raceways, to Trustees for the benefit of the creditors of Raceways. It is also apparent that the Trustees were given power to liquidate the assets of Raceways, if, in their judgment, that course of action should be for the best interests of the creditors.

But liquidation was not the real purpose of the conveyance. The conveyance contemplated that the Trustees might effectuate a composition of the debts, or a

---

[1] The first Act of Bankruptcy consists of having conveyed, transferred, concealed, removed or permitted to be concealed or removed any part of one's property, with intent to hinder, delay or defraud one's creditors or any of them. The fourth Act of Bankruptcy consists of having made a general assignment for the benefit of creditors. Bankruptcy Act of 1898, section 3, as amended, 11 U.S.C.A. § 21.

reorganization of the corporation. In either of those events there would be no liquidation, the property would revert to Raceways, and the Trust Mortgage would lapse.

The real and primary purpose of the Trust Mortgage is clearly disclosed in the provision made therein for the continued use of its assets in the enterprise, by Raceways itself or by the Trustees. Persons extending credit to Raceways, in connection with the operation of the enterprise, were given priority over assenting unsecured creditors. Raceways was given authority to sell merchandise in the usual course of the operation of this enterprise. Clearly, therefore, the Trust Mortgage did not necessarily contemplate the liquidation of the assets conveyed, even though provision was made for the equitable distribution of the proceeds of sale among the assenting creditors, in the event that liquidation should occur.

Moreover, by assenting to the Trust Mortgage, a creditor did not assure to himself any immediate dividend, or even an ultimate dividend, from the sale of assets. The assenting creditor merely agreed not to interfere with the control of the assets by the Trustees, during the continuation of efforts by Raceways to work its way out of its financial difficulties. During negotiations for this purpose, the Trust Mortgage contemplated that the operations of Raceways would continue. Liquidation would come only as a last resort, if all other efforts failed. This conclusion is supported by the letter of September 11, 1950, from the Trustees addressed to the creditors and stockholders of Raceways, which petitioners have put in the record. That letter indicates clearly that the Trust Mortgage was executed as a means of protecting the creditors while at the same time permitting Raceways to continue its operations.

Petitioners correctly point out that the approval of stockholders is not a necessary element of an act of bankruptcy by a corporation. *Royal Indemnity Co. v. American Bond Co.*, 1933, 289 U.S. 165, 53 S.Ct. 551, 77 L.Ed. 1100 (Considering application of Maine statute). Nevertheless, for what it may be worth, and as evidence of the intention of Raceways in executing the Trust Mortgage, it is to be noted that the Trust Mortgage was authorized by the stockholders of Raceways for the purpose of securing the creditors, as the record of the stockholders' meeting of July 17, 1950, demonstrates, and not for the purpose of liquidating the assets of the corporation.

With these facts in mind, a sufficient reason becomes apparent for the detailed provisions in the Trust Mortgage, relating to procedure for liquidation, should that be found necessary, and for the apportionment of the proceeds of liquidation among the creditors. Those provisions were made necessary by the fact that the mortgage was given, not to secure one debt, owed to a single mortgagee, but to secure many debts, owed to a large number of creditors. In such a situation it was obviously necessary to make careful provision for an equitable settlement of the estate, in the event that the basic purposes of the Trust Mortgage could not for any reason be successfully carried out.

After earnest consideration of the whole document, in the light of the very able and illuminating discussion of facts and law by counsel in their briefs, this Court is of the opinion that the Referee was correct in ruling that the Trust Mortgage was not a general assignment for the benefit of creditors. This Court adopts the discussion and conclusions of law with respect to this issue, contained in the Opinion of the Referee.

Brief notice may be made of the fourth allegation of error made by petitioners, with respect to the Referee's ruling limiting the evidence to be received at the hearing on the merits. From an examination of the pleadings, it is apparent that the issues defined by the Referee are the only issues raised by the pleadings, with the sole exception of the issue relating to the legal effect of the Trust Mortgage, discussed herein. It is the function of the Referee on motion for summary judgment to limit the issues of fact to be tried on the merits. Rule 56(d), Fed.Rules Civ.Proc. There was no abuse of his authority here.

Conclusion.

This court is of the opinion that the allegations of error numbered (1) and (2), above, refer to rulings of the Referee which are interlocutory; and that these alleged errors are, therefore, not properly before this Court at this time; that the Trust Mortgage did not constitute a general assignment for the benefit of creditors; and that the Referee was not in error in setting the matter for trial and limiting the evidence to be received at the hearing to the issues as set out by him.

It is therefore ORDERED, ADJUDGED, and DECREED, that the Petition for Review be and hereby is denied.

NOTES AND QUESTIONS

(1) One court recently summarized the New York assignment for the benefit of creditors procedure as follows:

> A general assignment for the benefit of creditors has been defined as "a voluntary transfer by a debtor of all his property, to a trustee of his own selection, for administration, liquidation, and equitable distribution among his creditors." 28 N.Y.Jur., Insolvency § 7 at 569. It is distinguishable from a federal bankruptcy proceeding in that no discharge from the assignor's debts is obtainable in an assignment for the benefit of creditors. See *Pavone Textile Corporation v. Bloom*, 195 Misc. 702, 90 N.Y.S.2d 785 (Sup. Ct. 1949), *aff'd* 302 N.Y. 206, 97 N.E.2d 755, *aff'd*. 342 U.S. 912, 72 S. Ct. 357, 96 L. Ed. 682. After a claim is allowed the debtor–assignor continues to remain liable for the unpaid balance of the debt, and the creditor may resort to and pursue such remedies as may be available. *Delta Trading Corp. v. Kohn & Son Co., Inc.*, 28 Misc. 2d 894, 215 N.Y. S.2d 607 (Sup. Ct. 1961); *Kay Mfg. Corp. v. Weiss*, 11 Misc. 2d 164, 168 N.Y.S.2d 330 (Sup. Ct.1957); 28 N.Y. Jur., Insolvency § 19 at 586. Upon assignment the assignee takes title to the debtor's estate as trustee for all the creditors under the court's supervision and the estate is in custodia legis. *In re John C. Creveling & Son Corporation*, 259 App. Div. 351, 19 N.Y.S.2d 378 (2d Dept. 1940) *aff'd* 283 N.Y. 760, 28 N.E.2d 975.

Freeman v. Marine Midland Bank of New York, 419 F. Supp. 410, 447 (E.D.N.Y. 1976).

(2) If creditors are dissatisfied with the assignment, it is usually easy to upset it by filing an involuntary bankruptcy petition against the debtor under 11 U.S.C. § 303(h)(2) (appointment of "custodian" who takes charge of more than substantially all of the property of the debtor, a ground for involuntary relief if petition filed "within 120 days"). The Bankruptcy Code defines "custodian" to mean, among other things, an "assignee under a general assignment for the benefit of the debtor's creditors." 11 U.S.C. § 101(11)(B). Creditors must act within 120 days of the assignee's being appointed or his taking possession. If they fail to move within the 120–day period, they may still seek involuntary relief by proving the debtor's general nonpayment of its debts as they become due, the alternative ground for involuntary relief, which has no 120–day time limitation. *See* 11 U.S.C.§ 303(h)(1). Apparently, the 120–day period begins on the later of the assignee's appointment or the taking of possession by the assignee. Section 543 of the Bankruptcy Code establishes an orderly transition procedure from assignee to bankruptcy trustee by (1) requiring a custodian to deliver property of the debtor to the trustee and to file an accounting; (2) providing for the payment of obligations incurred by the custodian; (3) providing for the payment of reasonable compensation for services rendered and costs incurred by the custodian; and (4) permitting the bankruptcy court to abstain from exercising jurisdiction and authorizing, after notice and hearing, the custodian to proceed under state law. *See also* Fed. R. Bankr. P. 6002 (Accounting by Prior Custodian of Property of the Estate).

(3) An assignment for the benefit of creditors also will trigger the application of 31 U.S.C. § 3713, the federal priority statute, discussed in Chapter 5, *supra.*

(4) As previously noted, liquidation is the objective in an assignment. When the assignment provides for the carrying on of the debtor's business, however, with no provision for a prompt liquidation and distribution among creditors until after the business has been discontinued, the assignment may be viewed as a fraudulent attempt to hinder and delay creditors. *F. H. Roberts Co. v. Hopkins, Inc.*, 296 Mass. 519, 6 N.E.2d 837 (1937).

(5) Why would creditors want to upset an assignment for the benefit of creditors? They may distrust the assignee, usually because he has been chosen by the debtor, and not elected by the creditors, as would be the case under the Bankruptcy Code. *See* 11 U.S.C. § 702. Creditors may also want to have preferences or other voidable transfers set aside by their elected representative under the Bankruptcy Code because such transfers may not be voidable under state law. *See Pritchett v. Tolbert*, 210 N.C. 644, 188 S.E. 71 (1936); *First Federal Savings & Loan Ass'n v. Marsh*, 19 Wash. 2d 438, 143 P.2d 297 (1943).

(6) Creditor distrust of assignments has been partially alleviated in the more than forty states that have comprehensive statutory procedures providing for safeguards in the assignee's disposition of assets, allowance fees, filing of lists of assets and liabilities, notice to parties in interest, resolution of disputed claims, marshalling and distribution of estate assets, and in the assignee's accounting to the court. Nevertheless, unless the more aggressive creditors are content with the assignment, bankruptcy will probably ensue.

(7) *See City of New York v. United States*, 283 F.2d 829 (2d Cir. 1960), which illustrates the relationships among the federal tax lien law, the federal priority statute, the federal bankruptcy laws and state assignment laws.

INTERNATIONAL SHOE CO. v. PINKUS

United States Supreme Court
278 U.S. 261, 49 S. Ct. 108, 73 L. Ed. 318 (1929)

Mr. Justice BUTLER delivered the opinion of the Court.

In an action in the common pleas court of Chicot County, Arkansas, August 24, 1925, plaintiff in error obtained judgment against Pinkus for $463.43. The debtor was an insolvent merchant doing business in that county. He had 46 creditors; his debts amounted to more than $10,000, and his assets were less than $3,000. On the day judgment was entered, the insolvent, invoking c. 93 of Crawford and Moses' Digest, commenced a suit in the chancery court of that county praying to be adjudged insolvent and for the appointment of a receiver to take and distribute his property as directed by that statute. On the same day, the court adjudged him insolvent and appointed a receiver, with directions to take the property and liquidate it and direct creditors to make proof of their claims "with the necessary stipulation that they will participate in the proceeds in full satisfaction of their demands." And, in pursuance of the statute, the court ordered the receiver, after the expiration of 90 days, first to pay costs, next salaries earned within 90 days, then "the claims of those who have duly filed their claims with the above stipulation, if enough funds are in your hands to pay the same, and lastly . . . to pay any and all other claims of creditors, or so much as the funds . . . will pay, all creditors of the same class receiving an equal percentage of the funds." The receiver sold the property for $2659, and gave Pinkus $500 as his exemption. The court allowed $250 as compensation for the receiver.

November 18, 1925, plaintiff in error caused execution to issue for collection of the judgment. The sheriff, being unable to find property on which to levy, returned the writ unsatisfied. Thereupon, plaintiff in error brought this suit. The complaint alleged the facts aforesaid, asserted that c. 93 had been superseded and suspended by the passage of the Bankruptcy Act, and prayed that the judgment be paid out of the funds in the hands of the receiver. The chancery court overruled the contention, held that the complaint failed to state a cause of action, and dismissed the case. Its judgment was affirmed by the highest court of the State. 173 Ark. 316. The case is here under § 237 (a), Judicial Code.

The question is whether, in the absence of proceedings under the Bankruptcy Act, what was done in the chancery court protects the property in the hands of the receiver from seizure to pay the judgment held by plaintiff in error.

A State is without power to make or enforce any law governing bankruptcies that impairs the obligation of contracts or extends to persons or property outside its jurisdiction or conflicts with the national bankruptcy laws. *Sturges v. Crowninshield*, 4 Wheat. 122. *Ogden v. Saunders*, 12 Wheat. 213, 369. *Baldwin v. Hale*, 1 Wall. 223, 228, *et seq. Gilman v. Lockwood*, 4 Wall. 409. *Denny v. Bennett*, 128 U.S. 489 497–498. *Brown v. Smart*, 145 U.S. 454, 457. *Stellwagen v. Clum*, 245 U.S. 605, 613.

The Arkansas statute is an insolvency law. It is so designated in its title (Acts of Arkansas, 1897) and in the revision. C. 93, *supra*. The supreme court of the State treats it as such. *Hickman v. Parlin–Orendorff Co.*, 88 Ark. 519. *Baxter County Bank v. Copeland*, 114 Ark. 316, 322. *Morgan v. State*, 154 Ark. 273, 279, 281. This case, 173 Ark. 316. *Friedman & Sons v. Hogins*, 175 Ark. 599. It provides for surrender by insolvent of all his unexempt property (§ 5885) to be liquidated by a trustee for the payment of debts under the direction of the court. It classifies creditors, prescribes the order of payment of their claims and gives preference to those fully discharging the debtor in consideration of pro rata distribution (§ 5888). *Mayer v. Hellman*, 91 U.S. 496, 502. *Stellwagen v. Clum, supra. Segnitz v. Garden City Co.*, 107 Wis. 171. *In re Weedman Stave Co.*, 199 Fed. 948, and cases cited.

The state enactment operates within the field occupied by the Bankruptcy Act. The insolvency of Pinkus was covered by its provisions. He could have filed a voluntary petition. His application to the state court for the appointment of a receiver was an act of bankruptcy, § 3(a), U.S.C., Tit. 11, § 21(a); and, at any time within four months thereafter, three or more creditors having claims amounting to $500 or over could have filed an involuntary petition. § 59(b), U.S.C., Tit. 11, § 95(b). We accept the statement made in the brief submitted on behalf of Pinkus that he had been discharged in voluntary proceedings within six years prior to the filing of the petition in the chancery court. Therefore he could not have obtained discharge under the Bankruptcy Act, § 14. U.S.C., Tit. 11, § 32, and in proceedings under that Act, all his creditors would have been entitled to participate in distribution without releasing the insolvent as to unpaid balances.

The power of Congress to establish uniform laws on the subject of bankruptcies throughout the United States is unrestricted and paramount. Constitution, Art. I, § 8, cl. 4. The purpose to exclude state action for the discharge of insolvent debtors may be manifested without specific declaration to that end; that which is clearly implied is of equal force as that which is expressed. *New York Central R. R. Co. v. Winfield*, 244 U.S. 147, 150, *et seq. Erie R. R. Co. v. Winfield*, 244 U.S. 170. *Savage v. Jones*, 225 U.S. 501, 533. The general rule is that an intention wholly to exclude state action will not be implied unless, when fairly interpreted, an Act of Congress is plainly in conflict with state regulation of the same subject. *Savage v. Jones, supra. Illinois Central R. R. Co. v. Public Utilities Comm'n*, 245 U.S. 493, 510. *Merchants Exchange v. Missouri*, 248 U.S. 365. In respect of bankruptcies the intention of Congress is plain. The national purpose to establish uniformity necessarily excludes state regulation. It is apparent, without comparison in detail of the provisions of the Bankruptcy Act with those of the Arkansas statute, that intolerable inconsistencies and confusion would result if that insolvency law be given effect while the national Act is in force. Congress did not intend to give insolvent debtors seeking discharge, or their creditors seeking to collect claims, choice between the relief provided by the Bankruptcy Act and that specified in state insolvency laws. States may not pass or enforce laws to interfere with or complement the Bankruptcy Act or to provide additional or auxiliary regulations. *Prigg v. Pennsylvania*, 16 Pet. 539, 617, 618. *Northern Pacific Ry. v. Washington*, 222 U.S. 370, 378, *et seq. St. Louis, Iron Mt. & S. Ry. v. Edwards*, 227 U.S. 265. *Erie R. R. Co. v. New York*, 233 U.S. 671, 681, *et seq. New York Central R. R. Co. v. Winfield, supra. Erie R. R. Co. v. Winfield, supra. Oregon–Washington Co. v. Washington*, 270 U.S. 87, 101. It is clear that the provisions of the Arkansas law governing the distribution of property of insolvents for the payment of their debts and providing for their discharge, or that otherwise relate to the subject of bankruptcies, are within the field entered by Congress when it passed the Bankruptcy Act, and therefore such provisions must be held to have been superseded. In *Boese v. King*, 108 U.S. 379, this Court, referring to the effect of the national Act upon a state insolvency law similar to the Arkansas statute under consideration, said (p. 385): "Undoubtedly the local statute was, from the date of the passage of the Bankrupt Act, inoperative in so far as it provided for the discharge of the debtor from future liability to creditors who came in under the assignment and claimed to participate in the distribution of the proceeds of the assigned property." And *see Foley–Bean Lumber Co. v. Sawyer*, 76 Minn. 118. *Parmenter Manufacturing Co. v. Hamilton*, 172 Mass. 178. *In re Bruss–Ritter Co.*, 90 Fed. 651.

In the opinion of the state supreme court, it is said that the effect of the proceedings in the chancery court was the same as if the insolvent had made an assignment for the benefit of his creditors. But the property was not handed over simply for the purpose of the payment of debts as far as it would go; it was transferred pursuant to a statute and decree imposing conditions intended to secure the debtor's discharge. As its claim was less than $500, plaintiff in error could not invoke the jurisdiction of the bankruptcy court without cooperation of other creditors. It was shown by insolvent's petition that his property was less than one–third of his debts. The amount remaining after deducting his exemption and the costs was not sufficient to pay 20 per cent of the claims. All creditors except plaintiff in error agreed fully to release insolvent in consideration of the distribution directed by the decree. And, as their claims were much in excess of the fund, plaintiff in error could have obtained nothing on account of its claim without giving insolvent a full release.

The decision below is not supported by *Boese v. King, supra*. In that case there was an assignment under the New Jersey insolvency law. Some years later creditors obtained judgment against the assignor in New York. A receiver appointed in supplementary proceedings sued the assignees in New York to compel payment of the judgment out of funds they had on deposit there. The highest court of the State denied relief, and the case was brought here on writ of error. This Court held that the assignment was sufficient to pass title; and, as the Bankruptcy Act had superseded the New Jersey insolvency law, all the creditors were entitled unconditionally to share in pro rata distribution. The receiver was held not entitled to recover because the judgment creditors could have secured equal distribution by the institution of bankruptcy proceedings, but instead they waited until after the expiration of the time allowed for that purpose, and then by the New York suit sought to obtain preference and full payment. In the course of the opinion, it is said (p. 386): "It can hardly be that the court is obliged to lend its aid to those who, neglecting or refusing to avail themselves of the provisions of the act of Congress, seek to accomplish ends inconsistent with that equality among creditors which those provisions were designed to secure." The case now before us is essentially different. Plaintiff in error could not invoke jurisdiction of the bankruptcy court. The insolvent commenced proceedings under the Arkansas insolvency law on the day that judgment was obtained against him. His purpose was to delay plaintiff in error and to secure full releases as provided by the statute. The state court did not treat the proceedings under the state law as a transfer of insolvent's property for unconditional distribution as was done in *Boese v. King*. On the contrary, the decree was the same as if the Bankruptcy Act had not been passed, and the court held that, without giving any effect to the statute, the insolvent by what was done in the chancery court could compel the same distribution and obtain for himself the same advantages as were contemplated by the insolvency law. We are of opinion that the proceedings in the chancery court cannot be given that effect. The enforcement of state insolvency systems, whether held to be in pursuance of statutory provisions or otherwise, would necessarily conflict with the national purpose to have uniform laws on the subject of the bankruptcies throughout the United States.

As all the proceedings were had under the Arkansas insolvency law, we need not decide whether, independently of statute, an assignment for the benefit of creditors on the conditions specified in the decree would protect the property of the insolvent from seizure to pay the judgment. And, as the passage of the Bankruptcy Act superseded the state law, at least insofar as it relates to the distribution of property and releases to be given, plaintiff in error is entitled to have its judgment paid out of the fund in the hands of the receiver.

Decree reversed.

Mr. Justice McREYNOLDS, Mr. Justice BRANDEIS and Mr. Justice SANFORD are of opinion that the decree should be affirmed.

NOTES AND QUESTIONS

(1) What was the basis for the court's decision in *International Shoe Co. v. Pinkus, supra*?

(2) The Supreme Court has upheld state statutory provisions which resemble common law assignments for the benefit of creditors and do not grant the debtor a discharge from debts. *See, e.g., Straton v. New*, 283 U.S. 318 (1931); *Stellwagen v. Clum*, 245 U.S. 605 (1918); *Mayer v. Hellman*, 91 U.S. 496 (1875). The Supreme Court of Wisconsin described the uncertainty and confusion caused by the sweeping language of *International Shoe, supra*, and offered some guidance in *In re Mader's Store for Men, Inc.*, 77 Wis. 2d 578, 254 N.W.2d 171, 180–82 (1977):

> It is settled in this regard that state statutes providing for the discharge of a debtor, or exacting from creditors a stipulation of discharge as a condition of participating in the distribution of the debtor's assets, are invalid so long

as national legislation is in effect. *International Shoe Co. v. Pinkus*, 278 U.S. 261, 49 S.Ct. 108, 73 L.Ed. 318 (1929); *Voluntary Assignment of Tarnowski*, 191 Wis. 279, 210 N.W. 836 (1926). It also appears to be generally conceded that the presence or absence of a discharge provision is not the sole determining criterion.[7] However, what the additional criteria are or ought to be is a matter of considerable confusion and uncertainty. Courts and commentators have been led into a variety of efforts to define the essence of bankruptcy legislation, the premise being that state laws which are "tantamount to bankruptcy" are suspended.[8] The results have not been satisfactory; after a period of nearly eighty years in which national bankruptcy legislation has been continuously in effect, the doctrinal basis of the distinction sought to be drawn remains unclear.

Some of the uncertainty in the area is traceable to the sweeping language used by the United States Supreme Court in *International Shoe Co. v. Pinkus*, *supra*.[9] Courts have examined state legislation with an eye to determining

---

[7] A number of decisions in the lower federal courts have held legislation in respect of insolvents to have been suspended notwithstanding the absence of discharge provisions. *See* for example, *In re Wisconsin Builders Supply Co.*, 239 F.2d 649 (7th Cir. 1956); *First National Bank of Albuquerque v. Robinson*, 107 F.2d 50 (10th Cir. 1939); *In re Weedman Stave Co.*, 199 F. 948 (E.D.Ark. 1912); *In re Smith*, 92 F. 135 (D.Ind. 1899).

In *Stellwagen v. Clum*, 245 U.S. 605, 616, 38 S.Ct. 215, 218, 62 L.Ed. 507 (1918), the court said:

> [W]hile it is not necessary to decide that there may not be state insolvent laws which are suspended although not providing for a discharge of indebtedness, all the cases lay stress upon the fact that one of the principal requisites of a true bankruptcy law is for the benefit of the debtor in that it discharges his future acquired property from the obligation of existing debts.

[8] A number of proposed tests are collected in a note at 14 Rutgers L.Rev. 800 (1960). *See also* Comment, *A Challenge to the Validity of Certain Sections of Wisconsin's Chapter 128*, 45 Marq.L.Rev. 403 (1962); McCarty, *Federal Bankruptcy or State Court Receivership*, 48 Marq.L.Rev. 340 (1965); Williston, *The Effect of a National Bankruptcy Law Upon State Laws*, 22 Harv.L.Rev. 547 (1909).

[9] " . . . In respect of bankruptcies the intention of Congress is plain. The national purpose to establish uniformity necessarily excludes state regulation. It is apparent, without comparison in detail of the provisions of the Bankruptcy Act with those of the Arkansas statute, that intolerable inconsistencies and confusion would result if that insolvency law be given effect while the national Act is in force. Congress did not intend to give insolvent debtors seeking discharge, or their creditors seeking to collect claims, choice between the relief provided by the Bankruptcy Act and that specified in state insolvency laws. States may not pass or enforce laws to interfere with or complement the Bankruptcy Act or to provide additional or auxiliary regulations. [citations] It is clear that the provisions of the Arkansas law governing the distribution of property of insolvents for the payment of their debts and providing for their discharge, or that otherwise relate to the subject of bankruptcies, are within the field entered by Congress when it passed the Bankruptcy Act, and therefore such provisions must be held to have been superseded. [278 U.S. at 265, 266, 49 S.Ct. at 110]

" . . .

" . . . The enforcement of state insolvency systems, whether held to be in pursuance of statutory provisions or otherwise, would necessarily conflict with the national purpose to have uniform laws on the subject of bankruptcies throughout the United States." *Id.* at 268, 49 S.Ct. at 111.

whether it "occupies the same field" as the federal Act or offers a competitive alternative thereto.[10] However, in *Pobreslo v. Joseph M. Boyd Co.*, 287 U.S. 518, 53 S.Ct. 262, 77 L.Ed. 469 (1933), a case decided after *Pinkus, supra,* the court upheld the provisions governing assignments for the benefit of creditors then contained in ch. 128, Wis.Stats., noting in the process that if creditors of the corporation so desired, they could put an end to the state assignment proceedings by instituting bankruptcy proceedings within the statutory four–month period. An assignment for the benefit of creditors results in the ratable distribution of non–exempt assets of an insolvent debtor among his creditors just as do proceedings in bankruptcy, and the bankruptcy court is available, as an alternative to the assignment proceedings, to the debtor and in most cases to his creditors as well. It is apparent that state legislation does not encroach in a forbidden way upon the field occupied by the Bankruptcy Act merely because it provides for a distribution of the assets of an insolvent corporation among its creditors, and we think this is true whether the proceeding is voluntary or involuntary in its inception. *Pinkus* must be read in the light of the *Pobreslo Case*, and the fact that the condemned Arkansas statutes provided for discharge of the debtor.

Both before and after the *Pinkus* decision, the United States Supreme Court has said that state legislation is suspended "only to the extent of actual conflict with the system provided by the Bankruptcy Act of Congress." *Stellwagen v. Clum*, 245 U.S. 605, 613, 38 S.Ct. 215, 217, 62 L.Ed. 507 (1918); *Chicago Title & Trust Co. v. Forty–One Thirty–Six Wilcox Building Corp.*, 302 U.S. 120, 126, 58 S.Ct. 125, 82 L.Ed. 147 (1937). In our opinion the appropriate focus of analysis is the effect of operation of the challenged state laws upon access of the debtor or his creditors to the bankruptcy courts, administration of proceedings therein, and rights and liabilities created by the federal Act.

> [T]he basic impropriety to be avoided in state insolvency legislation is interference with the orderly administration of the constitutionally authorized uniform national bankruptcy laws.

In re Distillers Factors Corp., supra, 187 F.2d at 687.

(3) In some states, the statutory scheme for assignments continues without the impermissible discharge provisions. In New York, for example, "the provisions of the Debtor and Creditor Law dealing with discharges in assignment proceedings [are] not presently effective, in view of the existence of the National Bankruptcy Act, 11 U.S.C.A. § 1 *et seq.*" *In re Hughes & Co.*, 172 N.Y.S.2d 441, 442, 9 Misc. 2d 16 (Sup. Ct. 1957), but assignments are strictly regulated by statute.

(4) Because the debtor may not receive a discharge for all of its debts in a state assignment proceeding, individual debtors will receive far greater protection in a liquidation case under chapter 7 of the Bankruptcy Code. *See* section 524 of the Bankruptcy Code, 11 U.S.C. § 524. For the corporate debtor that is not concerned with continuation of its business, however, the lack of a discharge is not an impediment to proceeding under a state law assignment.

---

[10] *See* for example *First National Bank of Albuquerque* and *In re Wisconsin Builders Supply Co.*, note 7, *supra.*

§ 9.03 Debt–Pooling for Consumer Debtors

"Debt–pooling," or consumer debt adjustment, once offered the financially distressed consumer debtor a method for dealing with his or her creditors collectively. The debtor would typically pay part of the wages to an agent who, for a fee, would try to persuade creditors to accept installment payments over a period of time. As the following two cases show, the agent would purport to advise the debtor on how to manage finances. Consider why this technique is either undesirable or, at the very least, ineffective, as you read these cases.

HOME BUDGET SERVICE INC. v. BOSTON BAR ASSOCIATION

Massachusetts Supreme Judicial Court
335 Mass. 228, 139 N.E.2d 387 (1957)

WILKINS, Chief Justice.

The plaintiffs, two Massachusetts corporations and an individual resident in the Commonwealth, bring this bill of complaint against Boston Bar Association and Massachusetts Bar Association and seek a declaratory decree as to the constitutionality of St.1955, c. 697, entitled "An Act relative to debt pooling plans." The defendants counterclaim asking injunctive relief against the plaintiffs. *See Growers' Outlet, Inc., v. Stone*, 333 Mass. 437, 441, 131 N.E.2d 210. The facts are agreed. A judge of the Superior Court with the consent of the parties reported the case without decision. G.L.(Ter.Ed.) c. 214, § 30.

Statute 1955, c. 697, has two sections. Section 1 inserts in G.L.(Ter.Ed.) c. 221, the following new section 46C: "The furnishing of advice or services for and in behalf of a debtor in connection with any debt pooling plan, whereby such debtor deposits any funds for the purposes of making pro rata payments or other distributions to his creditors, shall be deemed to be the practice of law within the provisions of sections forty–six and forty–six A. Any person who, not being a member of the bar of the commonwealth, furnishes or offers to furnish any such advice or services, shall be punished by a fine of not more than five hundred dollars or by imprisonment for not more than six months or both." Section 2 brings section 46C within the scope of G.L.(Ter.Ed.) c. 221, §46B, as amended by St.1947, c. 75, thereby causing section 46B to read: "The supreme judicial court and the superior court shall have concurrent jurisdiction in equity, upon petition of any bar association within the commonwealth, or of three or more members of the bar of the commonwealth, or of the attorney general, or of the district attorney within his district, to restrain violations of section forty–six, forty–six A or forty–six C."

Neither the individual plaintiff nor any officer, director, or employee of the corporate plaintiffs is a member of the bar of the Commonwealth. All three plaintiffs are engaged, within the meaning of St.1955, c. 697, in furnishing advice or services for and in behalf of debtors in connection with debt pooling plans whereby debtors deposit funds for the purpose of making pro rata payments or other distributions to their creditors.

Each plaintiff runs newspaper advertisements aimed at debtors who find themselves in such financial distress that they cannot meet their obligations with their creditors. A debtor who gets in touch with a plaintiff is requested to disclose his total income, basic living expenses, total indebtedness, the nature and balance of each creditor's claim, and the steps any creditor has taken to collect. The debt pooler works out a plan or budget under which a certain amount is to be deposited each week or month with the debt pooler for distribution. The amount each creditor will receive weekly or monthly depends upon the nature and amount of his claim, the amount of any security, and the extent of pressure exerted for payment. Creditors in the strongest positions receive the largest payments proportionately. Thus, a conditional vendor may receive the full payments called for by his contract.

A debtor engaging the services of a debt pooler enters into a written agreement whereby he undertakes to make the weekly or monthly deposits; and the debt pooler undertakes to use its best efforts to persuade creditors to accept payments according to the plan, and if successful, to distribute such payments. The agreement states the amount of the debt pooler's service fee, normally not more than six per cent of the total indebtedness, to be collected from deposits made by the debtor. There is also an administration charge of from ten to fifteen cents per creditor per week. The agreement may be terminated by the debtor at any time, but by the debt pooler only if the debtor fails to make the agreed deposits. Debtors are instructed to refer all communications from creditors or their attorneys to the debt pooler, which will endeavor to work out satisfactory terms of adjustment.

After an agreement is signed, the debt pooler writes the creditors or their attorneys, stating that it has been engaged to assist the debtor in the adjustment and liquidation of his debts; that the debtor is anxious to meet his obligations but is unable to do so upon the terms contracted for; and that under the proposed new plan of payment the debt pooler will forward to a particular creditor or his attorney a stated amount weekly or monthly which represents the maximum which the debtor can pay on that creditor's claim consistently with the orderly liquidation of all his obligations. The letter points out the advantages of the plan, urges cooperation, and advises that the debt pooler will commence and continue to make payments under the plan unless it hears from the creditor or his attorney.

In cases where creditors or their attorneys refuse to agree to accept payment on the proposed terms, the debt pooler attempts a compromise of the amount of the weekly or monthly payments. It is not the practice of the debt pooler to contest the validity of claims or amounts except as to the extension of time for payment. If a creditor or his attorney agrees with the debt pooler to a compromise figure of weekly or monthly payments higher than originally proposed, the plan and the amount of the debtor's deposits are revised accordingly.

After the plan is in operation, debtors refer dunning letters, telephone calls, complaints, threats, and other communications from their creditors or their creditors' attorneys to the debt pooler, which then negotiates in an effort to persuade a creditor not to attempt to collect his claim independently of the plan. Among the situations in which the debt pooler so acts are where a creditor refuses to agree to the plan or becomes dissatisfied and demands payment on the original terms; or, being secured, threatens to foreclose his lien; or threatens to approach the debtor's employer; or institutes legal proceedings; or, holding a judgment, seeks to enforce it. In negotiating in any of these situations the debt pooler again attempts to persuade the creditor to accept payments under the plan, or offers to increase payments, or even to pay a claim in full. In some instances the plaintiffs have continued to negotiate after suit has been brought. If the debt pooler is unable to reach an agreement with a creditor as to the terms of payment, the debtor is informed of the creditor's attitude, and is told to deal direct, or, if he prefers, to withdraw from the plan. He is also told if necessary to engage an attorney of his own choosing or, in an appropriate case, to go to a legal aid society. The debt poolers do not make court appearances or prepare legal documents.

The conduct of the plaintiffs presents features of the practice of law, and viewed as a whole, amounts substantially to that. An important difference between their conduct and that of lawyers is in the inception of the relationship, which arises in a manner not permitted to the legal profession. The distressed debtor unable to look out for his financial affairs is importuned through the public press to engage for a consideration the services of a skilled handler. If he responds, there then comes into being a basic relationship of trust and confidence. To the hired negotiator the debtor makes a complete disclosure of his financial secrets, his income, and an account of his indebtedness to the last detail. Entrusted with such information, the debt pooler evolves a program which it advises the debtor to accept as one which under its administration might free him from financial embarrassment. Authorized in writing, the debt pooler enters into direct negotiation at the sources of the debtor's distress, dealing indiscriminately with creditors or their attorneys, undeterred by judgments, pending suits, or attachments. Indeed the greater the pressure, legal and otherwise, the greater the percentage of the entrusted fund the debt pooler will in its own discretion allocate to the reduction of a given claim. In a situation of insolvency—for the debtor is unable to pay his debts as they mature—the debt pooler is engaged to develop and carry out a series of compromises, which, irrespective of litigation, will ward off bankruptcy. The antagonists may be members of the bar subject to the ethical standards and discipline of their profession. The plaintiffs, according to their own contention, are not subject to similar regulation, because they are business men engaged in arm's length dealings in the commercial arena. That the debt pooler neither enters the court room nor prepares legal documents does not save its conduct from classification as the practice of law. Nor is there escape in the fact that it does not advise as to the validity of claims; for, quite to the contrary, its omission to do so may be a surrender to some demands which a member of the bar perhaps ought to question and advise the debtor to contest. The debt pooler's plan and its administration thus exclude the debtor from skilled professional legal advice. So, where there is a conditional sale contract, the creditor may be paid, even in full, notwithstanding that there may have been no compliance with the applicable statutes. In this field the rules of law are most stringent, and the condition of the sale may be lost because of some departure in the contract from the prescribed statutory language. *See*, for example, *Lehan v. North Main Street Garage, Inc.*, 312

Mass. 547, 45 N.E.2d 945, 145 A.L.R. 1100; *Mogul v. Boston Acceptance Co., Inc.*, 328 Mass. 424, 104 N.E.2d 427; *Clark v. A & J Transportation Co., Inc.*, 330 Mass. 327, 113 N.E.2d 228; *Clark & White Inc., v. Fitzgerald*, 332 Mass. 603, 127 N.E.2d 172; *Nickerson v. Zeoli*, 332 Mass. 738, 127 N.E.2d 779.

From this analysis of the plaintiffs' methods it is apparent that they have "extended . . . operations beyond the legitimate field of lay business and into the field which public policy requires should be reserved for the professional practitioner." *Matter of Shoe Manufacturers Protective Association, Inc.*, 295 Mass. 369, 372, 3 N.E.2d 746, 748. Debt pooling as set forth in the agreed facts differs from mere bill collecting by a lay agent named by a creditor to present a claim to a debtor and to receive payment.

The statute here assailed is not unconstitutional as an interference with the purely judicial function to determine who may practice law but is a valid enactment in aid of the court's power to make such a determination. *Opinion of the Justices*, 279 Mass. 607, 611, 180 N.E. 725, 81 A.L.R. 1059; *Opinion of the Justices*, 289 Mass. 607, 612, 194 N.E. 313; *In re Keenan*, 310 Mass. 166, 177, 37 N.E.2d 516, 137 A.L.R. 766; *Matter of Keenan*, 313 Mass. 186, 196, 212, 47 N.E.2d 12; *Lowell Bar Association v. Loeb*, 315 Mass. 176, 179, 52 N.E.2d 27; *Creditors' Service Corp. v. Cummings*, 57 R.I. 291, 300, 190 A. 2.

The defendants' counterclaim seeks relief expressly authorized by St.1955, c. 697, § 2, *Board of Survey of Lexington v. Suburban Land Co.*, 235 Mass. 108, 113, 126 N.E. 360; *Commonwealth v. Stratton Finance Co.*, 310 Mass. 469, 474, 38 N.E.2d 640; *City of Malden v. Flynn*, 318 Mass. 276, 282, 61 N.E.2d 107.

A final decree will be entered declaring that St.1955, c. 697, is constitutional as applied to the plaintiffs and their debt pooling operations; enjoining the plaintiffs from violation of G.L.(Ter.Ed.) c. 221, § 46C, inserted by St.1955, c. 697, § 1, and of G.L.(Ter.Ed.) c. 221, § 46A, inserted by St.1935, c. 346, § 2; and enjoining the corporate plaintiffs from violation of G.L.(Ter.Ed.) c. 221, § 46, as appearing in St.1935, c. 346, § 1.

So ordered.

FERGUSON v. SKRUPA

United States Supreme Court
372 U.S. 726, 83 S. Ct. 1028, 10 L. Ed. 2d 93 (1963)

Mr. Justice BLACK delivered the opinion of the Court.

In this case, properly here on appeal under 28 U.S.C. § 1253, we are asked to review the judgment of a three–judge District Court enjoining, as being in violation of the Due Process Clause of the Fourteenth Amendment, a Kansas statute making it a misdemeanor for any person to engage "in the business of debt adjusting" except as an incident to "the lawful practice of law in this state."[1] The statute defines "debt adjusting" as "the making of a contract, express, or implied with a particular debtor whereby the debtor agrees to pay a certain amount of money periodically to the person engaged in the debt adjusting business who shall for a consideration distribute the same among certain specified creditors in accordance with a plan agreed upon."

The complaint, filed by appellee Skrupa doing business as "Credit Advisors," alleged that Skrupa was engaged in the business of "debt adjusting" as defined by the statute, that his business was a "useful and desirable" one, that his business activities were not "inherently immoral or dangerous" or in any way contrary to the public welfare, and that therefore the business could not be "absolutely prohibited" by Kansas. The three–judge court heard evidence by Skrupa tending to show the usefulness and desirability of his business and evidence by the state officials tending to show that "debt adjusting" lends itself to grave abuses against distressed debtors, particularly in the lower income brackets, and that these abuses are of such gravity that a number of States have strictly regulated "debt adjusting" or prohibited it altogether.[2] The court found that Skrupa's business did fall within the Act's proscription and concluded, one judge dissenting, that the Act was prohibitory, not regulatory, but that even if construed in part as regulatory it was an unreasonable regulation of a "lawful business," which the court held amounted to a violation of the Due Process Clause of the Fourteenth Amendment. The court accordingly enjoined enforcement of the statute.[3]

The only case discussed by the court below as support for its invalidation of the statute was *Commonwealth v. Stone*, 191 Pa. Super. 117, 155 A. 2d 453 (1959), in which the Superior Court of Pennsylvania struck down a statute almost identical to the Kansas act involved here. In *Stone* the Pennsylvania court held that the State could regulate, but could not prohibit, a "legitimate" business. Finding debt adjusting, called "budget planning" in the Pennsylvania statute, not to be "against the public interest" and concluding that it could "see no justification for such interference" with this business, the Pennsylvania court ruled that State's statute to be

---

[1] Kan. Gen. Stat. (Supp. 1961) § 21–2464.

[2] Twelve other States have outlawed the business of debt adjusting. Fla. Stat. Ann. (1962) §§ 559.10–559.13; Ga. Code Ann. (Supp. 1961) §§ 84–3601 to 84–3603; Me. Rev. Stat. Ann. (Supp. 1961) c. 137, §§ 51–53; Mass. Gen. Laws Ann. (1958) c. 221, § 46C; N. J. Stat. Ann. (Supp. 1962) 2A:99A–1 to 2A:99A–4; N. Y. Penal Law (Supp. 1962) §§ 410–412; Ohio Rev. Code Ann. (1962 Supp.) §§ 4710.01–4710.99; Okla. Stat. Ann. (Supp. 1962) Tit. 24, §§ 15–18; Pa. Stat. Ann. (Supp. 1961) Tit. 18, § 4899; Va. Code Ann. (1958) § 54–44.1; W. Va. Code Ann. (1961) § 6112(4); Wyo. Stat. Ann. (1957) §§ 33–190 to 33–192. Seven other States regulate debt adjusting. Cal. Fin. Code Ann. (1955 and Supp. 1962) §§ 12200–12331; Ill. Stat. Ann. (Supp. 1962) c. 16½, §§ 251–272; Mich. Stat. Ann. (Supp. 1961) §§ 23.630 (1)–23.630 (18); Minn. Stat. Ann. (1947 and 1962 Supp.) §§ 332.04–332.11; Ore. Rev. Stat. (1961) §§ 697.610–697.992; R. I. Gen. Laws (Supp. 1962) §§ 5–42–1 to 5–42–9; Wis. Stat. Ann. (1957) § 218.02. The courts of New Jersey have upheld a New Jersey statute like the Kansas statute here in question. *American Budget Corp. v. Furman*, 67 N.J. Super. 134, 170 A. 2d 63, aff'd *per curiam*, 36 N.J. 129, 175 A. 2d 622 (1961).

[3] *Skrupa v. Sanborn*, 210 F. Supp. 200 (D. C. D. Kan. 1961).

unconstitutional. In doing so, the Pennsylvania court relied heavily on *Adams v. Tanner*, 244 U.S. 590 (1917), which held that the Due Process Clause forbids a State to prohibit a business which is "useful" and not "inherently immoral or dangerous to public welfare."

Both the District Court in the present case and the Pennsylvania court in *Stone* adopted the philosophy of *Adams v. Tanner*, and cases like it, that it is the province of courts to draw on their own views as to the morality, legitimacy, and usefulness of a particular business in order to decide whether a statute bears too heavily upon that business and by so doing violates due process. Under the system of government created by our Constitution, it is up to legislatures, not courts, to decide on the wisdom and utility of legislation. There was a time when the Due Process Clause was used by this Court to strike down laws which were thought unreasonable, that is, unwise or incompatible with some particular economic or social philosophy. In this manner the Due Process Clause was used, for example, to nullify laws prescribing maximum hours for work in bakeries, *Lochner v. New York*, 198 U.S. 45 (1905), outlawing "yellow dog" contracts, *Coppage v. Kansas*, 236 U.S. 1 (1915), setting minimum wages for women, *Adkins v. Children's Hospital*, 261 U.S. 525 (1923), and fixing the weight of loaves of bread, *Jay Burns Baking Co. v. Bryan*, 264 U.S. 504 (1924). This intrusion by the judiciary into the realm of legislative value judgments was strongly objected to at the time, particularly by Mr. Justice Holmes and Mr. Justice Brandeis. Dissenting from the Court's invalidating a state statute which regulated the resale price of theatre and other tickets, Mr. Justice Holmes said,

> I think the proper course is to recognize that a state legislature can do whatever it sees fit to do unless it is restrained by some express prohibition in the Constitution of the United States or of the State, and that Courts should be careful not to extend such prohibitions beyond their obvious meaning by reading into them conceptions of public policy that the particular Court may happen to entertain.[4]

And in an earlier case he had emphasized that, "The criterion of constitutionality is not whether we believe the law to be for the public good."[5]

The doctrine that prevailed in *Lochner, Coppage, Adkins, Burns,* and like cases— that due process authorizes courts to hold laws unconstitutional when they believe the legislature has acted unwisely—has long since been discarded. We have returned to the original constitutional proposition that courts do not substitute their social and economic beliefs for the judgment of legislative bodies, who are elected to pass laws. As this Court stated in a unanimous opinion in 1941, "We are not concerned . . . with the wisdom, need, or appropriateness of the legislation."[6] Legislative bodies

---

[4] *Tyson & Brother v. Banton*, 273 U.S. 418, 445, 446 (1927) (dissenting opinion). Mr. Justice Brandeis joined in this dissent, and Mr. Justice Stone dissented in an opinion joined by Mr. Justice Holmes and Mr. Justice Brandeis. Mr. Justice Sanford dissented separately.

[5] *Adkins v. Children's Hospital*, 261 U.S. 525, 567, 570 (1923) (dissenting opinion). Chief Justice Taft, joined by Mr. Justice Sanford, also dissented. Mr. Justice Brandeis took no part.

[6] *Olsen v. Nebraska ex rel. Western Reference & Bond Assn.*, 313 U.S. 236, 246 (1941) (upholding a Nebraska statute limiting the amount of the fee which could be charged by private employment agencies).

have broad scope to experiment with economic problems, and this Court does not sit to "subject the State to an intolerable supervision hostile to the basic principles of our Government and wholly beyond the protection which the general clause of the Fourteenth Amendment was intended to secure."[7] It is now settled that States "have power to legislate against what are found to be injurious practices in their internal commercial and business affairs, so long as their laws do not run afoul of some specific federal constitutional prohibition, or of some valid federal law."[8]

In the face of our abandonment of the use of the "vague contours"[9] of the Due Process Clause to nullify laws which a majority of the Court believed to be economically unwise, reliance on *Adams v. Tanner* is as mistaken as would be adherence to *Adkins v. Children's Hospital*, over–ruled by *West Coast Hotel Co. v. Parrish*, 300 U.S. 379 (1937). Not only has the philosophy of *Adams* been abandoned, but also this Court almost 15 years ago expressly pointed to another opinion of this Court as having "clearly undermined" *Adams*.[10] We conclude that the Kansas Legislature was free to decide for itself that legislation was needed to deal with the business of debt adjusting. Unquestionably, there are arguments showing that the business of debt adjusting has social utility, but such arguments are properly addressed to the legislature, not to us. We refuse to sit as a "superlegislature to weigh the wisdom of legislation,"[11] and we emphatically refuse to go back to the time when courts used the Due Process Clause "to strike down state laws, regulatory of business and industrial conditions, because they may be unwise, improvident, or out of harmony with a particular school of thought."[12] Nor are we able or willing to draw lines by calling a law "prohibitory" or "regulatory." Whether the legislature takes for its textbook Adam Smith, Herbert Spencer, Lord Keynes, or some other is no concern of ours.[13] The Kansas debt adjusting statute may be

---

[7] *Sproles v. Binford*, 286 U.S. 374, 388 (1932). And Chief Justice Hughes, for a unanimous Court, added, "When the subject lies within the police power of the State, debatable questions as to reasonableness are not for the courts but for the legislature, which is entitled to form its own judgment, and its action within its range of discretion cannot be set aside because compliance is burdensome." *Id.*, at 388–389.

[8] *Lincoln Federal Labor Union v. Northwestern Iron & Metal Co.*, 335 U.S. 525, 536 (1949).

Mr. Justice Holmes even went so far as to say that "subject to compensation when compensation is due, the legislature may forbid or restrict any business when it has a sufficient force of public opinion behind it." *Tyson & Brother v. Banton*, 273 U.S. 418, 445, 446 (1927) (dissenting opinion).

[9] *See Adkins v. Children's Hospital*, 261 U.S. 525, 567, 568 (1923) (Holmes, J., dissenting).

[10] *Lincoln Federal Labor Union v. Northwestern Iron & Metal Co.*, 335 U.S. 525, 535 (1949), referring to *Olsen v. Nebraska ex rel. Western Reference & Bond Assn.*, 313 U.S. 236 (1941). Ten years later, in *Breard v. Alexandria*, 341 U.S. 622, 631–632 (1951), this Court again commented on the infirmity of *Adams*.

[11] *Day–Brite Lighting, Inc.*, v. *Missouri*, 342 U.S. 421, 423 (1952).

[12] *Williamson v. Lee Optical Co.*, 348 U.S. 483, 488 (1955).

[13] "The Fourteenth Amendment does not enact Mr. Herbert Spencer's Social Statics." *Lochner v. New York*, 198 U.S. 45, 74, 75 (1905) (Holmes, J., dissenting).

wise or unwise. But relief, if any be needed, lies not with us but with the body constituted to pass laws for the State of Kansas.[14]

Nor is the statute's exception of lawyers a denial of equal protection of the laws to nonlawyers. Statutes create many classifications which do not deny equal protection; it is only "invidious discrimination" which offends the Constitution.[15] The business of debt adjusting gives rise to a relationship of trust in which the debt adjuster will, in a situation of insolvency, be marshalling assets in the manner of a proceeding in bankruptcy. The debt adjuster's client may need advice as to the legality of the various claims against him, remedies existing under state laws governing debtor–creditor relationships, or provisions of the Bankruptcy Act—advice which a nonlawyer cannot lawfully give him. If the State of Kansas wants to limit debt adjusting to lawyers,[16] the Equal Protection Clause does not forbid it. We also find no merit in the contention that the Fourteenth Amendment is violated by the failure of the Kansas statute's title to be as specific as appellee thinks it ought to be under the Kansas Constitution.

Reversed.

Mr. Justice HARLAN concurs in the judgment on the ground that this state measure bears a rational relation to a constitutionally permissible objective. *See Williamson v. Lee Optical Co.*, 348 U.S. 483, 491.

NOTES AND QUESTIONS

(1) Is debt–pooling any more effective in gaining creditor cooperation than the out–of–court settlement technique used by business debtors?

(2) What protections, if any, exist for creditors who, like the debtor, may not be treated fairly by those giving debt–pooling advice to the debtor?

(3) As *Home Budget Service* and *Ferguson*, *supra*, show, many states have prohibited debt–pooling. Many others have closely regulated its practice with statutory requirements for licensing, inspection, accounting and service fees. *See* Shimm, *The Impact of State Law on Bankruptcy*, 1971 Duke L.J. 879, 884–888.

---

[14] *See Daniel v. Family Security Life Ins. Co.*, 336 U.S. 220, 224 (1949); *Secretary of Agriculture v. Central Roig Ref. Co.*, 338 U.S. 604, 618 (1950).

[15] *See Williamson v. Lee Optical Co.*, 348 U.S. 483, 488–489 (1955); *Lindsley v. Natural Carbonic Gas Co.*, 220 U.S. 61, 78–79 (1911).

[16] Massachusetts and Virginia prohibit debt pooling by laymen by declaring it to constitute the practice of law. Mass. Gen. Laws Ann. (1958) c. 221, § 46C; Va. Code Ann. (1958) § 54–44.1. The Massachusetts statute was upheld in *Home Budget Service, Inc.*, v. *Boston Bar Assn.*, 335 Mass. 228, 139 N.E.2d 387 (1957).

§ 9.04 Receiverships

Courts with general equity jurisdiction may appoint a receiver to administer the debtor's assets for the benefit of all creditors. *See* Note, 15 N.C.L. Rev. 199 (1936). Although a receiver may be appointed for a particular secured creditor in a mortgage foreclosure proceeding or for a judgment lien creditor (*e.g.*, N.Y. Civ. Prac. R. §§ 5106, 5228) (McKinney 1978 and Supp. 1983), courts have also appointed receivers to administer all of the assets of a financially distressed debtor. *See, e.g., Luhrig Collieries Co. v. Interstate Coal & Dock Co.*, 281 F. 265 (S.D.N.Y. 1922), *appeal dismissed*, 287 F. 711 (2d Cir. 1923).

The receivership can often delay a particular creditor's attempt to levy on the debtor's assets, and was used frequently before debtor–relief provisions were added to the federal bankruptcy laws in 1938. The receivership remedy was subject, however, to frequent abuse. *See, e.g., Shapiro v. Wilgus*, 287 U.S. 348 (1932), where the debtor formed a one–man corporation, and conveyed all of his property to it. He later arranged for the creation of an equity receivership in federal court, preventing creditors from proceeding against his assets. The Supreme Court held the transfer of assets and the ensuing receivership to constitute "a scheme" to hinder and delay creditors. 287 U.S. at 353–55. *See also* SEC Report on the Study and Investigation of the Work, Activities, Personnel and Functions of Protective and Reorganization Committees, Pt. VIII, § II B (1940); *First National Bank of Cincinnati v. Flershem*, 290 U.S. 504, 519 (1934) (solvent corporate debtor sought equity receivership "not to enforce rights of creditors, but to defeat them").

The receivership, like the assignment for the benefit of creditors, can be superseded by bankruptcy if the requisite number of creditors file an involuntary petition. *See* 11 U.S.C. §§ 303(h)(2), 101(10) ("custodian" defined to include "receiver" of any of the debtor's property "in a case . . . not under this title"). In any event, "the receivership does not appear to be well regarded as a liquidation method." D. Stanley & M. Girth, Bankruptcy: Problem, Process, Reform at 120 (1971).

INLAND EMPIRE INSURANCE CO. v. FREED

United States Court of Appeals, Tenth Circuit
239 F.2d 289 (1956)

MURRAH, Circuit Judge.

This is an appeal from an order of the District Court of Utah, appointing a receiver for Inland Empire Insurance Company, domiciled in Idaho, with its principal place of business in Salt Lake City, Utah. The receiver was appointed after a full hearing on complaint of a contract creditor, alleging due and unpaid indebtedness, insolvency and imminence of dissipation. Federal jurisdiction is based upon requisite diversity of citizenship and amount in controversy.

Prior to the filing of this complaint, an Idaho district court appointed the Insurance Commissioner of that State conservator of the Company on the Commissioner's complaint, to the effect that a detailed examination of the Company disclosed insolvency, mismanagement and dissipation of assets. The order of rehabilitation, pursuant to applicable Idaho law, directed the Insurance Commissioner to take possession of all assets of the Company, conduct all business; and restrained all other persons from transacting any business or disposing of any of the property or assets of the Company.

After the institution of this suit, however, the Idaho Insurance Commissioner, represented by the Attorney General of that State, was granted permission to intervene. In his answer, he admitted the past due indebtedness of the Company to the complainants and most of the material allegations of the complaint. It affirmatively alleged his appointment as conservator of the Company's assets in Idaho, the order of rehabilitation and application for an order of dissolution. It further specifically alleged his inability to rehabilitate the Company in Idaho courts by reason of the fact that most of the assets of the Company were outside the jurisdictional reach of the Idaho court; and that a receivership proceedings in the courts of the United States was the only competent procedure for the protection of the policyholders and creditors. Attached to the answer was the detailed report of the Chief Examiner of the Department of Insurance of the State of Idaho pursuant to an examination of the Company. In this report, the Examiner recommended action in the federal court "so as to secure jurisdiction wherever necessary to resolve the problem presented by the widespread and complex nature of the activities involved."

One attorney appearing for the Company at the direction of its Executive Vice–President and the Idaho Insurance Commissioner, filed an answer admitting the indebtedness and the affirmative allegations of the complaint. Before conclusion of the hearing, another attorney, representing the appellants here, filed an answer on behalf of the Company, challenging the legal sufficiency of the complaint, and alleging that in each of the states in which the Company had been doing business, state law provided for the appointment of commissioners, conservators, liquidators or supervisors, duly authorized and empowered to take over the assets of insolvent insurance companies doing business in the respective states; and to administer such assets and property for the benefit of policyholders, creditors and stockholders; that the commissioner, liquidator or director of insurance in each of the states in which the defendant was doing business could and would immediately take possession of all of the assets and property of the Company in the respective states and administer same for the benefit of the interested parties; that all such proceedings would be prosecuted to completion without cost or expense to the policyholders, creditors and stockholders; and that the appointment of a receiver in the Utah federal court was therefore unnecessary and not in the best interest of the parties concerned. When the trial court inquired whether testimony was indicated on the question of authority to represent the Company, the attorney for the appellants replied that none was necessary and the answer was thereupon filed without further inquiry.

The Director of Insurance of the State of Arizona, as receiver for the Trans–Pacific Insurance Company, was permitted to intervene in opposition to the appointment of the federal court receiver. The answer alleged that Trans–Pacific was the owner of ninety percent of the common stock of Inland Empire, and reiterated the appellant's answering allegations. The Utah Insurance Commissioner appeared amicus curiae by the Assistant Attorney General of that State to urge the appointment of the federal court receiver.

Thus, at the commencement of the hearing on the motion for the appointment of a receiver, the Insurance Commissioner of the domiciliary State of Idaho, with the Company assets in his actual or constructive custody, and the Insurance Commissioner of Utah, where the principal office was located, each appeared by his attorney general to urge the federal receivership. And, they were supported by an attorney purporting to represent the Company. Another insurance commissioner–receiver for another insurance company holding most of the stock of Inland Empire, appeared to oppose the receivership. And, he was supported by another attorney, also purporting to represent Inland Empire.

In view of the Idaho state court's injunction against the officers of the Company transacting any business of the Company, it may be seriously doubted whether either of the attorneys purporting to represent the Company in the federal court was authorized to do so in the absence of leave or authority of the Idaho court. Neither sought nor obtained permission. And, having no authority to represent the Company, they would of course be without standing to perfect or prosecute this appeal. The Arizona Director of Insurance was authorized and directed by the competent Arizona court to intervene as receiver for Trans–Pacific in opposition to the federal receivership, and such intervention was allowed in the trial court. But, he has perfected no appeal from the order appointing the receiver.

The former directors, who are also appellants here, are represented by the same attorney who purported to represent the Company in opposition to the receivership. They have served notice of appeal from the order appointing the receiver and they appear here by their attorney. They filed no formal pleadings in the trial court. But their attorney did enter a formal appearance in their behalf and resisted the appointment of the receiver throughout. In view of the disability of the corporation as a legal entity, we will assume that the directors, who are also stockholders, have a litigable interest in the proceedings; that they are in court by their attorney with standing to challenge the order of the District Court on appeal.

The power of the federal court to appoint a receiver on petition of this unsecured contract–creditor, is challenged on authority of *Pusey & Jones Co. v. Hanssen*, 261, U.S. 491, 43 S.Ct. 454, 67 L.Ed. 763. That case did withhold federal equity jurisdiction to appoint a receiver on petition of an unsecured creditor, saying that the appointment of a receiver was not an equitable right, but a remedy not available in federal court until after the establishment of the creditor's legal right in the property of the debtor. And, this is so, although the remedy is given by a state statute to a state court of concurrent jurisdiction. The jurisdictional disparity arises from the binding effect of substantive law in diversity cases on the one hand, and the inapplicability of state remedies on the other. Thus, the remedial right to proceed in a federal equity court cannot be enlarged or diminished by state statute. *Pusey & Jones Co. v. Hanssen, supra*, 261 U.S. at pages 497–498, 43 S.Ct. 454. If, therefore, the appointment of a receiver is merely the manner or means by which the federal court proceeds to enforce a state recognized substantive right, the remedy is not ordinarily available in the federal court. And, this rule is apparently unaffected by the conceptual impact of *Erie R. Co. v. Tompkins*, 304 U.S. 64, 58 S.Ct. 817, 82 L.Ed. 1188. *See* footnote 3, *Guaranty Trust Co. of New York v. York*, 326 U.S. 99, 106, 65 S.Ct. 1464, 89 L.Ed. 2079. And *see Beneficial Industrial Loan Corp. v. Smith*, 3 Cir., 170 F.2d 44. The Utah Procedural Rule, 66 (a) (5), Utah Rules of Civil Procedure, authorizing the state courts to appoint a receiver for a corporation which has been dissolved or is insolvent or in imminent danger of insolvency, cannot therefore add to the equitable powers of a federal equity court sitting in that State.

Section 754, Title 28 U.S.C.A., provides that a receiver appointed in the federal courts involving property situated in different districts shall, upon giving the required bond, "be vested with complete jurisdiction and control of all such property with the right to take possession thereof." But we do not construe that act to broaden the equitable grounds for the appointment of a receiver. It goes to the jurisdiction and control of the property once the receiver has been rightfully appointed.

But, *Pusey & Jones v. Hanssen, supra,* and the cases which followed it, leave no doubt that the restriction or limitation thus placed upon the federal equity courts in diversity cases, is a policy restriction which goes not to the jurisdiction of the court as such, but to the propriety of the exercise of a jurisdiction conferred by the Constitution and laws of the United States. *Kelleam v. Maryland Casualty Co.*, 312 U.S. 377, 61 S.Ct. 595, 85 L.Ed. 899; *Commonwealth of Pennsylvania v. Williams*, 294 U.S. 176, 55 S.Ct. 380, 79 L.Ed. 841; *Penn General Casualty Co. v. Commonwealth of Pennsylvania*, 294 U.S. 189, 55 S.Ct. 386, 79 L.Ed. 850. One of the great virtues of federal equity jurisdiction is the facility with which it may be exercised or withheld in the public interest. It is usually withheld to avoid unseemly conflicts between state and federal concurrent jurisdictions, *i.e. see Commonwealth of Pennsylvania v. Williams, supra; Penn General Casualty Co. v. Commonwealth of Pennsylvania, supra.* It is rarely, if ever, utilized to obstruct or interfere with the domestic policy of a state. *See Great Lakes Dredge & Dock Co. v. Huffman*, 319 U.S. 293, 63 S.Ct. 1070, 87 L.Ed. 1407; *Burford v. Sun Oil Co.*, 319 U.S. 315, 63 S.Ct. 1098, 87 L.Ed. 1424; *Alabama Public Service Commission v. Southern Railway Co.*, 341 U.S. 341, 71 S.Ct. 762, 95 L.Ed. 1002.

To that end, "Receiverships for conservation of property 'are to be watched with jealous eyes lest their function be perverted.' " *Kelleam v. Maryland Casualty Co., supra*, 312 U.S. at page 381, 61 S.Ct. at page 598. But, in the last analysis, the governing consideration is one of restraint or abstention, not want of authority. Authoritative decisions have undoubtedly laid a heavy hand on the exercise of federal equity jurisdiction to appoint receivers in diversity cases where the relief sought is readily available in the state courts or by state processes. But we do not interpret the admonishments of restraint as an absolute bar to the exercise of equity jurisdiction where the exigencies require it, or where its exercise is clearly in the public interest and will not conflict with state processes. Sometimes "Rules of comity or convenience must give way to constitutional rights." *Oklahoma Natural Gas Co. v. Russell*, 261 U.S. 290, 43 S.Ct. 353, 354, 67 L.Ed. 659.

It is clear from the record that the Company is hopelessly insolvent and must be liquidated. When disaster came, it was doing business in twenty–one states, where its assets and liabilities are to be found. The record shows that more than one and a half million dollars is due the Company from its agents in all of the states at the home office in Utah. The states of its domicile and principal place of business have freely conceded their inability to rehabilitate or to liquidate for the best interest of the Company, its creditors, policyholders and stockholders. The trial court observed that only six states in which the Company has been authorized to transact business had adopted the uniform liquidation act for insurance companies, and that the only alternative is independent receivership proceedings in each state for the liquidation of the Company and the distribution of the assets. The court said, and we agree, that it would be wholly impractical under existing state laws to liquidate the Company by local receiverships in the various states in which the defendant Company is doing business. It was this "very special set of circumstances indicating the necessity of a conservation and liquidation of the assets of the corporation in aid of the claim of the plaintiff" that the court deemed a receivership "proper."

As we have seen, federal law has made adequate provision for the acquisition and complete jurisdiction and control over the property of the Company wherever and in whatever district it may be located, with capacity to sue or be sued in any district without ancillary appointment, provided the receiver "shall, within ten days after entry of his order of appointment, file copies of the complaint and such order of appointment in the district court for each district in which property is located." 28 U.S.C.A. § 754.

The record shows that the receiver has qualified in each of the states where the property of the Company is located, and immediately thereafter has undertaken the defense or prosecution of many lawsuits involving the property or the assets of the Company. Other steps have been taken toward the conservation and adjudication of the rights and liabilities of the Company arising out of its business in all the states involved. While the appointment of the receiver may in one sense have been the end in view, the court expressly found that it was ancillary to the enforcement of the plaintiff's claim. It may well be that a number of the state insurance commissioners having authority and duty to act will assert the right to exclusively control the liquidation of the assets of the Company in their respective states. In these circumstances, it will of course be in the wise discretion of the trial court to avoid undue conflict with the state court processes. But this can be done, we think, within the framework of the federal court receivership. With these guiding principles firmly in mind, the order appointing the receiver is affirmed.

[Dissenting opinion omitted.]

NOTES

(1) General receiverships may, as a practical matter, no longer be important because of the flexible voluntary and involuntary reorganization procedure now

available under chapter 11 of the Bankruptcy Code. *See, e.g., New England Coal & Coke Co. v. Rutland R.R.*, 143 F.2d 179, 184–85 (2d Cir. 1944) (reorganization provisions of federal bankruptcy law "designed to prevent the notorious evils and abuses of consent receiverships"). The major practical function of the receiver today is the enforcement of a real property mortgagee's rights in a state court mortgage foreclosure proceeding. Moreover, the motion for a receiver seeks only ancillary relief incidental to a request for more substantive relief, such as foreclosure.

(2) The receiver is an officer of the state court, limited by that court's jurisdiction, with only the authority granted it by the court. *See generally* Clark, Law of Receivers (3d. rev. ed. 1968–1969); *Pusey & Jones Co. v. Hanssen*, 261 U.S. 491 (1923); Schwarz, *Termination of SEC Receiverships in the Federal Courts*, 43 Fordham L. Rev. 163 (1974). Moreover, general receivers are ordinarily available only for corporate debtors, and not individuals. *See, e.g., Davis v. Hayden*, 238 F. 734 (4th Cir. 1916) (equity receivership jurisdiction denied when debtor not a corporation). *See also Shapiro v. Wilgus*, 287 U.S. 348 (1932), where the court held it to be a fraudulent transfer for an individual to incorporate for the purpose of commencing a receivership.

CHAPTER 10

STRUCTURE OF THE BANKRUPTCY REFORM ACT OF 1978

The current statutory law relating to bankruptcy was enacted on November 6, 1978, after some eight years of pendency in the houses of Congress. The enactment was embodied in Pub. L. 95–598, 95th Congress, 2d Session, 92 Stat. 2551, *et seq.* (1978), which consisted of four titles. Unofficially, this law is also called the Bankruptcy Reform Act of 1978. It was substantially amended in 1984 by the Bankruptcy Amendments and Federal Judgeship Act of 1984, Pub. L. 98–353, 98th Congress, 2d Session, in 1986 by the Bankruptcy Judges, United States Trustees, and Family Farmer Bankruptcy Act of 1986, Pub. L. 99–554, 99th Congress, 2d Session, and again in 1994 by the Bankruptcy Reform Act of 1994, Pub. L. 103–394, 103d Congress, 2d Session.

Title I of the 1978 Reform Act was comprised of the substantive law of bankruptcy. On its effective date, October 1, 1979, (Pub. L. 95–598, § 402), it became, and remains, title 11 of the United States Code. Thus, references to sections of the bankruptcy law would accurately be referred to as, *e.g.,* 11 U.S.C. § 501. This part of the enacted legislation has come to be known, unofficially, as the Bankruptcy Code, with citations as Bankruptcy Code § 501 or even § 501 of the Code. The term "Code" is distinguishable from "Act." The earlier and repealed bankruptcy law[1] was officially known as the Bankruptcy Act. That was, by the way, the Bankruptcy Act of 1898.

Title II of Pub. L. 95–598 contained amendments to title 28 of the United States Code, otherwise known as the Judicial Code. All matters pertaining to the structure of the bankruptcy court, the jurisdiction of bankruptcy courts, proper venue for cases and proceedings before that court, the appellate process, and the like were contained in title II of the Reform Act. The most important of these provisions were changed by the 1984 amendments.

These first two titles of the Bankruptcy Reform Act contain the subject matter for the bankruptcy course. For purposes of completeness, however, the final two titles of the Reform Act will be described briefly.

Title III of Pub. L. 95–598 contained changes which were essentially conforming amendments to a myriad of federal statutes. Almost all statutes which had such words as trustee, receiver, trustee in bankruptcy, and the like required conforming changes to relate to the new bankruptcy law. Some little substantive change was effected in selected statutes.

Title IV does not find its way into any title of the United States Code. It contains provisions with respect to the effective date of the 1978 Code (it is made applicable

---

[1] The Bankruptcy Act of 1898 was repealed by § 401 of Pub. L. 95–598.

to all cases commenced on and after October 1, 1979) and the repeal of the Bankruptcy Act of 1898 (except as to cases pending on September 30, 1979).[2]

§ 10.01 The Bankruptcy Court

[A] Former Law

As it finally evolved under the 1898 Act, the bankruptcy court was part of the United States district court. The judicial officer was labeled "referee in bankruptcy" under the statute, but in 1973 that title was changed to "bankruptcy judge" by the rules promulgated by the Supreme Court (former Bankruptcy Rule 901). The change made by the rules was in keeping with the actual role played by that officer, which was in fact deciding litigated matters. The bankruptcy judge was appointed by the district court judges for a term of six years. Orders and judgments of the bankruptcy judge could be appealed to the district court, then to the U.S. court of appeals, and, by writ of certiorari, to the Supreme Court.

The bankruptcy judges in office on the enactment date of the Reform Act were to remain in office until April 1, 1984, unless, on expiration of their terms, they were found to be unqualified by the Chief Judge of the Circuit in consultation with a merit screening committee.[3]

[B] Current Law

To upgrade the bankruptcy court, and in recognition of the important judicial role it plays, the 1978 Reform Act made several changes which were not without controversy.

To take office on April 1, 1984, the bankruptcy judges[4] were to be appointed by the President with the advice and consent of the Senate; that is, after the transition period (October 1, 1979—March 31, 1984), the method of judicial appointment was to be the same as used for the federal district court. The term of office was set forth as 14 years. The 1984 Amendments retained the 14 year term of office but vested the appointing power in the court of appeals for each circuit.[5]

The intent of the statute was to rid the bankruptcy judge of all or mostly all administrative duties and delegate unto that judge an exclusively judicial role. This intent has, however, been substantially frustrated for purely political reasons. Nevertheless, an important manifestation of the purpose of the law was in effect for

---

[2] *See* Pub. L. 95–598, § 403(a).

[3] Pub. L. 95–598, § 404(b).

[4] 28 U.S.C. § 151(a): "There shall be in each judicial district, as an adjunct to the district court for such district a bankruptcy court which shall be a court of record known as the United States Bankruptcy Court for the district." This section was amended in 1984 to provide that " . . . the bankruptcy judges . . . shall constitute a unit of the district court to be known as the bankruptcy court for that district." Bankruptcy Amendments and Federal Judgeship Act of 1984, § 104.

[5] *See* 28 U.S.C. §§ 152, 153(a).

a brief period. The court had been given what may be called expanded or pervasive jurisdiction of all matters related to a pending case.[6]

The changes effected in the jurisdiction of the court and the appellate process will be taken up at a later time. Suffice it to note at this point that the structural change and jurisdictional improvements together constituted one of the most important purposes underlying the reform legislation and, in the legislative process, became the most controversial. Much of the improvement has been vitiated by the 1984 amendments.

The bankruptcy court was to remain part of the district court either as a department or as an adjunct of it. The purpose for the connection was to have the powers and jurisdiction of an Article III (constitutional) court flow through it to the Article I (legislative) court. A predecessor House bill provided for the bankruptcy court to be a separate, independent, Article III court, but this did not sit well politically and various compromises were effected. The constitutionality of its structure (expanded jurisdiction given to an Article I court) was quickly questioned and decided negatively. *Northern Pipeline Construction Co. v. Marathon Pipe Line Co.*, 458 U.S. 50 (1982), *infra.*

§ 10.02   The United States Trustee

It is simple to state that the judge should not perform an administrative function, but it then becomes difficult to place the role, important as it is, elsewhere. This, too, was the subject of much political controversy.

The House bill, H.R. 8200, proposed to place a United States trustee in each judicial district. General supervision of the United States trustees would be by an Assistant Attorney General in the Department of Justice. The U.S. trustees would not be judicial officers in any sense, but would be exclusively administrators. Probably because of the logic and good sense of the proposal, it did not sit well with the Senate or at least some of its staff. Thus, S. 2266 contained no similar provisions. Naturally, when the bills passed the respective legislative bodies, compromise was necessary. Additionally, the Attorney General (Bell) wanted no part of the program.[7]

In the last days of the 95th Congress, an experimental program was agreed upon to effect a compromise. As a pilot program, the U.S. trustee system would be put in place in 18 judicial districts (some districts being combined for this purpose).[8]

During the transition period the Attorney General was to report to Congress with respect to the program, and unless Congress enacted new legislation continuing it, the program was to expire of its own accord on March 31, 1984. The pilot program subsequently was extended until September 30, 1984, Pub. L. 93–166, 97 Stat. 1071

---

[6] 28 U.S.C. § 1471(b), (c).

[7] Testimony of Attorney General Griffin Bell, hearing before the Subcommittee on Civil and Constitutional Rights of the Committee on the Judiciary on H.R. 8200, pp. 218–223, 95th Congress, 1st Session (1977). *See generally* App. 2 Collier, Bankruptcy, v–xxv (15th rev. ed. 1983).

[8] *See* 11 U.S.C. § 1501.

(1983), and again until September 30, 1986, Bankruptcy Amendments and Federal Judgeship Act of 1984, § 323, Pub. L. 98–353, (1984). Finally, the 1986 Amendments made the U.S. trustee program permanent and nationwide, with some delayed transition provisions.

The provisions dealing with the U.S. trustee are contained in 28 U.S.C. §§ 581–589a.

§ 10.03 Structure of 11 U.S.C.

What has become title 11 of the United States Code, or as explained above, the Bankruptcy Code, was divided into eight odd numbered chapters, *i.e.*, chapters 1, 3, 5, 7, 9, 11, 13, and 15. The four operative chapters, those that provide the different forms of relief for debtors, are chapters 7, 9, 11, and 13. The remaining chapters contain provisions generally applicable in the different types of debtor relief chapters; thus, chapters 1, 3, and 5 will be applicable in cases for relief under chapter 7, 9, 11, or 13. *See* Code §§ 103 and 901. In 1986, another operative chapter, providing relief for the family farmer, was added to the Code as chapter 12.

[A] Chapter 7

Chapter 7 is entitled "Liquidation" and has for its purpose the surrender and marshalling of a debtor's non–exempt assets, the sale of such property and the distribution of the proceeds among the debtor's creditors; if the debtor operates a business, the business will cease to exist.

[B] Chapter 9

Chapter 9 is entitled "Adjustment of Debts of a Municipality" and it is available only by means of a voluntary petition filed by a municipality as defined in § 101. As the title states, the purpose is to work out a debt adjustment plan with creditors rather than to cause the liquidation of the assets of a municipality.

(a) Questions:

Is New York City a municipality?

Is the State of Michigan a municipality?

Is the Chicago Transit Authority a municipality?

May a municipality seek relief under any of the other operative chapters of the Code?

(b) Compare 11 U.S.C. § 109(c) with 11 U.S.C. § 109(b), (d), and (e).

[C] Chapter 11

Chapter 11, entitled "Reorganization," is essentially for the reorganization of a business, whether in the form of a sole proprietorship, partnership, or corporation. Its purpose is to enable the debtor to keep its assets and rehabilitate the business, if possible, by means of an extension or composition plan or both, agreed to by creditors and, if necessary, equity interest holders.

(a) Questions:

Who is an equity interest holder?

What is a composition plan?

[D]　Chapter 12

Chapter 12 is entitled "Adjustment of Debts of a Family Farmer with Regular Income." It was enacted in 1986 and was due to expire in 1998. It has been extended to 1998. Its purpose is to afford a means by which family farmers in dire straits can attempt to retain farm property and repay debts.

[E]　Chapter 13

Chapter 13 is entitled "Adjustment of Debts of an Individual with Regular Income." *See* § 101(24). The basic purpose of chapter 13 is to permit an individual, on his or her own volition, to pay his or her debts out of future income. It offers an alternative to the liquidation process contemplated by chapter 7.

(a) *Question:*

What have you read in the news media, heard on the radio, or seen on television with respect to chapter 13? What do you believe with respect to chapter 13?

[F]　Chapter 1

Chapter 1 is general, containing a lengthy and important basic definitions section (§ 101), rules of construction section (§ 102), and a few other important sections which shall be discussed in context. During the course of the semester (or the semester's course) there will be constant references to §§ 101 and 102; study them carefully. *See also* § 103 for general applicability of chapter 1.

[G]　Chapter 3

Chapter 3 contains many important sections such as the automatic stay (§ 362), use of collateral (§ 363), executory contracts (§ 365), commencement of cases (§§ 301–303), and some relatively unimportant sections, such as compensation of attorneys and other professionals (§§ 327 *et seq.*). *See also* § 103 for general applicability of chapter 3.

[H]　Chapter 5

Chapter 5 contains provisions relating to the debtor, creditors, and the estate. For example, the avoiding powers of the trustee are set forth in this part (§§ 544–549), what is property of the estate is controlled by § 541, and the effect of the discharge is covered by §§ 523–525. Chapter 5 is generally applicable; *see* § 103.

§ 10.04 Rules of Bankruptcy Procedure

Effective August 1, 1983, Rules of Bankruptcy Procedure became effective to prescribe the procedure to be followed in cases filed under the Code. They supersede the rules governing cases filed under the former Bankruptcy Act that were in effect since 1973. The rules are promulgated by the Supreme Court pursuant to rulemaking authority granted it by Congress in 28 U.S.C. § 2075. The process and many of the rules are the same as the Federal Rules of Civil Procedure. The Bankruptcy Amendments and Federal Judgeship Act of 1984 included an Official Form as well as amendments to a small number of the bankruptcy rules. The rules have subsequently been amended to take account of statutory changes.

CHAPTER 11

COMMENCEMENT OF CASES
UNDER THE CODE

§ 11.01 Introduction

In order for a case to be commenced seeking relief under chapter 7, 9, 11, 12, or 13, a petition must be filed. "Petition" is a word of art and is defined in § 101 of the Code which, in turn, refers to §§ 301, 302, 303, and 304. That word is distinguishable from other labels such as complaint, motion, and application and, similarly, these other words should be used as intended without substituting the word petition for any of them.

The "petition" commences the "case." "Case" also is a word of art and should be used selectively. The "case" is the entire chapter 7 matter pending in the bankruptcy court; it is not a proceeding. The term "proceeding" is used to delineate a matter arising within a pending case which may be raised by complaint (*see* Part VII of the Bankruptcy Rules with respect to adversary proceedings) or by motion (*see* Rules 9013 and 9014 with respect to contested matters). Accordingly, the Bankruptcy Code contemplates that a chapter 7 *case,* chapter 9 *case,* chapter 11 *case,* chapter 12 *case,* or chapter 13 *case* will be commenced only by the filing of a *petition. See* §§ 301, 303(b). *See also* Rule 1002, Advisory Committee's Note and Official Form No. 1.

§ 11.02 Eligibility

Before pursuing issues pertaining to the two types of petitions, voluntary and involuntary, some time should be spent on who may be debtors under the various relief chapters of the Code. The key provisions in this respect are found in § 109, but, as with many other sections, constant reference should be made to the definitions contained in § 101.

Pursuant to § 109, there are certain jurisdictional limitations regarding persons who may be debtors under the Code or under a particular chapter of the Code. An interesting exercise in statutory use arises with respect to the word "person" in § 109(a) and (b) on the issue of whether a city, water district, etc., may commence a case under chapter 7 or chapter 11.

(Matthew Bender & Co., Inc.) (Pub.094)

QUESTIONS

1. Should § 109(a) be considered as affecting the subject matter jurisdiction of the bankruptcy court? Does § 109(a) contemplate use of the Bankruptcy Code by a foreign domiciliary that has neither an address nor a place of business in the United States?

2. May a railroad utilize any part of the Code?

3. May domestic banks and insurance companies utilize any part of the Code? What happens if one becomes insolvent? What about foreign banks?

4. Who may be a debtor under chapter 11? Does this differ in any way from chapter 7?

5. What are the limitations of eligibility for relief under chapter 13? What is "regular income"? Is a business eligible for chapter 13 relief? A lawyer? Is a tort claim included in the $250,000 debt limitation? Similar, but not exactly the same, questions can be raised with respect to chapter 12. Note that partnerships and corporations are eligible for chapter 12 relief (*see* § 101), but they must be family controlled entities.

TOIBB v. RADLOFF

Supreme Court of the United States
111 S. Ct. 2197, 24 C.B.C. 2d 1179 (1991)

Justice BLACKMUN delivered the opinion of the Court:

In this case we must decide whether an individual debtor not engaged in business is eligible to reorganize under Chapter 11 of the Bankruptcy Code, 11 U.S.C. 1101 *et seq.*

I.

From March 1983 until April 1985, petitioner Sheldon Baruch Toibb, a former staff attorney with the Federal Energy Regulatory Commission, was employed as a consultant by Independence Electric Corporation (IEC), a company he and two others organized to produce and market electric power. Petitioner owns 24 percent of the company's shares. After IEC terminated his employment, petitioner was unable to find work as a consultant in the energy field; he has been largely supported by his family and friends since that time.

On November 18, 1986, petitioner filed in the United States Bankruptcy Court for the Eastern District of Missouri a voluntary petition for relief under Chapter 7 of the Code, 11 U.S.C. § 701 *et seq.* The Schedule of Assets and Liabilities accompanying petitioner's filing disclosed no secured debts, a disputed federal tax priority claim of $11,000, and unsecured debts of $170,605. Petitioner listed as nonexempt assets his IEC shares and a possible claim against his former business associates. He stated that the market value of each of these assets was unknown.

On August 6, 1987, the Chapter 7 Trustee appointed to administer petitioner's estate notified the creditors that the Board of Directors of IEC had offered to purchase petitioner's IEC shares for $25,000. When petitioner became aware that this stock had such value, he decided to avoid its liquidation by moving to convert his Chapter 7 case to one under the reorganization provisions of Chapter 11.

The Bankruptcy Court granted petitioner's conversion motion, App. 21, and on February 1, 1988, petitioner filed a plan of reorganization. *Id.*, at 70. Under the plan, petitioner proposed to pay his unsecured creditors $25,000 less administrative expenses and priority tax claims, a proposal that would result in a payment of approximately 11 cents on the dollar. He further proposed to pay the unsecured creditors, for a period of six years, 50 percent of any dividends from IEC or of any proceeds from the sale of the IEC stock, up to full payment of the debts.

On March 8, 1988, the Bankruptcy Court on its own motion ordered petitioner to show cause why his petition should not be dismissed because petitioner was not engaged in business and, therefore, did not qualify as a Chapter 11 debtor. App. 121. At the ensuing hearing, petitioner unsuccessfully attempted to demonstrate that he had a business to reorganize. Petitioner also argued that Chapter 11 should be available to an individual debtor not engaged in an ongoing business. On August 1, the Bankruptcy Court ruled that, under the authority of *Wamsganz v. Boatmen's Bank of De Soto*, 804 F.2d 503 (CA8 1986), petitioner failed to qualify for relief under Chapter 11. App. to Pet. for Cert. A–17 and A–19.

The United States District Court for the Eastern District of Missouri, also relying on *Wamsganz*, upheld the Bankruptcy Court's dismissal of petitioner's Chapter 11 case. App. to Pet. for Cert. A–8 and A–9. The United States Court of Appeals for the Eighth Circuit affirmed, holding that the Bankruptcy Court had the authority to dismiss the proceeding *Sua Sponte*, and that the Circuit's earlier *Wamsganz* decision was controlling. *In Re Toibb*, 902 F.2d 14 (1990). Because the Court of Appeals' ruling that an individual nonbusiness debtor may not reorganize under Chapter 11 clearly conflicted with the holding of the Court of Appeals for the Eleventh Circuit in *In Re Moog*, 774 F2d 1073 (1985), we granted certiorari to resolve the conflict. —U.S.—(1991).

II.

A.

In our view, the plain language of the Bankruptcy Code disposes of the question before us. Section 109, 11 U.S.C. § 109, defines who may be a debtor under the various chapters of the Code. Section 109(d) provides: "Only a person that may be a debtor under chapter 7 of this title, except a stockbroker or a commodity broker, and a railroad may be a debtor under chapter 11 of this title." Section 109(b) states: "A person may be a debtor under chapter 7 of this title only if such person is not—(1) a railroad; (2) a domestic insurance company, bank, . . .; or (3) a foreign insurance company, bank, . . . engaged in such business in the United States." The Code defines "person" as used in Title 11 to "include [an] individual." § 101(35). Under the express terms of the Code, therefore, petitioner is "a person who may be a debtor under chapter 7" and satisfies the statutory requirements for a Chapter 11 debtor.

The Code contains no ongoing business requirement for reorganization under Chapter 11, and we are loath to infer the exclusion of certain classes of debtors from the protections of Chapter 11, because Congress took care in § 109 to specify who qualifies—and who does not qualify—as a debtor under the various chapters of the Code. Section 109(b) expressly excludes from the coverage of Chapter 7 railroads and various financial and insurance institutions. Only municipalities are eligible for the protection of Chapter 9. § 109(c). Most significantly, § 109(d) makes stockbrokers and commodities brokers ineligible for Chapter 11 relief, but otherwise leaves that Chapter available to any other entity eligible for the protection of Chapter 7. Congress knew how to restrict recourse to the avenues of bankruptcy relief; it did not place Chapter 11 reorganization beyond the reach of a nonbusiness individual debtor.

B.

The *amicus curiae* in support of the Court of Appeals' judgment acknowledges that Chapter 11 does not expressly exclude an individual nonbusiness debtor from its reach. He echoes the reasoning of those courts that have engrafted an ongoing–business requirement onto the plain language of § 109(a) and argues that the statute's legislative history and structure make clear that Chapter 11 was intended for business debtors alone. *See, e.g., Wamsganz v. Boatmen's Bank of De Soto*, 804 F.2d at 505 ("The legislative history of the Bankruptcy Code, taken as a whole, shows that Congress meant for chapter 11 to be available to businesses and persons engaged in business, and not to consumer debtors"). We find these arguments unpersuasive for several reasons.

First, this Court has repeated with some frequency: "Where, as here, the resolution of a question of federal law turns on a statute and the intention of Congress, we look first to the statutory language and then to the legislative history if the statutory language is unclear." *Blum v. Stenson*, 465 U.S. 886, 896 (1984). The language of § 109 is not unclear. Thus, although a court appropriately may refer to a statute's legislative history to resolve statutory ambiguity, there is no need to do so here.

Second, even were we to consider the sundry legislative comments urged in support of a congressional intent to exclude a nonbusiness debtor from Chapter 11, the scant history on this precise issue does not suggest a "clearly expressed legislative intent . . . contrary . . ." to the plain language of § 109(d). *See Consumer Product Safety Comm'n v. GTE Sylvania, Inc.*, 447 U.S. 102, 108 (1980). The *amicus* does point to the following statement in a House report:

> "Some consumer debtors are unable to avail themselves of the relief provided under chapter 13. For these debtors, straight bankruptcy is the only remedy that will enable them to get out from under the debilitating effects of too much debt." H.R. Rep. No. 95–595, p. 125 (1977).

Petitioner responds with the following excerpt from a later Senate report:

"Chapter 11, Reorganization, is primarily designed for businesses, although individuals are eligible for relief under the chapter. The procedures of chapter 11, however, are sufficiently complex that they will be used only in a business case and not in the consumer context." S. Rep. No. 95–989, p. 3 (1978).

These apparently conflicting views tend to negate the suggestion that the Congress enacting the current Code operated with a clear intent to deny Chapter 11 relief to an individual nonbusiness debtor.

Finally, we are not persuaded by the contention that Chapter 11 is unavailable to a debtor without an ongoing business because many of the Chapter's provisions do not apply to a nonbusiness debtor. There is no doubt that Congress intended that a business debtor be among those who might use Chapter 11. Code provisions like the ones authorizing the appointment of an equity security holders' committee, § 1102, and the appointment of a trustee "for cause, including fraud, dishonesty, incompetence, or gross mismanagement of the affairs of the debtor by current management . . .," § 1104(a)(1), certainly are designed to aid in the rehabilitation of a business. It does not follow, however, that a debtor whose affairs do not warrant recourse to these provisions is ineligible for Chapter 11 relief. Instead, these provisions—like the references to debtor businesses in the Chapter's legislative history—reflect an understandable expectation that Chapter 11 would be used primarily by debtors with ongoing businesses; they do not constitute an additional prerequisite for Chapter 11 eligibility beyond those established in § 109(d).

III.

Although the foregoing analysis is dispositive of the question presented, we deal briefly with *amicus'* contention that policy considerations underlying the Code support inferring a congressional intent to preclude a nonbusiness debtor from reorganizing under Chapter 11. First, it is said that bringing a consumer debtor within the scope of Chapter 11 does not serve Congress' purpose of permitting business debtors to reorganize and restructure their debts in order to revive the debtors' businesses and thereby preserve jobs and protect investors. This argument assumes that Congress had a single purpose in enacting Chapter 11. Petitioner suggests, however, and we agree, that Chapter 11 also embodies the general Code policy of maximizing the value of the bankruptcy estate. *See Commodity Futures Trading Comm'n v. Weintraub,* 471 U.S. 343, 351–354 (1985). Under certain circumstances a consumer debtor's estate will be worth more if reorganized under Chapter 11 than if liquidated under Chapter 7. Allowing such a debtor to proceed under Chapter 11 serves the congressional purpose of deriving as much value as possible from the debtor's estate.

Second, *amicus* notes that allowing a consumer debtor to proceed under Chapter 11 would permit the debtor to shield both disposable income and nonexempt personal property. He argues that the legislative history of Chapter 11 does not reflect an intent to offer a consumer debtor more expansive protection than he would find under Chapter 13, which does not protect disposable income, or Chapter 7, which does not protect nonexempt personal assets. As an initial matter, it makes no difference whether the legislative history affirmatively reflects such an intent, because the plain language of the statute allows a consumer debtor to proceed under Chapter 11. Moreover, differences in the requirements and protections of each Chapter reflect Congress' appreciation that various approaches are necessary to address effectively the disparate situations of debtors seeking protection under the Code.

Amicus does not contend that allowing a consumer debtor to reorganize under Chapter 11 will leave the debtor's creditors in a worse position than if the debtor were required to liquidate. *See Tr.* of Oral Arg. 29–31. Nor could he. Section 1129(a)(7) provides that a reorganization plan may not be confirmed unless all the debtor's creditors accept the plan or will receive not less than they would receive under a Chapter 7 liquidation. Because creditors cannot be expected to approve a plan in which they would receive less than they would from an immediate liquidation of the debtor's assets, it follows that a Chapter 11 reorganization plan usually will be confirmed only when creditors will receive at least as much as if the debtor were to file under Chapter 7. Absent some showing of harm to the creditors of a nonbusiness debtor allowed to reorganize under Chapter 11, we see nothing in the allocation of "burdens" and "benefits" of Chapter 11 that warrants an inference that Congress intended to exclude a consumer debtor from its coverage. *See* Herbert, *Consumer Chapter 11 Proceedings: Abuse or Alternative?*, 91 Com. L. J. 234, 245–248 (1986).

Amicus also warns that allowing consumer debtors to proceed under Chapter 11 will flood the bankruptcy courts with plans or reorganization that ultimately will prove unworkable. We think this fear is unfounded for two reasons. First, the greater expense and complexity of filing under Chapter 11 likely will dissuade most consumer debtors from seeking relief under this Chapter. *See* S. Rep. No. 95–989, at 3; *see also* Herbert, *supra,* at 242–243. Second, the Code gives bankruptcy courts substantial discretion to dismiss a Chapter 11 case in which the debtor files an untenable plan of reorganization. *See* §§ 1112(b) and 1129(a).

Finally, *amicus* asserts that extending Chapter 11 to consumer debtors creates the risk that these debtors will be forced into Chapter 11 by their creditors under § 303(a), a result contrary to the intent reflected in Congress' decision to prevent involuntary bankruptcy proceedings under Chapter 13. In particular, he suggests that it would be unwise to force a debtor into a Chapter 11 reorganization, because an involuntary debtor would be unlikely to cooperate in the plan of reorganization—a point that Congress noted in refusing to allow involuntary Chapter 13 proceedings. *See* H.R. Rep. No. 95–595, at 120.

We find these concerns overstated in light of the Code's provisions for dealing with recalcitrant Chapter 11 debtors. If an involuntary Chapter 11 debtor fails to cooperate, this likely will provide the requisite "cause" for the bankruptcy court to convert the Chapter 11 case to one under Chapter 7. *See* § 1112(b). In any event, the argument overlooks Congress' primary concern about a debtor's being forced into bankruptcy under Chapter 13: that such a debtor, whose future wages are not exempt from the bankruptcy estate, § 1322(a)(1), would be compelled to toil for the benefit of creditors in violation of the Thirteenth Amendment's involuntary servitude prohibition. See H.R. Rep. No. 95–595, at 120. Because there is no comparable provision in Chapter 11 requiring a debtor to pay future wages to a creditor,

Congress' concern about imposing involuntary servitude on a Chapter 13 debtor is not relevant to a Chapter 11 reorganization.

IV.

The plain language of the Bankruptcy Code permits individual debtors not engaged in business to file for relief under Chapter 11. Although the structure and legislative history of Chapter 11 indicate that this Chapter was intended primarily for the use of business debtors, the Code contains no "ongoing business" requirement for Chapter 11 reorganization, and we find no basis for imposing one. Accordingly, the judgment of the Court of Appeals is reversed.

It is so ordered.

Justice STEVENS, dissenting:

The Court's reading of the statute is plausible. It is supported by the omission of any prohibition against the use of Chapter 11 by consumer debtors and by the excerpt from the introduction to the Senate Report, quoted *ante,* at 5–6. Nevertheless, I am persuaded that the Court's reading is incorrect. Two chapters of the Bankruptcy Code—Chapter 7, entitled "Liquidation," 11 U.S.C. § 701 *et seq.,* and Chapter 13, entitled "Adjustment of Debts of an Individual With Regular Income," § 1301 *et seq.*—unquestionably and unambiguously authorize relief for individual consumer debtors. Chapter 11, entitled "Reorganization," § 1101 *et seq.,* was primarily designed to provide relief for corporate debtors but also unquestionably authorizes relief for individual proprietors of business enterprises. When the statute is read as a whole, however, it seems quite clear that Congress did not intend to authorize a "reorganization" of the affairs of an individual consumer debtor.

Section 109(d) places a limit on the class of persons who may be a debtor under Chapter 11, but it does not state that all members of that class are eligible for Chapter 11 relief. It states that "*only* a person that may be a debtor under Chapter 7 . . . may be a debtor under Chapter 11 . . . ." (Emphasis added.) It does not, however, state that *every* person entitled to relief under Chapter 7 is also entitled to relief under Chapter 11. In my judgment, the word "only" introduces sufficient ambiguity to justify a careful examination of other provisions of the Act, as well as the legislative history.

This examination convinces me that consumer debtors may not avail themselves of Chapter 11. The repeated references to the debtor's "business, the operation of the debtor's business," and the "current or former management of the debtor" make it abundantly clear that the principal focus of the chapter is upon business reorganizations. This conclusion is confirmed by the discussion of Chapter 11 in the Senate Report, which describes the provision as a "chapter for *business* reorganization" and repeatedly refers to a "business" as the subject of Chapter 11 relief. *See also* 124 Cong. Rec. 34007 (1978) (Chapter 11 is a "consolidated approach to business rehabilitation") (statement of Sen. DeConcini).

The House Report, however, is more significant because it emphasizes the relationship between different chapters of the Code. The Report unambiguously states that a Chapter 7 liquidation is "the only remedy" for "consumer debtors [who] are unable to avail themselves of the relief provided under chapter 13." H.R. Rep. No. 95–595, p. 125 (1977). *See also* 124 Cong. Rec., at 32392, 32405 (Chapter 11 is "a consolidated approach to business rehabilitation" and a "new commercial reorganization chapter") (statement of Rep. Edwards). The accuracy of the statement in the House Report is confirmed by a comparison of the text of Chapter 11 with the text of Chapter 13.

Above, I noted the striking difference between the chapter titles—"Reorganization" for Chapter 11 as opposed to "Adjustment of Debts of an Individual With Regular Income" for Chapter 13. Also significant is the conspicuous omission from Chapter 11 of both an important limit and an important protection included in Chapter 13. Chapter 13 relief is only available to individuals whose unsecured debts amount to less than $100,000 and whose secured debts are less than $350,000. See U.S.C. § 109(e). Chapter 11 contains no comparable limit. Congress would have accomplished little in imposing this limit on the adjustment of individual consumer debt through Chapter 13 if Congress at the same time allowed the individual to avoid the limitation by filing under Chapter 11.

More important, the Code expressly provides that involuntary proceedings can only be instituted under Chapter 7 and Chapter 11. *See* 11 U.S.C. § 303(a). A creditor therefore may not force an individual consumer debtor into an involuntary Chapter 13 proceeding. Under the Court's reading of the Act, however, a creditor could institute an involuntary proceeding under Chapter 11 against any individual with regular income. It seems highly unlikely that Congress intended to subject individual consumer debtors, such as pensioners, to involuntary Chapter 11 proceedings while at the same time prohibiting involuntary Chapter 13 proceedings against the same class of debtors.

For these reasons, notwithstanding the excerpt from the Senate Report on which the Court relies, I would, in accordance with the clear statement in the House Report, read the statute as a whole to limit Chapter 11 relief to business debtors. I therefore respectfully dissent.

NOTES AND QUESTIONS

If the majority or the dissent found the Code to be ambiguous with respect to the issue before the Court, can either say that the legislative history is any less ambiguous? Would it not make more sense to conclude that Congress actually contemplated use of chapter 11 by an individual who was not engaged in business if one was silly enough to attempt such use? Can you think of any specific individuals for whom chapter 11 might make sense?

The individual debtor has an option, subject to §§ 707(b) and 109, to seek relief under chapter 7, 11, or 13. For most individuals, relief is sought, as a practical matter, under either chapter 7 or 13. What are the key differences between chapters 13 and 11 that would render chapter 11 of less utility for the ordinary individual debtor?

What considerations would dictate use of chapter 13 over chapter 7 or vice versa? *See, e.g.,* §§ 1102, 705, 1325, 1126, 1129(a)(8), 1302, 726, 523(a), 1328(a).

§ 11.03   Voluntary Petitions

See §§ 301, 302 of the Bankruptcy Code. *See also* Bankruptcy Rules 1002, 1004, 1005 and Official Form No. 1.

A voluntary petition, in addition to commencing the case, also constitutes an order for relief. Section 301. There is no need for the court to enter such an order; it is automatic. Under the former Bankruptcy Act, the filing of a voluntary petition constituted, automatically, an adjudication in bankruptcy, or an adjudication that the debtor was a bankrupt. Notice that thus far the term "bankrupt" has not been used in the Code; also, "order for relief" has been substituted for "adjudication." Why? *See* House and Senate Committee Reports at pages 321 and 31, respectively.[1]

Pursuant to § 302, a joint case is commenced by filing a single petition.

QUESTIONS

1. Who may commence a joint case? What is the effect of commencing a joint case?

2. Must the debtor be "insolvent" (defined in 11 U.S.C. § 101) to file a voluntary petition under chapter 7 or chapter 11? Why?

3. What allegations must a voluntary petition seeking relief under chapter 7 contain? Who may file an answer to a voluntary petition? On what grounds, if any, may the court dismiss a voluntary petition? *See* §§ 305, 707. What is the purpose of § 707(b), added in 1984? Why in 1986 was § 707(b) amended to allow a U.S. trustee to move for dismissal? Is this further evidence of a Congressional intent to bar creditors from so moving? *See also* § 342(b) requiring the clerk to notify debtors of their right to use chapter 13 before a case is commenced. How does the clerk do this? Official Form No. 1 was amended by § 322 of the 1984 Bankruptcy Amendments. If the petition is dismissed by the court or the debtor, may a new one be filed? *See* § 109(g).

---

[1] H.R. No. 95–595, 95th Cong., 1st Sess. (1977); S. Rep. No. 95–989, 95th Cong., 2d Sess. (1978).

PROBLEM

Sandy Simmons, a well known female vocalist, has not sold many records in the last two years and her concerts have not generated much interest (or ticket sales). She has, however, found no respite from her monetary obligations and because of reduced income, her number of unpaid obligations has increased dramatically. On visiting your office for advice, you learn that she is expecting to sign a contract to co–star in a motion picture with the hottest property currently about, Magnes Magnuson, and the prospects for rejuvenation of her career are more than just encouraging. You and she discuss the possibility of using chapter 7 of the Code to alleviate her current problems and to give her the possibility of a fresh start. What, if any, concerns do you have in going forward with a chapter 7 petition?

MATTER OF JAMES WILSON ASSOCIATES

United States Court of Appeals, Seventh Circuit
965 F.2d 160 (1992)

POSNER, Circuit Judge:

We have consolidated five (!) appeals by Metropolitan Life Insurance Company from adverse orders in a bankruptcy proceeding in which Metropolitan is the principal creditor. The debtor, James Wilson Associates (JWA), is a limited partnership that built and operates an office building in Madison, Wisconsin, and that in 1973 had borrowed $3.9 million from Metropolitan, secured by a first mortgage, with an assignment of rents as additional collateral. Later it borrowed more money, against a second mortgage (and assignment of rents) now held by First Nationwide Bank. The balance outstanding on the two mortgages is roughly $4.6 million. In 1976 JWA sold the building for $7 million under a land contract to JWP Investors, another and (despite the similarity in names, or at least initials) unrelated limited partnership, which leased the building back to JWA. Although the purpose of the sale and lease back was to finance JWA's operation of the building rather than to transfer control, the transaction created a genuine lease under Wisconsin law because it did not vest title in JWA at the lease's termination. *In re Spring Valley Meats, Inc.,* 94 Wis. 2d 600, 609–10, 288 N.W.2d 852, 856 (1980); *American Industrial Leasing Co. v. Moderow,* 147 Wis. 2d 64, 70–71, 432 N.W.2d 617, 620 (Ct. App. 1988).

JWP Investors did not assume the mortgages; JWA remained liable under them, and eventually defaulted. In 1990 the two mortgagees brought foreclosure suits in a Wisconsin state court, which at the request of both appointed a receiver to collect the rents from the building's tenants and enjoined the tenants from paying rent to anyone else. Three weeks later JWA filed for bankruptcy under Chapter 11 of the Bankruptcy Code, and in its new status as debtor in possession resumed collecting the tenants' rents because the bankruptcy filing automatically stayed all judicial proceedings against the debtor, including the receivership. 11 U.S.C. § 362(a).

Metropolitan moved to lift the stay with regard to the receivership, arguing that the lease was not an asset of the bankrupt estate.

*   *   *

We must consider, however, the bearing of section 1109(b) of the Bankruptcy Code, which provides that a "party in interest [in a bankruptcy proceeding], including . . . a creditor . . . may raise and may appear and be heard on any issue in a case under this chapter." Provided that the creditor has a stake in the issue, as Metropolitan does, there could be no objection founded on Article III to such a grant of standing. But we do not think that this section was intended to waive other limitations on standing, such as that the claimant be within the class of intended beneficiaries of the statute that he is relying on for his claim, although a literal reading of section 1109(b) would support such an interpretation. We think all the section means is that anyone who has a legally protected interest that could be affected by a bankruptcy proceeding is entitled to assert that interest with respect to any issue to which it pertains, thus making explicit what is implicit in an *in rem* proceeding—that everyone with a claim to the *res* has a right to be heard before the *res* is disposed of since that disposition will extinguish all such claims. Cf. 5 *Collier on Bankruptcy* ¶ 1109.02, at pp. 1109–16 to 1109–32 (Lawrence P. King ed., 15th ed. 1991); *United States v. Tit's Cocktail Lounge,* 873 F.2d 141, 143 (7th Cir. 1989) (per curiam). Section 365(b)(4) confers no legally protected interest on Metropolitan in the lease between JWP Investors and the bankrupt, and section 1109(b) therefore does not entitle Metropolitan to make an issue of the assumption of the lease.

We have not, however, considered the possible bearing of the receivership on Metropolitan's standing. Remember that a receiver was appointed to enforce JWA's assignment of rents to Metropolitan. The receivership was enjoined when the petition for bankruptcy was filed, but if by virtue of the receivership JWP Investors was ousted as the lessor in favor of Metropolitan, then Metropolitan could reject the lease and would have standing to appeal if the rejection were not honored. Although Metropolitan does not argue for standing on this ground, its brief does contain a suggestion that the receivership by terminating JWP Investors' interest cancelled any lease that JWA could have assumed. The suggestion is insufficiently developed to require us to consider it, for a merely skeletal argument does not preserve an issue for review. *United States v. Harvey,* No. 90–3569, slip op. at 8 (7th Cir. March 10, 1992); *United Rope Distributors, Inc. v. Seatriumph Marine Corp.,* 930 F.2d 532, 536 (7th Cir. 1991); *United States v. Dunkel,* 927 F.2d 955, 956 (7th Cir. 1991) (per curiam); *United States v. Giovannetti,* 919 F.2d 1223, 1230 (7th Cir. 1990). That principle has particular bite in a case such as this where the merits of the skeletal argument are difficult to assess. Even if (and this is unclear) the receiver stepped into the shoes of the landlord, JWP Investors, as well as the lessee, JWA, the receivership was enjoined when the bankruptcy petition was filed. The natural inference is that the receiver stepped out of whatever shoes he had stepped into and JWP Investors resumed its landlordship—and it was after that that JWA assumed the lease. But all this assumes that the automatic stay can operate in favor not only of the debtor (JWA) but also of a third party (JWP Investors), and the rule is *contra. Pitts v. Unarco Industries, Inc.,* 698 F.2d 313 (7th Cir. 1983) (per curiam); *In re K & L Ltd.,* 741 F.2d 1023, 1030 (7th Cir. 1984). There may, however, be an exception where the debtor is an indispensable party to the litigation, as suggested in *United States v. Nicolet, Inc.,* 857 F2d 202, 203 (3d Cir. 1988), and *In re Comcoach Corp.,* 698 F2d 571, 574 (2d Cir. 1983), which JWA might or might not be. Compare *id.* at 574 with *Wisconsin Finance Corp. v. Garlock,* 140 Wis. 2d 506, 512, 410 N.W.2d 649, 651 (Ct. App. 1987). The thinking here is that if the debtor is an indispensable party, protected by the stay from involvement in the litigation, the litigation cannot proceed in his absence and therefore must be stayed as against the third party, here JWP Investors, as well. However all this may be, Metropolitan would have had to move to lift the stay as to JWP Investors, and it did not.

Obviously this is a richly complex issue, and it was Metropolitan's burden to develop it in adequate depth to enable its opponent and this court to evaluate it. A very large corporation, Metropolitan is well able to afford the best counsel. It has filed five appeals in this case and hundreds of pages of briefs. We won't rewrite its appeal briefs for it.

Our resolution of the question of standing brings to the fore Metropolitan's argument that the entire bankruptcy proceeding is an abuse of the Bankruptcy Code because the sole purpose is to squirrel away the rents where the receiver can't get at them. In so arguing Metropolitan is appealing to section 1112(b) of the Code, which authorizes the bankruptcy judge to dismiss a bankruptcy proceeding for want of good faith. What should count as bad faith in this setting is unclear. It is not bad faith to seek to gain an advantage from declaring bankruptcy—why else would one declare it? One might have supposed that the clearest case of bad faith would be filing for bankruptcy knowing that one was not bankrupt, but the Bankruptcy Code permits an individual or firm that has debts to declare bankruptcy even though he (or it) is not insolvent. *In re Johns–Manville Corp.,* [9 C.B.C.2d 1179] 36 B.R. 727, 732 (Bankr. S.D.N.Y. 1984); *Baird & Jackson, supra,* at 86–219. (These are usually cases of impending insolvency.) The clearest case of bad faith is where the debtor enters Chapter 11 knowing that there is no chance to reorganize his business and hoping merely to stave off the evil day when the creditors take control of his property. *Carolin Corp. v. Miller,* 886 F.2d 693, 700–03 (4th Cir. 1989). There is no indication of that here. JWA defaulted on its mortgage payments, and when Metropolitan procured the appointment of a receiver to receive the rents this precipitated JWA into insolvency; it had no income outside of the tenants' rentals now to be handed over to the receiver out of which to pay its other creditors, and no unencumbered assets out of which to pay them either. Could it be that JWA defaulted on its mortgages in order to set in motion a chain of events that would lead to the specific actions of which Metropolitan complains—the automatic stay, the diversion of rents to lawyers and to the second mortgagee, and now the plan of reorganization that relieves JWA, for a time anyway, from the consequences of its defaulting on the first mortgage? Maybe so, but Metropolitan has presented no evidence that it is so.

* * *

MATTER OF LITTLE CREEK DEVELOPMENT CO.

United States Court of Appeals, Fifth Circuit
779 F.2d 1068 (1986)

JONES, Circuit Judge:

The debtor, Little Creek Development Company (Little Creek), appeals from an order of the bankruptcy court lifting the automatic stay so that the secured creditor, Commonwealth Mortgage Corporation (Commonwealth), could foreclose on Little Creek's single asset, two parcels of undeveloped real estate. The principal issue on appeal is whether the bankruptcy court was clearly erroneous in finding that "cause" to lift the stay pursuant to 11 U.S.C. § 362(d)(1) could be based solely on the remarks of counsel for Little Creek that the bankruptcy petition was filed in order to escape the necessity of posting a substantial bond in an ongoing state court proceeding. We find that more evidence was necessary to support the bankruptcy court's conclusions, and we therefore remand with instructions.

I. Background

Little Creek obtained a loan from Commonwealth for the purpose of developing town homes on two tracts of land in Hurst, Texas, a suburb of Dallas. In March 1984, the parties signed promissory notes, deeds of trust, and other financing documents that would commit Commonwealth to fund up to $4.7 million for the project. Little Creek purchased the tracts of land for $675,000, but was unexpectedly delayed in obtaining building permits from the City of Hurst. Little Creek has not yet broken ground on the project. In January 1985, Commonwealth informed Little Creek of its intention to accelerate the debt and foreclose its mortgages, based on Little Creek's failure to obtain building permits and a satisfactory replacement guarantor.

Little Creek preempted foreclosure proceedings in March by filing a wide-ranging complaint in state court, alleging causes of action based upon the Texas Deceptive Trade Practices Act, breach of contract, and unconscionability. An *ex parte* temporary restraining order was issued against foreclosure. In early May, Little Creek obtained a preliminary injunction, conditioned upon its posting a bond for $50,000 to forestall foreclosure during the month of May, and thereafter, a bond for $1,250,000 pending the conclusion of the litigation. Little Creek could not post the required larger bond in June.

Again staving off foreclosure, Little Creek filed a petition for reorganization under Chapter 11 of the Bankruptcy Code. Commonwealth moved in the bankruptcy court for relief from the automatic stay, 11 U.S.C. § 362(d), seeking to foreclose the property. Little Creek's response to that motion defensively raised most of the issues presented in the pending state court action. Little Creek also sought leave to take numerous depositions and to engage in extensive discovery.

The bankruptcy court held two hearings on the motion for relief from the stay. In the first hearing, Commonwealth claimed that Little Creek's debt exceeded

$1,400,000, and that its mortgage was perfected. Through an appraiser Commonwealth claimed that the value of Little Creek's property was only $775,000. Due to the court's time constraints, Little Creek neither pursued its questions concerning the amount of the debt nor completed its cross–examination of Commonwealth's appraiser. By the time of the second stay hearing, the bankruptcy court had granted a motion to strike Little Creek's defenses, finding them inappropriate for consideration in that context, where upon counsel for Little Creek uttered candid remarks. In attempting to explain why Little Creek should be allowed to present evidence of alleged modification of the loan agreements, counsel stated:

> "The Debtor in this case has already sought and obtained an injunction in State Court against the foreclosure sale and was unable to continue that by virtue of an increasing bond requirement. And that was the reason it [precipitated] this filing in this court. * * * And we feel like this is the proper [forum] to consider the issues relative to a proper acceleration of the debt and foreclosure sale because we don't feel like there's any other [forum] available to the Debtor in this case."

Co–counsel then reiterated the debtor's position:

> "Now, if we were able to carry forward with that type of bond, we'd still be in State Court. The reason we're in Bankruptcy Court is because the sole asset of the corporation is [jeopardized] by the fact that the lenders committed some acts, which we've alleged to this court. The same reasoning by going to State Court for our remedy–going to State Court for our remedy isn't applicable here. Because State Court has granted our remedy, we're not able to bond the amount in State Court and that's why we're in Bankruptcy Court seeking our remedy here."

Based on these representations, which Little Creek's counsel later sought to modify, the court *sua sponte* found that

> "the admissions of counsel coupled with Little Creek's prior attempts to incorporate the state court causes of action into the stay litigation make it readily apparent that Little Creek simply wanted to transfer the litigation from state court to bankruptcy court where it could have an automatic injunction and escape the state court's bond requirement."

These actions, in the bankruptcy court's view, rendered the debtor's petition for reorganization a "bad faith" proceeding. The court subsequently entered an order granting Commonwealth relief from the stay for "cause," finding that Little Creek lacked good faith in filing the petition. The district court affirmed the bankruptcy court's disposition.

This court temporarily stayed the lift pending expedited appeal, and our jurisdiction to review the final order of the bankruptcy court derives from 28 U.S.C. § 158(d). Because we have concluded that the record was insufficiently developed to justify the bankruptcy court's conclusion, it is desirable to provide guidance for the court's benefit on remand.

II. The Good Faith Principle As "Cause" For Lifting The Stay

Bankruptcy is an equitable remedy whereby a debtor is clothed with the protection of an automatic stay, preventing his creditors from acting against him for a period of time, in order to facilitate rehabilitation or reorganization of his finances and to promote a "fresh start" through the orderly disposition of assets to satisfy his creditors. *See GATX Aircraft Corp. v. M/V Courtney Leigh*, 768 F.2d 711, 716 (5th Cir. 1985); *In re Sun Country Dev., Inc.*, 764 F.2d 406, 408 (5th Cir. 1985); *In re Winshall Settlor's Trust*, 758 F.2d 1136, 1137 (6th Cir. 1985); *Browning v. Navarro*, 743 F.2d 1069, 1083 (5th Cir. 1984). Every bankruptcy statute since 1898 has incorporated literally, or by judicial interpretation, a standard of good faith for the commencement, prosecution, and confirmation of bankruptcy proceedings. *See In re Victory Constr. Co.*, 9 B.R. 549, 551–60 (Bankr. C.D. Cal. 1981) (containing an excellent historical survey). *See, e.g., Fidelity Assur. Assoc. v. Sims*, 318 U.S. 608, 621, 63 S. Ct. 807, 87 L.Ed. 1032 (1943); *A–COS Leasing Corp v. Wheless*, 422 F.2d 522, 523–25 & n. 1 (5th Cir. 1970). Such a standard furthers the balancing process between the interests of debtors and creditors which characterizes so many provisions of the bankruptcy laws and is necessary to legitimize the delay and costs imposed upon parties to a bankruptcy. Requirement of good faith prevents abuse of the bankruptcy process by debtors whose overriding motive is to delay creditors without benefitting them in any way or to achieve reprehensible purposes. Moreover, a good faith standard protects the jurisdictional integrity of the bankruptcy courts by rendering their powerful equitable weapons (*i.e.*, avoidance of liens, discharge of debts, marshalling and turnover of assets) available only to those debtors and creditors with "clean hands." The Supreme Court aptly summarized the bankruptcy court's responsibility to enforce a standard of good faith when it stated:

> " 'A court of equity may in its discretion in the exercise of the jurisdiction committed to it grant or deny relief upon performance of a condition which will safeguard the public interest.' . . . These principles are a part of the control which the court has over the whole process of formulation and approval of plans of composition or reorganization."

. . .*American Ins. Co. v. Avon Park*, 311 U.S. 138, 145, 61 S. Ct. 157, 85 L.Ed. 91 (1940) (quoting *SEC v. United States Realty & Improvement Co.*, 310 U.S. 434, 455, 60 S. Ct. 1044, 84 L.Ed. 1239 (1940)).

Like its predecessor statutes, and based on the foregoing considerations, the Bankruptcy Code of 1978 has been endowed with requirements of good faith in the construction of many of its provisions. *See* Ordin, *The Good Faith Principle in the Bankruptcy Code: A Case Study*, 38 Bus. Law. 1795 (1983). *See also Winshall Settlor's Trust*, 758 F.2d at 1137; *In re Moog*, 774 F.2d at 1077; *Coastal Cable T.V.*, 709 F.2d at 764–65. Litigation concerning good faith which is pertinent to this case has arisen under § 362(d) of the Bankruptcy Code, 11 U.S.C § 362(d)(1), governing relief from the automatic stay, and under 11 U.S.C. § 1112(b), which permits dismissal or conversion of a reorganization case. Both of these provisions allow relief to be granted "for cause," a term not defined in the statute so as to afford flexibility to the bankruptcy courts. *See e.g., Victory Constr.*, 9 B.R. at 558–60 ("cause" is any reason cognizable to the equity power and conscience of the court as constituting an abuse of the bankruptcy process). Numerous cases have found a lack of good faith to constitute "cause" for lifting the stay to permit foreclosure or for dismissing the case.

Determining whether the debtor's filing for relief is in good faith depends largely upon the bankruptcy court's on–the–spot evaluation of the debtor's financial condition, motives, and the local financial realities. Findings of lack of good faith in proceedings based on §§ 362(d) or 1112(b) have been predicated on certain recurring but non–exclusive patterns, and they are based on a conglomerate of factors rather than on any single datum. Several, but not all, of the following conditions usually exist. The debtor has one asset, such as a tract of undeveloped or developed real property. The secured creditors' liens encumber this tract. There are generally no employees except for the principals, little or no cash flow, and no available sources of income to sustain a plan of reorganization or to make adequate protection payments pursuant to 11 U.S.C. §§ 361, 362(d)(1), 363(e), or 364(d)(1). Typically, there are only a few, if any, unsecured creditors whose claims are relatively small. The property has usually been posted for foreclosure because of arrearages on the debt and the debtor has been unsuccessful in defending actions against the foreclosure in state court. Alternatively, the debtor and one creditor may have proceeded to a standstill in state court litigation, and the debtor has lost or has been required to post a bond which it cannot afford. Bankruptcy offers the only possibility of forestalling loss of the property. There are sometimes allegations of wrongdoing by the debtor or its principals. The "new debtor syndrome," in which a one–asset entity has been created or revitalized on the eve of foreclosure to isolate the insolvent property and its creditors, exemplifies, although it does not uniquely categorize, bad faith cases.

Resort to the protection of the bankruptcy laws is not proper under these circumstances because there is no going concern to preserve, there are no employees to protect, and there is no hope of rehabilitation, except according to the debtor's "terminal euphoria." The Sixth Circuit in *Winshall Settlor's Trust,* 758 F.2d at 1137 aptly noted that

> "[t]he purpose of Chapter 11 reorganization is to assist financially distressed business enterprises by providing them with breathing space in which to return to a viable state. *See In re Dolton Lodge Trust No. 35188,* 22 B.R. 918, 922 (Bankr. N.D. Ill. 1982). [I]f there is not a potentially viable business in place worthy of protection and rehabilitation, the Chapter 11 effort has lost its *Raison D'etre . . . . In re Ironsides, Inc.,* 34 B.R. 337, 339 (Bankr. W.D. Ky. 1983)."

Neither the bankruptcy courts nor the creditors should be subjected to the costs and delays of a bankruptcy proceeding under such conditions.

III.   Whether The Bankruptcy Court's Findings Were Clearly Erroneous

Standing alone, the conclusions of the bankruptcy court in this case, based solely on the statements of the debtor's counsel and the litigation tactic of attempting to retry the state court action in the course of the hearing on the motion for relief from the stay, did not provide sufficient evidence to show lack of good faith. *See, e.g., In re* Route 202 Corp., 37 B.R. 367, 373 (Bankr. E.D. Pa. 1984) (filing a bankruptcy petition on the eve of a scheduled foreclosure sale is not, by itself, sufficient to constitute bad faith). When compared with the several general indicia of bad faith previously discussed, these facts do not rise to the level of egregiousness necessary to conclude that the reorganization process is being perverted in this case. *See, e.g., American Property Corp.,* 44 B.R. at 182–83; *Corp. Deja Vu,* 34 B.R. at 848–51; *Lotus Inv.,* 16 B.R. at 595; *Eden Assoc.,* 13 B.R. at 584–85.

The entire course of the bankruptcy court's consideration of the good faith issue, from the quoted remarks of debtor's counsel through a brief argument on oral motion for rehearing, occupies only a few pages of trial transcript. No witnesses were presented. The debtor was afforded no prior notice of the issue, which had not been specifically raised by Commonwealth in its motion for relief from the stay.

The abrupt ruling of the bankruptcy court here contrasts with the approach of the Ninth Circuit Bankruptcy Appellate Panel in *Thirtieth Place,* which "consider[s] the determination of this question [whether to dismiss a case for bad faith] to require an examination of all the particular facts and circumstances in each case." 30 B.R. at 505. In reversing a bankruptcy court determination that had rejected a creditor's motion to dismiss the case or lift the stay, the Bankruptcy Appellate Panel thoroughly analyzed the debtor's condition, which amounted to a "new debtor" bankruptcy filing on the eve of foreclosure, and concluded:

> "The predominant purpose in filing the petition was to prevent foreclosure upon the heavily encumbered property. It must be noted that there was no plan contemplated for the infusion of capital, no gain in managerial expertise, no history of past business conduct, no employees and indeed, no current business activity on the date of the commencement of the case nor are there any reasonable prospects for the conduct of future business."

Id.

We do not, in reversing the bankruptcy court's somewhat hasty conclusion in this case, imply that a finding of lack of good faith would be improper after fuller consideration of the issue on remand. Unless facts appear in the record that clearly warrant a finding of bad faith, however, a debtor should ordinarily be given an opportunity to respond to a charge of abuse of the bankruptcy process.

From the foregoing discussion, it should be clear that a debtor may not counter allegations of bad faith solely with an attempt to relitigate the issues presented in its state court case. If the circumstances surrounding Little Creek's filing demonstrate that the goals of the bankruptcy laws cannot be fulfilled by permitting Little Creek to stave off foreclosure by Commonwealth, then it makes no difference whether Little Creek had, or has, a cause of action for damages against Commonwealth in state court. Additionally, as the issue of good faith arose during a hearing on a motion to lift the stay, Little Creek will not be permitted to undermine the expedited treatment of this motion, *see* 11 U.S.C. § 362(e), by interposing the state court issues. *See In re Johnson,* 756 F.2d 738, 740 (9th Cir.), cert. denied, 106 S. Ct. 88 (1985); *In re Born,* 10 B.R. 43, 48–50 (Bankr. S.D. Tex. 1981). The bankruptcy court was correct in striking the extrinsic state law defenses from the debtor's response to the motion to lift the stay.

For these reasons, the judgments of the bankruptcy court and the district court are *reversed* and this cause is *remanded* for further proceedings not inconsistent herewith.

NOTES AND QUESTIONS

1. There is no specific provision in the Code, and particularly in chapter 11, that requires the court to make a finding of good faith in the filing of a petition or that permits anyone to object to the filing on the ground of a lack of good faith. As a matter of fact, under the prior law, Chapter X of the Bankruptcy Act of 1898 required the court specifically to find that the petition was filed in good faith. *See In re Victory Construction Co.,* 9 B.R. 549, 3 C.B.C.2d 655 (Bankr. C.D. Cal. 1981).

2. In 1994, paragraph (3) was added to § 362(d) to deal specifically with single asset real estate cases involving realty worth $4,000,000 or less. If such a chapter 11 case were filed, at what point could the petition be dismissed on good faith grounds?

3. Is chapter 11 appropriate to avoid posting an appeal bond when the bond would disrupt the debtor's business? *See In re Marsch,* 36 F.2d 825, 828 (9th Cir. 1994). *See also In re Texaco, Inc.,* 17 C.B.C.2d 169 (Bankr. S.D.N.Y. 1987).

---

§ 11.04 Involuntary Petitions

A case commenced by an involuntary petition is a rather drastic form of debt collection by creditors. If the involuntary petition is well founded and the bankruptcy court sustains it, the case proceeds thereafter the same as if a voluntary petition had been filed. Thus, for example, if the case is under chapter 7, the assets of the debtor would be obtained by a trustee and sold, and the proceeds distributed among creditors, all without the volition of the debtor. It is not surprising therefore that § 303 contains restrictions, requirements and penalties pertaining to involuntary petitions.

Pursuant to § 303(a), an involuntary petition may be filed to commence a chapter 7 or a chapter 11 case. It may not be used for chapter 9, 12, or 13, which are cases that may be commenced only by the debtor and not by creditors. Even if a chapter 7 case is commenced by means of an involuntary petition, the debtor may voluntarily convert the case to chapter 11 (12 or 13) pursuant to § 706.

An involuntary petition not only commences a case, it also is the institution of a contested proceeding on the petition itself. The order for relief is not automatic as it is with a voluntary petition. The Code presupposes that the involuntary petition will or certainly may be contested by the debtor, but it spells out very little by way of procedural detail. The bankruptcy rules, however, contain specific provisions with respect to that procedure. Rule 1010 concerns the issuance of a summons and the method of service of the summons and the involuntary petition; Rule 1011 deals with responsive pleadings, the time within which an answer or motion must be filed, the defenses that are available, and, in conjunction with § 303(d), who may contest the petition; Rules 1012 and 1013 deal with examination of the debtor on specific issues and with the hearing on and disposition of the involuntary petition; and, Rule 1018 incorporates by reference many of the adversary proceeding rules contained in Part VII of the rules which, in turn, incorporate wholly, partially, or with some change many of the Federal Rules of Civil Procedure.

MATTER OF BUSICK

United States Court of Appeals, Seventh Circuit
831 F.2d 745 (1987)

RIPPLE, Circuit Judge.

In this appeal, we are asked to review the judgment of the district court which reversed the bankruptcy court's grant of an involuntary petition in bankruptcy. The district court held that Mrs. Busick's contention that she was not liable to the petitioning creditors for certain debts incurred by her husband in business constituted a "bona fide dispute" over the debt which, under the terms of 11 U.S.C. §§ 303(b)(1) and (h)(1) precluded the granting of an involuntary petition in bankruptcy. For the following reasons, we affirm the judgment of the district court.

I.   Background

A.   Procedural History

On February 14, 1980, the appellants filed a joint petition for involuntary relief against Mrs. Busick and her husband. After rather extended proceedings which are not directly relevant here and which are summarized in an earlier appeal to this court, *Matter of Busick*, 719 F.2d 922 (7th Cir. 1983), the matter was tried before the bankruptcy court and judgment was entered on April 5, 1985. The bankruptcy court held that Mrs. Busick was indebted to the creditors and granted the involuntary petition. Mrs. Busick's motion to alter or amend the judgment was denied on March 11, 1986.

B.   *Statutory Scheme*

The statutory provision under which the creditors have proceeded is 11 U.S.C. § 303, which governs involuntary petitions in bankruptcy. While this suit was pending, the statute was amended by the Bankruptcy Amendments and Federal Judgeship Act of 1984, Pub. L. No. 98–353, 98 Stat. 392 (1984) (1984 amendments) which was passed on July 10, 1984.

The 1984 amendments to 11 U.S.C. § 303 imposed additional limitations upon the granting of an involuntary petition. First, in subsection (b), Congress added a requirement that, in order to have standing, the claim of each creditor must be one that is not subject to "a bona fide dispute." Under subsection (h), a claim which is the subject of "a bona fide dispute" must be eliminated from any calculation of whether the debtor generally was not paying his debts as they came due.

C. Orders of the Bankruptcy Court

1. Orders of April 5, 1985

In an order dated April 5, 1985, the bankruptcy court granted the creditors' involuntary petition. *See Matter of Busick,* No. 80–10502, order at 15–16 (Banker. N.D. Ind. Apr. 5, 1985). In finding that the record contained "sufficient evidence to support findings of express and implied agency, joint venture, and ratification," *id.* at 21, the bankruptcy court stated: "[I]t follows that Jane Busick's denial of affiliation with her husband in business transactions was not made in good faith. As a consequence, the Court now holds that she has not raised a good faith dispute with respect to the claims of petitioners herein." *Id.* at 22. Because the bankruptcy court found that Mrs. Busick's claims were not made in good faith, it held that they were not the subject of a bona fide dispute. Thus, apparently applying the 1984 amendments to 11 U.S.C. § 303, the court found that the petitioners had standing to file an involuntary petition under section 303(b) and that Mrs. Busick was generally not paying her debts as they became due as required by section 303(h).

2. Order of March 11, 1986

On March 11, 1986, the bankruptcy court issued an order amending part of the April 5, 1985 order. *Matter of Busick,* No. 80–10502, order at 3–4 (Banker. N.D. Ind. Mar. 11, 1985). Again, the court found that "Ms. Busick was integrally involved in her husband's business affairs." However, in this order, the bankruptcy court stated that the 1984 amendments to section 303 did not apply to the petition filed against Mrs. Busick. Furthermore, the court stated that, had those amendments been applicable, relief would be denied to the petitioners because Mrs. Busick's "dispute of these debts appears bona fide." *Id.* at 2. Thus, while substantially revising its rationale, the court declined to alter its original judgment and permitted the involuntary petition.

D. Order of the District Court

Mrs. Busick appealed the judgment of the bankruptcy court to the district court. In reversing the bankruptcy court's order, the district court first held that the 1984 amendments to section 303 applied to the petition. *Matter of Busick,* 65 B.R. 630, 635 (N.D. Ind. 1986). Next, the court discussed several cases which sought to apply the bona fide dispute requirement of subsections (b) and (h) of section 303. After examining *In re Lough,* 57 B.R. 993, 996–97 (E.D. Mich. 1986), *In re Stroop,* 51 B.R. 210, 212 (D. Colo. 1985), and *In re Johnston Hawks,* Ltd., 49 B.R. 823, 831 (D. Haw. 1985), the district court chose the standard used by the court in *In re Lough.* Thus, the court held that, " 'if there is either a genuine issue of material fact that bears upon the debtor's liability, or a meritorious contention as to the application of law to undisputed facts, then the petition must be dismissed.' " *Busick,* 65 B.R. at 637 (quoting *In re Lough,* 57 B.R. at 997). Moreover, the court stated that "a bona fide dispute as that term is used in 303(b) and 303(h) refers to a genuine issue of material fact that bears upon the debtor's liability, or a meritorious contention as to the application of law to undisputed facts." *Id.* The court held that, in this case, the facts were not disputed and "certainly not enough to warrant a finding that the bankruptcy court's findings were clearly erroneous." *Id.* Instead, the court indicated that the issue here turned upon "the identification of the proper legal standard and the application of the facts to it." *Id.* Because Mrs. Busick had raised "substantial questions" to the claims involved, the district court, applying the *Lough* standard, concluded that the claims were the subject of a bona fide dispute. *Id.* at 638. Finally, the district court noted that, although there was ample evidence of a lack of good faith on the part of Mrs. Busick and her husband, the term "bona fide" in the statute referred only to the dispute, and "not the moral character of those involved in it." *Id.* Therefore, the district court reversed the bankruptcy court's granting of the involuntary petition. *Id.*

· · ·

B. *The Appropriate Standard*

The statute does not define the term "bona fide dispute." We must therefore adopt an analysis which appropriately fulfills the Congressional intent. Like the district court, we have surveyed the various formulations which have been employed by the bankruptcy courts in deciding cases under the 1984 amendments.[1]

---

[1] The district court focused on three cases that discussed the appropriate definition of the term "bona fide.'

In *In re Stroop,* 51 B.R. 210 (D. Colo. 1985), the court adopted a summary judgment standard, stating: "If the defense of the alleged debtor to the claim of the petitioning creditor raises material issues of fact or law so that a summary judgment could not be rendered as a matter of law in favor of the creditor on a trial of the claim, the claim is subject to a bona fide dispute." *Id.* at 212.

In *In re Johnston Hawks, Ltd.,* 49 B.R. 823 (D. Haw. 1985), the court stated that, in considering whether a claim was subject to a bona fide dispute, the court should consider:

1. The nature of the dispute.

2. The nature and the extent of the evidence and allegations presented in support of the creditor's claim and in support of the debtor's contrary claims.

3. Whether the creditor's claim and the debtor's contrary claims are made in good faith and without fraud or deceit.

4. Whether on balance the interests of the creditor outweighs [sic] those of the debtor.

Id. at 831.

Finally, the district court discussed *In re Lough,* 57 B.R. 993 (E.D. Mich. 1986). The court in *Lough* criticized the *Stroop* standard because "its approach did not account for the possibility of undisputed facts but substantial dispute as to the proper application of law." *Matter of Busick,* 65 B.R. 630, 637 (N.D. Ind. 1986). The *Lough* court also criticized the *Johnston Hawks'* standard for two reasons. First, it found no basis in the statute for balancing the interests of the creditor with those of the debtor. *Second, the court in Lough* noted that the good faith, fraud, or deceit factor of Johnston Hawks' analysis would allow a claim with

We agree with the district court that the standard employed by the court in *Lough* is the formulation most compatible with the Congressional intent.[2]

Under that standard, "if there is a bona fide dispute as to either the law or the facts, then the creditor does not qualify and the petition must be dismissed." *Lough,* 57 B.R. at 997; *see In re Garland Coal & Mining Co.,* 67 B.R. 514 (W.D. Ark. 1986) (adopting the *Lough* standard). Under this standard, the bankruptcy court must determine whether there is an objective basis for either a factual or a legal dispute as to the validity of debt. However, "[t]he statute does not require the court to determine the outcome of any dispute, only its presence or absence. Only a limited analysis of the claims at issue is necessary." *Busick,* 65 B.R. at 637.

As noted by the district court, Mrs. Busick raised

> substantial legal questions regarding each of the creditors' claims. These claims arose almost exclusively through the actions of Jane's husband, Leo. Any liability for these debts flowing to Jane cannot be characterized as a foregone conclusion. Indeed, the creditors base their claims on theories of agency, quantum meruit, and joint venture. While their presentation of these theories in their arguments before the court presents a plausible case, Jane has raised substantial questions as to all of them.

Id. at 637–38.

Mrs. Busick has therefore raised claims which, when assessed by an objective standard, raise a reasonable contention "as to the application of law to undisputed facts." *Lough,* 57 B.R. at 997. Therefore, the claims upon which the involuntary

---

no objective basis to defeat an involuntary petition. As noted by the court, if the debtor held a good faith, but subjective, belief that his challenge to the creditor's claim was meritorious, the debtor could defeat the petition.

[2] In *Lough,* the court noted that in *In re Henry,* 52 B.R. 8 (S.D. Ohio 1985), the court had relied upon the following statement of the proponent of the amendment:

> The problem can be explained simply. Some courts have interpreted section 303's language on a debtor's general failure to pay debts as allowing the filing of involuntary petitions and the granting of involuntary relief even when the debtors' reason for not paying is a legitimate and good–faith dispute over his or her liability. This interpretation allows creditors to use the Bankruptcy Code as a club against debtors who have bona fide questions about their liability, but who would rather pay up than suffer the stigma of involuntary bankruptcy proceedings.

> My amendment would correct this problem. Under my amendment, the original filing of an involuntary petition could not be based on debts that are the subject of a good–faith dispute between the debtor and his or her creditors. In the same vein, the granting of an order of relief could not be premised solely on the failure of a debtor to pay debts that were legitimately contested as to liability or amount.

> I believe this amendment, although a simple one, is necessary to protect the rights of debtors and to prevent misuse of the bankruptcy system as a tool of coercion. I also believe it corrects a judicial misinterpretation of existing law and congressional intent as to the proper basis for granting involuntary relief. 30 Cong. Rec S7618 (June 19, 1984) (comments of Senator Baucus).

Lough, 57 B.R. at 996 (quoting *Henry,* 52 B.R. at 9–10).

petition is based are the "subject of a bona fide dispute" as that term is used in subsections (b) and (h) of section 303.

Conclusion

Because the district court correctly identified the legal standard and correctly assessed the facts of the case in light of that standard, we affirm its judgment.

REID v. SCHMID

United States Court of Appeals
Seventh Circuit 854 F.2d 156 (1988)

FLAUM, Circuit Judge.

Dale Schmid, D.D.S., Ralph Schmid, Katherine G. Dengler, and Michael Overfield (the "creditors") filed an involuntary petition in bankruptcy against Zaddock & Co. ("Zaddock") under § 303(b)(1) of the Bankruptcy Code of 1978. 11 U.S.C. § 303(b)(1). Shortly thereafter the creditors filed another involuntary petition against Zaddock's president and principal shareholder Zaddock Reid ("Reid"). The district court appointed an interim trustee to manage both Zaddock's estate and Reid's personal estate. Reid appealed the appointment of the interim trustee. We determined that at least on the basis of the evidence relied on by the district court, the creditors' claims against Reid were the subject of a bona fide dispute and therefore could not serve as the basis for an involuntary petition in bankruptcy. *In re Reid,* 773 F.2d 945 (7th Cir. 1985). Reid and his former attorneys, Arthur T. Susman and Marvin Temple (collectively "appellants"), now seek to recover $63,570 in attorneys' fees and expenses incurred in rectifying what the appellants characterize as the wrongful appointment of an interim trustee. The district court denied their fee petition. We affirm.

I.

On June 29, 1984, the creditors filed an involuntary petition in bankruptcy against Zaddock. On July 2, 1984 an interim trustee, Nathan Yorke, was appointed to manage the Zaddock business. Pursuant to his responsibilities as interim trustee, Yorke conducted a hearing at which Reid was examined. Reid invoked his fifth amendment right against self–incrimination and refused to answer any questions other than his name and legal residence.

On July 13, 1984, the creditors filed an involuntary petition against Reid individually. Four days later, the creditors filed an emergency application under 11 U.S.C. § 303(g) to have an interim trustee appointed to take possession of Reid's personal assets in order to prevent loss to his estate. Pursuant to § 303(g), the district court conducted a hearing and concluded that Reid controlled Zaddock and was improperly commingling Zaddock's assets with his own personal assets. As a result, the court appointed Yorke as interim trustee to manage Reid's personal estate and ordered the creditors to post a $10,000 bond to protect Reid against damages, including damages which might be recoverable under 11 U.S.C. § 303(i). Bankr. R. 2001(b).

Reid appealed, arguing that the appointment of the interim trustee was unlawful because the creditors' claims against him were subject to a bona fide dispute and therefore could not serve as the basis for an involuntary petition in bankruptcy. We reversed the district court in a divided opinion, each judge writing separately. *In re Reid,* 773 F.2d 945 (7th Cir. 1985).

Two judges found that the creditors failed to satisfy their burden under § 303(b)(1) which provides that an involuntary case in bankruptcy may be commenced by three or more creditors, "each of whom is a holder of a claim against such person that is not contingent as to liability or the subject of a bona fide dispute." 11 U.S.C. § 303(b)(1). Reid's alleged liability to the creditors was premised on the theory that the "corporate veil" should be "pierced"—that Reid should be held personally liable for Zaddock's obligations to the creditors because he commingled Zaddock's assets with his own and transferred them to foreign jurisdictions. These two judges determined that the evidence relied on by the district court was insufficient to conclude that Reid was commingling assets and therefore was also insufficient to support the conclusion that the creditors' claims against Reid were not the subject of a bona fide dispute. The lead opinion specifically stated that the creditors therefore lacked standing to file an involuntary petition against Reid and reversed "the district court's grant of the creditors' involuntary petition for the appointment of an interim trustee." *Reid,* 773 F.2d at 948. The case was remanded to the district court "for further proceedings consistent with [the] opinion." *Id.*

In his concurring opinion, Judge Cudahy stated:

> I agree that the petitioning creditors have not established the absence of a bona fide dispute with respect to their claims against Zaddock Reid. I would therefore expressly authorize the district court on remand to conduct further evidentiary proceedings to determine whether the dispute as to Reid's liability is bona fide.

Id. Judge Wood, Jr. dissented, reasoning that the evidence relied on by the district court was sufficient to support its conclusion.

On December 4, 1985, the appellants filed a joint petition for damages, fees, and costs related to the appointment of the interim trustee. The petition was captioned "Joint Petition of Alleged Debtor and His Attorneys Arthur T. Susman and Marvin W. Temple For Damages, Fees and Costs." The district court ruled that the motion was premature. The court interpreted our decision as requiring further consideration of the question of Reid's personal liability for Zaddock's obligations to the creditors. *In re Reid,* No. 84 B 8768, mem. op. at 3 (N.D. Ill. Jan. 14, 1986). The court therefore denied the petition without prejudice pending further proceedings. These further proceedings, however, were hampered by Reid's repeated failure to attend. Apparently not comforted by the success of his first appeal, it now appears that Reid is outside the country and the possibility of his return is uncertain at best.

On August 29, 1986 the appellants filed a "Joint Petition of Alleged Debtor's Attorneys, Arthur T. Susman and Marvin W. Temple, for Fees and Costs." Although the petition's caption did not specifically refer to Reid, the first sentence stated that "[t]his petition for fees and costs is submitted by the Debtor and the attorneys for Zadock Reid." The petition was substantially similar to the petition filed on December 4, 1985 except that it omitted the debtor's prior request for damages caused by the wrongful filing of the involuntary petition. The district court denied the fee petition. The appellants now renew their claim for $63,570 in fees (510 hours) and costs allegedly incurred in their effort to set aside the appointment of the interim trustee to manage Reid's estate.

II.

Appellants base their claim for fees and expenses in part on 11 U.S.C. 303(i). This section provides:

> If the court dismisses a petition under this section other than on consent of all petitioners and the debtor, and if the debtor does not waive the right to judgment under this subsection, the court may grant judgment—
>
> (1)   against the petitioners and in favor of the debtor for—
>
>   (A)   costs;
>
>   (B)   a reasonable attorney's fee; or
>
>   (C)   any damages proximately caused by the taking of possession of the debtor's property by a trustee appointed under [303(g)]; or
>
> (2)   against any petitioner that filed the petition in bad faith, for —
>
>   (A)   any damages proximately caused by such filing; or
>
>   (B)   punitive damages.

11 U.S.C. 303(i).

A degree of uncertainty in this case is attributable to the division within the panel that decided Reid's prior appeal. The district court interpreted the prior decision as an instruction to conduct a further inquiry into whether the creditors' claims against Reid were the subject of a bona fide dispute. Section 303(i) authorizes a district court to award fees if it *dismisses* an involuntary petition filed against a debtor. The appropriateness of dismissing the creditors' petition in this case depends on whether their claim that Reid was depleting Zaddock's assets for his personal use was the subject of a bona fide dispute under § 303(b)(1). The district court was not able to resolve this issue on remand because Reid never appeared for any of the scheduled proceedings. Accordingly, the district court ruled that the appellants were not entitled to fees under § 303(i) because the court had not dismissed the creditors' involuntary petition.

The appellants argue that the district court erred in its reading of our prior opinion. They reason that both the lead opinion and the concurring opinion state that the creditors failed to establish that their claims were not the subject of a bona fide dispute as required under § 303(b)(1). The creditors therefore lacked standing to bring the involuntary petition and it must be dismissed. Thus, in the appellants' view, all that remained for the district court to do on remand was to formally "dismiss the involuntary petition and entertain petitioners' petition for costs and attorneys' fees." Appellants' Br. at 9.

Even if we accept this view of our earlier opinion, it does not follow that the appellants must be awarded fees under § 303(i). The language of § 303(i) states that if the court dismisses an involuntary petition, it *"may grant judgment"* *in favor of the debtor.* (Emphasis added). The use of the word "may" indicates that fees do not have to be awarded in all cases. Whether fees and costs should be awarded is committed to the discretion of the district court. *In re: Gerald Nordbrock,* 772 F.2d 397, 400 (8th Cir. 1985). The district court did not abuse its discretion by denying appellants' fee petition in this case.

Neither party has directed us to, nor have we independently located, any authority which sets forth criteria to guide a district court's exercise of discretion when awarding fees under § 303(i). Appellants stress that the legislative history of § 303(i) demonstrates that it was enacted in recognition of the serious harm inflicted upon alleged debtors when involuntary petitions are wrongfully filed. Part of this harm includes the attorneys' fees and costs incurred in seeking to dismiss the involuntary petition. But the plain language of the statute clearly contemplates that fees and costs will not be awarded in all cases, even though a party will ordinarily incur attorneys' fees in seeking to dismiss the petition. The legislative history is therefore ultimately not helpful in identifying those cases in which a fee award under § 303(i) is appropriate.

One possible criterion for identifying such cases is the presence of bad faith on the part of the creditors in filing the involuntary petition. Section 303(i) distinguishes between good and bad faith petitions with respect to the type of recovery that may be awarded, but makes no similar distinction as to the district court's initial decision to make an award at all under this subsection. *See* 11 U.S.C. § 303(i)(2) (punitive damages and damages proximately caused by the filing are authorized if the involuntary petition is filed in bad faith). Because Congress specifically distinguished between good and bad faith petitions with respect to damages, but not in determining when the court should make a § 303(i) award, it may not have intended bad faith to be relevant to the award decision itself. Conceivably, Congress' focus was on the well–being of the debtor, which is not necessarily a function of the petitioning creditors' state of mind. This position, however, is difficult to reconcile with Congress' decision to authorize additional remedies when a petition is filed in bad faith. The more plausible reading of the provision is that Congress believed that an involuntary petition filed in bad faith was sufficiently offensive to justify an additional recover, but chose to reserve to the court the power to withhold an award in certain rare circumstances. Accordingly, we believe that the presence or absence of bad faith will inform the exercise of the district court's discretion under § 303(i). Appellants, however, have made no allegations of bad faith on the part of the creditors in this case.

Congress' decision to authorize fees under § 303(i) also suggests that bad faith on the part of the creditors is not the only situation in which fees may be awarded. *See Christiansburg Garment Co. v. E.E.O.C.,* 434 U.S. 412, 419, 98 S. Ct. 694, 699, 54 L. Ed. 2d 648 (1978) (statute providing that a "court, in its discretion, may" allow fees was interpreted to encompass more than bad faith conduct because the American Rule already provided a remedy for such conduct, making the statutory provision unnecessary). Thus, the district court should also consider the merit of a creditor's position that the petition was properly filed when determining whether a recovery should be awarded under § 303(i). In this case, Reid argued that the creditors'involuntary petition should be dismissed because § 303(b)(1) required that the creditors' claims not be the subject of a bona fide dispute.

This in turn hinged on whether Reid had commingled Zaddock's business assets with his own, thereby making Reid accountable for Zaddock's obligations to the creditors. This was a close question, as demonstrated by the differing outcomes reached by the courts which considered the issue. As the district court stated:

> Attorneys for the petitioning creditors sought a determination by the court that there was no bona fide dispute as to the commingling of Reid's assets with those of the involved corporation and, after hearing, this court so held. The Seventh Circuit thereafter disagreed, leaving this court in the uncomfortable position of addressing a petition to assess costs and fees against attorneys for advancing a position which this court was persuaded had merit.

In re Reid, No. 84 B 8768, mem. op. at 3 (N. D. Ill. May 5, 1987) (order denying attorneys' fees). On these facts, we hold that the district court did not abuse its discretion when it denied appellants' fee petition under § 303(i).

The appellants argue, however, that the appointment of the interim trustee to manage the debtor's business is both a drastic step and one which is potentially very detrimental to the debtor. The appellants contend that because this step was wrongfully taken against Reid, an award of attorneys' fees is particularly appropriate here. They rely on a policy codified in part by Bankruptcy Rule 2001(b). This rule provides that an interim trustee may not be appointed until the creditors furnish a bond "conditioned to indemnify the debtor for costs, attorney's fee, expenses, and damages allowable under § 303(i) of the Code." In addition, § 303(i)(1)(C) specifically provides that an award may include "any damages proximately caused by the taking of possession of the debtor's property by a trustee appointed under [§ 303(g)]."

The difficulty with the appellants' position is that Bankruptcy Rule 2001(b) references § 303(i) which, as we have noted, does not require the district court to award a recovery and is triggered by the dismissal of an involuntary petition. The appointment of an interim trustee is a supplemental remedy available after an involuntary case is commenced "if [it is] necessary to preserve the property of the estate or to prevent loss to the estate." 11 U.S.C. § 303(g). Because the appointment of an interim trustee depends in part on this independent test, there will be some cases where this standard is not met and the appointment will be wrongful even if the involuntary petition was properly filed. It is not obvious from the language of Bankruptcy Rule 2001(b) that attorneys' fees are authorized when the appointment of an interim trustee is set aside, but the involuntary petition is not dismissed. The rule speaks in terms of attorneys' fees "allowable under § 303(i)" and § 303(i) in turn depends on the dismissal of an involuntary petition. On the other hand, by requiring creditors to post a bond, the rule attempts to afford the debtor additional protection when an interim trustee is appointed. The focus of the rule is on the appointment of the interim trustee, not the filing of the involuntary petition, and a bond is required every time an appointment is sought. This suggests that the rule contemplates that fees incurred in having an interim trustee set aside might be recoverable regardless of whether the involuntary petition is dismissed.

We do not, however, have to resolve this issue because regardless of the rule's scope, its reliance on § 303(i) demonstrates that an award is not mandatory. Any hardship accompanying the appointment of the interim trustee in this case was minimal. First, although any damages to Reid proximately caused by the interim trustee's taking possession of his personal estate are specifically provided for in § 303(i)(1)(C), the appellants have not claimed such damages. Second, the appellants' claim that the interim trustee was wrongfully appointed was based in large part on the creditors' lack of standing to file the involuntary petition. If the creditors' claims against Reid were the subject of a bona fide dispute, their involuntary petition was unlawful and the appointment of the interim trustee, as a supplemental remedy, was by implication also unlawful. The effort required by Reid's counsel in attempting to have the involuntary petition dismissed and the appointment of the interim trustee set aside therefore substantially overlapped.

We hold that the district court did not abuse its discretion when it denied attorneys' fees and costs under § 303(i). The appellants have not alleged that the creditors' petition was filed in bad faith and we find that the creditors' position had merit, although it failed (if only temporarily). In addition, we conclude that an award of fees incurred in attempting to have the appointment of an interim trustee set aside, if recoverable at all, is not mandatory and on the facts of this case is not required.

III.

The appellants also argue that they are entitled to fees under the common law. They acknowledge that the "American Rule" generally prohibits the award of fees in favor of the prevailing party except in cases where the losing party has acted in bad faith, but they cite to authority in which courts have invoked their inherent equity powers to award fees in connection with removing a wrongfully appointed receiver. *See, e.g., First Federal Savings & Loan Assoc. of Coffeyville v. Moulds,* 202 Kan. 557, 451 P.2d 215 (1969); *Stella v. Mosele,* 305 Ill. App. 577, 27 N.E.2d 559 (1st Dist. 1940). They argue that the wrongful appointment of the interim trustee in this case is analogous.

We agree that the situations are analogous. The appellants have not, however, cited to any case where a court has relied on its equity powers to award attorneys' fees in connection with the wrongful appointment of an interim trustee under the Bankruptcy Code of 1978. The most plausible explanation for the absence of such authority is that Congress has specifically authorized the award of attorneys' fees in certain circumstances, including § 303(i), and has pre–empted the judiciary's equitable power to redistribute attorneys' fees in bankruptcy cases.

The pre–emption of the judiciary's power to award attorney's fees in situations other than those within the traditional exceptions to the American Rule was authoritatively set forth in *Alyeska Pipeline Service Co. v. Wilderness Society,* 421

U.S. 240, 95 S. Ct. 1612, 44 L. Ed. 2d 141 (1975). In *Alyeska* the Supreme Court reversed an award of fees based on the court of appeals' equitable power stating that "[the American Rule] is deeply rooted in history and in congressional policy; and it is not for us to invade the legislature's province by redistributing litigation costs in the manner suggested by respondents." *Id.* at 271, 95 S. Ct. at 1628 (footnote omitted). Specifically, the Court reasoned:

> [W]hat Congress has done, however, while fully recognizing and accepting the [American] rule, is to make specific and explicit provisions for the allowance of attorneys' fees under selected statutes granting or protecting various federal rights. Under this scheme of things, it is apparent that the circumstances under which attorneys' fees are to be awarded and the range of discretion of the courts in making those awards are matters for Congress to determine.

Id. at 260–63, 95 S. Ct. at 1623–25 (citations and footnotes omitted). The application of this principle is particularly clear in this case because § 303(i)(1)(C) plainly contemplates the wrongful appointment of an interim trustee. In view of the principles set forth in *Alyeska*, we hold that appellants' common law claim for attorneys' fees is preempted by § 303(i). The decision of the district court is Affirmed.

§ 11.05   Abstention in Cases and Proceedings; 11 U.S.C. § 305

Ajax Corporation is insolvent, and has no desire to continue its business. It makes an assignment for the benefit of its creditors under New York law on March 1. The assignee promptly takes charge of the debtor's assets and conducts an auction sale on April 3. The assignee distributes the cash proceeds of the auction sale to the debtor's creditors on May 1. Thereafter, three disgruntled creditors file an involuntary chapter 7 petition against Ajax. The debtor and the assignee answered the petition, arguing that no useful purpose would be served by administering the debtor's assets under the Bankruptcy Code. What result? Would it be at all significant if Ajax had made preferential payments to certain creditors prior to the filing of the involuntary petition and those payments could not have been challenged by the assignee under state law? *See, e.g., In re RAI Marketing Services, Inc.,* 20 B.R. 943, 945, 946 (Bankr. D. Kan. 1982) ("§ 305 should be strictly construed." Bankruptcy court would "sustain a § 305 motion *only* when: 1. The petition was filed by a few recalcitrant creditors and most creditors oppose bankruptcy; 2. There is a state insolvency proceeding or other equitable and concrete out–of–court arrangement pending; and 3. Dismissal or suspension is in the best interest of the debtor and all creditors"); *In re Michael S. Starbuck, Inc.,* 14 B.R. 134, 135 (Bankr. S.D.N.Y. 1981) (debtors were subjected to prepetition receivership filed by Securities and Exchange Commission in federal district court; when involuntary petitions filed, receiver and counsel had spent many hours and several thousand dollars in administering estate; held that best interests of debtors and creditors warranted dismissal of involuntary petition; the "receivership is providing for efficient and equitable distribution of [the debtors'] assets. Allowing this matter to continue as a debtor proceeding under the Bankruptcy Code would result in a terrible waste of time and resources. Many services, already rendered in the administration of the receivership estate, would have to be repeated at additional expense to the estate. No advantage would accrue to the creditors if this matter were to proceed in the bankruptcy court.").

Regardless of your answers to the above questions, does the Bankruptcy Code give the court the discretion not to enter an order for relief if it finds that the allegations of the involuntary petition are well–founded? *See International Shoe Co. v. Smith–Cole, Inc.*, 62 F.2d 972 (10th Cir. 1933).

BUFFINGTON v. FIRST SERVICE CORP.

United States Court of Appeals, Eighth Circuit
672 F.2d 687 (1982)

Before BRIGHT and ARNOLD, Circuit Judges, and DAVIES, Senior District Judge.

PER CURIAM

In this second appeal brought by appellants Dewey L. Buffington, *et al.* (debtors), appellants seek to raise a jurisdictional objection to successive orders of the bankruptcy court dismissing debtors' reorganization petitions under Chapter XI [sic] of the Bankruptcy Reform Act of 1978. In the prior appeal, *Buffington v. Adams*, 676 F.2d 703 (8th Cir. 1981 (unpublished)), we rejected the debtors' efforts to enjoin the dismissal by the bankruptcy judge. We noted in our prior opinion, however, that similar issues were pending in a separate appeal from an earlier order by another judge of the United States District Court for the Eastern District of Arkansas. In that order, the district court dismissed debtors' appeal from the bankruptcy judge's decision to abstain and dismiss debtors' reorganization petitions under 11 U.S.C. § 305. The district court concluded that the bankruptcy judge had properly abstained and that the statute bars review of the bankruptcy judge's decision.

We now have before us an appeal from that order of the district court. After reconsidering the jurisdictional challenge to the order of the bankruptcy court, we reject the debtors' contentions. Accordingly, we affirm the order of the district court.

We briefly review the relevant background of the present appeal, as set out in Judge Roy's memorandum and order of August 19, 1981:

> The instant appeal [in the United States District Court for the Eastern District of Arkansas form the bankruptcy judge's ruling] arises from the March 23, 1981, Memorandum and Order of the Honorable Arnold M. Adams, United States Bankruptcy Judge, who found that "it is to the best interest of the debtor and creditors that this Court should, and does hereby, abstain and dismiss," citing 11 U.S.C. § 305.

Presently pending before this Court is the Motion to Dismiss Appeal filed on behalf of the Twin City Bank, one of the creditors herein. As reflected by the pleadings which have been designated as part of the record on appeal, the present action originated with the filing of a foreclosure action in Pulaski County Chancery Court against the debtor herein, Dewey L. Buffington, Jr., by certain secured creditors who held mortgages upon unimproved and non–income producing real property of Buffington's. After Buffington had attempted unsuccessfully to dispose of the property named in the foreclosure suit, a hearing on the merits was scheduled in the Chancery Court for 9:00 a.m. on October 22, 1980. Upon that same date, at 8:14 a.m., Buffington filed in the Bankruptcy Court a Voluntary Petition for reorganization under Chapter XI, whereby the Chancery Court foreclosure proceedings were stayed. On January 14, 1981, First Service Corporation, the Twin City Bank, and the Metropolitan National Bank (secured creditors of Buffington who had been among those who filed the foreclosure action against him in state court) filed with the Bankruptcy Court a Complaint Seeking Relief from Stay and Abandonment of Property. On February 19, 1981, secured creditors John D. and Mary R. Toney (also parties in the Chancery Court suit) joined in the Complaint, in which it was contended that pursuant to 11 U.S.C. § 362(d)(2) the creditors were entitled either to have the court abstain or to grant relief from the stay against the Chancery Court proceedings. As reasons in support of their contention, the creditors alleged that Buffington had no equity in the property upon which they held mortgages; that the creditors' claims exceeded the market value of the property; that the accrual of daily interest was eroding the value of the collateral; and that the property in question was not necessary to an effective reorganization, citing Buffington's testimony at the December 29, 1980, first meeting of creditors to the effect that the property was undeveloped and generates no cash or income, that the property was ready to be sold, and that only by a sale would the creditors be able to make any recovery. The Complaint requested that the Bankruptcy Court abstain pursuant to 11 U.S.C. § 305, urging that the Chancery Court proceeding was ready for adjudication and that Chapter XI action had been filed by Buffington for the sole purpose of delay.

A hearing was held on March 16 and 20, 1981, during which the testimony of numerous witnesses was taken and arguments of counsel were heard. Subsequent to the hearing Judge Adams issued his Order and Memorandum Opinion, which contains a detailed discussion of the testimony and of the status of the various creditors' liens against Buffington's property. This Court agrees with Judge Adams' assessment of the issue which had to be decided by him, to wit, whether Buffington possessed any equity in the property in question. The inescapable conclusion is that he did not. It is likewise clear that Buffington had no means by which to provide anything even approaching adequate protection to the creditors, and that the continuation of the Chapter XI case would inevitably result in the diminution of the estate and in unreasonable prejudice to the creditors. As the Bankruptcy Judge properly noted, not all debtors who file Chapter XI cases are fit candidates for reorganization. Thus the invocation of 11 U.S.C. § 305, as per the prayer in the creditors' complaint, was proper. That section provides that,

Abstention.

> (a) The court, after notice and a hearing may dismiss a case under this title, or may suspend all proceedings in a case under this title [11 U.S.C. §§ 1, *et seq.*], at any time if—

> (1) The interests of creditors and the debtor would be better served by such dismissal or suspension;

Section 305 also provides in subsection (c) that,

> An order under subsection (a) of this section dismissing a case or suspending all proceedings in a case, or a decision not so to dismiss or suspend, is not reviewable by appeal or otherwise.

The Court finds that Judge Adams, who had the opportunity to observe the witnesses and hear the arguments of counsel firsthand, made the finding that in the instant case the interests of all parties concerned would best be served by abstention. The Court further finds from the record before it that such a conclusion was warranted and proper in all respects. [*Buffington v. First Service Corp.*, No. LR–C–81–135 (E.D.Ark., Aug. 20, 1981) (Memorandum and order) (footnotes omitted).]

The briefs and record clearly indicate that the bankruptcy court had entered its order after an adversary proceeding in which debtors asserted their own interests, as well as the interests of unsecured creditors. Furthermore, the chairman of the creditors' committee received notice of the proceedings and attended the hearing.

In this court, the debtors, nevertheless, attack the jurisdiction of the bankruptcy proceedings. Without citation to case authority, appellants assert in their brief that the bankruptcy court lacked jurisdiction to issue its abstention ruling, because the unsecured creditors did not receive twenty days' notice of the hearing pursuant to Interim Bankruptcy Rule 2002(b). Appellants did not present these contentions to the bankruptcy judge or to the district court.

We reject this contention as essentially frivolous for the following reasons:

1) The clerk of the bankruptcy court provided interested parties with notice of hearing on the secured creditors' complaint for relief from stay. No contention is made that such notice was not appropriate under the "particular circumstances," as required by 11 U.S.C. § 102(1)(A).

2) No challenge is made to the adequacy of the hearing under 11 U.S.C. § 362(d) for release from the automatic stay, or the notice thereof. The record discloses that interested persons, including the representative of the general creditors, received notice. The issue was decided in a contested hearing at which interested parties appeared, including the chairman of the (unsecured) creditors' committee. That sort of notice and hearing satisfies the requirements of 11 U.S.C. § 305(a)(1).

3) Appellants who have litigated and lost on the merits of the section 305 and section 362(e) contentions have no ground to assert the rights of unsecured creditors relating to the mortgaged real estate, when the bankruptcy court has found that the debtors possessed no equity in that real estate.

4) Finally, appellants did not challenge the bankruptcy court's jurisdiction either in the bankruptcy court or in the district court before Judge Roy. The alleged defect in service, if any, did not deprive any person or party in interest of property right without due process.

We reject the appeal as essentially frivolous and affirm the judgment of the district court.

Because of repetitious litigation, both here and in the district court, we think it appropriate to assess double costs against the appellant and his counsel.

Let the mandate issue forthwith, reserving the right of the appellants to move for a rehearing.

KIMREY v. DORSETT

Bankruptcy Court, Middle District of North Carolina
10 B.R. 466, 4 C.B.C.2d 254, 7 B.C.D. 625 (1981)

REYNOLDS, Bankruptcy Judge:

The above–captioned adversary proceeding was filed by the female debtor to recover property that allegedly belonged to the debtor. This matter came on for hearing before the undersigned United States Bankruptcy Judge after due and timely notice was given to the defendant and other interested parties, and was heard on March 17, 1981. After due consideration in this matter, and upon hearing evidence and testimony and arguments of counsel and reviewing briefs filed by both parties in this matter, the Court finds the following facts and applies the law accordingly.

Findings of Fact

1.   On July 16, 1980, Donald W. Kimrey and wife, Penny Kimrey, filed a petition for relief under Chapter 13 of the Bankruptcy Code.

2.   The female debtor, Penny Kimrey, is the daughter of B. William Rosenfeld. B. William Rosenfeld died in August, 1980. His death was within 180 days of the filing of the debtors' Chapter 13 petition and, therefore, any property the female debtor would be entitled to by reason of his death, would become property of her estate, pursuant to 11 U.S.C. § 541.

3.   On the date of his death, B. William Rosenfeld held a certificate of deposit in the amount of $13,000.00 from the Fidelity Bank of Biscoe, N.C. This certificate of deposit was issued in the name of B. William Rosenfeld or Penny Sue Kimrey or William C. Rosenfeld. These names were all typed on the front of the certificate. The back of the certificate of deposit had the following:

SIGNATURE OF REGISTERED HOLDER—ONE PERSON
TO THE FIDELITY BANK

The bank and the undersigned party or parties agree: We, the undersigned parties, agree and declare that all funds on deposit now or deposited at any time in this joint account are, and shall be our joint property, owned by us as joint tenants with the right of survivorship and not as tenants in common regardless of source of origin of these funds; and upon the death of one or more of us any balance remaining in said account shall become the property of the survivor or survivors subject, however, to the provision of Section 411(b) of the General Statutes of North Carolina. The entire account or any part thereof may be withdrawn by or upon the order of any one of us, the survivor or survivors and the withdrawal of funds by the survivor or survivors shall be binding upon us, our heirs, next of kin, legatees, assigns, creditors and personal representatives. This agreement is made subject to the provisions of Section 411 of the General Statutes of North Carolina.

SIGNATURE OF REGISTERED HOLDERS—JOINT ACCOUNT WITH RIGHT OF SURVIVORSHIP

B. William Rosenfeld
Signature
Signature
Signature

As noted, there was only one signature under the line of "Joint Account with Right of Survivorship." That is the signature of B. William Rosenfeld.

4. The defendant in this action is Charles H. Dorsett. He was duly appointed the Executor of the estate of B. William Rosenfeld. On September 30, 1980, Charles H. Dorsett as Executor, redeemed the certificate of deposit from Fidelity Bank and placed the proceeds in the decedent's estate for disbursement as a general asset of the estate.

5. The plaintiff, the female debtor, contends that a portion of the funds in the certificate of deposit are property of her estate by reason of an inter vivos gift from her father or in the alternative by reason that it was the usual and customary banking practice of Fidelity Bank to only require that the depositor sign a joint account with right of survivorship even if more than one registered holder is indicated on the face of the certificate of deposit.

6. The Executor contends that these funds belong to the decedent's estate as North Carolina has a statute which expressly governs joint bank accounts with right of survivorship. The defendant states that the provisions of N.C.G.S. § 41–2.1 have not been complied with and that the proceeds of the certificate of deposit are rightfully in the possession of the Executor. The Executor also contends that the Bankruptcy Court had no jurisdiction over this action pursuant to N.C.G.S. § 1–78.

7. Also involved in this case is the fact that the plaintiff is indebted to the estate of B. William Rosenfeld in the amount of $2,779.40. This indebtedness is based on a demand note and deed of trust executed by the female debtor. Plaintiff seeks to set off this debt under § 553 of the Bankruptcy Code and use the remaining funds allegedly due her to bring current the arrearage owed to Federal National Mortgage Association, holder of a note and deed of trust on the debtor's home.

The Court now finds the following to substantiate an order to abstain:

1. N.C.G.S. § 7A–241 provides "exclusive and original jurisdiction for the probate of wills and the administration of the decedent's estate is vested in the Superior Court Division."

2.   N.C.G.S. § 1–78 provides "all actions against an executor and administrator in their official capacity must be instituted in the county where the bonds were given."

3.   The North Carolina statutes have other restrictions in regard to claimants bringing an action against the personal representative. N.C.G.S. § 28A–19–18 prohibits the recovery of costs by the plaintiff under certain circumstances. N.C.G.S. § 28A–19–16 has a 90–day limitation on recovering on a claim where such claim has been denied by the personal representative. Therefore, this Court may not have jurisdiction over this adversary proceeding.

4.   Even if this Court does have jurisdiction over this adversary proceeding, the issue of ownership of the proceeds of the certificate of deposit is one which should be decided in state court. N.C.G.S. § 41–2.1 states that a "bank account may be established in the names of two or more persons, payable to either or the survivor or survivors when both or all parties have signed a written agreement, either on a signature card or by a separate instrument, expressly providing for the right of survivorship." The statute then goes on to state that "this section shall be governed by other applicable provisions of the law." The statute has many ambiguities and the case law in this state is not clear.

5.   The Executor, Charles H. Dorsett, has a claim consisting of a note and deed of trust against plaintiff in this action which will probably involve adjusting the rights of plaintiff against the defendant in the Probate Court.

6.   If it should be determined that the plaintiff, Penny Kimrey, is entitled to proceeds of the certificate of deposit under N.C.G.S. § 41–2.1(3)(1) the proceeds would be subject to the following claims listed below upon that portion of the unwithdrawn deposit which would belong to the deceased had the unwithdrawn deposit been divided equally between both or among all the joint tenants at the time of the death of the deceased:

(a) One–year's allowance to the surviving widow

(b) Funeral expenses

(c) Estate expenses

(d) Creditors of the deceased

(e) Government obligations, such as taxes.

This Court now makes the following

Conclusions of Law

1.   Although the Bankruptcy Court has jurisdiction over all claims and causes of action relating to bankruptcy matters under 28 U.S.C. § 1471, the Court is also given the authority to decline jurisdiction in the interest of justice under 28 U.S.C. § 1471(d), or to remand removal of cases on equitable grounds under 28 U.S.C. § 1478. Section 1471(d) provides "a bankruptcy court, in the interest of justice, (may) abstain from hearing a particular proceeding arising under Title 11 or arising in or related to a case under Title 11. Such abstention, or decision not to abstain, is not reviewable by appeal or otherwise."

2. The legislative history of § 1471(d) cites *Thompson v. Magnolia Petroleum,* 309 U.S. 478, 5 S.Ct.628, 84 L.Ed 876 (1940), as support for the decision to abstain. In *Thompson,* a case involving oil rights and land ownership, the Supreme Court held that it was appropriate for the bankruptcy court to abstain from hearing this matter as it involved the interpretation of instruments of conveyance which were governed by state law and because there were no state statutes or state court decisions which were on point. Therefore, the issue was one of unsettled state law and one in which the state court should make a ruling.

3. There were very few reported decisions under the 1979 Code with respect to § 1471(d). However, it seems clear that the legislators have incorporated the *Thompson* ruling in the Code. In a 1980 Code case, *Matter of Jewel Terrace Corporation,* 3 BR 36 (1980), the Bankruptcy Court of the Eastern District of New York held that "Where there has been a prior state court proceeding of issues involving state court expertise such as the landlord tenant area, it is proper to defer to the state court," 3 BR at page 39. There is no doubt that the rights of ownership in a joint bank account with the rights of survivorship is clearly a question of state law requiring state expertise.

This Court holds that a decision to abstain from deciding a particular issue in a case should only be exercised after due deliberation and discretion. It was the intent of Congress to give the court original jurisdiction over "all civil proceedings arising under Title 11 or arising in or related to cases under Title 11, 28 U.S.C. § 1471." However, this Court holds that it is in the best interests of all parties to abstain from hearing the matter that involves such an unsettled issue in North Carolina law.

Now, therefore, based on the foregoing Findings of Fact and Conclusions of Law, it is

Ordered that pursuant to the authority granted this Court under 28 U.S.C. § 1471(d) this Court abstains from exercising jurisdiction over this adversary proceeding and directs that this proceeding be commenced in state court as the state court is better able to respond to this particular issue.

It Is Further Ordered, Adjudged and Decreed that the stay afforded by 11 U.S.C. § 362 be, and hereby is, modified to permit a party of interest to commence a proceeding against the debtor that is substantially related to the proceeds of the certificate of deposit in question. For all other purposes the automatic stay of 11 U.S.C. § 362 is in full force and effect.

NOTES AND QUESTIONS

1. 28 U.S.C. § 1334(a), (b) replaced § 1471(a), (b) in 1984.

2. 28 U.S.C. § 1334(c) authorizes the district court to abstain from hearing a related matter. *See also* Rule 5011.

3. Under what circumstances must a court abstain pursuant to § 1334(c)?

4. In the *Maxwell Commmunication* chapter 11 case, the following occurred: a chapter 11 petition was filed in the bankruptcy court for the Southern District of New York and the court appointed an examiner pursuant to § 1104. Shortly thereafter, an administration proceeding of the debtor was commenced under the English reorganization law and administrators were appointed by the English court. The administrators commenced a proceeding in New York to recover allegedly preferential transfers made to several banks which they claimed were voidable under § 547(b) of the U.S. Bankruptcy Code. The bankruptcy court dismissed the complaint on the ground that because of the centrality of all the relevant facts, the English law and not the U.S. law should apply and the action should be brought under it in England. (In fact, the transfers were not voidable under the English law.) Consider the relevance of the following:

     a.   Section 109(a) of the Bankruptcy Code
     b.   Section 305 of the Bankruptcy Code
     c.   Section 304 of the Bankruptcy Code.

Do these sections evidence a Congressional intent to permit foreign debtors to use the Code? If it is used, are not all of its sections relevant and applicable? Of what import are doctrines of conflict of laws? Why were not §§ 305 and 304 utilized rather than having duplicate proceedings extant under two different laws?

CHAPTER 12

JURISDICTION AND VENUE OF CASES AND PROCEEDINGS

§ 12.01 Jurisdiction and Venue Generally

In discussing or even raising the issues of jurisdiction and venue, it is first necessary to delimit the circumstances under which they are relevant. To speak overly broadly is to create unmitigated confusion as Congress has seemed bent on doing. (*See* 1984 Bankruptcy Amendments.) This is particularly true because in bankruptcy cases, jurisdiction and even venue are unique concepts as compared with those relevant in the typical civil action brought either in state or federal court. Under the Bankruptcy Reform Act as enacted in 1978, classes in bankruptcy law could have covered jurisdiction matters in one hour whereas prior thereto, it could have taken eight hours. Since 1984, it can easily take eight hours once again.

It was mentioned in Chapter 10, *supra,* that the Bankruptcy Reform Act of 1978 gave the bankruptcy court expanded or pervasive jurisdiction. That differs from what it had been under the 1898 Bankruptcy Act by a considerable measure. The jurisdiction has, however, been cut back by the 1984 Bankruptcy Amendments, but it is still different from the earlier Act. The difference will be discussed in this chapter. For the moment, however, it should be recognized that jurisdiction as used in this context is exclusively related to the power of the bankruptcy court to *hear* disputes that arise in cases pending before that court. Hence, the distinction between the terms "proceedings" and "cases" is necessary.

But there is another and equally important facet to the concept of jurisdiction which has, essentially, already been discussed. This relates to the subject matter jurisdiction of the bankruptcy court with respect to the chapter 7, 9, 11, 12, or 13 case itself. *See* § 109(a) of the Code.

QUESTIONS

1. Other than § 109(a), what other provisions of the Code would go to the subject matter jurisdiction of the court?

2. *See* 28 U.S.C. § 1408. Is this a jurisdiction or venue section? What is the difference between the two? How do you compare 11 U.S.C. § 109(a) and 28 U.S.C. § 1408?

3. Suppose the debtor is employed by the Kansas Farm Bank & Trust Co. as a teller. The bank is located in Kansas City, Kansas, and the debtor's house is

(Matthew Bender & Co., Inc.) (Pub.094)

in the same city. Not wishing to cause any unnecessary stir, commotion, or anxiety, the debtor files a chapter 7 petition in the bankruptcy court located in Kansas City, Missouri. What are the court's options? What are the creditors' options? *See* 28 U.S.C. § 1412 and F.R.B.P. 1014. May the bankruptcy court in Kansas City, Missouri retain the case if a motion challenging venue is timely made? Suppose, instead of a bankruptcy petition, a complaint commencing a civil action were similarly filed in a federal court that did not have venue. What options would that court have? *See* 28 U.S.C. § 1406.

[A] Venue for Filing Petition

HADER LEASING INTERNATIONAL CO. v . D.H. OVERMYER TELECASTING CO.
(In re Hadar Leasing International Co.)

United States District Court
14 B.R. 819, 7 BCD 686 (S.D.N.Y. 1981)

GAGLIARDI, District Judge.

Since all parties are familiar with the events leading up to this appeal there is no need for me to recount in detail those events.

When the parties appeared before me last week, they agreed on a briefing schedule to which all parties have substantially adhered. At that time, Judge Galgay's order transferring this case to the Northern District of Ohio was effective as of April 21st, and I ordered a stay of that order until today, with the understanding that if at all possible I would render my decision on this appeal today. Although the briefing schedule was extended for one additional day, I have nonetheless concluded that the interests of all concerned would be best served by a prompt decision, thereby alleviating the need for a further extension of the stay.

A threshold question before reaching the merits is whether Judge Galgay's order transferring venue, pursuant to 28 U.S.C. § 1475, is appealable. This court, of course, has jurisdiction over all *final* orders from the Bankruptcy Court under 28 U.S.C. § 1334(a). A bankruptcy order transferring venue, though, is an interlocutory order, similar to an order transferring venue under § 1404(a). This does not, however, preclude judicial review of the order, since an interlocutory order may be appealed with leave of the court to which the appeal is taken under 28 U.S.C. § 1334(b). Subsection (d) of Rule 8004 of the Suggested Interim Bankruptcy Rules, adopted in this district, permits the court to waive the required application for leave to appeal if a timely notice of appeal is filed. I will consider Hadar's timely notice of appeal an application for leave to appeal. Collier suggests, at § 3.02[g], that unlike a 1404 order, where there is little prejudice by deferring appeal until the conclusion of the case, there is good reason to grant leave to appeal freely from a bankruptcy venue transfer order. Accordingly, I grant, *nunc pro tunc,* Hadar's motion for leave to appeal as of April 20th.

The parties appear to be in agreement on the applicable legal standards for the bankruptcy court's consideration of a motion to transfer venue, as well as on this court's standard of review from that order. Pursuant to Fed.R.Bank. 810, unless I find that Judge Galgay's findings were clearly erroneous, I must affirm his order of transfer.

The two applicable statutes on a motion to transfer venue are 28 U.S.C. § 1475 which contains the relevant language governing the exercise of the bankruptcy court's discretion: a case may be transferred "in the interest of justice and for the convenience of the parties," and Bankruptcy Rule 116(b), which repeats the same standard and adds the procedural requirement that the court may transfer a case "after hearing on notice to petitioner and such other persons as it may direct." Rule 116 goes on to state that "the transfer may be ordered at or before the first meeting of creditors."

In order to refine the broad and somewhat nebulous terms "convenience of witnesses" and "interest of justice", courts have considered five concrete standards. These are 1) proximity of creditors of every kind to the court; 2) proximity of the debtor to the court; 3) proximity of witnesses necessary to administration of the estate; 4) location of assets and 5) economic administration of the estate. *Matter of Commonwealth Oil Refining Co.*, 596 F.2d 1239, 1247 (5th Cir. 1979). Occasionally, courts have applied a sixth standard; whether the intertwined relationship of debtors requires proceedings in one district. *See In re Banker's Trust*, 403 F.2d 16 (7th Cir. 1968), citing *In re Hudick–Ross*, 198 F.Supp. 695 (S.D.N.Y.1961).

Judge Galgay made eleven specific findings after hearing argument on the motion. Contrary to appellant's arguments, I find that there was adequate support for these findings, based solely on uncontroverted facts on the record before him, primarily in Hadar's Chapter 11 petition. These findings, as they relate to the standards I have outlined, are: first, that the majority of Hadar's creditors are located in the Northern District of Ohio or in adjacent districts. I have reviewed the creditors' list attached to the Chapter 11 petition and I conclude that there was a valid basis for Judge Galgay's finding. Of the nineteen creditors listed, eight are located in Ohio or Michigan. An additional six are in states other than New York and five are listed with New York addresses. I have eliminated Hundred East Credit from this calculation, the secured creditor joining in the motion to transfer. It is true, of course, that Judge Galgay did not consider the motion of the intervening creditors which is now before me. I first note that according to the Rules, it was not error for Judge Galgay to proceed with the argument on the motion without notice to creditors. Rule 116(b) states that notice shall be given to those whom the court directs, and I have found no explicit authority, nor have the intervenors cited any, which mandates notice to creditors on a motion to transfer venue. Since Rule 116 authorizes transfer before the first meeting of creditors, it permits transfer before the creditors are heard. Furthermore, as one court stated in denying a motion to transfer despite the overwhelming support of creditors in favor of transfer, "[i]f creditors' committees would be permitted to select the venue in an arrangement proceeding, it would completely thwart the venue provision of the Rules." *Matter of Distributors Warehouse, Inc.*, 1 B.R. 539, 542 (M.D. Fla.1979) (Bankruptcy Court). The governing standard is the proximity of the creditors to the court, not the creditors' choice of forum. Four of the six intervening creditors are in Ohio, and the remaining two in Michigan, they are indeed in greater proximity to Ohio than to New York.

The next factor is the proximity of the Bankrupt to the court. This consideration of course anticipates that it would be more convenient for the debtor, and would provide for ease of administration of the estate if the officers and directors were located in close proximity to the court. Judge Galgay found that Hadar is incorporated in Ohio, and further that it is not licensed to do business in New York. He further relied on Hadar's own admission that it intended to litigate in Ohio, which could fairly lead to the inference that its officers expected to appear before the Ohio court. Even without accepting the assertions of the movants at argument that Hadar's operation in New York is comprised of a staff of three persons occupying space rented to an Overmyer entity, there was sufficient support for finding that Hadar could be available without hardship in Ohio.

Finally, the factor which overwhelmingly militates in favor of transfer was Judge Galgay's finding, again by Hadar's own admission, that substantially all of its assets are in Ohio. The relationships between Hadar, Telecasting and Hundred East arise from the equipment which is in Ohio and under the jurisdiction of the Ohio court. The most economic administration of the estate will occur where one court can consider the intertwining relationships and the rights of Hadar to payment under those leases, which will in turn affect all its creditors. In its petition, Hadar asserted that its expectations of a successful arrangement depended on the resumption of lease payments to it by Telecasting. Since those payments terminated by order of the Ohio court, it seems clear and logical that the Ohio court should administer this estate.

I have considered carefully Hadar's arguments that it was not afforded an opportunity to present witnesses before Judge Galgay, and that he did not consider the affidavits of several creditors. In light of my findings that Judge Galgay had sufficient evidence on the record on which to base his ruling, it would be a waste of judicial resources to remand for the purposes of a hearing. The Second Circuit stated in *Corke v. Sameiet M.S. Song of Norway,* 572 F.2d 77, 81 (1978), "[b]ecause transfer is so clearly warranted by the facts at hand, it is unnecessary to waste the district court's valuable time by requiring a hearing on transferability." Although there is no statutory mandate under § 1404 or § 1406, at issue in *Corke,* as there is under Rule 116, the same considerations of judicial economy are applicable. Even had witnesses testified as to Hadar's activities in New York, they could not controvert Hadar's own statements as to the primary nature of its business activity, the leasing of equipment to Telecast, the location of nearly all its assets in Ohio and its expectations that successful reorganization would require a determination concerning the validity of the leases.

I have addressed the intervening creditors' argument that the ruling was in error because made without notice to creditors or before a creditors' meeting. The only remaining issue is whether the moving parties, Telecasting and Hundred East, had standing to move for a change of venue. The intervening creditors contend that since the interests of Telecasting, one of the moving parties, are adverse to the interests of the estate, it is an improper party to seek the venue transfer. In support of the argument, the creditors assert that Telecasting would not be entitled to vote at a creditors' meeting pursuant to Rule 207(d) and should thus be similarly precluded from moving to transfer venue. Although the creditors claim "they have been unable to find even one case in which a motion to transfer in such circumstances was granted," they have unfortunately failed to cite even one case in which a motion to transfer under such circumstances was denied. It is doubtful, as appellees argue, whether Rule 207(d) eliminates Telecasting from participating in all proceedings; however, that is not the issue before me. The court considering a venue transfer motion is not concerned with the identity of the moving party but rather with the standards which have to be met before granting such a motion. Judge Galgay addressed those issues and I affirm his ruling. Even if Telecasting were an improper moving party, there is no reason why Hundred East, a creditor could not bring on this motion. It is not motives which a court should consider but rather the objective standards applied by Judge Galgay.

Judge Galgay's order is affirmed.

So Ordered.

NOTE

Because this case was decided prior to the 1984 amendments, the statutory citations are not accurate. The substance of the references, however, continues to apply. The basic section permitting a change of venue of either a case or a proceeding is 28 U.S.C. § 1412 (rather than § 1475). 28 U.S.C. § 158 now contains the provisions dealing with appeals in bankruptcy matters. The reference to § 1334 in the decision was to its earlier version when it controlled bankruptcy appeals. In its present form, it is the basic jurisdiction section. The rule concerning venue is Rule 1014, which replaced former Rule 116.

Proper venue for a petition commencing a case under the Code is set forth in 28 U.S.C. § 1408. If, however, a petition is not filed in the proper venue, what is the remedy available to a complainant? What occurs if no one objects? May the U.S. trustee object? *See* § 307. May the court take any action *sua sponte? See* § 105(a).

Proper venue for a proceeding in a case is governed by 28 U.S.C. § 1409 and transfer of venue of a proceeding is governed by § 1412 and F.R.B.P. 7087.

IN RE CHARLES C. GREINER

Bankruptcy Court, District of North Dakota
12 C.B.C.2d 363 (1985)

HILL, Bankruptcy Judge:

The Trustee in the above captioned case, on September 18, 1984, commenced an adversary action seeking recovery from the Defendant of an alleged preferential payment in the sum of $238.96. On January 3, 1985, the Trustee moved for entry of a default judgment against the Defendant for the reason that no answer or other appearance had been made within the time specified by statute.

The Defendant, Seattle First National Bank, is a resident of Seattle, Washington, and was served at that location. The instant case was commenced and is venued in North Dakota. The provisions of the 1984 Bankruptcy Code Amendments with regards to venue are generally the same as the provisions of the former 1978 Act. The Code provides that proceedings arising under Title 11 or arising in or related to a case under Title 11 be commenced in the district court in which such case is pending. 28 U.S.C. § 1409. Section 1409, which became effective on July 10, 1984, replaces former 28 U.S.C. § 1473. Section 1409 contains a mandatory exception in the case of recovery of small claims by a trustee. Subsection (b) of the statute states that suits to recover property or a money judgment worth less than $1,000 or less than $5,000 if a consumer debt, may be commenced *only* in the district court for the district in which the defendant resides. Thus, in the case of a suit to recover a preferential payment received by a creditor, the only venue available is the district court for the district in which the creditor resides, even if that district is remote from the debtor's state of residency.

Under the 1978 Act, improper venue did not impair the jurisdiction of the bankruptcy court where a party had not interposed a timely or sufficient objection to venue. Under former section 1477(b), venue was deemed waived by the failure to object. Thus, in cases of improper venue where no objection had been raised, the bankruptcy court could retain the case for disposition. But, unfortunately, section 1477 is no longer in effect pursuant to section 113 of P.L. 98–353, and no statute has replaced that provision. Under the 1984 Amendments, when venue is in the wrong district, a court may no longer retain the case. The only options available to the court is to either dismiss the case or transfer it to another district as provided in 28 U.S.C. § 1412. Section 1412 provides that only the district court may transfer an improperly venued case. The only avenue available to the bankruptcy court in such instance is to dismiss the case. Accordingly, and for the reasons herein stated, the Trustee's Motion for Default Judgment is *Denied* and the case is *Dismissed* without prejudice.

[B] Jurisdiction Over Proceedings; Bankruptcy Act

Under the former law, the bankruptcy court could resolve a dispute between the estate's representative, usually the trustee in bankruptcy, and a third party only if the court had "summary" jurisdiction over the matter. If the court did not have summary jurisdiction, the trustee was relegated to a plenary action, that is, the trustee would have to bring suit in the forum in which the bankrupt could have sued had there been no bankruptcy case. That forum would normally be the state court, but if an independent basis of jurisdiction existed such as diversity of citizenship and amount in controversy, the federal district court could have been used. Therefore, the preeminent issue raised in many cases was whether the bankruptcy court had summary jurisdiction. Summary jurisdiction would attach when:

1. the property in issue was in the actual or constructive possession of the bankruptcy court (*in custodia legis*); or

2. the adverse claimant (defendant usually) consented to the exercise of summary jurisdiction by the court, either expressly or impliedly with implied consent arising through

    i. failure to object timely to jurisdiction, or

    ii. creating a counterclaim situation by filing a proof of claim as a creditor in the case.

For full discussion of summary–plenary jurisdiction, *see* 2 Collier, Bankruptcy ¶ 23.02 *et seq.* (14th rev. ed. 1974); 1 Collier, Bankruptcy c. 3 (15th ed.); Seligson & King, *Jurisdiction and Venue in Bankruptcy,* 36 J. Nat'l. Ass'n. Ref. in Bankr. 36 (April 1962), 73 (July 1962).

Too often suit would be brought in the bankruptcy court and instead of litigating the merits of the action, much time and money would be spent in contesting the jurisdiction of the court. Only after that was resolved, often through layers of appeals, would the merits of the action come to the fore. To cure this inefficiency, the 1978 Bankruptcy Reform Act eliminated the dichotomy between summary and plenary jurisdiction and invested the court with pervasive jurisdiction. *See* 28 U.S.C. § 1471 as contained in the Reform Act. *See* § 1334(b), which replaced § 1471(b), *infra.*

QUESTIONS

1. Suppose an action by the debtor was commenced in state court before the chapter 7 case was filed. What happens? *See* Bankruptcy Rule 6009.

2. What does pervasive jurisdiction mean? May the bankruptcy court hear a treble damage antitrust action? Action for personal injuries resulting from an automobile accident? Grant a divorce?

3. If the court desires not to resolve a particular dispute, what may it do? *See* 28 U.S.C. § 1334(c).

4. What role, if any, does the issue of right to trial by jury play? *See* 28 U.S.C. §§ 1411, 157(e).

---

[1] Bankruptcy Amendments and Federal Judgeship Act of 1984

Pursuant to 28 U.S.C. 1334(b), the district court is given original but not exclusive jurisdiction of all civil proceedings arising under title 11 or arising in or related to cases under title 11. But subsection (c) permits the district court in the "interest of justice, or in the interest of comity with State courts or respect for State law" to abstain from a particular proceeding. Moreover, subsection (c) requires abstention, called mandatory abstention, on timely motion if the proceeding is based on a State law claim or cause of action and is related to a case under title 11 but does not arise under title 11 or in a case under title 11.

Is a proof of claim filed by a creditor for breach of contract, *e.g.,* nonpayment for delivered goods, a claim that arises in a title 11 case or is it "merely" related to a case? What about a claim based on injuries sustained in an automobile accident?

A claim against a former employer based on injuries sustained from long–term exposure to cancer–causing material?

28 U.S.C. § 157(a) provides that district courts *may* permit cases and proceedings to be referred to the bankruptcy judges for the district. They, in turn, can hear and determine cases and "core" proceedings to final judgment. Core proceedings are defined in § 157(b)(2).

Are all non–core proceedings subject to mandatory abstention? Section 157(b)(4) provides that they are not. But non–core proceedings certainly include related proceedings. Presumably, therefore, some related proceedings are subject to mandatory abstention and some are not.

28 U.S.C. § 157(b)(5) requires the *district court* to order that personal injury tort and wrongful death claims be tried in the district court where the bankruptcy case is pending or in the *district court* in the district in which the claim arose. May the district court use its referral powers of 28 U.S.C. § 157(a) for personal injury tort and wrongful death claims?

A bankruptcy court may hear a non–core proceeding but not render final judgment. It is to submit findings of fact and conclusions of law and a final order is to be rendered by the district court after a *de novo* review (not necessarily a hearing) of matters to which a party has objected. *See* Rule 9033. But, by consent of the parties, the bankruptcy judge may enter a final order. 28 U.S.C. § 157(c). How is consent to the exercise of such jurisdiction manifested? *See* Rules 7008, 7012.

Pursuant to 28 U.S.C. § 158, the general outline for taking an appeal is as follows: from final orders of the bankruptcy courts to the district courts and then to the courts of appeals. There is one possible exception to this route. When the judicial council of the circuit creates an appellate panel consisting of bankruptcy judges, the appeal would not necessarily go to the district court. It could go to the panel and then to the court of appeals. However, the parties must consent to use of the panel, and the district court by majority vote must authorize such referral of appeals. 28 U.S.C. § 158.

Appeals from interlocutory orders are appealable only to the district court (or appellate panel, where appropriate), and then only by leave of the appellate court. 28 U.S.C. § 158(a). What is an interlocutory order in a case under title 11?

The court of appeals has jurisdiction of appeals from final orders of the district court or appellate panel. 28 U.S.C. § 158(d). As mentioned, the district court or appellate panel has appellate jurisdiction over final orders of the bankruptcy court. 28 U.S.C. § 158(a), (b). But the district court does not hear an appeal in a related non–core matter; the district court enters the final order, not the bankruptcy court. Is the court of appeals without jurisdiction to hear an appeal from this type of order? *See* 28 U.S.C. §§ 1291, 1292; *Connecticut National Bk. v. Germain*, 112 S.Ct. 1146, 26 C.B.C.2d 175 (1992).

What procedure is to be followed when taking an appeal to the district court or appellate panel? *See* 28 U.S.C. § 158(c). What is the standard of review to be used?

§ 12.02   Jurisdiction Over Proceedings; Bankruptcy Code

NORTHERN PIPELINE CONSTRUCTION CO. v . MARATHON PIPELINE CO.

United States Supreme Court
458 U.S. 50, 102 S. Ct. 2858, 73 L. Ed 2d 598 (1982)

Justice BRENNAN, announced the judgment of the Court and delivered an opinion in which Justice MARSHALL, Justice BLACKMUN, and Justice STEVENS joined.

The question presented is whether the assignment by Congress to bankruptcy judges of the jurisdiction granted in § 241(a) of the Bankruptcy Act of 1978, 28 U.S.C. § 1471 (1976 ed., Supp. III), violates Art. III of the Constitution.

I.

A.

In 1978, after almost ten years of study and investigation, Congress enacted a comprehensive revision of the bankruptcy laws. The Bankruptcy Act of 1978 (Act)[1] made significant changes in both the substantive and procedural law of bankruptcy. It is the changes in the latter that are at issue in this case.

Before the Act, federal district courts served as bankruptcy courts and employed a "referee" system. Bankruptcy proceedings were generally conducted before referees,[2] except in those instances in which the district court elected to withdraw a case from a referee. *See* Bkrptcy. Rule 102. The referee's final order was appealable to the district court. Bkrptcy. Rule 801. The bankruptcy courts were vested with "summary jurisdiction" — that is, with jurisdiction over controversies involving property in the actual or constructive possession of the court. And, with consent, the bankruptcy court also had jurisdiction over some "plenary" matters—such as disputes involving property in the possession of a third person.

The Act eliminates the referee system and establishes "in each judicial district, as an adjunct to the district court for such district, a bankruptcy court which shall be a court of record known as the United States Bankruptcy Court for the district." 28 U.S.C. § 151(a) (1976 ed., Supp. III). The judges of these courts are appointed to office for 14–year terms by the President, with the advice and consent of the Senate. §§ 152, 153(a). They are subject to removal by the "judicial council of the circuit" on account of "incompetence, misconduct, neglect of duty or physical or mental disability." § 153(b). In addition, the salaries of the bankruptcy judges are set by statute and are subject to adjustment under the Federal Salary Act, 2 U.S.C. §§ 351–361. 28 U.S.C. § 154 (1976 ed., Supp. III).

The jurisdiction of the bankruptcy courts created by the Act is much broader than that exercised under the former referee system. Eliminating the distinction between

---

[1] Pub. L. 95–598, 92 Stat. 2549. The Act became effective October 1, 1979.

[2] Bankruptcy referees were redesignated as "judges" in 1973. Bkrptcy. Rule 901(7). For purposes of clarity, however, we refer to all judges under the old Act as "referees."

"summary" and "plenary" jurisdiction, the Act grants the new courts jurisdiction over all "civil proceedings arising under title 11 [the Bankruptcy title] or arising in or *related to* cases under title 11." 28 U.S.C. § 1471(b) (1976 ed., Supp. III) (emphasis added).[3]

This jurisdictional grant empowers bankruptcy courts to entertain a wide variety of cases involving claims that may affect the property of the estate once a petition has been filed under title 11 of the Act. Included within the bankruptcy courts' jurisdiction are suits to recover accounts, controversies involving exempt property, actions to avoid transfers and payments as preferences or fraudulent conveyances, and causes of action owned by the debtor at the time of the petition for bankruptcy. The bankruptcy courts can hear claims based on state law as well as those based on federal law. *See* 1 Collier on Bankruptcy, ¶ 3.01, at 3–47 to 3–48 (15th ed. 1981).[4]

The judges of the bankruptcy courts are vested with all of the "powers of a court of equity, law and admiralty," except that they "may not enjoin another court or punish a criminal contempt not committed in the presence of the judge of the court or warranting a punishment of imprisonment." 28 U.S.C. § 1481 (1976 ed., Supp. III). In addition to this broad grant of power, Congress has allowed bankruptcy judges the power to hold jury trials, § 1480; to issue declaratory judgments, § 2201; to issue writs of habeas corpus under certain circumstances, § 2256; to issue all writs necessary in aid of the bankruptcy court's expanded jurisdiction, § 451; *See* 28 U.S.C. § 1651 (1976 ed.); and to issue any order, process or judgment that is necessary or appropriate to carry out the provisions of title 11, 11 U.S.C. § 105(a) (1976 ed., Supp. III).

The Act also establishes a special procedure for appeals from orders of bankruptcy courts. The circuit council is empowered to direct the Chief Judge of the circuit to designate panels of three bankruptcy judges to hear appeals. 28 U.S.C. § 160 (1976 ed., Supp. III). These panels have jurisdiction of all appeals from final judgments,

---

[3] Although the Act initially vests this jurisdiction in district courts, 28 U.S.C. § 1471(a) (1976 ed., Supp. III), it subsequently provides that "[t]he bankruptcy court for the district in which a case under title 11 is commenced shall exercise *all* of the jurisdiction conferred by this section on the district courts," § 1471(c) (emphasis added). Thus the ultimate repository of the Act's broad jurisdictional grant is the bankruptcy courts. *See* 1 Collier on Bankruptcy ¶ 3.01, at 3–37, 3–44 to 3–49 (15th ed. 1981).

[4] With respect to both personal jurisdiction and venue, the scope of the Act is also expansive. Although the Act does not in terms indicate the extent to which bankruptcy judges may exercise personal jurisdiction, it has been construed to allow the constitutional maximum. *See, e.g., In re Whippany Paper Board Co.,* 15 B.R. 312, 314–315 (Bkrptcy. Ct. D NJ 1981). With two exceptions not relevant here, the venue of "a proceeding arising in or related to a case under title 11 [is] in the bankruptcy court in which such case is pending." 28 U.S.C. § 1473(a) (1976 ed., Supp. III). Furthermore, the Act permits parties to remove many kinds of action to the bankruptcy court. Parties "may remove any claim or cause of action in a civil action, other than a proceeding before the United States Tax Court or a civil action by a Government unit to enforce such governmental unit's police or regulatory power" . § 1478. The bankruptcy court may, however, remand such actions "on any equitable ground" ; the decision to remand or retain an action is unreviewable. § 1478(b).

orders, and decrees of bankruptcy courts, and, with leave of the panel, of interlocutory appeals. § 1482. If no such appeals panel is designated, the district court is empowered to exercise appellate jurisdiction. § 1334. The court of appeals is given jurisdiction over appeals from the appellate panels or from the district court. § 1293. If the parties agree, a direct appeal to the court of appeals may be taken from a final judgment of a bankruptcy court. § 1293(b).[5]

The Act provides for a transition period before the new provisions take full effect in April 1984. Bankruptcy Act of 1978, §§ 401–411, 92 Stat. 2682–2688. During the transition period, previously existing bankruptcy courts continue in existence. § 404(a), 92 Stat. 2683. Incumbent bankruptcy referees, who served six–year terms for compensation subject to adjustment by Congress, are to serve as bankruptcy judges until March 31, 1984, or until their successors take office. § 404(b), 92 Stat. 2683.[6]

During this period they are empowered to exercise essentially all of the jurisdiction and powers discussed above. See §§ 404, 405, 92 Stat. 2683–2685. See generally 1 Collier on Bankruptcy §§ 7.04–7.05, 7–23 to 7–65 (15th ed. 1981). The procedure for taking appeals is similar to that provided after the transition period. See § 405(c)(1), 92 Stat. 2685.[7]

B.

This case arises out of proceedings initiated in the United States Bankruptcy Court for the District of Minnesota after appellant Northern Pipeline Construction Co. (Northern) filed a petition for reorganization in January 1980. In March 1980 Northern, pursuant to the Act, filed in that court a suit against appellee Marathon Pipeline Co. (Marathon). Appellant sought damages for alleged breaches of contract and warranty, as well as for alleged misrepresentation, coercion, and duress. Marathon sought dismissal of the suit, on the ground that the Act unconstitutionally conferred Art. III judicial power upon judges who lacked life tenure and protection against salary diminution. The United States intervened to defend the validity of the statute.

The bankruptcy judge denied the motion to dismiss. App. to Juris. Statement 27a–36a. But on appeal the District Court entered an order granting the motion, on the ground that "the delegation of authority in 28 U.S.C. § 1471 to the Bankruptcy Judges to try cases otherwise relegated under the Constitution to Article III judges"

---

[5] Although no particular standard of review is specified in the Act, the parties in the present case seem to agree that the appropriate one is the clearly erroneous standard, employed in the old Bankruptcy Rule 801 for review of findings of fact made by a referee. See Brief for the United States 41; Tr. of Oral Arg. 27. See also In re Rivers,—B. R.—(Bkrptcy. Ct. ED Tenn. 1982); 1 Collier on Bankruptcy ¶ 3.03, at 3–315 (15th ed. 1981).

[6] Under the old Bankruptcy Act, referees could be removed by the district court for "incompetency, misconduct, or neglect of duty," 11 U.S.C. § 62(b) (1976 ed.); the same grounds for removal apply during the transition period, see § 404(d), 92 Stat. 2684.

[7] It appears, however, that during the transition period an appeal of a bankruptcy judge's decision may be taken to the district court even if an appellate panel of bankruptcy judges has been established.

was unconstitutional. *Id.,* at 1a. Both the United States and Northern filed notices of appeal in this Court.[8]

We noted probable jurisdiction. — U.S. — (1981).[9]

II.

A.

Basic to the constitutional structure established by the Framers was their recognition that "The accumulation of all powers, legislative, executive, and judiciary, in the same hands, whether of one, a few, or many, and whether hereditary, self–appointed, or elective, may justly be pronounced the very definition of tyranny." The Federalist No. 47 (J. Madison), p. 300 (H. Lodge ed. 1888). To ensure against such tyranny, the Framers provided that the Federal Government would consist of three distinct Branches, each to exercise one of the governmental powers recognized by the Framers as inherently distinct. "The Framers regarded the checks and balances that they had built into the tripartite Federal Government as a self–executing safeguard against the encroachment or aggrandizement of one branch at the expense of the other." *Buckley v. Valeo,* 424 U.S. 1, 122 (1976) (*per curiam*).

The Federal Judiciary was therefore designed by the Framers to stand independent of the Executive and Legislature—to maintain the checks and balances of the constitutional structure, and also to guarantee that the process of adjudication itself remained impartial. Hamilton explained the importance of an independent Judiciary:

> Periodical appointments, however regulated, or by whomsoever made, would, in some way or other, be fatal to [the courts'] necessary independence. If the power of making them was committed either to the Executive or legislature, there would be danger of an improper complaisance to the branch which possessed it; if to both, there would be an unwillingness to hazard the displeasure of either; if to the people, or to persons chosen by them for the special purpose, there would be too great a disposition to consult popularity, to justify a reliance that nothing would be consulted but the Constitution and the laws.

The Federalist no. 78, p. 489 (H. Lodge ed. 1888). The Court has only recently reaffirmed the significance of this feature of the Framers' design: "A Judiciary free from control by the Executive and Legislature is essential if there is a right to have claims decided by judges who are free from potential domination by other branches of government." *United States v. Will,* 449 U.S. 200, 217–218 (1980).

As an inseparable element of the constitutional system of checks and balances, and as a guarantee of judicial impartiality, Art. III both defines the power and protects the independence of the Judicial Branch. It provides that "The judicial Power of the United States, shall be vested in one supreme Court, and in such inferior Courts as the Congress may from time to time ordain and establish." Art. III, § 1.

---

[8] After Northern docketed an appeal in this Court, the District Court supplemented its order with a memorandum. App. to Juris. Statement 3a–26a.

[9] Two other bankruptcy courts have considered the constitutionality of § 1471: The Bankruptcy Court for the District of Puerto Rico determined it to be constitutional, *In re Segarra,* 14 B.R. 870 (1981), while the Bankruptcy Court for the Eastern District of Tennessee reached the opposite conclusion, *In re Rivers, supra.*

The inexorable command of this provision is clear and definite: The judicial power of the United States must be exercised by courts having the attributes prescribed in Art. III. Those attributes are also clearly set forth:

> The Judges, both of the supreme and inferior Courts, shall hold their Offices during good Behaviour, and shall, at stated Times, receive for their Services, a Compensation, which shall not be diminished during their Continuance in Office. Art. III, § 1.

The "good Behaviour" Clause guarantees that Art. III judges shall enjoy life tenure, subject only to removal by impeachment. *Toth v. Quarles,* 350 U.S. 11, 16 (1955). The Compensation Clause guarantees Art. III judges a fixed and irreducible compensation for their services. *United States v. Will, supra,* at 218–221. Both of these provisions were incorporated into the Constitution to ensure the independence of the judiciary from the control of the executive and legislative branches of government.[10]

As we have only recently emphasized, "The Compensation Clause has its roots in the longstanding Anglo–American tradition of an independent Judiciary," *id.,* at 217, while the principle of life tenure can be traced back at least as far as the Act of Settlement in 1701, *Id., at 218.* To be sure, both principles were eroded during the late colonial period, but that departure did not escape notice and indignant rejection by the Revolutionary generation. Indeed, the guarantees eventually included in Art. III were clearly foreshadowed in the Declaration of Independence, "which, among the injuries and usurpations recited against the King of Great Britain, declared that he had 'made judges dependent on his will alone, for the tenure of their offices, and the amount and payment of their salaries." *O'Donoghue v. United States,* 289 U.S. 516, 531 (1933). The Framers thus recognized that

> Next to permanency in office, nothing can contribute more to the independence of the judges than a fixed provision for their support. In the general course of human nature, *a power over a man's subsistence amounts to a power over his will.*

The Federalist No. 79 (A. Hamilton), p. 491 (H. Lodge ed. 1888) (emphasis in original).[11]

---

[10] These provisions serve other institutional values as well. The independence from political forces that they guarantee helps to promote public confidence in judicial determinations. *See* The Federalist No. 78 (A. Hamilton). The security that they provide to members of the Judicial Branch helps to attract well qualified persons to the federal bench. *Ibid..* The guarantee of life tenure insulates the individual judge from improper influences not only by other branches but by colleagues as well, and thus promotes judicial individualism. *See* Kaufman, *Chilling Judicial Independence,* 88 Yale L. J. 681, 713 (1979). *See generally* Note, *Article III Limits on Article I Courts: The Constitutionality of the Bankruptcy Court and the 1979 Magistrate Act,* 80 Colum. L. Rev. 560, 583–585 (1980).

[11] Further evidence of the Framers' concern for assuring the independence of the judicial branch may be found in the fact that the Constitutional Convention soundly defeated a proposal to allow the removal of judges by the executive and legislative branches. *See* 2 Farrand, Records of the Federal Convention 428–429 (1911); P. Bator, P. Mishkin, D. Shapiro, & H. Wechsler, Hart and Wechsler's The Federal Courts and the Federal System

In sum, our Constitution unambiguously enunciates a fundamental principle—that the "judicial Power of the United States" must be reposed in an independent Judiciary. It commands that the independence of the Judiciary be jealously guarded, and it provides clear institutional protections for that independence.

B.

It is undisputed that the bankruptcy judges whose offices were created by the Bankruptcy Act of 1978 do not enjoy the protections constitutionally afforded to Art. III judges. The bankruptcy judges do not serve for life subject to their continued "good Behaviour." Rather, they are appointed for 14-year terms, and can be removed by the judicial council of the circuit in which they serve on grounds of "incompetence, misconduct, neglect of duty or physical or mental disability." Second, the salaries of the bankruptcy judges are not immune from diminution by Congress. *See supra,* at 2. In short, there is no doubt that the bankruptcy judges created by the Act are not Art. III judges.

That Congress chose to vest such broad jurisdiction in non–Art. III bankruptcy courts, after giving substantial consideration to the constitutionality of the Act, is of course reason to respect the congressional conclusion. *See Fullilove v. Klutznick,* 448 U.S., 448 472–473 (1980) (opinion of Burger, C. J.); *Palmore v. United States,* 411 U.S. 389, 409 (1973). *See also National Ins. Co. v. Tidewater Co.,* 337 U.S. 582, 655 (1949) (Frankfurter, J., dissenting).[12]

---

7 (2d ed. 1973). Mr. Wilson, of Pennsylvania, commented that "The Judges would be in a bad situation if made to depend on every gust of faction which might prevail in the two branches of our Govt." 2 Farrand, *supra,* at 429.

[12] It should be noted, however, that the House of Representatives expressed substantial doubts respecting the constitutionality of the provisions eventually included in the Act. The House Judiciary Committee and its Subcommittee on Civil and Constitutional Rights gave lengthy consideration to the constitutional issues surrounding the conferral of broad powers upon the new bankruptcy courts. The committee, the subcommittee, and the House as a whole initially concluded that Art. III courts were constitutionally required for bankruptcy adjudications. *See* H. R. 8200, 95th Cong., 1st Sess. (1977); hearings on H. R. 31 and H. R. 32 before the Subcommittee on Civil and Constitutional Rights of the House Committee on the Judiciary, 94th Cong., 2d Sess., 2081–2084 (1976); *id.,* at 2682, 2706; H.R. Rep. No. 95, 595, p. 39 (1977) ("Article III is the constitutional norm, and the limited circumstances in which the courts have permitted departure from the requirements of Article III are not present in the bankruptcy context"); *id.,* at 21–38; Subcomm. on Civil and Constitutional Rights of the House Committee on the Judiciary, Constitutional Bankruptcy Courts, 95th Cong., 2d Sess., 33 (Comm. Print No. 3 1977) (concluding that the proposed bankruptcy courts should be established "under Article III, with all of the protection that the Framers intended for an independent judiciary"); Subcomm. on Civil and Constitutional Rights of the House Comm. on the Judiciary, Report on Hearings on the Court Administration Structure for Bankruptcy Cases, 95th Cong., 2d Sess., 5 (Comm. Print No. 13 1978) (same); *see generally* Klee, *Legislative History of the New Bankruptcy Law,* 28 De Paul L. Rev. 941, 945–949, 951 (1979). The Senate bankruptcy bill did not provide for life tenure or a guaranteed salary, instead adopting the concept of a bankruptcy court with similarly broad powers but as an "adjunct" to an Art. III court. S. 2266, 95th Cong., 2d Sess. (1978). The bill that was finally enacted, denying bankruptcy judges the tenure and compensation protections of Art. III, was the result of a series of last minute conferences and compromises between the managers of both houses. *See* Klee, *supra,* at 952–956.

But at the same time,

> Deciding whether a matter has in any measure been committed by the Constitution to another branch of government, or whether the action of that branch exceeds whatever authority has been committed, is itself a delicate exercise in constitutional interpretation, and is a responsibility of this Court as ultimate interpreter of the Constitution.

Baker v. Carr, 369 U.S. 186, 211 (1962). With these principles in mind, we turn to the question presented for decision: whether the Bankruptcy Act of 1978 violates the command of Art. III, that the judicial power of the United States must be vested in courts whose judges enjoy the protections and safeguards specified in that Article.

Appellants suggest two grounds for upholding the Act's conferral of broad adjudicative powers upon judges unprotected by Art. III. First, it is urged that "pursuant to its enumerated Article I powers, Congress may establish legislative courts that have jurisdiction to decide cases to which the Article III judicial power of the United States extends." Brief for the United States 9. Referring to our precedents upholding the validity of "legislative courts," appellants suggest that "the plenary grants of power in Article I permit Congress to establish non–Article III tribunals in 'specialized areas having particularized needs and warranting distinctive treatment," such as the area of bankruptcy law. *Ibid.,* quoting *Palmore v. United States,* 411 U.S. 389, 408 (1973). Second, appellants contend that even if the Constitution does require that this bankruptcy–related action be adjudicated in an Art. III court, the Act in fact satisfies that requirement. "Bankruptcy jurisdiction was vested in the district court" of the judicial district in which the bankruptcy court is located, "and the exercise of that jurisdiction by the adjunct bankruptcy court was made subject to appeal as of right to an Art. III court." *Id.,* at 12. Analogizing the role of the bankruptcy court to that of a special master, appellants urge us to conclude that this "adjunct" system established by Congress satisfies the requirements of Art. III. We consider these arguments in turn.

III.

Congress did not constitute the bankruptcy courts as legislative courts.[13]

Appellants contend, however, that the bankruptcy courts could have been so constituted, and that as a result the "adjunct" system in fact chosen by Congress does not impermissibly encroach upon the judicial power. In advancing this argument, appellants rely upon cases in which we have identified certain matters that "congress may or may not bring within the cognizance of [Art. III] courts, as it may deem proper." *Murray's Lessee v. Hoboken Land and Improvement Co.,* 18 How. 272, 284 (1855).[14]

---

[13] The Act designates the bankruptcy court in each district as an "adjunct" to the district court. 28 U.S.C. § 151(a) (1976 ed., Supp. III). Neither House of Congress concluded that the bankruptcy courts should be established as independent legislative courts. *See* n. 12, *supra.*

[14] At one time, this Court suggested a rigid distinction between those subjects that could be considered only in Art. III courts and those that could be considered only in legislative courts. *See Williams v. United States,* 289 U.S. 553 (1933). But this suggested dichotomy

But when properly understood, these precedents represent no broad departure from the constitutional command that the judicial power of the United States must be vested in Art. III courts.[15]

Rather, they reduce to three narrow situations not subject to that command, each recognizing a circumstance in which the grant of power to the Legislative and Executive Branches was historically and constitutionally so exceptional that the congressional assertion of a power to create legislative courts was consistent with, rather than threatening to, the constitutional mandate of separation of powers. These precedents simply acknowledge that the literal command of Art. III, assigning the judicial power of the United States to courts insulated from Legislative or Executive interference, must be interpreted in light of the historical context in which the Constitution was written, and of the structural imperatives of the Constitution as a whole.

Appellants first rely upon a series of cases in which this Court has upheld the creation by Congress of non–Art. III "territorial courts." This exception from the general prescription of Art. III dates from the earliest days of the Republic, when it was perceived that the Framers intended that as to certain geographical areas, in which no State operated as sovereign, Congress was to exercise the general powers of government. For example, in *American Ins. Co. v. Canter,* 1 Pet. 511 (1828), the Court observed that Art. IV bestowed upon Congress alone a complete power of government over territories not within the States that comprised the United States. The Court then acknowledged Congress' authority to create courts for those territories that were not in conformity with Art. III. Such courts were

> created in virtue of the general right of sovereignty which exists in the govern-
> ment, or in virtue of that clause which enables Congress to make all needful
> rules and regulations, respecting the territory belonging to the United States.
> The jurisdiction with which they are invested is conferred by Congress, in the
> execution of those general powers which that body possesses over the territories
> of the United States. Although admiralty jurisdiction can be exercised in the

---

has not withstood analysis. *See* Wright, Law of the Federal Courts 33–35 (3d ed. 1976). Our more recent cases clearly recognize that legislative courts may be granted jurisdiction over some cases and controversies to which the Art. III judicial power might also be extended. *E.g., Palmore v. United States,* 411 U.S. 389 (1973). *See Glidden v. Zdanok,* 370 U.S. 530, 549–551 (1962) (Opinion of Harlan, J.).

[15] Justice White's dissent finds particular significance in the fact that Congress could have assigned all bankruptcy matters to the state courts. *Post,* at 25. But, of course, virtually all matters that might be heard in Art. III courts could also be left by Congress to state courts. This fact is simply irrelevant to the question before us. Congress has no control over state court judges; accordingly the principle of separation of powers is not threatened by leaving the adjudication of federal disputes to such judges. *See* Krattenmaker, *Article III and Judicial Independence: Why the New Bankruptcy Courts are Unconstitutional,* 70 Geo. L J. 297, 304–305 (1981). The Framers chose to leave to Congress the precise role to be played by the lower federal courts in the administration of justice. *See* Hart and Wechsler's The Federal Courts and the Federal System, *supra,* at 11. But the Framers did not leave it to Congress to define the character of those courts—they were to be independent of the political branches and presided over by judges with guaranteed salary and life tenure.

states in those Courts, only, which are established in pursuance of the 3d article of the Constitution; the same limitation does not extend to the territories. In legislating for them, Congress exercises the combined powers of the general, and of a state government.

1 Pet., at 546. The Court followed the same reasoning when it reviewed Congress— creation of non–Art. III courts in the District of Columbia. It noted that there was in the District

no division of powers between the general and state governments. Congress has the entire control over the district for every purpose of government; and it is reasonable to suppose, that in organizing a judicial department here, all judicial power necessary for the purposes of government would be vested in the courts of justice.

Kendall v. United States, 12 Pet. 524, 619 (1838).**16**

Appellants next advert to a second class of cases—those in which this Court has sustained the exercise by Congress and the Executive of the power to establish and administer courts martial. The situation in these cases strongly resembles the situation with respect to territorial courts: It too involves a constitutional grant of power that has been historically understood as giving the political branches of Government extraordinary control over the precise subject matter at issue. Art. I, § 8, cls. 13, 14, confer upon Congress the power "to provide and maintain a Navy," and "to make Rules for the Government and Regulation of the land and naval Forces." The Fifth Amendment, which requires a presentment or indictment of a grand jury before a person may be held to answer for a capital or otherwise infamous crime, contains an express exception for "cases arising in the land or naval forces." And Art. II, § 2, cl. 1, provides that "The President shall be Commander in Chief of the Army and Navy of the United States, and of the Militia of the several States, when called into the actual Service of the United States." Noting these constitutional directives, the Court in *Dynes v. Hoover,* 20 How. 65 (1858), explained:

These provisions show that Congress has the power to provide for the trial and punishment of military and naval offences in the manner then and now practiced by civilized nations; and that the power to do so is given without any connection between it and the 3d article of the Constitution defining the judicial power of the United States; indeed, that the two powers are entirely independent of each other.

---

16 We recently reaffirmed the principle, expressed in these early cases, that Art. I, § 8, cl. 17, provides that Congress shall have power "[t]o exercise exclusive legislation in all cases whatsoever, over" the District of Columbia. *Palmore v. United States,* 411 U.S. 389, 397 (1973). *See also Wallace v. Adams,* 204 U.S. 415, 423 (1907) (recognizing Congress' authority to establish legislative courts to determine questions of tribal membership relevant to property claims within Indian territory); *In re Ross,* 140 U.S. 453 (1891) (same, respecting consular courts established by concession from foreign countries). *See generally* 1 Moore, Federal Practice 46–49, 53–54 (2d. ed. 1982). *But see Reid v. Covert,* 354 U.S. 1 (1957).

Id., at 79.[17]

Finally, appellants rely on a third group of cases, in which this Court has upheld the constitutionality of legislative courts and administrative agencies created by Congress to adjudicate cases involving "public rights."[18]

The "public rights" doctrine was first set forth in *Murray's Lessee v. Hoboken Land & Improvement Co.,*18 How. 272 (1855):

> [W]e do not consider congress can either withdraw from judicial cognizance any matter which, from its nature, is the subject of a suit at the common law, or in equity, or admiralty; nor, on the other hand, can it bring under the judicial power a matter which, from its nature, is not a subject for judicial determination. At the same time there are matters, involving public rights, which may be presented in such form that the judicial power is capable of acting on them, and which are susceptible of judicial determination, but which congress may or may not bring within the cognizance of the courts of the United States, as it may deem proper.

Id., at 284.

This doctrine may be explained in part by reference to the traditional principle of sovereign immunity, which recognizes that the Government may attach conditions to its consent to be sued. *See id.* at 283–285; see also *Ex parte Bakelite Corp.,* 279 U.S. 438, 452 (1929). But the public–rights doctrine also draws upon the principle of separation of powers, and an historical understanding that certain prerogatives were reserved to the political branches of government. The doctrine extends only to matters arising "between the Government and persons subject to its authority in connection with the performance of the constitutional functions of the executive or legislative departments," *Crowell v. Benson,* 285 U.S. 22, 50 (1932), and only to matters that historically could have been determined exclusively by those departments, *see Ex parte Bakelite Corp., supra,* at 458. The understanding of these cases is that the Framers expected that Congress would be free to commit such matters completely to non–judicial executive determination, and that as a result there can be no constitutional objection to Congress' employing the less drastic expedient of committing their determination to a legislative court or an administrative agency. *Crowell v. Benson, supra,* at 50.[19]

The public–rights doctrine is grounded in a historically recognized distinction between matters that could be conclusively determined by the Executive and

---

[17] *See also Burns v. Wilson,* 346 U.S. 137, 139–140 (1953). But this Court has been alert to ensure that Congress does not exceed the constitutional bounds and bring within the jurisdiction of the military courts matters beyond that jurisdiction, and property within the realm of "judicial power." *See, e.g., Reid v. Covert, supra; Toth v. Quarles,* 350 U.S. 11 (1955).

[18] Congress' power to create legislative courts to adjudicate public rights carries with it the lesser power to create administrative agencies for the same purpose, and to provide for review of those agency decisions in Art. III courts. *See, e.g., Atlas Roofing Co. v. Occupational Safety Comm'n,* 430 U.S. 442, 450 (1977).

[19] *See Oceanic Nav. Co. v. Stranahan,* 214 U.S. 320, 339 (1909); Katz, *Federal Legislative Courts,* 43 Harv. L. Rev. 894, 915 (1930).

Legislative Branches and matters that are "inherently judicial." *Ex parte Bakelite Corp., supra,* at 458. *See Murray's Lessee v. Hoboken Land & Improvement Co., supra,* at 280–282. For example, the Court in Murray's Lessee looked to the law of England and the States at the time the Constitution was adopted, in order to determine whether the issue presented was customarily cognizable in the courts. *Ibid.* Concluding that the matter had not traditionally been one for judicial determination, the Court perceived no bar to Congress' establishment of summary procedures, outside of Art. III courts, to collect a debt due to the Government from one of its customs agents.[20]

On the same premise, the Court in *Ex parte Bakelite Corp., supra,* held that the Court of Customs Appeals had been properly constituted by Congress as a legislative court:

> The full province of the court under the act creating it is that of determining matters arising between the Government and others in the executive administration and application of the customs laws. The appeals include nothing which inherently or necessarily requires judicial determination, but only matters the determination of which may be, and at times has been, committed exclusively to executive officers.

279 U.S., at 458.[21]

The distinction between public rights and private rights has not been definitively explained in our precedents.[22] *Id.,* at 51 (footnote omitted).

Nor is it necessary to do so in the present case, for it suffices to observe that a matter of public rights must at a minimum arise "between the government and others." *Ex Parte Bakelite Corp., supra,* at 451.[23]

---

[20] Doubtless it could be argued that the need for independent judicial determination is greatest in cases arising between the government and an individual. But the rationale for the public–rights line of cases lies not in political theory, but rather in Congress' and this Court's understanding of what power was reserved to the Judiciary by the Constitution as a matter of historical fact.

[21] *See also Williams v. United States,* 289 U.S. 553 (1933) (holding that Court of Claims was a legislative court and that salary of a judge of that court could therefore be reduced by Congress).

[22] *Crowell v. Benson,* 285 U.S. 22 (1932), attempted to catalogue some of the matters that fall within the public–rights doctrine:

> Familiar illustrations of administrative agencies created for the determination of such matters are found in connection with the exercise of the congressional power as to interstate and foreign commerce, taxation, immigration, the public lands, public health, the facilities of the post office, pensions, and payments to veterans.

[23] Congress cannot "withdraw from [Art. III] judicial cognizance any matter which, from its nature, is the subject of a suit at common law, or in equity or admiralty." *Murray's Lessee v. Hoboken Land & Improvement Co.,* 18 How., at 284. It is thus clear that the presence of the United States as a proper party to the proceeding is a necessary but not sufficient means of distinguishing "private rights" from "public rights." And it is also clear that even with respect to matters that arguably fall within the scope of the public rights doctrine, the presumption is in favor of Art. III courts. *See Glidden v. Zdanok,* 370 U.S. 530, 548–549,

In contrast, "the liability of one individual to another under the law as defined," *Crowell v. Benson,* 285 U.S., at 51, is a matter of private rights. Our precedents clearly establish that only controversies in the former category may be removed from Art. III courts and delegated to legislative courts or administrative agencies for their determination. *See Atlas Roofing Co. v. Occupational Safety Comm'n,* 430 U.S., at 450, n. 7; *Crowell v. Benson, supra,* at 50–51. *See also Katz, Federal Legislative Courts.* 43 Harv. L. Rev. 894, 917–918 (1930).[24]

Private–rights disputes, on the other hand, lie at the core of the historically recognized judicial power.

In sum, this Court has identified three situations in which Art. III does not bar the creation of legislative courts. In each of these situations, the Court has recognized certain exceptional powers bestowed upon Congress by the Constitution or by historical consensus. Only in the face of such an exceptional grant of power has the Court declined to hold the authority of Congress subject to the general prescriptions of Art. III.[25]

Although the dissent recognizes that the Framers had something important in mind when they assigned the judicial power of the United States to Art. III courts, it concludes that our cases and subsequent practice have eroded this conception. Unable to find a satisfactory theme in our precedents for analyzing this case, the dissent rejects all of them, as well as the historical understanding upon which they were based, in favor of an ad hoc balancing approach in which Congress can essentially determine for itself whether Art. III courts are required. *See post,* at 14–25. But even the dissent recognizes that the notion that Congress rather than the Constitution should determine whether there is a need for independent federal courts cannot be what the Framers had in mind. See *post,* at 22.

We discern no such exceptional grant of power applicable in the case before us. The courts created by the Bankruptcy Act of 1978 do not lie exclusively outside

---

and n. 21 (1962) (opinion of Harlan, J.). *See also* Currie, *The Federal Courts and the American Law Institute,* pt. 1, 36 U. Chi. L. Rev. 1, 13–14, n. 67 (1968). Moreover, when Congress assigns these matters to administrative agencies, or to legislative courts, it has generally provided, and we have suggested that it may be required to provide, for Art. III judicial review. *See Atlas Roofing Co. v. Occupational Safety Comm'n,* 430 U.S. 442, 455, n. 13 (1977).

[24] Of course, the public–rights doctrine does not extend to any criminal matters, although the government is a proper party. *See, e.g., Toth v. Quaries,* 350 U.S. 11 (1955).

[25] The "unifying principle" that Justice White's dissent finds lacking in all of these cases, *see post,* at 14, is to be found in the exceptional constitutional grants of power to Congress with respect to certain matters. Although the dissent is correct that these grants are not explicit in the language of the Constitution, they are nonetheless firmly established in our historical understanding of the constitutional structure. When these three exceptional grants are properly constrained, they do not threaten the Framers' vision of an independent federal judiciary. What clearly remains subject to Art. III are all private adjudications in federal courts within the States—matters from their nature subject to "a suit at common law or in equity or admiralty" —and all criminal matters, with the narrow exception of military crimes. There is no doubt that when the Framers assigned the "judicial Power" to an independent Art. III branch, these matters lay at what they perceived to be the protected core of that power.

the States of the Federal Union, like those in the District of Columbia and the territories. Nor do the bankruptcy courts bear any resemblance to courts martial, which are founded upon the Constitution's grant of plenary authority over the Nation's military forces to the Legislative and Executive Branches. Finally, the substantive legal rights at issue in the present action cannot be deemed "public rights." Appellants argue that a discharge in bankruptcy is indeed a "public right," similar to such congressionally created benefits as "radio station licenses, pilot licenses, and certificates for common carriers" granted by administrative agencies. *See* Brief for the United States 34. But the restructuring of debtor–creditor relations, which is at the core of the federal bankruptcy power, must be distinguished from the adjudication of state–created private rights, such as the right to recover contract damages that is at issue in this case. The former may well be a "public right," but the latter obviously is not. Appellant Northern's right to recover contract damages to augment its estate is—one of private right, that is, of the liability of one individual to another under the law as defined. *Crowell v. Benson,* 285 U.S., at 51.[26]

Recognizing that the present case may not fall within the scope of any of our prior cases permitting the establishment of legislative courts, appellants argue that we should recognize an additional situation beyond the command of Art. III, sufficiently broad to sustain the Act. Appellants contend that Congress' constitutional authority to establish "uniform Laws on the subject of Bankruptcies throughout the United States," Art. I, § 8, cl. 4, carries with it an inherent power to establish legislative courts capable of adjudicating "bankruptcy related controversies." Brief for the United States 14. In support of this argument, appellants rely primarily upon a quotation from the opinion in *Palmore v. United States,* 411 U.S. 389 (1973), in which we stated that

> both Congress and this Court have recognized that the requirements of Art. III, which are applicable where laws of national applicability and affairs of national concern are at stake, must in proper circumstances give way to accommodate plenary grants of power to Congress to legislate with respect to specialized areas having particularized needs and warranting distinctive treatment.

Id., 407–408. Appellants cite this language to support their proposition that a bankruptcy court created by Congress under its Art. I powers is constitutional, because the law of bankruptcy is a "specialized area," and Congress has found a "particularized need" that warrants "distinctive treatment." Brief for the United States 20–33.

Appellants' contention, in essence, is that pursuant to any of its Art. I powers, Congress may create courts free of Art. III's requirements whenever it finds that

---

26 This claim may be adjudicated in federal court on the basis of its relationship to the petition for reorganization. *See Williams v. Austrian,* 331 U.S. 642 (1947); *Schumacher v. Beeler,* 293 U.S. 367 (1934). *See also National Ins. Co. v. Tidewater Co.,* 337 U.S. 582, 611–613 (1949) (Rutledge, J., concurring); *Textile Workers v. Lincoln Mills,* 353 U.S. 448, 472 (1957) (Frankfurter, J., dissenting). *Cf. Osborn v. United States Bank,* 9 Wheat. 738 (1824). But this relationship does not transform the state–created right into a matter between the Government and the petitioner for reorganization. Even in the absence of the federal scheme, the plaintiff would be able to proceed against the defendant on the state–law contractual claims.

course expedient. This contention has been rejected in previous cases. *See, e.g., Atlas Roofing Co. v. Occupational Safety Comm'n, supra,* at 450, n. 7; *Toth v. Quarles,* 350 U.S. 11 (1955). Although the cases relied upon by appellants demonstrate that independent courts are not required for all federal adjudications, those cases also make it clear that where Art. III does apply, all of the legislative powers specified in Art. I and elsewhere are subject to it. *See, e.g., Ex parte Bakelite Corp.,* 279 U.S., at 449; *Toth v. Quarles, supra; American Ins. Co. v. Canter,* 1 Pet., at 546; *Murray's Lessee,* 18 How., at 284. *Cf. Crowell v. Benson, supra,* at 51.

The flaw in appellants' analysis is that it provides no limiting principle. It thus threatens to supplant completely our system of adjudication in independent Art. III tribunals and replace it with a system of "specialized" legislative courts. True, appellants argue that under their analysis Congress could create legislative courts pursuant only to some "specific" Art. I power, and "only when there is a particularized need for distinctive treatment." Brief for the United States 22–23. They therefore assert, that their analysis would not permit Congress to replace the independent Art. III judiciary through a "wholesale assignment of federal judicial business to legislative courts." *Ibid.* But these "limitations" are wholly illusory. For example, Art. I, § 8, empowers Congress to enact laws, *inter alia,* regulating interstate commerce and punishing certain crimes. Art. I, § 8, cls. 3, 6. On appellants' reasoning Congress could provide for the adjudication of these and "related" matters by judges and courts within Congress' exclusive control.[27]

The potential for encroachment upon powers reserved to the Judicial Branch through the device of "specialized" legislative courts is dramatically evidenced in the jurisdiction granted to the courts created by the Act before us. The broad range of questions that can be brought into a bankruptcy court because they are "related to cases under title 11," 28 U.S.C. § 1471(b) (1976 ed., Supp. III), *see supra,* at 3, is the clearest proof that even when Congress acts through a "specialized" court, and pursuant to only one of its many Art. I powers, appellants' analysis fails to provide any real protection against the erosion of Art. III jurisdiction by the unilateral action of the political branches. In short, to accept appellants' reasoning would require that we replace the principles delineated in our precedents, rooted in history and the Constitution, with a rule of broad legislative discretion that could

---

[27] Nor can appellants' analysis logically be limited to Congress' Art. I powers. For example, appellants' reasoning relies in part upon analogy to our approval of territorial courts in *American Ins. Co. v. Canter,* 1 Pet. 511 (1828), and of the use of an administrative agency in *Crowell v. Benson,* 285 U.S. 22 (1932). Brief for the United States 15; Brief for Northern Pipeline Construction Co. 10. In those cases the Court recognized the right of Congress to create territorial courts pursuant to the authority granted under Art. IV, § 3, cl. 2 and to create administrative tribunals to adjudicate rights in admiralty pursuant to the federal authority in Art. III § 2 over admiralty jurisdiction. *See American Ins. Co. v. Canter, supra, at 546; Crowell v. Benson, supra,* at 39. This reliance underscores the fact that appellants offer no principled means of distinguishing between Congress' Art. I powers and any of Congress' other powers—including, for example, those conferred by the various amendments to the Constitution, *e.g.,* U.S. Const. Amdt. XIII, XIV, XV, XVI, XIX, XXIII, XXIV, XXVI.

effectively eviscerate the constitutional guarantee of an independent Judicial Branch of the Federal Government.[28]

Appellants' reliance upon Palmore for such broad legislative discretion is misplaced. In the context of the issue decided in that case, the language quoted from the Palmore opinion, supra, at 21, offers no substantial support for appellants' argument. Palmore was concerned with the courts of the District of Columbia, a unique federal enclave over which "Congress has entire control for every purpose of government." *Kendall v. United States,* 12 Pet. 524, 619 (1838). The "plenary authority" under the District of Columbia clause, Art. I, § 8 cl. 17, was the subject of the quoted passage and the powers granted under that clause are obviously different in kind from the other broad powers conferred on Congress: Congress' power over the District of Columbia encompasses the *full* authority of government, and thus, necessarily, the executive and judicial powers as well as the legislative. This is a power that is clearly possessed by Congress only in limited geographic areas. *Palmore* itself makes this limitation clear. The quoted passage distinguishes the congressional powers at issue in *Palmore* from those in which the Art. III command of an independent Judiciary must be honored: where "laws of national

---

[28] Justice White's suggested "limitations" on Congress' power to create Art. I courts are even more transparent. Justice White's dissent suggests that Art. III "should be read as expressing one value that must be balanced against competing constitutional concerns and legislative responsibilities," and that the Court retains the final word on how the balance is to be struck. *Post,* at 22–23. The dissent would find the Art. III "value" accommodated where appellate review to Art. III courts is provided and where the Art. I courts are "designed to deal with issues likely to be of little interest to the political branches." *Post,* at 24–25. But the dissent's view that appellate review is sufficient to satisfy either the command or the purpose of Art. III is incorrect. *See* n. 39, *infra.* And the suggestion that we should consider whether the Art. I courts are designed to deal with issues likely to be of interest to the political branches would undermine the validity of the adjudications performed by most of the administrative agencies, on which validity the dissent so heavily relies.

In applying its ad hoc balancing approach to the facts of this case, the dissent rests on the justification that these courts differ from standard Art. III courts because of their "extreme specialization." As noted above, "extreme specialization" is hardly an accurate description of bankruptcy courts designed to adjudicate the entire range of federal and state controversies. *See infra,* at 34–35. Moreover, the special nature of bankruptcy adjudications is in no sense incompatible with performance of such functions in a tribunal afforded the protection of Art. III. As one witness pointed out to Congress:

> Relevant to that question of need, it seems worth noting that Article III itself permits much flexibility; so long as tenure during good behavior is granted, much room exists as regards other conditions. Thus it would certainly be possible to create a special bankruptcy court under Article III and there is no reason why the judges of that court would have to be paid the same salary as district judges or any other existing judges. It would also be permissible to provide that when a judge of that court retired pursuant to statute, a vacancy for new appointment would not automatically be created. And it would be entirely valid to specify that the judges of that court could not be assigned to sit, even temporarily, on the general district courts or courts of appeals.

Hearings on H. R. 31 and H. R. 32 before the Subcommittee on Civil and Constitutional Rights of the House Committee on the Judiciary, 94th Cong., 2d Sess., 2697 (letter of Paul Mishkin).

applicability and affairs of national concern are at stake." 411 U.S., at 408. Laws respecting bankruptcy, like most laws enacted pursuant to the national powers catalogued in Art. I, § 8, are clearly laws of national applicability and affairs of national concern. Thus our reference in *Palmore* to "specialized areas having particularized needs" referred only to *geographic* areas, such as the District of Columbia or territories outside the States of the Federal Union. In light of the clear commands of Art. III, nothing held or said in *Palmore* can be taken to mean that in every area in which Congress may legislate, it may also create non–Art. III courts with Art. III powers.

In sum, Art. III bars Congress from establishing legislative courts to exercise jurisdiction over all matters related to those arising under the bankruptcy laws. The establishment of such courts does not fall within any of the historically recognized situations in which the general principle of independent adjudication commanded by Art. III does not apply. Nor can we discern any persuasive reason, in logic, history, or the Constitution, why the bankruptcy courts here established lie beyond the reach of Art. III.

IV.

Appellants advance a second argument for upholding the constitutionality of the Act: that "viewed within the entire judicial framework set up by Congress," the bankruptcy court is merely an "adjunct" to the district court, and that the delegation of certain adjudicative functions to the bankruptcy court is accordingly consistent with the principle that the judicial power of the United States must be vested in Art. III courts. *See* Brief for the United States 11–13, 37–45. As support for their argument, appellants rely principally upon *Crowell v. Benson, supra,* and *United States v. Raddatz,* 447 U.S. 667 (1980), cases in which we approved the use of administrative agencies and magistrates as adjuncts to Art. III courts. Brief for the United States at 40–42. The question to which we turn, therefore, is whether the Act has retained "the essential attributes of the judicial power," *Crowell v. Benson, supra,* at 51, in Art. III tribunals.[29]

The essential premise underlying appellants' argument is that even where the Constitution denies Congress the power to establish legislative courts, Congress possesses the authority to assign certain factfinding functions to adjunct tribunals. It is, of course, true that while the power to adjudicate "private rights" must be vested in an Art. III court, *See* Part III, *supra,*

> "this Court has accepted factfinding by an administrative agency, as an adjunct to the Art. III court, analogizing the agency to a jury or a special master and

---

[29] Justice White's dissent fails to distinguish between Congress' power to create adjuncts to Art. III courts, and Congress' power to create Art. I courts in limited circumstances. *See Post,* at 12–13. Congress' power to create adjuncts and assign them limited adjudicatory functions is in no sense an "exception" to Art. III. Rather, such an assignment is consistent with Art. III, so long as "the essential attributes of judicial power" are retained in the Art. III court, *Crowell v. Benson,* 285 U.S., at 51, and so long as Congress' adjustment of the traditional manner of adjudication can be sufficiently linked to its legislative power to define substantive rights, *see infra,* at 32–33. *Cf. Atlas Roofing Co. v. Occupational Safety Comm'n.,* 430 U.S., at 450, n. 7.

permitting it in admiralty cases to perform the function of a special master. *Crowell v. Benson*, 285 U.S. 22, 51–65 (1932)." *Atlas Roofing Co. v. Occupational Safety Comm'n*, 430 U.S. 442, 450, n. 7 (1977).

The use of administrative agencies as adjuncts was first upheld in *Crowell v. Benson, supra*. The congressional scheme challenged in Crowell empowered an administrative agency, the United States Employees' Compensation Commission, to make initial factual determinations pursuant to a federal statute requiring employers to compensate their employees for work–related injuries occurring upon the navigable waters of the United States. The Court began its analysis by noting that the federal statute administered by the Compensation Commission provided for compensation of injured employees "irrespective of fault," and that the statute also prescribed a fixed and mandatory schedule of compensation. *Id.*, at 38. The agency was thus left with the limited role of determining "questions of fact as to the circumstances, nature, extent and consequences of the injuries sustained by the employee for which compensation is to be made." *Id.*, at 54. The agency did not possess the power to enforce any of its compensation orders: On the contrary, every compensation order was appealable to the appropriate federal district court, which had the sole power to enforce it or set it aside, depending upon whether the court determined it to be "in accordance with law" and supported by evidence in the record. *Id.*, at 44–45, 48. The Court found that in view of these limitations upon the Compensation Commission's functions and powers, its determinations were "closely analogous to findings of the amount of damages that are made, according to familiar practice, by commissioners or assessors." *Id.*, at 54. Observing that "there is no requirement that, in order to maintain the essential attributes of the judicial power, all determinations of fact in constitutional courts shall be made by judges." *id.*, at 51, the Court held that Art. III imposed no bar to the scheme enacted by Congress, *id.*, at 54.

Crowell involved the adjudication of congressionally created rights. But this Court has sustained the use of adjunct fact–finders even in the adjudication of constitutional rights—so long as those adjuncts were subject to sufficient control by an Art. III district court. In *United States v. Raddatz, supra*, the Court upheld the 1978 Federal Magistrates Act, which permitted district court judges to refer certain pretrial motions, including suppression motions based on alleged violations of constitutional rights, to a magistrate for initial determination. The Court observed that the magistrate's proposed findings and recommendations were subject to *de novo* review by the district court, which was free to rehear the evidence or to call for additional evidence. *Id.*, at 676–677, 681–683. Moreover, it was noted that the magistrate considered motions only upon reference from the district court, and that the magistrates were appointed, and subject to removal, by the district court. *Id.*, at 685 (Blackmun, J., concurring).[30]

---

[30] Thus in *Raddatz* there was no serious threat that the exercise of the judicial power would be subject to incursion by other branches. "The only conceivable danger of a 'threat' to the 'independence' of the magistrate comes from within, rather than without the judicial department." 447 U.S., at 685. (Blackmun, J., concurring).

In short, the ultimate decisionmaking authority respecting all pretrial motions clearly remained with the district court. *Id.,* at 682. Under these circumstances, the Court held that the Act did not violate the constraints of Art. III. *Id.,* at 683–684.[31]

Together these cases establish two principles that aid us in determining the extent to which Congress may constitutionally vest traditionally judicial functions in non–Art. III officers. First, it is clear that when Congress creates a substantive federal right, it possesses substantial discretion to prescribe the manner in which that right may be adjudicated—including the assignment to an adjunct of some functions historically performed by judges.[32]

---

[31] Appellants and Justice White's dissent also rely on the broad powers exercised by the bankruptcy referees immediately before the Bankruptcy Act of 1978. *See post,* at 4–12. But those particular adjunct functions, which represent the culmination of years of gradual expansion of the power and authority of the bankruptcy referee, see 1 Collier on Bankruptcy ¶ 3.02 (15th ed. 1981), have never been explicitly endorsed by this Court. In *Katchen v. Landy,* 382 U.S. 323 (1966), on which the dissent relies, there was no discussion of the Art. III issue. Moreover, when *Katchen* was decided the 1973 Bankruptcy Rules had not yet been adopted, and the District Judge, after hearing the report of magistrate, was free to "modify it or reject it in whole or in part or receive further evidence or recommit it with instructions." Gen. Order in Bankruptcy No. 47, 305 U.S. 679 (1935).

We note, moreover, that the 1978 Act made at least three significant changes from the bankruptcy practice that immediately preceded it. First, of course, the jurisdiction of the bankruptcy courts was "substantially expanded by the Act." H. R. Rep. No. 95–595, *supra,* p. 13 (1977). Before the Act the referee had no jurisdiction, except with consent, over controversies beyond those involving property in the actual or constructive possession of the court. 11 U.S.C. § 46(b) (repealed). *See MacDonald v. Plymouth Trust Co.,* 296 U.S. 263, 266 (1932). It cannot be doubted that the new bankruptcy judges, unlike the referees, have jurisdiction far beyond that which can be even arguably characterized as merely incidental to the discharge in bankruptcy or a plan for reorganization. Second, the bankruptcy judges have broader powers than those exercised by the referees. *See infra* at 34–35; H. R. Rep. 95–595, *supra,* p. 12 and nn. 63–68. Finally, and perhaps most significantly, the relationship between the district court and the bankruptcy court was changed under the 1978 Act. Before the Act, bankruptcy referees were "subordinate adjuncts of the district courts." *Id.,* at 7. In contrast, the new bankruptcy courts are "independent of the United States district courts." *Ibid.;* Collier on Bankruptcy, ¶ 1.03, at 1–9 (15th ed. 1981). Before the Act, bankruptcy referees were appointed and removable only by the district court. 11 U.S.C. § 62 (repealed). And the district court retained control over the reference by his power to withdraw the case from the referee. Bkrptcy. Rule 102. Thus even at the trial stage, the parties had access to an independent judicial officer. Although Congress could still lower the salary of referees, they were not dependent on the political branches of government for their appointment. To paraphrase Justice Blackmun's observation in *Raddatz, supra,* the primary "danger of a threat" to the independence of the [adjunct came] from within, rather than without the judicial department." 447 U.S., at 685 (concurring opinion).

[32] Contrary to Justice White's suggestion, we do not concede that "Congress may provide for initial adjudications by Article I courts or administrative judges of all rights and duties arising under otherwise valid federal laws." *See post,* at 3. Rather we simply reaffirm the holding of *Crowell*—that Congress may assign to non–Art III bodies some adjudicatory functions. Crowell itself spoke of "specialized" functions. This case does not require us to specify further any limitations that may exist with respect to Congress' power to create adjuncts to assist in the adjudication of federal statutory rights.

Thus *Crowell* recognized that Art. III does not require "all determinations of fact [to] be made by judges," 285 U.S., at 51; with respect to congressionally created rights, some factual determinations may be made by a specialized factfinding tribunal designed by Congress, without constitutional bar, *Id.*, at 54. Second, the functions of the adjunct must be limited in such a way that "the essential attributes" of judicial power are retained in the Art. III court. Thus in upholding the adjunct scheme challenged in Crowell, the Court emphasized that "the reservation of full authority to the court to deal with matters of law provides for the appropriate exercise of the judicial function in this class of cases." *Ibid.* And in refusing to invalidate the Magistrates Act at issue in *Raddatz,* the Court stressed that under the congressional scheme "[t]he authority—and the responsibility—to make an informed, final determination remains with the judge," 447 U.S., at 682, quoting *Mathews v. Weber,* 423 U.S. 261, 271 (1976); the statute's delegation of power was therefore permissible, since "the ultimate decision is made by the district court," 447 U.S., at 683.

These two principles assist us in evaluating the "adjunct" scheme presented in this case. Appellants assume that Congress' power to create "adjuncts" to consider all cases related to those arising under title 11 is as great as it was in the circumstances of *Crowell.* But while *Crowell* certainly endorsed the proposition that Congress possesses broad discretion to assign factfinding functions to an adjunct created to aid in the adjudication of congressionally created statutory rights, *Crowell* does not support the further proposition necessary to appellants' argument– that Congress possesses the same degree of discretion in assigning traditionally judicial power to adjuncts engaged in the adjudication of rights not created by Congress. Indeed, the validity of this proposition was expressly denied in *Crowell,* when the Court rejected "the untenable assumption that the constitutional courts may be deprived in all cases of the determination of facts upon evidence even though a constitutional right may be involved," 285 U.S., at 60–61,[33] and stated that

> the essential independence of the exercise of judicial power of the United States in the enforcement of *constitutional* rights requires that the Federal court should determine an issue [of agency jurisdiction] upon its own record and the facts elicited before it. *Id.,* at 64 (emphasis added).[34]

---

[33] The Court in *Crowell* found that the requirement of *de novo* review as to certain facts was not "simply the question of due process in relation to notice and hearing," but was "rather a question of the appropriate balance of Federal judicial power." 285 U.S., at 56. The dissent agreed that some factual findings cannot be made by adjuncts, on the ground that "under certain circumstances, the constitutional requirement of due process is a requirement of [Art. III] judicial process." *Id.,* at 87 (Brandeis, J., dissenting).

[34] *Crowell's* precise holding, with respect to the review of "jurisdictional" and "constitutional" facts that arise within ordinary administrative proceedings, has been undermined by later cases. *See St. Joseph Stock Yards Co. v. United States,* 298 U.S. 38, 53 (1936). *See generally* 4 K. Davis, Administrative Law Treatise §§ 29.08, 29.09 (1st ed. 1958). But the general principle of *Crowell*—distinguishing between congressionally created rights and constitutionally recognized rights—remains valid, as evidenced by the Court's recent approval of *Ng Fung Ho v. White,* 259 U.S. 276 (1922), on which *Crowell* relied. *See Agosto v. INS,* 436 U.S. 748, 753 (1978) (*de novo* judicial determination required for claims of American citizenship in deportation proceedings). *See also United States v. Raddatz,* 447 U.S., at 682–684; *id.,* at 707–712 (Marshall, J., dissenting).

Appellants' proposition was also implicitly rejected in *Raddatz*. Congress' assignment of adjunct functions under the Federal Magistrates Act was substantially narrower than under the statute challenged in *Crowell*. Yet the Court's scrutiny of the adjunct scheme in *Raddatz*—which played a role in the adjudication of *constitutional* rights—was far stricter than it had been in *Crowell*. Critical to the Court's decision to uphold the Magistrates Act was the fact that the ultimate decision was made by the district court. 447 U.S., at 683.

Although *Crowell* and *Raddatz* do not explicitly distinguish between rights created by Congress and other rights, such a distinction underlies in part *Crowell's* and *Raddatz's* recognition of a critical difference between rights created by federal statute and rights recognized by the Constitution. Moreover, such a distinction seems to us to be necessary in light of the delicate accommodations required by the principle of separation of powers reflected in Art. III. The constitutional system of checks and balances is designed to guard against "encroachment or aggrandizement" by Congress at the expense of the other branches of government. *Buckley v. Valeo,* 424 U.S., at 122. But when Congress creates a statutory right, it clearly has the discretion, in defining that right, to create presumptions, or assign burdens of proof, or prescribe remedies; it may also provide that persons seeking to vindicate that right must do so before particularized tribunals created to perform the specialized adjudicative tasks related to that right.[35]

Such provisions do, in a sense, affect the exercise of judicial power, but they are also incidental to Congress' power to define the right that it has created. No comparable justification exists, however, when the right being adjudicated is not of congressional creation. In such a situation, substantial inroads into functions that have traditionally been performed by the judiciary cannot be characterized merely as incidental extensions of Congress' power to define rights that it has created. Rather, such inroads suggest unwarranted encroachments upon the judicial power of the United States, which our Constitution reserves for Art. III courts.

We hold that the Bankruptcy Act of 1978 carries the possibility of such an unwarranted encroachment. Many of the rights subject to adjudication by the Act's bankruptcy courts, like the rights implicated in *Raddatz,* are not of Congress' creation. Indeed, the case before us, which centers upon appellant Northern's claim for damages for breach of contract and misrepresentation, involves a right created

---

[35] Drawing the line between permissible extensions of legislative power and impermissible incursions into judicial power is a delicate undertaking, for the powers of the Judicial and Legislative Branches are often overlapping. As Justice Frankfurter noted in a similar context, "To be sure the content of the three authorities of government is not to be derived from an abstract analysis. The areas are partly interacting, not wholly disjointed." *Youngstown Co. v. Sawyer,* 343 U.S. 579, 610 (1952) (concurring opinion). The interaction between the Legislative and Judicial Branches is at its height where courts are adjudicating rights wholly of Congress' creation. Thus where Congress creates a substantive right, pursuant to one of its broad powers to make laws, Congress may have something to say about the proper manner of adjudicating that right.

by *state* law, a right independent of and antecedent to the reorganization petition that conferred jurisdiction upon the bankruptcy court.[36]

Accordingly, Congress' authority to control the manner in which that right is adjudicated, through assignment of historically judicial functions to a non–Art. III "adjunct," plainly must be deemed at a minimum. Yet it is equally plain that Congress has vested the "adjunct" bankruptcy judges with powers over appellant's state–created right that far exceed the powers that it has vested in administrative agencies that adjudicate only rights of Congress' own creation.

Unlike the administrative scheme that we reviewed in *Crowell,* the Act vests all "essential attributes" of the judicial power of the United States in the "adjunct" bankruptcy court. First, the agency in *Crowell* made only specialized, narrowly confined factual determinations regarding a particularized area of law. In contrast, the subject matter jurisdiction of the bankruptcy courts encompasses not only traditional matters of bankruptcy, but also "all civil proceedings arising under title 11 or arising in or related to cases arising under title 11." 28 U.S.C. § 1471(b) (1976 ed., Supp. III). Second, while the agency in *Crowell* engaged in statutorily channeled factfinding functions, the bankruptcy courts exercise "all of the jurisdiction" conferred by the Act on the district courts, § 1471(b) (emphasis added). Third, the agency in *Crowell* possessed only a limited power to issue compensation orders pursuant to specialized procedures, and its orders could be enforced only by order of the district court. By contrast, the bankruptcy courts exercise all ordinary powers of district courts, including the power to preside over jury trials, 28 U.S.C. § 1480 (1976 ed., Supp. III), the power to issue declaratory judgments, § 2201, the power to issue writs of habeas corpus, § 2256, and the power to issue any order, process or judgment appropriate for the enforcement of the provisions of title 11, 11 U.S.C. § 105(a) (1976 ed., Supp. III).[37]

Fourth, while orders issued by the agency in *Crowell* were to be set aside if "not supported by the evidence," the judgments of the bankruptcy courts are apparently subject to review only under the more deferential "clearly erroneous" standard. *See* n. 5, *supra.* Finally, the agency in *Crowell* was required by law to seek enforcement of its compensation orders in the district court. In contrast, the bankruptcy courts issue final judgments, which are binding and enforceable even in the absence of an appeal.[38]

---

[36] Of course, bankruptcy adjudications themselves, as well as the manner in which the rights of debtors and creditors are adjusted, are matters of federal law. Appellant Northern's state–law contract claim is now in federal court because of its relationship to appellant's reorganization petition. *See* n. 26, *supra.* But Congress has not purported to prescribe a rule of decision for the resolution of appellant's contractual claims.

[37] The limitations that the judges "may not enjoin another court or punish a criminal contempt not committed in the presence of the judge of the court or warranting a punishment of imprisonment," 28 U.S.C. § 1481 (1976 ed., Supp. III), are also denied to Art. III judges under certain circumstances. *See* 18 U.S.C. §§ 401, 402, 3691; 28 U.S.C. § 2283.

[38] Although the entry of an enforcement order is in some respects merely formal, it has long been recognized that

"The award of execution is a part, and an essential part of every judgment passed by a court exercising judicial power. It is no judgment in the legal sense of the term, without it."

In short, the "adjunct" bankruptcy courts created by the Act exercise jurisdiction behind the facade of a grant to the district courts, and are exercising powers far greater than those lodged in the adjuncts approved in either *Crowell* or *Raddatz.*[39]

We conclude that § 241(a) of the Bankruptcy Act of 1978 has impermissibly removed most, if not all, of "the essential attributes of the judicial power" from the Art. III district court, and has vested those attributes in a non–Art. III adjunct. Such a grant of jurisdiction cannot be sustained as an exercise of Congress' power to create adjuncts to Art. III courts.

V.

Having concluded that the broad grant of jurisdiction to the bankruptcy courts contained in § 241(a) is unconstitutional, we must now determine whether our holding should be applied retroactively to the effective date of the Act.[40]

ICC v. Brimson, 154 U.S. 447, 484 (1894), quoting Chief Justice Taney's memorandum in *Gordon v. United States,* 117 U.S. 697, 702 (1864).

[39] Appellants suggest that *Crowell* and *Raddatz* stand for the proposition that Art. III is satisfied so long as some degree of appellate review is provided. But that suggestion is directly contrary to the text of our Constitution: "The Judges, *both* of the supreme and inferior Courts, shall hold their Offices during good Behaviour, and shall receive [undiminished] Compensation." Art. III, § 1 (emphasis added). Our precedents make it clear that the constitution requirements for the exercise of the judicial power must be met at all stages of adjudication, and not only on appeal, where the court is restricted to considerations of law, as well as the nature of the case as it has been shaped at the trial level. The Court responded to a similar suggestion in *Crowell* by stating that to accept such a regime,

> would be to sap the judicial power as it exists under the Federal Constitution, and to establish a government of bureaucratic character alien to our system, wherever fundamental rights depend, as not infrequently they do depend, upon the facts, and finality as to facts becomes in effect finality in law.

285 U.S., at 57. *Cf. Ward v. Village of Monroeville,* 409 U.S. 57, 61–62 (1972); *Osborn v. Bank of the United States,* 9 Wheat. 738, 883 (1824).

Justice White's dissent views the function of the Third Branch as interpreting the Constitution in order to keep the other two branches in check, and would accordingly find the purpose, if not the language, of Art. III satisfied where there is an appeal to an Art. III court. *See post,* at 24. But in the Framers' view, Art. III courts would do a great deal more than, in an abstract way, announce guidelines for the other two branches. While "expounding" the Constitution was surely one vital function of the Art. III courts in the Framers' view, the tasks of those courts, for which independence was an important safeguard, included the mundane as well as the glamorous, matters of common law and statute as well as constitutional law, issues of fact as well as issues of law. As Hamilton noted, "it is not with a view to infractions of the Constitution only, that the independence of the judges may be an essential safeguard against the effects of occasional ill humors in the society." The Federalist No. 78, p. 488 (H. Lodge ed. 1888). In order to promote the independence and improve the quality of federal judicial decision making in all of these areas, the Framers created a system of independent federal courts. *See* The Federalist Nos, 78–82.

[40] It is clear that, at the least, the new bankruptcy judges cannot constitutionally be vested with jurisdiction to decide this state–law contract claim against Marathon. As part of a comprehensive restructuring of the bankruptcy laws, Congress has vested jurisdiction over this and all matters related to cases under title 11 in a single non–Art III court, and has done

Our decision in *Chevron Oil Co. v. Huson,* 404 U.S. 97 (1971), sets forth the three considerations recognized by our precedents as properly bearing upon the issue of retroactivity. They are, first, whether the holding in question "decid[ed] an issue of first impression whose resolution was not clearly foreshadowed" by earlier cases, *Id.,* at 106; second, "whether retrospective operation will further or retard [the] operation" of the holding in question, *Id.,* at 107, and third, whether retroactive application "could produce substantial inequitable results" in individual cases, *ibid.* In the present case, all of these considerations militate against the retroactive application of our holding today. It is plain that Congress' broad grant of judicial power to non–Art. III bankruptcy judges presents an unprecedented question of interpretation of Art. III. It is equally plain that retroactive application would not further the operation of our holding, and would surely visit substantial injustice and hardship upon those litigants who relied upon the Act's vesting of jurisdiction in the bankruptcy courts. We hold, therefore, that our decision today shall apply only prospectively.[41]

The judgment of the District Court is affirmed. However, we stay our judgment until October 4, 1982. This limited stay will afford Congress an opportunity to reconstitute the bankruptcy courts or to adopt other valid means of adjudication, without impairing the interim administration of the bankruptcy laws. *See Buckley v. Valeo,* 424 U.S. 1, 143 (1976); *cf. Georgia v. United States,* 411 U.S. 526, 541 (1973); *Fortson v. Morris,* 385 U.S. 231, 235 (1966); *Maryland Comm. v. Tawes,* 377 U.S. 656, 675–676 (1964).

It is so ordered.

Justice REHNQUIST, with whom Justice O'CONNOR, joins, concurring in the judgment.

Were I to agree with the plurality that the question presented by this case is "whether the assignment by Congress to bankruptcy judges of the jurisdiction granted in § 241(a) of the Bankruptcy Act of 1978 violates Art. III of the Constitution," *ante,* at 1, I would with considerable reluctance embark on the duty of deciding this broad question. But appellee Marathon Pipe Line Co. has not been

---

so pursuant to a single statutory grant of jurisdiction. In these circumstances we cannot conclude that if Congress were aware that the grant of jurisdiction could not constitutionally encompass this and similar claims, it would simply remove the jurisdiction of the bankruptcy court over these matters, leaving the jurisdictional provision and adjudicatory structure intact with respect to other types of claims, and thus subject to Art. III constitutional challenge on a claim–by–claim basis. Indeed, we note that one of the express purposes of the Act was to ensure adjudication of all claims in a single forum and to avoid the delay and expense of jurisdictional disputes. *See* H.R. Rep. No. 95–595, *supra,* p. 43–48; S. Rep. No. 95–989, p. 17 (1978). Nor can we assume, as The Chief Justice suggests, *post,* at 2, that Congress' choice would be to have this case "routed to the United States district court of which the bankruptcy court is an adjunct." We think that it is for Congress to determine the proper manner of restructuring the Bankruptcy Act of 1978 to conform to the requirements of Art. III, in the, way that will best effectuate the legislative purpose.

[41] *See also Buckley v. Valeo,* 424 U.S., at 142; *Chicot County Drainage Dist. v. Bank,* 308 U.S. 371, 376–377 (1940); *Insurance Corp. v. Compagnis des Bauxites,* — U.S. —, —, n. 9 (1982).

subjected to the full range of authority granted Bankruptcy Courts by § 241(a). It was named as a defendant in a suit brought by appellant in a United States Bankruptcy Court. The suit sought damages for, *inter alia,* breaches of contract and warranty. Marathon moved to dismiss the action on the grounds that the Bankruptcy Act of 1978, which authorized the suit, violated Art. III of the Constitution insofar as it established Bankruptcy Judges whose tenure and salary protection do not conform to the requirements of Art. III.

With the case in this posture, Marathon has simply been named defendant in a lawsuit about a contract, a lawsuit initiated by appellant Northern after having previously filed a petition for reorganization under the Bankruptcy Act. Marathon may object to proceeding further with this lawsuit on the grounds that if it is to be resolved by an agency of the United States, it may be resolved only by an agency which exercises "the judicial power of the United States" described by Art. III of the Constitution. But resolution of any objections it may make on this ground to the exercise of a different authority conferred on Bankruptcy Courts by the 1978 Act, *see ante,* at 2–4, should await the exercise of such authority.

> This Court, as is the case with all federal courts, "has no jurisdiction to pronounce any statute, either of a State or of the United States, void, because irreconcilable with the Constitution, except as it is called upon to adjudge the legal rights of litigants in actual controversies. In the exercise of that jurisdiction, it is bound by two rules, to which it has rigidly adhered, one, never to anticipate a question of constitutional law in advance of the necessity of deciding it; the other never to formulate a rule of constitutional law broader than is required by the precise facts to which it is to be applied." *Liverpool, New York & Philadelphia S.S. Co. v. Commissioners of Emigration,* 113 U.S. 33, 39.

United States v. Raines, 362 U.S. 17, 21 (1960). Particularly in an area of constitutional law such as that of "Art. III Courts," with its frequently arcane distinctions and confusing precedents, rigorous adherence to the principle that this Court should decide no more of a constitutional question than is absolutely necessary accords with both our decided cases and with sound judicial policy.

From the record before us, the lawsuit in which Marathon was named defendant seeks damages for breach of contract, misrepresentation, and other counts which are the stuff of the traditional actions at common law tried by the courts at Westminster in 1789. There is apparently no federal rule of decision provided for any of the issues in the lawsuit; the claims of Northern arise entirely under state law. No method of adjudication is hinted, other than the traditional common law mode of judge and jury. The lawsuit is before the Bankruptcy Court only because the plaintiff has previously filed a petition for reorganization in that Court.

The cases dealing with the authority of Congress to create courts other than by use of its power under Art. III do not admit of easy synthesis. In the interval of nearly 150 years between *American Insurance Co. v. Canter,* 1 Pet. 511 (1828), and *Palmore v. United States,* 411 U.S. 389 (1973), the Court addressed the question infrequently. I need not decide whether these cases in fact support a general proposition and three tidy exceptions, as the plurality believes, or whether instead they are but landmarks on a judicial "darkling plain" where ignorant armies have clashed by night, as Justice White apparently believes them to be. None of the cases has gone so far as to sanction the type of adjudication to which Marathon will be subjected against its will under the provisions of the 1978 Act. To whatever extent different powers granted under that Act might be sustained under the "public rights" doctrine of *Murray's Lessee v. Hoboken Land & Improvement Co.,* 18 How. 272 (1855), and succeeding cases, I am satisfied that the adjudication of Northern's lawsuit cannot be so sustained.

I am likewise of the opinion that the extent of review by Art. III courts provided on appeal from a decision of the Bankruptcy Court in a case such as Northern's does not save the grant of authority to the latter under the rule espoused in *Crowell v. Benson,* 285 U.S. 22 (1932). All matters of fact and law in whatever domains of the law to which the parties' dispute may lead are to be resolved by the Bankruptcy Court in the first instance, with only traditional appellate review apparently contemplated by Art. III courts. Acting in this manner the Bankruptcy Court is not an "adjunct" of either the District Court or the Court of Appeals.

I would, therefore, hold so much of the Bankruptcy Act of 1978 as enables a Bankruptcy Court to entertain and decide Northern's lawsuit over Marathon's objection to be violative of Art. III of the United States Constitution. Because I agree with the plurality that this grant of authority is not readily severable from the remaining grant of authority to Bankruptcy Courts under § 241(a), *see ante,* at 37 n. 40, I concur in the judgment. I also agree with the discussion in Part V of the plurality opinion respecting retroactivity and the staying of the judgment of this Court.

Chief Justice BURGER, dissenting.

I join Justice White's dissenting opinion, but I write separately to emphasize that, notwithstanding the plurality opinion, the Court does *not* hold today that Congress' broad grant of jurisdiction to the new bankruptcy courts is generally inconsistent with Article III of the Constitution. Rather, the Court's holding is limited to the proposition stated by Justice Rehnquist in his concurrence in the judgment—that a "traditional" state common–law action, not made subject to a federal rule of decision, and related only peripherally to an adjudication of bankruptcy under federal law, must, absent the consent of the litigants, be heard by an "Article III court" if it is to be heard by any court or agency of the United States. This limited holding, of course, does not suggest that there is something inherently unconstitutional about the new bankruptcy courts; nor does it preclude such courts from adjudicating all but a relatively narrow category of claims "arising under" or "arising in or related to cases under" the Bankruptcy Act.

It will not be necessary for Congress, in order to meet the requirements of the Court's holding, to undertake a radical restructuring of the present system of bankruptcy adjudication. The problems arising from today's judgment can be resolved simply by providing that ancillary common–law actions, such as the one involved in this case, be routed to the United States district court of which the bankruptcy court is an adjunct.

Justice WHITE, with whom THE CHIEF JUSTICE, and Justice POWELL, join, dissenting.

Article III, § 1 of the Constitution is straightforward and uncomplicated on its face: The judicial Power of the United States, shall be vested in one supreme Court, and in such inferior Courts as the Congress may from time to time ordain and establish. The Judges, both of the supreme and inferior Courts, shall hold their Offices during good Behavior, and shall at stated Times, receive for their Services a Compensation, which shall not be diminished during their Continuance in Office.

Any reader could easily take this provision to mean that although Congress was free to establish such lower courts as it saw fit, any court that it did establish would be an "inferior" court exercising "judicial power of the United States" and so must be manned by judges possessing both life–tenure and a guaranteed minimal income. This would be an eminently sensible reading and one that, as the plurality shows, is well–founded in both the documentary sources and the political doctrine of separation of powers that stands behind much of our constitutional structure. *Ante,* at 6–9.

If this simple reading were correct and we were free to disregard 150 years of history, this would be an easy case and the plurality opinion could end with its observation that "[i]t is undisputed that the bankruptcy judges whose offices were created by the Bankruptcy Reform Act of 1978 do not enjoy the protections constitutionally afforded to Art. III judges." *Ante,* at 9. The fact that the plurality must go on to deal with what has been characterized as one of the most confusing and controversial areas of constitutional law [1] itself indicates the gross oversimplification implicit in the plurality's claim that "our Constitution unambiguously enunciates a fundamental principle—that the "Judicial Power of the United States must be reposed in an independent Judiciary [and] provides clear institutional protections for that independence." *Ante,* at 9. While this is fine rhetoric, analytically it serves only to put a distracting and superficial gloss on a difficult question.

That question is what limits Article III places on Congress' ability to create adjudicative institutions designed to carry out federal policy established pursuant to the substantive authority given Congress elsewhere in the Constitution. Whether fortunate or unfortunate, at this point in the history of constitutional law that question can no longer be answered by looking only to the constitutional text. This Court's cases construing that text must also be considered. In its attempt to pigeon–hole these cases, the plurality does violence to their meaning and creates an artificial structure that itself lacks coherence.

I.

There are, I believe, two separate grounds for today's decision. First, non–Article III judges, regardless of whether they are labelled "adjuncts" to Article III courts or "Article I judges," may consider only controversies arising out of federal law. Because the immediate controversy in this case—Northern Pipeline's claim against Marathon—arises out of state law, it may only be adjudicated, within the federal system, by an Article III court.[2] Second, regardless of the source of law that governs

---

[1] *Glidden Co. v. Zdanok,* 370 U.S. 530, 534 (1962) (Harlan, J., plurality opinion).

[2] Because this is the sole ground relied upon by the concurring Justices, this is the effective basis for today's decision.

the controversy, Congress is prohibited by Article III from establishing Article I courts, with three narrow exceptions. Adjudication of bankruptcy proceedings does not fall within any of these exceptions. I shall deal with the first of these contentions in this section.

The plurality concedes that Congress may provide for initial adjudications by Article I courts or administrative judges of all rights and duties arising under otherwise valid federal laws. Ante, at 30. There is no apparent reason why this principle should not extend to matters arising in federal bankruptcy proceedings. The Court attempts to escape the reach of prior decisions by contending that the bankrupt's claim against Marathon arose under state law. Non–Article III judges, in its view, cannot be vested with authority to adjudicate such issues. It then proceeds to strike down § 241(a) on this ground. For several reasons, the Court's judgment is unsupportable.

First, clearly this ground alone cannot support the Court's invalidation of § 241(a) on its face. The plurality concedes that in adjudications and discharges in bankruptcy, "the restructuring of debtor–creditor relations, which lies at the core of the federal bankruptcy power," ante, at 21, and "the manner in which the rights of debtors and creditors are adjusted," ante, at 34, n. 36, are matters of federal law. Under the plurality's own interpretation of the cases, therefore, these matters could be heard and decided by Article I judges. But because the bankruptcy judge is also given authority to hear a case like that of petitioner against Marathon, which the Court says is founded on state law, the Court holds that the section must be stricken down on its face. This is a grossly unwarranted emasculation of the scheme Congress has adopted. Even if the Court is correct that such a state law claim cannot be heard by a bankruptcy judge, there is no basis for doing more than declaring the section unconstitutional as applied to the claim against Marathon, leaving the section otherwise intact. In that event, cases such as this one would have to be heard by Article III judges or by state courts—unless the defendant consents to suit before the bankruptcy judge—just as they were before the 1978 Act was adopted. But this would remove from the jurisdiction of the bankruptcy judge only a tiny fraction of the cases he is now empowered to adjudicate and would not otherwise limit his jurisdiction.[3]

---

[3] The plurality attempts to justify its sweeping invalidation of § 241(a), because of its inclusion of state–law claims, by suggesting that this statutory provision is nonseverable. Ante, at n. 40. The concurring Justices specifically adopt this argument as the reason for their decision to join the judgment of the Court. The basis for the conclusion of nonseverability, however, is nothing more than a presumption: "Congress has vested jurisdiction over this and all matters related to cases under title 11 in a single non–Art. III court, and has done so pursuant to a single statutory grant of jurisdiction. In these circumstances, we cannot conclude that if Congress were aware that the grant of jurisdiction could not constitutionally encompass this and similar claims, it would simply remove the jurisdiction of the bankruptcy court over these matters." Ibid. Although it is possible, as a historical matter, to find cases of this Court supporting this presumption, see e.g., Williams v. Standard Oil Co., 278 U.S. 235, 242 (1929), I had not thought this to be the contemporary approach to the problem of severability, particularly when dealing with federal statutes. I would follow the approach taken by the Court in Buckley v. Valeo, 424 U.S. 1, 108 (1976): "Unless it is evident that the Legislature

Second, the distinction between claims based on state law and those based on federal law disregards the real character of bankruptcy proceedings. The routine in ordinary bankruptcy cases now, as it was before 1978, is to stay actions against the bankrupt, collect the bankrupt's assets, require creditors to file claims or be forever barred, allow or disallow claims that are filed, adjudicate preferences and fraudulent transfers, and make pro rata distributions to creditors, who will be barred by the discharge from taking further actions against the bankrupt. The crucial point to be made is that in the ordinary bankruptcy proceeding the great bulk of creditor claims are claims that have accrued under state law prior to bankruptcy—claims for goods sold, wages, rent, utilities and the like. "[T]he word debt as used by the Act is not confined to the technical common law meaning but extends to liabilities arising out of breach of contract to torts and to taxes owing to the United States or state or local governments." 1 Collier on Bankruptcy ¶¶ (14th ed. 1976). Every such claim must be filed and its validity is subject to adjudication by the bankruptcy court. The existence and validity of such claims recurringly depends on state law. Hence, the bankruptcy judge is constantly enmeshed in state law issues.

The new aspect of the Bankruptcy Act of 1978, in this regard, therefore, is not the extension of federal jurisdiction to state law claims, but its extension to particular kinds of state law claims, such as contract cases against third parties or disputes involving property in the possession of a third person.[4]

Prior to 1978, a claim of a bankrupt against a third party, such as the claim against Marathon in this case, was not within the jurisdiction of the bankruptcy judge. The old limits were based, of course, on the restrictions implicit within the concept of *in rem* jurisdiction; the new extension is based on the concept of in personam jurisdiction. "The bankruptcy court is given *in personam* jurisdiction as well as in rem jurisdiction to handle everything that arises in a bankruptcy case." H.R. Rep. No. 595, 95th Cong., 1st Sess. 445 (1977). The difference between the new and old Act, therefore, is not to be found in a distinction between state law and federal law matters; rather, it is in a distinction between *in rem* and *in personam* jurisdiction. The majority at no place explains why this distinction should have constitutional implications.

Third, all that can be left of the majority's argument in this regard is that state law claims adjudicated within the federal system must be heard in the first instance by Article III judges. I shall argue below that any such attempt to distinguish Article

---

would not have enacted those provisions which are within its power, independently of that which is not, the invalid part may be dropped if what is left is fully operative as a law." Quoting *Champlin Refining Co. v. Corporation Commission,* 286 U.S. 210 (1932). This presumption seems particularly strong when Congress has already "enacted those provisions which are within its power, independently of that which is not" —*i.e.,* in the old Bankruptcy Act.

[4] Even this is not entirely new. Under the old Act, in certain circumstances, the referee could actually adjudicate and order the payment of a claim of the bankrupt estate against another. In *Katchen v. Landy,* 382 U.S. 323 (1966), for example, we recognized that when a creditor files a claim, the referee is empowered to hear and decide a counter–claim against that creditor arising out of the same transaction. A similar situation could arise in adjudicating setoffs under former § 68 of the Bankruptcy Act.

I from Article III courts by the character of the controversies they may adjudicate fundamentally misunderstands the historical and constitutional significance of Article I courts. Initially, however, the majority's proposal seems to turn the separation of powers doctrine, upon which the majority relies, on its head: Since state law claims would ordinarily not be heard by Article III judges—*i.e.,* they would be heard by state judges—one would think that there is little danger of a diminution of, or intrusion upon, the power of Article III courts, when such claims are assigned to a non–Article III court. The plurality misses this obvious point because it concentrates on explaining how it is that federally created rights can ever be adjudicated in Article I courts—a far more difficult problem under the separation of powers doctrine. The plurality fumbles when it assumes that the rationale it develops to deal with the latter problem must also govern the former problem. In fact, the two are simply unrelated and the majority never really explains the separation of powers problem that would be created by assigning state law questions to legislative courts or to adjuncts of Article III courts.

One need not contemplate the intricacies of the separation of powers doctrine, however, to realize that the majority's position on adjudication of state law claims is based on an abstract theory that has little to do with the reality of bankruptcy proceedings. Even prior to the present Act, bankruptcy cases were generally referred to bankruptcy judges, previously called referees. Bankruptcy Rule 102(a). Section 66 of Title 11 described the jurisdiction of the referees. Their powers included the authority to

> consider all petitions referred to them and make the adjudications or dismiss the petition grant, deny or revoke discharges, determine the dischargeability of debts, and render judgments thereon [and] perform such of the duties as are by this Title conferred on courts of bankruptcy, including those incidental to ancillary jurisdiction, and as shall be prescribed by rules or orders of courts of bankruptcy of their respective districts, except as herein otherwise provided.

The bankruptcy judge possessed "complete jurisdiction of the proceedings." 1 Collier on Bankruptcy 65 (14th ed. 1976). The referee would initially hear and decide practically all matters arising in the proceedings, including the allowance and disallowance of the claims of creditors.[5]

If a claim was disallowed by the bankruptcy judge and the decision was not reversed on appeal, the creditor was forever barred from further action against the bankrupt. As pointed out above, all of these matters could and usually did involve state law issues. Initial adjudication of state law issues by non–Article III judges is, then, hardly a new aspect of the 1978 Act.

Furthermore, I take it that the Court does not condemn as inconsistent with Article III the assignment of these functions—i.e., those within the summary jurisdiction of the old bankruptcy courts—to a non–Article III judge, since, as the plurality says, they lie at the core of the federal bankruptcy power. *Ante,* at 21. They also happen

---

[5] "The judicial act of allowance is one, of course, that is performed by the referee where the proceedings have been generally referred." 3 Collier on Bankruptcy 229 n. 3 (14th ed. 1977).

to be functions that have been performed by referees or bankruptcy judges for a very long time and without constitutional objection. Indeed, we approved the authority of the referee to allow or disallow claims in *Katchen v. Landy,* 382 U.S. 323 (1966). There, the referee held that a creditor had received a preference and that his claim could therefore not be allowed. We agreed that the referee had the authority not only to adjudicate the existence of the preference, but also to order that the preference be disgorged. We also recognized that the referee could adjudicate counterclaims against a creditor who files his claim against the estate. The 1973 Bankruptcy Rules make similar provision. *See* Rule 306(c), Rule 701, and Advisory Committee Note to Rule 701. Hence, if Marathon had filed a claim against the bankrupt in this case, the trustee could have filed and the bankruptcy judge could have adjudicated a counterclaim seeking the relief that is involved in this case.

Of course, all such adjudications by a bankruptcy judge or referee were subject to review in the District Court, on the record. *See* 11 U.S.C. § 67(c) (1976). Bankruptcy Rule 810, transmitted to Congress by this Court, provided that the District Court "shall accept the referee's findings of fact unless they are clearly erroneous." As the plurality recognizes, *ante,* at 4, the 1978 Act provides for appellate review in Article III courts and presumably under the same "clearly erroneous standard." In other words, under both the old and new act, initial determinations of state law questions were to be made by non–Article III judges, subject to review by Article III judges. Why the differences in the provisions for appeal in the two Acts are of unconstitutional dimension remains entirely unclear.

In theory and fact, therefore, I can find no basis for that part of the majority's argument that rests on the state–law character of the claim involved here. Even if prior to 1978, the referee could not generally participate in cases aimed at collecting the assets of a bankrupt estate, he nevertheless repeatedly adjudicated issues controlled by state law. There is very little reason to strike down § 241(a) on its face on the ground that it extends, in a comparatively minimal way, the referee's authority to deal with state law questions. To do so is to lose all sense of proportion.

II.

The plurality unpersuasively attempts to bolster its case for facial invalidity by asserting that the bankruptcy courts are now "exercising powers far greater than those lodged in the adjuncts approved in either *Crowell* or *Raddatz.*" *Ante,* at 35. In support of this proposition it makes five arguments in addition to the "state–law" issue. Preliminarily, I see no basis for according standing to Marathon to raise any of these additional points. The state–law objection applies to the Marathon case. Only that objection should now be adjudicated.[6]

I also believe that the major premise of the plurality's argument is wholly unsupported: There is no explanation of why *Crowell* and *Raddatz* define the outer limits of constitutional authority. Much more relevant to today's decision are first, the practice in bankruptcy prior to 1978, which neither the majority nor any authoritative case has questioned, and second, the practice of today's administrative

---

[6] On this point I am in agreement with the concurring Justices.

agencies. Considered from this perspective, all of the plurality's arguments are unsupportable abstractions, divorced from the realities of modern practice.

The first three arguments offered by the plurality, *ante,* at 34–35, focus on the narrowly defined task and authority of the agency considered in *Crowell:* The agency made only "specialized, narrowly confined factual determinations" and could issue only a narrow class of orders. Regardless of whether this was true of the Compensation Board at issue in Crowell, it certainly was not true of the old bankruptcy courts, nor does it even vaguely resemble current administrative practice. As I have already said, general references to bankruptcy judges, which was the usual practice prior to 1978, permitted bankruptcy judges to perform almost all of the functions of a bankruptcy court. Referees or bankruptcy judges not only exercised summary jurisdiction but could also conduct adversary proceedings to:

> (1) recover money or property. (2) determine the validity, priority, or extent of a lien or other interest in property, (3) sell property free of a lien or other interest for which the holder can be compelled to make a money satisfaction, (4) object to or revoke a discharge, (5) obtain an injunction, (6) obtain relief from a stay (7) determine the dischargeability of a debt.

Bankruptcy Rule 701. Although there were some exceptions to the referee's authority, which have been removed by the 1978 Act, the additions to the jurisdiction of the bankruptcy judges were of marginal significance when examined in the light of the overall functions of those judges before and after 1978. In my view, those changes are not sufficient to work a qualitative change in the character of the bankruptcy judge.

The plurality's fourth argument fails to point to any difference between the new and old bankruptcy acts. While the administrative orders in *Crowell* may have been set aside by a court if "not supported by the evidence," under both the new and old acts at issue here, orders of the bankruptcy judge are reviewed under the "clearly erroneous standard." *See* Bankruptcy Rule 810. Indeed, judicial review of the orders of bankruptcy judges is more stringent than that of many modern administrative agencies. Generally courts are not free to set aside the findings of administrative agencies, if supported by substantial evidence. But more importantly, courts are also admonished to give substantial deference to the agency's interpretation of the statute it is enforcing. No such deference is required with respect to decisions on the law made by bankruptcy judges.

Finally, the plurality suggests that, unlike the agency considered in *Crowell*, the orders of a post–1978 bankruptcy judge are final and binding even though not appealed. Ante, at 35. To attribute any constitutional significance to this, unless the plurality intends to throw into question a large body of administrative law, is strange. More directly, this simply does not represent any change in bankruptcy practice. It was hornbook law prior to 1978 that the authorized judgments and orders of referees, including turnover orders, were final and binding and res judicata unless appealed and overturned:

> The practice before the referee should not differ from that before the judge of the court of bankruptcy and, apart from direct review within the limitation of

§ 39(c), the orders of the referee are entitled to the same presumption of validity, conclusiveness and recognition in the court of bankruptcy or other courts.

1 Collier on Bankruptcy 65 (14th ed. 1976).

Even if there are specific powers now vested in bankruptcy judges that should be performed by Article III judges, the great bulk of their functions are unexceptionable and should be left intact. Whatever is invalid should be declared to be such; the rest of the 1978 Act should be left alone. I can account for the majority's inexplicably heavy hand in this case only by assuming that the Court has once again lost its conceptual bearings when confronted with the difficult problem of the nature and role of Article I courts. To that question I now turn.

III.

A.

The plurality contends that the precedents upholding Article I courts can be reduced to three categories. First, there are territorial courts, which need not satisfy Article III constraints because "the Framers intended that as to certain geographical areas. Congress was to exercise the general powers of government."[7]

Ante, at 13. Second, there are courts martial, which are exempt from Article III limits because of a constitutional grant of power that has been "historically understood as giving the political branches of Government extraordinary control over the precise subject matter at issue." *Ante,* at 15. Finally, there are those legislative courts and administrative agencies that adjudicate cases involving public rights—controversies between the government and private parties—which are not covered by Article III because the controversy could have been resolved by the executive alone without judicial review. *See ante,* at 17. Despite the plurality's attempt to cabin the domain of Article I courts, it is quite unrealistic to consider these to be only three "narrow," *ante,* at 13, limitations on or exceptions to the reach of Article III. In fact, the plurality itself breaks the mold in its discussion of "adjuncts" in Part IV, when it announces that "when Congress creates a substantive federal" right, it possesses substantial discretion to prescribe the manner in which that right may be adjudicated." Ante, at 30. Adjudications of federal rights may, according to the plurality, be committed to administrative agencies, as long as provision is made for judicial review.

The first principle introduced by the plurality is geographical: Article I courts presumably are not permitted within the states.[8]

---

[7] The majority does not explain why the constitutional grant of power over the territories to Congress is sufficient to overcome the strictures of Article III, but presumably not sufficient to overcome the strictures of the Presentment Clause or other executive limits on congressional authority.

[8] Had the plurality cited only the territorial courts, the principle relied on perhaps could have been the fact that power over the territories is provided Congress in Article IV. However, Congress' power over the District of Columbia is an Article I power. As such, it does not seem to have any greater status than any of the other powers enumerated in Art. I, § 8.

The problem, of course, is that both of the other exceptions recognize that Article I courts can indeed operate within the States. The second category relies upon a new principle: Article I courts are permissible in areas in which the Constitution grants Congress "extraordinary control over the precise subject matter." *Ante,* at 15. Preliminarily, I do not know how we are to distinguish those areas in which Congress' control is "extraordinary" from those in which it is not. Congress' power over the armed forces is established in Art. I, § 8, cls. 13, 14. There is nothing in those clauses that creates congressional authority different in kind from the authority granted to legislate with respect to bankruptcy. But more importantly, in its third category, and in its treatment of "adjuncts", the plurality itself recognizes that Congress can create Article I courts in virtually all the areas in which Congress is authorized to act, regardless of the quality of the constitutional grant of authority. At the same time, territorial courts or the courts of the District of Columbia, which are Article I courts, adjudicate private, just as much as public or federal, rights.

Instead of telling us what it is Article I courts can and cannot do, the plurality presents us with a list of Article I courts. When we try to distinguish those courts from their Article III counterparts, we find—apart from the obvious lack of Article III judges—a series of non–distinctions. By the plurality's own admission, Article I courts can operate throughout the country, they can adjudicate both private and public rights, and they can adjudicate matters arising from congressional actions in those areas in which congressional control is "extraordinary." I cannot distinguish this last category from the general "arising under" jurisdiction of Article III courts.

The plurality opinion has the appearance of limiting Article I courts only because it fails to add together the sum of its parts. Rather than limiting each other, the principles relied upon complement each other; together they cover virtually the whole domain of possible areas of adjudication. Without a unifying principle, the plurality's argument reduces to the proposition that because bankruptcy courts are not sufficiently like any of these three exceptions, they may not be either Article I courts or adjuncts to Article III courts. But we need to know why bankruptcy courts can not qualify as Article I courts in their own right.

B.

The plurality opinion is not the first unsuccessful attempt to articulate a principled ground by which to distinguish Article I from Article III courts. The concept of a legislative, or Article I, court was introduced by an opinion authored by Chief Justice Marshall. Not only did he create the concept, but at the same time he started the theoretical controversy that has ever since surrounded the concept:

The Judges of the Superior Courts of Florida hold their offices for four years. These Courts, then, are not constitutional Courts, in which the judicial power conferred by the Constitution on the general government, can be deposited. They are incapable of receiving it. They are legislative Courts, created in virtue of the general right of sovereignty which exists in the government, or in virtue of that clause which enables Congress to make all needful rules and regulations, respecting the territory belonging to the United States. The jurisdiction with which they are invested is not a part of that judicial power which is defined in the 3d article of the

Constitution, but is conferred by Congress, in the execution of those general powers which that body possesses over the territories of the United States.

Note: "Materials and Preparations" instructions are grouped by exercise. Some materials may be used in more than one exercise. *American Insurance Co. v. Canter,* 1 Pet. 511, 546 (1828). The proposition was simple enough: Constitutional courts exercise the judicial power described in Article III of the Constitution; legislative courts do not and cannot.

There were only two problems with this proposition. First, *Canter* itself involved a case in admiralty jurisdiction, which is specifically included within the "judicial power of the United States" delineated in Article III. How, then, could the territorial court not be exercising Article III judicial power? Second, and no less troubling, if the territorial courts could not exercise Article III power, how could their decisions be subject to appellate review in Article III courts, including this one, that can exercise only Article III "judicial" power? Yet from early on this Court has exercised such appellate jurisdiction. *Benner v. Porter,* 9 How. 235, 243 (1850); *Clinton v. Englebrecht,* 13 Wall. 434 (1872); *Reynolds v. United States,* 98 U.S 145, 154 (1878); *United States v. Coe,* 155 U.S. 76, 86 (1894); *Balzac v. Porto Rico,* 258 U.S. 298, 312–313 (1922). The attempt to understand the seemingly unexplainable was bound to generate "confusion and controversy." This analytic framework, however—the search for a principled distinction—has continued to burden the Court.

The first major elaboration on the Canter principle was in *Murray's Lessee v. Hoboken Land & Improvement Co.,* 18 How. 272 (1856). The plaintiff in that case argued that a proceeding against a customs collector for the collection of moneys claimed to be due to the United States was an exercise of "judicial power" and therefore had to be carried out by Article III judges. The Court accepted this premise: "It must be admitted that, if the auditing of this account, and the ascertainment of its balance, and the issuing of this process, was an exercise of the judicial power of the United States, the proceeding was void; for the officers who performed these acts could exercise no part of that judicial power." *Id.,* at 275. Having accepted this premise, the Court went on to delineate those matters which could be determined only by an Article III court, i.e., those matters that fall within the nondelegable "judicial power" of the United States. The Court's response to this was twofold. First, it suggested that there are certain matters which are inherently "judicial": "[W]e do not consider congress can either withdraw from judicial cognizance any matter which, from its nature, is the subject of a suit at the common law, or in equity, or admiralty." *Id.,* at 284. Second, it suggested that there is another class of issues that, depending upon the form in which Congress structures the decision making process, may or may not fall within "the cognizance of the courts of the United States." *Ibid.* This latter category consisted of the so–called "public rights." Apparently, the idea was that Congress was free to structure the adjudication of "public rights" without regard to Article III.

Having accepted the plaintiff's premise, it is hard to see how the Court could have taken too seriously its first contention. The Court presented no examples of such issues that are judicial "by nature" and simply failed to acknowledge that Article

I courts already sanctioned by the Court—e.g., territorial courts—were deciding such issues all the time. The second point, however, contains implicitly a critical insight; one that if openly acknowledged would have undermined the entire structure. That insight follows from the Court's earlier recognition that the term "judicial act" is broad enough to encompass all administrative action involving inquiry into facts and the application of law to those facts. *Id.,* at 280. If administrative action can be characterized as "judicial" in nature, then obviously the Court's subsequent attempt to distinguish administrative from judicial action on the basis of the manner in which Congress structures the decision cannot succeed. There need be no Article III court involvement in any adjudication of a "public right", which the majority now interprets as any civil matter arising between the Federal Government and a citizen. In that area, whether an issue is to be decided by an Article III court depends, finally, on congressional intent.

Although *Murray's Lessee* implicitly undermined Chief Justice Marshall's suggestion that there is a difference in kind between the work of Article I and that of Article III courts, it did not contend that the Court must always defer to congressional desire in this regard. The Court considered the plaintiff's contention that removal of the issue from an Article III court must be justified by "necessity." Although not entirely clear, the Court seems to have accepted this proposition: "[I]t seems to us that the just inference from the entire law is, that there was such a necessity for the warrant." *Id.,* at 285.[9]

The Court in *Murray's Lessee* was precisely right: Whether an issue can be decided by a non–Article III court does not depend upon the judicial or nonjudicial character of the issue, but on the will of Congress and the reasons Congress offers for not using an Article III court. This insight, however, was completely disavowed in the next major case to consider the distinction between Article I and Article III courts, *Ex Parte Bakelite Corp.,* 279 U.S. 438 (1929), in which the Court concluded that the Court of Customs Appeals was a legislative court. The Court there directly embraced the principle also articulated in *Murray's Lessee* that Article I courts may not consider any matter "which inherently or necessarily requires judicial determination," but only such matters as are "susceptible of legislative or executive determination." 279 U.S., at 453. It then went on effectively to bury the critical insight of Murray's Lessee, labelling as "fallacious" any argument that "assumes that whether a court is of one class or the other depends on the intention of Congress, whereas the true test lies in the power under which the court was created and in the jurisdiction conferred." *Id.,* at 459.[10]

---

[9] By stating that "of this necessity congress alone is the judge," 18 How., at 285, the Court added some serious ambiguity to the standard it applied. Because this statement ends the Court's analysis of the merits of the claim, it does not seem to mean that the Court will simply defer to congressional judgment. Rather, it appears to mean that the Court will review the legislative record to determine whether there appeared to Congress to be compelling reasons for not establishing an Article III court.

[10] The Court did not, however, entirely follow this principle, for it stated elsewhere that "there is propriety in mentioning the fact that Congress always has treated [the Court of Claims as an Article I court]." 279 U.S., at 454.

The distinction between public and private rights as the principle delineating the proper domains of legislative and constitutional courts respectively received its death blow, I had believed, in *Crowell v. Benson,* 285 U.S. 22 (1932). In that case, the Court approved an administrative scheme for the determination, in the first instance, of maritime employee compensation claims. Although acknowledging the framework set out in *Murray's Lessee* and *Ex Parte Bakelite,* the Court specifically distinguished this case: "The present case does not fall within the categories just described but is one of private right, that is, of the liability of one individual to another under the law as defined."[11] *Id.,* at 51. Nevertheless, the Court approved of the use of an Article I adjudication mechanism on the new theory that "there is no requirement that, in order to maintain the essential attributes of the judicial power, all determinations of fact in constitutional courts shall be made by judges." *Ibid.* Article I courts could deal not only with public rights, but also, to an extent, with private rights. The Court now established a distinction between questions of fact and law: "The reservation of full authority to the court to deal with matters of law provides for the appropriate exercise of the judicial function in this class of cases."[12] *Id.,* at 54.

Whatever sense *Crowell* may have seemed to give to this subject was exceedingly shortlived. One year later, the Court returned to this subject, abandoning both the public/private and the fact/law distinction and replacing both with a simple literalism. In *O'Donoghue v. United States,* 289 U.S. 516 (1933), considering the courts of the District of Columbia, and in *Williams v. United States,* 289 U.S. 553 (1933), considering the Court of Claims, the Court adopted the principle that if a federal court exercises jurisdiction over cases of the type listed in Art. III, § 2 as falling within the "judicial power of the United States," then that court must be an Article III court:

> The provision of this section of the article is that the "judicial power shall extend" to the cases enumerated, and it logically follows that where jurisdiction over these cases is conferred upon the courts of the District, the judicial power, since they are capable of receiving it, is ipso facto, vested in such courts as inferior courts of the United States. *O'Donoghue, supra,* at 545.[13]

In order to apply this same principle and yet hold the Court of Claims to be a legislative court, the Court found it necessary in *Williams, supra,* to conclude that

[11] The plurality is clearly wrong in citing *Crowell* in support of the proposition that matters involving private, as opposed to public, rights may not be considered in a non–Article III court. *Ante,* at 19.

[12] *Crowell* also suggests that certain facts—constitutional or jurisdictional—must also be subject to *de novo* review in an Article III court. I agree with the plurality that this aspect of *Crowell* has been "undermined by later cases," *ante,* at 32 n. 34. As a matter of historical interest, however, I would contend that *Crowell's* holding with respect to these "facts" turned more on the questions of law that were inseparably tied to them, than on some notion of the inadequacy of a non–Article III factfinder.

[13] *O'Donoghue* does not apply this principle wholly consistently: It still recognizes a territorial court exception to Article III's requirements. It now bases this exception, however, not on any theoretical difference in principle, but simply on the "transitory character of the territorial governments." 289 U.S., at 536.

the phrase "controversies to which the United States shall be a party" in Article III must be read as if it said "controversies to which the United States shall be a party plaintiff or petitioner."[14]

By the time of the *Williams* decision, this area of the law was mystifying to say the least. What followed helped very little, if at all. In the next two major cases the Court could not agree internally on a majority position. In *National Insurance Co. v. Tidewater Co.*, 337 U.S. 582 (1949), the Court upheld a statute giving federal district courts jurisdiction over suits between citizens of the District of Columbia and citizens of a State. A majority of the Court, however, rejected the plurality position that Congress had the authority to assign Article I powers to Article III courts, at least outside of the District of Columbia. Only Chief Justice Vinson in dissent reflected on the other side of this problem: whether Article I courts could be assigned Article III powers. He entirely disagreed with the conceptual basis for *Williams* and *O'Donoghue*, noting that to the extent that Article I courts consider non–Article III matters, appellate review by an Article III court would be precluded. Or conversely, since appellate review is exercised by this Court over Article I courts, Article I courts must "exercise federal question jurisdiction." *Id.*, at 643. Having gone this far, the Chief Justice was confronted with the obvious question of whether in fact "the distinction between constitutional and legislative courts is meaningless." *Id.*, at 644. Although suggesting that outside of the territories or the District of Columbia there may be some limits on assignment to Article I courts of matters that fall within Article III jurisdiction—apart from federal question jurisdiction—for the most part the Chief Justice ends up relying on the good will of Congress: "[W]e cannot impute to Congress an intent now or in the future to transfer jurisdiction from constitutional to legislative courts for the purpose of emasculating the former." *Ibid.*

Another chapter in this somewhat dense history of a constitutional quandary was provided by Justice Harlan's plurality opinion in *Glidden Company v. Zdanok*, 370 U.S. 530 (1962), in which the Court, despite *Bakelite* and *Williams*—and relying on an Act of Congress enacted since those decisions—held the Court of Claims and the Court of Customs and Patent Appeals to be Article III courts. Justice Harlan continued the process of intellectual repudiation begun by Chief Justice Vinson in *Tidewater*. First, it was clear to him that Chief Justice Marshall could not have meant what he said in Cantor on the inability of Article I courts to consider issues within the jurisdiction of Article III courts: "Far from being 'incapable of receiving" federal–question jurisdiction, the territorial courts have long exercised a jurisdiction commensurate in this regard with that of the regular federal courts and have been subjected to the appellate jurisdiction of this Court precisely because they do so." *Id.*, at 545 n. 13. Second, exceptions to the requirements of Article III, he thought, have not been founded on any principled distinction between Article I issues and Article III issues; rather, a "confluence of practical considerations," *Id.*, at 547, account for this Court's sanctioning of Article I courts:

> The touchstone of decision in all these cases has been the need to exercise the jurisdiction then and there and for a transitory period. Whether constitutional

---

[14] *See* Hart & Wechsler, The Federal Courts and The Federal System 399 (reviewing the problems of the *Williams* case and characterizing it as an "intellectual disaster").

limitations on the exercise of judicial power have been held inapplicable has depended on the particular local setting, the practical necessities, and the possible alternatives.

Id., at 547–548. Finally, recognizing that there is frequently no way to distinguish between Article I and Article III courts on the basis of the work they do, Justice Harlan suggested that the only way to tell them apart is to examine the "establishing legislation" to see if it complies with the requirements of Article III. This, however, comes dangerously close to saying that Article III courts are those with Article III judges; Article I courts are those without such judges. One hundred and fifty years of constitutional history, in other words, had led to a simple tautology.

IV.

The complicated and contradictory history of the issue before us leads me to conclude that Chief Justice Vinson and Justice Harlan reached the correct conclusion: There is no difference in principle between the work that Congress may assign to an Article I court and that which the Constitution assigns to Article III courts. Unless we want to overrule a large number of our precedents upholding a variety of Article I courts—not to speak of those Article I courts that go by the contemporary name of "administrative agencies"—this conclusion is inevitable. It is too late to go back that far; too late to return to the simplicity of the principle pronounced in Article III and defended so vigorously and persuasively by Hamilton in The Federalist Nos. 78–82.

To say that the Court has failed to articulate a principle by which we can test the constitutionality of a putative Article I court, or that there is no such abstract principle, is not to say that this Court must always defer to the legislative decision to create Article I, rather than Article III, courts. Article III is not to be read out of the Constitution; rather, it should be read as expressing one value that must be balanced against competing constitutional values and legislative responsibilities. This Court retains the final word on how that balance is to be struck.

Despite the principled, although largely mistaken, rhetoric expanded by the Court in this area over the years, such a balancing approach stands behind many of the decisions upholding Article I courts. Justice Harlan suggested as much in *Glidden,* although he needlessly limited his consideration to the "temporary" courts that Congress has had to set up on a variety of occasions. In each of these instances, this Court has implicitly concluded that the legislative interest in creating an adjudicative institution of temporary duration outweighed the values furthered by a strict adherence to Article III. Besides the territorial courts approved in *Canter, supra,* these courts have included the Court of Private Land Claims, *United States v. Coe,* 155 U.S. 76 (1894), the Choctaw and Chickasaw Citizenship Court, *Stephens v. Cherokee Nation,* 174 U.S. 445 (1899); and consular courts established in foreign countries, *In re Ross,* 140 U.S. 453 (1891). This same sort of "practical" judgment was voiced, even if not relied upon, in *Crowell, supra,* with respect to the Employees' Compensation Claims Commission, which was not meant to be of limited duration: "[W]e are unable to find any constitutional obstacle to the action of the Congress in availing itself of a method shown by experience to be essential in order to apply its standards to the thousands of cases involved." 285 U.S., at 54. And even in *Murray's Lessee,* there was a discussion of the "necessity" of Congress' adopting an approach that avoided adjudication in an Article III court. 18 How., at 285.

This was precisely the approach taken to this problem in *Palmore v. United States,* 411 U.S. 389 (1973), which, contrary to the suggestion of the majority, did not rest on any theory of territorial or geographical control. Ante, at 24. Rather, it rested on an evaluation of the strength of the legislative interest in pursuing in this manner one of its constitutionally assigned responsibilities—a responsibility not different in kind from numerous other legislative responsibilities. Thus, *Palmore* referred to the wide variety of Article I courts, not just territorial courts. It is in this light that the critical statement of the case must be understood:

> [T]he requirements of Article III, which are applicable where laws of national applicability and affairs of national concern are at stake, must in proper circumstances give way to accommodate plenary grants of power to Congress to legislate with respect to specialized areas having particularized needs and warranting distinctive treatment.

Id., at 407–408.

I do not suggest that the Court should simply look to the strength of the legislative interest and ask itself if that interest is more compelling than the values furthered by Article III. The inquiry should, rather, focus equally on those Article III values and ask whether and to what extent the legislative scheme accommodates them or, conversely, substantially undermines them. The burden on Article III values should then be measured against the values Congress hopes to serve through the use of Article I courts.

To be more concrete: *Crowell, supra,* suggests that the presence of appellate review by an Article III court will go a long way toward insuring a proper separation of powers. Appellate review of the decisions of legislative courts, like appellate review of state court decisions, provides a firm check on the ability of the political institutions of government to ignore or transgress constitutional limits on their own authority. Obviously, therefore, a scheme of Article I courts that provides for appellate review by Article III courts should be substantially less controversial than a legislative attempt entirely to avoid judicial review in a constitutional court.

Similarly, as long as the proposed Article I courts are designed to deal with issues likely to be of little interest to the political branches, there is less reason to fear that such courts represent a dangerous accumulation of power in one of the political branches of government. Chief Justice Vinson suggested as much when he stated that the Court should guard against any congressional attempt "to transfer jurisdiction for the purpose of emasculating" constitutional courts. *National Insurance Co. v. Tidewater Co.,* 337 U.S., at 644.

V.

I believe that the new bankruptcy courts established by the Bankruptcy Reform Act of 1978, 28 U.S. § 1471 (1976 ed., supp. III), satisfy this standard.

First, ample provision is made for appellate review by Article III courts. Appeals may in some circumstances be brought directly to the district courts. 28 U.S.C. § 1334. Decisions of the district courts are further appealable to the court of appeals. § 1293. In other circumstances, appeals go first to a panel of bankruptcy judges, § 1482, and then to the court of appeals. § 1293. In still other circumstances—when the parties agree—appeals may go directly to the court of appeals. In sum, there is in every instance a right of appeal to at least one Article III court. Had Congress decided to assign all bankruptcy matters to the state courts, a power it clearly possesses, no greater review in an Article III court would exist. Although I do not suggest that this analogy means that Congress may establish an Article I court wherever it could have chosen to rely upon the state courts, it does suggest that the critical function of judicial review is being met in a manner that the Constitution suggests is sufficient.

Second, no one seriously argues that the Bankruptcy Reform Act represents an attempt by the political branches of government to aggrandize themselves at the expense of the third branch or an attempt to undermine the authority of constitutional courts in general. Indeed, the congressional perception of a lack of judicial interest in bankruptcy matters was one of the factors that led to the establishment of the bankruptcy courts: Congress feared that this lack of interest would lead to a failure by federal district courts to deal with bankruptcy matters in an expeditious manner. H.R. Rep. No. 95–595, 95th Cong., 1st Sess. 14 (1977). Bankruptcy matters are, for the most part, private adjudications of little political significance. Although some bankruptcies may indeed present politically controversial circumstances or issues, Congress has far more direct ways to involve itself in such matters than through some sort of subtle, or not so subtle, influence on bankruptcy judges. Furthermore, were such circumstances to arise, the Due Process Clause might very well require that the matter be considered by an Article III judge: Bankruptcy proceedings remain, after all, subject to all of the strictures of that constitutional provision.[15]

Finally, I have no doubt that the ends that Congress sought to accomplish by creating a system of non–Article III bankruptcy courts were at least as compelling as the ends found to be satisfactory in *Palmore, supra,* or the ends that have traditionally justified the creation of legislative courts. The stresses placed upon the old bankruptcy system by the tremendous increase in bankruptcy cases were well documented and were clearly a matter to which Congress could respond.[16]

I don't believe it is possible to challenge Congress' further determination that it was necessary to create a specialized court to deal with bankruptcy matters. This was the nearly uniform conclusion of all those that testified before Congress on the

---

[15] *See Crowell v. Benson* 285 U.S. 22, 87 (Brandeis, J., dissenting) ("If there be any controversy to which the judicial power extends that may not be subjected to the conclusive determination of administrative bodies or federal legislative courts, it is not because of any prohibition against the diminution of the jurisdiction of the federal district courts as such, but because, under the circumstances, the constitutional requirement of due process is a requirement of judicial process.")

[16] "During the past 30 years, the number of bankruptcy cases filed annually has increased steadily from 10,000 to over 254,000." H.R. Rep. No. 95–595, at 21.

question of reform of the bankruptcy system, as well as the conclusion of the Commission on Bankruptcy Laws established by Congress in 1970 to explore possible improvements in the system.[17]

The real question is not whether Congress was justified in establishing a specialized bankruptcy court, but rather whether it was justified in failing to create a specialized, Article III bankruptcy court. My own view is that the very fact of extreme specialization may be enough, and certainly has been enough in the past,[18] to justify the creation of a legislative court. Congress may legitimately consider the effect on the federal judiciary of the addition of several hundred specialized judges: We are, on the whole, a body of generalists.[19]

The addition of several hundred specialists may substantially change, whether for good or bad, the character of the federal bench. Moreover, Congress may have desired to maintain some flexibility in its possible future responses to the general problem of bankruptcy. There is no question that the existence of several hundred bankruptcy judges with life–tenure would have severely limited Congress' future options. Furthermore, the number of bankruptcies may fluctuate producing a substantially reduced need for bankruptcy judges. Congress may have thought that, in that event, a bankruptcy specialist should not as a general matter serve as a judge in the countless nonspecialized cases that come before the federal district courts. It would then face the prospect of large numbers of idle federal judges. Finally, Congress may have believed that the change from bankruptcy referees to Article I judges was far less dramatic, and so less disruptive of the existing bankruptcy and constitutional court systems, than would be a change to Article III judges.

For all of these reasons, I would defer to the congressional judgment. Accordingly, I dissent.

NOTE

See King, *The Unmaking of a Bankruptcy Court: Aftermath of Northern Pipeline,* 40 Wash. & Lee L. Rev. 99 (1983).

SALOMON v . KAISER
(In re Kaiser)

United States Court of Appeals, Second Circuit
722 F.2d 1574 (1983)

MESKILL, Circuit Judge:

This is an appeal from a decision of the United States District Court for the Southern District of New York, Werker, J., dated April 11, 1983, 32 B.R. 701,

---

[17] See H.R. Doc. No. 93–137 (Pt1), 93d Cong., 1st Sess. 85–96 (1973).

[18] Consider, for example, the Court of Customs and Patent Appeals considered in *Ex Parte Bakelite, supra,* or the variety of specialized administrative agencies that engage in some form of adjudication.

[19] In 1977, there were approximately 190 full–time and 30 part–time bankruptcy judges throughout the country. H.R. Rep. 95–595, at 9.

affirming a decision by the United States Bankruptcy Court for the Southern District of New York, Lifland, J., dated January 17, 1983.

The bankruptcy judge below denied appellant Gerald Kaiser a discharge in bankruptcy on the grounds that (a) he transferred property with intent to hinder, delay or defraud his existing and future creditors within one year before the filing of the bankruptcy petition in violation of 11 U.S.C. § 727(a)(2)(A) (1982); and (b) he knowingly, willfully and fraudulently made false oaths in his petition and schedules in contravention of 11 U.S.C. § 727(a)(4)(A) (1982). In addition, the judge impressed a constructive trust on Florida property held in the name of appellant Joan Kaiser to avoid unjust enrichment of Gerald Kaiser to the detriment of his creditors.

Appellants challenge these decisions and the jurisdiction of both the bankruptcy court and the district court to hear this dispute. We reject all of appellants' contentions and affirm.

II.

Appellants contend initially that the bankruptcy judge had no jurisdiction to hear the instant dispute and to render a final judgment. They assert that the Supreme Court's decision in *Northern Pipeline Construction Co. v. Marathon Pipe Line Co.,* 458 U.S. 50, 102 S.Ct. 2858, 73 L.Ed.2d 598 (1982) (*Marathon*), invalidated the bankruptcy jurisdiction of both the bankruptcy courts and the district courts granted in 28 U.S.C. § 1471 (Supp. IV 1980). They claim that even if the Court did not strike down the jurisdictional grant to the district courts, those courts could not enact Emergency Bankruptcy Rule I (Rule) to "revive" the bankruptcy courts and empower them to hear bankruptcy disputes and related matters. They argue that even if the Rule is valid as a general proposition, a bankruptcy judge cannot constitutionally enter a final judgment. Finally, they claim that even if the bankruptcy judge could enter a final judgment in a traditional bankruptcy matter, the instant case is one involving a "related proceeding" and thus cannot be finally determined by the bankruptcy judge in accordance with both *Marathon* and the Rule. In particular, they contest the bankruptcy judge's jurisdiction to issue a final judgment that imposes a constructive trust upon the Florida property in favor of the trustee in bankruptcy where the debtor was not the record owner of the property. We deal with these contentions individually.

A.

Appellants make the all–too–familiar claim that *Marathon* declared 28 U.S.C. § 1471 unconstitutional *in toto,* leaving the district courts without jurisdiction to hear bankruptcy matters. 28 U.S.C. § 1471 provides in pertinent part:

(a) Except as provided in subsection (b) of this section, the district courts shall have original and exclusive jurisdiction of all cases under title 11.

(b) Notwithstanding any Act of Congress that confers exclusive jurisdiction on a court or courts other than the district courts, the district courts shall have original but not exclusive jurisdiction of all civil proceedings arising under title 11 or arising in or related to cases under title 11.

(c) The bankruptcy court for the district in which a case under title 11 is commenced shall exercise all of the jurisdiction conferred by this section on the district courts. Marathon in no way involved the jurisdiction of the district courts. The issue in the case was whether Congress could constitutionally invest the bankruptcy courts, as non–Article III courts, with the power to hear a case involving a state law claim extraneous to the bankruptcy action and to issue a final judgment therein. The plurality found that Congress could not constitutionally grant the bankruptcy court jurisdiction over the state law claim. Because the plurality could not conclude that Congress would have been willing to retain the jurisdictional grant only for some of the claims in section 1471 if the remainder of the jurisdictional grant was found unconstitutional, it simply struck down on separability grounds the entire grant of jurisdiction over bankruptcy matters to the bankruptcy court.

The plurality thus noted in *Marathon* that "the broad grant of jurisdiction to the bankruptcy courts contained in 28 U.S.C. § 1471 is unconstitutional." 458 U.S. at 87, 102 S.Ct. at 2880. It did not declare that the district courts had no jurisdiction in bankruptcy matters. Appellants cite language from the following passage to support their proposition that no federal court has bankruptcy jurisdiction:

It is clear that, at the least, the new bankruptcy judges cannot constitutionally be vested with jurisdiction to decide this state–law contract claim against Marathon. As part of a comprehensive restructuring of the bankruptcy laws, Congress has vested jurisdiction over this and all matters related to cases under title 11 in a single non–Art. III court, and has done so pursuant to a single statutory grant of jurisdiction. In these circumstances we cannot conclude that if Congress were aware that the grant of jurisdiction could not constitutionally encompass this and similar claims, it would simply remove the jurisdiction of the bankruptcy court over these matters, leaving the jurisdictional provision and adjudicatory structure intact with respect to other types of claims, and thus subject to Art. III constitutional challenge on a claim–by–claim basis. Indeed, we note that one of the express purposes of the Act was to ensure adjudication of all claims in a single forum and to avoid the delay and expense of jurisdictional disputes . Nor can we assume, as The Chief Justice suggests, that Congress' choice would be to have this case "routed to the United States district court of which the bankruptcy court is an adjunct." We think that it is for Congress to determine the proper manner of restructuring the Bankruptcy Act of 1978 to conform to the requirements of Art. III, in the way that will best effectuate the legislative purpose.

458 U.S. at 87–88 n. 40, 102 S.Ct. at 2880–2881 n. 40 (citations omitted). But this language only refers to the question of whether the unconstitutional grant of authority to the bankruptcy courts can be severed from the remainder of the jurisdictional grant. It does not refer to the constitutionality of district court jurisdiction either explicitly or implicitly.

Justice Rehnquist's concurrence and Chief Justice Burger's dissent, *See* note 2 infra, also focused solely on the jurisdiction of the bankruptcy courts. Justice Rehnquist, joined by Justice O'Connor, agreed with the plurality that the unconstitutional part of the grant of jurisdiction to the bankruptcy courts could not be separated from the constitutional part:

> I would hold so much of the Bankruptcy Act of 1978 as enables a Bankruptcy Court to entertain and decide Northern's lawsuit over Marathon's objection to be violative of Art. III of the United States Constitution. Because I agree with the plurality that this grant of authority is not readily severable from the remaining grant of authority *to Bankruptcy Courts under* § 1471, *See* n. 40, I concur in the judgment.

458 U.S. at 91–92, 102 S.Ct. at 2881–2882 (emphasis added). Justice Rehnquist's concurrence did not question district court jurisdiction. Similarly, Chief Justice Burger's dissent stated explicitly that the plurality's holding was limited to the breadth of the jurisdictional grant to the bankruptcy courts. Id. at 92, 102 S.Ct. at 2882 (Burger, C.J., dissenting). It also stated that neither the bankruptcy courts nor their adjudication of most bankruptcy claims was unconstitutional and it did not attack the jurisdiction of the district courts at all.

It is thus clear that the Court invalidated only the section 1471(c) jurisdictional grant to the bankruptcy courts and not the jurisdictional grant to the district courts under section 1471(a) and (b). "The difficulty was *not* in separating § 1471(c) from § 1471(a) and (b), but in separating jurisdiction over 'this case," *i.e.* a case like *Marathon,* requiring an Art. III court, from the other appropriate jurisdiction of the bankruptcy court over non–Art. III matters, all of which were combined in the words 'all of the jurisdiction" in 28 U.S.C. § 1471(c)." *In re Braniff Airways, Inc.,* 27 B.R. 231, 234 (N.D. Tex.), *aff'd,* 700 F.2d 214 (5th Cir.), *cert. denied,* — U.S. —, 103 S.Ct. 2122, 77 L.Ed.2d 1302 (1983). Other courts agree that the Supreme Court did not invalidate the jurisdictional grant to the district courts. *E.g., White Motor Corp. v. Citibank, N.A.,* 704 F.2d 254, 259–60 (6th Cir. 1983); *In re Hansen,* 702 F.2d 728, 729 (8th Cir.1983); *In re Q1 Corp.,* 28 B.R. 647, 652 (E.D.N.Y.1983). *But see Rhodes v. Stewart,* 705 F.2d 159, 160 (6th Cir.1983) (section 1471 declared unconstitutional in toto in Marathon) (dicta).

Thus, section 1471(a) and (b) still explicitly vests jurisdiction in the district courts in "all cases under title 11" and "all civil proceedings arising under title 11 or arising in or related to cases under title 11." In addition, *Marathon* did not invalidate 28 U.S.C. § 1334 (1976) (old section 1334), which provides that "[t]he district courts shall have original jurisdiction, exclusive of the courts of the States, of all matters and proceedings in bankruptcy." This provision is effective until April 1, 1984 when the new system for bankruptcy adjudication was to have permanently taken effect. Therefore, we conclude that the district courts retain broad original jurisdiction to entertain bankruptcy and related cases, under both section 1471(a) and (b) and old section 1334. See In re Boileau, 30 B.R. 795, 796 (S.D. Cal.1983); *In re Lear Colorprint,* 29 B.R. 438, 440–41 (N.D. Ill.1983).

B.

Appellants contend that even if the district courts retain jurisdiction over bankruptcy matters, they cannot constitutionally delegate this power to the bankruptcy judges by creating rules for bankruptcy adjudication. They therefore challenge the promulgation of Emergency Bankruptcy Rule I.

The Rule, relating to the powers of bankruptcy judges and district court review of judgments and proposals of bankruptcy judges, was recommended to the judicial districts of the Second Circuit by the Judicial Council by memorandum dated October 21, 1982[1] because of the Supreme Court's refusal to stay the effective date of *Marathon* beyond December 24, 1982. The Board of Judges for the United States District Court for the Southern District of New York adopted the Rule on December 21, 1982.

The district court's promulgation of the Rule is not inherently suspect. The Supreme Court has authorized the district courts to promulgate bankruptcy rules and regulations: Circuit councils which have authorized bankruptcy appellate panels pursuant to 28 U.S.C. § 160 and the district courts in districts in which an appellate panel has not been authorized may by action of a majority of the judges of the council or district court make and amend rules governing practice and procedure for appeals from the bankruptcy courts to the respective bankruptcy appellate panel or district court, not inconsistent with the rules of this Part VIII . In all cases not provided for by rule, the district court or the bankruptcy appellate panel may regulate its practice in any manner not inconsistent with these rules.

Bkrtcy. R. 8018, 51 U.S.L.W. 4484–85 (U.S. Apr. 25, 1983).

This provision was part of proposed bankruptcy rules the Supreme Court transmitted to Congress pursuant to 28 U.S.C. § 2075 (Supp. V 1981) in April 1983. With one exception not relevant here Congress did not act upon them and they became effective on August 1,1983. *See* Bkrtcy. R. 927, 411 U.S. 1103, 93 S.Ct. 3173, 37 L.Ed.2d lxxx (1973) (no longer in force, but identical in substance). These bankruptcy rules can be presumed to be constitutional. *See Hanna v. Plumer,* 380 U.S. 460, 85 S.Ct. 1136, 14 L.Ed.2d 8 (1965) (Federal Rules of Civil Procedure). Also, it is unlikely that the Supreme Court would promulgate procedural bankruptcy rules for the bankruptcy courts and the district courts in 1983 if its 1982 decision in Marathon invalidated the jurisdiction of both the bankruptcy courts and the district courts.

Furthermore, promulgation of the Rule is within the district courts' power pursuant to 28 U.S.C. § 2071 (1976), which provides that the district courts "may from time to time prescribe rules for the conduct of their business." *See* also Fed.R.Civ.P. 83. The district courts have used their rulemaking power not to create bankruptcy courts but to use the structure for bankruptcy adjudication left intact by Marathon and to sustain life in the congressionally mandated bankruptcy scheme. *See In re Herrera,* 29 B.R. 49, 50–51 (D. Colo.1983); *In re Braniff Airways, Inc.,* 27 B.R. at 235. *But see In re South Portland Shipyard and Marine Railways Corp.,* 32 B.R. 1012 (D.Maine 1983) (Emergency Bankruptcy Rule violates Fed.R.Civ.P. 53); *In re United Grocers Corp.,* 29 B.R. 309, 314 (Bkrtcy. D.N.J. 1983) (only

---

[1] In so doing, the Judicial Council of the Second Circuit was acting pursuant to the power vested in it by 28 U.S.C. §§ 331 and 332(d) (1976 & Supp. V 1981). The parties do not question the power of the Judicial Council to make this recommendation.

Congress may promulgate the Rule); *In re Williamson,* 28 B.R. 276, 281 (Bkrtcy. M.D.Ga.1983) (same).

To support their position that the district courts cannot delegate power to the bankruptcy judges, appellants point to the plurality's statement in Marathon that "[w]e think that it is for Congress to determine the proper manner of restructuring the Bankruptcy Act of 1978 to conform to the requirements of Art. III, in the way that will best effectuate the legislative purpose." 458 U.S. at 88 n. 40, 102 S.Ct. at 2880 n. 40. Certainly any permanent restructuring of the federal bankruptcy jurisdiction is solely a matter for congressional action. It cannot be fairly argued, however, that the Court in Marathon intended to hamstring the district courts in the exercise of their bankruptcy jurisdiction. As we explained earlier, the plurality's statement was made in the context of its refusal to separate the exercise of jurisdiction by the bankruptcy court in Marathon from the general grant of jurisdiction found in section 1471(c). The plurality noted that it could not determine what the congressional response would be to Marathon. As such, the plurality decided to strike down all of section 1471(c), leaving the response up to Congress. At no point did the plurality suggest that the district courts were powerless to sustain proper bankruptcy court jurisdiction until the time that Congress chooses to act.

C.

Having determined that the district courts acted properly by promulgating rules for bankruptcy adjudication, we now turn our attention to the validity of the Rule itself.

The Rule is virtually identical to the Sixth Circuit's emergency bankruptcy rule, which has been described as follows:

> First, the bankruptcy judges may not issue binding judgments in "related" proceedings. In these cases, the bankruptcy judges are limited to submitting findings of fact and proposed rulings which must be reviewed de novo by the district court whether or not an appeal has been taken by the parties. *See* Rule (e)(2)(A)(iii)
>
> Second, the interim rule institutes several protective changes in the procedures for the adjudication of all bankruptcy cases, "related" and traditional. The district courts have specific authority to revoke the referral of any case to the bankruptcy court upon the district court's own motion or upon the request of a party for any reason. Thus, the district courts can ensure that the parties receive a just resolution of bankruptcy cases within the limitations established by Art. III.
>
> Third, even in traditional bankruptcy cases, the district courts may hold a hearing and receive evidence in cases first adjudicated by the bankruptcy court. The district court need give no deference to the bankruptcy judge's factual findings or interpretations of the law. The district court may modify, in whole or in part, any order or judgment issued by the bankruptcy judge. *See* Rule (e)(2)(B).

White Motor Corp., 704 F.2d at 263.

Appellants contend that, even assuming the correctness of the determination by the courts below that the instant dispute is not "related," section (d)(2) of the Rule, which permits the bankruptcy judge to render a final judgment in a traditional dispute, is unconstitutional because of *Marathon*. This argument is also without merit.

Marathon only invalidated the jurisdiction of the bankruptcy court to make final determinations in matters that could have been brought in a district court or a state court (*i.e.*, "related proceedings"). *See In re Turner*, 29 B.R. 419, 421–22 (N.D.N.Y.1983). In no way did *Marathon* implicate the jurisdiction of the bankruptcy courts in other matters within the "traditional" bankruptcy jurisdiction. The Court's invalidation of the jurisdictional grant was on separability grounds, not on the grounds that bankruptcy courts could not adjudicate traditional bankruptcy matters.[2]

As the court in White Motor Corp. noted, "[T]he referees under the Chandler Act and the bankruptcy judges after the 1973 Amendments have adjudicated traditional bankruptcy matters without constitutional challenge for over a century." 704 F.2d at 263. *See also In re Color Craft Press, Ltd.*, 27 B.R. 962, 966 (D. Utah 1983) ("[s]uch a device did yeoman service in the bankruptcy field from at least 1898 until 1978 and does yeoman service in other fields as well").

There are also strong policy reasons for allowing bankruptcy judges to enter final judgments in traditional bankruptcy disputes. First, the practice eliminates the need for the district courts to enter every bankruptcy case at the beginning. District courts are thus free to attend to the other matters on their crowded calendars, giving all litigants a better opportunity to have their day in court. Second, all cases are not appealed. There should be at least one adjudication made by a judge with expertise in bankruptcy law. There is no assurance that a better initial determination would be made by a district court.

In addition, the Rule provides for district court review as a safeguard against bankruptcy court abuses. Section (e)(2)(B) of the Rule permits a district court to make a *de novo* review of the bankruptcy judge's findings. Any abuses may be rectified by the district court *without* applying the stringent "clearly erroneous" test.

---

[2] Indeed, the plurality in *Marathon* stated that "the restructuring of debtor–creditor relations, which is at the core of the federal bankruptcy power, may well be a public right" and thus subject to adjudication in an Article I court. 458 U.S. at 71, 102 S.Ct. at 2871. *See also* 458 U.S. at 92, 102 S.Ct. at 2882 (Burger, C.J., dissenting) ("I write separately to emphasize that, notwithstanding the plurality opinion, the Court does not hold today that Congress" broad grant of jurisdiction to the new bankruptcy courts is generally inconsistent with Article III. Rather, the Court's holding is limited to the proposition stated by Justice Rehnquist in his concurrence in the judgment—that a traditional" state common–law action, not made subject to a federal rule of decision, and related only peripherally to an adjudication of bankruptcy under federal law, must, absent consent of the litigants, be heard by an Article III court' if it is to be heard by any court or agency of the United States. This limited holding, of course, does not suggest that there is something inherently unconstitutional about the new bankruptcy courts; nor does it preclude such courts from adjudicating all but a relatively narrow category of claims arising under "or arising in or related to cases under' the Bankruptcy Act.").

See United States v. Raddatz, 447 U.S. 667, 100 S.Ct. 2406, 65 L.Ed.2d 424 (1980). Section (e)(1) of the Rule grants an appeal of the final judgment of the bankruptcy judge as a matter of right.

The disposition of cases by bankruptcy judges is also under the control and supervision of the district courts. Section (c)(2) of the Rule provides that even in a traditional case "[t]he reference to a bankruptcy judge may be withdrawn by the district court at any time on its own motion or on timely motion by a party." Section (d)(2) also permits a district court to stay the final judgment of a bankruptcy judge.

Given the policy considerations supporting the bankruptcy courts' power to issue final judgments in a traditional bankruptcy case, and absent a Supreme Court decision denying that power, we conclude that the Rule is constitutional. *Accord White Motor Corp.,* 704 F.2d at 263–65; *In re Hansen,* 702 F.2d at 729; *In re Braniff Airways, Inc.,* 27 B.R. at 236, *aff'd,* 700 F.2d at 215; *In re Pioneer Ford Sales, Inc.,* 30 B.R. 458, 461 (D. R.I.1983); *In re Lear Colorprint,* 29 B.R. at 441; *In re Color Craft Press, Ltd.,* 27 B.R. at 965–66. *But cf. In re Matlock Trailer Corp.,* 27 B.R. 318, 328 (M.D. Tenn.1983) (bankruptcy court cannot constitutionally enter a final judgment) (overruled *sub silentio* by *White Motor Corp.*).

D.

Appellant's final claim is that the present case is a "related proceeding." In an attempt to conform to the stricture of *Marathon,* the Rule provides that the bankruptcy judge may not enter a final judgment in a related proceeding. Section (d)(3)(B). Thus, if this case is a related proceeding, the final order of the bankruptcy court is unconstitutional according to *Marathon* and also violates section (d)(3)(B) of the Rule; if it is not, the final order is constitutional and satisfies the requirements of section (d)(2) of the Rule.

Our analysis of whether the instant case presents a related claim must start with appellee's demand for relief. In his first complaint, dated February 22, 1982 and amended on September 23, 1982, the trustee sought to deny the debtor's discharge on the ground that the debtor (a) transferred property with intent to hinder, delay or defraud his creditors within one year prior to the filing of his petition; and (b) knowingly and fraudulently made false oaths. The trustee's second complaint, dated March 31, 1982, sought to impose a constructive trust in favor of the trustee on real property held by the debtor's wife because of the debtor's fraudulent transfers concerning the property and to avoid fraudulent transfers made by the debtor.

Appellants argue that the trustee could have brought an action to impose a constructive trust in state court. Therefore, under section (d)(3)(A) of the Rule, which defines a related proceeding as one that "could have been brought in a district court or state court," the instant dispute is a related proceeding. Section (d)(3)(A) of the Rule states in full, however, that: Related proceedings are those civil proceedings that, in the absence of a petition in bankruptcy, could have been brought in a district court or state court. Related proceedings include, but are not limited to, claims brought by the estate against parties who have not filed claims against the estate. Related proceedings do not include: orders to turn over property of the estate; proceedings to set aside preferences and fraudulent conveyances; proceedings to object to the discharge. A proceeding is not a related proceeding merely because the outcome will be affected by state law.

The Rule thus explicitly states that an action to impose a constructive trust is not a related proceeding, although an action to impose a constructive trust, viewed by itself, is one that could be brought in a state court. It is certainly true that state courts commonly impose constructive trusts. What appellant ignores, however, is that this action was brought as a result of his fraudulent transfers in light of the bankruptcy laws. This action is inextricably tied to the creation of the estate in bankruptcy for the benefit of Gerald Kaiser's creditors; there would be no cause of action without the federal bankruptcy statutes that authorize it. In other words, federal law provides the *right* upon which the remedy of the constructive trust sought here is based. In contrast, the action in *Marathon* was independent of the bankruptcy laws. There, the debtor, Northern Pipeline Co., would have had an action based on state contract law against Marathon Pipe Line Co. irrespective of whether Northern filed for bankruptcy; that Northern had so filed had no bearing whatsoever on the issues involved or the outcome of the case.

The present action is not a "traditional" action to impose a constructive trust upon real estate. It has no life of its own in either state or federal common law or statute independent of the federal bankruptcy laws. This action is not a related proceeding for the purposes of section (d)(3)(A) of the Rule or for constitutional purposes. *See Moody v. Amoco Oil Co.*, 31 B.R. 224, 225 n. 1 (W.D. Wis.1983) ("the question of whether a proceeding is 'related' or not depends upon whether the party opposing the debtor is a creditor").

> *The judgment of the district court is affirmed.*

NOTES

1. In addition to the Fifth Circuit in the Braniff case cited in the *Hansen* opinion, other circuits upholding the validity of the emergency rule were: *Oklahoma Health Services Federal Credit Union v. Webb*, 726 F.2d 624 (10th Cir. 1984); *In re Hansen* 702 F.2d 728 (8th Cir.), *cert. denied*, — U.S. — , (1983); *White Motor Corp. v. Citibank, N.A.*, 704 F.2d 254 (6th Cir. 1983).

2. The Supreme Court stayed the effect of its judgment in *Northern Pipeline* until October 4, 1982, to give Congress an opportunity to resolve the court problem legislatively. Congress failed to act even though a bill to make the bankruptcy court an Article III court was introduced in the House. The Court extended the stay until December 25, 1982, and again Congress failed to act. It was still politically unpalatable to give the bankruptcy judges Article III status. The emergency rule came into effect on December 25 for the avowed purpose of enabling the bankruptcy courts to function. As indicated in the Statement of the National Bankruptcy Conference in Opposition to Proposed Judicial Conference

Rule, 97th Cong., 2d Sess., 128 Cong. Rec. H9640–H9643 (1982), the validity of the emergency rule was an open question: first, because of a lack of authority in the district court to adopt such a rule and second, because the district court itself had no jurisdiction to exercise in bankruptcy cases (28 U.S.C. § 1471(c)).

Nevertheless, the district courts and the courts of appeals without exception upheld the validity of the emergency rule. Why? *See* the *Kaiser* case, *supra.*

3. Finally, in 1984 Congress passed the Bankruptcy Amendments and Federal Judgeship Act of 1984 which has resolved the jurisdictional issue to date. The issue has not been revisited by the Supreme Court and, while Congress attempted to buttress the constitutionality of the bankruptcy judicial system in various ways, the attempt has not been officially blessed (or condemned) by the Court. It did take Congress from 1982 until 1984 to respond to the *Northern Pipeline* plurality decision.

4. This period of trying to respond to the Supreme Court's decision in *Northern Pipeline* saw a variety of lobbying groups attempting to change the substantive law of bankruptcy for private interest purposes. Many were successful in having amendments attached to S. 1013 and H.R. 5174, such as, the consumer finance industry, farmers who wanted to control insolvencies of grain elevators, fishermen who wanted to control insolvencies of fish storage facilities, landlords who owned shopping centers, and others too numerous to mention. *See* also the *Bildisco* case, *infra,* and § 1113.

5. In reading the Court's opinion, and the dissenting opinion of Justice White, should any form of Article I court be able to withstand constitutional attack?

6. The Magistrate's Act provides that the parties to a dispute may, by express consent, permit the magistrate judge to enter final judgment. All courts of appeal that have ruled on the issue have held it constitutional to permit such jurisdiction by consent. Interestingly, all of these decisions were rendered during the turmoil surrounding the validity of the emergency rule controlling the bankruptcy courts and Congress' attempts to respond to the *Northern Pipeline* case. *See Pacemaker Diagnostic Clinic of America, Inc. v. Instromedix Inc.,* 725 F.2d 537 (9th Cir. 1984) (en banc), *rev'g,* 712 F.2d 1305 (9th Cir. 1983); *Wharton–Thomas v. United States,* 721 F.2d 922 (3d Cir. 1983); *Collins v. Foreman,* 729 F.2d 108 (2d Cir. 1984); *Goldstein v. Kelleher,* 728 F.2d 32 (1st Cir. 1984).

§ 12.03 Procedure Under the 1984 Act

[A] Core and Non–Core Proceedings

The provisions dealing with the bankruptcy judicial system were completely revised in 1984. The key jurisdictional grant is contained in 28 U.S.C. § 1334(a) and (b). In fact, the language of these subsections is exactly the same as the language in former § 1471 of the 1978 Bankruptcy Reform Act. The major difference is found in subsection (c). While it was that subsection in § 1471 that the Supreme Court found objectionable, present § 1334(c) is not a grant of jurisdiction but only deals with matters of abstention.

To follow through the procedure, it is necessary to go from the jurisdictional grant in § 1334(a) and (b), which is to the federal *district courts,* to the *reference* of authority to the bankruptcy judges of the district. The discretion placed in the district court to make the reference is found in 28 U.S.C. § 157(a).

1.   What is the difference between former § 1471(c) which enabled the bankruptcy court to act, and present § 157(a), which enables the bankruptcy court to act? How does the difference impact on the constitutionality issue?

2.   28 U.S.C. § 157(b)(1) permits the bankruptcy court to hear and determine core proceedings. What does "determine" mean? What may be the next step in the judicial process after the bankruptcy court "determines" a proceeding?

3.   Non–core proceedings are provided for in § 157(c)(1) and (2). Under (c)(1), the bankruptcy judge may hear a non–core proceeding but may not determine it. It must submit proposed findings of fact and conclusions of law to the district judge who is to enter a final order. What is a non–core proceeding?

4.   What standard should be used by the district court in deciding whether to enter a final order? What is the difference, if any, between what the district judge does under § 157(c)(1) and what it may do under § 157(b)(1)? Consider the applicability of FRBP 9033.

5.   Core proceedings are listed in § 157(b)(2). This list is not exclusive or exhaustive. As shall be seen, it may not even be wholly accurate. Some preliminary issues follow.

6.   How many catchalls can be found in § 157(b)(2)?

7.   It is not uncommon for a trustee in a chapter 7 case or a debtor in possession in a chapter 11 case to seek to recover accounts receivables that were owing to the debtor prepetition. These are, generally, amounts owing for goods delivered on credit. Quite often, when a petition under the Bankruptcy Code has been filed, these account debtors are slow in paying, hoping that delay will provide some reasons for settling with the estate for less that full price.

(a)   When a lawsuit against the account debtor is necessary, may it be brought in the bankruptcy court? Under what jurisdictional provision?

(b)   If it can be brought in the bankruptcy court, will it be a proceeding under § 157(b) or § 157(c)? May it be considered a turnover proceeding under § 157(b)(2)(E) or may it come under (b)(2)(O)?

(c)   If it is concluded that it is a core proceeding, is § 157 (b)(1) constitutional under *Northern Pipeline*? What is the difference, if any, between the suit to recover an account receivable and a suit to recover damages for breach of contract? If it is not as core proceeding, does the bankruptcy court have jurisdiction to entertain it in the first place?

8.   Does the bankruptcy court have jurisdiction over the following matters and, if so, are they core or non–core proceedings?

(a)   Action against debtor's insurer by father of boy who witnessed crash of debtor's airplane, alleging boy suffered post–traumatic stress disorder: *Coar v. National: Union Fire Ins. Co.*, 19 F.3d 247, 249 (5th Cir. 1994)("related to" jurisdiction).

(b)   Action to enjoin postconfirmation products liability suit even though prior orders retained jurisdiction in bankruptcy court. *Zerand–Bernal Group, Inc. v. Cox*, 23 F.3d 159 (7th Cirt. 1994)(not "related to" jurisdiction).

(c)   Issue of breach of contract when debtor sought to assume contract was non–core. *In re Orion Pictures Corp., infra.*

CELOTEX CORPORATION v. EDWARDS

Supreme Court of the United States
115 S. Ct. 1493, 32 C.B.C. 2d 685 (1995)

Chief Justice REHNQUIST:

The United States Court of Appeals for the Fifth Circuit held that respondents should be allowed to execute against petitioner's surety on a supersedeas bond posted by petitioner where the judgment which occasioned the bond had become final. It so held even though the United States Bankruptcy Court for the Middle District of Florida previously had issued an injunction prohibiting respondents from executing on the bond without the Bankruptcy Court's permission. We hold that respondents were obligated to obey the injunction issued by the Bankruptcy Court.

I.

In 1987 respondents Bennie and Joann Edwards filed suit in the United States District Court for the Northern District of Texas against petitioner Celotex (and others) alleging asbestos–related injuries. In April 1989 the District Court entered a $281,025.80 judgment in favor of respondents and against Celotex. To stay execution of the judgment pending appeal, Celotex posted a supersedeas bond in the amount of $294,987.88, with Northbrook Property and Casualty Insurance Company serving as surety on the bond. As collateral for the bond, Celotex allowed Northbrook to retain money owed to Celotex under a settlement agreement resolving insurance coverage disputes between Northbrook and Celotex.

The United States Court of Appeals for the Fifth Circuit affirmed, issuing its mandate on October 12, 1990, and thus rendering "final" respondents' judgment against Celotex. *Edwards (Edwards I) v. Armstrong World Industries, Inc.*, 911 F.2d 1151 (1990). That same day, Celotex filed a voluntary petition for relief under Chapter 11 of the Bankruptcy Code in the United States Bankruptcy Court for the Middle District of Florida.[1]

---

[1] For purposes of this case, we assume respondents' judgment became final before Celotex filed its petition in bankruptcy.

The filing of the petition automatically stayed both the continuation of "proceeding[s] against" Celotex and the commencement of "any act to obtain possession of property" of Celotex.[2] 11 U.S.C. §§ 362(a)(1) and (3).

On October 17, 1990, the Bankruptcy Court exercised its equitable powers under 11 U.S.C. § 105(a) and issued an injunction (the "Section 105 Injunction") to augment the protection afforded Celotex by the automatic stay. In pertinent part, the Section 105 Injunction stayed all proceedings involving Celotex "regardless of whether the matter is on appeal and a supersedeas bond has been posted by [Celotex]." App. to Pet. for Cert. A–28.[3]

Respondents, whose bonded judgment against Celotex had already been affirmed on appeal, filed a motion pursuant to Federal Rule of Civil Procedures 65.1 in the District Court seeking permission to execute against Northbrook on the supersedeas bond. Both Celotex and Northbrook opposed this motion, asserting that all proceedings to enforce the bonds had been enjoined by the Bankruptcy Court's Section 105 Injunction. Celotex brought to the District Court's attention the fact that, since respondents had filed their Rule 65.1 motion, the Bankruptcy Court had reaffirmed the Section 105 Injunction and made clear that the injunction prohibited judgment creditors like respondents from proceeding against sureties without the Bankruptcy Court's permission:

> "Where at the time of filing the petition, the appellate process between Debtor and the judgment creditor had been concluded, the judgment creditor is precluded from proceeding against any supersedeas bond posted by Debtor without first seeking to vacate the Section 105 stay entered by this Court." *In re Celotex (Celotex I),* 128 B.R. 478, 485 (Bkrtcy. Ct. MD Fla. 1991).

Despite the Bankruptcy Court's reaffirmation and clarification of the Section 105 Injunction, the District Court allowed respondents to execute on the bond against Northbrook.[4]

---

[2] As of the filing date, more than 141,000 asbestos–related bodily injury lawsuits were pending against Celotex, and over 100 asbestos–related bodily injury cases were in some stage of appeal, with judgments totaling nearly $70 million being stayed by supersedeas bonds that Celotex had posted.

[3] The Bankruptcy Court noted that, upon request of a party in interest and following 30 days written notice and a hearing, it would "consider granting relief from the restraints imposed" by the Section 105 Injunction. App. to Pet. for Cert. A–28. Several of Celotex' bonded judgment creditors whose cases were still on appeal filed motions requesting that the Bankruptcy Court lift the Section 105 Injunction (1) to enable their pending appellate actions to proceed and (2) to permit them to execute upon the bonds once the appellate process concluded in their favor. The Bankruptcy Court granted the first request but denied the second. *In re Celotex (Celotex I),* 128 B.R. 478, 484 (Bkrtcy. Ct. MD Fla. 1991).

[4] Two days after the District Court entered its order, the Bankruptcy Court ruled on motions to lift the Section 105 Injunction that had been filed by several bonded judgment creditors who, like respondents, had prevailed against Celotex on appeal. The Bankruptcy Court again reaffirmed the Section 105 Injunction and it again explained that the injunction prohibited judgment creditors like respondents from executing on the supersedeas bonds against third parties without its permission. *In re Celotex (Celotex II),* 140 B.R. 912, 914 (Bkrtcy. Ct. MD Fla. 1992). It refused to lift the Section 105 Injunction at that time, finding that Celotex would

Celotex appealed, and the Fifth Circuit affirmed. *Edwards (Edwards II) v. Armstrong World Industries, Inc.,* 6 F.3d 312 [30 C.B.C.2d 148] (1993). It first held that, because the appellate process for which the supersedeas bond was posted had been completed, Celotex no longer had a property interest in the bond and the automatic stay provisions of 11 U.S.C. § 362 therefore did not prevent respondents from executing against Northbrook. *Edwards II, supra,* at 315–317. The Court then acknowledged that "[t]he jurisdiction of bankruptcy courts has been extended to include stays on proceedings involving third parties under the auspices of 28 U.S.C. § 1334(b)," 6 F.3d at 318, and that the Bankruptcy Court itself had ruled that the Section 105 Injunction enjoined respondents' proceeding against Northbrook to execute on the supersedeas bond. *Ibid.* The Fifth Circuit nevertheless disagreed with the merits of the Bankruptcy Court's Section 105 Injunction, holding that "the integrity of the estate is not implicated in the present case because the debtor has no present or future interest in this supersedeas bond." *Id.,* at 320. The Court reasoned that the Section 105 Injunction was "manifestly unfair" and an "unjust result" because the supersedeas bond was posted "to cover precisely the type of eventuality which occurred in this case, insolvency of the judgment debtor." *Id.* at 319. In concluding that the Section 105 Injunction was improper, the Fifth Circuit expressly disagreed with the reasoning and result of *Willis v. Celotex Corp.,* 978 F.2d 146 (CA4 1992), *cert. denied,* 507 U.S. (1993), where the Court of Appeals for the Fourth Circuit, examining the same Section 105 Injunction, held that the Bankruptcy Court had the power under 11 U.S.C. § 105(a) to stay proceedings against sureties on the supersedeas bonds. 6 F.3d at 320.

Celotex filed a petition for rehearing, arguing that the Fifth Circuit's decision allowed a collateral attack on an order of the Bankruptcy Court sitting under the

suffer irreparable harm. It reasoned that if the judgment creditors were allowed to execute against the sureties on the supersedeas bonds, the sureties would in turn seek to lift the Section 105 Injunction to reach Celotex' collateral under the settlement agreements, possibly destroying any chance of a successful reorganization plan. *See id.* at 914–915.

To protect the bonded judgment creditors, the Bankruptcy Court ordered that: (1) the sureties involved, including Northbrook, establish escrow accounts sufficient to insure full payment of the bonds; (2) Celotex create an interest–bearing reserve account or increase the face amount of any supersedeas bond to cover the full amount of judgment through confirmation; and (3) Celotex provide in any plan that the bonded claimants' claims be paid in full unless otherwise determined by the court or agreed by the claimant. *Id.* at 917. The Bankruptcy Court also directed Celotex to file "any preference action or any fraudulent transfer action or any other action to avoid or subordinate any judgment creditor's claim against any judgment creditor or against any surety on any supersedeas bond within 60 days of the entry" of its order. *Ibid.* Accordingly, Celotex filed an adversary proceeding against respondents, 227 other similarly situated bonded judgment creditors in over 100 cases, and the sureties on the supersedeas bonds, including Northbrook. See Second Amended Complaint in *Celotex Corp. v. Allstate Ins. Co.,* Adversary No. 92–584 (Bkrtcy. Ct. MD Fla.). In that proceeding, Celotex asserts that the bonded judgment creditors should not be able to execute on their bonds because, by virtue of the collateralization of the bonds, the bonded judgment creditors are beneficiaries of Celotex asset transfers that are voidable as preferences and fraudulent transfers. *See ibid.* Celotex also contends that the punitive damages portions of the judgments can be voided or subordinated on other bankruptcy law grounds. *See ibid.* This adversary proceeding is currently pending in the Bankruptcy Court.

jurisdiction of the Court of Appeals for the Eleventh Circuit. The Fifth Circuit denied the petition, stating in part that "we have not held that the bankruptcy court in Florida was necessarily wrong; we have only concluded that the district court, over which we do have appellate jurisdiction, was right." *Id.* at 321. Because of the conflict between the Fifth Circuit's decision in this case and the Fourth Circuit's decision in *Willis,* we granted certiorari. 511 U.S. We now reverse.

II.

Respondents acknowledge that the Bankruptcy Court's Section 105 Injunction prohibited them from attempting to execute against Northbrook on the supersedeas bond posted by Celotex. Brief in Opposition 6, n. 2 (recognizing that the Section 105 Injunction "was intended to, and did, enjoin collection attempts like those made by [respondents] against Northbrook in this case"). In *GTE Sylvania, Inc. v. Consumers Union of United States, Inc.,* 445 U.S. 375, 386 (1980), we reaffirmed the well established rule that "persons subject to an injunctive order issued by a court with jurisdiction are expected to obey that decree until it is modified or reversed, even if they have proper grounds to object to the order." In *GTE Sylvania,* we went on to say:

> "There is no doubt that the Federal District Court in Delaware had jurisdiction to issue the temporary restraining orders and preliminary and permanent injunctions. Nor were those equitable decrees challenged as only a frivolous pretense to validity, although of course there is disagreement over whether the District Court erred in issuing the permanent injunction. Under these circumstances, the CPSC was required to obey the injunctions out of respect for judicial process." *Id.* at 386–387 (internal quotation marks, citations, and footnote omitted).

This rule was applied in the bankruptcy context more than 60 years ago in *Oriel v. Russell,* 278 U.S. 358 (1929), where the Court held that turnover orders issued under the old bankruptcy regime could not be collaterally attacked in a later contempt proceeding. Respondents acknowledge the validity of the rule but contend that it has no application here. They argue that the Bankruptcy Court lacked *jurisdiction* to issue the Section 105 Injunction, though much of their argument goes to the correctness of the Bankruptcy Court's decision to issue the injunction rather than to its jurisdiction to do so.

The jurisdiction of the bankruptcy courts, like that of other federal courts, is grounded in and limited by statute. Title 28 U.S.C. § 1334(b) provides that "the district courts shall have original but not exclusive jurisdiction of all civil proceedings arising under title 11, or arising in or related to cases under title 11." 28 U.S.C. § 1334(b). The district courts may, in turn, refer "any or all proceedings arising under title 11 or arising in or related to a case under title 11 to the bankruptcy judges for the district." 28 U.S.C. § 157(a). Here, the Bankruptcy Court's jurisdiction to enjoin respondents' proceeding against Northbrook must be based on the "arising under," "arising in," or "related to" language of §§ 1334(b) and 157(a).

Respondents argue that the Bankruptcy Court had jurisdiction to issue the Section 105 Injunction only if their proceeding to execute on the bond was "related to" the

Celotex bankruptcy. Petitioner argues the Bankruptcy Court indeed had such "related to" jurisdiction. Congress did not delineate the scope of "related to"[5] jurisdiction, but its choice of words suggests a grant of some breadth. The jurisdictional grant in § 1334(b) was a distinct departure from the jurisdiction conferred under previous acts, which had been limited to either possession of property by the debtor or consent as a basis for jurisdiction. *See* S. Rep. No. 95–989, pp. 153–154 (1978). We agree with the views expressed by the Court of Appeals for the Third Circuit in *Pacor, Inc. v. Higgins,* 743 F.2d 984 (1984), that "Congress intended to grant comprehensive jurisdiction to the bankruptcy courts so that they might deal efficiently and expeditiously with all matters connected with the bankruptcy estate," *id.* at 994; see also H. Rep. No. 95–595, pp. 43–48 (1977), and that the "related to" language of § 1334(b) must be read to give district courts (and bankruptcy courts under § 157(a)) jurisdiction over more than simply proceedings involving the property of the debtor or the estate. We also agree with that Court's observation that a bankruptcy court's "related to" jurisdiction cannot be limitless. See *Pacor, supra,* at 994; cf. *Board of Governors v. MCorp Financial,* 502 U.S. 32, 40 (1991) (stating that Congress has vested "limited authority" in bankruptcy courts).[6]

---

[5] Proceedings "related to" the bankruptcy include (1) causes of action owned by the debtor which become property of the estate pursuant to 11 U.S.C. § 541, and (2) suits between third parties which have an effect on the bankruptcy estate. *See* 1 Collier on Bankruptcy ¶ 3.01[1][c][iv], p. 3–28 (15th ed. 1994). The first type of "related to" proceeding involves a claim like the state law breach of contract action at issue in *Northern Pipeline Constr. Co. v. Marathon Pipe Line Co.,* 458 U.S. 50 [6 C.B.C.2d 785] (1982). The instant case involves the second type of "related to" proceeding.

[6] In attempting to strike an appropriate balance, the Third Circuit in *Pacor, Inc. v. Higgins,* 743 F.2d 984 (1984), devised the following test for determining the existence of "related to" jurisdiction:

"The usual articulation of the test for determining whether a civil proceeding is related to bankruptcy is whether *the outcome of that proceeding could conceivably have any effect on the estate being administered in bankruptcy.* Thus, the proceeding need not necessarily be against the debtor or against the debtor's property. An action is related to bankruptcy if the outcome could alter the debtor's rights, liabilities, options, or freedom of action (either positively or negatively) and which in any way impacts upon the handling and administration of the bankrupt estate." *Id.* at 994 (emphasis in original; citations omitted).

The First, Fourth, Fifth, Sixth, Eighth, Ninth, Tenth and Eleventh Circuits have adopted the *Pacor* test with little or no variation. *See In re G.S.F. Corp.,* 938 F.2d 1467, 1475 [25 C.B.C.2d 112] (CA1 1991); *A.H. Robins Co. v. Piccinin,* 788 F.2d 994, 1002, n. 11 (CA4), *cert. denied,* 479 U.S. 876 (1986); *In re Wood,* 825 F.2d 90, 93 [17 C.B.C.2d 743] (CA5 1987); *Robinson v. Michigan Consol. Gas Co.,* 918 F.2d 579, 583–584 [24 C.B.C.2d 49] (CA6 1990); *In re Dogpatch U.S.A., Inc.,* 810 F.2d 782, 786 (CA8 1987); *In re Fietz,* 852 F.2d 455, 457 (CA9 1988); *In re Gardner,* 913 F.2d 1515, 1518 (CA10 1990); *In re Lemco Gypsum, Inc.,* 910 F.2d 784, 788, and n.19 [23 C.B.C.2d 999] (CA11 1990). The Second and Seventh Circuits, on the other hand, seem to have adopted a slightly different test. *See In re Turner,* 724 F.2d 338, 341 [10 C.B.C.2d 782] (CA2 1983); *In re Xonics, Inc.,* 813 F.2d 127, 131 [17 C.B.C.2d 230] (CA7 1987); *Home Ins. Co. v. Cooper & Cooper, Ltd.,* 889 F.2d 746, 749 (CA7 1989). But whatever test is used, these cases make clear that bankruptcy courts have no jurisdiction over proceedings that have no effect on the debtor.

We believe that the issue of whether respondents are entitled to immediate execution on the bond against Northbrook is at least a question "related to" Celotex' bankruptcy.[7]

Admittedly, a proceeding by respondents against Northbrook on the supersedeas bond does not directly involve Celotex, except to satisfy the judgment against it secured by the bond. But to induce Northbrook to serve as surety on the bond, Celotex agreed to allow Northbrook to retain the proceeds of a settlement resolving insurance coverage disputes between Northbrook and Celotex. The Bankruptcy Court found that allowing respondents—and 227 other bonded judgment creditors—to execute immediately on the bonds would have a direct and substantial adverse effect on Celotex' ability to undergo a successful reorganization. It stated:

> "[I]f the Section 105 stay were lifted to enable the judgment creditors to reach the sureties, the sureties in turn would seek to lift the Section 105 stay to reach Debtor's collateral, with corresponding actions by Debtor to preserve its rights under the settlement agreements. Such a scenario could completely destroy any chance of resolving the prolonged insurance coverage disputes currently being adjudicated in this Court. The settlement of the insurance coverage disputes with all of Debtor's insurers may well be the linchpin of Debtor's formulation of a feasible plan. Absent the confirmation of a feasible plan, Debtor may be liquidated or cease to exist after a carrion feast by the victors in a race to the courthouse." *In re Celotex* (Celotex II), 140 B.R. 912, 915 (MD Fla. 1992).

In light of these findings by the Bankruptcy Court, it is relevant to note that we are dealing here with a reorganization under Chapter 11, rather than a liquidation under Chapter 7. The jurisdiction of bankruptcy courts may extend more broadly in the former case than in the latter. Cf. *Continental Illinois Nat. Bank & Trust Co. v. Chicago, R.I. & P.R. Co.*, 294 U.S. 648, 676 (1935). And we think our holding—that respondents' immediate execution on the supersedeas bond is at least "related to" the Celotex bankruptcy—is in accord with representative recent decisions of the Courts of Appeals. See *American Hardwoods, Inc. v. Deutsche Credit Corp.*, 885

---

[7] The dissent agrees that respondents' proceeding to execute on the supersedeas bond is "related to" Celotex' bankruptcy, *post*, at 6 n. 5, but noting that "only the district court has the power [under 28 U.S.C. § 157(c)(1)] to enter "any final order or judgment" " in related "non–core proceedings," *post*, at 9, the dissent concludes that the Bankruptcy Court here did not possess sufficient "related to" jurisdiction to issue the Section 105 Injunction. *Post*, at 10. The Section 105 Injunction, however, is only an *interlocutory stay* which respondents have yet to challenge. See *infra*, at 13. Thus, the Bankruptcy Court did not lack jurisdiction under § 157(c)(1) to issue the Section 105 Injunction because that injunction was not a "final order or judgment."

In any event, respondents have waived any claim that the granting of the Section 105 Injunction was a "non–core" proceeding under § 157(c)(1). Respondents base their arguments solely on 28 U.S.C. § 1334, and concede in their brief that the "bankruptcy court had subject matter jurisdiction to issue orders affecting the bond, then, only if the proceedings on the bond were 'related' to the Celotex bankruptcy itself within the meaning of § 1334(b)." Brief for Respondent 22. We conclude, and the dissent agrees, that those proceedings are so related. *See post*, at 5–6, and n. 5. We thus need not (and do not) reach the question whether the granting of the Section 105 Injunction was a "core" proceeding.

F.2d 621, 623 (CA9 1989) finding "related to" jurisdiction where enforcement of state court judgment by creditor against debtor's guarantors would affect administration of debtor's reorganization plan); *cf. MacArthur Co. v. Johns–Manville Corp.,* 837 F.2d 89, 93 [18 C.B.C.2d 316] (CA2) (noting that a bankruptcy court's injunctive powers under § 105(a) allow it to enjoin suits that "might impede the reorganization process"), cert. denied, 488 U.S. 868 (1988); *In re A.H. Robins Co.,* 828 F.2d 1023, 1024–1026 [17 C.B.C.2d 526] (CA4 1987) (affirming bankruptcy court's § 105(a) injunction barring products liability plaintiffs from bringing actions against debtor's insurers because such actions would interfere with debtor's reorganization), cert. denied *sub nom.,* 485 U.S. 969 (1988).[8]

Respondents, relying on our decision in *Board of Governors v. MCorp Financial,* 502 U.S. 32 (1991), contend that § 1334(b)'s statutory grant of jurisdiction must be reconciled and harmonized with Federal Rule of Civil Procedure 65.1, which provides an expedited procedure for executing on supersedeas bonds. In MCorp, we held that the grant of jurisdiction in § 1334(b) to district courts sitting in bankruptcy did not authorize an injunction against a regulatory proceeding, but there we relied on "the specific preclusive language" of 12 U.S.C. § 1818(i)(1) which stated that "no court shall have jurisdiction to affect by injunction or otherwise the issuance or enforcement of any [Board] notice or order." *MCorp, supra,* at 39, 42. There is no analogous statutory prohibition against enjoining the maintenance of a proceeding under Rule 65.1. That Rule provides:

> "Whenever these rules require or permit the giving of security by a party, and security is given in the form of a bond or stipulation or other undertaking with one or more sureties, each surety submits to the jurisdiction of the court and irrevocably appoints the clerk of the court as the surety's agent upon whom any papers affecting the surety's liability on the bond or undertaking may be served. The surety's liability may be enforced on motion without the necessity of an independent action." Fed. Rule Civ. Proc. 65.1.

This rule outlines a streamlined *procedure* for executing on bonds. It assures judgment creditors like respondents that they do not have to bring a separate action against sureties, and instead allows them to collect on the supersedeas bond by merely filing a motion. Just because the rule provides a simplified procedure for collecting on a bond, however, does not mean that such a procedure, like the more complicated procedure of a full–fledged law suit, cannot be stayed by a lawfully entered injunction.

Much of our discussion dealing with the jurisdiction of the Bankruptcy Court under the "related to" language of §§ 1334(b) and 157(a) is likewise applicable in determining whether or not the Bankruptcy Court's Section 105 Injunction has "only a frivolous pretense to validity." *GTE Sylvania,* 445 U.S. at 386 (internal

---

8 We recognize the theoretical possibility of distinguishing between the proceeding to execute on the bond in the Fifth Circuit and the § 105 stay proceeding in the Bankruptcy Court in the Eleventh Circuit. One might argue, technically, that though the proceeding to execute on the bond is "related to" the title 11 case, the stay proceeding "arises under" title 11, or "arises in" the title 11 case. See *In re Monroe Well Serv., Inc.,* [15 C.B.C.2d 1341] 67 B.R. 746, 753 (Bkrtcy. Ct. ED Pa. 1986). We need not and do not decide this question here.

quotation marks and citation omitted). The Fourth Circuit has upheld the merits of the Bankruptcy Court's Section 105 Injunction, see *Willis,* 978 F.2d at 149–150, and even the Fifth Circuit in this case did not find "that the bankruptcy court in Florida was necessarily wrong." *See Edwards II,* 6 F.3d at 321. But we need not, and do not, address whether the Bankruptcy Court acted properly in issuing the Section 105 Injunction.[9]

We have made clear that "[i]t is for the court of first instance to determine the question of the validity of the law, and until its decision is reversed for error by orderly review, either by itself or by a higher court, its orders based on its decision are to be respected." *Walker v. Birmingham,* 388 U.S. 307, 314 (1967) (quoting *Howat v. Kansas,* 258 U.S. 181, 189–190 (1922)). If respondents believed the Section 105 Injunction was improper, they should have challenged it in the Bankruptcy Court, like other similarly situated bonded judgment creditors have done. *See* Celotex II, 140 B.R. at 912. If dissatisfied with the Bankruptcy Court's ultimate decision, respondents can appeal "to the district court for the judicial district in which the bankruptcy judge is serving," *See* 28 U.S.C. § 158(a), and then to the Court of Appeals for the Eleventh Circuit. *See* § 158(d). Respondents chose not to pursue this course of action, but instead to collaterally attack the Bankruptcy Court's Section 105 Injunction in the Federal courts in Texas. This they cannot be permitted to do without seriously undercutting the orderly process of the law.

The judgment of the Court of Appeals, accordingly, is *reversed.*

It is so ordered.

Justice STEVENS, with whom Justice GINSBURG, joins, dissenting.

Today the majority holds that an Article III court erred when it allowed plaintiffs who prevailed on appeal to collect on a supersedeas bond in the face of an injunction issued by a non–Article III judge. Because, in my view, the majority attaches insufficient weight to the fact that the challenged injunction was issued by a non–Article III judge, I respectfully dissent.

I.

The outlines of the problems I perceive are best drawn by starting with an examination of the injunctions and opinions issued by the bankruptcy judge in this case. As the majority notes, Bennie and Joann Edwards (the Edwards) won a tort judgment against Celotex for damages Bennie Edwards suffered as a result of exposure to asbestos. To stay the judgment pending appeal, Celotex arranged for Northbrook

---

[9] The dissent contends that Celotex' attempts to set aside the supersedeas bond are "patently meritless" because none of Celotex' claims can impair Northbrook's obligation to respondents. See *post,* at 14. That premise, however, is not so clear as to give the Section 105 Injunction "only a frivolous pretense to validity.' There is authority suggesting that, in certain circumstances, transfers from the debtor to another for the benefit of a third party may be recovered from that third party. *See In re Air Conditioning, Inc. of Stuart,* 845 F.2d 293, 296–299 (CA11), *cert. denied,* 488 U.S. 993 (1988); *In re Compton Corp.,* 831 F.2d 586, 595 [17 C.B.C.2d 98] (1987), modified on other grounds, 835 F.2d 584 [18 C.B.C.2d 273] (CA5 1988). Although we offer no opinion on the merits of that authority or on whether it fits the facts here, it supports our conclusion that the stay was not frivolous.

Property and Casualty Insurance Company (Northbrook) to post a supersedeas bond to cover the full amount of the judgment. On October 12, 1990, before Celotex filed its voluntary petition under Chapter 11 of the Bankruptcy Code, the Court of Appeals for the Fifth Circuit affirmed the Edwards' judgment against Celotex. It is undisputed that, when the Edwards' judgment was affirmed, any property interest that Celotex retained in the supersedeas bond was extinguished.

The filing of Celotex's bankruptcy petition on October 12, 1990, triggered the automatic stay provisions of the Bankruptcy Code. *See* 11 U.S.C. § 362(a). On October 17, 1990, the bankruptcy judge, acting pursuant to 11 U.S.C.§ 105(a),[1] supplemented the automatic stay provisions with an emergency order staying, *inter alia,* all proceedings "involving any of the Debtors [*i.e.,* Celotex]." App. to Pet. for Cert. 28. The supersedeas bond filed in the Edwards' case, however, evidences an independent obligation on the part of Northbrook. For that reason, neither the automatic stay of proceedings against the debtor pursuant to § 362(a) of the Bankruptcy Code nor the bankruptcy judge's October 17, § 105(a) stay restrained the Edwards from proceeding against Northbrook to enforce Northbrook's obligations under the bond. As the Court of Appeals correctly held, the October 17 order enjoined the prosecution of proceedings involving "the Debtors," but did not expressly enjoin the Edwards from proceeding against Northbrook. *See* 6 F.3d 312, 315 [30 C.B.C.2d 148] (CA5 1993).

On May 3, 1991, the Edwards commenced their proceeding against Northbrook by filing a motion pursuant to Rule 65.1 of the Federal Rules of Civil Procedure[2] to enforce the supersedeas bond. Several weeks later—on June 13, 1991—the Bankruptcy Court entered a new three–paragraph order enjoining all of Celotex's judgment creditors from collecting on their supersedeas bonds. Paragraph 1 of the order addressed creditors whose appellate process had not yet concluded. Paragraph 2 addressed creditors whose appellate process concluded only after Celotex had filed for bankruptcy. Paragraph 3 applied to judgment creditors, such as the Edwards, whose appeals had concluded before the filing of the bankruptcy petition. Paragraph 3 expressly precluded those creditors from proceeding against any bond "without first seeking to vacate the Section 105 stay entered by this Court." *In re Celotex Corp.,* 128 B.R. 478, 485 (Bkrtcy. Ct. MD Fla. 1991).

---

[1] Title 11 U.S.C. § 105(a) provides:

"The court may issue any order, process, or judgment that is necessary or appropriate to carry out the provisions of this title. No provision of this title providing for the raising of an issue by a party in interest shall be construed to preclude the court from, sua sponte, taking any action or making any determination necessary or appropriate to enforce or implement court orders or rules, or to prevent an abuse of process."

[2] Federal Rule of Civil Procedure 65.1 states:

"Whenever these rules require or permit the giving of security by a party, and security is given in the form of a bond or stipulation or other undertaking with one or more sureties, each surety submits to the jurisdiction of the court and irrevocably appoints the clerk of the court as the surety's agent upon whom any papers affecting the surety's liability on the bond or undertaking may be served. The surety's liability may be enforced on motion without the necessity of an independent action."

The opinion supporting that order explains that Paragraphs 1 and 2 rest in part on the theory that the debtor retains a property interest in the supersedeas bonds until the appellate process is complete, and any attempt to collect on those bonds is therefore covered in the first instance by § 362(a)'s automatic stay provisions. The opinion recognized that that rationale did not cover supersedeas bonds posted in litigation with judgment creditors, such as the Edwards, whose appellate process was complete. The bankruptcy judge concluded, however, that § 105(a) gave him the power to stay the collection efforts of such bonded judgment creditors. The bankruptcy judge contended that other courts had utilized the § 105(a) stay "to preclude actions which may 'impede the reorganization process,' " *id.* at 483, quoting *In re Johns–Manville Corp.*, 837 F.2d 89, 93 (CA2), cert. denied, 488 U.S. 868 (1988), or "which will have an adverse impact on the Debtor's ability to formulate a Chapter 11 plan." 128 B.R. at 483, quoting *A.H. Robins Co. v. Piccinin*, 788 F.2d 994 (CA4), cert. denied, 479 U.S. 876 (1986). But cf. n. 12, *infra.* Apparently viewing his own authority as virtually limitless, the bankruptcy judge described a general bankruptcy power "to stop ongoing litigation and to prevent peripheral court decisions from dealing with issues without first allowing the bankruptcy court to have an opportunity to review the potential effect on the debtor." 128 B.R., at 484. He concluded that in "mega" cases in which "potential conflicts with other judicial determinations" might arise, "the powers of the bankruptcy court under Section 105 must in the initial stage be absolute." *Ibid.*

I do not agree that the powers of a bankruptcy judge, a non–Article III judge, "must be absolute" at the initial stage or indeed at any stage. Instead, the jurisdiction and the power of bankruptcy judges are cabined by specific and important statutory and constitutional constraints that operate at every phase of a bankruptcy. In my view, those constraints require that the judgment of the Court of Appeals be affirmed.

The majority concludes that the Court of Appeals must be reversed because the bankruptcy judge had jurisdiction to issue the injunction and because the injunction had more than a "frivolous pretense to validity." *Ante,* at 13. Even applying the majority's framework, I would affirm the Court of Appeals. As I will demonstrate, the constraints on the jurisdiction and authority of the bankruptcy judge compel the conclusion that the bankruptcy judge lacked jurisdiction to issue the challenged injunction, and that the injunction has only a "frivolous pretense to validity." I will also explain, however, why the majority's deferential approach seems particularly inappropriate as applied to this particular injunction, now in its fifth year of preventing enforcement of supersedeas bonds lodged in an Article III court.

II.

In my view, the bankruptcy judge lacked jurisdiction to issue an injunction that prevents an Article III court from allowing a judgment creditor to collect on a supersedeas bond posted in that court by a nondebtor. In reaching the contrary conclusion, the majority relies primarily on the bankruptcy judge's "related to" jurisdiction, and thus I will address that basis of jurisdiction first. The majority properly observes that, under 28 U.S.C. § 1334(b), the district court has broad bankruptcy jurisdiction, extending to "all civil proceedings arising under title 11, or arising in or related to cases under title 11."**3**

The majority also notes correctly that the Edwards' action to enforce the supersedeas bond is within the district court's "related to" jurisdiction,**4** because allowing creditors such as the Edwards "to execute immediately on the bonds would have a direct and substantial adverse effect on Celotex's ability to undergo a successful reorganization." *Ante,* at 10.**5**

---

3 The full text of § 1334 reads as follows:

"(a) Except as provided in subsection (b) of this section, the district courts shall have original and exclusive jurisdiction of all cases under title 11.

"(b) Notwithstanding any Act of Congress that confers exclusive jurisdiction on a court or courts other than the district courts, the district courts shall have original but not exclusive jurisdiction of all civil proceedings arising under title 11, or arising in or related to cases under title 11.

"(c)(1) Nothing in this section prevents a district court in the interest of justice, or in the interest of comity with State courts or respect for State law, from abstaining from hearing a particular proceeding arising under title 11 or arising in or related to a case under title 11.

"(2) Upon timely motion of a party in a proceeding based upon a State law claim or State law cause of action, related to a case under title 11 but not arising under title 11 or arising in a case under title 11, with respect to which an action could not have been commenced in a court of the United States absent jurisdiction under this section, the district court shall abstain from hearing such proceeding if an action is commenced, and can be timely adjudicated, in a State forum of appropriate jurisdiction. Any decision to abstain or not to abstain made under this subsection is not reviewable by appeal or otherwise by the court of appeals under section 158(d), 1291, or 1292 of this title or by the Supreme Court of the United States under section 1254 of this title. This subsection shall not be construed to limit the applicability of the stay provided for by section 362 of title 11, United States Code, as such section applies to an action affecting the property of the estate in bankruptcy.

"(d) The district court in which a case under title 11 is commenced or is pending shall have exclusive jurisdiction of all of the property, wherever located, of the debtor as of the commencement of such case, and of property of the estate." 28 U.S.C. § 1334 (1988 ed. and supp. V).

4 As § 1334(b) indicates, the district court's "related to" jurisdiction is "original but not exclusive."

5 I do not take issue with the conclusion that the Edwards' attempt to collect on the supersedeas bond falls within the "related to" jurisdiction of the district court. *Cf.* 1 L. King, Collier on Bankruptcy ¶ 3.01[1][c][iv], p. 3–29 (15th ed. 1994) (hereinafter Collier) (" Related" proceedings which involve litigation between third parties, which could have some effect on the administration of the bankruptcy case, are illustrated by suits by creditors against guarantors"). Despite the Edwards' argument to the contrary, it seems to me quite clear that allowing the Edwards to recover from Northbrook on the supersedeas bond would have an adverse impact on Celotex because Northbrook would then be able to retain the insurance proceeds that Celotex pledged as collateral when the bond was issued. Indeed, I am willing to assume that if all of the bonds were enforced, the reorganization efforts would fail and Celotex would have to be liquidated. In my judgment, however, the specter of liquidation is not an acceptable basis for concluding that a bankruptcy judge, and not just the district

The majority then observes that, under 28 U.S.C. § 157(a), the district court may "refe[r]" to the bankruptcy judge "any or all cases under title 11 and any or all proceedings arising under title 11 or arising in or related to a case under title 11."[6]

Thus, the majority concludes that, because the Edwards' action to enforce the supersedeas bond was within the District Court's "related to" jurisdiction and because the District Court referred all matters to the bankruptcy judge, the bankruptcy judge had jurisdiction over the Edwards' action.

In my view, the majority's approach pays insufficient attention to the remaining provisions of § 157, and, more importantly, to the decision of this Court that gave rise to their creation. The current jurisdictional structure of the Bankruptcy Code reflects this Court's decision in *Northern Pipeline Constr. Co. v. Marathon Pipe Line Co.*, 458 U.S. 50 [6 C.B.C.2d 785] (1982), which in turn addressed the Bankruptcy Reform Act of 1978, 92 Stat. 2549. The 1978 Act significantly restructured the Bankruptcy Code. The Act created "bankruptcy courts" and vested in them "jurisdiction over all 'civil proceedings arising under title 11 [the Bankruptcy title] or arising in or related to cases under title 11.'" *Northern Pipeline*, 458 U.S. at 54, quoting 28 U.S.C. § 1471(b) (1976 ed. Supp. IV). As the plurality opinion in *Northern Pipeline* observed, "[t]his jurisdictional grant empowers bankruptcy courts to entertain a wide variety of cases, 'involving' claims based on state law as well as those based on federal law." 458 U.S., at 54. The Act also bestowed upon the judges of the bankruptcy courts broad powers to accompany this expanded jurisdiction. *See infra, Northern Pipeline*, 458 U.S., at 55. The Act did not, however, make the newly empowered bankruptcy judges Article III judges. In

---

court, has jurisdiction to interfere with the performance of a third party's fixed obligation to a judgment creditor. I also agree with the majority, ante, at 8, n. 6, that the facts of this case do not require us to resolve whether *Pacor v. Higgins,* 743 F.2d 984 (CA3 1984), articulates the proper test for determining the scope of the district court's "related to" jurisdiction.

[6] The text of 28 U.S.C. § 157 reads in relevant part as follows:

"(a) Each district court may provide that any or all cases under title 11 and any or all proceedings arising under title 11 or arising in or related to a case under title 11 shall be referred to the bankruptcy judges for the district.

"(b)(1) Bankruptcy judges may hear and determine all cases under title 11 and all core proceedings arising under title 11, or arising in a case under title 11, referred under subsection (a) of this section, and may enter appropriate orders and judgments, subject to review under section 158 of this title.

"(c)(1) A bankruptcy judge may hear a proceeding that is not a core proceeding but that is otherwise related to a case under title 11. In such proceeding, the bankruptcy judge shall submit proposed findings of fact and conclusions of law to the district court, and any final order or judgment shall be entered by the district judge after considering the bankruptcy judge's proposed findings and conclusions and after reviewing *de novo* those matters to which any party has timely and specifically objected.

"(2) Notwithstanding the provisions of paragraph (1) of this subsection, the district court, with the consent of all the parties to the proceeding, may refer a proceeding related to a case under title 11 to a bankruptcy judge to hear and determine and to enter appropriate orders and judgments, subject to review under section 158 of this title."

particular, it denied bankruptcy judges the life tenure and salary protection that the Constitution requires for Article III judges. *See* U.S. Const., Art. III., § 1.

In *Northern Pipeline,* this Court held that the Act was unconstitutional, at least insofar as it allowed a non–Article III court to "entertain and decide" a purely state law claim. 458 U.S., at 91 (Rehnquist, J., concurring in judgment); *see also Id.,* at 86 (plurality opinion). The plurality opinion distinguished the revamped bankruptcy courts from prior district court "adjuncts" which the Court had found did not violate Article III. The plurality noted that, in contrast to the narrow, specialized jurisdiction exercised by these prior adjuncts, "the subject–matter jurisdiction of the bankruptcy courts encompasses not only traditional matters of bankruptcy, but also 'all civil proceedings arising under title 11 or arising in or related to cases under title 11." *Id.,* at 85. In addition, prior adjuncts "engaged in statutorily channeled factfinding functions," while the bankruptcy courts "exercis[e] 'all of the jurisdiction' conferred by the Act on the district courts."[7] *Ibid.*

In response to *Northern Pipeline,* Congress passed the Bankruptcy Amendments and Federal Judgeship Act of 1984 (1984 amendments), 98 Stat. 333. Section 157 was passed as part of the 1984 amendments. Section 157 establishes two broad categories of proceedings: "core proceedings" and "non–core proceedings." For "all core proceedings arising under title 11, or arising in a case under title 11 referred under [§ 157(a)]," § 157(b)(1) permits bankruptcy judges to "hear and determine" the proceedings and to "enter appropriate orders and judgments." For noncore proceedings "otherwise related to a case under title 11", § 157(c)(1) permits the bankruptcy court only to "hear" the proceedings and to "submit proposed findings of fact and conclusions of law to the district court." *See* 1 Collier ¶ 3.01[1][c][iv], at 3–28 ("Civil proceedings 'related to cases under title 11' are 'excluded from being treated as "core proceedings" by 28 U.S.C. § 157(b)(1), and are the subject of special procedures contained in section 157(c)(1) and (c)(2)"). For these "related proceedings," 1 Collier ¶ 3.01[1][c][iv], at 3–28, only the district court has the power to enter "any final order or judgment."[8]

In my view, the distinction between the jurisdiction to "hear and determine" core proceedings on the one hand and the jurisdiction only to "hear" related proceedings on the other hand is critical, if not dispositive. I believe that the jurisdiction to hear (and yet not to determine) a case under § 157(c)(1) provides insufficient jurisdiction to a bankruptcy judge to permit him to issue a binding injunction that prevents an Article III court from exercising its conceded jurisdiction over the case.[9]

---

[7] The plurality also noted that, in contrast to the limited powers possessed by prior adjuncts, "the bankruptcy courts exercise all ordinary powers of district courts." 458 U.S. at 85.

[8] The district court may enter judgment only after *de novo* review of the bankruptcy judge's recommendation with respect to any matters to which one of the parties has raised a timely objection. *See* 28 U.S.C. § 157(c)(1).

[9] It should be noted that the bankruptcy judge's order cannot be upheld on the ground that it purported to enjoin only the Edwards and thus did not enjoin directly the Article III court. First, the bankruptcy judge's orders cannot be interpreted so narrowly. The October 17 order enjoined, *inter alia,* "all Entities" from "commencing or continuing any judicial, administrative or other proceeding involving any of the Debtors." App. to Pet. for Cert. 28. In my view, the word "entities" includes courts. Indeed, the bankruptcy judge's order tracks § 362(a)'s

The unambiguous text of § 157(c)(1) requires that the bankruptcy judge's participation in related proceedings be merely advisory rather than adjudicative. In my view, having jurisdiction to grant injunctions over cases that one may not decide is inconsistent with such an advisory role. An injunction is an extraordinary remedy whose impact on private rights may be just as onerous as a final determination. The constitutional concerns that animate the current jurisdictional provisions of the Bankruptcy Code and that deny non–Article III tribunals the power to determine private controversies apply with equal force to the entry of an injunction interfering with the exercise of the admitted jurisdiction of an Article III tribunal.**10**

In sum, my view on the sufficiency of "related to" jurisdiction to sustain the injunction in this case can be stated quite simply: If a bankruptcy judge lacks jurisdiction to "determine" a question, the judge also lacks jurisdiction to issue an injunction that prevents an Article III court, which concededly does have jurisdiction, from determining that question.**11**

---

automatic stay provisions, which provide, in part, that the automatic stay is applicable "to all entities" and which enjoin "the commencement or continuation of a judicial, administrative, or other proceeding against the debtor." 11 U.S.C. § 362(a)(1). The Courts of Appeals have uniformly held that "entities," as used in § 362, include courts. *See, e.g., Maritime Electric Co. v. United Jersey Bank,* 959 F.2d 1194, 1206 (CA3 1991) ("§ 362's stay is mandatory and applicable to all entities, including state and federal courts"); *Pope v. Manville Forest Products Corp.,* 778 F.2d 238, 239 (CA5 1985) ("just the entry of an order of dismissal, even if entered *sua sponte,* constitutes a judicial act toward the disposition of the case and hence may be construed as a continuation 'of a judicial proceeding' "); *Ellis v. Consolidated Diesel Electric Corp.,* 894 F.2d 371, 372–373 (CA10 1990) (district court's entry of summary judgment violated § 362(a)'s automatic stay); see also *Maritime Electric Co. v. United Jersey Bank,* 959 F.2d at 1206 (collecting cases). *Cf.* 2 Collier ¶ 101.15 at 101–62 to 101–63 ("Entity" is the broadest of all definitions which relate to bodies or units").

More importantly, though the bankruptcy judges' June 13 order enjoins " the judgment creditor," " *In re Celotex Corp.,* 128 B.R. 478, 485 (Bkrtcy. Ct. MD Fla. 1991), the order clearly has the same practical effect as if it enjoined the court directly. My objection to the majority's approach does not at all depend on whether the order that prevents the Article III court from exercising its jurisdiction does so directly or indirectly. Instead, my view is simply that a bankruptcy judge who lacks jurisdiction to decide an issue may not prevent an Article III court that is ready and willing to exercise its conceded jurisdiction from doing so.

10 In addition, 28 U.S.C. § 1334(c)(2) provides for mandatory abstention in cases involving state law claims for which the sole basis of bankruptcy jurisdiction is "related to" jurisdiction. That provision thus makes clear that no order could have been entered over the Edwards' objection if their tort action had been tried in a state rather than a federal court. The bankruptcy judge's order, which does not distinguish proceedings to enforce supersedeas bonds that were posted in state court proceedings, fails to address the implications of this mandatory abstention provision.

I also believe that Congress would have expected bankruptcy judges to show the same deference to federal courts adjudicating state law claims under diversity jurisdiction, at least when the bankruptcy judge purports to act on the basis of his "related to" jurisdiction and when the federal action can be "timely adjudicated." *Ibid.*

11 I agree with the majority that the bankruptcy judge's order is a temporary injunction, and thus it is not a "final order or judgment." *Ante,* at 9., n. 7. The temporary nature of the

Any conclusion to the contrary would trivialize the constitutional imperatives that shaped the Bankruptcy Code's jurisdictional provisions.[12]

III.

Petitioners and the majority rely primarily on "related to" jurisdiction. Indeed, the Court's holding appears to rest almost entirely on the view that a bankruptcy judge has jurisdiction to enjoin proceedings in Article III courts whenever those proceedings are "related to" a pending Title 11 case. *See ante,* at 7–11. Two footnotes in the Court's opinion, however, might be read as suggesting alternative bases of jurisdiction. See ante, at 3, n. 4, 11, n. 8. Those two footnotes require a brief response.

In footnote 4 of its opinion, the Court refers to two different claims advanced by Celotex in the bankruptcy proceedings: a claim that "the bonded judgment creditors should not be able to execute on their bonds because, by virtue of the collateralization of the bonds, the bonded judgment creditors are beneficiaries of Celotex asset transfers that are voidable as preferences and fraudulent transfers"; and a claim that "the punitive damages portions of the judgments can be voided or subordinated." There is little doubt that those claims are properly characterized as ones "arising under" Title 11 within the meaning of 28 U.S.C. § 1334(b);[13] however, it does not

---

injunction, however, is irrelevant. As I have stated repeatedly in the text, I believe that a statutory scheme that deprives a bankruptcy judge of jurisdiction to "determine" a case also deprives that judge of jurisdiction to issue binding injunctions—even temporary ones—that would prevent an Article III court with jurisdiction over the case from determining it.

[12] The cases on which the bankruptcy judge relied are entirely consistent with my approach, and they provide at most indirect support for his order. In *A.H. Robins Co.,* the challenged injunction was issued by an Article III court, see *A.H. Robins Co. v. Piccinin,* 788 F. 2d 994, 997 (CA4), cert. denied, 479 U.S. 876 (1986) ("the district court granted Robins' request for a preliminary injunction"); and in *In re Johns–Manville Corp.,* the Court of Appeals found that the bankruptcy judge had jurisdiction to enter the injunction in a core proceeding because the insurance policies that were the subject of the injunction were property of the bankruptcy estate, *see* 837 F. 2d 89, 91–92 (CA2), *cert. denied,* 488 U.S. 868 (1988). Thus, those cases do not support the present injunction, which was issued by a non–Article III judge and which affects supersedeas bonds that are concededly not property of the debtor's estate.

I also note that in *Willis v. Celotex Corp.,* 978 F. 2d 146 (1992), *cert. denied,* 507 U.S.— (1993), though upholding the very injunction at issue in this case, the Fourth Circuit engaged in no detailed jurisdictional analysis and entirely omitted any discussion of the significance of the bankruptcy judge's non–Article III status.

[13] "[W]hen a cause of action is one which is created by title 11, then that civil proceeding is one arising under title 11." 1 Collier ¶ 3.01[1][c][iii], at 3–26. A perusal of the complaint reveals that Celotex seeks relief under causes of action created by the Bankruptcy Code. *See, e.g.,* Count I (11 U.S.C. § 547(b) (seeking to avoid preferential transfers)); Count III (11 U.S.C. § 548(a)(2)(A) (seeking to avoid constructively fraudulent transfers)); Count IV (11 U.S.C. § 544 (seeking to avoid transactions that would constitute constructively fraudulent transfers under state law)); Count VII (11 U.S.C. § 502 (seeking to disallow punitive damage awards); Count VII (11 U.S.C. § 510(c)(1) (seeking equitable subordination for pending punitive damages awards to the claims of unsecured creditors)). *Cf. e.g.,* 1 Collier ¶ 3.01[1][c][iii], at 3–27 ("[C]ourts interpreting this language have held that arising under title 11 includes causes of action to recover fraudulent conveyances"). My acknowledgement of these claims, of course, is not intended as a suggestion that they have merit.

necessarily follow from that characterization that the bankruptcy judge had jurisdiction to issue the injunction in support of the prosecution of those claims. Celotex's complaint was not filed until months after the bankruptcy judge's injunction issued. The claims raised in that complaint cannot retroactively provide a jurisdictional basis for the bankruptcy judge's injunction.

Moreover, Celotex's attempts to set aside the Edwards' supersedeas bond are patently meritless. It strains credulity, to suggest that a supersedeas bond, posted almost a year and a half before the bankruptcy petition was filed, could be set aside as a preference or as a fraudulent transfer for the benefit of Celotex's adversaries in bitterly contested litigation. Conceivably, Celotex's provision of security to Northbrook might be voidable, but that possibility could not impair the rights of the judgment creditors to enforce the bond against Northbrook even though they might be unwitting beneficiaries of the fraud. That possibility, at most, would be relevant to the respective claims of Northbrook and Celotex to the pledged collateral. Similarly, the fact that the Edwards' judgment included punitive as well as compensatory damages does not provide even an arguable basis for reducing Northbrook's obligations under the supersedeas bond. Even if there is a basis for subordinating a portion of Northbrook's eventual claim against Celotex on "bankruptcy law grounds," that has nothing to do with the Edwards' claim against Northbrook. It thus seems obvious that, at least with respect to the Edwards, Celotex has raised frivolous claims in an attempt to manufacture bankruptcy jurisdiction and thereby to justify a bankruptcy judge's injunction that had been issued over one year earlier. Cf. Siler v. Louisville & Nashville R. Co., 213 U.S. 175, 191 (1909) ("Of course, the Federal question must not be merely colorable or fraudulently set up for the mere purpose of endeavoring to give the court jurisdiction").

In its footnote 8, the Court appears to suggest that the injunction prohibiting the Edwards from proceeding against Northbrook (described in the footnote as the "stay proceeding" may "aris[e] under" Title 11 or may "arise in" the Title 11 case. Perhaps this is accurate in a literal sense; the injunction did, of course, "arise under" Title 11 because 11 U.S.C. § 105(a) created whatever power the bankruptcy judge had to issue the injunction. Similarly, the injunction "arises in" the Title 11 case because that is where it originated. It cannot be the law, however, that a bankruptcy judge has jurisdiction to enter any conceivable order that a party might request simply because § 105(a) authorizes some injunctions or because the request was first made in a pending Title 11 case. Cf. 2 Collier ¶ 105.01[1], at 105–2 (Section 105 "is not an independent source of jurisdiction, but rather it grants the courts flexibility to issue orders which preserve and protect their jurisdiction"). The mere filing of a motion for a § 105 injunction to enjoin a proceeding in another forum cannot be a jurisdictional bootstrap enabling a bankruptcy judge to exercise jurisdiction that would not otherwise exist.

IV.

Even if I believed that the bankruptcy judge had jurisdiction to issue its injunction, I would still affirm the Court of Appeals because in my view the bankruptcy judge's injunction has only a "frivolous pretense to validity."

In 1898, Congress codified the bankruptcy laws. Under the 1898 Bankruptcy Act, most bankruptcy proceedings were conducted by "referees" who resolved controversies involving property in the actual or constructive possession of the court, as well as certain disputes involving property in the possession of third parties. In § 2(a)(15) of the 1898 Act, Congress vested in bankruptcy courts the power to:

> "[M]ake such orders, issue such process, and enter such judgments in addition to those specifically provided for as may be necessary for the enforcement of the provisions of this Act." Act of July 1, 1898, 30 Stat. 546.

In 1938, Congress clarified both the powers and the limitations on the injunctive authority of referees in bankruptcy by adding to the end of § 2(a)(15), "*Provided, however,* That an injunction to restrain a court may be issued by the judge only." 52 Stat. 843 (emphasis in original).

In 1978, through the Bankruptcy Reform Act, Congress significantly revised the Bankruptcy Code and the role of bankruptcy referees.[14]

Though stopping short of making bankruptcy referees Article III judges, Congress significantly increased the status, the duties, and the powers of those referees. For example, as we noted in *Northern Pipeline,* the expanded powers under the new Act included "the power to hold jury trials, to issue declaratory judgments, [and] to issue writs of habeas corpus under certain circumstances." 458 U.S., at 55. In addition, Congress again provided for broad injunctive powers. Thus, for example, in the place of § 2(a)(15), Congress added 11 U.S.C. § 105, which provided in relevant part: "The bankruptcy court may issue any order, process, or judgment that is necessary or appropriate to carry out the provisions of this title." *See also* 458 U.S., at 55 ("Congress has allowed bankruptcy judges the power to issue all writs necessary in aid of the bankruptcy court's jurisdiction"). Once again, however, along with both this marked expansion of the power of bankruptcy judges and the broad delegation of injunctive authority, Congress indicated its intent to limit the power of those judges to enjoin other courts: Although Congress provided that "[a] bankruptcy court shall have the powers of a court of equity, law, and admiralty," it also provided that bankruptcy courts "may not enjoin another court." 28 U.S.C. § 1481 (1982 ed.).[15]

Thus, for well over 50 years prior to the adoption of the 1984 amendments to the Bankruptcy Code, it was clear that Congress intended to deny bankruptcy judges the power to enjoin other courts.

The 1984 amendments, *inter alia,* repealed § 1481 (and its express limitation on injunctive authority), leaving § 105 as the only source of the bankruptcy judge's injunctive authority.[16] Given that *Northern Pipeline* required a contraction in the

---

[14] In 1973, bankruptcy "referees" were redesignated as "judges." *See Northern Pipeline Constr. Co. v. Marathon Pipe Line Co.,* 458 U.S. 50, 53 n.2 [6 C.B.C.2d 785] (1982). As did the plurality opinion in Northern Pipeline, *see ibid.,* I will continue to refer to all judges under the pre–1978 Act as "referees."

[15] Congress also limited the power of bankruptcy courts to "punish a criminal contempt not committed in the presence of the judge of the court or warranting a punishment of imprisonment." 28 U.S.C. § 1481 (1982 ed.).

[16] The 1984 amendments also repealed the authorization of bankruptcy judges to act pursuant to the All Writs Act. *See* 2 Collier ¶ 105.01[1], at 105–3.

authority of bankruptcy judges,[17] and given that the 1984 amendments regarding the powers of the bankruptcy courts were passed to comply with *Northern Pipeline,*[18] it would be perverse—and in my view "frivolous"—to contend that Congress intended the repeal of § 1481 to operate as an authorization for those judges to enjoin proceedings in other courts, thus significantly expanding the powers of bankruptcy judges.

My view of the consequence of the 1984 amendments is reinforced by the structure of § 1481. When Congress placed restrictions on the injunctive power of the bankruptcy courts, it did so in § 1481, right after the clause granting those courts "the powers of a court of equity, law, and admiralty." In my view, this suggests that Congress saw § 1481—and not § 105(a)—as the source of any power to enjoin other courts. Thus, the removal of § 1481 by the 1984 amendments is properly viewed as eliminating the sole source of congressionally–granted authority to enjoin other courts. Cf. *In re Hipp,* 895 F.2d 1503, 1515–1516 [22 C.B.C.2d 876] (CA5 1990) (concluding on similar reasoning that § 1481, not § 105(a), was the source of the bankruptcy court's power to punish criminal contempt under the 1978 Act).

Nor does anything in the 1986 amendments to the Bankruptcy Code alter my analysis.[19]

The primary effect of those amendments was to give the bankruptcy judges the power to issue orders *sua sponte.*[20]

The 1986 amendments, therefore, do not reflect any expansion of the power of bankruptcy judges to enjoin other courts.

The bankruptcy judge's error with respect to this injunction thus seems clear, and the injunction falls, therefore, within the exception recognized by the majority for injunctions with only a "frivolous pretense to validity." I recognize, of course, that one may legitimately question the "frivolousness" of the injunction in light of the Fourth Circuit's upholding the very injunction at issue in this case, see *Willis v. Celotex Corp.,* 978 F.2d 146 (1992), cert. denied, 507 U.S. (1993), and the disagreement of a substantial number of my colleagues. In my view, however, the bankruptcy judge's error is sufficiently plain that the Court of Appeals was justified in allowing the Edwards to collect on their bond.[21]

---

[17] The plurality opinion expressly noted its concerns about the bankruptcy judge's exercise of broad injunctive powers. See n. 7, *supra.*

[18] *See, e.g.,* 130 Cong. Rec. 20089 (1984) ("*Northern Pipeline* held that the broad powers granted to bankruptcy judges under the Bankruptcy Act of 1978 were judicial powers and violated Article III of the Constitution. The present Bill attempts to cure the problem").

[19] *See* Bankruptcy Judges, United States Trustees, and Family Farmer Bankruptcy Act of 1986, Pub L. 99–554, 100 Stat. 3088. With respect to 11 U.S.C. § 105, the 1986 amendments added the second sentence of the current version of § 105(a). *See* 100 Stat., at 3097.

[20] The only relevant legislative history regarding the changes to § 105(a) is contained in Senator Hatch's view that the amendment "allows a bankruptcy court to take any action on its own, or to make any necessary determination to prevent an abuse of process and to help expedite a case in a proper and justified manner." 132 Cong. Rec. 28610 (1986).

[21] Neither of the cases cited by the majority, *ante,* at 13, n. 9, provides any reason to conclude otherwise. As the majority notes, those cases hold that the bankruptcy trustee may

V.

The Court's holding today rests largely on its view that the Edwards' proper remedy is to appeal the bankruptcy judge's injunction, first to the District Court and then to the Court of Appeals for the Eleventh Circuit. The Court concedes, however, that the Edwards need not do so if the bankruptcy judge exceeded his jurisdiction, or if the injunction is supported by nothing more than "a frivolous pretense to validity." *Ante,* at 6. For the reasons already stated, I think both of those conditions are satisfied in this case. The non–Article III bankruptcy judge simply lacked both jurisdiction and authority to prevent an Article III court from exercising its unquestioned jurisdiction to decide a matter that is related only indirectly to the bankruptcy proceeding. I think it important, however, to add a few brief words explaining why I find this injunction especially troubling and why the injunction should be viewed with a particularly critical eye.

First, the justification offered by the bankruptcy judge should give the court pause. As originally articulated, the jurisdiction for this injunction was that emergency relief was required lest the reorganization of Celotex become impossible and liquidation follow. Apart from the fact that the "emergency" rationale is plainly insufficient to support an otherwise improper injunction that has now lasted for more than four years, the judge's reasoning reveals reliance on the misguided notion that a good end is a sufficient justification for the existence and exercise of power. His reference to the need to exercise "absolute" power to override "potential conflicts with other judicial determinations" that might have a "potential impact on the debtor" should invite far more exacting scrutiny of his order than the Court deems appropriate.

Second, that the subject of the injunction was a supersedeas bond makes the injunction suspect. A supersedeas bond may be viewed as putting the integrity of the Court in which it is lodged on the line. As the Court of Appeals noted, the Edwards were "promised by the court" that the supersedeas bond would be available if they prevailed on appeal. 6 F.3d, at 320. For that reason, in my opinion, questions relating to the enforceability of a supersedeas bond should generally be answered in the forum in which the bond is posted.

Moreover, whenever possible, such questions should be resolved before the court accepts the bond as security for collection of the judgment being appealed. After a debtor has benefitted from the postponement of collection of an adverse judgment,

---

recover from a third party (*e.g.,* the Edwards) funds transferred from the debtor (*e.g.,* Celotex) to another (*e.g.,* Northbrook) for the benefit of that third party. Both cases, however, make clear that the obligation of the Northbrook–like guarantor (a bank in each case) to pay the third party was not at issue. *See In re Compton Corp.,* 831 F.2d 586, 590 [17 C.B.C.2d 987] (1987) ("[T]he trustee is not attempting to set aside the post petition payments by [the bank] to [the third party] under the letter of credit as a preference"), modified on other grounds, 835 F.2d 584 [18 C.B.C.2d 273] (CA5 1988); *In re Air Conditioning, Inc., of Stuart,* 845 F.2d 293, 295–296, (CA11), *cert. denied sub nom. First Interstate Credit Alliance v. American Bank of Martin County,* 488 U.S. 993 (1988). Thus, in my view, those cases cannot form the basis for any nonfrivolous argument that Northbrook may avoid its obligation to pay the Edwards.

both that debtor and its successors–in–interest should normally be estopped from asserting that the judgment creditors who relied to their detriment on the validity of the bond had no right to do so. The very purpose of a supersedeas bond is to protect judgment creditors from the risk that insolvency of the debtor may impair their ability to enforce the judgment promptly. When the bond has served the purpose of forestalling immediate levies on the judgment debtor's assets—levies that might have precipitated an earlier bankruptcy—it is inequitable to postpone payment merely because the risk against which the bond was intended to provide protection has actually occurred. *See id.* at 319 ("It is manifestly unfair to force the judgment to delay the right to collect with a promise to protect the judgment only to later refuse to allow that successful plaintiff to execute the bond because the debtor has sought protection under the laws of bankruptcy"); *In re Southmark,* 138 B.R. 820, 827–828 (Bkrtcy. Ct. ND Tex. 1992) (internal quotation marks omitted) ("The principal risk against which such bonds are intended as a protection is insolvency. To hold that the very contingency against which they guard shall, if it happens, discharge them, seems to us bad law and worse logic"). The inequity that the Court today condones does not, of course, demonstrate that its legal analysis is incorrect. It does, however, persuade me that the Court should not review this case as though it presented an ordinary collateral attack on an injunction entered by an Article III court.[22] Instead, the Court should, I believe, more carefully consider which of the two competing tribunals is guilty of trespassing in the other's domain.

Accordingly, I respectfully dissent.

MATTER OF WOOD

United States Court of Appeals, Fifth Circuit
825 F.2d 90 (1987)

WISDOM, Circuit Judge:

This appeal calls upon us to decipher the jurisdictional provisions of the Bankruptcy Amendments and Federal Judgeship Act of 1984. A brief history of the Act may cast some light on the nature of our task.

Years of effort to reform the bankruptcy laws culminated with the enactment of the Bankruptcy Reform Act of 1978.[1]

As part of its overall goal to create a more efficient procedure for administering bankruptcies, the 1978 Act vested broad powers in the bankruptcy courts. This

------

[22] Indeed, one wonders if the same analysis would apply to a bankruptcy judge's injunction that purported to prevent this Court from allowing a successful litigant to enforce a supersedeas bond posted by a nondebtor in this Court pursuant to our Rule 23.4.

[1] Pub. L. 95–598, 92 Stat. 2549.

reform was short–lived. In 1982 the Supreme Court decided *Marathon v. Northern Pipeline.*[2]

The Court declared the jurisdictional provision of the 1978 Act unconstitutional because, in short, it vested Article III judicial power in Article I judges. Courts were left to their own devices while Congress deliberated a response to *Marathon.* With prompting from bench, bar, and law professors with expertise in bankruptcy, Congress responded with the Bankruptcy Amendments and Federal Judgeship Act of 1984. Essentially, Congress reenacted the 1978 Act, but divided its jurisdictional grant into "core" proceedings, over which the bankruptcy courts exercise full judicial power—and "otherwise related" or "non–core" proceedings—over which the bankruptcy courts exercise only limited power. In this case, we must decide two issues: first, whether bankruptcy jurisdiction exists; second, if jurisdiction does exist, whether the bankruptcy court may proceed over this matter as a "core" or a "non–core" proceeding.

I.

This case results from a dispute among the directors/stockholders of a medical clinic. In 1981, Dr. James Wood and Dr. Arthur Wood, III, formed the Wayne Clinic, P.A., each becoming the owner of 1000 shares of stock. In March of 1984, Dr. James Wood and his wife, Carol Wood, filed a Chapter 11 bankruptcy petition in the Southern District Court of Mississippi. In May of 1985, Dr. Arthur Wood filed a complaint in the same court is [sic] alleging that in November of 1984, Dr. and Mrs. James Wood and Woodrow Barham, acting to together as directors of the clinic, wrongfully issued additional stock to Dr. James Wood. The complaint stated that in the Spring of 1985, Dr. James Wood received a disproportionate distribution from the clinic as the result of the wrongful stock issuance in violation of the agreement between Dr. James Wood and Dr. Arthur Wood that they were to be equal partners in the clinic. The complaint seeks damages and declaratory relief.

The bankruptcy judge of the district denied the defendants' motion to dismiss for lack of subject–matter jurisdiction and held that the matter was a core proceeding. On appeal to the district court, the court held that the matter was neither a "core" proceeding, over which the bankruptcy judge had full judicial power, nor an "otherwise related" or "non–core" proceeding, over which the bankruptcy judge has limited judicial power. The court dismissed the complaint for lack of subject–matter jurisdiction. The plaintiffs appealed to this Court.

II.

The starting point in our analysis is 28 U.S.C. § 1334. In relevant part this provision provides:

(a) Except as provided in subsection (b) of this section, the district court shall have original and exclusive jurisdiction of all cases under title 11.

---

[2] 458 U.S. 50, 102 S.Ct. 2858, 73 L. Ed. 2d 598 (1982). *Marathon* provided the impetus for the new Act. *See* King, *Jurisdiction and Procedure Under the Bankruptcy Amendments of 1984,* 38 Vand. L. Rev. 625 (1985); Note, *The Bankruptcy Act of 1984; Marathon Revisited,* 3 Yale L. & Pol. Rev. 231 (1984).

(b) Notwithstanding any Act of Congress that confers exclusive jurisdiction on a court or courts other than the district courts, the district courts shall have original but not exclusive jurisdiction of all civil proceedings arising under title 11, or arising in or related to cases under title 11.[3]

Section 1334 lists four types of matters over which the district court has jurisdiction:

1. "cases under title 11",

2. "proceedings arising under title 11",

3. proceedings "arising in" a case under title 11, and

4. proceedings "related to" a case under title 11.

The first category refers merely to the bankruptcy petition itself, over which district courts (and their bankruptcy units) have original and exclusive jurisdiction. Our concern, however, is with the other proceedings listed in subsection 1334(b), over which the district courts have original, but not exclusive, jurisdiction.

There is almost no legislative history to guide us in interpreting the 1984 Act. Subsection 1334(b), however, was taken verbatim from subsection 1471(b) of the 1978 Act.[4]

The legislative history and judicial interpretations of that Act therefore are instructive.[5]

Legislative history indicates that the phrase "arising under title 11, or arising in or related to cases under title 11" was meant, not to distinguish between different matters, but to identify collectively a broad range of matters subject to the bankruptcy jurisdiction of federal courts.[6]

Congress was concerned with the inefficiencies of piecemeal adjudication of matters affecting the administration of bankruptcies and intended to give federal courts the power to adjudicate all matters having an effect on the bankruptcy.[7]

Courts have recognized that the grant of jurisdiction under the 1978 Act was broad.[8]

Nothing in *Marathon* suggests that we should read the corresponding provisions of the 1984 Act differently. The jurisdictional provision of the 1978 Act, section

---

[3] Pub. L. 98–353, 98 Stat. 333.

[4] Section 1471(b) of the 1978 Act read, in pertinent part:

the district courts shall have original but not exclusive jurisdiction of all civil proceedings arising under title 11 or arising in or related to cases under title 11.

[5] *Carlton v. BAWW, Inc.,* 751 F.2d 781, 787 n. 7 (5th Cir. 1985); *In re Salem Mortgage Co.,* 783 F.2d 626, 632–34 (6th Cir. 1986); *In re Cemetery Development Corp.,* 59 B.R. 115, 119–21 (Bankr. M.D. La.1986).

[6] S. Rep. No. 989, 95th Cong., 2d Sess., 153–54 (1978), *reprinted in* 1978 U.S. Code Cong. & Admin. News 5787, 5939–40.

[7] *Id.*

[8] *Pacor, Inc. v. Higgins,* 743 F.2d 984, 994 (3d Cir. 1984); *In re Salem Mortgage Co.,* 783 F.2d 626, 633–34 (6th Cir. 1986); *In re Cemetery Development Corp.,* 59 B.R. 115, 121 (Bankr. M.D. La. 1986).

1471, accomplished two things. First, subsection (b) vested an expansive bankruptcy jurisdiction in the district courts.[9]

Second, subsection (c) conferred the power to exercise that jurisdictional grant in the bankruptcy courts.[10]

The issue in *Marathon* was not the constitutionality of subsection (b), but the constitutionality of subsection (c). *Marathon* held that Congress could not vest the whole of bankruptcy jurisdiction in bankruptcy courts because the jurisdictional grant encompassed proceedings too far removed from the "core" of traditional bankruptcy powers to allow them to be adjudicated by non–Article III judges.[11]

The holding in *Marathon* suggests no concern over the constitutionality of the scope of bankruptcy jurisdiction defined by Congress; its concern is with the *placement* of that jurisdiction in non–Article III courts. In response to *Marathon*, Congress altered the placement of bankruptcy jurisdiction by creating a statutory distinction between core and non–core proceedings and restricting the power of bankruptcy courts to adjudicate the latter. Because *Marathon* did not compel Congress to reduce the scope of bankruptcy jurisdiction, it seems plain that Congress intended no change in the scope of jurisdiction set forth in the 1978 Act when it later enacted section 1334 of the 1984 Act.

The district court expressed its concern that an overbroad interpretation of section 1334 would bring into federal court matters that should be left to state courts to decide. We have also expressed the same concern.[12]

There is no necessary reason why that concern must be met by restrictive interpretations of the statutory grant of jurisdiction under section 1334. The Act grants the district court broad power to abstain whenever appropriate "in the interest of justice, or in the interest of comity with State courts or respect for State law".[13]

The abstention provisions of the Act demonstrate the intent of Congress that concerns of comity and judicial convenience should be met, not by rigid limitations on the jurisdiction of federal courts, but by the discretionary exercise of abstention when appropriate in a particular case.[14]

Here, the possibility of abstention was not raised in the district court.[15]

For the purpose of determining whether a particular matter falls within bankruptcy jurisdiction, it is not necessary to distinguish between proceedings "arising under", "arising in a case under", or "related to a case under", title 11. These references operate conjunctively to define the scope of jurisdiction. Therefore, it is necessary only to determine whether a matter is at least "related to" the bankruptcy. The Act

---

[9] *See* note 4.

[10] Section 1471(c) of the 1978 Act read:

The bankruptcy court for the district in which a case under title 11 is commenced shall exercise all of the jurisdiction conferred by this section on the district courts.

[11] *See Marathon*, 458 U.S. at 71, 102 S.Ct. at 2871, 73 L.Ed.2d at 615.

[12] *See 12–66*, 755 F.2d 421, 425 (5th Cir. 1985).

[13] 28 U.S.C. § 1334(c)(1).

[14] *In re Salem Mortgage Co.*, 783 F.2d 626, 635 (6th Cir. 1986).

[15] On remand the district court may, of course, consider the abstention issue.

does not define "related" matters. Courts have articulated various definitions of "related", but the definition of the Court of Appeals for the Third Circuit appears to have the most support: "whether the outcome of that proceeding could *conceivably* have any effect on the estate being administered in bankruptcy."[16]

This definition comports with the legislative history of the statutory predecessor to section 1334. Neither *Marathon* nor general concerns of comity counsel against its use. We adopt it as our own.

Applying this test to the case before us, we find that the complaint is sufficiently related to the pending bankruptcy to allow the district court to exercise jurisdiction under section 1334. The complaint against the bankruptcy debtors could have a *conceivable* effect on their bankruptcy. The plaintiff seeks to recover stock and monies that the debtors allegedly appropriated from the clinic. They seek to resolve the disputed allocation of interest in the clinic. To the extent that the debtors' interest in the clinic, their stock holdings, or their withdrawals are now property of the estate, the complaint against them has a potential effect on their estate.

The debtors argue that the complaint raises a post–petition claim that will not affect their bankruptcy.[17]

Generally, post–petition claims are not dischargeable in bankruptcy and, therefore, do not affect the estate.[18]

To fall within the court's jurisdiction, the plaintiffs' claims must affect the estate, not just the debtor.[19]

Although we acknowledge the possibility that this suit may ultimately have no effect on the bankruptcy, we cannot conclude, on the facts before us, that it will have no conceivable effect. First, the complaint raises a dispute over the division of ownership of the clinic. Because the debtors held their stock in the clinic before filing for bankruptcy, the disputed share is now part of the estate.[20]

Second, the complaint seeks to recover stock and cash withdrawals made after the filing of the petition. Although post–petition acquisitions of the debtor are generally not part of the estate, they may be estate property in this case if considered income from pre–petition property.[21]

---

16 *Pacor, Inc. v. Higgins,* 743 F.2d 984, 994 (3d Cir. 1984) (emphasis added); *accord In re Dogpatch U.S.A., Inc.,* 810 F.2d 782, 786 (8th Cir. 1987); *In re Salem Mortgage Co.,* 783 F.2d 626, 634 (6th Cir. 1986); *In re Globe Parcel Service,* 71 B.R. 323, 326 (E.D. Pa. 1987); *In re World Financial Services Center, Inc.,* 64 B.R. 980, 988 (Bankr. S.D. Cal. 1986); *In re Cemetery Development Corp.,* 59 B.R. 115, 121 (Bankr. M.D. La. 1986).

17 The complaint challenges the issuance of stock in November of 1984 and the withdrawal of money in Spring of 1985, both of which occurred after the filing of the bankruptcy petition in March of 1984.

18 *See* Weintraub & Resnick, *Bankruptcy Law Manual* ¶ 5.07 (1986).

19 *See In re Cemetery Development Corp.,* 59 B.R. 115, 121 & n. 13 (Bankr. M.D. La.1986).

20 *See* 11 U.S.C. § 541.

21 *See Id.* § 541(a)(6), 541(a)(7).

We raise these possibilities, not to resolve them, for that matter is left to the district and bankruptcy courts to decide under federal law,[22] but to illustrate the conceivable effect of the complaint on the administration of the bankruptcy.

Defendant Woodrow Barham argues that even if the court has jurisdiction over the claims against Dr. James Wood and his wife, it does not have jurisdiction over him because he is not a debtor–in–bankruptcy. The Bankruptcy Rules incorporate the joinder provisions of the Federal Rules of Civil Procedure allowing the joinder of other defendants.[23]

Joinder is allowed, however, only if an independent basis of federal jurisdiction exists to support the joined claim.[24]

We find that the claim against Woodrow Barham is "related to" the Wood's bankruptcy and, thus, its joinder is jurisdictionally supported.

The plaintiff has filed one complaint against the defendants seeking liability for their joint conduct. Success against any of the defendants will have a potential effect on the estate. For example, if Dr. Wood and his wife are held liable but Barham is not, the bankrupt estate may bear the entire burden of the judgment. If, on the other hand, Barham is found jointly liable, the estate may bear only a portion of the judgment. Moreover, in filing the complaint, the plaintiff challenged the combined actions of both the debtors and Barham, a non–debtor. Resolution of the dispute will necessarily involve, therefore, consideration of Barham's involvement in those actions. We find support in the Court of Appeals for the Sixth Circuit and lower courts, which have held that when the plaintiff alleges liability resulting from the joint conduct of the debtor and non–debtor defendants, bankruptcy jurisdiction exists over all claims under section 1334.[25]

III.

We have decided that subject–matter jurisdiction exists over this proceeding. We must now determine the placement of that jurisdiction. Our analysis turns to 28 U.S.C. § 157, the response of Congress to *Marathon* and its replacement for subsection 1471(c) of the 1978 Act. In contrast to subsection 1471(c), section 157 does not give bankruptcy courts full judicial power over all matters over which the district courts have jurisdiction under section 1334. With respect to proceedings other than the bankruptcy petition itself, section 157 divides all proceedings into two categories. Subsection 157(b)(1) gives bankruptcy judges the power to deter-mine "all core proceedings arising under title 11, or arising in a case under title 11" and to enter appropriate orders and judgments. Subsection 157(c)(2) gives the bankruptcy judge the limited power to hear "a proceeding that is not a core proceeding but that is otherwise related to a case under title 11" and to submit proposed findings of fact and conclusions of law to the district court, subject to de

---

[22] *See* 28 U.S.C. § 1334(d); *Texas v. Wellington Resource Corp.,* 706 F.2d 533, 536 (5th Cir. 1983).

[23] *See Bankr. Rules* 7018–7020.

[24] *Pacor, Inc. v. Higgins,* 743 F.2d 984, 994 (3d Cir. 1984).

[25] *In re Salem Mortgage Co.,* 783 F.2d 626, 634 (6th Cir. 1986); *In re Zamost,* 7 B.R. 859 (Bankr. S.D. Cal. 1980).

novo review. The essential distinction that must be made, therefore, is whether this action is a core or non–core proceeding.

The statute does not define core proceedings. Subsection (b)(2) does provide a non–exclusive list of examples, three of which are arguably relevant here:

(A)   matters concerning the administration of the estate;

(B)   allowance or disallowance of claims against the estate;

and . . .

(O)   other proceedings affecting the liquidation of the assets of the estate or the adjustment of the debtor–creditor or the equity security holder relationship.

We note that the last example is broadly worded; indeed, "proceedings affecting the estate" is similar in scope to the test of jurisdiction: proceedings having a "conceivable effect on the estate". We decline, however, to give such a broad reading to subsection 157(b)(2)(O); otherwise, the entire range of proceedings under bankruptcy jurisdiction would fall within the scope of core proceedings, a result contrary to the ostensible purpose of the 1984 Act. That purpose is to conform the bankruptcy statute to the dictates of Marathon.[26]

Specifically, *Marathon* involved an adversarial proceeding brought by the debtor–in–bankruptcy on a pre–petition claim arising under state substantive law against a defendant who had not filed a claim in bankruptcy. A plurality of the Supreme Court held that the proceeding could not be adjudicated by the bankruptcy court. The exact extent of *Marathon's* holding is subject to debate. Certain principles can be extracted from its opinions, principles that apparently have been incorporated into the 1984 Act.

Justice Brennan, writing for the plurality, held that only controversies involving "public rights", rights provided to an individual by Congress under one of its exceptional powers under the Constitution, may be removed from Article III courts and delegated to non–Article III tribunals.[27]

Justice Brennan implicitly recognized that the exceptional powers of Congress under the bankruptcy clause may sometimes allow for such delegations of judicial power:

> But the restructuring of debtor–creditor relations, which is at the *core* of the federal bankruptcy power, must be distinguished from the adjudication of state–created private rights, such as the right to recover contract damages that is at issue in this case. The former may well be a "public right," but the latter obviously is not.[28]

Concerning the latter controversy, he noted:

---

[26] Numerous courts have noted the necessity of defining core proceedings narrowly so as to conform to the constitutional proscription of *Marathon. E.g., Piombo Corp. v. Castlerock Properties,* 781 F.2d 159, 162 (9th Cir. 1986); *In re Satelco, Inc.,* 58 B.R. 781, 788 (Bankr. N.D. Tex. 1986); *In re American Energy, Inc.,* 50 B.R. 175, 178 (Bankr. D.N.D. 1985).

[27] 458 U.S. at 69–70, 102 S. Ct. at 2870–71, 73 L. Ed.2d at 614.

[28] *Id.* at 71, 102 S. Ct. at 2871, 73 L. Ed.2d at 615.

This claim may be adjudicated in federal court on the basis of its relationship to the petition for reorganization. But this relationship does not transform the state–created right into a matter between the Government and the petitioner for reorganization. Even in the absence of the federal scheme, the plaintiff would be able to proceed against the defendant on the state–law contractual claims.[29]

Two points are suggested by this language. First, bankruptcy judges may exercise full judicial power over only those controversies that implicate the peculiar rights and powers of bankruptcy or, in Justice Brennan's words, controversies "at the core of the federal bankruptcy power". Second, controversies that do not depend on the bankruptcy laws for their existence—suits that could proceed in another court even in the absence of bankruptcy—are not core proceedings. These points are echoed by Chief Justice Burger in his dissent in which he characterized the plurality opinion as follows:

the Court's holding is limited to the proposition that a "traditional" state common–law action, not made subject to a federal rule of decision, and related only peripherally to an adjudication of bankruptcy under federal law, must, absent the consent of the litigants, be heard by an "Article III court".[30]

Justice White expressed concern, however, that the plurality's holding placed too much emphasis on the existence of state law issues in the proceeding before bankruptcy court:

Second, the distinction between claims based on state law and those based on federal law disregards the real character of bankruptcy proceedings. The crucial point to be made is that in the ordinary bankruptcy proceeding the great bulk of creditor claims are claims that have accrued under state law prior to bankruptcy—claims for goods sold, wages, rent, utilities, and the like. Every such claim must be filed and its validity is subject to adjudication by the bankruptcy court. The existence and validity of such claims recurringly depend on state law. Hence, the bankruptcy judge is constantly enmeshed in state–law issues.[31]

Section 157 of the 1984 Act incorporates the principles suggested in the language of the *Marathon* opinions. The reference in the Act to "core" proceedings is taken directly from Justice Brennan's description of matters that involve the peculiar powers of bankruptcy courts. The Act describes non–core proceedings as "otherwise related", an apparent reference to Chief Justice Burger's description of the *Marathon* proceeding as "related only peripherally to an adjudication of bankruptcy". Mindful of the limitations of the plurality's holding and of Justice White's observations concerning state law, Congress added: "A determination that a proceeding is not a core proceeding shall not be made solely on the basis that its resolution may be affected by State law."[32]

---

[29] *Id.* at 72 n. 26, 102 S. Ct. at 2872 n. 26, 73 L. Ed. 2d at 615 n. 26.
[30] *Id.* at 92, 102 S. Ct. at 2882, 73 L. Ed.2d at 628 (Burger, C. J., dissenting).
[31] *Id.* at 96–97, 102 S. Ct. at 2884–85, 73 L. Ed.2d at 631 (White, J., dissenting).
[32] 28 U.S.C. § 157(b)(3).

The meaning of core proceedings is illuminated also by the textual context in which it appears. Subsection 157(b)(1) vests full judicial power in bankruptcy courts over "core proceedings *arising under title 11, or arising in a case under title 11.*" The prepositional qualifications of core proceedings are taken from two of the three categories of jurisdiction set forth in section 1334(b): proceedings "arising under" title 11, "arising in" title 11 cases, and "related to" title 11 cases. Although the purpose of this language in section 1334(b) is to define conjunctively the scope of jurisdiction, each category has a distinguishable meaning. These meanings become relevant because section 157 apparently equates core proceedings with the categories of "arising under" and "arising in" proceedings.

Congress used the phrase "arising under title 11" to describe those proceedings that involve a cause of action created or determined by a statutory provision of title 11.[33]

Apparently, the phrase was taken from 28 U.S.C. § 1331, conferring federal question jurisdiction in which it carries a similar and well–accepted meaning. The meaning of "arising in" proceedings is less clear, but seems to be a reference to those "administrative" matters that arise *only* in bankruptcy cases.[34]

In other words, "arising in" proceedings are those that are not based on any right expressly created by title 11, but nevertheless, would have no existence outside of the bankruptcy.

As defined above, the phrases "arising under" and "arising in" are helpful indicators of the meaning of core proceedings. If the proceeding involves a right created by the federal bankruptcy law, it is a core proceeding; for example, an action by the trustee to avoid a preference. If the proceeding is one that would arise only in bankruptcy, it is also a core proceeding; for example, the filing of a proof of claim or an objection to the discharge of a particular debt. If the proceeding does not invoke a substantive right created by the federal bankruptcy law and is one that could exist outside of bankruptcy it is not a core proceeding; it may be *related* to the bankruptcy because of its potential effect, but under section 157(c)(1) it is an "otherwise related" or non–core proceeding.

Finally, the interpretation of core proceeding based on its equation with "arising under" and "arising in" proceedings comports with the interpretation suggested by *Marathon.* Justice Brennan's description of "core" matters parallels that of matters "arising under" title 11—matters invoking a substantive right created by federal bankruptcy law. Moreover, his comment that the matter could have proceeded absent the bankruptcy suggests a contrast with "arising in" proceedings—matters that could arise only in bankruptcy.

We hold, therefore, that a proceeding is core under section 157 if it invokes a substantive right provided by title 11 or if it is a proceeding that, by its nature, could arise only in the context of a bankruptcy case. The proceeding before us does not meet this test and, accordingly, is a non–core proceeding. The plaintiff's suit is not

---

[33] *See* 1 Collier on Bankruptcy ¶ 3.01 at 3–23 (1987).

[34] *Id.* at 3–27.

based on any right created by the federal bankruptcy law. It is based on state–created rights.[35]

Moreover, this suit is not a proceeding that could arise only in the context of a bankruptcy. It is simply a state contract action that, had there been no bankruptcy, could have proceeded in state court.

The plaintiff argues that his action is literally a claim against the estate, which is expressly defined as a core proceeding by section 157(b)(2)(B).[36]

We disagree. In determining the nature of a proceeding for purposes of determining core status, the court must look to both the form and the substance of the proceeding.[37]

The form of this action is not that of a "claim" as that term is used in bankruptcy law. A claim against the estate is instituted by filing a proof of claim as provided by the bankruptcy rules.[38]

The filing of the proof invokes the special rules of bankruptcy concerning objections to the claim, estimation of the claim for allowance purposes, and the rights of the claimant to vote on the proposed distribution.[39]

Understood in this sense, a claim filed against the estate is a core proceeding because it could arise only in the context of bankruptcy. Of course, the state–law right underlying the claim could be enforced in a state court proceeding absent the bankruptcy, but the nature of the state proceeding would be different from the nature of the proceeding following the filing of a proof of claim. Here, the plaintiff has not filed a proof of claim and has not invoked the peculiar powers of the bankruptcy court.

The substance of this action does not support a finding of core status. The essential issue in the proceeding is whether the defendants are liable to the plaintiff under state law. The suit does not raise as primary issues such matters as dischargeability, allowance of the claim, or other bankruptcy matters.[40]

Conceivably, a final judgment in this proceeding in the plaintiff's favor may lead to proceedings to allow the claim or to discharge the debt. At this juncture, however, these concerns are speculative and insubstantial issues in the proceeding. The plaintiff's suit is not a core proceeding.

---

[35] We are mindful that, alone, this circumstance should not be dispositive. 28 U.S.C. § 157(b)(3).

[36] "Core proceedings include (B) allowance or disallowance of claims against the estate." 28 U.S.C. § 157(b)(2)(B).

[37] *See In re World Financial Services Center, Inc.,* 64 B.R. 980, 984–87 (Bankr. S.D. Cal. 1986); *In re Satelco, Inc.,* 58 B.R. 781 786–89 (Bankr. N.D. Tex. 1986).

[38] *See* Bankr. Rules 3001–3002.

[39] *See In re Criswell,* 44 B.R. 95 (Bankr. E.D. Va. 1984); *Distinguishing Core from Non–Core Proceedings,* Norton Bankr. L. Adviser, No. 1, Jan. 1985, p. 2.

[40] *Cf. Matter of Colorado Energy Supply,* 728 F.2d 1283, 1285–86 (10th Cir. 1984) in which the court held that a claim for rents under state law was not a "traditional state claim" within the meaning of *Marathon* because the plaintiff sought also preferred status under the bankruptcy laws.

The judgment of the district court is vacated and the case is remanded to the district court for further proceedings consistent with this opinion.

HUFFMAN v. PERKINSON
(In re Harbour)

United States Court of Appeals, Fourth Circuit
18 C.B.C. 2d 627 (1988)

SPROUSE, Circuit Judge:

Diana M. Perkinson and her husband, Frank N. Perkinson, Jr., appeal from the district court's order denying their demand for a jury trial in this action against them by Donald W. Huffman, trustee in bankruptcy for the estate of Billy H. Harbour, and Bluefield Holding Company (hereafter Huffman or the trustee). The trustee seeks to recover funds that he alleges Diana Perkinson received from Harbour in transactions voidable as fraudulent transfers and illegal preferences under federal bankruptcy laws, and as voluntary conveyances voidable under Virginia state law. 11 U.S.C. §§ 543, 547, 548; Va. Code § 55–81.

Harbour's creditors placed him in involuntary bankruptcy on February 11, 1982.[1]

Harbour remained as the debtor in possession during the Chapter 11 proceedings until the court appointed Huffman trustee on February 8, 1983. On October 21, 1984, Huffman as trustee initiated this action to recover payments Harbour made to Diana Perkinson allegedly as legal fees. The trustee asserts Diana Perkinson received payments totalling $125,713.49 either within one year prior to Harbour being placed in bankruptcy or while he remained as debtor in possession.[2]

Diana Perkinson had represented Harbour and Bluefield Holding Company, a company wholly owned by Harbour, and had served as Secretary and registered agent of the company. Frank Perkinson was joined as a co–defendant in the trustee's action because he and his wife practiced law as a partnership, and she had deposited the disputed funds into their joint account.

The district court denied the Perkinsons' motion for a jury trial but certified its order for interlocutory appeal. 28 U.S.C. § 1292(b). We granted the Perkinsons' petition for interlocutory appeal. The merits of the trustee's attempt to avoid the transfers and obtain the funds, of course, have not been determined. The issues on appeal involve the jurisdiction of the bankruptcy court and whether the Perkinsons

---

[1] 11 U.S.C. § 303. Chapter 11 is codified at 11 U.S.C. § 1101 *et seq.* The bankruptcy was converted to a Chapter 7 proceeding on September 13, 1983. 11 U.S.C. § 701 *et seq.*

[2] Huffman filed a second complaint against the Perkinsons on February 7, 1985, seeking to recover an additional $144,060.81. This sum includes $24,500 as the value of diamond earrings, a Rolex ring and wristwatch, and clothing Harbour allegedly gave Diana Perkinson. The proceedings in that action have been stayed pending the outcome in this appeal of the district court's denial of the jury trial motion made pursuant to the first complaint.

are constitutionally or statutorily entitled to a jury trial to determine the parties' respective rights under 11 U.S.C. §§ 543, 547, and 548 and Va. Code § 55–81.

The Perkinsons first assert, in effect, that the funds Mrs. Perkinson received from Harbour were for fees earned under Virginia law so that the federal bankruptcy court has no jurisdiction to entertain the trustee's action, *Northern Pipeline Co. v. Marathon Pipe Line Co.*, 458 U.S. 50, 73 L. Ed. 2d 598, 102 S. Ct. 2858 [6 C.B.C.2d 785] (1982). They also assert that both the seventh amendment to the United States Constitution and the Bankruptcy Amendments and Federal Judgeship Act of 1984, Pub. L. No. 98–353, 98 Stat. 333 (hereafter the 1984 Bankruptcy Act or the 1984 Act) grant them a right to a trial by jury.[3]

We hold that the bankruptcy court has jurisdiction over these actions and that neither the seventh amendment nor the 1984 Act require a jury trial. We discuss seriatim the jurisdiction issue, the seventh amendment question and whether, apart from the constitutional requirements, the 1984 Act entitles the Perkinsons to a jury trial in the trustee's action against them.

I.

The Perkinsons advance three related arguments in support of their contention that the bankruptcy court has no jurisdiction over the trustee's actions. First, they assert that under *Northern Pipeline* a non–Article III bankruptcy judge has no jurisdiction over the trustee's avoidance action based on alleged fraudulent or preferential transfers because the actions involve only rights created by the substantive law of Virginia. They assert that any action involving the sums paid to Mrs. Perkinson is not a "case under Title 11," did not "arise under Title 11"; nor did the issues "arise in a case under Title 11." 28 U.S.C. § 1334.[4]

---

[3] The Perkinsons inexplicably cite both the 1978 and 1984 Acts. The 1984 Act controls the outcome of this case, however. Section 122 of the 1984 Act provides that "amendments made by this title [title I—Bankruptcy Jurisdiction and Procedure] shall take effect on the date of the enactment of this Act [July 10, 1984]," with certain exceptions. Pub. L. No. 98–353, § 122(a), 98 Stat. 333, 346 (1984). Section 553(a) provides that "the amendments made by this title [title III—Amendments to Title 11 of the United States Code] shall become effective to cases filed 90 days after the date of enactment of this Act." Pub. L. No. 98–353, § 553(a), 98 Stat. 333, 392 (1984). We have held that the jurisdictional provisions of the 1984 Act apply to any case pending on July 10, 1984. *Creasy v. Coleman Furniture Corp.*, 763 F.2d 656, 660 [12 C.B.C.2d 1238] (4th Cir. 1985); *see also In re Hudson Shipbuilders, Inc.*, 794 F.2d 1051, 1054 n.4 (5th Cir. 1986); *In re Castlerock Properties*, 781 F.2d 159, 161 [15 C.B.C.2d 20] (9th Cir. 1986); *Carlton v. Baww, Inc.*, 751 F.2d 781, 787 n.6 [12 C.B.C.2d 457] (5th Cir. 1985). Most, if not all, issues involved in this appeal relate to jurisdictional disputes that had not arisen or were pending on July 10, 1984. The only non–jurisdictional matter relates to the possible application of 11 U.S.C. § 544, which became effective for cases filed 90 days after July 10, 1984, or October 9, 1984. Here, although the petition was filed in February 1982, the trustee's complaint was filed October 12, 1984. In any event, the provisions of § 544 are essentially the same under both the 1978 and 1984 Acts.

[4] Section 101 of the 1984 Act provides in pertinent part:

(a) Except as provided in subsection (b) of this section, the district courts shall have original and exclusive jurisdiction of all cases under title 11.

They argue instead that, at most, the issues in this case only "relate to a case under Title 11" and possess the same characteristics as Northern Pipeline's suit against Marathon Pipe Line, which could not be tried by a bankruptcy judge. Second, they argue that if Congress intended to include actions to litigate rights created by state substantive law as "core" proceedings, section 157(b) of the 1984 Act violates the principles of *Northern Pipeline*. [5]

Third, the Perkinsons stress that Harbour transferred some of the property more than a year prior to the filing of the bankruptcy petition and, as to those transfers, the Virginia avoidance law, and not the federal bankruptcy law, provides the essential procedural mechanism under which the trustee can proceed. [6]

Assuming these factual contentions are correct, we think neither of these classes of transfers are within the proscription of the Supreme Court's holding in *Northern Pipeline*.

Initially, the Perkinsons maintain that their right to legal fees was created by the substantive law of Virginia, so the trustee's attack of that right can only be determined in a state forum or by an Article III judge. They urge that the trustee's action is similar to Northern Pipeline's action against Marathon, which the Supreme Court reviewed in *Northern Pipeline*. The trustee, on the other hand, insists that his action

---

(b) Notwithstanding any Act of Congress that confers exclusive jurisdiction on a court or courts other than the district courts, the district courts shall have original but not exclusive jurisdiction of all civil proceedings arising under title 11, or arising in or related to cases under title 11.

28 U.S.C. § 1334.

[5] Section 104 of the 1984 Act, codified at 28 U.S.C. § 157 (hereafter § 157 of the 1984 Act), provides:

(a) Each district court may provide that any or all cases under title 11 and any or all proceedings arising under title 11 or arising in or related to a case under title 11 shall be referred to the bankruptcy judges for the district.

(b) (1) Bankruptcy judges may hear and determine all cases under title 11 and all core proceedings arising under title 11, or arising in a case under title 11, referred under subsection (a) of this section, and may enter appropriate orders and judgments, subject to review under section 158 of this title.

Section 157(b)(2) provides as follows:

Core proceedings include, but are not limited to—

. . .

(F) proceedings to determine, avoid, or recover preferences;

. . .

(H) proceedings to determine, avoid, or recover fraudulent conveyances.

[6] The trustee filed two actions against the Perkinsons. *See supra* note 2. The first action sought to set aside transfers of money to Diana Perkinson for legal fees, and this appeal involves only the district court's denial of a jury trial in that action. The complaint reflects that all of the transfers were made within one year of bankruptcy. In view of the record's sparsity and the Perkinsons' contentions on appeal, however, we will assume that some transfers were made more than one year prior to bankruptcy, but within a time frame permitting an action under § 55–81 of the Virginia Code.

is a "core" proceeding "arising in a case under title 11" that, under *Northern Pipeline,* can be determined by a bankruptcy judge.

In *Northern Pipeline,* the Supreme Court held that a jurisdictional provision of the Bankruptcy Reform Act of 1978, Pub. L. No. 95–598, 92 Stat. 2549, violated the separation of powers doctrine by conferring Article III judicial power on non–Article III bankruptcy judges with respect to proceedings that included those only "related to cases under Title 11." The Court found no constitutional objections to the congressional exercise of its Article I § 8 bankruptcy powers in assigning jurisdiction over traditional bankruptcy matters to bankruptcy courts. Although not so stated by the Court, those proceedings presumably were matters "arising under title 11, or arising in a case under title 11." 28 U.S.C. § 1334 (replacing 28 U.S.C. § 1471); *see* 1 Collier on Bankruptcy ¶ 3.01[l][c][ii]—[iv] (15th ed. 1987) (hereafter Collier). It held, however, that a contract action based on state law must be resolved in a state court or by an Article III judge. *See Thomas v. Union Carbide Agricultural Products Co.,* 105 S. Ct. 3325, 3334–35 (1985).

Our first task is to identify the jurisdictional restrictions applied to bankruptcy courts in *Northern Pipeline* and to determine if the trustee's action against the Perkinsons comes within them. In the aftermath of *Northern Pipeline,* the limitations encompassed in the phrase "related to cases under title 11" are not entirely clear. It generally has been held, however, that the *Northern Pipeline* restriction is limited to actions by the bankrupt or his trustee over the disposition of state–created substantive rights.[7]

As Justice Rehnquist said in his concurring opinion to *Northern Pipeline:*

> [T]he lawsuit in which Marathon was named defendant seeks damages for breach of contract, misrepresentation, and other counts which are the stuff of the traditional actions at common law. There is apparently no federal rule of decision provided for any of the issues in the lawsuit; the claims of Northern arise entirely under state law.

458 U.S. at 90 (Rehnquist, J., concurring).

In his dissent, Chief Justice Burger added:

> [T]he Court's holding is limited to the proposition that a "traditional" state common–law action, not made subject to a federal rule of decision, and related only peripherally to an adjudication of bankruptcy under federal law, must, absent the consent of the litigants, be heard by an "Art. III court" if it is to be heard by any court or agency of the United States.

Id. at 92 (Burger, C. J., dissenting).

If there was any question that these statements reflect the limits of Northern Pipeline's holding, it was dispelled by the Court's decision in *Thomas v. Union Carbide Agriculture Products Co.,* 105 S. Ct. at 3334–35, in which the Court noted:

---

[7] *Northern Pipeline,* 458 U.S. at 87 n.40; *see also id.* at 92 (Burger, C. J., dissenting); 1 Collier ¶ 3.01[1][c][iv] (15th ed.); *Thomas v. Union Carbide Agricultural Products Co.,* 105 S. Ct. 3325, 3334–35 (1985); *1616 Reminc Limited Partnership v. Atchison & Keller,* 704 F.2d 1313, 1318 n.15 [8 C.B.C.2d 467] (4th Cir. 1983).

[Our] holding in [*Northern Pipeline*] establishes only that Congress may not vest in a non–Article III court the power to adjudicate, render final judgment, and issue binding orders in a traditional contract action arising under state law, without consent of the litigants, and subject only to ordinary appellate review. (Citations omitted).

Here, Harbour, the bankrupt, transferred a large amount of money to Mrs. Perkinson. The dispute between the trustee and Mrs. Perkinson over the right to this money does not depend upon the substantive law of Virginia, rather it is governed by federal bankruptcy laws. It is a dispute involving the restructuring of debtor–creditor relations. As the *Northern Pipeline* plurality opinion noted:

> the restructuring of debtor–creditor relations, which is at the core of the federal bankruptcy power, must be distinguished from the adjudication of state–created private rights, such as the right to recover contract damages that is at issue in this case.

458 U.S. at 71.

In this case, the transfers that were made within a year prior to the filing of Harbour's bankruptcy petition[8] present very little analytical difficulty; actions to recover them are specifically identified as "core" matters in section 157(b)(2)(F) ("proceedings to determine, avoid, or recover preferences") and (H) ("proceedings to determine, avoid, or recover fraudulent conveyances") of the 1984 Act. Mrs. Perkinson claims she earned the money transferred to her as legal fees. Her contractual right to receive the funds is no doubt a right that existed by virtue of Virginia law. It does not belong, however, to the same species of legal rights involved in *Northern Pipeline*. Northern Pipeline's action was based on its claim for breach of contract and warranty—a traditional common law action based on no federal rule of decision. The trustee's action is a core proceeding arising under title 11, or arising in a case under title 11,[9] in which Congress gave bankruptcy courts *in personam*

---

[8] Under 11 U.S.C. § 547(b), the trustee can avoid as preferences certain transfers made within 90 days before the bankruptcy petition is filed, or one year if the transferee is an insider. Mrs. Perkinson was Secretary of Bluefield Holding Company, so for purposes of this appeal we assume, without deciding, that she was an insider. Section 548(a) grants the trustee the authority to avoid fraudulent transfers made by the debtor within one year before the bankruptcy petition was filed. Without considering the merits of the trustee's attempt to avoid the transfers, we consider them as two groups: those made within one year prior to the filing of Harbour's petition and those made more than one year prior to it.

[9] *See* 1 Collier ¶ 3.01[2][b][ii] (15th ed.) (equating the jurisdictional provision declared invalid in *Northern Pipeline* to the provisions in the 1984 Act treating proceedings relating to a case under title 11 and stating that under the 1984 Act "there is no such thing as a core matter which is only related to cases under title 11"). *See also* Taggart, *The New Bankruptcy Court System,* 59 Am. Bankr. L.J. 231, 241–42 (1985) (hereafter Taggart), to the effect that the drafters of the 1984 Act dealt with *Northern Pipeline* by omitting matters only "related to a case under the Code" from the matters over which a bankruptcy judge could exercise jurisdiction. *Compare* King, *Jurisdiction and Procedure Under the Bankruptcy Amendments of 1984,* 38 Vand. L. Rev. 675, 689 (1985) (hereafter King). The author said:

> One could argue that [a case only related to cases arising under title 11] would be a core proceeding. It certainly affects the liquidation of the assets of the estate. The

jurisdiction over Mrs. Perkinson and summary jurisdiction to decide this dispute between her and the trustee.

In their brief, however, the Perkinsons make the additional argument that some of the involved funds were paid to Mrs. Perkinson more than one year prior to Harbour's bankruptcy and the trustee can only recover those funds under section 55–81 of the Virginia Code.[10]

They contend that actions based solely on Virginia's avoidance law only peripherally relate to the administration of Harbour's bankruptcy and are the equivalent of Northern Pipeline's action against Marathon. We are unable to determine from the record if, in fact, some funds were paid to her beyond the controlling bankruptcy time frame. Assuming her factual contentions are correct, however, we are not persuaded that the trustee's recovery under section 55–81 of the Virginia Code should be treated differently from recovery under 11 U.S.C. §§ 547 and 548 of funds transferred within one year of bankruptcy.

First, the language of section 157(b)(2)(F) and (H) does not limit the proceedings to avoid preferences and fraudulent transfers only to those proceedings authorized by sections 547 and 548 of the Bankruptcy Code. It embraces state avoidance laws and includes them as part of the bankruptcy proceedings. 1 Collier ¶ 3.01[2] [b] [ii] (15th ed.); Taggart, at 247. The legislative history of section 157(b) certainly demonstrates that this was the intent of Congress.[11]

Chapter 11 debtor in *Northern Pipeline* sued for breach of contract. The cause of action (a chose in action) was an asset of the estate and had to be liquidated. It is therefore likely that the proceeding also affected the adjustment of the debtor–creditor relationship. If the breach of contract action would be a core proceeding under the 1984 amendments, Congress has not complied with the Supreme Court's mandate and has enacted a constitutionally invalid statute.

The author also listed in note 44 a number of bankruptcy court holdings indicating that the distinction between these categories of bankruptcy matters is a difficult one to make. *But cf.* Taggart, at 947 *et seq.;* Kamp, *Court Structure Under the Bankruptcy Code,* 90 Com. L.J. 203, 207 (1985).

[10] Va. Code § 55–81 provides:

Voluntary gifts, etc., void as to prior creditors.—Every gift, conveyance, assignment, transfer or charge which is not upon consideration deemed valuable in law, or which is upon consideration of marriage, shall be void as to creditors whose debts shall have been contracted at the time it was made, but shall not, on that account merely, be void as to creditors whose debts shall have been contracted or as to purchasers who shall have purchased after it was made; and though it be decreed to be void as to a prior creditor, because voluntary or upon consideration of marriage, it shall not, for that cause, be decreed to be void as to subsequent creditors or purchasers.

[11] Representative Kastenmeier, who introduced the legislation containing § 157, had this to say:

In this respect, State law rights arising in core bankruptcy proceedings are functionally equivalent to congressionally created rights, because Congress has the power to modify State law rights in bankruptcy proceedings. Unlike the States, Congress may impair the obligations of contracts through the bankruptcy clause. Indeed, the very purpose of bankruptcy is to modify the rights of the debtors and creditors, and the bankruptcy code

Moreover, section 544(b) gives trustees in bankruptcy the same authority to avoid transfers that an unsecured debtor would have under state law.[12]

In *Carlton v. Baww, Inc.*, 751 F.2d 781 [12 C.B.C.2d 457] (5th Cir. 1985), for example, the Fifth Circuit held that an action by the trustee to avoid a fraudulent conveyance under state law, as authorized by section 544(b), is a proceeding arising under title 11 and the district court (and presumably the bankruptcy court) has jurisdiction over the action.[13]

Finally, section 157(b)(3) provides that "a determination that a proceeding is not a core proceeding shall not be made solely on the basis that its resolution may be affected by state law." 28 U.S.C.§ 157(b)(3). In short, the portion of this dispute that must be resolved by the bankruptcy court's interpretation of Va. Code § 55–81 likewise falls within the dispute resolution mechanism of section 157(b). This dispute does not involve the type of state–created substantive rights that *Northern Pipeline* ruled must be resolved by Article III judges.[14]

I.

The Perkinsons next contend that the seventh amendment of the United States Constitution guarantees them a jury trial. The seventh amendment provides:

> In Suits at common law, where the value in controversy shall exceed twenty dollars, the right of trial by jury shall be preserved, and no fact tried by jury, shall be otherwise re–examined in any Court of the United States, than according to the rules of the common law.

The nature of the seventh amendment inquiry has been so thoroughly and universally stated that extensive case citation is not necessary.[15]

---

authorizes the bankruptcy court to abrogate or modify State–created obligations in many ways.

130 Cong. Rec. H1110 (daily ed. March 20, 1984).

12 Section 544(b) provides:

(b) The trustee may avoid any transfer of an interest of the debtor in property or any obligation incurred by the debtor that is voidable under applicable law by a creditor holding an unsecured claim that is allowable under section 502 of this title or that is not allowable only under section 502(e) of this title.

11 U.S.C. § 544(b).

13 *But see* King, at 693, where the author states:

It is difficult, if not impossible, to perceive any conceptual difference between the trustee's use of an individual creditor's right to sue under section 544(b) and the debtor suing for breach of contract as it did in *Northern Pipeline*.

14 *But see id.*, at 689, where the author postulates that some *Northern Pipeline*–type "related to" matters might be core proceedings under § 157 and, if so, the section would be unconstitutional as violating the principles of *Northern Pipeline*.

15 As one noted commentator remarks:

The Seventh Amendment preserved the right of trial by jury "in suits at common law." Inevitably this calls for some historical inquiry. If the issue in the context in which it arises would have been heard at common law in 1791, when the Seventh Amendment was adopted, or, more accurately, in 1938 when law and equity were merged, it is now

Simply stated, the essence of our seventh amendment inquiry is whether the underlying issues to be ascertained and determined in this proceeding are legal or equitable. If the action is to enforce legal rights, then it falls within the seventh amendment grant of a right to a trial by jury. *Curtis v. Loether*, 415 U.S. 189, 195 (1974); *see also Ross v. Bernhard*, 396 U.S. 531 (1970); *Dairy Queen Inc. v. Wood*, 369 U.S. 469 (1962); *Beacon Theatres, Inc. v. Westover*, 359 U.S. 500 (1959). In deciding this question, courts have traditionally employed a historical test looking to the custom that existed with respect to the action under English common law at the time the seventh amendment was adopted. *Baltimore & Carolina Line, Inc. v. Redman*, 295 U.S. 654, 657 (1935); *Damsky v. Zavatt*, 289 F.2d 46, 48–51 (2d Cir. 1961). *See also Ross v. Bernhard*, 396 U.S. at 533–34.[16]

Our analytical chore, however, has been abbreviated by the Supreme Court's decisions in *Schoenthal v. Irving Trust Co.*, 287 U.S. 93 (1932), and *Katchen v. Landy*, 382 U.S. 323 (1966), and the congressional enactment of the Bankruptcy Act of 1984. Our inquiry is directed at determining whether the underlying issues in this case are legal or equitable, but we focus on the Supreme Court's decision in *Schoenthal, Katchen* and Congress' enactment of the 1984 Act.

The universal rule under the Bankruptcy Act of 1898[17] and its predecessors[18] had been that actions to set aside the bankrupt's transfers as fraudulent or preferential

---

triable of right to a jury. There is no right to jury trial if viewed historically the issue would have been tried in courts of equity or if otherwise it would have been tried without a jury.

Wright & Miller, Federal Practice and Procedure, § 2302, at 14–15 (1971) (footnotes omitted).

[16] Since the merger of law and equity in 1938, Fed. R. Civ. P. 2, however, the Supreme Court has not adhered rigidly to a historical test. *See Beacon Theatres, Inc., v. Westover*, 359 U.S. 500 (1959); *Dairy Queen, Inc. v. Wood*, 369 U.S. 469 (1962); *Ross v. Bernhard*, 396 U.S. 351 (1970). *See also Whitlock v. Hause*, 694 F.2d 861, 863 (1st Cir. 1982). 5 Moore's Federal Practice ¶ 38.09[5–4] (2d ed. 1982); Wright and Miller, Federal Practice and Procedure, § 2302, at 18 (1971). *Compare Tull v. United States*, 55 U.S.L.W. 4571 (April 28, 1987), where Justice Brennan, in the majority opinion, described one important approach to resolving the question of whether an issue is legal or equitable for seventh amendment purposes:

Our search is for a single historical analogue, taking into consideration the nature of the cause of action and the remedy as two important factors.

Id. at 4574 (citing Pernell v. Southall Realty, 416 U.S. 363, 375 (1974), and *Curtis*, 415 U.S. at 195–96).

[17] 30 Stat. 544 (1898).

[18] Congress enacted the first national bankruptcy act in 1800. 2 Stat. 19–21. It was to be in effect for five years, but was repealed in 1803. Congress enacted a second act, the Bankruptcy Act of 1841, 5 Stat. 440, but repealed it in 1843. 1 Collier ¶ 0.04 (14th ed.). Financial stress following the Civil War prompted the Bankruptcy Act of 1867, 14 Stat. 517, which was repealed in 1878. *Id.* at ¶ 0.05. Congress ultimately enacted the Bankruptcy Act of 1898, which remained in effect until superseded by the Bankruptcy Reform Act of 1978. The 1898 Act was amended extensively by the Bankruptcy Act of 1938, commonly known as the Chandler Act, *id.* at ¶ 0.07, and was also amended in 1903, 1906, 1910, 1914, 1916, 1917, 1922, 1926, 1932, 1933, 1934 (on four occasions), 1935 (on five occasions), 1936 (on

were actions outside the bankruptcy proceeding and were to be resolved by plenary proceedings in a different forum.[19]

Schoenthal, recognizing that rule in the seventh amendment context,[20] unequivocally had determined that actions such as this one were to be considered outside the bankruptcy proceedings, were legal in nature and were under the aegis of the seventh amendment. As in *Schoenthal,* the Court in *Katchen* considered (under the Bankruptcy Act of 1898) an action similar to the one we review. It held emphatically that bankruptcy proceedings were equitable. Although the case cast some doubt on the vitality of *Schoenthal,* the Court refrained from overruling it. The 1984 Act, by designating actions to avoid preferences and fraudulent transfers as core proceedings, mandated that these actions be resolved within the bankruptcy forum by the bankruptcy judge, a legislative mandate that has a direct bearing on the seventh amendment jury question.[21]

The combined effect of judicial and legislative actions, we think, is to cast the trustee's claim against the Perkinsons as a bankruptcy proceeding entirely within the traditionally equitable bankruptcy forum[22] and free of the seventh amendment's requirement that in all suits at common law the right to trial by jury shall be preserved.

In *Schoenthal,* the Court stated that "[s]uits to recover preferences constitute no part of the proceedings in bankruptcy but concern controversies arising out of it." 287 U.S. at 94–95. It said, therefore, that "[t]he question whether remedy must be by action at law or may be pursued in equity notwithstanding objection by defendants depends upon the facts stated in the bill." *Id.* at 95. The Court referred

---

four occasions), 1937 (on two occasions), 1938, 1939, and 1946. *Id.* at ¶¶ 0.06 n.6, 0.08, 0.09.

19 1 Collier ¶ 3.01[7][b][i] (15th ed.).

20 In *Schoenthal,* the Court actually construed a provision of the judicial code, 28 U.S.C. § 384, not the seventh amendment. The Court noted, however, that the provision "guard[s] the right of trial by jury preserved by the Seventh Amendment ." 287 U.S. at 94.

21 *See In Re O'Bannon,* 49 B.R. 763, 766 n.5 (Bankr. M.D. La. 1985), where the bankruptcy court says:

> If *Katchen v. Landy* stands for the proposition that cases with a clear bankruptcy focus do not involve a Seventh Amendment right to jury, then parties in core matters would have no *constitutional* jury rights.

(emphasis in original).

22 The early English bankruptcy statutes were administered through the Court of Chancery at the direction of the Lord Chancellor. For a discussion of those statutes *see,* Jones, *The Foundations of English Bankruptcy: Statutes and Commissions in the Early Modern Period,* 69 Transactions of the Am. Phil. Soc'y, Part 3 (1979); Levinthal, *The Early History of English Bankruptcy,* 67 U. Pa. L. Rev. 1 (1919). For a comparison of English and American law and procedures governing the granting of discharges in a historical and modern context, which demonstrates the equitable nature of the proceedings, *see* Boshkoff, *Limited, Conditional, and Suspended Discharges in Anglo–American Bankruptcy Proceeding,* 131 U. Pa. L. Rev. 69 (1982).

both to the historical English practice and to the then current American practice in suits by bankrupts to recover preferential payments.[23]

Although *Schoenthal* dealt with suits to recover preferences, there is little doubt that, under the 1898 Act, the same reasoning would have applied with equal force to an action by a trustee to set aside the transfer as a fraudulent conveyance.

A noted commentator has stated:

> It follows that whether the trustee's suit should be at law or in equity is to be judged by the same standards that are applied to any other owner of property which is wrongfully withheld. If the subject matter is a chattel, and is still in the grantee's possession, an action in trover or replevin would be the trustee's remedy; and if the fraudulent transfer was of cash, the trustee's action would be for money had and received. Such actions at law are as available to the trustee today as they were in the English courts of long ago.

Glenn, *Fraudulent Conveyances and Preferences,*§ 98 (1940) (footnote omitted). He went on to say with reference to the Supreme Court's decision in *Schoenthal*:

> The actual decision was that in the case of a preference the trustee's suit must be at law unless he needs equitable relief for any reason as above suggested. But what is true of a preference, which essentially is an offense against a bankruptcy law as such, is a *fortiori* true of a fraudulent conveyance, and hence the Supreme Court's decision should be accepted as final for all purposes.

Id. It seems clear then that under the doctrine announced in *Schoenthal* and at least until the Supreme Court's decision in *Katchen*, adverse claimants like the Perkinsons would have had a right to a jury trial in a trustee's action to avoid and recover the fraudulent or preferential conveyance.

Katchen was decided in 1966, thirty–four years after *Schoenthal*. In it, the Supreme Court reviewed a holding that a bankruptcy court had summary jurisdiction to order a creditor to surrender property that the bankrupt had preferentially transferred to him. The Court upheld the summary jurisdiction of the bankruptcy court and emphasized that the creditor had subjected himself to the jurisdiction of the bankruptcy court by filing a claim in the bankruptcy proceeding. Justice White's opinion stated, with great emphasis, that bankruptcy courts are "essentially courts of equity" and "characteristically proceed in summary fashion." 382 U.S. at 327 (citations omitted). The Court also stated:

> When Congress enacted general revisions of the bankruptcy laws in 1898 and 1938, it gave special attention to the subject of making [the bankruptcy laws] inexpensive in [their] administration. Moreover, this Court has long recognized that a chief purpose of the bankruptcy laws is to secure a prompt

---

[23] The 1898 Act, as amended when *Schoenthal* was decided, provided two types of jurisdiction. Section 2 of the Act conferred upon the courts of bankruptcy original jurisdiction at law and equity over proceedings under the Act, which included administrative matters, disputes over property in the actual or constructive property of the court, and disputes over the bankrupt's discharge. This was considered summary jurisdiction. Section 23 governed the district court's plenary jurisdiction over controversies at law and in equity. *See In re Boss–Linco Lines, Inc.,* 55 B.R. 299, 302–04 (Bankr. W.D.N.Y. 1985). *See infra* note 25.

and effectual administration and settlement of the estate of all bankrupts within a limited period, and that provision for summary disposition, "without regard to usual modes of trial attended by some necessary delay," is one of the means chosen by Congress to effectuate that purpose.

Id. at 328–29 (citations omitted).

The *Katchen* decision, of course, addressed an action by a trustee against an adverse claimant who had filed a claim in the bankruptcy proceeding and thus submitted to the jurisdiction of the bankruptcy court. The Court stopped short of overruling *Schoenthal*, however, stating:

> But although petitioner might be entitled to a jury trial on the issue of preference if he presented no claim in the bankruptcy proceeding and awaited a federal plenary action by the trustee, when the same issue arises as part of the process of allowance and disallowance of claims, it is triable in equity. *Id.* at 336 (citation omitted).

If this language connoted a reticence by the Court to overrule *Schoenthal*,[24] its reluctance is understandable. *Schoenthal* was based on solid precedent and historical judicial treatment of actions by debtors or trustees to set aside preferential transfers.[25]

---

[24] Some writers were of the opinion that on the authority of *Katchen*, even before Congress passed the 1984 Act, there was no seventh amendment right to a jury trial in any bankruptcy proceedings. 1 Collier ¶ 3.01[7][b][i] at 3–86 (15th ed.). For cases holding to the contrary, *see id.* at 3–87 n.178.

[25] Firmly implanted in the structure of all the congressional enactments listed in note 18 was the longstanding English and American principle that actions to avoid preferential and fraudulent conveyances were not a part of the proceedings in bankruptcy, but were part of controversies arising out of it.

The Bankruptcy Acts of 1841 and 1867 gave federal district courts concurrent jurisdiction with state courts to conduct plenary trials involving suits by the trustee (assignee) against an adverse third party. Congress deleted that provision in the original Act of 1898, but reinserted it by amendments in 1903 and 1910. *Bardes v. First National Bank of Hawarden,* 178 U.S. 524 (1900). *See Schumacher v. Beeler,* 293 U.S. 367 (1934) (discussing federal court jurisdiction following the 1903 and 1910 amendments). Each bankruptcy act until the 1978 Act, however, provided that actions to avoid preferential and fraudulent conveyances were to be tried outside the bankruptcy forum.

As explained by the Court's historical analysis in *Bardes,* that rule was strictly a creature of various congressional acts. Prior to the 1903 amendment, section 23(b) of the 1898 Act provided:

> (b) Suits by the trustee shall only be brought or prosecuted in the courts where the bankrupt might have brought or prosecuted them if proceedings in bankruptcy had not been instituted, unless by consent of the proposed defendant.

In reviewing the jurisdiction of federal trial courts to entertain, in a bankruptcy proceeding, an action to set aside preferential or fraudulent transfers, the Court in *Bardes* said that under the 1867 Act federal trial courts had two types of jurisdiction in bankruptcy matters:

> First, jurisdiction, as a court of bankruptcy, over the proceedings in bankruptcy ending in the distribution of assets amongst the creditors, and the discharge of the bankrupt; secondly, jurisdiction, as an ordinary court, of suits at law or in equity brought by or

Short of congressional action dramatically altering the structure of bankruptcy administration that was established in the early bankruptcy acts, it seems likely that the principle announced in *Schoenthal* would have remained a permanent fixture in the law of bankruptcy.

An essential key to the Court's ruling in *Schoenthal* that suits to recover preferences were legal in nature was the well–founded concept that Congress intended actions against third parties in general and avoidance actions in particular not to be part of bankruptcy proceedings.**26**

---

against the assignee in reference to alleged property of the bankrupt, or to claims alleged to be due from or to him.

Bardes, 178 U.S. at 531 (quoting *Lathrop v. Drake,* 91 U.S. 516 (1975)).

The Court went on to note that in its original form, the 1898 Act omitted the second type of jurisdiction, and only state courts could at that time entertain actions to set aside preferences or fraudulent conveyances.

Under the act of 1867, then, the distinction between proceedings in bankruptcy, properly so–called, and independent suits, at law or in equity, between the assignee in bankruptcy and an adverse claimant, was distinctly recognized and emphatically declared.

Id. at 533.

The Court also said:

It was also repeatedly held by this court that the right of an assignee in bankruptcy to assert a title in property transferred by the bankrupt before the bankruptcy to a third person who now claimed it adversely to the assignee could only be enforced by a plenary suit at law or in equity, under the 2d section of the act of 1867; and not by summary proceedings under the 1st section thereof.

Id. at 532.

Proceedings in bankruptcy generally are in the nature of proceedings in equity; "at law," in the opening sentence may have been inserted to meet clause 4, authorizing the trial and punishment of offenses.

Id. at 535.

The Court, again speaking of the 1867 jurisdiction before it was temporarily removed by Congress in the 1898 Act, said:

The 1st clause provides that "the United States circuit courts shall have jurisdiction of all controversies at law and in equity, as distinguished from proceedings in bankruptcy" (thus clearly recognizing the essential difference between proceedings in bankruptcy, on the one hand, and suits at law or in equity, on the other), "between trustees as such and adverse claimants, concerning the property acquired or claimed by the trustees," restricting that jurisdiction, however, by the further words, "in the same manner and to the same extent only as though bankruptcy proceedings had not been instituted and such controversies had been between the bankrupts and such adverse claimants." *Id.* 536. In its § 23 analysis, the Court went on to say that an adverse third party claimant "shall not be brought within the jurisdiction of the national courts solely because the rights of the bankrupt and of his creditors have been transferred to the trustee in bankruptcy." *Id. See also Schumacher v. Beeler,* 293 U.S. 367 (1934) (discussing the effect of the 1903 and 1910 amendments on federal court jurisdiction over suits by the trustee against adverse third parties to recover property as preferences or fraudulent conveyances).

26 Types of bankruptcy actions that the bankruptcy court could resolve by summary disposition as "bankruptcy proceedings" have varied in the different acts. In *Bardes,* the Court set

Congress dramatically changed this rule, however, in the 1984 Act. It directed that bankruptcy courts may now hear, determine, and enter orders and judgments in all proceedings under Title 11, and all core proceedings arising under Title 11 or arising in a case under Title 11. 28 U.S.C. § 157(b)(1). From the unmistakable language of the Act, it is manifest that Congress intended bankruptcy courts to have jurisdiction over "proceedings to determine, avoid, or recover preferences," 11 U.S.C. § 157(b)(2)(F), and "proceedings to determine, avoid, or recover fraudulent conveyances," 11 U.S.C. § 157(b)(2)(H).

Relying on *Schoenthal* and precedent involving common law actions to avoid transfers, the Perkinsons contend, however, that

> [i]f the bankruptcy statutes must be interpreted to categorize the adversary suits by the Trustee against the Perkinsons as "core" proceedings and if the bankruptcy statutes must further be interpreted to require core proceedings be tried by the bankruptcy judge and if the Constitution is interpreted to prohibit bankruptcy judges from conducting jury trials, then the appropriate provisions of 28 U.S.C. § 157 are unconstitutional by denying the Perkinsons the right of trial by jury.

We disagree.

Schoenthal went no further than to hold that a preferential transfer action under the 1898 Act must be tried in a non–bankruptcy forum and that its characterization as being either legal or equitable in the seventh amendment context must, therefore, be determined independently of the bankruptcy proceeding—*i.e.*, its legal or equitable nature must be judged as if it were a unitary common law action to avoid a transfer without any connection to a bankruptcy proceeding.[27]

It based its holding, however, on its recognition that avoidance actions were not part of the bankruptcy proceedings and, when judged under the practice of litigating those cases, were considered to be legal in nature.[28]

The Court reasserted, moreover, the conventional jurisprudence that bankruptcy proceedings are equitable. Thirty–four years later, *Katchen* reasserted with even greater force the ancient principle that bankruptcy proceedings are equitable.

---

forth these categories and noted that the 1898 Act differed from the 1867 Act in that "[i]t specifies in greater detail matters which are, in the strictest sense, proceedings in bankruptcy." *Bardes,* 178 U.S. at 534. The 1898 Act specified nineteen such types of actions, including the appointing of receivers and trustees; authorizing them to conduct the bankrupt's business; exercising administrative control over cases; extraditing bankrupts; transferring cases to other bankruptcy courts; deciding substantive issues in some proceedings (such as adjudging persons to be bankrupt); allowing or disallowing claims; causing the estate to be collected and distributed to creditors; reviewing findings of the referee; discharging the bankrupt; and enforcing its orders through contempt powers. 1898 Act § 2. This jurisdiction has varied. For a summary of modern jurisdiction, *see* Countryman, *Scrambling to Define Bankruptcy Jurisdiction: The Chief Justice, the Judicial Conference, and the Legislative Process,* 22 Harv. J. on Legis. 1,35 (1985).

27 *See supra* note 25.

28 The fact that they were not part of the bankruptcy proceedings at any given time, however, was simply dependent on federal statutory law. 1 Collier ¶ 3.01[2][b][iii] at 3–36.1 (15th ed.). *See also supra* note 25.

More importantly for our purposes, *Katchen* explained the somewhat subtle, but imminently [sic] logical, reasoning of seventh amendment jurisprudence relating to bankruptcy controversies. Justice White carefully explained how actions that are, and always have been considered to be, legal for seventh amendment or other purposes, become equitable when merged into bankruptcy proceedings.**29**

So, in cases of bankruptcy, many incidental questions arise in the course of administering the bankrupt estate, which would ordinarily be pure cases at law, and in respect of their facts triable by jury, but, as belonging to the bankruptcy proceedings, they become cases over which the bankruptcy court, which acts as a court of equity, exercises exclusive control. Thus a claim of debt or damages against the bankrupt is investigated by chancery methods.

382 U.S. at 337 (quoting *Barton v. Barbour,* 104 U.S. 126, 134 (1881)).

The Bankruptcy Act, passed pursuant to the power given to Congress by Art. I, § 8, of the Constitution to establish uniform laws on the subject of bankruptcy, converts the creditor's legal claim into an equitable claim to a pro rata share of the res.

Id. at 336.

Justice White, in answering the creditors' argument that the exercise of summary jurisdiction would violate the Court's holding in *Dairy Queen,* said:

---

29 The successive bankruptcy statutes themselves have changed actions from plenary to summary proceedings. For example, under § 58 of the Bankruptcy Act of 1800, claims of creditors could be tried before a jury. 2 Stat. 19–21, § 58, *reprinted in* 10 Collier, Appendix at 1736 (14th ed.). Under § 1 of the Bankruptcy Act of 1841, debtors who were declared a bankrupt involuntarily could petition for a jury trial. *Id.* at 1738. Under § 4 of that Act, bankrupts who did not receive a full discharge could demand a jury trial. As in § 58 of the 1800 Act, a jury trial was available under § 7 of the 1841 Act "to ascertain the validity and amount of debts or other claims" against the estate. Id. at 1743. Under § 41 of the Bankruptcy Act of 1867, the debtor retained the right to demand a jury trial in an involuntary bankruptcy proceeding to determine if an act of bankruptcy had been committed. *Id.* at 1773–74. However, there was no provision for jury trials over the grant of discharges or allowance of claims. Section 2 of the 1898 Act specifically included in its grant of jurisdiction to courts of bankruptcy the authority to adjudge persons bankrupt, to allow or disallow claims against the estate, and to discharge (or not) bankrupts. These matters were within the bankruptcy proceedings, which would be summary. *Id.* at 1785–86. Section 19, however, retained the right to a jury trial with respect to the question of insolvency in an involuntary proceeding. *Id.* at 1797. Between the 1800 and 1898 Acts, therefore, the boundaries of plenary versus summary jurisdiction were altered by legislative enactments as formerly plenary proceedings were changed to summary proceedings.

The Chandler Act of 1938, 52 Stat. 840 (1938), further increased the summary jurisdiction of the bankruptcy court. Section 50n provided for summary proceedings in suits over breach of an obligation of a bond furnished pursuant to the Act.

Section 571 provided for summary jurisdiction over actions by the trustee to recover excess payments on claims or payments made on disallowed claims. The 1938 Act also provided for summary jurisdiction over a trustee's suit to recover property held pursuant to a lien voidable under § 67, even absent consent of the adverse party. *See* 2 Collier § 23.04[4] (14th ed.). The 1978 and 1984 Acts continued that trend of increasing the bankruptcy court's summary jurisdiction.

Such a result is not consistent with the equitable purposes of the Bankruptcy Act nor with the rule of *Beacon Theatres* and *Dairy Queen*, which is itself an equitable doctrine. In neither *Beacon Theatres* nor *Dairy Queen* was there involved a specific statutory scheme contemplating the prompt trial of a disputed claim without the intervention of a jury.

Id at 39 (citations omitted).

In a different context, the Court in *Northern Pipeline* said:

the interaction between the Legislative and Judicial Branches is at its height where courts are adjudicating rights wholly of Congress' creation. Thus where Congress creates a substantive right, pursuant to one of its broad powers to make laws, Congress may have something to say about the proper manner of adjudicating that right.

Id. at 83 n.35.

The Court recognized in *Northern Pipeline* that the "reconstructing of debtor–creditor relations" is a pure bankruptcy matter in which Congress could assign jurisdiction to bankruptcy judges. *Id.* at 71. It can hardly be gainsaid that bankruptcy proceedings are equitable. In all the Bankruptcy Acts, at least from 1841 until the Bankruptcy Act of 1978, however, Congress purposefully excluded the actions of a trustee to avoid and recover fraudulent and preferential transfers from its designation of matters considered "pure" bankruptcy or "core" bankruptcy proceedings. *See Bardes,* 178 U.S. 534 (1900); 2 Collier ¶¶ 23.12, 23.13 (14th ed.); Taggart, at 233. It just as purposefully reversed this course of action when it enacted the 1978 and the 1984 Acts.

Granting bankruptcy courts broad jurisdictional powers to entertain actions aimed at resolving disputes between a trustee and an adverse third party resulted, in large measure, from the deleterious effect of disputes over whether a particular issue was subject to summary or plenary jurisdiction.[30]

The summary/plenary distinction and the judicial quagmires resulting from the disputes it generated were the by–products of the 1898 Act rule that third–party claims were to be tried independently of the bankruptcy forum. Congress, after studying this problem for almost ten years,[31] dramatically altered bankruptcy

---

[30] *See* 1 Collier ¶ 3.01 [1][b][iv] (15th ed); *see also* Countryman, at 6–7.

A major impetus underlying this reform legislation has been the need to enlarge the jurisdiction of the bankruptcy court in order to eliminate the serious delays, expense and duplications associated with the current dichotomy between summary and plenary jurisdiction.

It is the purpose of new section 164 of title 28, United States Code, in conjunction with 28 U.S.C. section 1334 to eliminate entirely the present jurisdictional dichotomy between summary and plenary jurisdiction.

S. Rep. No. 989, 95th Cong., 2d Sess. 17–18, reprinted in 1978 U.S. Code Cong. & Ad. News 5787, 5803–04.

[31] Congress created the Commission on the Bankruptcy Laws of the United States in 1970, Act of July 24, 1970, Pub. L. No. 91–354, 84 Stat. 468. For a discussion of the proposals developed by the Commission and leading to the 1978 Act, *see* 1 Collier ¶ 1.03 (15th ed.).

proceedings in the 1978 Act to correct these deficiencies. It not only reconstructed the mechanics of bankruptcy administration, but completely altered the philosophy underlying the litigation of bankruptcy issues. *See* Taggart, at 233; Countryman, at 7–12. After the Supreme Court declared the jurisdictional provision of the 1978 Act unconstitutional in *Northern Pipeline*, Congress obviously restructured the jurisdictional grant in the 1984 Act. The Jurisdictional features of both acts, however, were designed primarily to eliminate a major defect in bankruptcy litigation—the time, resources and efficiency wasted in deciding whether disputes were to be resolved by summary or plenary proceedings. In the 1978 Act, Congress accomplished this purpose in two ways. First, it expanded the bankruptcy courts' jurisdiction and, second, it allowed them to conduct jury trials in cases that previously had been routed to non–bankruptcy forums.[32]

In the 1984 Act, Congress achieved this purpose by granting bankruptcy courts summary jurisdiction over all civil proceedings except those only peripherally related to a case under title 11. By this action, Congress brought all but a very narrow category of cases[33] affecting the bankruptcy estate within the bankruptcy framework, to be litigated in the traditional equitable forum of the bankruptcy court.

It is true that in determining seventh amendment rights we examine issues rather than cases. *Ross v. Bernhard*, 396 U.S. at 538. Here, however, the issues we examine relate to the restructuring of the debtor–creditor relationship in bankruptcy. American courts have held core bankruptcy proceedings to be equitable from the beginning of our system of bankruptcy.[34]

Now, Congress also has determined that actions such as the trustee's in this case are core bankruptcy proceedings requiring summary disposition by a bankruptcy judge. As such, they assume the historical equitable posture of all such bankruptcy proceedings, and the litigants involved in these actions have no seventh amendment right to a trial by jury.[35]

III.

The Perkinsons contend that, even if the seventh amendment does not mandate that they receive a jury trial, provisions of the 1984 Act nevertheless require it.

Congress could have exceeded constitutional requirements, of course, and statutorily provided a right to trial by jury in all bankruptcy matters. In fact, as we previously noted, Congress took an expansive approach to jury trials in the 1978 Act. *See* King, at 705; *see also* Levy, at 10; Countryman, at 7–12; Note, *The*

---

[32] 28 U.S.C. §§ 1471, 1480 (repealed 1984). *See generally,* Levy, *Trial By Jury Under the Bankruptcy Reform Act of 1978,* 12 Conn. L. Rev. 1 (1979).

[33] 28 U.S.C. § 157(a), (b)(1), (c)(1). *See Northern Pipeline,* 458 U.S. at 92 (Burger, C.J., dissenting); *see generally,* King, *supra.*

[34] *See Barton v. Barbour,* 104 U.S. 126, 134 (1881); *Bardes v. First National Bank of Hawarden,* 178 U.S. 524, 535 (1900); *Local Loan Co. v. Hunt,* 292 U.S. 234, 240 (1934); *Pepper v. Litton,* 308 U.S. 295, 304 (1939); *Katchen v. Landy,* 382 U.S. 323, 337 (1966).

[35] *See* 1 Collier ¶ 3.01[7][b][1] at 3–87 (15th ed.); *Matter of McLouth Steel Corp.,* [14 C.B.C.2d 22] 55 B.R. 357, 362–63 (Bankr. E.D. Mi. 1985); *In re American Energy, Inc.,* 50 B.R. 175, 180 (Bankr. D.N.D. 1985); O'Bannon, 49 B.R. at 766.

Bankruptcy Amendments and Federal Judgeship Act of 1984: The Impact on the Right of Jury Trial in Bankruptcy Court, 16 Tex. Tech L. Rev. 535, 541 (1985) (hereafter Note). Section 241 (a) of that Act, 28 U.S.C. § 1471, provided in part:

(a) Except as provided in subsection (b) of this section, the district courts shall have original and exclusive jurisdiction of all cases under title 11.

(b) Notwithstanding any Act of Congress that confers exclusive jurisdiction on a court or courts other than the district courts, the district courts shall have original but not exclusive jurisdiction of all civil proceedings arising under title 11 or arising in or related to cases under title 11.

(c) The bankruptcy court for the district in which a case under title 11 is commenced shall exercise all of the jurisdiction conferred by this section on the district courts.

Title 28, section 1480, also part of section 241(a) of the 1978 Act, provided in part:

(a) Except as provided in subsection (b) of this section, this chapter and title 11 do not affect any right to trial by jury, in a case under title 11 or in a proceeding arising under title 11 or arising in or related to a case under title 11, that is provided by any statute in effect on September 30, 1979.

Rather than expand existing rights to jury trials in bankruptcy proceedings, the 1984 Act drastically restricted such rights. For reasons not completely apparent either in the language of the Act or from its legislative history, Congress went beyond those faults identified by the Supreme Court in Northern Pipeline in restructuring the 1978 Act to eliminate its constitutional faults. 1 Collier ¶ 3.01[7][b][i] (15th ed.). The pervasive jury trial rights contained in section 1480 under the 1978 Act were eliminated. In its stead, Congress provided in part:

§ 1411. Jury trials

(a) Except as provided in subsection (b) of this section, this chapter and title 11 do not affect any right to trial by jury that an individual has under applicable nonbankruptcy law with regard to a personal injury or wrongful death tort claim. Pub. L. No. 98–353, § 102(a) (codified at 28 U.S.C. § 1411).

Congress, in the 1984 Act, granted bankruptcy courts the authority to "hear and determine" matters that previously could only be determined in plenary proceedings, as well as matters that could be determined in summary proceedings. 28 U.S.C. § 157(b)(1). Considered against the background of congressional effort to eliminate the systematic problems caused by the plenary/summary distinction, it seems logical to infer from the structure of the 1984 Act that Congress intended all core proceedings to be determined by exercise of summary jurisdiction. *See* King, at 703; Taggart, at 248. Apart from that, the plain language of section 1411 indicates almost conclusively that litigants such as the Perkinsons have no statutory right to a trial by jury under the 1984 Act.[36]

A comparison of section 1480 of the 1978 Act with the cryptic language of section 1411 in the 1984 Act reinforces that conclusion. The general structure of the

---

[36] *See* 1 Collier ¶ 3.01[7][b][i] (15th ed.); *McLouth Steel,* 55 B.R. at 362; *In re American Energy,* 50 B.R. at 180; King, at 702–06. *But see* Note, at 545 *et seq.;* Taggart, at 260–61.

jurisdiction sections of the 1984 Act, the absence in it of the broad jury trial provision contained in the 1978 Act, and the 1984 language specifically limiting the right to a jury trial to negligence and wrongful death actions effectively forecloses any argument that Congress intended issues such as are involved there to be tried by jury.

The judgment of the district court is affirmed.

Affirmed.

WIDENER, Circuit Judge, dissenting: Since I believe that the Perkinsons are entitled to trial by jury, I respectfully dissent.

Huffman, as a trustee in bankruptcy, commenced adversary proceedings against the Perkinsons to avoid allegedly preferential and fraudulent transfers or voluntary conveyances. The trustee relied both upon federal law to set aside the transfers as preferential and fraudulent,[1] and also upon Virginia state law which allows for the voiding of voluntary conveyances. Va. Code § 55–81. The trustee seeks repayment or judgment.[2]

There is no property in the hands of the Perkinsons which the trustee seeks to recover. The Perkinsons, who have not filed any claim in the bankruptcy case, challenge the court's jurisdiction and demand trial by jury on the claims asserted by the trustee. The district court did not refer these proceedings to a bankruptcy judge, and this appeal is from an interlocutory order of the district court denying trial by jury.

My concern is not with the trustee's ability to press for the recovery of preferential, fraudulent or voluntary transfers; rather, it is with the determination that the exercise of all avoiding powers at the trustee's disposal are "core proceedings" subject to summary adjudication by the bankruptcy court and free of the Seventh Amendment's jury requirement.

I.

I agree with the majority that the district court has jurisdiction, although my reasons differ from those given in the majority opinion.

Congress has the undoubted power to create federal question causes of action, as it has done here, in 11 U.S.C. § 547 for preferences and § 548 for fraudulent transfers. It also has the undoubted power to authorize a trustee in bankruptcy to proceed against the beneficiary of a preferential or fraudulent transfer under federal

---

[1] 11 U.S.C. §§ 547, 548.

[2] As noted by the court, there were two such proceedings instituted by the trustee, one alleging voidable transfer of money and seeking an order requiring repayment or judgment for the transferred amount. The second complaint alleges voidable transfer of negotiable instruments, personal property and services. The relief sought in this second proceeding is judgment for the aggregate value of the transfers. Nowhere does the trustee seek reconveyance of property. Only the first of the two proceedings is here on appeal. The trustee and his co–plaintiff, Bluefield Holding Co., were treated as one by the parties and the district court. No question is made of Bluefield's participation in this proceeding.

substantive law or of a voluntary conveyance under Virginia Code § 55–81 as it has done in 11 U.S.C. § 544(b).

Following the 1978 amendments to the Bankruptcy Code as amended in 1984, the trustee has the power to bring into the bankruptcy case the beneficiaries of preferential, fraudulent or voluntary conveyances, even involuntarily as here. *Northern Pipeline* requires that when someone is made a party in a proceeding in a bankruptcy case involuntarily, as here, that he be brought into an Article III court. The district judge in this case prudently held to himself the decision in the adversary proceeding and did not refer it to a bankruptcy judge. By so doing, the district court wisely finessed the even more ticklish question than the one present here.

I can see nothing about bringing the Perkinsons into the case which is a violation of *Northern Pipeline* and the subsequent case dealing with the same subject, *Commodities Future Trading Comm. v. Schor,*— U.S. —, 106 S. Ct. 3245 (1986). Neither can I see in this case the exercise by Congress of any authority relating to jurisdiction which it did not have. Since the trustee proceeds against the Perkinsons on both federal and state substantive law grounds, it is a matter of indifference on which ground, if any, he may ultimately be successful for the grounds onwhich he proceeds must govern the procedure.

It is the nature of the federal and state causes of action which the trustee asserts, as well as the procedural aspect in which this case finds itself, which must determine whether or not the Perkinsons are entitled to trial by jury, which will be discussed below.

II.

The trustee seeks to use his avoiding powers to restore the value of the transferred assets to the debtor's estate.[3]

Although the distinction may sometimes be difficult to draw, preferences are generally permitted outside of bankruptcy law while fraudulent or voluntary conveyance law reaches actions taken by a debtor irrespective of the pendency of a bankruptcy case.[4]

The justification for fraudulent conveyance law is fundamentally broader than the reasons for a bankruptcy proceeding. The Supreme Court has long recognized the distinction between a fraudulent and preferential conveyance:

> One is inherently and always vicious; the other innocent and valid, except when made in violation of the express provisions of a statute. One is *malum per se* and the other *malum prohibitum,* — and then only to the extent that it is forbidden. A fraudulent conveyance is void regardless of its date; a preference is valid unless made within the prohibited period.

---

[3] The avoiding powers employed by this trustee are codified in 11 U.S.C. § 547 (Preferences); § 548 (Fraudulent transfers and obligations); and § 544 (Trustee as lien creditor and as successor to certain creditors and purchasers). 11 U.S.C. § 544(b) authorizes the trustee to fill the shoes of an unsecured creditor and to seek avoidance of "any" transfer voidable under "applicable law." It is by virtue of § 544(b) that the trustee can assert a claim under Virginia's voluntary conveyance statute.

[4] *See* Jackson, *Avoiding Powers in Bankruptcy,* 36 Stan. L. Rev. 725 (1984).

Van Iderstine v. National Discount Co., 227 U.S. 575, 582 (1912). And, we too have previously stated our understanding of the distinct natures of these causes of action. In considering the applicability of West Virginia preference and fraudulent conveyance law in a pre–Code bankruptcy case, a case dealing with § 544(b)'s statutory predecessor, we followed the distinction recited in *Van Iderstine, David v. Woolf,* 147 F.2d 629 (4th Cir. 1945).

Fraudulent conveyance law has its origins at least as early as the Statute of 13 Elizabeth and has survived essentially intact for four centuries.[5]

In England, well before our independence, the common law actions of trover and money had and received were used to recover preferential payments made by bankrupts. *Schoenthal v. Irving Trust Co.,*287 U.S. 92, 94 (1932). The claims allowed, indeed created, by these common law actions have long histories and existed at common law in 1791 when we adopted the Seventh Amendment.

The court today decides that federal bankruptcy law rather than the substantive rule of decision controls all procedural aspects of these adversary proceedings, since the dispute involves the restructuring of debtor–creditor relations. But, I should add, that consideration should not be of controlling moment here, for all bankruptcy cases involve such restructuring. It is the very purpose of bankruptcy. While federal law may provide the rule of decision with respect to the preference and fraudulent conveyance claims asserted under 11 U.S.C. §§ 547 and 548, it is clear that Virginia law provides the rule of decision in claims asserted under§ 544(b). It is § 544(b) which provides the trustee with authority to assert the state law claim. *See Glove v. Martin,*236 U.S. 288, 297 (1914); *Stellwagen v. Clum,* 245 U.S. 605, 614 (1917) (discussing § 70(e) of the Bankruptcy Act of 1898, the predecessor of § 544(b)). It is also true that the Article I, § 8 bankruptcy power allows Congress to suspend conflicting state laws, but suspension occurs only to the "extent of actual conflict with the bankruptcy act of Congress." *Stellwagen* at 613. These cases establish that § 544(b) works no such suspension but rather incorporates state law into the bankruptcy scheme, authorizing the trustee to stand in the shoes of unsecured creditors for purposes of asserting any claims available to them and existing under any law. I do not think that such a claim as here, assertible by creditors if there was no bankruptcy case, and to be determined by exclusive reference to state law, is transformed into a Congressionally created wholly federal claim to "restructure debtor–creditor relations." The historical nature of common or state law claims has been preserved by § 544(b). That section simply works no transformation of historically legal claims into purely equitable ones. Rather than being a "core proceeding" within the summary jurisdiction of the bankruptcy court, the claim pressed under Virginia Code § 55–81 is "a 'private right' for which state law provides the rule of decision. It is therefore a claim of the kind normally assumed to be at the 'core' of matters normally reserved to Article III courts." *Schor,* 54 U.S. L.W. at 5102.

---

[5] 13 Elizabeth ch. 5 (1571). *See* Kent's Commentaries v. 2, p. 439 (3rd Ed. 1836); Baird & Jackson, *Fraudulent Conveyance Law and its Proper Domain,* 38 Vand. L. Rev. 829 (1985).

The federal question claims of preference under § 547 and fraudulent transfer under § 548 fare no better. In *Schoenthal v. Irving Trust Co.*,287 U.S. 92 (1932), the Supreme Court examined whether or not a claim of preference asserted by a trustee in bankruptcy against the beneficiary of the preference was legal or equitable. In that case, the trustee had asserted his claim of preference in a plenary proceeding in a district court. The Court reversed the court of appeals which had held that a jury trial was not required because the proceeding was equitable and had affirmed the district court which had left the case on the equity side of the docket and tried it without a jury over the defendant's protest. The Court based its decision on the Seventh Amendment right of trial by jury in questions in which the remedy is by action at law. There, as here, "[t]he preferences sued for were money payments of ascertained and definite amounts." 287 U.S. at 95. So, *Schoenthal* is a precise ruling of the Supreme Court on the question at hand, that the substantive federal questions sought to be asserted by the trustee are actions at law, for, if a preference is an action at law when a money judgment is the relief sought, how may a fraudulent conveyance be otherwise when the same relief is asked for? Thus, all of the causes of action the trustee asserts in this case are legal rather than equitable, and to make the case even stronger, one of them is a cause of action under state law rather than federal.

Congress surely has the power to establish a federal bankruptcy scheme, but the bankruptcy power granted in Article I § 8 (clause 4) is not absolute and cannot be used to abrogate other constitutional guarantees. *See, e.g., Louisville Bank v. Radford*, 295 U.S. 555 (1934) (bankruptcy power subject to the Fifth Amendment). Indeed, the existence of a federal statutory scheme does not destroy the right to jury trial. *Simmons v. Avisco*, Local 713, Textile Workers Union, 350 F.2d 1012 (4th Cir. 1965) (Landrum–Griffin Act).

Civil trial by jury is guaranteed by the Seventh Amendment.[6]

While some trace jury trials from even earlier times, it is settled that clause 39 of Magna Carta preserved the right.[7]

Not only has the right a long history, it was a theme of our struggle for independence. There are numerous works which recount the role the right to jury trial in civil cases has played in our history. It was perhaps the only right universally guaranteed by state constitutions prior to the revolution; it was guaranteed in the Northwest Ordinance; and secured by the Articles of Confederation.[8]

In fact, the Seventh Amendment played a crucial role in ratification of the Constitution. This right, one of "deep interest and solicitude," is to be jealously

---

[6] The Seventh Amendment:

In suits at common law, where the value in controversy shall exceed twenty dollars, the right of trial by jury shall be preserved.

[7] *See, generally*, Pope, *The Jury*, 39 Tex. L. Rev. 426 (1961); Green, *Jury Trial and Mr. Justice Black*, 65 Yale L.J. 482 (1956); Howard, The Road from Runnymede: Magna Carta and Constitutionalism in America (1968 Univ. of Va. Press).

[8] *See* Wolfram, *The Constitutional History of the Seventh Amendment*, 57 Minn. L. Rev. 639 (1973); Goebel, History of the Supreme Court of the U.S., Vol. I (1971 Macmillan and Co.).

guarded against encroachment. *Parsons v. Bedford,*3 Pet, (28 U.S.) 433, 445–46 (1830). It is against this historical backdrop that the Supreme Court has considered the application of the amendment.

The historical test of the cause of action which governs Seventh Amendment jurisprudence was complicated by the merger of law and equity accomplished by the enactment of the Federal Rules of Civil Procedure in 1938. The effect, if any, of the merger, however, has been to enlarge rather than restrict the application of the right to jury trial. In *Beacon Theatres, Inc. v. Westover,* 359 U.S. 500 (1959), the Supreme Court held that where both legal and equitable issues are presented in a single cause, the right to jury trial is lost in only the most imperative circumstances. Three years later, the Court stated that there is a right to jury trial on issues material to both legal and equitable relief, even if the legal issues are "incidental" to the equitable issues. *Dairy Queen, Inc. v. Wood,*369 U.S. 469 (1962). Still grappling with the problem created by the merger effected by the Federal Rules, the Court emphasized that restrictive application of the Seventh Amendment is not encouraged in *Ross v. Bernhard,* 396 U.S. 532 (1970). Ross stated that the "seventh amendment question depends on the nature of the issue to be tried rather than the character of the overall action," *Id.* at 538, and specifically held that there was a right to jury trial on all legal claims in the historically equitable shareholder's derivative suit. The court has upheld the right to jury trial in actions to enforce Congressionally created statutory rights provided the action involves rights and remedies traditionally enforced in an action at law. *Curtis v. Loether,* 415 U.S. 189 (1974) (Seventh Amendment applies to actions for damages under Title VIII of the Civil Rights Act of 1968); *Pernell v. Southall Realty,* 416 U.S. 363 (1974) (Seventh Amendment applies to courts established by Congress in the District of Columbia in an action to recover possession of real property). *Tull v. United States,* 55 U.S.L.W. 4571 (April 28, 1987) (Seventh Amendment guarantees a jury trial to determine liability in actions by the Government seeking civil penalties and injunctive relief under the Clean Water Act). In Tull, the Court directed that examination of both the nature of the action and the remedy sought governs Seventh Amendment analysis. Absent consent, if the action is one comparable to those which were tried in courts of law in 18th century England, and the remedy sought is legal, the Seventh Amendment attaches. 55 L.W. at 4573.

The principal and perhaps the only difficulty the majority opinion finds with following the usual analysis of determining what is triable to a jury and what is not is *Katchen,* 382 U.S. 323 (1966). *Katchen* involved a trustee's plenary action in a federal district court to recover a money judgment for a preference. The beneficiary of the preference, however, had filed two claims in the proceeding, one for back rent, the other for payment he had made as endorser of a note of the bankrupt. Section 57g of the Bankruptcy Act required that the claim of creditors who had received a preference "should not be allowed unless such creditors shall surrender such preferences ." The trustee objected to the allowance of the creditor's claim, and the Court affirmed the referee's decision to proceed to try the question of whether or not there was a preference in order to ascertain whether or not to allow the creditor's claims. In *Katchen,* the creditor had submitted himself to the jurisdiction of the bankruptcy court by filing his claims. Thus, there was no question of his involuntarily being made a party to the proceeding, the key question on which *Northern Pipeline* turns. The Court noted its precedent, that *Schoenthal* and two of its other cases required a jury trial in a plenary proceeding on the question of whether or not a preference existed, and stated that the question put was whether "the situation is the same when the creditor files a claim and the trustee not only objected to the allowance of the claim but also demands surrender of the preference." 382 U.S. at 328. The Court held specifically that the situation was not the same. The Court based its decision on the power of the bankruptcy court to allow or disallow claims, which it stated was the full power to inquire into the validity of any alleged debt of the bankrupt upon which a demand or claim against the estate was based. 382 U.S. at 329. So, far from holding that a jury trial was not required on the question of the existence of the preference, the holding of *Katchen* is that jury trial is not required on the question of existence of a preference when the creditor has filed his claim and the trustee objects to the allowance of the claim. The Court distinguished the situation in which the creditor had filed a claim and the situation in which the creditor "presented no claim in the bankruptcy proceeding and awaited a federal plenary action by the trustee," 382 U.S. at 336, which is the precise situation existing in the case before us. To repeat, the Court based the authority for its decision on § 57g which required the bankruptcy court to necessarily determine the amount of the preference so as to ascertain whether the claimant, should he return the preference, had satisfied the condition imposed by § 57g on allowance of the claim. 382 U.S. at 334. Thus, I do not perceive *Katchen* to be any stumbling block in applying the regular test of whether or not the cause of action asserted is historically legal or equitable. It is obvious that an Article III judge, sitting in a bankruptcy proceeding, may do just that. It is the "district courts" which have jurisdiction in bankruptcy cases under 28 U.S.C. § 1334, not bankruptcy courts. Under 28 U.S.C. § 157(a), a "district court" "may" refer cases and proceedings to "bankruptcy judges," not bankruptcy courts, who under § 157(b) "may" hear and determine the matters referred (italics added). It would be rather futile to hold, I think, that under *Northern Pipeline,* if a party is involuntarily brought into a bankruptcy proceeding he must be brought before an Article III court if the Article III court does not have its attendant protections, notably the right to trial by jury.

Finally, I cannot leave the subject without calling attention to the fact that the Supreme Court has expressly rejected the notion that there is some necessary inconsistency between the desire for speedy justice and the right to trial by jury. Pernell, 416 U.S. at 383–84.

The claims asserted by the trustee in this proceeding are historically legal in nature. A money judgment is asked for. The case is pending in a United States district court. I see no reason to deny the Perkinsons their demanded trial by jury.

GRANFINANCIERA, S.A. v. NORDBERG

Supreme Court of the United States
492 U.S. 33, 20 C.B.C.2d 1216 (1989)

Justice BRENNAN Delivered the Opinion of the Court:

The question presented is whether a person who has not submitted a claim against a bankruptcy estate has a right to a jury trial when sued by the trustee in bankruptcy to recover an allegedly fraudulent monetary transfer. We hold that the Seventh Amendment entitles such a person to a trial by jury, notwithstanding Congress' designation of fraudulent conveyance actions as "core proceedings" in 28 U.S.C. § 157(b)(2)(H) (1982 ed., Supp. IV).

I.

The Chase & Sanborn Corporation filed a petition for reorganization under Chapter 11 in 1983. A Plan of Reorganization approved by the United States Bankruptcy Court for the Southern District of Florida vested in respondent Nordberg, the trustee in bankruptcy, causes of action for fraudulent conveyances. App. to Pet. for Cert. 37. In 1985, respondent filed suit against petitioners Granfinanciera, S.A. and Medex, Ltda. in the United States District Court for the Southern District of Florida. The complaint alleged that petitioners had received $1.7 million from Chase & Sanborn's corporate predecessor within one year of the date its bankruptcy petition was filed, without receiving consideration or reasonably equivalent value in return. *Id.,* at 39–40. Respondent sought to avoid what it alleged were constructively and actually fraudulent transfers and to recover damages, costs, expenses, and interest under 11 U.S.C. § § 548(a)(1) and (a)(2), 550(a)(1) (1982 ed. and Supp. V). App. to Pet. for Cert. 41. The District Court referred the proceedings to the Bankruptcy Court. Over five months later, and shortly before the Colombian Government nationalized Granfinanciera, respondent served a summons on petitioners in Bogota, Columbia. In their answer to the complaint following Granfinanciera's nationalization, both petitioners requested a "trial by jury on all issues so triable." App. 7. The Bankruptcy Judge denied petitioners' request for a jury trial, deeming a suit to recover a fraudulent transfer "a core action that originally, under the English common law, as I understand it, was a non–jury issue." App. to Pet. for Cert. 34. Following a bench trial, the court dismissed with prejudice respondent's actual fraud claim but entered judgment for respondent on the constructive fraud claim in the amount of $1,500,000 against Granfinanciera and $180,000 against Medex. *Id.,* at 24–30. The District Court affirmed, without discussing petitioners' claim that they were entitled to a jury trial. *Id.,* at 18–23.

The Court of Appeals for the Eleventh Circuit also affirmed. 835 F.2d 1341 (1988). The court found that petitioners lacked a statutory right to a jury trial, because the constructive fraud provision under which suit was brought—11 U.S.C. § 548(a)(2) (1982 ed., Supp. V)—contains no mention of a right to a jury trial and 28 U.S.C. § 1411 (1982 ed., Supp. IV) "affords jury trials only in personal injury or wrongful death suits." 835 F.2d, at 1348. The Court of Appeals further ruled that the Seventh Amendment supplied no right to a jury trial, because actions to recover fraudulent conveyances are equitable in nature, even when a plaintiff seeks only monetary relief, *Id.*, at 1348–1349, and because "bankruptcy itself is equitable in nature and thus bankruptcy proceedings are inherently equitable." *Id.*, at 1349. The court read our opinion in *Katchen v. Landy*, 382 U.S. 323 (1966), to say that "Congress may convert a creditor's legal right into an equitable claim and displace any seventh amendment right to trial by jury," and held that Congress had done so by designating fraudulent conveyance actions "core proceedings" triable by bankruptcy judges sitting without juries. 835 F.2d, at 1349.

We granted certiorari to decide whether petitioners were entitled to a jury trial, 486 U.S.–(1988), and now reverse.

II.

Before considering petitioners' claim to jury trial, we must confront a preliminary argument. Respondent contends that the judgment below should be affirmed with respect to Granfinanciera—though not Medex—because Granfinanciera was a commercial instrumentality of the Colombian Government when it made its request for a jury trial. Respondent argues that the Seventh Amendment preserves only those jury trial rights recognized in England at common law in the late 18th century, and that foreign sovereigns and their instrumentalities were immune from suit at common law. Suits against foreign sovereigns are only possible, respondent asserts, in accordance with the Foreign Sovereign Immunities Act of 1976 (FSIA), Pub. L. 94–583, 90 Stat. 2891, 28 U.S.C. § § 1330, 1602–1611, and respondent reads § 1330(a)[1] to prohibit trial by jury of a case against a foreign state. Respondent concludes that Granfinanciera has no right to a jury trial, regardless of the merits of Medex' Seventh Amendment claim.

We decline to address this argument because respondent failed to raise it below and because the question it poses has not been adequately briefed and argued. Without cross–petitioning for certiorari, a prevailing party may, of course, "defend its judgment on any ground properly raised below whether or not that ground was relied upon, rejected, or even considered by the District Court or the Court of Appeals," *Washington v. Yakima Indian Nation*, 439 U.S. 463, 476, n. 20 (1979), provided that an affirmance on the alternate ground would neither expand nor contract the rights of either party established by the judgment below. *See, e.g., Blum v. Bacon*, 457 U.S. 132, 137, n. 5 (1982); *United States v. New York Telephone Co.*, 434 U.S. 159, 166, n. 8 (1977). Respondent's present defense of the judgment, however, is not one he advanced below.[2] Although "we could consider ground

---

[1] Section 1330(a) provides:

"The district courts shall have original jurisdiction without regard to amount in controversy of any *nonjury civil action* against a foreign state as defined in section 1603(a) of this title as to any claim for relief in personam with respect to which the foreign state is not entitled to immunity either under sections 1605–1607 of this title or under any applicable international agreement." (Emphasis added.)

[2] Indeed, respondent strenuously supported the Court of Appeals' conclusion, which echoed that of the District Court, see App. to Pet. for Cert. 22, that the "FSIA is inapplicable to the case at bar," 835 F.2d 1341, 1347 (CA11 1988), not only on the court's rationale that

supporting [the] judgment different from those on which the Court of Appeals rested its decision," "where the ground presented here has not been raised below we exercise this authority 'only in exceptional cases.' " *Heckler v. Campbell,* 461 U.S. 458, 468, n. 12 (1983), quoting *McGoldrick v. Compagnie Generale Transatlantique,* 309 U.S. 430, 434 (1940).

This is not such an exceptional case. Not only do we lack guidance from the District Court or the Court of Appeals on this issue, but it remains a difficult question whether a jury trial is available to a foreign state upon request under 28 U.S.C. § 1330 and, if not, under what circumstances a business enterprise that has since become an arm of a foreign state may be entitled to a jury trial. *Compare Gould, Inc. v. Pechiney Ugine Kuhlmann,* 853 F.2d 445, 450 (CA6 1988) (jurisdiction under 28 U.S.C. § 1330 determined by party's status when act complained of occurred); *Morgan Guaranty Trust Co. of N.Y. v. Republic of Palau,* 639 F. Supp. 706, 712–716 (SDNY 1986) (status at time complaint was filed is decisive for § 1330 jurisdiction), with *Calejo v. Bancomer, S.A.,* 764 F.2d 1101, 1106–1107 (CA5 1985) (FSIA applies even though bank was nationalized after suit was filed); *Wolf v. Banco Nacional de Mexico, S.A.,* 739 F.2d 1458, 1460 (CA9 1984) (same), cert. denied, 469 U.S. 1108 (1985). Moreover, petitioners alleged in their reply brief, without contradiction by respondent at oral argument, that affirmance on the ground that respondent now urges would "unquestionably enlarge the respondent's rights under the circuit court's decision and concomitantly decrease those of the petitioner" by "open[ing] up new areas of discovery in aid of execution" and by allowing respondent, for the first time, to recover any judgment he wins against Granfinanciera from Colombia's central banking institutions and possibly those of other Colombian governmental instrumentalities. Reply Brief for Petitioners 19. Whatever the merits of these claims, their plausibility, coupled with respondent's failure to offer rebuttal, furnishes an additional reason not to consider respondent's novel argument in support of the judgment at this late stage in the litigation. We therefore leave for another day the questions respondent's argument raises under the FSIA.

III.

Petitioners rest their claim to a jury trial on the Seventh Amendment alone.[3] The Seventh Amendment provides: "In Suits at common law, where the value in

---

"the transfers in question and the suit to recover those transfers occurred before Granfinanciera was nationalized," *Ibid.,* but on the more sweeping rationale that Granfinanciera never proved that it was an instrumentality of a foreign state because it had never really been nationalized. *See* Brief for Appellee in No. 86–5738 (CA11), pp. 21–30; Brief for Appellee in No. 86–1292 (SD Fla.), pp. 32–36. Admittedly, respondent's present position that the FSIA does not confer immunity on Granfinanciera because it was not an instrumentality of a foreign state when the alleged wrongs occurred or when respondent filed suit is not necessarily incompatible with its claim that Granfinanciera cannot qualify for a jury trial under the FSIA because it requested a jury trial after it was nationalized. Respondent has not attempted, however, to reconcile these views and did not make the second claim until he filed his merits brief in this Court.

[3] The current statutory provision for jury trials in bankruptcy proceedings—28 U.S.C. § 1411 (1982 ed., Supp. IV), enacted as part of the Bankruptcy Amendments and Federal Judgeship

controversy shall exceed twenty dollars, the right of trial by jury shall be preserved
. . . " We have consistently interpreted the phrase "Suits at common law" to refer
to "suits in which legal rights were to be ascertained and determined, in contradis-
tinction to those where equitable rights alone were recognized, and equitable
remedies were administered." *Parsons v. Bedford,* 3 Pet. 433, 447 (1830). Although
"the thrust of the Amendment was to preserve the right to jury trial as it existed in
1791," the Seventh Amendment also applies to actions brought to enforce statutory
rights that are analogous to common–law causes of action ordinarily decided in
English law courts in the late 18th century, as opposed to those customarily heard
by courts of equity or admiralty. *Curtis v. Loether,* 415 U.S. 189, 193 (1974).

The form of our analysis is familiar. "First, we compare the statutory action to
18th–century actions brought in the courts of England prior to the merger of the
courts of law and equity. Second, we examine the remedy sought and determine
whether it is legal or equitable in nature." *Tull v. United States,* 481 U.S. 412,
417–418 (1987) (citations omitted). The second stage of this analysis is more
important than the first. Id., at 421. If, on balance, these two factors indicate that
a party is entitled to a jury trial under the Seventh Amendment, we must decide

---

Act of 1984 (1984 Amendments), Pub: L. 98–353, 98 Stat. 333—is notoriously ambiguous.
Section 1411(a) provides: "[T]his chapter and title 11 do not affect any right to trial by jury
that an individual has under applicable nonbankruptcy law with regard to a personal injury
or wrongful death tort claim." Although this section might suggest that jury trials are available
only in personal injury and wrongful death actions, that conclusion is debatable. Section
1411(b) provides that "[t]he district court may order the issues arising [in connection with
involuntary bankruptcy petitions] to be tried without a jury," suggesting that the court lacks
similar discretion to deny jury trials on at least some issues presented in connection with
involuntary petitions. The confused legislative history of these provisions has further puzzled
commentators. *See, e.g.,* Gibson, *Jury Trials in Bankruptcy: Obeying the Commands of
Article III and the Seventh Amendment,* 72 Minn. L. Rev. 967, 989–996 (1988) (hereinafter
Gibson); Note, *The Bankruptcy Amendments and Federal Judgeship Act of 1984; The Impact
on the Right of Jury Trial in Bankruptcy Court,* 16 Tex. Tech. L. Rev. 535, 543–546 (1985).
Whatever the proper construction of § 1411, petitioners concede that this section does not
entitle them to a jury trial. Section 122(b) of the 1984 Amendments, 98 Stat. 346, bars
application of § 1411 to "cases under title 11 of the United States Code that are pending on
the date of enactment of this Act or to proceedings arising in or related to such cases," and
Chase & Sanborn's petition for reorganization was pending on that date. Nor does § 1411's
predecessor—28 U.S.C. § 1480(a), which stated that "this chapter and title 11 do not affect
any right to trial by jury, in a case under title 11 or in a proceeding arising under title 11
or arising in or related to a case under title 11, that is provided by any statute in effect on
September 30, 1979"—seem to afford petitioners a statutory basis for their claim. As they
recognize, § 1480 was apparently repealed by the 1984 Amendments. *See* Gibson 989, and
n. 96; King, *Jurisdiction and Procedure Under the Bankruptcy Amendments, of 1984,* 38
Vand. L. Rev. 675, 703 and n. 79 (1985); Brief for Respondent 5, n. 11. Petitioners therefore
appear correct in concluding that, "absent any specific legislation in force providing jury trials
for cases filed before July 10, 1984, but tried afterwards, [their] right to jury trial in this
proceeding must necessarily be predicated entirely on the Seventh Amendment." Brief for
Petitioners 33, n. 7. *See also* Brief for Respondent 10, and n. 15.

whether Congress may assign and has assigned resolution of the relevant claim to a non–Article III adjudicative body that does not use a jury as factfinder.[4]

A.

There is no dispute that actions to recover preferential or fraudulent transfers were often brought at law in late 18th–century England. As we noted in *Schoenthal v. Irving Trust Co.*, 287 U.S. 92, 94 (1932) (footnote omitted), "[i]n England, long prior to the enactment of our first Judiciary Act, common law actions of trover and money had and received were resorted to for the recovery of preferential payments by bankrupts." *See, e.g., Smith v. Payne*, 6 T.R. 152, 101 Eng. Rep. 484 (1795) (trover); *Barnes v. Freeland*, 6 T.R. 80, 101 Eng. Rep. 447 (1794) (trover); *Smith v. Hodson*, 4 T.R. 211, 100 Eng. Rep. 979 (1791) (assumpsit; goods sold and delivered); *Vernon v. Hanson*, 2 T.R. 287, 100 Eng. Rep. 156 (1788) (assumpsit; money had and received); *Thompson v. Freeman,*1 T.R. 155, 99 Eng. Rep. 1026 (1786) (trover); *Rust v. Cooper*, 2 Cowp. 629, 98 Eng. Rep. 1277 (1777) (trover); *Harman v. Fishar*, 1 Cowp. 117, 98 Eng. Rep. 998 (1774) (trover); *Martin v. Pewtress*, 4 Burr. 2477, 98 Eng. Rep. 299 (1769) (trover); *Alderson v. Temple*, 4 Burr. 2235, 98 Eng. Rep. 165 (1768) (trover). These actions, like all suits at law, were conducted before juries.

Respondent does not challenge this proposition or even contend that actions to recover fraudulent conveyances or preferential transfers were more than occasionally tried in courts of equity. He asserts only that courts of equity had concurrent jurisdiction with courts of law over fraudulent preference actions. Brief for Respondent 37–38. While respondent's assertion that courts of equity sometimes provided relief in fraudulent preference actions is true, however, it hardly suffices to undermine petitioners' submission that the present action for monetary relief would not have sounded in equity two hundred years ago in England. In *Parsons v. Bedford, supra,* at 447, we contrasted suits at law with "those where equitable rights alone were recognized" in holding that the Seventh Amendment right to a jury trial applies to all but the latter actions. Respondent adduces no authority to buttress the claim that suits to recover an allegedly fraudulent transfer of money, of the sort that he has brought, were typically or indeed ever entertained by English

---

[4] This quite distinct inquiry into whether Congress has permissibly entrusted the resolution of certain disputes to an administrative agency or specialized court of equity, and whether jury trials would impair the functioning of the legislative scheme, appears to be what the Court contemplated when in *Ross v. Bernhard*, 396 U.S. 531, 538, n. 10 (1970), it identified "the practical abilities and limitations of juries" as an additional factor to be consulted in determining whether the Seventh Amendment confers a jury trial right. *See Tull v. United States,* 481 U.S. 412, 418, n. 4 (1987); *Atlas Roofing Co. v. Occupational Safety and Health Review Comm'n,* 430 U.S. 442, 454–455 (1977). We consider this issue in Part IV, *infra.* Contrary to Justice White's contention, *see Post,* at 9–10, we do not declare that the Seventh Amendment provides a right to a jury trial on all legal rather than equitable claims. If a claim that is legal in nature asserts a "public right," as we define that term in Part IV, then the Seventh Amendment does not entitle the parties to a jury trial if Congress assigns its adjudication to an administrative agency or specialized court of equity. *See infra,* at 16–18. The Seventh Amendment protects a litigant's right to a jury trial only if a cause of action is legal in nature and it involves a matter of "private right."

courts of equity when the Seventh Amendment was adopted. In fact, prior decisions of this Court, *see, e.g., Buzard v. Houston,* 119 U.S. 347, 352–353 (1886), and scholarly authority compel the contrary conclusion:

> "[W]hether the trustee's suit should be at law or in equity is to be judged by the same standards that are applied to any other owner of property which is wrongfully withheld. If the subject matter is a chattel, and is still in the grantee's possession, an action in trover or replevin would be the trustee's remedy; and if the fraudulent transfer was of cash, the trustee's action would be for money had and received. Such actions at law are as available to the trustee to-day as they were in English courts of long ago. If, on the other hand, the subject matter is land or an intangible, or the trustee needs equitable aid for an accounting or the like, he may invoke the equitable process, and that also is beyond dispute." 1 G. Glenn, Fraudulent Conveyances and Preferences § 98, pp. 183–184 (rev. ed. 1940).

The two cases respondent discusses confirm this account of English practice. *Ex parte Scudamore,* 3 Ves. Jun. 85, 30 Eng. Rep. 907 (1796), involved the debtor's assignment of his share of a law partnership's receivables to repay a debt shortly before the debtor was declared bankrupt. Other creditors petitioned chancery for an order directing the debtor's law partner to hand over for general distribution among creditors the debtor's current and future shares of the partnership's receivables, which he held in trust for the assignee. The Chancellor refused to do so, finding the proposal inequitable. Instead, he directed the creditors to bring an action at law against the assignee if they thought themselves entitled to relief. Although this case demonstrates that fraudulent conveyance actions could be brought in equity, it does not show that suits to recover a definite sum of money would be decided by a court of equity when a petitioner did not seek distinctively equitable remedies. The creditors in *Ex parte Scudamore* asked the Chancellor to provide injunctive relief by ordering the debtor's former law partner to convey to them the debtor's share of the partnership's receivables that came into his possession in the future, along with receivables he then held in trust for the debtor. To the extent that they asked the court to order relinquishment of a specific preferential transfer rather than ongoing equitable relief, the Chancellor dismissed their suit and noted that the proper means of recovery would be an action at law against the transferee. Respondent's own cause of action is of precisely that sort.

Hobbs v. Hull, 1 Cox 445, 29 Eng. Rep. 1242 (1788), also fails to advance respondent's case. The assignees in bankruptcy there sued to set aside an alleged fraudulent conveyance of real estate in trust by a husband to his wife, in return for her relinquishment of a cause of action in divorce upon discovering his adultery. The court dismissed the suit, finding that the transfer was not fraudulent, and allowed the assignees to bring an ejectment or other legal action in the law courts. The salient point is that the bankruptcy assignees sought the traditional equitable remedy of setting aside a conveyance of land in trust, rather than the recovery of money or goods, and that the court refused to decide their legal claim to ejectment once it had ruled that no equitable remedy would lie. The court's sweeping statement that "Courts of Equity have most certainly been in the habit of exercising a concurrent jurisdiction with the Courts of Law on the statutes of Elizabeth respecting fraudulent conveyances," *Id.,* at 445–446, 30 Eng. Rep., at 1242, is not supported by reference to any cases that sought the recovery of a fixed sum of money without the need for an accounting or other equitable relief. Nor has respondent repaired this deficit.[5] We therefore conclude that respondent would have had to bring his action to recover an alleged fraudulent conveyance of a determinate sum of money at law in 18th–century England, and that a court of equity would not have adjudicated it.[6]

---

[5] Rather than list 18th–century English cases to support the contention that fraudulent monetary transfers were traditionally cognizable in equity, respondent cites three recent cases from the Courts of Appeals. These cases, however, weaken rather than bolster respondent's argument. *In Re Graham,* 747 F.2d 1383 (CA11 1984), held that there was no Seventh Amendment jury trial right in a suit for the *equitable* remedy of setting aside an alleged fraudulent conveyance of *real estate* by a bankrupt. With respect to suits like respondent's, the court expressly noted that "an action by a creditor or trustee–in–bankruptcy seeking money damages is an action at law." *Id.,* at 1387 (citations omitted). *Damsky v. Zavatt,* 289 F.2d 46 (CA2 1961), also involved a conveyance of real estate. And there, too, the court acknowledged that the jury trials are ordinarily available with respect to monetary claims. *See Id.,* at 54. Both of these holdings are questionable, moreover, to the extent that they are in tension with our decision in *Whitehead v. Shattuck,* 138 U.S. 146 (1891). Although there is scholarly support for the claim that actions to recover real property are quintessentially equitable actions, see 1 G. Glenn, Fraudulent Conveyances and Preferences § 9, pp. 183–184 (rev. ed. 1940), in *Whitehead* we stated:

> "[W]here an action is simply for the recovery and possession of specific real or personal property, or for the recovery of a money judgment, the action is one at law. An action for the recovery of real property, including damages for withholding it, has always been of that class. The right which in this case the plaintiff wishes to assert is his title to certain real property; the remedy which he wishes to obtain is its possession and enjoyment; and in a contest over the title both parties have a constitutional right to call for a jury." 138 U.S., at 151.

See also Pernell v. Southall Realty, 416 U.S. 363, 370–374 (1974).

Finally, respondent misreads *In Re Harbour,* 840 F.2d 1165, 1172–1173 (CA4 1988). The Fourth Circuit relied in that case on the same authorities to which we have referred, distinguishing between suits to recover fraudulent transfers and other bankruptcy proceedings. The court's holding that the Seventh Amendment right to a jury trial no longer extends to such actions was based not on its historical analysis, which accords with our own, but on its erroneous belief that Congress possesses the power to assign jurisdiction over all fraudulent conveyance actions to bankruptcy courts sitting without juries. The case therefore lends no support to respondent's historical argument.

[6] Citing several authorities, Justice White contends that "[o]ther scholars have looked at the same history and come to a different conclusion." *Post,* at 15, and n. 7. This assertion, however, lacks the support it claims. With the exception of Justice Gray's opinion in *Drake v. Rice,* 130 Mass. 410, 412 (1881), and Robert's treatise, none of the authorities cited so much as mentions 18th–century English practice. Although Collier offers as its opinion that actions to set aside fraudulent transfers are equitable in nature, 4 Collier on Bankruptcy ¶ 548.10, p. 548–125 (15th ed., 1989), it refers only to recent cases in defending its opinion, while acknowledging that some courts have disagreed. Wait and Bump both limit their citations to state court decisions, refusing to analyze earlier English cases. See O. Bump, Conveyances Made By Debtors to Defraud Creditors § 532 (4th ed. 1896); F. Wait, Fraudulent Conveyances and Creditors' Bills §§ 56–60 (1884). To be sure, in *Drake v. Rice,*

B.

The nature of the relief respondent seeks strongly supports our preliminary finding that the right he invokes should be denominated legal rather than equitable. Our decisions establish beyond peradventure that "[i]n cases of fraud or mistake, as under any other head of chancery jurisdiction, a court of the United States will not sustain a bill in equity to obtain only a decree for the payment of money by way of damages, when the like amount can be recovered at law in an action sounding in tort or for money had and received." *Buzard v. Houston,* 119 U.S., at 352, citing *Parkersburg v. Brown,* 106 U.S. 487, 500 (1883); *Ambler v. Choteau,* 107 U.S. 586 (1883); *Litchfield v. Ballou,*114 U.S. 190 (1885). *See also Atlas Roofing Co. v. Occupational Safety and Health Review Comm'n,* 430 U.S. 442, 454, n. 11 (1977) ("the otherwise legal issue of voidable preferences"); *Pernell v. Southall Realty,* 416 U.S. 363, 370 (1974) (" [W]here an action is simply for the recovery. . . of a money judgment, the action is one at law' "), quoting *Whitehead v. Shattuck,* 138 U.S. 146, 151 (1891); *Dairy Queen, Inc. v. Wood,*369 U.S. 469, 476 (1962) ("Petitioner's contention . . . is that insofar as the complaint requests a money judgment it presents a claim which is unquestionably legal. We agree with that contention"); *Gaines v. Miller,* 111 U.S. 395, 397–398 (1884) ("Whenever one person has in his hands money equitably belonging to another, that other person may recover it by assumpsit for money had and received. The remedy at law is adequate and complete.") (citations omitted).

Indeed, in our view *Schoenthal v. Irving Trust Co.,*287 U.S. 92 (1932), removes all doubt that respondent's cause of action should be characterized as legal rather than as equitable. In *Schoenthal,* the trustee in bankruptcy sued in equity to recover alleged preferential payments, claiming that it had no adequate remedy at law. As in this case, the recipients of the payments apparently did not file claims against the bankruptcy estate. The Court held that the suit had to proceed at law instead, because the long–settled rule that suits in equity will not be sustained where a complete remedy exists a law, then codified at 28 U.S.C. § 384, "serves to guard the right of trial by jury preserved by the Seventh Amendment and to that end it should be liberally construed." *Id.,* at 94. The Court found that the trustee's suit—indistinguishable from respondent's suit in all relevant respects—could not go forward in equity because an adequate remedy was available at law. There, as here, "[t]he preferences sued for were money payments of ascertained and definite

---

supra, at 412, Justice Gray says that "[b]y the law of England before the American Revolution, . . . fraudulent conveyances of choses in action, though not specified in the statute [of Elizabeth], were equally void, but from the nature of the subject the remedy of the creditor must be sought in equity." But the reason why suits to recover fraudulent transfers of choses in action had to be brought in equity, Justice Gray points out, is that they could not be attached or levied upon. *Id.,* at 413. *See also* O. Bump, *supra,* at § 531 ("[T]here is no remedy at law when the property can not be taken on execution or by attachment"). Justice Gray's summary of 18th–century English practice does not extend to cases, such as those involving monetary transfers, where an adequate remedy existed at law. The passage Justice White cites from Roberts' treatise is obscure, and does not speak squarely to the question whether 18th–century English courts of equity would hear cases where legal remedies were sufficient. See W. Roberts, Voluntary and Fraudulent Conveyances 526–527 (1845).

amounts," and "[t]he bill discloses no facts that call for an accounting or other equitable relief." *Id.*, at 95. Respondent's fraudulent conveyance action plainly seeks relief traditionally provided by law courts or on the law side of courts having both legal and equitable dockets.[7] Unless Congress may and has permissibly withdrawn jurisdiction over that action by courts of law and assigned it exclusively to non–Article III tribunals sitting without juries, the Seventh Amendment gurantees petitioners a jury trial upon rquest.

IV.

Prior to passage of the Bankruptcy Reform Act of 1978, Pub. L. 95–598, 92 Stat. 2549 (1978 Act), "[s]uits to recover preferences constitute[d] no part of the proceedings in bankruptcy." *Schoenthal v. Irving Trust Co., supra,* at 94–95. Although related to bankruptcy proceedings, fraudulent conveyance and preference actions brought by a trustee in bankruptcy were deemed separate, plenary suits to which the Seventh Amendment applied. While the 1978 Act brought those actions within the jurisdiction of the bankruptcy courts, it preserved parties' rights to trial by jury as they existed prior to the effective date of the 1978 Act. 28 U.S.C. § 1480(a) (repealed). The Bankruptcy Amendments and Federal Judgeship Act of 1984 (1984 Amendments), Pub. L. 98–353, 98 Stat. 333, however, designated fraudulent conveyance actions "core proceedings," 28 U.S.C. § 157(b)(2)(H) (1982 ed., Supp. IV), which bankruptcy judges may adjudicate and in which they may issue final judgments, § 157(b)(1), if a district court has referred the matter to them. § 157(a). We are not obliged to decide today whether bankruptcy courts may conduct jury trials in fraudulent conveyance suits brought by a trustee against a person who has not entered a claim against the estate, either in the rare procedural posture of this case, see supra, at 6, n. 3, or under the current statutory scheme. *See* 28 U.S.C. § 1411 (1982 ed., Supp. IV). Nor need we decide whether, if Congress has authorized bankruptcy courts to hold jury trials in such actions, that authorization comports with Article III when non–Article III judges preside over them subject to

---

[7] Respondent claims to seek "avoidance" of the allegedly fraudulent transfers and restitution of the funds that were actually transferred, but maintains that petitioners have made restitution impossible because the transferred funds cannot be distinguished from the other dollars in petitioners' bank accounts. *See* Brief for Respondent 39–44. Because avoidance and restitution are classical equitable remedies, he says, petitioners are not entitled to a trial by jury. We find this strained attempt to circumvent precedent unpersuasive. Because dollars are fungible and respondent has not requested an accounting or other specifically equitable form of relief, a complete remedy is available at law, and equity will not countenance an action when complete relief may be obtained at law. *See, e.g., Schoenthal v. Irving Trust Co.,* 287 U.S., at 94–95. Moreover, because a plaintiff is entitled to return of any funds transferred in violation of 11 U.S.C. § 548 (1982 ed., Supp. V), and because a judge lacks equitable discretion to refuse to enter an award for less than the amount of the transfer, any distinction that might exist between "damages" and monetary relief under a different label is purely semantic, with no relevance to the adjudication of petitioners' Seventh Amendment claim. *Cf. Albemarle Paper Co. v. Moody,* 422 U.S. 405, 442–443 (1975) (Rehnquist, J., concurring). Indeed, even if the checks respondent seeks to recover lay untouched in petitioners' offices, legal remedies would apparently have sufficed. *See, e.g., Adams v. Champion,* 294 U.S. 231, 234 (1935); *Whitehead v. Shattuck, supra,* at 151.

review in or withdrawal by the district courts. We also need not consider whether jury trials conducted by a bankruptcy court would satisfy the Seventh Amendment's command that "no fact tried by a jury, shall be otherwise re-examined in any Court of the United States, than according to the rules of the common law," given that district courts may presently set aside clearly erroneous factual findings by bankruptcy courts. Bkrtcy. Rule 8013. The sole issue before us is whether the Seventh Amendment confers on petitioners a right to a jury trial in the face of Congress' decision to allow a non–Article III tribunal to adjudicate the claims against them.

A.

In *Atlas Roofing,* we noted that "when Congress creates new statutory 'public rights,'" it may assign their adjudication to an administrative agency with which a jury trial would be incompatible, without violating the Seventh Amendment's injunction that jury trial is to be "preserved' in 'suits at common law.' " 430 U.S., at 455 (footnote omitted). We emphasized, however, that Congress' power to block application of the Seventh Amendment to a cause of action has limits. Congress may only deny trials by jury in actions at law, we said, in cases where "public rights" are litigated: "Our prior cases support administrative factfinding in only those situations involving 'public rights,' *e.g.,* where the Government is involved in its sovereign capacity under an otherwise valid statute creating enforceable public rights. Wholly private tort, contract, and property cases, as well as a vast range of other cases, are not at all implicated." *Id.,* at 458.[8]

We adhere to that general teaching. As we said in *Atlas Roofing:* " 'On the common law side of the federal courts, the aid of juries is not only deemed appropriate but is required by the Constitution itself.' " *Id.,* at 450, n. 7, quoting *Crowell v. Benson,* 285 U.S. 22, 51 (1932). Congress may devise novel causes of action involving public rights free from the strictures of the Seventh Amendment if it assigns their adjudication to tribunals without statutory authority to employ juries as factfinders.[9] But it lacks the power to strip parties contesting matters of

---

[8] Although we left the term "public rights" undefined in *Atlas Roofing Co. v. Occupational Safety and Health Review Comm'n,* 430 U.S., at 450, 458, we cited *Crowell v. Benson,* 285 U.S. 22 (1932), approvingly. In *Crowell,* we defined "private right" as "the liability of one individual to another under the law as defined," *Id.,* at 51, in contrast to cases that "arise between the Government and persons subject to its authority in connection with the performance of the constitutional functions of the executive or legislative departments." *Id.,* at 50.

[9] This proposition was firmly established in *Atlas Roofing Co. v. Occupational Safety and Health Review Comm'n, supra,* 455 (footnote omitted):

> "Congress is not required by the Seventh Amendment to choke the already crowded federal courts with new types of litigation or prevented from committing some new types of litigation to administrative agencies with special competence in the relevant field. This is the case even if the Seventh Amendment would have required a jury where the adjudication of those rights is assigned to a federal court of law instead of an administrative agency."

private right of their constitutional right to a trial by jury. As we recognized in *Atlas Roofing,* to hold otherwise would be to permit Congress to eviscerate the Seventh Amendment's guarantee by assigning to administrative agencies or courts of equity all causes of action not grounded in state law, whether they originate in a newly fashioned regulatory scheme or possess a long line of common–law forebears. 430 U.S., at 457–458. The Constitution nowhere grants Congress such puissant authority. "[L]egal claims are not magically converted into equitable issues by their presentation to a court of equity," *Ross v. Bernhard,* 396 U.S. 531, 538 (1970), nor can Congress conjure away the Seventh Amendment by mandating that traditional legal claims be brought there or taken to an administrative tribunal.

In certain situations, of course, Congress may fashion causes of action that are closely analogous to common–law claims and place them beyond the ambit of the Seventh Amendment by assigning their resolution to a forum in which jury trials are unavailable. *See, e.g., Atlas Roofing,* 430 U.S., at 450–461 (workplace safety regulations); *Block v. Hirsh,* 256 U.S. 135, 158 (1921) (temporary emergency regulation of rental real estate). *See also Pernell v. Southall Realty,* 416 U.S., at 382–383 (discussing cases); *Murray's Lessee v. Hoboken Land and Improvement Co.,* 18 How. 272, 284 (1856) (Congress "may or may not bring within the cognizance of the courts of the United States, as it may deem proper," matters involving public rights). Congress' power to do is limited, however, just as its power to place adjudicative authority in non–Article III tribunals is circumscribed. *See Thomas v. Union Carbide Agricultural Products Co.,* 473 U.S. 568, 589, 593–594 (1985); *Id.,* at 598–600 (Brennan, J., concurring in judgment); *Northern Pipeline Construction Co. v. Marathon Pipe Line Co.,* 458 U.S. 50, 73–76 (1982) (opinion of Brennan, J.); *Id.,* at 91 (Rehnquist, J., concurring in judgment). Unless a legal cause of action involves "public rights," Congress may not deprive parties litigating over that right of the Seventh Amendment's guarantee to a jury trial.

In *Atlas Roofing, supra,* at 458, we noted that Congress may effectively supplant a common–law cause of action carrying with it a right to a jury trial with a statutory cause of action shorn of a jury trial right if that statutory cause of action inheres in or lies against the Federal Government in its sovereign capacity. Our case law makes plain, however, that the class of "public rights" whose adjudication Congress may assign to administrative agencies or courts of equity sitting without juries is more expansive than *Atlas Roofing's* discussion suggests. Indeed, our decisions point to the conclusion that, if a statutory cause of action is legal in nature, the question whether the Seventh Amendment permits Congress to assign its adjudication to a tribunal that does not employ juries as factfinders requires the same answer as the question whether Article III allows Congress to assign adjudication of that cause of action to a non–Article III tribunal. For if a statutory cause of action, such as respondent's right to recover a fraudulent conveyance under 11 U.S.C. § 548(a)(2), is not a "public right" for Article III purposes, then Congress may not assign its adjudication to a specialized non–Article III court lacking "the essential attributes of the judicial power." *Crowell v. Benson, supra,* at 51. And if the action must be tried under the auspices of an Article III court, then the Seventh Amendment affords the parties a right to a jury trial whenever the cause of action is legal in nature. Conversely, if Congress may assign the adjudication of a statutory cause of action to a non–Article III tribunal, then the Seventh Amendment poses no independent bar to the adjudication of that action by a nonjury factfinder. *See, e.g., Atlas Roofing, supra,* at 453–455, 460; *Pernell v. Southall Realty, supra,* at 383; *Block v. Hirsh, supra,* at 158. In addition to our Seventh Amendment precedents, we therefore rely as well on our decisions exploring the restrictions Article III places on Congress' choice of adjudicative bodies to resolve disputes over statutory rights to determine whether petitioners are entitled to a jury trial.

In our most recent discussion of the "public rights" doctrine as it bears on Congress' power to commit adjudication of a statutory cause of action to a non–Article III tribunal, we rejected the view that "a matter of public rights must at a minimum arise 'between the government and others.'" *Northern Pipeline Construction Co., supra,* at 69 (opinion of Brennan, J.), quoting *Ex Parte Bakelite Corp.,* 279 U.S. 438, 451 (1929). We held, instead, that the Federal Government need not be a party for a case to revolve around "public rights." *Thomas v. Union Carbide Agricultural Products Co.,* 473 U.S., at 586; *Id.,* at 596–599 (Brennan, J., concurring in judgment). The crucial question, in cases not involving the Federal Government, is whether "Congress, acting for a valid legislative purpose pursuant to its constitutional powers under Article I, [has] create[d] a seemingly 'private' right that is so closely integrated into a public regulatory scheme as to be a matter appropriate for agency resolution with limited involvement by the Article III judiciary." *Id.,* at 593–594. *See Id.,* at 600 (Brennan, J., concurring in judgment) (challenged provision involves public rights because "the dispute arises in the context of a federal regulatory scheme that virtually occupies the field"). If a statutory right is not closely intertwined with a federal regulatory program Congress has power to enact, and if that right neither belongs to nor exists against the Federal Government, then it must be adjudicated by an Article III court.[10] If the right is

---

10 In *Atlas Roofing,* 430 U.S., at 442, 450, n. 7, we stated that "[i]n cases which do involve only private rights', this Court has accepted factfinding by an administrative agency, without intervention by a jury, only as an adjunct to an Art. III court, analogizing the agency to a jury or a special master and permitting it in admiralty cases to perform the function of the special master.' That statement, however, must be read in context. First, we referred explicitly only to Congress' power, where disputes concern private rights, to provide administrative factfinding instead of jury trials in *admiralty* cases. Civil causes of action in admiralty, however, are not suits at common law for Seventh Amendment purposes, and thus no constitutional right to a jury trial attaches. *Waring v. Clark,* 5 How. 441, 460 (1847). Second, our statement should not be taken to mean that Congress may assign at least the initial factfinding in all cases involving controversies entirely between private parties to administrative agencies or other tribunals not involving juries, so long as they are established as adjuncts to Article III courts. If that were so, Congress could render the Seventh Amendment a nullity. Rather, that statement, citing *Crowell v. Benson,* 285 U.S., at 51–65, means only that in *some* cases involving "private rights" *as that term was defined in Crowell and used in Atlas Roofing*—namely, as encompassing all disputes to which the Federal Government is not a party in its sovereign capacity—may Congress dispense with juries as factfinders through its choice of adjudicative forum. Those cases in which Congress may decline to provide jury trials are ones involving statutory rights that are integral parts of a public regulatory scheme and whose adjudication Congress has assigned to an administrative agency or specialized court of equity. Whatever terminological distinctions *Atlas Roofing* may have suggested, we now refer to those rights as "public" rather than "private."

legal in nature, then it carries with it the Seventh Amendment's guarantee of a jury trial.

B.

Although the issue admits of some debate, a bankruptcy trustee's right to recover a fraudulent conveyance under 11 U.S.C. § 548(a)(2) seems to us more accurately characterized as a private rather than a public right as we have used those terms in our Article III decisions. In *Northern Pipeline Construction Co.,* 458 U.S., at 71, the plurality noted that the restructuring of debtor–creditor relations in bankruptcy "may well be a 'public right.' "**11** But the plurality also emphasized that state–law causes of action for breach of contract or warranty are paradigmatic private rights, even when asserted by an insolvent corporation in the midst of Chapter 11 reorganization proceedings. The plurality further said that "matters from their nature subject to 'a suit at common law or in equity or admiralty' " lie at the "protected core" of Article III judicial power, *Id.,* at 71, n. 25; *see Id.,* at 90 (Rehnquist, J., concurring in judgment)—a point we reaffirmed in *Thomas, supra,* at 587. There can be little doubt that fraudulent conveyance actions by bankruptcy trustees—suits which, we said in *Schoenthal v. Irving Trust Co.,* 287 U.S., at 94–95 (citation omitted), "constitute no part of the proceedings in bankruptcy but concern controversies arising out of it"—are quintessentially suits at common law that more nearly resemble state–law contract claims brought by a bankrupt corporation to augment the bankruptcy estate than they do creditors' hierarchically ordered claims to a pro rata share of the bankruptcy res. *See Gibson* 1022–1025. They therefore appear matters of private rather than public right.**12**

Our decision in *Katchen v. Landy,* 382 U.S. 323 (1966), under the Seventh Amendment rather than Article III, confirms this analysis. Petitioner, an officer of a bankrupt corporation, made payments from corporate funds within four months of bankruptcy on corporate notes on which he was an accommodation maker. When petitioner later filed claims against the bankruptcy estate, the trustee counterclaimed, arguing that the payments petitioner made constituted voidable preferences because they reduced his potential personal liability on the notes. We held that the bankruptcy court had jurisdiction to order petitioner to surrender the preferences and that it could rule on the trustee's claim without according petitioner a jury trial. Our holding did

---

11 We do not suggest that the restructuring of debtor–creditor relations is in fact a public right. This thesis has met with substantial scholarly criticism, *see, e.g.,* Gibson 1041, n. 347; Currie, *Bankruptcy Judges and the Independent Judiciary,* 16 Creighton L. Rev. 441, 452 (1983); Baird, *Bankruptcy Procedure and State–Created Rights: The Lessons of Gibbons and Marathon,* 1982 Sup. Ct. Rev. 25, 44, and we need not and do not seek to defend it here. Our point is that even if one accepts this thesis, the Seventh Amendment entitles petitioners to a jury trial.

12 *See Northern Pipeline Construction Co. v. Marathon Pipe Line Co.,* 458 U.S. 50, 71 (1982) (opinion of Brennan, J.):

> "[T]he restructuring of debtor–creditor relations, which is at the core of the federal bankruptcy power, must be distinguished from the adjudication of state–created private rights, such as the right to recover contract damages that is at issue in this case. The former may well be a 'public right,' but the latter obviously is not."

not depend, however, on the fact that "[bankruptcy] courts are essentially courts of equity" because "they characteristically proceed in summary fashion to deal with the assets of the bankrupt they are administering." *Id.,* at 327. Notwithstanding the fact that bankruptcy courts "characteristically" supervised summary proceedings, they were statutorily invested with jurisdiction at law as well, and could also oversee plenary proceedings. *See Altas Roofing,* 430 U.S., at 454, n. 11 *Katchen* rested "on the ground that a bankruptcy court, exercising its summary jurisdiction, was a specialized court of equity"); *Pepper v. Litton,* 308 U.S. 295, 304 (1939) ("[F]or many purposes 'courts of bankruptcy are essentially courts of equity' "). Our decision turned, rather, on the bankruptcy court's having "actual or constructive possession" of the bankruptcy estate, 382 U.S., at 327, and its power and obligation to consider objections by the trustee in deciding whether to allow claims against the estate. *Id.,* at 329–331. Citing *Schoenthal v. Irving Trust Co., supra,* approvingly, we expressly stated that, if petitioner had not submitted a claim to the bankruptcy court, the trustee could have recovered the preference only by a plenary action, and that petitioner would have been entitled to a jury trial if the trustee had brought a plenary action in federal court. *See* 382 U.S., at 327–328. We could not have made plainer that our holding in *Schoenthal* retained its vitality: "[A]lthough petitioner might be entitled to a jury trial on the issue of preference if he presented no claim in the bankruptcy proceeding and awaited a federal plenary action by the trustee, *Schoenthal v. Irving Trust Co.,* 287 U.S. 92, when the same issue arises as part of the process of allowance and disallowance of claims, it is triable in equity." 382 U.S., at 336.[13]

Unlike Justice White, see *Post,* at 3–5, 8, we do not view the Court's conclusion in *Katchen* as resting on an accident of statutory history. We read *Schoenthal* and *Katchen* as holding that, under the Seventh Amendment, a creditor's right to a jury trial on a bankruptcy trustee's preference claim depends upon whether the creditor has submitted a claim against the estate, not upon Congress' precise definition of the "bankruptcy estate" or upon whether Congress chanced to deny jury trials to creditors who have not filed claims and who are sued by a trustee to recover an alleged preference. Because petitioners here, like the petitioner in *Schoenthal,* have not filed claims against the estate, respondent's fraudulent conveyance action does not arise "as part of the process of allowance and disallowance of claims." Nor is that action integral to the restructuring of debtor–creditor relations. Congress therefore cannot divest petitioners of their Seventh Amendment right to a trial by

---

[13] Although we said in *Katchen v. Landy,* 382 U.S., at 336, that the petitioner *might* have been entitled to a jury trial had he presented no claim against the bankruptcy estate, our approving references not only to *Schoenthal* but also to *Adams v. Champion,* 294 U.S. 231, 234 (1935), and *Buffum v. Barceloux Co.,* 289 U.S. 227, 235–236 (1933), *see* 382 U.S., at 327–328, demonstrate that we did not intend to cast doubt on the proposition that the petitioner in *Katchen* would have been entitled to a jury trial had he not entered a claim against the estate and had the bankruptcy trustee requested solely legal relief. We merely left open the possibility that a jury trial might not be required because in some cases preference avoidance actions are equitable in character.

jury. *Katchen* thus supports the result we reach today; it certainly does not compel its opposite.[14]

The 1987 Act abolished the statutory distinction between plenary and summary bankruptcy proceedings, on which the Court relied in *Schoenthal* and *Katchen*. Although the 1978 Act preserved parties' rights to jury trials as they existed prior to the day it took effect, 28 U.S.C. § 1480(a) (repealed), in the 1984 Amendments Congress drew a new distinction between "core" and "non–core" proceedings and classified fraudulent conveyance actions as core proceedings triable by bankruptcy

---

[14] In *Katchen v. Landy, supra,* at 335, we adopted a rationale articulated in *Alexander v. Hillman,* 296 U.S. 222, 241–242 (1935) (citations omitted):

> " By presenting their claims respondents subjected themselves to all the consequences that attach to an appearance . . .
>
> " Respondents' contention means that, while invoking the court's jurisdiction to establish their right to participate in the distribution, they may deny its power to require them to account for what they misappropriated. In behalf of creditors and stockholders, the receivers reasonably may insist that, before taking aught, respondents may by the receivership court be required to make restitution. That requirement is in harmony with the rule generally followed by courts of equity that having jurisdiction of the parties to controversies brought before them, they will decide all matters in dispute and decree complete relief."

It warrants emphasis that this rationale differs from the notion of waiver on which the Court relied in *Commodity Futures Trading Comm'n v. Schor,* 478 U.S. 833 (1986). The Court ruled in *Schor*—where no Seventh Amendment claims were presented—that the Commodities Futures Trading Commission could adjudicate state–law counterclaims to a federal action by investors against their broker consistent with Article III. The Court reached this conclusion, however, not on the ground that the Commission had possession of a disputed *res,* to which the investors laid claim, but on the ground that Congress did not require investors to avail themselves of the remedial scheme over which the Commission presided. The investors could have pursued their claims, albeit less expeditiously, in federal court. By electing to use the speedier, alternative procedures Congress had created, the Court said, the investors waived their right to have the state–law counterclaims against them adjudicated by an Article III court. *See Id.,* at 847–850. Parallel reasoning is unavailable in the context of bankruptcy proceedings, because creditors lack an alternative forum to the bankruptcy court in which to pursue their claims. As *Katchen* makes clear, however, by submitting a claim against the bankruptcy estate, creditors subject themselves to the court's equitable power to disallow those claims, even though the debtor's opposing counterclaims are legal in nature and the Seventh Amendment would have entitled creditors to a jury trial had they not tendered claims against the estate.

It hardly needs pointing out that Justice White's assertion, *see Post,* at 2–3, that this case is controlled by the Court's statement in *Katchen* that "it makes no difference, so far as petitioner's Seventh Amendment claim is concerned, whether the bankruptcy trustee urges only a § 57g objection or also seeks affirmative relief," 382 U.S., at 337–338, is entirely unfounded. Read in context, the Court's statement merely means that once a creditor has filed a claim against the estate, the bankruptcy trustee may recover the full amount of any preference received by the creditor–claimant, even if that amount exceeds the amount of the creditor's claim. The Court's statement says nothing about a creditor's Seventh Amendment right to a jury trial on a trustee's preference action when the creditor has *not* entered a claim against the estate.

judges. 28 U.S.C. § 157(b)(2)(H) (1982 ed., Supp. IV). Whether 28 U.S.C. § 1411 (1982 ed., Supp. IV) purports to abolish jury trial rights in what were formerly plenary actions is unclear, and at any rate is not a question we need decide here. *See supra,* at 6, n. 3. The decisive point is that in neither the 1978 Act nor the 1984 Amendments did Congress "creat[e] a new cause of action, and remedies therefore, unknown to the common law," because traditional rights and remedies were inadequate to cope with a manifest public problem. *Atlas Roofing,* 430 U.S., at 461. Rather, Congress simply reclassified a pre–existing common–law cause of action that was not integrally related to the reformation of debtor–creditor relations[15] and that apparently did not suffer from any grave deficiencies. This purely taxonomic change cannot alter our Seventh Amendment analysis. Congress cannot eliminate a party's Seventh Amendment right to a jury trial merely by relabelling the cause of action to which it attaches and placing exclusive jurisdiction in an administrative agency or a specialized court of equity. *See Gibson* 1022–1025.

Nor can Congress' assignment be justified on the ground that jury trials of fraudulent conveyance actions would "go far to dismantle the statutory scheme," *Atlas Roofing,* 430 U.S., at 454, n. 11, or that bankruptcy proceedings have been placed in "an administrative forum with which the jury would be incompatible." *Id.,* at 450. To be sure, we owe some deference to Congress' judgment after it has given careful consideration to the constitutionality of a legislative provision. *See Northern Pipeline Construction Co.,* 458 U.S., at 61 (opinion of Brennan, J.). But respondent has adduced no evidence that Congress considered the constitutional implications of its designation of all fraudulent conveyance actions as core proceedings. Nor can it seriously be argued that permitting jury trials in fraudulent conveyance actions brought by a trustee against a person who has not entered a claim against the estate would "go far to dismantle the statutory scheme," as we used that phrase in *Atlas Roofing,* when our opinion in that case, following *Schoenthal,* plainly assumed that such claims carried with them a right to a jury trial.[16] In addition, one cannot easily

---

[15] The adventitious relation of a trustee's fraudulent conveyance actions to the reorganization proceedings themselves, which we recognized in *Schoenthal* and *Katchen,* which federal bankruptcy legislation acknowledged until 1978 by treating them as plenary actions when the defendant had not made a claim against the estate, and for which Congress expressly provided jury trial rights until 1984, is further evidenced by the events in this case. Respondent's fraudulent conveyance action was not filed until well *after* the bankruptcy court had approved the plan or reorganization and Chase & Sanborn's tangible assets and business had been liquidated. Reply Brief for Petitioner 9.

[16] Of course, the 1984 Amendments altered the statutory scheme that formed the backdrop to our discussion in *Atlas Roofing.* But in this connection they did so only by depriving persons who have not filed claims against the estate of a statutory right to a jury trial when the trustee sues them to recover an alleged fraudulent conveyance or preferential transfer. The 1984 Amendments did not alter the nature of the trustee's claim or the relief to which he was entitled. To say that our failure to respect Congress' reclassification of these causes of action would "go far to dismantle the statutory scheme" simply because they partly define the new statutory scheme would be to render this test an empty tautology.

This is not to say, of course, contrary to Justice White's assertion, *see Post,* at 6, n. 4, that we regard Congress' amendments to the bankruptcy statutes as an "act of whimsy." The sweeping changes Congress instituted in 1978 were clearly intended to make the reorganiza-

say that "the jury would be incompatible" with bankruptcy proceedings, in view of Congress' express provision for jury trials in certain actions arising out of bankruptcy litigation. *See* 28 U.S.C. § 1411 (1982 ed., Supp. IV); Gibson 1024–1025; Warner, *Katchen Up in Bankruptcy: The New Jury Trial Right,* 63 Am. Bankr. L.J. 1, 48 (1989) (hereinafter Warner). And Justice White's claim that juries may serve usefully as checks only on the decisions of judges who enjoy life tenure, see *Post,* at 13, overlooks the extent to which judges who are appointed for fixed terms may be beholden to Congress or executive officials, and thus ignores the potential for juries to exercise beneficial restraint on their decisions.

It may be that providing jury trials in some fraudulent conveyance actions—if not in this particular case, because respondent's suit was commenced after the bankruptcy court approved the debtor's plan of reorganization—would impede swift resolution of bankruptcy proceedings and increase the expense of Chapter 11 reorganizations.[17] But "these considerations are insufficient to overcome the clear command of the Seventh Amendment." *Curtis v. Loether,* 415 U.S., at 198. *See also*

---

tion process more efficient, as Justice White's quotation from a Senate Report indicates. But the radical reforms of 1978, on whose legislative history his dissent relies, did not work the slightest alteration in the right to a jury trial of alleged recipients of fraudulent conveyances. That change came in 1984. Although enhanced efficiency was likely Congress' aim once again, neither Justice White nor Justice Blackmun points to any statement from the legislative history of the 1984 Amendments confirming this supposition with respect to preference actions in particular. More important, they offer no evidence that Congress considered the propriety of its action under the Seventh Amendment. The House Report cited by Justice Blackmun, *see Post,* at 3, advocated conferring Article III status on bankruptcy judges. Its favored approach would therefore have eliminated the problem before us by clearly *entitling* petitioners to a jury trial under the Seventh Amendment. See H.R. Rep. No. 98–9, pt. 1, pp. 7, 9, 16 (1983). This approach was rejected by the senate. In defending an alternative proposal that ultimately prevailed, however, the Senate Report to which Justice Blackmun refers neglects to discuss specifically the inclusion of preference actions in the class of core proceedings or potential difficulties under the Seventh Amendment to which that assignment might give rise. See S. Rep. No. 98–40, pp. 32–40 (1983). Apparently, the Senate Judiciary Committee overlooked this problem entirely. Thus, the 1984 Amendments' denial of the right to a jury trial in preference and fraudulent conveyance actions can hardly be said to represent Congress' considered judgment of the constitutionality of this change.

[17] Respondent argues, for example, that the prompt resolution of fraudulent transfer claims brought by bankruptcy trustees is often crucial to the reorganization process and that if, by demanding a jury trial, a party could delay those proceedings, it could alter the negotiating framework and unfairly extract more favorable terms for itself. Brief for Respondent 35. It warrants notice, however, that the provision of jury trials in fraudulent conveyance actions has apparently not been attended by substantial difficulties under previous bankruptcy statutes; that respondent has not pointed to any discussion of this alleged serious problem in the legislative history of the 1978 Act or the 1984 Amendments; that in many cases defendants would likely not request jury trials; that causes of action to recover preferences may be assigned pursuant to the plan of reorganization rather than pursued prior to the plan's approval, as was done in this very case; and that Congress itself, in enacting 28 U.S.C. § 1411, explicitly provided for jury trials of personal injury and wrongful death claims, which would likely take much longer to try than most preference actions and which often involve large sums of money.

Bowsher v. Synar, 478 U.S. 714, 736 (1986) (" '[T]he fact that a given law or procedure is efficient, convenient, and useful in facilitating functions of government, standing alone, will not save it if it is contrary to the Constitution' "), quoting *Ins v. Chada,* 462 U.S. 919, 944 (1983); *Pernell v. Southall Realty,* 416 U.S., at 383–384 (discounting arguments that jury trials would be unduly burdensome and rejecting "the notion that there is some necessary inconsistency between the desire for speedy justice and the right to jury trial").[18]

V.

We do not decide today whether the current jury trial provision—28 U.S.C. § 1411 (1982 ed., Supp. IV)—permits bankruptcy courts to conduct jury trials in fraudulent conveyance actions like the one respondent initiated. Nor do we express any view as to whether the Seventh Amendment or Article III allows jury trials in such actions to be held before non–Article III bankruptcy judges subject to the oversight provided by the district courts pursuant to the 1984 Amendments. We leave those issues for future decisions.[19] We do hold, however, that whatever the answers to these questions, the Seventh Amendment entitles petitioners to the jury trial they requested. Accordingly, the judgment of the Court of Appeals is reversed, and the case is remanded for further proceedings consistent with this opinion.

It Is So Ordered.

Justice SCALIA, concurring in Part and Concurring in the Judgment:

I join all but Part IV of the Court's opinion. I make that exception because I do not agree with the premise of its discussion: that "the Federal Government need not be a party for a case to revolve around 'public rights.' " *Ante,* at 19, quoting *Thomas v. Union Carbide Agricultural Products Co.,* 473 U.S. 568, 586 (1986). In my view a matter of "public rights," whose adjudication Congress may assign to tribunals

---

[18] One commentator has noted:

> "[T]he interpretation of *Katchen* as a 'delay and expense' exception to the seventh amendment is negated by the Court's rejection of the argument that delay, or even the more significant problem of jury prejudice, an override the seventh amendment. *Katchen's* reference to 'delay and expense' must, therefore, be read as part of the Court's consideration of whether the legal remedy had become sufficiently adequate to result in a shifting of the boundaries of law and equity. At a minimum, the delay and expense language of *Katchen* must be read in light of the petitioner's demand for a stay of the bankruptcy action and the institution of a separate suit in a different court. That is a qualitatively different type of delay and expense from the delay and expense of providing a jury trial in the same action. The latter could never override Beacon [*Theaters, Inc. v. Westover,* 359 U.S. 500 (1959),] and *Dairy Queen [Inc. v. Wood,* 369 U.S. 469 (1962)]." Warner 39 (footnotes omitted); *see Id.,* at 42, 48.

[19] Justice White accuses us of being "rather coy" about which statute we are invalidating, *Post,* at 1, n. 2, and of "preferring to be obtuse" about which court must preside over the jury trial to which petitioners are entitled. *Id.,* at 11. But however helpful it might be for us to adjudge every pertinent statutory and constitutional issue presented by the 1978 Act and the 1984 Amendments, we cannot properly reach out and decide the matters not before us. The only question we have been called upon to answer in this case is whether the Seventh Amendment grants petitioners a right to a jury trial. We hold unequivocally that it does.

lacking the essential characteristics of Article III courts, "must at a minimum arise between the government and others." *Northern Pipeline Construction Co. v. Marathon Pipe Line Co.*, 458 U.S. 50, 69 (1982) (plurality opinion). Until quite recently this has also been the consistent view of the Court. *See Id.*, at 69, n. 23 ("[T]he presence of the United States as a proper party . . .is a necessary but not sufficient means of distinguishing 'private rights' from 'public rights' "); *Atlas Roofing Co. v. Occupational Safety and Health Review Comm'n*, 430 U.S. 442, 450 (1977) (public rights cases are "cases in which the Government sues in its sovereign capacity to enforce public rights created by statutes"); *Id.*, at 457 (noting "distinction between cases of private right and those which arise between the Government and persons subject to its authority"); *Id.*, at 458 (situations involving "public rights" are those "where the Government is involved in its sovereign capacity under an otherwise valid statute creating enforceable public rights"); *Crowell v. Benson*, 285 U.S. 22, 50–51 (1932) (public rights are "those which arise between the Government and persons subject to its authority in connection with the performance of the constitutional functions of the executive or legislative departments"); *Ex parte Bakelite Corp.*, 279 U.S. 438, 451 (1929) (public rights are those "arising between the government and others, which from their nature do not require judicial determination and yet are susceptible of it"); *Murray's Lessee v. Hoboken Land & Improvement Co.*, 18 How. 272, 283 (1856) (plaintiff's argument that a controversy susceptible of judicial determination must be a "judicial controversy" heard in an Article III court "leaves out of view the fact that the United States is a party").

The notion that the power to adjudicate a legal controversy between two private parties may be assigned to a non–Article III, yet federal, tribunal is entirely inconsistent with the origins of the public rights doctrine. The language of Article III itself, of course, admits of no exceptions; it directs unambiguously that the "judicial Power of the United States, shall be vested in one supreme Court, and in such inferior Courts as the Congress may from time to time ordain and establish." In *Murray's Lessee, supra,* however, we recognized a category of "public rights" whose adjudication, though a judicial act, Congress may assign to tribunals lacking the essential characteristics of Article III courts. That case involved the Act of May 15, 1820, 3 Stat. 592, which established a summary procedure for obtaining from collectors of federal revenue funds that they owed to the Treasury. Under that procedure, after a federal auditor made the determination that the funds were due, a "distress warrant" would be issued by the Solicitor of the Treasury, authorizing a United States marshal to seize and sell the personal property of the collector, and to convey his real property, in satisfaction of the debt. The United States' lien upon the real property would be effective upon the marshal's filing of the distress warrant in the district court of the district where the property was located. The debtor could, however, bring a challenge to the distress warrant in any United States district court, in which judicial challenge "every fact upon which the legality of the extra–judicial remedy depends may be drawn in[to] question," 18 How., at 284. *Murray's Lessee* involved a dispute over title to lands that had been owned by a former Collector of Customs whom the Treasury auditor had adjudged to be deficient in his remittances. The defendant had purchased the land in the marshal's sale pursuant to a duly issued distress warrant (which had apparently not been contested by the

Collector in any district court proceeding). The plaintiff, who had acquired the same land pursuant to the execution of a judgment against the Collector, which execution occurred *before* the marshal's sale, but *after* the marshal's filing of the distress warrant to establish the lien, brought an action for ejectment to try title. He argued, *inter alia,* that the process by which the defendant had obtained title violated Article III because adjudication of the Collector's indebtedness to the United States was inherently a judicial act, and could not lawfully have been performed by a Treasury auditor, but only by an Article III court. We rejected this contention by observing that although "the auditing of the accounts of a receiver of public moneys may be, in an enlarged sense, a judicial act," *Id.,* at 280, the English and American traditions established that it did not, without consent of Congress, give rise to a judicial "controversy" within the meaning of Article III.

It was in the course of answering the plaintiff's rejoinder to this holding that we uttered the words giving birth to the public rights doctrine. The plaintiff argued that if we were correct that the matter was "not in its nature a judicial controversy, congress could not make it such, nor give jurisdiction over it to the district courts" in the bills permitted to be filed by collectors challenging distress warrant—so that "the fact that congress has enabled the district court to pass upon it, is conclusive evidence that it is a judicial controversy." *Id.,* at 282. That argument, we said, "leaves out of view the fact that the United States is a party." *Id.,* at 283. Unlike a private party who acts extrajudicially to recapture his property, the marshal who executes a distress warrant "cannot be made responsible in a judicial tribunal for obeying the lawful command of the government; and the government itself, which gave the command, cannot be sued without its own consent," even though the issue in question is an appropriate matter for a judicial controversy. *Ibid* Congress could, however, waive this immunity, so as to permit challenges to the factual bases of officers' actions in Article III courts; and this waiver did not have to place the proceeding in the courts unconditionally or *ab initio,* for the "United States may consent to be sued, and may yield this consent upon such terms and under such restrictions as it may think just." *Ibid.* Thus, we summed up, in the oft–quoted passage establishing the doctrine at issue here:

> [T]here are matters, *involving public rights,* which may be presented in such form that the judicial power is capable of acting on them, and which are susceptible of judicial determination, but which Congress may or may not bring within the cognizance of the courts of the United States, as it may deem proper."
> *Id.,* at 284 (emphasis added).

It is clear that what we meant by public rights were not rights important to the public, or rights created by the public, but rights of the public—that is, rights pertaining to claims brought by or against the United States. For central to our reasoning was the device of waiver of sovereign immunity, as a means of converting a subject which, though its resolution involved a "judicial act," could not be brought before the courts, into the stuff of an Article III "judicial controversy." Waiver of sovereign immunity can only be implicated, of course, in suits where the Government is a party. We understood this from the time the doctrine of public rights was born, in 1856, until two Terms ago, saying as recently as 1982 that the suits to which it applies "must at a minimum arise 'between the government and others,' " *Northern Pipeline Construction Co. v. Marathon Pipe Line Co.,* 458 U.S., at 69, quoting *Ex parte Bakelite,* 279 U.S., at 451. *See also,* in addition to the cases cited *supra,* at 1–2, *Williams v. United States,* 289 U.S. 553, 581 (1933) (noting sovereign immunity origins of legislative courts); *Ex parte Bakelite, supra,* at 453–454 (same). *Cf. McElrath v. United States,* 102 U.S. 426, 440 (1880).

In *Thomas v. Union Carbide Agricultural Products Co.,* 473 U.S. 568 (1986), however, we decided to interpret the phrase "public rights" as though it had not been developed in the context just discussed and did not bear the meaning just described. We pronounced, as far as I can tell by sheer force of our office, that it applies to a right "so closely *integrated into a public regulatory scheme* as to be a matter appropriate for agency resolution with limited involvement by the Article III judiciary." *Id.,* at 593–594 (emphasis added). The doctrine reflects, we announced, "simply a pragmatic understanding that when Congress selects a quasi–judicial method of resolving mattters that 'could be conclusively determined by the Executive and Legislative Branches,' the danger of encroaching on the judicial powers is reduced," *Id* at 589, quoting *Northern Pipeline, supra,* at 68—without pointing out, as had *Murray's Lessee,* that the only adjudications of private rights that "could be conclusively determined by the Executive and Legislative Branches" were a select category of private rights vis–a–vis the Government itself. We thus held in *Thomas,* for the first time, that a purely private federally created action did not require Article II courts.

There was in my view no constitutional basis for that decision. It did not purport to be faithful to the origins of the public rights doctrine in *Murray's Lessee;* nor did it replace the careful analysis of that case with some other reasoning that identifies a discrete category of "judicial acts" which, at the time the Constitution was adopted, were not thought to implicate a "judicial controversy." The lines sought to be established by the Constitution did not matter. "Pragmatic understanding" was all that counted—in a case–by–case evaluation of whether the danger of "encroaching" on the "judicial powers" (a phrase now drained of constnt content) is too much. The Term after *Thomas,* in *Commodity Futures Trading Comm'n v. Schor,* 478 U.S. 833 (1986), we reconfirmed our error, embracing the analysis of *Thomas* and describing at greater length the New Article III standard it established, which seems to me no standard at all:

> "[I]n reviewing Article III challenges, we have weighed a number of factors, none of which has been deemed determinative, with an eye to the practical effect that the congressional action will have on the constitutionally assigned role of the federal judiciary . . . Among the factors upon which we have focused are the extent to which the 'essential attributes of judicial power' are reserved to Article III courts, and, conversely, the extent to which the non–Article III forum exercises the range of jurisdiction and powers normally vested only in Article III courts, the origins and importance of the right to be adjudicated, and the concerns that drove Congress to depart from the requirements of Article III." 478 U.S., at 851, citing *Thomas, supra,* at 587, 589–593.

I do not think one can preserve a system of separation of powers on the basis of such intuitive judgments regarding "practical effects," no more with regard to the assigned functions of the courts, see *Mistretta v. United States,* 488 U.S. —, — (1989) (Scalia, J., dissenting), than with regard to the assigned functions of the Executive, see *Morrison v. Olson,* 487 U.S.—, — (1988) (Scalia, J., dissenting). This central feature of the Constitution must be anchored in rules, not set adrift in some multifactored "balancing test"—and especially not in a test that contains as its last and most revealing factor "the concerns that drove Congress to depart from the requirements of Article III." *Schor, supra, at 851.*

I would return to the longstanding principle that the public rights doctrine requires, at a minimum, that the United States be a party to the adjudication. On that basis, I concur in the Court's conclusion in Part IV of its opinion that the Article III concomitant of a jury trial could not be eliminated here. Since I join the remainder of the Court's opinion, I concur in its judgment as well.

Justice WHITE, Dissenting:

The Court's decision today calls into question several of our previous decisions,[1] strikes down at least one federal statute,[2] and potentially concludes for the first time that the Seventh Amendment[3] guarantees litigants in a specialized non–Article III forum the right to a jury trial. Because I cannot accept these departures from established law, I respectfully dissent.

I.

Before I explore the Court's approach to analyzing the issues presented in this case, I first take up the question of the precedent that the Court most directly disregards today, *Katchen v. Landy,* 382 U.S. 323 (1966). Though the Court professes not to overrule this decision, and curiously, to be acting in reliance on it,

---

[1] As I will discuss more fully below, the Court's opinion can be read as overruling or severely limiting the relevant portions of the following cases: *Atlas Roofing Co. v. Occupational Safety and Health Review Comm'n,* 430 U.S. 442 (1977); *Katchen v. Landy,* 382 U.S. 323 (1966); *Block v. Hirsh,* 256 U.S. 135 (1921); and *Barton v. Barbour,* 104 U.S. 126 (1881), plus perhaps some others as well.

[2] Like much else about its opinion, the Court is rather coy about disclosing which federal statute it is invalidating today. Perhaps it is 28 U.S.C. § 157(b)(2)(H) (1982 ed., Supp. V), the statute which includes actions to avoid or recover fraudulent conveyances among core bankruptcy proceedings; or 28 U.S.C. § 157(b)(1), which permits bankruptcy judges to enter final judgments in core proceedings (given the inclusion of fraudulent conveyance actions among these proceedings); or perhaps it is 28 U.S.C. § 1411(b) (1982 ed., Supp. V), limiting jury trial rights in bankruptcy; or perhaps some part of Title 11 itself—or some combination of the above.

There is no way for Congress, or the lower Article III courts, or the bankruptcy courts—or creditors or debtors for that matter—to know how they are expected to respond to the Court's decision, even if they wish to be diligent in conforming their behavior to today's mandate. *See especially* Part V, *ante,* at 29. Though the Court denies that it is being "coy" or "obtuse," it steadfastly refuses to the end to disclose which statute it finds unconstitutional today. *See ante,* at 29–30, n. 19.

[3] The Seventh Amendment provides that "[i]n Suits at common law, where the value in controversy shall exceed twenty dollars, the right of trial by jury shall be preserved." U.S. Const., Amdt. 7.

see ante, at 22–25, there is simply no way to reconcile our decision in *Katchen* with what the Court holds today.

In *Katchen,* the petitioner filed a claim in the bankruptcy proceeding to recover funds that he alleged were due to him from a bankrupt estate; respondent, the trustee, resisted paying the claims based on § 57g of the old Bankruptcy Act, which forbade payments to creditors holding "void or voidable" preferences. Petitioner claimed, much as petitioners here do, that the question whether prior payments to him were preferences was a matter that could not be adjudicated without the benefit of a jury trial. We rejected this claim, holding that "there is no Seventh Amendment right to a jury trial" on claims such as Katchen's. *Katchen,* 382 U.S., at 337. Not only could the issue of preference be tried without a jury for the purpose of denying the filed claim pursuant to § 57g, but a money judgment for the amount of the preference could be entered without a jury trial: "It makes no difference, so far as petitioner's Seventh Amendment claim is concerned, whether the bankruptcy trustee urges only a § 57g objection or also seeks affirmative relief." *Id.,* at 337–338. This holding dispositively settles the question before us today: like the petitioner in *Katchen,* petitioners in this case have no Seventh Amendment right to a jury trial when respondent trustee seeks to avoid the fraudulent transfers they received.

In order to escape the force of *Katchen's* holding, the Court exploits the circumstances under which that decision was made. Most notably, at the time *Katchen* was decided, the Bankruptcy Act then in force (the 1898 Act) did not include actions to set aside voidable preferences among those proceedings covered by the Act. Thus, the clause of our opinion in *Katchen, supra,* at 336, on which the Court today puts so much weight—"petitioner might be entitled to a jury trial on the issue of preference if he presented no claim in the bankruptcy proceeding and awaited a federal plenary action by the trustee,"*see ante,* at 23—simply stated the truism that, under the 1898 Act in force at that time, if petitioner had not presented his claim to the bankruptcy court, that court would have had no jurisdiction to perform a summary adjudication of the preference.

That entitlement, however, on which the Court so heavily relies, was solely the product of the statutory scheme in existence at the time. If it were not, the next phrase appearing in the *Katchen* decision would make little sense: "[W]hen the same issue [*i.e.,* validity of a preference] arises as part of the process of allowance and disallowance of claims, it is triable in equity." *Katchen, supra,* at 336. *Katchen* makes it clear that when Congress does commit the issue and recovery of a preference to adjudication in a bankruptcy proceeding, the Seventh Amendment is inapplicable. Only the limits of the 1898 Act prevented this from being the case in all instances, and thereby, left Katchen with the possibility of a jury trial right.

Today's Bankruptcy Code is markedly different. Specifically, under the 1984 Act, an action to recover fraudulently transferred property has been reclassified as a "core" bankruptcy proceeding. *See* 28 U.S.C. § 157(b)(2)(H) (1982 ed., Supp. V). While in Katchen's day, it was only in special circumstances that adjudicating a preference was committed to bankruptcy proceedings, today, Congress has expressly designated adjudication of a preference or a fraudulent transfer a "core" bankruptcy proceeding. The portion of *Katchen* on which the Court relies—"petitioner might be entitled to a jury trial on the issue of preference if he presented no claim in the bankruptcy proceeding and awaited a federal plenary action by the trustee," *see ante,* at 23—is therefore a relic of history. The same is true of the decision in *Schoenthal v. Irving Trust Co.,* 287 U.S. 92, 94–95 (1932), which, in holding that "[s]uits to recover preferences constitute no part of the proceedings in bankruptcy," merely reflected the then–existing statutory scheme.

The Court recognizes the distinction between the earlier law and the present Code, but calls the change a "purely taxonomic" one that "cannot alter our Seventh Amendment analysis." *Ante,* at 26. I disagree for two reasons. First, the change is significant because it illustrates the state of the law at the time of *Katchen,* and explains why that case came out as it did. It is hypocritical for the Court to rely on *Katchen's* statement as to the existence of a jury trial entitlement for the petitioner's claim there, but then dismiss as "taxonomic" the change that wiped out that jury entitlement—or, at the very least, profoundly shifted the basis for it.

More fundamentally, the inclusion of actions to recover fraudulently conveyed property among core bankruptcy proceedings has meaning beyond the taxonomic. As I explain in more detail below, *see* Part II–A, *infra,* we have long recognized that the forum in which a claim is to be heard plays a substantial role in determining the extent to which a Seventh Amendment jury trial right exists. As we put it in *Katchen:*

> " '[I]n cases of bankruptcy, many incidental questions arise in the course of administering the bankrupt estate, which would ordinarily be pure cases at law, and in respect of their facts triable by jury, but, as belonging to bankruptcy proceedings, they become cases over which the bankruptcy court, which acts as a court of equity, exercises exclusive control. Thus a claim of debt or damages against the bankrupt is investigated by chancery methods.' " *Katchen,* 382 U.S. at 337 (quoting *Barton v. Barbour,* 104 U.S. 126, 133–134 (1881)).

The same is true here, and it counsels affirmance under our holding in *Katchen.*

In essence, the Court's rejection of *Katchen*—and its classification of the change effected by the 1984 Act as "taxonomic"—comes from its conclusion that the fraudulent conveyance action at issue here is not " 'part of the process of allowance and disallowance of claims.' " *Ante,* at 24 (quoting *Katchen, supra,* at 336). The Court misses *Katchen's* point, however: it was the fact that *Congress* had committed the determination and recovery of preferences to bankruptcy proceedings that was determinative in that case, not just the bare fact that the action "happened" to take place in the process of adjudicating claims. And the same determinative element is present here, for under the 1984 Act, Congress unmistakably intended to have fraudulent conveyances adjudicated and recovered in the Bankruptcy Court in accordance with that Court's usual procedures.

Perhaps in this respect the Court means something more akin to its later restatement of its position; namely, that the 1984 Act simply "reclassified a pre–existing common–law cause of action that was not integrally related to the reformation of debtor–creditor relations." *Ante,* at 26. The Court further indicates that it will pay little heed to the congressional inclusion of avoidance and recovery proceedings in core bankruptcy jurisdiction because that choice was not made "because [Congress found that] traditional rights and remedies were inadequate to cope with a manifest public problem."[4] *Ibid.* This misguided view of the congressional enactment is the crux of the problem with the Court's approach.

How does the Court determine that an action to recover fraudulently conveyed property is not "integrally related" to the essence of bankruptcy proceedings? Certainly not by reference to a current statutory definition of the core of bankruptcy proceedings—enacted by Congress under its plenary constitutional power, see U.S. Const., Art. I, § 8, to establish bankruptcy laws. As discussed in the preceding paragraph, this vision of what is "integrally related" to the resolution of creditor–debtor conflicts includes the sort of action before us today. *See* 28 U.S.C. § 157(b)(2)(H) (1982 ed., Supp. V). Nor does the Court find support for its contrary understanding in petitioners' submission, which concedes that the action in question

---

[4] In addition to the points I make below, I disagree with the Court's portrayal of Congress' expansion of bankruptcy jurisdiction to include actions such as this one as an act of whimsy. In fact, when (in 1978) Congress first swept proceedings like the fraudulent conveyance suit before us into the jurisdiction of the bankruptcy courts, it was legislating out of a sense that "traditional rights and remedies were inadequate to cope with a manifest public problem." *Cf. ante,* at 26:

> "A major impetus underlying this reform legislation has been the need to enlarge the jurisdiction of the bankruptcy court in order to eliminate the serious delays, expense and duplications associated with the current dichotomy between summary and plenary jurisdiction . . . [T]he jurisdictional limitations presently imposed on the bankruptcy courts have embroiled the court and the parties in voluminous litigation . . . " S. Rep. No. 95–899, p. 17 (1978).

This rather plain statement by Congress makes it clear that it found the system in place at the time grossly inadequate, and perceived a "manifest public" need for change. *See also* H.R. Rep. No. 95–595, p. 445 (1977).

In response to this legislative history, the Court makes two points. First, the Court observes that these reports concerned the 1978 Code, and not the 1984 Act; it was the latter, the Court notes, that stripped petitioners of their jury–trial right. *Ante,* at 27, n. 16. While the Court's analysis is technically correct, it ignores the fact that the 1978 Code undertook—to use the Court's own description—a "radical refor[m]" of bankruptcy law, *ibid.,* including the absorption of fraudulent preference actions into what used to be the plenary jurisdiction of bankruptcy courts. It was this change which laid the groundwork for the post–*Northern Pipeline* Act at issue here.

Second, and more importantly, the Court acknowledges that when Congress adopted the 1984 Act, it was motivated by the same "efficiency" concerns that were the basis for the 1978 legislation. *Ante,* at 27, n. 16. Thus, the Court concedes the fundamental point that Congress modified the traditional jurisdictional scheme concerning fraudulent conveyance actions because Congress found that this traditional approach was "inadequate to cope with a manifest public problem" ; under *Atlas Roofing*—even under the Court's own description of that case, *ante* at 26—this should suffice to permit Congress to limit jury trial rights on such claims.

Instead of so concluding, however, the Court retreats from *Atlas Roofing* and its earlier analysis, and holds that Congress' enactments do not control here because, in adopting them, Congress failed to make a "considered judgment of the constitutionality of [these] change[s]." *Ante,* at 28, n. 16. As I observe below, *infra,* at 17–18, elevating this inquiry to bellwether status is unprecedented in our Seventh Amendment cases—and unwise.

here is brought to "recover monies that are properly part of the debtor's estate and should be ratably distributed among creditors," and that fraudulent transfers put at risk "the basic policy of non–discriminatory distribution that underlies the bankruptcy law." Brief for Petitioners 12. This, too, seems to belie the Court's view that actions to set aside fraudulent conveyances are not "integrally related" to reforming creditor–debtor relations.

Nor is the Court's conclusion about the nature of actions to recover fraudulently transferred property supportable either by reference to the state of American bankruptcy law prior to adoption of the 1978 Code, or by reference to the pre–1791 practice in the English courts. If the Court draws its conclusions based on the fact that these actions were not considered to be part of bankruptcy proceedings under the 1800 or 1898 Bankruptcy Acts (or, more generally, under federal bankruptcy statutes predating the 1978 Code), it has treated the power given Congress in Art. I, § 8, as if it were a disposable battery, good for a limited period only—once the power in it has been consumed by use, it is to be discarded and considered to have no future value. The power of Congress under this clause is plainly not so limited: merely because Congress *once* had a scheme where actions such as this one were solely heard in plenary proceedings in Article III courts—where the Seventh Amendment attached—does not impugn the legality of every other possible arrangement. *See also* Part II–B, *infra*.

Perhaps instead the Court rests its conclusion on the practice of the 18th–century English courts. I take issue with this view of the old English law, below. But even if this were correct, I do not see why the Article I, § 8, power should be so restricted. *See Ibid.*

One final observation with respect to *Katchen*. The Court attempts to distinguish Katchen by saying that a jury trial was not needed there because the funds in dispute were part of the "bankruptcy estate." *Ante*, at 23. "Our decision [in *Katchen*] turned . . . on the bankrupty court's having 'actual or constructive possession' of the bankruptcy estate," the Court writes. *Ibid.* But obviously in this case, the bankruptcy court similarly had " 'actual or constructive possession' of the bankruptcy estate;" certainly it had as much constructive possession of the property sought as it had of the preference recovered in *Katchen*. Thus, it is as true here as it was in *Katchen* that the funds in dispute are part of the "bankruptcy estate." The Bankruptcy Code defines that estate to be comprised of "all the following property, wherever located and by whomever held," including "[a]ny interest in property that the trustee recovers under" the provision authorizing actions to recover fraudulently transferred property. 11 U.S.C. § § 541(a)(3), 550 (1982 ed., Supp. V). Consequently, even if the Court is accurate in pinpointing the dispositive fact in the *Katchen* decision, that fact equally points towards a ruling for the trustee here.

In sum, I find that our holding in *Katchen*, and its underlying logic, dictate affirmance. The court's decision today amounts to nothing less than a *sub silentio* overruling of that precedent.

II.

Even if the question before us were one of first impression, however, and we did not have the decision in *Katchen* to guide us, I would dissent from the Court's decision. Under our cases, the determination of whether the Seventh Amendment guarantees a jury trial on petitioners' claims must turn on two questions: first, in what forum will those claims be heard; and second, what is the nature of those claims. A weighing of both of these factors must point towards application of the Seventh Amendment before that guarantee will attach.[5]

A.

To read the Court's opinion, one might think that the Seventh Amendment is concerned only with the nature of a claim. If a claim is legal, the Court announces, then the Seventh Amendment guarantees a jury trial on that claim. *Ante*, at 7–8, n. 4. This is wrong. "[H]istory and our cases support the proposition that the right to a jury trial turns not solely on the nature of the issue to be resolved but also on the forum in which it is to be resolved," *Atlas Roofing Co. v. Occupational Safety and Health Review Comm'n*, 430 U.S. 442, 460–461 (1977). Perhaps like *Katchen*, *Atlas Roofing* is no longer good law after today's decision. A further examination of the issue before us reveals, though, that it is the Court's decision today, and not our prior rulings, that is in error.

In the most obvious case, it has been held that the Seventh Amendment does not apply when a "suit at common law" is heard in a state court. *Minneapolis & St. L.R. Co. v. Bombolis*, 241 U.S. 211, 217 (1916); *Woods v. Holy Cross Hospital*, 591 F.2d 1164, 1171, n. 12 (CA5 1979). Even with its exclusive focus on the claim at issue here, the Court does not purport to hold that a fraudulent conveyance action brought in state court would be covered by the Seventh Amendment, becauses that action was one at "common law" in the Court's view.

Nor does the Seventh Amendment apply in all federal forums. "[T]he Seventh Amendment is not applicable to administrative proceedings," for example. *Tull v. United States*, 481 U.S. 412, 418, n. 4 (1987). In these forums " 'where jury trials

---

[5] Since both of the relevant factors point against application of the Seventh Amendment here, resolving this case does not require offering some comprehensive view of how these factors are to be balanced. The ambiguity, however, is not of my creation, but rather, comes from the apparent inconsistency of our case law. For example, cases brought in state courts are *never* subject to the Seventh Amendment, no matter the nature of the claim; conversely, under the Court's decision in *Northern Pipeline Construction Co. v. Marathon Pipe Line Co.*, 458 U.S. 50 (1982), the sort of state–law contract claim at issue there could *never* be assigned by Congress to anything other than an Article III tribunal, in which the Seventh Amendment would apply. See also *ante*, at 3–4 (Blackmun, J., concurring). Other cases look at both factors, without being altogether clear on their relative import.

Whatever the shortcomings of this opinion for failing to resolve the difficult balancing question, it remains superior to the Court's method of "balancing" these concerns, which amounts to no balancing at all—and instead focuses solely on the nature of claim (*i.e.*, whether it is legal, and whether it concerns a public right, *see ante*, at 8, n. 4) in determining if the Seventh Amendment applies.

would be incompatible with the whole concept of administrative adjudication,' " the Seventh Amendment has no application. Atlas Roofing Co., *supra*, at 454 (quoting *Pernell v. Southall Realty*, 416 U.S. 363, 383 (1974)). Thus, we have often looked at the character of the federal forum in which the claim will be heard, asking if a jury has a place in that forum, when determining if the Seventh Amendment's guarantee of a jury trial will apply there.

Most specifically relevant for this case, we have indicated on several previous occasions that bankruptcy courts—by their very nature, courts of equity—are forums in which a jury would be out of place. "[A] bankruptcy court . . . [is] a specialized court of equity . . . a forum before which a jury would be out of place," *Atlas Roofing, supra*, at 454, n. 11; consequently, the Seventh Amendment has no application to these courts. "[T]he Court [has] recognized that a bankruptcy court has been traditionally viewed as a court of equity, and that jury trials would 'dismember' the statutory scheme of the Bankruptcy Act." *Curtis v. Loether*, 415 U.S. 189, 195 (1974). *Atlas Roofing, Curtis*, and countless other cases have recognized that Congress has the power to "entrust enforcement of statutory rights to [a] . . . specialized court of equity free from the strictures of the Seventh Amendment." *Curtis, supra*, at 195. Prior cases emphatically hold that bankruptcy courts are such specialized courts of equity. Indeed, we have stated that "bankruptcy courts are inherently proceedings in equity." *Katchen v. Landy*, 382 U.S., at 336; *see also Local Loan Co. v. Hunt*, 292 U.S. 234, 240 (1934).

Before today, this Court has never held that a party in a bankruptcy court has a Seventh Amendment right to a jury trial on its claims. Of course, the Court does not actually so hold today, preferring to be obtuse about just where petitioners are going to obtain the jury trial to which the Court deems them entitled. *See ante*, at 29–30. But in blithely ignoring the relevance of the forum Congress has designated to hear this action—focusing instead exclusively on the "legal" nature of petitioner's claim—the Court turns its back on a long line of cases that have rested, in varying degrees, on that point. The Court's decision today ignores our statement in *Atlas Roofing* that "even if the Seventh Amendment would have required a jury where the adjudication of [some types of] rights is assigned to a federal court of law instead of an administrative agency," this constitutional provision does not apply when Congress assigns the adjudication of these rights to specialized tribunals where juries have no place. *Atlas Roofing* 430 U.S., at 455. Indeed, we observed in *Atlas Roofing* that it was even true in "English or American legal systems at the time of the adoption of the Seventh Amendment [that] the question whether a fact would be found by a jury turned to a considerable degree on the nature of the forum in which a litigant found himself." *Id.*, at 458.

The Court's decision also substantially cuts back on Congress' power to assign selected causes of action to specialized forums and tribunals (such as bankruptcy courts), by holding that these forums will have to employ juries when hearing claims like the one before us today—a requirement that subverts in large part Congress' decision to create such forums in the first place. Past decisions have accorded Congress far more discretion in making these assignments. Thus, *Block v. Hirsh*, 256 U.S. 135, 158 (1921), found that a Seventh Amendment "objection amount[ed] to little" when Congress assigned what was, in essence, a common–law action for ejectment to a specialized administrative tribunal. We reiterated the vitality of *Block v. Hirsh* as recently as our decision in *Pernell v. Southall Realty, supra,* at 383, and the principle was reaffirmed in several cases between these two decisions. *See* n. 10, *infra.* In *Pernell,* referring to *Block v. Hirsh,* we stated that "the Seventh Amendment would not be a bar to a congressional effort to entrust landlord–tenant disputes, including those over the right to possession, to an administrative agency." *Pernell, supra,* at 383. Yet to the extent that such disputes involve matters that are "legal" in nature—as they clearly do—the Court's decision today means that Congress cannot do what we said in *Block* and *Pernell* that it could.[6]

Finally, the Court's ruling today ignores several additional reasons why juries have no place in bankruptcy courts and other "specialized courts of equity" like them. First, two of the principal rationales for the existence of the Seventh Amendment guarantee—the notions of "jury equity," and of juries serving as popular checks on life–tenured judges—are inapt in bankruptcy courts. As one scholar noted:

> "We have kept the civil jury . . . as a check on the federal judge whose life tenure makes [him] suspect [under] . . . the Populist traditions of this country. The function of the civil jury is to diffuse the otherwise autocratic power and authority of the judge.

> "This . . . function . . . has little application to nontraditional civil proceedings such as those which occur in bankruptcy. . . . The condition of autocracy which would bring the underlying values of the Seventh Amendment [into force] is not present; the right to jury trial therefore has no application." Hearings on § 558 before the Subcommittee on the Constitution of the Senate Committee on Judiciary, 100th Cong., 1st. Sess., 572–573 (1987) (Statement of Paul Carrington).

Others have made this same observation. See, *e.g., id.,* at 684–685 (statement of Prof. Rowe). *Cf., e.g., In re Japanese Electronic Products Antitrust Litigation,* 631 F.2d 1069, 1085 (CA3 1980). As respondent put it: "A jury in an equitable tribunal such as a bankruptcy court would in a sense be redundant." Brief for Respondent 22.

Beyond its redundancy, a requirement that juries be used in bankruptcy courts would be disruptive, and would unravel the statutory scheme that Congress has created. The Court dismisses this prospect, and scoffs that it "can[not] seriously be argued that permitting jury trials" on this sort of claim would undermine the statutory bankruptcy scheme. *Ante,* at 26. Yet this argument has not only been "seriously" made, it was actually accepted by this Court in *Curtis v. Loether,* 415 U.S. 189 (1974). In *Curtis,* we observed that *Katchen* had rejected a Seventh Amendment

---

[6] Our decision in *Katchen,* 382 U.S., at 336—which described the 1898 Act as "convert[-ing] [a] legal claim into an equitable claim" —is often cited for the same principle; *i.e.,* as upholding "the power of Congress to take some causes of action outside the scope of the Seventh Amendment by providing for their enforcement . . . in a specialized court." *See* J. Friedenthal, M. Kane, & A. Miller, Civil Procedure 498 (1985).

claim (similar to the one before us today), due to our "recogni[tion] that a bankruptcy court has been traditionally viewed as a court of equity, and that jury trials would 'dismember' the statutory scheme of the Bankruptcy Act." *Curtis, supra,* at 195; *see also Atlas Roofing Co. v. Occupational Safety and Health Review Comm'n,* 430 U.S., at 454, n. 11. I fear that the Court's decision today will have the desultory effect we feared when *Curtis* was decided.

B.

The above is not to say that Congress can vitiate the Seventh Amendment by assigning any claim that it wishes to a specialized tribunal in which juries are not employed. *Cf. Atlas Roofing, supra,* at 461, n. 16. Our cases require a second inquiry—the one that the Court focuses exclusively upon—concerning the nature of the claim so assigned.

To resolve this query, the Court properly begins its analysis with a look at English practice of the 18th century. *See ante,* at 8–12. After conducting this review, the Court states with confidence that "in 18th–century England . . . a court of equity would not have adjudicated" respondent's suit. *Ante,* at 12. While I agree that this action could have been brought at law—and perhaps even that it might have been so litigated in the most common case—my review of the English cases from the relevant period leaves me unconvinced that the chancery court would have refused to hear this action—the Court's conclusion today.

The Court itself confesses that "courts of equity sometimes provided relief in fraudulent preference actions." *Ante,* at 9. The Chancery Court put it stronger, though: "Courts of Equity have most certainly been in the habit of exercising a concurrent jurisdiction with the Courts of Law on the statutes of *Elizabeth* respecting fraudulent conveyances." *Hobbs v. Hull,* 1 Cox 445, 445–446, 29 Eng. Rep. 1242 (1788). Rarely has a more plain statement of the prevailing English practice at the time of ratification of the Seventh Amendment been discovered than this one; this alone should be enough to make respondent's case. Yet instead of accepting the pronouncement of the equity court about its own jurisdiction, this Court assumes the role of High Court of Historical Review, questioning the soundness of *Hobbs'* decision because it was issued without adequate supporting citations. *Ante,* at 11. A similar criticism is levied against another case from the same period, Ex parte Scudamore, 3 Ves. jun. 85, 30 Eng. Rep. 907 (1796), which, as even the Court concedes, "demonstrates that fraudulent conveyance actions could be brought in equity." *Ante* at 10.

In addition to nitpicking respondent's supporting case law into oblivion, the Court's more general rejection of respondent's claim rests on two sources: a passing citation to a wholly inapposite case, *Buzard v. Houston,* 119 U.S. 347 (1886); and a more lengthy quotation from Professor Glenn's treatise on fraudulent conveyances. *See Ante,* at 9. I will not deny that Professor Glenn's work supports the historical view that the Court adopts today. But notwithstanding his scholarly eminence, Professor Glenn's view of what the 18th–century English equity courts would have done with an action such as this one is not dispositive. Other scholars have looked at the same history and come to a different conclusion.[7] Still others have questioned the soundness of the distinction that Professor Glenn drew—between suits to set side monetary conveyances and suits to avoid the conveyances of land—as unwise or unsupported. *See, e.g., In re Wencl,* 71 B.R. 879, 883, n. 2 (Bkrtcy Ct., DC Minn. 1987). Indeed, just a few pages after it rests its analysis of the 18th–century case law on Professor Glenn's writing, the Court itself dismisses this aspect of Professor Glenn's historical conclusions. *See Ante,* at 11, n. 5. The Court embraces Professor Glenn's treatise where it agrees with it and calls it authoritative, while rejecting the portions it finds troublesome.

Trying to read the ambiguous history concerning fraudulent conveyance actions in equity—a task which the Court finds simple today—has perplexed jurists in each era, who have come to conflicting decisions each time that the question has found relevance. Even in Schoenthal's time, and under the statutory regime applicable when that case was decided, many courts reviewing the same historical sources considered by us today had concluded that actions such as this one sounded in equity. *See Schoenthal v. Irving Trust Co.,* 287 U.S., at 96, n. 3; Note, 42 Yale L.J. 450, 450–452 (1933). In more recent times, an impressive collection of courts have come to a similar conclusion, finding that actions to avoid fraudulent conveyances were historically considered equitable in nature.[8]

In sum, I do not think that a fair reading of the history—our understanding of which is inevitably obscured by the passage of time and the irretrievable loss of subtleties in interpretation—clearly proves or disproves that respondent's action would have sounded in equity in England in 1791.[9]

---

[7] *See, e.g.,* 4 Collier on Bankruptcy ¶ 548.10, p. 548–125 (15th ed. 1989); O. Bump, Conveyances Made by Debtors to Defraud Creditors § 532 (4th ed. 1896); F. Wait, Fraudulent Conveyances §§ 56–60 (1884); *Drake v. Rice,* 130 Mass. 410, 412 (1881) (Gray, C.J.); W. Roberts, Voluntary and Fraudulent Conveyances 525–526 (3d Am. ed. 1845).

[8] *See, e.g., In Re Graham,* 747 F.2d 1383, 1387 (CA7 1984); *Damsky v. Zavatt,* 289 F.2d 46, 53 (CA2 1961) (Friendly, J.) (an action by a bankruptcy trustee to "set aside a fraudulent conveyance has long been cognizable in equity"); *Johnson v. Gardner,* 179 F.2d 1114, 116–117 (CA9 1949). *See also In Re Harbour,* 840 F.2d 1165, 1172–1178 (CA4 1988); *In Re I.A. Durbin, Inc.,* 62 B.R. 139, 145 (SD Fla. 1986); *In Re Herndon Pools of Michigan, Inc.,* 57 B.R. 801, 802–803 (ED Mich. 1986); *In Re Southern Industrial Banking Corp.,* 66 B.R. 370, 372–375 (Bkrtcy Ct., ED Tenn. 1986).

[9] Nor do I think it clear, as the Court seems to, that simply because the remedy sought by respondent can be expressed in monetary terms, the relief he seeks is therefore "legal" in nature, and not equitable. *Ante,* at 12–14.

This Court has not accepted the view that "any award of monetary relief must necessarily be 'legal relief.' " *Curtis v. Loether,* 415 U.S. 189, 196 (1974). We have previously recognized that actions to disgorge improperly gained profits, *Tull v. United States,* 481 U.S. 412, 424 (1987), to return funds rightfully belonging to another, *Curtis, supra,* at 197, or to submit specific funds wrongfully withheld, *Bowen v. Massachusetts,* 487 U.S.—,— (1988) (slip op., at —), are all equitable actions—even though the relief they seek is monetary—because they are restitutionary in nature. Respondent's action against petitioners is of the same class, seeking a similar remedy.

Here the trustee is simply "ask[ing] the court to act in the public interest by restoring the status quo and ordering the return of that which rightfully belongs" to the estate; "[s]uch

With the historical evidence thus in equipoise—and with the nature of the relief sought here not dispositive either, see n. 8, *supra*—we should not hesitate to defer to Congress' exercise of its power under the express constitutional grant found in Art. I, § 8, cl. 4, authorizing Congress "[t]o establish . . . uniform Laws on the subject of Bankruptcies." Congress has exercised that power, defining actions such as the one before us to be among the "core" of bankruptcy proceedings, triable in a bankruptcy court before a bankruptcy judge, and without a jury. I would defer to these decisions.

The Court, however, find that some (if not all) of these congressional judgments are constitutionally suspect. While acknowledging that "[t]o be sure, we owe some deference to Congress' judgment after it has given careful consideration to" such a legislative enactment, the Court declines to defer here because "respondent has adduced no evidence that Congress considered the constitutional implications of its designation of all fraudulent conveyance actions as core proceedings." *Ante,* at 26–27. *See also Ante,* at 27–28, n. 16. This statement is remarkable, for it should not be assumed that Congress in enacting 28 U.S.C. § 157(b)(2)(H) ignored its constitutional implications.[10] The Court does not say where it draws its requirement that the Congress must provide us with some indication that it considered the constitutional dimensions of its decision before acting, as a prerequisite for obtaining our deference to those enactments.[11]

---

action is within . . . the highest tradition of a court of equity." *Porter v. Warner Co.,* 328 U.S. 395, 402 (1946). It should not matter whether respondent is seeking to have returned the precise cashier's checks that petitioner Medex had in its possession at one time, or the funds yielded to Medex by cashing those checks. To turn the case on this distinction would only give entities in Medex's position an incentive to consummate fraudulent transfers as quickly as possible: hardly a desirable one. A host of bankruptcy courts have recognized as much. *See, e.g., In Re Wencl,* 71 B.R. 879, 883–884, and n. 2 (DC Min. 1987); *In Re Reda, Inc.,* 60 B.R. 178, 181 (ND Ill. 1986).

10 An irony of the Court's rebuke of Congress is that Congress' decision to include actions to avoid or recover fraudulent conveyances among "core" bankruptcy proceedings found its inspiration in the "Emergency Rule" drafted and issued by the Administrative Office of the United States Courts on December 3, 1982, to govern practice in the Bankruptcy Courts following our decision in *Northern Pipeline. See* Emergency Rule § d(3)(A) ("Related proceedings do not include . . . proceedings to set aside preferences and fraudulent conveyances"); *see also Addison v. O'Leary,* 68 B.R. 487, 491 (ED Va. 1986) ("the jurisdictional provisions of the 1984 [Act] closely parallel the Emergency Reference Rule"); G. Treister, J. Trost, L. Forman, K. Klee, & R. Levin, Fundamentals of Bankruptcy Law § 2.01(a), p. 31 (2d ed. 1988) (describing this portion of the Emergency Rule as the "forerunner" of the 1984 Act).

We learn today that, in retrospect, the Emergency Rule, too, was unconstitutional in its failure to include a jury trial right for actions to avoid fraudulent conveyances. It appears that it was not only Congress that failed in its duty to give adequate "consider[ation] [to] the constitutional implications of its' actions." *Cf. ante,* at 28, n. 16.

11 This is particularly unfortunate because today's ruling may be the first time ever that the Court has struck down a congressional designation of a particular cause of action as "equitable" in nature. *See* Note, *Congressional Provision for Nonjury Trials,* 83 Yale L.J. 401, 414–415 (1973) ("[T]he Court has never rejected a congressional indication that an

Moreover, the Court's cramped view of Congress' power under the Bankruptcy Clause to enlarge the scope of bankruptcy proceedings, ignoring that changing times dictate changes in these proceedings, stands in sharp contrast to a more generous view expressed some years ago:

> "The fundamental and radically progressive nature of [congressional] extensions [in the scope of bankruptcy laws] becomes apparent upon their mere statement . . . . Taken altogether, they demonstrate in a very striking way the capacity of the bankruptcy clause to meet new conditions as they have been disclosed as a result of the tremendous growth of business and development of human activities from 1800 to the present day. And these acts, far–reaching though they may be, have not gone beyond the limit of congressional power; but rather have constituted extensions into a field whose boundaries may not yet be fully revealed." *Continental Illinois National Bank v. Chicago*, R.I. & P.R. Co., 294 U.S. 648, 671 (1935).

See also Katchen v. Landy, 382 U.S., at 328–329.

One of that period's leading constitutional historians expressed the same view, saying that the Framers of the Bankruptcy Clause "clearly understood that they were not building a straight–jacket to restrain the growth and shackle the spirits of their decedents for all time to come," but rather, were attempting to devise a scheme "which, while firm, was nevertheless to be flexible enough to serve the varying social needs of changing gnerations." C. Warren, Bankruptcy in United States History 4 (1935). Today, the Court ignores these lessons and places a straightjacket on Congress' power under the Bankruptcy Clause: a straightjacket designed in an era, as any reader of Dickens is aware, that was not known for its enlightened thinking on debtor–creditor relations.

Indeed, the Court calls into question the long–standing assumption of our cases and the bankruptcy courts that the equitable proceedings of those courts, adjudicating creditor–debtor disputes, are adjudications concerning "public rights." *See Northern Pipeline Construction Co. v. Marathon Pipe Line Co.*, 458 U.S. 50, 71 (1982); *Id.*, at 91 (Rehnquist, J., concurring in judgment); *Id.*, at 92 (Burger, C. J., dissenting); *Id.*, at 108–118 (White, J., dissenting). The list of lower court opinions that have reasoned from this assumption is so lengthy that I cannot reasonably include it in the text; a mere sampling fills the margin.[12] Yet today the Court calls

---

action is equitable in nature"); *but cf. Curtis v. Loether, supra* ("re–interpreting" congressional enactment to respond to Seventh Amendment "concerns").

In the past, we have been far more deferential to Congress' designations in this regard. *See, e.g., Mitchell v. Robert Demario Jewelry, Inc.*, 361 U.S. 288, 290–295 (1960); *Porter v. Warner, supra*, at 397–402.

[12] Such cases decided since *Northern Pipeline*, from the Court of Appeals alone, include *In Re Harbor*, 840 F.2d, at 1177–1178; *In Re Wood*, 825 F.2d 90, 95–98 (CA5 1987); *In Re Mankin*, 823 F.2d 1296, 1307–1308 (CA9 1987), *cert. denied sub nom. Munn v. Duck*, 485 U.S. 1006 (1988); *In Re Arnold Print Works*, 815 F.2d 165, 168–170 (CA1 1987); *Briden v. Foley*, 776 F.2d 379, 381 (CA1 1985); and *In Re Kaiser* 722 F.2d 1574, 1580, and n. 2. (CA2 1983). Many more such cases are found in the reports of the decisions of the District Courts and the Bankruptcy Courts.

all of this into doubt merely because these cases have been subjected to "substantial scholarly criticism." *Ante,* at 21, n. 11.[13] If no part of bankruptcy proceedings involve the adjudication of public rights, as the Court implies today, then *all* bankruptcy proceedings are saved from the strictures of the Seventh Amendment only to the extent that such proceedings are the decedents of earlier analogues heard in equity in 18th–century England. Because, as almost every historian has observed, this period was marked by a far more restrictive notion of equitable jurisdiction in bankruptcies, see, *e.g.,* Warren, *supra,* at 3–5, the Court's decision today may threaten the efficacy of bankruptcy courts as they are now constituted. I see no reason to use the Seventh Amendment as a tool to achieve this dubious result.

III.

Because I find the Court's decision at odds with our precedent, and peculiarly eager to embark on an unclear course in Seventh Amendment jurisprudence, I respectfully dissent.[14]

Justice BLACKMUN, with whom Justice O'CONNOR joins,

I agree generally with what Justice White has said, but write separately to clarify, particularly in my own mind, the nature of the relevant inquiry.

Once we determine that petitioners have no statutory right to a jury trial, we must embark on the Seventh Amendment inquiry set forth in *Atlas Roofing Co. v. Occupational Safety and Health Review Comm'n,* 430 U.S. 442 (1977). First, we must determine whether the matter to be adjudicated is "legal" rather than "equitable" in nature, a determination which turns on the nature of the claim and of the relief sought. If the claim and the relief are deemed equitable, we need go no further: the Seventh Amendmen's jury–trial right applies only to actions at law.

In this case, the historical inquiry is made difficult by the fact that, before the Federal Rules of Civil Procedure unified law and equity, parties might have been

---

[13] This is indicative of the Court's approach throughout its opinion: virtually every key holding announced today rests on a citation to scholarly authority, and not to any precedent of the Court. This includes the Court's holdings that the action at issue here was cognizable only at law in 18th–century England, *ante,* at 9; that fraudulent conveyance actions "more nearly resemble state–law contract claims . . . than they do creditors' hierarchically ordered claims to a pro rata share of the bankruptcy *res,*" *ante,* at 22; and that Congress could not eliminate a jury trial right in this sort of action by placing it in "a specialized court of equity," *ante,* at 26—in short, the three critical holdings issued by the Court in its opinion.

Like the Court, I think the analysis of learned commentators is a useful tool to enhance our understanding of the law in a field such as bankruptcy. Unlike the Court, however, I would not use the views of these scholars as *the* basis for disposing of the case before us— particularly where those views counsel rejection of otherwise viable strains in our case law. *See, e.g.,* Gibson, *Jury Trials in Bankruptcy,* 72 Minn. L. Rev. 967, –1040–1041, n. 347 (1988) (cited *ante,* at 21, n. 11).

[14] Because I do not believe that either petitioner is entitled to a jury trial under the Seventh Amendment, I do not reach the question whether petitioner Granfinanciera is deprived of any Seventh Amendment rights it might otherwise have due to its status as an instrument of a foreign sovereign. Like the Court, I would "leave for another day" the resolution of this difficult question. *Ante,* at 5–6.

drawn to the equity side of the court because they needed its procedural tools and interim remedies: discovery, accounting, the power to clear title, and the like. In light of the frequency with which these tools were likely needed in fraud cases of any kind, it is no surprise that, as Justice White points out, fraudulent conveyance actions, even if cognizable at law, often would be found on the equity docket. *See generally* O. Bump, Conveyances Made by Debtors to Defraud Creditors § 532 (1896); F. Wait, Fraudulent Conveyances and Creditors' Bills §§ 59–60 (1884); W. Roberts, Voluntary and Fraudulent Conveyances 525–526 (1845). This procedural dimension of the choice between law and equity lends a tentative quality to any lessons we may draw from history.

The uncertainty in the historical record should lead us, for purposes of the present inquiry, to give the constitutional right to a jury trial the benefit of the doubt. Indeed, it is difficult to do otherwise after the Court's decision in *Schoenthal v. Irving Trust Co.,* 287 U.S. 92 (1932). *Schoenthal* turned on the legal nature of the preference claim and of the relief sought, *Id.,* at 94–95, rather than upon the legal nature of the tribunal to which "plenary proceedings" were assigned under the 1898 Bankruptcy Act.

"With the historical evidence thus in equipoise," *ante,* at 17 (White, J., dissenting), but with *Schoenthal* weighing on the "legal" side of the scale, I then would turn to the second stage of the *Atlas Roofing* inquiry: I would ask whether, assuming the claim here is of a "legal" nature, Congress has assigned it to be adjudicated in a special tribunal "with which the jury would be incompatible." *Atlas Roofing,* 430 U.S., at 450; *see also Tull v. United States,* 481 U.S. 412, 418, n. 4 (1987). Here, I agree with Justice White that *Katchen v. Landy,* 382 U.S. 323 (1966), as interpreted in *Atlas Roofing,* requires the conclusion that courts exercising core bankruptcy functions are equitable tribunals, in which "a jury would be out of place and would go far to dismantle the statutory scheme." *Atlas Roofing,* 430 U.S., at 454, n. 11.

Having identified the tribunal to which Congress has assigned respondent's fraudulent conveyance claim as equitable in nature, the question remains whether the assignment is one Congress may constitutionally make. Under *Atlas Roofing,* that question turns on whether the claim involves a "public right." *Id.,* at 455. When Congress was faced with the task of divining the import of our fragmented decision in *Northern Pipeline Construction Co. v. Marathon Pipe Line Co.,* 458 U.S. 50 (1982), it gambled and predicted that a statutory right which is an integral part of a pervasive regulatory scheme may qualify as a "public right." Compare H.R. Rep. No. 98–9, pt. 1, pp. 6, 13 (1983) (House Report), with S. Rep. No. 98–55, pp. 33–40 (1983) (Senate Report); *see Thomas v. Union Carbide Agricultural Products Co.,* 473 U.S. 568, 586, 594 (1985); *see also Id.,* at 599 (Brennan, J., concurring in the judgment) ("a bankruptcy adjudication, though technically a dispute among private parties, may well be properly characterized as a matter of public rights"). Doing its best to observe the constraints of *Northern Pipeline* while at the same time preserving as much as it could of the policy goals of the major program of bankruptcy reform the decision in *Northern Pipeline* dismantled, see House Report, at 7, Senate Report, at 6–7, Congress struck a compromise. It identified those proceedings which it viewed as integral to the bankruptcy scheme as "core" (doing its best to exclude "*Marathon*–type State law cases"), and assigned them to a special-ized equitable tribunal. *Id.,* at 2.

I agree with Justice White, *ante,* at 18–19, that it would be improper for this Court to employ, in its Seventh Amendment analysis, a century–old conception of what is and is not central to the bankruptcy process, a conception that Congress has expressly rejected. To do so would, among other vices, trivialize the efforts Congress has engaged in for more than a decade to bring the bankruptcy system into the modern era.

There are, nonetheless, some limits to what Congress constitutionally may desig-nate as a "core proceeding," if the designation has an impact on constitutional rights. Congress, for example, could not designate as "core bankruptcy proceedings" state–law contract actions brought by debtors against third parties. Otherwise, *Northern Pipeline* would be rendered a nullity. In this case, however, Congress has not exceeded these limits.

Although causes of action to recover fraudulent conveyances exist outside the federal bankruptcy laws, the problems created by fraudulent conveyances are of particular significance to the bankruptcy process. Indeed, for this reason, the Bankruptcy Code long has included substantive legislation regarding fraudulent conveyances and preferences. And the cause of action respondent brought in this case arises under federal law. *See* 11 U.S.C.§§ 548(a)(2) and 550(a). This substantive legislation is not a jurisdictional artifice. It reflects, instead, Congress' longstanding view that fraudulent conveyances and preferences on the eve of bankruptcy are common methods through which debtors and creditors act to under-mine one of the central goals of the bankruptcy process: the fair distribution of assets among creditors. Congress' conclusion that the proper functioning of the bankruptcy system requires that expert judges handle these claims, and that the claims be given higher priority than they would receive on a crowded district court's civil jury docket (*see* Senate Report, at 3; House Report, at 7–8), is entitled to our respect.

The fact that the reorganization plan in this case provided that the creditor's representatives would bring fraudulent conveyance actions only after the plan was approved does not render the relationship between fraudulent conveyance actions and the bankruptcy process "adventitious." *Ante,* at 26, n. 15 (majority opinion). Creditors would be less likely to approve a plan which forced them to undertake the burden of collecting fraudulently transferred assets if they were not assured that their claims would receive expert and expedited treatment.

In sum, it must be acknowledged that Congress has legislated treacherously close to the constiutional line by denying a jury trial in a fraudulent conveyance action in which the defendant has no claim against the estate. Nonetheless, given the significant federal interests involved, and the importance of permitting Congress at long last to fashion a modern bankruptcy system which places the basic rudiments of the bankruptcy process in the hands of an expert equitable tribunal, I cannot say that Congress has crossed the constitutional line on the facts of this case. By holding otherwise, the Court today throws Congress into still another round of bankruptcy court reform, without compelling reason. There was no need for us to rock the boat in this case. Accordingly, I dissent.

LANGENKAMP v. CULP

Supreme Court of the United States
498 U.S. 42, 111 S. Ct. 330, 112 L. Ed. 2d 343

PER CURIAM:

This case presents the question whether creditors who submit a claim against a bankruptcy estate and are then sued by the trustee in bankruptcy to recover allegedly preferential monetary transfers are entitled to jury trial under the Seventh Amendment. This action was brought by petitioner Langenkamp, successor trustee to Republic Trust & Savings Company and Republic Financial Corporation (collectively debtors). Debtors were uninsured, nonbank financial institutions doing business in Oklahoma. Debtors filed Chapter 11 bankruptcy petitions on September 24, 1984. At the time of the bankruptcy filings, respondents held thrift and passbook savings certificates issued by the debtors, which represented the debtors' promise to repay moneys the respondents had invested. Within the 90–day period immediately preceding debtors' Chapter 11 filing, respondents redeemed some, but not all, of the debtors' certificates which they held. Thus, upon the bankruptcy filing, respondents became creditors of the now–bankrupt corporations. Respondents timely filed proofs of claim against the bankruptcy filing, the trustee instituted adversary proceedings under 11 U.S.C. § 547(b) to recover, as avoidable preferences, the payments which respondents had received immediately prior to the September 24 filing. A bench trial was held, and the Bankruptcy Court found that the money received by respondents did in fact constitute avoidable preferences. Republic Trust & Savings Co., CCH Bkrptcy. L. Rep. ¶ 73281 (1990). The United States District Court for the Northern District of Oklahoma affirmed. On appeal, the United States Court of Appeals for the Tenth Circuit upheld the District court's judgment on three grounds, but reversed on the issue of the holders' entitlement to a jury trial on the trustee's preference claims. *Langenkamp v. Hackler*, 897 F.2d 1041 [22 C.B.C.2d 824) (1990). Relying on our decisions in Granfinanciera, *S.A. v. Nordberg*, 492 U.S. — [20 C.B.C.2d 1216] (1989), and *Katchen v. Landy*, 382 U.S. 323 (1966), the Tenth Circuit correctly held that "those appellants that did not have or file claims against the debtors' estates undoubtedly [were] entitled to a jury trial on the issue whether the payments they received from the debtors within ninety days of the latter's bankruptcy constitute[d] avoidable preferences." *Langenkamp, supra,* at 1046. The Court of Appeals went further, however, concluding:

> "[A]lthough some of the appellants did file claims against the estates because they continued to have monies invested in the debtors at the time of bankruptcy, . . . we believe they likewise are entitled to a jury trial under the rationale of *Granfinanciera* and *Katchen*. Despite these appellants' claims, the trustee's actions to avoid the transfers, consolidated by the bankruptcy court, were plenary rather than a part of the bankruptcy court's summary proceedings involving the 'process of allowance and disallowance of claims.' " 897 F.2d, at 1046–1047.

Petitioner contends that the Tenth Circuit erred in holding that those creditors of the debtors who had filed claims against the estate were entitled to a jury trial. We agree.

In *Granfinanciera* we recognized that by filing a claim against a bankruptcy estate the creditor triggers the process of "allowance and disallowance of claims," thereby subjecting himself to the bankruptcy court's equitable power. 492 U.S., at —, and n.14 (slip op. 22–24) (citing *Katchen, supra,* at 336). If the creditor is met, in turn, with a preference action from the trustee, that action becomes part of the claims–allowance process which is triable only in equity. *Ibid.* In other words, the creditor's claim and the ensuing preference action by the trustee become integral to the restructuring of the debtor–creditor relationship through the bankruptcy court's equity jurisdiction. *Granfinanciera, supra* at — (slip op. 22–23). As such, there is no Seventh Amendment right to a jury trial. If a party does not submit a claim against the bankruptcy estate, however, the trustee can recover allegedly preferential transfers only by filing what amounts to a legal action to recover a monetary transfer. In those circumstances the preference defendant is entitled to a jury trial. 492 U.S., at — (slip op. 23).

Accordingly, "a creditor's right to a jury trial on a bankruptcy trustee's preference claim depends upon whether the creditor has submitted a claim against the estate." *Id.* at — (slip op. 23–24). Respondents filed claims against the bankruptcy estate, thereby bringing themselves within the equitable jurisdiction of the bankruptcy court. Consequently, they were not entitled to a jury trial on the trustee's preference action. The decision by the Court of Appeals overlooked the clear distinction which our cases have drawn and in so doing created a conflict among the circuits on this issue. For this reason we grant the petition for certiorari, reverse the judgment of the Court of Appeals for the Tenth Circuit and remand for further proceedings consistent with this opinion.

It is so ordered.

BEN COOPER, INC. v. THE INSURANCE COMPANY OF THE STATE OF PENNSYLVANIA
(In Re Ben Cooper, Inc.)

United States Court of Appeals, Second Circuit
896 F.2d 1394, 22 C.B.C.2d 729 (1990)

TIMBERS, Circuit Judge:

Appellant Ben Cooper, Inc. ("Cooper") appeals from an oral decision from the bench on July 11, 1989, in the Southern District of New York, Louis L. Stanton, District Judge. The district court reversed an order of the bankruptcy court, Cornelius Blackshear, Bankruptcy Judge, filed on June 15, 1989. The bankruptcy court held that the adversary proceeding filed by Cooper against appellees Insurance Company of the State of Pennsylvania ("ICSP"), Kalvin–Miller International, Inc. ("KM") and Kerwick & Curran, Inc. ("K & C") was "core" within the meaning of 28 U.S.C. § 157(b)(2) (1988). It retained jurisdiction. The district court disagreed, holding that the adversary proceeding was merely "related" to Cooper's underlying Chapter 11 petition, and withdrew the reference to the bankruptcy court. The district court also held that withdrawal was required because appellees were entitled to a jury trial on at least some of their affirmative defenses and on some of Cooper's claims. The district court then abstained from addressing the merits of Cooper's claims in favor of ongoing proceedings based on the same operative facts, commenced by ICSP in New York Supreme Court, New York County. Cooper timely appealed to this Court.

On appeal, Cooper asserts that the proceeding is core and that appellees are not entitled to a jury trial. Appellees, in turn, assert that the proceeding is non–core and that their jury demand should be honored. For the reasons stated below, we hold that the proceeding is core, and therefore we reverse the district court. We also hold that appellees are entitled to a jury trial, and that such trial should be in the bankruptcy court. We therefore remand the case to the bankruptcy court.

We reach our determination of the issue of core jurisdiction in light of In re Manville Forest Products Corp., No. 89–5019, —2d — Cir. 1990), also decided today, and assume familiarity with that opinion.

I.

We summarize only those facts and prior proceedings believed necessary to an understanding of the issues raised on appeal.

Cooper is a toy and costume manufacturer and importer. Facing economic difficulties, it filed a voluntary petition for reorganization under Chapter 11 of the Bankruptcy Code in April 1988. Pursuant to that petition, Cooper submitted a reorganization plan under which, among other things, it covenanted to "keep all of its respective properties adequately insured at all times with responsible insurance carriers against loss or damage by fire and other hazards."

Acting to fulfill its responsibility under the plan (which was finally confirmed by the bankruptcy court on April 4, 1989), Cooper retained KM, an insurance broker, to obtain coverage for his various facilities. KM enlisted K & C, another broker, to assist in finding coverage for Cooper. In October 1988 the brokers procured from ICSP a standard commercial property insurance policy for one of Cooper's facilities, located in Georgia. Appellees do not dispute that they were aware of Cooper's Chapter 11 status.

On January 6, 1989, the Georgia facility was hit by fire, resulting in damage that, Cooper claimed, totaled over $2 million. After an extended investigation, ICSP determined that it was not liable for the loss because of alleged misrepresentation and omissions by Cooper in the policy application; specifically, that Cooper failed to disclose in its application that the facility was used for manufacturing rather than as a warehouse. Moreover, ICSP determined that Cooper exaggerated its loss in the fire when it submitted the claim. That dispute underlies the instant appeal but is not before us directly. We express no view as to its proper disposition.

On April 18, 1989, ICSP formally cancelled its policy with Cooper. That same day, ICSP commenced an action in the New York Supreme Court, New York County. Its complaint alleged three causes of action: (1) that the policy was void *ab initio* due to the misrepresentations in Cooper's application; (2) that it was not liable for the fire loss because of those misrepresentations; and (3) that it was not liable under the policy because of Cooper's exaggerated claim of loss. Cooper sought and, on May 9, received from the bankruptcy court a stay of the state court action and a preliminary injunction requiring ICSP to maintain the policy.

Almost simultaneously, Cooper commenced, in the bankruptcy court, the adversary proceeding that is the subject of the instant appeal. Cooper's complaint contained three counts. The first, against ICSP, requested a declaration that the policy remained in effect, a declaration that ICSP was liable for all losses sustained in the fire, and punitive damages from ICSP of $5 million. The second count, against KM, alleged negligent conduct in obtaining the policy, and requested, if ICSP were found not liable under the policy, that KM be held responsible for the fire and consequential losses. The third count, against K & C, essentially mirrored the second. ICSP's answer set forth five affirmative defenses. Three of them repeated, almost to the word, the three causes of action in ICSP's state court complaint.

Appellees opposed the bankruptcy court's jurisdiction over the adversary proceeding, and moved the district court for withdrawal of the reference. They also moved to have the state court stay and the preliminary injunction lifted. Rather than rule on the merits of the motion, the district court, Hon. John M. Walker, remanded the case to the bankruptcy court on May 31 for a determination of the question whether the claims in the proceeding were core.

On June 15 the bankruptcy court entered an order holding that the proceeding was core, and retained jurisdiction. It relied primarily on § 157(b)(2)(A) (estate administration) and secondarily on § 157(b)(2)(L) (confirmation of plans).

Appellees then moved in the district court to reverse that order. The court did so in an oral ruling dated July 11, holding that, while the statutory provisions were relevant to the adversary proceeding, the statutory provisions were not sufficiently broad to render the proceeding core. Moreover, the court held that appellees were entitled to a jury trial on at least some of the issues raised. The court also granted the ancillary relief appellees sought: withdrawal of the reference to the bankruptcy court, abstaining from exercising its own jurisdiction, and lifting the stay of the state court proceedings. This appeal followed.

On appeal, the parties agree that the primary issues are (1) whether the adversary proceeding is core, and (2) whether appellees are entitled to a jury trial, as they have demanded. Cooper does not raise the other issues on which the district court ruled–the decisions to lift the state court stay and to abstain from exercising jurisdiction.

II.

We turn first to the question whether the adversary proceeding is core within the meaning of 28 U.S.C. § 157(b)(2) (1988). As a question of law, we review de novo the district court's determination that the proceeding is non–core. *Brunner v. New York State Higher Ed. Servs.*, 831 F.2d 395, 396 (2 Cir. 1987).

A.

The jurisdiction of the bankruptcy court over core proceedings is set forth in 28 U.S.C. § 157(b)(1) (1988), which provides that "[b]ankruptcy judges may hear and determine . . . all core proceedings arising under title 11 . . . and may enter appropriate orders and judgments." By contrast, any determinations by the bankruptcy court in a non–core proceeding, upon timely objection, are subject to de novo review by the district court. 28 U.S.C. § 157(c)(1) (1988).

In § 157(b)(2), Congress provided a non–exclusive list of proceedings which it deemed core. Like the bankruptcy court, our analysis will focus on § 157(b)(2)(A) ("matters concerning the administration of the estate"). The language of that sub–section could be construed to include almost any matter relating to bankruptcy, but the structure of the statute as a whole does not permit such a construction. Matters that merely concern the administration of the bankrupt estate tangentially are related, non–core proceedings. *In re Wood*, 825 F.2d 90, 96 [17 C.B.C.2d 743] (5 Cir. 1987) (Wisdom, J.).

Our attempt to make the general language of § 157(b)(2)(A) more concrete begins with the Supreme Court's plurality opinion in *Northern Pipeline Constr. Co. v. Marathon Pipe Line Co.*, 458 U.S. 50 [6 C.B.C.2d 785] (1982). At issue in *Marathon* was the provision of the Bankruptcy Act of 1978 which gave the bankruptcy court "jurisdiction over all 'civil proceeding arising under . . . or arising in or related to cases under title 11.' " *Id.* at 54 (quoting 28 U.S.C. § 1471(b) (Supp. IV 1980)). In order to exercise that jurisdiction, the statute vested bankrutpcy courts with "all of the 'powers of a court of equity, law, and admiralty,' " with only very limited exceptions. *Id.* at 55 (quoting 28 U.S.C. § 1481 (Supp. IV 1980)). Despite that broad jurisdictional grant, however, the Act did not give bankruptcy judges Article III status.

In *Marathon*, the underlying cause of action, as here, was breach of contract. The cause of action arose before Northern Pipeline, the debtor, petitioned the bankruptcy court for Chapter 11 reorganization. The debtor, however, did not initiate the action until after the Chapter 11 petition was filed. Under the 1978 Act, therefore, the bankruptcy court had full jurisdiction over the dispute.

The Supreme Court held that while Congress, pursuant to its power under the Bankruptcy Clause of the Constitution, U.S. Const., art. I, § 8, cl. 4, could grant the bankruptcy courts the right to issue final orders in proceedings that were at the core of bankruptcy jurisdiction, primarily the restructuring of the debtor–creditor relationship, it could not give the right to issue such orders in "private right" claims (*e.g.,* tort and contract), merely because those claims involved a debtor. *Marathon, supra,* 458 U.S. at 71. Those traditional common law claims, the Court held, were reserved for Article III courts.

The congressional response to *Marathon* is set forth in § 157. We employ the "traditional tools of statutory construction," *INS v. Cardoza–Fonseca,* 480 U.S. 421, 446 (1987), to interpret that response. Neither the House nor the Senate issued a report regarding the Bankruptcy Amendments and Federal Judgeship Act of 1984, of which § 157 is a part. The statements of several influential legislators, however, indicate that bankruptcy jurisdiction was to be construed as broadly as possible within the constitutional constraints of *Marathon*. We agree with the First Circuit's analysis of the legislative history. As that court stated,

> "the legislative history of [§ 157] indicates that Congress intended that 'core proceedings' would be interpreted broadly, close to or congruent with constitutional limits. The sponsors repeatedly said that 95 percent of the proceedings brought before bankruptcy judges would be core proceedings. *See* 130 Cong. Rec. E1108–1110 (daily ed. March 20, 1984) (statement of Representative Kastenmeier); *Id.* at H1848, H1850 (daily ed. March 21, 1984) (statement of Representative Kindness). They used arguments strongly suggesting that they were pressing the notion to its constitutional bounds. They referred to the suits in the non–core category as '*Marathon*–type' cases, *see, e.g., id.* at E1108, E1109 (daily ed. March 20, 1984) (prepared statement of Representative Kastenmeier); *Id.* at H1848 (daily ed. March 21, 1984) (statement of Representative Kindness), which they understood to be proceedings of 'a very limited kind,' *Id.* at H1848 (daily ed. March 21, 1984) (statement of Representative Kindness)."

In re Arnold Print Works, Inc.,M 815 F.2d 165, 168 [16 C.B.C.2d 944] (1 Cir. 1987) (Breyer, J.).

Moreover, § 157(b)(3) provides additional support for our conclusion that Congress intended a narrow reading of *Marathon*. That section provides in relevant part that "[a] determination that a proceeding is not a core proceeding shall not be made solely on the basis that its resolution may be affected by State law." We read that as a demonstration of Congress' intent that bankruptcy courts are not precluded from adjudicting state–law claims when such claims are at the heart of the administration of the bankrupt estate.

B.

With this in mind, our task is to determine whether this adversary proceeding, which arose after Cooper filed its Chapter 11 petition and which is founded on state contract law, falls within "the core of the federal bankruptcy power." *Marathon, supra,* 458 U.S. at 71.

Section 301 of the Bankruptcy Code provides:

> "A voluntary case under a chapter of this title is commenced by the filing with the bankruptcy court of a petition under such chapter by an entity that may be a debtor under such chapter. The commencement of a voluntary case under a chapter of this title constitutes an order for relief under such chapter."

11 U.S.C. § 301 (1988). The filing of the petition sets in motion several events. Most significant, from the standpoint of the instant appeal, it creates the "estate" for bankruptcy purposes. 11 U.S.C. § 541(a) (1988). The Supreme Court has stated, in construing the direct predecessor to § 541(a), that

" 'the purpose of the law was to fix the line of cleavage with reference to the condition of the bankrupt estate as of the time at which the petition was filed and that the property which vests in the trustee at the time of adjudication is that which the bankrupt owned at the time of the filing of the petition.' "

Goggin v. Division of Labor Law Enforcement, 336 U.S. 118, 125–26 (1949) (quoting *Everett v. Judson,* 228 U.S. 474, 479 (1913)); *see also Kohn v. Myers,* 266 F.2d 353, 355 (2 Cir. 1959); *Lockhart v. Garden City Bank & Trust Co.,* 116 F.2d 658, 661 (2 Cir. 1940). Moreover, in addition to creating estate property, the filing date adjusts "the rights of others connected with the proceeding." King, 4 Collier on Bankruptcy ¶ 541.04, at 541–22 (15th ed. 1989). Logically, a post–petition contract that has as its subject matter an estate asset must be analyzed differently than one arising pre–petition.

The First Circuit, in *Arnold Print Works, supra,* recently held that post–petition contract claims are core. *Arnold Print Works* observed that, historically, trustees and debtors–in–possession (Cooper's status) have been viewed for various purposes as officers of the bankruptcy court. 815 F.2d at 169–70. Post–petition contracts with the debtor–in–possession, therefore, are integral to the estate administration from the date they are entered into. *Id.; In re Baker & Getty Financial Servs. Inc.,* 88 B.R. 137, 139–40 (Bankr. N.D. Ohio 1988); *In re Franklin Computer Corp.,* 60 B.R. 795, 800–01 (Bankr. E.D. Pa. 1986). We find the reasoning of *Arnold Print Works* especially persuasive in light of the facts of the instant appeal: the Georgia facility was an asset of the estate; Cooper's reorganization plan promised adequate insurance for the estate assets; the bankruptcy court's confirmation of the plan was premised on adequate insurance; and appellees were aware that they were dealing with a debtor–in–possession and that the subject matter of the policy was an asset of the estate. *Cf. In re Mike Burns Inn, Inc.,* 70 B.R. 863 (Bankr. D. Mass. 1987) (post–petition claim on insurance policy acquired post–petition is core); *In re Heaven Sent, Ltd.,* 50 B.R. 636 (Bankr. E.D. Pa. 1985) (action to maintain insurance is core). It is difficult to conceive of a claim, at least one arising outside of the substantive law of bankruptcy, that would be more intrinsic to estate administration.

We hold, therefore, that the bankruptcy court has core jurisdiction, pursuant to § 157(b)(2)(A), over contract claims under state law when the contract was entered into post–petition. The adjudication of such claims is an essential part of administering the estate. We read Marathon to apply to claims arising *pre–petition,* and decline to apply that ruling to claims involving contracts entered into post–petition. Similarly, we distinguish those lower court cases cited by appellees that, relying on *Marathon,* hold pre–petition claims to be non–core. *E.g., In re Pied Piper Casuals, Inc.,* 65 B.R. 780 (S.D.N.Y. 1986); *In re Blue Point Carpet, Inc.,* 86 B.R. 327 (Bankr. E.D.N.Y. 1988); *Acolyte Electric Corp. v. City of New York,* 69 B.R. 155 (Bankr. E.D.N.Y. 1986), aff'd, No. 86–0329 (E.D.N.Y. 1987).

We are aware that language from opinions of two other circuits may be read to disagree with our holding. In one, *In re Castlerock Properties,* 781 F.2d 159 [15 C.B.C.2d 20] (9th Cir. 1986), the contract apparently existed pre–petition. It is therefore unlikely that its holding that the proceeding in question was non–core conflicts with our holding on the instant appeal. In any event, we decline to follow the sweeping statement in Castlerock that "state law contract claims that do not specifically fall within the categories of core proceedings enumerated in 28 U.S.C. § 157(b)(2)(B)–(N) are related proceedings under 157(c) even if they arguably fit within the literal wording of the two catch–all provisions, sections § [sic]157(b)(2)(A) and (O)."

Id. at 162. Such a reading of the statute in our view would render the general provisions null.

The Fifth Circuit stated in *In re Wood, Supra,* 825 F.2d at 97, that "a proceeding is core under section 157 if it invokes a substantive right provided by title 11 or if it is a proceeding that, by its nature, could arise only in the context of a bankruptcy case." The court held that a claim under state law arising from a post–petition dispute did not fit either category. The instant appeal does not fit in the first category. We hold that the timing of a dispute may render it uniquely a bankruptcy case. To the extent that *Wood* conflicts with our holding, we decline to follow it.

III.

Having held that the bankruptcy court has jurisdiction over the adversary proceeding as a core matter, we turn to the question whether appellees are entitled to a jury trial on the factual issues raised, *i.e.,* whether Cooper misrepresented the nature of the facility in its insurance application and whether it exaggerated its loss from the fire.

A.

In its decision, the district court stated that "[t]he defendants are entitled to a jury trial with respect to at least some of the debtor's claims and their affirmative defenses." That ruling made no reference to *Granfinanciera, S.A. v. Nordberg,* 109 S.Ct. 2782 [20 C.B.C.2d 1216] (1989), decided only two weeks earlier. Since that case weighs heavily on the instant appeal, we address it in depth.

In *Granfinanciera,* the respondent, a Chapter 11 trustee, sued the petitioners in the bankruptcy court to recover fraudulent transfers allegedly made by the bankrupt corporation. Section 157(b)(2)(H) explicitly provides that actions to recover fraudulent conveyances are core proceedings. The bankruptcy court therefore held that it could hear the action without a jury, despite the petitioners' demand for a jury trial. The district court and the court of appeals both affirmed. The Supreme Court, however, in a somewhat opaque opinion, reversed.

One aspect of the Supreme Court opinion is clear–that is, when a party makes a jury demand for a claim that is inherently legal, "Congress cannot eliminate [that] party's Seventh Amendment right to a jury trial merely by relabeling the cause of action to which it attaches and placing exclusive jurisdiction in an administative agency or a specialized court of equity." *Id.* at 2800. In other words, we are required to analyze the underlying nature of the claim without regard to Congress' designation of that claim as core.

The aspect of *Granfinanciera* that we find difficult to decipher is its expression of the Court's view whether the bankruptcy court can hold jury trials in proceedings that are both legal and, at the same time, core pursuant to § 157(b). To be sure, the

Court explicitly left that question open. *Id.* at 2802. But in its discussion of the questions it did address, there are several passages that can be construed as affecting the determination of that question.

One such passage is the discussion of the "public rights–private rights" dichotomy. To review, Marathon appeared to hold that Article I courts could adjudicate claims at the core of bankruptcy because such claims were public rights, and central to Congress' constitutional bankruptcy power. *Marathon, supra,* 458 U.S. at 71; *see also in re Kaiser,* 722 F.2d 1574, 1580 & n.2 [9 C.B.C.2d 910] (2 Cir. 1983). We say "appeared" only because *Granfinanciera* equivocated on that statement. 109 S.Ct. at 2797–98 & n.11. *Granfinanciera,* in turn, premised its holding that a fraudulent conveyance action carries a Seventh Amendment right to a jury trial, at least in part, on its conclusion that such action is a private right. *Id* at 2795–98. If, therefore, the Supreme Court held that all adversary proceedings sounding in law are private rights of action, a determination that the instant action is legal would compel us to hold that the proceeding is not core.

Fortunately, we need not read *Granfinanciera*so broadly. That opinion also contains several passages indicating the Court's contemplation that its holding may result in jury trials in the bankruptcy court. For example, the Court stated that

> "one cannot easily say that 'the jury would be incompatible' with bankruptcy proceedings, in view of Congress' express provision for jury trials in certain actions arising out of bankruptcy litigation. And Justice White's claim that juries may serve usefully as checks only on the decisions of judges who enjoy life tenure overlooks the extent to which judges who are appointed for fixed terms may be beholden to Congress or executive officials, and thus ignores the potential for juries to exercise beneficial restraint on their decisions."

Id. at 2801 (citations omitted). As this passage indicates, Justice White's dissenting opinion understood the majority as leaving the door open for jury trials in bankruptcy and criticized the majority for doing so. *Id.* at 2810–12 (White, J., dissenting).

In view of the foregoing, we find that *Granfinanciera* does not foreclose the possibility of jury trials in the bankruptcy court. We therefore will analyze the question anew; addressing first whether the claims on the instant appeal are inherently legal, and second whether any statutory or constitutional provision bars the bankruptcy court from conducting jury trials.

B.

In any action commenced in a federal court, "the right to a jury trial . . . is to be determined as a matter of federal law." *Simler v. Conner,* 372 U.S. 221, 222 (1963) (per curiam). Before we analyze the federal law applicable to the issues raised on the instant appeal, we will review briefly the relevant facts. The parties do not dispute that, due to the fire, ICSP's alleged obligation under the policy has matured. ICSP believes that Cooper defrauded it, and accordingly has sued in the state court to have the policy rescinded and to have its obligations declared void. Cooper then sued in the bankruptcy court for a declaration that the policy was still valid and that ICSP is liable for the damages Cooper claims. Alternatively, Cooper claims that if the policy is declared void, the fault lies with KM and K & C, rendering them liable for Cooper's losses.

We reject Cooper's contention that, merely because ICSP arguably is seeking rescission, the nature of the action is equitable. We agree with Professor Moore, who states that when

> "the insurer's liability under the policy has matured, the basic issues are legal. This is true whether the insurer sues to cancel the policy and the beneficiary counterclaims for recovery on the policy, or the beneficiary sues for recovery on the policy and the insurer defends and/or counterclaims for cancellation on the ground of fraud."

5 Moore's Federal Practice ¶ 38.23, at 38–200–01 (2d ed. 1988) (footnotes omitted); *See American Life Ins. Co. v. Stewart,* 300 U.S. 203, 212 (1937); *Woods v. National Life and Accident Ins. Co.,* 347 F.2d 760, 767 (3d Cir. 1965); *Ettelson v. Metropolitan Life Ins. Co.,* 137 F.2d 62, 65 (3d Cir.), cert. denied, 320 U.S. 777 (1943).

That the claim may be construed as a request for a declaratory judgment does not change matters. It is settled law that in a declaratory action, "the nature of the underlying dispute determines whether a jury trial is available." *In re Petition of Rosenman & Colin,* 850 F.2d 57, 60 (2 Cir. 1988).

The argument of KM and K & C in favor of a jury trial is even more compelling. Cooper seeks damages from them for alleged negligence and malpractice. It is difficult to imagine a claim that is more inherently legal. Cooper makes little attempt to assert the contrary. The conclusion that "in an ordinary tort action . . . the right of trial by jury is guaranteed by the Constitution," *United States v. Fotopulos,* 180 F.2d 631, 634 (9 Cir. 1950), is so obvious that it hardly needs belaboring.

C.

Since appellees have a right to a jury trial in this core proceeding, this brings us to the issue whether the bankruptcy court has statutory and constitutional authority to conduct such trials.

The relevant statutory provision, 28 U.S.C. § 1411 (1988), offers almost no guidance. The part of the statute applicable to voluntary petitions provides only that "this chapter and title 11 do not affect any right to trial by jury that an individual has under applicable non–bankruptcy law with regard to a personal injury or wrongful death tort claim." *Id.* at § 1411(a). This provision does not even make clear whether jury trials are afforded for other actions, let alone the proper forum for those trials. Of course, *Granfinanciera* has clarified the former issue, holding that jury trials are to be afforded for all legal actions.

Despite the lack of a specific statutory provision, we nevertheless hold that the bankruptcy courts may conduct jury trials in core proceedings. This is the position taken by the majority of courts which have considered the issue. Gibson, *Jury Trials in Bankruptcy: Obeying the Commands of Article III and The Seventh Amendment,* 72 Minn. L. Rev. 967, 1027–34 (1988) (citing cases). The cases in support of this view are too numerous to cite; we mention only a few of the more comprehensive ones. *Daily v. First Peoples Bank of N.J.,* 76 B.R. 963 (D.N.J. 1987); *In re*

McCormick, 67 B.R. 838 (D. Nev. 1986); *In re Kroh,* 1989 WL 153045 (Bankr. W.D. Mo., Dec. 18, 1989); *In re Data Compass Corp.,* 92 B.R. 575 (Bankr. E.D.N.Y. 1988).

Our holding rests on two separate but related provisions. The first provision is 28 U.S.C. § 151 (1988), which states that "[e]ach bankruptcy judge, as a judicial officer of the district court, may exercise the authority conferred under this chapter with respect to any action, suit or proceeding." The second provision is § 157(b), which, as stated previously, gives bankruptcy judges the authority to conduct trials and issue final orders in core proceedings. *Granfinanciera* teaches that such proceedings, if legal in nature, are subject to the Seventh Amendment, but that opinion does not alter Congress' intent that they be heard by a bankruptcy court with authority to issue final orders. Construing the Bankruptcy Code to allow jury trials in the bankruptcy court is the only way to reconcile these various concerns.

At present, there is no specific procedure in the Bankruptcy Rules providing for jury trials. For several years Rule 9015 prescribed a procedure for trials, but that rule was withdrawn in 1987 because bankruptcy courts were relying on it for substantive support for their right to conduct the trials. The Committee noted that " '[i]n the event the courts of appeals or the Supreme Court define a right to jury trial in any bankruptcy mattes [sic], a local rule in substantially the form of Rule 9015 can be adopted pending amendment of these rules.' " Gibson, *supra,* 72 Minn. L. Rev. at 1030 n.296 (quoting Committee Note to Abrogation of Bankr. R. 9015). In the interim, many courts have relied on local rules or Rule 38, the analogous Federal Rule of Civil Procedure. *E.g., In re Kroh, supra; In re 222 Liberty Assocs.,* [20 C.B.C.2d 1608] 99 B.R. 639, 643 (Bankr. E.D. Pa. 1989); *In re W.G.M.C., Inc.,* [20 C.B.C.2d 889] 96 B.R. 5, 6 (Bankr. D. Me. 1989); *In re Jackson,* [19 C.B.C.2d 619] 90 B.R. 126, 133 (Bankr. E.D. Pa. 1988).

D.

The first possible constitutional hurdle to jury trials in the bankruptcy court is the Seventh Amendment, specifically the requirement that "no fact tried by a jury, shall be otherwise reexamined in any Court of the United States, than according to the rules of the common law." U.S. Const. amend. VII. No reviewing court therefore may "redetermine facts found by the jury." *Atlantic & Gulf Stevedores, Inc. v. Ellerman Lines, Ltd.,* 369 U.S. 355, 359 (1962). Thus, the Seventh Amendment may well render unconstitutional jury trials in non–consensual non–core proceedings, because of the requirement that findings of fact by the bankruptcy court be reviewed de novo by the district court. 28 U.S.C. § 157(c)(1). District court review of final orders in Core proceedings, however, is limited to the analogous review that courts of appeals have over district courts. 28 U.S.C. § 158 (1988); *In re Daniels–Head & Assocs.,* 819 F.2d 914, 918–19 (9 Cir. 1987). Since the jury verdict in a core proceeding is subject only to the traditional standards of appellate review, such proceeding does not violate the Seventh Amendment.

E.

Finally, we reach the question whether jury trials in the bankruptcy court violate Article III of the Constitution. The essential predicate question, even more fundamental, is whether the statutory authority of bankruptcy judges to enter final judgments in core proceedings runs afoul of Article III. The parties did not raise this issue on appeal, limiting themselves to the question of the interpretation of § 157(b). The conclusion that core jurisdiction is constitutional, however, is implicit in our analysis in Section II of this opinion. That is particularly true in light of our holding that *Marathon,* a case decided under Article III, is to be distinguished from the instant appeal. We therefore assume for the sake of this appeal that § 157(b) passes muster under Article III. *Cf. Arnold Print Works, supra,* 815 F.2d at 169 (holding explicitly that Article III "permits a non–Article III bankruptcy court to adjudicate post–petition claims related to administration or liquidation of a debtor's estate because the claims are both historically and factually distinguishable from those at issue in *Marathon*").

If bankruptcy courts have the power to enter final judgments without violating Article III, it follows that jury verdicts in the bankruptcy courts do not violate Article III. The primary purpose of this Article is to ensure a federal judiciary free from pressure from the other branches of government. *E.g., Commodity Futures Trading Comm'n v. Schor,* 478 U.S. 833, 848 (1986); *United States v. Will,* 449 U.S. 200, 218 (1980). If anything, jurors are less likely to feel pressure from the executive and legislative branches than are bankruptcy judges, who depend on the other branches for reappointment to office. *Granfinanciera, supra,* 109 S.Ct. at 2801. Additionally, the practice of jury trials in Article I courts has been upheld when the authority of the Article I judges does not otherwise run afoul of Article III. *Pernell V. Southall Realty,* 416 U.S. 363 (1974) (local District of Columbia judges); *Collins v. Foreman,* 729 F.2d 108 (2 Cir.) (federal magistrates), *cert. Denied,* 469 U.S. 870 (1984). We hold, therefore, that jury trials in core proceedings in the bankruptcy court do not violate Article III.

IV.

To summarize:

We hold that the adversary proceeding between Cooper and appellees is core within the meaning of § 157(b), and that the proceeding is properly before the bankruptcy court. We further hold that the issues underlying the proceeding are legal, entitling appellees to a jury trial, as they have demanded. Finally, finding no statutory or constitutional bar, we hold that the jury trial should be in the bankruptcy court.

Reversed and remanded.

NOTES AND QUESTIONS

The only statutory reference to a right to jury trial in a bankruptcy case is in 28 U.S.C. § 1411(a) and (b) but neither subsection applies in the preceding cases. In the pre–1984 law, the bankruptcy judge was authorized to conduct jury trials. This was part of the 1978 Reform Act that the Supreme Court struck down in *Northern Pipeline*. Accordingly, it is difficult to conclude, as a matter of proper statutory interpretation, that Congress continued such authority in the 1984 amendments. All of the other circuits that ruled on the issue have disagreed with the Second Circuit's decision in *Ben Cooper*. There is neither statutory authority nor is the issue free of constitutional doubt for a non–Article III judge to conduct a jury trial mandated by the Seventh Amendment. *In 1994, subsection (e) was added to 28 U.S.C. § 157 to permit the bankruptcy judge to conduct the jury trial. But this grant is conditioned on (1) the bankruptcy judge being specially designated with authority to do so by the district court, and (2) the express consent of the parties to the litigation.*

1. Why does § 157(e) require express consent of the parties?

2. By requiring express consent, has the mischief caused by upholding the right to jury trial been continued? What is the mischief?

3. Of what effect is the addition of § 157(e) on the issues of the existence of the right to jury trial and waiver?

4. Since filing a proof of claim by the defendant constitutes a waiver of the right to jury trial under Langencamp, what other activity would also constitute a waiver?

5. If the parties do not consent to jury trial before the bankruptcy judge in a non–core proceeding, and one of them has rightfully demanded trial by jury, must the district court withdraw the proceeding under 28 U.S.C. § 157(d), first sentence, and conduct the trial? Incidentally, what is the meaning or application of the second sentence?

[B] Appeals

DUBIN v. SECURITIES AND EXCHANGE COMMISION
(In re Johns–Manville Corp.)

United States Court of Appeals, Second Circuit
824 F.2d 176 (1987)

JON O. NEWMAN, Circuit Judge:

This appeal presents the question whether an order denying a request for a shareholder committee in a bankruptcy proceeding is appealable to the court of appeals or only reviewable upon appeal from a confirmation of a reorganization plan. Just before the submission of a plan of reorganization in the Johns–Manville bankruptcy proceeding, a joint shareholder committee representing common and preferred shareholders was disbanded by the Bankruptcy Court because of a divergence of interests between the classes of shareholders. Chief Bankruptcy Judge Burton R. Lifland denied the motion of a group representing approximately 300 common shareholders ("Wright Group") to appoint a committee for common shareholders. The Wright Group appealed this ruling to the District Court for the Southern District of New York (Shirley Wohl Kram, Judge), which affirmed the order of the Bankruptcy Court. 68 B.R. 155. On appeal to the Second Circuit, Johns–Manville Corporation, the debtor in bankruptcy, moved to dismiss on the ground that the denial of the request to form a shareholder committee was not a "final" order as required by 28 U.S.C. § 158(d) (Supp. III 1985). Because orders denying requests for shareholder committees do not satisfy the finality requirement of 28 U.S.C. § 158(d) and because the present order does not meet the requirements of the collateral order doctrine, *see Cohen v. Beneficial Industrial Loan Corp.*, 337 U.S. 541, 546, 69 S. Ct. 1221, 1225, 93 L. Ed. 1528 (1949), we dismiss the appeal.

Background

This appeal concerns the bankruptcy proceeding for Johns–Manville Corporation. The circumstances of this enormous Chapter 11 bankruptcy proceeding are discussed in *In re Johns–Manville Corp.*, 36 B.R. 727 (Bankr. S.D.N.Y) *appeal denied,* 39 B.R. 234 (S.D.N.Y. 1984). At the outset of the reorganization proceeding in 1982, certain preferred and common shareholders, joined by the Securities and Exchange Commission (SEC), moved for the appointment of separate official committees to represent common and preferred shareholders. Under the Bankruptcy Reform Act of 1978, Pub. L. No. 95–598, 92 Stat. 2626, *as amended by* Pub. L. No. 99–554, 100 Stat. 3101 (1986), unsecured creditors are the only group entitled to appointment of an official committee in all reorganizations. 11 U.S.C.A. § 1102(a) (West Supp. 1987). With respect to other interested parties, the Act provides that the bankruptcy court "may order the appointment of additional committees of creditors or of equity security holders if necessary to assure adequate representation of creditors or of equity security holders." 11 U.S.C. § 1102(a)(2). Acting pursuant to this authority, the Bankruptcy Court on November 5, 1982, denied the applications for separate common and preferred shareholder committees and directed the appointment of a single committee to represent all shareholders. This order was upheld by the District Court. *In re Johns–Manville Corp.*, 38 B.R. 331, 332 (S.D.N.Y. 1983). The Equity Committee was formed shortly after the Bankruptcy Court issued its November 5 order.

Negotiations among the several official committees progressed slowly through mid–1985. In August 1985, a proposal by the legal representative for future victims—which called for the establishment of a trust for asbestos health victims to be funded substantially by common stock of the reorganized corporation—was favorably received by all of the represented interests except the common shareholders. On April 21, 1986, Johns–Manville announced a proposed plan of reorganization that had been agreed to by the asbestos health claimants, the asbestos property damage claimants, the unsecured creditors, and the preferred shareholders. At that point, the official shareholder committee became deadlocked by the divergence of the interests of common and preferred stockholders; consequently, the committee requested that it be disbanded and that separate official committees be appointed to represent preferred and common shareholders respectively. On July 31, 1986, Chief Judge Lifland disbanded the shareholder committee and deferred consideration of new appointments pending application by appropriate parties. The Wright

Group, approximately 300 shareholders who collectively own approximately 10% of the outstanding Johns–Manville common stock, and one other common shareholder moved for the appointment of an official committee to represent common shareholders. On October 9, 1986, Chief Judge Lifland denied both motions. The Wright Group appealed to the District Court. Judge Kram affirmed denial of the Wright Group's motion on November 20, 1986. 68 B.R. 155. The Wright Group, joined by the SEC as a statutory party, 11 U.S.C. § 1109(a)(1982); *see Manville Corp. v. Equity Security Holders Committee,* 801 F.2d 60, 61 n.2 (2d Cir. 1986), has appealed this determination.

It bears mentioning that the bankruptcy proceeding has not been stayed during the pendency of this appeal. On December 16, 1986, the Bankruptcy Court held a confirmation hearing. The proposed plan of reorganization was confirmed on December 22, 1986, and is presently on appeal to the District Court.

Discussion

Johns–Manville has moved to dismiss the appeal for lack of finality. Our jurisdiction to hear this appeal is governed by 28 U.S.C. § 158(d). "While subsection (a) of [section 158] permits [district courts to] hear appeals from interlocutory orders of bankruptcy courts, subsection (d) permits no such discretionary review by the courts of appeals." *In re Stable Mews Associates,* 778 F.2d 121, 122 (2d Cir. 1985). Rather, the courts of appeals' jurisdiction "is more narrowly limited to 'appeals from all final decisions, judgments, orders, and decrees' of the bankruptcy court." *Id.* (quoting 28 U.S.C. § 158(d)).

By the standards of finality applied in the typical civil case, *see generally* 9 Moore's Federal Practice ¶¶ 110.06–08 (1987), the order appealed from clearly is not final. Denial of a request to appoint an official common shareholder committee does not fully and finally resolve the case, even with regard to the common shareholders. Shareholders are statutorily authorized to participate in the bankruptcy proceeding and to challenge the reorganization plan at the confirmation stage. 11 U.S.C. § 1109(b). The Bankruptcy Court's ruling only denies them the advantages of official committee status, see 11 U.S.C.A. § 330(a) (West Supp. 1987); 11 U.S.C. § 1103 (1982 & Supp. III 1985).

It is important to recognize, however, that the finality requirement is less rigidly applied in bankruptcy than in ordinary civil litigation. *See In re Saco Local Development Corp.,* 711 F.2d 441, 444–46 (1st Cir. 1983); 16 Wright, Miller & Cooper, Federal Practice and Procedure § 3926 at 69–73 (Supp. 1986). In *In re Saco,* Judge Breyer points out that "Congress has long provided that orders in bankruptcy cases may be immediately appealed if they finally dispose of *discrete disputes within the larger case,*" *id.* at 444 (emphasis in original), and that "a 'final judgment, order, or decree' under 28 U.S.C. § 1293(b) includes an order that conclusively determines a separable dispute over a creditor's claim or priority." *Id.* at 445–46.[1]

---

[1] Title I of the Bankruptcy Reform Act of 1984, Pub. L. No. 98–353, 98 Stat. 333, 341, 343, promulgated 28 U.S.C. § 158 and repealed 28 U.S.C. § 1293. Although the language of 28 U.S.C. § 158(d) and 28 U.S.C. § 1293(b) differs slightly, the analysis of the availability of appellate review in *In re Saco Local Development Corp., supra,* is applicable to the

Nonetheless, we do not believe that a bankruptcy court's denial of a request to appoint an official committee for shareholders is final even under the more flexible standard of finality applied in bankruptcy cases. The greater flexibility in allowing bankruptcy appeals reflects two special attributes of bankruptcy proceedings—their ongoing nature, frequently over long time periods, and the fact that discrete claims are often resolved at various points during these lengthy proceedings. *See In re Saco Local Development Corp., supra,* 711 F.2d at 445 (noting that the legislative history of the Bankruptcy Act of 1978 indicates that Congress intended "the relevant 'judicial unit' to remain the traditional 'proceeding' *within* the overall bankruptcy case, not the overall case itself" (emphasis in original)). To require that appeals of dispositions of discrete claims be forestalled until the completion of the entire bankruptcy proceeding would seriously delay adjudication of individual claims without significantly advancing final resolution of the larger proceeding. Thus, Judge Meskill's comment in *In re Stable Mews Associates, supra,* 778 F.2d at 122, that there need only be "a final decision on the discrete issue at bar" is properly understood as limiting appellate review in bankruptcy cases to issues resolving particular disputes. Orders denying shareholder requests for official committee status do not resolve particular disputes within the overall bankruptcy case; they simply affect the committee structure within which various disputes in the reorganization proceeding will be considered. We conclude that such orders are not appealable to the courts of appeals. Such orders remain reviewable upon appeal from any final order resolving a dispute concerning the group denied appointment of a committee. In this proceeding, such a final order would normally be the order confirming a plan of reorganization.

The Wright Group and the SEC contend that this case is similar to *In re Amatex Corp.,* 755 F.2d 1034 (3d Cir. 1985), in which the Third Circuit held that an order denying a request to appoint a legal representative for future asbestos claimants was appealable. The Court based its decision on the fact that the bankruptcy court's order excluded future asbestos claimants from any participation in the bankruptcy proceeding. *Id.* at 1040. By contrast, an order denying a request by shareholders for appointment of an official committee does not exclude shareholders from participation in the proceeding; it merely denies them the advantages of official committee status. We do not believe that this is tantamount to exclusion from participation in the proceeding.

There exist adequate avenues of immediate appellate review for denial of motions to appoint shareholder committees without automatic, immediate access to the courts of appeals during the pendency of a bankruptcy proceeding. Under 28 U.S.C. § 158(a), district courts are authorized to review interlocutory orders of the bankruptcy courts. Moreover, district courts may certify for appeal to the courts of appeals any interlocutory order meeting the statutory criteria of 28 U.S.C. § 1292(b) (Supp. III 1985). *Cf. Coopers & Lybrand v. Livesay,* 437 U.S. 463, 474–75, 98 S. Ct. 2454, 2460–61, 57 L. Ed. 2d 351 (1978).

availability of review under 28 U.S.C. § 158(d). *See In re Stable Mews Associates, supra,* 778 F.2d at 123; *In re American Colonial Broadcasting Corp.,* 758 F.2d 794, 799–800 (1st Cir. 1985).

As a backstop position, the Wright Group argues that the Bankruptcy Court's order is appealable under the collateral order doctrine, *see Cohen v. Beneficial Industrial Loan Corp.*, 337 U.S. 541, 69 S. Ct. 1221, 93 L. Ed. 1528 (1949). Under this doctrine, a court of appeals may review an interlocutory order that (1) conclusively determines a disputed question, (2) resolves an important issue completely separable from the merits of the action, and (3) is effectively unreviewable on appeal from a final judgment. *Id.* at 546, 69 S. Ct. at 1225; *Coopers & Lybrand v. Livesay, supra,* 437 U.S. at 468, 98 S. Ct. at 2457.

Even if we accept the Wright Group's contention that the first two requirements of the *Cohen* test are satisfied, it is clear that the Bankruptcy Court's denial of the Wright Group's request to appoint an official shareholder committee fails the third requirement. The Supreme Court has recently emphasized that *Cohen's* exception to the final judgment rule is confined to "trial court orders affecting rights that will be irretrievably lost in the absence of an immediate appeal." *Richardson–Merrell Inc. v. Koller,* 472 U.S. 424, 430–31, 105 S. Ct. 2757, 2761, 86 L. Ed. 2d 340 (1985) (holding that effective review of order disqualifying counsel is available on appeal after trial). The Wright Group will be able to challenge the denial of its request for official committee status separately from the validity of the confirmed plan at the conclusion of the bankruptcy proceeding. *Cf. id.* at 438, 105 S.Ct. at 2765. Of course, even if the Wright Group were to establish that the Bankruptcy Court erred in denying its request for an official common shareholder committee, the reviewing court could still find that such error was harmless. Fed. R. Civ. P. 61; *see In re Westgate–California Corp.,* 634 F.2d 459, 462 (9th Cir. 1980). However, this is not a sufficient basis for establishing that an interlocutory order is effectively unreviewable after completion of the case. *Cf. Richardson–Merrell Inc. v. Koller, supra,* 472 U.S. at 437–38, 105 S. Ct. at 2764–65.[2]

---

[2] In *Richardson–Merrell,* the Supreme Court repeated its analysis, set forth in *Flanagan v. United States,* 465 U.S. 259, 104 S. Ct. 1051, 79 L. Ed. 2d 288 (1984), concerning the unavailability of an interlocutory appeal of a disqualification order regardless of whether prejudice was required to obtain a reversal of the ultimate judgment. In *Flanagan* the Court noted that if prejudice is not required, the disqualification ruling is effectively reviewable on appeal from a final judgment. *Id.* at 268, 104 S. Ct. at 1056. On the other hand, if prejudice is required, then the disqualification ruling fails to satisfy the requirement that an appealable interlocutory ruling must be completely separate from the merits. *Id.* This analysis might be read to suggest that if prejudice is a requirement for reversal, a disqualification ruling *would* satisfy the test of being effectively unreviewable on appeal from a final judgment, but would fail only the test of separability from the merits. We think this reading is unwarranted. In *Flanagan* the Court made clear that it was not deciding whether a challenge to the final judgment would provide plainly ineffective review of a disqualification order. *Id.* The Court noted that the absence of a prejudice requirement would cause the disqualification ruling to fail the test of effective unreviewability, not that a prejudice requirement would necessarily demonstrate effective unreviewability. In any event, we see no basis to conclude that a ruling denying appointment of a shareholders' committee in a bankruptcy proceeding can be considered effectively unreviewable on appeal from a final judgment simply because reversal would require both a determination that the committee was erroneously denied and that the denial adversely affected the substantial rights of the shareholders.

Accordingly, notwithstanding the inferences drawn by the Court of Appeals, the legislative history is not only consistent with petitioner's interpretation of the statute, but also actually

Conclusion

Having determined that the Bankruptcy Court's denial of the Wright Group's motion for appointment of an official common shareholder committee is not a final order under 28 U.S.C. § 158(d) nor appealable under the collateral order doctrine, we dismiss the appeal.

NOTES AND QUESTIONS

1. How much time does an appellant have to file a notice of appeal from the bankruptcy court to the district court? From the district court to the court of appeals? *See* Bankruptcy Rule 8002; Fed. R. App. P. 4.

2. Can the parties stipulate to give the court of appeals jurisdiction over an appeal from an interlocutory order? *See Maiorino v. Branford Savings Bank,* 691 F.2d 89 (2d Cir. 1982); *In re Kutner,* 656 F.2d 1107 (5th Cir. 1981), *cert. denied,* 455 U.S. 945 (1982). If the parties mistakenly stipulate to give the court of appeals jurisdiction over an appeal and the appeal is dismissed on jurisdictional grounds, is the appellant thus deprived of an appellate forum? *See* Bankruptcy Rule 8001(d). Is there any way for the appellant's counsel to protect the client against such a possibility? *See* Levin, *Bankruptcy Appeals,* 58 N.C.L. Rev. 967 (1980).

3. In the *Johns–Manville Corp.* case, at what subsequent point in time would there be the possibility to appeal the order denying a request to appoint a shareholders' committee? Would that point in time permit any effective relief to the appellant? If the point in time is after entry of the order confirming the plan of reorganization, and the appeal is attached to the appeal from the order of confirmation, would the appellant have to post a bond to get a stay of consummation of the confirmation order? In the absence of a stay and after commencement of consummation, would the appeal become moot, requiring dismissal? If so, is there any effective appellate relief under the Second Circuit's interpretation of finality?

---

supports it. For this reason, and because I agree with the Court's textual analysis, I concur in its judgment.

CONNECTICUT NATIONAL BANK v. GERMAIN

Supreme Court of the United States
112 S.Ct. 1146, 26 C.B.C.2d 175 (1992)

Justice THOMAS delivered the opinion of the court:

In this case, we determine the appealability of an interlocutory order issued by a district court sitting as a court of appeals in bankruptcy.

I

In 1984, O'Sullivan's Fuel Oil Co. filed a bankruptcy petition in the United States Bankruptcy Court for the District of Connecticut. Although the case began as a reorganization under Chapter 11 of the Bankruptcy Code, in 1986 the Bankruptcy Court converted it into a liquidation under Chapter 7. Petitioner Connecticut National Bank (CNB) is successor in interest to one of O'Sullivan's creditors. Respondent Thomas M. Germain is trustee of O'Sullivan's estate.

On June 1, 1987, Germain sued CNB in Connecticut state court, seeking to hold the bank liable for various torts and breaches of contract. CNB removed the suit to the United States District Court for the District of Connecticut, which, pursuant to local rule, automatically referred the proceeding to the Bankruptcy Court overseeing the liquidation. Germain then filed a demand for a jury trial. CNB moved to strike Germain's demand. The Bankruptcy Court denied CNB's motion, *In re O'Sullivan's Fuel Oil Co.,* [21 C.B.C.2d 646] 103 B.R. 388 (Conn. 1989), and the District Court affirmed, *Germain v. Connecticut Nat. Bank,* [22 C.B.C.2d 1394] 112 B.R. 57 (Conn. 1990).

CNB then tried to appeal to the Court of Appeals for the Second Circuit, but the court dismissed for lack of jurisdiction. 926 F.2d 191 [24 C.B.C.2d 1236] (1991). The Second Circuit held that a court of appeals may exercise jurisdiction over interlocutory orders in bankruptcy only when a district court issues the order after having withdrawn a proceeding or case from a bankruptcy court, and not when the district court acts in its capacity as a bankruptcy court of appeals. We granted certiorari, 502 U.S.—(1991), and now reverse and remand.

II

Courts of appeals have jurisdiction over "interlocutory orders of the district courts of the United States" under 28 U.S.C. § 1292. CNB contends that § 1292(b) applies by its terms in this case, and that the Second Circuit therefore could have exercised discretionary jurisdiction over its appeal. Germain argues that § 1292 does not apply at all in this case because Congress limited § 1292 through 28 U.S.C. § 158(d), which deals with bankruptcy jurisdiction. CNB responds that nothing in § 158(d) limits § 1292. We agree with CNB.

Bankruptcy appeals are governed for the most part by 28 U.S.C. § 158. This section comprises four subsections, three of which concern us here. Subsection (a) gives the district courts authority to hear appeals from final and interlocutory orders of the bankruptcy courts. The District Court, as we have noted, had jurisdiction under this provision to hear CNB's appeal from the Bankruptcy Court. Subsection (b) permits the judicial council of any circuit to establish a bankruptcy appellate panel to fill the role of the district courts under subsection (a). Subsection (d), which is pivotal in this case, provides:

> "The courts of appeals shall have jurisdiction of appeals from all final decisions, judgments, orders, and decrees entered under subsections (a) and (b) of this section."

Neither this subsection nor any other part of § 158 mentions interlocutory orders entered by the district courts in bankruptcy. The parties agree, as they must, that § 158 did not confer jurisdiction on the Court of Appeals.

Germain contends that the Court of Appeals did not have jurisdiction under § 1292 either, for § 158(d), in his view, precludes jurisdiction under § 1292 by negative implication. Germain reasons as follows: Although 28 U.S.C. § § 1291 and 1292 appear to cover the universe of decisions issued by the district courts—with § 1291 conferring jurisdiction over appeals from final decisions of the district courts, and § 1292 conferring jurisdiction over certain interlocutory ones—that cannot in fact be so. If § 1291 did cover all final decisions by a district court, he argues, that section would render § 158(d) superfluous, since a final decision issued by a district court sitting as a bankruptcy appellate court is still a final decisions of a district court. If § 158(d) is to have effect, Germain contends, then that section must be exclusive within its own domain, which he defines as the universe of orders issued by district courts sitting pursuant to § 158(a) as courts of appeals in bankruptcy. When a district court enters an order in that capacity, Germain concludes, only § 158(d) can confer jurisdiction, and if it does not, nothing else can. Germain claims to find support for his view in his reading of the legislative history of § 158(d).

Contrary to Germain's contention, we need not choose between giving effect on the one hand to § 1291 and on the other to § 158(d), for the statutes do not pose an either–or proposition. Section 1291 confers jurisdiction over appeals from "final decisions of the district courts" acting in any capacity. Section 158(d), in contrast, confers jurisdiction over appeals from final decisions of the district courts when they act as bankruptcy appellate courts under § 158(a), and also confers jurisdiction over final decisions of the appellate panels in bankruptcy acting under § 158(b). Sections 1291 and 158(d) do overlap, therefore, but each section confers jurisdiction over cases that the other section does not reach.

Redundancies across statutes are not unusual events in drafting, and so long as there is no "positive repugnancy" between two laws, *Wood v. United States,* 16 Pet. 342, 363 (1842), a court must give effect to both. Because giving effect to both § § 1291 and 158(d) would not render one or the other wholly superfluous, we do not have to read § 158(d) as precluding courts of appeals, by negative implication, from exercising jurisdiction under § 1291 over district courts sitting in bankruptcy. We similarly do not have to read § 158(d) as precluding jurisdiction under § 1292. While courts should disfavor interpretations of statutes that render language superfluous, in this case that canon does not apply.

In any event, canons of construction are no more than rules of thumb that help courts determine the meaning of legislation, and in interpreting a statute a court should always turn first to one, cardinal canon before all others. We have stated time and again that courts must presume that a legislature says in a statute what it means and means in a statute what it says there. *See, e.g., United States v. Ron Pair Enterprises, Inc.,* 489 U.S. 235, 241–242 [20 C.B.C.2d 267] (1989); *United States v. Goldenberg,* 168 U.S. 95, 102–103 (1897); *Oneale v. Thornton, 6 Cranch 53,* 68 (1810). When the words of a statute are unambiguous, then, this first canon is also the last: "judicial inquiry is complete." *Rubin v. United States,* 449 U.S. 424, 430 (1981); *see also Ron Pair Enterprises, supra,* at 241.

Germain says that legislative history points to a different result. But we think that judicial inquiry into the applicability of § 1292 begins and ends with what § 1292 does say and with what § 158(d) does not. Section 1292 provides for review in the courts of appeals, in certain circumstances, of "[i]nterlocutory orders of the district courts of the United States." Section 158(d) is silent as to review of interlocutory orders. Nowhere does 1292 limit review to orders issued by district courts sitting as trial courts in bankruptcy rather than appellate courts, and nowhere else, whether in 158(d) or any other statute, has Congress indicated that the unadorned words of § 1292 are in some way limited by implication. "It would be dangerous in the extreme to infer . . . that a case for which the words of an instrument expressly provide, shall be exempted from its operation." *Sturges v. Crowninshield,* 4 Wheat. 122, 202 (1819); *see also Regents of Univ. Of Cal. v. Public Employment Relations Bd.,* 485 U.S. 589, 598 (1988). There is no reason to infer from either § 1292 or § 158(d) that Congress meant to limit appellate review of interlocutory orders in bankruptcy proceedings. So long as a party to a proceeding or case in bankruptcy meets the conditions imposed by § 1292, a court of appeals may rely on that statute as a basis for jurisdiction.

The judgment of the Court of Appeals for the Second Circuit is reversed and this case remanded for proceedings consistent with this opinion. It is so ordered.

Justice STEVENS, concurring in the Judgment:

Whenever there is some uncertainty about the meaning of a statute, it is prudent to examine its legislative history.[1]

Rejecting petitioner's position, the Court of Appeals concluded that in enacting the current system of bankruptcy appeals, Congress limited the scope of 28 U.S.C. § 1292(b), excluding review by the courts of appeals of certain interlocutory bankruptcy orders. If Congress had intended such a significant change in the scheme

---

[1] In this case, such an examination is appropriate because petitioner's interpretation of 28 U.S.C. § 158(d) creates an unusual overlap with 28 U.S.C. § 1291.
Section 1330(a) provides:

"The district courts shall have original jurisdiction without regard to amount in controversy of any nonjury civil action against a foreign state as defined in section 1603(a) of this title as to any claim for relief in personam with respect to which the foreign state is not entitled to immunity either under sections 1605–1607 of this title or under any applicable international agreement.'

of appellate jurisdiction, some indication of this purpose would almost certainly have found its way into the legislative history. The legislative record, however, contains no mention of an intent to limit the scope of § 1292(b). This silence tends to support the conclusion that no such change was intended.

Justice O'CONNOR, with whom Justice WHITE and Justice BLACKMUN join, concurring in the judgment:

I agree that when Congress enacted 28 U.S.C. § 158(d) as part of the Bankruptcy Amendments and Federal Judgeship Act of 1984, Congress probably did not intend to deprive the Courts of Appeals of their longstanding jurisdiction over interlocutory appeals in bankruptcy cases. But I think we should admit that this construction of the statutes does render § 158(d) largely superfluous, and that we do strive to interpret statutes so as to avoid redundancy. *Cf. Ante,* at 4–5. In this case, I think it far more likely that Congress inadvertently created a redundancy than that Congress intended to withdraw appellate jurisdiction over interlocutory bankruptcy appeals by the roundabout method of reconferring jurisdiction over appeals from final bankruptcy orders. I would reverse the judgment below only for this reason.

NOTES AND QUESTIONS

Since the Supreme Court did not find § 158(d) to be the exclusive jurisdictional grant to the courts of appeals in bankruptcy matters, the broader provisions in 28 U.S.C. § § 1291 and 1292 apply. It should be noted that distinguishing between final orders and interlocutory orders is more difficult in bankruptcy cases than in non–bankruptcy civil actions.

In 1994, § 158(b) was amended, seeemingly to require the judicial councils to establish bankruptcy appellate panels. It is not quite mandatory because several other options are available for the judicial council that prefers not to have a bankruptcy appellate panel. It is quite likely that the greater majority of circuits will not establish such panels. Is there any good reason not to do so?

Would it make sense to create a single appellate court composed of Article III judges to hear appeals from bankruptcy courts? This would eliminate appeals from one trial judge to another trial judge as now happens when the appeal goes to the district court, and it would alleviate the burdens on the courts of appeals. A single court could have an appropriate number of judges who, in effect, would "ride circuit." This system would also have the additional benefit of establishing a more uniform application of the bankruptcy law across the United States and make it more predictable.

CHAPTER 13

BANKRUPTCY COURT STAYS, ADEQUATE PROTECTION AND POSTPETITION FINANCING

§ 13.01 Introduction

Under prior law, bankruptcy courts routinely stayed the commencement or continuation of suits against the debtor, the enforcement of judgments against the debtor, and foreclosure proceedings on property of the debtor. The automatic stay contained in § 362(a) of the Bankruptcy Code is not only broad, but also becomes effective upon the mere filing of a petition commencing a case under any of the Code's operative chapters, that is, chapters 7, 9, 11, 12, and 13. Reinforced by the Rules of Bankruptcy Procedure, the Code also contains procedural safeguards for the secured creditor. *See* 11 U.S.C. § 362(d), (e); Bankruptcy Rule 4001.

Generally speaking, the automatic stay prevents the piecemeal depletion of the debtor's estate and enables the trustee to dispose of the debtor's property in an orderly manner. In reorganization cases under chapter 11, the § 362 stay permits the trustee to use the debtor's property, although it may be subject to a lien, and thus continue the debtor's business. In liquidation cases under chapter 7, however, the trustee's use of property subject to a lien–the collateral–will be much more limited. The reason is simple: liquidation of the debtor's assets is the statutory objective. *See* 11 U.S.C. § 704(1).

[A] The Automatic Stay: Scope and Duration

The automatic stay of § 362, as previously noted, becomes effective upon the filing of the petition. Moreover, in chapter 13 individual debt adjustment cases, § 1301 provides an additional limited stay of actions, effective "after the order for relief," "to collect all or any part of a consumer debt of the [chapter 13] debtor from any individual that is liable on such debt with the debtor, or that secured such debt." 11 U.S.C. § 1301(a). *See also* § 1201(a). Thus, in a marked change from prior law and the Code's other operative chapters, certain guarantors of a chapter 13 or chapter 12 debtor's obligations will get the benefit of a limited automatic stay.

What is the jurisdictional basis of the bankruptcy court's injunctive power? First, 28 U.S.C. § 1334(e) gives the district court "exclusive jurisdiction of all of the property, wherever located, of the debtor, as of the commencement of the case." Section 362 of the Code merely implements that jurisdiction. Section 105(a) of the Code, which further authorizes the court to "issue any order, process, or judgment that is necessary or appropriate to carry out the provisions of " the Code, supplements § 362. With this broad jurisdictional base, the court thus has the inherent power to protect property within its jurisdiction and prevent any impairment of that jurisdiction (*e.g.*, enforcement of a prepetition judgment against property of the estate).

The court's injunctive power is intended to insulate property belonging to the debtor. As noted in Chapter 14, *infra*, commencement of a case under title 11 creates an "estate" comprised of all legal or equitable interests of the debtor in property, wherever located. 11 U.S.C. § 541(a)(1). In addition, other interests, such as "[p]roceeds, products, offspring, rents, and profits of or from property of the estate," are included as part of the debtor's estate. 11 U.S.C. § 541(a)(6).

Section 362(a) is broad in scope. The filing of a petition for relief will automatically stay, among other things, commencement or continuation of a suit on a prepetition claim against the debtor; enforcement of a prepetition judgment against the debtor or its property; "any act" to obtain possession of the debtor's property; any act to create, perfect or enforce any lien against the debtor's property; and setoff of any prepetition debt owing to the debtor. Note, however, that the § 362 automatic stay is not applicable to postpetition claims arising out of the routine operation of the debtor's business by the trustee. *See* 28 U.S.C. § 959(a).

The automatic stay of § 362(a) applies "to all entities," including any "person, estate, trust, governmental unit." 11 U.S.C. § 101. This broad definition eliminates the need to define who is a "creditor," "secured creditor" or other person affected by the stay. Must a person seeking relief from the stay be a creditor? *See In re Comcoach Corp., infra,* 698 F.2d 571 (2d Cir. 1983).

The automatic stay will continue to protect the debtor's property until it is no longer part of the estate. The stay of all other acts, (*e.g.*, suits) will continue until the case is closed or dismissed, or, if the debtor is an individual, until the debtor is granted or denied a discharge. 11 U.S.C. § 362(c)(2).

[1] Exceptions to the Automatic Stay

Section 362(b) of the Code contains significant exceptions to the automatic stay. For example, (1) the commencement or continuation of criminal proceedings against the debtor; (2) the collection of alimony, maintenance or support from the debtor; and (3) the commencement or continuation by a governmental unit to enforce its police or regulatory powers (*e.g.*, environmental protection laws, consumer protection laws, safety violations) will not be stayed by the filing of the petition. Nevertheless, by relying on § 105(a), the court may still stay any of these acts on an appropriate factual showing.

[2] Obtaining Relief from the Automatic Stay

The Bankruptcy Code in § 362(d) merely refers to a "request" for relief from the stay, leaving the appropriate procedure to the Bankruptcy Rules. Bankruptcy Rule 4001(a) requires the request to "be made in accordance with Rule 9014." Rule 9014 provides that such relief must be "requested by motion," with "reasonable notice and opportunity for hearing." In other words, to get relief from a stay, the affected party must move in the bankruptcy court. After an appropriate hearing, if the court decides to grant relief, § 362(d) gives the court discretion to terminate, annul, modify or condition the stay.

Requests for relief from the automatic stay will ordinarily be made on notice to the trustee. Nevertheless, the court has the power to grant relief "to prevent irreparable damage to the interest of an entity in property, if such interest will suffer damage before there is an opportunity for notice and a hearing." 11 U.S.C. § 362(f). Despite the availability of such ex parte relief from the stay, the plaintiff should describe to the court all of the efforts made at giving notice to the trustee and state why notice should not be required as a precondition to relief from the stay. *See also* Bankruptcy Rule 4001(a)(3). As a practical matter, therefore, ex parte relief from the stay will be rare. *See, e.g., In re Sullivan Ford Sales,*1 C. B. C. 2d 397 (Bankr. D. Me. 1980).

Section 362(e) provides a meaningful procedural safeguard to secured creditors. The court must hold at least a preliminary hearing and disposition within 30 days after the secured creditor seeks relief from the stay. The automatic stay will be "terminated unless the court, after notice and a hearing, orders such stay continued in effect pending, or as a result of, a final hearing and determination." 11 U.S.C. § 362(e). This hearing may be a "preliminary hearing, or may be consolidated with the final hearing" to determine whether the stay should be terminated, annulled, modified, or conditioned.

The court may continue the stay after a preliminary hearing if it finds that "there is a reasonable likelihood that the party opposing relief from the stay will prevail at the final hearing." Any such "final hearing" must then be "concluded within thirty days after [the] preliminary hearing." 11 U.S.C. § 362(e)(1), (2). Although § 362(e) requires the final hearing to be "concluded" within 30 days from the preliminary hearing, it fails to set a deadline for the rendition of the court's decision.

What are the standards for obtaining relief from the automatic stay? Section 362(d) permits a modification of the stay upon a showing of "cause," or that the debtor has no equity in the property that is the subject of the motion and that the property is not necessary "to an effective reorganization." In a chapter 7 liquidation, therefore, the secured creditor need only show that there is no equity because, by definition, the property will not be necessary for "an effective reorganization." In reorganization cases, however, the mere absence of an equity, without more, will not be sufficient for a modification of the stay. The secured creditor in a reorganization case will have to show, in addition, that the property is not needed to reorganize the debtor.

Lack of "adequate protection" may constitute "cause" under § 362(d)(1) and this is the most common basis for seeking relief from the stay. The concept of "adequate protection" of an interest in property is referred to in § 361, but it is not defined. The statute, in § 361, provides alternative methods for giving such protection to secured creditors against a decrease in the value of their collateral: periodic or a single cash payment to compensate for any depreciation during the pendency of the stay; "an additional or replacement lien"; or any other relief that would give the secured creditor the "indubitable equivalent" of its property interest. The mere granting of a priority administrative claim under § 507(a)(1), however, will not be sufficient, for § 361(3) expressly provides that such a claim will not amount to "adequate protection." In sum, if the party seeking relief from the automatic stay can show that its property interest is not being adequately protected while the stay is in effect, the court may terminate or otherwise modify the stay, unless the trustee provides adequate protection.

What happens if the "adequate protection" ordered by the court later proves to be inadequate? See 11 U.S.C. § 507(b) ("superpriority" over all other expenses of administration, including fees for the trustee's attorney). Is this remedy sufficient protection for the inadequately secured creditor? What other instances are there in which "cause" for modification of the stay may exist?

Who has the burden of proving that the secured creditor is adequately protected? Section 362(g) places the burden of proof for all issues regarding the automatic stay, except the issue of whether the debtor has an equity in collateral, upon the trustee. Nevertheless, what is the precise nature of the secured creditor's burden? *See* 11 U.S.C. § 362(d)(1).

[B] Use of Collateral

The automatic stay provisions of § 362 must be read together with § 363, which authorizes the trustee to use the debtor's property, except for cash collateral ("cash, negotiable instruments, documents of title, securities, deposit accounts, or other cash equivalents"). 11 U.S.C. § 363(a). Unless the court imposes conditions, the debtor's noncash collateral may be used "in the ordinary course of business without notice or a hearing" if the debtor's business "is authorized to be operated." 11 U.S.C. § 363(c). The automatic stay of § 362(a) thus prevents extrajudicial interference from secured creditors while the trustee is using collateral. Unless the secured creditor objects, the trustee's ability to use noncash collateral in the ordinary course of the debtor's business will no longer be an issue. (The secured creditor has the burden of proof concerning the validity of its security interest; thus, the validity is a proper defense that may be raised by the trustee; *ibid.*)

What limitations are there on the trustee's use of "cash collateral"? Without the court's authorization to use cash collateral or the consent of the affected secured creditor, the trustee must "segregate and account for any cash collateral in [his] possession, custody or control." 11 U.S.C. § 363(c)(4).

Note the relationship among § § 361, 362 and 363 of the Code. Under § 363(e) an objecting party has the right to request protection "at any time," and, with or without a hearing, the court must "prohibit or condition [the trustee's] use as is necessary to provide adequate protection of " the secured creditor's interest. In any challenge asserting lack of adequate protection, the trustee "has the burden of proof on the issue of adequate protection." 11 U.S.C. § 363(e).

The secured creditor seeking "adequate protection" under § 363(e) will also probably seek relief from the § 362 automatic stay. Granting relief under § 362 is subject to specific time limitations, whereas determinations of "adequate protection" under § 363 are not. In any event, the trustee's use of the secured creditor's collateral under § 363 must be consistent with any relief granted under § 362. *See* 11 U.S.C. § 363(d).

REFERENCES

2 Collier on Bankruptcy, ¶ 362.01 et seq. (15th ed.).

Kennedy, *The Automatic Stay in Bankruptcy,* 11 U. Mich. J. L. Ref. 175–266 (1978).

§ 13.02 Scope and Duration of Automatic Stay

PITTS v. UNARCO INDUSTRIES, INC.

United States Court of Appeals, Seventh Circuit
698 F.2d 313 (1983)

PER CURIAM.

This matter comes before the Court on the filing of the following documents:

1. "Notice Of Stay And Motion For Suspension Of Pleadings" by counsel for defendant–appellee Armstrong World Industries, Inc., on August 20, 1982;

2. "Brief In Support Of Notice Of Stay And Motion For Suspension Of Pleadings" by counsel for defendant–appellee Armstrong World Industries, Inc., on August 20, 1982; and

3. "Reply Of Plaintiff–Appellant To Motion For Suspension Of Pleadings" by counsel for plaintiff–appellant on August 27, 1982.

4. "Supplemental Memorandum" of defendant–appellee GAF Corporation on January 12, 1983.

5. "Supplemental Memorandum" of plaintiff–appellant on January 17, 1983.

The underlying appeal involves several defendants who are manufacturers and distributors of asbestos products. On August 20, 1982, co–defendant Armstrong World Industries, Inc. (Armstrong), filed its "Notice Of Stay And Motion For Suspension Of Pleadings" seeking to stay the disposition of the appeal. Armstrong argues that because co–defendant Unarco Industries, Inc. (Unarco) filed its Petition for Reorganization under Chapter 11 of the Bankruptcy Reform Act of 1978, Section 362 of the Bankruptcy Code automatically suspends all further proceedings against all parties to this appeal. In her response to Armstrong's motion, plaintiff Pitts contends that Section 362 of the Bankruptcy Code stays the proceedings in this appeal only with respect to the bankruptcy debtor and not all co–defendants.

The clear language of Section 362(a)(1) extends the automatic stay provision only to the debtor filing bankruptcy proceedings and not to nonbankrupt co–defendants. This interpretation has been adopted by several reviewing courts. *In Re: Related Asbestos Cases,* 23 B.R. 523 (N.D. Cal.1982); *Clutter v. Johns–Manville et al.,* No. C1229 (N.D. Ohio August 2, 1982); *Royal Truck & Trailer v. Armadora Martina Salvadorean,* 10 B.R. 488 (N.D. Ill. 1981); *In re Dino Smith,* 14 B.R. 956 (Bkrtcy.

D.C. Conn. 1981); *In re Aboussie Brothers Construction Co.*, 8 B.R. 302, 3 C.B.C.2d 684 (E.D. Mo. 1981).

We are particularly guided by the well–reasoned decision in *Royal Truck & Trailer v. Armadora Martina Salvadorean,*10 B.R. 488 (N.D. Ill. 1981). In *Royal Truck,* the district court carefully examined the Congressional intent surrounding the new Bankruptcy Code and highlighted the distinction between Chapter 13 and Chapter 11 of the Code. Chapter 13 expressly provides for the stay of an action against a co–debtor but Chapter 11 does not. The district court concluded that such Congressional silence would seem to indicate that the automatic stay provisions of Section 362(a) operate in favor of the bankrupt debtor only. This conclusion is supported by the legislative history of Section 362.

Appellee Armstrong disagrees with our interpretation of the scope of Section 362, and cites *In re: White Motor Credit Corp.,*11 B.R. 294 (Bkrtcy. N.D. Ohio 1981), and *Federal Life Insurance Co. v. First Financial Group of Texas, Inc.,*3 B.R. 375 (S.D. Tex.1980), to support its motion for stay. These decisions, however, are not persuasive. In both *Federal Life* and *White Motor,* the respective bankruptcy courts failed to analyze the clear language of Section 362. This language unambiguously states that the stay operates only as "against the debtor." Additionally, neither decision contains an analysis of the Congressional intent underlying the phrase "against the debtor" as set forth in Section 362 and examined in *Royal Truck.*

The issue raised by this motion is a question of first impression on the federal appellate level. We find the district court's extensive analysis in *Royal Truck & Trailer, Inc. v. Armadora Maritima Salvadoreana,*10 B.R. 488 (N.D. Ill. 1981), persuasive. Because we agree with the *Royal Truck*court's conclusion that the automatic stay provisions of Section 362(a) operate only in favor of the bankrupt debtor, Appellee's "Notice Of Stay And Motion For Suspension Of Pleadings ", which we construe as a motion for stay, is Denied.

WEDGEWORTH v. FIBREBOARD CORP.

United States Court of Appeals, Fifth Circuit
706 F.2d 541 (1983)
recalled, vacated, modified in part, 9 C.B.C. 2d 725

POLITZ, Circuit Judge:

These consolidated appeals concern the effect of stays granted to Johns–Manville Corporation (Johns–Manville) and UNR Industries, Inc. (Unarco), pending disposition of their proceedings in bankruptcy, upon their co–defendants in suits alleging liability for asbestosis caused by defendants' products. We hold that: (1) the automatic stay of all litigation against Johns–Manville and Unarco does not mandate that claims against their co–defendants be likewise stayed, (2) the co–defendants are not entitled to a discretionary stay pending resolution of the bankruptcy claims, and (3) the district court in the *Wedgeworth*case improperly denied leave to amend to allow direct action against the liability insurers of Johns–Manville and Unarco.

Background Facts

The plaintiffs in these three actions, like the plaintiffs in thousands of similar suits filed across the nation, allege that the inhalation of asbestos fibers from defendants' products caused asbestosis, a pneumoconiosis or progressive lung disease. Defendants manufactured asbestos–related products and products containing asbestos fibers. A large number of these suits have been pending for years. Extensive discovery has been accomplished. Some suits have been concluded. A developing tactic has been to use in subsequent trials evidence developed in earlier litigation.

Against this ground swell of litigation, threatening to engulf all in its path, on July 29, 1982, Unarco filed an application for reorganization under Chapter 11 of the Bankruptcy Code in the bankruptcy court in the Northern District of Illinois. Less than a month later, on August 26, 1982, Johns–Manville petitioned for a Chapter 11 reorganization in bankruptcy court in the Southern District of New York. All legal proceedings, in whatever jurisdiction and forum, were automatically stayed against Unarco and Johns–Manville in accordance with 11 U.S.C. § 362(a).

In the cases before us the co–defendants asked that the pending litigation against them be stayed until the bankruptcy proceedings initiated by Johns–Manville and Unarco are concluded.

On September 14, 1982, the district court in *Fontenot v. Fibreboard Corp.*,Nos. 82–4386 and 82–9270 (W.D. La., Hunter, J.), denied the motion of the remaining 14 co–defendants for an indefinite stay.

On September 28, 1982, the district court in *Wedgeworth v. Fibreboard Corp.*, Nos. 82–3612 and 82–9295 (M.D. La., Polozola, J.), took the opposite tack, granting a stay of the entire litigation, including the claims against the co–defendants. The court also denied plaintiffs leave to amend to assert a direct cause of action against the liability insurers of Johns–Manville and Unarco.

On October 12, 1982, the district court in *Davis v. Johns–Manville Products*, No. 82–3687 (E.D. La., Arceneaux, J.), granted a stay as to all parties in nearly 200 claims, although Johns–Manville had been released as a party defendant eight months before.

Appeals were filed in the first two cases; the third comes before us by writ. The matters were ordered consolidated under our appellate and supervisory jurisdiction. Today we attempt to provide at least a measure of uniformity in an area where little exists. Indeed, one district judge characterized the nationwide situation as one of "unbelievable confusion."

Automatic Stay

Plaintiffs maintain that a stay of proceedings against the co–defendants is not mandated by 11 U.S.C. § 362(a), which merely provides for the automatic stay of any judicial "proceeding against the debtor," § 362(a)(1). Although judicial interpretation is checkered as to the extent of this statutorily required stay, resolution of the question presented requires a walk down a path as yet unblazed by this court. At trail's end we conclude that § 362 does not operate as an automatic stay of claims against the co–defendants of Johns–Manville and Unarco.

We begin our inquiry by examining the plain language of the statute. That language clearly focuses on the insolvent party. There are repeated references to the debtor. The stay envisioned is "applicable to all entities," § 362(a), but only in the sense that it stays all entities proceeding against the debtor. To read the "all entities" language as protecting co–debtors would be inconsistent with the specifically defined scope of the stay "against the debtor," § 362(a)(1). Continuing, we note that the remaining clauses of § 362(a) carefully list the kinds of proceedings stayed, in each instance explicitly or implicitly referring to "the debtor."

This literal interpretation of § 362(a) is bolstered by language which is notably absent from its provisions. By way of comparison, Chapter 13 specifically authorizes the stay of actions against co–debtors. 11 U.S.C. § 1301(a) ("a creditor may not commence or continue any civil action [against] any individual that is liable on such debt with the debtor "). No such shield is provided Chapter 11 co–debtors by § 362(a).

Further, the legislative history of § 362 supports this distinction between debtors and co–debtors. The automatic stay was intended to protect the debtor's assets and give it a "breathing spell." *See* S.Rep. No. 989, 95th Cong., 2d Sess., 54–55, reprinted in [1978] U.S.Code Cong. & Admin. News 5787, 5840–41. The provision concomitantly protects creditors by preventing a race for the debtor's assets. *See* H.R. Rep. No. 595, 95th Cong., 2d Sess., 340, reprinted in [1978] U.S. Code Cong. & Admin. News 5787, 6297. Neither purpose is advanced by application of the stay rule to co–defendants.

Finally, the bankruptcy court considering the Johns–Manville reorganization has refused to interpret its stay to include co–defendants, *In re Johns–Manville Corp.,*26 B.R. 405 (Bkrtcy. S.D.N.Y. 1983), as has the bankruptcy court considering Unarco's reorganization, *In re UNR Industries, Inc.,* 23 B.R. 144 (Bkrtcy. N.D. Ill.1982) (citing *Royal Truck & Trailer v. Armadora Maritima Salvadoreana,*10 B.R. 488 (D.C.N.D. Ill. 1981)). *See also Austin v. Unarco Industries, Inc.,* 705 F.2d 1 (1st Cir. 1983); *Pitts v. Unarco Industries, Inc.,* 698 F.2d 313 (7th Cir.1983);

CITIZENS BANK OF MARYLAND v. STRUMPF

Supreme Court of the United States
— U.S. — , Sup. Ct., C.B.C. 2d (1995)

Justice SCALIA delivered the opinion of the court.

We must decide whether the creditor of a debtor in bankruptcy may, in order to protect its setoff rights, temporarily withhold payment of a debt that it owes to the debtor in bankruptcy without violating the automatic stay imposed by 11 U.S.C. § 362(a).

I.

On January 25, 1991, when respondent filed for relief under Chapter 13 of the Bankruptcy Code, he had a checking account with petitioner, a bank conducting business in the State of Maryland. He also was in default on the remaining balance of a loan of $5,068.75 from the bank. Under 11 U.S.C. § 362(a), respondent's bankruptcy filing gave rise to an automatic stay of various types of activity by his creditors, including "the setoff of any debt owing to the debtor that arose before the commencement of the [bankruptcy case] against any claim against the debtor." 11 U.S.C. § 362(a)(7).

On October 2, 1991, petitioner placed what it termed an "administrative hold" on so much of respondent's account as it claimed was subject to setoff—that is, the bank refused to pay withdrawals from the account that would reduce the balance below the sum that it claimed was due on respondent's loan. Five days later, petitioner filed in the Bankruptcy Court, under § 362(d), a "Motion for Relief from Automatic Stay and for Setoff." Respondent then filed a motion to hold petitioner in contempt, claiming that petitioner's administrative hold violated the automatic stay established by § 362(a).

The Bankruptcy Court ruled on respondent's contempt motion first. It concluded that petitioner's "administrative hold" constituted a "setoff" in violation of § 362(a)(7) and sanctioned petitioner. Several weeks later, the Bankruptcy Court granted petitioner's motion for relief from the stay and authorized petitioner to set off respondent's remaining checking account balance against the unpaid loan. By that time, however, respondent had reduced the checking account balance to zero, so there was nothing to set off.

The District Court reversed the judgment that petitioner had violated the automatic stay, concluding that the administrative hold was not a violation of § 362(a). The Court of Appeals reversed. "[A]n administrative hold," it said, "is tantamount to the exercise of a right of setoff and thus violates the automatic stay of § 362(a)(7)." 37 F.3d 155, 158 [32 C.B.C.2d 1080] (CA4 1994). We granted certiorari. 514 U. S. — (1995).

II.

The right of setoff (also called "offset") allows entities that owe each other money to apply their mutual debts against each other, thereby avoiding "the absurdity of making A pay B when B owes A." *Studley v. Boylston Nat. Bank*, 229 U.S. 523, 528 (1913). Although no federal right of sctoff is created by the Bankruptcy Code, 11 U.S.C. § 553(a) provides that, with certain exceptions, whatever right of setoff otherwise exists is preserved in bankruptcy. Here it is undisputed that, prior to the bankruptcy filing, petitioner had the right under Maryland law to set off the defaulted loan against the balance in the checking account. It is also undisputed that under § 362(a) respondent's bankruptcy filing stayed any exercise of that right by petitioner. The principal question for decision is whether petitioner's refusal to pay its debt to respondent upon the latter's demand constituted an exercise of the setoff right and hence violated the stay.

In our view, petitioner's action was not a setoff within the meaning of § 362(a)(7). Petitioner refused to pay its debt, not permanently and absolutely, but only while it sought relief under § 362(d) from the automatic stay. Whether that temporary refusal was otherwise wrongful is a separate matter—we do not consider, for example, respondent's contention that the portion of the account subjected to the "administrative hold" exceeded the amount properly subject to setoff. All that concerns us here is whether the refusal *was a setoff.* We think it was not, because—as evidenced by petitioner's "Motion for Relief from Automatic Stay and for Setoff"—petitioner did not purport permanently to reduce respondent's account balance by the amount of the defaulted loan. A requirement of such an intent is implicit in the rule followed by a majority of jurisdictions addressing the question, that a setoff has not occurred until three steps have been taken: (i) a decision to effectuate a setoff, (ii) some action accomplishing the setoff, and (iii) a recording of the setoff. See, *e.g., Baker v. National City Bank of Cleveland,* 511 F.2d 1016, 1018 (CA6 1975) (Ohio law); *Normand Josef Enterprises, Inc. v. Connecticut Nat. Bank,* 230 Conn. 486, 504–505, 646 A.2d 1289, 1299 (1994). But even if state law were different, the question whether a setoff *under § 362(a)(7)* has occurred is a matter of federal law, and other provisions of the Bankruptcy Code would lead us to embrace the same requirement of an intent permanently to settle accounts.

Section 542(b) of the Code, which concerns turnover of property to the estate, requires a bankrupt's debtors to "pay" to the trustee (or on his order) any "debt that is property of the estate and that is matured, payable on demand, or payable on order . . . *except to the extent that such debt may be offset under section 553 of this title against a claim against the debtor.*" 11 U.S.C. § 542(b) (emphasis added). Section 553(a), in turn, sets forth a general rule, with certain exceptions, that any right of setoff that a creditor possessed prior to the debtor's filing for bankruptcy is not affected by the Bankruptcy Code. It would be an odd construction of § 362(a)(7) that required a creditor with a right of setoff to do immediately that which § 542(b) specifically excuses it from doing as a general matter: pay a claim to which a defense of setoff applies.

Nor is our assessment of these provisions changed by the fact that § 553(a), in generally providing that nothing in the Bankruptcy Code affects creditors' prebankruptcy setoff rights, qualifies this rule with the phrase "[e]xcept as otherwise provided in this section and in sections 362 and 363." This undoubtedly refers to § 362(a)(7), but we think it is most naturally read as merely recognizing that provision's restriction upon *when* an *actual setoff* may be effected—which is to say, not during the automatic stay. When this perfectly reasonable reading is available, it would be foolish to take the § 553(a) "except" clause as indicating that § 362(a)(7) requires immediate payment of a debt subject to setoff. That would render § 553(a)'s general rule that the Bankruptcy Code does not affect the right of setoff meaningless, for by forcing the creditor to pay *its* debt immediately, it would divest the creditor of the very thing that supports the right of setoff. Furthermore, it would, as we have stated, eviscerate § 542(b)'s exception to the duty to pay debts. It is an elementary rule of construction that "the act cannot be held to destroy itself." *Texas & Pacific R. Co. v. Abilene Cotton Oil Co.,* 204 U.S. 426, 446 (1907).

Finally, we are unpersuaded by respondent's additional contentions that the administrative hold violated § 362(a)(3) and § 362(a)(6). Under these sections, a bankruptcy filing automatically stays "any act to obtain possession of property of the estate or of property from the estate or to exercise control over property of the estate," 11 U.S.C. § 362(a)(3), and "any act to collect, assess, or recover a claim against the debtor that arose before the commencement of the case under this title," 11 U.S.C. § 362(a)(6). Respondent's reliance on these provisions rests on the false premise that petitioner's administrative hold took something from respondent, or exercised dominion over property that belonged to respondent. That view of things might be arguable if a bank account consisted of money belonging to the depositor and held by the bank. In fact, however, it consists of nothing more or less than a promise to pay, from the bank to the depositor, see *Bank of Marin v. England*, 385 U. S. 99, 101 (1966); *Keller v. Frederickstown Sav. Institution*, 193 Md. 292, 296, 66 A.2d 924, 925 (1949); and petitioner's temporary refusal to pay was neither a taking of possession of respondent's property nor an exercising of control over it, but merely a refusal to perform its promise. In any event, we will not give §§ 362(a)(3) or (6) an interpretation that would proscribe what § 542(b)'s "except[ion]" and § 553(a)'s general rule were plainly intended to permit: the temporary refusal of a creditor to pay a debt that is subject to setoff against a debt owed by the bankrupt.*

> * We decline to address respondent's contention, not raised below, that the confirmation of his Chapter 13 Plan under 11 U.S.C. § 1327 precluded petitioner's exercise of its setoff right. See *Granfinanciera, S.A. v. Nordberg*, 492 U.S. 33, 39 (1989).

The judgment of the Court of Appeals for the Fourth Circuit is reversed.

It is so ordered.

———————

DAVIS v. SHELDON
(In re Davis)

United States Court of Appeals, Third Circuit
691 F.2d 176 (1982)

ADAMS, Circuit Judge

This appeal presents the question whether a bankruptcy court erred in declining to enjoin pending state criminal prosecutions because of their possible impact on federal bankruptcy proceedings. Because of the traditional concerns of equity and comity implicated when a federal court considers a request to enjoin state criminal proceedings, we conclude that the district court properly upheld the denial of the injunction in this case.

I. Background

Chapter 7 of the Bankruptcy Code authorizes the liquidation of the assets of an insolvent debtor to pay creditors at least a portion of what they are owed. When a petition is filed in a Chapter 7 case, a trustee is appointed by the court; the debtor then submits to the trustee schedules listing his debts and assets; the trustee then distributes the property of the estate; and the debts are eventually discharged.

Marvin and Linda Davis, the appellants in this proceeding, purchased goods by check at various times from each of the four appellees. These checks were dishonored by the Davises' bank. Dana Lane, one of the appellees, instituted a criminal complaint against Mr. Davis on April 13, 1981, for issuing a bad check. The next day, the Davises filed a Chapter 7 petition in the bankruptcy court. Their initial schedule of unsecured creditors did not list the other three appellees. After the filing, these appellees instituted criminal bad check complaints against Mr. Davis.

Issuing bad checks is a Class A misdemeanor under Delaware law. 11 Del.C. § 900. The Delaware criminal code appears to require that a defendant convicted under § 900, in addition to other sanctions, must make restitution to the person or persons to whom bad checks were issued. 11 Del.C. § 4206(a). The criminal actions at issue here were originally brought in a justice of the peace court, but were transferred at the request of Marvin Davis to the Court of Common Pleas of Delaware, where cases are prosecuted by the Attorney General of the State of Delaware rather than by the complaining witnesses.

On June 24, 1981, the bankruptcy judge issued, at the request of the Davises, a temporary restraining order enjoining the State of Delaware and the individual claimants from proceeding with the criminal charges. None of the claimants exercised his right to object in the bankruptcy court to the discharge of his debt and the Davises were granted a discharge on July 28, 1981. On August 19, the bankruptcy judge held a hearing to determine whether the state court criminal proceedings should be permanently enjoined on the ground that, because of the restitution requirement upon conviction, such proceedings would subvert the bankruptcy court's grant of a discharge of those debts. The bankruptcy judge refused, on November 10, 1981, to issue the injunction, and the Davises appealed to the district court.

The district court, 18 B.R. 701, affirmed the decision of the bankruptcy court and the Davises filed the present appeal.

The bankruptcy court denied the request for an injunction for two reasons: First, a bankruptcy court "should rarely, if ever, issue a permanent injunction against the enforcement of the criminal law." *Davis v. Sheldon, (In re Davis),*15 B.R. 442 at 443 (Bkrtcy., D.Del. 1981). Second, "[t]he mere possibility that a creditor may recover all or part of a discharged debt after a debtor's conviction does not thwart the purposes of the bankruptcy laws." *Id.* at 443. On appeal, the district judge upheld the bankruptcy court, but based his decision on the Supreme Court's opinion in *Younger v. Harris,*401 U.S. 37, 91 S.Ct. 746, 27 L.Ed.2d 639 (1971). The judgment of the district court will be affirmed. Because of the importance of the issue that has been presented, we have set forth the reasons for our decision in some detail.

II. Considerations in Enjoining State Criminal Proceedings

Under most circumstances, a federal court has no power to enjoin state court proceedings. The Anti–Injunction Act, 28 U.S.C. § 2283, provides:

> A court of the United States may not grant an injunction to stay proceedings in a State court except as expressly authorized by Act of Congress, or where necessary in aid of its jurisdiction, or to protect or effectuate its judgments.

The Bankruptcy Code, however, is an "expressly authorized" exception to the statute.

11 U.S.C. § 105(a). See S. Rep.No. 95–989, 95th Cong., 2d Sess., reprinted in 1978 U.S. Code Cong. & Ad. News 5787, 5815. Prior to 1948, the Anti–Injunction Act contained only one exception, for "cases where such injunction may be authorized by any law relating to proceedings in bankruptcy." Judicial Code § 265, 36 Stat. 1162. In 1948, this passage was expanded to cover all statutory exceptions. *See* Reviser's Comments to 28 U.S.C. § 2283, 1948 U.S. Code Cong. & Ad. News Special Compilation of Legislative History of Revision of Title 28, 80th Cong., 2d Sess. 1910. Therefore, under proper circumstances, a bankruptcy court may issue an injunction to prevent a state prosecution.

The Supreme Court has held that the type of statutory exception set forth in the Anti–Injunction Act does not put into "question or qualify in any way the principles of equity and comity that must restrain a federal court when asked to enjoin a state court proceeding." *Mitchum v. Foster,* 407 U.S. 225, 243, 92 S.Ct. 2151, 2162, 32 L.Ed.2d 705 (1972). *See also O'Shea v. Littleton,* 414 U.S. 488, 94 S.Ct. 669, 38 L.Ed.2d 674 (1974). These principles were discussed at length in the Court's opinion in *Younger v. Harris,* 401 U.S. 37, 91 S.Ct. 746, 27 L.Ed.2d 639 (1971), a case involving a non–statutory exception to the Act. The Davises have failed to prove that their request for an injunction is justified under either principle.

As the Supreme Court stated in *Younger,* it is a "basic doctrine of equity jurisprudence that courts of equity should not act, and particularly should not act to restrain a criminal prosecution, when the moving party has an adequate remedy at law and will not suffer irreparable injury if denied equitable relief." 401 U.S. at 43–44, 91 S.Ct. at 750. The Davises contend that the legal remedy is inadequate because, if Marvin Davis is convicted of issuing bad checks, the state court would impose a mandatory restitution penalty in contravention of the bankruptcy court's discharge order and the Bankruptcy Code policy of providing debtors with a fresh start. The imposition of such a penalty may indeed raise serious questions under the Supremacy Clause of the United States Constitution, although we do not reach that question today. The Davises, however, have put forth no evidence that Marvin Davis will be unable to raise the Supremacy Clause challenge in the state court. We decline to presume that the judges of Delaware will disregard the obligation imposed upon them by the federal Constitution. *Cf. Kugler v. Helfant,* 421 U.S. 117, 127, 95 S.Ct. 1524, 1532, 44 L.Ed.2d 15 (1975).

The Davises also appear to argue that they will suffer irreparable injury from the state proceedings. However, the "cost, anxiety, and inconvenience" of defending oneself in a good faith criminal prosecution does not constitute irreparable injury.

Younger v. Harris, 401 U.S. at 46, 91 S.Ct. at 751. *See also, Watson v. Buck,* 313 U.S. 387, 400, 61 S.Ct. 962, 966, 85 L.Ed. 1416 (1941); *Beal v. Missouri Pacific Railroad Corp.,* 312 U.S. 45, 49, 61 S.Ct. 418, 420, 85 L.Ed. 557 (1941); *Ex parte Young,* 209 U.S. 123, 28 S.Ct. 441, 52 L.Ed. 714 (1908). If a state prosecution is brought in bad faith or for purposes of harassment, the federal court can, under *Younger,* enjoin the criminal proceedings. 401 U.S. at 54, 91 S.Ct. at 755; *Kugler v. Helfant,* 421 U.S. at 124, 95 S.Ct. at 1530. The bankruptcy court found that "[t]he mandatory restitution aspect of 11 Del. C. § 4206(a) was the principal reason each individual creditor filed a criminal complaint." *Davis v. Sheldon (In re Davis), supra,* at 443. The Davises contend that inasmuch as the creditors were motivated by a desire to collect on a dischargeable debt, rather than by a sense of public duty, the criminal proceedings were brought in bad faith and thus are fatally tainted.

The Davises do not argue that the state lacks a legitimate interest in protecting its citizens against the issuance of bad checks, nor do they allege that the state Attorney General, who is prosecuting this case, is proceeding in bad faith. They assert that it was improper for the state to act upon these claims because there was no state interest being protected; only the financial interest of the creditors was furthered. The State, however, is prosecuting the criminal actions on behalf of all of the citizens of Delaware, to protect the integrity of commercial transactions within the state. The Davises have made no showing that the Attorney General had any reason to doubt the validity of the charges, that he failed to exercise independent judgment in continuing these prosecutions, or that the complaining witnesses had insufficient evidence to support their allegations. We cannot require a prosecutor to conduct a searching inquiry into the public spirit of the victim of a crime before proceeding with what appears to be an otherwise valid criminal prosecution. Under these circumstances the intentions of the complaining witnesses are not controlling in judging the good faith of a criminal prosecution. *See generally, Allee v. Medrano,*416 U.S. 802, 836–38, 94 S.Ct. 2191, 2210–11, 40 L.Ed.2d 566 (1974) (opinion of Chief Justice Burger); *Lewis v. Kugler,* 446 F.2d 1343, 1348–49 (3d Cir. 1971). The processing of a bona fide criminal proceeding does not itself constitute irreparable injury in this case. If an order of restitution is ultimately issued against Marvin Davis, it will be appealable. If no such order is issued, the rights of the Davises under the Bankruptcy Code will not have been affected. Furthermore, in response to the Davises' contentions, it is highly doubtful that an order of restitution at this time would constitute an unlawful preference since none of the money that might have gone to repay creditors was reserved in the estate to pay the possible restitutionary penalty.

In addition to principles of equity, a federal court must consider "the notion of 'comity,' that is, a proper respect for state functions, a recognition of the fact that the entire Country is made up of a Union of separate state governments, and a continuance of the belief that the National Government will fare best if the States and their institutions are left free to perform their separate functions in their separate ways." *Younger v. Harris,*401 U.S. at 44, 91 S.Ct. at 750. A federal court should be especially cautious in enjoining state criminal proceedings, because of the state's paramount interest in protecting its citizens through its police power. In this case, there has been no showing that Delaware has acted in bad faith in its prosecution, nor any allegation that the Delaware courts have inadequate procedures for hearing the federal challenges to a judgment of restitution. Therefore, we cannot say that the bankruptcy court erred in refusing to interfere with the state court proceedings.

III. Conclusion

Federalism in this nation relies in large part on the proper functioning of two separate court systems. The integrity of each must be preserved so that both can serve as effective forums for protecting individual rights and societal interests. Therefore, federal courts must remain vigilant not to diminish the rightful prerogatives of their state counterparts, and should exercise their power to enjoin state criminal proceedings only with considerable caution and indeed only when proper cause has been shown. The appellants in this proceeding failed to demonstrate why the concerns of equity or comity would require, or even permit, the issuance of an injunction. As a consequence, the bankruptcy judge did not err in denying the motion for an injunction and the district judge was correct in upholding that denial. Accordingly, the judgment of the district court, 18 B.R. 701, will be affirmed.

NOTES AND QUESTIONS

See In re Van Riper, 25 B.R. 972 (Bankr. W.D. Wis. 1982) (threat of criminal prosecution is not prosecution itself and within exception to stay; it does not absolve contempt sanction for having debtor sign note and mortgage postpetition in violation of automatic stay).

Sections 362(b)(4) and 362(b)(5) except from the automatic stay actions of a governmental unit to enforce its police or regulatory power. These exceptions have wreaked some havoc in the environmental law area, causing courts to draw fine lines between a state enforcing its regulatory power and collecting on a claim. In this regard, consideration should be given to 28 U.S.C. § 959(b) which requires a business being operated under the Bankruptcy Code to comply with state and federal laws. If, for example, the state has a claim to recover for prepetition pollution, it should be treated like any other creditor and the exception to the automatic stay should not apply. If, postpetition, the pollution is ongoing, the business should be required, under § 959(b), to comply with the applicable state law. In neither situation is section 362(b)(4), (5) necessary. *See* "Reforming the Bankruptcy Code," Final Report of the National Bankruptcy Conference's Code Review Project 36–38, 252–261 (1994). *See also United States v. Whizzo*, 841 F.2d 147 (6th Cir. 1988) (government had right to an injunction for cleanup of prepetition waste which was held to be subject to the bankruptcy discharge since it required expenditure of money by debtor); *Penn Terra Ltd. v. Pennsylvania Dep't of Environ. Resources*, 733 F.2d 267 (3d Cir. 1984) (cleanup injunction is not a money judgment and is within the § 362(b)(5) exception; accordingly, in this liquidation case, the government would get the meager resources of the debtor at the expense of other creditors).

§ 13.03 Relief from the Stay: Procedural Considerations

ROSLYN SAVINGS BANK v. COMCOACH CORP.
(In re Comcoach Corp.)

United States Court of Appeals, Second Circuit
698 F.2d 571 (1983)

CARDAMONE, Circuit Judge:

Plaintiff Roslyn Savings Bank (Bank) seeks modification of the automatic stay occasioned by the filing of a bankruptcy petition by defendant–debtor Comcoach Corporation. The United States Bankruptcy Court (Lifland, J.) refused to modify the stay, and the United States District Court for the Southern District of New York (Loew, J.) affirmed. We affirm.

I.

In the spring of 1979 the Bank loaned Jon–Rac Associates a sum of money secured by a mortgage on certain premises. Later that year, and with the consent of the Bank, Jon–Rac Associates conveyed the mortgaged premises to Rhone Holdings Nominee Corporation (Rhone). The Bank simultaneously entered into a written agreement with Rhone under which Rhone agreed to pay the mortgage, and at the same time Rhone leased the property to Comcoach subject to the Bank's mortgage.

On August 1, 1981 Rhone defaulted on its mortgage payments and the Bank instituted a foreclosure proceeding against Rhone in New York State Supreme Court, Suffolk County. Comcoach, the tenant in possession of the mortgaged premises, was neither named as a party–defendant nor served with process. On October 26, 1981 Comcoach filed a reorganization petition to institute Chapter 11 proceedings pursuant to the United States Bankruptcy Code (the "Code"), 11 U.S.C. § § 1101–74. Since that date the debtor has not paid any rent.

Arguing that it was barred from conducting the state foreclosure action by virtue of the Code's automatic stay provision, 11 U.S.C. § 362(a)(1) (Supp. V 1981), the Bank commenced the present action in federal court asking that the automatic stay be lifted under 11 U.S.C. § 362(d)(1), (2) (Supp. V 1981) to enable it to name Comcoach as a party–defendant in the pending state foreclosure action. The Bankruptcy Court denied plaintiff's request for relief on the ground that the Bank was not a "party in interest" entitled to seek modification of the stay under the Code. An appeal was then taken to the District Court which affirmed the Bankruptcy Court's decision. Subsequently, the bankruptcy was converted from a Chapter 11 reorganization to a Chapter 7 liquidation of the debtor Comcoach.

II.

The automatic stay in bankruptcy is governed by Code section 362 which stays, among other things, the commencement of a lawsuit against the debtor, 11 U.S.C. § 362(a)(1), and any act to obtain possession of property of or from the estate, 11 U.S.C. § 362(a)(3). The statute contains a mechanism for terminating, annulling, modifying or conditioning the stay. Section 362(d) states that a party in interest may request relief from the stay for cause, 11 U.S.C. § 362(d)(1) or, in reorganization cases, when the property is not necessary to an effective plan, 11 U.S.C. § 362(d)(2)(B). Inasmuch as this case was converted from a Chapter 11 reorganization to a Chapter 7 liquidation, the latter section is inapplicable.

To qualify for the "for cause" relief provided in section 362(d)(1), it is necessary that the party seeking such relief be "a party in interest." 11 U.S.C. § 362(d). The term "party in interest" is not defined in the Code. Generally, the "real party in interest" is the one who, under the applicable substantive law, has the legal right which is sought to be enforced or is the party entitled to bring suit. *Coe v. United States District Court for the District of Colorado,* 676 F.2d 411, 415 (10th Cir. 1982); *see Lubbock Feed Lots, Inc. v. Iowa Beef Processors, Inc.,* 630 F.2d 250, 256–57 (5th Cir. 1980); *Virginia Electric & Power Co. v. Westinghouse Electric Corp.,*485 F.2d 78, 83 (4th Cir. 1973), *cert. denied,*415 U.S. 935, 94 S.Ct. 1450, 39 L.Ed.2d 493 (1974); *Weniger v. Union Center Plaza Associates,*387 F.Supp. 849, 855 (S.D.N.Y. 1974); *see generally,* 3A J. Moore & J. Lucas, Moore's Federal Practice ¶ 17.07 (2d ed. 1979); 6 C. Wright & A. Miller, Federal Practice and Procedure § § 1543–1544 (1971).

Whether or not the Bank qualifies as a "party in interest" as that term is generally defined, we agree with the courts below that the Bank was not a "party in interest" within the meaning of the Bankruptcy Code. When interpreting the meaning of Code terms such as "party in interest," we are governed by the Code's purposes. *See Kokoszka v. Belford,* 417 U.S. 642,–645–46, 94 S.Ct. 2431, 2433–34, 41 L.Ed.2d 374 (1974). One of those purposes is to convert the bankrupt's estate into cash and distribute it among creditors. *See Burlingham v. Crouse,* 228 U.S. 459, 473, 33 S.Ct. 564, 568, 57 L.Ed. 920 (1913); *In re Thompson's Estate,* 192 F.2d 451, 453 (3d Cir. 1951); *Coulter v. Blieden,*104 F.2d 29, 34 (8th Cir.) (chief purpose of bankruptcy is protection of creditors), cert. denied, 308 U.S. 583, 60 S.Ct. 106, 84 L.Ed. 488 (1939); *cf. In re Pen–Dixie Industries,*6 B.R. 832, 836 (S.D.N.Y. 1980) (the purpose of the automatic stay is the protection of the debtor and his estate from creditors). Bankruptcy courts were established to provide a forum where creditors and debtors could settle their disputes and thereby effectuate the objectives of the statute. Necessarily, therefore, the Bank must be either a creditor or a debtor to invoke the court's jurisdiction.

Support for this view is found in the Code's legislative history which suggests that, notwithstanding the use of the term "party in interest", it is only creditors who may obtain relief from the automatic stay. *See H.R. Rep. No. 95–595, 95th Cong., 1st Sess. 175 (1977), U.S.Code & Admin. News 1978, p. 5787 ("Creditors may obtain relief from the stay if their interests would be harmed by continuance of the stay."). While the case law is scant, it also supports this position. In *In re Toar Train*

Partnership, 15 B.R. 401 (Bkrtcy. D. Vt.1981), the court held that a judgment creditor of a creditor of the bankrupt was not a "party in interest" because the judgment creditor was not itself a direct creditor of the bankrupt. *See* 15 B.R. at 402. As a stranger to the proceeding the judgment creditor did not qualify to seek modification of the stay which had been imposed when the debtor filed for bankruptcy.

Turning to the particular facts of this case, the Bank is clearly not a debtor. Nor is the Bank a "creditor" of the bankrupt. The Code in pertinent part defines a creditor as an entity that has a claim against either the debtor or the estate, arising at certain specified times. 11 U.S.C. § 101(9)(A), (B) (Supp. V 1981). A claim means a right to payment, *id.* at § 101(4)(A) (Supp. V 1981), or "a right to an equitable remedy for breach of performance if such breach gives rise to a right to payment," *id.* at § 101(4)(B). The Bank here has no right to payment from the bankrupt, since the bankrupt has no obligation on the mortgage and the bankrupt's duty to pay rent on its lease runs only to Rhone, not the Bank. Moreover, the Bank lacks any right to equitable relief against the bankrupt arising out of a breach of performance giving rise to a right to payment. Consequently, the Bank possesses no claim against the debtor or the estate, lacks "creditor" status, and cannot move to lift the automatic stay.

III.

The Bank further expresses concern that if it is not a "party in interest" entitled to seek modification of the stay, it will be barred from continuing its foreclosure action in state court and left without a remedy to enforce its rights under the mortgage. As noted by both lower courts these concerns are premised upon an erroneous view of the law. First, the state foreclosure action, as presently constituted, is not stayed. Until the debtor is named as a party–defendant the action does not affect the bankrupt estate. New York law provides that lessees are necessary parties in foreclosure actions. *See Flushing Savings Bank v. CCN Realty Corp.,* 73 A.D.2d 945, 424 N.Y.S.2d 27 (2d Dep't 1980); *G.B. Seely's Son, Inc. v. Fulton–Edison, Inc.,* 52 A.D.2d 575, 576, 382 N.Y.S.2d 516 (2d Dep't 1976); N.Y. Real Prop. Acts. Law § 1311(1) (McKinney 1979). Necessary parties are not always indispensable parties, however, whose absence mandates dismissal of the action. *See* N.Y. Civ. Prac. Law § 1001(b) (McKinney 1976). The absence of a necessary party in a foreclosure action simply leaves such party's rights to the premises unaffected. *See Douglas v. Kohart,* 196 A.D. 84, 88, 187 N.Y.S. 102 (2d Dep't 1921); *Home Life Insurance Co. v. O'Sullivan,* 151 A.D. 535, 537, 136 N.Y.S. 105 (2d Dep't 1912). By failing to name Comcoach as a party–defendant in its foreclosure action, the Bank has left the debtor in exactly the same position as it was in prior to commencement of the suit. Since no interest of the bankrupt estate has been affected, no automatic stay prohibiting the continuance of the state foreclosure action exists.

Our disposition of the Bank's first argument appears to be of small or no solace for the Bank. After all, its only source of income from this property is the bankrupt tenant in a building rendered nearly unmarketable. But, in response to the Bank's second concern, we find that it has not been left without a remedy. The Bank has the right to the appointment of a receiver in the state court action. For reasons already noted, plaintiff is not stayed from seeking such an appointment. A court–appointed receiver *would*qualify as a party–in–interest for purposes of section 362(d), since under New York law a receiver steps into the shoes of the mortgagor–debtor, in this case Rhone. The receiver becomes vested with Rhone's property right and acts as an arm of the court for the creditor–Bank's benefit. *See United States v. Mr. Hamburg Bronx Corp.,* 228 F.Supp. 115, 124–25 (S.D.N.Y. 1964) (quoting *Smith v. Meader Pen Corp.,*255 A.D. 397, 399, 8 N.Y.S.2d 39 (1st Dep't 1938)). It would then have rights against Comcoach under applicable substantive law including the right to sue for rent and, therefore, the right to move to lift the automatic stay.

For the foregoing reasons we hold that the Bank is not a party–in–interest in the bankruptcy proceeding and cannot seek to have the automatic stay vacated or modified so as to name debtor Comcoach a party–defendant in the pending state foreclosure action.

NOTE

See Matter of James Wilson Associates, 965 F.2d 160, 169–170, 173 (7th Cir. 1992) (concurring opinion), *supra:*"We have not considered the possible bearing of the receivership on Metropolitan's [mortgagee's] standing . . . . Obviously this is a richly complex issue, and it was Metropolitan's burden to develop it in adequate depth to enable its opponent and this court to evaluate it. A very large corporation, Metropolitan is well able to afford the best counsel. It has filed five appeals in this case and hundreds of pages of briefs. We won't rewrite its appeal briefs for it."

§ 13.04   Adequate Protection, § 361; Use of Collateral, § 363

[A]   What Is Adequate Protection? What Is to Be Protected?

UNITED SAVINGS ASSOCIATION OF TEXAS v. TIMBERS OF INWOOD FOREST ASSOCIATES, LTD.

United States Supreme Court
484 U.S. 365, 108 S. Ct. 626, 98 L. Ed. 2d 740, 17 C.B.C. 2d 1368 (1988)

Justice SCALIA delivered the opinion of the Court.

Petitioner United Savings Association of Texas seeks review of an en banc decision of the United States Court of Appeals for the Fifth Circuit, holding that petitioner was not entitled to receive from respondent debtor, which is undergoing reorganization in bankruptcy, monthly payments for the use value of the loan collateral which the bankruptcy stay prevented it from possessing. *In re Timbers of Inwood Forest Assocs.,*808 F.2d 363 [16 C.B.C.2d 1] (1987). We granted certiorari, 481 U.S. — (1987), to resolve a conflict in the Courts of Appeals regarding application of § § 361 and 362(d)(1) of the Bankruptcy Code, 11 U.S.C. § § 361 and 362(d)(1) (1982 ed. and Supp. IV). *Compare Grundy Nat. Bank v. Tandem Mining Corp.,* 754 F.2d 1436, 1440–1441 [12 C.B.C.2d 264] (CA4 1985); *In re American Mariner Indus., Inc.,* 734 F.2d 426, 432–435 [10 C.B.C.2d 910] (CA9 1984); *see also In re Briggs Transp. Co.,*780 F.2d 1339, 1348–1351 [13 C.B.C.2d 1289] (CA8 1985).

I.

On June 29, 1982, respondent Timbers of Inwood Forest Associates, Inc. executed a note in the principal amount of $4,100,000. Petitioner is the holder of the note as well as of a security interest created the same day in an apartment project owned by respondent in Houston, Texas. The security interest included an assignment of rents from the project. On March 4, 1985, respondent filed a voluntary petition under Chapter 11 of the Bankruptcy Code, 11 U.S.C. § 101 *et seq.*(1982 ed. and Supp. IV), in the United States Bankruptcy Court for the Southern District of Texas.

On March 18, 1985, petitioner moved for relief from the automatic stay of enforcement of liens triggered by the petition, *see* 11 U.S.C. § 362(a), on the ground that there was lack of "adequate protection" of its interest within the meaning of 11 U.S.C. § 362(d)(1). At a hearing before the Bankruptcy Court, it was established that respondent owed petitioner $4,366,388.77, and evidence was presented that the value of the collateral was somewhere between $2,650,000 and $4,250,000. The collateral was appreciating in value, but only very slightly. It was therefore undisputed that petitioner was an undersecured creditor. Respondent had agreed to pay petitioner the postpetition rents from the apartment project (covered by the after–acquired property clause in the security agreement), minus operating expenses. Petitioner contended, however, that it was entitled to additional compensation. The Bankruptcy Court agreed and on April 19, 1985, it conditioned continuance of the stay on monthly payments by respondent, at the market rate of 12% per annum, on the estimated amount realized on foreclosure, $4,250,000—commencing six months after the filing of the bankruptcy petition, to reflect the normal foreclosure delays. *In re Bear Creek Ministorage, Inc.*, [12 C.B.C.2d 1099] 49 B.R. 454 (1985) (editorial revision of earlier decision). The court held that the postpetition rents could be applied to these payments. *See id.* at 460. Respondent appealed to the District Court and petitioner cross–appealed on the amount of the adequate protection payments. The District Court affirmed but the Fifth Circuit en banc reversed.

We granted certiorari to determine whether undersecured creditors are entitled to compensation under 11 U.S.C. § 362(d)(1) for the delay caused by the automatic stay in foreclosing on their collateral.

II.

When a bankruptcy petition is filed, § 362(a) of the Bankruptcy Code provides an automatic stay of, among other things, actions taken to realize the value of collateral given by the debtor. The provision of the Code central to the decision of this case is § 362(d), which reads as follows:

On request of a party in interest and after notice and a hearing, the court shall grant relief from the stay provided under subsection (a) of this section, such as by terminating, annulling, modifying, or conditioning such stay —

(1) for cause, including the lack of adequate protection of an interest in property of such party in interest; or

(2) with respect to a stay of an act against property under subsection (a) of this section, if—

(A) the debtor does not have an equity in such property; and

(B) such property is not necessary to an effective reorganization.

The phrase "adequate protection" in paragraph (1) of the foregoing provision is given further content by § 361 of the Code, which reads in relevant part as follows:

When adequate protection is required under section 362 of this title of an interest of an equity in property, such adequate protection may be provided by—

(1) requiring the trustee to make a cash payment or periodic cash payments to such entity, to the extent that the stay under section 362 of this title results in a decrease in the value of such entity's interest in such property;

(2) providing to such entity an additional or replacement lien to the extent that such stay results in a decrease in the value of such entity's interest in such property; or

(3) granting such other relief as will result in the realization by such entity of the indubitable equivalent of such entity's interest in such property.

It is common ground that the "interest in property" referred to by § 362(d)(1) includes the right of a secured creditor to have the security applied in payment of the debt upon completion of the reorganization; and that that interest is not adequately protected if the security is depreciating during the term of the stay. Thus, it is agreed that if the apartment project in this case had been declining in value petitioner would have been entitled, under § 362(d)(1), to cash payments or additional security in the amount of the decline, as § 361 describes. The crux of the present dispute is that petitioner asserts, and respondent denies, that the phrase "interest in property" also includes the secured party's right (suspended by the stay) to take immediate possession of the defaulted security, and apply it in payment of the debt. If that right is embraced by the term, it is obviously not adequately protected unless the secured party is reimbursed for the use of the proceeds he is deprived of during the term of the stay.

The term "interest in property" certainly summons up such concepts as "fee ownership," "life estate," "co–ownership," and "security interest" more readily than it does the notion of "right to immediate foreclosure." Nonetheless, viewed in the isolated context of § 362(d)(1), the phrase could reasonably be given the meaning petitioner asserts. Statutory construction, however, is a holistic endeavor. A provision that may seem ambiguous in isolation is often clarified by the remainder of the statutory scheme—because the same terminology is used elsewhere in a context that makes its meaning clear, see, e.g., Sorenson v. Secretary of Treasury, 475 U.S. 851, 860 (1986), or because only one of the permissible meanings produces a substantive effect that is compatible with the rest of the law, see, e.g., Pilot Life Ins. Co. v. Dedeaux, 480 U.S. — , — (1987); Weinberger v. Hynson, Westcott & Dunning, Inc., 412 U.S. 609, 631–632 (1973); Jarecki v. G. D. Searle & Co.,367 U.S. 303, 307–308 (1961). That is the case here. Section 362(d)(1) is only one of a series of provisions in the Bankruptcy Code dealing with the rights of secured creditors. The language in those other provisions, and the substantive dispositions that they effect, persuade us that the "interest in property" protected by § 362(d)(1) does not include a secured party's right to immediate foreclosure.

Section 506 of the Code defines the amount of the secured creditor's allowed secured claim and the conditions of his receiving postpetition interest. In relevant part it reads as follows:

(a) An allowed claim of a creditor secured by a lien on property in which the estate has an interest . . . is a secured claim to the extent of the value of such creditor's interest in the estate's interest in such property, . . . and is an unsecured claim to the extent that the value of such creditor's interest is less than the amount of such allowed claim . . .

(b) To the extent that an allowed secured claim is secured by property the value of which . . . is greater than the amount of such claim, there shall be allowed to the holder of such claim, interest on such claim, and any reasonable fees, costs or charges provided for under the agreement under which such claim arose.

In subsection (a) of this provision the creditor's "interest in property" obviously means his security interest without taking account of his right to immediate possession of the collateral on default. If the latter were included, the "value of such creditor's interest" would increase, and the proportions of the claim that are secured and unsecured would alter, as the stay continues–since the value of the entitlement to use the collateral from the date of bankruptcy would rise with the passage of time. No one suggests this was intended. The phrase "value of such creditor's interest" in § 506(a) means "the value of the collateral." H.R. Rep. No. 95–595, pp. 181, 356 (1977); *see also* S. Rep. No. 95–989, p. 68 (1978). We think the phrase "value of such entity's interest" in § 361(1) and (2), when applied to secured creditors, means the same.

Even more important for our purposes than § 506's use of terminology is its substantive effect of denying undersecured creditors postpetition interest on their claims–just as it denies *over*secured creditors postpetition interest to the extent that such interest, when added to the principal amount of the claim, will exceed the value of the collateral. Section 506(b) provides that *"[t]o the extent that* an allowed secured claim is secured by property the value of which is greater than the amount of such claim, there shall be allowed to the holder of such claim, interest on such claim." (Emphasis added.) Since this provision permits postpetition interest to be paid only out of the "security cushion," the undersecured creditor, who has no such cushion, falls within the general rule disallowing postpetition interest. *See* 11 U.S.C. § 502(b)(2). If the Code had meant to give the undersecured creditor, who is thus denied interest on his *claim*, interest on the value of his *collateral*, surely this is where that disposition would have been set forth, and not obscured within the "adequate protection" provision of § 362(d)(1). Instead of the intricate phraseology set forth above, § 506(b) would simply have said that the secured creditor is entitled to interest "on his allowed claim, or on the value of the property securing his allowed claim, whichever is lesser." Petitioner's interpretation of § 362(d)(1) must be regarded as contradicting the carefully drawn disposition of § 506(b).

Petitioner seeks to avoid this conclusion by characterizing § 506(b) as merely an alternative method for compensating oversecured creditors, which does not imply that no compensation is available to undersecured creditors. This theory of duplicate protection for oversecured creditors is implausible even in the abstract, but even more so in light of the historical principles of bankruptcy law. Section 506(b)'s denial of postpetition interest to undersecured creditors merely codified pre–Code bankruptcy law, in which that denial was part of the conscious allocation of reorganization benefits and losses between undersecured and unsecured creditors. "To allow a secured creditor interest where his security was worth less than the value of his debt was thought to be inequitable to unsecured creditors." *Vanston Bondholders Protective Committee v. Green,*329 U.S. 156, 164 (1946). It was considered unfair to allow an undersecured creditor to recover interest from the estate's unencumbered assets before unsecured creditors had recovered any principal. *See id.,* at 164, 166; *Ticonic Nat. Bank v. Sprague,* 303 U.S. 406, 412 (1938). We think it unlikely that § 506(b) codified the pre–Code rule with the intent, not of achieving the principal purpose and function of that rule, but of providing oversecured creditors an alternative method of compensation. Moreover, it is incomprehensible why Congress would want to favor undersecured creditors with interest if they move for it under § 362(d)(1) at the inception of the reorganization process–thereby probably pushing the estate into liquidation–but not if they forbear and seek it only at the completion of the reorganization.

Second, petitioner's interpretation of § 362(d)(1) is structurally inconsistent with 11 U.S.C. § 552. Section 552(a) states the general rule that a prepetition security interest does not reach property acquired by the estate or debtor postpetition. Section 552(b) sets forth an exception, allowing postpetition "proceeds, product, offspring, rents, or profits" of the collateral to be covered only if the security agreement expressly provides for an interest in such property, and the interest has perfected under "applicable nonbankruptcy law." *See, e.g., In re Casbeer,*793 F.2d 1436, 1442–1444 (CA5 1986); *In re Johnson,* [15 C.B.C.2d 367] 62 B.R. 24, 28–30 (CA9 Bkrtcy. App. 1986); *cf. Butner v. United States,* 440 U.S. 48, 54–56 (1979) (same rule under former Bankruptcy Act). Section 552(b) therefore makes possession of a perfected security interest in postpetition rents or profits from collateral a condition of having them applied to satisfying the claim of a secured creditor ahead of the claims of unsecured creditors. Under petitioner's interpretation, however, the undersecured creditor who lacks such a perfected security interest in effect achieves the same result by demanding the "use value" of his collateral under § 362. It is true that § 506(b) gives the *over*secured creditor, despite lack of compliance with the conditions of § 552, a similar priority over unsecured creditors; but that does not compromise the principle of § 552, since the interest payments come only out of the "cushion" in which the oversecured creditor *does have* a perfected security interest.

Third, petitioner's interpretation of § 362(d)(1) makes nonsense of § 362(d)(2). On petitioner's theory, the undersecured creditor's inability to take immediate possession of his collateral is always "cause" for conditioning the stay (upon the payment of market rate interest) under § 362(d)(1), since there is, within the meaning of that paragraph, "lack of adequate protection of an interest in property." But § 362(d)(2) expressly provides a different standard for relief from a stay "of an act against property," which of course includes taking possession of collateral. It provides that the court shall grant relief "if (A) the debtor does not have an equity in such property [*i.e.*, the creditor is undersecured]; and (B) such property is not necessary to an effective reorganization." By applying the "adequate protection of an interest in property" provision of § 362(d)(1) to the alleged "interest" in the earning power of collateral, petitioner creates the strange consequence that § 362 entitles the secured creditor to relief from the stay (1) if he is undersecured (and thus not eligible for interest under § 506(b)), *or* (2) if he is undersecured *and* his collateral "is not necessary to an effective reorganization." This renders § 362(d)(2) a practical nullity and a theoretical absurdity. If § 362(d)(1) is interpreted in this fashion, an undersecured creditor would seek relief under § 362(d)(2) only if its collateral was not depreciating (or it was being compensated for depreciation) and it was receiving market rate interest on its collateral, but nonetheless wanted to foreclose. Petitioner offers no reason why Congress would want to provide relief for such an obstreperous and thoroughly unharmed creditor.

Section 362(d)(2) also belies petitioner's contention that undersecured creditors will face inordinate and extortionate delay if they are denied compensation for interest lost during the stay as part of "adequate protection" under § 362(d)(1). Once the movant under § 362(d)(2) establishes that he is an undersecured creditor, it is the burden of the *debtor* to establish that the collateral at issue is "necessary to an effective reorganization." *See* § 362(g). What this requires is not merely a showing that if there is conceivably to be an effective reorganization, this property will be needed for it; but that the property is essential for an effective reorganization *that is in prospect.* This means, as many lower courts, including the en banc court in this case, have properly said, that there must be "a reasonable possibility of a successful reorganization within a reasonable time." 808 F.2d, at 370–371, and nn.12–13, and cases cited therein. The cases are numerous in which § 362(d)(2) relief has been provided within less than a year from thefiling of the bankruptcy petition.

And while the bankruptcy courts demand less detailed showings during the four months in which the debtor is given the exclusive right to put together a plan, *see* 11 U.S.C. § § 1121(b), (c)(2), even within that period lack of any realistic prospect of effective reorganization will require § 362(d)(2) relief.

III.

A.

Petitioner contends that denying it compensation under § 362(d)(1) is inconsistent with sections of the Code other than those just discussed. Petitioner principally relies on the phrase "indubitable equivalent" in § 361(3), which also appears in 11 U.S.C. § 1129(b)(2)(A)(iii). Petitioner contends that in the latter context, which sets forth the standards for confirming a reorganization plan, the phrase has developed a well–settled meaning connoting the right of a secured creditor to receive present value of his security–thus requiring interest if the claim is to be paid over time. It is true that under § 1129(b) a secured claimant has a right to receive under a plan the present value of his collateral. This entitlement arises, however, not from the phrase "indubitable equivalent" in § 1129(b)(2)(A)(iii), but from the provision of § 1129(b)(2)(A)(i)(II) that guarantees the secured creditor "deferred cash payments of a value, *as of the effective date* of the plan, of at least the value of such [secured claimant's] interest in the estate's interest in such property." (Emphasis added.) Under this formulation, even though the undersecured creditor's "interest" is regarded (properly) as solely the value of the collateral, he must be rendered payments that assure him that value *as of the effective date of the plan.* In § 361(3), by contrast, the relief pending the stay need only be such "*as will result in the realization* of the indubitable equivalent" of the collateral. (Emphasis added.) It is obvious (since § § 361 and 362(d)(1) do not entitle the secured creditor to immediate payment of the principal of his collateral) that this "realization" is to "result" not at once, but only upon completion of the reorganization. It is *then* that he must be assured "realization of the indubitable equivalent" of his collateral. To put the point differently: similarity of outcome between § 361(3) and § 1129 would be demanded only if the former read "such other relief as will give such entity, *as of the date of the relief,* the indubitable equivalent of such entity's interest in such property."

Nor is there merit in petitioner's suggestion that "indubitable equivalent" in § 361(3) connotes reimbursement for the use value of collateral because the phrase is derived from *In re Murel Holding Corp.,* 75 F.2d 941 (CA2 1935), where it bore that meaning. *Murel* involved a proposed reorganization plan that gave the secured creditor interest on his collateral for 10 years, with full payment of the secured principal due at the end of that term; the plan made no provision, however, for amortization of principal or maintenance of the collateral's value during the term. In rejecting the plan, *Murel* used the words "indubitable equivalence" with specific reference not to interest (which was assured), but to the jeopardized principal of the loan:

> Interest is indeed the common measure of the difference [between payment now and payment 10 years hence], but a creditor who fears the safety of his principal will scarcely be content with that; he wishes to get his money or at least the property. We see no reason to suppose that the statute was intended to deprive him of that in the interest of junior holders, unless by a substitute of the most indubitable equivalence.

Id., at 942.

Of course *Murel,* like § 1129, proceeds from the premise that in the confirmation context the secured creditor is entitled to present value. But no more from *Murel* than from § 1129 can it be inferred that a similar requirement exists as of the time of the bankruptcy stay. The reorganized debtor is supposed to stand on his own two feet. The debtor in process of reorganization, by contrast, is given many temporary protections against the normal operation of the law.

Petitioner also contends that the Code embodies a principle that secured creditors do not bear the costs of reorganization. It derives this from the rule that general administrative expenses do not have priority over secured claims. *See* §§ 506(c); 507(a). But the general principle does not follow from the particular rule. That secured creditors do not bear one kind of reorganization cost hardly means that they bear none of them. The Code rule on administrative expenses merely continues pre–Code law. But it was also pre–Code law that undersecured creditors were not entitled to postpetition interest as compensation for the delay of reorganization. *See supra,* at 7; *see also infra,* at 14–15. Congress could hardly have understood that the readoption of the rule on administrative expenses would work a change in the rule on postpetition interest, which is also readopted.

Finally, petitioner contends that failure to interpret § 362(d)(1) to require compensation of undersecured creditors for delay will create an inconsistency in the Code in the (admittedly rare) case when the debtor proves solvent. When that occurs, 11 U.S.C. § 726(a)(5) provides that postpetition interest is allowed on unsecured claims. Petitioner contends it would be absurd to allow postpetition interest on unsecured claims but not on the secured portion of undersecured creditor's claims. It would be disingenuous to deny that this is an apparent anomaly, but it will occur so rarely that it is more likely the product of inadvertence than are the blatant inconsistencies petitioner's interpretation would produce. Its inequitable effects, moreover, are entirely avoidable, since an undersecured creditor is entitled to "surrender or waive his security and prove his entire claim as an unsecured one." *United States Nat. Bank v. Chase Nat. Bank,* 331 U.S. 28, 34 (1947). Section 726(a)(5) therefore requires no more than that undersecured creditors receive postpetition interest from a solvent debtor on equal terms with unsecured creditors rather than ahead of them–which, where the debtor is solvent, involves no hardship.

B.

Petitioner contends that its interpretation is supported by the legislative history of § § 361 and 362(d)(1), relying almost entirely on statements that "[s]ecured creditors should not be deprived of the benefit of their bargain." H.R. Rep. No. 95–595, at 339; S. Rep. No. 95–989, at 53. Such generalizations are inadequate to overcome the plain textual indication in § § 506 and 362(d)(2) of the Code that Congress did not wish the undersecured creditor to receive interest on his collateral during the term of the stay. If it is at all relevant, the legislative history tends to subvert rather than support petitioner's thesis, since it contains not a hint that § 362(d)(1) entitles the undersecured creditor to postpetition interest. Such a major change in the existing rules would not likely have been made without specific provision in the text of the statute, *cf. Kelly v. Robinson,* 479 U.S. — , — [15 C.B.C.2d 890] (1987); it is most improbable that it would have been made without even any mention in the legislative history.

Petitioner makes another argument based upon what the legislative history does not contain. It contends that the pre–Code law gave the undersecured creditor relief from the automatic stay by permitting him to foreclose; and that Congress would not have withdrawn this entitlement to relief without any indication of intent to do so in the legislative history, unless it was providing an adequate substitute, to wit, interest on the collateral during the stay.

The premise of this argument is flawed. As petitioner itself concedes, Brief for Petitioner 20, the undersecured creditor had no absolute entitlement to foreclosure in a Chapter X or XII case; he could not foreclose if there was a reasonable prospect for a successful rehabilitation within a reasonable time. *See, e.g., In re Yale Express System, Inc.,* 384 F.2d 990, 991–992 (CA2 1967) (Chapter X); *In re Nevada Towers Assocs.,* 14 Collier Bankr. Cas. (MB) 146, 151–156 (Bkrtcy. Ct. SDNY 1977) (Chapter XII); *In re Consolidated Motor Inns,* 6 Collier Bankr. Cas. (MB) 18, 31–32

(Bkrtcy. Ct. ND Ga. 1975) (same). Thus, even assuming petitioner is correct that the undersecured creditor has an absolute entitlement to relief under Chapter XI, Congress would have been faced with the choice between adopting the rule from Chapters X and XII or the asserted alternative rule from Chapter XI, because Chapter 11 of the current Code "replaces chapters X, XI and XII of the Bankruptcy Act" with a "single chapter for all business reorganizations." S. Rep. No. 95–989, at 9; *see also* H.R. Rep. No. 95–595, at 223–224. We think § 362(d)(2) indicates that Congress adopted the approach of Chapters X and XII. In any event, as far as the silence of the legislative history on the point is concerned, that would be no more strange with respect to alteration of the asserted Chapter XI rule than it would be with respect to alteration of the Chapters X and XII rule.

Petitioner's argument is further weakened by the fact that it is far from clear that there was a distinctive Chapter XI rule of absolute entitlement to foreclosure. At least one leading commentator concluded that "a Chapter XI court's power to stay lien enforcement is as broad as that of a Chapter X or XII court and that the automatic stay rules properly make no distinctions between the Chapters." Countryman, *Real Estate Liens in Business Rehabilitation Cases,*50 Am. Bankr. L.J. 303, 315 (1976). Petitioner cites dicta in some Chapter XI cases suggesting that the undersecured creditor was automatically entitled to relief from the stay, but the courts in those cases uniformly found in addition that reorganization was not sufficiently likely or was being unduly delayed.

See, e.g., In re Bric of America, Inc.,*4 Collier Bankr. Cas. (MB) 34, 39–40 (Bkrtcy. Ct. MD Fla. 1975); *In re O. K. Motels,*1 Collier Bankr. Cas. (MB) 416, 419–420 (Bkrtcy. Ct. MD Fla. 1974). Moreover, other Chapter XI cases held undersecured creditors not entitled to foreclosure under reasoning very similar to that used in Chapters X and XII cases. *See In re Coolspring Estates, Inc.,* 12 Collier Bankr. Cas. (MB) 55, 60–61 (Bkrtcy. Ct. ND Ind. 1977); *In re The Royal Scot, Ltd.,* 2 Bankr. Ct. Dec. (CRR) 374, 376–377 (Bkrtcy. Ct. WD Mich. 1976); *In re Mesker Steel, Inc.,*1 Bankr. Ct. Dec. (CRR) 235, 236–237 (Bkrtcy. Ct. SD Ind. 1974). The at best divided authority under Chapter XI removes all cause for wonder that the alleged departure from it should not have been commented upon in the legislative history.

. . .

The Fifth Circuit correctly held that the undersecured petitioner is not entitled to interest on its collateral during the stay to assure adequate protection under 11 U.S.C. § 362(d)(1). Petitioner has never sought relief from the stay under § 362(d)(2) or on any ground other than lack of adequate protection. Accordingly, the judgment of the Fifth Circuit is *Affirmed.*

NOTES AND QUESTIONS

What, in effect, did the Supreme Court suggest in *Timbers* that bankruptcy judges do with respect to case management techniques? *See* § 105 as amended in 1994.

The 1994 Bankruptcy Reform Act added paragraph (3) to § 362(d) to deal with what is called the single asset real estate case. That term is defined in § 101. When § 362(d)(3) applies and its conditions are not met, the automatic stay is lifted and the mortgagee can take steps to foreclose under nonbankruptcy law. Parse through the conditions to revisit a question propounded earlier concerning the effect of the provision on courts which were dismissing such chapter 11 cases as not having been filed in good faith. It may be asked at this time whether the amendment has any effect on the ruling in the *Timbers case, supra.*

[B]   Use, Sale, and Lease of Property; § 363

Pursuant to § 363(c)(1), the trustee may use, sell, or lease property of the estate in the ordinary course of business without notice and hearing, *i.e.,*without a court order. The only qualification is that the trustee is authorized to operate the business in the first place. In a chapter 11 case, since that is the norm, § 1108 presumes the continued operation of the business and a court order to that effect is not necessary. In a chapter 7 case, however, since liquidation is the relief, continued operation is not the norm, and a specific court order is necessary if it is to be continued for a (brief) period of time. § 721.

The trustee may also use, sell, or lease property not in the ordinary course of business but notice is required as is the opportunity for a hearing. § 363(b)(1); *see* § 102(1). *See also* Rules 2002(a)(2), 6004. In a chapter 7 case, the norm will be to sell property, assuming the existence of some nonexempt assets, because the proceeds of the sale are the source of distributions to creditors. Special provisions are contained in § 363 which permit, *inter alia,* the trustee to sell property that is jointly owned as, for example, by tenants in the entireties, and allow a secured creditor to bid in at the sale of its collateral.

As regards the secured creditor, property that is "cash collateral" (defined in § 363(a)), may not be used by the trustee unless the secured creditor consents or adequate protection is approved by the court. § 363(c)(2). Section 363(a) should be read with § 552(a) which provides that an after acquired property clause in a security agreement is not effective in a case under the Bankruptcy Code. Compare U.C.C. § 9–204. Section 552(b), however, allows the security interest to continue in proceeds except as the court may find that the equities of the case dictate otherwise. Thus, § 363(a) will encompass proceeds that come within the definition of cash collateral.

PROBLEM

Ajax Corp. is a manufacturer of men's and women's clothing. It has given Bank a security interest in all of the suits, dresses, and overcoats that it makes including those in existence and those that will be made in the future. In the ordinary course of Ajax's business, orders are accepted from retailers such as Macys and Bloomingdales, who generally are given 30 days after receipt of the invoice to pay for their goods. Ajax files a chapter 11 petition. Its books show several millions of dollars of delivered orders for which payment was not received prior to the petition, and checks coming in postpetition in payment of other orders. Ajax, the debtor in possession, is in need of money for various business expenses, such as meeting a payroll imminently, and paying its suppliers. What should (may) Ajax do?

§ 13.05   Postpetition Financing

IN RE SULLIVAN FORD SALES

Bankruptcy Court, District of Maine
2 B.R. 350, 1 C.B.C.2d 397 (1980)

CONRAD K. CYR, Bankruptcy Judge.

Sullivan Ford Sales, the Largest Ford dealership in Maine, filed a voluntary chapter 11 petition on November 23, 1979, whereupon reorganization relief was ordered by operation of law. On December 5, 1979, the debtor in possession caused three applications to be filed with the court for authorization to enter into various financial arrangements. These applications requested that the debtor be permitted (1) to borrow $200,000 on certificates of indebtedness, (2) to borrow $500,000 from The Merrill Trust Company to finance its 1980 automobile floor plan, and (3) to use "cash collateral" generated from sales of encumbered automobile parts.

The applications recited that due to the urgency of the need for operating capital written notice of the applications for relief was impractical. The United States trustee had not yet designated a creditors' committee by the time these applications were filed with the court on December 5, 1979. Informal telephonic notification of the hearing scheduled for December 6, 1979 at 11:00 a.m. was provided by the debtor in possession on December 5, 1979. Approximately one hour before the scheduled hearing, the United States trustee designated a committee of creditors. Counsel for the creditors' committee was appointed December 10, 1979. The application for authorization to enter into the 1980 floor plan financing arrangement with The Merrill Trust Company was amended at the hearing.

. . .

At the hearing on December 6, 1979, a secured claim holder and several holders of unsecured claims interposed objections to the adequacy of the notice afforded by the debtor in possession. While conceding that the 24–hour interval between the telephonic notification and the hearing was indeed brief, counsel for the debtor in possession maintained that nothing more was either appropriate or necessary in the circumstances due to the urgent nature of the operating capital needs of the debtor. The debtor in possession presented uncontroverted evidence that it was operating at a negative cash flow, as well as at a pretax loss; that it was without funds with which to defray current and future operating expenses; and that earlier notification of the requests for relief was impracticable, due to the fact that agreement on the specific terms of its financing arrangements with The Merrill Trust Company was not achieved until shortly before the filing of the applications.

The adequacy of the notice provided by the debtor in possession is to be determined with reference to an important statutory rule of construction which defines "after notice and a hearing" as meaning

> . . . after such notice as is appropriate in the particular circumstances, and such opportunity for a hearing as is appropriate in the particular circumstances, but [after notice and a hearing] authorizes an act without an actual hearing if such notice is given properly and if–
>
> (i) such a hearing is not requested timely by a party in interest; or
>
> (ii) there is insufficient time for a hearing to be commenced before such act must be done, and the court authorizes such act . . .

The primary thrust of section 102(1), defining "after notice and a hearing," is to give practical effect to the separation of administrative and judicial functions, by eliminating direct involvement on the part of the court in the approval of requests for relief absent a dispute. "After notice and a hearing" has a much different meaning than does such plain language as "the court shall hold a hearing," appearing elsewhere in the Code. There was complete awareness on the part of the principal congressional architect of the Code that "after notice and a hearing" did not contemplate a hearing in every instance. Indeed, that result was fully intended.

. . .

Subparagraph 102(1)(B)(i) authorizes relief without hearing where "hearing is not requested timely by a party in interest . . . " It would torture its purpose to use this provision to license action without a hearing where the parties entitled to be heard were afforded no notice of the request for relief. Subparagraph 102(1)(B)(ii) permits the court to authorize relief, without actual hearing, if "there is insufficient time for a hearing to be commenced before such act must be done . . . ," but only after notice "appropriate in the particular circumstances."

The court must determine the notice "appropriate in the particular circumstances," giving due consideration to the notice opportunity available. In the present case, notice consisted of an informal oral notification communicated by counsel for the debtor in possession by telephone to a few holders of secured and unsecured claims on the day before the hearing. The creditors' committee was not designated until an hour before the hearing and its counsel was not appointed until several days later. Virtually all holders of unsecured claims received no notification of the request for relief. In the circumstances of this case, each unsecured claim holder is a party in interest entitled to appropriate notice. In the absence of a duly constituted committee of creditors, there was no alternative but to provide each individual holder with whatever notice was appropriate in the particular circumstances, thus underscoring the importance of prompt performance by the United States trustee of the duty imposed by section 102(a). The notice to the committee, once constituted, was plainly insufficient to enable effective representation of its own interests, much less the interests of individual holders of unsecured claims.

The timing of requests for ex parte relief generally rests within the control of the party requesting relief. The court must be alert to the need to prevent the moving party, whether by design or neglect, from denying adequate notice to other parties in interest, which would only serve to encourage the deferment of requests for relief until an emergency had become self–evident. The time of the request for relief was within the control of Sullivan Ford Sales, although the designation of a committee of creditors was not. The evidence adduced at the hearing on December 6, 1979 established that Sullivan Ford Sales and other parties in interest joining in the application for relief were aware of its serious financial condition and of the need for working capital at least a month before the commencement of the chapter 11 case. In any event, the debtor was fully cognizant, at least by November 23, 1979 when its chapter 11 petition was filed, that it would require relief of the nature requested on December 5, 1979. The debtor in possession was in a position, no later than November 23, 1979, therefore, to provide notice of the general nature of the relief requested, although the details of its financial arrangements with The Merrill Trust Company were yet to be finally agreed upon.

It is not necessary, in these particular circumstances, to determine the extent, if any, to which it would be appropriate to probe the pre–petition past in evaluating whether the debtor made sufficient use of the opportunity to provide adequate notice of the relief requested through the prompt filing of its chapter 11 petition. The 12–day delay between the commencement of the chapter 11 case and the filing of these applications squandered an ample opportunity to provide formal, written notice of the relief requested to all parties in interest. In these circumstances, judicial emphasis should be placed upon protecting the rights of parties in interest to adequate advance notice of requests for relief whose filing was not within their control. A different or more relaxed rule would facilitate dilatory filing of requests for relief with a view to abbreviating the occasion for advance notice. Delay in requesting the relief and in designating the committee of creditors deprived parties in interest in these proceedings of the advance notice appropriate in the particular circumstances. Although section 102(1) dispenses with an evidentiary hearing in certain circumstances, nowhere does it expressly annul the requirement of "notice . . . appropriate in the particular circumstances."

The matter may not be left there, however, unless the bankruptcy court is to abort reorganization proceedings ab initio by withholding ex parte relief essential to the survival of the business of the debtor pending evaluation of the reorganization prospects. Thus, while notice appropriate in the particular circumstances must always be provided, it remains to be determined whether relief may be granted without *advance* notice where there is insufficient time for notice before action must be taken. Boiled down to doublethink the question becomes whether action permitted only "after notice and a hearing" may be taken before either notice or hearing?

There are two primary factors competing for emphasis in the present context. First, ex parte relief under section 364(c)(1) may jeopardize significant property interests of the holders of subordinated claims. Extraordinary legal safeguards are therefore required to minimize the potentially drastic consequences of ex parte relief in these and similar circumstances. Second, in certain circumstances the entire reorganization effort may be thwarted if emergency relief is withheld. Reorganization under either the Bankruptcy Code or the Bankruptcy Act is a perilous process, seldom more so than at the outset of the proceedings when the debtor is often without sufficient cash flow to fund essential business operations.

The remedy under consideration bears a close resemblance to ex parte injunctive relief in federal civil proceedings generally.

. . .

The court can conceive of no competent rationale applicable in all reorganization cases upon which to withhold emergency ex parte relief essential to the preservation of the reorganizability of the debtor pending an opportunity to provide effective final relief.

The procedural problems presented are closely analogous to those confronted in ex parte injunctive relief proceedings under Federal Rule 65(b). The procedural safeguards mandated by Federal Rule 65(b) may therefore suggest standards appropriate for consideration by the court in the context of proceedings for ex parte relief in chapter 11 reorganization cases.

Where parties in interest are not afforded appropriate notice in the particular circumstances, considering the opportunity for notice and the nature of the relief requested, ex parte relief should nonetheless be available upon a sufficient showing that immediate and irreparable injury, loss, or damage will result to the moving party *or to the reorganization effort* before adverse parties or their counsel can be notified. Counsel for the moving party should be required to certify in writing the efforts made to provide notice and the reasons supporting the claim that advance notice should not be required.

The extraordinary nature of ex parte relief requires exceptional scrutiny on the part of the court as the only real protection against loss or damage to the property interests of innocent parties. *See Austin v. Altman,* 332 F.2d 273, 275 (2d Cir. 1964); *Arvida Corp. v. Sugarman,* 259 F.2d 428, 429 (2d Cir. 1958) *(per curiam).* Any order granting ex parte relief without advance notice should include an endorsement reflecting the date and hour of its issuance and should be entered of record in the office of the clerk of the bankruptcy court forthwith. The order should remain in effect not more than ten days from its issuance, unless extended by the court within the ten–day period for good cause shown or by agreement of all adverse parties. The court should proceed to notify and hear adverse parties at the earliest possible time following ex parte relief, and should hear any request for dissolution of the ex parte order on two days' notice or less to the party that obtained it.

It does not seem advisable that the security provisions of Federal Rule 65(c) be considered mandatory in a reorganization context. *See* Rule of Bankruptcy Procedure 765. *See also* Wright & Miller, Federal Practice and Procedure: Civil § 2954, at 535. *Compare In re Lustron Corp.*, 184 F.2d 789 (7th Cir. 1950), *cert. denied*, 340 U.S. 946, 71 S.Ct. 531, 95 L.Ed. 682 (1951), with *Magidson v. Duggan*, 180 F.2d 473 (8th Cir.), *cert. denied*, 339 U.S. 965, 70 S.Ct. 1000, 94 L.Ed. 1374 (1950). An order for ex parte reorganization relief should comport with the requirements of Federal Rule 65(d) in respect of the particularity of its findings and conclusions and of its duration and scope.

Ex parte relief is not warranted in the present circumstances. The reorganization effort is no more immediately threatened by whatever brief deferment is required to afford advance notice to parties in interest than by the 12–day delay already occasioned by the failure of the debtor to request relief on or about November 23, 1979. There is no evidence that the business operations of the debtor must cease in the absence of immediate relief, only that the debtor may be without an adequate 1980 model car inventory to enable the continuation of its business on a normal basis. Although the debtor asserts that it is without funds with which to defray current operating expenses, it has been experiencing that problem for some time without any interruption of its business. The court is satisfied that no immediate or irreparable injury will result either to the debtor or to the reorganization effort as a result of whatever brief delay is occasioned by the need to provide appropriate advance notice of the relief requested to parties in interest.

The pending applications for relief were therefore ordered noticed and heard within five days.

IN RE GARLAND CORP.

United States Court of Appeals, Bankruptcy Appellate Panel, First Circuit
6 B.R. 456, 3 C.B.C.2d 24 (1980)

CYR, Bankruptcy Judge:

An emergency appeal has been taken from various orders of the bankruptcy judge entered during the early stages of these chapter 11 reorganization proceedings. The Garland Corporation and its subsidiaries [debtor] manufacture and sell clothing, principally knitted goods and sportswear for women. From its earliest beginnings, the debtor achieved financial success as a sweater manufacturer. Severe financial difficulties later developed in the wake of its operation of thirty–six retail stores and a factory producing clothing principally for Levi Strauss, and its entry into the field of sportswear design and manufacture.

Upon the commencement of its reorganization proceedings, the debtor sought authorization to borrow operating funds from New England Merchants Bank [Bank] and Prudential Insurance Company [Prudential]. Following an ex parte hearing the same day the bankruptcy judge authorized an immediate borrowing from the Bank and Prudential, fixing May 7, 1980, after the formation of the Creditors' Committee, for further hearing on the application. At the conclusion of the May 7 hearing, the Creditors' Committee having appeared without interposing objection, the bankruptcy judge authorized the debtor to borrow an additional $700,000 and to enter into a line–of–credit agreement with the Bank and Prudential for up to $1.4 million in postpetition borrowings. These postpetition loans were later deemed priority costs of administration under Bankruptcy Code § 507(b) and a first encumbrance on all assets of the debtor.

On May 16, the Creditors' Committee appeared in opposition to the request of the debtor to borrow an additional $500,000, and filed a motion to convert the proceedings to chapter 7. After hearing, the bankruptcy judge approved the $500,000 borrowing, increased the line of credit to $1.7 million, declined to convert the proceedings to chapter 7, and granted a motion by the U.S. trustee to appoint a trustee. The Creditors' Committee appeals.

The Appellate Panel authorized an expedited appeal, while denying a stay pending appeal. Immediately following oral argument, the Appellate Panel affirmed the orders of the bankruptcy judge declining to convert the proceedings to chapter 7 and appointing a reorganization trustee. The Panel deferred its decision on the remaining issue in response to Bankruptcy Code § 364(e).

The appellant challenges the May 16 order authorizing a third borrowing in the amount of $500,000 on grounds that the evidence did not demonstrate a reasonable likelihood that the debtor could be successfully rehabilitated, and because the borrowing of operating funds secured by theretofore unencumbered assets requires adequate protection of the interests of unsecured creditors, within the meaning of Bankruptcy Code § 361, in the absence of which the borrowing constituted a taking of property without just compensation, contrary to the fifth amendment to the Constitution of the United States. The decision of the bankruptcy judge permitting the continued operation of the debtor under the direction of a trustee was challenged on the same grounds.

The refusal to convert the case to chapter 7 and the approval of the motion to appoint a trustee to operate the business were based on findings, adequately supported by the record, that the future financial condition and business prospects of the debtor would be significantly enhanced were it to dispose of its retail stores and the Georgia plant, terminate all but its sweater manufacturing operation, reduce its topheavy payroll, and bring in new management. The appellant did not deny that significant reductions in employee and executive payrolls and the sale of the retail outlets would produce beneficial results. The likelihood that substantial benefits would result from an aggressive implementation of these initiatives was substantiated by the appellant's own witness. There was uncontroverted evidence that current management had erred seriously in the past, particularly in its cash flow projections and unprofitable business undertakings. The appellant mounts no serious challenge to these findings, but believes it would be better for the estate and creditors were the debtor liquidated under chapter 7.

The only basis for converting an embryonic reorganization proceeding under section 1112(b)(1) is a sufficient showing that the debtor would continue to sustain losses or diminish the estate if the reorganization effort is permitted to proceed *and* that there exists no reasonable likelihood of rehabilitation. Bankruptcy Code § 1112(b)(1). While the debtor's own projections clearly evidenced the near certainty of short–term operating losses, the bankruptcy judge concluded, appropriately in our view, that there existed a reasonable likelihood that the debtor could be rehabilitated. *See* 5 Collier on Bankruptcy, ¶ 1112.03[c][i] (15th Ed. 1980) at 1112–14. Where there is a reasonable prospect of a successful rehabilitation, a motion to convert under section 1112(b)(1) must be denied. *Id.*

The appropriateness of the decision to appoint a reorganization trustee under Bankruptcy Code §§ 1104 & 151104 turns upon whether there was a sufficient showing of cause, including incompetence or gross mismanagement of the affairs of the debtor by current management, either before or after the commencement of the case, or, in the alternative, a showing that the appointment would be in the best interests of the creditors and the estate. *See, e.g., In re Hotel Associates, Inc.,*3 B.R. 343, 1 CBC 2d 733, 6 BCD 160 (E.D. Penn. 1980). There is a presumption in a chapter 11 case that the debtor is to continue in control and possession of its business. *LaSherene, Inc. d/b/a The Sunshine Corporation,* 3 B.R. 169, 174, 1 CBC 2d 685, 692, 6 BCD 153, 156 (N.D. Georgia 1980).

The Appellate Panel must accept the findings of the bankruptcy judge unless clearly erroneous. First Circuit Rules Governing Appeals From Bankruptcy Judges to District Courts, Appellate Panels and Court of Appeals, Rule 16. *In re Multiponics, Inc.,* 622 F.2d 709, 713 (5th Cir. 1980); *Boston and Maine Corp. v. First National Bank of Boston,* 618 F.2d 137, 141 (1st Cir. 1980). The findings of fact are amply supported by the record, and the conclusions of law, freely reviewable on appeal, *In re Multiponics, Inc., supra,* comport with the legislative prescriptions of sections 1104(a) [151104(a)] and 1112(b)(1).

Appellant next challenges the authorization under section 364(c)(2) to borrow operating funds secured by unencumbered assets. The appellant insists that it was an abuse of discretion to permit the May 16 loan to be secured by unencumbered assets of the debtor, without first determining that the debtor was unable to obtain unsecured credit, as required by Bankruptcy Code § 364(c).

The May 16 borrowing was another in a series arranged pursuant to a line–of–credit agreement among the debtor, the Bank and Prudential, approved by the bankruptcy judge on May 1, 1980. The May 1 order contains an express finding that unsecured financing was not available to the debtor. A review of the sufficiency of the evidence supporting this finding is severely hampered by the failure of the appellant to include the April 30 hearing transcript in the record on appeal. Without such a transcript we decline to review. *In re Colonial Realty Investment,* 516 F.2d 154, 160 (1st Cir. 1975). The May 1 order was not appealed and is not, therefore, before us. Neither is there any evidence before us that the ability to obtain unsecured financing improved between May 1 and May 16.

Appellant is the official Creditors' Committee representing the holders of unsecured claims against the debtor. The Creditors' Committee is concerned that the satisfaction of unsecured claims may be delayed, diminished or rendered impossible as a result of the authorization to encumber "free" assets as security for postpetition operating loans. Its position appears to be that holders of unsecured claims whose recoveries may be thus materially impaired are entitled, by statute as well as by constitutional guarantee, to adequate protection in advance of the fixing of liens on unencumbered assets as a means of obtaining postpetition operating loans to finance the future operations of the reorganization debtor.

The May 16 borrowing was authorized under Bankruptcy Code § 364(c)(2), after notice and a hearing, upon a sufficient showing that the debtor was unable to obtain unsecured credit. The debtor was in urgent need of operating funds with which to meet its payroll. Its 1,300 employees had been instructed not to report for work without calling in advance to learn if the plant would open. The appellant's own witnesses and committee members confirmed that essential raw materials were available only on a cash–on–delivery basis and that other trade creditors would not produce the needed yarns without assurances of payment. The record substantiates the finding that the urgently needed operating monies were otherwise unavailable.

There is no express statutory requirement that holders of unsecured claims be provided "adequate protection." Adequate protection within the meaning of Bankruptcy Code § 361 need be provided only as expressly required under section 362, section 363, or section 364. There is no requirement of adequate protection in respect to credit obtained under Bankruptcy Code § 364(c)(2).

The authorization to use previously unencumbered assets as collateral for postpetition operating loans is further challenged as an unconstitutional deprivation of the fifth amendment rights of unsecured creditors.

The bankruptcy power conferred by the Constitution upon the Congress is subject to fifth amendment guarantees against the taking of private property without just compensation. *Louisville Joint Stock Land Bank v. Radford,* 295 U.S. 555, 589 (1935). The fifth amendment guarantees protection against any taking of private property, even for a purpose wholly public in nature, without just compensation. 295 U.S. at 602. Therefore, no taking of private property, in reorganization proceedings or otherwise, can be countenanced by the court in contravention of the "just compensation" clause.

Although our attention has not been invited to any authority for the proposition that holders of unsecured claims possess constitutionally protected substantive rights in property of the estate of a reorganization debtor, it is at least arguable that the fixing of a lien on property of the estate under the bankruptcy laws in certain circumstances may constitute a taking within the meaning of the "just compensation" clause. It is in the area of collateral impairment, however, that such constitutional concerns more frequently arise in a reorganization context. It seems generally agreed in broad outline at least that Congress in the exercise of its bankruptcy power cannot deprive a creditor of substantial preexisting property rights in specific collateral, without just compensation. *Armstrong v. U.S.,* 364 U.S. 40, 44, 48–49 (1960); 295 U.S. at 602. Nevertheless, there are no constitutional constraints inhibiting Congress in the exercise of its bankruptcy power from extinguishing the recovery rights of holders of unsecured claims, because an unsecured claim confers no right in specific property of the obligor. 295 U.S. at 588. Congress may rearrange the order of distribution of the property of a bankrupt estate without infringing the constitutional rights of the holders of claims thereby deprived of recoveries otherwise available under the preexisting scheme of priority. *See, e.g., New York Credit Men's Adjustment Bureau, Inc. v. Jesse Goldstein & Co.,* 276 F.2d 886, 888 (2d Cir. 1960); *City of Chelsea v. Dolan,* 24 F.2d 522, 523 (1st Cir. 1928).

Appellant represents the interests of holders of unsecured claims against the debtor. Their constitutional rights do not rise to the level accorded lien creditors, *id.*at 523, and their claims are subject to discharge under federal bankruptcy laws, inasmuch as the constitutional proscription against impairing the obligation of contracts applies to the states alone. *Louisville Joint Stock Land Bank v. Radford,* 295 U.S. 555, 589 (1935).

Any impairment of the recoupment anticipated by holders of unsecured claims from unencumbered assets of the estate is dependent for its redress upon congressional rather than constitutional prescription. *See New York Men's Adjustment Bureau v. Jessie Goldstein & Co.,*276 F.2d 886, 888 (2d Cir. 1960); *City of Chelsea v. Dolan*24 F.2d 522, 523 (1st Cir. 1928). Congress has chosen to exercise its substantive bankruptcy power so as not to require "adequate protection" of the interests of the holders of unsecured claims under the Bankruptcy Code in circumstances where the debtor obtains postpetition credit on the strength of a lien on previously unencumbered property of the estate theretofore available in whatever measure for the satisfaction of unsecured claims. *See* Bankruptcy Code § § 361 & 364(c)(2). The only criteria mandated by Congress for the fixing of a lien on free assets pursuant to section 364(c)(2) are that such action be authorized by the court, after notice and a hearing, upon showing that unsecured credit cannot be obtained. Since there are no other constitutional or legislative requirements, the court may permit the use of unencumbered assets as collateral to secure postpetition indebtedness upon compliance with section 364(c)(2).

Affirmed.

MATTER OF SAYBROOK MANUFACTURING CO., INC.

United States Court of Appeals, Eleventh Circuit
963 F.2d 1490, 27 C.B.C.2d 277 (1992)

COX, Circuit Judge:

Seymour and Jeffrey Shapiro, unsecured creditors, objected to the bankruptcy court's authorization for the Chapter 11 debtors to "cross–collateralize" their pre–petition debt with unencumbered property from the bankruptcy estate. The bankruptcy court overruled the objection and also refused to grant a stay of its order pending appeal. The Shapiros appealed to the district court, which dismissed the case as moot under section 364(e) of the Bankruptcy Code because the Shapiros had failed to obtain a stay, 127 B.R. 494. We conclude that this appeal is not moot and that cross–collateralization is not authorized under the Bankruptcy Code. Accordingly, we reverse and remand.

I. Facts and Procedural History

Saybrook Manufacturing Co., Inc., and related companies, (the "debtors") initiated proceedings seeking relief under Chapter 11 of the Bankruptcy Code on December 22, 1988. On December 23, 1988, the debtors filed a motion for the use of cash collateral and for authorization to incur secured debt. The bankruptcy court entered an emergency financing order that same day. At the time the bankruptcy petition was filed, the debtors owed Manufacturers Hanover approximately $34 million. The value of the collateral for this debt, however, was less than $10 million. Pursuant to the order, Manufacturers Hanover agreed to lend the debtors an additional $3 million to facilitate their reorganization. In exchange, Manufacturers Hanover received a security interest in all of the debtors' property–both property owned prior to filing the bankruptcy petition and that which was acquired subsequently. This security interest not only protected the $3 million of post–petition credit but also secured Manufacturers Hanover's $34 million pre–petition debt.

This arrangement enhanced Manufacturers Hanover's position vis–a–vis other unsecured creditors, such as the Shapiros, in the event of liquidation. Because Manufacturers Hanover's pre–petition debt was undersecured by approximately $24 million, it originally would have shared in a pro rata distribution of the debtors' unencumbered assets along with the other unsecured creditors. Under the financing order, however, Manufacturers Hanover's pre–petition debt became fully secured by all of the debtors' assets. If the bankruptcy estate were liquidated, Manufacturers Hanover's entire debt–$34 million pre–petition and $3 million post–petition–would have to be paid in full before any funds could be distributed to the remaining unsecured creditors.

Securing pre–petition debt with pre– and post–petition collateral as part of a post–petition financing arrangement is known as cross–collateralization. The Second Circuit aptly defined cross–collateralization as follows:

> [I]n return for making new loans to a debtor in possession under Chapter XI, a financing institution obtains a security interest on all assets of the debtor, both those existing at the date of the order and those created in the course of the Chapter XI proceeding, not only for the new loans, the propriety of which is not contested, but [also] for existing indebtedness to it.

Otte v. Manufacturers Hanover Commercial Corp. (In re Texlon Corp.), 596 F.2d 1092, 1094 (2d Cir. 1979).

Because the Second Circuit was the first appellate court to describe this practice in *In re Texlon*, it is sometimes referred to as *Texlon*–type cross–collateralization. Another form of cross–collateralization involves securing post–petition debt with pre–petition collateral. *See, e.g., In re Antico Manufacturing Co.*, 31 B.R. 103, 105 (Bankr. E.D.N.Y. 1983). This form of non–*Texlon*–type cross–collateralization is not at issue in this appeal. *See*Appellant's Brief at 8–9. The Shapiros challenge only the cross–collateralization of the lenders' pre–petition debt, not the propriety of collateralizing the post–petition debt. *Id.* at 10.

The Shapiros filed a number of objections to the bankruptcy court's order on January 13, 1989. After a hearing, the bankruptcy court overruled the objections. The Shapiros then filed a notice of appeal and a request for the bankruptcy court to stay its financing order pending appeal. The bankruptcy court denied the request for a stay on February 23, 1989.

The Shapiros subsequently moved the district court to stay the bankruptcy court's financing order pending appeal; the court denied the motion on March 7, 1989. On May 20, 1989, the district court dismissed the Shapiros' appeal as moot under 11 U.S.C. § 364(e) because the Shapiros had failed to obtain a stay of the financing order pending appeal, rejecting the argument that cross–collateralization is contrary to the Code. *Shapiro v. Saybrook Mfg. Co. (In re Saybrook Mfg. Co.),* 127 B.R. 494 (M.D. Ga. 1991). The Shapiros then appealed to this court.

II. Issues on Appeal

1. Whether the appeal to the district court and the appeal to this court are moot under section 364(e) of the Bankruptcy Code because the Shapiros failed to obtain a stay of the bankruptcy court's financing order.

2. Whether cross–collateralization is authorized under the Bankruptcy Code.

III. Contentions of the Parties

The lenders argue that this appeal is moot under section 364(e) of the Bankruptcy Code. That section provides that a lien or priority granted under section 364 may not be overturned unless it is stayed pending appeal. Even if this appeal were not moot, the Shapiros are not entitled to relief. Cross–collateralization is a legitimate means for debtors to obtain necessary financing and is not prohibited by the Bankruptcy Code.

The Shapiros contend that their appeal is not moot. Because cross–collateralization is not authorized under bankruptcy law, section 364(e) is inapplicable. Permitting cross–collateralization would undermine the entire structure of the Bankruptcy Code by allowing one unsecured creditor to gain priority over all other unsecured creditors simply by extending additional credit to a debtor.

IV. Standard of Review

Conclusions of law by the bankruptcy and district courts are reviewed *de novo.* *Equitable Life Assurance Society v. Sublett (In re Sublett),* 895 F.2d 1381, 1383 [22 C.B.C.2d 868] (11th Cir. 1990).

V. Discussion

A.   Mootness

We begin by addressing the lenders' claim that this appeal is moot under section 364(e) of the Bankruptcy Code. Section 364(e) provides that:

The reversal or modification on appeal of an authorization under this section to obtain credit or incur debt, or of a grant under this section of a priority or a lien, does not affect the validity of any debt so incurred, or any priority or lien so granted, to an entity that extended such credit in good faith, whether or not such entity knew of the pendency of the appeal, unless such authorization and the incurring of such debt, or the granting of such priority or lien, were stayed pending appeal.

11 U.S.C. § 364(e). The purpose of this provision is to encourage the extension of credit to debtors in bankruptcy by eliminating the risk that any lien securing the loan will be modified on appeal.

The lenders suggest that we assume cross–collateralization is authorized under section 364 and then conclude the Shapiros' appeal is moot under section 364(e). This is similar to the approach adopted by the Ninth Circuit in *Burchinal v. Central Washington Bank (In re Adams Apple, Inc.)*, 829 F.2d 1484 [17 C.B.C.2d 1132] (9th Cir. 1987). That court held that cross–collateralization was "authorized" under section 364 for the purposes of section 364(e) mootness but declined to decide whether cross–collateralization was illegal per se under the Bankruptcy Code. *Id.* at 1488 n.6. *See also Unsecured Creditors' Committee v. First National Bank & Trust Co. (In re Ellingsen Maclean Oil Co.)*, 834 F.2d 599 [17 C.B.C.2d 1402] (6th Cir. 1987), *cert. denied*, 488 U.S. 817, 109 S.Ct. 55, 102 L.Ed.2d 33 (1988).

We reject the reasoning of *In re Adams Apple* and *In re Ellingsen* because they "put the cart before the horse." By its own terms, section 364(e) is only applicable if the challenged lien or priority was authorized under section 364. *See* Charles J. Tabb, *Lender Preference Clauses and the Destruction of Appealability and Finality: Resolving a Chapter 11 Dilemma*, 50 Ohio St.L.J. 109, 116–35 (1989) (criticizing *In re Adams Apple, In re Ellingsen*, and the practice of shielding cross–collateralization from appellate review via mootness under section 364(e)); *See also In re Ellingsen*, 834 F.2d at 607 (Merritt, dissenting) (arguing that section 364(e) was not designed to prohibit creditors from challenging pre–petition matters and that "[l]enders should not be permitted to use their leverage in making emergency loans in order to insulate their prepetition claims from attack"). We cannot determine if this appeal is moot under section 364(e) until we decide the central issue in this appeal–whether cross–collateralization is authorized under section 364. Accordingly, we now turn to that question.

B.   Cross–Collateralization and Section 364

Cross–collateralization is an extremely controversial form of Chapter 11 financing. Nevertheless, the practice has been approved by several bankruptcy courts. *See, e.g., In re Vanguard Diversified, Inc.*, 31 B.R. 364 (Bankr. E.D.N.Y. 1983); *In re Roblin Indus., Inc.*, 52 B.R. 241 (Bankr. W.D.N.Y. 1985); *In re Beker Indus. Corp.*, 58 B.R. 725 (Bankr. S.D.N.Y. 1986). *Contra In re Monach Circuit Indus., Inc.*, [11 C.B.C.2d 312] 41 B.R. 859 (Bankr. E.D. Pa. 1984). Even the courts that have allowed cross–collateralization, however, were generally reluctant to do so. *See McLemore v. Citizens Bank (In re Tom McCormick Enterprises, Inc.)*, [7 C.B.C.2d 1288] 26 B.R. 437, 439–40 (Bankr. M.D. Tenn. 1983).

In *In re Vanguard,* for example, the bankruptcy court noted that cross–collateralization is "a disfavored means of financing" that should only be used as a last resort. *In re Vanguard,* 31 B.R. at 366. In order to obtain a financing order including cross–collateralization, the court required the debtor to demonstrate (1) that its business operations would fail absent the proposed financing, (2) that it is unable to obtain alternative financing on acceptable terms, (3) that the proposed lender will not accept less preferential terms, and (4) that the proposed financing is in the general creditor body's best interest. *Id.* This four–part test has since been adopted by other bankruptcy courts which permit cross–collateralization. *See, e.g., Roblin,* 52 B.R. at 244–45.

The issue of whether the Bankruptcy Code authorizes cross–collateralization is a question of first impression in this court. Indeed, it is essentially a question of first impression before any court of appeals. Neither the lenders' brief nor our own research has produced a single appellate decision which either authorizes or prohibits the practice.

The lenders claim that the Sixth Circuit's decision in *In re Ellingsen* endorses cross–collateralization. Like *In re Adams Apple,* the issue in *In re Ellingsen* was whether section 364(e) rendered an appeal moot because the appellants failed to obtain a stay. Judge Wellford's opinion for the court notes that, while cross–collateralization is controversial, it appears to have been used and approved in the past. Therefore, "Congress would not have intended to exclude all cross–collateralization orders categorically from section 364(e)'s protection." *In re Ellingsen,* 834 F.2d at 602. The court concluded that the appeal was moot under section 364(e) because the bankruptcy court did not issue a stay of its cross–collateralization order. The court, however, did not hold that cross–collateralization itself was authorized under the Bankruptcy Code. In fact, Judge Nelson concurred separately to emphasize the limited scope of the court's decision, stating that he was uncertain as to whether section 364 permitted cross–collateralization. *Id.* at 606.

As noted above, the Ninth Circuit reached a similar conclusion in *In re Adams Apple. In re Adams Apple* held that the appeal was moot under section 364(e) but expressly declined to decide whether cross–collateralization was illegal per se under the Bankruptcy Code. *In re Adams Apple,* 829 F.2d at 1488 n. 6. The Ninth Circuit reaffirmed this holding in *Transamerica Commercial Finance Corp. v. Citibank (In re Sun Runner Marine, Inc.),* 945 F.2d 1089 [25 C.B.C.2d 1054] (9th Cir. 1991).

The court in *Adams Apple* held only that where the bankruptcy court grants cross–collateralization under § 364, post–petition credit is extended to the debtor in reliance thereon, an appeal is taken, and no stay pending appeal is sought, § 364(e) renders the appeal moot because even reversal would not affect the post–petition lender's rights. The court explicitly declined to rule whether the Bankruptcy Code authorizes cross–collateralization.

We also decline to rule whether cross–collateralization is appropriate in this case, or whether as a matter of law it is ever permissible. *Id.* at 1094. *See also Official Committee of Creditors v. Union Bank (In re Texas Research, Inc.),* 862 F.2d 1161, 1164 (5th Cir. 1989) (declining to decide whether the Bankruptcy Code prohibits cross–collateralization because, under the facts of the case, no cross–collateralization could have occurred).

The Second Circuit expressed criticism of cross–collateralization in *In re Texlon.* The court, however, stopped short of prohibiting the practice altogether. At issue was the bankruptcy court's *ex parte* financing order granting the lender a security interest in the debtor's property to secure both pre–petition and post–petition debt. The court, in an exercise of judicial restraint, concluded that:

> In order to decide this case we are not obliged, however, to say that under no conceivable circumstances could "cross–collateralization" be authorized. Here it suffices to hold that . . . a financing scheme so contrary to the spirit of the Bankruptcy Act should not have been granted by an *ex parte* order, where the bankruptcy court relies solely on representations by a debtor in possession that credit essential to the maintenance of operations is not otherwise obtainable.

In re Texlon,

596 F.2d at 1098. *See also In re Monach,*41 B.R. at 862 (arguing that, if the *Texlon* court were faced with the merits of cross–collateralization, it would hold that the practice is forbidden). Although *In re Texlon* was decided under the earlier Bankruptcy Act, the court also considered whether cross–collateralization was authorized under the Bankruptcy Code. "To such limited extent as it is proper to consider the new Bankruptcy Act, which takes effect on October 1, 1979, in considering the validity of an order made in 1974, we see nothing in § 364(c) or in other provisions of that section that advances the case in favor of "cross–collateralization.' " *In re Texlon,* 596 F.2d at 1098 (citations omitted).

Cross–collateralization is not specifically mentioned in the Bankruptcy Code. *See, e.g., In re Beker,* 58 B.R. at 741 (conceding that cross–collateralization is not expressly permitted by the Code). We conclude that cross–collateralization is inconsistent with bankruptcy law for two reasons. First, cross–collateralization is not authorized as a method of post–petition financing under section 364. Second, cross–collateralization is beyond the scope of the bankruptcy court's inherent equitable power because it is directly contrary to the fundamental priority scheme of the Bankruptcy Code. *See generally* Charles J. Tabb, *A Critical Reappraisal of Cross–Collateralization in Bankruptcy,* 60 S. Cal. L. Rev. 109 (1986).

Section 364 authorizes Chapter 11 debtors to obtain secured credit and incur secured debt as part of their reorganization. It provides, in relevant part, that:

> (c) If the trustee is unable to obtain unsecured credit allowable under section 503(b)(1) of this title as an administrative expense, the court, after notice and a hearing, may authorize the obtaining of credit or the incurring of debt–

> (1) with priority over any or all administrative expenses of the kind specified in section 503(b) or 507(b) of this title;

> (2) secured by a lien on property of the estate that is not otherwise subject to a lien; or

> (3) secured by a junior lien on property of the estate that is subject to a lien.

(d)(1) The court, after notice and a hearing, may authorize the obtaining of credit or incurring of debt secured by a senior or equal lien on property of the estate that is subject to a lien only if–

(A) the trustee is unable to obtain such credit otherwise; and

(B) there is adequate protection of the interest of the holder of the lien on the property of the estate on which such senior or equal lien is proposed to be granted.

(2) In any hearing under this subsection, the trustee has the burden of proof on the issue of adequate protection.

11 U.S.C. § 364(c) & (d). By their express terms, sections 364(c) & (d) apply only to future–*i.e.*,post–petition–extensions of credit. They do not authorize the granting of liens to secure pre–petition loans.

The bankruptcy court for the Eastern District of Pennsylvania reached this same conclusion regarding section 364(c) in *In re Monach*. "[T]he terms of § 364(c) appear to limit the extent of the priority or lien to the amount of the credit obtained or debt incurred *after* court approval." *In re Monach*, 41 B.R. at 862 (emphasis in original). *See also In re Ellingsen*, 834 F.2d at 601 (noting that "the express language of [section 364(c)] suggests that the priority or lien granted thereunder is limited to securing the newly incurred debt authorized by that provision"). Similarly, the bankruptcy court for the District of New Hampshire held that section 364(d) was limited to future credit or debt. "Section 364(d) speaks only of the granting of liens as security for *new credit* authorized by the Court." *In re Tenney Village Co.*, 104 B.R. 562, 570 (D.N.H. 1989) (emphasis added).

Given that cross–collateralization is not authorized by section 364, we now turn to the lenders' argument that bankruptcy courts may permit the practice under their general equitable power. Bankruptcy courts are indeed courts of equity, *See, e.g., Young v. Higbee Co.*, 324 U.S. 204, 65 S.Ct. 594, 89 L.Ed. 890 (1945); 11 U.S.C. § 105(a), and they have the power to adjust claims to avoid injustice or unfairness. *Pepper v. Litton*, 308 U.S. 295, 60 S.Ct. 238, 84 L.Ed.2d 281 (1939). This equitable power, however, is not unlimited.

[T]he bankruptcy court has the ability to deviate from the rules of priority and distribution set forth in the Code in the interest of justice and equity. The Court cannot use this flexibility, however, merely to establish a ranking of priorities within priorities. Furthermore, absent the existence of some type of inequitable conduct on the part of the claimant, which results in injury to the creditors of the bankrupt or an unfair advantage to the claimant, the court cannot subordinate a claim to claims within the same class.

In re FCX, Inc., [14 C.B.C.2d 1281] 60 B.R. 405, 409 (E.D.N.C. 1986) (citations omitted).

Section 507 of the Bankruptcy Code fixes the priority order of claims and expenses against the bankruptcy estate. 11 U.S.C. § 507. Creditors within a given class are to be treated equally, and bankruptcy courts may not create their own rules of superpriority within a single class. 3 Collier on Bankruptcy ¶ 507.02[2] (15th ed.

1992). Cross–collateralization, however, does exactly that. *See, e.g., In re FCX*, 60 B.R. at 410. As a result of this practice, post–petition lenders' unsecured pre–petition claims are given priority over all other unsecured pre–petition claims. The Ninth Circuit recognized that "[t]here is no . . . applicable provision in the Bankruptcy Code authorizing the debtor to pay certain pre–petition unsecured claims in full while others remain unpaid. To do so would impermissibly violate the priority scheme of the Bankruptcy Code." *In re Sun Runner*, 945 F.2d at 1094 (citations omitted). *See also In re Tenney Village*, 104 B.R. at 570 (holding that § 364 does not authorize bankruptcy courts to change the priorities set forth in § 507.)

The Second Circuit has noted that, if cross–collateralization were initiated by the bankrupt while insolvent and shortly before filing a petition, the arrangement "would have constituted a voidable preference." *In re Texlon*, 596 F.2d at 1097. The fundamental nature of this practice is not changed by the fact that it is sanctioned by the bankruptcy court. We disagree with the district court's conclusion that, while cross–collateralization may violate some policies of bankruptcy law, it is consistent with the general purpose of Chapter 11 to help businesses reorganize and become profitable. *In re Saybrook,*127 B.R. at 499. Rehabilitation is certainly the primary purpose of Chapter 11. This end, however, does not justify the use of any means. Cross–collateralization is directly inconsistent with the priority scheme of the Bankruptcy Code. Accordingly, the practice may not be approved by the bankruptcy court under its equitable authority.

VI. Conclusion

Cross–collateralization is not authorized by section 364. Section 364(e), therefore, is not applicable and this appeal is not moot. Because *Texlon*-type cross–collateralization is not explicitly authorized by the Bankruptcy Code and is contrary to the basic priority structure of the Code, we hold that it is an impermissible means of obtaining post–petition financing. The judgment of the district court is *reversed* and the case is *remanded*for proceedings not inconsistent with this opinion.

Reversed and remanded.

QUESTIONS

1. Earlier, it was seen that when adequate protection ordered under § 362 (or §§ 363 or 364(d)) proves to be inadequate, the shortfall is given priority over all administrative expenses by § 507(b). This may be called a super priority. Now it is seen that § 364(c)(1) permits the court to approve a postpetition financing agreement giving the lender a priority over not only all expenses of administration but also over the § 507(b) super priority. What may this priority be called?

2. Does § 364(c)(1) really mean what it says? Suppose a chapter 11 debtor cannot be reorganized and, instead, liquidation results. The attorney for the debtor in

possession and the attorney for the committee of unsecured creditors file applications under § 330 for compensation which is a cost of administration entitled to first priority under § § 507(a)(1) and 503(b)(2). Bank had extended postpetition financing to debtor and the court approved agreement gave it § 364(c)(1) protection. The liquidation proceeds are insufficient to repay Bank in full and it objected to the attorneys' applications for compensation. What result?

3. For assistance on the preceding question, *see In re Flagstaff Foodservice Corp.,*which follows.

IN RE FLAGSTAFF FOODSERVICE CORP.

United States Court of Appeals, Second Circuit
739 F.2d 73, 10 C.B.C.2d 1309 (1984)

VAN GRAAFEILAND, Circuit Judge:

General Electric Credit Corporation (GECC) appeals from an order of the United States District Court for the Southern District of New York (Broderick, J.) which affirmed a bankruptcy court order awarding appellees interim compensation for professional services and disbursements and directing that payment thereof be made from assets of the debtors in possession in which GECC had a security interest. For reasons hereafter discussed, we reverse.

On July 21, 1981, Flagstaff Foodservice Corporation and its related companies (Flagstaff) filed petitions for reorganization under chapter 11 of the Bankruptcy Reform Act of 1978 (the Code), 11 U.S.C. § § 1101 *et seq.* As permitted by the Code, 11 U.S.C. § § 1107, 1108, the companies continued to operate their businesses as debtors in possession.

GECC had been financing Flagstaff's operations since 1978 by making loans and advances on accounts receivable and inventory. As of July 21, 1981, Flagstaff owed GECC approximately $22 million, which was secured by assets worth $42 million. Shortly before commencement of the chapter 11 proceedings, Flagstaff's attorneys met with representatives of GECC to obtain immediate short–term financing in order to maintain sufficient cash flow to support Flagstaff's operations. These negotiations resulted in an order which permitted Flagstaff to use up to $750,000 of GECC's collateral for the limited period of five days. Flagstaff's attorneys also prepared an application for a more permanent financing arrangement with GECC. An order (the "Financing Order") was issued by the bankruptcy court authorizing Flagstaff to borrow additional money from GECC, the loans to be secured by a super–priority interest in all present and future property of the estate. In pertinent part, the order provided that:

"any and all obligations and Liabilities of Borrowers and debtors in possession to GECC (as defined in the Loan Agreement and the Security Agreement) shall have priority in payment over any other debts or obligations now in existence or incurred hereafter of Borrowers and debtors in possession and over all administrative expenses of the kind specified in Section 503(b) or 507(b) of the Bankruptcy Code, and said Liabilities and obligations of Borrowers and debtors in possession to GECC shall be secured by a first and prior lien on all property of whatever kind and nature of the Borrowers and debtors in possession, and proceeds thereof, until all such obligations and Liabilities of the Borrowers and debtors in possession to GECC shall have been paid in full."

By December 21, 1981, Flagstaff had generated enough income from its accounts receivable to pay all of GECC's pre–petition liabilities. However, during the chapter 11 proceedings, GECC advanced an additional $9 million to Flagstaff pursuant to the Financing Order. Despite this infusion of funds, the Flagstaff reorganization ultimately failed. No chapter 11 plan ever was proposed; no bulk purchaser appeared; and no buyer emerged to take over any of the debtor companies. Accordingly, although Flagstaff's indebtedness to GECC had been reduced substantially, the realizable value of the collateral which remanded was insufficient to satisfy the unpaid balance.

The issue before us is whether, despite the super–priority lien given GECC in the Financing Order, the bankruptcy court subsequently might direct that interim fees and disbursements of attorneys and accountants be paid from the encumbered collateral. The bankruptcy court awarded Levin & Weintraub, attorneys for the debtor, $57,403.57; Bell, Wolkowitz, Kalnick, Klee, Green & Beckman, co–counsel to the Levin firm, $130,479.77; Angel & Frankel, attorneys for the Committee of Unsecured Creditors, $38,388.40; and Ernst & Whinney, the Committee's accountants, $22,966. In each instance, the award was 70% of the amount claimed. These awards were affirmed by the district court. We hold this to be error. Section 364(c)(1) of the Code authorizes the issuance of a financing order, such as the one secured by Flagstaff, which will have "priority over any or all administrative expenses of the kind specified in section 503(b) or 507(be) of [the Code]." Among the administrative expenses listed in section 503(b), and thus reduced in priority by the Flagstaff Financing Order, are "compensation and reimbursement awarded under section 330 of [the Code]." Section 330 is the section that authorizes the bankruptcy court to make awards for services and expenses to attorneys and professional persons representing debtors or creditors' committees, which awards may be made on an interim basis pursuant to section 331.

Looking to the plain language of these sections, as we are bound to do, *Comminetti v. United States,* 242 U.S. 470, 485 (1917), we conclude that GECC's security interest has priority over appellees' claims for professional services, *In re Malaspina,* 30 B.R. 267, 270 (Bankr. W.D. Pa. 1983); 3 Collier on Bankruptcy ¶ 507.05 at 507–44 (15th ed. 1984). To the extent that *In re Callister,* [5 C.B.C.2d 1058] 15 B.R. 521 (Bankr. D. Utah 1981), *appeal dismissed,* 673 F.2d 305 [6 C.B.C.2d 147] (10th Cir. 1982), relied upon by appellees, is to the contrary, we decline to follow it. Where, as here, the statutory language clearly expresses the congressional intent, a court may not read another meaning into the statute in order to arrive at a result which the court deems preferable. *Central Trust Co. v. Official Creditors' Committee of Geiger Enterprises, Inc.,* 454 U.S. 354, 359–60 [5 C.B.C.2d 1085] (1982);

In re Fidelity Mortgage Investors, 690 F.2d 35, 39–40 (2d Cir. 1982). Attorneys may, as Levin & Weintraub did here, secure a portion of their fee in advance. *See Matter of Arlan's Dep't Stores, Inc.*, 615 F.2d 925, 935–37 (2d Cir. 1979). If attorneys need more encouragement than this to participate in chapter 11 proceedings, Congress, not the courts, must provide it. Under the law as it presently exists, knowledgeable bankruptcy attorneys must be aware that the priority ordinarily given to administration expenses may "prove illusive in light of the various provisions in the Code for competing or superiorities." 2 Collier on Bankruptcy ¶ 364.02, at 364–6 (15th ed. 1984). Section 364(c)(1) is such a provision.

We conclude that the district court erred in holding that section 330 "empower[ed] the Bankruptcy Judge to make awards without reference to any schedule of priorities, without reference to any contractual agreement with respect to those priorities and on the basis of his assessment in the course of supervising the bankruptcy proceeding that if actual and necessary services have been rendered, they should be compensated for." We hold, instead, that any fees payable from GECC's collateral must be for services which were for the benefit of GECC rather than the debtor or other creditors. *See Matter of Trim–X, Inc.*, 695 F.2d 296, 301 [7 C.B.C.2d 955] (7th Cir. 1983). Provision for such allowance is made in section 506(c), which provides: "The trustee [debtor in possession] may recover from property securing an allowed secured claim the reasonable, necessary costs and expenses of preserving, or disposing of, such property to the extent of any benefit to the holder of such claim." Congress's express intent in enacting section 506(c) was to ensure that, any time a debtor in possession "expends money to provide for the reasonable and necessary cost and expenses of preserving or disposing of a secured creditor's collateral, the . . . debtor in possession is entitled to recover such expenses from the secured party or from the property securing an allowed secured claim held by such party." 124 Cong. Rec. H11089 (daily ed., Sept. 28, 1978) (Statement of Rep. Edwards), *reprinted in* 1978 U.S. Code Cong. & Ad. News 6436, 6451. That is not the situation disclosed in appellees' affidavits.

It is undisputed that the chapter 11 proceedings were initiated with the hope of effectuating Flagstaff's rehabilitation and with optimism that this could be accomplished. Indeed, a less forthright purpose in seeking chapter 11 relief might preclude the awarding of any fees at all. *See In re Casco Fashions, Inc.*, 490 F.2d 1197, 1204 (2d Cir. 1973). Such benefits as might be said to have accrued to GECC from the attempt to reorganize were incidental to the reorganization efforts and did not fall within the intended scope of section 506(c). *See Matter of Trim–X, supra*, 695 F.2d at 301; *In re Codesco, Inc.*, [6 C.B.C. 2D 395] 18 B.R. 225, 228–30 (Bankr. S.D.N.Y. 1982).

As a matter of fact, it requires rather strained logic to conclude that GECC actually benefited from appellees' services. At the outset of the chapter 11 proceedings, GECC's $22 million claim against Flagstaff was secured by $42 million in collateral. When the chapter 11 proceedings aborted, the indebtedness had been reduced to $4 million but this balance was substantially under–collateralized. In return for this "benefit," appellees now seek to reduce the remaining collateral another quarter of a million dollars to pay their interim fee allowances.

Although GECC requested a hearing in connection with the fee applications, none was held, appellees being content to rest on their written applications. We are as well equipped as the district court to evaluate these documents. *See Forts v. Ward,* 566 F.2d 849, 852 n.8 (2d Cir. 1977). Having done so, we are satisfied that, conclusory allegations aside, they do not justify the allowances made herein. For example, Angel & Frankel's application, which is not atypical, states that "[a]ll of the professional services for which an interim allowance is being sought were rendered solely on behalf of the Committee in connection with the Debtors' Chapter 11 proceedings, pursuant to the responsibility of Applicant as attorneys for the Committee, and in accordance with the instructions of the Committee, and not on behalf of any other person, as such term is defined in Section 101(30) of the Code." The application then outlines the steps which Angel & Frankel took to carry out their duties to the Committee, including, among other things, an extensive court challenge to the "validity, extent and priority" of GECC's security interest. Angel & Frankel contend that they "performed services which benefited all creditors of the estate including GECC." Angel & Frankel's Brief 17. The district court, whose opinion contains no reference whatever to section 506(c), adopted this argument, holding that the "context" of the case "necessarily imports" that appellees' service benefited GECC "by preserving or enhancing the bankrupt estate."

Approval of the fee award on this basis was error. Payment of administration expenses traditionally has been the responsibility of the debtor's estate, not its secured creditors.

Matter of Trim–X, Inc., supra, 695 F.2d at 301; *Seaboard Nat. Bank v. Rogers Milk Products Co.,* 21 F.2d 414, 417 (2d Cir. 1927). However, if expenses for the preservation of disposition of property are incurred primarily for the benefit of a creditor holding a security interest in the property, such expenses, properly identified, may be charged against the secured creditor. *Matter of Trim–X, Inc., supra,* 695 F.2d at 301; *In re Korupp Associates, Inc.,* [8 C.B.C.2d 87] 30 B.R. 659, 661 (Bankr. D. Me. 1983). Appellees had the burden of proving that the administration expenses for which they sought recovery were covered by section 506(c). *Id.* They failed to sustain that burden.

We find no merit in appellees' alternative argument that GECC impliedly consented to bearing the costs of their professional services by employing the chapter 11 procedure to effect the disposition of its collateral. *See In re Hotel Associates, Inc.,*[2 C.B.C. 2d 1162] 6 B.R. 108, 113–114 (Bankr. E.D. Pa. 1980). Appellees assert that GECC's active involvement in devising a program aimed at reducing its secured claims justified resorting to the secured assets for payment of the interim fees. Although a secured creditor may consent to bearing the costs of professional fees incurred by a debtor in possession, "such consent is not to be lightly inferred." *In re S & S Indus., Inc.,* [8 C.B.C. 2d 947] 30 B.R. 395, 398 (Bankr. E.D. Mich. 1983). "It is not to be inferred merely because a secured creditor cooperates with the debtor." *Id.; See Law Research Service, Inc. v. Crook,*524 F.2d 301, 310 (2d Cir. 1975). We find no evidence of such consent in appellees' fees applications. Moreover, the existence of consent is negatived by the provisions of the Financing Order.

Saddling unconsenting secured creditors with professional fees, such as are sought by appellees, would discourage those creditors from supporting debtors' reorganization efforts. "To hold that mere cooperation with the debtor exposes a secured creditor to payment of all expenses of administration would . . . make it difficult, if not impossible, to induce new lenders to finance a chapter 11 operation." *In re S & S Indus., Inc., supra,* 30 B.R. at 398. The Financing Order granting GECC a super–priority position was intended to give GECC protection against the very awards made herein. The lack of sufficient unencumbered assets to pay appellees' fees is not an adequate basis for denying GECC its super–priority status. *See Seaboard Nat. Bank v. Roger Milk Products Co., supra,* 21 F.2d at 417. Although it has been well said that "professionals should not be expected to finance the administration of liquidation or reorganization cases," 2 Collier on Bankruptcy ¶ 331.01, at 331–3 (15th ed. 1984), "it does not follow that in the event the estate has no unencumbered funds from which to pay such expenses, the secured creditor becomes obligated to satisfy these obligations." *In re S & S Indus., Inc., supra,* 30 B.R. at 399.

As stated above, GECC, alone, sought a hearing in connection with appellees' fee applications. Appellees have been content to rest on their written submissions. Because those documents do not warrant the allowances made herein, the order of the district court is *reversed.*The district court is instructed to direct the bankruptcy court to disallow payment of appellees' claims from the assets of the estate in which GECC has a security interest covered by the Financing Order.

COMMENT

Subsequently, the bankruptcy court permitted payroll taxes to be paid to the government. Another appeal was taken with the following result.

IN RE FLAGSTAFF FOODSERVICE CORP.

United States Court of Appeals, Second Circuit
762 F.2d 10, 12 C.B.C. 2d 1019 (1985)

VAN GRAAFEILAND, Circuit Judge:

This appeal raises for the second time the question whether the super–priority security interest held by General Electric Credit Corporation (GECC) in all of the assets of the debtors in possession, Flagstaff Foodservice Corporation and its related companies (Flagstaff), may be subordinated to certain administrative expenses. In an earlier opinion, 739 F.2d 73 [10 C.B.C. 2d 1309] (2d Cir. 1984) (referred to hereafter as *Flagstaff I*), we reversed an order authorizing funds subject to GECC's lien to be used in payment of interim fees and disbursements of the attorneys for the debtors in possession and the Committee of Unsecured Creditors. The issue now before us is whether the district court erred in affirming the bankruptcy court's order that payment of outstanding payroll taxes incurred during Flagstaff's attempted reorganization be made either from those same funds or directly by GECC. Because we conclude that the district court did err, we again reverse.

Many of the pertinent facts were discussed in our prior opinion. *See* 739 F.2d at 74–75. As stated in that opinion, a financing order which was issued shortly after Flagstaff filed its chapter 11 petition authorized Flagstaff to borrow additional funds from GECC pursuant to a security agreement annexed to the order. GECC was given a security interest that would cover all present and future property of the estate and would have priority over all existing and future debts of Flagstaff and "all administrative expenses of the kind specified in Sections 503(b) or 507(b) of the Bankruptcy Code." The order further provided that neither Flagstaff nor its successors could apply again for permission to use any property subject to GECC's lien.

Despite this last provision, representatives of Flagstaff informed GECC on September 17, 1981 that Flagstaff would require additional cash to pay various operating expenses, including payroll taxes. Relying upon Flagstaff's cash needs projections, GECC agreed to make certain "overadvances" in addition to the amounts authorized in the original financing order. This "overadvance" agreement was incorporated in an order of the bankruptcy court dated October 29, 1981.

At some time, the exact date being disputed, it became obvious that the reorganization attempt was doomed. In the meantime, however, Flagstaff continued to operate its businesses and incurred an obligation for payroll taxes totalling $290,000 for the last quarter of 1981 and the first quarter of 1982. Apparently, these taxes were not paid because Flagstaff's management mistook the payroll figures in its cash needs projections for those periods to be gross amounts when, in fact, they were net figures. As a result, the amount which GECC agreed to advance was not sufficient to pay the taxes. In September of 1982, Flagstaff's attorneys informed GECC for the first time of the unpaid taxes and asked it to advance additional funds to satisfy the liability. GECC refused.

By this time, all of Flagstaff's pre–petition obligations to GECC, which at the time the petition was filed amounted to approximately $22 million and were secured by collateral worth about $42 million, had been repaid. However, pursuant to the financing arrangements described above, Flagstaff had borrowed another $9 million. By late 1982, "the indebtedness had been reduced to $4 million, but this balance was substantially under–collateralized." 739 F.2d at 76.

In November, 1982, several officers of the debtor, alleging that they might be held personally liable for the unpaid payroll taxes, asked the bankruptcy court to compel GECC to pay the taxes or to allow them to use Flagstaff's encumbered assets to do so. The court refused GECC's request to hold an evidentiary hearing, finding that, while some of the facts were disputed, none of the disputed facts was determinative. In a decision dated April 12, 1983, 29 B.R. 215, the court rejected GECC's argument that the officers lacked standing. It then analyzed the claim under section 506(c) of the Bankruptcy Code, which allows a trustee to "recover from property securing an allowed secured claim the reasonable, necessary costs and expenses of preserving, or disposing of, such property to the extent of any benefit to the holder of such claim." Finding that GECC had benefited from the chapter 11 proceedings or, in the alternative, that it had consented to the payment of all reasonable and necessary expenses of the liquidation, the bankruptcy court granted the relief sought. On April 2, 1984 the district court affirmed.

GECC's first argument for reversal is that the officers lacked standing to bring the motion, because, GECC says, section 506(c) may be invoked only by a trustee or debtor in possession. *See, e.g., Gravel, Shea & Wright v. New England Carpet Co.,* [10 C.B.C. 2d 1265] 38 B.R. 703, 704 (D. Vt. 1983), *aff'd per curiam,* 744 F.2d 16 (2d Cir. 1984); *In re Codesco, Inc.,* [6 C.B.C. 2d 395] 18 B.R. 225, 230 (Bkrtcy. S.D.N.Y. 1982). Since Flagstaff, the debtor in possession, joined in the officers' motion, 29 B.R. at 216, and since reversal is required on other grounds, we need not address this issue.

In concluding that GECC benefited directly from Flagstaff's attempted reorganization and subsequent liquidation, the bankruptcy court found that GECC "received an actual return of millions of dollars." 29 B.R. at 219. It also found that GECC's conduct in allowing the chapter 11 liquidation to proceed and in withdrawing its motion to convert the case to a chapter 7 proceeding demonstrated that GECC found the chapter 11 proceeding beneficial to it. The district court agreed with these findings and added that GECC was collaterally estopped from contesting the court's earlier determination that GECC was the sole beneficiary of the chapter 11 proceedings.

In *Flagstaff I,* however, we rejected this view. We held there that any benefits accruing to GECC from the attempted reorganization were incidental to the reorganization efforts and beyond the scope of section 506(c). 739 F.2d at 76. We also said that

> "it requires rather strained logic to conclude that GECC actually benefited from appellees' services. At the outset of the Chapter 11 proceedings, GECC's $22 million claim against Flagstaff was secured by $42 million in collateral. When the chapter 11 proceedings aborted, the indebtedness had been reduced to $4 million, but this balance was substantially under–collateralized." *Id.*

Appellees contend that the value ascribed to GECC's collateral as of the commencement of the chapter 11 proceedings was based on a going concern valuation of the assets and that Flagstaff's reorganization attempt helped preserve most of this value. Assuming for the argument that this is so, it does not suffice to warrant section 506(c) recovery. The debtor in possession also must show that its funds were expended primarily for the benefit of the creditor and that the creditor directly benefited from the expenditure. *Brookfield Production Credit Ass'n v. Borron,* 738 F.2d 951, 952 [10 C.B.C. 2d 14] (8th Cir. 1984) (quoting the district court's opinion, 36 B.R. 445, 448 (E.D. Mo. 1983)). A debtor does not meet this burden of proof by suggesting possible or hypothetical benefits. *Brookfield Production Credit Ass'n v. Borron, supra,* 36 B.R. at 449. Proof of direct benefits sought and received by GECC is completely lacking in this case. Indeed, appellees never requested an evidentiary hearing for the purpose of tendering such proof.

There is no merit in appellees' contention that GECC impliedly consented to the payment of the disputed payroll taxes when it agreed to make "overadvances" intended to be used in part to pay a limited amount of projected taxes. A secured creditor's consent to the payment of designated expenses limited in amount will not be read as a blanket consent to being charged with additional administrative expenses not included in the consent agreement. *See In re West Post Road Properties Corp.,*44 B.R. 244, 247–48 (Bkrtcy. S.D.N.Y. 1984); *In re Roamer Linen Supply, Inc.,* [9 C.B.C.2d 218] 30 B.R. 932, 836 (Bkrtcy. S.D.N.Y. 1983). Implied consent, as distinguished from actual consent, generally is limited to cases where the creditor has in some way caused the additional expense. *See Matter of Trin–X, Inc.,* 695 F.2D 296, 301 (7th Cir. 1982); *In re AFCO Enterprises, Inc.,* [9 C.B.C.2d 1127] 35 B.R. 512, 517 (Bkrtcy. D. Utah 1983). Neither actual nor implied consent to the payment of unanticipated payroll taxes has been shown to exist in the instant case.

Finally, we reiterate the concern expressed in *Flagstaff I* that rulings such as those made by the lower courts in this case would discourage creditors from supporting debtors' reorganization efforts. 739 F.2d at 77. We are not impressed by appellees' counterargument that a rule other than that adopted below will discourage experienced management "with the ability to turn an ailing company around or who can get the highest return on a secured creditor's collateral." Experienced management would not try to make unauthorized use of a secured creditor's collateral. Congress certainly could not have intended that such collateral be used simply to protect management from the consequences of its own wrongful or negligent acts.

The order of the district court is *reversed*. The matter is *remanded* to that court with instructions to direct the bankruptcy court to disallow payment of the payroll taxes from GECC's collateral and to vacate its order requiring GECC to pay the taxes.

QUESTIONS

In the above decisions, the court speaks of knowledgeable attorneys. In light of the decisions, are professionals retained by debtors in possession and creditors' committees at risk for their compensation? If you are asked to represent a debtor who will become a debtor in possession, how will you react to the above problem? If you are asked to represent a creditors' committee how will you proceed as related to the above problem?

CHAPTER 14

EXECUTORY CONTRACTS

§ 14.01 Introduction

The Supreme Court of the United States long ago permitted a trustee in bankruptcy to discard property of the debtor that would burden the estate during its administration. *See Dushane v. Beall,* 161 U.S. 513 (1896). The Court's doctrine enabled trustees to abandon worthless property of the debtor so as to expedite the liquidation process. The courts eventually permitted trustees to abandon not only burdensome property, but also onerous executory contracts and leases.

The Bankruptcy Code contains significant substantive provisions governing the treatment of executory contracts. In all cases, for example, § 365(a) of the Code permits the trustee to "assume or reject any executory contract or unexpired lease of the debtor," subject to court approval. In a chapter 7 liquidation case, however, executory contracts and unexpired leases of residential real property and personalty will be deemed rejected 60 days after the order for relief, unless assumed by the trustee before then. In other words, if the trustee does not affirmatively assume an executory contract within 60 days (unless extended by the court) of the commencement of a voluntary case (i.e., the order for relief), it will automatically be "deemed rejected" in a chapter 7 liquidation case. 11 U.S.C. § 365(d)(1). Pursuant to § 365(d)(2) such contracts and leases may be assumed or rejected at any time prior to confirmation of a plan, in a case other than chapter 7.

But, under § 365(d)(4), a lease of nonresidential real property is subject to the 60–day rule in all cases and, on rejection, the trustee is required to surrender the property to the lessor. In a chapter 11 case (or chapter 7) what will the routine be if the debtor is lessee of space in a shopping center?

What does "rejection" mean? What is an "executory contract" in the context of the Bankruptcy Code? Rejection is merely a statutory breach of the contract that relates back to the commencement of the case. 11 U.S.C. § 365(g). Although the terms of § 365(a) suggest that an "unexpired lease of the debtor" is an executory contract, the provisions are not limited to real property leases. The Code permits the rejection of any kind of lease or contract, including leases of personal property and equipment, as well as employment and personal service contracts.

Congress intentionally declined to define "executory contract." Accordingly, decisions under the former Bankruptcy Act remain relevant in determining whether a contract is executory for bankruptcy purposes. One court, for example, found unused airline tickets to be executory contracts and required the trustee to affirm or reject them. It noted that neither party (the airline or the debtor–purchaser) had received any benefit or performed any obligation under the contract. In reaching its conclusion, the court found that both parties faced substantial future obligations, and the failure of either to perform would have constituted a material breach. *Northwest Airlines, Inc. v. Klinger (In re Knutson),* 563 F.2d 916, 917–18 (8th Cir. 1977).

Other appellate courts and Congress, in the legislative history accompanying § 365, followed the Eighth Circuit's reasoning in *Northwest Airlines, supra.* In effect, they adopted Professor Countryman's definition of an executory contract as "a contract under which the obligation [sic] of both the debtor and other party to the contract are so far unperformed that the failure of either to complete performance would constitute a material breach excusing the performance of the other." Countryman, *Executory Contracts in Bankruptcy (pt. 1),* 57 Minn. L. Rev. 439, 460 (1973). For the possibility that this definition may not be all–encompassing, *see* 4 Collier Bankruptcy Practice Guide ¶ 68.02.

The Countryman definition is essentially pragmatic. The trustee's rejection or disaffirmance of an executory contract ordinarily gives the other party to the contract a claim for damages that is treated as if it had arisen prior to the commencement of the case. *See* 11 U.S.C. § 502(g). Conversely, the trustee's assumption of an executory contract gives the other contracting party a priority claim for administrative expenses should the trustee later fail to meet outstanding contractual obligations or fail to cure a prepetition default by the debtor. *See* 11 U.S.C. § 365(b)(1).

A claim arising from the rejection of an executory contract is ordinarily treated as a prepetition general unsecured claim. Section 502(g) of the Code provides that such a claim will either be allowed or disallowed "the same as if such claim had arisen before the date of the filing of the petition." Thus, although the trustee's rejection may occur two months after the commencement of the case, it will still be deemed a prepetition claim for purposes of allowance or disallowance.

§ 14.02 Limitations on Rejection and Assumption

The terms of § 365(a) give a trustee the right, subject to the court's approval, to assume or reject an executory contract or unexpired lease of the debtor. The balance of § 365 contains limitations on the trustee's power. Amendments made in 1984 place greater restrictions on the ability to assume and assign shopping center leases. Sections 765 and 766 of the Code, dealing with commodity broker liquidations, will control in the event of any conflict with the terms of § 365. Similarly, utility service contracts are specifically dealt with in § 366.

What limitations exist on the trustee's assuming a contract that has been breached? Despite the existence of a default, the trustee may, under certain conditions, assume an executory contract or lease. Under § 365(b), the trustee must (a) cure or provide "adequate assurance" that the default will be promptly cured; (b) compensate the other party to the contract for any actual pecuniary loss resulting from the default, or provide adequate assurance that it will be promptly done; *and* (c) give "adequate assurance" of future performance under the contract or lease. These conditions precedent, however, do not apply to defaults based upon the breach of an ipso facto or "bankruptcy termination" clause. 11 U.S.C. § 365(b)(2). In a significant departure from prior law, subsections (b)(2) and (e)(1), when read together with (a), make bankruptcy termination clauses unenforceable during the pendency of a bankruptcy case.

What does "adequate assurance" mean? The Code does not define the term. Nevertheless, the court will have to exercise discretion so as to protect the interests of the debtor and the nondebtor contracting party. In fact, Congress urged the courts to be sensitive to the rights of the nondebtor party and make sure that it gets the benefit of its bargain. Will the trustee's granting of an administrative expense priority claim constitute adequate assurance of payment for future services? If you were representing the nondebtor contracting party, such as a real property lessor, what would you insist on to protect your client adequately?

Congress went out of its way to define "adequate assurance" with respect to the trustee's future performance under a real property lease in a shopping center. But it did not define "shopping center." In any event, § 365(b)(3) contains several specific provisions designed to protect the lessor's rights when the debtor–lessee's trustee assumes a shopping center real property lease. To find adequate assurance, the court must be satisfied that (a) the source of rent and other consideration under the lease will be adequate and any assignee is situated similarly to the lessee at the time of entering into the lease; (b) any percentage rent will not decline substantially; (c) assumption or assignment is subject to all terms thereof and will not breach any provision, "such as a radius, location, use, or exclusivity provision," in this or "any other lease, financing agreement, or master agreement relating to such shopping center" ; and that (d) the assumption or assignment will not disrupt any tenant mix or balance in the shopping center. (With respect to breach of provisions and disruption, the word "substantially" was deleted by the 1984 amendments. Why? At whose behest?) Whenever the trustee seeks to assume any contract or lease that is not a shopping center lease, imaginative counsel will try to apply the criteria set forth in § 365(b)(3). Why would a chapter 7 trustee assume the debtor's lease? Section 365(h)(1)(C) was added by the 1994 amendments to give added protection to lessees.

What about personal service contracts? If applicable nonbankruptcy law would excuse the nondebtor party from rendering further performance under an executory contract or lease, § 365(c)(1) prohibits the trustee from assuming that contract or lease. This limitation on the trustee's power of assumption applies only when the nondebtor party's excuse for nonperformance is "independent of any restrictive language in the contract or lease itself." *See Report of the Committee on the Judiciary, Bankruptcy Law Revision,* H.R. Rep. No. 595, 95th Cong., 1st Sess. 348 (1977). What does this statement mean? Of course, the nondebtor party may still consent to the trustee's assumption or assignment.

Perhaps the most common instance of a party's being excused from performance is the socalled "personal service contract." Courts have routinely held, for example, that a trustee in bankruptcy may not assume "personal service contracts." If the debtor were a popular recording artist under contract with a recording company, the trustee could not assume this contract and require the recording company to continue paying under the contract, regardless of the quality of the trustee's voice (for a variation on this theme, *see In re Noonan,* 17 B.R. 793 (Bankr. S.D.N.Y.) *aff'd* No.

82–5011 (2d Cir. April 19, 1982)). In short, if the debtor's unperformed duties are nondelegable under applicable nonbankruptcy law, the nondebtor party may not be required to accept performance by the trustee or by the trustee's assignee, particularly when the contract in question entails a special skill or a trust relationship.

What about a contract to make a loan or extend credit to the debtor? Section 365(c)(2) also prohibits the trustee from assuming or assigning such a contract. In this way, the trustee will not be able to require a lender, for example, to make new loans to the debtor.

§ 14.03   Unenforceability of Certain Contractual Provisions

As previously noted, § 365(e)(1) makes bankruptcy termination clauses unenforceable "at any time after the commencement of the case." This provision is particularly important in reorganization cases, when a debtor could be forced to give up its operating quarters or other premises that are essential to the reorganization. Bankruptcy termination clauses are also generally unenforceable in liquidation cases. Why? In the *W.T. Grant* bankruptcy liquidation case, for example, the debtor occupied store premises under approximately 1200 leases throughout the country. Many of these locations were valuable, and, if assignable, could yield substantial amounts of money for creditors of the estate. Had the bankruptcy termination clauses contained in the vast majority of these leases been enforced, creditors would have been deprived of whatever value existed in these leases.

If bankruptcy termination clauses are not enforceable during the pendency of the case, what about contractual provisions prohibiting or restricting the assignment of a contract or lease? Again, under § 365(f)(1), the trustee will not be prevented from assigning the executory contract to a third party as long as the trustee assumes the contract or lease and gives adequate assurance of future performance by the assignee. 11 U.S.C. § 365(f)(2)(A), (B). To facilitate assignment, § 365(f)(3) also invalidates contractual provisions that permit the nondebtor party to terminate or modify the contract because of an assignment. Is the trustee liable for any defaults by the assignee after the assignment of an assumed contract or lease? *See* 11 U.S.C. § 365(k). Suppose the prospective assignee is a shell corporation?

§ 14.04   Real Property Leases

Perhaps the most common form of executory contract rejection arises when the debtor is the lessee of real property. The Code adopts a policy of limiting lessors' damage claims. Damages arising out of a long term real property lease might give the landlord a claim so large that other general unsecured creditors would not be able to share meaningfully in the assets of the estate. Under §§ 502(b)(7) of the Code, a real property lessor's damage claim resulting from breach of a lease (including rejection) may not exceed the rent reserved by the lease for the greater of (a) one year, *or* (b) 15 percent of the remaining term of the lease, not to exceed three years, *plus* any rent arrears. *See Oldden v. Tonto Realty Corp., infra,* 143 F.2d

916 (2d Cir. 1944). Note that the statutory limitation is not applied to the rent arrears due the landlord, but only to the landlord's damage claim. What is the limitation on damages if the lease covers equipment? An employment contract?

What happens when the debtor is the *lessor* of real property and the trustee rejects the lease? There is no limitation on the nondebtor lessee's damage claim. Under § 365(h)(1)(A), if the trustee of a debtor–lessor rejects an unexpired lease, the lessee may either treat the lease as terminated and vacate the premises, or remain in possession for the balance of the term, including any renewal term enforceable by the lessee under applicable nonbankruptcy law. Should these provisions apply when the debtor is a sublessor?

The nondebtor tenant who remains in possession of the leased premises after rejection of the lease by the debtor–lessor's trustee will be legally obligated to pay, at most, the rental reserved in the lease. Section 365(h)(1)(B) also provides that a tenant "may offset against the rent reserved under such lease for the balance of the term' any damages occurring after rejection as long as such damages are caused by the nonperformance of any obligation of the debtor. Thus, if, as a result of the debtor–lessor's rejection, the tenant is deprived of services required under the lease, such as heat, electricity, elevator service, or garbage removal, it may obtain this service elsewhere and deduct the cost from future rent payments. The right of offset is the tenant's only remedy. Section 365(h)(1)(B) expressly provides that the tenant shall have no other "rights against the estate on account of any damages arising . . . from . . . rejection."

Section 365(d)(10) was added in 1994 to conform the requirements in (d)(3) with respect to leases of real property to leases of personal property (equipment leases). What differences exist between (d)(3) and (d)(10)? Why?

In 1984, §§ 365(d)(3) and 365(d)(4) were amended to give added protection to nondebtor landlords of nonresidential real property. Pursuant to (d)(4), if such a lease is not assumed by the lessee's trustee within 60 days after the order for relief or within any extension granted within that period, the lease is deemed rejected. This automatic rejection is applicable in all cases and was inserted particularly to be applicable in chapter 11 cases. (Why?) Thus, as the Code reads, either the trustee must assume the lease within 60 days or the court must grant an extension within the same 60 days for the trustee to assume or reject. It appears from the Code that if the court does not act within the 60 day period, an extension cannot be granted beyond that time. It also appears that only one extension can be granted since any purported additional one would perforce be granted beyond the 60–day period.

Can the debtor in possession make a meaningful decision within the first 60 days? Suppose it is the operator of a chain or retail stores throughout the United States?

In the first case to interpret §§ 365(d)(4) that went to the court of appeals, the attorney for the debtor in possession filed a motion to extend the time on the 57th day. The court did not, within the last 3 days, hold a hearing and grant the motion. On the basis of the Code, the motion was later denied but the court of appeals reversed. *In re Southwest Aircraft Services, Inc.,* which follows.

IN RE SOUTHWEST AIRCRAFT SERVICES, INC.

United States Court of Appeals, Ninth Circuit
831 F.2d 848, 17 C.B.C.2d 976 (1987)

REINHARDT, Circuit Judge:

We are asked here to resolve a question of first impression in the circuit courts regarding the interpretation of section 365(d)(4) of the Bankruptcy Code. 11 U.S.C. § 365(d)(4) (Supp. 1985).1 The Code permits a debtor in bankruptcy to assume or reject any unexpired lease it may have. *Id.* § 365(a). Under section 365(d)(4), a nonresidential lease is deemed rejected by a debtor–lessee unless that party assumes the lease within 60 days after filing for Chapter 11 protection or within such additional period as is fixed by the bankruptcy court. In the case before us, the debtor–lessee moved, before the initial 60–day period had expired, for an extension of time within which to assume or reject a commercial lease, but the bankruptcy court did not hear the motion until after that period had ended. The court held that the lease was deemed rejected immediately upon the expiration of the sixtieth day, and that it was without authority to grant the timely filed motion for extension. The bankruptcy appellate panel affirmed; we reverse.

I. Facts

Southwest Aircraft Services, Inc., is an aircraft maintenance company located at the Long Beach Airport. Southwest leases its business premises from the City of Long Beach under a long–term lease it assumed in 1976. Several years later, commercial jet flights into the airport increased, and Long Beach leased a vacant parcel adjoining Southwest's to Atlantic Aviation, which built a jet facility on the newly leased property. Evidently the existence of the new facility resulted in a significant increase in the value of Southwest's parcel.

Southwest filed for Chapter 11 relief on April 18, 1985, and received permission to operate its business as debtor–in–possession. It then closed its pre–bankruptcy checking accounts and opened a new one in its new capacity. The March and April 1985 rent checks which were written on an old checking account, were returned to Long Beach unpaid. After filing for Chapter 11 protection, Southwest made no further rent payments to the city.

On June 14, 57 days after filing for Chapter 11, Southwest filed a motion to extend the 60–day deadline for assuming or rejecting its lease with Long Beach. The bankruptcy court did not hear Southwest's motion until July 17, 90 days after the bankruptcy filing, and 30 days after the 60–day period had ended. At the hearing, Southwest tendered checks to Long Beach for all outstanding rent, which the city refused.

While the bankruptcy judge declared that he would be inclined to grant the extension motion, he concluded that he no longer had the authority to do so, ruling that the lease was deemed rejected pursuant to section 365(d)(4) of the Bankruptcy

Code. The court found that in order for a debtor–lessee to obtain an extension of time under that section, not only must that party move for an extension within 60 days of filing for Chapter 11 protection, but the court must hear and grant the motion within that period. *In re Southwest Aircraft Servs., Inc.,* [13 C.B.C.2d 979] 53 Bankr. 805 (Bankr. C.D. Cal. 1985). Under the bankruptcy judge's view, rejection was automatic since the 60–day deadline passed before he had held any hearing or issued any ruling on the motion. The Bankruptcy Appellate Panel affirmed, holding that the language of section 365(d)(4) "is precise and leaves no room for arguing that an extension may be granted or confirmed after 60 days have elapsed." *.In re Southwest Aircraft Servs., Inc.,* [15 C.B.C.2d 1285] 66 Bankr. 121, 123 (Bankr. 9th Cir. 1986). Southwest promptly appealed.

II. Legal Discussion

A.   The Proper Interpretation of Section 365(d)(4)

The interpretation of a statute is a question of law which we review *de novo. e.g., United States v. Roberts,* 747 F.2d 537, 546 (9th Cir. 1984). A court's objective in interpreting a federal statute is to ascertain the intent of Congress and to give effect to its legislative will. *E.g., Philbrook v. Glodgett,* 421 U.S. 707, 713 (1975). The first place a court looks in determining legislative intent is the language of the statute itself. *E.g., United States v. James,* 106 S. Ct. 3116, 3121 (1986); *Blum v. Stenson,* 465 U.S. 886, 896 (1984).

Here, the meaning of the words of section 365(d)(4) is not entirely clear. The section is not plainly susceptible to only one interpretation, and bankruptcy courts are divided on how the statute should be applied. Section 365(d)(4) provides that any unexpired nonresidential lease is deemed rejected unless the debtor–lessee assumes it "within 60 days after the date of the order for relief, *or within such additional time as the court, for cause, within such 60–day period, fixes . . .* " 11 U.S.C. § 365(d)(4) (emphasis added). Under the section, the court's ability to extend the 60–day period is limited by a clause which includes three successive terms: "for cause," "within such 60–day period," and "fixes." It is not entirely clear whether the second term—"within such 60–day period" —modifies the term that precedes it or the term that follows it. If we read it as modifying "fixes," then a bankruptcy court would not under the literal words of the statute have the authority to grant a timely motion to extend after the sixtieth day. That is the interpretation advanced by Long Beach, as well as by some bankruptcy courts in this and other cases. *See In re House of Deals of Broward, Inc.,* 67 Bankr. 23, 24 (Bankr. E.D.N.Y. 1986); *In re Coastal Indus., Inc.,* 58 Bankr. 48, 49 (Bankr. D.N.J. 1986); *In re Taynton Freight Sys., Inc.,* 55 Bankr. 668, 671 (Bankr. M.D. Pa. 1985). If, however, the 60–day term modifies "for cause," then while the cause must arise within 60 days (and implicitly the debtor must file its motion to show cause within that period), there is no express limit on when the bankruptcy court must hear and decide the motion. This more liberal reading of the statute would allow the bankruptcy courts to operate with greater freedom and flexibility. It is the one we adopt.

Several bankruptcy courts have held that the more restrictive interpretation of the statute would lead to arbitrary and fortuitous results and have rejected it for that reason. *See In re Wedtech Corp.,* [17 C.B.C.2d 10] 72 Bankr. 464, 468 (Bankr. S.D.N.Y. 1987); *In re Musikahn Corp.,* [14 C.B.C.2d 314] 57 Bankr. 938, 942 (Bankr. E.D.N.Y. 1986); *In re Unit Portions of Del., Inc.,* [13 C.B.C.2d 706] 53 Bankr. 83, 84 (Bankr. E.D.N.Y. 1985). While we recognize that were we to look only to the face of the statute Long Beach's argument would by far be the stronger one, we cannot say with certainty that it is the only plausible interpretation of section 365(d)(4). There is another possible interpretation of the statutory language, one that permits a more reasonable construction—a construction that is more consistent with the normal concepts that govern the functioning of the judiciary. Thus, we turn to the legislative purpose and history for whatever guidance they may provide. *See, e.g., Blum v. Stenson,* 465 U.S. at 896.

Like the language of section 365(d)(4), the legislative purpose and history of the section do not provide a definitive answer to the question before us; however, they do offer some support for Southwest's view. Before 1984, debtors in Chapter 11 reorganizations had no fixed deadline to assume or reject unexpired leases, although any party could request the court to fix a time limit. 11 U.S.C. § 365(d)(2) (1983). Congress became concerned about the practical consequences of Chapter 11 filings by tenants of shopping centers. It was particularly concerned that mall operators were facing periods of extended vacancies, that would last until such time as the bankruptcy courts would finally decide to take the initiative and force debtors to make a choice whether to assume or reject the leases. It was also concerned about the effects the extended vacancies were having on other tenants. *See* 130 Cong. Rec. S8891, S8894–95 (daily ed. June 29, 1984) (statement of Sen. Hatch), reprinted in 1984 U.S. Code Cong. & Admin. News 590, 598–99.

To address this problem, Congress added two provisions dealing specifically with nonresidential leases in Chapter 11 proceedings. Subsection (d)(3) requires the debtor to perform all lease obligations while deciding whether to assume, but permits the court to delay the debtor's performance during the first 60 days after filing for reorganization. Subsection (d)(4) establishes the 60–day deadline for assumption or rejection, and imposes on the debtor the burden of petitioning the bankruptcy court for a change in the deadline.

According to the legislative history, the so–called Shopping Center Amendments were expressly intended to

> lessen the problems caused by extended vacancies and partial operation of tenant space by requiring that the trustee decide whether to assume or reject nonresidential real property lease [sic] within 60 days after the order for relief in a case under any chapter. This time period could be extended by the court for cause, such as in exceptional cases involving large numbers of leases.

1984 U.S. Code Cong. & Admin. News at 599. This is the sole passage in the legislative history that addresses extensions of time. The second sentence discusses the requirement that the court find "cause" for the extension; there is no reference to any requirement that the bankruptcy judge make his finding within any particular period of time. Congress' emphasis on cause for an extension, and its failure to mention any deadline within which the court must act, is fairly indicative of its intent. Congress was concerned that a properly supported motion for extension, *i.e.,* one for good cause, should be permitted under the provision and not that the bank-ruptcy court should be stripped of its authority to grant an extension if it did not act within a prescribed time period.

We recognize that while the legislative history does not specifically mention that the debtor must file its motion for an extension within 60 days, such a requirement may be fairly implied in the section. It is frequently the case that if an act must be undertaken within a particular time period a request for an extension must be made before that period has expired. Such a rule can hardly be said to be unusual or worthy of special discussion in the legislative history. On the other hand, a rule that forfeits a party's rights, benefits, privileges or opportunities simply because a court fails to act within a particular time period would be quite extraordinary. We think that Congress would not adopt any such rule without clearly indicating in the legislative history its intention to do so and explaining its reasons. *Cf. Logan v. Zimmerman Brush Co.*, 455 U.S. 422 (1982), discussed *infra*, note 6.

We, and other circuits, have previously considered whether to construe another deadline–setting provision in a manner that would deprive a court of jurisdiction to act if it failed to consider a timely filed motion within a prescribed time period. The issue was squarely presented in a series of cases involving the former version of Fed. R. Crim. P. 35 (governing reduction in sentence). One major difference was that Rule 35, unlike section 365(d)(4), was unambiguous. The rule explicitly afforded district courts only 120 days within which to act in order to reduce a sentence. Had the circuit courts given the language of the Rule its literal meaning, we would have been forced to hold that district courts had no jurisdiction to act on pending sentence reduction motions once the 120–day period had expired. However, five of the six circuits that considered the issue refused to do so. This circuit was firmly in the majority. Typical of the circuit courts' reasoning was Chief Judge Haynsworth's analysis in his opinion for the Fourth Circuit:

> We need not give the Rule so literal a reading, however, and we can not assume that such a reading was intended when the consequences would be so devastatingly and arbitrarily fortuitous. For any number of reasons it may be impossible or impractical for a judge to act promptly upon a motion for reduction of sentence filed with the court long before the expiration of the 120 day period.

United States v. Stollings, 516 F.2d 1287, 1288 (4th Cir. 1975).

Similarly here, Long Beach's interpretation of section 365(d)(4) would produce arbitrary and fortuitous results. Under the city's view, a diligent debtor with an unexpired lease oftentimes an asset critical to a successful reorganization who moved for an extension of time immediately upon filing his petition for relief would nevertheless automatically lose the lease if the bankruptcy court failed, for whatever reason, to decide the motion within a 60–day period. Also, a debtor who diligently attempted to determine whether he could prudently assume the lease, and sought an extension only after he had determined that more time was in actuality required, might find his leasehold interest forfeited if the bankruptcy judge took even a minimal amount of time to conduct a hearing and reach a decision. The results in both instances would be manifestly unjust and so might the result here. The bankruptcy judge said that he was inclined to the view that Southwest *had* demonstrated cause for the grant of an extension; yet, under Long Beach's interpretation, the court would be unable to act, Southwest would be deprived of its place of doing business, and Long Beach might well obtain an undeserved windfall.

Bankruptcy courts, like district courts, may have numerous reasons that make it impractical or impossible for them to act within a fairly short time deadline. Construing Congress' action in adopting section 365(d)(4) as an attempt by the legislative branch to force bankruptcy courts to act at an earlier time than they would otherwise deem proper would not only result in hasty, ill–considered decisions by bankruptcy courts but might in addition exacerbate rather than alleviate the judicial backlog problem. Such an interpretation would also encourage debtors to make *pro forma* motions for extension of time before they had a full opportunity to consider whether an extension was necessary–conceivably as soon as the petition for reorganization was filed–simply to minimize the possibility that the vagaries of bankruptcy court scheduling would deny them a timely hearing. *See In re Wedtech Corp.,* [17 C.B.C.2d 10] 72 Bankr. at 470; *In re Musikahn Corp.,* 57 Bankr. at 941–42. Bankruptcy courts would then be burdened with numerous unnecessary show cause hearings. Moreover, extensions would undoubtedly be granted in cases in which, but for the restrictive interpretation of the provision, requests for extensions would not ever have been made. The cumulative effect might well be even greater delays in deciding assumption of lease issues than previously existed. In any event, Long Beach's interpretation would impose an arbitrary and unreasonable restriction on bankruptcy courts as well as work an injustice on many debtors.

Our holdings with respect to former Rule 35 are pertinent here. While in our case, unlike the Rule 35 cases, we need not reject the only possible literal reading of the provision at issue in order to reach a reasonable result, we are nevertheless influenced in our decision by the rule announced almost one hundred years ago by the Supreme Court: "If a literal construction of the words of a statute be absurd, the act must be so construed as to avoid the absurdity." *Church of the Holy Trinity v. United States,* 143 U.S. 457, 460 (1892). This is still good law today. "It is a familiar rule that a thing may be within the letter of the statute and yet not within the statute, because not within its spirit nor within the intention of its makers." *Philbrook v. Glodgett,* 421 U.S. at 714 (quoting *Church of the Holy Trinity, 143 U.S. at 459); See INS v. Cardoza–Fonseca,* 107 S. Ct. at 1213 n.12; *United States v. James,* 106 S. Ct. at 3121, *Consumer Prod. Safety Comm'n v. GTE Sylvania, Inc.,* 447 U.S. at 108.

Long Beach's interpretation of section 365(d)(4) would produce fortuitous and inequitable results. It would also require us to assume that Congress intended to take the most unusual and highly questionable step of interfering with the normal operation of the judicial branch by ordering the termination of jurisdiction over a particular issue whenever a court failed to make a ruling within a brief period. In light of those circumstances, we cannot conclude that the more restrictive interpretation of the section accurately reflects the intent of Congress.

Rather, the interpretation we believe best comports with congressional intent is the one that preserves the authority of the bankruptcy court to rule on timely filed motions. It strikes the balance between creditor protection and debtor relief that Congress intended, and is eminently reasonable, fair and sensible. We fully agree with the bankruptcy courts that have previously adopted that view. *In re Wedtech Corp.*, [17 C.B.C.2d 10] 72 Bankr. at 469–71; *In re Musikahn Corp.*,. 57 Bankr. at 942; *In re Unit Portions of Del., Inc.*, [13 C.B.C.2d 706] 53 Bankr. at 84–85.

For all the above reasons, we hold that if cause for extension arises within the 60–day period and a motion for an extension is made within that period, a bankruptcy court may, even after the 60–day period has expired, consider the debtor's motion and, if it finds there was sufficient cause at the time the motion was filed, grant the requested extension.

B.　The Effect of Violating Section 365(d)(3)

Long Beach makes one other argument beyond its reliance on section 365(d)(4). The city asserts that because Southwest violated section 365(d)(3), by failing to perform its obligations under the lease after filing for Chapter 11 relief, the lease should be deemed rejected as a penalty for the violation. As the bankruptcy court noted, subsection (d)(3) does not expressly state what consequences follow from a debtor's violation of its terms. Only its companion provision, subsection (d)(4), addresses the circumstances in which a debtors' nonresidential lease is deemed rejected–and it does not include any reference to a violation of the earlier subsection. Nothing in either subsection, in any other part of the Bankruptcy Code, or in the legislative history of that Code suggests a reading such as is suggested by the city. Of the two cases Long Beach cites in support of its position, *In re Barrister of Del., Ltd.*, 49 Bankr. 446 (Bankr. D. Del. 1985), and *In re Condominium Admin. Servs.*, 55 Bankr. 792 (Bankr. M.D. Fla. 1985), the former does not hold or even suggest— directly or impliedly—that non–performance under subsection (d)(3) leads to automatic rejection, while the latter does so without citation of authority except for a wholly unsupported reference to "legislative history."

Long Beach's interpretation is a draconian one that, like its view of subsection (d)(4), would serve to deprive the court of the ability to make fair and just evaluations of the circumstances. We believe that Congress intended the bankruptcy courts to have the discretion to consider all of the particular facts and circumstances involved in each bankruptcy case and to decide whether the consequence of a violation of subsection (d)(3) should be forfeiture of the unassumed lease, some other penalty, or no penalty at all. Accordingly, we hold that the failure to make payments under subsection (d)(3) constitutes simply one element to be considered, along with all the other relevant factors, in determining whether cause exists under subsection (d)(4) to extend the 60–day period for assumption or rejection. *See In re Beker Indus. Corp.*, 64 Bankr. 890, 898 (Bankr. S.D.N.Y. 1986). Thus on remand the bankruptcy court shall take Southwest's failure to make rental payments into account when it hears its motion for extension of time. However, at that time, the court should also consider the fact that Southwest tendered its past due rent at the bankruptcy court hearing on the extension motion.

III. Conclusion

Application of our views on the proper interpretation of sections 365(d)(3) and 365(d)(4) to this case is a straightforward matter. The bankruptcy court retains the authority to decide Southwest's motion for an extension of time. We reverse and remand so that the court may hear that motion. Southwest's failure to make proper rental payments does not require that the bankruptcy court deem the lease rejected. That failure should, however, be considered at the hearing, along with all other relevant factors, including Southwest's previous tender of all sums due.

Reversed and remanded.

ANDERSON, Circuit Judge, Dissenting:

In my view, dissents should be sparing. We should strive for open–minded unanimity. In this case, try though I have, it is not possible to make that decision. Respectfully, my disagreement seems to demand a dissent from the majority opinion.

The Bankruptcy Appellate Panel was eminently correct when it observed that the language of section 365(d)(4) "is precise and leaves no room for arguing that an extension may be granted or confirmed after the 60 days has elapsed." *In re Southwest Aircraft Services, Inc.,* 66 Bankr. 121, 123 (Bankr. 9th Cir. 1986).

The majority attempts to find a "possible" ambiguity in order to allow more freedom and flexibility. That ambiguity simply does not exist. The majority ignores the plain meaning and the structure of the pertinent portions of section 365(d)(4). Webster's Third International Dictionary, Unabridged, 1978, defines "within" in several different ways: "on the inside or the inner side," "internally," "inside the bounds of a place or region," and "used as a function word to indicate enclosure or containment." In any definition of the word, in any application, there is not the slightest hint that something within the parameters of containment can also, at the same time, be "without."

The majority complains that 60 days is a short period of time to act and uses that as a reason for creating an exception or extension that clearly was not contemplated by Congress. The assertion is also made that a plain reading renders the section harsh and inequitable.

Sixty days is really not that short. It is six times longer than that fixed to take a criminal appeal. It is twice as long as that fixed for taking a civil appeal. It is one–sixth of a year. Significant and important decisions are often made in those time frames. It may be safely assumed that debtors, their lawyers and accountants are familiar with this time frame and have (or should have) already assessed the pros and cons of accepting or rejecting a nonresidential lease prior to filing a bankruptcy petition so that they may act or advise the trustee.

In my experience, judges at all levels are quick to respond to urgent and emergency situations. An ex parte emergency motion for extension of time is clearly an option open to the debtor or the trustee in this situation. It simply was not done.

While the majority does mention and pay some lip service to the legislative history concerning the problems Congress was addressing, it fails to acknowledge that Congress, as it has the undoubted power to do, was attempting to correct a "harsh" and "inequitable" situation that was perceived as chaotic for lessors of nonresidential properties. The plain and intended meaning of section 365(d)(4) is also supported by this same legislative history. As pointed out by the bankruptcy judge in *In re Bernard,* 69 B.R. 13, 14 (Bankr. Haw. 1986):

> The legislative history of § 365(d)(4) shows that it was the result of heavy lobbying by the [sic] lessors. Previous to the enactment of the 1984 statute, the lessors were often frustrated by the long delay in regaining possession of their property from the debtors–lessees. As a result, many leased premises were often–times left vacant while the debtors–lessees delayed in determining whether to assume or reject a lease.

The purpose of the section was clearly intended to provide protection to lessors by requiring the trustee or debtor in possession to make prompt decisions (if not already made) to either assume, reject, or to file to extend the period in which the debtor or trustee must do one or the other. The majority decision is unsupported and unsupportable. "The Court would truly be gazing with a jaundiced eye were it to perceive some ambiguity within § 365(d)(4)." *In re Coastal Industries, Inc.,* [15 C.B.C.2d 435] 58 B.R. 48, 50 (Bankr. D.N.J. 1986).

It may be trite, but underlying most trite expressions there is a vast well of human experience. Harshness or inequity is all too often in the mind and eye of the beholder. Or, as my livestockman grandfather used to say, "It just depends on whose ox is being gored!"

This statute clearly and positively demands a *fixing* of additional time within the sixty–day time frame, and that requirement was not satisfied.

The majority opinion relies on a line of cases interpreting former Rule 35, Fed. R. Crim. P. Whatever else may be said for that line of authority as support for the majority conclusion, it should be noted that Congress corrected the problem. That is the avenue of relief to be pursued in this case. Additionally, it is significant to point out that former Rule 35 contained no provision for an extension of time. Section 365(d)(4) does have that safety valve. Research fails to disclose any cases upsetting similar deadline setting rules. This leads me to believe that such judicial determinations are the exception rather than the rule justifying the assertion of a power to do so. As was stated by the Supreme Court in *Crooks v. Harrelson,* 282 U.S. 55, 60 (1930):

> Courts have sometimes exercised a high degree of ingenuity in the effort to find justification for wrenching from the words of a statute a meaning which literally they did not bear in order to escape consequences thought to be absurd or to entail great hardship. But an application of the principle so nearly approaches the boundary between the exercise of the judicial power and that of the legislative power as to call rather for great caution and circumspection in order to avoid usurpation of the latter. [cite omitted]. It is not enough merely that hard and objectionable or absurd consequences, which probably were not within the contemplation of the framers, are produced by an act of legislation. Laws enacted with good intention, when put to the test, frequently, and to the surprise of the law maker himself, turn out to be mischievous, absurd or

otherwise objectionable. But in such case the remedy lies with the law making authority, and not with the courts.

The reasons were sufficient to persuade Congress to act. We do not sit to second–guess the wisdom of their choices and "the course Congress has set." *Heckler v. Turner*, 470 U.S. 184, 212 (1985).

We should affirm the Bankruptcy Appellate Panel. In my view, the majority opinion leads to unprincipled decision making.

NOTES AND QUESTIONS

The court states that "the meaning of the words in section 365(d)(4) is not entirely clear." What is unclear? Does the fact that bankruptcy courts are divided necessarily mean that there is more than one possible interpretation, or can it mean that some courts are plainly wrong? Is the statute directed at making the bankruptcy judge act in a short time or is it directed at the lawyers to file their motions in sufficient time for the judge to hold a hearing and rule?

Does the subsection permit successive extensions of time? If the motion has to be filed in the first 60 days, a second extension is not possible. But see *In re Channel Home Centers, Inc.*, 989 F.2d 682 (1993):

> "We agree that a strictly literal reading of the words of the statute leads to these results [once the 60–day period ends, no further extension may be granted], but we do not believe that *we are bound to accept such an interpretation in this case.. . .* [Emphasis added.] The statutory language certainly does not prohibit such extensions in so many words; yet it would have been easy for Congress to do so had that been its intent.. . . Section 365(d)(4) simply neglected to address the question of second extensions.

> "*Moreover, even unambiguous statutory language need not be followed in those rare cases* [in which] the literal application of a statute will produce a result demonstrably at odds with the intentions of its drafters' [citing cases]."

If the unambiguous language of the statute can be changed by the judiciary rather than by Congress, how does the lawyer counsel a client? What is the effect on the predictability of commercial transactions, or other transactions? Would the Third Circuit be willing to grant declaratory relief whenever a transaction was being structured? In accord with *Channel Home* are *Matter of Healthcare Management, Inc.*, 900 F.2d 827 (5th Cir. 1990)(second extension may be granted if motion is made within first extended period); *In re Victoria Station, Inc.*, 875 F.2d 1380 (9th Cir. 1989)(same). Another analysis is contained in *In re Horwitz*, 167 B.R. 237 (Bankr. W.D. Okla. 1994).

§ 14.05　Rejection of Executory Contracts for the Sale of Real Property by the Debtor

The Code protects persons who, prepetition, enter into contracts to purchase real property from the debtor. Under § 365(i)(1), if the trustee rejects an executory contract for the sale of real property, a purchaser in possession of the property may either treat the contract as terminated or, alternatively, remain in possession. If the purchaser does remain in possession, it must make all payments due under the contract, but may offset damages that occur after rejection. The offset remedy is exclusive; the purchaser has no other rights based on post–rejection damages. Although the trustee must deliver title to the purchaser under the terms of the contract, the trustee is relieved of all the contractual obligations.

A purchaser of a debtor's real property who is *not* in possession, or a purchaser in possession who elects to treat the rejected contract as terminated, will not be entitled to specific performance from the trustee. 11 U.S.C. § 365(g). Rather, the purchaser's remedy is limited to its acquiring a lien on the real property to secure any portion of the purchase price already paid. As a practical matter, this means that if the purchaser has made a down payment, it has a lien against the real property for that amount. Although the trustee may transfer the property to a third person, the transfer will be subject to the prior purchaser's lien.

Since 1984, purchasers of timeshare interests under timeshare plans are treated similarly to lessees and purchasers. Are they the same? What is their legal interest?

PROBLEMS

1. Your client operates a number of commercial office buildings in New York City. Each building is operated as a separate corporation, with separate books and records, and with all of the corporate formalities observed. The client tells you that it operates a building located at 40th Street and Broadway, and that the building is in the name of a wholly owned corporation known as 1430 Equities, Inc. One tenant ("Lovelace") occupies 43 percent of the building under a 10–year lease that will expire in six months. Lovelace has a renewal option for another 10 years as long as (a) the original lease is "in full force and effect" on the expiration of the original term, (b) the tenant is not then "in default," and (c) the tenant gives advance written notice of its intention to exercise the option. Lovelace has given the required notice, and there are presently no defaults in the lease.

   The lease with Lovelace is very advantageous to it, but is disadvantageous to your client. For example, the lease contains no escalation charges for an increase in real estate taxes, operating costs, and expenses. To make matters even worse, the current lease rental is $3 per square foot, at a time when the average market rental for similar space is $10 per square foot. Even worse, the renewal option will permit the tenant to occupy the same space at $2 a square foot for the next 10 years. The client comes to you and reports that 1430 Equities, Inc. is now solvent, but will soon be insolvent because of ongoing losses. The client asks you whether 1430 Equities, Inc. should seek relief under the Bankruptcy Code, and tells you that another bankruptcy lawyer has recommended that the corporation file a petition for reorganization relief under chapter 11. Is bankruptcy relief appropriate? If so, would you recommend chapter 11 or chapter 7? Why? Can the lease be rejected? Under what circumstances? What are the practical problems for the debtor–lessor and the nondebtor–lessee upon rejection? *See In re 1430 Equities Inc.,* 4 B.C.D. 806 (S.D.N.Y. 1978).

2. Nemo Real Estate owns a shopping center in downtown Detroit, Michigan. The "anchor" tenant is Interstate Drygoods, Inc., which occupies store premises of 100,000 square feet, pursuant to a 25–year lease, dated January 1, 1988. The lease contains a damage clause providing for a complete indemnity by Interstate against losses arising out of a subsequent breach: if Interstate breaches the lease, it will be required to compensate Nemo for all damages it sustains, including the difference between the rental provided for under the lease and any rental that Nemo may obtain from another tenant. The lease also requires Interstate to indemnify Nemo against the cost of all "alterations and necessary repairs" incurred by Nemo in obtaining a new tenant. The monthly rental is $8,333 per month, or $100,000 per year, for the entire 25–year lease term.

Interstate filed a chapter 7 petition on January 1, 1993. At that time, it had already owed Interstate two months' rent. The trustee in bankruptcy occupies the store premises for the next three months (January, February, and March) for the purpose of selling off the debtor's inventory, but does not surrender possession of the premises to Nemo until May 1, 1993.

Nemo conducted an intensive search for a new tenant for the entire store premises. It finally obtains a supermarket to occupy the space on June 1, 1993, but, as a condition of the new lease, must "alter" the space to convert it to a supermarket. The cost of this conversion work is $750,000. The new supermarket tenant agrees to pay Nemo the same rental when the premises are suitable for occupancy, which is January 1, 1994, one year after Interstate filed its bankruptcy petition.

Nemo filed a claim against the Interstate estate. It seeks the prepetition rental arrears of approximately $16,000; damages for breach of its lease; reimbursement of the cost of altering the premises for the new tenant; and reimbursement for the trustee's use and occupancy of the premises.

Nemo retains you to represent its interests. Advise it as to the most effective manner in which to assert its claim, and discuss the potential legal problems. What portion of the claim, if any, is entitled to priority? Why? What limitation, if any, exists on the allowability of the claim under the Bankruptcy Code? To what extent must you refer to applicable nonbankruptcy law? Was the lease rejected on the basis of the facts given? Explain. What difference, if any, would there be in your answers to the foregoing questions if Nemo had a $25,000 security deposit?

REFERENCES

Cook, *Judicial Standards for Rejection of Executory Contracts in Bankruptcy Code Reorganization Cases,* 1980 Ann. Survey of American Law 689.

Countryman, *Executory Contracts in Bankruptcy: Part I,* 57 Minn. L. Rev. 439 (1973).

Creedon & Zinman, *Landlord's Bankruptcy: Laissez Les Lessees,* 26 Bus. Law 1391 (1971).

Shanker, *The Treatment of Executory Contracts and Leases in the 1978 Bankruptcy Code,* 25 Prac. Law. 11 (October 15, 1979).

Silverstein, *Rejection of Executory Contracts in Bankruptcy and Reorganization,* 31 U. Chi. L. Rev. 467 (1964).

§ 14.06   Collective Bargaining Agreements

NATIONAL LABOR RELATIONS BOARD v. BILDISCO & BILDISCO

United States Supreme Court
465 U.S. 513, 104 S. Ct. 1188, 79 L. Ed. 2d 482 (1984)

Justice REHNQUIST delivered the opinion of the court.

Two important and related questions are presented by these petitions for certiorari: (1) under what conditions can a Bankruptcy Court permit a debtor–in–possession to reject a collective–bargaining agreement; (2) may the National Labor Relations Board find a debtor–in–possession guilty of an unfair labor practice for unilaterally terminating or modifying a collective–bargaining agreement before rejection of that agreement has been approved by the Bankruptcy Court. We decide that the language "executory contract" in 11 U.S.C. § 365 of the Bankruptcy Code includes within it collective–bargaining agreements subject to the National Labor Relations Act, and that the Bankruptcy Court may approve rejection of such contracts by the debtor–in–possession upon an appropriate showing. We also decide that a debtor–in–possession does not commit an unfair labor practice when, after the filing of a bankruptcy petition but before court–approved rejection of the collective–bargaining agreement, it unilaterally modifies or terminates one or more provisions of the agreement. We therefore affirm the judgment of the Court of Appeals for the Third Circuit in these cases.

I.

A.

On April 14, 1980, respondent Bildisco and Bildisco ("Bildisco"), a New Jersey general partnership in the business of distributing building supplies, filed a voluntary petition in bankruptcy for reorganization under Chapter 11 of the Bankruptcy Code, 11 U.S.C. § 1101 *et seq.*

Bildisco was subsequently authorized by the Bankruptcy Court to operate the business as debtor–in–possession under 11 U.S.C. § 1107.

At the time of the filing of the petition in bankruptcy, approximately 40 to 45 percent of Bildisco's labor force was represented by Local 408 of the International Brotherhood of Teamsters, Chauffeurs, Warehousemen and Helpers of America ("Union"). Bildisco had negotiated a three–year collective–bargaining agreement with the Union that was to expire on April 30, 1982, and which expressly provided that it was binding on the parties and their successors even though bankruptcy should supervene. Beginning in January, 1980, Bildisco failed to meet some of its obligations under the collective–bargaining agreement, including the payment of health and pension benefits and the remittance to the Union of dues collected under the agreement. In May, 1980, Bildisco refused to pay wage increases called for in the collective–bargaining agreement.

In December, 1980, Bildisco requested permission from the Bankruptcy Court, pursuant to 11 U.S.C. § 365(a), to reject the collective–bargaining agreement. At the hearing on Bildisco's request the sole witness was one of Bildisco's general partners, who testified that rejection would save his company approximately $100,000 in 1981. The Union offered no witnesses of its own, but cross–examined the witness for Bildisco. On January 15, 1981, the Bankruptcy Court granted Bildisco permission to reject the collective–bargaining agreement and allowed the Union 30 days in which to file a claim for damages against Bildisco stemming from the rejection of the contract. The District Court upheld the order of the Bankruptcy Court, and the Union appealed to the Court of Appeals for the Third Circuit.

B.

During mid–summer 1980, the Union filed unfair labor practice charges with the National Labor Relations Board ("Board"). The General Counsel of the Board issued a complaint alleging that Bildisco had violated § 8(a)(5) and § 8(a)(1) of the National Labor Relations Act ("NLRA"), 28 U.S.C. § 158(a)(5) and § 158(a)(1), by unilaterally changing the terms of the collective–bargaining agreement, in failing to pay certain contractually mandated fringe benefits and wage increases and to remit dues to the Union. Ultimately the Board found that Bildisco had violated § 8(a)(5) and § 8(a)(1) of the NLRA by unilaterally changing the terms of the collective–bargaining agreement and by refusing to negotiate with the Union. Bildisco was ordered to make the pension, health, and welfare contributions and to remit dues to the Union, all as required under the collective–bargaining agreement. The Board petitioned the Court of Appeals for the Third Circuit to enforce its order.

C.

The Court of Appeals consolidated the Union's appeal and the Board's petition for enforcement of its order. *In re Bildisco,* 682 F.2d 72 (CA3 1982). That court held that a collective–bargaining agreement is an executory contract subject to rejection by a debtor–in–possession under § 365(a) of the Bankruptcy Code. The authority of the debtor–in–possession to seek rejection of the collective–bargaining agreement was not qualified by the restrictions of § 8(d) of the NLRA, which established detailed guidelines for mid–term modification of collective–bargaining agreements, because in the court's view, the debtor–in–possession was a "new entity" not bound by the labor agreement. The Court of Appeals concluded, however, that given the favored status Congress has accorded collective–bargaining agreements, a debtor–in–possession had to meet a more stringent test than the usual business judgment rule to obtain rejection. The Court of Appeals accepted the standard applied by the Court of Appeals for the Second Circuit in *Shopmen's Local Union No. 455 v. Kevin Steel Products, Inc.*, 519 F.2d 698, 707 (CA2 1975), and required the debtor–in–possession to show not only that the collective–bargaining agreement is burdensome to the estate, but also that the equities balance in favor of rejection. The case was remanded to the Bankruptcy Court for reconsideration in light of the standards enunciated.

The Court of Appeals refused to enforce the Board's order, rejecting the Board's conclusion that Bildisco, as debtor–in–possession, was the alter–ego of the pre–petition employer. Under the Bankruptcy Code, a debtor–in–possession was deemed a "new entity" not bound by the debtor's prior collective–bargaining agreement. Because rejection relates back to the filing of a petition, the Court of Appeals held that if Bildisco were permitted to reject the contract, the Board was precluded from premising an unfair labor practice on Bildisco's rejection of the labor contract. The Court of Appeals implied that if the Bankruptcy Court determined that the collective–bargaining agreement should not be rejected, the Board could find a violation of § 8(d) of the NLRA.

We granted certiorari to review the decision of the Court of Appeals because of the apparent conflict between that decision and the decision of the Court of Appeals for the Second Circuit in *Brotherhood of Railway Employees v. REA Express, Inc.*, 523 F.2d 164, *cert. denied*, 423 U.S. 1019 (1975).

II.

Section 365(a) of the Bankruptcy Code, 11 U.S.C. § 365, provides in full:

(a) Except as provided in sections 765 and 766 of this title and in subsections (b), (c), and (d) of this section, the trustee, subject to the court's approval, may assume or reject any executory contract or unexpired lease of the debtor.

This language by its terms includes all executory contracts except those expressly exempted, and it is not disputed by the parties that an unexpired collective–bargaining agreement is an executory contract.

Any inference that collective–bargaining agreements are not included within the general scope of § 365(a) because they differ for some purposes from ordinary contracts, *see John Wiley & Sons, Inc. v. Livingston*, 376 U.S. 543, 550 (1964), is rebutted by the statutory design of § 365(a) and by the language of § 1167 of the Bankruptcy Code. The text of § 365(a) indicates that Congress was concerned about the scope of the debtor–in–possession's power regarding certain types of executory contracts, and purposely drafted § 365(a) to limit the debtor–in–possession's power of rejection or assumption in those circumstances.

Yet none of the express limitations on the debtor–in–possession's general power under § 365(a) apply to collective–bargaining agreements. Section 1167, in turn, expressly exempts collective–bargaining agreements subject to the Railway Labor Act, but grants no similar exemption to agreements subject to the NLRA.

Obviously, Congress knew how to draft an exclusion for collective–bargaining agreements when it wanted to; its failure to do so in this instance indicates that Congress intended that § 365(a) apply to all collective–bargaining agreements covered by the NLRA.

None of the parties to this case dispute the foregoing proposition. But the Board contends that the standard by which the Bankruptcy Court must judge the request of a debtor–in–possession to reject a collective–bargaining contract must be stricter than the traditional "business judgement" standard applied by the courts to authorize rejection of the ordinary executory contract. *See Group of Institutional Investors v. Chicago, Milwaukee, St. Paul & Pacific R. Co.*, 318 U.S. 523, 550 (1943); *see also In re Minges*, 602 F.2d 38, 42 (CA2 1979); *In re Tilco, Inc.*, 558 F.2d 1369, 1372 (CA10 1977). The Union also contends that the debtor–in–possession must comply with the procedural requirements of § 8(d) of the NLRA, or at a minimum, bargain to impasse before it may request the Bankruptcy Court either to assume or to reject the collective–bargaining agreement.

Although there is no indication in § 365 of the Bankruptcy Code that rejection of collective–bargaining agreements should be governed by a standard different from that governing other executory contracts, all of the Courts of Appeals which have considered the matter have concluded that the standard should be a stricter one. *See In re Brada–Miller Freight System, Inc.*, 702 F. 2d 890 (CA11 1983); *In re Bildisco*, 682 F. 2d 72 (CA3 1982); *see also Local Joint Executive Board v. Hotel Circle*, 613 F. 2d 210 (CA9 1980) (rejection under the Bankruptcy Act); *Shopmen's Local Union No. 455 v. Kevin Steel Products, Inc.*, 519 F. 2d 698 (CA2 1975) (same). We agree with these Courts of Appeals that because of the special nature of a collective–bargaining contract, and the consequent "law of the shop" which it creates, *see John Wiley & Sons, supra; United Steelworkers v. Warrior & Gulf Navigation Co.*, 363 U.S. 574, 578–579 (1960), a somewhat stricter standard should govern the decision of the Bankruptcy Court to allow rejection of a collective–bargaining agreement.

The Union and the Board argue that in light of the special nature of rights created by labor contracts, Bildisco should not be permitted to reject the collective–bargaining agreement unless it can demonstrate that its reorganization will fail unless rejection is permitted. This very strict standard was adopted by the Second Circuit in *Brotherhood of Railway and Airline Clerks v. REA Express, Inc.*, 523 F. 2d 164, 167–169 (CA2), *cert. denied*, 423 U.S. 1017 (1975), decided under the former Bankruptcy Act three years before § 365(a) was passed by Congress. Under the canon of statutory construction that Congress is presumed to be aware of judicial interpretations of a statute, the Board argues that Congress should be presumed to have adopted the interpretation of the Second Circuit when it enacted § 365(a). *See Merrill, Lynch, Pierce, Fenner & Smith, Inc. v. Curran*, 456 U.S. 353, 379–382 (1982); *Lorillard v. Pons*, 434 U.S. 575, 580–581 (1978). The Board makes a related argument that Congress was fully aware of the strict standard for rejection established in *REA Express* and approved that standard when enacting § 365(a) of the Bankruptcy Code. In the legislative history accompanying § 82 of the Bankruptcy Act, a provision relating to municipal bankruptcies, the report of the House Committee on the Judiciary referred to *Kevin Steel Products, supra,* and *REA Express, supra,* as authority for the proposition that a stricter showing than the business judgment test was necessary to reject a collective–bargaining agreement. See H. R. Rep. No. 94–686, p. 17–18 (1975). Since Congress made § 365(a) applicable to municipal bankruptcies, *see* 11 U.S.C. § 901(a), the Board argues that this reference to *REA Express* supports an inference that Congress adopted the *REA Express* standard for rejecting collective–bargaining agreements when it enacted § 365(a).

These arguments are wholly unconvincing. Quite simply, *Kevin Steel* and *REA Express* reflect two different formulations of a standard for rejecting collective–bargaining agreements. Congress cannot be presumed to have adopted one standard over the other without some affirmative indication of which it preferred. The reference in the House report to *Kevin Steel* and *REA Express* also cannot be considered a congressional endorsement of the stricter standard imposed on rejection of collective–bargaining agreements by the Second Circuit in *REA Express,* since the report indicates no preference for either formulation. At most, the House report supports only an inference that Congress approved the use of a somewhat higher standard than the business judgment rule when appraising a request to reject a collective–bargaining agreement.

The standard adopted by the Court of Appeals for the Second Circuit in *REA Express* is fundamentally at odds with the policies of flexibility and equity built into Chapter 11 of the Bankruptcy Code. The rights of workers under collective–bargaining agreements are important, but the *REA Express* standard subordinates the multiple, competing considerations underlying a Chapter 11 reorganization to one issue: whether rejection of the collective–bargaining agreement is necessary to prevent the debtor from going into liquidation. The evidentiary burden necessary to meet this stringent standard may not be insurmountable, but it will present difficulties to the debtor–in–possession that will interfere with the reorganization process.

We agree with the Court of Appeals below, and with the Court of Appeals for the Eleventh Circuit in a related case, *In re Brada–Miller Freight System, Inc.,* 702 F. 2d 929 (1983), that the Bankruptcy Court should permit rejection of a collective–bargaining agreement under § 365(a) of the Bankruptcy Code if the debtor can show that the collective–bargaining agreement burdens the estate, and that after careful scrutiny, the equities balance in favor of rejecting the labor contract. The standard which we think Congress intended is a higher one than that of the "business judgment' rule, but a lesser one than that embodied in the *REA Express* opinion of the Court of Appeals for the Second Circuit.

Before acting on a petition to modify or reject a collective–bargaining agreement, however, the Bankruptcy Court should be persuaded that reasonable efforts to negotiate a voluntary modification have been made and are not likely to produce a prompt and satisfactory solution. The NLRA requires no less. Not only is the debtor–in–possession under a duty to bargain with the union under § 8(a)(5) of the

NLRA, 29 U.S.C. § 158(a)(5), *see* post, at 18–19, but the national labor policies of avoiding labor strife and encouraging collective bargaining, *id.,* § 1, 29 U.S.C. § 151, generally require that employers and unions reach their own agreements on terms and conditions of employment free from governmental interference. *See, e.g., Howard Johnson Co. v. Hotel Employees,* 417 U.S. 249 (1974); *NLRB v. Burns Security Services,* 406 U.S. 272, 282–294 (1972). The Bankruptcy Court need step into this process only if the parties' inability to reach an agreement threatens to impede the success of the debtor's reorganization. If the parties are unable to agree, a decision on the rejection of the collective–bargaining agreement may become necessary to the reorganization process. At such a point, action by the Bankruptcy Court is required, while the policies of the Labor Act have been adequately served since reasonable efforts to reach agreement have been made. That court need not determine that the parties have bargained to impasse or make any other determination outside the field of its expertise. *See post,* at 18.

Since the policy of Chapter 11 is to permit successful rehabilitation of debtors, rejection should not be permitted without a finding that that policy would be served by such action. The Bankruptcy Court must make a reasoned finding on the record why it has determined that rejection should be permitted. Determining what would constitute a successful rehabilitation involves balancing the interests of the affected parties—the debtor, creditors, and employees. The Bankruptcy Court must consider the likelihood and consequences of liquidation for the debtor absent rejection, the reduced value of the creditors' claims that would follow from affirmance and the hardship that would impose on them, and the impact of rejection on the employees. In striking the balance, the Bankruptcy Court must consider not only the degree of hardship faced by each party, but also any qualitative differences between the types of hardship each may face.

The Bankruptcy Court is a court of equity, and in making this determination it is in a very real sense balancing the equities, as the Court of Appeals suggested. Nevertheless, the Bankruptcy Court must focus on the ultimate goal of Chapter 11 when considering these equities. The Bankruptcy Code does not authorize free–wheeling consideration of every conceivable equity, but rather only how the equities relate to the success of the reorganization. The Bankruptcy Court's inquiry is of necessity speculative and it must have great latitude to consider any type of evidence relevant to this issue.

III.

The second issue raised by this case is whether the NLRB can find a debtor–in–possession guilty of an unfair labor practice for unilaterally rejecting or modifying a collective–bargaining agreement before formal rejection by the Bankruptcy Court. Much effort has been expended by the parties on the question of whether the debtor is more properly characterized as an "alter ego" or a "successor employer" of the prebankruptcy debtor, as those terms have been used in our labor decisions. *See Howard Johnson Co. v. Detroit Local Joint Executive Board,* 417 U.S. 249, 259 n. 5 (1974); *NLRB v. Burns Security Services, Inc.,* 406 U.S. 272 (1972); *Southport Petroleum Co. v. NLRB,* 315 U.S. 100, 106 (1942). We see no profit in an exhaustive effort to identify which, if either, of these terms represents the closest analogy to the debtor–in–possession. Obviously if the latter were a wholly "new entity,' it would be unnecessary for the Bankruptcy Code to allow it to reject executory contracts, since it would not be bound by such contracts in the first place. For our purposes, it is sensible to view the debtor–in–possession as the same "entity" which existed before the filing of the bankruptcy petition, but empowered by virtue of the Bankruptcy Code to deal with its contracts and property in a manner it could not have done absent the bankruptcy filing.

The fundamental purpose of reorganization is to prevent a debtor from going into liquidation, with an attendant loss of jobs and possible misuse of economic resources. *See* H. R. Rep. No. 95–595, p. 220 (1977). In some cases reorganization may succeed only if new creditors infuse the ailing firm with additional capital. We recognized the desirability of an analogous infusion of capital in *Burns, supra,* at 288; a similarly beneficial recapitalization could be jeopardized if the debtor–in–possession were saddled automatically with the debtor's prior collective–bargaining agreement. Thus, the authority to reject an executory contract is vital to the basic purpose to a Chapter 11 reorganization, because rejection can release the debtor's estate from burdensome obligations that can impede a successful reorganization.

While all parties to this case ultimately concede that the Bankruptcy Court may authorize rejection of a collective–bargaining agreement, the Board and the Union nonetheless insist that a debtor–in–possession violates § 8(a)(5) and § 8(d) of the NLRA if it unilaterally changes the terms of the collective–bargaining agreement between the date of filing the bankruptcy petition and the date on which the Bankruptcy Court authorizes rejection of the agreement.

But acceptance of such a contention would largely, if not completely, undermine whatever benefit the debtor–in–possession otherwise obtains by its authority to request rejection of the agreement. In a Chapter 11 reorganization, debtor–in–possession has until a reorganization plan is confirmed to decide whether to accept or reject an executory contract, although a creditor may request the Bankruptcy Court to make such a determination within a particular time. 11 U.S.C. § 365(d)(2). In contrast, during a Chapter 7 liquidation the trustee has only 60 days from the order for relief in which to decide whether to accept or reject an executory contract. 11 U.S.C. § 365(d)(1). It seems to us that this difference between the two types of proceedings reflects the considered judgment of Congress that a debtor–in–possession seeking to reorganize should be granted more latitude in deciding whether to reject a contract than should a trustee in liquidation.

Under the Bankruptcy Code proof of claims must be presented to the Bankruptcy Court for administration, or be lost when a plan of reorganization is confirmed. *See* 11 U.S.C. § 501, § 502, and § 1141.

Actions on claims that have been or could have been brought before the filing of a bankruptcy petition are, with limited exceptions not relevant here, stayed through the automatic stay provisions of the Bankruptcy Code. 11 U.S.C. § 362(a). The Bankruptcy Code specifies that the rejection of an executory contract which had not been assumed constitutes a breach of the contract which relates back to the date immediately preceding the filing of a petition in bankruptcy. 11 U.S.C. § 365(g)(1).

Consequently, claims arising after filing, such as result from the rejection of an executory contract, must also be presented through the normal administration process by which claims are estimated and classified. *See* 11 U.S.C. § 502(g); *In re Hoe & Co., Inc.,* 508 F. 2d 1126, 1132 (CA2 1974); *Workman v. Harrison,* 282 F. 2d 693, 699 (CA10 1960). Thus suit may not be brought against the debtor–in–possession under the collective–bargaining agreement; recovery may be had only through administration of the claim in bankruptcy.

While the Board insists that § 365(g)(1) deals only with priorities of payment, the implications from the decided cases are that the relation back of contract rejection to the filing of the petition in bankruptcy involves more than just priority of claims.

Damages on the contract that result from the rejection of an executory contract, as noted, must be administered through bankruptcy and receive the priority provided general unsecured creditors. *See* 11 U.S.C. § 502(g), 507. If the debtor–in–possession elects to continue to receive benefits from the other party to an executory contract pending a decision to reject or assume the contract, the debtor–in–possession is obligated to pay for the reasonable value of those services, *Philadelphia Co. v. Dipple,* 312 U.S. 168, 174 (1941), which, depending on the circumstances of a particular contract, may be what is specified in the contract, *see In re Public Ledger,* 161 F. 2d 762, 770–771 (CA3 1947). *See also In re Mammoth Mart, Inc.,* 536 F. 2d 950, 954–955 (CA1 1976). Should the debtor–in–possession elect to assume the executory contract, however, it assumes the contract *cum onere, In re Italian Cook Oil Corp.,* 190 F. 2d 994, 996 (CA3 1951), and the expenses and liabilities incurred may be treated as administrative expenses, which are afforded the highest priority on the debtor's estate, 11 U.S.C. § 503(b)(1)(A).

The necessary result of the foregoing discussion is that the Board is precluded from, in effect, enforcing the contract terms of the collective–bargaining agreement by filing unfair labor practices against the debtor–in–possession for violating § 8(d) of the NLRA. Though the Board's action is nominally one to enforce § 8(d) of that Act, the practical effect of the enforcement action would be to require adherence to the terms of the collective–bargaining agreement. But the filing of the petition in bankruptcy means that the collective–bargaining agreement is no longer immediately enforceable, and may never be enforceable again. Consequently, Board enforcement of a claimed violation of § 8(d) under these circumstances would run directly counter to the express provisions of the Bankruptcy Code and to the Code's overall effort to give a debtor–in–possession some flexibility and breathing space. *See* H. R. Rep. No. 95–595, p. 340 (1977). We conclude that from the filing of a petition in bankruptcy until formal acceptance, the collective–bargaining agreement is not an enforceable contract within the meaning of NLRA § 8(d). *Cf. Allied Chemical Workers, supra,* at 187; *Dowd Box Co. v. Courtney,* 368 U.S. 502, 510–513 (1962).

The Union, but not the Board, also insists that the debtor–in–possession must comply with the mid–term contract modification procedures set forth in § 8(d) of the NLRA, 29 U.S.C. § 158(d). *See ante,* at n. 5. Because the collective–bargaining agreement is not an enforceable contract within the meaning of § 8(d), it follows that the debtor–in–possession need not comply with the provisions of § 8(d) prior to seeking the Bankruptcy Court's permission to reject the agreement.

Section 8(d) applies when contractual obligations are repudiated by the unilateral actions of a party to the collective–bargaining agreement. We have recognized that Congress's central purpose in enacting § 8(d) was to regulate the modification of collective–bargaining agreements and to facilitate agreement in place of economic warfare. *Allied Chemical & Alkali Workers of America, Local Union No. 1 v. Pittsburgh Plate Glass Co.,* 404 U.S. 157, 187 (1971); *see also* H. R. Rep. No. 510, 80th Cong., 1st Sess., p. 34 (1947) (Report of the Conference). In a Chapter 11 case, however, the "modification" in the agreement has been accomplished not by the employer's unilateral action, but rather by operation of law. Since the filing of a petition in bankruptcy under Chapter 11 makes the contract unenforceable, § 8(d) procedures have no application to the employer's unilateral rejection of an already unenforceable contract. Indeed, even the Board concedes that the cumbersome and rigid procedures of § 8(d) need not be imported into bankruptcy proceedings. Brief of NLRB, at 41.

The Union maintains, as a fall–back position, that even if § 8(d) procedures do not apply fully, the debtor–in–possession should be required to "bargain to impasse" prior to seeking rejection from the Bankruptcy Court. We interpret this contention to mean that the debtor–in–possession should not be permitted to seek rejection unless the duty to bargain has been excused because further negotiations would be fruitless, a standard little different from that imposed on all employers subject to the NLRA. *See NLRB v. American National Insurance Co.,* 343 U.S. 395, 404 (1952); *Taft Broadcasting Co.,* 163 N. L. R. B. 475, 478 (1967); *enforced,* 395 F. 2d 622 (CADC 1968). Our rejection of the need for full compliance with § 8(d) procedures of necessity means that any corresponding duty to bargain to impasse under § 8(a)(5) and § 8(d) before seeking rejection must also be subordinated to the exigencies of bankruptcy.

Whether impasse has been reached generally is a judgment call for the Board to make; imposing such a requirement as a condition precedent to rejection of the labor contract will simply divert the Bankruptcy Court from its customary area of expertise into a field in which it presumably has little or none.

Our determination that a debtor–in–possession does not commit an unfair labor practice by failing to comply with § 8(d) prior to formal rejection of the collective–bargaining agreement does undermine the policy of the NLRA, for that policy, as we have noted, is to protect the process of labor negotiations, not to impose particular results on the parties. *See H.K. Porter Co. v. NLRB,* 397 U.S. 99, 105 (1970); *NLRB v. Jones & Laughlin Steel Corp.,* 301 U.S. 1, 45 (1937). Nevertheless, it is important to note that the debtor–in–possession is not relieved of all obligations under the NLRA simply by filing a petition for bankruptcy. A debtor–in–possession is an "employer" within the terms of the NLRA, 11 U.S.C. § 152(1) and (2), and is obligated to bargain collectively with the employees' certified representative over the terms of a new contract pending rejection of the existing contract or following formal approval of rejection by the Bankruptcy Court. *See NLRB v. Burns Security Services, Inc.,* 406 U.S. 272, 281 (1972). But while a debtor–in–possession remains obligated to bargain in good faith under NLRA § 8(a)(5) over the terms and conditions of a possible new contract, it is not guilty of an unfair labor practice by unilaterally breaching a collective–bargaining agreement before formal Bankruptcy Court action.

Accordingly, the judgment of the Court of Appeals is

Affirmed.

Justice BRENNAN, with whom Justice WHITE, Justice MARSHALL, and Justice BLACKMUN join, concurring in part and dissenting in part.

The Court holds that under § 365 of the Bankruptcy Code, a Bankruptcy Court should permit a debtor in possession to reject a collective–bargaining agreement upon a showing that the agreement "burdens the estate, and that after careful scrutiny, the equities balance in favor of rejecting the labor contract." *Ante,* at 11. This test properly accommodates the policies of the National Labor Relations Act (NLRA) and the Bankruptcy Code, and I therefore join Parts I and II of the Court's opinion. But I cannot agree with the Court's holding in Part III that a debtor in possession does not commit an unfair labor practice if he unilaterally alters the terms of an existing collective–bargaining agreement after a bankruptcy petition has been filed, but before a Bankruptcy Court has authorized the rejection of that agreement. *Ante,* at 17. In so holding, the Court has completely ignored important policies that underlie the NLRA, as well as Parts I and II of its own opinion.

I.

Two sections of the NLRA govern the alteration of existing collective–bargaining agreements. Section 8(a)(5) makes it an unfair labor practice for an employer "to refuse to bargain collectively with the representatives of his employees." Section 8(d) defines the § 8(a)(5) duty to "bargain collectively" as "the performance of the mutual obligation of the employer and the representative of the employees to meet at reasonable times and confer in good faith with respect to wages, hours, and other terms and conditions of employment." When a collective–bargaining agreement is "in effect," § 8(d) adds four additional requirements to the duty to bargain collectively: "no party to [a collective–bargaining contract] shall terminate or modify such contract unless' he (1) provides the other party to the contract with timely written notice of the proposed modification, (2) "offers to meet and confer with the other party," (3) provides timely notice to the Federal Mediation and Conciliation Service and any similar state agencies, and (4) "continues in full force and effect all the terms and conditions of the existing contract for a period of sixty days after such notice is given or until the expiration date of such contract, whichever occurs later." Because § 8(d) defines the duty to bargain collectively that is imposed by § 8(a)(5), an employer who terminates or modifies a collective–bargaining agreement without complying with the requirements of § 8(d) violates § 8(a)(5). *See National Labor Relations Board v. Lion Oil Co.,* 352 U.S. 282, 285 (1956) (employer who violates § 8(d)(4) violates § 8(a)(5)). A unilateral modification of an existing collective–bargaining agreement is, therefore, a violation of § 8(d) and § 8(a)(5). *See Allied Chemical Workers v. Pittsburgh Plate Glass Co.,* 404 U.S. 157, 159, 185 (1971); *Lion Oil, supra,* at 285.

In this case, the National Labor Relations Board (Board) held that Bildisco had violated § 8(a)(5) of the NLRA by unilaterally altering the terms of its collective–bargaining agreement with Local 408 of the International Brotherhood of Teamsters, Chauffeurs, Warehousemen, and Helpers of America. Specifically, the Board found that Bildisco violated the terms of that agreement by its failure to (1) increase wages, (2) make pension, health, and welfare contributions, (3) remit dues to the union that were withheld from employees' wages, and (4) pay vacation benefits. Some of these activities occurred after Bildisco filed a voluntary petition in bankruptcy under Chapter 11 of the Bankruptcy Code, 11 U.S.C. § 1101 *et seq*, but before the Bankruptcy Court authorized Bildisco to reject its agreement with Local 408. During this period, Bildisco was operating its business as a debtor in possession. This aspect of the case, therefore, presents the question whether a debtor in possession violates § 8(d) and, as a result, § 8(a)(5) if he unilaterally modifies the terms of a collective–bargaining agreement in the interim between the filing of a bankruptcy petition and the rejection of that agreement.

II.

The Court today rejects the Board's finding that Bildisco's unilateral modifications of its collective–bargaining agreement violated § 8(a)(5). The Court supports this conclusion by asserting that enforcement of § 8(d) in the post–filing period "would run directly counter to the express provisions of the Bankruptcy Code." *Ante*, at 17. Yet, the Court points to no provision of that Code that purports to render § 8(d) inapplicable, and to no provision of the NLRA that would preclude the application of § 8(d). Indeed, the Court concedes that a debtor in possession generally must comply with the provisions of the NLRA. *Ante*, at 19.

Accordingly, in order to achieve its desired result, the Court is forced to infer from the Bankruptcy Code's general treatment of executory contracts, and from the policies that underlie that treatment, that Congress must have intended the filing of a bankruptcy petition to render § 8(d) inapplicable. *Ante*, at 14–17. The Court observes that during the post–petition period, the nondebtor party to an executory contract may not sue the debtor in possession to enforce the contract terms, *ante*, at 15, but rather can only recover the reasonable value of any benefits conferred on the estate. *Ante*, at 16.

By contrast, "though the Board's action is nominally one to enforce § 8(d) the practical effect of the enforcement action would be to require adherence to the terms of the collective–bargaining agreement." *Ante*, at 17. Because the Court finds that suspending the enforceability of executory contracts serves the goals of providing the debtor in possession with "flexibility and breathing space," the Court concludes that Congress could not have intended § 8(d) to remain applicable once a bankruptcy petition has been filed.

This argument is unpersuasive. However correct the Court may be in its description of the manner in which the Bankruptcy Code treats executory contracts generally and the policies that underlie that treatment, there is an unavoidable conflict between the Code and the NLRA with which the Court has simply failed to grapple. Permitting a debtor in possession unilaterally to alter a collective–bargaining agreement in order to further the goals of the Bankruptcy Code seriously undermines the goals of the NLRA. We thus have the duty to decide the issue before us in a way that accommodates the policies of *both* federal statutes. That cannot properly be done, in the Court's fashion, by concentrating on the Bankruptcy Code alone; under that approach, a holding that § 8(d) is inapplicable once a bankruptcy petition has been filed must obviously follow. One could as easily, and with as little justification, focus on the policies and provisions of the NLRA alone and conclude the Congress must have intended that § 8(d) remain applicable. Rather, it is necessary to examine the policies and provisions of both statutes to answer the question presented to the Court.

The Court's concentration on the Bankruptcy Code and its refusal to accommodate that statute with the NLRA is particularly incongruous since the analysis in Part II of its opinion rests almost exclusively on the recognition that the two statutes must be accommodated. In that Part, the Court concludes that "because of the special nature of a collective–bargaining contract a somewhat stricter standard should govern the decision of the Bankruptcy Court to allow rejection of a collective–bargaining agreement." *Ante,* at 9. Surely, the "special nature of a collective–bargaining contract" must also be considered when determining whether Congress intended a debtor in possession to be able unilaterally to alter its terms. I can only conclude that the Court does not do so because an examination of the policies and provisions of both statutes inexorably leads to the conclusion that Congress did not intend the filing of a bankruptcy petition to affect the applicability of § 8(d), and that, as a result, a debtor in possession commits an unfair labor practice when he unilaterally alters the terms of an existing collective–bargaining agreement after a bankruptcy petition has been filed but prior to rejection of that agreement.

III.

A.

Because the issue in this case centers on the effect of filing a bankruptcy petition on the obligations of a debtor in possession under NLRA § 8(d), it is appropriate to begin by examining whether that provision would apply even in the absence of the countervailing provisions and policies of the Bankruptcy Code. In undertaking this threshold analysis, we must remember that we have previously recognized that § 8(d) must be construed flexibly to effectuate the purposes of the NLRA. *See e.g., NLRB v. Lion Oil Co.,* 352 U.S. 282, 290 (1956); *Mastro Plastics Corp. v. NLRB,* 350 U.S. 270 (1955). As we stated in *Lion Oil,* a construction that does not serve the goals of the statute "is to be avoided unless the words chosen by Congress clearly compel it."

In addition, in resolving this threshold question we must be mindful of the deference to the Board's construction of the NLRA required by our decisions. *See e.g., NLRB v. Ironworkers,* 434 U.S. 335, 350 (1978); *NLRB v. Weingarten, Inc.,* 420 U.S. 251, 267 (1974); *NLRB v. Erie Resistor Corp.,* 373 U.S. 221, 236 (1962). It is the Board's position that filing a bankruptcy petition does not affect the applicability of § 8(d). *See, e.g., ISG Extrusion Toolings, Inc.,* 262 NLRB 114 (1982) (debtor in possession violates § 8(d) by unilaterally altering terms of collective–bargaining agreement); Airport Limousine Service, Inc., 231 NLRB 932

(1977) (receiver violates § 8(d)). Plainly, the Court's position that § 8(d) is inapplicable once a bankruptcy petition has been filed is contrary to the goals of the NLRA, and a careful examination of "the words Congress has chosen" reveals that they do not "clearly compel" this result.

By their terms, the notice and cooling–off requirements of § 8(d) apply when "there is in effect a collective–bargaining contract' and a "party to such contract" seeks to "terminate or modify" it. The Court of Appeals held that § 8(d) was inapplicable because the "debtor–in–possession is [a] new entity created with its own rights and duties, subject to the supervision of the bankruptcy court." 682 F.2d, at 82, quoting *Shopmen's Local Union No. 455 v. Kevin Steel Products, Inc.,* 519 F.2d 698, 704 (CA2 1975). As a result, the Court of Appeals concluded that the debtor in possession is not a "party" to a collective–bargaining agreement within the meaning of § 8(d).

The Court today properly rejects the "new entity" theory, conceding that the debtor in possession is a party within the meaning of § 8(d). *Ante,* at 13. The Court nevertheless reaches an equally unsupportable result by concluding that once a bankruptcy petition has been filed, "the collective–bargaining agreement is not an enforceable contract within the meaning of NLRA § 8(d)." *Ante,* at 17. Of course, the phrase "enforceable contract" does not appear in § 8(d), so the Court's point must be that the collective–bargaining agreement is not "in effect" within the meaning of that section. Surely, the plain language of the statute does not compel this result. Perhaps the Court's omission of any specific reference to this phrase indicates that it agrees that the language is not dispositive. In any event, it is simply incorrect to suggest that the collective–bargaining agreement does not retain sufficient vitality after a bankruptcy petition has been filed to be reasonably termed "in effect" within the meaning of the statute.

Although enforcement of the contract is suspended during the interim period, the contract clearly has other characteristics that render it "in effect" during the interim period. For example, if the debtor in possession assumes the contract, that assumption relates back to the time that the bankruptcy petition was filed. 2 Collier on Bankruptcy ¶ 365.03, at 365–24 (15th ed. 1983). As a result, "any compensation earned by and payable to the employee under the contract" after the petition is filed is a first priority administrative expense. Countryman, *Executory Contracts in Bankruptcy:* Part II, 58 Minn. L. Rev. 479, 484 (1974). *See also* Fogel, *Executory Contracts and Unexpired Leases in The Bankruptcy Code,* 64 Minn. L. Rev. 341, 376 (1980). If the contract is eventually rejected, rejection constitutes a breach effective immediately before the date of the filing of the petition. 11 U.S.C. § 365(g). The employees will have general unsecured claims for damages resulting from that breach. 3 Collier on Bankruptcy, ¶ 502.07, at 502–99 (15th ed. 1983); Note, *The Bankruptcy Law's Effect on Collective Bargaining Agreements,* 81 Colum. L. Rev. 391 (1981). Some of these damages will stem from the employer's obligations under the contract in the post–filing period. Therefore, whether the contract is accepted or rejected, it will support a claim that arises out of the debtor's obligations in the post–petition period.

Additionally, even under the Court's approach, *see ante,* at 16, during the interim between filing and rejection or assumption, the estate will be liable to the employees for the reasonable value of any services they perform. The contract rate frequently will be the measure of the reasonable value of those services. *See, e.g., In re Chase Commissary,* 11 F. Supp. 288 (SDNY 1935) (rental in lease presumed to be reasonable value of use and occupancy); Fogel *supra,* at 370 (generally courts presume lease rentals reasonable). For these reasons, it is inaccurate to say that the collective–bargaining agreement may not reasonably be considered "in effect" for purposes NLRA § 8(d). Other provisions of the NLRA, as well as the policies underlying that statute require that such a contract be considered "in effect."

The definitional sections of the NLRA plainly support the conclusion that Congress did not intend the filing of a bankruptcy petition to affect the applicability of § 8(d). As the Court notes, a debtor in possession is an "employer" within the meaning of the NLRA. *Ante,* at 19. Because § 8(a)(5) imposes the duty to bargain on employers, the Court properly concludes that § 8(a)(5) applies to debtors in possession. *Ibid.* And because definition of the duty to bargain includes the notice and "cooling–off" requirements of § 8(d), *Lion Oil, supra,* 352 U.S., at 285, the logical inference is that Congress intended these restrictions of unilateral alterations to apply to debtors in possession as well. It is most unlikely that Congress intended that the obligation to bargain apply to debtors in possession but not the definition of that duty.

B.

The policies underlying the NLRA in general, and § 8(d) in particular, also strongly support the application of the notice and cooling–off requirements of § 8(d) in this context. As we explained in *First National Maintenance Corp. v. NLRB,* 452 U.S. 666 (1980), "[a] fundamental aim of the National Labor Relations Act is the establishment and maintenance of industrial peace to preserve the flow of interstate commerce. Central to achievement of this purpose is the promotion of collective bargaining as a method of defusing and channelling conflict between labor and management." *Id.,* at 674 (citations omitted). *See also* NLRA § 1, 29 U.S.C. § 152. Because of the central role played by collective bargaining in achieving the goals of the NLRA, "[e]nforcement of the obligation to bargain collectively is crucial to the statutory scheme." *NLRB v. American National Insurance Co.,* 343 U.S. 395, 402 (1951). The notice and cooling–off requirements of § 8(d), which are components of the duty to bargain, are specifically designed to prevent labor strife resulting from unilateral modifications and terminations of collective–bargaining agreements. In *Allied Chemical Workers v. Pittsburgh Plate Glass Co.,* 404 U.S. 157 (1971), we explained that "[t]he purpose of the proscription of unilateral mid–term modifications and terminations in 8(d) cannot be, therefore, simply to assure adherence to contract terms. The conditions for a modification or termination set out in paragraphs (1) through (4) plainly are designed to regulate modifications and terminations so as to facilitate agreement in place of economic warfare. [T]he provision "seeks to bring about the termination and modification of collective–bargaining agreements without interrupting the flow of commerce or the production of goods." *Id.,* at 187, quoting *Mastro Plastics, supra,* at 284.

Plainly, the need to prevent "economic warfare" resulting from unilateral changes in terms and conditions of employment is as great after a bankruptcy petition has been filed as it is prior to that time. I do not think that there is any question that the threat to labor peace stemming from a unilateral modification of a collective–bargaining agreement is as great one day after a bankruptcy petition is filed as it was one day before the petition was filed. We cannot ignore these realities when construing the reach of the NLRA. *Cf. NLRB v. Erie Resistor Corp.*, 373 U.S. 221, 236 (1962) (citing Board's function in applying the "general provisions of the Act to the complexities of industrial life" as a reason to defer to its judgment). Nor can we ignore the judgment of the Board that § 8(d) should remain applicable after a bankruptcy petition has been filed, because that judgment stems from the Board's "special understanding of 'the actualities of industrial relations,' " *NLRB v. Erie Resistor Corp.*, 373 U.S. 221, 236 (1962), quoting *NLRB v. United Steelworkers*, 357 U.S. 357, 362–363 (1962).

The basis for 8(d)'s prohibition against unilateral modifications is a congressional judgment that such modifications would be antithetical to labor peace. As we explained in a somewhat different context in *Fibreboard Paper Products Corp. v. NLRB*, 379 U.S. 203, 211 (1964), "[t]he Act was framed with an awareness that refusals to confer and negotiate had been one of the most prolific causes of industrial strife." Permitting unilateral modifications of collective–bargaining agreements, therefore, seriously undermines policies that lie at the very heart of § 8(d) and the NLRA. In sum, were one to consider only the policies and provisions of the NLRA, there could be no question that Congress intended that § 8(d) remain applicable after a bankruptcy petition has been filed.

C.

When we turn to the relevant provisions and policies of the Bankruptcy Code, we find nothing that alters this conclusion. As I have said, *supra,* at —, the Court is unable to point to any provision of the Bankruptcy Code that by its terms renders § 8(d) inapplicable. Nor does the Court argue that there is anything in the Code that would forbid the debtor in possession from complying with the requirements of § 8(d). The question then is whether application of § 8(d) would so undermine the goals of the Bankruptcy Code that, despite the deleterious effect on the policies of the NLRA, Congress could not have intended that § 8(d) remain applicable once a bankruptcy petition has been filed.

As the Court correctly points out, the primary goal of Chapter 11 is to enable a debtor to restructure his business so as to be able to continue operating. *Ante,* at 13. Unquestionably, the option to reject an executory contract is essential to this goal. But the option to violate a collective–bargaining agreement before it is rejected is scarcely vital to insuring successful reorganization. For if a contract is so burdensome that even temporary adherence will seriously jeopardize the reorganization, the debtor in possession may seek the Bankruptcy Court's permission to reject that contract. Under the test announced by the Court today, his request should be granted. Indeed, because labor unrest is inimical to the prospects for a successful reorganization, and because unilateral modifications of a collective–bargaining agreement will often lead to labor strife, such unilateral modifications may more likely *decrease* the prospects for a successful reorganization.

The Court claims that requiring the debtor in possession to adhere to the terms of a collective–bargaining agreement conflicts with the "Code's overall effort to give the debtor in possession some flexibility and breathing space." *Ante,* at 17. Again the Court does not explain how enforcement of § 8(d) interferes with these policies; but I assume that the Court expects that the financial pressures created by requiring adherence to the collective–bargaining agreement would put pressure on the debtor in possession to reach a rapid and possibly premature judgment about whether to assume or reject a contract. It is apparent, however, that Congress did not believe that providing the debtor in possession with unlimited time to consider his options should outweigh all other considerations. For example, although Chapter 11 permits a debtor in possession to accept or reject a contract "at any time before the confirmation of the plan," the nondebtor party to such a contract is permitted to request that the Court order the debtor in possession to assume or reject the contract within a specified period. 11 U.S.C. § 365(d)(2). Congress thus clearly concluded that, in certain circumstances, the rights of the nondebtor party would outweigh the need of the debtor in possession for unlimited flexibility and breathing space.

More importantly, I do not believe that the pressure to seek early rejection will frequently impede the reorganization process. As noted above, when a collective–bargaining agreement will seriously impede the reorganization, the debtor in possession should be able to obtain permission to reject the agreement. The major danger to the reorganization that stems from premature rejection of collective–bargaining agreements is that the debtor in possession will reject an agreement he would not have rejected upon further deliberation. If that agreement contains terms more favorable than any that he is later able to obtain through renegotiation the reorganization may be impaired. In the case of a collective–bargaining agreement, however, this danger is largely illusory. Because the union members will lose their jobs if the reorganization fails, it is highly likely that the debtor in possession will be able to negotiate a contract that is at least as favorable as the contract that he has rejected. *Cf. First National Maintenance Corp. v. NLRB,* 452 U.S. 666, 681 n. 19 (1980) (noting instances in which unions have aided employers to save failing businesses); New York Times, October 9, 1983, § 3, p. 1, 12 (reporting instances of employees agreeing to wage reductions in response to threatened bankruptcy or plant closings). In addition, because unions have a strong incentive to avoid rejection of contracts, they frequently may be willing to enter into negotiated settlements for the interim period that will at least forestall rejection. Consequently, in many cases, requiring the debtor in possession to adhere to the terms of an existing agreement will not lead to early rejection at all. In sum, because the debtor in possession may apply to the bankruptcy court for rejection of executory contracts, holding § 8(d) applicable to the reorganization period will not seriously undermine the chances for a successful reorganization.

IV.

My conclusion that Congress intended that a debtor in possession adhere to the terms of a collective–bargaining agreement in the post–petition period, when he is free to disregard all other contracts, is supported by our consistent recognition that collective–bargaining agreements are not like other agreements. What Justice Douglas wrote in 1960 remains true today:

> The collective bargaining agreement is more than a contract; it is a generalized code to govern a myriad of cases which the draftsmen cannot wholly anticipate. A collective bargaining agreement is an effort to erect a system of industrial self–government. When most parties enter into contractual relationship, they do so voluntarily, in the sense that there is no real compulsion to deal with one another, as opposed to dealing with other parties. This is not true of the labor agreement. The choice is generally not between entering or refusing to enter into a relationship, for that in all probability preexists the negotiations. Rather, it is between having the relationship governed by an agreed–upon rule of law or leaving each and every matter subject to a temporary resolution dependent solely upon the relative strength, at any given moment, of the contending forces.

United Steelworkers v. Warrior & Gulf Navigation Co., 363 U.S. 574, 578–580 (1960) (citations and footnotes omitted). *See also John Wiley & Sons, Inc. v. Livingston*, 376 U.S. 543, 550 (1963).

The Court's holding that an employer, without committing an unfair labor practice, may disregard the terms of a collective–bargaining agreement after a bankruptcy petition has been filed deprives the parties to the agreement of their "system of industrial government." Without this system, resolution of the parties' disputes will indeed be left to "the relative strength of the contending forces.' *Steelworkers, supra,* at 580. Of course, there is some tension between the policies underlying the Bankruptcy Code and a holding that § 8(d) remains applicable after a bankruptcy petition has been filed. Holding § 8(d) inapplicable in these circumstances, however, strikes at the very heart of the policies underlying that section and the NLRA, and will, I believe, spawn precisely the type of industrial strife that NLRA § 8(d) was designed to avoid. By contrast, I do not think that the prospects for a successful reorganization will be seriously impaired by holding that § 8(d) continues to apply. For this reason, I conclude that filing a bankruptcy petition does not affect the applicability of § 8(d), and that, as a result, a debtor in possession who unilaterally alters the terms of a collective–bargaining agreement commits an unfair labor practice.

IN RE MAXWELL NEWSPAPERS, INC.

United States Court of Appeals, Second Circuit
981 F.2d 85, 28 C.B.C.2d 352 (1992)

CARDAMONE, Circuit Judge:

This appeal is part of the final acts in a drama—whose denouement is unknown—that will determine whether the Daily News, one of New York City's four venerable newspapers, survives. Nearly 20 years ago the typesetters' union, faced with the reality that technological advances necessary for the continued viability of a modern newspaper had made their skilled craft obsolete, consented to automation. In return, the typesetters obtained a guarantee of lifetime employment.

That July 1974 guarantee was provided for in a collective bargaining agreement and assumed by the Daily News, now a debtor in bankruptcy reorganization. It is at the heart of the litigation before us. As a debtor the newspaper is awash in red ink, having lost over $100 million in the past ten years. It has asked the bankruptcy court to modify the labor contract by eliminating the lifetime guarantees given its 167 typesetters. The typographers' union asks us what such guarantees mean, if they are not honored. All but 15 of these employees, under the debtor's proposal, will lose their jobs over time. To this question there is no convincing answer except perhaps that nothing is forever today.

The circumstances confronting the debtor and the printers are like those facing a Navy ship torpedoed at sea. Drastic damage control instituted at the site seals off that portion of the vessel, with a disproportionate loss of those ill–fated to be in that section. These measures are necessary so that the ship and its remaining crew might survive. The present debtor, like the ship, is in danger of foundering, eliminating not only the typesetters' jobs, but also costing the 1850 other employees their livelihoods as well. Modification of the collective bargaining agreement, like naval damage control, is not something good or pleasing to contemplate, but without it this newspaper will sink.

The New York Typographical Union No. 6 (Local No. 6 or union) and Maxwell Newspapers, Inc., doing business as the Daily News (debtor or Maxwell) cross–appeal from an order of the United States District Court for the Southern District of New York (McKenna, J.), which affirmed in part and reversed in part an order of the Southern District Bankruptcy Court (Brozman, J.). Maxwell is the debtor in a bankruptcy proceeding where a buyer of the newspaper is sought, and Mortimer Zuckerman is the prospective buyer. After filing these appeals on December 10, 1992, the parties moved to consolidate and expedite them so that they could be heard and decided before December 31, 1992 when the issues, if still unresolved, will be rendered moot. On Tuesday, December 15 the motion to consolidate and expedite was granted and the appeals were heard on Thursday, December 17, 1992.

Background

A. Overview of Negotiations

This procedurally complex case arises from the effort by the debtor Maxwell to find a buyer for the Daily News with sufficient resources to satisfy not only its creditors and its employees, but also to modernize the Daily News' printing plant so that it can compete in the New York metropolitan market. In September 1992 Mortimer Zuckerman—through his affiliate New DN Company—entered negotiations with the Daily News to buy its assets. These negotiations included a so–called "stand–alone plan of reorganization" that was conditioned on union support. One crucial component of the plan was concessions by Local No. 6 with respect to the

July 28, 1974 collective bargaining agreement that guaranteed the printers lifetime employment.

On October 1, 1992 the debtor, in tandem with Zuckerman, proposed to the union that the collective bargaining agreement be modified to eliminate: (1) any obligation of Maxwell to require the purchaser of the assets of the Daily News to employ any member of the union, (2) any obligation of Maxwell to continue to employ any member of the union if Maxwell ceases publication or ceases publication and sells the Daily News pursuant to the bankruptcy proceeding, and (3) any obligation to arbitrate any controversy regarding these matters. Maxwell also provided documentation of the impact of the union's collective bargaining agreement on the financial stability of the Daily News and asserted that it had sought in vain prospective purchasers who would honor the labor agreement.

The union made a counter–proposal on October 14 in which it expressed a willingness to forego the lifetime job guarantees. The union proposed a progressive reduction in the number of shifts worked conditioned upon a cash buyout for each union member, three years' contribution to the pension and welfare funds, and an early retirement enhancement. The parties bargained in terms of shifts rather than jobs. Five shifts per week equals one full–time job; 200 shifts equal 40 full–time jobs. The full–time jobs of the 167 members of Local No. 6 are represented by 835 shifts. The progressive reduction proposed by the union began with an immediate reduction from 835 shifts to 540, then to 425 in 1996, to 300 in 1999, and to 200 in 2002. Translated into jobs that is 108, 85, 60 and finally 40. The initial cut to 540 shifts was designed to induce union members age 62 or older to retire. Although not acceptable to the debtor, Maxwell found this a constructive approach.

The next day, October 15, Maxwell responded with a proposal that hastened the reduction in shifts. The debtor's proposed modification contemplated an immediate cut to 400, a reduction to 300 once a proposed new color printing plant was operational, and then in one year intervals reductions to 250, to 200, and finally to 150. Translated into jobs that is 80, 60, 50, 40 and finally 30. Maxwell's proposal did not provide for any cash buyout or payment to the pension and welfare funds, but it offered an early retirement subsidy that would take the form of adding five years to the age at retirement and five years to the working time at the Daily News (referred to as $5+5$). On October 19, the union made a counter–proposal that stood firm on the first shift reduction remaining at 540 (or 108 jobs) but accelerated the dates and times of all later reductions down to 200 shifts (40 jobs). It agreed tentatively to Maxwell and Zuckerman's "$5+5$" proposal. It did not address the other changes, awaiting resolution of differences on guaranteed shifts, buyouts, and the publisher's jurisdiction over work assignments.

Negotiations continued on October 21 when the union revised its October 19 offer by dropping the buyout, increasing the "$5+5$" retirement enhancements to 6 years, that is "$6+6$," adding a $10,000 cash payment to retiring employees, and lowering the first shift reduction from 540 to 500 (from 108 to 100 jobs) and the second to 350 (70 jobs). The union also demanded a guarantee that remaining employees would receive at least four shifts per week, but then retreated from this demand in the face of Zuckerman's strong opposition.

Late in the evening of that same day, Zuckerman delivered a final proposal reacting to the union's revised offer. Zuckerman's offer reduced the guaranteed shifts immediately to 400 (80 positions), to 300 (60 jobs) when the new printing plant opened, to 150 (30 jobs) one year later, and to 75 (15 jobs) a year after that. These remaining 15 jobs would be guaranteed for the remainder of the 13 year contract. Zuckerman withdrew his "5 + 5" proposal and did not propose any other continued payments to the pension and welfare fund. He did agree to make one immediate contribution of $1 million, which equals 18 months of continuing coverage.

At oral argument before us it was conceded that the total value of the package offered by Zuckerman to Local No. 6 amounts to approximately $30 million, and that Zuckerman has now reinstated its earlier "5 + 5" offer.

B. Prior Judicial Proceedings

These negotiations between the union, the Daily News, and Zuckerman broke down when the union rejected Zuckerman's final offer to modify the collective bargaining agreement. Zuckerman's final offer came on the eve of an October 22, 1992 hearing in bankruptcy court to consider the debtor's motion to reject Local No. 6's contract and to consider whether the sale to Zuckerman should be approved. The bankruptcy court on October 27, 28 and 29, 1992 issued four orders that are the subject of the cross–appeals before us. It (1) granted Maxwell's motion pursuant to 11 U.S.C. § 1113 to reject the union's collective bargaining agreement (rejection order); (2) approved the sale of certain assets that comprise the Daily News as an ongoing business to New DN Company pursuant to 11 U.S.C. § 363 (sale order); (3) denied the union's motion under 11 U.S.C. § 1104(b) for appointment of an examiner (examiner order); and (4) dismissed as moot the union's adversary proceeding to compel arbitration (adversary dismissal order).

The union appealed these four orders to the district court, which on December 3, 1992 affirmed the sale order, the examiner order, and the adversary dismissal order. It reversed the bankruptcy court's rejection order on the ground that under § 1113(c)(2) the union had "good cause" to reject Zuckerman's final offer. The district court held therefore that the Daily News had not satisfied those requirements of the Bankruptcy Code necessary to empower a bankruptcy judge to approve rejection of a collective bargaining agreement. The debtor appeals from this order.

Discussion

I. 11 U.S.C. § 1113

We first analyze whether the union in fact had "good cause" to refuse Zuckerman's final offer. In order to do that we must consider the scope of our review. The district court order is subject to plenary review. *See In re Ionosphere Clubs, Inc.*, 922 F.2d 984, 988 (2d Cir. 1990), cert. denied, 112 S. Ct. 50 (1991). We employ the same standard of review over the district court's holding as it exercised over the bankruptcy court's. In deciding issues involving 11 U.S.C. § 1113, we review conclusions of law *de nova* and findings of fact under a clearly erroneous standard. *See Truck Drivers Local 807 v. Carey Transp., Inc.*, 816 F.2d 82, 88 [16 C.B.C.2d 799] (2d Cir. 1987).

Section 1113 of the Bankruptcy Code "controls the rejection of collective bargaining agreements in Chapter 11 proceedings." *In re Century Brass Prods., Inc.,* 795 F.2d 265, 272 (2d Cir.), cert, denied, 479 U.S. 949 (1986). The statute put in place "safeguards designed to insure that employers did not use Chapter 11 as medicine to rid themselves of corporate indigestion." *Id.* Employers may only propose "those necessary modifications in the employees benefits and protections that are necessary to permit' the effective reorganization of the debtor. § 1113(b)(1)(A). A debtor may sell the assets of the business unencumbered by a collective bargaining agreement if that agreement has been rejected pursuant to § 1113. This statute requires unions to face those changed circumstances that occur when a company becomes insolvent, and it requires all affected parties to compromise in the face of financial hardship. At the same time, § 1113 also imposes requirements on the debtor to prevent it from using bankruptcy as a judicial hammer to break the union. Rejection of a collective bargaining agreement is permitted only if the debtor fulfills the requirements of § 1113(b)(1), the union fails to reject the debtor's proposal with good cause, and the balance of the equities clearly favors rejection. § 1113(c)(1)–(3).

Most importantly, the statute imposes the obligation on the parties to negotiate in good faith. This obligation is properly analyzed under § 1113(c)(2), which permits rejection of a labor agreement only when the union has rejected the debtor's proposal without good cause. *See In re Royal Composing Room, Inc.,* 848 F.2d 345, 349 (2d Cir. 1988), *cert.denied,* 489 U.S. 1078 (1989). The district court believed the bankruptcy court's view of "good cause" under § 1113(c)(2) was too narrow. The bankruptcy court had held that a union would have good cause to refuse an employer's proposal only in two cases: where its members are "unfairly burdened relative to the other parties," and where the employer's "proposal is not necessary for the debtor's reorganization." This interpretation, as the district court noted, makes the "good cause' requirement of § 1113(c)(2) depend entirely upon the satisfaction of the requirements of § 1113(b)(1)(A), which are incorporated into the rejection standard at § 1113(c)(1). This renders "good cause" surplusage because it would add nothing to the existing substantive requirements of § 1113(c)(1) of the statute. *See Carey,* 816 F.2d at 91–92.

The district court reasoned, in addition, that the statute covers not only the contents of an employer's proposed modification of a labor contract, but also how the offer is made. It ruled because the offer was made on October 21—on the eve of the bankruptcy hearing—and on a take–it–or–leave–it basis, the union had no meaningful opportunity to consider and make a counter–proposal.

II. Section 1113 Applied

We turn to apply § 1113 to the instant facts. Here, although the bankruptcy court perhaps took a too narrow view of § 1113(c)(2), its findings of fact under that section were not clearly erroneous. Prompted by the bankruptcy judge's view of the statute, the district court ruled that the bankruptcy court's findings of fact also were erroneous. In this conclusion, the district court erred.

What "good cause" means is difficult to answer in the abstract apart from the moorings of a given case. A more constructive and perhaps more answerable inquiry is why this term is in the statute. We think good cause serves as an incentive to the debtor trying to have its labor contract modified to propose in good faith only those changes necessary to is successful reorganization, while protecting it from the union's refusal to accept the changes without a good reason.

To that end, the entire thrust of § 1113 is to ensure that well–informed and good faith negotiations occur in the market place, not as part of the judicial process. Reorganization procedures are designed to encourage such a negotiated voluntary modification. *See* Joseph L. Cosetti & Stanley A. Kirshenbaum, *Rejecting Collective Bargaining Agreements Under Section 1113 of the Bankruptcy Code—Judicial Precision or Economic Reality?*, 26 Duq. L. Rev. 181, 221 (1987). Knowing that it cannot turn down an employer's proposal without good cause gives the union an incentive to compromise on modifications of the collective bargaining agreement, so as to prevent its complete rejection. Because the employer has the burden of proving its proposals are necessary, the union is protected from an employer whose proposals may be offered in bad faith. *See* Jeffrey W. Berkman, Note, *Nobody Likes Rejection Unless You're a Debtor in Chapter 11: Rejection of Collective Bargaining Agreements Under 11 U.S.C. § 1113*, 34 N.Y.L. Sch. L. Rev. 169, 187–88 (1989).

Thus, for example, a union will not have good cause to reject an employer's proposal that contains *only* those modifications essential for the debtor's reorganization, that is, the union's refusal to accept it will be held to be without good cause. On the other hand, as we have noted, where the union makes compromise proposals during the negotiating process that meet its needs while preserving the debtor's savings, its rejection of the debtor's proposal would be with good cause. *See Royal Composing Room*, 848 F.2d at 349.

Whether or not the bankruptcy court may have misstated the good cause rule, its findings clearly were not wrong. For example, it found the debtor measures its workforce by calculating "full time equivalents" (FTEs) derived from dividing payroll expenses by five, which is the number of days in a week worked by a full–time employee. The bankruptcy judge further found that from September 1990 to August 1992, FTEs for debtor's employees declined as follows: for managers 58 percent, guild members 34 percent, drivers 46 percent, pressmen 47 percent, mailers 45 percent, paperhandlers 54 percent, machinists and electricians 21 percent, engravers and stereotypers 27 percent. In stark contrast, the Local 6 typographers workforce declined only 13 percent, and these employees are by far the highest hourly paid employees of the debtor. No other employees or unions suffered so small an FTE cut as Local No. 6.

Moreover, unsecured creditors, the court observed, are estimated to obtain only 13 to 18 cents on the dollar and the value of stockholders' equity is nearly worthless. Yet, the bankruptcy judge declared, the union did not offer an alternative that focused on the needs of its employer's reorganization, but instead adhered to its position that Local 6's excess employees had to be given an incentive to induce them to leave. Neither the debtor or purchaser could fund this demand. Where there is a plausible view of the evidence, considering the entire record, a factfinder's determination to adopt that view may not be held clearly erroneous. *See Anderson v. City of Bessemer*, 470 U.S. 564, 573–74 (1985).

We reverse the district court's ruling not only on the contents of the rejection order but also concerning the manner in which Zuckerman made his final offer to the union. First, Local No. 6 did not complain that it had too little time to respond to the employer's proposal made on October 21. In addition, parties to collective bargaining agreements routinely negotiate for many hours under imperative deadlines. In that negotiating universe, ten hours is ample time to consider and respond to a proposal. Consequently, the bankruptcy court correctly concluded that Local No. 6 rejected the employer's proposal without good cause.

III.   Other Issues

Local No. 6 appeals from the three orders of the bankruptcy court affirmed by the district court, that is, the sale order, examiner order, and adversary dismissal order. The union raises several issues, none of which have merit. It contends that the debtor has not shown that a collective bargaining agreement may be rejected to serve the interests of a purchaser of assets. The two lower courts believed that 11 U.S.C. § 1113 applied to this transaction because what is to emerge, if the sale is consummated, is the Daily News reorganized as an ongoing business. We agree.

The union also contends that the order approving the sale and finding Zuckerman a good faith purchaser was in error. Section 363 of the Bankruptcy Code provides that a debtor–in–possession may, among other actions, "sell" property of the estate, after notice and a hearing. 11 U.S.C. § 363(b)(1) (1988). In the case at hand, the business reasons for the sale were uncontested, only the purchaser's good faith was put in issue. The bankruptcy court held an in camera hearing on this subject. It authorized the creditors' committee to conduct a confidential examination to determine whether allegations of improprieties in the form of bonuses or other payments to the pressmen's and drivers' unions were well founded. The modest age increase to the pressmen was effected in the normal process of negotiating a new collective bargaining agreement. There were no payments made or promised to be made outside those contained within the four corners of the final collective bargaining agreement, which the creditors' committee examined.

The drivers' union received a first–year bonus based on improvements in returns of newspapers, a matter largely under the drivers' control. The lack of returns results in significant losses annually to the Daily News. In subsequent years, there will be additional bonuses for each percentage of improvement for returns. After consulting labor counsel the committee concluded this kind of payment is proper under a labor contract. Here, too, there were no payments outside the collective bargaining agreement. The creditors' committee therefore supported the sale to Zuckerman because it was assured of the integrity of the sale process. After reading the transcript of this investigation, we are satisfied—as was the bankruptcy court—that the purchaser has acted in good faith in pursuing its offer to buy the Daily News.

The other orders the union appealed from were either well within the bankruptcy court's "broad administrative power" , *In re Lionel Corp.*, 722 F.2d 1063, 1069 [9 C.B.C.2d 941] (2d Cir. 1983); *Accord, In re Chateaugay Corp.*, 973 F.2d 141, 144 (2d Cir. 1992), were fully supported by findings not clearly erroneous, or are now moot.

Conclusion

Having ruled in debtor's favor, we hasten to add that our judgment is conditioned on the continuation of offers recently negotiated between the parties, represented to us in open court at the time of the oral argument, which include the offer of 5 + 5. That is, those offers the debtor made to the union that were on the bargaining table as of December 17, 1992 are not now to be withdrawn.

The judgment appealed from is reversed as to the rejection order, conditioned upon terms consistent with this opinion, and otherwise *affirmed.*

QUESTIONS

1. The 1984 Act amendments added § 1113 to chapter 11 after much wrangling and lobbying between labor (unions) and management (NAM, U.S. Chamber of Commerce). Who won?

2. In 1988, § 1114 was added to provide similar procedures if a trustee attempts to modify medical benefit commitments made to current retirees. Is this sound legislation?

3. The *Bildisco* opinion refers to *In re Minges*, decided by the Second Circuit. In determining whether to assume an executory contract generally, what standard is the trustee expected to use? *See also* discussion of *Minges* in *In re Orion Pictures Corp., infra.* Why is a different standard used when a collective bargaining agreement is the subject of assumption or rejection?

4. Describe briefly the procedure that § 1113 prescribes for the parties to follow when the debtor in possession desires to reject a collective bargaining agreement. What is the status of the agreement until it is assumed or rejected? In this context, what does rejection really contemplate?

5. Under § 1113, may a collective bargaining agreement be rejected unilaterally?

§ 14.07 Executory Contracts Generally

IN RE ORION PICTURES CORP.

United States Court of Appeals, Second Circuit
21 F.3d 24, 30 C.B.C.2d 1819 (1994)

PRATT, Circuit Judge:

This appeal requires us to examine, in the context of a bankruptcy proceeding, the presumptive right of public access to court records and the boundaries of that right. Plaintiff, Video Software Dealers Association ("VSDA"), appeals from a judgment of the United States District Court for the Southern District of New York, Thomas P. Griesa, Chief Judge, that affirmed Bankruptcy Judge Burton R. Lifland's denial of its motion to modify a protective order that had sealed all documents relating to a promotional agreement between the debtor, Orion Pictures Corporation ("Orion"), and McDonald's Corporation ("McDonald's"). For the reasons set forth below, we affirm.

Background

Orion granted McDonald's a license to reproduce, manufacture, distribute, and sell videocassettes of three films, including the extremely popular "Dances With Wolves." Since Orion was in a Chapter 11 reorganization, the parties sought and obtained from the bankruptcy court approval to enter into the transaction. Because the parties agreed that the transaction should remain confidential, Orion moved to seal all documents filed with the court, including the licensing agreement itself. Bankruptcy Judge Lifland granted the motion under 11 U.S.C. § 107(b) of the Bankruptcy Code and Bankruptcy Rule 9018.

After a news release revealed information about the Orion/McDonald's transaction, VSDA, whose members had earlier purchased from Orion approximately 500,000 videocassettes of "Dances With Wolves" at $72 per copy, $64 more per copy than McDonald's was selling them for, moved to unseal the agreement and related documents. On December 18, 1992, the bankruptcy court denied VSDA's motion, finding "that good cause exists to maintain the sealing order." The bankruptcy court noted that

> [d]isclosing the sealed information, including the overall structure, terms and conditions of the McDonald's Agreement, renders very likely a direct and adverse impairment to Orion's ability to negotiate favorable promotion agreements with future customers, thereby giving Orion's competitors an unfair advantage.

In re Orion Pictures Corp., et al., No. 91 B 15635, Memorandum at 7 (Bankr. S.D.N.Y., filed Dec. 18, 1992).

VSDA appealed to the district court, arguing that the bankruptcy court had relied on conclusory allegations that were insufficient to show serious injury to Orion and McDonald's, and that commercial information must rise to the level of a trade secret before it can be protected under § 107(b). The district court affirmed after concluding that: (1) § 107(b)(1) of the Bankruptcy Code creates an exception to the general rule that court records are open for public examination; (2) confidential commercial information does not have to rise to the level of a trade secret in order to be protected under § 107(b)(1); and (3) the bankruptcy court did not abuse its discretion by sealing the confidential materials. VSDA has appealed and we affirm. Because we have not previously been required to interpret § 107(b), we write to explain our view on this problem.

Discussion

A. The Common Law Right of Access

In this country, courts have recognized a strong presumption of public access to court records. *See, e.g., Nixon v. Warner Communications Inc.,* 435 U.S. 589, 597–98

(1978). This preference for public access is rooted in the public's first amendment right to know about the administration of justice. It helps safeguard "the integrity, quality, and respect in our judicial system" , *In re Analytical Sys.*, 83 B.R. 833, 835 (Bankr. N.D. Ga. 1987), and permits the public to "keep a watchful eye on the workings of public agencies." *Nixon*, 435 U.S. at 598.

This policy of open inspection, codified generally in § 107(a) of the Bankruptcy Code, evidences congress's strong desire to preserve the public's right of access to judicial records in bankruptcy proceedings. 11 U.S.C. § 107(a) of the Bankruptcy Code provides

> (a) *Except as provided in subsection* of this section, a paper filed in a case under this title and the dockets of a bankruptcy court are public records and open to examination by an entity at reasonable times without charge.

11 U.S.C. § 107(a) (emphasis added).

In its legislative history congress confirmed its general intent under § 107(a) to keep access open to judicial records. Senate Report No. 989 states that § 107(a)

> makes all papers filed in a bankruptcy case and the dockets of the bankruptcy court public and open to examination at reasonable times without charge.

S. Rep. No. 989, 95th Cong., 2d Sess. 30, *reprinted in* 1978 U.S.C.C.A.N. 5787, 5816.

Moreover, on a purely practical level, the sealing of court records inflicts a costly nuisance on the judicial system. *City of Hartford v. Chase*, 942 F.2d 130, 137 (2d Cir. 1991) (Pratt, J., concurring). Mechanical and logistical problems of sealing the files, finding extra space in the vault, satisfying all the handling requirements, plus the related direct and indirect costs, impose substantial burdens on the clerk's office and on a judge's staff. All these factors argue strongly for open access to court records in the bankruptcy court. *Id.*

B.   Countervailing Interests

Although the right of public access to court records is firmly entrenched and well supported by policy and practical considerations, the right is not absolute. 2 Collier on Bankruptcy ¶ 107.01, at 107-2 (15th ed. 1993). In limited circumstances, courts must deny access to judicial documents–generally where open inspection may be used as a vehicle for improper purposes. *See, e.g., Nixon*, 435 U.S. at 597 (citing to *In re Caswell*, 29 A. 259 (R.I. 1893) (court can insure that its records are not used to promote public scandal through publication of disgusting details of a divorce), and *Schmedding v. May*, 48 N.W. 201, 202 (Mich. 1891) (court refused to permit its records to be used as sources of business information that might harm litigant's competitive standing).

Congress, itself, has recognized that under compelling or extraordinary circumstances, an exception to the general policy of public access is necessary. *See, e.g.,* Fed. R. Crim. P. 6(e)(2) (secrecy of grand jury proceedings); 5 U.S.C. § 552(b)(1) (provision of FOIA that exempts from disclosure material affecting the national defense); Fed. R. Civ. P. 26(c)(5)–(8) (sealing of depositions and restrictions on revealing trade secrets or other confidential information).

Section 107(b) of the Bankruptcy Code, a statutory exception to the broad principle of § 107(a), also responds to this need. Derived from former Bankruptcy Rule 918, it provides in part:

> (b) On request of a party in interest, the bankruptcy court shall, and on the bankruptcy court's own motion, the bankruptcy court may—

>> (1) protect an entity with respect to a trade secret or confidential research, development, or commercial information.

11 U.S.C. § 107(b).

In most cases, a judge must carefully and skeptically review sealing requests to insure that there really is an extraordinary circumstance or compelling need. *Chase,* 942 F.2d at 135–36. In the bankruptcy area, however, congress has established a special rule for trade secrets and confidential research, development, and commercial information. As explained in Senate Report No. 989, § 107(b) "permits the court, on its own motion, and requires the court, on the request of a party in interest, to protect trade secrets, confidential research, development, or commercial information." S. Rep. No. 989, *supra,* ¶ 107.01, at 107–2. Thus, if the information fits any of the specified categories, the court is required to protect a requesting interested party and has no discretion to deny the application. 2 Collier on Bankruptcy, *supra,* ¶ 107.01, at 107–2 ("Protection is mandatory when requested by an [interested party]").

C.   Application to this Case

The bankruptcy court reviewed *in camera* the information that Orion requested be sealed, found that it qualified as confidential commercial information, and therefore ordered the material sealed as required by the mandatory language of § 107(b). The district court reviewed the bankruptcy court record and found that "there is ample support for the Bankruptcy court's findings." *In Re Orion Pictures Corp.,* 1993 U.S. Dist. LEXIS 11734, at *2 (S.D.N.Y. Aug. 25, 1993).

The district court recognized the manifest congressional intent that a paper filed in a case under Title 11 (Bankruptcy), and the dockets of the bankruptcy court, constitute public records and are open to examination by an entity at reasonable times without charge. At the same time, the district court acknowledged that "§ 107(b) of the Bankruptcy Code establishes the exception to the general rule that court documents are open for public inspection." *Id.* Under this exception, Orion, an interested party, had to show only that the information is sought to seal was "confidential" and "commercial" in nature.

Commercial information has been defined as information which would cause "an unfair advantage to competitors by providing them information as to the commercial operations of the debtor." *Ad Hoc Protective Comm. for 10 1/2% Debenture Holders V. Intel Corp. (In Re Intel Corp.),* [6 C.B.C.2d 4] 17 B.R. 942, 944 (Bankr. 9th Cir. 1982). Here, the bankruptcy court properly found, after reviewing the licensing agreement and other relevant material, that "[d]isclosing the sealed information, including the overall structure, terms and conditions of the McDonald's Agreement, renders very likely a direct and adverse impairment to Orion's ability to negotiate favorable promotion agreements * * *, thereby giving Orion's competitors an unfair advantage." *In Re Orioin Pictures Corp.,* No. 91 B 15635, Memorandum at 7.

VSDA argues that the district court misinterpreted § 107(b) by not invoking a principle applied in *United States v. Ibm Corp.,* 67 F. R. D. 40, 46 (S.D.N.Y. 1975)—involving discovery under the Federal Rules of Civil Procedure—that confidential commercial information must rise to the level of a trade secret to be entitled to protection.

VSDA is wrong, however, because § 107(b) is carefully drafted to avoid merging "trade secrets" with "confidential commercial information." By authorizing protection for trade secrets *or* confidential commercial information, *In re Lomas Fin. Corp.,* No. 90–7827, WL 21231 (S.D.N.Y. Feb. 11, 1991); *See also In re Epic Assocs.,* [13 C.B.C.2d 952] 54 B.R. 445, 449–50 (Bankr. E.D. Va. 1985), the statute flatly rejects the very concept that VSDA is advancing.

Similarly, Bankruptcy Rule 9018, the procedural rule related to § 107, provides that the

> court may make any order which justice requires * * * to protect the estate or any entity in respect of a trade secret OR other confidential research, development, or commercial information. Bankruptcy Rule 9018 (1993).

In short, this clear and unambiguous usage of "or" neither equates "trade secret" with "commercial information" nor requires the latter to reflect the same level of confidentiality as the former. Therefore, the district court properly held that courts interpreting § 107(b) need not require that commercial information be the equivalent of a trade secret before protecting such information.

VSDA also claims that Orion did not show good cause for issuing the sealing order. It argues that the standard embodied in Federal Rules of Civil Procedure 26(c)(7)—that a court may issue a protective order for a trade secret or confidential commercial information, only for good cause shown—should apply in bankruptcy court, as well. According to VSDA, good cause was not shown here because the information offered to the district court was already known as a result of other similar transactions in which McDonald's had been involved. VSDA's argument lacks merit. When congress addressed the secrecy problem in § 107(b) of the Bankruptcy Code it imposed no requirement to show "good cause" as a condition to sealing confidential commercial information. This omission is particularly significant because FRCP 26(c), from which the language of § 107(b) appears to have been drawn, expressly required "good cause" to be established before a discovery protective order could be granted–even when the material sought to be protected was "a trade secret or other confidential research, development, or commercial information."

Finally, VSDA argues that McDonald's and Orion waived their claims of confidentiality because they had previously disclosed several of the terms in their agreement in order to rebut VSDA's claim of an antitrust violation. We see no waiver here. Disclosing a limited amount of information in opposition to the motion to unseal the agreement, information designed to rebut VSDA's allegations of misconduct, did not waive the protection of § 107(b) for the other confidential commercial information contained in their agreement and motion papers. *See In re von Bulow*, 828 F.2d 94, 102 (2d Cir. 1987) (attorney's publication of book did not result in waiver of attorney–client privilege as to any undisclosed portions of such communications or as to any other related communications on same subject matter). None of the arguments or cases cited by VSDA undermines the broad protection in bankruptcy proceedings that § 107(b) contemplates for confidential commercial information.

Affirmed.

NOTES AND QUESTIONS

1. Is a motion to assume an executory contract a core or a non–core proceeding?

2. Is a breach of contract action by the debtor a core or a non–core proceedilng?

3. Would the debtor in possession have been better off if it had only filed a motion to assume the contract and sought no other relief? Might this have left Showtime to raise the defense of breach of contract, requiring a cure, if possible, before there could be an assumption? In this posture could the disputed facts be tried by the basnkruptcy court under the guise of a motion to assume?

4. Did the Second Circuit back off from its earlier pronouncement in Ben Cooper, supra, about the bankruptcy court's authority to conduct a jury trial?

GENERAL QUESTIONS

1. If a lease is assumed and subsequently rejected by the debtor in possession, it should be black letter law that the resulting damage claim is entitled to first priority as an expense of administration. *In re Multech Corp.*, 47 B.R. 747 (Bankr. N.D.Ia. 1985); § 365(g)(2). Inexplicably, it was otherwise held in *In re Klein Sleep Products, Inc.*, 173 B.R. 96 (S.D.N.Y. 1994)(no benefit to estate).

2. What is the status of an executory contract before it is assumed or rejected? Is it enforceable by the debtor in possession? Against the debtor? *U.S. on Behalf of Postal Serv. v. Dewey Freight*, 31 F.3d 620 (8th Cir. 1994).

3. General reading: Andrew, *Executory Contracts in Bankruptcy: Understanding "Rejection*, 59 U. Colo. L. Rev. 895 (1988); Westbrook, *A Functional Analysis of Executory Contracts*, 74 Minn. L. Rev. 227 (1989).

IN RE PIONEER FORD SALES, INC.

United States Court of Appeals, First Circuit
729 F.2d 27 (1984)

BREYER, Circuit Judge

The Ford Motor Company appeals a federal district court decision, 30 B.R. 458, allowing a bankrupt Ford dealer (Pioneer Ford Sales, Inc.) to assign its Ford franchise over Ford's objection to a Toyota dealer (Toyota Village, Inc.). The district court decided the case on the basis of a record developed in the bankruptcy court. The bankruptcy court, 26 B.R. 116, had approved the transfer, which ran from Pioneer to Fleet National Bank (Pioneer's principal secured creditor) and then to Toyota Village. Fleet sought authorization for the assignment because Toyota Village will pay $10,000 for the franchise and buy all parts and accessories in Pioneer's inventory at fair market value (about $75,000); if the franchise is not assigned, Ford will buy only some of the parts for between $45,000 and $55,000. Thus, the assignment will increase the value of the estate. Fleet is the appellee here.

The issue that the case raises is the proper application of 11 U.S.C. § 365(c)(1)(A), an exception to a more general provision, 11 U.S.C. § 365(f)(1), that allows a trustee in bankruptcy (or a debtor in possession) to assign many of the debtor's executory contracts even if the contract itself says that it forbids assignment. The exception at issue reads as follows:

> (c) The trustee [or debtor in possession] may not assume or assign an executory contract of the debtor, whether or not such contract prohibits assignment if—

> (1)(A) applicable law excuses [the other party to the contract] from accepting performance from an assignee whether or not [the] contract prohibits assignment.

The words "applicable law" in this section mean "applicable non–bankruptcy law." *See* H. R. Rep. No. 95–595, 95th Cong., 1st Sess. 348 (1977), *reprinted in* [1978] U.S.Code Cong. & Ad. News 5787, 5963, 6304; S.Rep. No. 95–989, 95th Cong., 2d Sess. 59 (1978), reprinted in [1978] U.S.Code Cong. & Ad.News 5787, 5845. Evidently, the theory of this section is to prevent the trustee from assigning (over objection) contracts of the sort that contract law ordinarily makes nonassignable, i.e. contracts that cannot be assigned when the contract itself is silent about assignment. At the same time, by using the words in (1)(A) "whether or not the contract prohibits assignment," the section prevents parties from using contractual language to prevent the trustee from assigning contracts that (when the contract is silent) contract law typically makes assignable. *Id.* Thus, we must look to see whether relevant nonbankruptcy law would allow Ford to veto the assignment of its basic franchise contract whether or not that basic franchise contract itself specifically prohibits assignment.

The nonbankruptcy law to which both sides point us is contained in Rhode Island's "Regulation of Business Practices Among Motor Vehicle Manufacturers, Distributors and Dealers" Act, R.I. Gen.Laws /st 31 5.1 4(C)(7). It states that

[N]o dealer shall have the right to assign the franchise without the consent of the manufacturer, except that such consent shall not be unreasonably withheld.

The statute by its terms allows a manufacturer to veto an assignment where the veto is reasonable but not otherwise. The statute's language also indicates that it applies "whether or not" the franchise contract itself restricts assignment. Thus, the basic question that the case presents is whether Ford's veto was reasonable in terms of the Rhode Island law.

Neither the district court nor the bankruptcy court specifically addressed this question. Their failure apparently arose out of their belief that 11 U.S.C. § 365(c)(1)(A) refers only to traditional personal service contracts. But in our view they were mistaken. The language of the section does not limit its effect to personal service contracts. It refers *generally* to contracts that are not assignable under nonbankruptcy law. State laws typically make contracts for personal services nonassignable (where the contract itself is silent); but they make other sorts of contracts nonassignable as well. *See, e.g.,* N.Y. State Finance Law § 138 (1974) (making certain government contracts unassignable); N.Y. General Municipal Law § 109 (1977) (same); N.C. Gen. Stat. § 147–62 (1978) (same). The legislative history of § 365(c) says nothing about "personal services." To the contrary, it speaks of letters of credit, personal loans, and leases—instances in which assigning a contract may place the other party at a significant disadvantage. The history thereby suggests that (c)(1)(A) has a broader reach.

The source of the "personal services" limitation apparently is a bankruptcy court case, *In re Taylor Manufacturing, Inc.,* 6 B.R. 370 (Bkrtcy. N.D. Ga. 1980), which other bankruptcy courts have followed. The Taylor court wrote that (c)(1)(A) should be interpreted narrowly, in part because it believed that (c)(1)(A) conflicted with another section, (f)(1), which states in relevant part:

Except as provided in subsection (c), notwithstanding a provision in applicable law that prohibits the assignment of [an executory] contract the trustee may assign [it].

As a matter of logic, however, we see no conflict, for (c)(1)(A) refers to state laws that prohibit assignment "whether or not" the contract is silent, while (f)(1) contains no such limitation. Apparently (f)(1) includes state laws that prohibit assignment only when the contract is not silent about assignment; that is to say, state laws that enforce contract provisions prohibiting assignment. *See* 1 Norton, Bankruptcy Law and Practice § 23.14. These state laws are to be ignored. The section specifically excepts (c)(1)(A)'s state laws that forbid assignment even when the contract is silent; they are to be heeded. Regardless, we fail to see why a "conflict" suggests that (c)(1)(A) is limited to "personal services."

The *Taylor* court cites 2 Collier on Bankruptcy § 365.05 and the Commission Report, H.R.Doc. No. 93–137, 93rd Cong., 1st Sess. 199 (1973), in support. Both of these sources speak of personal services. However, they do not say that (c)(1)(A) was intended to be *limited* to personal services. Indeed, since it often is difficult to decide whether or not a particular duty can be characterized by the label "personal service," it makes sense to avoid this question and simply look to see whether state law would, or would not, make the duty assignable where the contract is silent. Thus, the Fifth Circuit has found no reason for limiting the scope of (c)(1)(A) to personal service contracts. *In re Braniff Airways, Inc.,* 700 F.2d 935, 943 (5th Cir.1983). Fleet concedes in its brief that "the exception to assignment [of § 365(c)(1)(A)] is not limited to personal services contracts." We therefore reject the district court's conclusion in this respect.

Although the district court did not explicitly decide whether Ford's veto was reasonable, it decided a closely related question. Under other provisions of § 365 a bankruptcy court cannot authorize assignment of an executory contract if 1) the debtor is in default, unless 2) there is "adequate assurance of future performance." § 365(b)(1)(C). Pioneer is in default, but the bankruptcy and district courts found "adequate assurance." For the sake of argument, we shall assume that this finding is equivalent to a finding that Ford's veto of the assignment was unreasonable. And, we shall apply a "clearly erroneous" standard in reviewing the factual element in this lower court finding. Fed.R.Civ.P. 52. On these assumptions, favorable to Fleet, we nonetheless must reverse the district court, for, in our view, any finding of unreasonableness, based on this record, is clearly erroneous.

Our review of the record reveals the following critical facts. First, in accordance with its ordinary business practice and dealer guidelines incorporated into the franchise agreement, Ford would have required Toyota Village, as a dealer, to have a working capital of at least $172,000, of which no more than half could be debt. Toyota Village, however, had a working capital at the end of 1981 of $37,610; and its net worth was $31,747. Although the attorney for Fleet at one point in the bankruptcy proceedings said Toyota Village could borrow some of the necessary capital from a bank, he made no later reference to the point, nor did he ever specifically state how much Toyota Village could borrow. Since the tax returns of Toyota Village's owner showed gross income of $27,500 for 1981, there is no reason to believe that the owner could readily find the necessary equity capital.

Second, at a time when Japanese cars have sold well throughout the United States, Toyota Village has consistently lost money. The financial statements in the record show the following operating losses:

	1977	1978	1979	1980	1981
Loss	($7,522)	($7,552)	($13,938)	($12,684)	($21,317)

At the same time, the record contains no significant evidence tending to refute the natural inference arising from these facts. The bankruptcy court mentioned five factors that it said showed that Toyota Village gave "adequate assurance" that it could do the job.

1. Toyota Village was an established dealership.

2. Toyota Village was "located within 500 yards of the present Ford dealership."

3. Toyota Village had a proven track record for selling cars.

4. Toyota Village was willing and able to pay $15,000 that Pioneer still owed Ford.

5. The owner and sole stockholder of Toyota Village testified that he was willing and able to fulfill the franchise agreement.

We do not see how the few positive features about Toyota Village that the record reveals can overcome the problem of a history of losses and failure to meet Ford's capital requirements. In these circumstances, Ford would seem perfectly reasonable in withholding its consent to the transfer. Thus, Rhode Island law would make the franchise unassignable.

Reversed

OLDDEN v. TONTO REALTY CORP.

United States Court of Appeals, Second Circuit
143 F.2d 916 (1944)

Before AUGUSTUS N. HAND, CLARK, and FRANK, Circuit Judges.

When the bankrupt, B. Westermann Company, Inc., filed its bankruptcy petition on March 5, 1942, the Tonto Realty Corporation, although itself only a lessee from the owner of the fee, was landlord of certain space on premises 18–20 West 48th Street, New York City, under a lease with the bankrupt expiring January 31, 1948. By the time of the bankruptcy the rental had become, by adjustment, $22,769.95 per year and there was owing the sum of $4,904.38 in back rent. This latter sum, however, included rent for the month of March; and since the trustee in bankruptcy occupied the premises, along with a subtenant and at the agreed rental, until June 20, 1942, the net amount of arrears, after deducting the rent paid for the overlapping period in March, was $3,313.70. Thereafter Tonto rerented the premises at a rental substantially lower than that reserved in the lease with the bankrupt. The new tenant defaulted, however, after two months, and Tonto itself was dispossessed for nonpayment of rent to its landlord in January, 1943. It then filed a claim for back rent and for damages.

Under an "ipso facto clause" of the lease (Paragraph 21), Tonto and the bankrupt had agreed that upon the latter's bankruptcy the lease should "expire ipso facto cease and come to an end," in which event there should be due the landlord as liquidated damages a sum to be computed as therein provided representing the difference between the cash value of the future rent as reserved and the cash rental value for the balance of the term, not exceeding any limit set by a governing statute. Applying the formula stated in this clause the bankruptcy referee found that the liquidated damages—before application of a statutory limitation—would be $40,307.81, from which should be deducted the sum of $3,000 held by Tonto as security under the lease, leaving a total of $37,307.81. By amendment of the Bankruptcy Act in 1934, now § 63, sub. a(9), 11 U.S.C.A. § 103, sub. a(9), however, there were added to the allowable claims in bankruptcy claims for anticipatory breach of contract, including unexpired leases of realty, but with the limitation that a landlord's claim for damages upon the rejection of an unexpired lease or "for damages or indemnity under a covenant contained in such lease shall in no event be allowed in an amount exceeding the rent reserved by the lease, without acceleration, for the year next succeeding the date of the surrender of the premises to the landlord or the date of reentry of the landlord, whichever first occurs, whether before or after bankruptcy, plus an amount equal to the unpaid rent accrued, without acceleration, up to such date." Because of this statutory provision, the referee reduced the total claim as allowed to one year's rent, $22,769.95, plus back rent of $3,313.70, or $26,083.65. On the trustee's petition to review, the district court held that the $3,000 deposited as security should be deducted not from the provable claim of $43,621.51, but from the allowable claim of $26,083.65, and hence modified the referee's order to allow Tonto's claim in the sum of $23,083.65. D.C.S.D.N.Y., 51 F.Supp. 776. Both parties have appealed, the trustee contending that nothing is due except the arrears of rent, less the security, *i.e.,* $313.70, and the creditor asserting that the deposit should be deducted from the total damages claimed, rather than from the allowable claim, and hence that the referee's, rather than the court's, computation should be followed.

The trustee's contention that no damages for breach of the lease should be allowed has as its premise the admitted fact that bankruptcy was a limitation, terminating the lease before the demised term, but requires also the further step that no provision should have been made for the payment of damages in the event of such termination. Since this is so obviously just what the parties were attempting to do in Paragraph 21, the trustee's construction of the language is tortured, to say the least, justifying the "scant consideration" of the referee and the total ignoring of the point by the court, of which the trustee so vigorously complains. Thus he asserts that there could be no damages "for the unexpired portion of the term hereby demised," since the term had expired by its terms; but the first line of the paragraph—quoted above in the footnote—shows that the "term" intended was the original term of ten years. Under the relevant state authorities, as well as the substantially identical case of *In re Outfitters' Operating Realty Co.,* 2 Cir., 69 F.2d 90, *affirmed Irving Trust Co. v. A. W. Perry, Inc.,* 293 U.S. 307, 55 S.Ct. 150, 79 L.Ed. 379, an express provision that bankruptcy is a breach, for which damages are provided, is concededly valid; but the attempted distinction here that the provision for damages fails because of lack of the word "breach" seems to us altogether too thin to justify thwarting so clear an intent, particularly when the paragraph does speak of "liquidated damages caused by such breach of the provisions of this lease." We are clear that Tonto had a valid claim under § 63, sub. a(9), subject to the latter's specified limitations. *See* 3 Collier on Bankruptcy, 14th Ed. 1941, 1898.

The landlord's appeal, however, presents an interesting and novel question. As far as we can determine, there are no decisions prior to the present case specifically deciding whether a landlord is required to deduct the amount of security held under a lease from the total damages provided by the lease or from the total claim allowable under § 63, sub. a(9) of the Bankruptcy Act. Some consideration of the background and history of the legislation is, therefore, necessary.

The Bankruptcy Act of 1898 as originally enacted was silent as to the provability of claims for rent to accrue in the future. The courts, however, were virtually unanimous in deciding that rent destined to accrue after the filing of a petition was not capable of proof, since there was no fixed liability absolutely owing, but merely a demand contingent upon uncertain events . This was not a matter of logic, but "of history that has not forgotten Lord Coke" (per Holmes, J., in *Gardiner v. William S. Butler & Co.,* 245 U.S. 603, 605, 38 S.Ct. 214, 62 L.Ed. 505), for rationally it was most difficult to reconcile this doctrine with the generally liberal treatment in bankruptcy cases of other types of anticipatory breaches of contracts. Hence the result was often harsh as to the landlord, though it did prevent the exhaustion of bankrupt estates for disproportionately large lease claims.

Beyond the fact that landlords' claims for future rent were not provable in any event, the earlier cases also held that the bankruptcy of the tenant constituted an absolute termination of the lease, so that no further claim of any kind remained to the landlord. *In re Jefferson,* D.C.Ky., 93 F. 948; *In re Hays, Foster & Ward Co.,* D.C.W.D.Ky., 117 F. 879. This rule was soon supplanted, however, by the majority view that bankruptcy had no effect at all on such claims; they were not provable, and the debtor did not receive a discharge therefrom. The landlord thus retained a valid claim for damages as long as he did not terminate the obligations of the lease by re-entering; but unless there was a specific stipulation for damages contained in the lease, a re-entry did release the tenant from liability for future rents A natural consequence was that landlords sought to discover some means of protecting themselves against the event of the tenant's bankruptcy. A first expedient was the reservation in the lease of a right of re-entry in the landlord and the inclusion of a covenant of indemnity by the lessee for all loss of future rent occasioned by bankruptcy. But the courts branded this also a contingent claim incapable of proof, since at the time of the filing of the bankruptcy petition there still remained uncertainty as to whether or not the option would be exercised by the landlord. Resort was then had to the so-called ipso facto clause, in which the lease automatically terminates upon the filing of the petition, as exemplified by Paragraph 21 of the instant lease. This covenant eventually received judicial approval, as we have seen, in *Irving Trust Co. v. A. W. Perry, Inc., supra,* which was not decided until after the passage of the 1934 amendment.

Although this result could be easily justified on technical legal grounds, its consequence presented distinctly unattractive elements from the standpoint of policy. It made landlords' claims depend on the niceties of ancient property law, rather than on the practical aspects of modern business. Then landlords, especially in the depression years from 1929 on, when there was a tremendous depreciation of rental values, were particularly hard hit by the bankruptcies of corporate tenants; for even though their claims for damages survived bankruptcy, the corporate entities in most cases did not and the landlords were left holding valid claims against permanently defunct corporations. Moreover, the main object of the Bankruptcy Act to afford means of rehabilitation of an honest bankrupt through discharge of his debts was thwarted by the nondischargeable character of these large rent claims. *See Central Trust Co. of Illinois v. Chicago Auditorium Ass'n,* 240 U.S. 581, 591, 36 S.Ct. 412, 60 L.Ed. 811. But allowance in full of such claims did not seem the appropriate answer, since other general creditors would suffer proportionately, and the claims themselves would often be disproportionate in amount to any actual damage suffered, particularly in the event of a subsequent rise in rental values. In truth, the landlord is not in the same position as other general creditors, and there is no very compelling reason why he should be treated on a par with them. For, after all, he has been compensated up until the date of the bankruptcy petition, he regains his original assets upon bankruptcy and the unexpired term in no way really benefits the assets of the bankrupt's estate. *See Trust Co. of Georgia v. Whitehall Holding Co.,* 5 Cir., 53 F.2d 635; *In re Metropolitan Chain Stores, Inc., supra.*

This, then, was the state of affairs when in 1934 Congress adopted the amendment to § 63, sub. a, making claims for future rent specifically provable. The amendment was an obvious compromise between the various conflicting interests outlined above, and was reached only after serious research and study on the part of the legislators. *City Bank Farmers' Trust Co. v. Irving Trust Co.,* 299 U.S. 433, 57 S.Ct. 292, 81 L.Ed. 324; *Kuehner v. Irving Trust Co.,* 299 U.S. 445, 453, 57 S.Ct. 298, 81 L.Ed. 340. As Professor Moore states, "The statutory solution represented a happy medium and imposed on the creditors a limited sacrifice in order to achieve the desirable end of facilitating the debtor's rehabilitation by extending the scope of his discharge." 3 Collier on Bankruptcy, 14th Ed. 1941, 1894. In the light of this history and purpose of the statutory provision and its clearly expressed intent, we should construe it so as to give it full force and effect, and not allow it to be nullified by crafty draftsmanship in particular leases. *See* 3 Collier on Bankruptcy, *op. cit.* 1900. Nor should a landlord obtain an advantage beyond that usually accorded under the statute merely because he has been shrewd or economically powerful enough to have obtained a substantial deposit as security. The contrary result would mean that a landlord with security would be able to exceed the statutory limit by as much as the security he holds, and that landlords would receive different treatment in bankruptcy proceedings, depending upon the existence and size of the security in their possession. Thus the two primary objectives of § 63, sub. a(9), would be flaunted. *Compare* Newman, *Rent Claims in Bankruptcy and Corporate Reorganization,* 43 Col. L. Rev. 317, 322—324. And all this would be deduced from a statute purporting to define provable claims, but saying nothing about security, of which, of course, the landlord gets full benefit through its application to his claim, thus affording him, so far forth, full payment in place of the usual small dividend.

Persuasive to this result is also the analogy of the decisions dealing with guaranty or surety contracts for rent. *In Hippodrome Bldg. Co. v. Irving Trust Co.,* 2 Cir., 91 F.2d 753, 756, *certiorari denied* 302 U.S. 748, 58 S.Ct. 265, 82 L.Ed. 578, we held that a lessor's claim in a reorganization proceeding against a corporation which had guaranteed payment of the rent reserved in the lease and performance of the lessee's covenants, the lease having been rejected by the lessee's trustee in bankruptcy and the premises having been relet at a loss, was subject to the three–year provision of § 77B(b) (10), 11 U.S.C.A. § 207(b)(10). We said that if this were not so "a guarantor in reorganization is liable for more than his principal; that cannot be the meaning of the statute; the guaranty is a secondary obligation and must be subject to the same limitations as the primary." Then, in *In re Schulte Retail Stores Corp.,* 2 Cir., 105 F.2d 986, we extended this doctrine to the case of a surety under similar circumstances, even though a surety is a primary obligor himself. Although the instant case is admittedly different in that the tenant here pledged his own property to cover the possibility of default, and the rights of a third party are in no way involved, yet in both situations there is an attempt on the part of the landlord to insure performance by the tenant. The difference is purely technical, *viz.*, that in one case the insurance is security put up by the tenant himself, while in the other it is the credit standing of a third party procured by the tenant; this difference is insufficient to justify divergent rules as to the respective allowable claims. If the total damages are limited in the one instance, they should likewise be limited in the other instance.

It may be suggested that this renders anomalous the situation where the landlord, by virtue of obtaining an unusually large deposit in advance, has still a balance in his hands after deducting the claim for one year's rent allowed by the statute. Any question here may be academic, for apparently the security ordinarily obtained by landlords seems to vary from one to six months' advance rent only; we have discovered no reported case where it even approaches the statutory limit of one year's rent. But it does not seem to us that the situation should be considered anomalous. If we are correct that the statute sets a limit on damages for breach of a lease by bankruptcy, then the landlord should be entitled only to that sum and not more; otherwise the security would be in the nature of a forfeiture in the event of bankruptcy, and forfeitures are not favored by the courts. *Seattle Rialto Theatre Co. v. Heritage*, 9 Cir., 4 F.2d 668. It is clear that when the lease is at an end, and no damages can thereafter be due, the security must be returned. *Cannon v. Fifty–Sixth St. Garage, Inc.*, 2 Cir., 45 F.2d 110. Hence, even before the 1934 amendment, the security could be retained only as against possible claims, and the cases assumed that upon complete termination of the lease upon bankruptcy, any surplus over damages allowable in bankruptcy was returnable to the trustee. The statute now makes the termination of the lease complete, and the damages fixed; and anything in excess should go to the trustee for the general creditors.

Judgment affirmed.

CHAPTER 15

THE BANKRUPTCY TRUSTEE

In a chapter 7 liquidation case, a trustee will be appointed by the U.S. trustee immediately after the order for relief, *i.e.*, in a voluntary case that date would be the filing of the petition. (In Alabama and North Carolina, the trustee is appointed by the court.) At this stage of the case, the statutory label affixed to this officer is "interim trustee" (§ 701(a)), which denotes that at some later stage a "permanent" trustee will take office. The structure, stated simply, is that the Code bows somewhat in the direction of creditor participation by permitting the creditor body to elect a trustee if a sufficient number of creditors so desire. (§ 702.)

The trustee's duties are to marshal the assets of the debtor, convert them to cash, and to pay out the money to the creditors according to the distribution scheme of the Code. *See* 11 U.S.C. § 704. Within this brief statement are encompassed many sections of the Code and principles of bankruptcy law. They will be discussed in the context of this chapter.

§ 15.01   Interim Trustee

See 11 U.S.C. § 701. The interim trustee is appointed from a panel of private trustees established and supervised by the U.S. trustee (28 U.S.C. § 586(a)(1)) in all districts except in Alabama and North Carolina.

(a)   What are the duties of the interim trustee?

(b)   How does the interim trustee get paid?

(c)   Can you become an interim trustee?

(d)   When are interim trustees appointed in chapter 11, 12, or 13 cases?

§ 15.02   Trustee

There is no label for the one who becomes the trustee later in the case to distinguish that person from the interim trustee. *See* §§ 701(b),(c), 702, 546(a). *See also* questions raised above.

IN RE BLANCHARD MANAGEMENT CORP.

Bankruptcy Court, Southern District of New York
10 B.R. 186, 4 C.B.C.2d 91, 7 B.C.D. 528 (1981)

RYAN, Bankruptcy Judge:

On November 28, 1980, an involuntary petition under Chapter 7 of the Bankruptcy Code was filed against the above–named debtor. Thereafter, an order for relief was entered by this court on January 13, 1981, and Barbara Balaber–Strauss was appointed interim trustee pursuant to 11 U.S.C. § 15701(a).

Although the debtor filed no schedules, the attorneys for the petitioning creditors filed a list of names and addresses of six creditors with claims against the debtor. However, this list did not indicate the amount claimed to be due each creditor, nor any approximation thereof.

A meeting of creditors was held before the United States Trustee on February 20, 1981, in accordance with 11 U.S.C. § 341. Pursuant to 28 U.S.C. § 586(a) and Interim Bankruptcy Rule X–1003(d)[now Rule 2003(d)], the United States Trustee filed with this court a Report of Election following the meeting of creditors which, among other informative matters, related the following:

At the meeting, a request for the election of a trustee was made by Neal M. Rosenbloom, Esq., who, representing one creditor, Hunter Paper Co., Inc. ("Hunter"), presented a proof of claim on behalf of Hunter indicating $40,114.90 due and owing by the debtor. Marvin Schrier of H. Schrier & Co., Inc., requested that an election be held; however, neither did Mr. Schrier have a proof of claim to present nor had a proof of claim been filed with the clerk of the bankruptcy court prior to the meeting of creditors, as required by Bankruptcy Rule 207(a) and Interim Bankruptcy Rule X–1003(b)(3). Nevertheless, at the Section 341(a) meeting, Mr. Rosenbloom and Mr. Schrier nominated and voted for Lawrence Sarf, 2365 Boston Post Road, Larchmont, New York, to serve as trustee.

On March 18, 1981, the attorneys for the petitioning creditors made an application to this court for an order resolving an election dispute and certifying Lawrence Sarf as the duly elected trustee.

At the March 18 hearing on the motion for certification Mr. Rosenbloom appeared for the petitioning creditors in support of the motion and application, and Cornelius Blackshear, Esq., appeared representing the United States Trustee in opposition to the proposed certification of Lawrence Sarf. The United States Trustee recommended that the election not be certified because there was no showing of the composition of the creditor body.

The court accepts the position of the United States Trustee, and denies the application for certification.

This decision turns on the provisions of 11 U.S.C. § 702 of the Bankruptcy Code. Under the Bankruptcy Act election of the person nominated to be trustee at the creditors meeting required a consensus of a majority in number and amount of the creditors who appeared to vote at the meeting. However, under the provisions of the Code, to elect a trustee it is necessary that creditors holding at least 20 percent in amount of the type of claims referred to in 11 U.S.C. § 702(a) first request that an election be held; then that creditors holding at least 20 percent in amount of such claims actually vote; and, finally, that the candidate for trustee receive a majority in amount of votes actually cast.

Since no schedules of liabilities were ever filed, nor were any amounts (either exact or approximate) demonstrated by the attorneys for the petitioning creditors in the list that they filed, it was not possible to determine whether the claim voted by Mr. Rosenbloom on behalf of Hunter met the 20 percent requisite majority of creditors holding the types of claims referred to in 11 U.S.C. § 702(a) necessary to request that an election be held or to determine whether the increased amount satisfied either statutory requirement.

At the March 18 hearing, the petitioning creditors contended that this was a unique situation since there were no assurances that schedules would ever be filed by the debtor or even that books and records of the debtors existed.

Relying for legal argument solely upon some thoughts expressed by another bankruptcy judge in another case in this district, the attorney for the petitioning creditors urged that this court certify the election of Lawrence Sarf as trustee. These arguments are not at all persuasive.

The petitioning creditors had available to them and failed to utilize measures under [former] Rule 205 of the Rules of Bankruptcy Procedure [now Rule 2004] (*e.g.*, a subpoena seeking production of the debtor's books and records or a deposition of an officer or bookkeeper of the debtor) which measures would have assisted the United States Trustee in determining the approximate amount of claims for § 702 purposes.

The attorneys for the petitioning creditors could have estimated and given at least a ballpark figure on the amounts claimed by the six creditors who were named in the list filed with this court by said attorneys.

The debtor need not file his schedules first; the petitioning creditors could have estimated the other debts and provided the United States Trustee with some means of verifying compliance with 11 U.S.C. § 702. However, since the petitioning creditors utterly failed in supplying necessary information to the United States Trustee, the latter was not able to report to this court that the proceedings which took place at the meeting of creditors satisfied the statutory requirements of § 702. Consequently, this court denies the application seeking confirmation of Lawrence Sarf as trustee in bankruptcy.

A purpose of the Bankruptcy Reform Act is to discourage the old fashioned type of electioneering associated with the election of a trustee. Often, the actual issue in the election of a trustee is who will be the attorney for the trustee, not who shall be the trustee. Here, as in *In Re Ira Haupt & Co.*, there is no question as to the competence of the trustee now in office. In the *Haupt* case, there was nothing in the record to suggest that the trustee was incompetent or otherwise disqualified from efficiently performing his duties of office. The Court of Appeals remarked, at 886, that:

> Behind the facade of protestation of deep concern for the creditors of Haupt (the New York Stock Exchange and the Banks account for $18,735,186 out of filed claims totaling $22,541,767.36), one can observe a defeated candidate seeking a recount in an election which may involve the prospect of a substantial fee to the successful candidate.

Often, under the Act, and especially when the return to creditors from the estate promised to be small there was little real creditor interest and attorneys would move in to control the case.

The procedure under the Code makes it more difficult for a trustee to be elected unless there is actual creditor interest in the case.

The Code's 20 percent requirement discourages attorney control and attempts to revitalize the idea of true creditor control.

Since the creditors failed at the first meeting to elect a trustee, they have exhausted their opportunity to do so and the interim trustee Barbara Balaber–Strauss shall continue to serve as the trustee in this case. 11 U.S.C. § 702(d).

Settle an appropriate order.

NOTES AND QUESTIONS

1. In *Blanchard, supra,* Bankruptcy Judge Ryan stated that "The procedure under the Code makes it more difficult for a trustee to be elected unless there is actual creditor interest in the case." Why should the procedure make it more difficult? If creditor interest is lacking, what other interest would exist in the election or appointment of a trustee? What abuse, if any, was the Code attempting to cure? Under the former bankruptcy law, creditors could elect a trustee absent any of the requirements presently in § 702; in a Chapter XI arrangement case, creditors elected a committee of unsecured creditors. Under chapter 11 of the Code, the committee is appointed by the U.S. trustee. Throughout, therefore, the democratic process has been restricted rather than fostered and the appointment procedure is more generally used. The so–called precept of "creditor control" in the bankruptcy process, while theoretically sound, meant all too often "attorney control" by those seeking fees from the estates undergoing liquidation or reorganization. "Creditor control" thus turned out to be more myth than reality and a major purpose of the appointment provisions in the Code was to "clean up" the practice.

2. In *In re Tartan Construction Co.,* 2 C.B.C. 2d 295 (Bankr. D. Neb. 1980), the court held that Interim Rule 2003(b)(3), which requires a creditor to file a claim in order to vote, was inconsistent with § 702(a)(1) of the Code. What is the inconsistency found by the court? If the rule is inconsistent, does the Code or rule control? *See* 28 U.S.C. § 2075.

The interim rules were superseded on August 1, 1983, when the bankruptcy rules promulgated by the Supreme Court became effective. Rule 2003(b)(3) now provides that a creditor may vote if a proof of claim was filed or if a writing is filed evidencing a right to vote. Does the revision of the rule cure whatever defect the *Tartan* court found in the interim rule?

3. In a chapter 11 case, a trustee may be appointed or elected but only pursuant to § 1104. Who may the U.S. trustee appoint as trustee? On whose motion? For what reason? The possibility of electing a trustee in a chapter 11 case was added to the Code in 1994. *See* § 1104(b). If cause is shown for a trustee, and creditors have 30 days to ask for an election, what may happen to the estate property in the interim?

§ 15.03   Trustee's Avoiding Powers

In furtherance of its ideal to promote an equitable distribution of a debtor's property among the creditors, the Code provides the trustee with an arsenal of weapons with which to attack and invalidate prebankruptcy transfers. Thus, for example, if the debtor had conveyed property fraudulently to another, the trustee may be able to recover the property for the estate under either § 544(b) or § 548. If security interests have not been properly perfected pursuant to applicable state law, they may be invalidated under either § 544(a) or § 547. The powers given a trustee may also be utilized by the debtor in possession in a chapter 11 case when a trustee is not appointed. *See* § 1107(a).

This part of the materials will treat the various avoiding powers given a trustee.

[A]   Trustee as Judicial Lien Creditor or Good Faith Purchaser

Pursuant to § 544(a), the trustee is invested with the powers of (1) a creditor holding a judicial lien on personal property of the debtor and (2) a bona fide purchaser of real property from the debtor. Essentially, the purpose is to test the validity under state law of prebankruptcy transfers as against a judicial lien creditor (if personal property was transferred) or as against a bona fide purchaser (if the transfer was of realty). The date of testing for § 544(a) purposes is the date of the commencement of a case under the Code.

A judicial lien creditor is a creditor who has obtained a lien on property of the debtor through the judicial process. A common type of judicial lien is the judgment lien which arises after a money judgment is obtained and the procedural steps, dictated by State law, are followed to create the judgment lien. These steps may be the delivery of a writ of execution to the sheriff or other enforcement officer empowered to seize property and sell it in satisfaction of judgment debts. Another alternative in some State laws requires the sheriff to make a levy on personal property, which is the actual taking of physical possession, before the judgment lien is created. Other forms of judicial liens are attachment and garnishment which may be obtained pre–judgment. Pursuant to § 544(a) of the Bankruptcy Code, the trustee has, on the date of the filing of the petition commencing a case under the Code, the rights and powers of a judicial lien creditor. Section 544(a) does not spell out those rights and powers; only State law does. Accordingly, resort must be had to appropriate State law related to the transfer of property under consideration for avoidance. If, for example, a security interest in personal property is involved, resort would be to § 9–301(1)(b) of Article 9 of the Uniform Commercial Code as enacted in the particular State, or other comparable law.

IN RE CARTER

Bankruptcy Court, District of Colorado
2 B.R. 321, 1 C.B.C.2d 381, 5 B.C.D. 1236 (1980)

KELLER, Bankruptcy Judge:

This matter came before the Court upon the Debtors' "Objection to Claim of Security Interest on Property Belonging to Debtor by Reliable Sewing Machine Company." Reliable Sewing Machine Company filed claim herein on November 30, 1979, in the amount of $2,271.00 claiming a security interest in a certain group of household furnishings. The lien claimed is a purchase money security interest, and the security agreement is attached to the proof of claim as required. The objection of the Debtors in total states:

> The debtors hereby object to the claim of a secured interest by the claimant in any property belonging to the debtors, as the purported security instrument filed with the Court is invalid against the debtor.

At the hearing, it appeared that the creditor had failed to file a financing statement within the time required under the Uniform Commercial Code, even though an attempted filing was returned by the filing officer upon grounds not relating to the validity of the financing statement. At the time of the filing of the Chapter 13 petition herein, the creditor again filed the financing statement, and it remains of record. The Debtors assert the right in these proceedings to avoid the security interest pursuant to the provisions of 11 U.S.C. § 544. Section 544 is the so–called "strong–arm clause" which has been incorporated into the new Bankruptcy Code.

There is some question whether the Chapter 13 trustee has strong–arm powers under the new Code. It was settled in this Circuit that the trustee was so empowered under former law. *City National Bank v. Oliver*, 230 F.2d 686 (10th Cir. 1956). All of the provisions of Chapter 5, including the strong–arm clause, appear to apply in Chapter 13 cases under the provisions of 11 U.S.C. 103(a). It is clear, however, that 11 U.S.C. 1302(b) does not give the Chapter 13 trustee all the duties of a liquidating trustee in Chapter 7. Conspicuously absent is the duty to "collect and reduce to money the property of the estate." *See* 11 U.S.C. § 1104(1). The avoidance of liens under the strong–arm clause might well constitute collection of property of the estate. Thus, it could be argued that § 1302(b) is inconsistent with and, therefore, overrides § 103(a). A decision on this question is not necessary to address these issues.

It is not the Trustee who seeks here to use § 544. Rather, it is the Debtors. The contract creating the security interest remained valid as between the Debtors and the creditor on the day of the filing of the Chapter 13 petition. The Debtors assert, however, that they are armed with the powers of the Chapter 13 Trustee by operation of law. No Code section supports that view. Various powers of the trustee pursuant to 11 U.S.C. § 363 granted to the debtor exclusive of the trustee pursuant to 11 U.S.C. § 1303. In addition, 11 U.S.C. § 1304 adds various other powers for a Chapter 13 debtor engaged in business. None of the powers accorded the trustee in Chapter 5 are given to the debtor by these Sections. The legislative history of § 1303 indicates that some powers may be concurrently held by the trustee and the debtor. S. Rep. No. 95–98, 95th Cong., 2nd Sess. 140 (1978). That legislative history does not authorize concurrent debtor access to the lien avoidance powers specifically granted to the trustee in Chapter 5 of the Code. The congressional example of a concurrently held power is the right to sue and be sued. Obviously, the recognition of that power does no violence to the role of the Chapter 13 trustee. Were lien avoidance powers concurrently held, the trustee would effectively lose control over lien avoidance litigation. That result should be avoided, particularly if it is reachable only by implication. When Congress intended debtors to exercise the powers of a trustee in Chapter 11, it explicitly so stated in § 1107(a). Presumably, a section analogous to § 1107(a) would be present in Chapter 13 if that were the congressional intent. The Court concludes that a Chapter 13 debtor has no "strong arm" power under the Code. Now, therefore, *It Is Ordered* that the objection of the Debtors to the claim of Reliable Sewing Machine Company insofar as that objection extends to the assertion of a security interest in certain household goods is *Denied*.

McCANNON v. MARSTON

United States Court of Appeals, Third Circuit
679 F.2d 13 (1982)

GIBBONS, Circuit Judge:

Among the provisions of the Bankruptcy Reform Act of 1978, 11 U.S.C. § 101 *et seq.* (Supp. III 1979) (the Code), that require reference to state law is the "strong arm clause" of Section 544. This section grants the trustee the state law defined rights and powers of certain creditors and transferees of property. In this case, both the bankruptcy and district courts interpreted the language of the Code to permit a trustee to avoid an equitable interest in real property (arising from a purchase agreement) of a person whose possession of that property provided constructive notice of her rights under state law. Concluding that Section 544 does not contemplate such a result, we reverse.

I.

On March 19,1973, Miriam H. McCannon entered into an agreement with a partnership doing business as The Drake Hotel (the debtor) for the sale of a condominium apartment and of a certain percentage of the common areas in that hotel. The agreement contained a contingency that the hotel, located in Philadelphia, be declared a valid condominium according to the terms of the then applicable Unit Property Act, Pa. Stat. Ann. tit. 68, § 700.101 *et seq.* (Purdon 1965) (repealed). That contingency was satisfied later in 1973.

Pursuant to the agreement, McCannon paid a deposit of $500 toward the purchase price of $17,988. She began residence in the apartment in April of 1975 and resides there presently. The bankruptcy court found, however, that "[f]or a variety of reasons, settlement on the property has never taken place." *In re Hotel Associates, Inc.,* [4 C.B.C.2d 523] 10 B.R. 668, 669 (Bk. E.D. Pa. 1981). McCannon never recorded her agreement for sale.

In November of 1979, the debtor filed a petition under Chapter XI of the Code, 11 U.S.C. § 1101 *et seq.* McCannon filed a complaint in February of 1981 seeking relief from the automatic stay imposed by Section 362 of the Code and requesting specific performance of the agreement to purchase the apartment. Holding that the trustee, as a bona fide purchaser without regard to any knowledge on his part, may avoid McCannon's interest in the property pursuant to Pennsylvania law and to Section 544(a)(3) of the Code, the bankruptcy court granted the trustee's motion for judgment at the close of the plaintiff's case. *In re Hotel Associates, Inc., supra.* The district court affirmed the bankruptcy court's judgment, employing the same interpretation of Section 544 and concluding that Section 365(i) did not apply. *McCannon v. Marston,* No. 81–1451 (E.D.Pa. Aug. 1, 1981). This appeal followed.

II.

The Code provides:

"Trustee as lien creditor and as successor to certain creditors and purchasers.

(a) The trustee shall have, as of the commencement of the case, and without regard to any knowledge of the trustee or of any creditor, the rights and powers of, or may avoid any transfer of property of the debtor or any obligation incurred by the debtor that is voidable by—

(1) a creditor that extends credit to the debtor at the time of the commencement of the case, and that obtains, at such time and with respect to such credit, a judicial lien on all property on which a creditor on a simple contract could have obtained a judicial lien, whether or not such a creditor exists;

>   (2) a creditor that extends credit to the debtor at the time of
>   the commencement of the case, and obtains, at such time and
>   with respect to such credit, an execution against the debtor that
>   is returned unsatisfied at such time, whether or not such a
>   creditor exists; and

>   (3) a bona fide purchaser of real property from the debtor,
>   against whom applicable law permits such transfer to be per-
>   fected, that obtains the status of a bona fide purchaser at the time
>   of the commencement of the case, whether or not such a
>   purchaser exists.

11 U.S.C. § 544(a). At issue in this case is the interrelationship of the third clause concerning the rights of transferees of real property and the prepositional phrase "without regard to any knowledge of the trustee or of any creditor," an interrelationship of state and federal law.

The law of Pennsylvania considers a purchaser under a written agreement for the sale of real property to be the equitable owner of that property. *E.g., Allardice v. McCain*, 375 Pa. 528, 101 A.2d 385 (1953); *Dubin Paper Co. v. Insurance Co. of North America*, 361 Pa. 68, 63 A.2d 85 (1949). After reviewing the contract, we find no fault with the conclusion of the bankruptcy court that McCannon acquired such an equitable interest once the condition that a valid condominium be created was satisfied.

Pennsylvania law gives subsequent purchasers of real property priority over the rights of prior purchasers if the subsequent purchasers are bona fide purchasers for value without notice. Record notice defeats the claims of a subsequent purchaser. McCannon's equitable interest was unrecorded. However, in Pennsylvania, clear and open possession of real property generally constitutes constructive notice to subsequent purchasers of the rights of the party in possession. Such possession, even in the absence of recording, obliges any prospective subsequent purchaser to inquire into the possessor's claimed interests, equitable or legal, in that property. *See, e.g., Finch v. Fluke*, 311 Pa. 405, 166 A. 905 (1933); *Long John Silver's, Inc. v. Fiore*, 255 Pa. Super. 183, 386 A.2d 569 (1978). Thus in Pennsylvania the rights of a subsequent purchaser do not take priority over those of one in clear and open possession of real property.

The bankruptcy and district courts, however, concluded that any notice which might be imputed to the trustee from possession is irrelevant because of the language of the above–quoted prepositional phrase in Section 544: "without regard to any knowledge of the trustee or of any creditor." Equating "knowledge" with "notice," both courts ruled that the trustee assumes the powers of a bona fide purchaser without notice, whether or not a transferee has given the rest of the world actual or constructive notice by possession.

Although the word "knowledge" is not defined in the Code and the legislative history of its inclusion is scant, in our view Congress cannot have intended such an interpretation. Once a transferee of real property in Pennsylvania has given all potential subsequent purchasers actual or constructive notice of an interest in that property, nothing else need be done to protect against claims of future purchasers. According to the bankruptcy and district courts, however, nothing can be done to protect against the claims of a future trustee in bankruptcy who assumes the role of a hypothetical bona fide purchaser without actual knowledge. The trustee, under that interpretation of Section 544, has been clothed not only with the rights of a bona fide purchaser, but has been granted as well a substantial additional mantle of power not available to any actual subsequent purchaser in Pennsylvania. Such a conclusion is not to be lightly inferred.

That the words "without regard to any knowledge" were not meant by Congress to nullify all state law protections of holders of equitable interests is suggested both by the history of its inclusion in the statutory language and by other language within Section 544(a)(3). The reference to the trustee's or creditors' knowledge appears to have originated out of a concern that actual knowledge might affect the trustee's status as a hypothetical judicial lien creditor. In a draft bankruptcy act prepared in 1973 by the Commission on Bankruptcy Laws of the United States, a note by the Commission explained that the trustee's status as hypothetical lien creditor should not be affected by any knowledge which he, personally, or any or all creditors may have. Report of the Commission on the Bankruptcy Laws of the United States, H.R. Doc. No. 93–137, Part II, 93rd Cong., 1st Sess. 160–61 & n.3 (1973). The note referred to an article by Professor Vern Countryman criticizing cases construing both the "strong arm" provision of the former Bankruptcy Act, Section 70c, and Article 9 of the Uniform Commercial Code, holding that a trustee with actual knowledge of unperfected security interests could not avoid those interests despite his status as hypothetical lien creditor. *See* Countryman, *The Use of State Law in Bankruptcy Cases*, 47 N.Y.U. L. Rev. 631, 652–55 (1972). In 1977 Congress first provided the trustee with the status of bona fide purchaser of real property. At that time it inserted the clarification regarding the trustee's actual knowledge. *See* H.R. 6, 95th Cong., 1st Sess. (1977).

Viewed in the context of this history, congressional desire to disregard the trustee's knowledge of the debtor's previous transactions with various claimants is appropriately understood to respond to the Article 9 problems referred to by Professor Countryman, rather than to obliterate the rights of equitable owners in possession of real property. Further evidence that the latter result was not intended by Congress is found in the language of Section 544(a)(3). Congress was careful to modify the status of bona fide purchasers by inserting the words "against whom applicable law permits such transfer to be perfected." As explained in statements made by Representative Edwards of California and Senator DeConcini of Arizona, sponsors of the proposed Code:

> Section 544(a)(3) modifies similar provisions contained in the House bill and Senate amendment so as not to require a creditor to perform the impossible in order to perfect his interest. Both the lien creditor test in section 544(a)(1), and the bona fide purchaser test in section 544(a)(3) should not require a transferee to perfect a transfer against an entity with respect to which applicable law does not permit perfection.

124 Cong. Rec. H. 11097 (daily ed. Sept. 28, 1978); 124 Cong. Rec. S. 17413 (daily ed. October 6, 1978). Such solicitude for transferees subject to laws not permitting perfection as to certain purchasers is not consistent with an interpretation of Section 544(a) that would ignore constructive notice under governing state law when a trustee was appointed.

One further point of dispute must be addressed. The trustee argues that the circumstances of McCannon's possession, as the occupant of one of many condominium apartments, a number of which were leased, are not constructive notice obliging a subsequent purchaser to inquire as to her interests. The only Pennsylvania cases cited, however, find no obligation to inquire in circumstances where the grantor was both record owner and in possession and where the one in possession was sharing possession with the record owner. *Salvation Army Incorporated Trustees v. Lawson*, 293 Pa. 459, 143 A. 113 (1928); *Overly v. Hixon*, 169 Pa. Super. 187, 82 A.2d 573 (1951). We believe that were the Pennsylvania Supreme Court asked to consider whether a subsequent purchaser *of a condominium building* had a duty to make inquiry as to the rights of persons in possession of apartments in that building, it would hold that such possession provides constructive notice, as a matter of law, no different than in the case of possession of a single family home.

III.

There is further evidence of Congressional intent in Section 544(a)(3) involving a Code section not directly at issue in this appeal. Section 365 deals with the trustee's power to assume or reject executory contracts and unexpired leases of the debtor. It contains a subsection dealing specifically with executory contracts of the debtor for the sale of real property. Section 365(i) permits a purchaser who is in possession under such an executory contract that has been rejected by the trustee the choice of treating the contract as terminated or remaining in possession. In the latter case, the purchaser is obliged to continue making all payments due under the contract and the trustee must deliver title to the purchaser in accordance with the terms of the contract.

On this appeal, McCannon refers to this provision not as a separate ground for her specific performance request, since the trustee has not yet explicitly chosen to reject the contract, but as evidence of congressional concern for purchasers in possession. We agree that it is highly unlikely Congress would enact Section 365(i) while at the same time allowing the trustee to avoid, under Section 544(a)(3), the equitable interests of buyers in possession.

The district court held that Section 365(i) does not apply because McCannon's agreement of sale is not executory, and because, in any event, Section 365(i) was intended to protect only purchasers under land installment contracts. We disagree with both reasons.

The second sentence of the notes concerning Section 365 states that "[t]hough there is no precise definition of what contracts are executory, it generally includes contracts on which performance remains due to some extent on both sides." Notes of Committee on the Judiciary, S. Rep. No. 95–989, 95th Cong., 2d Sess. 58 (1978). Under the agreement for purchase and sale of the apartment, McCannon has yet to furnish the amount of the purchase price above her $500 deposit, and the debtor has yet to transfer title. Plainly, some performance remains due on both sides.

Section 365(i) specifically concerns the case in which "the trustee rejects an executory contract of the debtor for the sale of real property under which the purchaser is in possession." The committee note regarding that subsection does begin with mention of installment sales contracts for the purchase of real property: "Subsection (i) gives a purchaser of real property under a land installment sales contract similar protections [to those of subsection (h) concerning unexpired leases of real property]." S. Rep. No. 95–989, *supra*, at 60. This reference to installment sales contracts, however, cannot be read as limiting the application of the general language in this subsection. It is understandable that a committee note would single out such contracts for mention, since they are common instances in which the purchaser would come into possession before the contract is fully executed. But nothing in either the language of the subsection or the obvious policy behind it, of obviating the hardship involved in forcing a purchaser already in possession to leave, suggests that the section is inapplicable to McCannon.

IV.

The judgment of the district court will be *Reversed*, and the case *remanded* for consideration of other objections to granting specific performance of McCannon's agreement with the debtor which were not considered in the bankruptcy court.

NOTES AND QUESTIONS

1. The ability to avoid prebankruptcy transfers pursuant to § 544(a) is limited to the "trustee" by the very wording of the section. As the court points out in the *Carter* case, for purposes of chapter 11 cases, the debtor in possession is given the same powers. Section 1107(a) translates "trustee" to mean "debtor in possession" for this purpose. The same is true for all of the other sections containing powers of avoidance. The instant case also points out that the debtor in a chapter 13 case does *not* have the powers of a trustee, and the court raises, without answering, the question of whether a trustee in a chapter 13 case has such powers. Were the court to hold that a chapter 13 trustee does not have powers of avoidance under § 544(a) or the other sections, how could preferences, fraudulent transfers and the like be recovered? Or could they not be recovered? Is there any legislative policy that would be served by such a ruling? Where would the court find a limitation on the meaning of the word "trustee" to support such a ruling? *In re Reeves*, 17 B.R. 383 (Bankr. W.D.La. 1982), held that the chapter 13 trustee has the powers under § 544 to avoid a lien on

property. See 5 Collier on Bankruptcy ¶ 1300.93 (15th ed.): the chapter 13 trustee may assert all of the avoiding powers set forth in chapter 5 of the Code.

2. Why was it thought necessary to include the provision in § 544(a) that the trustee is a creditor who "extends credit to the debtor at the time of the commencement of the case"? As long as the trustee is given the rights of a judicial lien creditor it would appear unnecessary to add this additional gloss on such status. The legislative history tells us that § 544(a)(1) overrules *Pacific Finance Corp. v. Edwards*, 304 F.2d 224 (9th Cir. 1962), and *In re Federals, Inc.*, 553 F.2d 509 (6th Cir. 1977), "insofar as those cases held that the trustee did not have the status of a creditor who extended credit immediately prior to the commencement of the case." 124 Cong. Rec. H11,097 (Sept. 28, 1978); S17,413 (Oct. 6, 1978).

Earlier, the Court of Appeals for the Second Circuit had held that if the trustee had the rights of a judicial lien creditor as of the date of the commencement of the case, perforce the trustee had to be classified as an unsecured creditor at some prior date. One does not become a judicial lien creditor unless one is first owed a debt or has a cause of action. As an unsecured creditor, the trustee was entitled to avoid a chattel mortgage which had been perfected, albeit tardily, prior to bankruptcy. *Constance v. Harvey*, 215 F.2d 571 (2d Cir. 1954), *cert. denied* 348 U.S. 913 (1955). This matter was set right in *Lewis v. Manufacturers National Bank*, 364 U.S. 603 (1961) (the Bankruptcy Act in § 70c, forerunner to § 544(a)(1), gave the trustee a purely hypothetical status and it was erroneous to attribute any other rights that would flow logically).

3. Section 544(a)(1) has its main force in testing the validity of security interests in personal property. This section gives the trustee the rights of a judicial lien creditor. What rights are in fact obtained are provided for in the relevant state law. Thus, Article 9 of the Uniform Commercial Code is called into play, and § 9–301(1)(b) thereof subordinates an unperfected security interest to an intervening judicial lien creditor. Suppose that a security interest is obtained by Bank in Debtor's equipment and Bank fails completely to file a financing statement as required by U.C.C. § § 303 and 302 to perfect the security interest. Debtor files a petition for relief under chapter 7 of the Bankruptcy Code. May the trustee, without proving any other facts, invalidate the security interest, relegate Bank to unsecured creditor status, and use the proceeds from the sale of the purported collateral for the benefit of all creditors? Suppose the Bank filed the financing statement the day before Debtor filed the chapter 7 petition?

4. Paragraph (3) in § 544(a) was nowhere contained in the former Bankruptcy Act. Previously the trustee could avoid transfers of realty only if they were considered voidable as preferences. For purposes of conformity, the strong–arm provision now clothes the trustee with the rights of a bona fide purchaser to test the validity of real property transfers against local recording statutes.

[B] Trustee as Successor to Creditors' Rights

Under § 544(b), the trustee is given the rights, if any, of actual, existing unsecured creditors to avoid prebankruptcy transfers, usually under state law. For example, § 544(b) serves to incorporate the state law of fraudulent transfers, such as the Uniform Fraudulent Transfer Act. But *see also* § 548, *infra*. It may also be used by a trustee to avoid a bulk transfer which is ineffective under Article 6 of the Uniform Commercial Code as against at least one existing creditor. Under what circumstances would the trustee prefer to rely on § 544(b) to avoid a fraudulent transfer, rather than § 548?

Under § 544(b), the trustee's rights are strictly derivative rather than hypothetical. Accordingly, if a defense such as the running of the statute of limitations would bar the creditor's action, the trustee's action would similarly be barred. The Supreme Court held, in construing § 70e of the Act, from which § 544(b) is derived, that when a trustee is successful, the entire transfer is avoided (regardless of the amount of the creditor's claim), and the proceeds are to be distributed generally (not only to the creditor into whose shoes the trustee stepped). *Moore v. Bay*, 284 U.S. 4 (1931). *See also* H.R. Rep. No. 95–595, 95th Cong., 1st Sess. 370 (1977).

HADLEY v. ACQUAFREDDA
(In re Acquafredda)

Bankruptcy Court, Middle District of Florida

26 B.R. 909 (1983)

ALEXANDER L. PASKAY, Chief Judge.

This is a Chapter 7 case and the matter under consideration is a claim asserted by George Hadley, the Trustee of the estate, against the several defendants named in the above captioned adversary proceeding. The Trustee's claim for relief is based on Sec. 544(b) of the Bankruptcy Code. The complaint asserts that Vincent Acquafredda and Joan B. Acquafredda, his wife, (the Debtors) fraudulently transferred certain assets to Gulf Coast Sanitation, Inc. (Sanitation) and Gulf Coast Disposal, Inc. (Disposal). The Debtors were principals of Sanitation and Disposal, Florida corporations which were dissolved in 1977 and 1979, respectively. Defendant Michael Acquafredda is the son of the Debtors and sole stockholder of Gulf Coast Carting, Inc. (Carting), a Florida corporation which was dissolved in 1980. While Industrial Waste Service, Inc. (Industrial) was originally named a Defendant, a Motion to Dismiss was granted as to this corporation on the condition that all payments owed by Industrial to any other Defendants would be paid into the Court registry pending final disposition of this proceeding.

From the evidence adduced at trial, the Court finds and concludes as follows:

In July of 1974, the Debtors purchased certain assets from Community Disposal, Inc., including at least two trucks and commercial trash accounts producing revenues of $8,000 to $9,000 per month. The Debtors made a down payment in the amount of $10,000 and executed a promissory note in the principal amount of $70,000. This obligation earns interest at an annual rate of 7%. The promissory note was ultimately .assigned to Joseph Messina by Community Disposal, Inc., the previous owner of the assets involved. The Debtors paid only $800 on this note, and there is no dispute that the Debtors remain indebted to Mr. Messina, to the extent of the remaining balance.

It further appears that the Debtors transferred all the assets acquired from Community Disposal, Inc. to Sanitation and Disposal. These two newly formed corporations, in which the Debtors were the sole stockholders, paid no consideration to the Debtors for the transfer. Michael Acquafredda, the son of the Debtors, was employed by these two corporations until they were dissolved. In 1979, Michael Acquafredda formed Carting and commenced doing business with the assets used in the business previously conducted by Sanitation and Disposal. There was no consideration furnished by Carting either to Sanitation or to Disposal, or to the Debtors for the assets transferred to Carting. The assets included approximately 300 trash containers, commonly known as dumpsters; the business routes, *i.e.*, customer lists, which consisted of between 200 and 300 stops. The business income at that time was between $9,000 and $12,000 per month.

In July of 1981, Carting sold substantially the same assets to Industrial Waste Service, Inc. (Industrial) for $200,000. Industrial paid $50,000 in cash and gave a promissory note for the balance. The note is to be paid in installments of $2,500 per month. It is unclear whether the note was made payable to Gulf Coast Carting or Michael Acquafredda or both, but it is clear that Carting is no longer in business having been dissolved in December of 1980.

The Debtors filed their petitions for relief under Chapter 7 of the Bankruptcy Code on February 14, 1982. The Trustee instituted this adversary proceeding pursuant to Sec. 544(b), based on the contention that the transfers by the Debtors were in fraud of their creditors. He does not seek to set aside the transfers, but seeks a judgment against Michael Acquafredda for $50,000 (the amount received in cash from Industrial), assignment to the Trustee of the note executed by Industrial Waste and turnover of all monies already received on the installment payments on the note.

Section 544(b) provides that a Trustee in Bankruptcy may avoid any transfer of an interest of the Debtor in property that is voidable under applicable non–bankruptcy laws by a creditor holding an allowable unsecured claim. In order to prevail under this Section, the Trustee must establish first that, at the time that the transaction under attack occurred, there was, in fact, a creditor in existence who was holding an unsecured claim which is allowable under Section 502 of the Code. Second, the Trustee must establish that the transaction could have been avoided by such creditor under the applicable local law, in this instance, under the laws of the State of Florida.

There is no serious dispute that there were, in fact, creditors who held unsecured claims against the Debtors at the time relevant. Joseph Messina was holding and still holds the promissory note executed by the Debtor in connection with the acquisition of the assets from Community Disposal. Tanner and Associates, Inc., also held a claim which was reduced to judgment in the amount of $14,831.92 on April 26, 1978. This leaves for consideration whether the transfers of the assets by the Debtors to the various defendants were voidable under the laws of Florida.

The transfer under attack is the initial transfer by the Debtors to Disposal and Sanitation, the corporations formed by them and in which they were the sole stockholders. These two corporate entities continued to operate the business in the same manner in which it was operated by the Debtors as sole proprietors. While it is true that this transfer of assets by the Debtors to the newly formed corporation was not supported by any consideration whatsoever, it ostensibly was a transfer in exchange for all the outstanding stock in these two corporations. However, unless the Trustee's right of recovery under Section 544 is not limited to recovery against the immediate transferees, in this case, against Disposal and Sanitation, the Trustee's right to prevail cannot be recognized. This result is inevitable because all subsequent transfers, *i.e.*, the transfers by Sanitation and Disposal to Carting, were transfers by two non–debtor entities of property in which these Debtors ostensibly no longer had any interest. Of course, the same conclusion is equally applicable to the ultimate transfer, that is, the transfer by Carting to Industrial, the transfer proceeds of which the Trustee now seeks to recover.

Thus, the extent of the Trustee's rights of recovery under Section 544 must be determined before one can address the question of a fraudulent transfer. The answer to this initial issue is found in Section 550(a) of the Code which provides *inter alia* that

> to the extent that a transfer is voided under Sections 544, 545, 547, 548, 549, or 724(a) of this title, the Trustee may recover for the benefit of the estate, the property transferred, or, if the court so orders, the value of such property, from
>
> (2) any immediate or mediate transferee of such initial transferee.

This leaves for consideration the true character of these transfers. The several transactions involved here were not transactions commonly recognized as ones conducted at arms length. In each instance, with the exception of the transfer to Industrial, both the transferors and the transferees, although operating under a corporate name, were corporate entities that were family–owned and controlled by either the transferors or transferees. There is hardly any question that the very same assets changed hands as a result of each exchange, but all assets remained within the same family and were controlled by the same family members.

Fla. Stat. Sec. 726.01 provides, *inter alia*, that every conveyance or transfer of property made with intent to delay, hinder or defraud creditors is void and of no effect. Intent to defraud within the meaning of the statute is the Debtor's intention to prevent his creditors from satisfying their debts. *Wimmers v. Blackburn*, 151 Fla. 236, 9 So.2d 505 (1942). The intent must exist at the time of the transfer which is under attack. *Bay View Estates Corp. v. Southerland*, 114 Fla. 635, 154 So. 894

(1934). However, when the legal effect of the conveyance is to delay or hinder creditors, it is fraud in law regardless of the actual motives of the Debtor. *Whetstone v. Coslick*, 117 Fla. 203, 157 So. 666 (1934); *Livesay Industries, Inc. v. Window Co.*, 305 F.2d 934 (5th Cir. 1962).

Certain facts and circumstances have been recognized as indicia or "badges" of fraud. The Florida Supreme Court in *Cleveland Trust Company v. Foster*, 93 So. 2d 112 (Fla. 1957) listed the most important indicators of fraud as follows:

(a)   Relationship between the debtor and the transferee.

(b)   Lack of consideration for the conveyance.

(c)   Insolvency or indebtedness of the debtor.

(d)   The transfer of the debtor's entire estate.

(e)   Reservation of benefits, control or dominion by the Debtor.

(f)   Secrecy or concealment of the transaction.

(g)   Pendency or threat of litigation at the time of the transfer.

Each of the above–mentioned badges of fraud has evidentiary force in establishing the fraudulent character of a transfer. Although the badges of fraud may be inconclusive to establish fraud when considered separately, if they exist in combination, they "may by their number and joint consideration be sufficient to constitute conclusive proof" of fraud. *Florida National Bank of Gainsville v. Sherouse*, 80 Fla. 405, 86 So. 279 (1920). In this State, it is a well–established proposition of law that the transferee, for no consideration, will not be permitted to benefit to the detriment of the creditors of the transferors. *In re Flanzbaum*, 10 B.R. 420 (Bkrtcy. S.D. Fla. 1981); *In re Kassuba*, 10 B.R. 309 (D.C.S.D. Fla. 1981).

Applying the foregoing legal principles to the record as established at the final evidentiary hearing, this Court is satisfied that the initial transfers by the Debtors to Sanitation and Disposal were not bona fide arms length transactions. None of the transfers were conducted in an acceptable business manner and none are supported by an actual Bill of Sale or other documentation. The end result after each transfer was that the assets still remained in the use and under the control of the transferors, all of which belies the claim that these were legitimate and proper transfers, and that the Debtors effectively divested themselves of ownership in the assets ultimately sold to Industrial.

Michael Acquafredda claims that he furnished support to the Debtors as part of the consideration for the assets he acquired from them and that he also paid substantial sums to them from his savings. This contention defies credibility and finds no competent evidentiary support. It is without dispute that Michael Acquafredda never earned in his adult life any monies of any consequence which would have enabled him to furnish support to his parents, let alone accumulate substantial monies which would have enabled him to furnish actual monetary consideration for the purchase of these assets.

Having found that the transfers were fraudulent, this leaves for consideration the remedy available to the Trustee. Industrial did give substantial consideration in exchange for the assets. Given its status as a bona fide purchaser, the sale to Industrial cannot be set aside. However, it is clear that by virtue of Sec. 550 of the Bankruptcy Code, the trustee may recover the fruits of the transfer from any immediate or mediate transferee. In addition, this Court is sitting as a court of equity and may fashion an appropriate remedy to correct a wrong and, to that end, to impose any equitable liens in favor of the Trustee on the proceeds of the transfer by Carting to Industrial.

Accordingly, it appears to be appropriate to award a money judgment against Michael Acquafredda in the amount of $50,000, to direct him to turn over to the Trustee all monies paid by Industrial under the promissory note, and to direct him to assign said note to the Trustee, and to direct Industrial to make all future payments to the Debtors' estate.

This is not a related proceeding within the meaning of the definition furnished by Emergency Rule (d)(3)(A). Therefore, the judgment entered herein in accordance with the foregoing shall be effective upon entry by the clerk of the Bankruptcy Court, unless stayed by the Bankruptcy Judge or by a District Judge, pursuant to Emergency Rule (d)(2).

A separate final judgment will be entered in accordance with the foregoing.

[C] Preferences

The forerunner of § 547 was § 60a and b of the Act. It is meant, basically, to prevent a debtor from disposing of assets shortly before bankruptcy in a way that favors one or more creditors over others.

The elements of a voidable preference are set forth in § 547(b). To avoid a transfer, the trustee must prove the existence of each element, although § 547(f) assists by providing a presumption of insolvency. A major difference from the former act is the elimination of the requirement that a creditor, when receiving the transfer, had reason to know that the debtor was insolvent. Many preference actions were defended on the ground of lack of reasonable cause to believe that the debtor was insolvent. The effect, however, of omitting that element is to make every payment on a debt within 90 days of the petition a preference. This created the need for a § 547(c).

It is first necessary to parse out the elements of a voidable preference as listed in subsection (b). For example, what is a transfer? Why include the requirement that it be of the debtor's property? What is an antecedent debt? As distinguished from what? Note the two critical time periods. Who is an insider? What is the preferential effect of a transfer?

NOTES AND QUESTIONS

1. An important factual determination that must be made, firstly by the trustee, is when, on what specific date, was the transfer made? Why is this fact so

essential? Suppose a check in payment of goods is delivered to Supplier on November 18 and is honored by the drawee bank on November 20. Which of the two dates is the date of transfer? Read *Barnhill v. Johnson, infra.*

2. Supplier is owed $20,000 for goods sold and delivered to Acme Mfg. Co., Inc. Miriam Farr and Robert Farr, each of whom owns 50 percent of the stock of Acme, guaranteed payment to Supplier for all orders placed by Acme. On May 12, Acme paid debt in full to Supplier. On the following July 20, Acme filed a chapter 7 petition. May the chapter 7 trustee sue Miriam and Robert to recover the $20,000? *See* generally, Pitts, *Insider Guaranties and the Law of Preferences,* 55 Am. Bankr. L.J. 343 (1981).

3. Same facts as in (2) above, except that the chapter 7 petition was filed on the following December 15. May the trustee recover from Robert and Miriam? May the trustee recover from Supplier instead? *See Levit v. Ingersoll Rand Fin. Corp. (In re Deprizio Constr. Co.),* 874 F.2d 1186 (7th Cir. 1989). In 1994, § 550 was amended to abrogate the rule of that case. Why?

4. Should the butcher, baker, and computer store, if extending credit, be required to disgorge payments received within the 90–day period? Section 547(c) contains a list of exceptions to avoidance. Thus, the trustee must prove the existence of a voidable preference under subsection (b) but, after that, the creditor may avoid liability by proving the existence of one of the exceptions in subsection (c).

    (a) Bank makes an unsecured loan in the morning and learns in the afternoon that borrower is having financial difficulties. Bank immediately calls borrower in and requires it to sign an agreement securing the loan. Is the grant of the security interest substantially contemporaneous for subsection (c) purposes? No: *National City Bank v,. Hotchkiss,* 231 U.S. 50 (1913). Suppose the parties originally intended the loan to be secured but did not do the documentation until the afternoon? *See Dean v. Davis,* 242 U.S. 438 (1917).

    (b) Prior to 1984, subsection (c)(2) required the ordinary course payment to have been made within 45 days after the debt was incurred. The legal analysis centered on defining when a debt is incurred. In 1984, that requirement was deleted. Since then the legal analysis centers on the meaning of "ordinary course of business." Read *Union Bank v. Wolas (In re ZZZZ Best Co.), infra.*

5. As indicated above, it is important to determine when the transfer was made. The key elements of a preference have one fact in common that must be learned: when did the transfer take place? If a security interest was created by an agreement signed by the debtor on March 1, covering all of the debtor's equipment, and a financing statement was filed on June 6 and a chapter 11 case was commenced on August 15, was there a voidable preference? How can one determine when the transfer was made? *See* § 547(e).

6. Suppose the security agreement is entered into and the financing statement is filed in 1995 and the chapter 11 case is commenced in 1997. The collateral is

all of the debtor's present and future inventory. Is the security interest attaching to inventory acquired by the debtor within 90 days before the commencement of the case voidable under § 547(e)(3)? If so, what effect would the Bankruptcy Code have on both inventory and receivables financing? Section 547(c)(5) should be read with § 547(e)(3). The House Committee Report, H. Rep. No. 95–595, 95th Cong., 1st Sess. 374–75 (1977) states that § 547(e)(3) was meant to abrogate the rule in *DuBay v. Williams*, 417 F.2d 1277 (9th Cir. 1969) and *Grain Merchants, Inc. v. Union Bank*, 408 F.2d 209 (7th Cir.), cert. den., 396 U.S. 827 (1969), but § 547(c)(5) codifies 98 percent of the rule in those cases. *See*, for discussion of § 547(c)(5), 4 Collier on Bankruptcy ¶ 547.13 (15th ed.).

BARNHILL v. JOHNSON

Supreme Court of the United States
112 S.Ct. 1386, 26 C.B.C.2d 323 (1992)

REHNQUIST, C.J., delivered the opinion of the Court, in which WHITE, O'CONNOR, SCALIA, KENNEDY, SOUTER, and THOMAS, JJ., joined. STEVENS, J., filed a dissenting opinion, in which Blackmun, J., joined.

Under the Bankruptcy Code's preference avoidance section, 11 U.S.C. § 547, the trustee is permitted to recover, with certain exceptions, transfers of property made by the debtor within 90 days before the date the bankruptcy petition was filed. We granted certiorari to decide whether, in determining if a transfer occurred within the 90–day preference period, a transfer made by check should be deemed to occur on the date the check is presented to the recipient or on the date the drawee bank honors it. We hold that the latter date is determinative.

The relevant facts in this case are not in dispute. The debtor1 made payment for a bona fide debt to petitioner Barnhill. The check was delivered to petitioner on November 18. The check was dated November 19, and the check was honored by the drawee bank on November 20. The debtor later filed a Chapter 11 bankruptcy petition. It is agreed by the parties that the 90th day before the bankruptcy filing was November 20.

Respondent Johnson was appointed trustee for the bankruptcy estate. He filed an adversary proceeding against petitioner, claiming that the check payment was recoverable by the estate pursuant to 11 U.S.C. § 547(b). That section generally permits the trustee to recover for benefit of the bankruptcy estate transfers of the debtor's property made within 90 days of the bankruptcy filing. Respondent asserted that the transfer occurred on November 20, the date the check was honored by the drawee bank, and therefore was within the 90–day period. Petitioner defended by claiming that the transfer occurred on November 18, the date he received the check (the so–called date of delivery rule), and that it therefore fell outside the 90–day period established by § 547(b)(4)(A).

The Bankruptcy Court concluded that a date of delivery rule should govern and therefore denied the trustee recovery. The trustee appealed and the District Court affirmed. The trustee then appealed to the Court of Appeals for the Tenth Circuit.

The Court of Appeals for the Tenth Circuit reversed, concluding that a date of honor rule should govern actions under § 547(b). *In re Antwell*, 931 F.2d 689 [24 C.B.C.2d 1772] (1991). It distinguished a prior decision, *In re White River Corp.*, 799 F.2d 631 [15 C.B.C.2d 617] (1986), in which it held that, for purposes of § 547(c), a date of delivery rule should govern when a transfer occurs. The Tenth Circuit concluded that § 547(b) and § 547(c) have different purposes and functions, justifying different rules for each. It further concluded that a date of honor rule was appropriate because such a rule was consistent with provisions of the Uniform Commercial Code, was capable of easier proof, and was less subject to manipulation. We granted certiorari to resolve a Circuit split.3 502 U.S. (1991).

In relevant part, § 547(b) provides:

"(b) Except as provided in subsection (c) of this section, the trustee may avoid any transfer of an interest of the debtor in property –

. . .

"(4) made –

"(A) on or within 90 days before the date of the filing of the petition . . . Title 11 U.S.C. § 101(54) (1988 ed. Supp. II)4 defines "transfer" to mean

"every mode, direct or indirect, absolute or conditional, voluntary or involuntary, of disposing of or parting with property or with an interest in property, including retention of title as a security interest and foreclosure of the debtor's equity of redemption." Section 547(e) provides further guidance on the meaning and dating of a transfer. For purposes of § 547, it provides

"[(e)(1)](B) a transfer of a fixture or property other than real property is perfected when a creditor on a simple contract cannot acquire a judicial lien that is superior to the interest of the transferee.

"[(e)](2) For the purposes of this section, except as provided in paragraph (3) of this subsection, a transfer is made–

"(A) at the time such transfer takes effect between the transferor and the transferee, if such transfer is perfected at, or within 10 days after, such time;

"(B) at the time such transfer is perfected, if such transfer is perfected after such 10 days . . .

Our task, then, is to determine whether, under the definition of transfer provided by § 101(54), and supplemented by § 547(e), the transfer that the trustee seeks to avoid can be said to have occurred before November 20.

"What constitutes a transfer and when it is complete" is a matter of federal law. *McKenzie v. Irving Trust Co.*, 323 U.S. 365, 369–370 (1945). This is unsurprising since, as noted above, the statute itself provides a definition of "transfer." But that definition in turn includes references to parting with "property and interests in property." In the absence of any controlling federal law, "property" and "interest in property" are creatures of state law. *Id.* at 370; *Butner v. United States*, 440 U.S. 48, 54 (1979) ("Congress has generally left the determination of property rights in the assets of a bankrupt's estate to state law"). Thus it is helpful to sketch briefly the rights and duties enjoyed under state law by each party to a check transaction.

A person with an account at a bank enjoys a claim against the bank for funds in an amount equal to the account balance. Under the U.C.C., a check is simply an order to the drawee bank to pay the sum stated, signed by the maker and payable on demand. U.C.C. § st/.3–104(1), (2)(b), 2 U.L.A. 224 (1991). Receipt of a check does not, however, give the recipient a right against the bank. The recipient may present the check but, if the drawee bank refuses to honor it, the recipient has no recourse against the drawee. U.C.C. § 3–409(1), 2A U.L.A. 189 (1991).6

That is not to say, however, that the recipient of a check is without any rights. Receipt of a check for an underlying obligation suspends the obligation "pro tanto until the instrument['s] . . . presentment[;] . . . discharge of the underlying obligor on the instrument also discharges him on the obligation." U.C.C. § 3–802(1)(b), 2A U.L.A. 514 (1991). But should the drawee bank refuse to honor a check, a cause of action against the drawer of the check accrues to the recipient of a check "upon demand following dishonor of the instrument." U.C.C. § 3–122(3), 2 U.L.A. 407 (1991); *see also*, U.C.C. § 3–413(2), 2A U.L.A. 208 (1991). And the recipient of a dishonored check, received in payment on an underlying obligation, may maintain an action on either the check or on the obligation. U.C.C. § 3–802(1)(b), 2A U.L.A. 514 (1991).

With this background we turn to the issue at hand. Petitioner argues that the Court of Appeals erred in ignoring the interest that passed from the debtor to the petitioner when the check was delivered on a date outside the 90–day preference period. We disagree. We begin by noting that there can be no assertion that an unconditional transfer of the debtor's interest in property had occurred before November 20. This is because, as just noted above, receipt of a check gives the recipient no right in the funds held by the bank on the drawer's account. Myriad events can intervene between delivery and presentment of the check that would result in the check being dishonored. The drawer could choose to close the account. A third party could obtain a lien against the account by garnishment or other proceedings. The bank might mistakenly refuse to honor the check.

The import of the preceding discussion for the instant case is that no transfer of any part of the debtor's claim against the bank occurred until the bank honored the check on November 20. The drawee bank honored the check by paying it. U.C.C. § 1–201(21) (defining honor), 1 U.L.A. 65 (1989); U.C.C. § 4–213(a), 2B U.L.A.

222 (1991). At that time, the bank had a right to "charge" the debtor's account, U.C.C. § 4–401, 2B U.L.A. 307 (1991)—*i.e.*, the debtor's claim against the bank was reduced by the amount of the check—and petitioner no longer had a claim against the debtor. Honoring the check, in short, left the debtor in the position that it would have occupied if it had withdrawn cash from its account and handed it over to petitioner. We thus believe that when the debtor has directed the drawee bank to honor the check and the bank has done so, the debtor has implemented a "mode, direct or indirect . . . of disposing of property or an interest in property." 11 U.S.C. § 101(54). For the purposes of payment by ordinary check, therefore, a "transfer" as defined by § 101(54) occurs on the date of honor, and not before. And since it is undisputed that honor occurred within the 90–day preference period, the trustee presumptively may avoid this transfer.

In the face of this argument, petitioner retreats to the definition of "transfer" contained in § 101(54). Petitioner urges that rather than viewing the transaction as involving two distinct actions—delivery of the check, with no interest in property thereby being transferred, and honoring of the check, with an interest being transferred—that we instead should view delivery of the check as a "conditional" transfer. We acknowledge that § 101(54) adopts an expansive definition of transfer, one that includes "every mode . . . absolute or conditional . . . of disposing of or parting with property or with an interest in property." There is thus some force in petitioner's claim that he did, in fact gain something when he received the check. But at most, what petitioner gained was a chose in action against the debtor. Such a right, however, cannot fairly be characterized as a conditional right to "property or an interest in property," § 101(54), where the property in this case is the account maintained with the drawee bank. For as noted above, until the moment of honor the debtor retains full control over disposition of the account and the account remains subject to a variety of actions by third parties. To treat petitioner's nebulous right to bring suit as a "conditional transfer" of the property would accomplish a near–limitless expansion of the term "conditional." In the absence of any right against the bank or the account, we think the fairer description is that petitioner had received no interest in debtor's property, not that his interest was "conditional."

Finally, we note that our conclusion that no transfer of property occurs until the time of honor is consistent with § 547(e)(2)(A). That section provides that a transfer occurs at the time the transfer "takes effect between the transferor and the transferee . . . " For the reasons given above, and in particular because the debtor in this case retained the ability to stop payment on the check until the very last, we do not think that the transfer of funds in this case can be said to have "taken effect between the debtor and petitioner" until the moment of honor.

Recognizing, perhaps, the difficulties in its position, petitioner places his heaviest reliance not on the statutory language but on accompanying legislative history. Specifically, he points to identical statements from Representative Edwards and Senator DeConcini that "payment of a debt by means of a check is equivalent to a cash payment, unless the check is dishonored. Payment is considered to be made when the check is delivered for purposes of sections 547(c)(1) and (2)." 124 Cong. Rec. 32400, (1978) and *Id.*, at 34000. We think this appeal to legislative history unavailing.

To begin, we note that appeals to statutory history are well–taken only to resolve "statutory ambiguity." *Toibb v. Radloff*, 501 U.S. – [24 C.B.C.2d 1179] (1991) (slip op. at 5). We do not think this is such a case. But even if it were, the statements on which petitioner relies, by their own terms, apply only to § 547(c), not § 547(b). Section 547(c), in turn, establishes various exceptions to § 547(b)'s general rule permitting recovery of preferential transfers. Subsection (c)(1) provides an exception for transfers that are part of a contemporaneous exchange of new value between a debtor and creditor; subsection (c)(2) provides an exception for transfers made from debtor to creditor in the ordinary course of business. These sections are designed to encourage creditors to continue to deal with troubled debtors on normal business terms by obviating any worry that a subsequent bankruptcy filing might require the creditor to disgorge as a preference an earlier received payment. But given this specialized purpose, we see no basis for concluding that the legislative history, particularly legislative history explicitly confined by its own terms to § 547(c), should cause us to adopt a "date of delivery" rule for purposes of § 547(b).

For the foregoing reasons, the judgment of the Court of Appeals is

Affirmed.

Justice STEVENS, with whom Justice BLACKMUN joins, dissenting:

In my opinion, a "transfer" of property occurs on the date the check is delivered to the transferee, provided that the check is honored within 10 days. This conclusion is consistent with the traditional commercial practice of treating the date of delivery as the date of payment when a payment is made by a check that is subsequently honored by the drawee bank. It is also consistent with the treatment of checks in tax law. A taxpayer may deduct expenses paid by a check delivered on or before December 31 against that year's income even though the drawee bank does not honor the check until the next calendar year. Insofar as possible, it is wise to interpret statutes regulating commercial behavior consistently with established practices in the business community. The custom that treats the delivery of a check as payment should not be rejected unless Congress has unequivocally commanded a contrary result. In the Bankruptcy Code, Congress has done no such thing. On the contrary, the Code is entirely consistent with the normal practice.

The definition of the term "transfer" in § 101(54) is plainly broad enough to encompass the conditional transfer of the right to funds in the debtor's bank account that occurs when the debtor delivers a check to a creditor. Section 101(54) defines a "transfer" as "every mode, direct or indirect, absolute or conditional, voluntary or involuntary, of disposing of or parting with property or with an interest in property . . . " 11 U.S.C. § 101(54) (1988 ed., Supp. II). A check is obviously a "mode" through which the debtor may "par[t] with property."

Of course, the fact that delivery of a check effects a "transfer" within the meaning of the Code does not answer the question whether the trustee may avoid the transfer by check in this case because § 547(b) only authorizes the trustee to avoid transfers made "on or within 90 days before the date of the filing of the [bankruptcy] petition." 11 U.S.C. § 547(b)(4)(A). That raises the question: when did the "transfer" occur?

Section 547(e)(2) provides the answer. It states that for purposes of the preference avoidance section, 11 U.S.C. § 547, a transfer is made

> "(A) at the time such transfer takes effect between the transferor and the transferee, if such transfer is perfected at, or within 10 days after, such time;

> "(B) at the time such transfer is perfected, if such transfer is perfected after such 10 days . . . " § 547(e)(2)."

The Court interprets this section as supporting its conclusion that the transfer does not occur until the check is honored by the drawee bank because, it reasons, a transfer cannot take effect between the transferor and transferee as long as the transferor retains the ability to stop payment on the check. Ante, at 8. But that reasoning is foreclosed by § 101(54), which states that even a conditional transfer is a transfer for purposes of the Code. Because delivery of a check effects a conditional transfer from the transferor to the transferee, the "transfer" is made, for purposes of § 547, on the date of delivery, provided that the transfer is "perfected" within 10 days as required by § 547(e)(2).

As the Court of Appeals for the Seventh Circuit recognized, the use of the term "perfected" is "jarring" because the meaning of the word "perfected" is not immediately apparent in this context. *Global Distribution Network, Inc. v. Star Expansion Co.*, 949 F.2d 910, 913 (1991). "Debtors transfer assets; creditors perfect security interests." *Ibid.* The answer lies in the fact that the term perfected has a broader meaning in § 547(e) than it does in the Uniform Commercial Code. Section 547(e)(1)(B) states that "a transfer of . . . property other than real property is perfected when a creditor on a simple contract cannot acquire a judicial lien that is superior to the interest of the transferee." Under this definition, a transfer by check is "perfected" when the check is honored because after that time no one can acquire a judicial lien superior to the interest of the transferee.

Thus § § 101(54) and 547, when read together, plainly indicate that a "transfer" by check occurs on the date the check is delivered to the transferee, provided that the drawee bank honors the check within 10 days. If, however, the check is not honored within 10 days, the "transfer" occurs on the date of honor.

An additional consideration reinforces this interpretation of the statutory text. The Courts of Appeals are unanimous in concluding that the date of delivery of a check is controlling for purposes of § 547(c), and the Court does not dispute that conclusion for the purposes of its decision today. Ante, at 9, n. 9. These Courts of Appeals decisions are consistent with the legislative history, which, though admittedly not conclusive, identifies the date of delivery of a check as the date of transfer for purposes of § 547(c). Normally, we assume that the same terms have the same meaning in different sections of the same statute. See, e.g., *Sullivan v. Stroop*, 496 U.S. 478, 484 (1990). That rule is not inexorable, but nothing in the structure or purpose of § 547(b) and § 547(c) suggests a reason for interpreting these adjacent subsections differently.

I would therefore reverse the judgment of the Court of Appeals.

NOTES AND QUESTIONS

1. The Barnhill case involved application of § 547(b). If, instead, the check was delivered on May 3 to a department store for a television set purchased and received on the same day, would the transfer fall within the exception of § 547(c)(1) if the check was honored by the bank on May 5?

2. Can any principle of statutory construction be gleaned from the Barnhill decision? *See also*, the *Wolas case, infra.*

UNION v. WOLAS

Supreme Court of the United States
112 S. Ct. 527, 25 C.B.C.2d 1011 (1991)

Justice STEVENS delivered the opinion of the Court:

Section 547(b) of the Bankruptcy Code, 11 U.S.C. 547(b), authorizes a trustee to avoid certain property transfers made by a debtor within 90 days before bankruptcy. The Code makes an exception, however, for transfers made in the ordinary course of business, 11 U.S.C. § 547(c)(2). The question presented is whether payments on long–term debt may qualify for that exception.

On December 17, 1986, ZZZZ Best Co., Inc. (Debtor) borrowed seven million dollars from petitioner, Union Bank (Bank). On July 8, 1987, the Debtor filed a voluntary petition under Chapter 7 of the Bankruptcy Code. During the preceding 90–day period, the Debtor had made two interest payments totalling approximately $100,000 and had paid a loan commitment fee of about $2,500 to the Bank. After his appointment as trustee of the Debtor's estate, respondent filed a complaint against the Bank to recover those payments pursuant to § 547(b).

The Bankruptcy Court found that the loans had been made "in the ordinary course of business or financial affairs" of both the Debtor and the Bank, and that both interest payments as well as the payment of the loan commitment fee had been made according to ordinary business terms and in the ordinary course of business. As a matter of law, the Bankruptcy Court concluded that the payments satisfied the requirements of § 547(c)(2) and therefore were not avoidable by the trustee. The District Court affirmed the Bankruptcy Court's summary judgment in favor of the Bank.

Shortly thereafter, in another case, the Court of Appeals held that the ordinary course of business exception to avoidance of preferential transfers was not available to long–term creditors. *In re CHG International, Inc.*, 897 F.2d 1479 (CA9 1990). In reaching that conclusion, the Court of Appeals relied primarily on the policies underlying the voidable preference provisions and the state of the law prior to the enactment of the 1978 Bankruptcy Code and its amendment in 1984. Thus, the Ninth Circuit concluded, its holding in CHG International, Inc. dictated a reversal in this case. 921 F.2d 968, 969 (1990). The importance of the question of law decided by the Ninth Circuit, coupled with the fact that the Sixth Circuit had interpreted § 547(c)(2) in a contrary manner, *In re Finn,* 909 F.2d 903 (1990), persuaded us to grant the Bank's petition for certiorari. 500 U.S.—(1991).

I.

We shall discuss the history and policy of § 547 after examining its text. In subsection (b), Congress broadly authorized bankruptcy trustees to "avoid any transfer of an interest of the debtor in property" if five conditions are satisfied and unless one of seven exceptions defined in subsection (c) is applicable. In brief, the five characteristics of a voidable preference are that it (1) benefit a creditor; (2) be on account of antecedent debt; (3) be made while the debtor was insolvent; (4) be within 90 days before bankruptcy; and (5) enable the creditor to receive a larger share of the estate than if the transfer had not been made. Section 547 also provides that the debtor is presumed to have been insolvent during the 90–day period preceding bankruptcy. 11 U.S.C. § 547(f). In this case, it is undisputed that all five of the foregoing conditions were satisfied and that the interest and loan commitment fee payments were voidable preferences unless excepted by subsection (c)(2).

The most significant feature of subsection (c)(2) that is relevant to this case is the absence of any language distinguishing between long–term debt and short–term debt. That subsection provides:

"The trustee may not avoid under this section a transfer–

"(2) to the extent that such transfer was–

"(A) in payment of a debt incurred by the debtor in the ordinary course of business or financial affairs of the debtor and the transferee;

"(B) made in the ordinary course of business or financial affairs of the debtor and the transferee; and

"(C) made according to ordinary business terms."

Instead of focusing on the term of the debt for which the transfer was made, subsection (c)(2) focuses on whether the debt was incurred, and payment made, in the "ordinary course of business or financial affairs" of the debtor and transferee. Thus, the text provides no support for respondent's contention that § 547(c)(2)'s coverage is limited to short–term debt, such as commercial paper or trade debt. Given the clarity of the statutory text, respondent's burden of persuading us that Congress intended to create or to preserve a special rule for long–term debt is exceptionally heavy. *United States v. Ron Pair Enterprises, Inc.,* 489 U.S. 235, 241–241 (1989). As did the Ninth Circuit, respondent relies on the history and the policies underlying the preference provision.

II.

The relevant history of § 547 contains two chapters, one of which clearly supports, and the second of which is not inconsistent with, the Bank's literal reading of the statute. Section 547 was enacted in 1978 when Congress overhauled the Nation's bankruptcy laws. The section was amended in 1984. For purposes of the question presented in this case, the original version of § 547 differed in one significant respect from the current version: it contained a provision that the ordinary course of business exception did not apply unless the payment was made within 45 days of the date the debt was incurred. That provision presumably excluded most payments on long–term debt from the exception. In 1984 Congress repealed the 45–day limitation but did not substitute a comparable limitation. *See* Bankruptcy Amendments and Federal Judgeship Act of 1984, Pub. L. 98–353, § 462(c), 98 Stat. 333, 378.

Respondent contends that this amendment was intended to satisfy complaints by issuers of commercial paper and by trade creditors that regularly extended credit for periods of more than 45 days. Furthermore, respondent continues, there is no evidence in the legislative history that Congress intended to make the ordinary course of business exception available to conventional long–term lenders. Therefore, respondent argues, we should follow the analysis of the Ninth Circuit and read § 547(c)(2) as protecting only short–term debt payments. *Cf. In re CHG International*, 897 F.2d at 1484.

We need not dispute the accuracy of respondent's description of the legislative history of the 1984 amendment in order to reject his conclusion. For even if Congress adopted the 1984 amendment to redress particular problems of specific short–term creditors, it remains true that Congress redressed those problems by entirely deleting the time limitation in § 547(c)(2). The fact that Congress may not have foreseen all of the consequences of a statutory enactment is not a sufficient reason for refusing to give effect to its plain meaning. *Toibb v. Radloff*, 501 U.S. [24 C.B.C.2d 1178] (1991).

Respondent also relies on the history of voidable preferences prior to the enactment of the 1978 Bankruptcy Code. The text of the preference provision in the earlier Bankruptcy Act did not specifically include an exception for payments made in the ordinary course of business. The courts had, however, developed what is sometimes described as the "current expense" rule to cover situations in which a debtor's payments on the eve of bankruptcy did not diminish the net estate because tangible assets were obtained in exchange for the payment. *See Marshall v. Florida National Bank of Jacksonville*, 112 F.2d 380, 382 (CA5 1940); 3 Collier on Bankruptcy ¶ 60.23, p. 873 (14th ed. 1977). Without such an exception, trade creditors and other suppliers of necessary goods and services might have been reluctant to extend even short–term credit and might have required advance payment instead, thus making it difficult for many companies in temporary distress to have remained in business. Respondent argues that Congress enacted § 547(c)(2) in 1978 to codify that exception, and therefore the Court should construe § 547(c)(2) as limited to the confines of the current expense rule.

This argument is not compelling for several reasons. First, it is by no means clear that § 547(c)(2) should be construed as the statutory analogue of the judicially crafted current expense rule because there are other exceptions in § 547(c) that explicitly cover contemporaneous exchanges for new value. Those provisions occupy some (if not all) of the territory previously covered by the current expense rule. Nor has respondent directed our attention to any extrinsic evidence suggesting that Congress intended to codify the current expense rule in § 547(c)(2).

The current expense rule developed when the statutory preference provision was significantly narrower than it is today. To establish a preference under the Bankruptcy Act, the trustee had to prove that the challenged payment was made at a time when the creditor had "reasonable cause to believe that the debtor [was] insolvent." 11 U.S.C. § 96(b) (1976 ed.). When Congress rewrote the preference provision in the 1978 Bankruptcy Code, it substantially enlarged the trustee's power to avoid preferential transfers by eliminating the reasonable cause to believe requirement for transfers made within 90 days of bankruptcy and creating a presumption of insolvency during that period. See 11 U.S.C. § § 547(b), (c)(2), (f); H.R. Rep. No. 95–595, p. 178 (1977). At the same time, Congress created a new exception for transfers made in the ordinary course of business, 11 U.S.C. § 547(c)(2). This exception was intended to "leave undisturbed normal financial relations, because it does not detract from the general policy of the preference section to discourage unusual action by either the debtor or his creditors during the debtor's slide into bankruptcy." H.R. Rep. No. 95–595, at 373.

In light of these substantial changes in the preference provision, there is no reason to assume that the justification for narrowly confining the "current expense" exception to trade creditors before 1978 should apply to the ordinary course of business exception under the 1978 Code. Instead, the fact that Congress carefully reexamined and entirely rewrote the preference provision in 1978 supports the conclusion that the text of § 547(c)(2) as enacted reflects the deliberate choice of Congress.

III.

The Bank and the trustee agree that § 547 is intended to serve two basic policies that are fairly described in the House Committee Report. The Committee explained:

> "A preference is a transfer that enables a creditor to receive
> payment of a greater percentage of his claim against the debtor
> than he would have received if the transfer had not been made
> and he had participated in the distribution of the assets of the
> bankrupt estate. The purpose of the preference section is two–fold.
> First, by permitting the trustee to avoid prebankruptcy transfers
> that occur within a short period before bankruptcy, creditors are
> discouraged from racing to the courthouse to dismember the
> debtor during his slide into bankruptcy. The protection thus
> afforded the debtor often enables him to work his way out of
> a difficult financial situation through cooperation with all of his

> creditors. Second, and more important, the preference provisions facilitate the prime bankruptcy policy of equality of distribution among creditors of the debtor. Any creditor that received a greater payment than others of his class is required to disgorge so that all may share equally. The operation of the preference section to deter 'the race of diligence' of creditors to dismember the debtor before bankruptcy furthers the second goal of the preference section–that of equality of distribution." *Id.*, at 177–178.

As this comment demonstrates, the two policies are not entirely independent. On the one hand, any exception for a payment on account of an antecedent debt tends to favor the payee over other creditors and therefore may conflict with the policy of equal treatment. On the other hand, the ordinary course of business exception may benefit all creditors by deterring the "race to the courthouse" and enabling the struggling debtor to continue operating its business.

Respondent places primary emphasis, as did the Court of Appeals, on the interest in equal distribution. *See In re CHG International,* 897 F.2d, at 1483–1485. When a debtor is insolvent, a transfer to one creditor necessarily impairs the claims of the debtor's other unsecured and undersecured creditors. By authorizing the avoidance of such preferential transfers, § 547(b) empowers the trustee to restore equal status to all creditors. Respondent thus contends that the ordinary course of business exception should be limited to short–term debt so the trustee may order that preferential long–term debt payments be returned to the estate to be distributed among all of the creditors.

But the statutory text which makes no distinction between short–term debt and long–term debt precludes an analysis that divorces the policy of favoring equal distribution from the policy of discouraging creditors from racing to the courthouse to dismember the debtor. Long–term creditors, as well as trade creditors, may seek a head start in that race. Thus, even if we accept the Court of Appeals' conclusion that the availability of the ordinary business exception to long–term creditors does not directly further the policy of equal treatment, we must recognize that it does further the policy of deterring the race to the courthouse and, as the House Report recognized, may indirectly further the goal of equal distribution as well. Whether Congress has wisely balanced the sometimes conflicting policies underlying § 547 is not a question that we are authorized to decide.

IV.

In sum, we hold that payments on long–term debt, as well as payments on short–term debt, may qualify for the ordinary course of business exception to the trustee's power to avoid preferential transfers. We express no opinion, however, on the question whether the Bankruptcy Court correctly concluded that the Debtor's payments of interest and the loan commitment fee qualify for the ordinary course of business exception, § 547(c)(2). In particular, we do not decide whether the loan involved in this case was incurred in the ordinary course of the Debtor's business and of the Bank's business, whether the payments were made in the ordinary course of business, or whether the payments were made according to ordinary business terms. These questions remain open for the Court of Appeals on remand.

The judgment of the Court of Appeals is reversed and the case is remanded for further proceedings consistent with this opinion.

It is so ordered.

Justice SCALIA, concurring:

I join the opinion of the Court, including Parts II and III, which respond persuasively to legislative–history and policy arguments made by respondent. It is regrettable that we have a legal culture in which such arguments have to be addressed (and are indeed creditor by a Court of Appeals), with respect to a statute utterly devoid of language that could remotely be thought to distinguish between long–term and short–term debt. Since there was here no contention of a "scrivener's error" producing an absurd result, the plain text of the statute should have made this litigation unnecessary and unmaintainable.

NOTES AND QUESTIONS

What does "ordinary course of business" mean? Is it limited to that which is ordinary in the particular industry or type of business? Or does it mean that which is ordinary to the particular debtor and creditor in the course of their dealing with each other? Or both? Suppose the supply contract calls for payment by the buyer within 10 days of the invoice date but over the last two years the payments were regularly made and received without objection on an average of 35 days late. Would payments made 36, 38, and 40 days late during the 90 days preceding the commencement of a case be voidable? *See In re Tolona Pizza Products Corp.*, 3 F.3d 1029 (7th Cir. 1993); *In re Graphic Productions Corp.*, 176 B.R. 65 (Bankr. S.D. Fla. 1994).

INDEPENDENCE LAND TITLE CORP. OF ILLINOIS v. NATIONAL BANK AND TRUST CO. OF SYCAMORE
(In re Independence Land Title Corp.)

Bankruptcy Court, Northern District of Illinois
9 B.R. 394, 4 C.B.C.2d 118 (1981)

EISEN, Bankruptcy Judge:

This matter came to be heard on the trustee's application to avoid a lien on a motor vehicle. The National Bank and Trust Company of Sycamore contends the lien is valid and perfected while the trustee contends the lien is null and void as a preference. The court having researched the issues presented and being fully advised in the premises makes the following findings of fact and conclusions of law.

Findings of Fact

1. In February 1980 the debtor assigned its interest in the car to Mr. Wade, President of the debtor corporation.

2. Mr. Wade, as President of the debtor, endorsed the back of the certificate of title, thereby assigning the car to himself individually. Mr. Wade took possession of the car but failed to send the certificate of title to the Secretary of State for the issuance of a new certificate of title

3. On March 18, 1980 the debtor applied to the Bank for a loan so that the debtor could repurchase the car from Mr. Wade.

    a. On March 18, 1980 the debtor and the Bank executed an installment note and a Motor Vehicle Security Agreement whereby the parties attempted to grant the Bank a security interest in the car.

    b. On March 18, 1980 the debtor gave Mr. Wade the loan proceeds.

    c. On March 18, 1980 Mr. Wade gave the Bank the certificate of title which showed the debtor as the owner and then showed the assignment of ownership from the debtor to Mr. Wade.

    d. On March 18, 1980 there was no room on the back of the certificate of title for further assignments so the Bank, with Mr. Wade's cooperation, mailed the certificate of title to the Secretary of State requesting a new certificate of title showing Mr. Wade as the car's owner.

4. On March 27, 1980 the debtor filed a petition under Chapter 11.

5. On or about April 24, 1980 the Bank received the new certificate of title showing Mr. Wade as the car's owner.

6. On or about May 15, 1980 Mr. Wade endorsed the new certificate of title thereby assigning the car to the debtor.

7. The Bank subsequently sent the certificate of title, as assigned, to the Secretary of State requesting a new certificate of title showing the debtor as the owner and the Bank as the lienholder.

8. On June 5, 1980 the Secretary of State issued a certificate of title indicating the debtor's and the Bank's respective interests in the car.

Issue

Does the transfer fall within an exception to the trustee's avoiding powers?

Discussion

The Bank contends it has a valid and perfected security interest in the car. The trustee contends the transfer is voidable as a preference. The Bank does not deny that the transfer created a preference voidable under 11 U.S.C. § 547(b). The Bank, however, does contend that the transfer falls within the exception to the trustee's avoiding powers. The exceptions to the trustee's avoiding powers appear in 11 U.S.C. § 547(c) which states that:

The trustee may not avoid under this section a transfer—

1. to the extent that such transfer was (a) intended by the debtor and creditor to be a contemporaneous exchange for new value given to the debtor; and (b) in fact a substantially contemporaneous exchange;

3. of a security interest in property acquired by the debtor—(a) to the extent such security interest secures new value that was—

and (b) that is perfected before 10 days after such security interest attaches.

Section 547(c)(1) will be referred to as the "substantially contemporaneous exchange" exception and § 547(c)(3) will be referred to as the "enabling loan" exception. The Bank argues in the alternative that either the transfer comes within the "substantially contemporaneous exchange" exception or that it comes within the "enabling loan" exception. Section 547(c)(1) will be referred to as the "substantially contemporaneous exchange" exception and § 547(c)(3) will be referred to as the "enabling loan" exception. The Bank argues in the alternative that either the transfer comes within the "substantially contemporaneous exchange" exception or that it comes within the "enabling loan" exception.

The first issue considered is whether the creation of the security interest was "substantially contemporaneous" with the giving of the loan. The transfer in question is the giving of the security interest in exchange for the loan. 11 U.S.C. § 101(40). The transfer is made when the security interest is perfected. 11 U.S.C. § 547(e)(2). This court holds that the transfer was not perfected until subsequent to May 15, 1980 at the earliest. The Illinois Vehicle Code holds that a security interest in a car is perfected when the certificate of title is delivered to the Secretary of State with an application containing the name and address of the lienholder as well as the required fee. S.H.A., Chp. 95 1/2, § 3–202(b). The debtor did not have rights in the car until May 15, 1980 so it was impossible for the Bank to perfect a security interest before that date. 11 U.S.C. § 547(e)(3). Contemporaneous is defined as "originating, arising or being formed or made at the same time" Webster's Third International Dictionary, Unabridged (1961). The Bank submits no case authorities holding that a two–month gap between a loan and the perfection of a security interest constitutes a "substantially contemporaneous exchange." The court therefore finds that the exchange was not substantially contemporaneous and thus not within the exception to the trustee's avoiding power set forth in § 547(c)(1). The court cites *In re Kelly*,

3 B.R. 651; C.C.H. ¶ 67,688, p. 78,217 (E.D.Tenn. 1980) and *In re Poteet,* 5 B.R. 631 (E.D. Tenn. 1980) in support of the instant holding. As the *Poteet* court stated:

> "Delayed perfection of the security interest thus resulted in a transfer avoidable by the trustee as preferential." *Id.* at 636.

Alternatively, the Bank contends that the transfer is within the "enabling loan" exception of § 547(c)(3). The Bank contends that the security interest first attached on May 15, 1980 when the debtor acquired rights in the collateral S.H.A. ch. 26, § 9–203. Then the Bank contends the security interest was perfected within 10 days of attachment. S.H.A. ch. 95 1/2, § 3–202(b). Section 547(e) of the Bankruptcy Code determines when a transfer is made for the purposes of the preference section of the Code. The Code states that:

> for the purposes of this section, a transfer is not made until the debtor has acquired rights in the property transferred.

11 U.S.C. § 547(e)(3). For the purposes of the preference section, the transfer was not made until May 15, 1980. Thus the transfer was a post–petition transaction. The loan was made March 18, 1980 and the Chapter 11 petition was filed March 27, 1980. The certificate of title showing the debtor as owner and the Bank as lienholder was not issued until June 5, 1980. The court holds that the transaction was not within the "enabling loan" exception to the trustee's avoiding powers. 11 U.S.C. § 547(c)(3), and as further support states that:

> (a) the trustee may avoid a transfer of property of the estate—(1) that occurs after the commencement of the case; and
>
> (2)(B) that is not authorized under this title or by the court.

11 U.S.C. § 549. The transfer occurred after the case was commenced and it was not authorized by the Code or the Court.

It is therefore concluded that the disputed transaction is not within either the "substantially contemporaneous exchange" or the "enabling loan" exceptions to the trustee's avoiding power. Furthermore, the transaction may be avoided pursuant to 11 U.S.C. § 549. *Wherefore, It Is Hereby Ordered* that the lien of the National Bank and Trust Company of Sycamore on the 1978 Dodge Magnum, Serial No. XS22K8R206107, owned by the debtor is null and void and that possession of the car is hereby awarded to the trustee.

———————

WALDSCHMIDT v. RANIER & ASSOCIATES
(In re Fulghum Construction Corp.)

United States Court of Appeals, Sixth Circuit
706 F.2d 171 (1983)
cert. denied, 464 U.S. 935 (1983)

KRUPANSKY, Circuit Judge.

This action joins inquiry into the longstanding judicially evolved application of the "net result rule" as the criteria for determining a preferential transfer as defined in 11 U.S.C. § 547 of the Bankruptcy Reform Act of 1978. An involuntary petition in bankruptcy was filed against Fulghum Construction Corporation (Fulghum) whereupon the trustee initiated the instant proceeding to, *inter alia*, avoid as preferential transfers certain monetary transactions which transpired between Fulghum and its sole shareholder, Ranier & Associates (Ranier), during the one year period immediately preceding the filing of the bankruptcy petition. Both the bankruptcy court and reviewing district court adjudged that application of the net result rule, incorporated into 11 U.S.C. § 547(b)(5) as a judicial gloss, foreclosed a finding that the transfers were preferential. *See: In re Fulghum Construction Corp.*, 7 B.R. 629 (Bankr. M.D. Tenn.1980); *In re Fulghum Construction Corp.*, 14 B.R. 293 (M.D.Tenn.1981). The operative facts, detailed in the lower courts' opinions, disclose that approximately 100 transactions occurred between Ranier and Fulghum during the year immediately preceding the filing of the bankruptcy petition. The aggregate amount of the payments by Ranier to Fulghum exceeded the aggregate amount of the payments tendered by Fulgham to Ranier during this period and the value of the estate was accordingly appreciated.

Preferential transfers which may be avoided by the trustee are defined in 11 U.S.C. § 547(b):

> (b)   Except as provided in subsection (c) of this section, the trustee may avoid any transfer of property of the debtor—

> (1)   to or for the benefit of a creditor;

> (2)   for or on account of an antecedent debt owned by the debtor before such transfer was made;

> (3)   made while the debtor was insolvent;

> (4)   made—

>> (A)   on or within 90 days before the date of filing of the petition; or

>> (B)   between 90 days and one year before the date of the filing of the petition, if such creditor, at the time of such transfer—

>>> (i)   was an insider; and

>>> (ii)   had reasonable cause to believe the debtor was insolvent at the time of such transfer; and

> (5)   that enables such creditor to receive more than such creditor would receive if—

(A) the case were a case under chapter 7 of this title;

(B) the transfer had not been made; and

(C) such creditor received payment of such debt to the extent provided by the provision of this title.

As is facially evident from this provision, all five enumerated criteria must be satisfied before a trustee may avoid any transfer of property as a preference. *See: In re Bishop*, 17 B.R. 180, 181–82 (Bkrtcy. N.D. Ga.1982). Section 547(b) is proscribed by its own terms to the numerous "defenses" available to creditors which appear in § 547(c) and which, if applicable, preclude the trustee from avoiding the § 547(b) preferential transfer. Particularly, § 547(c)(4) provides:

(c) The trustee may not avoid under this section a transfer—

(4) to or for the benefit of a creditor, to the extent that, after such transfer, such creditor gave new value to or for the benefit of the debtor—

(A) not secured by an otherwise unavoidable security interest; and

(B) on account of which new value the debtor did not make an otherwise unavoidable transfer to or for the benefit of such creditor

Section 547(c)(4) is perhaps most accurately characterized as a "subsequent advance rule." Preferential transfers as defined in § 547(b) may not be avoided by the trustee if " after such transfer, such creditor gave new value". *Id. See: In re Bishop, supra; In re Garland,* 19 B.R. 920 (Bkrtcy. E.D.Mo.1982); *In re Rustia,* 20 B.R. 131, 135 (Bkrtcy. S.D.N.Y. 1982); *In re Fabric Buys of Jericho,* 22 B.R. 1013, 1016–17 (Bkrtcy. S.D.N.Y. 1982); *In re Hersman,* 20 B.R. 569 (Bkrtcy. N.D. Ohio 1982).

In the action *sub judice*, the district court adjudged, and the parties do not dispute on appeal, that the criteria of § 547(b)(1) through (b)(4) have been satisfied. In addressing the application of § 547(b)(5) to the facts of the case at bar, however, the district court relied upon its equitable powers to justify its application of the net result with the following rationale:

> [T]his Court must agree with the Bankruptcy Court that two "net results rules" actually exist in bankruptcy law. One, that of section 547(c)(4) and insisted upon by the trustee, is statutory. The other, that applied by the Bankruptcy Court, is nonstatutory, a judicial gloss upon the requirements of section 547(b).

14 B.R. at 303. Applying the net result rule as a condition implicitly incorporated into § 547(b)(5) and, correspondingly, a threshold requirement to support a preferential transfer, the district court observed that the net effect of all the transactions between the debtor, Fulghum, and the creditor, Ranier, appreciated the value of the estate and, accordingly, the transfers could not be avoided by the trustee as preferences. Upon concluding that no preferential transfers existed it was unnecessary for the district court to identify the defenses available to the creditor under § 547(c).

The net result rule is a judicially created doctrine, predicated upon principles of equity, which evolved shortly after the enactment of the Bankruptcy Act of 1898 to presumably rectify what was judicially perceived to be inequities in bankruptcy law. *See: In re Garland, supra*, 19 B.R. at 922–25 (artfully documenting development of this doctrine); *In re Bishop supra*, 17 B.R. at 183–85 (same). As an equitable doctrine its application, of necessity, must "comport to and remain compatible with the prevailing legislative intent." *In re Bell*, 700 F.2d 1053, 1057 (6th Cir. 1983); *United States v. Killoren*, 119 F.2d 364, 366 (8th Cir. 1941). Logic dictates that judicial interposition of the net result rule into § 547(b)(5) vitiates the congressional intent clearly reflected both on the face of § 547 and in the legislative history of the enactment.

Since the net result rule is "broader" in scope than the subsequent advance rule of § 547(c)(4), engrafting the former doctrine upon § 547(b)(5) as a threshold requirement for the qualifying preference would render the defense incorporated in § 547(c)(4) impotent. The broader scope of the net result rule permits its utilization by the creditor irrespective of whether the value furnished by the creditor to the debtor is advanced either before or after the transfer from the debtor to the creditor. Contrawise, the subsequent advance rule of § 547(c)(4) is more circumscribed in application and forecloses avoidance of the transfer by the trustee only if the creditor provides additional value after the transfer from the debtor to the creditor. A "judicial gloss" which significantly restricts the statutory definition of "preference" and pragmatically emasculates the creditor defense thereto as intended by Congress in § 547(c)(4) constitutes nothing less than legislation by judicial decree.

Moreover, judicial interposition of the net result rule into § 547(b)(5) finds no sanction in the legislative history of the Bankruptcy Reform Act of 1978. The legislative proceedings attendant to the promulgation of § 547(b)(5) are significantly devoid of any allusion to the net result rule. Contrawise, the House Report discussing the subsequent advance rule, § 547(c)(4), incorporates concise language reflecting the intent of Congress:

> The fourth exception [§ 547(c)(4)] codifies the net result rule in section 60c of current law. If the creditor and the debtor have more than one exchange during the 90–day period, the exchanges are *netted out according to the formula in paragraph (4)*. Any new value that the creditor advances must be unsecured in order for it to qualify under this exception. (Emphasis added).

H.R.Rep. No. 95–595, 95th Cong., 1st Sess. 374, reprinted in 1978 U.S. Code Cong. & Ad. News 5787, 6330. The Senate Report is identical. S. Rep. No. 95–989, 95th Cong., 2d Sess. 88, reprinted in 1978 U.S. Code Cong. & Ad. News 5874. Thus, it would appear that the "net result rule" is an anachronism of § 547(c). As has been noted,

> Whatever the net result rule may have been under the prior Bankruptcy Act, Congress has indicated that, under the Bankruptcy Code, the rule is to be applied accordingly to the formula set forth in section 547(c)(4).

In re Garland, supra, 19 B.R. at 926. Congressional metamorphosis has transformed the judicially created net result rule into what may be characterized as a subsequent advance rule and has codified this augmented version into § 547(c)(4) rather than

§ 547(b)(5). *See also: In re Bishop, supra*, referencing: 2 Norton Bankr. L. & Prac. § 32.20 (net result rule "is of doubtful current validity"); 4 Collier on Bankruptcy § 547.40 (seriously questioning continuing vitality of the net result rule in the wake of the Bankruptcy Reform Act of 1978); Report of the Commission on the Bankruptcy Laws of the United States, H. Doc. No. 93–137, 93rd Cong., 1st Sess., Pt. 1, 210–211 (1973) ("A true 'net result' rule would total all payments and all advances and offset the one against the other. This is not allowed under the Commission's recommendation, since the advance to be offset must be subsequent to the preference.").

Section 547(b) deliberately defines a preference as a "transfer," rather than as an aggregate of transfers or netting of transactions between the creditor and debtor, and § 547(c) artfully articulates equitable "defenses" whereby the trustee may be foreclosed from avoiding the preference. In particular, § 547(c)(4) permits a netting procedure to be applied when the debtor and creditor are both recipients and initiators of transactions. Construed *in pari materia*, § 547(b) and (c) disclose a calculated legislative scheme and intent to implement equitable considerations which the judiciary at the turn of this century adjudged as lacking and responded by evolving the net result rule. This legislative response reflected in the promulgation of § 547(b) and particularly § 547(c)(4) mirror the congressional version of equitable principles, expressed as the subsequent advance rule, to be incorporated into the 1978 revision of the Bankruptcy Act.

Accordingly, the judgment of the district court dismissing the trustee's complaint to avoid transfers from Fulghum to Ranier as preferential is hereby *vacated* and this case is remanded for further proceedings consistent with this opinion. The judgment of the district court is affirmed in all other respects, including the dismissal of (1) the trustee's amended complaint seeking to set aside the sale of construction equipment, and seeking to pierce Fulghum's corporate veil and (2) Ranier's claim for damages arising from the trustee's alleged improper retention of construction equipment, for the reasons articulated in the district court's memorandum opinion.

[D] Fraudulent Transfers

Section 548 is adapted from § 67d of the Act and is the Code's own version of the Uniform Fraudulent Conveyance Act, now the Uniform Fraudulent Transfer Act in many states, but the trustee may avoid such transfers only if made within one year of the filing of the petition. On the other hand, the trustee's power is not derivative as it is under § 544(b). *See generally* Cook, *Fraudulent Transfer Liability Under the Bankruptcy Code*, 17 Hous. L. Rev. 263 (1980).

GRAY v. SNYDER

United States Court of Appeals, Fourth Circuit
704 F.2d 709 (1983)

PHILLIPS, Circuit Judge:

Upon suit by the trustee in bankruptcy, the bankruptcy court for the Western District of North Carolina found a conveyance of property from a debtor to his wife, in exchange for the release of marital rights of support and inheritance, to be fraudulent and voidable under 11 U.S.C. § 548. This appeal is from the district court's judgment affirming the bankruptcy court. We vacate in part and remand for further factual development of the issue whether the wife's release of her marital rights constituted "reasonably equivalent value" within the meaning of § 548.

I.

After being married for more than thirty years, Jerald and Irma Snyder entered into a separation agreement whereby Jerald would transfer to Irma his half–interest in their residence in exchange for her release of any claims against him for support, alimony, or inheritance. Seven days later, on April 29, 1980, the Snyders conveyed the residence to a third party for $80,000, and Jerald fulfilled his obligation under the separation agreement by assigning his portion of the proceeds to his wife. Thereafter, the Snyders have lived separately, although they have never been divorced.

On October 10, 1980, Jerald Snyder filed a voluntary petition for bankruptcy pursuant to 11 U.S.C. § 301. The trustee in bankruptcy then instituted suit in the bankruptcy court for the Western District of North Carolina, seeking pursuant to 11 U.S.C. § 548 to avoid the transfer by Snyder of his half–interest in the residence. The bankruptcy judge determined that, as a matter of law, there was no "reasonably equivalent value" given by Irma Snyder in exchange for her husband's half–interest. A jury to whom the issue was submitted by the bankruptcy judge found as fact that Jerald Snyder "became insolvent" as a result of the transfer. These two determinations having satisfied the statutory predicates for avoidability under § 548(a)(2)(A), 2(B)(i), the bankruptcy judge entered judgment in favor of the trustee avoiding the transfer and the district court affirmed that judgment. Irma Snyder then brought this appeal, challenging the jurisdiction of the bankruptcy court, the legal ruling that she had not given her husband "reasonably equivalent value," and the jury finding of insolvency. We address these contentions seriatim.

III.

A trustee in bankruptcy may avoid a transfer of a debtor's interest in property, made within one year of the filing in bankruptcy, if the debtor "received less than a reasonably equivalent value in exchange for such transfer," 11 U.S.C. § 548(a)(2)(A), and was insolvent on the date of transfer "or became insolvent as a result" of it, *id.* § 548(a)(2)(B)(i). Section 548(d)(2)(A) provides that " 'value' means property, or satisfaction or securing of a present or antecedent debt of the debtor, but does not include an unperformed promise to furnish support to the debtor." A critical principle, therefore, is that "reasonably equivalent value" under § 548 "excludes future considerations, at least to the extent not actually performed." 4 Collier on Bankruptcy Para. 548.07, at 548–66 (15th ed. 1982).

Faced with this statutory formulation, both the bankruptcy court and the district court concluded as a matter of law that Irma Snyder had not given "value" in exchange for her husband's half–interest in the residence. The district court drew "a distinction between cases where there is a divorce or court order and the cases where there is only an agreement between husband and wife," reasoning that "value" within the statutory meaning required in this circumstance a release of court–mandated alimony or support payments. Under this view, the conveyance between the Snyders was voidable because Jerald was under no judicial compulsion at the time of transfer to make payments to his wife, so that her release of rights to support and inheritance did not satisfy a "present or antecedent debt."

This rationale construes too narrowly the statutory meaning of "value." If, at the time of transfer, Jerald Snyder owed a presently enforceable legal obligation of support to his wife, her release of that obligation—whether or not the obligation was manifested in a judicial decree—in exchange for the transfer of his half–interest in the residence would—to that extent—constitute satisfaction of a "present or antecedent debt." *Cf. In re Chappel*, 243 F. Supp. 417, 420 (S.D. Cal. 1965) (waiver of alimony by wife could be fair consideration for husband's transfer of community property).

To determine whether there existed such an obligation of support, we look to North Carolina law. That law clearly imposes a continuing legal duty upon a husband to support his wife. *See* 2 R. Lee, *supra* note 3, § 128. This duty is enforceable in a variety of ways: through criminal sanctions imposed for willful abandonment coupled with nonsupport, N.C. Gen. Stat. § 14–322 (1981), and through civil decrees granting alimony, alimony pendente lite, or alimony without divorce, *see id.* § § 50–16.1, 50–16.8 (1976), on the basis of misconduct or failure to support, see id. § 50–16.2. It is a duty considered to be so fraught with a public interest that any contractual undertaking between a husband and wife living together and not contemplating imminent separation which purports to quantify or limit the duty is, under North Carolina law, void as against public policy. *Motley v. Motley*, 255 N.C. 190, 120 S.E.2d 422 (1961); 2 R. Lee, supra note 3, § 183.

On the other hand, North Carolina law has long recognized that the husband's duty of support may be discharged by a valid separation agreement between the spouses under which fixed benefits are provided the wife in consideration of the discharge. *Archbell v. Archbell*, 158 N.C. 408, 74 S.E. 327 (1912). *See generally* R. Lee, *supra* note 3, § 183; Merritt, *supra* note 4, at 97. To be valid such an agreement must (1) be made between spouses either actually separated or intending immediately to separate, 2 R. Lee, *supra* note 3, § 187, at 460, 463, and (2) be executed in accordance with statutory formality requirements, *see* N.C. Gen. Stat. § 52–10.1 (Supp. 1981).

Applying these principles to the matter at hand, it would appear on the face of the record on appeal that the Snyders may indeed have entered into a valid, enforceable separation agreement the effect of which under state law could be the satisfaction of a present obligation of support owed by the bankrupt to his wife. We recognize, however, that the basis of decision in the bankruptcy and district courts did not necessitate inquiry into the validity and enforceability under state law of the separation agreement. This must therefore be considered an open question for resolution upon remand. If it be determined that the separation agreement was a valid and enforceable one under state law, this would necessarily satisfy the requirement of § 548 that Irma's release of support rights under it was—to that extent—in satisfaction of a "present or antecedent debt" of the bankrupt spouse. There would still remain for resolution, however, the second–level issue under § 548 whether the release of support rights constituted "reasonably equivalent" value for the transfer of the bankrupt's one–half interest in the residence. These issues must be addressed in the first instance upon the remand we order.

IV.

Irma Snyder challenges as well the jury finding that her husband "became insolvent," within the meaning of § 548(a)(2)(B)(i), as a result of the transfer of his half–interest in the residence. We cannot accept her argument that her husband's misstatement of assets on his bankruptcy petition misled the jury and thus fatally infected the jury verdict; the question of the bankrupt's assets and liabilities was fully presented and argued in detail to the jury, and there was no error which would justify setting aside its factual finding. Accordingly, we affirm this portion of the proceedings.

V.

The jury finding that the bankrupt became insolvent as a result of the transfer at issue is affirmed. In all other respects, we vacate the judgment and remand the case to the district court for further proceedings consistent with this opinion. We note that further proceedings must be in conformity with the Interim Bankruptcy Rules now in effect, see 51 U.S.L.W. 2382 (Jan. 4, 1983).

BFP v. RESOLUTION TRUST CORPORATION

Supreme Court of the United States
30 C.B.C.2d 345 (1994)

SCALIA, J., delivered the opinion of the Court, in which REHNQUIST, C.J., and O'CONNOR, KENNEDY, and THOMAS, JJ., joined. SOUTER, J., filed a dissenting opinion, in which BLACKMUN, STEVENS, and GINSBURG, JJ., joined.

This case presents the question whether the consideration received from a noncollusive, real estate mortgage foreclosure sale conducted in conformance with applicable state law conclusively satisfies the Bankruptcy Code's requirement that transfers of property by insolvent debtors within one year prior to the filing of a bankruptcy petition be in exchange for "a reasonably equivalent value." 11 U.S.C. § 548(a)(2).

I.

Petitioner BFP is a partnership, formed by Wayne and Marlene Pedersen and Russell Barton in 1987, for the purpose of buying a home in Newport Beach, California, from Sheldon and Ann Foreman. Petitioner took title subject to a first deed of trust in favor of Imperial Savings Association (Imperial) to secure payment of a loan of $356,250 made to the Pedersens in connection with petitioner's acquisition of the home. Petitioner granted a second deed of trust to the Foremans as security for a $200,000 promissory note. Subsequently, Imperial, whose loan was not being serviced, entered a notice of default under the first deed of trust and scheduled a properly noticed foreclosure sale. The foreclosure proceedings were temporarily delayed by the filing of an involuntary bankruptcy petition on behalf of petitioner. After the dismissal of that petition in June 1989, Imperial's foreclosure proceeding was completed at a foreclosure sale on July 12, 1989. The home was purchased by respondent Paul Osborne for $433,000.

In October 1989, petitioner filed for bankruptcy under Chapter 11 of the Bankruptcy Code, 11 U.S.C. § § 1101–1174. Acting as a debtor in possession, petitioner filed a complaint in bankruptcy court seeking to set aside the conveyance of the home to respondent Osborne on the grounds that the foreclosure sale constituted a fraudulent transfer under § 548 of the Code, 11 U.S.C. § 548. Petitioner alleged that the home was actually worth over $725,000 at the time of the sale to Osborne. Acting on separate motions, the bankruptcy court dismissed the complaint as to the private respondents and granted summary judgment in favor of Imperial. The bankruptcy court found, *inter alia*, that the foreclosure sale had been conducted in compliance with California law and was neither collusive nor fraudulent. In an unpublished opinion, the District Court affirmed the bankruptcy court's granting of the private respondents' motion to dismiss. A divided bankruptcy appellate panel affirmed the bankruptcy court's entry of summary judgment for Imperial. 132 B.R. 748 (1991).

Applying the analysis set forth in *In re Madrid*, [6 C.B.C.2d 1133] 21 B.R. 424 (Bkrtcy. App. Pan. CA9 1982), affirmed on other grounds, 725 F.2d 1197 [10 C.B.C.2d 347] (CA9), cert. denied, 469 U.S. 833 [11 C.B.C.2d 1067] (1984), the panel majority held that a "non–collusive and regularly conducted nonjudicial foreclosure sale . . . cannot be challenged as a fraudulent conveyance because the consideration received in such a sale establishes 'reasonably equivalent value' as a matter of law." 132 B.R., at 750.

Petitioner sought review of both decisions in the Court of Appeals for the Ninth Circuit, which consolidated the appeals. The Court of Appeals affirmed. *In re BFP*,

974 F.2d 1144 [27 C.B.C.2d 1417] (1992). BFP filed a petition for certiorari, which we granted. 508 U.S. — (1993).

II.

Section 548 of the Bankruptcy Code, 11 U.S.C. § 548, sets forth the powers of a trustee in bankruptcy (or, in a Chapter 11 cse, a debtor in possession) to avoid fraudulent transfers. It permits to be set aside not only transfers infected by actual fraud but certain other transfers as well–so–called constructively fraudulent transfers. The constructive fraud provision at issue in this case applies to transfers by insolvent debtors. It permits avoidance if the trustee can establish (1) that the debtor had an interest in property; (2) that a transfer of that interest occurred within one year of the filing of the bankruptcy petition; (3) that the debtor was insolvent at the time of the transfer or became insolvent as a result thereof; and (4) that the debtor received "less than a reasonably equivalent value in exchange for such transfer." 11 U.S.C. § 548(a)(2)(A). It is the last of these four elements that presents the issue in the case before us.

Section 548 applies to any "transfer," which includes "foreclosure of the debtor's equity of redemption." 11 U.S.C. § 101(54) (1988 ed., Supp. IV). Of the three critical terms "reasonably equivalent value," only the last is defined: "value" means, for purposes of § 548, "property, or satisfaction or securing of a . . . debt of the debtor," 11 U.S.C. § 548(d)(2)(A). The question presented here, therefore, is whether the amount of debt (to the first and second lien holders) satisfied at the foreclosure sale (*viz.*, a total of $433,000) is "reasonably equivalent" to the worth of the real estate conveyed. The Courts of Appeals have divided on the meaning of those undefined terms. In *Durrett v. Washington Nat. Ins. Co.*, 621 F.2d 201 (1980), the Fifth Circuit, interpreting a provision of the old Bankruptcy Act analogous to § 548(a)(2), held that a foreclosure sale that yielded 57% of the property's fair market value could be set aside, and indicated in dicta that any such sale for less than 70% of fair market value should be invalidated. *Id.* at 203–204. This *"Durrett* rule" has continued to be applied by some courts under § 548 of the new Bankruptcy Code. *See In re Littleton*, 888 F.2d 90, 92, n. 5 [21 C.B.C.2d 1155] (CA11 1989). In *In re Bundles*, 856 F.2d 815, 820 (1988), the Seventh Circuit rejected the *Durrett* rule in favor of a case–by–case, "all facts and circumstances" approach to the question of reasonably equivalent value, with a *rebuttable* presumption that the foreclosure sale price is sufficient to withstand attack under § 548(a)(2). *Id.*, at 824–825; *see also In re Grissom*, 955 F.2d 1440, 1445–1446 [26 C.B.C.2d 1002] (CA11 1992). In this case the Ninth Circuit, agreeing with the Sixth Circuit, see *In re Winshall Settler's Trust*, 758 F.2d 1136, 1139 [12 C.B.C.2d 605] (CA6 1985), adopted the position first put forward in *In re Madrid*, 21 B.R. 424 [6 C.B.C.2d 1133] (Bkrtcy. App. Pan. CA9 1982), affirmed on other grounds, 725 F.2d 1197 (CA9), cert. denied, 469 U.S. 833 (1984), that the consideration received at a noncollusive, regularly conducted real estate foreclosure sale constitutes a reasonably equivalent value under § 548(a)(2)(A). The Court of Appeals acknowledged that it "necessarily part[ed] from the positions taken by the Fifth Circuit in *Durrett* . . . and the Seventh Circuit in *Bundles*." 974 F.2d at 1148.

In contrast to the approach adopted by the Ninth Circuit in the present case, both *Durrett* and *Bundles* refer to fair market value as the benchmark against which determination of reasonably equivalent value is to be measured. In the context of an otherwise lawful mortgage foreclosure sale of real estate, such reference is in our opinion not consistent with the text of the Bankruptcy Code. The term "fair market value," though it is a well–established concept, does not appear in § 548. In contrast, § 522, dealing with a debtor's exemptions, specifically provides that, for purposes of that section, " 'value' means fair market value as of the date of the filing of the petition." 11 U.S.C. § 522(a)(2). "Fair market value" also appears in the Code provision that defines the extent to which indebtedness with respect to an equity security is not forgiven for the purpose of determining whether the debtor's estate has realized taxable income. § 346(j)(7)(B). Section 548, on the other hand, seemingly goes out of its way to avoid that standard term. It might readily have said "received less than fair market value in exchange for such transfer or obligation," or perhaps "less than a reasonable equivalent of fair market value." Instead, it used the (as far as we are aware) entirely novel phrase "reasonably equivalent value." "[I]t is generally presumed that Congress acts intentionally and purposely when it includes particular language in one section of a statute but omits it in another," *Chicago v. Environmental Defense Fund*, 511 U.S. — (1994) (slip op., at 9) (internal quotation marks omitted), and that presumption is even stronger when the omission entails the replacement of standard legal terminology with a neologism. One must suspect the language means that fair market value cannot—or at least cannot *always*—be the benchmark.

That suspicion becomes a certitude when one considers that market value, as it is commonly understood, has no applicability in the forced–sale context; indeed, it is the very *antithesis* of forced–sale value. "The market value of . . . a piece of property is the price which it might be expected to bring if offered for sale in a fair market; not the price which might be obtained on a sale at public auction or a sale forced by the necessities of the owner, but such a price as would be fixed by negotiation and mutual agreement, after ample time to find a purchaser, as between a vendor who is willing (but not compelled) to sell and a purchaser who desires to buy but is not compelled to take the particular . . . piece of property." Black's Law Dictionary 971 (6th ed. 1990). In short, "fair market value" presumes market conditions that, by definition, simply do not obtain in the context of a forced sale. *See, e.g., East Bay Municipal Utility District v. Kieffer*, 99 Cal. App. 240, 255, 278 P. 476, 482 (1929), overruled on other grounds by *County of San Diego v. Miller*, 13 Cal.3d 684, 532 P.2d 139 (1975) (in banc); *Nevada Nat. Leasing Co. v. Hereford*, 36 Cal.3d 146, 152, 680 P.2d 1077, 1080 (1984) (in banc); *Guardian Loan Co. v. Early*, 47 N.Y.2d 515, 521, 392 N.E.2d 1240, 1244 (1979).

Neither petitioner, petitioner's amici, nor any federal court adopting the *Durrett* or the *Bundles* analysis has come to grips with this glaring discrepancy between the factors relevant to an appraisal of a property's market value, on the one hand, and the strictures of the foreclosure process on the other. Market value cannot be the criterion of equivalence in the foreclosure sale context. The language of § 548(a)(2)(A) ("received less than a reasonably equivalent value in exchange") requires judicial inquiry into whether the foreclosed property was sold for a price that approximated its worth at the time of sale. An appraiser's reconstruction of "fair market value" could show what similar property would be worth if it did not have to be sold within the time and manner strictures of state–prescribed foreclosure. But property that must be sold within those strictures is simply *worth less*. No one would pay as much to own such property as he would pay to own real estate that could be sold at leisure and pursuant to normal marketing techniques. And it is no more realistic to ignore that characteristic of the property (the fact that state foreclosure law permits the mortgagee to sell it at forced sale) than it is to ignore other price–affecting characteristics (such as the fact that state zoning law permits the owner of the neighboring lot to open a gas station). Absent a clear statutory requirement to the contrary, we must assume the validity of this state–law regulatory background and take due account of its effect. "The existence and force and function of established institutions of local government are always in the consciousness of lawmakers and, while their weight may vary, they may never be completely overlooked in the task of interpretation." *Davies Warehouse Co. v. Bowles*, 321 U.S. 144, 154 (1944). *Cf. Gregory v. Ashcroft*, 501 U.S. — , — (1991) (slip op., at 6–8).

There is another artificially constructed criterion we might look to instead of "fair market price." One might judge there to be such a thing as a "reasonable" or "fair" forced–sale price. Such a conviction must lie behind the *Bundles* inquiry into whether the state foreclosure proceedings "were calculated . . . to return to the debtor–mortgagor his equity in the property." 856 F.2d, at 824. And perhaps that is what the courts that follow the *Durrett* rule have in mind when they select 70% of fair market value as the outer limit of "reasonably equivalent value" for forecloseable property (we have no idea where else such an arbitrary percentage could have come from). The problem is that such judgments represent policy determinations which the Bankruptcy Code gives us no apparent authority to make. How closely the price received in a forced sale is likely to approximate fair market value depends upon the terms of the forced sale–how quickly it may be made, what sort of public notice must be given, etc. But the terms for foreclosure sale are not *standard*. They vary considerably from State to State, depending upon, among other things, how the particular State values the divergent interests of debtor and creditor. To specify a federal "reasonable" foreclosure–sale price is to extend federal bankruptcy law well beyond the traditional field of fraudulent transfers, into realms of policy where it has not ventured before. Some sense of history is needed to appreciate this.

The modern law of fraudulent transfers had its origin in the Statute of 13 Elizabeth, which invalidated "covinous and fraudulent" transfers designed "to delay, hinder or defraud creditors and others." 13 Eliz., ch. 5 (1570). English courts soon developed the doctrine of "badges of fraud": proof by a creditor of certain objective facts (for example, a transfer to a close relative, a secret transfer, a transfer of title without transfer of possession, or grossly inadequate consideration) would raise a rebuttable presumption of actual fraudulent intent. *See Twyne's* Case, 3 Coke Rep. 80b, 76 Eng. Rep. 809 (K.B. 1601); O. Bump, Fraudulent Conveyances: A Treatise upon Conveyances Made by Debtors to Defraud Creditors 31–60 (3d ed. 1882). Every American bankruptcy law has incorporated a fraudulent transfer provision;

the 1898 Act specifically adopted the language of the Statute of 13 Elizabeth. Bankruptcy Act of July 1, 1898, ch. 541, § 67(e), 30 Stat. 564–565.

The history of foreclosure law also begins in England, where courts of chancery developed the "equity of redemption"—the equitable right of a borrower to buy back, or redeem, property conveyed as security by paying the secured debt on a later date than "law day," the original due date. The courts' continued expansion of the period of redemption left lenders in a quandary, since title to forfeited property could remain clouded for years after law day. To meet this problem, courts created the equitable remedy of foreclosure: after a certain date the lender would be forever foreclosed from exercising his equity of redemption. This remedy was called strict foreclosure because the borrower's entire interest in the property was forfeited, regardless of any accumulated equity. See G. Glenn, 1 Mortgages 3–18, 358–362, 395–406 (1943); G. Osborne, Mortgages 144 (2d ed. 1970). The next major change took place in 19th century America, with the development of foreclosure by sale (with the surplus over the debt refunded to the debtor) as a means of avoiding the draconian consequences of strict foreclosure. Osborne, *supra*, at 661–663; Glenn, *supra*, at 460–462, 622. Since then, the States have created diverse networks of judicially and legislative crafted rules governing the foreclosure process, to achieve what each of them considers the proper balance between the needs of lenders and borrowers. All States permit judicial foreclosure, conducted under direct judicial oversight; about half of the States also permit foreclosure by exercising a private power of sale provided in the mortgage documents. See Zinman, Houle, & Weiss, *Fraudulent Transfers According to Alden, Gross and Borowitz: A Tale of Two Circuits*, 39 Bus. Law. 977, 1004–1005 (1984). Foreclosure laws typically require notice to the defaulting borrower, a substantial lead time before the commencement of foreclosure proceedings, publication of a notice of sale, and strict adherence to prescribed bidding rules and auction procedures. Many States require that the auction be conducted by a government official, and some forbid the property to be sold for less than a specified fraction of a mandatory presale fair–market–value appraisal. *See Id.*, at 1002, 1004–1005; Osborne, *supra*, at 683, 733–735; G. Osborne, G. Nelson, & D. Whitman, Real Estate Finance Law 9, 446–447, 475–477 (1979). When these procedures have been followed, however, it is "black letter" law that mere inadequacy of the foreclosure sale price is no basis for setting the sale aside, though it may be set aside (under state foreclosure law, rather than fraudulent transfer law) if the price is so low as to "shock the conscience or raise a presumption of fraud or unfairness." Osborne, Nelson, & Whitman, *supra*, at 469; *see also Gelfert v. National City Bank of New York*, 313 U.S. 221, 232 (1941); *Ballentyne v. Smith*, 205 U.S. 285, 290 (1907).

Fraudulent transfer law and foreclosure law enjoyed over 400 years of peaceful coexistence in Anglo–American jurisprudence until the Fifth Circuit's unprecedented 1980 decision in *Durrett*. To our knowledge no prior decision had ever applied the "grossly inadequate price" badge of fraud under fraudulent transfer law to set aside a foreclosure sale. To say that the "reasonably equivalent value" language in the fraudulent transfer provision of the Bankruptcy Code requires a foreclosure sale to yield a certain minimum price beyond what state foreclosure law requires, is to say, in essence, that the Code has adopted *Durrett* or *Bundles*. Surely

Congress has the power pursuant to its constitutional grant of authority over bankruptcy, U.S. Const., Art. I, § 8, cl. 4, to disrupt the ancient harmony that foreclosure law and fraudulent–conveyance law, those two pillars of debtor–creditor jurisprudence, have heretofore enjoyed. But absent clearer textual guidance than the phrase "reasonably equivalent value"—a phrase entirely compatible with pre–existing practice–we will not presume such a radical departure. *See United Savings Assn. Of Texas v. Timbers of Inwood Forest Associates, Ltd.*, 484 U.S. 365, 380 [17 C.B.C.2d 1368] (1988), *Midlantic Nat. Bank v. New Jersey Dept. of Environmental Protection*, 474 U.S. 494, 501 [13 C.B.C.2d 1355] (1986); *cf. United States v. Texas*, 507 U.S. — , — (1993) (slip op., at 4) (statutes that invade common law must be read with presumption favoring retention of long–established principles absent evident statutory purpose to the contrary).

Federal statutes impinging upon important state interests "cannot . . . be construed without regard to the implications of our dual system of government . . . [W]hen the Federal Government takes over . . . local radiations in the vast network of our national economic enterprise and thereby radically readjusts the balance of state and national authority, those charged with the duty of legislating [must be] reasonably explicit." F. Frankfurter, *Some Reflections on the Reading of Statutes*, 47 Colum. L. Rev. 527, 539–540 (1947), quoted in *Kelly v. Robinson*, 479 U.S. 36, 49–50 n. 11 [15 C.B.C.2d 890] (1986). It is beyond question that an essential state interest is at issue here: we have said that "the general welfare of society is involved in the security of the titles to real estate" and the power to ensure that security "inheres in the very nature of [state] government." *American Land Co. v. Zeiss*, 219 U.S. 47, 60 (1911). Nor is there any doubt that the interpretation urged by petitioner would have a profound effect upon that interest: the title of every piece of realty purchased at foreclosure would be under a federally created cloud. (Already, title insurers have reacted to the *Durrett* rule by including specially crafted exceptions from coverage in many policies issued for properties purchased at foreclosure sales. *See, e.g.,* L. Cherkis & L. King, Collier Real Estate Transactions and the Bankruptcy Code 5–18 to 5–19 (1992). To displace traditional State regulation in such a manner, the federal statutory purpose must be "clear and manifest," *English v. General Electric Co.*, 496 U.S. 72, 79 (1990). *Cf. Gregory v. Ashcroft*, 501 U.S., at — (1991) (slip op., at 7). Otherwise, the Bankruptcy Code will be construed to adopt, rather than to displace, pre–existing state law. *See Kelly, supra,* at 49; *Butner v. United States*, 440 U.S. 48, 54–55 (1979); *Vanston Bondholders Protective Comm. v. Green*, 329 U.S. 156, 171 (1946) (Frankfurter, J., concurring).

For the reasons described, we decline to read the phrase "reasonably equivalent value" in § 548(a)(2) to mean, in its application to mortgage foreclosure sales, either "fair market value" or "fair foreclosure price" (whether calculated as a percentage of fair market value or otherwise). We deem, as the law has always deemed, that a fair and proper price, or a "reasonably equivalent value," for foreclosed property, is the price in fact received at the foreclosure sale, so long as all the requirements of the State's foreclosure law have been complied with.

This conclusion does not render § 548(a)(2) superfluous, since the "reasonably equivalent value" criterion will continue to have independent meaning (ordinarily a meaning similar to fair market value) outside the foreclosure context. Indeed, § 548(a)(2) will even continue to be an exclusive means of invalidating some foreclosure sales. Although *collusive* foreclosure sales are likely subject to attack under § 548(a)(1), which authorizes the trustee to avoid transfers "made . . . with actual intent to hinder, delay, or defraud" creditors, that provision may not reach foreclosure sales that, while not intentionally fraudulent, nevertheless fail to comply with all governing state laws. *Cf.* 4 L. King, Collier on Bankruptcy ¶ 548.02, p. 548–35 (15th ed. 1993) (contrasting subsections (a)(1) and (a)(2)(A) of § 548). Any irregularity in the conduct of the sale that would permit judicial invalidation of the sale under applicable state law deprives the sale price of its conclusive force under § 548(a)(2)(A), and the transfer may be avoided if the price received was not reasonably equivalent to the property's actual value at the time of the sale (which we think would be the price that would have been received if the foreclosure sale had proceeded according to law).

III.

A few words may be added in general response to the dissent. We have no quarrel with the dissent's assertion that where the "meaning of the Bankruptcy Code's text is itself clear," *post*, at 19, its operation is unimpeded by contrary state law or prior practice. Nor do we contend that Congress must override historical state practice "expressly or not at all," *ibid.* The Bankruptcy Code can of course override by implication when the implication is unambiguous. But where the intent to override is doubtful, our federal system demands deference to long established traditions of state regulation.

The dissent's insistence that here no doubt exists—that our reading of the statute is "in derogation of the *straightforward language* used by Congress," *post*, at 1 (emphasis added)—does not withstand scrutiny. The problem is not that we disagree with the dissent's proffered "plain meaning" of § 548(a)(2)(A) ("the bankruptcy court must compare the price received by the insolvent debtor and the worth of the item when sold and set aside the transfer if the former was substantially ('[un]reasonabl[y]') 'less than' the latter," *post*, at 4–5)—which indeed echoes our own framing of the question presented ("whether the amount of debt . . . satisfied at the foreclosure sale . . . is 'reasonably equivalent' to the worth of the real estate conveyed," *supra*, at 4). There is no doubt that this provision directs an inquiry into the relationship of the value received by the debtor to the worth of the property transferred. The problem, however, as any "ordinary speaker of English would have no difficulty grasping," *post*, at 4, is that this highly generalized reformulation of the "plain meaning" of "reasonably equivalent value" continues to leave unanswered the one question central to this case, wherein the ambiguity lies: *what is a foreclosed property worth?* Obviously, until that is determined, we cannot know whether the value received in exchange for foreclosed property is "reasonably equivalent." We have considered three (not, as the dissent insists, only two, see *post*, at 1) possible answers to this question–fair market value, *supra*, at 5–8, reasonable forced–sale price, *supra*, at 8, and the foreclosure sale price itself—and have settled on the last. We would have expected the dissent to opt for one of the other two, or perhaps even to concoct a fourth; but one searches Justice Souter's opinion in vain for any alternative response to the question of the transferred property's worth. Instead, the dissent simply reiterates the "single meaning" of "reasonably equivalent value" (with which we entirely agree): "a court should discern the 'value' of the property transferred and determine whether the price paid was, under the circumstances, 'less than reasonabl[e].' " *Post*, at 11–12. Well and good. But what is the "value"? The dissent has no response, evidently thinking that, in order to establish that the law is clear, it suffices to show that "the eminent sense of the natural reading," *Post*, at 18, provides an unanswered question.

Instead of answering the question, the dissent gives us hope that someone else will answer it, exhorting us "to believe that [bankruptcy courts], familiar with these cases (and with local conditions) as we are not, will give ["reasonably equivalent value"] sensible content in evaluating particular transfers on foreclosure." *Post*, at 13. While we share the dissent's confidence in the capabilities of the United States Bankruptcy Courts, it is the proper function of *this* Court to give "sensible content" to the provisions of the United States Code. It is surely the case that bankruptcy "courts regularly make . . . determinations about the 'reasonably equivalent value' of assets transferred through other means than foreclosure sales," *Ibid.* But in the vast majority of those cases, they can refer to the traditional common–law notion of fair market value as the benchmark. As we have demonstrated, this generally useful concept simply has no application in the foreclosure–sale context, *supra*, at 5–8.

Although the dissent's conception of what constitutes a property's "value" is unclear, it does *seem* to take account of the fact that the property is subject to forced sale. The dissent refers, for example, to a reasonable price "under the circumstances," *post*, at 12, and to the "worth of the item *when sold*," *post*, at 4 (emphasis added). But just as we are never told how the broader question of a property's "worth" is to be answered, neither are we informed how the lesser included inquiry into the impact of forced sale is to be conducted. Once again, we are called upon to have faith that bankruptcy courts will be able to determine whether a property's foreclosure sale price falls unreasonably short of its "optimal value," *post*, at 12, whatever that may be. This, the dissent tells us, is the statute's plain meaning.

We take issue with the dissent's characterization of our interpretation as carving out an "exception" for foreclosure sales, *post*, at 1, or as giving "two different and inconsistent meanings," *post*, at 10, to "reasonably equivalent value." As we have emphasized, the inquiry under § 548(a)(2)(A)—whether the debtor has received value that is substantially comparable to the worth of the transferred property—is the same for all transfers. But as we have also explained, the fact that a piece of property is legally subject to forced sale, like any other fact bearing upon the property's use or alienability, necessarily affects its worth. *Unlike* most other legal restrictions, however, foreclosure has the effect of completely redefining the market in which the property is offered for sale; normal free–market rules of exchange are replaced by the far more restrictive rules governing forced sales. Given this altered reality, and the concomitant inutility of the normal tool for determining what property is worth (fair market value), the only legitimate evidence of the property's value at the time it is sold is the foreclosure sale price itself.

For the foregoing reasons, the judgment of the Court of Appeal for the Ninth Circuit is *affirmed.*

Justice SOUTER, with whom Justice BLACKMUN, Justice STEVENS, and Justice GINSBURG join, dissenting:

The Court today holds that by the terms of the Bankruptcy Code Congress intended a peppercorn paid at a noncollusive and procedurally regular foreclosure sale to be treated as the "reasonabl[e] equivalent" of the value of a California beachfront estate. Because the Court's reasoning fails both to overcome the implausibility of that proposition and to justify engrafting a foreclosure–sale exception onto 11 U.S.C. § 548(a)(2)(A), in derogation of the straightforward language used by Congress, I respectfully dissent.

I.

A.

The majority presents our task of giving meaning to § 548(a)(2)(A) in this case as essentially entailing a choice between two provisions that Congress might have enacted, but did not. One would allow a bankruptcy trustee to avoid a recent foreclosure–sale transfer from an insolvent debtor whenever anything less than fair market value was obtained, while the second would limit the avoidance power to cases where the foreclosure sale was collusive or had failed to comply with state–prescribed procedures. The Court then argues that, given the unexceptionable proposition that forced sales rarely yield as high a price as sales held under ideal, "market" conditions, Congress's "omission" from § 548(a)(2)(A) of the phrase "fair market value" means that the latter, narrowly procedural reading of § 548(a)(2)(A) is the preferable one.

If those in fact were the interpretive alternatives, the majority's choice might be a defensible one. The first, equating "reasonably equivalent value" at a foreclosure sale with "fair market value" has little to recommend it. Forced–sale prices may not be (as the majority calls them) the "very antithesis" of market value, see *ante*, at 6, but they fail to bring in what voluntary sales realize, and rejecting such a reading of the statute is as easy as statutory interpretation is likely to get. On the majority's view, laying waste to this straw man necessitates accepting as adequate value whatever results from noncollusive adherence to state foreclosure requirements. Because properties are "simply worth less," *ante*, at 7, on foreclosure sale, the Court posits, they must have been "worth" whatever price was paid. That, however, is neither a plausible interpretation of the statute, nor its only remaining alternative reading.

The question before the Court is whether the price received at a foreclosure sale after compliance with state procedural rules in a non collusive sale must be treated conclusively as the "reasonably equivalent value" of the mortgaged property and in answering that question, the words and meaning of § 548(a)(2)(A) are plain. *See*

Patterson v. Shumate, 504 U.S. — , — (slip op., at 7) (1992) (party seeking to defeat plain meaning of Bankruptcy Code text bears an "exceptionally heavy burden") (internal quotations marks omitted); *Perrin v. United States*, 444 U.S. 37, 42 (1979) (statutory words should be given their ordinary meaning). A trustee is authorized to avoid certain recent pre–bankruptcy transfers, including those on foreclosure sales, that a bankruptcy court determines were not made in exchange for "a reasonably equivalent value." Although this formulation makes no pretense to mathematical precision, an ordinary speaker of English would have no difficulty grasping its basic thrust: the bankruptcy court must compare the price received by the insolvent debtor and the worth of the item when sold and set aside the transfer if the former was substantially ("[un]reasonabl[y]") "less than" the latter. Nor would any ordinary English speaker, concerned to determine whether a foreclosure sale was collusive or procedurally irregular (an enquiry going exclusively to the process by which a transaction was consummated), direct an adjudicator, as the Court now holds Congress did, to ascertain whether the sale had realized "less than a reasonably equivalent value" (an enquiry described in quintessentially substantive terms).

Closer familiarity with the text, structure, and history of the disputed provision (and relevant amendments), confirms the soundness of the plain reading. Before 1984, the question whether foreclosure sales fell within bankruptcy courts' power to set aside transfers for "too little in return" was, potentially, a difficult one. Then, it might plausibly have been contended that § 548 was most concerned with "fraudulent" conduct by debtors on the brink of bankruptcy, misbehavior unlikely to be afoot when an insolvent debtor's property is sold, against his wishes, at foreclosure. Indeed, it could further have been argued, again consonantly with the text of the earlier version of the Bankruptcy Code, that Congress had not understood foreclosure to involve a "transfer" within the ambit of § 548, see, *e.g., Abramson v. Lakewood Bank & Trust Co.*, 647 F.2d 547, 549 (CA5 1981) (Clark, J., dissenting), cert. denied, 454 U.S. 1164 (1982) (Bankruptcy Act case), on the theory that the "transfer" from mortgagor to mortgagee occurs, once and for all, when the security interest is first created. *See generally In re Madrid*, 725 F.2d 1197 [10 C.B.C.2d 347] (CA9), cert. denied, 469 U.S. 833 (1984).   ·

In 1984, however, Congress pulled the rug out from under these previously serious arguments, by amending the Code in two relevant respects. *See* Bankruptcy Amendments and Federal Judgeship Act of 1984, Pub. L. 98–353 §§ 401(1), 463(a), 98 Stat. 368, 370. One amendment provided expressly that "involuntar[y]" transfers are no less within the trustee's § 548 avoidance powers than "voluntar[y]" ones, and another provided that the "foreclosure of the debtor's equity of redemption" itself is a "transfer" for purposes of bankruptcy law. *See* 11 U.S.C. § 101(54) (1988 ed., Supp. IV). Thus, whether or not one believes (as the majority seemingly does not) that foreclosure sales rightfully belong within the historic domain of "fraudulent conveyance" law, that is exactly where Congress has now put them, *cf. In re Ehring*, 900 F.2d 184, 187 (CA9 1990), and our duty is to give effect to these new amendments, along with every other clause of the Bankruptcy Code. *See, e.g., United States v. Nordic Village, Inc.*, 503 U.S. — , — (1992) (slip op., at 6); *United Savings Assn. Of Texas v. Timbers of Inwood Forest Associates, Ltd.*, 484 U.S. 365, 374–75 [17 C.B.C.2d 1368] (1988); *see also Dewsnup v. Timm*, 502 U.S. — , —

(1992) (slip op., at 7) (Scalia, J., dissenting). The Court's attempt to escape the plain effect of § 548(a)(2)(A) opens it to some equally plain objections.

The first and most obvious of these objections is the very enigma of the Court's reading. If a property's "value" is conclusively presumed to be whatever it sold for, the "less than reasonabl[e] equivalen[ce]" question will never be worth asking, and the bankruptcy avoidance power will apparently be a dead letter in reviewing real estate foreclosures[.] *Cf.* 11 U.S.C. § 361(3) ("indubitable equivalent"). The Court answers that the section is not totally moribund: it still furnishes a way to attack collusive or procedurally deficient real property foreclosures, and it enjoys a vital role in authorizing challenges to other transfers than those occurring on real estate foreclosure. The first answer, however, just runs up against a new objection. If indeed the statute fails to reach noncollusive, procedurally correct real estate foreclosures, then the recent amendments discussed above were probably superfluous. There is a persuasive case that collusive or seriously irregular real estate sales were already subject to avoidance in bankruptcy, *see, e.g., In re Worcester*, 811 F.2d 1224, 1228, 1232 [16 C.B.C.2d 589] (CA9 1987) (interpreting § 541(a)), and neither the Court nor the respondents and their amici identify any specific case in which a court pronounced itself powerless to avoid a collusive foreclosure sale. *But cf. Madrid*, 725 F.2d at 1204 (Farris, J., concurring). It would seem peculiar, then, that for no sound reason, Congress would have tinkered with these closely–watched sections of the Bankruptcy Code, for the sole purpose of endowing bankruptcy courts with authority that had not been found wanting in the first place.

The Court's second answer to the objection that it renders the statute a dead letter is to remind us that the statute applies to all sorts of transfers, not just to real estate foreclosures, and as to all the others, the provision enjoys great vitality, calling for true comparison between value received for the property and its "reasonably equivalent value." (Indeed, the Court has no trouble acknowledging that something "similar to" fair market value may supply the benchmark of reasonable equivalence when such a sale is not initiated by a mortgagee, *ante*, at 14.) This answer, however, is less tenable than the first. A common rule of construction calls for a single definition of a common term occurring in several places within a statute, *see Bray v. Alexandria Women's Health Clinic*, 506 U.S. — , — (1993) (slip op., at 19); *Dewsnup v. Timm*, 502 U.S. — , — (slip op., at 3) (Scalia, J., dissenting) (" 'normal rule[s] of statutory construction'" require that " '*identical words used in the same section of the same enactment*'" must be given the same effect) (emphasis in original), and the case for different definitions within a single text is difficult to make, *cf. Bray, supra*, at — (slip op., at 5) (Souter, J., concurring in part). But to give a single term two different and inconsistent meanings (one procedural, one substantive) for a single occurrence is an offense so unlikely that no common prohibition has ever been thought necessary to guard against it. *Cf. Owen v. Owen*, 500 U.S. 305, 313 (1991) (declining to "create a distinction [between state and federal exemptions] that the words of the statute do not contain"); *Union Bank v. Wolas*, 502 U.S. — , — (1991) (slip op., at 11) the "statutory text . . . makes no distinction between short–term debt and long–term debt"). Unless whimsy is attributed to Congress, the term in question cannot be exclusively procedural in one class of cases and entirely substantive in all others. To be sure, there are real differences between sales on mortgage foreclosures and other transfers, as Congress no doubt understood, but these differences may be addressed simply and consistently with the statute's plain meaning.

The "neologism," *ante*, at 6, "reasonably equivalent value" (read in light of the amendments confirming that foreclosures are to be judged under the same standard as are other transfers) has a single meaning in the one provision in which it figures: a court should discern the "value" of the property transferred and determine whether the price paid was, under the circumstances, "less than reasonabl[e]." There is thus no reason to rebuke the courts of appeals for having failed to "come to grips," *ante*, at 7, with the implications of the fact that foreclosure sales cannot be expected to yield fair market value. The statute has done so for them. As courts considering nonforeclosure transfers often acknowledge, the qualification "reasonably equivalent" itself embodies both an awareness that the assets of insolvent debtors are commonly transferred under conditions that will yield less than their optimal value and a judgment that avoidance in bankruptcy (unsettling as it does the expectations of parties who may have dealt with the debtor in good faith) should only occur when it is clear that the bankruptcy estate will be substantially augmented. *See, e.g., In re Southmark Corp.*, 138 B.R. 820, 829–830 (Bkrtcy. Ct. ND Tex. 1992) (court must compare "the value of what went out with value of what came in," but the equivalence need not be "dollar for dollar") (citation omitted), *In re Countdown*, 115 B.R. 18 (Bkrtcy. Ct. Conn. 1990) (". . . [S]ome disparity between the value of the collateral and the value of the debt does not necessarily lead to a finding of lack of reasonably equivalent value.").

B.

I do not share in my colleagues' apparently extreme discomfort at the prospect of vesting bankruptcy courts with responsibility for determining whether "reasonably equivalent value" was received in cases like this one, nor is the suggestion well taken that doing so is an improper abdication. Those courts regularly make comparably difficult (and contestable) determinations about the "reasonably equivalent value" of assets transferred through other means than foreclosure sales, *see, e.g., Covey v. Commercial Nat. Bank*, 960 F.2d 657, 661–662 [26 C.B.C.2d 1046] (CA7 1992) (rejecting creditor's claim that resale price may be presumed to be "reasonably equivalent value" when that creditor "seiz[es] an asset and sell[s] it for just enough to cover its loan (even if it would have been worth substantially more as part of an ongoing enterprise)"); *In re Morris Communications N.C., Inc.*, 914 F.2d 458 [23 C.B.C.2d 1456] (CA4 1990) (for "reasonably equivalent value" purposes, worth of entry in cellular phone license "lottery" should be discounted to reflect probability of winning); *cf. In re Royal Coach Country, Inc.*, 125 B.R. 668, 673–674 (Bkrtcy. Ct. MD Fla. 1991) (avoiding exchange of 1984 truck valued at $2,800 for 1981 car valued at $500), and there is every reason to believe that they, familiar with these cases (and with local conditions) as we are not, will give the term sensible content in evaluating particular transfers on foreclosure, *cf. United States v. Energy Resources Co.*, 495 U.S. 545, 549 [22 C.B.C.2d 1093] (1990); *NLRB v. Bildisco*

& *Bildisco*, 465 U.S. 513, 527 [9 C.B.C.2d 1219] (1984); *Rosen v. Barclays Bank of N.Y.*, 115 B.R. 433 (E.D.N.Y. 1990). As in other § 548(a)(2) cases, a trustee seeking avoidance of a foreclosure–sale transfer must persuade the bankruptcy court that the price obtained on pre–bankruptcy transfer was, "unreasonabl[y]" low, and as in other cases under the provision, the gravamen of such a claim will be that the challenged transfer significantly and needlessly diminished the bankruptcy estate, *i.e.*, that it extinguished a substantial equity interest of the debtor and that the foreclosing mortgagee failed to take measures which (consistently with state law, if not required by it) would have augmented the price realized.

Whether that enquiry is described as a search for a benchmark " 'fair' forced–sale price," *ante*, at 9, or for the "price that was reasonable under the circumstances," *cf. ante*, n. 4, is ultimately, as the Court itself seems to acknowledge, see *ante*, at 9, of no greater moment than whether the rule the Court discerns in the provision is styled an "exception," an "irrebuttable presumption," or a rule of per se validity. The majority seems to invoke these largely synonymous terms in service of its thesis that the provision's text is "ambiguous" (and therefore ripe for application of policy–based construction rules), but the question presented here, whether the term "less than reasonably equivalent value" may be read to forestall all enquiry beyond whether state law foreclosure procedures were adhered to, admits only two answers, and only one of these, in the negative, is within the "apparent authority," *ante*, at 9 conferred on courts by the text of the Bankruptcy Code.

C.

What plain meaning requires and courts can provide, indeed, the policies underlying a national bankruptcy law fully support. This case is a far cry from the rare one where the effect of implementing the ordinary meaning of the statutory text would be "patent absurdity," *see Ins v. Cardoza–Fonseca*, 480 U.S. 421, 452 (1987) (Scalia, J., concurring in judgment), or "demonstrably at odds with the intentions of its drafters," *United States v. Ron Pair Enterprises, Inc.*, 489 U.S. 235, 244 (1989) (internal quotation marks omitted). Permitting avoidance of procedurally regular foreclosure sales for low prices (and thereby returning a valuable asset to the bankruptcy estate) is plainly consistent with those policies of obtaining a maximum and equitable distribution for creditors and ensuring a "fresh start" for individual debtors, which the Court has often said are at the core of federal bankruptcy law. *See Stellwagen v. Clum*, 245 U.S. 605, 617 (1918); *Williams v. United States Fidelity & Guaranty Co.*, 236 U.S. 549, 554–555 (1915). They are not, of course, any less the policies of federal bankruptcy law simply because state courts will not, for a mortgagor's benefit, set aside a foreclosure sale for "price inadequacy" alone. The unwillingness of the state courts to upset a foreclosure sale for that reason does not address the question of what "reasonably equivalent value" means in bankruptcy law, any more than the refusal of those same courts to set aside a contract for "mere inadequacy of consideration," see Restatement (Second) of Contracts § 79 (1981), would define the scope of the trustee's power to reject executory contracts. *See* 11 U.S.C. § 365 (1988 ed. and Supp. IV). On the contrary, a central premise of the bankruptcy avoidance powers is that what state law plainly allows as acceptable or "fair," as between a debtor and a particular creditor, may be set aside because of its impact on other creditors or on the debtor's chances for a fresh start.

When the prospect of such avoidance is absent, indeed, the economic interests of a foreclosing mortgagee often stand in stark opposition to those of the debtor himself and of his other creditors. At a typical foreclosure sale, a mortgagee has no incentive to bid any more than the amount of the indebtedness, since any "surplus" would be turned over to the debtor (or junior lienholder), and, in some states, it can even be advantageous for the creditor to bid less and seek a deficiency judgment. *See generally* Washburn, *The Judicial and Legislative Response to Price Inadequacy in Mortgage Foreclosure Sales*, 53 S. Cal. L. Rev. 843, 847–851 (1980); Ehrlich, *Avoidance of Foreclosure Sales as Fraudulent Conveyances: Accommodating State and Federal Objectives*, 71 Va. L. Rev. 933, 959–962 (1985); G. Osborne, G. Nelson & D. Whitman, Real Estate Finance Law § 8.3, p. 528. (1979) And where a property is obviously worth more than the amount of the indebtedness, the lending mortgagee's interests are served best if the foreclosure sale is poorly attended; then, the lender is more likely to take the property by bidding the amount of indebtedness, retaining for itself any profits from resale. While state foreclosure procedures may somewhat mitigate the potential for this sort of opportunism (by requiring for publication of notice, for example), it surely is plausible that Congress, in drafting the Bankruptcy Code, would find it intolerable that a debtor's assets be wasted and the bankruptcy estate diminished, solely to speed a mortgagee's recovery.

II.

Confronted with the eminent sense of the natural reading, the Court seeks finally to place this case in a line of decisions, *e.g., Gregory v. Ashcroft*, 501 U.S. 452 (1991), in which we have held that something more than mere plain language is required. Because the stability of title in real property may be said to be an "important" state interest, the Court suggests, see *ante*, at 13, the statute must be presumed to contain an implicit foreclosure–sale exception, which Congress must override expressly or not at all. Our cases impose no such burden on Congress, however. To be sure, they do offer support for the proposition that when the Bankruptcy Code is truly silent or ambiguous, it should not be read as departing from previous practice, *see, e.g., Dewsnup v. Timm*, 502 U.S. — (1992); *Butner v. United States*, 440 U.S. 48, 54 (1979). But we have never required Congress to supply "clearer textual guidance" when the apparent meaning of the Bankruptcy Code's text is itself clear, as it is here. *See Ron Pair*, 489 U.S. at 240 ("[I]t is not appropriate or realistic to expect Congress to have explained with particularity every step it took. Rather, as long as the statutory scheme is coherent and consistent, there generally is no reason to inquire beyond the plain language of the statute"); *cf. Dewsnup*, 502 U.S., — (slip op., at 15) (Scalia, J.) (Court should not "venerat[e] 'pre–Code law' " at the expense of plain statutory meaning).

We have, on many prior occasions, refused to depart from plain Code meaning in spite of arguments that doing that would vindicate similar, and presumably equally "important," state interests. *In Owen v. Owen*, 500 U.S. 305 (1991), for example, the Court refused to hold that the state "opt–out" policy embodied in § 522(b)(3) required immunity from avoidance under § 522(f) for a lien binding under Florida's exemption rules. We emphasized that "[n]othing in the text of § 522(f) remotely justifies treating the [state and federal] exemptions differently." 500 U.S. at, 313. And in *Johnson v. Home State Bank*, 501 U.S. 78 (1991), we relied on plain Code language to allow a debtor who had "stripped" himself of personal mortgage liability under Chapter 7 to reschedule the remaining indebtedness under Chapter 13, notwithstanding a plausible contrary argument based on Code structure and a complete dearth of precedent for the manoeuver under state law and prior bankruptcy practice.

The Court has indeed given full effect to Bankruptcy Code terms even in cases where the Code would appear to have cut closer to the heart of state power than it does here. No "clearer textual guidance" than a general definitional provision was required, for example, to hold that criminal restitution could be a "debt" dischargeable under Chapter 13, see *Davenport*, 495 U.S., at 563–564 (declining to "carve out a broad judicial exception" from statutory term, even to avoid "hamper[ing] the flexibility of state criminal judges"). Nor, in *Perez v. Campbell*, 402 U.S. 637 (1971), did we require an express reference to state highway safety laws before construing the generally–worded discharge provision of the Bankruptcy Act to bar application of a state statute suspending the driver's licenses of uninsured tortfeasors.

Rather than allow state practice to trump the plain meaning of federal statutes, *cf. Adams Fruit Co. v. Barrett*, 494 U.S. 638, 648 (1990), our cases describe a contrary rule: whether or not Congress has used any special "preemptive" language, state regulation must yield to the extent it actually conflicts with federal law. This is no less true of laws enacted under Congress's power to "establish . . . uniform Laws on the subject of Bankruptcies," U.S. Const., Art. I, § 8, cl. 4., than of those passed under its Commerce Clause power. See generally *Perez v. Campbell, supra; cf. id.*, at 651–652 (rejecting the "aberrational doctrine . . . that state law may frustrate the operation of federal law as long as the state legislature in passing its law had some purpose in mind other than one of frustration"); *Cipollone v. Liggett Group, Inc.*, 505 U.S. — , — (1992) (slip op., at 2–3) (Scalia, J., concurring in part) (arguing against a "presumption against preemption" of "historic police powers").

Nor, finally, is it appropriate for the Court to look to "field preemption" cases, see *ante*, at 13–14, to support the higher duty of clarity it seeks to impose on Congress. As written and as applied by the majority of courts of appeals to construe it, the disputed Code provision comes nowhere near working the fundamental displacement of the state law of foreclosure procedure that the majority's rhetoric conjures. To the contrary, construing § 548(a)(2)(A) as authorizing avoidance of an insolvent's recent foreclosure–sale transfer in which "less than a reasonably equivalent value" was obtained is no more preemptive of state foreclosure procedures than the trustee's power to set aside transfers by marital dissolution decree, see *Britt v. Damson*, 334 F. 2d 896 (CA9 1964), cert. denied (1965); *In re Lange*, 35 B.R. 579 (Bkrtcy. Ct. ED MO. 1983), "preempts" state domestic relations law, or the power to reject executory contracts, see 11 U.S.C. § 365, "displaces" the state law of voluntary obligation. While it is surely true that if the provision were accorded its plain meaning, some States (and many mortgagees) would take steps to diminish the risk that particular transactions would be set aside, such voluntary action should not be cause for dismay: it would advance core Bankruptcy Code purposes of augmenting the bankruptcy estate and improving the debtor's prospects for a "fresh start," without compromising lenders' state–law rights to move expeditiously against the property for the money owed. To the extent, in any event, that the respondents and their numerous amici are correct that the "important" policy favoring security of title should count more and the "important" bankruptcy policies should count less, Congress, and not this Court, is the appropriate body to provide a foreclosure–sale exception. *See Wolas*, 502 U.S., at — (slip op., at 11). *See also S.* 1358, 100th Cong., 1st Sess. (1987) (proposed amendment creating foreclosure–sale exception).

III.

Like the Court, I understand this case to involve a choice between two possible statutory provisions: one authorizing the trustee to avoid "involuntar[y] . . . transfers [including foreclosure sales] . . . [for] less than a reasonably equivalent value," see 11 U.S.C. § 548(a), and another precluding such avoidance when "[a] secured party or third party purchaser . . . obtains title to an interest of the debtor in property pursuant to a good faith prepetition foreclosure . . . proceeding . . . permitting . . . the realization of security upon default of the borrower," see S. 445, 98th Cong., 1st Sess., § 360 (1983). But that choice is not ours to make, for Congress made it in 1984, by enacting the former alternative into law and not the latter. Without some indication that doing so would frustrate Congress's clear intention or yield patent absurdity, our obligation is to apply the statute as Congress wrote it. Doing that in this case would produce no frustration or absurdity, but quite the opposite.

NOTE

During the process of amending the Code in 1984, an attempt was made to overrule legislatively *Durrett* and adopt the conclusion reached in the Uniform Fraudulent Transfer Act that the price paid at a non–collusive and properly conducted foreclosure sale would be deemed to be for an equivalent value. At the same time, amendments would be placed in the Code recognizing that the foreclosure itself was a transfer. In the late minutes of the legislative process, because a senior Senator from Ohio had to rethink a problem he had not thought about before or since, it was decided by these great minds to delete the provision and come back to it another day. In following through, however, the Senatorial staff, with its usual competence in bankruptcy matters, took out the UFTA provision validating the sale but forgot to take out the amendments to § 101 and § 548 deeming the transfer to be the later foreclosure sale. The upshot was to enact the rule of *Durrett* and to overrule *Madrid*. Several months after enactment of the 1984 amendments, Senators Dole and DeConcini engaged in a colloquy on the floor of the Senate in which they asserted that there was no Congressional intent so to do. *See* 130 Cong. Rec. 13771–72 (Oct. 5, 1984). Such types of legislative history should be worth about as much as the paper the Congressional Record is printed on.

CONSOVE v. COHEN
(In re Roco Corp.)

United States Court of Appeals, First Circuit
701 F.2d 978 (1983)

BOWNES, Circuit Judge.

Appellant Edward Consove (Consove) appeals from a judgement of the United States Bankruptcy Appellate Panel, 21. B. R. 429, which affirmed a decision of the United States Bankruptcy Court, 15 B. R. 813 for the District of Rhode Island. This decision concerned two transfers of funds to Consove from Roco Corporation (Roco), a corporation subject to an involuntary proceeding under chapter 7 of the Bankruptcy Code. Consove maintains that the bankruptcy court erred in finding that a $300,000 note and security interest he received from Roco in exchange for stock constituted a fraudulent transfer and in finding that $26,158.95 he received from Roco was a voidable preference. For the reasons discussed below we affirm the bankruptcy court's judgment as affirmed by the appellate panel.

I. Facts and Proceedings Below

Consove and his partner Arthur Rosen incorporated Roco in 1946; each one owned fifty percent of the company's outstanding stock. Roco, doing business as Standard Supply Company, operated a hardware supply business. Consove was the "inside man" who took care of purchases and accounts receivable while Rosen handled sales. The company appears to have been a marginal one, but generally paid its bills as they came due and provided reasonable salaries for Consove and Rosen.

Rosen died in February 1978 and Roco redeemed his stock for approximately $130,000, funded in part by insurance proceeds. As a result of this redemption Consove became the sole shareholder of Roco. Soon thereafter Consove and his son Gerald discussed the possibility of Gerald taking over the business and Consove retiring. Gerald had been a full–time employee of Roco since 1979 and a part–time employee before that. During these years Rosen had displayed little confidence in Gerald's ability to manage the company and Gerald had not been given any position of responsibility or ownership.

The discussions between Consove and Gerald resulted in a series of transactions executed on November 1, 1979. Consove sold his 100 shares of Roco, representing all of the company's outstanding stock, back to the company in exchange for a $300,000 note. The note provided for interest at ten percent annually payable on a monthly basis or, at Roco's option, on a weekly basis at $600 per week plus a year–end adjustment. This weekly amount approximated Consove's salary and expense benefits before retirement. During the first five years only interest was due on the note, with principal to be amortized thereafter over fifteen years by monthly payments. Along with the note Consove took a security interest in all of Roco's personal property, including inventory, accounts receivable, and equipment; a financing statement was filed with the Rhode Island Secretary of State. Roco also executed a secured note to Consove for $29,558.13 to cover an earlier loan Consove had made to the company. On the same date Gerald became the sole shareholder of Roco by purchasing a single share for $3,000 and also became the sole officer and director, Consove resigned as director and president. Consove and his wife signed a letter to Gerald stating that they would not transfer the $300,000 note and that any outstanding balance would be given to Gerald at the death of the surviving parent.

Consove and his wife then retired to Florida. He apparently had little contact with Roco, other than receiving $600 weekly interest payments, until January 1980 when Gerald telephoned to request a $15,000 loan to cover the company's cashflow shortfalls caused by slow collections of accounts receivable. Consove loaned Roco the amount requested. Apparently this situation was not unusual: Consove had made such loans to the company during the years he had managed it. He cashed a check in full payment of this latest loan on June 13, 1980.

A fire in June 1980 forced Roco to close its warehouse. Consove returned to Rhode Island in July when his weekly payments of $600 stopped; up to this point he had received interest payments totalling $21,600. Consove took back control of the business from Gerald and soon confirmed his suspicion that his son had been mismanaging Roco and diverting its funds for personal use. Consove confronted Gerald about this diversion of funds and had him execute a personal note of $27,000 to the order of Roco. In his capacity as Roco's president Gerald endorsed this note to Consove. It has not been paid.

Between the time Consove reassumed control of Roco and September 23, 1980, the date an involuntary bankruptcy petition was filed, he caused the corporation to issue him six checks totalling $36,886.69. According to Roco's books, $26,159.95 of this amount was applied to the balance due Consove for officer loans and the remaining $10,727.74 was applied to reduce the principal balance on the $300,000 note to $289,272.26.

After the filing of the bankruptcy petition, Consove filed a complaint to modify the 11 U.S.C. § 362 automatic stay to permit him to continue exercising his rights as a secured creditor, specifically to reclaim Roco's assets. In his answer the Trustee asserted several affirmative defenses and counterclaims. The bankruptcy court rendered a judgment for the Trustee based on the affirmative defense of fraudulent transfer and on his counterclaim seeking avoidance of preferential transfers under 11 U.S.C. § 547. The appellate panel affirmed the bankruptcy court's findings and conclusions on the issues of the fraudulent transfer and preferences. The panel vacated the court's order that Consove turn over to the Trustee Gerald's $27,000 note because there was no support for it in the record and remanded that issue for appropriate proceedings. The Trustee has conducted a public auction of Roco's hardware inventory and is holding the proceeds as well as the estate's remaining assets pending the outcome of this case.

II. Fraudulent Transfer

The bankruptcy court held that the transfer by Roco of the $300,000 note and security interest in redeeming its stock was a fraudulent transfer under 11 U.S.C. § § 548(a)(1) & (a)(2) (Supp. V 1981). Section 548(a)(1) enables a trustee to avoid any transfer that the debtor made with "actual intent to hinder, delay, or defraud" creditors. Section 548(a)(2) in relevant part provides a standard of constructive fraud which enables the trustee to avoid any transfer in which the debtor "received less than a reasonably equivalent value in exchange for such transfer" and "was insolvent on the date [of such transfer] or became insolvent as a result of such transfer."

The clearly erroneous standard of review provided by Rule 16 of the First Circuit Rules Governing Appeals from Bankruptcy Judges to District Courts, Appellate Panels and Court of Appeals (effective Mar. 1, 1980) seems to apply to our review of the bankruptcy court's findings with respect to both sections 548(a)(1) and 548(a)(2). Consove concedes that there is clear authority for the proposition that the court's finding of actual fraud is a factual finding. See Collier on Bankruptcy ¶ 548–02, at 548–26 (15th ed. 1982) ("The approach under section 548(a)(1) is to be purely factual." (footnote omitted)). The review standard under section 548(a)(2) is not quite as straightforward; that section and its predecessors have been analyzed as intending to provide "a test of a fraud in law as distinguished from fraud in fact." 4 Collier on Bankruptcy, *supra*, ¶ 548.03, at 548–43. At least one court has treated the issue of fair equivalent value as one of law, *see Durrett v. Washington National Insurance*, 621 F.2d 201, 203 (5th Cir.1980). The court stated, however, that it would have reached the same result under the clearly erroneous standard. *Id.* at 204. There is support for viewing the less than reasonably equivalent value and insolvency determinations required by section 548(a)(2) as factual determinations. *See, e.g., Klein v. Tabatchnick*, 610 F.2d 1043, 1047–48 (2d Cir.1979) ("Fairness of consideration is generally a question of fact" and "[i]nsolvency is also a factual question."); *Braunstein v. Massachusetts Bank & Trust*, 443 F.2d 1281, 1284 (1st Cir.1971) (insolvency on date of transfer a question of fact); 4 Collier on Bankruptcy, *supra*, ¶ 548.09, at 548–96 to 97 ("Whether the transfer is for 'reasonably equivalent value' in every case is largely a question of fact, as to which considerable latitude must be allowed to the trier of the facts."). In this case the question of reasonably equivalent value appears to us to be a factual issue to be reviewed under the clearly erroneous standard and the question of insolvency appears at best to be a mixed question. In any event, we would affirm the bankruptcy court's finding on these two issues under either standard of review.

In finding that the redemption of Consove's shares of Roco was a fraudulent transfer under section 548(a)(2), the bankruptcy court held that Roco received less than reasonably equivalent value for the $300,000 note and security interest it gave Consove. Indeed, Roco received nothing but all of its outstanding stock. We agree with the bankruptcy court that this stock was virtually worthless to Roco. Under generally accepted accounting principles this treasury stock would be reported on the balance sheet of Roco as a reduction of stockholders' equity, not as an asset. *See generally* R. Anthony & J. Reese, Accounting Principles 215 (4th ed. 1979) ("Treasury stock is clearly not an 'economic resource' of an entity."). As the appellate panel noted, treasury stock is a form of shareholder distribution from which the corporation receives no assets. When a corporation purchases treasury stock it reduces its capitalization. Consove argues that the implication of this accounting theory when incorporated into the section 548(a)(2)(A) analysis is that no stock redemption could pass muster under this section. We disagree. It is possible, for example, that a publicly traded corporation with many shares outstanding could redeem a fraction of these shares, perhaps to fund an executive benefits plan or to use in converting convertible bonds or preferred stocks, and receive value as defined in the Bankruptcy Code that would be reasonably equivalent to what it transferred. The implication of the bankruptcy court's holding is merely that when a corporation with one shareholder redeems all of its outstanding stock, the value of this stock in the hands of the corporation is at best questionable.

Consove argues that the only proper measure of the value of the shares transferred to Roco in this redemption is the value of the ownership interest that he forfeited. Even if we were to accept this proposition, and ignore the clear language of section 548(a)(2) that the value to be considered is that received by the debtor and not that forfeited by the transferee, we would still hold that the district court properly found that Roco received less than reasonably equivalent value. Consove points to the Rosen redemption in 1978 as evidence of the value of Consove's ownership interest on November 1, 1979. If we assume that the value of Rosen's stock was $130,000 the maximum value of Roco at the time of this redemption would have been $260,000, and after paying for Rosen's shares the value would have fallen to $130,000. Financial statements included in the appendix to Consove's brief filed with this court indicate that Roco's net income for the next two fiscal years totalled less than $30,000—not nearly enough to raise the value of the corporation to the $300,000 face value of the note. Despite Consove's statements to the contrary, we have seen no evidence to rebut the Trustee's prima facie case that reasonably equivalent value is lacking here. Perhaps the best available evidence as to the true worth of Roco on November 1, 1979, when Consove redeemed his shares and retired from active management of the company, was the $3,000 supposedly paid by Gerald for 100% control.

We turn next to the bankruptcy court's finding that the redemption of Roco's shares rendered the corporation insolvent. The Bankruptcy Code defines "insolvency" with respect to a corporate entity as a "financial condition such that the sum of such entity's debts is greater than all of such entity's property, at a fair valuation, exclusive of property transferred, concealed, or removed with intent to hinder, delay, or defraud such entity's creditors." 11 U.S.C. § 101(26) (Supp. V 1981). The bankruptcy court relied upon expert testimony and the unaudited financial statements of Roco in finding that the corporation was insolvent. The unaudited balance sheet as of October 31, 1979, the day before the redemption, reported assets of $683,503.55 and liabilities of $501,032.98. The redemption increased the liabilities by $300,000 to $801,032.98, substantially higher than the total assets.

Consove maintains that the court erred in its reliance on unaudited financial statements because these statements did not accurately reflect the fair value of the company's assets. We have held, however, that unaudited financial statements may be admissible as the best available evidence and that it is for the trier of fact to assess the accuracy of such statements. *Braunstein*, 443 F.2d at 1284. Consove argues that the unaudited balance sheet is inaccurate for the purpose of determining insolvency because it reflects historical costs and not fair values. For several reasons, however, this historical cost balance sheet approximated the fair value of Roco's assets with sufficient accuracy. First, the balance sheet of Roco was dominated by current assets; for example, cash, accounts receivable, and inventory amounted to over $726,000 of the total assets of $756,439.54 on January 31, 1980. The balance sheet reflected no fixed assets, those assets most affected by the inaccuracies of historical cost accounting. Second, the accounts receivable may actually have been overvalued as there did not appear to have been a reserve for doubtful accounts. Third, and most importantly, there was evidence that the inventory, which amounted to $529,647.08, was not valued at the lower of cost or market as required by generally accepted accounting principles. Instead, the inventory was reported at either retail sales price or the prior year's cost, whichever more accurately reflected fair market value. The bankruptcy court clearly did not err in relying on Roco's unaudited balance sheet to determine that the company was insolvent.

Finally, Consove argues that the court erred by not including $100,000 for goodwill in the value of Roco's assets. He correctly states that the fact that goodwill was not disclosed on Roco's balance sheet does not mean that the company did not possess goodwill. Typically goodwill will not be reported on a balance sheet unless there is hard evidence of its existence and value—for example, a balance sheet might reflect the goodwill of a subsidiary which a parent corporation has purchased by paying an amount in excess of the fair value of the subsidiary's assets in an arms' length transaction. *See generally* Anthony & Reese, *supra*, at 24–25. Although goodwill might exist even though not recorded in Roco's accounts, Consove provided nothing more than mere self–serving statements to back his goodwill claims. Typical indicators of goodwill, such as a record of highly profitable operation over a period of years, a valuable customer list, or a trade name developed by the company, are not present in this case.

Having found that the bankruptcy court did not err in holding that the redemption of Consove's shares of Roco was a fraudulent transfer under section 548(a)(2), we would not normally reach the issue of actual fraud under section 548(a)(1). Like the appellate panel, however, we find that we must address this issue because it plays an integral role in analyzing Consove's claim that he has a valid lien under section 548(c) for any value he actually transferred to Roco. There is a question of whether we should consider this section 548(c) issue because it was not raised before the bankruptcy court; Consove argues that it is not a new issue and that the bankruptcy court should have considered it sua sponte once it found the redemption to be a fraudulent transfer. In any event, we have little trouble finding that the bankruptcy court did not err in its finding of actual fraud and, as a result, that Consove does not have a valid lien under section 548(c).

A court may make a finding of fraudulent intent under section 548(a)(1) on the basis of circumstantial evidence; direct proof of the transferor's fraudulent intent will rarely be available. 4 Collier on Bankruptcy, *supra*, § 548.02, at 548–33. We may impute any fraudulent intent of Consove to the transferor Roco because, as the company's president, director, and sole shareholder, he was in a position to control the disposition of its property. *See id.* at 548–30. The substance of the redemption was that the father passed along the ownership interest of Roco to his son and secured for himself a steady retirement income at his prior salary level, all at the expense of the corporation's creditors. As the appellate panel noted, the stockholder's claim became superior to the claims of trade creditors with the latter receiving no value, but instead having their interests severely impaired. The large discrepancy in value between the note transferred and the stock received strengthens the inference of fraud. *See id.* at 548–37. We cannot say that the bankruptcy court was clearly erroneous in its factual finding of actual fraud. Consove's argument that his $15,000 loan to the corporation in January 1980 evidences his lack of fraudulent intent with respect to creditors is unpersuasive. At this time Consove had a strong motivation to assure the continued operation of Roco because it represented his source of retirement income and his son's source of employment. Fraudulent intent does not require an intent to run the company aground; it requires merely an intent to hinder or defraud creditors.

Consove's claim that he is entitled to the saving benefit of section 548(c) must fail once we have found that the bankruptcy court was not clearly erroneous in its finding of actual fraud. Good faith is an "indispensable element" of this saving benefit provision. *Id.* ¶ 548.07, at 548–61. Although the good faith requirement here is not susceptible of precise definition, *id.*, surely a finding of actual fraud under section 548(a)(1) precludes any opportunity for a lien under section 548(c) to the extent of any value given.

III. Preferences

As noted earlier, between the time he regained control of Roco and the date the bankruptcy petition was filed, Consove had the corporation issue him checks totalling $36,886.69. The bankruptcy court held that the $26,158.55 of this amount that was applied to the balance due Consove for officer loans was a preference under section 547(b). It follows from our finding that the bankruptcy court did not err on the fraudulent transfer and section 548(c) issues that it also did not err in its conclusion that the payments here constituted a preference; these payments clearly fall within section 547(b) because they enabled Consove to receive more than he would have otherwise received under chapter 7.

IV. Conclusion

We affirm the bankruptcy court's finding, as affirmed by the appellate panel, that the redemption of Consove's shares of Roco resulted in a fraudulent transfer under both the constructive and actual fraud provisions of the Bankruptcy Code and that subsequent payments of $26,158.95 constituted an avoidable preference. Accordingly, the court properly ordered Consove to turn over to the Trustee $21,600 he received as interest and $10,727.74 he received as principal on the $300,000 note as well as the $26,158.95 preference item. In trying to establish the existence of goodwill in the company, Consove at one point testified that he thought he was entitled to $100,000 as the price for his thirty–four years devoted to the business. This overlooks the fact that he could have provided for his retirement throughout his working years either through personal savings and investment or some type of corporate retirement package fully disclosed on the company's financial records. Having failed to do this, he cannot suddenly create for himself a stream of retirement income at the expense of the company's creditors.

Affirmed.

[E]   Statutory Liens

See § 101(47). Section 545 invalidates statutory liens which are (i) disguised priorities, (ii) not perfected against bona fide purchasers at the date of the petition, and (iii) for rent.

NOTES AND QUESTIONS

1. Give three examples of a statutory lien. Can you distinguish a statutory lien from a judicial lien and from a consensual lien? Can a statutory lien be avoided by the trustee as a preference pursuant to § 547? What about pursuant to § 544(a)(1)?

2. Is there any language difference in the bona fide purchaser test as contained in § 545(2) from that in § § 544(a)(3), 547(e)(1), 548(d)(1), and 549(c)?

3. Suppose a federal tax lien is properly perfected before bankruptcy under § § 6321–6323 of the Internal Revenue Code. The IRC provides that it is subordinate to an existing perfected security interest on the same property. Assume that Debtor owes Bank $75,000 which is secured by a perfected security interest on Debtor's equipment. Subsequently, IRS assesses Debtor for income tax deficiency in the amount of $400,000. Debtor files a petition under chapter 7 of the Code. Among its other debts, $35,000 is owed to employees, the total amount of which is payable as a third priority under § 507(a), and approximately $50,000 will be required to pay expenses of administration. Debtor's only realizable asset is its equipment and on its sale by the trustee, $200,000 is obtained. Pursuant to the IRC, the federal government has a lien which it

perfected by filing before the chapter 7 petition on all of the property of Debtor. How should the $200,000 be distributed? *See* § 724. If Bank's security interest had been perfected after notice of the tax lien was filed, and was thus subordinate to it, how should the money be distributed? Instead of the tax lien, suppose an ERISA lien were involved; any change in result? What about a lien held by the Small Business Administration for a loan it guaranteed and paid?

[F]   Rights of Reclaiming Seller

Before the Uniform Commercial Code was adopted, sellers of goods to insolvent buyers were able to rescind the purchase contract if they could prove they had been defrauded. Rescission resulted in a revesting of title in the seller of the delivered goods. The remedy of rescission was generally allowed in a bankruptcy case even though the seller was obviously being preferred over other creditors. *See, e.g., In re Stridacchio,* 107 F. Supp. 486 (D. N. J. 1952); *Bateman v. Patterson,* 212 Ga. 284, 92 S.E.2d 8 (1956). The difficulty and the area of disagreement among the state courts was the degree of fraud or misrepresentation the seller had to prove to be entitled to rescind the contract. The Uniform Commercial Code in § 2–702 codified this common law right, made proof of fraud unnecessary, and simply required that a seller who delivered goods on credit to a buyer who it subsequently learned was insolvent could reclaim the goods by making demand therefor within ten days after their receipt by the buyer. Several cases immediately were brought in the courts for a determination of the trustee's rights as a lien creditor relative to the reclaiming seller's rights. Generally, these cases held for the seller on the ground that under pre–U.C.C. law the seller would have prevailed over the lien creditor or trustee in bankruptcy. *In re Kravitz,* 278 F.2d 820 (3d Cir. 1960); *In re Mel Golde Shoes, Inc.,* 403 F.2d 658 (6th Cir. 1968); *In re PFA Farmers Market Association,* 583 F.2d 992 (8th Cir. 1978); *In re Daylin,* 596 F.2d 853 (9th Cir. 1979).

Bankruptcy courts then began holding the right of the reclaiming seller to be a statutory lien that first became effective on the buyer's insolvency and was therefore invalid as against the trustee pursuant to §§ 67(c) and 64 of the former Act, which are the forerunners of §§ 545 and 507. These holdings were repudiated by the Courts of Appeals that adjudicated the issue. *In re Federal's, Inc.,* 553 F.2d 509 (6th Cir. 1977); *In re Telemart Enterprises, Inc.,* 524 F.2d 761 (9th Cir. 1975), cert. denied 424 U.S. 969 (1976), *In re Daylin, supra.*

For fuller discussion of the history and exposition of these issues, *see* Duesenberg & King, Sales and Bulk Transfers under the Uniform Commercial Code, 3A Bender's U.C.C. Service, § 13.13.

Against this background, § 546(c) of the Bankruptcy Code was developed. The obvious intent was to validate the seller's right of reclamation as long as the Code requirements were fulfilled. It restricts the trustee's use of the strong arm provision of § 544, the statutory lien provision of § 545, and the preference provision of § 547 and permits a seller to obtain the goods, a lien for the purchase price or an administration expense priority if the seller conforms to § 546(c). Such conformity merely requires that the seller makes a demand in writing for the goods within ten days after they have been received by the buyer or within 20 days if the ten day period had not expired before the commencement of the bankruptcy case. Note that the demand must be in writing, a more stringent requirement than in § 2–702 of the U.C.C. Note also that the written demand is not made unnecessary if the seller received a written misrepresentation of solvency within 90 days of delivery as in the U.C.C.

Is the remedy of § 546(c) exclusive? Could seller claim a right under § 2–702 if the bankruptcy case is in the 9th or 6th Circuit? Some courts have held § 546 to be exclusive. *See* 4 Collier, Bankruptcy ¶ 546.04[2] (15th ed.). How would you read § 546(c). Exclusive? Or concurrent with § 2–702 in jurisdictions that have permitted reclamation in the face of a trustee's assertion of the various avoiding powers?

IN RE ORIGINAL AUTO PARTS DISTRIBUTORS, INC.

Bankruptcy Court, Southern District of New York
9 B.R. 469, 3 C.B.C.2d 933, 7 B.C.D. 490 (1981)

SCHWARTZBERG, Bankruptcy Judge:

The determination of this controversy hinges upon whether or not a seller's demand for reclamation of goods sold to a debtor must always be made in writing before ten days after receipt of the goods by the debtor. In this case, the seller did not learn of the debtor's insolvency until more than ten days after receipt of the goods.

The seller, TR–3 Chemical Corporation, filed a complaint objecting to the discharge of the obligation owed to it by the debtor, Original Auto Parts Distributors, Incorporated. In addition, TR–3 seeks an order directing Original to turn over and surrender certain goods which it has in its possession. The Official Creditors' Committee has moved for an order pursuant to Rules 12(b) and (c) and 56(b) of the Federal Rules of Civil Procedure granting summary judgment as to counts three and four of TR–3's complaint; the counts dealing with the turn over of goods sold by TR–3 to Original. In response, TR–3 filed a cross–motion seeking an order granting it partial summary judgment on counts three and four of its complaint and denying the Creditors' Committee motion.

The debtor filed its petition under Chapter 11 of the Bankruptcy Code, 11 U.S.C. § 1101 et seq., on June 27, 1980; TR–3 filed a proof of claim in the amount of $50,137.50 on August 8th, 1980. In its complaint TR–3 alleges the following facts:

1. In January, 1980 the debtor communicated with TR–3 to request the purchase of 2,000 cases of auto cleaner and glaze manufactured by TR–3.

2. Based upon the request of the debtor and upon the debtor's representations that it had the ability to pay for the goods, TR–3 delivered the goods on credit.

3. The goods, which had a value of $50,137.50, were received by the debtor on March 7, 1980.

4. The debtor obtained the goods by false pretenses and false representations in light of the fact that it had ordered the goods during a period when it knew that it was insolvent and had been negotiating with its creditors.

5. The debtor now has in its possession approximately 1,000 cases of the goods delivered by TR–3, each case worth $25.80.

6. On or about June 23, 1980 TR–3 mailed and served a notice of reclamation of the goods upon the debtor.

7. On or about June 23, 1980 TR–3 caused a Telex to be served upon the debtor by Western Union, demanding reclamation of the goods.

In its answer the Creditors' Committee denies knowledge or information sufficient to form a belief with respect to the course of events in question. However, in its statement pursuant to Rule 9(g) of the General Rules of the Southern and Eastern Districts of New York the Creditors' Committee states that there are no genuine issues to be tried with respect to the following facts:

1. On March 7, 1980 TR–3 sold and delivered to the debtor 2,000 cases of auto cleaner and glaze having an agreed value of $50,137.50.

2. On June 23, 1980 TR–3 mailed and served a notice of reclamation of the goods upon the debtor.

3. On June 24, 1980 TR–3 caused a Telex to be served upon the debtor by Western Union demanding reclamation of the goods.

In its Rule 9(g) statement TR–3 denies selling the goods to the debtor on March 7, 1980 but admits delivering the goods on March 7th. In addition, TR–3 reasserts its allegations concerning the debtor's false representations as to its solvency at the time of the transaction.

Summary judgment is a procedural device which cuts off a party's right to trial, therefore the court must resolve all ambiguities in favor of the party which opposes a summary judgment motion, *Heyman v. Commerce and Industry Insurance Co.*, 524 F.2d 1317, 1319–20 (2d Cir. 1975). However, the reclamation aspect of this adversary proceeding is one which can be decided on the merits since there clearly exist no genuine issues of material fact which need to be tried. *See, Schwartz v. Assoc. Musicians of Greater N.Y., Local 802*, 340 F.2d 228, 233 (2d Cir. 1964).

The issue to be resolved is whether or not TR–3 has a right to reclaim the goods from the debtor based upon the fact that it delivered the goods on March 7, 1980 and sought to reclaim them by written notice on June 23, 1980.

Section 546(c) of the Bankruptcy Code, 11 U.S.C. § 546(c), which deals with the reclamation rights of a seller, states in part:

> The rights and powers of the trustee under sections 544(a), 545, 547, and 549 of this title are subject to any statutory right or common–law right of a seller, in the ordinary course of such

seller's business, of goods to the debtor to reclaim such goods if the debtor has received such goods while insolvent, but—

(1) such a seller may not reclaim any such goods unless such seller demands in writing reclamation of goods before ten days after receipt of such goods by the debtor.

The Creditors' Committee admits that Code § 546(c) recognizes the rights of a seller to reclaim either under common law principles or pursuant to U.C.C. § 2–702. However, the Committee argues that before reclamation may be allowed the conditions prescribed in subsection (1) of § 546(c) must be met, and since TR–3 did not make a written demand for reclamation within ten days of the receipt of the goods by the debtor, it is precluded from reclaiming the goods.

TR–3 argues that a careful reading of § 546(c) and its legislative history mandates the conclusion that a seller who has not complied with subsection (1) of § 546(c) is not barred from seeking reclamation pursuant to its common law rights since § 546(c) states that the rights and powers of a trustee are subject to any common–law rights of a seller. The plaintiff concedes, for the purposes of this motion, that § 2–702(2) of the Uniform Commercial Code is inapplicable to this controversy. A determination of whether or not U.C.C. § 2–702(2) precludes reliance on a common law right of reclamation under New York law is not required at this time since Code § 546(c) expressly permits the assertion of a common law right of reclamation in a bankruptcy proceeding.

Both the Second Circuit Court of Appeals and the New York State Court of Appeals have recognized a seller's right to reclaim goods sold on credit when the buyer fraudulently misrepresented his solvency, credit status, or intent to pay. *See, California Conserving Co. v. D'Avanzo*, 62 F.2d 528 (2d Cir. 1933); *In re Meiselman*, 105 F.2d 995 (2d Cir. 1939); *Hotchkin v. Third National Bank*, 127 N.Y. 329, 27 N.E. 1050 (1891); *Baldwin v. Childs*, 249 N.Y. 212, 163 N.E. 737 (1928). Therefore, the sole question to be determined by this court is whether TR–3 may reclaim the goods from the debtor, in spite of the fact that it did not comply with the requirements of Code § 546(c)(1).

In support of its argument TR–3 relies upon an article written by Professors Mann and Phillips appearing in The American Bankruptcy Law Journal; Mann, Phillips, *Section 546(c) of the Bankruptcy Reform Act: An Imperfect Resolution of the Conflict Between the Reclaiming Seller and the Bankruptcy Trustee*, 54 Am. Bankr. L. J. 239 (1980). TR–3 cites the article for the proposition that § 546(c) does not preclude a seller from reclaiming goods pursuant to a common law fraud claim, despite the fact that it did not demand reclamation in writing within ten days of the debtor's receipt of the goods. After a careful review of the Mann–Phillips article this court cannot agree with TR–3's interpretation of the author's conclusion.

The authors do not believe that § 546(c) is the exclusive bankruptcy provision governing a seller's reclamation rights but that a seller who does not comply with the requirements of § 546(c) would have the right to defend itself against the trustee's avoiding powers. 54 Am. Bankr. L. J., *supra*, at 265, 267. Notwithstanding the accuracy of this conclusion, TR–3's reliance upon it is misplaced. TR–3 is not seeking to override an avoiding power but is attempting instead to assert a nonbankruptcy cause of action, common law fraud, in a setting where its assertion is limited by the specific language of Code § 546(c). Indeed, Professors Mann and Phillips recognize this argument and state:

> [A] seller who is unable to utilize section 2–702(2) for [proce-dural reasons] will also usually be unable to employ section 546(c) in which case *the availability of common law fraud remedies will be of little avail also, because they too depend upon these requirements under section 546(c).*

[emphasis added]. 54 Am. Bankr. L. J., *supra*, at 261 n.107. *See*, Schneyer, *Statutory Liens Under the New Bankruptcy Code—Some Problems Remain*, 55 Am. Bankr L. J. 1 (1981). Further, the legislative history of Code § 546(c) states, "[A] demand for reclamation must be made in writing anytime before ten days after receipt of the goods by the debtor." 124 Cong. Rec. H11,097 (Sept. 28, 1978); S17,413–17,414 (Oct. 6, 1978). Therefore, it is clear that a seller who seeks to reclaim goods delivered to a debtor, whether relying upon U.C.C. § 2–702(2) or common law fraud, must comply with the requirements of Code § 546(c). TR–3's failure to give written notice of its demand for reclamation before ten days after receipt of the goods is fatal; it may not now prevail under its complaint seeking a turn over or surrender of these goods.

Accordingly, TR–3's cross–motion for summary judgment as to counts three and four of its complaint must be denied. Conversely, the debtor's motion for summary judgment on the same counts is *Granted* and that aspect of the complaint is *Dismissed.*

KELLER v. TIME CREDIT CORP.
(In re Keller)

Bankruptcy Court, Northern District of Ohio
24 B.R. 720 (1982)

WALTER J. KRASNIEWSKI, Bankruptcy Judge.

This matter is before the Court upon the Motion of Plaintiff for reconsideration of this Court's Orders of August 14, 1981 and August 20, 1981 which dismissed Debtor's Complaint to Avoid a Judicial Lien pursuant to 11 U.S.C. § 522(f)(1) and denied Plaintiff's/Debtor's Application to reopen her bankruptcy case. Upon consideration of the memoranda submitted by the parties and recent developments in the case law since the Court first considered the issue, the Court finds that, absent the proof of equitable considerations which would dictate a contrary result, the Court should vacate its initial Order dismissing the complaint as untimely. Reconsideration of the application to reopen, however, for reasons more fully discussed below, is denied.

After filing a petition under Chapter 7 of the Bankruptcy Code Plaintiff/Debtor received a discharge on March 2, 1981. The case was closed on April 30, 1981. On May 11, 1981 Plaintiff filed her complaint to avoid Defendant's judicial lien which complaint was dismissed on Defendant's motion by order entered August 14, 1981. The instant motion for reconsideration was filed on August 25, 1981.

The issue raised by the motion for reconsideration is whether or not a § 522(f) complaint filed after the discharge order has been entered and the case is closed is timely filed. In granting Defendant's motion to dismiss the Court relied upon *In re Adkins*, 7 B.R. 325, 6 B.C.D. 997 (Bkrtcy. S.D. Cal.1980) and *Associates Financial Services v. Porter*, 11 B. R. 578, 7 B. D. C. 959 (Bkrtcy. W.D. Okla.1981) in holding that a § 522(f) complaint must be filed at or before the discharge hearing in order to be considered timely. Since *Adkins and Porter*, however, the majority of the Courts that have considered the question have found no bar to the exercise of § 522(f) lien avoidance rights after either the granting of a discharge or the administrative closing of a case. *See, e.g., Tarrant v. Spenard Builders Supply, Inc.*, 19 B. R. 360, 9 B. C. D. 413 (Bkrtcy. D. Ala.1982); *Modern Supply Co. v. Lee*, 21 B. R. 774 (Bkrtcy. E.D. Tenn. 1982); *In re Hall*, 22 B. R. 701, 9 B. C. D. 588 (Bkrtcy. E.D. Pa. 1982); *Russell v. United States*, 20 B. .R 537 (Bkrtcy. W.D. Penn.1982); *Barner v. Associates Financial Services Co.*, 20 B. R. 428 (Bkrtcy. E.D. Wis.1982); *Johnson v. First and Merchants National Bank*, 18 B. R. 555 (Bkrtcy. D. Md.1982); *Schneider v. Beneficial Finance Co.*, 18 B. R. 274, 8 B. C. D. 1084 (Bkrtcy. D. N.D.1982); *In re Conley*, 17 B. R. 387 (Bkrtcy. S.D. Ohio 1982); *Montney v. Beneficial Finance Co.*, 17 B. R. 353, 8 B. C. D. 931 (Bkrtcy. E.D. Mich.1982); *Baskins v. Household Finance Corp.*, 14 B. R.110, 8 B. C. D. 161 (Bkrtcy. E.D. N.C.1981); *Gortmaker v. Avco Financial Services*, 14 B. R. 66, 8 B. C. D. 67 (Bkrtcy. D. S.D.1981); *Associates Financial Services v. Swanson*, 13 B. R. 851, 8 B. C. D. 13 (Bkrtcy. D. Idaho 1981). *Cf., Brown v. Morris Plan*, 18 B. R. 323 (Bkrtcy. E.D. Cal.1982) (Congress did not intend to limit the time for debtor to file a complaint as long as case is pending).*Contra Penco Corp. v. Andrews*, 22 B. R. 623, 9 B.C.D. 589 (Bkrtcy. D. Del.1982). *Cf. In re Coomes*, 20 B. R. 290 (Bkrtcy. W.D. Ky.1982) (Local Rule required filing of lien avoidance action at least 5 days prior to scheduled discharge). Upon reconsideration, this Court now concurs in the majority view and holds that, absent equitable considerations to the contrary, neither the granting of a discharge nor the administrative closing of a case should be a bar to the debtor's exercise of his lien avoidance rights.

Section 522(f) places no time limitation on the assertion of lien avoidance rights. Similarly, there is nothing in the Bankruptcy Rules, the Interim Rules, or the Local Rules of Court of this district which limits a debtor's rights under § 522(f). As one court has noted. The right to avoid liens is a personal right given to a debtor, independent of case administration. It is fundamentally no different than any other legal right available to an individual. Congress has not placed any statutory limitation on the exercise of the right and I know of no legal doctrine at common law or equity which would allow this court to create an arbitrary time limitation on the exercise of this legal right.

Advocates Financial Services v. Swanson, 13 B. R. at 854, 8 B. C. D. at 14.

In Adkins, supra, the Court relied on the following reasoning to support its conclusion that a § 522(f) complaint must be filed at or before the discharge hearing.

> It seems to me that debtors in order to comply with the purpose and intent of § 524(c), must know with some degree of certainty whether a reaffirmation agreement may have to be negotiated in order to permit the retention of property pledged as security before the grant of the discharge. Otherwise it may be too late to negotiate a reaffirmation agreement.
>
> Therefore, in order to effectively carry out the provisions of the Code and to obtain finality of a determination of the rights of all parties, it seems to me that a debtor must file a complaint to avoid a lien under § 522(f) at or before the discharge hearing. At that point there is sufficient time to negotiate a reaffirmation agreement or continue the discharge hearing to permit such negotiation.

7 B. R. at 327, 6 B. C. D. at 998.

This is "no justification", however, "for arbitrarily equating the date fixed for the discharge hearing pursuant to § 524(d) with the time within which a debtor must file a § 522(f) complaint." *Montney v. Beneficial Finance Co.,* 17 B. R. at 356, 8 B. C. D. at 933. The fact that it may be in a debtor's best interest to avoid liens under 522(f) before his time to reaffirm passes, is not a valid reason for saying he must do so before discharge or forfeit the right to do so. In most cases the exemption covers the security in its entirety and no need to reaffirm arises.

Associates Financial Services v. Swanson, 13 B. R. at 853, 8 B. C. D. at 14. In addition, the failure of the debtor to make use of one remedy given him by Congress does not justify the barring of a second independent remedy. *Tarrant v. Spenard Builders Supply, Inc.,* 19 B. R. 360, 9 B. C. D. 413, 415 (Bkrtcy. D. Ala.1982).

Finally the other reason for limiting a debtor's lien avoidance rights expressed in *Adkins,* the interest in finality in a bankruptcy proceeding, although certainly compelling, is not adequate reason for arbitrarily setting time limits on legislatively created rights. If limits are to be imposed, it should be done by statute or by duly promulgated bankruptcy rule. *Schneider v. Beneficial Finance Co.,* 18 B. R. 274, 276, 8 B. C. D. 1084, 1085 (Bkrtcy. D. N.D.1982).

The notion that the administrative closing of a case should impose a time limit on the debtor's exercise of his lien avoidance rights has its roots in *Associates Financial Services v. Porter, supra.* In *Porter* the Court linked the limitations placed on the trustee's rights to recover, for the benefit of the estate, property transferred to a third party by an avoidable transfer found in § 550, through § 522(i)(1), to the debtor's lien avoidance rights under § 522(f).

On the basis of the statutory provisions [§§ 552(i)(1); 550(a), (e)] the court in *Porter* then concluded that:

> [i]f, under § § 522(i)(1) and 550(e), an action to recover property from a transferee in an avoided transfer cannot be

commenced after a case is closed, it naturally follows that the initial action to avoid the transfer also cannot be commenced after the case is closed.

11 B.R. at 581, 7 B.C.D. at 961.

The Court in *Montney v. Beneficial Finance Co.*, 17 B. 0R. 353, 357, 8 B. C. D. 931, 933 (Bkrtcy. E.D. Mich.1982) and *Associates Financial Services v. Swanson*, 13 B. R. 851, 854, 8 B. C. D. 13, 14 (Bkrtcy. D. Idaho 1981) have rejected this reasoning concluding that § 550 is only a limitation on the right to recover property from a transferee, not a statutory limitation on the right of the debtor to avoid liens under § 522(f). Both Courts have in part relied on the fact that whereas a time limit on the trustee's right to avoid liens is stated in § 546, no similar limitation on the debtor's avoidance power is found in § 522(f). The Court in *Montney v. Beneficial Finance Co.*, 17 B. R. at 357–358, 8 B. C. D. at 934 concluded as follows:

> If Congress had intended to impose a time limit within which debtors had to institute a section 522(f) action, it could have done so either by so stating in section 522(f) or by referring to the time limit prescribed by section 546(a) in section 522(i)(1), as it did with reference to section 550(e). Congress did not do so. The omission is not unintentional. The drafters of the Code consciously omitted any reference to the time within which a section 522(f) action had to be instituted. They intended that if a time limit was to be imposed, it was to be imposed by the Rules of Bankruptcy Procedure to be promulgated, or by local rule. H.R. Rep. No. 95–595, 95th Cong., 1st Sess. 293, 297 (1977), U.S. Code Cong. & Admin. News 1978, pp. 6250, 6254. Rules of Bankruptcy Procedure for the Code have not as yet been promulgated, and this court has not adopted a local rule requiring a debtor to institute a section 522(f) action within a stated time. A debtor may, therefore, rely on section 522(f) even after a case is closed unless equitable considerations dictate otherwise.

(footnote omitted)

This Court agrees with the courts in *Montney v. Beneficial Finance Co.*, 17 B. R. 353, 8 B. C. D. 931 (Bkrtcy. E.D. Mich.1982) and *Associates Financial Services v. Swanson*, 13 B. R. 851, 8 B. C. D. 13 (Bkrtcy. D. Idaho 1981) in concluding that the closing of a bankruptcy case, absent equitable considerations to the contrary, is no bar to the commencement of a § 522(f) lien avoidance action. Defendant in this case, however, at the trial on the merits, should be permitted to introduce proof of such equitable circumstances that could bar relief.

Finally, this Court concurs with the view in *Schneider v. Beneficial Finance Co.*, 18 B. R. 274, 276, 8 B. C. D. 1084, 1085 that, as the jurisdiction of the Court is presently constituted, it is not necessary that a closed bankruptcy case be reopened in order for the debtor to bring an action to avoid liens under § 522(f). As the jurisdiction of the Court is presently constituted under 28 U.S.C. § 1471, the Court has jurisdiction over all civil proceedings arising under or related to a case under Title 11. Since the Court agrees with the reasoning in *Associates Financial Services v. Swanson, supra,* that a lien avoidance action under § 522(f) does not affect the administration of a bankruptcy case but only a personal right of the debtor, there should be no reason to require a bankruptcy case to be reopened for the Court to consider a matter merely related to a bankruptcy case.

For the foregoing reasons, it is hereby,

Ordered that this Court's Order of August 14, 1981 dismissing Plaintiff's complaint be, and it hereby is, vacated. It is further,

Ordered that reconsideration of this Court's Order of August 20, 1981 which denied Plaintiff's application to reopen her bankruptcy case be, and it hereby is, denied. It is further;

Ordered that a trial on Plaintiff's Complaint is hereby set

§ 15.04   Setoff of Claims; Section § 553

The law of setoff as it existed under § 68 of the Act was essentially retained in the Code but with some important modifications. *See* § 533. In general, a creditor who owes a prepetition debt to the debtor may set that debt off against the prepetition debt owing to the creditor by the debtor. To the extent of such setoff, the creditor is receiving dollar for dollar on the claim instead of the lower percentage usually obtained in a bankruptcy distribution. Section 553, however, places some restrictions on the right of setoff. In particular, there is a provision somewhat similar to § 547(c)(5) providing a two–prong test to determine if the deficiency of the creditor is increased during the 90–day period. Since a setoff is not a preference under § 547 (where does one find support for this conclusion?), § 553(b) provides its own power of avoidance to the trustee which is analogous to a preference. See generally 4 Collier on Bankruptcy, § 553.01 et seq. (15th ed.), Freeman, *Setoff Under the New Bankruptcy Code: The Effect on Bankers*, 97 Banking L.J. 484 (1980). *See Citizens Bank of Maryland v. Strumpf*, Chapter 13, *supra.*

BIG BEAR SUPER MARKET NO. 3 v . PRINCESS BAKING CORP.
(In re Princess Baking Corp.)

Bankruptcy Court, Southern District of California
5 B.R. 587, 2 C.B.C.2d 1071, 6 B.C.D.842 (1980)

JAMES, W. MEYERS, Bankruptcy Judge.

I.

On May 9, 1980, the plaintiff, Big Bear Super Market No. 3 ("Big Bear") filed this complaint naming the debtor, Princess Baking Corporation, ("Princess"), as defendant, seeking relief from the automatic stay, an accounting, a determination as to the dischargeability of debt, and rescission. On May 22, 1980, this Court issued an order setting a hearing on the defendant's motion to show cause why Big Bear should not be compelled to release funds. The hearing was held before this Court on June 27, 1980, at which time the parties submitted the issues presented on the declarations and exhibits files and the argument of counsel. This memorandum decision is filed to announce this Court's findings and conclusions.

II.

Facts

On April 24, 1980, Princess filed a petition seeking protection under Chapter 11 of the United States Bankruptcy Code ("Code"). As of the date the petition was filed there existed various obligations between the parties.

Under two leases signed on October 29, 1979, Big Bear leased to Princess space to operate retail bakery businesses in its stores at 7611 Fay Avenue and 2707 Via de la Valle, both in San Diego County. As part of its responsibilities under these leases, Big Bear collected for Princess' retail sales of baked goods and remitted these receipts to Princess within four days after the close of the business week, less six and one half percent of the sales as a rental charge. As of April 24, 1980, Big Bear owed Princess $5,583.74 for the week ending April 20, and $2,033.08 for the subsequent three days through April 23. In turn Princess owed rental payments of $495.09, which is 6.5% of the total gross sales receipts then due to Princess. In addition, Big Bear admits it owed Princess an additional $4,357.82 for purchases of goods. Thus, as of the day Princess filed its petition, Big Bear owed it a total of $11,974.64 for outstanding sales collections and purchases.

Against these, Princess had several obligations to Big Bear. First, there was the remaining principal balance of approximately $235,000.00 due on a promissory note dated October 29, 1979. Payments under this note commenced on December 5, 1979 and were current through March of 1980. This note was in conjunction with the sale to Princess of certain of Big Bear's bakery stock, fixtures and equipment. While this note was intended to be secured by the same goods and equipment, Big Bear concedes it is now in an unsecured status since it did not perfect its security interest in these assets prior to the petition being filed. Princess also owed $5,500 as the balance on inventory that it had also purchased from Big Bear. In addition, Princess was responsible for $1,854.05 in NSF checks, mainly payroll, it had issued and which were cashed by Big Bear.

On May 1, 1980, Princess made demands on Big Bear for payment of the amounts due as it needed funds to pay its employees. Big Bear apparently claimed a right of setoff, but on May 2, 1980 did advance $7,500 to Princess so it could make its payroll.

III.

Discussion

A. Automatic Stay

In this dispute Princess has demanded payment from Big Bear of those amounts due it as of April 24, 1980. Big Bear has informed Princess that it has chosen to exercise its rights of setoff as of that date.

As a preliminary matter Princess contends that all creditor rights to setoff mutual obligations have been stayed under Section § 362(a)(7) and exercise of this right must await judicial determination. 11 U.S.C. § 362(a)(7). In this Princess is correct, for Big Bear did not exercise any setoff prior to the petition being filed and therefore it must obtain relief from the automatic stay. 4 Collier on Bankruptcy, § 553.05[2], at 553–37 (15th ed. 1979). *See* Ahart, *Bank Setoff Under the Bankruptcy Reform Act of 1978*, 53 Am. Bankr. L.J. 205, 207 (1979). Any setoffs accomplished by Big Bear after the petition was filed are of no effect pending resolution of the issues presented in this motion to show cause.

B. Statutory Basis for Setoff

In considering this question of setoff we are directed to Section 553 of the recently enacted Code which is entitled "Setoff." 11 U.S.C. § 553. This section preserves, with some changes, the right of setoff in bankruptcy cases as was found in Section 68 of the former Bankruptcy Act ("Act"). H. R. Rep. No. 595, 95th Cong., 1st Sess. 377 (1977) (*"House Report"*). *See also* S. Rep. No. 989, 95th Cong., 2d Sess. 91 (1978), U.S.Code Cong. & Admin. News 1978, p. 5787.

1.   Under the Bankruptcy Act

Under the Act it has been noted that the right of setoff violates one of the basic impulses of bankruptcy law by not treating creditors equally in that it allows one creditor to receive more than another. *Bohack Corp. v. Borden, Inc.*, 599 R.2d 1160, 1165 (2d Cir. 1979). *See In re Applied Logic Corp.*, 576 F.2d 952, 957 (2d Cir. 1978). But the right of setoff is of ancient derivation and has been embodied in every bankruptcy law the United States has enacted. *See* 4 Collier on Bankruptcy, *supra*, § 553.01, at 553–3–8. This recognizes the longstanding belief that an injustice would result from compelling a creditor to file its claim in full with the hope of fair treatment, while at the same time paying in full its indebtedness to the estate. *See Matter of Progressive Wallpaper Co.*, 240 F. 807, 811 (N.Y. 1917).

In applying setoff provisions the courts have held that they are permissive rather than mandatory and they are placed within the control of the Bankruptcy Court, which exercises its discretion in these cases upon the general principles of equity. *Cumberland Glass Mfg. Co. v. DeWitt*, 237 U.S. 447, 445, 35 S.Ct. 636, 639, 59 L.Ed. 1042 (1915); *Tuscon House Construction Company v. Fulford*, 378 F.2d 734, 737 (9th Cir. 1967); *Riggs v. Government Emp. Financial Corp.*, 623 F.2d 68, 73

(9th Cir. 1980). Now this discretion was not intended to preclude setoff simply because the result would be "unjust." *In re Applied Logic Corp., supra,* 576 F.2d at 957. Instead the Court will disallow setoff only where the creditor has been guilty of a kind of conduct which is morally unsound and tending to undermine the integrity of modern business. *See Palmer v. Stokely,* 259 F.Supp. 776, 779 (W.Okla.1966). Whether setoff will be disallowed is dependent on the particular facts presented in each case. *In re Duplan Corp.,* 455 F.Supp. 926, 933 (S.N.Y.1978).

The application of these principles to operating cases presented considerable difficulty under the Act for the purpose of reorganization is to save a sick business, not to bury it and divide up its belongings. *Susquehanna Chemical Corp. v. Producers Bank & Tr. Co.,* 174 F.2d 783, 787 (3d Cir. 1949) (Chap. X). *See Baker v. Gold Seal Liquors,* 417 U.S. 467, 470, 94 S.Ct. 2504, 2506, 41 L.Ed.2d 243 (1974) (Railroad Reorganization). A debtor in a reorganization must keep its precarious cash inflow sufficient for operating purposes in order to survive. *Bohack Corp. v. Borden, Inc. supra,* 599 F.2d at 1166. Yet setoff has been allowed in numerous cases under Chapter XI. *In Matter of Olins Leasing Inc.,* 3 B.C.D. 605, 607 (S.N.Y.1977). This is because Section 302 of the Act made the provisions of Section 68 applicable to Chapter XI proceedings "insofar as they are not inconsistent with or in conflict with the provisions of [this] Chapter." *Western Land Planning v. Midland Nat. Bank,* 434 F.Supp. 616, 617 (E.Wis.1977). See 6 Collier on Bankruptcy, § 9.09, at 1588 (14th ed. 1978). But on many occasions the courts have considered the compulsory application of Section 68 inappropriate to Chapter XI situations. *See e.g., In Matter of Olins Leasing, Inc., supra,* 3 B.C.D. at 608. These cases seem to be motivated by a desire to protect the financial status of the debtor and its ability to reorganize. *See DiversaGraphics v. Management & Technical, Etc.,* 561 F.2d 725, 728 (8th Cir. 1977); *Western Land Planning v. Midland Nat. Bank, supra,* 434 F.Supp. at 617–18; *In re U.S.N. Co., Inc.,* 2 B. R. 468 (S.N.Y.1979). However, the only credible basis articulated for these decisions disallowing setoff in Chapter XI cases, is that in some cases allowance of setoff would undermine the debtor's ability to reorganize which in itself is inconsistent with the provisions of Chapter XI as it conflicts with the basic purposes of the Chapter. *See Bohack Corp. v. Borden, Inc., supra,* 599 F.2d at 1166; *Susquehanna Chemical Corp. v. Producers Bank & Tr. Co., supra,* 174 F.2d at 787.

2. Under the Bankruptcy Code

Under the Code the Congress recognized that:

> [t]he situation for the treatment of setoff in a reorganization case is very different than in a liquidation case. In order to accomplish a successful reorganization, it is important that business proceed as usual for the debtor. Setoff is an interruption in the conduct of business, and may have detrimental effects on the attempted reorganization.
>
> *House Report*, at 183, U.S.Code Cong. & Admin. News 1978 at 6144. Given this sympathetic attitude it was assumed that the new Code would have at least retained discretion in the courts

to bar setoff when it tends to frustrate the rehabilitation of the debtor. However, Section 553 is made applicable to Chapter 11 proceedings without specific regard for the unique problems associated with entities fighting for their financial lives. See 11 U.S.C. § 103(a)(Applicability of Chapters).

Congress clearly intended that the amount that may be setoff should be treated as tantamount to a perfected security interest. Ahart, *Bank Setoff Under The Bankruptcy Reform Act of 1978, supra*, 53 Am. Bankr. L.J. at 210; *House Report*, at 184–85, U.S.Code Cong. & Admin. News 1978 at 6145. Like any secured creditor under the Code, an entity with a right to setoff is assured that the automatic stay will be lifted unless it is adequately protected. See 11 U.S.C. §§ 361, 362; *In re Applied Logic Corp., supra*, 576 F.2d at 958 n.15; Orr & Klee, *Secured Creditors Under the New Bankruptcy Code*, 11 Unif. Com. C. L. J. 312, 335 36 (1979); *House Report*, at 185, U.S. Code Cong. & Admin. News 1978 at 6145.

C. Big Bear's Right to Setoff for Mutual Pre–petition Debts

Within this general statutory framework we can examine Big Bear's entitlement to setoff. Under the terms of Section 553 a creditor may offset mutual debts owing to the debtor against claims of the creditor due from the debtor. These mutual debts must be owing when the petition is filed commencing the bankruptcy proceeding. 11 U.S.C. § 553(a). *See Avant v. United States*, 165 F.Supp. 802, 805 (E.Va.1958). Big Bear would argue that as of April 24, 1980, it should be allowed to setoff the entire $11,974.64 it then owed Princess. To be a proper setoff we must review the mutual debts owed by the debtor. The $5,500 balance due on the inventory purchases appear to satisfy the requirements of Section 553. The entire amount of the principal balance of the promissory note is likewise available for setoff even though only one monthly installment was due on the day the petition was filed. This is because bankruptcy proceedings operate to accelerate the principal amounts of all claims against the debtor, with the result that setoff may be asserted even though one of the debts involved is absolutely owing, but not then presently due. 4 Collier on Bankruptcy, *supra*, § 553.10[2] at 553–49; *House Report. supra*, at 353, U.S. Code Cong. & Admin. News 1978 at 6308. Thus, the entire amount due Big Bear is covered by mutual debts owed by Princess.

It should be noted that the $1,854.05 due for NSF checks issues by Princess and cashed by Big Bear appears to run afoul of Section 553(a)(2)(B). 11 U.S.C. § 553(a)(2)(B). This new provision bars setoff for claims against the debtor that were transferred to the creditor by a third party within 90 days of filing and while the debtor was insolvent. 4 Collier on Bankruptcy, *supra*, § 553.08[2] at 553–44. This is certainly an ironic result given the considerable benefit conferred by Big Bear when it cashed the payroll checks. If these checks had been returned to Princess' employees, most of them being hourly wage earners, then great harm may have been done to staff morale with its negative effect on the chances for eventual reorganization.

It would appear, then, that Big Bear has a total of $11,974.64 which is eligible for setoff. But whether the automatic stay should be lifted to allow the setoff to take place requires consideration of Section 362(d). 11 U.S.C. § 362(d). Under this provision relief must be granted unless Big Bear's interest in the property is adequately protected. What constitutes adequate protection is stated in Section 361, which details several means available to fulfill this requirement. However, it is not an exclusive nor exhaustive listing. 11 U.S.C. § 361. The burden is on the debtor in possession to propose the protection method. *House Report*, at 338, U.S.Code Cong. & Admin. News at 6294. But Princess offers no alternative method to be used to adequately protect Big Bear, so the Court must conclude that relief must be granted given the lack of adequate protection. 11 U.S.C. § § 362(d)(1), 363(d). In addition, the stay must be lifted under the alternative standard stated in Section 362(d)(2), as the debtor has no equity in the property and it is not necessary to an effective reorganization since there is no evidence that there is a reasonable possibility of a successful reorganization. 11 U.S.C. § 362(d)(2). *See In Matter of Terra Mar Associates*, 3 B. R. 462, 466, 6 B. C. D. 150, 152 (Conn.1980).

D. Big Bear's Right To Setoff of Post–petition Obligations

The parties have also presented the question of whether Big Bear has any right to continue to exercise the privilege of setoff on obligations arising subsequent to the commencement of the reorganization proceedings.

It appears that the question, in part, deals with Big Bear's right to setoff the amounts due the debtor from post–petition collections made by Big Bear, against the obligations, such as the promissory note, due Big Bear when the case was commenced. Here Big Bear clearly has no right of setoff as to this pre–petition obligation and the corresponding post–petition obligation as no mutuality would exist. *See e.g., Mutual Trust Life Insurance Company v. Wemyss*, 309 F.Supp. 1221, 1232 n. 18 (Me. 1970).

The remaining question presented concerns itself with the right of setoff of exclusively post–petition debts which are mutual. The proper rule to be applied as to these obligations is not clearly stated in the Code. The Court, however, need not resolve this issue, for although mutual obligations do exist between the parties it has not been shown that a right of setoff has in fact matured with respect to these debts. That is to say, there has been no justification asserted which would occasion the right to setoff those obligations. *See Highsmith v. Lair,* 44 Cal.2d 298, 302, 281 P.2d 865 (1955); *Advance Industrial Finance Co. v. Western Equities, Inc.*, 173 Cal.App.2d 420, 426–27, 343 P.2d 408 (1959). *See also* 4 Collier on Bankruptcy, *supra*, at § 553.06.

Undoubtedly the rights Big Bear has in receiving rent for its bakery space and on the promissory note created at the sale of the bakery equipment will be fully determined when final judgement is issued on the remaining issues reserved for trial on the complaint. Of course, the $7,500 payment made on May 2, 1980, will be credited in favor of Big Bear against any debts to Princess it incurred after the petition was filed. And finally, Big Bear can deduct the rental assessment on the retail sales at the two retail outlets as this recoupment procedure was fully contemplated in the lease agreements and the rental is obviously a necessary cost of the administration of this case.

IV.

Conclusions

1. On April 24, 1980, the date the petition was filed in this case there existed $11,974.64 in mutual obligations between Princess and Big Bear.

2. These mutual obligations formed the basis for the proper exercise of a setoff by Big Bear.

3. Since the Princess has not proposed a means to assure that Big Bear will be adequately protected as required under Section 362(d), then the automatic stay issued under Section 362(a)(7) must be lifted.

4. Big Bear may not offset mutual postpetition obligations, except for the 6.5% rental assessments on Princess' retail sales handled by Big Bear.

5. Big Bear shall prepare a proposed order within 10 days of the filing of this decision.

§ 15.05 Property of the Estate

Section 541 describes that which becomes property of the estate. Title is not transferred from the debtor to the trustee as it formerly was under § 70a of the Act. Rather, an estate is created. Essentially any and every interest of the debtor at the date of the petition becomes property of the estate. (See discussion of "Exemptions.") Accordingly, §§ 549, 542, and 543 treat the situations of postpetition transfers and turnover of a debtor's property in the possession of a third person.

As a general rule, only interests held on the petition date move into the estate. Section 541, however, contains some exceptions with respect to what property acquired after the petition also becomes part of the estate.

NOTES AND QUESTIONS

1. What is the position of the Code with respect to spendthrift trusts? (What is a spendthrift trust?)

2. What is the position of the Code with respect to property of a debtor held as a tenant by the entirety? What is a tenancy by the entirety? Tenancy in common? Joint tenancy? May property held in any such form be sold by the trustee? Can any statutory authority be located for a response?

UNITED STATES v . WHITING POOLS, INC.

United States Supreme Court
462 U.S. 198, 103 S. Ct. 2309 (1983)

Justice BLACKMUN

Promptly after the Internal Revenue Service (IRS or Service) seized respondent's property to satisfy a tax lien, respondent filed a petition for reorganization under the Bankruptcy Reform Act of 1978, hereinafter referred to as the "Bankruptcy Code." The issue before us is whether § 542(a) of that Code authorized the Bankruptcy Court to subject the IRS to a turnover order with respect to the seized property.

I.

A.

Respondent Whiting Pools, Inc., a corporation, sells, installs, and services swimming pools and related equipment and supplies. As of January 1981, Whiting owed approximately $92,000 in Federal Insurance Contribution Act taxes and federal taxes withheld from its employees, but had failed to respond to assessments and demands for payment by the IRS. As a consequence, a tax lien in that amount attached to all of Whiting's property.

On January 14, 1981, the Service seized Whitings's tangible personal property—equipment, vehicles, inventory, and office supplies—pursuant to the levy and distraint provision of the Internal Revenue Code of 1954.

According to uncontroverted findings, the estimated liquidation value of the property seized was, at most, $35,000, but its estimated going–concern value in Whiting's hands was $162,876. The very next day, January 15, Whiting filed a petition for reorganization, under the Bankruptcy Code's Chapter 11, 11 U.S.C. § § 1101 *et seq.* (1976 ed., Supp. V), in the United States Bankruptcy Court for the Western District of New York. Whiting was continued as debtor–in–possession.

The United States, intending to proceed with a tax sale of the property, moved in the Bankruptcy Court for a declaration that the automatic stay provision of the Bankruptcy Code, § 362(a), is inapplicable to the IRS or, in the alternative, for relief from the stay. Whiting counterclaimed for an order requiring the Service to turn the seized property over to the bankruptcy estate pursuant to § 542(a) of the Bankruptcy Code. Whiting intended to use the property in its reorganized business.

B.

The Bankruptcy Court determined that the IRS was bound by the automatic stay provision. *In re Whiting Pools, Inc.*, 10 B. R. 755 (1981). Because it found that the seized property was essential to Whiting's reorganization effort, it refused to lift the stay. Acting under § 543(b)(1) of the Bankruptcy Code, rather than under § 542(a), the court directed the IRS to turn the property over to Whiting on the condition that Whiting provide the Service with specified protection for its interests. 10 B. R., at 760–761.7

The United States District Court reversed, holding that a turnover order against the Service was not authorized by either § 542(a) or § 543(b)(1). App. to Pet. for Cert. 46a. The United States Court of Appeals for the Second Circuit, in turn, reversed the District Court. 674 F.2d 144 (1982). It held that a turnover order could issue against the Service under § 542(a), and it remanded the case for reconsideration of the adequacy of the Bankruptcy Court's protection conditions. The Court of Appeals acknowledged that its ruling was contrary to that reached by the United States Court of Appeals for the Fourth Circuit in *Cross Electric Co. v. United States*, 664 F.2d 1218 (1981), and noted confusion on the issue among bankruptcy and district courts. 674 F.2d, at 145 and n. 1. We granted certiorari to resolve this conflict in an important area of the law under the new Bankruptcy Code. 459 U.S.—(1982).

II.

By virtue of its tax lien, the Service holds a secured interest in Whiting's property. We first examine whether § 542(a) of the Bankruptcy Code generally authorizes the turnover of a debtor's property seized by a secured creditor prior to the commencement of reorganization proceedings. Section 542(a) requires an entity in possession of "property that the trustee may use, sell, or lease under § 363" to deliver that property to the trustee. Subsections (b) and (c) of § 363 authorize the trustee to use, sell, or lease any "property of the estate," subject to certain conditions for the protection of creditors with an interest in the property. Section 541(a)(1) defines the "estate" as "comprised of all the following property, wherever located: (1) all legal or equitable interests of the debtor in property as of the commencement of the case." Although these statutes could be read to limit the estate to those "interests of the debtor in property" at the time of the filing of the petition, we view them as a definition of what is included in the estate, rather than as a limitation.

A.

In proceedings under the reorganization provisions of the Bankruptcy Code, a troubled enterprise may be restructured to enable it to operate successfully in the future. Until the business can be reorganized pursuant to a plan under 11 U.S.C. §§ 1121–1129 (1976 ed., Supp. V), the trustee or debtor–in–possession is authorized to manage the property of the estate and to continue the operation of the business. *See* § 1108. By permitting reorganization, Congress anticipated that the business would continue to provide jobs, to satisfy creditors' claims, and to produce a return for its owners. H. R. Rep. No. 95–595, p. 220 (1977). Congress presumed that the assets of the debtor would be more valuable if used in a rehabilitated business than if "sold for scrap." *Ibid.* The reorganization effort would have small chance of success, however, if property essential to running the business were excluded from the estate. *See* 6 J. Moore & L. King, Collier on Bankruptcy ¶ 3.05, p. 431 (14th ed. 1978). Thus, to facilitate the rehabilitation of the debtor's business, all the debtor's property must be included in the reorganization estate.

This authorization extends even to property of the estate in which a creditor has a secured interest. § 363(b) and (c); see H. R. Rep. No. 95–595, p. 182 (1977). Although Congress might have safeguarded the interests of secured creditors outright by excluding from the estate any property subject to a secured interest, it chose instead to include such property in the estate and to provide secured creditors with "adequate protection for their interests." § 363(e), quoted in n. 7, *supra*. At the secured creditor's insistence, the bankruptcy court must place such limits or conditions on the trustee's power to sell, use, or lease property as are necessary to protect the creditor. The creditor with a secured interest in property included in the estate must look to this provision for protection, rather than to the nonbankruptcy remedy of possession.

Both the congressional goal of encouraging reorganizations and Congress' choice of methods to protect secured creditors suggest the Congress intended a broad range of property to be included in the estate.

B.

The statutory language reflects this view of the scope of the estate. As noted above, § 541(a) provides that the "estate is comprised of all the following property, wherever located: all legal or equitable interests of the debtor in property as of the commencement of the case." 11 U.S.C. § 541(a)(1).

The House and Senate Reports on the Bankruptcy Code indicate that § 541(a)(1)'s scope is broad.

Most important, in the context of this case, § 541(a)(1) is intended to include in the estate any property made available to the estate by other provisions of the Bankruptcy Code. *See* H. R. Rep. No. 95–595, p. 367 (1977). Several of these provisions bring into the estate property in which the debtor did not have a possessory interest at the time the bankruptcy proceedings commenced.

We do not now decide the outer boundaries of the bankruptcy estate. We note only that Congress plainly excluded property of others held by the debtor in trust at the time of the filing of the petition. *See* § 541(b); H. R. Rep. No. 95–595, p. 368 (1977); S. Rep. No. 95–989, p. 82 (1978). Although it may well be that funds that the IRS can demonstrate were withheld for its benefit pursuant to 26 U.S.C. § 7501 (employee withholding taxes), are excludable from the estate, see 124 Cong. Rec. 32417 (1978) (remarks of Rep. Edwards)(Service may exclude funds it can trace), the IRS did not attempt to trace the withheld taxes in this case. *See* Tr. of Oral Arg. 18, 28–29.

Section 542(a) is such a provision. It requires an entity (other than a custodian) holding any property of the debtor that the trustee can use under § 363 to turn that property over to the trustee.

Given the broad scope of the reorganization estate, property of the debtor repossessed by a secured creditor falls within this rule, and therefore may be drawn into the estate. While there are explicit limitations on the reach of § 542(a) none requires that the debtor hold a possessory interest in the property at the commencement of the reorganization proceedings.

As does all bankruptcy law, § 542(a) modifies the procedural rights available to creditors to protect and satisfy their liens.

See Wright v. Union Central Life Ins. Co., 311 U.S. 273, 278–279 (1940). *See generally* Nowak, *Turnover Following Prepetition Levy of Distraint Under Bankruptcy Code § 542*, 55 Am. Bankr. L. J. 313, 332–333 (1981). In effect, § 542(a) grants to the estate a possessory interest in certain property of the debtor that was not held by the debtor at the commencement of reorganization proceedings.

The Bankruptcy Code provides secured creditors various rights, including the right to adequate protection, and these rights replace the protection afforded by possession.

C.

This interpretation of § 542(a) is supported by the section's legislative history. Although the legislative reports are silent on the precise issue before us, the House and Senate hearings from which § 542(a) emerged provide guidance. Several witnesses at those hearings noted, without contradiction, the need for a provision authorizing the turnover of property of the debtor in the possession of secured creditors.

Section 542(a) first appeared in the proposed legislation shortly after these hearings. *See* H. R. 6, § 542(a), 95th Cong., 1st Sess., introduced January 4, 1977. *See generally* Klee, *Legislative History of the New Bankruptcy Code*, 54 Am. Bankr. L. J. 275, 279–281 (1980). The section remained unchanged through subsequent versions of the legislation.

Moreover, this interpretation of § 542 in the reorganization context is consistent with judicial precedent predating the Bankruptcy Code. Under Chapter X, the reorganization chapter of the Bankruptcy Act of 1878, as amended, § § 101–276, 52 Stat. 883 (1938) (formerly codified as 11 U.S.C. § § 501–676 (1976 ed.)), the bankruptcy court could order the turnover of collateral in the hands of a secured creditor. *Reconstruction Finance Corp. v. Kaplan*, 185 F.2d 791, 796 (CA1 1950); *see In re Third Ave. Transit Corp.*, 198 F.2d 703, 706 (CA2 1952); 6A J. Moore & L. King, Collier on Bankruptcy ¶ 14.03, p. 741–742 (14th ed. 1977); Murphy, *Use of Collateral in Business Rehabilitations: A Suggested Redrafting of Section 7–203 of the Bankruptcy Reform Act*, 63 Calif. L. Rev. 1483, 1492–1495 (1975). Nothing in the legislative history evinces a congressional intent to depart from that practice. Any other interpretation of § 542(a) would deprive the bankruptcy estate of the assets and property essential to its rehabilitation effort and thereby would frustrate the congressional purpose behind the reorganization provisions.

We conclude that the reorganization estate includes property of the debtor that has been seized by a creditor prior to the filing of a petition for reorganization.

III.

A.

We see no reason why a different result should obtain when the IRS is the creditor. The Service is bound by § 542(a) to the same extent as any other secured creditor. The Bankruptcy Code expressly states that the term "entity," used in § 542(a), includes a governmental unit § 101(14). *See* Tr. of Oral Arg. 16. Moreover, Congress carefully considered the effect of the new Bankruptcy Code on tax collection, *see generally* S. Rep. No. 95–1106 (1978)(report of Senate Finance Committee), and decided to provide protection to tax collectors, such as the IRS, through grants of enhanced priorities for unsecured tax claims, 507(a)(6), and by the nondischarge of tax liabilities, § 523(a)(1). S. Rep. No. 95–989, pp. 14–15 (1978). Tax collectors also enjoy the generally applicable right under § 363(e) to adequate protection for property subject to their liens. Nothing in the Bankruptcy Code or its legislative history indicates that Congress intended a special exception for the tax collector in the form of an exclusion from the estate of property seized to satisfy a tax lien.

B.

Of course, if a tax levy or seizure transfers to the IRS ownership of the property seized, § 542(a) may not apply. The enforcement provisions of the Internal Revenue Code of 1954, 26 U.S.C. §§ 6321–6326 (1976 ed. and Supp. V), do grant to the Service powers to enforce its tax liens that are greater than those possessed by private secured creditors under state law. *See United State v. Rodgers,*—U.S.—,— (1983) (slip op. 4); id., at—,—, n. 7 (dissenting opinion) (slip op. 1, 6, n. 7); *United States v. Bess,* 357 U.S. 51, 56–57 (1958). But those provisions do not transfer ownership of the property to the IRS.

The Service's interest in seized property is its lien on that property. The Internal Revenue Code's levy and seizure provisions, 26 U.S.C. §§ 6331 and 6332, are special procedural devices available to the IRS to protect and satisfy its liens, *United States v. Sullivan,* 333 F.2d 100, 116 (CA3 1964), and are analogous to the remedies available to private secured creditors. *See* Uniform Commercial Code § 9–503, 3A U. L. A. 211–212 (1981); n. 14, *supra.* They are provisional remedies that do not determine the Service's rights to the seized property, but merely bring the property into the Service's legal custody. *See* 4 Bittker, Federal Taxation of Income, Estates and Gifts ¶ 111.5.5, p. 111–108 (1981). *See generally* Plumb, *Federal Tax Collection and Lien Problems,* pt. 1, 13 Tax L. Rev. 247, 272 (1958). At no point does the Service's interest in the property exceed the value of the lien. *United States v. Rodgers,* — U.S., at —, — (slip op. 12); id., at — (dissenting opinion)(slip op. 12); *see United States v. Sullivan,* 333 F.2d, at 116 ("the Commissioner acts pursuant to the collection process in the capacity of lienor as distinguished from owner"). The IRS is obligated to return to the debtor any surplus from a sale. 26 U.S.C. § 6342(b). Ownership of the property is transferred only when the property is sold to a bona fide purchaser at a tax sale. *See Bennett v. Hunter*, 9 Wall. 326, 336 (1870); 26 U.S.C. § 6339(a)(2); Plumb, 13 Tax. L. Rev., at 274–275. In fact, the tax sale provision itself refers to the debtor as the owner of the property after the seizure but prior to the sale.

Until such a sale takes place, the property remains the debtor's and thus is subject to the turnover requirement of 542(a).

IV.

When property seized prior to the filing of a petition is drawn into the Chapter 11 reorganization estate, the Service's tax lien is not dissolved; nor is its status as a secured creditor destroyed. The IRS, under § 363(e), remains entitled to adequate protection for its interests, to other rights enjoyed by secured creditors, and to the specific privileges accorded tax collectors. Section 542(a) simply requires the Service to seek protection of its interest according to the congressionally established bankruptcy procedures, rather than by withholding the seized property from the debtor's efforts to reorganize.

The judgment of the Court of Appeals is affirmed.

It is so ordered.

NOTES AND QUESTIONS

1. What broader implications may be derived from the *Whiting Pools* decision? Is its scope limited to recovering property from an IRS levy? Would a creditor in possession of property serving as security for a debt pursuant to voluntary agreement be subject to a turnover order under § 542? What about property upon which levy has been made at the instance of a person who obtained a judgment against the debtor?

2. What is the distinction between § 542 and § 543? In Whiting Pools, was the IRS considered to be a custodian? What are some examples of a custodian? Why in § 543(c)(3) is 120 days selected rather than some other time period?

3. On September 17, Drawer remits check as payment to Supplier for delivered goods. On September 19, immediately on receipt, Supplier endorses and deposits check in its bank. On September 20, Drawer files a petition for relief under chapter 7 of the Bankruptcy Code. On September 21, Drawer's bank receives check and determines to pay it. Check is not returned by drawee bank within legal time for returning checks unpaid. Drawer's checking account was debited with amount of check on September 21. May trustee require bank to

recredit its account? The Supreme Court in Bank of Marin v. England, 385 U.S. 99 (1966), decided under the 1898 Act, held that the bank without notice of the bankruptcy filing was not liable to the trustee (although a literal reading of the Act could have led to the opposite conclusion). Is the rule of this case abrogated by § 549(a)? § 542?

PATTERSON v. SHUMATE

Supreme Court of the United States
504 U.S. —, 112 S.Ct. 2042, 119 L. Ed. 2d 519, 26 C.B.C.2d 1119 (1992)

Justice BLACKMUN, delivered the opinion of the Court

The Bankruptcy Code excludes from the bankruptcy estate property of the debtor that is subject to a restriction on transfer enforceable under "applicable nonbankruptcy law." 11 U.S.C. § 541(c)(2). We must decide in this case whether an anti–alienation provision contained in an ERISA–qualified pension plan constitutes a restriction on transfer enforceable under "applicable nonbankruptcy law," and whether, accordingly, a debtor may exclude his interest in such a plan from the property of the bankruptcy estate.

I.

Respondent Joseph B. Shumate, Jr., was employed for over 30 years by Coleman Furniture Corporation, where he ultimately attained the position of president and chairman of the board of directors. Shumate and approximately 400 other employees were participants in the Coleman Furniture Corporation Pension Plan (Plan). The Plan satisfied all applicable requirements of the Employee Retirement Income Security Act of 1974 (ERISA) and qualified for favorable tax treatment under the Internal Revenue Code. In particular, Article 16.1 of the Plan contained the anti–alienation provision required for qualification under § 206(d)(1) of ERISA, 29 U.S.C. § 1056(d)(1) ("Each pension plan shall provide that benefits provided under the plan may not be assigned or alienated"). App. 342. Shumate's interest in the plan was valued at $250,000. App. 93–94.

In 1982, Coleman Furniture filed a petition for bankruptcy under Chapter 11 of the Bankruptcy Code. The case was converted to a Chapter 7 proceeding and a trustee, Roy V. Creasy, was appointed. Shumate himself encountered financial difficulties and filed a petition for bankruptcy in 1984. His case, too, was converted to a Chapter 7 proceeding, and petitioner John R. Patterson was appointed trustee.

Creasy terminated and liquidated the Plan, providing full distributions to all participants except Shumate. Patterson then filed an adversary proceeding against Creasy in the Bankruptcy Court for the Western District of Virginia to recover Shumate's interest in the Plan for the benefit of Shumate's bankruptcy estate.

Shumate in turn asked the United States District Court for the Western District of Virginia, which already had jurisdiction over a related proceeding, to compel Creasy to pay Shumate's interest in the Plan directly to him. The bankruptcy proceeding subsequently was consolidated with the district court action. App. to Pet. for Cert. 53a–54a.

The District Court rejected Shumate's contention that his interests in the Plan should be excluded from his bankruptcy estate. The court held that § 541(c)(2)'s reference to "nonbankruptcy law" embraced only state law, not federal law such as ERISA. *Creasy v. Coleman Furniture Corp.*, 83 B. R. 404, 406 (1988). Applying Virginia law, the court held that Shumate's interest in the Plan did not qualify for protection as a spendthrift trust. *Id.*, at 406–409. The District Court also rejected Shumate's alternative argument that even if his interest in the Plan could not be excluded from the bankruptcy estate under § 541(c)(2), he was entitled to an exemption under 11 U.S.C. § 522(b)(2)(A), which allows a debtor to exempt from property of the estate "any property that is exempt under Federal law." *Id.*, at 409–410. The District Court ordered Creasy to pay Shumate's interest in the Plan over to his bankruptcy estate. App. to Pet. For Cert. 54a–55a.

The Court of Appeals for the Fourth Circuit reversed. 943 F.2d 362 (1991). The court relied on its earlier decision in *Anderson v. Raine (In re Moore)*, 907 F.2d 1476 [23 C.B.C.2d 390] (1990), in which another Fourth Circuit panel was described as holding, subsequent to the District Court's decision in the instant case, that "ERISA–qualified plans, which by definition have a non–alienation provision, constitute 'applicable nonbankruptcy law' and contain enforceable restrictions on the transfer of pension interests." 943 F.2d at 365. Thus, the Court of Appeals held that Shumate's interest in the Plan should be excluded from the bankruptcy estate under § 541(c)(2). *Ibid.* The court then declined to consider Shumate's alternative argument that his interest in the Plan qualified for exemption under § 522(b). *Id.*, at 365–366.

We granted certiorari,—U.S.—(1992), to resolve the conflict among the Courts of Appeals as to whether an anti–alienation provision in an ERISA–qualified pension plan constitutes a restriction on transfer enforceable under "applicable nonbankruptcy law" for purposes of the § 541(c)(2) exclusion of property from the debtor's bankruptcy estate.

II.

A.

In our view, the plain language of the Bankruptcy Code and ERISA is our determinant. *See Toibb v. Radloff*, 501 U.S. [24 C.B.C.2d 1179] (1991) (slip op. 3). Section 541(c)(2) provides the following exclusion from the otherwise broad definition of "property of the estate" contained in § 541(a)(1) of the Code:

> "A restriction on the transfer of a beneficial interest of the debtor
> in a trust that is enforceable under applicable nonbankruptcy law
> is enforceable in a case under this title."

The natural reading of the provision entitles a debtor to exclude from property of the estate any interest in a plan or trust that contains a transfer restriction enforceable under any relevant nonbankruptcy law. Nothing in § 541 suggests that the phrase "applicable nonbankruptcy law" refers, as petitioner contends, exclusively to state law. The text contains no limitation on "applicable nonbankruptcy law" relating to the source of the law.

Reading the term "applicable nonbankruptcy law" in § 541(c)(2) to include federal as well as state law comports with other references in the Bankruptcy Code to sources of law. The Code reveals, significantly, that Congress, when it desired to do so, knew how to restrict the scope of applicable law to "state law" and did so with some frequency. *See, e.g.*, 11 U.S.C. § 109(c)(2) (entity may be a debtor under chapter 9 if authorized "by State law"); 11 U.S.C. § 522(b)(1) (election of exemptions controlled by "the State law that is applicable to the debtor"); 11 U.S.C. § 523(a)(5) (a debt for alimony, maintenance, or support determined "in accordance with State or territorial law" is not dischargeable); 11 U.S.C. § 903(1) ("a State law prescribing a method of composition of indebtedness" of municipalities is not binding on nonconsenting creditors); *see also* 11 U.S.C. §§ 362(b)(12) and § 1145(a). Congress' decision to use the broader phrase "applicable nonbankruptcy law" in § 541(c)(2) strongly suggests that it did not intend to restrict the provision in the manner that petitioner contends.

The text of § 541(c)(2) does not support petitioner's contention that "applicable nonbankruptcy law" is limited to state law. Plainly read, the provision encompasses any relevant nonbankruptcy law, including federal law such as ERISA. We must enforce the statute according to its terms. *See United States v. Ron Pair Enterprises, Inc.*, 489 U.S. 235, 241 [20 C.B.C.2d 267] (1989).

B.

Having concluded that "applicable nonbankruptcy law" is not limited to state law, we next determine whether the anti–alienation provision contained in the ERISA–qualified plan at issue here satisfies the literal terms of § 541(c)(2).

Section 206(d)(1) of ERISA, which states that "[e]ach pension plan shall provide that benefits provided under the plan may not be assigned or alienated," 29 U.S.C. § 1056(d)(1), clearly imposes a "restriction on the transfer" of a debtor's "beneficial interest" in the trust. The coordinate section of the Internal Revenue Code, 26 U.S.C. § 401(a)(13), states as a general rule that "[a] trust shall not constitute a qualified trust under this section unless the plan of which such trust is a part provides that benefits provided under the plan may not be assigned or alienated," and thus contains similar restrictions. *See also* 26 CFR 1.401(a)–13(b)(1) (1991).

Coleman Furniture's pension plan complies with these requirements. Article 16.1 of the Plan specifically stated: "No benefit, right or interest" of any participant "shall be subject to alienation, sale, transfer, assignment, pledge, encumbrance or charge, seizure, attachment or other legal, equitable or other process." App. 342.

Moreover, these transfer restrictions are "enforceable," as required by § 541(c)(2). Plan trustees or fiduciaries are required under ERISA to discharge their duties "in accordance with the documents and instruments governing the plan." 29 U.S.C. § 1104(a)(1)(D). A plan participant, beneficiary, or fiduciary, or the Secretary of Labor may file a civil action to "enjoin any act or practice" which violates ERISA or the terms of the plan. 29 U.S.C. § § 1132(a)(3) and (5). Indeed, this Court itself vigorously has enforced ERISA's prohibition on the assignment or alienation of pension benefits, declining to recognize any implied exceptions to the broad statutory bar. *See Guidry v. Sheet Metal Workers Pension Fund*, 493 U.S. 365 (1990).

The anti–alienation provision required for ERISA qualification and contained in the Plan at issue in this case thus constitutes an enforceable transfer restriction for purposes of § 541(c)(2)'s exclusion of property from the bankruptcy estate.

III.

Petitioner raises several challenges to this conclusion. Given the clarity of the statutory text, however, he bears an "exceptionally heavy" burden of persuading us that Congress intended to limit the § 541(c)(2) exclusion to restrictions on transfer that are enforceable only under state spendthrift trust law. *Union Bank v. Wolas*, 502 U.S. — , — [25 C.B.C.2d 1011] (1991) (slip op. 4).

A.

Petitioner first contends that contemporaneous legislative materials demonstrate that § 541(c)(2)'s exclusion of property from the bankruptcy estate should not extend to a debtor's interest in an ERISA–qualified pension plan. Although courts "appropriately may refer to a statute's legislative history to resolve statutory ambiguity," *Toibb v. Radloff*, 501 U.S. at — (slip op. 5), the clarity of the statutory language at issue in this case obviates the need for any such inquiry. *See ibid.; United States v. Ron Pair Enterprises, Inc.*, 489 U.S. at 241; *Davis v. Michigan Dept. Of Treasury*, 489 U.S. 803, 809, n. 3 (1989).

Even were we to consider the legislative materials to which petitioner refers, however, we could discern no "clearly expressed legislative intention" contrary to the result reached above. *See Consumer Product Safety Comm'n v. GTE Sylvania, Inc.*, 447 U.S. 102, 108 (1980). In his brief, petitioner quotes from House and Senate reports accompanying the Bankruptcy Reform Act of 1978 that purportedly reflect "unmistakable" congressional intent to limit § 541(c)(2)'s exclusion to pension plans that qualify under state law as spendthrift trusts. Brief for Petitioner 38. Those reports contain only the briefest of discussions addressing § 541(c)(2). The House Report states: "Paragraph (2) of subsection (c) . . . preserves restrictions on transfer of a spendthrift trust to the extent that the restriction is enforceable under applicable nonbankruptcy law." H.R. Rep. No. 95–595, p. 369 (1977); *see also* S. Rep. No. 95–989, p. 83 (1978) (§ 541(c)(2) "preserves restrictions on a transfer of a spendthrift trust"). A general introductory section to the House Report contains the additional statement that the new law "continues over the exclusion from property of the estate of the debtor's interest in a spendthrift trust to the extent the trust is protected from creditors under applicable State law." H. R. Rep. No. 95–595, p 176.

These meager excerpts reflect at best congressional intent to include state spendthrift trust law within the meaning of "applicable nonbankruptcy law." By no means do they provide a sufficient basis for concluding, in derogation of the statute's clear language, that Congress intended to exclude other state and federal law from the provision's scope.

B.

Petitioner next contends that our construction of § 541(c)(2), pursuant to which a debtor may exclude his interest in an ERISA–qualified pension plan from the bankruptcy estate, renders § 522(d)(10)(E) of the Bankruptcy Code superfluous. Brief for Petitioner 24–33. Under § 522(d)(10)(E), a debtor who elects the federal exemptions set forth in § 522(d) may exempt from the bankruptcy estate his right to receive "a payment under a stock bonus, pension, profitsharing, annuity, or similar plan or contract . . . , to the extent reasonably necessary for the support of the debtor and any dependent of the debtor." If a debtor's interest in a pension plan could be excluded in full from the bankruptcy estate, the argument goes, then there would have been no reason for Congress to create a limited exemption for such interests elsewhere in the statute.

Petitioner's surplusage argument fails, however, for the reason that § 522(d)(10)(E) exempts from the bankruptcy estate a much broader category of interests than § 541(c)(2) excludes. For example, pension plans established by governmental entities and churches need not comply with Subchapter I of ERISA, including the anti–alienation requirement of § 206(d)(1). *See* 29 U.S.C. §§ 1003(b)(1) and (2); 26 CFR 1.401(a)–13(a) (1991). So, too, pension plans that qualify for preferential tax treatment under 26 U.S.C. § 408 (individual retirement accounts) are specifically excepted from ERISA's anti–alienation requirement. *See* 29 U.S.C. § 1051(6). Although a debtor's interest in these plans could not be excluded under § 541(c)(2) because the plans lack transfer restrictions enforceable under "applicable nonbankruptcy law," that interest nevertheless could be exempted under § 522(d)(10(E). Once petitioner concedes that § 522(d)(10)(E)'s exemption applies to more than ERISA–qualified plans containing anti–alienation provisions, *see* Tr. of Oral Arg. 10–11; Brief for Petitioner 31, his argument that our reading of § 541(c)(2) renders the exemption provision superfluous must collapse.

C.

Finally, petitioner contends that our holding frustrates the Bankruptcy Code's policy of ensuring a broad inclusion of assets in the bankruptcy estate. *See* Brief for Petitioner 37; 11 U.S.C. § 541(a)(1) (estate comprised of "all legal and equitable interests of the debtor in property as of the commencement of the case"). As an initial matter, we think that petitioner mistakes an admittedly broad definition of includable property for a "policy" underlying the Code as a whole. In any event, to the extent that policy considerations are even relevant where the language of the statute is so clear, we believe that our construction of § 541(c)(2) is preferable to the one petitioner urges upon us.

First, our decision today ensures that the treatment of pension benefits will not vary based on the beneficiary's bankruptcy status. *See Butner v. United States*, 440 U.S. 48, 55 (1978) (observing that "[u]niform treatment of property interests" prevents "a party from 'receiving a windfall merely by reason of the happenstance of bankruptcy,'" quoting *Lewis v. Manufacturers National Bank*, 364 U.S. 603, 609 (1961)). We previously have declined to recognize any exceptions to ERISA's anti–alienation provision outside the bankruptcy context. *See Guidry v. Sheet Metal Workers Pension Fund*, 493 U.S. 365 (1990) (labor union may not impose constructive trust on pension benefits of union official who breached fiduciary duties and embezzled funds). Declining to recognize any exceptions to that provision within the bankruptcy context minimizes the possibility that creditors will engage in strategic manipulation of the bankruptcy laws in order to gain access to otherwise inaccessible funds. *See* Seiden, *Chapter 7 Cases: Do ERISA and the Bankruptcy Code Conflict as to Whether a Debtor's Interest in or Rights Under a Qualified Plan Can be Used to Pay Claims?*, 61 Am. Bankr. L.J. 301, 317 (1987) (noting inconsistency if "a creditor could not reach a debtor–participant's plan right or interest in a garnishment or other collection action outside of a bankruptcy case but indirectly could reach the plan right or interest by filing a petition . . . to place the debtor in bankruptcy involuntarily").

Our holding also gives full and appropriate effect to ERISA's goal of protecting pension benefits. *See* 29 U.S.C. § § 1001(b) and (c). This Court has described that goal as one of ensuring that "if a worker has been promised a defined pension benefit upon retirement–and if he has fulfilled whatever conditions are required to obtain a vested benefit–he actually will receive it." *Nachman Corp. v. Pension Benefit Guaranty Corp.*, 446 U.S. 359, 375 (1980). In furtherance of these principles, we recently declined in *Guidry*, notwithstanding strong equitable considerations to the contrary, to recognize an implied exception to ERISA's anti–alienation provision that would have allowed a labor union to impose a constructive trust on the pension benefits of a corrupt union official. We explained:

> "Section 206(d) reflects a considered congressional policy choice, a decision to safeguard a stream of income for pensioners (and their dependents, who may be, and perhaps usually are, blameless), even if that decision prevents others from securing relief for the wrongs done them. If exceptions to this policy are to be made, it is for Congress to undertake that task." 493 U.S., at 376.

These considerations apply with equal, if not greater, force in the present context.

Finally, our holding furthers another important policy underlying ERISA: uniform national treatment of pension benefits. *See Fort Halifax Packing Co. v. Coyne*, 482 U.S. 1, 9 (1987). Construing "applicable nonbankruptcy law" to include federal law ensures that the security of a debtor's pension benefits will be governed by ERISA, not left to the vagaries of state spendthrift trust law.

IV.

In light of our conclusion that a debtor's interest in an ERISA–qualified pension plan may be excluded from the property of the bankruptcy estate pursuant to § 541(c)(2), we need not reach respondent's alternative argument that his interest in the Plan qualifies for exemption under § 522(b)(2)(A).

The judgment of the Court of Appeals is affirmed.

It is so ordered.

Justice SCALIA, concurring:

The Court's opinion today, which I join, prompts several observations.

When the phrase "applicable nonbankruptcy law" is considered in isolation, the phenomenon that three Courts of Appeals could have thought it a synonym for "state law" is mystifying. When the phrase is considered together with the rest of the Bankruptcy Code (in which Congress chose to refer to state law as, logically enough, "state law"), the phenomenon calls into question whether our legal culture has so far departed from attention to text, or is so lacking in agreed–upon methodology for creating and interpreting text, that it any longer makes sense to talk of "a government of laws, not of men."

Speaking of agreed–upon methodology: It is good that the Court's analysis today proceeds on the assumption that use of the phrases "state law" and "applicable nonbankruptcy law" in other provisions of the Bankruptcy Code is highly relevant to whether "applicable nonbankruptcy law" means "state law" in § 541(c)(2), since consistency of usage within the same statute is to be presumed. *Ante,* at 4–5, and n. 2. This application of a normal and obvious principle of statutory construction would not merit comment, except that we explicitly rejected it, in favor of a one–subsection–at–a–time approach, when interpreting another provision of this very statute earlier this Term. *See Dewsnup v. Timm,* — U.S. — , — , 112 S. Ct. 773, [25 C.B.C.2d 1297] (slip op. at 6–7); *Id.,* at — (slip op. at 1–4) (Scalia, J.). "[W]e express no opinion," our decision said, "as to whether the words [at issue] have different meaning in other provisions of the Bankruptcy Code." *Id.,* at 7, n. 3. I trust that in our search for a neutral and rational interpretive methodology we have now come to rest, so that the symbol of our profession may remain the scales, not the see–saw.

NOTES AND QUESTIONS

1. Would IRA accounts come within the holding of *Patterson?*

2. Can any principle of statutory interpretation be gleaned from this case? *See Barnhill* and *Wolas supra.* Any other cases?

CHAPTER 16

CREDITORS' BENEFITS

§ 16.01 Meeting of Creditors

Shortly after a case is commenced, the Code mandates the convening of a creditors' meeting by the U.S. trustee (§ 341(a)), but it does not specify any precise time, or provide for a complete agenda. Much of the detail with respect to the meeting of creditors is left to the Federal Rules of Bankruptcy Procedure.

Bankruptcy Rule 2003 requires the meeting of creditors to be held between 20 and 40 days of the order for relief in chapter 7 and 11 cases. The times are different in chapter 12 and 13 cases. Subdivision (b)(1) of the Rule provides for the United States trustee to preside at the meeting but Rule 9001(11) defines United States trustee to include the designee of the United States trustee. Accordingly, except in chapter 11 cases, the interim trustee or trustee will preside at the meeting. In the judicial districts in Alabama and North Carolina, the bankruptcy administrator or designee will preside at the meeting of creditors. Bankruptcy Reform Act of 1994, Pub. L. No. 103–394, § 105. These districts are not part of the United States Trustee System.

Section 341(c) is new to the bankruptcy code and represents a marked change from former practice. It does not permit the bankruptcy judge to preside at or attend the meeting of creditors. What is the purpose of such a strange statutory provision? May the judge discuss the substance of the meeting with creditors outside the meeting room? *See In re Parr Meadows Racing Association, Inc., infra. See also* Rule 5001 (*ex parte* contacts with bankruptcy judge concerning matters in case are prohibited).

Some agenda items are included in the Code. For example, § 343 requires the debtor to appear at the meeting and submit to examination by the creditors and the trustee. In this connection, *see also* § 344 with respect to self–incrimination and immunity. Other agenda items that may or may not occur are the election of a trustee under § 702 and the election of a committee under § 705. In 1994, subsection (d) was added to § 341 to include another agenda item. This addition requires, in a chapter 7 case, the trustee to examine the debtor orally "to ensure' that the debtor is aware of the availability of other relief chapters (like chapter 13), the consequences of obtaining a discharge, the effect of receiving a discharge, and the effect of reaffirming a debt as well as the debtor's knowledge of § 524(d). No sanction seems to be imposed if the debtor fails this law school type examination.

NOTES AND QUESTIONS

1. The "debtor" specified in § 341(d) is not limited to the individual. What is the purpose of requiring this type of oral examination of a partnership or corporate debtor? Did Congress mean to require it? Did Congress know what it was doing in the first place? What is the underlying purpose of the subsection? See also § 342(b).

2. Is § 341(d) applicable in the judicial districts in Alabama and North Carolina? Why or why not?

Generally speaking, the meeting of creditors sparks about as much interest as a funeral. It theoretically gives creditors the opportunity to question the debtor with respect to the causes of insolvency and, more importantly in chapter 7 cases, the location of assets which were perhaps not reported on the schedules, if filed. In practice, since most chapter 7 cases are individual no–asset cases, there is generally no attendance of creditors at the meeting. Usually, only the interim trustee is present.

RUSCH FACTOR DIVISION, BVA CREDIT CORP. v. MILLER
(In re Mission Carpet Mills, Inc.)

United States Bankruptcy Appellate Panel, Ninth Circuit
10 B. R. 494, 4 C. B. C. 2d 502, (1981)

GEORGE: Bankruptcy Judge:

The instant appeal comes from a determination of Bankruptcy Judge Barry Russell, of the Central District of California, that an August 13, 1980 meeting of creditors called pursuant to Section 341(a) of the Code be reopened for the purpose of allowing one creditor, Avondale Mills, to file a new proof of claim and/or power of attorney with respect to the election of a trustee in the above–entitled Chapter 7 case. In so doing, Judge Russell noted that the intentions of Avondale at that time were unclear to the Court.

Plaintiff/Appellant has requested that the Panel 1) reverse Judge Russell's decision to reopen the Section 341(a) meeting which allowed Avondale to file a new proof of claim and/or a power of attorney, 2) remove the elected trustee, and 3) deem the alternate nominee to have been elected as trustee.

Upon review, we find that Judge Russell was justified in his decision to allow the reopening of the Debtor's Section 341(a) meeting for the purpose of allowing Avondale to file a final proof of claim and/or power of attorney and to thereby cast its vote for the permanent trustee.

I. Background

At the August 13, 1980 Section 341(a) meeting of creditors for Mission Carpet Mills, Inc., an election of trustee was properly requested and a sufficient number of creditors, with the requisite amount of claims, were present. The following claims were voted:

For Garry Miller (the Interim Trustee)

> Warn Brothers, dba Crescent Truck Lines $ 3,708.07

> Calspun Mills 415,538.72

> Citizens and Southern Bank 320,716.80

> California Carpet Finishing 8,088.00

> Multitex Corp. of California 43,785.00

> The Total Vote for Gary Miller $791,836.59

For Carlyle Michaelman (Alternate Nominee)

> National Services $56,253.87

> Allied Chemical Fibers 190,076.69

> Avondale Mills 325,157.03

> Martin Processing 100,785.66

> Rusch Factors 79,160.24

> The Total Vote for Carlyle Michaelman $751,433.49

An issue was raised prior to the vote relating to Multitex's status as both a secured and unsecured creditor. The United States Trustee conducting the Section 341(a) meeting allowed Multitex to vote the unsecured portion of its claim. Subsequent litigation between Multitex and the Debtor's estate removed this issue from consideration in the instant appeal.

Avondale's representative, prior to the vote, filed a power of attorney, which was voted for the alternate trustee, Carlyle Michaelman. After the vote was taken, the representative of Citizens and Southern Bank informed the United States Trustee that he had spoken with an officer of Avondale and that another power of attorney had been given to an entity known as A. C. I. The United States Trustee then certified the interim trustee, Gary Miller, as permanent trustee. It was later determined that this second power of attorney went to the same representative as the first power of attorney. Because the exclusion of Avondale from the computation would not have affected the results, with Multitex included, no further inquiry was made at that time. However, Avondale's vote becomes critical with the exclusion of Multitex's vote.

At the time of the hearing on the Application for Resolution of Election Dispute before Judge Russell, Avondale's second power of attorney, the existence of which had been raised at the conclusion of the Debtor's Section 341(a) meeting, was shown to have been signed by a different corporate official giving authority to the same representative as the first power of attorney. Based on the arguments of counsel, the court below concluded that there was confusion regarding the claim of Avondale.

To resolve that matter, the court voided all prior powers of attorney executed by Avondale and required Avondale to file a new power of attorney and to inform the United States Trustee, by affidavit, which candidate for trustee was to receive their vote.

II. Issue

The issue presented is, whether given this set of facts, Judge Russell was bound by the initial vote at the Section 341(a) meeting which, with the eventual exclusion of Multitex's vote, would have resulted in the election of Carlyle Michaelman, the alternate trustee, as the permanent trustee.

III. Discussion

At the time of the Section 341(a) meeting there was evidence of confusion relating to Avondale's power of attorney and vote in the election of a permanent trustee. The issue was not pursued as the outcome of the election, at that time, would not have been affected by a change in Avondale's vote.

Avondale is the second largest creditor of the debtor, Mission Carpet Mills, Inc., by virtue of its $325,157.03 claim. A creditor of such magnitude should not be ignored and should be allowed a reasonable opportunity to cast a vote based upon adequate information and knowledge.

Judge Russell, by reopening the Section 341(a) meeting for the limited purpose of allowing Avondale to present an informed choice, provided a reasonable opportunity for all sides to present their positions to Avondale and thereby eliminate any confusion Avondale may have had. Judge Russell, in reviewing the issue presented him, was not precluded from considering a variety of factors which would affect the expedient and orderly administration of the Debtor's affairs.

Pursuant to Section 105(a) of the Code, and in the exercise of the equitable powers granted him, Judge Russell had ample authority to support his actions in the present matter.

It should be noted that the qualifications of the interim trustee, Gary Miller, have not been questioned at any time during these proceedings.

IV. Conclusion

Given the facts as presented before the court, the Panel finds no authority which would preclude Judge Russell from reopening the Debtor's Section 341(a) meeting to allow Avondale the opportunity to file a new power of attorney and/or proof of claim.

Affirmed.

IN RE PARR MEADOWS RACING ASSOCIATION

Bankruptcy Court, Eastern District of New York
5 B. R. 564, 2 C. B. C.2d 788 (1980),
aff'd in part, rev'd in part, 13 B. R. 1010, 5 C. B. C.2d 1039 (E.D.N.Y. 1981)

HALL, Bankruptcy Judge:

I.

Flushing Savings Bank ("Bank") has moved this Court for an Order Disqualifying Judge. For the reasons set forth below, the Bank's motion is denied.

II.

On January 11, 1980, the Bank moved in the District Court for an order recusing the above captioned cases from the bankruptcy judge. The motion was based, in part, on certain ex parte communications between the Court and participants in the proceedings. On February 1, 1980 the District Court denied the Bank's motion for withdrawal of the reference, and requested that the Court should determine whether the allegation concerning the Court's partiality required that the Court recuse itself from this proceeding. Thereafter, this Court sent a letter to counsel for the Bank requesting that the Court be given copies of all papers filed in the District Court, so that the Court could comply with the District Court's order. Counsel responded to the Court's letter by filing a motion to disqualify the Court.

The Bank contends that the Court has "engaged in ex parte conversation with the debtors' counsel, their confederates, and other adverse parties, thus creating a reasonable appearance of bias in favor of the debtors in these cases." The Bank does not allege that the Court received information regarding disputed issues.

> Although the record is clear that ex parte conversations did exist, the counsel for the Bank obviously cannot state what took place during these conversations. These ex parte conversations create the reasonable appearance of bias and impropriety.

Bank's affidavit in support of motion under 28 U.S.C. section 455(a) for Order Disqualifying Judge (hereinafter "Bank's affidavit") p. 6, ¶ 21.

The affidavits which were submitted in opposition to the Bank's motion, both in this Court and in the District Court, clearly state that the ex parte contacts involved either questions on the administrative aspect of bankruptcy cases, (not necessarily involving the Parr cases), or the exchanging of pleasantries. Indeed, counsel for the debtor in his affidavit stated that as a trustee, he has had many ex parte conversations with bankruptcy judges in Westbury concerning the administration of bankruptcy cases. Mr. Cook, counsel for the bank, in his response reveals the absurd nature of the Bank's motion:

> Mr. Speciner's candid admission of ex parte communications with Bankruptcy Judge Hall and the other two Bankruptcy Judges precludes, we submit, reassignment of these cases to any of the two Bankruptcy Judges in Westbury, New York.

Bank's reply affidavit in the District Court dated January [illegible] 1980 in support of a motion under Federal Law of Bankruptcy Procedure 102(b) for Withdrawal of Reference, p. 3, ¶ 4.

If Mr. Cook's position was correct, it would not be much of an overstatement to say that successful motions for recusal could be made in almost every case involving a "bankruptcy practitioner."

III.

The Bank contends that ex parte contacts between a bankruptcy judge and participants in a bankruptcy proceeding, regardless of the nature of those contacts, are grounds for recusal. The Bank's contention is wholly without merit.

Ex parte communications, in and of themselves, are not grounds for refusal under either 28 U.S.C. sections 144, 455(a) and (b)(1), the due process clause of the Fifth Amendment to the U.S. Constitution, or the Code of Judicial Conduct. *In the Matter of Georgia Paneling Supply, Inc.*, 581 F.2d 520, 522 (5th Cir. 1978) vacated 588 F.2d 93 (5th Cir. 1978); 607 F.2d 117, 118 (5th Cir. 1979) vacated and then reinstated 613 F.2d 137 (1979, 1980); *United States v. Haldeman*, 559 F.2d 31, 133 n.301 (D.C. Cir. 1976) cert. denied 431 U.S. 933 (1977); *Howell v. Jones*, 516 F.2d 53, 57 (5th Cir. 1975); *Glynn v. Donnelly*, 485 F.2d 692, 694 (1st Cir. 1973); *Bradley v. Milliken*, 426 F. Supp. 929, 941 (E.D. Mich. 1977); *Lazofsky v. Sommerset Bus Co., Inc.*, 389 F. Supp. 1041, 1044 (E.D.N.Y. 1975); *Martelli v. City of Sanoma*, 359 F. Supp. 397, 400 (N.D. Calif. 1973).

It has long been held that "[t]he alleged bias and prejudice to be disqualifying must stem from an extrajudicial source and result in an opinion on the merits on some basis other than what the judge learned from his participation in the case." *In re International Business Machines, Corp.*, 618 F.2d 923, 927 (2d Cir. 1980), quoting *United States v. Grinnell Corp.*, 384 U.S. 563, 583 (1966).

An ex parte communication which is occasioned by the exercise of "related judicial functions' does not stem from an extrajudicial source. Thus, a judge's ex parte communications with prosecutors arising from the judge's administrative duties did not stem from an extrajudicial source. *United States v. Haldeman*, 559 F.2d 13, 133 n.301 (D.C. Cir. 1976). Nor was a judge's attempt to persuade defense counsel to make stronger efforts with their clients to settle the case an extrajudicial source. *Lazofsky v. Sommerset Bus Co., Inc.*, 389 F.Supp. 1041 (E.D.N.Y. 1975).

Moreover, ex parte communications are not grounds for disqualification when there is a practical necessity for those contacts. *Glynn v. Donnelly*, 485 F.2d 592 (1st Cir. 1973). Certainly under the Bankruptcy Act there is a practical necessity for ex parte communications between the judge and the trustee, who are "co–administrators" of bankruptcy cases. *See In re Pacific Homes*, 611 F.2d 1253, 1257 (9th Cir. 1980).

In addition, ex parte contacts are not grounds for recusal when they do not involve discussions of either disputed issues or trial strategy. *Bradley v. Milliken*, 426 F. Supp. 929, 941 (E.D. Mich. 1977). The Bank has neither alleged nor shown that this court has reached an opinion on the merits on some basis other than this court's participation in this case. Nor has the Bank alleged that the ex parte contacts involved discussions of disputed issues or trial strategy. The Bank's counsel is ignoring the fact that the day to day administration of bankruptcy cases often requires bankruptcy judges to have ex parte contacts with various participants in a bankruptcy case. It is common knowledge that:

> The bankruptcy judge is often called upon to resolve disputes between the estate and adverse third parties. The estate is represented by the trustee, usually an appointee of the bankruptcy judge, serving in many cases that are before that judge, and continually being reappointed to new cases as they come in. There usually develops a close working relationship between the judge and "his' trustee, due to the necessity for frequent ex parte contacts between the judge and the trustee in the administration of the case. It is not uncommon to see a trustee enter a courtroom, for a hearing on a matter, from the judge's chambers, followed closely by the judge himself. As often as not, the trustee was working with the judge on a different matter than the one up for hearing. Nevertheless, the combined force of all of these factors seriously compromises the appearance of the bankruptcy judge as an impartial arbiter. They have worked to generate deep suspicion on the part of attorneys who practice in the bankruptcy court as to the fairness of the decisions of the bankruptcy court.

Report of the Committee of the Judiciary, Bankruptcy Law Revision H. R.Rep. No. 95–595, 95th Cong., 1st Sess. ("House Report") 89–90 (1977).

Furthermore, this district's local bankruptcy rules, promulgated by the learned judges of the District Court, do not merely condone, but command the bankruptcy judge to have some ex parte contact with the debtor and the debtor's counsel. Eastern District Court Local Bankruptcy Rule XI–4 provides, in pertinent part, that:

> As soon as practical after petition is filed the debtor, or if the debtor is a corporation, the president or principal operating officer of such corporation, and the debtor's attorney shall attend before the bankruptcy judge for an informal conference to discuss the petition and any matters pertinent thereto.

Certainly the court would not be justified in transferring the matter to another bankruptcy judge because fault is found with the system of administering a bankrupt estate. If the system is at fault, then it should be corrected not by judicial but congressional legislation. *In re Carburetor Corporation,* 91 F. Supp. 782 (E.D.N.Y. 1950).

Congress did *attempt* to correct the "bankruptcy system." The House Bill, H. R. 8200, proposed to solve the aforementioned problem by creating a system of United States Trustees. *House Report, supra,* at 99–100. The United States Trustee was to take over the supervising and appointing functions that were handled by the bankruptcy judges.

> The United States trustees will relieve the bankruptcy judges of their current administrative and supervisory role, and will become the principal administrative officers of the bankruptcy system. Bankruptcy judges, relieved of administrative responsibilities, will take a more passive role, consistent with their judicial responsibilities which will serve to eliminate the institutional bias that

exists in the bankruptcy system today. These changes in the present bankruptcy administrative system will accomplish the separation of judicial and administrative functions currently performed by the bankruptcy judges. The judges will become passive arbiters of disputes that arise in bankruptcy cases. The United States trustees will assume the bankruptcy judges' current supervisory roles over the conduct of bankruptcy cases and over individuals serving in the bankruptcy system.

House Report, supra, at 101.

However, the Senate did not favor the United States trustee system. A compromise was reached and a pilot program of United States trustees was established in certain districts for the transition period. 124 Cong. Rec. H11088 (daily ed. Sept. 28, 1978). The Eastern District of New York is not a pilot district and therefore, does not have a United States trustee. 11 U.S.C. section 1501.

The result of the attempted reform of the bankruptcy system has been described as follows:

> Despite Congress' ambitious attempts with the Reform Act, many of the bankruptcy court's duties will continue to be "administrative" in nature. Indeed, in those jurisdictions where United States Trustees will not be appointed, the bankruptcy judge's supervisory role often will remain as administrative as it has always been. Even in those jurisdictions in which a United States Trustee will be appointed, the court will retain many of its administrative duties.

Eisen and Smrtnik, *The Bankruptcy Reform Act of 1978—An Elevated Judiciary,* 28 DePaul L. Rev. 1007, 1022 (1979).

> In non–pilot project districts there is relatively little separation of administrative and judicial functions and the judges will continue to play an important role in supervising administration.

> In non United States trustee districts, the court's role in administration is necessarily larger and the involvement will continue to be substantial.

J. Trost, G. Treister, L. Forman, K. Klee & R. Levin, The New Federal Bankruptcy Code 30–31, 33 (1979). Accordingly, even under the Bankruptcy Code, bankruptcy judges in non U.S. trustee districts may be required to have certain ex parte contacts. The Bank contends that the court's ex parte communications with Sheldon Lowe, the reorganization trustee, requires the court to recuse itself. As with the other ex parte communications, the Bank does not allege that any substantive matters were discussed; for, indeed, none were. The first ex parte communication involved a chance meeting in the crowded hallway, in front of dozens of people, in which the court exchanged pleasantries with Mr. Lowe. But for certain statements made in the Bank's affidavit and memorandum of law, the court would not bother to elaborate on this matter. However, Paragraph 26 of the Bank's affidavit in support of its motion contains the following statement:

> Although affiant Werther did not hear the substance of the conversation between the Bankruptcy Judge and Mr. Lowe, the Bankruptcy Code provides that a bankruptcy judge "may not preside at, and may not attend, any meeting" of creditors.

11 U.S.C. section 341(c)

This statement is both inaccurate and misleading. First, 11 U.S.C. section 341(c) does not provide that a "bankruptcy judge may not attend any meeting of creditors." 11 U.S.C. section 341(c) provides that: "[t]he court may not preside at, and may not attend, any meeting under this section." The Bank's affidavit does not state that the court attended a meeting of creditors. However, ¶ 26 of the affidavit, by linking the conversation between the Judge and Mr. Lowe with the prohibition contained in 11 U.S.C. section 341, clearly implies that the court did attend a "meeting of creditors' in violation of section 341. The court, in fact, did not preside at or attend the section 341 meeting of creditors or any other meeting of creditors. Such attempts to obfuscate facts are to be deplored. *See In re Beck Industries,* 605 F.2d 624 (2d Cir. 1979).

In addition, in its memorandum of law in support of the instant motion, the Bank states

> *EX PARTE* communication Between The JUDGE AND THE CHAPTER 11 TRUSTEE IS *SPECIFICALLY PROHIBITED* BY THE NEW BANKRUPTCY CODE.

Bank's Memorandum of Law, p. 10.

This statement is false; nothing in the Bankruptcy Code *"specifically"* prohibits ex parte communications between a bankruptcy judge and a Chapter 11 trustee. Indeed, the Bank did not even attempt to support this statement. Instead, the memorandum of law refers to the House Judiciary Committee's attempt to separate the bankruptcy judge's judicial and administrative functions. As has previously been discussed, the proposed separation of these functions was not adopted in non–United States Trustee districts.

The Bank also states that on December 18, 1979 affiants Cook and Werther "saw and heard" the Bankruptcy Judge ask Sheldon Lowe to meet with the Judge in his chambers. This request was made to Mr. Lowe in open court, only after it was announced that the District Court had reversed this court's order appointing Mr. Lowe as trustee. The Bank's counsel were present when the request was made. The Bank's counsel could have voiced their objections at that time, or they could have requested to be present at the meeting.

However, the Bank's counsel remained silent. While Mr. Case, counsel for ITT, may have expressed his intention to appeal the aforementioned district court's order, he never did. The debtor, however, did take an appeal, which was later dismissed. In any event, on April 7, 1980, the Parrs were adjudicated bankrupts, and the Parr Meadows Racing Association, Inc. Chapter 11 case was converted to a Chapter 7 case. Mr. Lowe was not appointed as a "liquidation trustee" in any of these matters.

Conclusion

In view of the foregoing, it is clear that 28 U.S.C. sections 144, 455, the due process clause of the Fifth Amendment and the Code of Judicial Conduct do not require recusal under the circumstances extant in these cases. In addition, these cases have been before this court, in one form or another, for almost three years. Transferring these cases at this time would place an intolerable burden on the court which would receive them, and would only further prolong these lengthy proceedings. *cf. In re Schoenfield,* 608 F2d 47 (2d Cir. 1979). Accordingly, the Bank's motion is *Denied.*

IN RE EDWARDS

Bankruptcy Court, Southern District of Florida
2 B. R. 103, 1 C. B. C. 2d 440, 5 B. C. D. 1321 (1979)

BRITTON, Bankruptcy Judge:

These two cases were filed separately by a husband and wife. They have been consolidated. The husband appears to be in the military service, stationed in the Philippines and there is no present indication when he will return to this Country.

When these cases were filed, the debtors anticipated he would be here on leave in time to testify before his creditors. The leave was cancelled.

The debtors' counsel has called my attention to the provisions of the Civil Relief Act of 1940, 50 App. Section 521, which gives a serviceman a mandatory stay of any lawsuit filed by or against him:

> unless, in the opinion of the court, the ability of plaintiff to prosecute the action or the defendant to conduct his defense is not materially affected by reason of his military service.

I find only one reported case discussing the application of this provision to a bankruptcy case. *Gayle v. Jones,* D.C. La. 1945. 63 F.Supp. 481. That decision is not directly analogous here.

All of the assets and debts of this family are jointly owned and owed by the husband and wife. The wife is here and is in possession of all the assets. At the creditors' meeting she appeared and testified as to all matters pertinent to this case and stated that, to the best of her knowledge, the information furnished by her would be the same information to be furnished by her husband. No creditors attended the meeting. Notwithstanding the provisions of 11 U.S.C. § 343, I conclude that the husband's failure to appear and testify at the creditors' meeting in this instance may be excused.

NOTES AND QUESTIONS

1. The presiding officer at the § 341 meeting is not supposed to resolve disputes. What happens if a dispute arises at the meeting? Debtor refuses to answer a question? A challenge is made to a creditor's right to vote for a trustee?

2. In the *Parr* case the court quotes from the House Committee Report to substantiate its view that ex parte contacts are permissible. Does that quote not imply that such contacts are neither desirable nor legitimate? What would the decision have been if the case arose under the Code? *See* Rule 9003. The judge was affirmed by the district court, because *inter alia* "it would seem inequitable after four years of proceedings to disqualify the bankruptcy judge." 5 C.B.C.2d at 1049.

3. Section 343 is mandatory in its requirement that a debtor attend the meeting of creditors for examination. In *In re Rust,* 1 B. R. 656, 1 C. B. C.2d 318 (Bankr. M.D. Tenn. 1979), the court dismissed the petition because of failure to appear at the meeting. The excuse given was irregular work schedule; debtor was a truck driver and required to be out of town. Suppose debtor is confined to a hospital? To a penal institution?

4. During the examination, debtor refuses to answer a series of questions, claiming a right to refuse under the Fifth Amendment to the Constitution. Is that a right recognizable in bankruptcy? May the debtor be denied a discharge if there is a persistence in such refusal?

§ 16.02 Filing and Allowance of Claims

In chapter 7 cases, in order to participate in any distribution, it is necessary for the creditor to have an "allowed" claim. Whether a claim is allowable is set forth in § 502 of the Code. The first step, however, is that the claim must be filed. Section 502 provides that a timely filed claim is deemed allowed if no objection is made to it.

Section 501 provides that a creditor *may* file a claim. The House Committee Report states that filing of a claim is permissive and not mandatory. Of course, it is permissive if the creditor does not wish to obtain any distribution; if the desire is otherwise, filing of a claim is required as the first step in allowance. The Committee Report, while grammatically correct, is somewhat misleading.

Neither § 501 nor § 502 specifies within what time period claims must be filed to be timely. Under the former Act, § 57 required claims to be filed within six months after the first date set for the first meeting of creditors. The case law had construed this provision to be inflexible; if a creditor failed to meet the deadline, an extension of time could not be granted by the court.

This deadline was carried over into the former Bankruptcy Rules, and Rule 302(e) provided the same six–month deadline. That rule has been superseded by Rule 3002(c), which reduces the time period for filing claims to 90 days from the first date set for the meeting of creditors (§ 341, Rule 2003). The Official Form for the notice of the meeting of creditors is mailed to all creditors and among the information it carries is the deadline for filing claims.

As mentioned, § 502 deals with the allowance of claims. In essence, it sets forth the reasons why claims may be disallowed on proper objection. Normally, it is the trustee who will object to claims although creditors have standing to do so.

What are some common grounds for objecting to claims?

What is a claim? *See* § 101(5), (10) of the Code.

How are secured claims treated? *See* § 506. What does § 506(d) mean? *See also* §§ 524(a)(2) and 727(b).

IN RE ALLEGHENY INTERNATIONAL, INC.

United States Court of Appeals, Third Circuit
954 F.2d 167, 26 C.B.C.2d 663, 670 (1992)

The burden of proof for claims brought in the bankruptcy court under. . .[§ 502(a)] rests on different parties at different times. Initially, the claimant must allege facts sufficient to support the claim. If the averments in his filed claim meet this standard of sufficiency, it is "prima facie" valid, *In re Holm*, 931 F.2d 620 (9th Cir. 1991)(quoting L. King, Collier on Bankruptcy § 502.02, at 502–22 (15th ed. 1991)). In other words, a claim that alleges facts sufficient to support a legal liability to the claimant satisfies the claimant's initial obligation to go forward. The burden of going forward then shifts to the objector to produce evidence sufficient to negate the prima facie validity of the filed claim. It is often said that the objection must produce evidence equal in force to the prima facie case. . .. In practice, the objector must produce evidence which, if believed, would refute at least one of the allegations that is essential to the claim's legal sufficiency. If the objector produces sufficient evidence to negate one or more of the sworn facts in the proof of claim, the burden reverts to the claimant to prove the validity of the claim by a preponderance of the evidence. . .. The burden of persuasion is always on the claimant [citing *Holm* and *Collier, supra*]. . ..

IN RE GRYNBERG

United States Court of Appeals, Tenth Circuit
986 F.2d 367, 28 C.B.C.2d 779 (1993)

LOGAN, Circuit Judge:

Plaintiffs Jack and Celeste Grynberg appeal the district court's affirmance of the bankruptcy court's order granting summary judgement in favor of defendants, the United States government and the Internal Revenue Service (IRS), and dismissing with prejudice plaintiffs' adversary proceeding against defendants.

The facts in this case are undisputed. In early 1981, plaintiffs filed petitions for reorganization under Chapter 11 of the Bankruptcy Code, 11 U.S.C. §§1101–1174. Their cases were jointly administered. As provided under § 521(1) and 1111(a), plaintiffs' bankruptcy schedules listed the United States as a disputed creditor, both for gift taxes and for income taxes. The disputed gift tax liability arose from intra–family transfers of mineral interests made in the year preceding the bankruptcy filings. Plaintiffs never filed gift tax returns on these transfers, contending that they were not taxable gifts.

On June 19, 1981, the bankruptcy court issued the following bar order:

> Creditors holding claims scheduled by Debtor as disputed, contingent, or unliquidated shall file a proof of claim with this Court on or before July 31, 1981. . ... Failure to file a proof of claim shall forever bar a creditor holding a disputed, contingent, or unliquidated claim from participation in this proceeding or in any distribution under a plan filed by the Debtor. . ..

Appellants' App. at 36. The IRS filed a timely proof of claim for the scheduled income tax liabilities, but not for the gift taxes. In April 1982, the bankruptcy court approved plaintiffs' joint reorganization plan, which made no reference to the disputed gift tax. The IRS did not object to the plan or to its accompanying disclosure statement.

In 1989, after the plan had been fully consummated, the IRS sent Jack Grynberg a notice of a proposed gift tax deficiency and penalties totalling nearly $5 million. In response, plaintiffs filed an adversary action in the bankruptcy court, seeking to enjoin the IRS from collecting the deficiency on the grounds that it had been disallowed under the bar order and discharged at the completion of the joint reorganization. The bankruptcy court granted defendants' motion for summary judgment and dismissed plaintiffs' complaint. The district court affirmed, and this appeal followed.

"We review the bankruptcy court's decision under the same standard used by the district court." *Citizens Nat'l Bank & Trust Co. v. Serelson (In re Burkart Farm & Livestock)*, 938 F.2d 1114, 1115 (10th Cir. 1991). Thus, we review legal conclusions, such as a grant of summary judgment, de novo and factual findings for clear error. *Unioil v. H.E. Elledge; 270 Corp. (In re Unioil)*, 962 F.2d 988, 990 [27 C. B. C.2d 83] (10th Cir. 1992).

Section 1141(d)(1)(A) of the Bankruptcy Code provides generally for discharge from any debt that arose before confirmation of the plan, even if no proof of claim was filed or the claim was disallowed. However, § 1141(d)(2) specifically provides that "confirmation of a plan does not discharge an individual debtor from any debt excepted from discharge under section 523 of this title."

Section 523, when read in conjunction with § 1141(d)(2), provides that confirmation of a reorganization plan for an individual debtor will not discharge recent excise taxes "whether or not a claim for such tax was filed or allowed," § 523(a)(1)(A), or taxes for which returns should have been but were not filed. The gift taxes at issue here fit within both categories.

Section 6019 of the Internal Revenue Code states that any individual making a transfer by gift in excess of $10,000, other than to a spouse "shall make a return for such year with respect to the gift tax imposed." Plaintiffs argue that there is no evidence in the record to support the district court's conclusion that their transfers were taxable gifts that required the filing of a return. The bankruptcy court has never ruled on the merits of the gift tax liability claim, which remains unresolved. However, plaintiffs cannot bootstrap their argument that returns were not required based on the absence of a ruling on the merits of the government's claim for such taxes. We emphasize that nothing in the district court's order purports to fix plaintiffs' gift tax liability; it merely establishes that whatever that liability may be, it has not been discharged.

In any event, these gift taxes fit within the § 523(a)(1)(A) exception to discharge that covers taxes entitled to priority under § 507(a)(7). Excise taxes include gift taxes, and the transfers at issue occurred within the three year statutory window. Although § 507(a)(7) refers to "allowed unsecured claims of governmental units," § 523(a)(1)(A) makes clear that these taxes remain nondischargeable "whether or not a claim for such tax was filed or allowed." Plaintiffs argue strenuously that the failure of the IRS to file a proof of claim before the bar date imposed by the bankruptcy court subjected their gift tax claim to discharge upon confirmation of the plan, and that the bankruptcy court's determination under the bar order is res judicata. This contention is contrary to the language of the bar order and to the operation of Bankruptcy Rule 3003 under which the bar order was issued.

Bankruptcy Rule 3003(c)(3) requires a bankruptcy court to fix a time for filing proofs of claims. The purpose of this deadline is to "enable a debtor and his creditors to know, reasonably promptly, what parties are making claims against the estate and in what general amounts." *United States v. Kolstad (In re Kolstad),* 928 F.2d 171, 173 (11th Cir.), *cert. denied,* 112 S. Ct. 419 (1991). However, as the language of the bar order itself states, failure to file a proof of claim before the bar date simply precludes a creditor from participating in the voting or distribution from the debtor's estate. Neither the rules nor the bar order prevents a creditor holding a nondischargeable debt who has not filed a proof of claim from collecting outside of bankruptcy. *See In re Olsen,* 123 B. R. 312, 314 (Bankr. N.D. Ill. 1991) ("the IRS's nondischargeable claim. . .would survive bankruptcy even if the IRS had never even filed a proof of claim"); *Kinney v. IRS (In re Kinney),* 123 B.R. 889, 891 (Bankr. D. Nev. 1991) ("[t]he IRS's failure to file timely a proof of claim would, at most, result in a loss of the right to payment under the plan"); *In re Howell,* 84 B. R. 834, 836 (Bankr. M.D. Fla. 1988) ("a creditor holding a non–dischargeable debt. . .may execute or collect on the balance of its nondischargeable debt without regard to the discharge provisions of the plan or the Code"); *Galbreath v. Illinois Dep't of Revenue (In re Galbreath),* 83 B. R. 549, 551 (Bankr. S.D. Ill. 1988) ("a creditor with a type of debt listed as nondischargeable under [§] 523(a)(1). . .may wait until the conclusion of the bankruptcy proceeding and then bring suit on its claim in the appropriate nonbankruptcy forum"). Plaintiffs cite numerous cases emphasizing the finality of bar orders and prohibiting the IRS for filing additional proofs of claim after the bar date has passed. These cases establish only that the IRS is bound to submit its proofs of claim like any other creditor or be foreclosed from participating in the debtor's reorganization. However, like any other holder of a nondischargeable debt, the IRS is also free to pursue the debtor outside bankruptcy.

Plaintiffs' argument that the bar order disallowed the gift tax claim is unconvincing. It is undisputed that defendant's failure to file a proof of claim for the gift taxes precluded it from participating in the voting and distribution under plaintiffs' Chapter 11 plan. It is equally clear, however, that a bankruptcy court's determination of a claim's untimeliness does not affect application of the § 523 exceptions to discharge. We agree with *Spruill v. South Atl. Prod. Credit Assoc. (In re Spruill),* 83 B.R. 359 (Bankr. E.D.N.C. 1988), which considered this issue and concluded that § 523(a)(1)(A) "was intended to prevent the discharge of tax claims which were never filed or filed late but which would otherwise have been allowable." *Id.* at 361. It held that while disallowance on the merits would have prevented the IRS from pursuing the gift tax claim postbankruptcy, disallowance for untimeliness does not act as a bar to asserting nondischargeability in subsequent litigation. *Id. See also Olsen,* 123 B. R. at 314 ("[t]he Bankruptcy Code makes it clear that the actual allowance of a tax claim as a priority debt and the nondischargeability of a tax claim are not related"); *Great Am. Ins. Co. v. Graziano (In re Graziano),* 35 B. R. 589, 592 (Bankr. E.D.N.Y. 1983) ("creditor's failure to file a proof of claim does not act as a bar to an action to determine dischargeability"); *Massoni v. District Director of IRS (In re Massoni),* [6 C. B. C.2d 1185] 20 B. R. 416, 419 (Bankr. D. Kan. 1982) ("the failure of the IRS to file a proof of claim does not affect the debt's dischargeability"). The clear provisions of Bankruptcy Rule 3003(c)(2) limit the rights of a creditor failing to file a proof of claim only with respect to voting and distribution under the plan. Bar orders issued pursuant to this rule have no other effect.

Although allowing the IRS to pursue its claim after the confirmation and consummation of a Chapter 11 plan admittedly conflicts with the "fresh start" policy animating the Code's discharge provisions, "it is apparent to us that Congress has made the choice between collection of revenue and rehabilitation of the debtor by making it extremely difficult for a debtor to avoid payment of taxes under the Bankruptcy Code." *United States v. Gurwitch (In re Gurwitch),* 794 F.2d 584, 585–86 (11th Cir. 1986). This is an express congressional policy judgment that we are bound to follow. *See United States v. Sotelo,* 436 U.S. 268, 279–80 (1978).

Finally, plaintiffs maintain that to be excepted from discharge under § 523, the disputed gift tax must be a "debt." The Code defines debt as "liability on a claim." § 101(12). Because the IRS never filed a proof of claim for the gift tax, the argument goes, it does not have a debt, and without a debt there is nothing to be deemed nondischargeable. Although this syllogism is semantically creative, it disregards the broader purposes and logic of the Code. Plaintiffs neglected to include in their argument the definition of "claim," which means a "right to payment, whether or not such right is reduced to judgment, liquidated, unliquidated, fixed, contingent, matured, unmatured, disputed, undisputed, legal, equitable, secured, or unsecured." § 101(5)(A). The Supreme Court has held that the language of § 101(5)(A) "reflects Congress' broad rather than restrictive view of the class of obligations that qualify as a claim' giving rise to a debt." *Pennsylvania Dep't of Pub. Welfare v. Davenport,* 495 U.S. 552, 558 [22 C.B.C.2d 1067] (1990). Nothing in the definition of the term requires the submission of proof to establish a claim's existence. Proof is required only to ensure the creditor's participation in the reorganization. In view of this expansive definition of the term "claim," we have no difficulty characterizing the gift taxes as a disputed right to payment, thus qualifying as a "debt" that can be excepted from discharge under § 523.

Plaintiffs' difficulties might easily have been averted. The Bankruptcy Code includes a mechanism specifically to protect debtors in those situations in which the creditor's debt is non–dischargeable. Section 501(c) provides that "[i]f a creditor does not timely file a proof of such creditor's claim, the debtor or the trustee may file a proof of such claim." Bankruptcy Rule 3004 gives the debtor or trustee thirty days after the bar date to file such claims. Together, § 501(c) and Rule 3004 afford the debtor the broadest relief possible in bankruptcy by allowing the debtor to bring in all known claimants and, through payment under the plan, to reduce the amount of nondischargeable debt owed after the closing of the case. Had plaintiffs taken advantage of this provision, § 1129(a)(9)(C) would have permitted confirmation of a plan that included deferred cash payments for excise taxes on transfers made within the three year window specified in § 507(a)(7)(E). *See generally Kolstad*, 928 F.2d at 174. Because the IRS declined to file the claim and hence did not participate in plaintiffs' reorganization with respect to this claim, and because plaintiffs failed to use the statutory mechanism for mandatory participation available to them, the IRS is now free to recover outside bankruptcy. *In re Kloeble*, 112 B. R. 379, 381 (Bankr. S.D. Cal. 1990) ("[t]he apparent consequence of the debtor's failure to file for the creditor within the time allotted under Rule 3004 is that the debtor remains burdened with the debt post–discharge to the extent the debt was nondischargeable").

Affirmed.

MATTER OF PENROD

United States Court of Appeals, Seventh Circuit
50 F.3d 459 (1995)

POSNER, Chief Judge

This appeal raises an issue of bankruptcy law that one might have supposed had been settled long ago. It is whether, when a plan of reorganization makes provision for the payment of a secured creditor's claim but does not say whether the creditor's security interest (lien) is extinguished, the security interest survives, in accordance with the old saw that "liens pass through bankruptcy unaffected."

Hog farmers named Penrod executed a promissory note to Mutual Guaranty Corporation (actually to its predecessor, but we can ignore that detail) for $150,000, secured by the Penrods' hogs. A year later, the Penrods filed for bankruptcy under Chapter 11, owing Mutual Guaranty $132,000. Mutual Guaranty filed a proof of claim in the bankruptcy proceeding. The Penrods, neither objecting to the claim nor questioning the validity of Mutual Guaranty's lien, filed a plan of reorganization which designated Mutual Guaranty as a "Class 3 creditor" in fact as the only Class 3 creditor. Class 3 creditors, the plan states, "will be paid in full, with interest at the rate of eleven percent (11%) per annum. Payments to this Class shall be paid on a monthly basis commencing sixty (60) days after Confirmation. Furthermore, said payments shall be based upon a seven (7) year amortization." That is all that the plan, or the order confirming it, says about Mutual Guaranty's interest.

Shortly after the plan went into effect, the Penrods' hogs became infected with "pseudo–rabies" virus, a disease of the reproductive system that causes the females infected with it to miscarry. Hogs so stricken cannot be kept for breeding purposes; all they are good for is food (human food, we note with some anxiety). So the Penrods sold their hogs for slaughter without remitting the proceeds to Mutual Guaranty, as the security agreement accompanying the promissory note had required. Mutual Guaranty brought suit in a state court to enforce a lien in the proceeds. The Penrods responded by asking the bankruptcy court to hold Mutual Guaranty in contempt for violating the order confirming the plan of reorganization, which the Penrods claim extinguished Mutual Guaranty's lien. The bankruptcy court agreed that the lien had been extinguished and enjoined (the court's term was "precluded,' but as far as we can tell it meant the same thing) Mutual Guaranty from attempting to enforce it. The district court affirmed.

A secured creditor can bypass his debtor's bankruptcy proceeding and enforce his lien in the usual way, which would normally be by bringing a foreclosure action in a state court. This is the principle that liens pass through bankruptcy unaffected. *Long v. Bullard,* 117 U.S. 617, 620–21 (1886); *Dewsnup v. Timm,* 502 U.S. 410 (1992); *In re James Wilson Associates,* 965 F.2d 160, 167 [26 C.B.C.2d 1673] (7th Cir. 1992). If the creditor follows this route, the discharge in bankruptcy will not impair his lien. *Dewsnup v. Timm, supra,* 112 S.Ct. at 778; *In re Tarnow,* 749 F.2d 464 [12 C.B.C.2d 3] (7th Cir. 1984). Alternatively, he may decide to collect his debt in the bankruptcy proceeding, and to this end may file a proof of claim in that proceeding. 11 U.S.C. § 501(a). He will do this if he is undersecured, for in that case merely enforcing his lien would not enable him to collect the entire debt owed him. His only chance of recovering any part of the amount by which the debt exceeds the value of the lien would be to share in the distribution of the debtor's estate to the unsecured creditors. 11 U.S.C. § 506(a); *In re Tarnow, supra,* 749 F.2d at 465.

A secured creditor may be dragged into the bankruptcy involuntarily, because the trustee or debtor (if there is no trustee), or someone who might be liable to the secured creditor and therefore has an interest in maximizing the creditor's recovery, may file a claim on the creditor's behalf. 11 U.S.C. 501(b), (c); *In re Lindsey,* 823 F.2d 189, 191 [17 C.B.C.2d 363] (7th Cir. 1987). He may participate in the bankruptcy in order to try to get the automatic stay (11 U.S.C. § 362(d)) lifted to the extent of allowing him to enforce his lien; for the stay applies to the enforcement of liens. He may want to participate in the bankruptcy proceeding (and so may decide to file a claim) simply because he wants to make sure that the debtor's estate is not administered in a way that will diminish the value, as distinct from threatening the existence, of his lien. *In re CMC Heartland Partners,* 966 F.2d 1143, 1147 (7th Cir. 1992).

The secured creditor does not, by participating in the bankruptcy proceeding through filing a claim, surrender his lien. But this is not to say that the lien is sure to escape unscathed from the bankruptcy. We have mentioned the automatic stay. If the secured creditor's claim is challenged in the bankruptcy proceeding and the court denies the claim, the creditor will lose the lien by operation of the doctrine of collateral estoppel. 11 U.S.C. 506(d); *In re Tarnow, supra*, 749 F.2d at 465–66. He may be forced in the plan of reorganization to swap his lien for an interest that is an "indubitable equivalent" of the lien. 11 U.S.C. 1129(b)(2)(A)(iii); *In re James Wilson Associates, supra*, 965 F.2d at 172. And in some circumstances he may even be compelled to surrender his lien without receiving anything in return. *See* 11 U.S.C. 1126(d), 1129(a)(10), (b)(1). And, of course, he can consent to its discharge. The right is implicit in 11 U.S.C. § 1126, and is anyway obvious. It is a frequent element of a plan of reorganization, as we are about to see.

Nothing we have said so far is controversial, and we can take one more step without inviting controversy. A plan of reorganization can expressly preserve preexisting liens, such as that of Mutual Guaranty in this case. 11 U.S.C. § 1123(b)(1). Conversely, it can expressly abrogate some or all of those liens with the full consent of the lien–holders; and this is common. A reorganization alters the capital structure of the bankrupt enterprise. Bondholders and other creditors, along with shareholders, exchange their notes, claims, and shares for new securities in the reorganized firm. For recent examples, see *Sullivan & Long v. Scattered Corp.*, No. 94-2015, slip op. at 2 (7th Cir. Feb. 8, 1995); *In re Envirodyne Industries, Inc.*, 29 F.3d 301 (7th Cir. 1994). Bondholders often give up their bonds and associated security agreements in exchange for common stock in the reorganized corporation, thus exchanging a secured for an unsecured interest. By now it should be clear that like most generalizations about law, the principle that liens pass through bankruptcy unaffected cannot be taken literally.

The question we must decide in this case is whether preexisting liens survive a reorganization when the plan (or the order confirming it) does not mention the liens. What in other words is the default rule when the plan is silent? We acknowledge this to be a difficult question. Liens are property rights and the forfeiture of such rights is disfavored. But when lienholders participate in a bankruptcy proceeding, and especially in a reorganization, they know that their liens are likely to be affected, and indeed altered. The issue here, moreover, is what the proper rule for interpreting silence is rather than in what circumstances a lien can be taken away from someone who has expressed his desire to retain it.

We have concluded that the default rule for secured creditors who file claims for which provision is made in the plan of reorganization is extinction and is found in the Code itself. Section 1141(c) provides with immaterial exceptions that "except as provided in the plan or in the order confirming the plan, after confirmation of a plan, the property dealt with by the plan is free and clear of all claims and interests of creditors, equity security holders, and of general partners in the debtor." The term "interest" is not defined in the Code, but a "lien" is defined as an interest in property, 11 U.S.C. § 101(37), and there is no doubt that a security interest is an interest, and it is defined as a "lien created by an agreement." 11 U.S.C. § 101(51). So section 1141(c) must cover liens, *In re Arctic Enterprises, Inc.*, 68 B. R. 71, 79 (D. Minn. 1986), and must mean, therefore, that unless the plan of reorganization, or the order confirming the plan, says that a lien is preserved, it is extinguished by the confirmation. This is provided, we emphasize, that the holder of the lien participated in the reorganization. If he did not, his lien would not be "property dealt with by the plan,' and so the section would not apply. One could argue that the quoted phrase should be equated to "property of the estate," defined in section 541 to include "all legal or equitable interests of the debtor in property as of the commencement of the case", and that at the start of the bankruptcy proceeding the liens of the secured creditors are not the debtor's property which indeed they are not. *Moody v. Amoco Oil Co.*, 734 F.2d 1200, 1213 [11 C.B.C.2d 1] (7th Cir. 1984); *In re Interstate Motor Freight System*, [18 C.B.C.2d 1116, 86 B.R. 500, 505 (Bankr. W.D. Mich. 1988). But the suggested equation is not especially plausible. Property dealt with by the plan is property dealt with by the plan, whether it was part of the debtor's estate when bankruptcy was first declared or was tossed into the pot later. As we have said, secured creditors commonly give up their preexisting liens for other interests in the reorganized firm. A plan of reorganization that does this "deal[s] with" the liens. Or does it? For it could be argued that the plan in this case dealt with the secured creditor's claim, but not with its lien. But this interpretation would be inconsistent with the rest of section 1141(c) that the property dealt with by the plan is, after confirmation of the plan, to be "free and clear of all claims and interests of creditors" (and others). On the view pressed by Mutual Guaranty, the assets of the reorganized entity would continue to be burdened by secured creditors' claims by virtue of their liens even if the plan made provision for those claims.

Our suggested interpretation reconciles the language of section 1141(c) with the principle, which we have pointed out cannot be maintained without careful qualification, that liens pass through bankruptcy unaffected. They do unless they are brought into the bankruptcy proceeding and dealt with there. The interpretation makes practical sense as well. It lowers the costs of transacting with the reorganized firm, thus boosting the chances that the reorganization will succeed. By studying the plan of reorganization a prospective creditor of or investor in the reorganized firm can tell whether any liens that creditors whose interests in the new entity are defined in the plan may have had against its bankrupt predecessor survive as encumbrances on the assets of the new firm. The cases that support a contrary interpretation are cases in which the courts were, we respectfully suggest, mesmerized by a formula ("liens pass through bankruptcy unaffected"). *E.g., Relihan v. Exchange Bank,* 69 B. R. 122 (S. D. Ga. 1985); *United Presidential Life Ins. Co. v. Barker,* 31 B. R. 145 (N. D. Tex. 1983); *In re Eakin,* 153 B. R. 59 (Bankr. D. Idaho 1993). They are none of them appellate cases, and there are plenty of cases that take our view. *E.g., In re Arctic Enterprises, Inc., supra,* 68 B. R. at 80; *In re Johnson,* 139 B. R. 208, 216 (Bankr. D. Minn. 1992). Oddly, none of the cases on either side is an appellate case, the ones cited by Mutual Guaranty being readily distinguishable. The secured creditor in *In re Tarnow, supra,* did not participate in the reorganization, except to file a late claim against the debtor. The bankruptcy court disallowed the lien because the claim was late—an excessive punishment—not because the plan of reorganization had dealt with the property constituted by the creditor's lien. It had not; in fact no plan had yet been confirmed. Nor had the plan in *Estate of Lellock v. Prudential Ins. Co.,* 811 F.2d 186, 188–89 (3d Cir. 1987), made provision for the secured creditor; the debtor had never even listed the property subject to the lien as an asset of the estate. *In General Electric Credit Corp. v. Nardulli & Sons Inc.*, 836 F.2d 184, 188–89 (3d Cir. 1988), the plan denominated the creditor as a "secured creditor" and explicitly recognized its security interest. *In re Simmons*, 765 F.2d 547 (5th Cir. 1985), not cited by Mutual Guaranty—no doubt because it did not involve a plan of reorganization or cite section 1141(c)—is nevertheless its best case. It arose under an analogous provision of the Code, 11 U.S.C. § 1327(c), which governs plans under Chapter 13—a counterpart to Chapter 11, only for individuals rather than firms. *Simmons* relied heavily on our decision in *Tarnow*, but *Tarnow* did not involve the interpretation of a plan of reorganization: there was none. For other grounds of distinction between *Simmons* and the present case, see *In re Wolf*, [30 C.B.C.2d 730, 742 n.16] 162 B. R. 98, 108 n. 16 (Bankr. D. N. J. 1993).

There is nothing to Mutual Guaranty's suggestion that our interpretation raises a question under the due process or takings clauses of the Fifth Amendment because a lien is property within the meaning of the clause. It is, *United States v. Security Industrial Bank*, 459 U.S. 70, 76–77 (1982), but Mutual Guaranty could have protected it by appealing from the order confirming the plan of reorganization. We recognize that since the law was not clear with respect to the survival of the lien of a creditor who is provided for in the plan without mention of his lien, Mutual Guaranty may not have realized when the plan was adopted that its lien was in jeopardy. Conceivably this might give Mutual Guaranty an equitable defense to the complete extinction of the lien, but it has not presented such a defense. It has staked its all on persuading us that its lien survived the bankruptcy proceeding intact.

Affirmed.

CEN–PEN CORPORATION v. HANSON

United States Court of Appeals, Fourth Circuit
58 F. 3d 89 (1995)

WILKINSON, Circuit Judge

In this case we must address the effect of a bankruptcy court's confirmation of a Chapter 13 wage earner plan on a creditor's liens. Specifically, appellants contend that liens on their primary residence were avoided because the creditor received notice (by means of a copy of the proposed plan) that the underlying debt was being treated as unsecured but neither objected to confirmation of the plan nor filed a proof of its secured claim. Because we believe that appellants failed to take appropriate steps to avoid the creditor's liens, we hold that those liens survived confirmation. Accordingly, we affirm the judgment of the district court.

I.

From 1969 through 1985, appellants Walter and Loraine Hanson executed four promissory notes secured by deeds of trust on their Newport News residence. In 1985, the Hansons defaulted on the first two notes, thereby placing their residence at risk of foreclosure. In order to forestall foreclosure, the Hansons entered into a financing agreement with a non–party, Charles Carrithers, who was apparently acting on behalf of appellee Cen–Pen Corporation. Pursuant to this agreement, $58,000 plus interest; the agreement provided that Carrithers succeeded to the rights and remedies under the second and third deeds of trust.

In 1985 and 1986, Mr. and Mrs. Hanson filed separate Chapter 7 bankruptcy petitions and received discharges. In November 1986, Mr. Hanson and the trustee of Mrs. Hanson's bankruptcy estate filed suit in federal district court against Carrithers and Cen–Pen, alleging that the 1985 financing agreement violated the Truth in Lending Act, 15 U.S.C. § 1635, and regulations enacted pursuant thereto. In April 1987, the parties entered a settlement agreement resolving their disputes. According to this agreement, the Hansons were to refinance their outstanding indebtedness to Carrithers and Cen–Pen within 90 days. The settlement agreement included a release provision, which stated in pertinent part:

> Except as [to] the obligations created hereunder, or provided herein Cen–Pen, and Carrithers and the Trustee and the Hansons do hereby mutually release and forever discharge any claims Cen–Pen [or] Carrithers may have against the Hansons or the Trustee in connection with the second Deed of Trust, third Deed of Trust, or the loans.

Cen–Pen, however, believed the Hansons never fulfilled their part of the agreement because they neither obtained alternative financing nor executed any documents to refinance the $58,000 debt through Cen–Pen or Carrithers. Cen–Pen subsequently brought suit in the Circuit Court for the City of Newport News seeking entry of an order requiring the Hansons to execute a note and deed of trust or, alternatively, a determination that Cen–Pen retained valid liens against the Hanson residence.

In September 1992, the Hansons filed a Chapter 13 bankruptcy petition; the state court action was accordingly stayed. The Hansons served a Chapter 13 plan upon their creditors in October. In reliance on the release contained in the settlement agreement, the plan treated Cen–Pen as an unsecured creditor, entitling it to approximately 25 percent of its claim and objections to the plan within specified time periods; it further provided that the plan would be automatically confirmed if no such objections were received. Lastly, ¶ B–10(A) provided that "[a]ll claims to be allowed must be filed; to the extent that the holder of a secured claim does not file a proof of claim, the lien of such creditor shall be voided upon the entry of the Order of Discharge.' Cen–Pen did not file an objection to the plan, which was accordingly confirmed.

All creditors submitting allowable claims were paid pursuant to the plan, and the Hansons received their discharge in December 1993.

On February 2, 1994, Cen–Pen filed a complaint in the bankruptcy court to determine the validity of its liens on the Hanson residence. At a June hearing,

Cen–Pen maintained that the release provision in the April 1987 settlement agreement did not destroy its rights under the deeds of trust. The Hansons responded, first, that the settlement agreement plainly released them from any obligations under the deeds of trust, and second, that confirmation of the plan without objection from Cen–Pen invalidated the liens pursuant to § 1327(b) and (c) of the Bankruptcy Code.

The Bankruptcy Court declined to address the effect of the settlement agreement on Cen–Pen's security. It did, however, conclude that even assuming Cen–Pen possessed valid liens as of the date of the Hansons' petition, confirmation of the plan vested the residence in the Hansons free and clear of the liens.

The district court disagreed. It held that confirmation of the plan simply vested in the debtors the same interest in the residence that they had before filing a petition for bankruptcy relief—that is, an interest subject to Cen–Pen's liens. The Hansons appeal.

II.

A.

On appeal, the Hansons insist that, under the terms of 11 U.S.C. § 1327, confirmation of their Chapter 13 plan voided the liens held by Cen–Pen. Section 1327, entitled "Effect of Confirmation," provides:

(a) The provision of a confirmed plan bind the debtor and each creditor, whether or not the claim of such creditor is provided for by the plan, and whether or not such creditor has objected to, has accepted, or has rejected the plan.

(b) Except as otherwise provided in the plan or the order confirming the plan, the confirmation of a plan vests all of the property of the estate in the debtor.

(c) Except as otherwise provided in the plan or in the order confirming the plan, the property vesting in the debtor under subsection (b) of this section is free and clear of any claim or interest of any creditor provided for by the plan.

The Hansons note that Cen–Pen received a copy of the plan, which treated it as an unsecured creditor, but failed to object prior to confirmation. Nor did Cen–Pen file a proof of claim, despite notice in ¶ B–10(A) of the plan that such failure would result in avoidance of its liens. Confirmation of the plan, appellants contend, is *res judicata* by virtue of § 1327 as to Cen–Pen's present claim that it continues to hold valid liens against the residence.

We disagree. Although at first blush § 1327 appears to support appellants' argument, we are persuaded that other provisions of the Bankruptcy Code and Rules undercut it. To begin with, appellants' argument ignores the general rule that liens pass through bankruptcy unaffected. *See, e.g., Dewnsup v. Timm,* 502 U.S. 410, 418 (1992). A bankruptcy discharge extinguishes only *in personam* claims against the debtor(s), but generally has no effect on an in rem claim against the debtor's property. *See Johnson v. Home State Bank,* 501 U.S. 78, 84 (1991). For a debtor to extinguish or modify a lien during the bankruptcy process, some affirmative step must be taken toward that end. *See, e.g., Lee Servicing Co. v. Wolf (In re Wolf),*

162 B. R. 98, 107 n.14 (Bankr. D.N.J. 1993); *In re Glow,* 111 B. R. 209, 221 (Bankr. N.D. Ind. 1990). Unless the debtor takes appropriate affirmative action to avoid a security interest in property of the estate, that property will remain subject to the security interest following confirmation. *In re Honaker,* 4 B. R. 415, 417 (Bankr. E.D.Mich. 1980). The simple expedient of passing their residence through the bankruptcy estate could not vest in the Hansons a greater interest in the residence than they enjoyed prior to filing their Chapter 13 petition. *Id.*

Here the Hansons did not take a sufficient "affirmative step" to avoid Cen–Pen's liens. Bankruptcy Rule 7001(2) expressly requires initiation of an *adversary proceeding* "to determine the validity, priority, or extent of a lien or other interest in property," with one exception not applicable here. The procedural requirements of such an action, which include, *inter alia,* the filing of a complaint and service of a summons, are set out in the Bankruptcy Rules. Bankruptcy Rule 7004, for instance, governs the procedures for service of process in adversary proceedings. *See In re Linkous,* 990 F.2d 160, 162 (4th Cir. 1993) (adequate notice to affected secured creditor is prerequisite to according preclusive effect to confirmation order under § 1327).

The Hansons' reliance on § 1327 fails to appreciate the import of these Rules. Because confirmation of a Chapter 13 plan is *res judicata* only as to issues that can be raised in the less formal procedure for contested matters, *see In re Beard,* 112 B. R. 951, 955–56 (Bankr. N.D. Ind. 1990) (contrasting adversary proceedings with contested matters), confirmation generally cannot have preclusive effect as to the validity of a lien, which must be resolved in an adversary proceeding. In other words, "[i]f an issue must be raised through an adversary proceeding it is not part of the confirmation process and, unless it is actually litigated, confirmation will not have a preclusive effect. [A] secured creditor is not bound by the terms of the confirmed plan with respect to limitations upon the scope or validity of the lien securing its claim." *Id.* at 956.

Confirmation of the Hansons' Chapter 13 plan thus did not establish that Cen–Pen holds no valid liens as against the Hansons' residence. This is true despite the fact that Cen–Pen neither filed a proof of claim nor objected to confirmation of the plan. *Id.* Initiation of an adversary proceeding is a prerequisite to challenging "the validity or existence" of a lien against property of the estate in a Chapter 13 proceeding, *id.,* and no such proceeding was initiated here. Where such a proceeding "is required to resolve the disputed rights of third parties, the potential defendant has the right to expect that the proper procedures will be followed." *Id.* at 955 (citing *In re Commercial Western Finance Corp.,* 761 F.2d 1329, 1336–38 (9th Cir. 1985)).

B.

The Hansons point to ¶ B–10(A) as support for their contention that confirmation of their Chapter 13 plan voided Cen–Pen's liens. Paragraph B–10(A), which appeared on page 4 of appellants' proposed plan, provided as follows:

> All claims to be allowed must be filed; to the extent that the holder of a secured claim does not file a proof of claim, the lien of such creditor shall be voided upon the entry of the Order of Discharge in this case.

We do not think, however, that the Hansons' inclusion of this boiler–plate language in the plan avoided the liens, despite the fact that Cen–Pen did not file a proof of claim.

Several sections of the Code support this view. Section 506(d) voids a lien that secures a claim against the debtor which is not an allowed secured claim, unless the claim is not treated as an allowed secured claim simply because the creditor has elected not to file a proof of claim. 11 U.S.C. § 506(d)(2). Subsection (2) was intended "to make clear that the failure of the secured creditor to file a proof of claim is not a basis for avoiding the lien of the secured creditor." *In re Tarnow*, 749 F.2d 464, 467 (7th Cir. 1984) (quoting S. Rep. No. 65, 98th Cong., 1st Sess. 79 (1983)); *see also In re Levine*, 45 B. R. 333, 337 (N. D. Ill. 1984).

We also note that 11 U.S.C. § 501 provides for filing proofs of claim but it clearly does not make such a filing mandatory. *In re Thomas*, 883 F.2d 991, 996 (11th Cir. 1989); *cert. denied sub nom. Thomas v. SouthTrust Bank of Alabama*, 497 U.S. 1007 (1990). The language in ¶ B–10(A) of the Hansons' plan attempts to circumvent the clear import of this section. Because an unchallenged lien survives the bankruptcy discharge of a debtor, however, a creditor with a loan secured by a lien on the debtor's property is free to ignore the bankruptcy proceeding and look solely to the lien for satisfaction of the debt. *See Tarnow*, 749 F.2d at 465 (citing cases); *Washington v. Nissan Motor Acceptance Corp. (In re Washington)*, 158 B. R. 722, 723–24 (Bankr. S.D. Ohio 1993) (language in plan canceling liens of secured creditors who do not file proofs of claim cannot override § 506(d)(2)). In sum, the simple fact that Cen–Pen did not file a proof of claim cannot, without more, result in avoidance of its liens.

Moreover, the fact that Cen–Pen was listed as an unsecured creditor in the bankruptcy schedules does not suffice to avoid its liens. *In re Simmons*, 765 F.2d 547, 554–56 (5th Cir. 1985). "Even where confirmed without objection, a plan will not eliminate a lien simply by failing or refusing to acknowledge it or by calling the creditor unsecured." *Beard*, 112 B. R. at 954. The Hansons should not be entitled to eliminate otherwise valid liens on their residence simply characterizing Cen–Pen's claims in the plan as unsecured. *Simmons*, 765 F.2d at 556. Nor does the combination of Cen–Pen's treatment as an unsecured creditor plus its failure to file a proof of claim avoid its liens. *See, e.g., In re Willey*, 24 B. R. 369, 371 (Bankr. E.D. Mich. 1982).

The Hansons insist, however, that ¶ B–10, together with the listing of Cen–Pen as an unsecured creditor, "provided for" Cen–Pen's claim sufficiently to satisfy § 1327(c) and vest title to the residence in the Hansons free and clear of Cen–Pen's liens. We believe, to the contrary, that § 1327(c) does not permit the result appellants seek. As a general matter, a plan "provides for" a claim or interest when it acknowledges the claim or interest and makes explicit provision for its treatment. *In re Work*, 58 B. R. 868, 871 (Bankr. D. Or. 1986). If a Chapter 13 plan does not address a creditor's lien (for instance, by expressly providing for payment of an allowed secured claim and cancellation of the lien), that lien passes through the bankruptcy process intact, absent the initiation of an adversary proceeding, as discussed above. *Wolf*, 162 B. R. at 106, 108 n.16. Several courts have held that a plan "provides for" the lien held by a secured creditor only when it provides for payment to the creditor in an amount equal to its security. *In re Bradshaw*, 65 B. R. 556, 559 (Bankr. M.D.N.C. 1986); *In re Hines*, 20 B. R. 44, 49 (Bankr. S. D. Ohio 1982).

Bradshaw expressly rejected the argument, similar to the one the Hansons press here, that inclusion of a creditor in a plan "on the condition that the creditor timely file a proof of claim even if the creditor never file[s] and never receive[s] any payment on its claim amounts to " 'provision for' the creditor." *Bradshaw*, 65 B. R. at 559. We think that decision soundly reasoned. The Hansons' plan nowhere mentioned or otherwise acknowledges Cen–Pen's liens, and certainly did not "provide for" treatment of the liens or full payment of the underlying claim. Because listing Cen–Pen as an unsecured creditor would have entitled it only to approximately 25 percent of its claim, the plan did not "provide for' Cen–Pen's claim and its liens survived the Chapter 13 confirmation.

III.

For the foregoing reasons, the judgement of the district court is affirmed.

Dissenting opinion omitted.

BITTNER v. BORNE CHEMICAL CO.

United States Court of Appeals, Third Circuit
691 F.2d 134 (1982)

GIBBONS, Circuit Judge.

Stockholders of The Rolfite Company appeal from the judgment of the district court, affirming the decision of the bankruptcy court to assign a zero value to their claims in the reorganization proceedings of Borne Chemical Company, Inc. (Borne) under Chapter 11 of the Bankruptcy Code (Code), 11 U.S.C. ¶¶ 1–151326 (Supp. IV 1981). Since the bankruptcy court neither abused its discretionary authority to estimate the value of the claims pursuant to 11 U.S.C. § 502(c)(1) nor relied on clearly erroneous findings of fact, we affirm.

I.

Prior to filing its voluntary petition under Chapter 11 of the Code, Borne commenced a state court action against Rolfite for the alleged pirating of trade secrets and proprietary information from Borne. The Rolfite Company filed a counterclaim, alleging, *inter alia*, that Borne had tortiously interfered with a proposed merger between Rolfite and the Quaker Chemical Corporation (Quaker) by unilaterally terminating a contract to manufacture Rolfite products and by bringing its suit. Sometime after Borne filed its Chapter 11 petition, the Rolfite stockholders sought relief from the automatic stay so that the state court proceedings might be continued.

Borne then filed a motion to disallow temporarily the Rolfite claims until they were finally liquidated in the state court. The bankruptcy court lifted the automatic stay but also granted Borne's motion to disallow temporarily the claims, extending the time within which such claims could be filed and allowed if they should be eventually liquidated.

Upon denial of their motion to stay the hearing on confirmation of Borne's reorganization plan, the Rolfite stockholders appealed to the district court, which vacated the temporary disallowance order and directed the bankruptcy court to hold an estimation hearing. The parties agreed to establish guidelines for the submission of evidence at the hearing, and, in accordance with this agreement, the bankruptcy court relied on the parties' choice of relevant pleadings and other documents related to the state court litigation, and on briefs and oral argument. After weighing the evidence, the court assigned a zero value to the Rolfite claims and reinstated its earlier order to disallow temporarily the claims until such time as they might be liquidated in the state court, in effect requiring a waiver of discharge of the Rolfite claims from Borne. Upon appeal, the district court affirmed.

II.

Section 502(c) of the Code provides: There shall be estimated for purposes of allowance under this section—

> (1) any contingent or unliquidated claim, fixing or liquidation of which, as the case may be, would unduly delay the closing of the case.

The Code, the Rules of Bankruptcy Procedure, 11 U.S.C. app. (1977), and the Suggested Interim Bankruptcy Rules, 11 U.S.C.A. (1982), are silent as to the manner in which contingent or unliquidated claims are to be estimated. Despite the lack of express direction on the matter, we are persuaded that Congress intended the procedure to be undertaken initially by the bankruptcy judges, using whatever method is best suited to the particular contingencies at issue. The principal consideration must be an accommodation to the underlying purposes of the Code. It is conceivable that in rare and unusual cases arbitration or even a jury trial on all or some of the issues may be necessary to obtain a reasonably accurate evaluation of the claims. *See* 3 Collier on Bankruptcy ¶ 502.03 (15th ed. 1981). Such methods, however, usually will run counter to the efficient administration of the bankrupt's estate and where there is sufficient evidence on which to base a reasonable estimate of the claim, the bankruptcy judge should determine the value. In so doing, the court is bound by the legal rules which may govern the ultimate value of the claim. For example, when the claim is based on an alleged breach of contract, the court must estimate its worth in accordance with accepted contract law. *See, e.g.,* 3 Collier on Bankruptcy ¶ 57.15[3.2] (14th ed., 1977). However, there are no other limitations on the court's authority to evaluate the claim save those general principles which should inform all decisions made pursuant to the Code.

In reviewing the method by which a bankruptcy court has ascertained the value of a claim under section 502(c)(1), an appellate court may only reverse if the bankruptcy court has abused its discretion. That standard of review is narrow. The appellate court must defer to the congressional intent to accord wide latitude to the decisions of the tribunal in question. Section 502(c)(1) of the Code embodies Congress' determination that the bankruptcy courts are better equipped to evaluate the evidence supporting a particular claim within the context of a particular bankruptcy proceeding. Thus, an appellate court can impose its own judgment only when "the factors considered [by the bankruptcy court] do not accord with those required by the policy underlying the substantive right or if the weight given to those factors is not consistent with that necessary to effectuate that policy." *Gurmankin v. Costanzo*, 626 F.2d 1115, 1119–20 (3d Cir. 1980).

According to the Rolfite stockholders, the estimate which section 502(c)(1) requires is the present value of the probability that appellants will be successful in their state court action. Thus, if the bankruptcy court should determine as of this date that the Rolfite stockholders' case is not supported by a preponderance or 51% of the evidence but merely by 40%, they apparently would be entitled to have 40% of their claims allowed during the reorganization proceedings, subject to modification if and when the claims are liquidated in state court. The Rolfite stockholders contend that instead of estimating their claims in this manner, the bankruptcy court assessed the ultimate merits and, believing that they could not establish their case by a preponderance of the evidence, valued the claims at zero.

We note first that the bankruptcy court did not explicitly draw the distinction that the Rolfite stockholders make. Assuming however that the bankruptcy court did estimate their claims according to their ultimate merits rather than the present value of the probability that they would succeed in their state court action, we cannot find that such a valuation method is an abuse of the discretion conferred by section 502(c)(1).

The validity of this estimation must be determined in light of the policy underlying reorganization proceedings. In Chapter 11 of the Code, Congress addressed the complex issues which are raised when a corporation faces mounting financial problems.

> The modern corporation is a complex and multi–faceted entity. Most corporations do not have a significant market share of the lines of business in which they compete. The success, and even the survival, of a corporation in contemporary markets depends on three elements: First, the ability to attract and hold skilled management; second, the ability to obtain credit; and third, the corporation's ability to project to the public an image of vitality.

> One cannot overemphasize the advantages of speed and simplicity to both creditors and debtors. Chapter XI allows a debtor to negotiate a plan outside of court and, having reached a settlement with a majority in number and amount of each class of creditors, permits the debtor to bind all unsecured creditors to the terms of the arrangement. From the perspective of creditors, early confirmation of a plan of arrangement: first, generally reduces administrative expenses which have priority over the claims of unsecured creditors; second, permits creditors to receive prompt distributions on their claims with respect to which interest does not accrue after the filing date; and third, increases the ultimate recovery on creditor claims by minimizing the adverse effect on the

business which often accompanies efforts to operate an enterprise under the protection of the Bankruptcy Act.

124 Cong. Rec. H 11101–H 11102 (daily ed. Sept. 28, 1978) (statement of Rep. D. Edwards of California, floor manager for bankruptcy legislation in the House of Representatives). Thus, in order to realize the goals of Chapter 11, a reorganization must be accomplished quickly and efficiently.

If the bankruptcy court estimated the value of the Rolfite stockholders' claims according to the ultimate merits of their state court action, such a valuation method is not inconsistent with the principles which imbue Chapter 11. Those claims are contingent and unliquidated. According to the bankruptcy court's findings of fact, the Rolfite stockholders' chances of ultimately succeeding in the state court action are uncertain at best. Yet, if the court had valued the Rolfite stockholders' claims according to the present probability of success, the Rolfite stockholders might well have acquired a significant, if not controlling, voice in the reorganization proceedings. The interests of those creditors with liquidated claims would have been subject to the Rolfite interests, despite the fact that the state court might ultimately decide against those interests after the reorganization. The bankruptcy court may well have decided that such a situation would at best unduly complicate the reorganization proceedings and at worst undermine Borne's attempts to rehabilitate its business and preserve its assets for the benefit of its creditors and employees. By valuing the ultimate merits of the Rolfite stockholders' claims at zero, and temporarily disallowing them until the final resolution of the state action, the bankruptcy court avoided the possibility of a protracted and inequitable reorganization proceeding while ensuring that Borne will be responsible to pay a dividend on the claims in the event that the state court decides in the Rolfite stockholders' favor. Such a solution is consistent with the Chapter 11 concerns of speed and simplicity but does not deprive the Rolfite stockholders of the right to recover on their contingent claims against Borne.

III.

The Rolfite stockholders further contend that, regardless of the method which the bankruptcy court used to value their claims, the court based its estimation on incorrect findings of fact. Rule 810 of the Rules of Bankruptcy Procedure permits an appellate court to overturn a bankruptcy referee's findings of fact only when they are clearly erroneous. This standard of review is identical to that required by Rule 52(a) of the Federal Rules of Civil Procedure for findings of fact determined by a trial court sitting without a jury. As is the case when reviewing the discretionary decisions of the bankruptcy court, an appellate court does not have wide latitude to substitute its own judgment for the factual findings of such a court. Only when the appellate court is firmly convinced that the bankruptcy court erred in its findings may these findings be reversed. *United States v. United States Gypsum Co.*, 333 U.S. 364, 395, 68 S.Ct. 525, 542, 92 L.Ed. 746 (1948). A bankruptcy court may not, however, mask its interpretation of the law as findings of fact. In determining the legal merits of a case on which claims such as those of the Rolfite stockholders are based, the bankruptcy court should be guided by the applicable state law. The determination of such law is of course subject to plenary review.

The clearly erroneous standard of review is as applicable to a bankruptcy court's ultimate finding of fact as it is to the subsidiary facts on which such a finding is based. As recently noted by the United States Supreme Court:

> Rule 52 broadly requires that findings of fact not be set aside unless clearly erroneous. It does not make exceptions or purport to exclude certain categories of factual findings from the obligation of a Court of Appeals to accept a district court's findings unless clearly erroneous. It does not divide facts into categories; in particular, it does not divide findings of fact into those that deal with "ultimate" and those that deal with "subsidiary" facts.

Pullman–Standard v. Swint,—U.S.—,—,102 S.Ct. 1781, 1789, 72 L.Ed.2d 66 (1982).

The Rolfite stockholders urge that "[a]n application of [the clearly erroneous] rule is relaxed where, as here, the initial decision rests, not on the oral testimony of parties and witnesses, but on an examination of documentaries undisputed or stipulated evidence. This principle reflects sensible deference to the equal ability of the appeal court to review and evaluate such evidence." Brief for Appellants at 29–30. We question whether cases suggesting such an interpretation of Rule 52(a) have any continuing authority in light of the interpretation of that rule announced in *Pullman–Standard v. Swint*. That case recognizes that substituting the factual inferences of one tribunal for those drawn by another does not in any real sense increase the certainty of the factfinding process, but does impinge seriously upon society's interest in the finality of judgments. Only when the trial court's factual findings are clearly erroneous should an appellate court intervene. Then the need to maintain the credibility of judgments outweighs the interest in finality. But in any event, even treating the matter originally, we would draw the same inferences with respect to the value of the claims as did the bankruptcy court.

The Rolfite stockholders argue that in assessing the merits of its state court action for the purpose of evaluating their claims against Borne, the bankruptcy court erred both in finding the facts and in applying the law. In reviewing the record according to the standards we have just described, we cannot agree. The first such error to which they point is the bankruptcy court's conclusion that Borne had the right to unilaterally terminate its manufacturing contract upon reasonable notice. While the Rolfite stockholders may quarrel with the bankruptcy court's choice of cases to support this conclusion, the court correctly defined the applicable law. *See* N. J. Stat. Ann § 12A:2–309, New Jersey Study Comment 2, and Uniform Commercial Code Comment 7. The court's finding that Borne reasonably terminated its contract with Rolfite is amply supported by the record and thus not clearly erroneous.

The Rolfite stockholders also assert that the bankruptcy court erred both in its treatment of their legal theory in the state court and in its finding that Borne did not act with malice. Whether the Rolfite action is characterized as one for malicious prosecution or as one for malicious interference with prospective business advantage, the bankruptcy court correctly found that proof of Borne's malice is an essential element. Again, the record supports the court's factual inference that such malice did not exist. While the evidence does not necessarily compel one to find that Borne had a good faith claim to those materials which it accuses Rolfite of pirating, a reasonable factfinder has a substantial basis for such a conclusion.

Finally, the Rolfite stockholders take issue with the bankruptcy court's determination that the aborted merger with Quaker was not caused by the initiation of Borne's suit. Once again, in light of the several reasonable inferences which can be drawn from Quaker's internal memorandum, this finding is not clearly erroneous.

The court's ultimate finding of fact—that the Rolfite stockholders' claims in the reorganization proceeding were worth zero—must also be upheld since it too is not clearly erroneous. The subsidiary findings of the court plainly indicated that the Rolfite counterclaim in the state action lacked legal merit. Faced with only the remote possibility that the state court would find otherwise, the bankruptcy court correctly valued the claims at zero. On the basis of the court's subsidiary findings, such an estimation was consistent both with the claims' present value and with the court's assessment of the ultimate merits.

IV.

The judgment appealed from will be affirmed.

Fortgang & King, *The 1978 Bankruptcy Code: Some Wrong Policy Decisions*

56 N.Y.U. L. Rev. 1148, 1149–53 (1981)

Postpetition Interest

A routine principle that was developed under the case law construing the Bankruptcy Act of 1898 was that interest on claims ceased to accrue as of the date a bankruptcy petition was filed. Except for two subdivisions of section 63, there was no specific provision in the statute dealing with postpetition interest. The courts, however, developed a policy that the accrual of interest should cease as a matter of convenience and efficiency in the administration of bankrupt estates; cessation avoided the necessity for recomputation of interest each time a distribution of dividends was made to creditors. In cases in which the assets of the debtor were insufficient to pay all of the claims of creditors, cessation did not change the actual amounts paid to creditors, since claims were paid on a pro rata basis. This principle of convenience was a deviation from the more general principle that a creditor was entitled to be paid the full amount of the debt, including the principle amount owed and interest accrued to the date of payment.

The drafters of the new Bankruptcy Code were not content to permit the judicially developed principle of convenience to continue. Instead, several sections of the Code explicitly deal with postpetition interest in technical detail. Specifically, section 502(b)(2) of the Code provides that a claim for unmatured interest is not allowable.

The House and Senate committee reports accompanying the Code make clear that this provision requires disallowance of interest unmatured at the date of the filing of the petition, including both postpetition interest not yet due and any portion of prepaid interest that represents "an original discounting of the claim."

Postpetition interest under the Code, as distinguished from the Bankruptcy Act, explicitly is made a *nonallowable* part of a creditor's claim.

The nonallowability of such claims has important ramifications under the Bankruptcy Code, just as it did under the Bankruptcy Act. Nonallowed claims are not entitled to any distribution in a case, whether it be a chapter 7 liquidation case or a chapter 11 reorganization case. Section 726 of the Code, which establishes the order of distribution of property of the estate for liquidation cases, includes as the second rung of the payment ladder "any allowed unsecured claim." In chapter 11, only holders of allowed claims are entitled to accept or reject plans. Pursuant to the "cramdown" provisions of section 1129(b)(2)(B), an unaccepting class of unsecured claims may be forced to accept a plan even if a class lower than it is to receive a distribution, as long as the unaccepting class receives property under the plan "equal to the allowed amount" of the claims of that class. These sections are not exhaustive of the provisions that refer to the concept of allowability; the concept is one that permeates the entire Code.

Moreover, the concept of allowability is inflexible. Under the Bankruptcy Act, courts would invoke the general principle that a creditor is entitled to full payment if the convenience factor was not present. If an estate proved to be solvent, the notion that it would be inconvenient to recompute interest was not invoked. The rationale was that, in this instance, the nonpayment of postpetition interest would permit the return of property to the debtor while creditors were not being paid in full—a patently unjust result. Section 502(b)(2), on the other hand, appears absolute on its face. Section 502, read simply and applied exclusively, provides that postpetition interest is not an allowable part of a claim. This appears to be so even if the debtor's assets have a value in excess of all its liabilities including postpetition interest.

A. *Chapter 7 Liquidation Cases*

Under chapter 7, there is one exception, in section 726(a)(5), to the absolute rule of section 502(b)(2): If an estate is solvent, before the debtor is entitled to retain any property of the estate, creditors are required to receive postpetition interest in an amount computed at the "legal rate." Interestingly, neither the statute nor the legislative history defines "legal rate." Legal rate may mean (i) the rate set statutorily by each state to be paid on judgments of its courts; (ii) the rate agreed to contractually by the parties (as long as it is not usurious) or, if no rate has been agreed to, the rate set forth in (i) above; or (iii) the market rate of interest at the particular time.

Some courts have assumed that "legal rate' means the statutory rate applied by each state to the payment of judgments.

If that assumption ultimately is given judicial sanction, then the Code will produce inequitable results. For instance, assume that a creditor's claim is based on a loan agreement that provides for the payment of interest at the rate of 15% per annum, that the statutory rate applied to the payment of judgments in the particular state is 7%, and that the estate turns out to be solvent. If there were more than sufficient value to provide for the liabilities set forth in the first four levels of priority in section 726, then, under section 726(a)(5), the creditor's claim would be allotted 7% interest from the date of the filing of the petition until the date of payment, instead of the

15% interest for which the creditor had bargained. The allowed portion of the creditor's claim would also include the principal unpaid balance plus interest at the rate of 15% *up to* the date of the filing of the petition. But even if the bankruptcy case had been pending for eighteen months, the creditor would be entitled to recover interest of only 7% for the entire period after the date of filing.

Thus, the debtor would be permitted to retain value directly at the expense of the creditor. Ordinarily, bankruptcy laws and rules affect the rights of creditors in favor of or at the expense of other creditors by changing the rules that would prevail outside a bankruptcy court in order to more equitably allocate the values of the debtor among the creditors.

The alteration of a valid, binding, and legal contractual obligation, so that the debtor retains nonexempt property prior to the payment of its valid debts, is a legally startling and somewhat appalling result. Under this "legal rate' theory, the Bankruptcy Code effectively states that the statutory rate of interest is preferred to the rate of interest to which the parties have themselves agreed and that the difference should be retained by the debtor. There does not appear to be any substantial policy consideration that would sanction this result.

Another interplay of sections similarly indicates that the statutory provisions dealing with postpetition interest were not fully thought through. In the illustration above, it was posited that a surplus would be returned to the debtor even though unsecured creditors did not receive the full amount of postpetition interest to which they were contractually entitled. Section 727(a)(1) of the Code, however, bars a corporation or a partnership from receiving a discharge in a chapter 7 case. Thus, a creditor would retain a contractually enforceable claim with respect to such a debtor. The creditor presumably would be able to recover from the debtor—if not voluntarily, then through a lawsuit in the appropriate forum—the difference between the statutory rate of interest which had been paid and the original contractual rate of interest. In order to insure the availability of funds to satisfy any subsequent judgment, the creditor would likely seek to attach or garnish funds in the hands of the chapter 7 trustee before any surplus was returned to the debtor.

This somewhat tortuous result indicates that a more reasoned and appropriate construction of section 726(a)(5) is that the statutory rate of interest should apply only to those creditors who have not bargained for an alternative rate. This would protect those creditors by providing them the rate of interest to which they would have been entitled had they obtained a judgment at the commencement of the case. With respect to creditors who had bargained for a rate of interest, the section would have no application and the bargained–for rate would apply. In view of the discharge provisions of section 727, this construction is more plausible and tenable.

NOTES AND QUESTIONS

1. In a chapter 7 case, § 726(a)(2)(C) permits a late filed claim to share ratably with other claims if the creditor did not have timely notice of the case. This

provision represents a substantial change from the law developed under the Bankruptcy Act. Does § 726 apply in chapter 13 cases? Did the court in the Collins case infer its applicability?

Section 726(a)(3) allows payment to a late filed claim (not entitled to payment under § 726(a)(2)(C)) from any surplus remaining after full payment to timely filed claims. In a chapter 13 case, is there any surplus? When, under *Collins*, would such a creditor be paid? In a lump sum or in installments? In one year or three?

2. Section 501(c) permits the debtor or trustee to file a claim on behalf of a nonfiling creditor. Why? When? *See* Rule 3004. Does the Code or the Rule extend the 90–day period for filing claims?

3. In *In re Middle Planatation, Inc.*, 36 B. R. 873, 10 C. B. C.2d 191 (Bankr. E. D.Va. 1984), the court held that Bankruptcy Rule 3003 does not meet due process requirements and is unconstitutional to the extent that it does not mandate notice to creditors with disputed, contingent or unliquidated claims in chapter 11 cases. Section 1111(a) of the Code provides that holders of scheduled claims which are not listed as disputed, contingent or unliquidated need not file proofs of claim; rather, the claim is deemed to have been filed. Section 502 provides that a filed proof of claim is deemed allowed unless objection is made to it. Thus, the double deeming approach for chapter 11 cases makes some paperwork unnecessary. If there were no Rule 3003(c)(2), would the court have held § 1111(a) unconstitutional?

  a. The notice of the meeting of creditors in a chapter 11 case warns creditors about the application of § 1111(a). It explicitly tells them that if their claim is scheduled as disputed, contingent or unluiquidated, they must file a proof of claim before the bar date for it to be allowed. Thus, creditors are told to check the schedules on file in the clerk's office to determine how the claim is scheduled. Is this not sufficient to pass constitutional muster?

  b. In advising a creditor–client about filing a proof of claim, what would you suggest? Is there any downside to filing a proof of claim?

---

§ 16.03 Priorities

Not all unsecured claims are treated in the same manner; some are more equal than others. Congress has determined that some claims should sometimes, for good and sufficient policy reasons, be paid before other claims are paid.

Section 507 sets forth the order or priority of claims. If there is sufficient money in the estate to pay the first priority, *i.e.*, expenses of administration (*see* § 503), payment will then be made to the next or second priority, and so on until all claimants entitled to priority have been paid. In the event funds still exist, the general body of unsecured creditors will receive a dividend. To determine how claims are then paid, it is necessary to turn to § 726. All in all, at least 14 rungs on the priority ladder or ladder of distribution may be counted.

QUESTIONS

1. With respect to § 507 generally, if there is not sufficient money to satisfy all the claims entitled to the second priority but there is some money left after paying the first priority claims, what should be the distribution?

2. Can you count 14 rungs on the distribution ladder? Should § 510 be included in the count? § 503? § 726? § 724? § 364?

3. How are claims entitled to priority under § 507(a) treated in chapter 11 and 13 cases?

ARTUS v. ALASKA DEPARTMENT OF LABOR
(In re Anchorage International Inn, Inc.)

United States Court of Appeals, Ninth Circuit
718 F.2d 1446 (1983)

FLETCHER, Circuit Judge:

This appeal is from the bankruptcy court's ruling (affirmed by the district court) that the provisions of an Alaska statute requiring payment of creditors of a liquor establishment before transfer of a liquor license are preempted by federal bankruptcy law. We have jurisdiction under 11 U.S.C. § 47(a)(1976) (repealed 1978) and reverse.

I.

On March 28, 1979, Anchorage International Inn, Inc. (Inn), the owner of an Alaska liquor license, was adjudicated a bankrupt. Prior to bankruptcy, the Inn had incurred two substantial debts arising out of the operation of a tavern connected to the Inn: (1) approximately $20,000 in taxes and employee withholding contributions due the State of Alaska, Department of Labor; and (2) approximately $143,000 in employee benefit contributions owed to the Alaska Hotel and Restaurant Employees Health & Welfare Trust and Pension Trust (Trust Funds).

During the bankruptcy proceedings, the trustee of the Inn arranged and secured the bankruptcy court's approval of the sale of the assets of the Inn, contingent upon approval of the transfer of the liquor license by the Alaska Alcoholic Beverage

Control Board (ABC Board). Under Alaska law, the ABC Board has sole authority to issue and transfer liquor licenses; no license may be transferred without ABC Board approval. The Alaska statute requires that approval of a transfer be denied if

> (4) The transferor has not paid all debts or taxes arising from the conduct of the business licensed under [the] title [governing alcoholic beverages] unless
>
>> (A) he gives security for the payment of the debts or taxes satisfactory to the creditors or taxing authority.

Alaska Stat. § 04.11.360(4)(A)(1982).

Relying on section 04.11.360(4)(A), the ABC Board initially denied the trustee's request for a license transfer because no arrangement had been made to pay the creditors of the liquor–related portion of the business. In order to facilitate sale of the assets of the Inn on the favorable terms arranged, the Trust Funds, the State, and the trustee entered into a stipulation under which the trustee promised to hold the proceeds from the sale of the license pending a judicial determination of their proper distribution. This stipulation constituted "security satisfactory to the creditors" as required under section 04.11.360(4)(A), permitting the ABC Board to approve transfer of the license to the purchaser. The proceeds are presently held by the trustee, to abide the result of this appeal.

On December 31, 1981, the bankruptcy court ordered that the $20,000 in state tax and contribution claims be paid first from the license sale proceeds, but denied any preferred right to payments from the sale proceeds to other liquor–related creditors of the debtor, including the Trust Funds. The court concluded that, because the license had been created by the State of Alaska, the Alaska statute did not conflict with federal law insofar as the statute required payment of state tax claims prior to transfer of the license.

As to the claims of the Trust Funds, however, the court ruled that the requirement of section 04.11.360(4) "that all general debts of the business be paid before a license may be transferred interfere[s] with the Bankruptcy Act's priority distribution scheme.' The court concluded that under the Supremacy Clause, the Alaska statute "may not be enforced where the transferor has initiated bankruptcy proceedings." The court ruled that application of the statute "in bankruptcy situations would frustrate the Bankruptcy Act's purpose of providing an equitable distribution of the bankrupt's non–exempt property to all creditors of the same class" and "would also frustrate the purpose of Congress to establish unified federal priorities."

The district court affirmed the bankruptcy court's decision. The Trust Funds timely took this further appeal. The trustee has not cross–appealed from the decision in favor of the State of Alaska.

II.

Appellants challenge the judgment below asserting that the Alaska statute does *not* "establish priorities" in contravention of the general system of priorities pertaining to unsecured claims against the bankrupt estate. Rather, they argue, section 04.11.360(4) simply establishes in effect a lien on one asset of the bankrupt (the liquor license), in favor of those creditors whose claims arose out of the use of the license. This "lien," like any encumbrance, reduces the value of the asset and diminishes what is available for distribution in accordance with the general priority scheme of the federal bankruptcy law. But, liens are not void in bankruptcy simply because they favor secured creditors at the expense of general creditors.

The trustee, in defense of the judgment, argues that the state cannot substitute its distribution scheme for that established under the Bankruptcy Act. According to the trustee, permitting payment of the claims related to the liquor business prior to payment of other claims would unconstitutionally frustrate the "primary" objective of the Bankruptcy Act: to provide for an equitable distribution of assets among all creditors. *See, e.g., Hassen v. Jones*, 373 F.2d 880, 881, 884 (9th Cir. 1967). She decries the notion of permitting some creditors of the bankrupt (*e.g.*, persons earning wages in the operation of the tavern) to be paid ahead of other creditors (*e.g.*, bedding manufacturers). She relies on *In re Leslie*, 520 F.2d 761 (9th Cir. 1975).

A.

As a preliminary matter, we must determine whether the Alaska statute gives the creditors of the licensed business a claim against the liquor license superior to that of other creditors of the bankrupt or whether it seeks simply to regulate license transfers without providing priority to the creditors of the liquor business. If the Alaska statute does not create a priority, the Trust Funds would have no superior right in bankruptcy to payment from the license sale proceeds. We would stop our analysis there.

The creditor of an owner of an Alaska liquor license, unlike the holder of a security interest or a mechanic's lien, cannot enforce the lien by self–help or by execution on the license. *See C.Y., Inc. v. Brown*, 574 P.2d 1274, 1277 (Alaska 1978). Nevertheless, the creditor's interest in the license is an encumbrance superior to the rights of others. The Alaska statute assures the liquor–related creditor that the sale of the license will not occur until his debt is paid or security satisfactory to him is provided. Other creditors whose debts are not related to the licensed business receive no similar assurances. Under Alaska law, the creditors of the liquor business do have a superior right to payment from the license sale proceeds.

Although the lien interest created by Alaska Stat. § 04.11.360(4) differs in form from other more typical creditor–protection devices such as a security interest or a materialman's lien, all serve the same function. Regardless of its label, each encourages the extension of credit by providing that, upon the occurrence of certain conditions, the creditor has a priority right to payment from a particular asset.

B.

Ordinarily, an asset subject to a lien such as the license in this case passes into the hands of the trustee on the date of filing subject to the lien. In this case, however, the bankruptcy court concluded that, since the Alaska statute "creates statutory priorities, not statutory liens or encumbrances on property," the license passed into the estate unencumbered except for the taxes due the State of Alaska. This was error.

For its rationale, the bankruptcy court relied heavily on In re Leslie, in which we stated in broad terms that "[c]onflicting priorities established by state law must yield upon the intervention of bankruptcy to superior federal law" and ruled that a California statute regulating the transfer of California liquor licenses "creates statutory priorities, not statutory liens." 520 F.2d 761, 762 (9th Cir. 1975). We directed that the proceeds of the sale of a liquor business (the assets of which included a liquor license) be paid according to the distribution scheme for general unsecured claims established by the Bankruptcy Act and not according to the California statutory scheme for allocation of proceeds among creditors when a California liquor business is sold. *Id. See also In re Professional Bar Co.*, 537 F.2d 339, 340 (9th Cir. 1976).

Although *Leslie* and this case seem similar, there are significant differences. In *Leslie*, at the time the petition in bankruptcy was filed, the liquor license (as well as the related business assets of the debtor) had already been sold and the proceeds placed in an escrow account. *See* 520 F.2d at 762. Under California law, consent to the sale of the license by the liquor–related creditors is not required. Thus, what the trustee received in *Leslie* was the cash proceeds from a sale of a liquor business, not a license transferable only on the approval of creditors. Since, at the time of filing, creditors of the debtor were free to attach or levy against the proceeds, *see id.* at 763, the *Leslie* court correctly concluded that the trustee took unencumbered title to the proceeds, *id.* at 762; 11 U.S.C. § 110(a)(5).

The California statute differs from the Alaska statute in two other regards. The California statute attempted to determine priorities in the distribution of the proceeds of the sale not only of the liquor business but also of all other assets of the licensed business. *See* 520 F.2d at 762–63; Cal. Bus. & Prof. Code § 24074 (West Supp. 1975). The statute further specified the order of distribution among all claims against the debtor, regardless of whether the particular claim was related to the liquor business. *See* 520 F.2d at 762; Cal. Bus. & Prof. Code § 24074.

By contrast, the Alaska statute establishes priority for one particular group of creditors in one specific asset. *See* Alaska Stat. § 04.11.360(4). Moreover, the creditors of the license holder can prevent the sale of the license unless the license transferor provides security "satisfactory to the creditors." *Id.* In this case, the ABC Board initially refused to allow the license to be sold and finally did so only after the creditors had agreed that the proceeds of the license sale were "satisfactory" security.

Given the significant differences in scope and effect between the California and Alaska statutes, we do not find the holding in *Leslie* controlling.

See In re Professional Bar Co., 537 F.2d 339, 340 (9th Cir. 1976) (creditor that state authorizes to prevent license transfer has valid preferred right in bankruptcy). Nothing in *Leslie* compels us to strike down the Alaska statute simply because it attempts to give certain creditors a preferred right in a particular asset.

We recognize, of course, that Congress has the authority to make uniform laws governing the subject of bankruptcies, *see* U.S. Const. art. I, § 8, cl. 4, and, pursuant to that authority, might invalidate in bankruptcy any or all prebankruptcy entitlements encumbering the debtor's assets. But Congress has not done so. The mechanic's lien and the security interest under the Uniform Commercial Code are but two examples of interests in particular property, created pursuant to state statutes, that are fully respected by the general bankruptcy law. The trustee's contention that states cannot allow some creditors to receive more of the proceeds of the sale of a bankrupt's assets than others receive is thus incorrect. No statutory bankruptcy policy forbids a state from giving one creditor a greater right to payment of his claim from a given asset than that conferred on another.

Perez v. Campbell, 402 U.S. 637, 649 (1971), which holds that a state statute is invalid if it "stands as an obstacle to the accomplishment and execution of the full purposes and objective of Congress," does not contradict our conclusion. In *Perez,* an Arizona statute, that conditioned the issuance of a driver's license to a discharged debtor on the payment of pre–bankruptcy debts, was held to be preempted. *Id.* at 652. The Arizona statute directly conflicted with the discharge provisions of federal bankruptcy law. *Id.* at 648, 652.

Here by contrast, the Alaska statute does not conflict with the federal distribution scheme because there is no general federal policy against state–created liens that favor one class of creditors over others. Section 04.11.360(4) does not, as the bankruptcy court concluded, frustrate the Act's "purpose of providing an equitable distribution of a bankrupt's non–exempt property to all creditors of the same class." Creditors who hold prior rights under the Alaska statute are simply not in the "same class" as other creditors.

C.

Since federal bankruptcy law does override state–created priorities that apply only in the event of bankruptcy, we must examine the statute to determine whether it in fact has force and effect independent of the bankruptcy proceeding. *See* 11 U.S.C. § 107(c)(1)(A). We conclude that the creditors' rights created by the Alaska statute exist independent of the debtor's insolvency and accordingly should be recognized by the trustee.

Regardless of when a license holder seeks to transfer an Alaska liquor license, all liquor–related claims must be paid first. *See C.Y., Inc. v. Brown,* 574 P.2d 1274, 1277 (Alaska 1978). The transfer caused by the trustee's need to liquidate the assets of the estate is no different from any other transfer in or outside of bankruptcy. Under Alaska law, the encumbrance has its full restrictive effect on the transfer of the underlying security (the liquor license) regardless of whether the transferor is or is not insolvent or undergoing a general distribution or liquidation of his property. The Alaska statute is not a bankruptcy distribution scheme in disguise.

Therefore, we hold that the Trust Funds have a prior right to the proceeds of the license sale to the extent of claims arising from the conduct of the licensed business.

III.

We *Reverse* the district court's ruling that the Bankruptcy Act preempts Alaska Stat. § 04.11.360(4) conditioning the transfer of an Alaska liquor license on the payment of debts arising from the conduct of the licensed business. We conclude that the proceeds of the sale of the license are to be used first to pay debts related to the licensed business. We therefore *Remand* for a determination of what portion of the $143,000 owed the Trust Funds arose from the "conduct of the business licensed."

Reversed and Remanded.

READING CO. v. BROWN

United States Supreme Court
391 U.S. 471, 88 S.Ct. 1759, 20 L. Ed 2d 751 (1968)

Mr. Justice HARLAN delivered the opinion of the Court.

On November 16, 1962, I. J. Knight Realty Corporation filed a petition for an arrangement under Chapter XI of the Bankruptcy Act, 11 U.S.C. §§ 701–799. The same day, the District Court appointed a receiver, Francis Shunk Brown, a respondent here. The receiver was authorized to conduct the debtor's business, which consisted principally of leasing the debtor's only significant asset, an eight–story industrial structure located in Philadelphia.

On January 1, 1963, the building was totally destroyed by a fire which spread to adjoining premises and destroyed real and personal property of petitioner Reading Company and others. On April 3, 1963, petitioner filed a claim for $559,730.83 in the arrangement, based on the asserted negligence of the receiver. It was styled a claim for "administrative expenses' of the arrangement. Other fire loss claimants filed 146 additional claims of a similar nature. The total of all such claims was in excess of $3,500,000, substantially more than the total assets of the debtor.

On May 14, 1963, Knight Realty was voluntarily adjudicated a bankrupt and respondent receiver was subsequently elected trustee in bankruptcy. The claims of petitioner and others thus became claims for administration expenses in bankruptcy which are given first priority under § 64a (1) of the Bankruptcy Act, 11 U.S.C. § 104 (a)(1). The trustee moved to expunge the claims on the ground that they were not for expenses of administration. It was agreed that the decision whether petitioner's claim is provable as an expense of administration would establish the status of the other 146 claims. It was further agreed that, for purposes of deciding whether the claim is provable, it would be assumed that the damage to petitioner's property resulted from the negligence of the receiver and a workman he employed. The United States, holding a claim for unpaid prearrangement taxes admittedly superior to the claims of general creditors and inferior to claims for administration expenses, entered the case on the side of the trustee.

The referee disallowed the claim for administration expenses. He also ruled that petitioner's claim was not provable as a general claim against the estate, a ruling challenged by neither side. On petition for review, the referee was upheld by the

District Court. On appeal, the Court of Appeals for the Third Circuit, sitting *en banc*, affirmed the decision of the District Court by a 4–3 vote. We granted certiorari, 389 U.S. 895, because the issue is important in the administration of the bankruptcy laws and is one of first impression in this Court. For reasons to follow, we reverse.

Section 64a of the Bankruptcy Act provides in part as follows:

> The debts to have priority, in advance of the payment of dividends to creditors, and to be paid in full out of bankrupt estates, and the order of payment, shall be (1) the costs and expenses of administration, including the actual and necessary costs and expenses of preserving the estate subsequent to filing the petition.

It is agreed that this section, applicable by its terms to straight bankruptcies, governs payment of administration expenses of Chapter XI arrangements. Furthermore, it is agreed that for the purpose of applying this section to arrangements, the words "subsequent to filing the petition" refer to the period subsequent to the *arrangement* petition, and the words "preserving the estate" include the larger objective, common to arrangements, of operating the debtor's business with a view to rehabilitating it.

The question in this case is whether the negligence of a receiver administering an estate under a Chapter XI arrangement gives rise to an "actual and necessary' cost of operating the debtor's business. The Act does not define "actual and necessary," nor has any case directly in point been brought to our attention. We must, therefore, look to the general purposes of § 64a, Chapter XI, and the Bankruptcy Act as a whole.

The trustee contends that the relevant statutory objectives are (1) to facilitate rehabilitation of insolvent businesses and (2) to preserve a maximum of assets for distribution among the general creditors should the arrangement fail. He therefore argues that first priority as "necessary" expenses should be given only to those expenditures without which the insolvent business could not be carried on. For example, the trustee would allow first priority to contracts entered into by the receiver because suppliers, employees, landlords, and the like would not enter into dealings with a debtor in possession or a receiver of an insolvent business unless priority is allowed. The trustee would exclude all negligence claims, on the theory that first priority for them is not necessary to encourage third parties to deal with an insolvent business, that first priority would reduce the amount available for the general creditors, and that first priority would discourage general creditors from accepting arrangements.

In our view the trustee has overlooked one important, and here decisive, statutory objective: fairness to all persons having claims against an insolvent. Petitioner suffered grave financial injury from what is here agreed to have been the negligence of the receiver and a workman. It is conceded that, in principle, petitioner has a right to recover for that injury from their "employer," the business under arrangement, upon the rule of respondeat superior.

Respondents contend, however, that petitioner is in no different position from anyone else injured by a person with scant assets: its right to recover exists in theory but is not enforceable in practice.

That, however, is not an adequate description of petitioner's position. At the moment when an arrangement is sought, the debtor is insolvent. Its existing creditors hope that by partial or complete postponement of their claims they will, through successful rehabilitation, eventually recover from the debtor either in full or in larger proportion than they would in immediate bankruptcy. Hence the present petitioner did not merely suffer injury at the hands of an insolvent business: it had an insolvent business thrust upon it by operation of law. That business will, in any event, be unable to pay its fire debts in full. But the question is whether the fire claimants should be subordinated to, should share equally with, or should collect ahead of those creditors for whose benefit the continued operation of the business (which unfortunately led to a fire instead of the hoped–for rehabilitation) was allowed.

Recognizing that petitioner ought to have some means of asserting its claim against the business whose operation resulted in the fire, respondents have suggested various theories as alternatives to "administration expense" treatment. None of these has case support, and all seem to us unsatisfactory.

Several need not be pursued in detail. The trustee contends that if the present claims are not provable in bankruptcy they would survive as claims against the shell. He also suggests that petitioner may be able to recover from the receiver personally, or out of such bond as he posted. Without deciding whether these possible avenues are indeed open, we merely note that they do not serve the present purpose. The "master," liable for the negligence of the "servant" in this case was the business operating under a Chapter XI arrangement for the benefit of creditors and with the hope of rehabilitation. That benefit and that rehabilitation are worthy objectives. But it would be inconsistent both with the principle of *respondeat superior* and with the rule of fairness in bankruptcy to seek these objectives at the cost of excluding tort creditors of the arrangement from its assets, or totally subordinating the claims of those on whom the arrangement is imposed to the claims of those for whose benefit it is instituted.

The United States, as a respondent, suggests instead that tort claims arising during an arrangement are, if properly preserved, provable general claims in any subsequent bankruptcy under § 63a of the Act, 11 U.S.C. § 103 (a). That section reads as follows:

> Debts of the bankrupt may be proved and allowed against his estate which are founded upon (7) the right to recover damages in any action for negligence instituted prior to and pending at the time of the filing of the petition in bankruptcy.

It is agreed by all parties that this section will not avail the present petitioner who, it appears, did not file suit on its claim prior to the bankruptcy proper. This, the United States argues, is its own fault: it could have filed suit after the tort, during the arrangement, and before the petition in bankruptcy, and thus preserved its claim.

This was not the view of the District Court. Section 302 of the Act, the section which provides that Chapters I to VII of the Act (including §§ 63 and 64) shall be applicable to arrangements under Chapter XI as well as straight bankruptcies, contains the following provision:

For the purposes of such application the date of the filing of the petition in bankruptcy shall be taken to be the date of the filing of an original petition under section 722 of this title [§ 322 of the Act, 11 U.S.C. § 722, which provides for filing original petitions for arrangements].

Section 378 (2) of the Act, 11 U.S.C. § 278 (2), dealing with procedure when bankruptcy ensues upon an arrangement, provides that

in the case of a petition filed under section 722 of this title, the proceeding shall be conducted, so far as possible, in the same manner and with like effect as if a voluntary petition for adjudication in bankruptcy had been filed and a decree of adjudication had been entered on the day when the petition under this chapter [i.e., the petition for an arrangement] was filed.

The effect of these two sections is that, whether or not an arrangement is superseded by bankruptcy, for purposes of applying § 63 to arrangements the date of the arrangement petition is deemed to be the date of a petition in bankruptcy.

From this fact, the District Court concluded, and petitioner now argues, that a person negligently injured during the course of an arrangement could never have a provable general claim under § 63a. For that section requires that suit be filed before the filing of the petition in bankruptcy, and, when the section is applied to an arrangement, the date of the filing of the petition in bankruptcy is deemed to be the date of the filing of the arrangement petition.

In response, the United States notes that § 378 (2) is qualified by the words "so far as possible." The Government therefore suggests a holding that it is not "possible" to treat the date of the arrangement petition as the critical date in a case such as the present, because that point in time antedates the tort. On that theory, it is suggested that, for present purposes, § 63a's reference to the date of filing the bankruptcy petition be taken to refer to the date of the petition in bankruptcy proper.

We do not find this an acceptable alternative. The only thing that renders it not "possible" to follow the statutory scheme and meld the arrangement into the bankruptcy is the Government's insistence that petitioner's claim must be held to have been provable under § 63a if only petitioner had taken the proper steps. There is nothing "impossible" about construing the sections here involved to mean what they say: a tort claim arising during an arrangement, like a tort claim arising during a bankruptcy proceeding proper, is not provable as a general claim in the bankruptcy.

There are additional reasons for reading the sections literally in this case. In the first place, the United States' suggestion will not work where bankruptcy does not ensue upon the arrangement, for then there is no later date that can be used as the cutoff for § 63a (7) claims. In that case, it would be necessary either to hold that a tort claim arising during an arrangement is a provable general claim if bankruptcy ensues but is not a provable general claim in the arrangement itself, or to hold that there is no time limit on filing suit so long as the arrangement remains an arrangement. Nothing in the qualifying language of § 378 (2) grants permission to read the time limitation out of § 63a (7) of the Act.

An even greater difficulty is presented by the fact that § 63a refers to provable debts of the *bankrupt*, and distinguishes the bankrupt from his *estate*. Section 302 provides that in applying § 63a to arrangements, the word "bankrupts" shall be deemed to relate also to "debtors." Thus the natural reading of § 63a, when applied to arrangements as if they were bankruptcies, is that in order to be provable under 63a (7) a tort claim must be a claim against the debtor and not against the estate in a Chapter XI arrangement. Respondents might argue this question as they do the time limitation: that it would be preferable to deem the words "debts of the bankrupt" to mean "debts of the debtor or of his estate arising up to the time of bankruptcy proper." This argument is open, however, to the same objections as the argument on time limitations: it is a strained reading of the statute which makes no allowance for the occasions when straight bankruptcy does not ensue.

In any event, we see no reason to indulge in a strained construction of the relevant provisions, for we are persuaded that it is theoretically sounder, as well as linguistically more comfortable, to treat tort claims arising during an arrangement as actual and necessary expenses of the arrangement rather than debts of the bankrupt. In the first place, in considering whether those injured by the operation of the business during an arrangement should share equally with, or recover ahead of, those for whose benefit the business is carried on, the latter seems more natural and just. Existing creditors are, to be sure, in a dilemma not of their own making, but there is no obvious reason why they should be allowed to attempt to escape that dilemma at the risk of imposing it on others equally innocent.

More directly in point is the possibility of insurance. An arrangement may provide for suitable coverage, and the court below recognized that the cost of insurance against tort claims arising during an arrangement is an administrative expense payable in full under § 64a (1) before dividends to general creditors. It is of course obvious that proper insurance premiums must be given priority, else insurance could not be obtained; and if a receiver or debtor in possession is to be encouraged to obtain insurance in adequate amounts, the claims against which insurance is obtained should be potentially payable in full. In the present case, it is argued, the fire was of such incredible magnitude that adequate insurance probably could not have been obtained and in any event would have been foolish; this may be true, as it is also true that allowance of a first priority to the fire claimants here will still only mean recovery by them of a fraction of their damages. In the usual case where damages are within insurable limits, however, the rule of full recovery for torts is demonstrably sounder.

Although there appear to be no cases dealing with tort claims arising during Chapter XI proceedings, decisions in analogous cases suggest that "actual and necessary costs" should include costs ordinarily incident to operation of a business, and not be limited to costs without which rehabilitation would be impossible. It has long been the rule of equity receiverships that torts of the receivership create claims against the receivership itself; in those cases the statutory limitation to "actual and necessary costs" is not involved, but the explicit recognition extended to tort claims in those cases weighs heavily in favor of considering them within the general category of costs and expenses.

In some cases arising under Chapter XI it has been recognized that "actual and necessary costs" are not limited to those claims which the business must be able to pay in full if it is to be able to deal at all. For example, state and federal taxes accruing during a receivership have been held to be actual and necessary costs of an arrangement.

The United States, recognizing and supporting these holdings, agrees with petitioner that costs that form "an integral and essential element of the continuation of the business" are necessary expenses even though priority is not necessary to the continuation of the business. Thus the Government suggests that "an injury to a member of the public—a business invitee—who was injured while on the business premises during an arrangement would present a completely different problem [*i.e.*, could qualify for first priority]" although it is not suggested that priority is needed to encourage invitees to enter the premises.

The United States argues, however, that each tort claim "must be analyzed in its own context." Apart from the fact that it has been assumed throughout this case that all 147 claimants were on an equal footing and it is not very helpful to suggest here for the first time a rule by which lessees, invitees, and neighbors have different rights, we perceive no distinction: No principle of tort law of which we are aware offers guidance for distinguishing, within the class of torts committed by receivers while acting in furtherance of the business, between those "integral" to the business and those that are not.

We hold that damages resulting from the negligence of a receiver acting within the scope of his authority as receiver give rise to "actual and necessary costs" of a Chapter XI arrangement.

The judgment of the Court of Appeals is reversed, and the case remanded for further proceedings consistent with this opinion.

It is so ordered.

Mr. Justice MARSHALL took no part in the consideration or decision of this case.

Mr. Chief Justice WARREN, with whom Mr. Justice DOUGLAS joins, dissenting.

In my opinion, the Court has misinterpreted the term "costs and expenses of administration" as intended by § 64a (1) of the Bankruptcy Act and, by deviating from the natural meaning of those words, has given the administrative cost priority an unwarranted application. The effect of the holding in this case is that the negligence of a workman may completely wipe out the claims of all other classes of public and private creditors. I do not believe Congress intended to accord tort claimants such a preference. Accordingly, I would affirm the judgment below.

On other occasions, the Court has observed that "[t]he theme of the Bankruptcy Act is equality of distribution"; and if one claimant is to be preferred over others, the purpose should be clear from the statute." *Nathanson v. NLRB*, 344 U.S. 25, 29 (1952); *see Sampsell v. Imperial Paper Corp.*, 313 U.S. 215, 219 (1941). More particularly, the Act expressly directs that eligible negligence claims are to share equally with the unsecured claims in a pro rata distribution of the debtor's nonexempt assets. Bankruptcy Act § 63a (7), 65a, 11 U.S.C. § 103 (a)(7), 105(a). Departing from this statutory scheme, the Court today singles out one class of tort claims for special treatment. After today's decision, the status of a tort claimant depends entirely upon whether he is fortunate enough to have been injured after rather than before a receiver has been appointed. And if the claimant is in the select class, he may be permitted to exhaust the estate to the exclusion of the general creditors as well as of the wage claims and government tax claims for which Congress has shown an unmistakable preference. In my view, this result frustrates rather than serves the underlying purposes of a Chapter XI proceeding, and I would not reach it without a clear indication that Congress so intended.

Congress enacted Chapter XI as an alternative to straight bankruptcy for individuals and small businesses which might be successfully rehabilitated instead of being subjected to economically wasteful liquidation. The success of a Chapter XI proceeding depends largely on two factors: first, whether creditors will take the chance of permitting an arrangement; second, whether other businesses will continue to deal with the distressed business. With respect to the first of these considerations, today's decision will undoubtedly discourage creditors from permitting arrangements, because it subjects them to unpredictable and probably uninsurable tort liability. I do not believe the statutory language requires such an interpretation. I would construe § 64a (1) with reference to the second consideration mentioned above. In my opinion, the Court would reach a result more in line with congressional intent and the Bankruptcy Act generally by regarding as administrative costs only those costs required for a smooth and successful arrangement. Accordingly, the administrative cost priority should be viewed as a guaranty to the receiver and those who deal with or are employed by him that they will be paid for their goods and services. Any broader interpretation will discourage creditors from permitting use of the rehabilitative machinery of Chapter XI and tend to force distressed businesses into straight bankruptcy.

It is equitable, the Court believes, that the general creditors (and wage and tax claimants) bear the loss in this case because they have "thrust" an insolvent business upon petitioner for their own benefit. I respectfully submit that this is a most unfair characterization of arrangements. An economically distressed businessman seeks an arrangement for his own and not for his creditors' benefit.

Of course the creditors will benefit if the arrangement is successful, just as they would have benefited if the businessman had been successful without resorting to an arrangement. But a business in arrangement is no more thrust on the public than is any other business enterprise which is conducted for the mutual prosperity of the owners, the wage earners and the creditors. Realistically, the only difference is that a business administered under Chapter XI has not been prosperous. If the arrangement is successful, the owners, wage earners and creditors will all benefit; if it is not, they will all be injured. Thus, I would not distinguish in this case between petitioner and the other general creditors, none of whom was responsible for the catastrophe for which all of them must sustain some loss. Instead, in deciding this case, I would adhere to the Act's basic theme of equality of distribution.

The Court states that its decision will encourage Chapter XI receivers to obtain "adequate" insurance. The Court fairly well concedes, however, that in this case "adequate" insurance "probably could not have been obtained and in any event would have been foolish." In other words, so far as this Court knows, the insurance taken out by the receiver in this case was in fact "adequate," in the sense that no reasonable receiver could or should obtain fire insurance in the amount of $3,500,000 on the assumption that his workman might accidentally cause a fire of the proportions which occurred here. Moreover, quite apart from the case at bar, there is absolutely no indication that today's decision is needed to encourage receivers to obtain insurance. I see no basis in the Act or in sound policy for a ruling that the creditors of an estate under a Chapter XI arrangement become involuntary insurers against a liability which probably would not and should not be insurable by more traditional means.

The Court also relies, in my opinion mistakenly, upon analogies to equity receiverships. In reorganizations under Chapter X and § 77, Congress has directed the courts to apply the rules of priority developed in equity. However, arrangements under Chapter XI are governed strictly by the statutory priorities fixed by § 64a. These statutory priorities differ in many respects from those applicable to equity receiverships, and they have been amended repeatedly to narrow the class of claimants which may participate ahead of the general creditors. Furthermore, even in the case of § 77 reorganizations where the priorities developed in equity are controlling, Congress has specifically provided for one exception to the rule that tort claimants are to be treated as general creditors. Bankruptcy Act § 77(n), 11 U.S.C. § 205(n). That exception is in favor of a narrowly defined class of claimants. Congress has not expressly provided a similar exception to cover petitioner's tort claim, and I would not infer one.

Finally, the Court concludes, for two reasons, that it is "linguistically more comfortable" to treat petitioner's claim as an administrative cost rather than as a negligence claim which could have been proven under § 63a(7). First, § 63a refers to provable claims against the debtor and not against his estate. Second, § 63a(7) and 302 require that an action be commenced on the claim before the filing of the arrangement petition, and allowing claims like petitioner's would in effect toll the time limitation imposed by these sections. With respect to the first of the Court's reasons, I find no statutory or practical basis for distinguishing between the debtor and his estate in this case. Had the arrangement been successful, the debtor would have been liable for any damages occasioned during the administration under the line of cases relied upon by the Court. *Texas & Pacific R. Co. v. Bloom*, 164 U.S. 636 (1897). The suggested distinction between "debtor" and "estate" would be meaningful only if the two words pointed to different sources of liability. Here, petitioner's negligence claim, if allowed, would diminish the debtor's estate irrespective of whether it were treated as an administrative cost under § 64a or as an ordinary negligence claim under § 63a(7). With respect to the Court's second argument, Chapter XI provides that the straight bankruptcy provisions, including § 63a(7), are applicable to arrangement proceedings only "so far as possible." Bankruptcy Act § 378(2), 11 U.S.C. § 778(2). I have no difficulty in concluding that, where the claim does not arise until after the arrangement petition is filed, it is manifestly impossible for a lawsuit on that claim to precede the filing of the petition. Further, I know of no more complete way to the time limitation out of § 63a(7) of the Act than by treating certain negligence claims as administrative costs as the Court does in this case.

I see no basis in equity or in the statutory language or purpose for subjecting every class of creditors except petitioner's to a loss caused by the negligence of a workman. Consequently, I would construe "actual and necessary costs" as limited to those costs actually and necessarily incurred in preserving the debtor's estate and administering it for the benefit of the creditors. I would not include ordinary negligence claims within this class.

IN RE WILNOR DRILLING, INC.

United States District Court, Southern District of Illinois
29 B.R. 727, 8 C.B.C.2d 1045, 10 B.C.D. 457 (1983)

WILLIAM L. BEATTY, District Judge

Before the Court is an appeal of the Bankruptcy Court's order denying the motion of Securities and Exchange Commission for reconsideration, entered June 29, 1982. The Bankruptcy Court affirmed its earlier ruling that the fees and expenses of the Investors' Committee will be subordinated to the reasonable fees and expenses of the Creditors' Committee. The issue on appeal is whether the Bankruptcy Court erred in subordinating the fees and expenses of the Investors' Committee to the reasonable fees and expenses of the Creditors' Committee.

On or about November 2, 1981, Wilnor Drilling, Inc., Mason Oil Company, William R. and Elenora D. Mason, and William R. Mason Petroleum, Inc., filed voluntary petitions for a business reorganization pursuant to Chapter 11 of the United States Bankruptcy Code. 11 U.S.C. Section 1101 *et seq.* Subsequent to that date, on or about November 30, 1981, Teresella Petroleum, Inc. also filed for a voluntary petition for a business reorganization under Chapter 11. The Bankruptcy Court appointed a committee of creditors (the Official Creditors' Committee) as required by Section 1102(a)(1) of the Bankruptcy Code. 11 U.S.C. Section 1102(a)(1).

The Securities and Exchange Commission (Commission) filed a motion, on or about March 1, 1982, to appoint a committee of investors. The motion was filed pursuant to Section 1102(a)(2) of the Bankruptcy Code which allows the Court to appoint "additional committees of creditors or equity security holders if necessary to assure adequate representation of creditors or of equity security holders." 11 U.S.C. Section 1102(a)(2).

The Bankruptcy Court determined that the investors who sought to have a committee appointed had interests in various oil wells of the debtors. As a result of these interests, the Bankruptcy Court found that the investors were "creditors" of the debtors as defined in Section 101(9)(a) of the Bankruptcy Code, 11 U.S.C. Section 101(9). By the order of March 23, 1982, the Bankruptcy Court granted the motion of the Commission to allow a separate committee (the Official Investors' Committee) to assure adequate representation and protection of the investors' interests. However, the Bankruptcy Court held that the expenses and fees of the Investors' Committee should be subordinated to the reasonable fees and expenses of the Creditors' Committee to assure the proper functioning of the Creditors' Committee.

The Commission filed a motion to reconsider the portion of the March 23rd order subordinating the fees and expenses of the Investors' Committee. The Bankruptcy Court denied the motion for reconsideration by memorandum order issued June 29, 1982. The Court stated that the Creditors' Committee is a mandatory committee under the Code, while the Investment Committee is only discretionary. *See* 11 U.S.C. Section 1102(a)(1), (a)(2). The Court further noted that since it is Congress' intent to make the Creditors' Committee the principal committee, then it is reasonable to subordinate the fees and expenses of other committees to the reasonable fees and expenses of the Creditors' Committee. The Court held that "the only reason the fees and expenses of the Investors' Committee were subordinated to the reasonable fees and expenses of the Creditors' Committee was to admonish the Investors' Committee that the Court would *equitably subordinate* (emphasis added) their fees and expenses in the event there were not enough assets to cover all of the reasonable fees and expenses." June 29th Order.

We respectfully reverse the decision of the Bankruptcy Court to subordinate the fees and expenses of the Investors' Committee to the reasonable fees and expenses of the Creditors' Committee for two reasons. First, the Bankruptcy Court should not fix priorities of payment within the same class when Congress has not set up an order of priority. *In re Columbia Ribbon Co.*, 117 F.2d 999, 1001 (3rd Cir. 1941). Second, three conditions must be satisfied before a Court should equitably subordinate one claim to another claim. *Matter of Mobile Steel Co.*, 563 F.2d 692 (5th Cir. 1977).

It is well established that "the courts of bankruptcy are courts of equity and exercise all equitable powers unless prohibited by the Bankruptcy Act." *Young v. Higbee Company*, 324 U.S. 204 (1945). The proceedings of the Court are inherently proceedings in equity. *In re: Jewish Memorial Hospital* 13 B. R. 417 (Bankr. SD NY 1981). "The bankruptcy court has the power to shift the circumstances surrounding any claim to see that injustice or unfairness is not done in administration of the bankrupt estate." *Pepper v. Litton*, 308 U.S. 295 (1939). The priorities for payment of expenses and claims are set forth in Section 507(a) of the Bankruptcy Code. *See* 11 U.S.C. Section 507(a). While Congress has set the order of priorities payment under the Bankruptcy Act, strict adherence to the order is not always necessary. The Bankruptcy Act does not establish inexorable rules of priority and distribution. The Bankruptcy Court may deviate from the rules in the interest of justice and equity. *Home Indemnity Company v. F.H. Donovan Painting Company*, 325 F.2d 870 (8th Cir. 1963). However, the Court should not use this flexibility merely to establish a ranking of priorities within priorities. *In re: Jewish Memorial Hospital, supra* at 421.

The Bankruptcy Court appointed both the Creditors' Committee and the Investors' Committee. 11 U.S.C. 1102. The fees and expenses of both committees are included as administrative expenses defined by Section 503(b)(2) of the Bankruptcy Code. 11 U.S.C. Section 503(b)(2). As a result of being administrative expenses, the fees and expenses of both committees constitute the first priority of payment under the Bankruptcy Code. 11 U.S.C. Section 507(a)(1). Section 507(a)(1) of the Bankruptcy Code does not set forth a priority of payment within the first class. By subordinating the fees and expenses of the Investors' Committee to the reasonable fees and expenses of the Creditors' Committee, the Bankruptcy Court has set up a priority within the class of administrative expenses. "Since Congress has set up no order of priority within the first class the Court may not fix priorities within the class." *In re: Columbia Ribbon Company, supra* at 1001. The fact that the Creditors' Committee is a mandatory appointment while the Investors' Committee is only a discretionary appointment is not sufficient reason for equitable subordination. Since the fees and expenses of both committees are in the class of administrative expenses, they are a parity as to payment. *In re Western Farmers Association*, 13 B. R. 132. (Bankr. WD WA 1981). The Bankruptcy Code does not make any distinction between a mandatory committee (11 U.S.C. Section 1102(a)(1)) and a discretionary committee (11 U.S.C. Section 1102(a)(2)) when describing the powers and duties of the committees in Section 1103 of the Bankruptcy Code. 11 U.S.C. Section 1103. Thus, Congress' intention is not to differentiate between the two types of committees. This idea must be inferred to the payment of priorities. The two claims are of the single class of administrative expenses and are of equivalent priority in the class. *Missouri v. Ross*, 299 U.S. 72 (1936). Therefore, if there is the possibility that there are not sufficient assets to pay all the costs of administration, then it is legally improper to subordinate the fees and expenses of the Investors' Committee to the fees and expenses of the Creditors' Committee. *In re Western Farmers Association, supra* at 136.

The Bankruptcy Court has the equitable power to disallow or subordinate a particular claim because of the fraudulent nature of the claim or bad faith or improper conduct of the claimant. *In re Columbia Ribbon Company supra* at 1002. The Court must find that actions or conduct by the claimant has harmed the debtor or other creditors in some way so that equity and fairness justify equitable subordination. *In re Ahlswede* 516 F.2d 784 (9th Cir. 1975). Furthermore, a three part criteria has been promulgated as a guideline to use in deciding whether a claim should be subordinated:

> (i) The claimant must have engaged in some type of inequitable conduct. (ii) The misconduct must have resulted in injury to the creditors of the bankrupt or conferred an unfair advantage on the claimant. (iii) Equitable subordination of the claim must not be inconsistent with the provisions of the Bankruptcy Act (citations omitted).

Matter of Mobile Steel Co. 563 F.2d 692 (5th Cir. 1977).

The Court cannot find any reason that justice and equity will be served by subordinating the fees and expenses of the Investors' Committee to the reasonable fees and expenses of the Creditors' Committee. The Investors' Committee claim to reasonable fees and expenses is not fraudulently represented through bad faith or inequitable conduct. Similarly, the Investors' Committee did not engage in any conduct which caused harm or injury to the debtors or other creditors, rendering to them an unfair advantage. Finally, the Bankruptcy Code does not contain any express or implicit authority to subordinate the fees and expenses of a mandatory committee to the fees and expenses of a discretionary committee. In fact, the Bankruptcy Code does not differentiate between the two types of committees in any respect. *See* 11 U.S.C. Section 703. Thus, the Bankruptcy Court had no authority to subordinate the Investors' Committee's fees and expenses.

The Bankruptcy Court relied on the rules stated in *Home Indemnity Company v. F.H. Donovan Painting Company, supra* that "[A]ccording to controlling equitable principles, a surety may not share in a bankrupt's assets ahead of or on equal terms with any creditors who are members of the class the surety's bond had been given to protect." 325 F.2d at 875. Home Indemnity Company was surety for labor, material, and performance bonds which were executed by Donovan, a sub-contractor. Donovan subsequently went bankrupt and Home Indemnity Company had to pay $17,474.25 in past due wages to employees of Donovan. Home Indemnity Company's wage claim, a second priority, was subordinated to fourth priority tax claims because of its surety relationship with the debtor.

In the present case, the Investors' Committee is not a surety of Investors. The Bankruptcy Court did appoint the Investors' Committee to "protect" the interest of the investors. However, this did not establish a surety relationship between the two. The Investors' Committee is appointed to assure adequate representation of the investors. *See* 11 U.S.C. Section 1102(a)(2). The rule in the *Home Indemnity* case applies only when there is a surety relationship. Since the Investors' Committee is not a surety, the Bankruptcy Court erred in applying the rule in the *Home Indemnity* case pertaining to sureties to the present case. Accordingly, the Court reverses the portion of the Bankruptcy Court's order which subordinated the fees and expenses of the Investors' Committee to the reasonable fees and expenses of the Creditors' Committee. Since each claim is an administrative expense of the first priority, they will share in the distribution pro rata in the event that there are insufficient assets to satisfy in full all claims in that class. This case is hereby remanded to the Bankruptcy Court.

NOTES AND QUESTIONS

1. What is encompassed by the second priority?

2. The sixth priority is an addition made by the Bankruptcy Code. It benefits consumer creditors, but in the Senate bill, S. 2266 would have followed the tax priority. A compromise was reached between the Senate and House by reducing the amount but retaining it ahead of taxes.

3. In chapter 11 cases, the official creditors' committee is entitled to its expenses, *e.g.*, fees for its attorneys and other professionals as an expense of administration, *see* § 503. Suppose a committee member incurs expense in attending meetings, e.g., travel, food, lodging. Are these expenses reimbursable as expenses of administration? At all? *See* 1994 amendments adding § 503(b)(3)(F). May the attorney for the member be compensated from the estate?

§ 16.04   Subordination; § 510

§ 510(a) and (c) codifies case law developed under the 1898 Act. Subsection (b) is new to the code and is meant to clarify and provide a solution for problems that had arisen under the Act. The basic problem was whether a defrauded stockholder could, by asserting a fraud claim in a Chapter X case, bootstrap its position from equity to creditor and participate in a plan at a higher level. The Code adopts the argument and conclusions suggested in Slain & Kripke, *The Interface Between Securities Regulation and Bankruptcy—Allocating the Risks of Illegal Securities Issuance Between Securityholders and the Issuer's Creditors*, 48 N. Y. U. L. Rev. 261 (1973).

Pursuant to § 510(b), on what rung of the distributive latter would a defrauded common stockholder stand with respect to the damage claim held by the stockholder resulting from the purchase of the security?

IN RE EATON FACTORS CO.

Bankruptcy Court, Southern District of New York
3 B.R. 20, 1 C.B.C.2d 286, 5 B.C.D. 1205 (1980)

BABITT, Bankruptcy Judge:

The bankrupt, Eaton Factors Co., Inc., formerly in the factoring and financing business, was adjudged bankrupt following the filing against it of an involuntary petition.

The trustee, in keeping with the discharge of the duties imposed by Section 47a(8) of the 1898 Bankruptcy Act, 11 U.S.C. § 75a(8), and Rule 306(a), 411 U.S. 1046, to examine claims and take appropriate action, now moves for an order enforcing, as against the unsecured claimants affected, the subordination provisions of notes and debentures issued to them by the bankrupt in favor of the senior bank and financial lending institutional creditors. The trustee also asks the court to fix the class of senior creditors entitled to have dividends otherwise payable to the subordinated creditors distributed *pro rata* to that class.

Turning to the first part of the relief requested, the trustee plaintiff has submitted exhibits in support of his request for subordination and various affidavits from some of the senior leaders. Exhibit (or Schedule) "A" lists the claims of twenty creditors (excluding duplications) who timely filed against the estate but who are affected by this motion because they are holders of subordinated notes of Eaton Factors, in the aggregate amount of $168,970.00. Exhibit "B" is a sample copy of such notes, and contains, on its face, the following:

By acceptance of this note, the payee hereby agrees (1) that the payment of the principal sum or any part hereof, and the interest due thereon is and shall remain subject and subordinated to any indebtedness of Eaton Factors Co., Inc. to any lending institutions whether private or public, Bank, Finance or Discount Company.

Exhibit (or schedule) "C" lists the claims of 67 creditors (excluding duplications) who have timely filed claims in the aggregate amount of $566,757.03, based on debentures issued by the bankrupt and which debentures state that

Payment of this debenture, both principal and interest shall, in case of any bankruptcy or other similar proceedings, voluntary or otherwise, of or with respect to the Corporation, be subordinated to all liabilities and obligations of the Corporation then existing to any banks or lending institutions and, in order to effectuate such subordinations, the provisions hereof shall constitute an assignment of the amounts payable hereon to such banks and lending institutions, pro rata in accordance with the amounts of their respective claims; and such banks and lending institutions shall be entitled to prove or assert any and all claims with respect to the debentures, for their pro rate sic benefit, and to receive and apply to the payment in full of their respective claims against the Corporation all dividends and other distributions and payments which may be payable with respect thereto.

Thus, the trustee seeks the legal enforcement of the above–mentioned subordination provisions, and has been joined in his application by various senior lenders

A hearing was held before this court upon notice to all the affected creditors. Several affected creditors opposed the trustee at the hearing, including one who filed a letter of objection to the instant motion. The tenor of the objections was that the persons holding the notes and debentures involved were not aware of the subordination provisions when they purchased their shares, due in part to the casual manner in which the debentures issued by Eaton Factors were, unfairly, not uniform, in that some contained subordination provisions and others did not. Thus, "equitable" grounds are pressed to this court to deny the enforcement of the subordinations.

There can no longer be question that subordination agreements are enforced by bankruptcy courts. 3A Collier on Bankruptcy (14th edition 1975) ¶ 65.02[2] states that:

Section [64a] of the Bankruptcy Act, for reasons of public policy, creates priorities regardless of the parties' contracts and overrides inconsistent covenants. But this does not mean that the parties are prohibited from making contracts for a priority or subordination in so far as they do not impinge upon statutory priorities. Section 65a means no more than that dividends paid to creditors shall be pro rata except where there is a priority given by law or by lawful contractual arrangement between the parties. *Matter of Aktiebolaget Kreuger & Toll*, 96 F.2d 768 (2d Cir. 1938). *See also In re Credit Industrial Corp.*, 366 F.2d 402, 410 (2d Cir. 1966) and *S. E .C. v. White & Co., Inc.*, 546 F.2d 789, 792 (8th Cir. 1976).

The objections raised by some of the affected creditors to the enforcement of the subordination clauses have been voiced before in the bankruptcy context. *In re Credit Industrial Corp., supra; In the Matter of Stirling Homex Corp.,* 579 F.2d 206 (2d Cir. 1978); *In the Matter of Weis Securities, Inc.,* 425 F. Supp. 212 (S.D.N.Y. 1977), unreported affirmance (2d Cir. June 12, 1978).

In the *Credit Industrial Corp.* case, the bankrupt corporation (CIC) sought to enforce the subordination provision of its high–interest promissory notes for the benefit of its institutional lenders. Objecting creditors asserted, among other things, that the institutional lenders had not shown that they had advanced funds in reliance on the subordination agreements, and further that the agreements were invalid since CIC had fraudulently induced the noteholders to accept them. *Id.,* at 405.

The Court of Appeals stated that:

> In bankruptcy, the parties claiming rights to participate in the assets of the bankrupt must do so in accordance with such contractual rights against the debtor as they may have purchased or acquired. Attention, therefore, must be focused on the contract upon the basis of which the noteholders loaned various amounts to CIC.

Id., at 407. Looking to the contracts there involved, the CIC court held that the subordination agreements were lawful, their terms explicit and consensual, and that therefore equitable considerations, such as reliance, were not relevant to the enforceability of the provisions.

In *Matter of Stirling Homex Corp., supra,* a Chapter X case, the court held that tort claims of allegedly defrauded stockholders were subordinate to those of the debtor's general unsecured creditors on the premise that the loss to stockholders should not be reimbursed by innocent general creditors. While Stirling Homex is not controlling in the instant motion, the court did note that

> [a]s a general rule equity prefers the claims of innocent general creditors over the claims of shareholders or subordinated creditors deceived by officers of the corporation.

Id., at 213.

And, as stated by the Court of Appeals in *First National Bank of Hollywood v. American Foam Rubber Corp.,* 530 F.2d 450, 454 (2d Cir. 1976).

> Various theories have been advanced to support the enforcement of subordination agreements in bankruptcy: equitable lien, equitable assignment, constructive trust and enforcement of contractual rights. (Citations omitted). This circuit has favored the recognition of priorities based upon the "lawful contractual arrangements between the parties."

In short, the motion before the court clearly falls under the guiding principles of CIC, *et al.* The debenture and note holders here held contractually–based interests, the terms of which are clearly laid out on the face of the documents. Whether or not these investors were aware of what type of interest they were purchasing, there was no ambiguity as to the meaning or enforceability of these subordination provisions.

It is not inappropriate at this point to examine the language and intent of the 1978 Bankruptcy Reform Act, effective October 1, 1979. While the new Code does not control the administration of this case, Section 403(a), this court may construe the former Act in harmony with the Code, where no explicit inconsistent provision exists. *U.S. ex rel Hintopoulos v. Shaughnessy*, 353 U.S. 72, 78 (1957). *See also In re Stirling Homex Corp., supra*, at 214–215.

Section 510(a) of the new Code, 11 U.S.C. § 105(a), provides that:

> A subordination agreement is enforceable in a case under this title to the same extent that such agreement is enforceable under applicable nonbankruptcy law.

Thus, there can be no more question but that the agreements presented here in the form of lawful, written contracts, are enforceable in the administration of this bankrupt estate.

The only remaining question is the determination of the class of senior creditors entitled to the benefits of this enforcement of subordination agreements. According to the trustee, 13 senior claimants are entitled to enforce the subordination agreements. Their claims, though not yet finally determined for purposes of allowability, amount to just under $2 million.

Representatives of four of the senior leaders have submitted affidavits to this court showing the amount and timely filing of their claims, and establishing that they are "banks" or "lending institutions" within the meaning of the provisions contained in the notes and debentures. Such a showing on the part of all creditors claiming the right of subordination satisfies the court that they are indeed entitled thereto. Those other lenders claiming the benefit of the enforcement of these subordination agreements are to submit proof of their status to the trustee within ten days from entry of the order to be submitted in conformity with this decision, in such form as will satisfy him that they are entitled to the same position as those who filed affidavits on this motion.

WILSON v. HUFFMAN
(In re Missionary Baptist Foundation of America)

United States Court of Appeals, Fifth Circuit
712 F.2d 206 (1983)

POLITZ, Circuit Judge:

This appeal requires an examination of the "insider status" contemplated by Section 101(25) of the Bankruptcy Code of 1978, 11 U.S.C. § 101(25) (1978), and the subordination of an insider's claim pursuant to Section 510(c)(1) of the Code, 11 U.S.C. § 510(c)(1). We affirm the resolution of the insider status issue and remand for further findings and consideration of the subordination issue.

Facts

Land Wall, president, controller and director of Missionary Baptist Foundation of America, Inc. (MBFA), a religious non–profit corporation, filed a petition for reorganization of that corporation and its seven wholly–owned subsidiaries, together considered as one entity, under Chapter 11 of the Bankruptcy Code. The debtor's schedules included two promissory notes which are the subject of this appeal. These notes represent obligations of the debtor to Robert G. Huffman, claimant herein, and result from several transactions involving (1) Huffman, (2) Wall, (3) their partnership known as Wall and Huffman, (4) West Texas Home Health Care, Inc. (West Texas Homes), a nursing home management corporation owned by Huffman and Wall, and (5) one or more of MBFA's subsidiaries.

Huffman and Wall established both their partnership, Wall and Huffman, and their corporation, West Texas Homes, in 1975. The partnership purchased Dumas Convalescent Center, a nursing home in Dumas, Texas, borrowing $228,000 from a commercial lender to cover the downpayment and the costs of needed improvements. Huffman had no personal exposure on this loan. Shortly thereafter the partnership contracted with West Texas Homes for the operation of the facility. Wall handled the financial details; Huffman was involved exclusively in management.

In early 1977, Wall individually purchased the Crestview Home in Throckmorton, Texas. He entered into a management contract with West Texas Homes identical to that for the Dumas home. On February 1, 1977, Wall transferred his interest in Crestview to Pampas Enterprises, a partnership composed of himself and three family members. That same day Pampas subleased the property to West Texas Homes.

Crestview and Dumas were sold to MBFA in April 1977. Under the terms of this package sale, MBFA assumed all indebtedness encumbering the properties and agreed to pay $148,014 for the equity. Huffman and Wall, individually, each received a promissory note for $74,007, secured by a second lien on the Dumas property. Through this *en globo* transaction Huffman shared equally with Wall in the equity in Crestview, despite the former's apparent lack of a proprietary interest therein.

Contemporaneously with the sale of the Dumas and Crestview homes, West Texas Homes assigned its contractual rights in both homes to MBFA receiving therefor two unsecured promissory notes, each in the amount of $88,860. West Texas Homes was subsequently dissolved and in the distribution of its assets, its shareholders, Huffman and Wall, each received one of the $88,860 notes.

Through August of 1980, MBFA made periodic payments to Huffman on the $74,007 and $88,860 notes. When the petition in bankruptcy was filed, MBFA's books reflected a balance of $37,170.96 owed Huffman on the $74,007 note. Although the corporate books did not evidence the $88,860 note, MBFA's representatives acknowledged the existence of a debt in this amount to West Texas Homes. The debtor's schedules reflected an aggregate balance on the two notes in favor of Huffman of $119,005.

The trustee formally objected to Huffman's claim, contending that MBFA was not indebted to him on the $88,860 note nor for the $37,170.96 balance because the $74,007 note was invalid as the product of an arrangement by Huffman and Wall designed to improperly extract monies from the debtor. The bankruptcy court found, *inter alia*, that Wall's ownership or control of the debtor placed him within the definition of "insider of the debtor,' 11 U. S. C. § 101(25)(B). Recognizing that Huffman's connection with MBFA differed from Wall's, the bankruptcy court then addressed the question whether Huffman could be characterized as an insider because of his business relationship with Wall and his stock ownership in West Texas Homes.

The bankruptcy judge found that MBFA's acquisition of the Dumas and Crestview homes and West Texas Homes' contractual position were effected by Wall on a less than arms–length basis. The judge concluded that because West Texas Homes was an affiliate of the debtor under 11 U.S.C. § 101(2)(B), its conveyance of the $88,860 note to Huffman was an insider transaction. Further, the judge determined that the $74,007 indebtedness to Huffman, in his capacity as general partner of a partnership which controlled the debtor, likewise resulted from an insider transaction.

Based on these findings, the bankruptcy judge allowed the $119,005 claim but ordered it subordinated under 11 U.S.C. § 510(c)(1) to those of the general unsecured creditors. The district court affirmed the bankruptcy court in all respects, concluding that there had been sufficient findings to justify the subordination of Huffman's claim under the three–pronged test we enunciated in *Matter of Mobile Steel Co.*, 563 F.2d 692 (5th Cir. 1977).

On appeal, Huffman contends that the bankruptcy court erred in imputing insider status to him because of MBFA's association with West Texas Homes and the Wall and Huffman partnership. He further contends that there were insufficient findings to support the application of the equitable subordination doctrine outlined in *Matter of Mobile Steel Co.* We disagree with the first contention and agree with the second.

Standard of Review

Findings of fact made in a bankruptcy proceeding will not be set aside unless clearly erroneous. *See Northern Pipeline Construction Co. v. Marathon Pipeline Co.,*—U.S.—, 102 S.Ct. 2858, 73 L.Ed.2d 598 [6 C.B.C.2d 785] (1982); *In re Reed*, 700 F.2d 986 [8 C.B.C.2d 370] (5th Cir. 1983). A finding of fact is clearly erroneous "when although there is evidence to support it, the reviewing court on the entire evidence is left with a firm and definite conviction that a mistake has been committed." *United States v. United States Gypsum Co.*, 333 U.S. 364, 395, 68 S.Ct. 525, 542, 92 L.Ed. 746 (1948). Strict application of the clearly erroneous rule is particularly important, where, as here, the district court has affirmed the bankruptcy judge's findings. *In re Garfinkle*, 672 F.2d 1340 (11th Cir.1982) (citing *DeMet v. Harralson*, 399 F.2d 35 (5th Cir. 1968)). This rigorous standard does not constrain appellate scrutiny of conclusions of law, which are subject to plenary review. *In re Bubble Up Delaware Inc.*, 684 F.2d 1259 (9th Cir. 1982); *Matter of Multiponics, Inc.*, 622 F.2d 709 (5th Cir. 1980). *See Pullman–Standard v. Swint*, 456 U.S. 273,

102 S.Ct. 1781, 72 L.Ed.2d 66 (1982). When a finding of fact is premised on an improper legal standard, or a proper one improperly applied, that finding loses the insulation of the clearly erroneous rule. *Smith v. Hightower*, 693 F.2d 359 (5th Cir. 1982).

Huffman as an Insider

The district court considered the determination by the bankruptcy court that Huffman was an insider to be a finding of fact which was not shown to be clearly erroneous. Huffman argues that we should make an independent analysis of the finding and, regardless of the standard applied, he contends that there is insufficient evidence to establish his insider status on either of the subject notes. We perceive the insider determination to be a question of fact.

According to the legislative history, an insider under 11 U.S.C. § 101(25) is an entity or person with "a sufficiently close relationship with the debtor that his conduct is made subject to closer scrutiny than those dealing at arms length with the debtor." S. Rep. No. 95-989, 95th Cong., 2d Sess., reprinted in [1978] U.S. Code Cong. & Admin. News, pp. 5787, 5810. *See* Phillips, *Insider Provisions of the New Bankruptcy Code*, 55 Am. Bank L. J. 363 (1981). If the debtor is a corporation, its insiders may include any officer, director, controlling person, partnership in which the debtor is a general partner, general partner of the debtor, or relative of a general partner, director, officer, or controlling person. § 101(25)(B).

Use of the word "includes" in ¶ 101(25) evidences Congress' expansive view of the scope of the insider class, suggesting that the statutory definition is not limiting and must be flexibly applied on a case-by-case basis. S. Rep. No. 95-989, 95th Cong., 2d Sess., *reprinted in* [1978] U.S.Code Cong. & Admin.News, p. 5812; Note, *The Term "Insider" Within § 547(b)(4)(B) of the Bankruptcy Code*, 57 Notre Dame Law. 730 (1982). *See* 2 L. King, Collier on Bankruptcy § 101.25 (15th ed. 1983). *See also Matter of Montanino*, [4 CBC.2d 362] 15 B. R. 307 (D. N.J. Bkrtcy. 1981).

Encompassed within the insider concept are entities or persons who can be classified as affiliates of the debtor or insiders of an affiliate, § 101(25)(E), both groups being presumed to have a close relationship with the debtor. S. Rep. No. 95-989, 95th Cong., 2d Sess., *reprinted in* [1978] U.S. Code Cong. & Admin. News, p. 5807; H. Rep. No. 95-595, 95th Cong., 2d Sess., *reprinted in* [1978] U.S. Code Cong. & Admin. News, p. 6265; Phillips, *Insider Provisions*, 55 Am. Bank. L. J. at 363.Section 101(2) provides:

affiliate means—

    (A)   entity that directly or indirectly owns, controls, or holds with power to vote, 20 percent or more of the outstanding voting securities of the debtor, other than an entity that holds such securities—

    (i)   in a fiduciary or agency capacity without sole discretionary power to vote such securities; or

    (ii)   solely to secure a debt, if such entity has not in fact exercised such power to vote;

(B) corporation 20 percent or more of whose outstanding voting securities are directly or indirectly owned, controlled, or held with power to vote, by the debtor, or by an entity that directly or indirectly owns, controls, or holds with power to vote, 20 percent or more of the outstanding voting securities of the debtor, other than an entity that holds such securities—

(i) in a fiduciary or agency capacity without sole discretionary power to vote such securities; or

(ii) solely to secure a debt, if such entity has not in fact exercised such power to vote;

(C) person whose business is operated under a lease or operating agreement by a debtor, or person substantially all of whose property is operated under an operating agreement with the debtor, or

(D) entity that operates the business or all or substantially all of the property of the debtor under a lease or operating agreement;

By using the word "means" rather than "includes,' Congress enacted a precise and restricted definition. 2 L. King, Collier on Bankruptcy ¶ 101.00[2]; Note, *The Term "Insider,"* 57 Notre Dame Law. at 733 n. 52. As explained in the Senate Report, the phrase "directly or indirectly' envisions "situations in which there is an opportunity to control, and where the existence of that opportunity operates as an indirect control." S. Rep. No. 95–989, 95th Cong., 2d Sess., reprinted in [1978] U.S. Code Cong. & Admin. News, p. 5807.

In finding that West Texas' assignment of the $88,860 note was an insider transaction, the bankruptcy court held that West Texas Homes, a corporation 20 percent or more of whose outstanding voting securities were owned by Wall, was an affiliate within the intendment of § 101(2)(B). Having determined that Wall was an alter ego2 of the debtor, the bankruptcy court concluded that MBFA could thus be deemed to own or control 50 percent of West Texas Homes' stock. Huffman does not challenge the legal identification of Wall with the debtor for purposes of this action, but assigns error in the judge's reference to evidence offered in other proceedings and at other times in this reorganization case in arriving at the finding.

A court may take judicial notice of the record in prior related proceedings, and draw reasonable inferences therefrom. *See Kinnett Dairies, Inc. v. Farrow,* 580 F.2d 1260 (5th Cir. 1978); *State of Florida Board of Trustees v. Charley Toppino & Sons, Inc.,* 514 F.2d 700 (5th Cir. 1975). Here, the bankruptcy court referred to the record developed in the same case, albeit in different proceedings. Although we intend no blanket approval of this action, we cannot gainsay the bankruptcy court's "right to take notice of its own files and records and [the absence of] any duty [on its part] to grind the same corn a second time." *Aloe Creme Labs. v. Francine Co.,* 425 F.2d 1295, 1296 (5th Cir. 1970). Both parties were aware that the principal issue was whether Wall's predetermined role as an insider of the debtor could be imputed to Huffman. The case was thus presented. Huffman had ample opportunity to submit evidence on this issue.

We are persuaded that as to the $88,860 note, Huffman was an insider of an affiliate within the intendment of 11 U.S.C. § 101(2). By definition, an insider of an affiliate is an insider of the debtor under 11 U.S.C. § 101(25)(E). In light of the interrelationship of all transactions, this finding of Huffman's insider status with respect to the $88,860 note is dispositive as to the $74,007 note, inasmuch as the components of Huffman's claim are not sufficiently discrete to warrant separate treatment.

Equitable Subordination

Upon finding that Huffman played an insider's role in the pertinent transactions with the debtor, the bankruptcy court subordinated his $119,005 claim pursuant to § 510(c), assigning no specific reasons therefor. Huffman asserts that the trustee failed to establish an adequate evidentiary basis for equitable subordination.

Section 510(c) permits the bankruptcy court, in the exercise of its equitable jurisdiction, to apply pre–Code principles of equitable subordination. 3 Collier on Bankruptcy ¶ 510.04. The courts have recognized three general categories of conduct considered sufficient to warrant equitable subordination: (1) fraud, illegality, breach of fiduciary duties; (2) undercapitalization; and (3) claimant's use of the debtor as a mere instrumentality or alter ego. *See* Cohn, *Subordinated Claims: Their Classification and Voting Under Chapter 11 of the Bankruptcy Code*, 56 Am. Bank. L.J. 295 (1982); Note, *Deep Rock in the Deep South—Equitable Subordination of Claims in Fifth Circuit Bankruptcy Proceedings*, 11 Cum. L. Rev. 619 (1980).

We adopted a triad test for the equitable subordination of claims in bankruptcy in *Matter of Mobile Steel Co.*:

(i) The claimant must have engaged in some type of inequitable conduct.

(ii) The misconduct must have resulted in injury to the creditors of the bankrupt or conferred an unfair advantage on the claimant.

(iii) Equitable subordination of the claim must not be inconsistent with the provisions of the Bankruptcy [Code].

563 F.2d at 700 (citations omitted). *Accord, Matter of Multiponics, Inc.*

A claim filed pursuant to § 501 enjoys prima facie validity which may be overcome by the trustee's presentation of evidence. A claim arising out of dealings between a debtor and its fiduciaries is to be rigorously scrutinized by the courts, *Matter of Multiponics; Matter of Mobile Steel Co.*, but mere proof of a fiduciary relationship is insufficient to invalidate a transaction. To sustain an objection, the trustee must overcome the presumption of validity which attaches to all properly filed claims. Upon the trustee's submission of sufficient evidence to overcome the prima facie showing, the claimant is obliged to prove his good faith and fairness in the dealings. It is at this juncture that the fiduciary's claim is subject to the probing light of judicial inquiry. We observed in *Multiponics* that "[t]his proof allocation provides a proper balance of burdens, assuring that the trustee does not underprove his objections while, at the same time, assuring that the fiduciary need not overprove his good faith and fairness at the mere cry of inequity by the trustee." 622 F.2d at 714.

Notwithstanding the bankruptcy judge's failure to assign reasons, the district court discerned sufficient findings of fact corresponding to each of *Mobile's* three components to justify the order of subordination. Specifically, the district court stated that the following findings by the bankruptcy judge were supported by the evidence and fulfilled the requirements of our articulation of the equitable subordination doctrine: (1) Huffman and Wall engaged in inequitable conduct in 1977 in the context of MBFA's acquisition of the Dumas and Crestview Homes and West Texas Homes' contractual rights therein; (2) these transactions conferred an unfair advantage on both Huffman and Wall; and (3) the subordination of Huffman's claim was consistent with the Bankruptcy Code.

These findings, though perhaps inherent in the bankruptcy court's ruling, were not enunciated. Though we agree that Huffman's insider connection with the debtor compels close examination of his claim, we cannot conclude, in the absence of explicit findings by the bankruptcy court on each element of the *Mobile* test, that the trustee has discharged his burden of proof thereunder. Whether or not Huffman's insider status, coupled with his receipt of the fruits of Wall's manipulations, is tantamount to the unfairness, bad faith or unconscionable wielding of control for personal gain envisioned by *Mobile* and *Multiponics* is problematical, in light of our holding that "an objection on equitable grounds cannot be merely formal, but rather must contain some substantial factual basis to support its allegation of impropriety.' *Matter of Mobile Steel Co.*, 563 F.2d at 701.

Under the totality of the circumstances of this case, therefore, we are persuaded that a remand to the bankruptcy court for entry of the findings required for application of this circuit's equitable subordination test is necessary. On remand, the bankruptcy court should set forth its relevant findings and conclusions under each element of the test we impressed in *Matter of Mobile Steel Co.*

Affirmed in part, *Reversed* and *Remanded* for further proceedings.

CHAPTER 17

THE DEBTOR'S BENEFITS

§ 17.01   The Bankruptcy Discharge

As a generalization, the bankruptcy law has two basic purposes:

1. to provide an equitable distribution to unsecured creditors of the proceeds from the debtor's nonexempt property; and,

2. to provide the honest debtor with a discharge from the debts or, stated somewhat differently, to permit the honest debtor a new financial life. Many cases have referred to this as the "fresh start" doctrine.

This section will consider the second of the two listed purposes, the bankruptcy discharge. At the outset, it should be noted that the discharge granted to the debtor is not dependent on the first of the two listed purposes, that is, it is not necessary that the debtor have property available for distribution to creditors in order to be entitled to a discharge. There is no such *quid pro quo* requirement. As a matter of fact, it is this very lack which renders the United States law so radically different from the law in most other nations. Many countries either do not have the concept of the bankruptcy discharge at all, or require that the debtor pay a rather high percentage of the debts owed before becoming entitled to the discharge.

There are essentially three aspects to the bankruptcy discharge. Under what circumstances should it be denied? When it is granted, what debts nevertheless remain nondischarged? What is the effect of the discharge? These aspects will be considered separately.

The first section of this chapter is concerned with the discharge. Section 727 of the Bankruptcy Code specifies who is entitled to a discharge and under what circumstances one so entitled may be denied a discharge.

Section 727 is applicable in chapter 7 cases but not, generally, in chapter 11 cases. Is there a practical difference? In a chapter 11 case, which is available to corporations, partnerships and individuals, a discharge is obtained when the plan of reorganization is confirmed by the court. *See* §1141. Why is there a difference, as to the ability to obtain a discharge, between a chapter 7 case and a chapter 11 case?

In a chapter 13 case, a discharge may be obtained when all payments required by the plan to be made to creditors have been completed. *See* § 1328(a). Section 727(a) contains a variety of acts, any one of which may be used by creditors or the trustee to commence a proceeding to bar the debtor's discharge. Are these acts also applicable to bar a chapter 13 debtor's discharge? May the acts, or any one of them, be used to bar a chapter 11 debtor's discharge? What provision in § 727 extends or limits its applicability? *See* § 103.

(Matthew Bender & Co., Inc.)   (Pub.094)

A chapter 13 debtor may find that circumstances beyond the debtor's control render it extremely difficult or impossible to maintain the payment schedule called for by the confirmed plan. The debtor may apply for and obtain an order from the court excusing further compliance. *See* § 1328(b). In this situation, however, the debtor's discharge is not as broad as that provided for in § 1328(a). Why should there be this difference?

The acts that are contained in § 727 which would bar a discharge are, for the most part, acts of dishonesty or having a dishonest tinge. One that is not so tainted is set forth in § 727(a)(9). It provides, essentially, that a debtor may not obtain a discharge in bankruptcy more frequently than once every six years, a slight Congressional revision of the Biblical direction that debtors must be discharged every seven years. Why did Congress settle on six years? Under the Bankruptcy Act of 1898, § 14c(5) also prohibited the granting of discharge more frequently than once in six years.

The Commission on the Bankruptcy Laws of the United States recommended that the six–year period be reduced to five years and that the court have discretion to waive the five–year bar if the nonpayment of debts was due to causes beyond the debtor's control and payment out of future income or wealth would constitute an undue hardship. See Report of the Commission on the Bankruptcy Laws of the United States, Part II, § 4–505(a)(7)(1973). This suggestion was incorporated in S. 2565, 93d Cong., 1st Sess. (1973), as § 4–505(a)(7). In a later House bill, however, the period was set forth as seven years. H.R. 6, 95th Cong., 1st Sess. (1977), § 727(a)(8). In the course of compromises, the respective Houses of Congress settled on what had been the former law, six years.

In the materials that follow, other acts barring a discharge will be considered. In this context, you may wish to think about the role being played by the bankruptcy process as related to the criminal process. At the conclusion of this section, that relationship will be more fully explored.

BURTRUM v. LAUGHLIN
(In re Laughlin)

Bankruptcy Court, Western District of Missouri
7 B.R. 924, 3 C.B.C.2d 552 (1981)

STEWART, Bankruptcy Judge:

The plaintiff in this action complains that the defendant transferred property within a year preceding bankruptcy with the intent to hinder, delay, or defraud her within the meaning of § 727(a)(2)(A) of the Bankruptcy Code . . .

I.

The facts of this action are simple but quite compelling. The defendants owned, as of July 1979, a tract of land of considerable value. They also owed the plaintiff an unsecured indebtedness of considerable magnitude, which she had long but unsuccessfully attempted to collect from them. At length, on or about July 13, 1979, she filed suit to collect the indebtedness in the Circuit Court of McDonald County. After the defendants had been served with summons in that action and thereby had actual knowledge of its pendency (a fact which the defendant Melvin A. Laughlin initially denied in his testimony in this action, but eventually admitted) on August 1, 1979, Melvin A. Laughlin and his wife conveyed the subject real property to their son and daughter–in–law. The son and daughter–in–law subsequently transferred the property to the latter's parents. Now owned by them, according to the defendant's testimony, it is neither occupied nor used by them nor by anyone else.

The defendants do not deny any of the above and foregoing facts. But they contend that in undertaking this transfer within a year of the filing of the petition herein for relief (which was filed on May 7, 1980), they had no intention to hinder, delay or defraud any creditor or the estate herein in bankruptcy. Rather, the defendant Melvin A. Laughlin states that he had, some time prior to July 1979, given over effective control of the property to his son and daughter–in–law because of his inability to make the $109.80 per month mortgage payments. Accordingly, he states, his son took over the mortgage payments on the property far in advance of July 1979.

When asked why he chose August 1, 1979, (after he was served with summons in the state court action commenced by plaintiff), the defendant Melvin A. Laughlin answered that, previously, his wife had not been able to make the trip to the lawyer's office in town to execute the deed. In fact, as he explains it, she was not really well enough on August 1, 1979, to make this trip, but, at his urging, she did it anyway. When they arrived at the lawyer's office in town, it was necessary that the instruments be presented to her as she sat in the car, for she was unable to walk into the office. Admittedly, the only consideration which the defendant received for the property was $1, when the appraised value was forty times higher.

The transfer of the property involved an equity in the defendant which otherwise would have been available to creditors and subject to any judgment lien obtained by the plaintiff as the result of the state court action.

II.

On the basis of the foregoing facts, the applicable law requires that the discharge of the defendant in bankruptcy be denied. Section 727 of the Bankruptcy Code pertinently provides that it is grounds for denial of a discharge for a debtor, within the year next preceding bankruptcy, to have transferred property with the actual intent of hindering, delaying, or defrauding creditors.

When it is shown, as in the case at bar, that the transfer within the year preceding bankruptcy has been to a relative for inadequate consideration during the pendency of a lawsuit against the transferor and in the absence of an explanation by the transferor sufficient to dispel these badges of fraud, the court cannot escape the conclusion that the transfer was with intent to hinder, delay and defraud creditors and Ms. Burtrum in particular. Considering the appearance and demeanor of the defendant Melvin A. Laughlin in the course of his testimony, it must be concluded that this testimonial disavowal of any intent to hinder, delay, or defraud creditors is not worthy of credit. Neither do the factual contentions which he makes sensibly explain why he chose a date after the filing of plaintiff's state court action to make the conveyance (which he claims had actually been made before) a matter of official record. If anything, his testimony shows that his wife was ill on August 1, 1979, as she had been previously and that therefore, the decision to consummate the transfer must have been for another reason– and the filing of the state court action by plaintiff is the only palpable reason in evidence.

For the foregoing reasons, it must be concluded that the defendants transferred property within a year prior to bankruptcy with intent to hinder, delay and defraud a creditor within the meaning of § 727(a)(2)(A) of the Bankruptcy Code. The intentional character of the misconduct and the seriousness of its consequences require the denial of the defendant's discharge in bankruptcy . . .

It is therefore accordingly, *Ordered, Adjudged and Decreed* that the discharge of defendants in bankruptcy be, and it is hereby, denied.

NOTES AND QUESTIONS

1. Section 727(a)(2) renders a transfer with intent to hinder, delay or defraud creditors a bar to a discharge. Section 548 makes fraudulent conveyances voidable at the instance of the trustee. Section 544(b) incorporates by reference the state law of fraudulent conveyances, giving the trustee additional powers. What differences, if any, exist between and among these sections, *i.e.*, would all conveyances that are fraudulent pursuant to § 548 be a bar to a discharge under § 727(a)(2)?

2. To bar a discharge, the fraudulent conveyance must be made within one year before the filing of the petition. It is a simple matter to determine the date of the filing of the petition but how is the date of the conveyance determined?

3. Fraudulent concealment of property of the estate may also be a federal crime. *See* 18 U.S.C. § 152. What investigation should the debtor's attorney perform when counselling a debtor with respect to relief from great financial distress?

O'BRIEN v. TERKEL
(In re Terkel)

Bankruptcy Court, Southern District of Florida
7 B.R. 801, 3 C.B.C.2d 513 (1980)

GASSEN, Bankruptcy Judge:

This matter was tried before the court on October 15, 1980 upon the adversary complaint in which the plaintiff, George F. O'Brien, objected to the discharge of Roland Terkel, the defendant–debtor herein. The plaintiff asserts that the debtor must be denied a discharge under 11 U.S.C. § 727(a) because he concealed an income tax refund, he did not schedule as an asset the stock of a corporation wholly owned by him, he did not maintain adequate records for that corporation, he did not produce corporate records for the trustee, and he did not deliver to the trustee, proceeds from the sale of assets of that corporation.

The right to discharge is statutory, and the provisions for denying discharge to a debtor must be construed liberally in favor of the bankrupt and strictly against the objecting creditor. *Spach v. Strauss*, 373 F.2d 641 (5th Cir. 1967); *Jones v. Friendly Finance Discount Corp.*, 490 F.2d 452 (5th Cir. 1974).

I do not find that the failure of the defendant to deliver the income tax refund to the estate is basis for denying discharge to him. Defendant's 1979 federal income tax return was prepared and signed by his accountant on April 11, 1980 (Plaintiff's Exhibit No. 10) and according to the testimony of the defendant, was filed sometime between that date and April 15, 1980. The defendant–debtor also testified that he did not include the anticipated tax refund of $768 in his schedules prepared on April 28,1980 and filed in the main proceeding on May 5, 1980 because he had already received that refund prior to April 28, 1980 and used it in his ordinary living expenses and obligations. There was no countervailing evidence on this point and even though the period between April 11, 1980 and April 28, 1980 is short, it is not impossible that the refund would have been paid during that span of time and therefore the court cannot deny the defendant–debtor his discharge on the tax refund issue.

The facts underlying plaintiff's objections which relate to the corporation are more lengthy, but are essentially not in dispute. Prior to the petition under chapter 7 filed by the debtor in this court (Case No. 80–00518–BKC–JAG) on May 5, 1980, the debtor had acquired through a series of transactions with former associates one hundred percent of the capital stock of Modern Trend Imports, Inc. which operated a small telephone and mail order business. In mid 1979 the business needed financial and management assistance. The plaintiff, George F. O'Brien, seemed to be the answer to that need. He participated in the business, intending that he would become an equal shareholder with the debtor. However, that intent never came to fruition. Instead, the plaintiff advanced substantial sums of money to the debtor for the business, for which the debtor issued his personal promissory note to the plaintiff. An action on this obligation was commenced in the State Court of Florida in which the defendant apparently asserted a counterclaim. However, the defendant–debtor does not here make an issue of his obligation to the plaintiff. In fact, that obligation is listed in the schedules filed by the debtor in the main proceeding. He does refer to his counterclaim in the state court action without evaluating it.

The business of Modern Trend Imports, Inc. had become defunct prior to the debtor's petition in bankruptcy. As principal of the defunct corporation, the defendant–debtor stored the few remaining supplies consisting of cages, feed, and some miscellaneous items. The corporation itself is not in bankruptcy.

In his statement of affairs and schedules filed in the main proceeding, the defendant–debtor referred to the corporation but did not list his ownership of the capital stock of the corporation. Subsequent to the original filing of his schedules on May 5, 1980, he filed an amendment to schedule B–2 on June 16, 1980 which likewise made no reference to that stock. In the meantime, he had attended the meeting of creditors held pursuant to 11 U.S.C. § 341 and had answered under oath the questions asked of him regarding that corporation and acknowledging his ownership of it. The plaintiff herein at all times knew of the existence of the corporation and of the defendant debtor's position in it.

During the pendency of these proceedings, the tangible personal property of the corporation was sold for approximately $200 which the defendant personally kept. He made no report of this to any corporate creditor. The defendant also testified at the trial that he felt that the corporate customers list was worth in excess of $1,000, but that he had had no success in selling it.

The court has considered and discarded plaintiff's allegations that defendant's discharge ought to be denied for his failure to keep and maintain adequate financial records and produce such records for the trustee. Following the § 341 meeting, the debtor furnished such corporate financial records as did exist. They consisted primarily of a check register and a sporadically maintained payroll book. The court finds that for the very simple business operation of the corporation, the check register was probably a sufficient bookkeeping system. Furthermore, the plaintiff during the time that he was surveying the business and considering becoming an equal share-holder in it, became familiar with the corporate business operation and offered no evidence that other business records were in existence and being concealed. There is no evidence at all that defendant's personal records were not produced. Therefore, this provides no basis for denying the debtor his discharge.

Under 11 U.S.C. § 727(a)(4)(A), a discharge may be denied to a debtor who knowingly and fraudulently made a false oath in connection with the case. Plaintiff asserts that defendant's failure to schedule the stock of Modern Trend Imports, Inc. requires a denial of discharge. I do not so conclude. Although proof of the omission of an asset which ought to have been scheduled raises a presumption of fraud, the total context does not bear out such a conclusion in this case.

The pattern of actions by the defendant and his attorney, who prepared the sched-ules, suggests carelessness rather than fraudulent intent. Defendant revealed his ownership of the stock at the § 341 meeting. This was not a surprise to plaintiff, who already knew of defendant's ownership of the stock because of their previous dealings, which solely concerned that corporation. The corporation was defunct. Plaintiff did not carry his burden of demonstrating that the stock had any value, and it appears that the stock in fact had no value. At the time of defendant's petition, the corporation owned a couple hundred dollars worth of assets, and debtor's schedules allude to one debt of the corporation, which alone would probably equal the asset. It is apparent that the trustee could have realized no income from the sale of the stock. Because of the negligible, if not non–existent, value of the stock, defendant had little to gain from the nondisclosure, and plaintiff, or any other creditor, did not, in fact, suffer by it. Defendant's misrepresentation in his schedules was not a material one and does not justify denying him a discharge. *Cf. Jones v. Friendly Finance Discount Corp., supra; Kentile Floors, Inc. v. Winham,* 440 F.2d 1128 (9th Cir. 1971); *In re Topper,* 229 F.2d 691 (3rd Cir. 1956).

Plaintiff implies that defendant's pocketing of some $200 from the sale of corporate assets demonstrates that the stock did have value, and also brings defendant within the provisions of § 727(a)(2)(B) which authorizes denying a discharge on the basis of the debtor's transferring or concealing assets of the estate after the date of filing of the petition. Defendant's retention of the approximately $200 may well have been wrongful as to the corporation, and particularly its creditors. But, as discussed above, plaintiff has failed to prove that the $200 was net earnings which was to be distributed to the shareholder. There is insufficient evidence that this was indeed an asset of the estate.

Therefore, defendant will not be denied a discharge. This court does not condone carelessness in the preparation of bankruptcy schedules or in complying with all requirements, but the denial of discharge to a debtor is a step not to be lightly taken, and one not merited here. As required by B.R. 921(a), a Final Judgement pursuant to these findings and Conclusions is being entered this date.

TAVORMINA v. RESNICK
(In re Resnick)

Bankruptcy Court, Southern District of Florida
4 B.R. 602, 2 C.B.C.2d 992 (1980)

WEAVER, Bankruptcy Judge:

This is a matter concerning objections to the discharge of a natural person, pursuant to § 727 of the United States Bankruptcy Code. The Plaintiff is the duly qualified and acting Trustee of the Debtor and the Defendant is the Debtor. The Complaint upon which this matter was tried was brought on two grounds as follows:

> A. That the Debtor concealed, destroyed, mutilated, falsified or failed to keep or preserve any recorded information including books, documents, records and papers from which the Debtor's financial condition or business transactions might be ascertained and such act, or failure to act, is not justified under all the circumstances of the case; and

B. The Debtor has failed to explain the loss of assets or deficiency of assets sufficient to meet the Debtor's liabilities.

The Debtor answered generally denying these allegations. The facts are as follows:

This matter was commenced as an involuntary proceeding brought by various Creditors on November 26, 1979. Relief was ordered without objection on December 26, 1979.

The evidence discloses that the Debtor, Herman Resnick, was engaged as a general merchandiser in the Opa Locka area for some twelve years prior to the commencement of this matter. The Debtor's personal income tax records for the years 1976, 1977 and 1978, disclose that the Debtor had approximate annual sales, resulting from this business, of $145,000.00 with the approximate cost of the merchandise sold being in the amount of $105,000.00. The Debtor's average net income, after payment of other business expenses, was approximately $10,000.00 per year.

During the year 1979, the Debtor's bank account, to which, he testified, all proceeds of sales were deposited, reflects the sales of $416,000.00. The cancelled checks disclose that the majority of the money deposited was paid to Creditors. In addition to the monies that were paid, there remained scheduled unpaid Creditors in the amount of $523,016.67.

From the foregoing, it is clear and conclusive that there is a dissipation of assets of approximately $500,000.00.

The Debtor has no records other than his invoices, bank statements and cancelled checks. There is no general ledger or other books and records available to show the disposition of this inventory.

In addition, when called to explain the disposition of this property by the Plaintiff, the Debtor replied that he cannot remember what took place during the last year of business. The Debtor appears to be disoriented due to his advancing years, various illnesses and the recent death of his wife. The Debtor has not been formally declared incompetent or unable to manage his affairs.

Although the Court has compassion for the Debtor, in regards to his personal problems, the overriding reality of what actually happened, in this matter, leads the Court to conclude that the Debtor should be denied a discharge.

The foregoing facts clearly show that the Debtor, a man of advancing years and increasing disability, intentionally increased his inventory and purchases to a point where they were equal to the sum of $1,000,000.00 per year. During this time and with the same basic overhead that had been carried for many years prior thereto, the Debtor proceeded to "lose" some half a million dollars. A loss of this magnitude cannot be permitted to go unaccounted for nor unexplained. It appears to the Court that the Debtor practiced a fraudulent scheme and that the failure of the business known as *Fabulous Hermans* was an intentional and deliberate business failure. Accordingly, the Court concluded that under the facts of the entire case, the Debtor failed to preserve books and records of account, which finding is sufficient to sustain an objection to the discharge of the Debtor. A separate Judgment will be entered in accordance with these Findings and Conclusions. Notes and Questions

1. The fourth ground for denying discharge (§ 727(a)(4)) is the commission of a bankruptcy crime as listed in 18 U.S.C. § 152; in fact, § 14c of the Bankruptcy Act of 1898, from which § 727 is derived, incorporated by reference this section of the Criminal Code rather than spelling out its provisions. What are the differences, if any, in a proceeding before a court between these two statutes which prohibit the same acts?

a. Suppose a creditor files a complaint objecting to discharge on the ground that the debtor has concealed assets and the allegation is denied by the debtor. Is there any risk for the creditor to agree to withdraw the complaint and dismiss the proceeding on being offered full payment of its debt by the debtor from postpetition earnings? Any risk if the debtor made such a promise to induce the creditor not to file the complaint in the first place? May the trustee file the complaint if the creditor decides not to or withdraws it?

b. Section 727(a)(4)(D) proscribes withholding books and records, etc. from "an officer of the estate." Why does it specify "officer of the estate" instead of "trustee?" Can there be any other kind of officer of an estate? *See* § 105.

(i) The officer of the estate must be entitled to possession of the books and records.
To what books and records is the officer so entitled, and when? § § 541, 542.

2. The sixth act barring a discharge is contained in § 727(a)(6). In what circumstances will a debtor be questioned so as to raise the opportunity to refuse to answer a question or to assert the privilege against self–incrimination? *See* § 341, 343 and Bankruptcy Rule 2004. How is immunity granted or obtained if the trustee or creditors want to get the debtor to testify fully? § 344. How broad is the immunity if granted? The legislative history indicates that § 727(a)(6) is a change from former law pursuant to which the exercise of the constitutional privilege not to incriminate oneself could be used to bar a discharge in bankruptcy. H.R. Rep. No. 95–595, 95th Cong., 1st Sess. 384 (1977); S. Rep. No. 95–989, 95th Cong., 2d Sess. 98 (1978); reprinted in App. 2 and 3, respectively, Collier, Bankruptcy (15th ed.). Interestingly, no authority is cited for this statement. Is there logic to the contrary position?

3. Section 727(a)(7) makes the acts listed in clauses (2)–(6) bars to discharge if committed by the debtor in another case concerning an insider. Who or what is an insider? Can you envision the type of situation to which this provision is directed?

4. The ninth ground for barring discharge is if, *inter alia*, the debtor obtained a discharge under § 1328 in a case commenced within the preceding 6 years and the payments under the plan totaled less than 100% of the claims or did not meet the 70% requirements. What is the utility of this provision?

5. Finally, a written waiver of discharge approved by the court is effective. 11 U.S.C. § 727(a)(10). May a borrower effectively waive a discharge in bankruptcy in a loan agreement? May a borrower effectively agree, in a loan document, not to commence a case under the Bankruptcy Code? Is there anything in the Code responding to either question?

6. How does one commence a proceeding to object to a debtor's discharge? *See* Bankruptcy Rule 4004. May such a proceeding be instituted at any time? In what court must the proceeding be commenced?

7. Subsection (b) of § 727 provides that the discharge operates against all prepetition debts. What does the word "debt" mean? Does this provision contemplate that a debt secured by property of the debtor will be discharged and the security rendered valueless to the creditor? *See also* § § 524(a)(1), (2), 506(d).

8. If facts come to light after a discharge has been granted that could have been used to bar the discharge, may the discharge be revoked by the court? *See* subsections (d) and (e) of § 727.

§ 17.02 Nondischargeability of Particular Types of Debts

Section 523 lists the debts which remain nondischargeable when a debtor obtains a discharge. This represents a policy determination by the Congress that regardless of the desirability of permitting a fresh start, it is more important that creditors holding certain types of debts be paid. For example, in § 523(a)(1) Congress has assured that almost all tax debts will be paid regardless of bankruptcy; differently stated, bankruptcy will not be used to avoid the payment of taxes. The same can be said for alimony and child support liability. The point is, even if a debtor is granted a discharge, certain creditors as determined by Congress may look to the debtor's future income, or other property acquired postpetition, for the payment of their debts.

Section 523 of the Bankruptcy Code is an evolutionary product. Under the law of 1800 the only debts which were recognized as being excepted from the operation of a discharge were those owing to the United States or any of the states. The Act of 1841, however, excepted only fiduciary obligations, while the Act of 1867 further designated fraudulent debts as unaffected by a discharge.

Section 17 of the Act of 1898 was much more extensive in character and in its scope and was further expanded and clarified by various amendments in 1903, 1917, 1922, 1938, 1960 and 1966. . . .

Section 17 of the Bankruptcy Act had to be read together with section 63. . . . Section 17 provided for the release of those debts only which were defined as provable under section 63, and then excepted from the effects of a discharge certain classes of provable debts. . . .

The Code abolished the concept of provability of section 63 of the Bankruptcy Act that limited the kinds of obligations that are payable in a bankruptcy case. A "claim" is broadly defined in section 101(4). . . . By this broadest possible definition, the Code contemplates that all legal obligations, no matter how remote or contingent, will be able to be dealt with in the bankruptcy case. It permits the broadest possible relief in a bankruptcy case. The Code does not tie discharge to a concept of "provability" as it was so tied under the Act. The broad definition of "claim" permits a complete settlement of the affairs of a bankrupt debtor, and a complete discharge and fresh start. 3 Collier, Bankruptcy ¶¶523.01, 523.02 (15th ed.).

The types of debts that are nondischargeable are set forth in § 523(a)(1)–(16). The first category of nondischargeable debts consists of certain tax debts owing to governmental units. Among the kinds of taxes which cannot be discharged in a chapter 7 case are the taxes entitled to priority in payment pursuant to § 507(a)(8). It is interesting to note that such a tax (basically a delinquent income tax liability) remains nondischargeable even if the government does not file a proof of claim. However, by not filing a proof of claim, the government will not be entitled to any distribution from the estate either on a priority basis or on a nonpriority basis. It may, therefore, be to the benefit of the debtor for the government to file a proof of claim and be paid according to its rights as a priority creditor, thus reducing the amount of the nondischargeable debt that would remain as a burden on the future financial resources of the debtor. What can the debtor do if the government does not file a proof of claim? *See* § 501(c); Bankruptcy Rule 3004.

Until 1966, the Bankruptcy Act of 1898 rendered all tax debts nondischargeable. In 1966, the Act was amended to permit "stale" tax claims to be discharged; such claims were defined to be taxes which became due more than three years before the filing of the bankruptcy petition. The Code continues the philosophy that stale tax claims should be subject to the discharge while at the same time the discharge should not be permitted to be used as a tax avoidance scheme. Thus, § 523(a)(1)(B)(i) does not permit the discharge of taxes for which no return was ever filed. Clause (ii) renders nondischargeable taxes owing for years in which the return was due within two years before the filing of the petition. How does clause (ii) compare with clause (i) of § 507(a)(8)(A)? Unpaid taxes incur interest and penalty liability. Are amounts represented by these liabilities subject to the discharge? *See* § 523(a)(8).

QUESTION

Debtor was president, chairman of the board and majority stockholder of a now defunct corporation. Among the liabilities left unpaid by the corporation when it went out of business because of extreme insolvency (it had no money or other assets but plenty of debts) were debts owing to the federal government for taxes withheld from the wages of its employees and social security payments withheld from such wages for the two years preceding the actual demise of the corporation. Subsequent to the dissolution of the company, Debtor filed a petition seeking relief under chapter 7 of the Code. Are the above debts owing the government subject to the discharge granted Debtor?

The next category of nondischargeable debt is the debt created by fraud or by means of a false financial statement in writing on which the creditor extending the credit relied. This category has been the subject of much literature, case law and statutory amendment or attempts at amendment.

BLACKWELL v. DABNEY

United States Court of Appeals, Second Circuit.
702 F.2d 490 (1983)

CHAPMAN, Circuit Judge:

This appeal presents the question whether debtor John Thomas Blackwell should be granted a discharge in bankruptcy for the amount of certain loans made to the corporation, Studio–1 International Productions, Inc. (Studio–1). Blackwell, who served as president of Studio–1, concedes personal liability for these loans because he had guaranteed repayment of the loans. The district court agreed with the bankruptcy court that the debts were not dischargeable because Blackwell obtained the money by false representations. We reverse because 11 U.S.C. § 523(a)(2)(A) (Supp. 1979), while barring discharge for money obtained by false pretenses, false representations or actual fraud, provides an exception where representations made were "statement[s] respecting the debtor's or an insider's financial condition." *Id.* Such statements fall within the purview of 11 U.S.C. § 523(a)(2)(B) which expressly provides that the statements be written. Since Blackwell's statements to plaintiffs were oral and concerned the financial condition of the corporation, an insider under the law, they are not encompassed by § 523(a)(2) and may not be relied on by his creditors to prevent his discharge in bankruptcy.

I.

Blackwell filed a voluntary petition in bankruptcy in the fall of 1981. From about 1976 until 1980 he and other Studio–1 principals participated on a part–time basis in the activity of the corporation, the promotion of rock concerts. Studio–1 experienced financial problems from its beginning. Losses for 1976 amounted to $17,717; 1977, $17,984; 1978, $14,716; and 1979, $89,000. The company had several judgments entered against it and had contemplated bankruptcy in 1977. In April 1979, however, Studio–1 produced a profitable concert that netted over $20,000.

Plaintiffs are Ella Dabney (who alleges making loans that were not repaid amounting to $35,000), Edward Bynum ($3000), Joseph Mercer ($4900) and William Hurdle ($3000). The loans in question were made during a period from May 1979 until October 1979. Each of the plaintiffs initially made a short–term loan that was repaid at a substantial rate of interest (from 15% to 20%). A second loan made by Edward Bynum was also fully repaid with interest. Later loans were not repaid.

At trial, testimony was given concerning Blackwell's statements to the plaintiffs. Dabney testified that Blackwell convinced her that the business "was growing", that "he was very successful." She also testified that the debtor told her that Studio–1 was a "top–notch company" and that "they were just blooming." Other statements made by Blackwell were that "business was going great,' that the corporation was a "very successful company of some young black men and they were doing very, very good," and that it was a "striving business that was doing well.'

II.

Although holding that the debts were non–dischargeable because the debtor had made a continuing series of misrepresentations to the plaintiffs, the bankruptcy court found that there was no evidence of bad faith or improper withdrawals of funds. The bankruptcy court also rejected claims of fraud or false financial statements. In affirming the decision of the bankruptcy court, the district court found the issue to be whether the debtor's statements constituted puffing or representations of fact.

We find it unnecessary to reach the question of whether Blackwell's statements constituted false representations or puffing because the relevant statutory provision excepts oral statements concerning the debtor's or an insider's financial condition.

In the instant case, Studio–1 is defined as an "insider." Where an individual debtor is involved, the definition of "insider" includes a "corporation of which the debtor is a director, officer, or person in control." 11 U.S.C. § 101(25)(A)(iv) (Supp. 1979). *In re Bedard,* 19 B.R. 565, 567 (Bkrtcy. E.D. Pa. 1982).

All of the statements made by Blackwell to the plaintiffs were essentially statements concerning the financial condition of Studio–1. Further, all of Blackwell's statements were oral. The representations are therefore outside the scope of 11 U.S.C. § 523(a)(2) and can not be the basis for preventing discharge of the bankrupt. . . .

Accordingly, we reverse the district court and remand for the entry of an order discharging these debts.

NOTES AND QUESTIONS

The false financial statement exception has been used most often in the consumer loan context and has been the subject of serious abuse by lenders. The Congressional hearings in the 1970s are replete with instances of abuse, many of which were attempted to be cured by the 1970 amendments to the Act. Nevertheless, problems remain. One of the problems attempted to be resolved was that created by the refinancing of a consumer loan.

1. Suppose Consumer obtains a loan from Friendly Finance Co. of $3,500. Over the next two years the loan is paid down to $500 and Consumer seeks a new loan from Friendly. The application (financial statement) which Consumer filled

out contains some misstatements. Friendly loans Consumer $3,000, although only $2,500 was requested. Of the $3,000, Friendly immediately applies $500 to repay in full the prior loan and gives Consumer $2,500 in cash. Subsequently Consumer files a chapter 7 petition and Friendly files a complaint to have its debt of $3,000 determined to be nondischargeable because of the false financial statement. Among other defenses, Consumer contends that if the debt is nondischargeable, only $500 should be so considered. What result on this issue?

The statements of the floor managers of the Reform Act bill indicate that the addition of the words "refinance of credit" in § 523(a)(2) codifies the reasoning expressed . . . in In re Danns, 558 F.2d 114 (2d cir. 1977). 124 Cong. Rec. H11,096 (Sept. 28, 1978); S17,413 (Oct. 6, 1978). Are the Code and the legislative history in harmony? In 1984, the Bankruptcy Amendments effected a clarifying change to provide that the refinancing to the extent obtained by fraud, etc. was nondischargeable.

Under the Bankruptcy Amendments of 1984, certain nonessential debts based on the debtor's "loading up" within 40 days of bankruptcy since amended to 60 days are nondischargeable. *See* § 523(a)(2)(C). If a debtor actually schemed to "load up," how hard or easy would it be to avoid application of subparagraph C ? Prior to amendment, could § 523(a)(2) be used in similar circumstances?

2. When Debtor applies for a loan from Friendly Finance Co., she is told by Friendly's employee to fill out the application containing a financial statement, which she does. One of the directions is to list all debts owing by applicant, and Debtor lists a debt owing on her Visa credit card and to Mercy's department store. There is no more room in the space provided on the form for other debts and Debtor asks Friendly's clerk how to list a debt owing to her aunt. Debtor is told not to bother, the form has sufficient information, and to make sure she signs it. The loan is granted. Subsequently, Debtor files a chapter 7 petition. Friendly then files a complaint for a determination that its debt is nondischargeable. In the trial on the complaint, Friendly shows by the Debtor's schedules filed in the case and statements made during the Debtor's examination that Debtor's application did not contain the debt owing to her aunt, a debt owing to Bloomingdale's department store and an unpaid medical bill. What result?

3. John Dell is in severe financial straits and seeks legal advice. Through his statements and your questioning, you learn about all of his debts, what assets he has, and what his future business prospects are, which are not too bad. It appears to you that a chapter 7 case may well be the best opportunity for relief and so suggest to Dell. He agrees to your suggestion and you set about preparing the necessary papers, *e.g.*, the petition, a list of creditors and the schedule of assets and liabilities (*see* § 521, Bankruptcy Rule 1007, and Official Forms Nos. 6, 7, and 8). While you are preparing the list and schedules, Dell tells you not to include Jane Creditor's name at all because she will surely file a complaint objecting to his discharge or to determine that her debt is nondischargeable or both, and she will raise a bunch of facts that no other creditor now knows and probably would otherwise not find out. Dell hopes to avoid such unpleasantness and, by obtaining a discharge in the chapter 7 case, be relieved of the burden

of Jane Creditor's debt. What advice will you give Dell? What procedures should you follow in having the schedules completed? What advice should you give with respect to the meeting of creditors held pursuant to § 341 and Bankruptcy Rule 2003?

4. The fourth category of nondischargeable debts consists of fraud or defalcation while acting in a fiduciary capacity and also larceny or embezzlement. It is not always clear when one has acted in a fiduciary capacity; the term is not defined in the Code although it has been in the bankruptcy law since 1841. It has been consistently limited in application "to what may be described as technical or express trusts, and not to trusts *ex maleficio* that may be imposed because of the very act of wrongdoing out of which the contested debt arose." 3 Collier, Bankruptcy, ¶523.14[c] (15th ed.).

5. Debts for alimony and child support are nondischargeable under § 523(a)(5) and related debts were rendered nondischargeable in § 523(a)(15) which was added to the Code in 1994. While debts accruing under property settlement agreements are not included in clause (5), they should be within the language of clause (15). The addition of clause (15) also clarifies the law, which was subject to varying opinions, that debts for legal fees, hold harmless provisions and the like are nondischargeable. But clause (15) is considerably different from clause (5) in application. It is litigation producing because the debtor can defend against nondischargeability on the ground of lack of ability to pay or comparison of the relative benefit and injury to the parties.

RANKIN v. ALLOWAY
(In re Alloway)

Bankruptcy Court, Eastern District of Pennsylvania
37 B.R. 420 (1984)

EMIL F. GOLDHABER, Bankruptcy Judge:

The issue at bench is whether we should grant the husband/debtor's former spouse an exception to discharge under 11 U.S.C. § 523(a)(1) and (a)(5). For the reasons stated herein we will deny the requested relief.

The parties have expressly waived an evidentiay [sic] hearing on this matter, so the following evidence has been drawn from the parties' stipulation and uncontested statement of facts. Ruth Rankin ("Rankin") and her then husband, Walter Alloway ("the debtor"), moved toward dissolving their marriage by executing a property settlement agreement on January 11, 1980. In part, the agreement transferred the debtor's interest in a jointly held parcel of realty to the wife and further provided that the debtor would be responsible for the payment of several liens on the property held by the Internal Revenue Service ("IRS"). "[The debtor's] assumption of responsibility of the tax liability was necessary to permit [Rankin] to maintain the household for herself and her son.' Prior to the execution of the property settlement agreement Rankin received $25.00 per week from the debtor for her own mainte- nance and $125.00 for that of her child although after the agreement was signed she received only $85.00 per week for the child's maintenance. Rankin was compelled to sell the realty on April 10, 1981, due to her inability to maintain it because of insufficient income. To complete settlement, Rankin satisfied the IRS tax liens. She did not receive a written assignment from the taxing authority for the payment. At the time of the sale the debtor's wages had been garnisheed for payment of the tax. Shortly thereafter a state arbitration proceeding fixed the debtor's obligation at $11,710.86. The debtor filed a petition for relief under chapter 7 of the Code on September 28, 1982. Rankin commenced the action at bench seeking an exception to the debtor's discharge of the said debt pursuant to 11 U.S.C. § 523(a)(1) and (a)(5).

In addressing § 523(a)(1), Rankin asserts that under § 509(a) she became subrogated to the IRS's purportedly nondischargeable claim against the debtor upon her payment of his tax liability. The clear weight of authority holds that one who has paid the tax liability of another, subject to the limitations of § 509(a), may be subrogated to the claim of the taxing authority and may thus seek an exception to discharge based on that claim. *Western Surety Co. v. Waite,* 698 F.2d 1177 (11th Cir. 1983); *Thomas International Corp. v. Morris (In re Morris),* 31 B.R. 474 (Bankr. N.D. Ill. 1983); *Woerner v. Farmers Alliance Mutual Insurance Co. (In re Woerner),* 19 B.R. 708 (Bankr. D. Kan. 1982); *In re Co–Build Companies, Inc.,* 21 B.R. 635 (Bankr. E.D. Pa. 1982) (in which we reviewed the cases on subrogation of tax claims under the Bankruptcy Act of 1898);*contra National Collection Agency, Inc. v. Trahan,* 624 F.2d 906 (9th Cir. 1980) (holding debt to be dischargeable under the Bankruptcy Act of 1898 since exception to discharge undermines the "fresh start" afforded by a discharge in bankruptcy). Consequently, we hold that, under the Code, one who pays the tax claim of another may be subrogated to the right of the taxing authority to seek an exception to discharge. Notwithstanding, "[s]ubrogation is not a matter of strict right but is purely equitable in nature, dependent upon the facts and circumstances of each particular case." *Co–Build, supra,* 21 B.R. at 636. The nature of this equitable doctrine has been described as follows:

> [Subrogation] is now a mechanism so universally applied in new and un- known circumstances that it is easy to overlook that it originates in equity. Every facet, whether substantive or procedural, is controlled by the equitable origin and aim of subrogation. These principles, so well established that to cite cases would be an affectation, find expression in accepted texts, as the following excerpts reflect. "Legal subrogation is a creature of equity not depending upon contract, but upon the equities of the parties." 50 Am. Jr. Subrogation § 3 at 679. . . . It is "a consequence which equity attaches to certain conditions. It is not an absolute right, but one which depends upon the equities and attending facts and circumstances of each case." § 10 at 688. Because its object is "to do complete and perfect justice between the parties without regard to form of technicality, the remedy will be applied in all cases where demanded by the dictates of equity, good conscience, and public policy. Consequently,

relief by way of subrogation will not be granted where it would work injustice, or where innocent persons would suffer, or where the result would be inimical to a sound public policy." § 11 at 690. As "subrogation is administered upon equitable principles, it is only where an applicant has an equity to invoke that the courts will interfere. Moreover, the equity of the party seeking subrogation must be strong and his rights clear, and his equity must be superior to that of other claimants." § 12 at 690–91. And it "will not be enforced to the prejudice of other rights of equal or higher rank, or to displace an intervening right or title, or to overthrow the equity of another person."

Compania Anonima Venezolana De Navegacion v. A. J. Perez Export Co., 303 F.2d 692, 697 (5th Cir. 1962),*cert. denied* 371 U.S. 942. The debtor urges the application of an additional principle of subrogation which is that the remedy will not be applied to one who was a mere volunteer in paying the obligation of another. *United States v. Pennsylvania Department of Highways*, 349 F. Supp. 1370, 1379 (E.D. Pa. 1972). We find this principle to be inapplicable in the instant case since Rankin was secondarily liable on the tax obligation and consequently was not a volunteer in paying the debt.

Having dealt with the issue of subrogation Rankin briefly addresses the question of whether the tax claim at issue would be nondischargeable under § 523(a)(1) if it were still held by the IRS. She fails to present any legal or factual basis to support such a conclusion except for an argument apparently based on § 507(a)(6)(A)(i) as incorporated in § 523(a)(1). Rankin argues that an application of the "limitation that the claim is to be for a tax for which the return was last due within three years before the filing of the petition would be inequitable [under] the circumstances of this case and would defeat rather than further the legislative purpose behind the nondischargeable tax scheme established by Congress." Contrary to Rankin's assertion, we find no equities in the case which would compel us to ignore the three year limitation period of § 507(a)(6)(A)(i). Consequently, the discharge of the debt is not barred by § 523(a)(1) since Rankin has failed to prove that the tax is of one of the types enumerated in that subsection. . . .

As stated above Rankin also asserts that the debt is not dischargeable under § 523(a)(5) since the debtor's obligation to satisfy the tax lien was in the nature of alimony, maintenance or support. This section has four requirements: (1) the debt must be owed to a spouse, former spouse, or child of the debtor; (2) for alimony, maintenance or support; (3) arising under a separation agreement, divorce decree or property settlement agreement; and (4) it must not be assigned except under § 402(a)(26) of the Social Security Act. § 523(a)(5). Thus, § 523(a)(5) will not bar the discharge of an obligation from the debtor to his former spouse unless the debt is for alimony, maintenance or support. Whether in any given case such obligations are in fact for "support" and therefore not dischargeable in bankruptcy, is a question of fact to be decided by the Bankruptcy Court as the trier of the facts in light of all the facts and circumstances relevant to the intention of the parties. *Williams v. Williams*, 703 F.2d 1055, 1057–58 (8th Cir. 1983). This determination of intent is particularly difficult since the designations used by the parties or the divorce court in denominating whether a debt is alimony or part of a property settlement are not conclusive although due consideration to those labels is afforded her. *Id.; Stout v. Prussel,* 691 F.2d 859, 861 (9th Cir. 1982). Further compounding the problem is the fact that, at the time the alimony is awarded and the property divided, very often the parties have no intent to differentiate between an alimony debt and a property settlement debt and will view both merely as financial obligations arising from the separation or divorce. The parties would have no purpose or rationale in making the distinction without some awareness of the legal consequences of the choice such as that found in the disciplines of tax and bankruptcy law. Since the parties typically have no actual intent to make the distinction we must usually establish their constructive intent from the facts and circumstances of the case.

The case law reveals that the following factors, as well as others, are relevant in distinguishing alimony from a property settlement debt: the label given to the debt by the parties and the state court; the express terms of the debt provision at issue in the settlement agreement or decree and its placement in the context of the document; whether the obligation is payable in installments over a substantial period of time or is a lump sum payment; whether the obligation terminates on the occurrence of a condition such as the spouse's remarriage or death; whether the debt was allocated in lieu of a greater allowance of alimony; the relative income of the parties; the length of the marriage; children from the marriage who require support; whether the support award would be inadequate absent assumption of the debt; whether the debt was incurred for a necessity; and whether the debt is a past or future obligation. . . .

In determining the dischargeability of a debt under § 523(a)(5) we must be mindful of two competing federal policies. The first is that granting the debtor a fresh start with his discharge of debts is a fundamental goal of bankruptcy relief. *Hixson v. Hixson (In re Hixson),* 23 B.R. 492, 496 (Bankr. S.D. Ohio 1982). The second is that the former spouse rather than society should be responsible for the maintenance and support of members of the family which is split by divorce or separation. *Id.* These two considerations must be balanced with an eye toward the burden of proof on the dischargeability of a debt which is placed on the party seeking such relief.

In the case at bench Rankin asserts that the assumption of the IRS tax lien by the debtor was in the nature of alimony or support since the assumption was necessary for Rankin to maintain the house in light of the relative economic disparity of the parties. Rankin contends that the house was a necessity which the debtor agreed to help preserve solely by payment of the tax lien.

The record is less than replete with evidence for determining which of the two federal policies outlined above has primacy in the case before us. We have no documentation of record on the relative income of the parties, the cost of the housing at issue and the necessary expenses of each party. Although this information would not be necessary in every case under § 523(a)(5), it would be helpful here since the IRS tax debt does not bear the typical trappings of alimony, maintenance or support as the terms are typically used. It is a single lump sum obligation payable under all conditions rather than an obligation payable at periodic intervals for an uncertain period of time which would end at the death or remarriage of the spouse.

Although the debtor's assumption of the debt would have eased Rankin's financial burden and may have aided here in keeping the house, this is not determinative. A debtor's promise to hold the other spouse harmless in the repayment of any joint obligations would always tend to ameliorate the spouse's financial condition, but unless the spouse bears her burden of proving that the debt is more akin to alimony, maintenance or support rather than a mere distribution of property, the debt will be discharged. In this case we find that Rankin has failed to meet this burden and we will deny her request that the debt created by her payment to the IRS in satisfaction of the tax lien be excepted from the debtor's discharge.

NOTES AND QUESTIONS

1. In 1990, § 523(a) was amended by the addition of clause (9) to cover specifically debts for personal injury caused by operating a motor vehicle under the influence of alcohol or drugs. It is, thus, unnecessary to interpret clause (6) in such cases.

   a. If the debt is for damage to property, i.e., while driving under the influence the debtor caused another's car to be totalled, could such debt be nondischargeable under clause (9) or clause (6)?

   b. If that which was being operated under the influence was a motor boat or an airplane, would the debt be nondischargeable under clause (9) or (6)?

2. Clause (8) excepts from discharge educational loans, although some little relief is contained in the provisions.

3. Note that liability for criminal restitution is nondischargeable under clause (13).

4. What type of debt is covered by clause (14)? What lobbying group might have obtained that addition in 1994?

LONG v. GREENWELL
(In re Greenwell)

U.S. District Court, Southern District of Ohio
21 B.R. 419, 7 C.B.C.2d 492 (1982)

SPIEGEL, District Judge:

This is an appeal from the Bankruptcy Court of a decision of The Honorable Burton Perlman, holding that the bankrupt appellant's actions of driving while intoxicated, which resulted in injury to appellees, constituted willful and malicious conduct in contravention of 11 U.S.C. § 523(a)(6), and was therefore not a dischargeable debt. . . .

Judge Perlman's findings of fact were stated at the conclusion of the hearing, at page 85 and 86 of the transcript:

> The fact is that either the defendant was drunk when this happened or else he did what he did intentionally. Because, he was on the wrong side of the street and he came along and hit the Plaintiffs' car. I'm satisfied that the facts are that he was drunk, from the observations of the Officer; and the testimony of the young lady who was the first witness, Ms. Deem, I guess; that he was driving on the wrong side, that he struck the–that he ran the stop sign, without stopping. The only reasonable explanation for that conduct was that he was drunk.

> Now, then, that brings directly into question whether Briceson (sic) is a correct statement of law or not.

> It's as to that that I am reserving decision.

> I am indicating I have no problem about what the facts are. Those are my findings of facts as I have just stated them. And, I am reserving only the question of law. . . .

Our review of the transcript leads us to conclude that Judge Perlman's findings of fact are not clearly erroneous. The issue, therefore, for the Court to consider is whether the Bankruptcy Court was correct in not following *In re Bryson,* 6 BCD 199, 1 CBC 2d 1038, 3 B.R. 593 (Bkrtcy. N.D. Ill. 1980), which interpreted 11 U.S.C. § 523(a)(6) to mean that a debt arising from an accident involving driving while under the influence of alcohol was not a non–dischargeable debt. . . .

Judge Perlman's analysis of this Section which led him to the conclusion that the appellant's debt should not be discharged because it was for willful and malicious injury by him to the plaintiff–appellees is as follows:

> The main case applied in the interpretation of the now superseded Bankruptcy Act § 17(a)(8) was *Tinker v. Colwell,* [193] 139 U.S. 473 [24 S.Ct. 505, 48 L.Ed. 754] (1902). It is clear that in enacting the Bankruptcy Code, the Congress meant to change the way in which that case was being applied, as may be seen from a review of the legislative history of 11 U.S.C. § 523(a)(6). As it appeared in the original Bankruptcy Reform Act, § 523(a)(6) provided that a debt "for willful and malicious injury by the debtor to another entity or to the property of another entity' was nondischargeable. (H.R. 8200 95th Cong., 1st Sess. [1977]). The accompanying report (H.R.Rep.No.595, 1st Sess. [1977]) then elaborated upon this section as follows:

> [Paragraph] (6) except debt for willful and malicious injury by the debtor to another person or the property of another person. Under this paragraph, "willful" means deliberate or intentional. To the extent that *Tinker v. Colwell,* [193] 139 U.S. 473 [24 S.Ct. 505, 48 L.Ed. 754] (1902) held that a looser standard is intended, and to the extent that other cases have relied on Tinker to apply a "reckless disregard" standard, they are overruled.

> The Senate then modified this suggested language by adding "conversion or" after "willful and malicious." 523(a)(5), S.B. 2266 95th Cong. , 2d Sess.,

416 (1978). Its report in all other aspects echoed the House Report. S.Rep.No.989, 95th Cong. , 2d Sess. 79 (1978). The compromise bill, however, only contained the language of the House version. 124 Cong. Rec. H11509 (Daily Ed. Sept. 28 1978). The statements of the sponsors in the House 124 Cong. Rec. H11096 (Daily Ed. Sept. 28, 1978), and the Senate 124 Cong.Rec. § 17412 (Daily Ed. October 6, 1978) were likewise identical and referred exclusively to the language contained in the House version of the bill.

What is to be gleaned from this review is that Congress intended that it not be sufficient to classify an act as willful and malicious that it be one done for reckless disregard for consequences. An intentional act is required. It is not, however, necessary to find that personal ill will existed in order for there to be a finding of willful and malicious injury. *In Re Obermeyer,* 12 B.R. 26 (B.J., [Bkrtcy.] Ohio, 1981). In the case before us now, we hold that the voluntary drinking by defendant constituted an intentional act sufficient to support the conclusion that the injury caused by defendant was willful and malicious. That is, while the legislature meant to circumscribe the scope of the *Tinker* case, its holding that "willful and malicious" under the statute is satisfied where there is an intentional injury remains valid. Defendant's intentional drinking unleashed the unbroken causative chain which led to the injury to plaintiff's vehicle. It will not avail defendant in his effort to avoid this result to argue that he did not know plaintiff prior to the accident and therefore the injury could not have been intentionally caused. One is responsible under the law for the natural outcome of his actions. To the extent that *In Re Bryson,* [3 B.R. 593] 6 B.C.D. 199 (B.J., [Bkrtcy.] Ill., 1980) reaches a different conclusion, we respectfully disagree with its reasoning and decline to follow it.

We find no error in the conclusion of law arrived at by the Bankruptcy Court for the reasons set forth by the Bankruptcy Judge, which we adopt. For the foregoing reasons, the decision of the Bankruptcy Court is hereby affirmed.

NOTES AND QUESTIONS

1. Suppose a debtor has been involved in successive chapter 7 cases and in the first one was denied a discharge for having committed an act specified in § 727(a). Assume the debtor obtains a discharge in the second case. May debts existing at the time of the first case be discharged in the second case? If the debtor was denied a discharge in the second case because a discharge was obtained in a case commenced within the previous six years, may debts existing in the second case be discharged if the debtor files a third petition more than six years after the commencement of the first case?

2. If, in a prior case, the debtor did not obtain a discharge from a particular debt because it was not timely scheduled, would it be discharged in a subsequent chapter 7 case if it is timely scheduled? What about a tax debt? Alimony? Student loan? Why a distinction?

3. *Jurisdiction to Determine Dischargeability.* With respect to the nondischargeable debts listed in paragraphs (2), (4), (6) and (15), where, when and by whom must a complaint raising their nondischargeability or dischargeability be filed? *See* § 523(c)(1) and Bankruptcy Rule 4007. What about debts listed in the other paragraphs? Why is such a distinction contained in the Code?

4. Section 523(d) provides some disincentive to discourage lenders from bringing frivolous or unsubstantiated proceedings for a determination that their debts are nondischargeable. It also has some bearing on their leverage in obtaining a reaffirmation agreement from the debtor. You should consider this provision in connection with the discussion of reaffirmation agreements in the next section.

§ 17.03 Reaffirmation of Discharged Debts

See § 524.

Before 1970, the general rule of law was that the Bankruptcy Act and the bankruptcy court determined whether the debtor was entitled to a discharge, but the effect of the discharge was to be determined in the appropriate nonbankruptcy court. *Cf. Local Loan Co. v. Hunt,* 292 U.S. 234 (1934). Thus, after discharge, a creditor (normally a consumer loan company) would bring suit on the debt (loan) in state court. The bankruptcy discharge was treated as an affirmative defense (think statute of frauds, statute of limitations, etc.) which, if not pleaded, was deemed waived. Most bankrupts did not plead the discharge for a variety of reasons including sewer service (debtor never received summons and complaint in the state court action), or debtor believed bankruptcy had wiped out the debt and ignored the summons and complaint, or debtor could not afford again to retain an attorney. The next thing bankrupt knew, his or her employer was served with a new writ of garnishment and the wages were once more tied up.

Much of this abuse was cured by the 1970 amendments to the Bankruptcy Act, which gave the bankruptcy court jurisdiction to determine the effect of the discharge and exclusive jurisdiction to determine whether a debt was nondischargeable because it was incurred by means of a false financial statement. It also contained injunctive provisions to prevent suits on such discharged debts.

The 1970 amendments left one important area untouched. Another ploy of the consumer lending industry was to obtain from the bankrupt, after the filing of the petition, an agreement to pay the debt owing to the company. This was called a reaffirmation agreement. The Bankruptcy Act had no provision dealing with reaffirmation agreements, and the judicially developed principle was that their validity depended on state law. Under state law, such agreements were valid (while a discharge relieves the legal liability, a moral obligation remains which is sufficient to support the new promise to pay, *Zavelo v. Reeves,* 227 U.S. 625 (1913)), although many states required them to be in writing. Often debtors were coerced into signing such agreements by threats of repossessing household furniture. In any event, the bankruptcy court remained out of the picture.

Section 524 of the Code regulates and restricts the use of reaffirmation agreements. The original House bill would have made such agreements unenforceable totally while the Senate bill would have continued their validity. The Code represents a compromise which is more closely aligned to the House position.

NOTES AND QUESTIONS

Section 524(c) contains a number of provisions meant to regulate the use of reaffirmation agreements in an effort to provide some protection for the individual debtor. How effective might you imagine the provisions of § 524(c) are? Debtor has given a security interest on all of debtor's household furniture to secure a loan from ABC Finance Co. Debtor has two years' worth of monthly payments left on the loan when it files a chapter 7 petition. ABC Finance Co. meets debtor in the hallway after conclusion of the § 341 meeting of creditors and informs debtor that it would be in the debtor's interest to sign an agreement reaffirming the balance of the Debt owing in order to keep the furniture from being taken by the finance company. Will Debtor sign?

§ 17.04 Redemption and Reaffirmation

Section 722, applicable only in chapter 7 cases, was new in the 1978 Bankruptcy Code. It permits a consumer debtor to redeem property subject to a lien by paying to the secured creditor the value of the property. Suppose, for example, an automobile is worth only $1,500 but secures payment of the purchase price which at the time in question has an unpaid balance of $3,500. Section 722 allows the debtor who has filed a chapter 7 petition to keep the car by paying the lender $1,500.

NOTES AND QUESTIONS

1. In the above situation, what becomes of the remaining $2,000 owed the lender if the debtor redeems the car?

2. If the debtor desires to redeem, must the $1,500 be paid in a lump sum in cash or may the debtor require the lender to accept installment payments which would total that amount?

    a. What if the debtor cannot scrape up $1,500?

    b. If the full amount must be paid in a lump sum, what other option(s) does the debtor have?

3. Who determines, and how, that the value of the car is $1,500? *See* § 506(a).

4. What is the relationship between redemption under § 722 and reaffirmation under § 524?

IN RE DELANO

Bankruptcy Court, District of Maine
4 B.R. 305, 2 C.B.C.2d 259, 6 B.C.D. 436 (1980)

CYR, Bankruptcy Judge:

The debtor moves the court, under Bankruptcy Code § 524(c)(4)(A), for approval of an agreement for the reaffirmation of an installment sale contract between the debtor and Bill Dodge Oldsmobile, Inc. [seller] concerning a 1978 Oldsmobile station wagon. The seller retained a purchase–money security interest in the automobile to secure payment of the $8,228.64 installment balance. The rights of the seller were assigned to General Motors Acceptance Corporation [GMAC]. The debtor paid $4,108.75 under the contract prior to bankruptcy, leaving a $4,119.91 balance.

At the hearing held on July 15, 1980, the court was informed that the debtor is disabled and unemployed and that her entire gross monthly income consists of a $300 social security disability payment. The debtor needs the automobile, her only available means of transportation. No public transportation is available between her rural residence and the neighboring village where food, medical and other necessary supplies and services are obtained. To avoid the high replacement cost, the debtor wants to reaffirm a $4,119.91 debt, at the rate of $171.43 per month, in order to retain an automobile worth $2,400. Court approval of a reaffirmation agreement must be predicated on findings that it will not impose an undue hardship on the debtor or a dependent of the debtor, and that it is in the best interest of the debtor. Bankruptcy Code § 524(c)(4)(A)(i) & (ii)

The monthly payment to GMAC exceeds half the available gross monthly income, meager as it is. In these circumstances, virtually the only basis for determining that reaffirmation would not impose an *undue hardship* on the debtor, within the meaning of section 524(c)(4)(A)(i), is that a disabled person deprived of her only means of transportation may experience even greater hardship than reaffirmation represents. For a disabled chapter 7 debtor with $300 monthly gross income, it is almost inescapable that basic self–support will represent a real hardship. What is an "undue" hardship for such a debtor?

The legislative history is somewhat unrevealing, though the basic rationale of section 524(c)(4)(A) seems plain enough on its face. It was designed to prevent overreaching by holders of dischargeable debts and to preserve the "fresh start" for individual debtors. In the extraordinarily difficult circumstances of the present case, the court is not prepared to disapprove reaffirmation as an undue hardship, by imposing an even more unmanageable hardship than that which the debtor proposes to assume.

But the matter may not rest there. The debtor desires to reaffirm a debt for almost twice the fair market value of the automobile. It is her almost desperate dependence on her automobile which leaves the debtor disadvantaged in the reaffirmation process. Congress had made other provisions for individual debtors in such circumstances. Although the debtor cannot resort to Bankruptcy Code § 522(f) for the avoidance of a purchase–money security interest, redemption may be more appropriate in these circumstances than reaffirmation. The debtor has not attempted to redeem her automobile from the GMAC security interest by payment of the amount of the allowed secured claim, under Bankruptcy Code § 722, which was designed to afford relief in circumstances where the holder of an allowed secured claim may use the threat of foreclosure to force a reaffirmation in an amount greater than the value of its collateral. Redemption would enable the debtor to retain her automobile for its fair market value. Absent a showing that redemption is either unavailable or inappropriate in the circumstances, the court will not approve a reaffirmation agreement as being in the best interest of the debtor under Bankruptcy Code § 524(c)(4)(A)(ii).

Accordingly, counsel for the debtor is directed, within twenty days, either to initiate redemption proceedings under Bankruptcy Code § 722, or to make a sufficient written showing that redemption is unavailable or inappropriate in the circumstances.

GENERAL MOTORS ACCEPTANCE v. BELL CORP.
(In re Bell)

United States Court of Appeals, Sixth Circuit
700 F.2d 1053 (1983)

KRUPANSKY, Circuit Judge.

This action joins the legal issue of whether redemption of secured collateral in a Chapter 7 bankruptcy proceeding may be achieved through installment payments. Debtors, Thomas and Louise Bell (Bells), were parties to a purchase money security agreement with General Motors Acceptance Corporation (GMAC) covering a 1978 Chevrolet Van. The agreement contemplated that the Bells would pay the balance of the purchase price, approximately $6,000 together with financing charges, in equal monthly installments. At the time debtors filed a joint petition in Bankruptcy on March 28, 1980, under Chapter 7 of the Bankruptcy Reform Act of 1978 (Bankruptcy Act), 11 U.S.C. § 701 *et seq.*, the fair market value of the Van exceeded the outstanding balance on the agreement by approximately $1,000, the debtors had tendered all monthly installments on their obligation to GMAC and had otherwise not defaulted upon any term of the contract. The Van became property of the estate subsequent to which the debtors exempted their equity and the trustee abandoned the estate's interest. GMAC filed a complaint to reclaim the Van and debtors counterclaimed seeking authorization from the bankruptcy court to retain possession of the Van upon continued payment of monthly installments. The Bankruptcy Court permitted installment redemption, *In re Bell,* 8 B.R. 549 (Bkrtcy. E.D. Mich. 1981), and the District Court reversed, *In re Bell,* 15 B.R. 859, 7 B.C.D. 219 (E.D. Mich. 1981).

The Bankruptcy Reform Act of 1978 authorizes a Chapter 7 debtor to redeem certain secured property [§ 722]. . . . This provision generally permits a debtor to redeem tangible secured personal property by paying the creditor the approximate fair market value of said property, or the amount of the claim, whichever is less.*See In re Zimmerman,* 4 B.R. 739 (Bkrtcy. S.D. Calif. 1980); *In re Hart* 8 B.R. 1020 (N.D.N.Y. 1981). However, § 722 is facially silent as to the mechanics of redemption and, particularly, on whether the redemption may be accomplished through installment payments. The weight of authority has denied installment redemption. *See: In re Miller,* 4 B.R. 305 (Bkrtcy. E.D. Mich. 1980); *In re Zimmerman, supra; In re Schweitzer,* 19 B.R. 860 (Bkrtcy. E.D. N.Y. 1982);*In re Stewart,* 3 B.R. 24 (Bkrtcy. N.D. Ohio 1980); *In re Hart, supra; In re Whatley,* 16 B.R. 394 (Bkrtcy. N.D .Ohio 1982); *In re Cruseturner,* 8 B.R. 581 (Bkrtcy. D. Utah 1981); *In re Carroll,* 11 B.R. 725 (Bkrtcy. Panel 9th Cir. 1981), rev'ng 7 B.R. 907 (Bkrtcy.Ariz. 1981).*Contra: In re Clark,* 10 B.R. 605 (Bkrtcy. C.D. Ill. 1981).

The bankruptcy redemption provision, § 722, is a legislative derivative of the redemption provision of 9–506, Uniform Commercial Code. The official comment to 9–506 provides:

> "Tendering fulfillment" obviously means more than a new promise to perform the existing promise; it requires payment in full of all monetary obligations then due and performance in full of all other obligations then matured.

The legislative history of § 722 does not reflect a Congressional intent which contemplated anything other than an intent to incorporate the fundamental requirement of "lump sum" redemption as suggested in the underlying UCC provision upon which § 722 was predicated. . . .

More importantly, the redemption remedy of § 722 must be construed *in pari material with the reaffirmation provision,* 11 U.S.C. § 524(c). . . .

Section 524(c) authorizes a Chapter 7 debtor to seek renegotiation of the terms of the security agreement with the creditor thereby creating an alternative method pursuant to which a debtor may attempt to retain possession of secured collateral. Such an alternative, obviously attractive to the debtor financially unable to redeem the secured collateral through a lump–sum payment, is the equitable complement to § 722. *See: In re Cruseturner, supra,* 8 B.R. at 583 *et seq.* Simply, a debtor incapable or unwilling to tender a lump–sum redemption and redeem the secured collateral for its fair market value may reaffirm with the creditor, contrawise, a debtor confronted with a creditor unwilling to execute a renegotiation may retain the secured collateral by redeeming it for its fair market value, which value may be substantially less than the contractual indebtedness. However, § 524(c) facially contemplates that the creditor, for whatever reason, may reject any and all tendered reaffirmation offers; § 524(c) envisions execution of an "agreement" which, by definition, is a voluntary undertaking. *See: In re Whatley, supra,* 16 B.R. at 396.

Accordingly, if a debtor is authorized by the bankruptcy court to redeem by installments over the objection of the creditor, such practice would render the voluntary framework of § 524(c) an exercise in legislative futility. *See: In re Miller, supra,* 4 B.R. at 307–08. Phrased differently:

> Of course, if Section 722 payments could be made by installment, no debtor would ever have reason to reaffirm under Section 524(c)(4)(B)(ii), since, by right, he could obtain under Section 722 the same end–continuing possession of his property–under the same terms–payment by installment–for what would often be a significantly lower price. Thus, installment payments under Section 722 would render useless Congress' carefully laid scheme for voluntary agreement under Section 524–clearly indicating that Congress had no intention to allow such payments under Section 722. *In re Hart, supra,* 8 B.R. at 1022.

Further, authorization of installment redemption would interpose into Chapter 7 a procedure which Chapter 7 is ill–equipped to implement. A Chapter 7 proceeding, whereby the debtor is discharged through liquidation, may conclude prior to the expiration of the installment payment period. A default by the debtor subsequent to discharge–possibly predicated upon a waste of the collateral, inability to meet the monthly installments or lack of motivation to continue payments on a rapidly depreciating collateral such as a vehicle–would burden the creditor with the expense and effort of reapplying to the bankruptcy court for relief.

See: In re Hart, supra, 8 B.R. at 1022–23 (rapidly depreciating collateral). A bankruptcy court's inability to effectively monitor the installment program and to expeditiously and meaningfully enforce the installment redemption raises serious issues of adequate creditor protection. *See: In re Cruseturner, supra,* 8 B.R. at 588 ("Chapter 7 bankruptcies are just not equipped with the procedure to enforce redemptions in installments").

A Chapter 7 debtor may assume the anomalous position of being financially unable to redeem the secured collateral by a lump–sum payment and concurrently incapable of persuading a creditor to reaffirm. However, a debtor's inability to exercise the § 722 option of redemption, in the absence of installment redemption, cannot serve as a basis for the bankruptcy court to abdicate its judicial function of statutory interpretation and resort to legislation by judicial decree. *See: In re Miller, supra,* 4 B.R. at 309, citing *West Coast Hotel Co. v. Parrish,* 300 U.S. 379, 57 S.Ct. 578, 81 L.Ed. 703 (1937). As has been aptly observed:

> Congress was well aware that the typical debtor might well find lump sum redemption unavailable and therefore provided a mechanism for achieving an installment redemption, to wit, by consensual agreement. That this mechanism may well be imperfect cannot be gainsaid; it may well be short circuited by the recalcitrant creditor who refuses to come to terms. But those deficiencies are more properly directed to Congressional review, and consequently, provide a poor excuse for judicial legislation.

In re Schweitzer, supra, 19 B.R. at 864 (footnote omitted). While a bankruptcy court is invested with equity jurisprudence, application of that jurisdiction must comport to and remain compatible with the prevailing legislative intent. *United States v.*

Killoren, 119 F.2d 364, 366 (8th Cir. 1941). A bankruptcy court's imposition of installment redemption clearly contravenes the overall statutory scheme and destroys the delicate balance between § 722 and § 524(c), and therefore finds no sanction in principles of equity.

Debtors posit that preclusion of installment redemption will precipitate situations wherein a Chapter 7 debtor will possess no viable method of retaining possession of secured collateral. However, a debtor may avoid such an untenuous position by initially filing a petition for bankruptcy under Chapter 13 or converting an existing Chapter 7 proceeding to a Chapter 13 proceeding. Chapter 13 is designed to provide a debtor with a fresh start through rehabilitation, unlike Chapter 7 which provides a fresh start through liquidation. As such, Chapter 13 authorizes redemption by installment over an objection by the creditor (a "cram down"), the very result sought in the action at bar. 11 U.S.C. § 1325(a)(5). *See: In re Miller, supra,* 4 B.R. at 308; *In re Schweitzer, supra,* 19 B.R. at 864, note 7; *In re Stewart,* 3 B.R. at 25; *In re Whatley, supra,* 16 B.R. at 397. In sum, construction of Chapters 7 and 13 *in pari materia* discloses that within the overall statutory scheme a debtor desirous of retaining possession of secured collateral is accorded that election by filing a Chapter 13 petition.

Lastly, the debtors maintain that no default had occurred under the terms of the security agreement and that, upon the trustee's abandonment of the Van under 11 U.S.C. § 554, the debtors reacquired the collateral since they held the primary possessory interest. Debtors posit that they enjoyed the same rights after abandonment as before the filing of the bankruptcy petition including the right to continue monthly installments so long as no default, as defined by the security agreement, intervened. Under this theory, the right to continued possession of the secured collateral emanates from the security agreement rather than under a § 722 redemption. However, it has been recognized that a return of abandoned property to the party with the primary possessory interest (usually the debtor) merely provides that debtor with time to enforce his right to redeem the property under § 722 or to seek a reaffirmation of the agreement under § 524(c). The automatic stay of 11 U.S.C. § 362(a)(5) continues in effect, and prevents repossession by the creditor until the case is closed, dismissed, or discharge is granted or denied pursuant to 11 U.S.C. § 362(c)(2). Analyzing the relationship between § 362(a)(5) (debtors protection of the automatic stay) and § 554 (abandonment), the Court in *In re Cruseturner* has summarized:

> Accordingly, Section 362(a)(5) grants the debtor time to enforce rights in his property given him under Sections 722 and 524(c)
>
> The effect of Section 362(a)(5) is to provide the debtor with separate protection of his property. This enables him to exercise his right to redeem either by acquiring refinancing or by otherwise gathering the necessary funds, or to negotiate a reaffirmation. Unless earlier relief is requested by the creditor, the creditor may not repossess property, despite any abandonment by the trustee, until one of the three acts specified in Section 362(c)(2) occurs The application of Section 362 to exempt property and abandoned property is co–extensive with the redemption right given in Section 722, for this right

extends to exempt property as well as to non–exempt property which may be abandoned by the trustee. Likewise, the stay will cover property which may be the subject of reaffirmation agreements.

8 B.R. at 592.

Further, a serious issue exists as to whether the debtors held the primary possessory interest in the Van upon abandonment. The security agreement authorized GMAC to immediately repossess the Van upon the filing of a bankruptcy petition (bankruptcy clause). While this bankruptcy clause was initially inoperative under 11 U.S.C. § 541(c)(1), and the Van had become property of the estate under 11 U.S.C. § 544 irrespective of such clause, the § 541(c) prohibition against such a bankruptcy clause has been held inoperable once the asset has been abandoned from the estate. *See: In re Schweitzer, supra,* 19 B.R. at 865 *et seq.* Accordingly, the bankruptcy clause became effective upon abandonment, the debtors were in default of the security agreement and therefore no longer entitled to the primary possessory interest in the Van.

Further, a discharge of the debtor's personal liability on the security agreement through bankruptcy constructively vitiated Paragraph 6 of the security agreement which provides that "buyer shall be liable for a deficiency." Negation of the creditor's right to seek personal liability precipitated a default so as to empower GMAC with the primary possessory right to the Van.

In sum, this Court concludes that redemption and reaffirmation constituted the exclusive methods pursuant to which the Bells could retain possession of the secured collateral. The sole method of redemption available to a Chapter 7 debtor under § 722 is a lump–sum redemption. Accordingly, the judgement of the district court is *affirmed.*

IN RE BELANGER

United States Court of Appeals, Fourth Circuit
962 F.2d 345, 26 C.B.C.2d 1429 (1992)

BUTZNER, Senior Circuit Judge:

The issue in this appeal is whether the district court correctly construed 11 U.S.C. § 521(2)(A) in a Chapter 7 proceeding by holding that debtors, who were current in their secured consumer loan installment payments, could retain the collateral after discharge without either redeeming the collateral or reaffirming the debt.

Budd George Belanger and Janice Leigh Belanger purchased a mobile home financed by Home Owners Financing Corporation (Home). The Belangers filed for relief under Chapter 7 of the Bankruptcy Code. They subsequently filed a statement of intention pursuant to § 521(2)(A) indicating that they would retain the mobile home. The Belangers have remained current on their payments. Home moved the bankruptcy court to compel the Belangers to reaffirm the debt, redeem the collateral, or surrender it, arguing that § 521(2)(A) restricts debtors to these options. The court denied the motion and discharged the Belangers, holding that they had complied with § 521(2)(A) by giving notice of their intent to retain the property while continuing to make payments in accordance with their contract with Home. *In re Belanger,* [23 C.B.C.2d 909] 118 B.R. 368 (Bankr. E.D.N.C. 1990). On appeal, the district court affirmed the bankruptcy court's decision in a carefully reasoned opinion that fully dealt with the arguments of the parties. We affirm the district court's judgment.

I.

Congress added § 521(2) to the Bankruptcy Code when it passed the Bankruptcy Amendments and Federal Judgeship Act of 1984, Pub. L. No. 98–353, 98 Stat. 333 (1984). Section 521(2) provides:

> (2) if any individual debtor's schedule of assets and liabilities includes consumer debts which are secured by property of the estate–
>
>> (A) within thirty days after the date of the filing of a petition under chapter 7 of this title or on or before the date of the meeting of creditors, whichever is earlier, or within such additional time as the court, for cause, within such period fixes, the debtor shall file with the clerk a statement of his intention with respect to the retention or surrender of such property and, if applicable, specifying that such property is claimed as exempt, that the debtor intends to redeem such property, or that the debtor intends to reaffirm debts secured by such property;
>>
>> (B) within forty–five days after the filing of a notice of intent under this section, or within such additional time as the court, for cause, within such forty–five day period fixes, the debtor shall perform his intention with respect to such property, as specified by subparagraph (A) of this paragraph; and
>>
>> (C) nothing in subparagraphs (A) and (B) of this paragraph shall alter the debtor's or the trustee's rights with regard to such property under this title.

Courts do not agree about the meaning of § 521(2). In this case the bankruptcy court and the district court construed this subsection to mean that the debtor must give notice stating an intention either to retain or to surrender the property. If applicable, the notice must specify whether the debtor intends to exempt the property, redeem it, or reaffirm the debt. But if these options are not applicable, the notice need not specify one of them. The options stated in the statute are not exclusive. A debtor who is not in default may elect to retain the property and make the payments specified in the contract with the creditor. The district court held that by giving notice of retention and intent to continue paying the loan according to the contract, the debtor complied with § 521(2). In short, the bankruptcy court and the district court concluded that § 521(2) was a procedural provision requiring notice in order to inform the lien creditor promptly of the debtor's intention. This conclusion is consistent with § 521(2)(C), which provides that the subsection does not alter the debtor's rights with regard to the collateral. Before Congress enacted

§ 521(2), *In re Ballance*, [9 C.B.C.2d 595] 33 B.R. 89 (Bankr. E.D. Va. 1983), held that a debtor who was not in default need not reaffirm the debt or redeem the collateral. Instead the debtor could retain the property securing the debt while making payments required by the loan papers.

The district court's interpretation of § 521(2)(A) is supported by *Lowry Federal Credit Union v. West*, 882 F.2d 1543 (10th Cir. 1989), which held that a bankruptcy court has discretion to permit debtors to retain collateral without either redeeming it or reaffirming the underlying debt. The court stated that [w]hile a debtor may redeem property, subject to 11 U.S.C. § 722, or reaffirm a debt, subject to 11 U.S.C. § 524(c)(4), nothing within the Code makes either course exclusive. 882 F.2d at 1546. Accord *In re Berenguer*, 77 B.R. 959 (Bankr. S.D. Fla. 1987); *In re Peacock*, [19 C.B.C.2d 69] 87 B.R. 657 (Bankr. D. Colo. 1988); *In re Crouch*, 104 B.R. 770 (Bankr. S.D.W. Va. 1989); *In re Hunter*, 121 B.R. 609 (Bankr. N.D. Ala. 1990); *In re Manring*, 129 B.R. 198 (Bankr. W.D. Mo. 1991); *In re Donley*, 131 B.R. 193 (Bankr. N.D. Fla. 1991).

Matter of Edwards, 901 F.2d 1383 [23 C.B.C.2d 488] (7th Cir. 1990), reached a contrary conclusion. Accord *In re Stevens*, 85 B.R. 854 (Bankr. D. Colo. 1988); *In re Chavarria*, 117 B.R. 582 (Bankr. D. Idaho 1990). Edwards construed § 521(2)(A) to limit the debtor's options to surrendering the collateral to the creditor, reaffirming the debt, or redeeming the collateral. The court held the debtor could not retain the collateral while making the regularly scheduled installment payments stipulated in the loan agreement unless the debtor either reaffirmed or redeemed, even though the debtor was not in default.

Edwards relies on *In re Bell*, 700 F.2d 1053 [8 C.B.C.2d 199] (6th Cir. 1983). *Bell* holds that a debtor cannot redeem by installments under 11 U.S.C. § 722. To defeat the possessory interest in collateral of a debtor who is not in default, *Bell* holds that a clause in the loan papers making a debtor in default upon filing for bankruptcy becomes effective when the trustee abandons the collateral. The creditor then is allowed to repossess the collateral unless the debtor pays the entire indebtedness or reaffirms. 700 F.2d at 1058. Reaffirmation must be with the consent of the creditor. 700 F.2d at 1056.

One treatise, 3 Collier on Bankruptcy ¶521.09A, at 521–49 (Lawrence P. King ed., 15th ed. 1991), criticizes *Edwards* for failing to give effect to § 521(2)(C) and legislative history that disclosed Congress rejected a proposal to lift the automatic stay if the debtor did not timely redeem or reaffirm. *See* H.R. 4786, 97 Cong., 1st Sess. § 7 (1981) (misprinted in *Collier* as H.R. 4876, § 521.09A at 52149, nn.5,6). The treatise, in agreement with the views of the bankruptcy court and the district court in the case now before us, construes § 521(2) to "affect only procedure, and not substantive rights of the debtor." § 521.09A at 521–48. The treatise states:

> Nothing in section 521(2) requires the debtor to choose redemption, reaffirmation or surrender of the property to the exclusion of all other alternatives although no other alternatives are provided for in the Code. That section merely requires a statement of whether the debtor intends to choose any of those options, if applicable.

S 521.09A at 521–46 (footnote omitted).

Collier's interpretation of § 521(2)(A) complies with the canon that courts should give effect, if possible, to every word in a statute. *See Reiter v. Sonotone Corp.,* 442 U.S. 330, 339 (1979). The phrase "if applicable" is redundant if, contrary to Collier and the district court, the options given to the debtor are considered to be exclusive. If this were so, § 521(2)(A) would have simply provided: "and specifying that such property is claimed as exempt, that the debtor intends to redeem such, or that the debtor intends to reaffirm debts secured by such property." The fact that the statutory options are stated in the disjunctive shows that the words "if applicable" are unnecessary under a construction of the statute that makes the options exclusive. But if the phrase "if applicable" is given effect, it plays an important role. As Collier points out, the debtor must specify a choice of the options if applicable. But if these options are not applicable, the debtor need not specify them. *See also Crouch,* 104 B.R. at 772.

Edwards and Bell conflict with precedent in this circuit. In *Riggs Nat'l Bank v. Perry,* 729 F.2d 982 [10 C.B.C.2d 701] (4th Cir. 1984), we held that a default–on–filing clause in an installment loan contract was unenforceable as a matter of law. 729 F.2d at 984–85. In this respect our precedent conflicts with *Bell,* 700 F.2d at 1058. In *Riggs,* the lien creditor sought a modification of the automatic stay to compel the debtor to surrender collateral, contending that it would depreciate. This court, affirming the district court, denied the creditor's complaint and permitted the debtor, during the bankruptcy proceedings, to retain the collateral by making the installment payments if he otherwise avoided default. *Riggs,* 729 F.2d at 985. In this respect our precedent conflicts with *Edwards.*

The issue of the effect that a discharge would have on the respective rights of the creditor and debtor was not raised in *Riggs.* However, in response to the creditor's argument that the court should modify the stay because the debtor might be discharged from personal liability, the court said:

> If Perry's obligation is discharged, however, the bank retains a lien against the automobile to the extent of its value. The bank's sole legitimate concern, therefore, is that its lien exceeds the present value of the collateral. Allegedly, it is placed at even greater risk because of the highly depreciable character of its security. Nevertheless, appellant's position is no more fragile, due to the Chapter 7 filing alone, than that of any lender under an installment sales contract.

Riggs, 729 F.2d at 985 (citations omitted).

In the case under review, the district court considered the practicalities of the options mentioned in § 521(2)(A). It pointed out that a person who has filed bankruptcy is unlikely to be able to redeem the collateral in a lump sum as required by § 722. If the debtor seeks to retain the collateral, the only alternative to redemption, according to the creditor's argument, is reaffirmation. But reaffirmation requires the consent of the creditor in order to comply with § 524(C). This enables the creditor to compel the debtor either to meet the creditor's terms of reaffirmation or to surrender the property. This situation is illustrated by Home's brief, which describes reaffirmation in terms of an option "to persuade a secured creditor to renew a debt agreement." Br. at 8.

Home complains that the district court's interpretation of § 521(2) and the discharge of the Belangers permit them to retain the mobile home without exposing them to personal liability for any deficiency in event of default and sale of the mobile home for less than the balance due.

Home is no more vulnerable than any lender under a consumer installment sales contract. *See Riggs,* 729 F.2d at 985. A purchaser who cannot satisfy a deficiency judgment can generally file a bankruptcy petition and obtain a discharge. This is a risk the creditor takes on any installment loan. Similarly, if a debtor in default surrenders the collateral during bankruptcy proceedings, the creditor must sell it, and the discharge of the debtor will bar collection of any deficiency. The same result would follow a trustee's sale. *See generally Crouch,* 104 B.R. at 772–74; *Peacock,* 87 B.R. at 659–61.

When a nondefaulting debtor is discharged while retaining the collateral, the principal disadvantage to the creditor is the possibility that the value of the collateral will be less than the balance due on the secured debt. But this is a risk in all installment loans, and presumably the creditor has structured repayment to accommodate it. If the debtor defaults by, for example, omitting payment, allowing insurance to lapse, or failing to maintain the collateral properly, the creditor can repossess the collateral and sell it. *See Belanger,* 118 B.R. at 372. The bar to recovering any deficiency is the same after bankruptcy as it would have been had the collateral been sold during the bankruptcy proceedings. If the debtor does not default, the creditor receives the full benefit of the bargain despite bankruptcy.

We reject the argument that a debtor who wishes to retain the collateral and make installment payments as they come due should resort to Chapter 13 of the Bankruptcy Code. Chapter 13 envisions a new arrangement among the debtor and creditors, not a continuation of a contract to which the creditor an debtor have already agreed. We see no reason to require a debtor to opt for Chapter 13 simply because he or she wants to remain current on a contract. If Congress intended Chapter 13 to be the sole remedy for a debtor who wished to abide by contractual obligations, there would have been little reason for enacting § 521(2).

II.

We affirm the district court's judgment because we conclude that its construction of § 521(2) is supported by well–reasoned precedent and that it is faithful to the text of the Code.

Affirmed.

NOTES AND QUESTIONS

1. If the debtor can continue to make installment payments without reaffirming or redeeming, what is the purpose of § 524 and 722? And chapter 13?

2. If the debtor continues to make payments, receives a discharge, and then defaults, what results? Is the balance of the debt discharged? Does it remain alive in full? If the creditor repossesses and sells the collateral for less than the outstanding debt, what happens to the deficiency

3. It is rather obvious that the Code contains no answers to the above questions because it is clear that the procedure permitted by the *Belanger* case was neither contemplated nor condoned by the Code. Whether or not it is a desirable procedure, is not the point; the fact is that Congress laid out the procedure in § 524 (reaffirmation), 722 (redemption by paying a lump sum), c. 13 (paying installments out of future income), and 554 (abandonment of collateral for foreclosure by the secured creditor). The *Belanger* and other courts have engrafted an additional remedy through judicial fiat.

§ 17.05 Effect of Discharge

Section 525 provides that a governmental unit may not discriminate against anyone who has obtained a discharge under the Code by way of denying a license, refusing employment or the like. As mentioned in the Committee reports, the section is intended to codify the result in *Perez v. Campbell,* 402 U.S. 637 (1971). The reports also indicate that the section is not as broad as recommended by the Bankruptcy Commission, which would have extended the prohibition to private parties. The legislative intention, however, is to permit the courts to develop the parameters of the antidiscrimination concept.

Can a city discharge a police officer who is indebted to the Public Employees Credit Union, has obtained a discharge from all debts in bankruptcy, and refuses to reaffirm the debt to the Credit Union? *See Grimes v. Hoschler,* 12 Cal. 3d 305, 115 Cal. Rptr. 625, 525 P.2d 65 (1974), *cert. denied,* 426 U.S. 973 (1975); *Rutledge v. Shreveport,* 387 F. Supp. 1277 (W.D. La. 1975); *Henry v. Heyson,* 1 C.B.C.2d 552 (Bankr. E.D. Pa. 1980).

As amended in 1984, § 525 prohibits *private* persons from discriminating with respect to employment because of use of the Bankruptcy Code.

In 1994, subsection (c) was added to prohibit the denial of a student loan because of use of the Bankruptcy Code by the borrower. The section was imperfectly drafted and, as written, would bar the denial of any loan.

IN RE HEATH

Bankruptcy Court, Northern District of Illinois
3 B.R. 351, 1 C.B.C.2d 736, 6 B.C.D. 169 (1980)

EISEN, Bankruptcy Judge:

The movant, Calvin Heath (Heath), together with his wife, Michelle R. Heath, filed a Chapter 13 plan on October 11, 1979. The plan, which scheduled an unpaid student loan owed to the respondent, University of Illinois, Chicago Campus (University), was confirmed by this Court on January 21, 1980. Subsequent to the filing of the 10% composition plan, Heath requested the University to provide him with a transcript of his academic record. The University refused to issue a transcript to Heath until such time as the prepetition debt owed to the University is paid in full. Heath now moves this Court to compel the University to relinquish the requested transcript.

In support of his motion, Heath contends that the University's action: 1. discriminates against Heath as a debtor in violation of 11 U.S.C. sec. 525; 2. contravenes the automatic stay of 11 U.S.C. sec. 362; and 3. deprives him of property in violation of 11 U.S.C. sec. 1327. Insofar as this Court agrees with Heath's contentions relating to sections 525 and 362, it is unnecessary to determine whether Heath has a property interest in the transcript which would be subject to section 1327.

Before addressing Heath's arguments, it should be stressed that the University did not file an objection to confirmation of the debtor's plan as not having been "proposed in good faith' (Sec. 1325(a)); nor is it asserted that the debtor does not really need the relief provided by Chapter 13 and that he has filed the petition only to seek improper advantage over the University under the section 362 automatic stay or merely to gain a discharge of an otherwise non– dischargeable debt. Had allegations of bad faith been asserted, a hearing on the issue would have been necessary before entry of the order confirming plan. But since the issue of bad faith or dischargeability has not been raised, it is appropriate to proceed directly to a discussion of sections 525 and 362.

I. Application of 11 U.S.C. sec. 525

By enacting 11 U.S.C. sec. 525 Congress intended to codify the Supreme Court's decision in *Perez v. Campbell*, 402 U.S. 637 (1971). House Report No. 95–595, 95th Cong., 1st Sess. (1977) 366–7; Senate Report No. 95–989, 95th Cong., 2nd Sess. (1978) 81. *In Perez*, two bankrupts challenged an Arizona statute which provided for the suspension of an individual's drivers license if there existed an outstanding automobile collision judgement against the individual. The statute was expressly applicable to outstanding judgements which had been discharged in bankruptcy. Finding that the statute in issue was intended to provide a mechanism for the collection of discharged tort judgments, the Supreme Court found the Arizona statute in direct conflict with the Congressional policy to give debtors "a new opportunity in life and a clear field for future effort, unhampered by the pressure and discouragement of preexisting debt" 402 U.S. 637 at 643, 648; quoting from *Local Loan Co.*

v. Hunt, 292 U.S. 234 at 244 (1934). Holding that this irreconcilable conflict was inconsistent with the Supremacy Clause, the Court struck down the Arizona statute 402 U.S. 637 at 656.

The language of section 525 and its legislative history unequivocally indicate that the holding in *Perez* should not be limited to its facts. Rather, the prohibition of state discrimination against debtors in a manner inconsistent with bankruptcy policy is to be extended by the Courts. Thus, whereas *Perez* was solely concerned with a state statute, section 525 explicitly proscribes various forms of discretionary action by any governmental unit. Furthermore, the legislative history of section 525 invites the Courts to extend the list of prohibited activities enumerated in section 525 whenever state action appears to contravene bankruptcy policy:

> In addition, the section is not exhaustive. The enumeration of various forms of discrimination against former bankrupts is not intended to permit other forms of discrimination. The courts have been developing the *Perez* rule. This section permits further development to prohibit actions by governmental or quasi–governmental organizations that perform licensing functions, such as a State bar association or a medical society, or by other organizations that can seriously affect the debtors' livelihood or fresh start, such as exclusion from a union on the basis of discharge of a debt to the union's credit union The courts will continue to mark the contours of the anti–discrimination provision in pursuit of sound bankruptcy policy. House Report No. 95–595, 95th Cong., 1st Sess. (1977) 366–7; Senate Report No. 95–989, 95th Cong., 2d Sess.(1978) 81.

> In the instant case there is no question that the University, a state college, is subject to section 525. It is apparent from the legislative history quoted above that section 525 extends to action by quasi–governmental units. Consequently, the only issue to be resolved is whether the University's action in withholding Heath's transcript is inconsistent with the Bankruptcy Code.

Obviously, Heath's transcript, as such, has no intrinsic value to the University. Thus, the Court finds that the University is withholding Heath's transcript for the sole purpose of compelling Heath to pay a prepetition debt, which debt may ultimately be discharged in Heath's Chapter 13 proceeding. By holding Heath's transcript hostage, the University seeks to circumvent Heath's composition plan, which includes the debt owed to the University and has been confirmed by this Court. In this context, the holding in *Handsome v. State University of New Jersey,* 445 F.Supp. 1362 (1978), is precisely on point. The defendant in *Handsome,* a state university, refused to provide a transcript to the plaintiff, a former student, until the plaintiff paid off a student loan owed to the defendant. The defendant maintained this position despite the fact that the plaintiff had obtained a discharge of the student loan in a Chapter 7 proceeding. Finding that the defendant's action transgressed upon the fresh start provision of the Bankruptcy Act, the Court relying on *Perez,* held the defendant's conduct to be violative of the Supremacy Clause. 445 F.Supp. 1362 at 1367; accord, *Lee v. Board of Higher Education in City of New York,* 1 B.R. 781 at 787–8 (1979).

The University in the instant case seeks to distinguish *Handsome* on two grounds. First, the University contends that *Handsome* is only applicable after the debtor has been granted a discharge. Although Heath has submitted a composition plan, which has been confirmed by this Court, he cannot obtain a discharge until that plan is complied with. Second, the University contends that its action has not impaired Heath's fresh start. Thus, the strictures of *Perez* as well as those of *Handsome* are not applicable to the University's action.

Neither of these arguments is persuasive. The proscriptions of section 525 are applicable to discriminatory actions prompted by a debtor's recourse to the protection of the Bankruptcy laws regardless of whether the debtor has obtained a discharge. The legislative history to section 525 is unambiguous in this request:

> The prohibition extends only to discrimination or other action based solely on the basis of bankruptcy, on the basis of insolvency before or during a bankruptcy prior to a determination of discharge, or on the basis of non–payment of a debt discharged in the bankruptcy case. House Report No. 95–595, 95th Cong., 1st Sess. (1977) 366–7; Senate Report No. 95–989, 95th Cong., 2d Sess. (1978) 81.

Indeed, it would be anomalous to grant a debtor protection from discriminatory actions in a liquidation proceeding and deny him the same protection in a rehabilitation (Chapter 13) proceeding.

The University's second contention is more subtle. By arguing that its actions have not impaired Heath's fresh start, the University implicitly assumes that discriminatory actions must impair a debtor's fresh start in order to fall within the scope of section 525.

This assumption is erroneous. In *Perez* the Supreme Court did not predicate its decision on a finding that the Arizona statute was in conflict with specific "fresh start' provisions of Chapter 7. Rather, the Court found that the Arizona statute was in conflict with the general policies supporting the Bankruptcy Act, *one* of which was Congress's intent to allow debtors to proceed, subsequent to Bankruptcy, unhampered by preexisting debts. 402 U.S. 637 at 648. Consistent with this reasoning, section 525 prohibits discriminatory action which tends to frustrate Bankruptcy policy as a *whole.*

Insofar as section 525 protects a debtor from discrimination, no legitimate distinction can be drawn between the fresh start of straight bankruptcy and the rehabilitation of a Chapter 13 or Chapter 11 debtor. In the former case, the end result is the creation of a new life, while in the latter the end result is, or should be, a continuation of the debtor's life, albeit freed from and unhampered by the financial burdens of his past. A denial of protection from discriminatory action in the latter case could only serve to dissuade debtors from pursuing rehabilitation plans. Obviously, such a result would clearly conflict with Congress' intent to encourage debtor rehabilitation. Therefore, the Court concludes not only that section 525 applies equally to fresh start (liquidation) and rehabilitation (plans) but that case precedent involving the fresh start principle should be applied with equal force to the other statutory forms of debtor relief.

This Court has confirmed a composition plan submitted by Heath, the viabilityof which is, to a large extent, contingent upon Heath's ability to secure and maintain employment. This, in turn, is dependent upon the availability of the debtor's college transcript. Thus, the University's conduct, if allowed to persist, will tend to preclude Heath from fulfilling his obligation under the confirmed composition plan. It is beyond argument, therefore, that the University's conduct frustrates the policies underlying Chapter 13 and is, consequently, violative of section 525.

II. Application of 11 U.S.C. sec. 362

Heath maintains that the University's conduct amounts to an act to collect a debt in violation of the automatic stay set out in section 362. The University, in turn, maintains, citing *Girardier v. Webster College,* 563 F.2d 1267 (8th Cir. 1977) and *Handsome, supra,* that the automatic stay provision applies only to the initiation of formal legal proceedings for the collection of prepetition debts. Since the withholding of a transcript is simply an informal means of inducing Heath to pay the prepetition debt, such withholding does not fall within the scope of the automatic stay.

Although the University's reading of *Girardier* and *Handsome* on this issue is correct, both of these cases were decided prior to the enactment of the Bankruptcy Code, effective October 1, 1979. Section 362 of the Code provides:

> (a)(6) Except as provided in subsection (b) of this section, a petition filed under section 301, 302, or 303 of this title operates as a stay, applicable to all entities, of any act to collect, assess, or recover a claim against the debtor that arose before the commencement of the case under this title.

The legislative history to section 362(a)(6) clearly indicates that Congress intended to prohibit creditors from collecting a prepetition debt in any manner:

> Paragraph (6) prevents creditors from attempting in any way to collect a prepetition debt. Creditors in consumer cases occasionally telephone debtors to encourage repayment in spite of bankruptcy. Inexperienced, frightened, or ill–counseled debtors may succumb to suggestions to repay notwithstanding their bankruptcy. This provision prevents evasion of the purpose of the bankruptcy laws by sophisticated creditors. House Report No. 95–595, 95th Cong., 1st Sess. (1977) 340–2; Senate Report No. 95–989 95th Cong., 2d Sess. (1978) 49–51.

Thus, to the extent that *Girardier* and *Handsome* limited the automatic stay to legal proceedings for debt collection, they have been legislatively overruled.

As stated earlier in this opinion, it is the opinion of the Court that the sole purpose behind the University's conduct in withholding Heath's transcript is the collection of Heath's prepetition debt. As such, the University's conduct undeniably falls within the scope of section 362(a)(6) and clearly violates the automatic stay.

Therefore, University of Illinois Chicago Campus is hereby ordered to provide Calvin Heath with a transcript of his academic record upon receipt of the customary processing fee.

(Matthew Bender & Co., Inc.)   (Pub.094)

§ 17.06   Exemptions

Another of a debtor's benefits recognized by the Bankruptcy Act and the Bankruptcy Code is embodied in the word "exemptions." It is a recognition that a financially distressed debtor may have types of property which, as a matter of policy, should not be subject to seizure and sale by creditors. For example, the family bible would be of no monetary value to creditors or, if it would, the importance to the debtor outweighs such value. Theoretically, permitting the debtor to retain the family residence is of greater importance because the debtor and family must at least be housed. (This is the basis of the homestead exemption.) Naturally, there can be and are reasonable differences of opinion as to the balancing of a debtor's and debtor's family's needs against the rightful claims to payment of creditors.

Under the 1898 Act, § 6 incorporated and made applicable the appropriate state law of exemptions; it did not contain a uniform federal provision. Thus, if the debtor was domiciled in Connecticut, there would be a minimal amount of exempt property, perhaps a cow and sufficient feed for 30 days for the cow. If domiciled in Texas, the debtor could claim as exempt a residence worth $4,000,000 as a homestead, and an air–conditioned luxury car worth $75,000 (under the state's horse and buggy exemption). The states varied considerably in their treatment of debtors in the law of exemptions. *See* Chapter 7, supra.

During the legislative process leading to enactment of the Code, there was a proposal to delete the concept of § 6 and provide a federal law of exemptions for use in bankruptcy cases, thereby overriding state law. Report of the Commission on the Bankruptcy Laws of the U.S., Part II, § 4–503 (1973). The basic idea was to provide a middle ground between the hardly favorable approach of the Northeast and the overly generous attitude of such states as Texas, California, and Florida. It would also be consonant with the constitutional mandate for Congress to provide for a uniform law of bankruptcy. States' rights adherents were not enamored of this approach, however, and some rather influential citizens (from Texas) threatened to have their state secede from the Union. (There were those, on the other hand, who thought this would be no great loss.) In any event, the recommendation for a single law of exemptions did not prevail. S. 2266 proposed to retain the former system of § 6. H.R. 8200 provided debtors the option of selecting the state law of exemptions or a new federal law as set forth in § 522.

As enacted, § 522 of the Code creates almost a three–tiered system. In the first two tiers, a debtor (individuals only) may elect to claim either the exemptions allowed by the domiciliary state or the exemptions set forth in § 522(d) (the federal floor). Thus, if the state law were more beneficial, a debtor would elect that law; if the list of exempt property in § 522(d) were more beneficial, the debtor could select that list. A debtor is not permitted, however, to select from each list. The third tier is that state legislatures are given an option to opt out of the election, that is, they can prohibit their citizenry from selecting the federal system. Most states have enacted legislation so prohibiting their domiciliaries. For a state–by–state analysis *see* 7 Collier, Bankruptcy (15th ed.).

NOTES AND QUESTIONS

1. At whose behest would states, so early in the operation of the Bankruptcy Code, move to enact legislation barring debtors from using the federal exemptions?

2. Why would anyone want to so bar debtors?

3. Is § 522(b)(1) unconstitutional as an impermissible delegation of authority by Congress? *See* Koffler, *The Bankruptcy Clause and Exemption Laws: A Reexamination of the Doctrine of Geographic Uniformity,* 58 N.Y.U. L. Rev. 22 (1983). Section 522(d) contains the federal exemptions. Listed there are types of property, monetary value of property, and aggregate amounts to which a debtor may be entitled. There, for example, the homestead exemption is listed as well as the final homestead. Certain types of personal property are also specified.

4. Suppose the debtor is an apartment dweller under lease; may a homestead exemption be claimed? If not, may anything be claimed in lieu thereof?

5. Suppose the debtor has no homestead and none of the personal property specified in § 522(d); is it impossible for the debtor to claim anything as exempt?

6. If the debtor and the debtor's spouse have filed a joint chapter 7 petition, how much by way of minimum exemptions under § 522(d) may they claim in total? May each claim separately and elect state or federal law separately?

RHODES v. STEWART

United States Court of Appeals, Sixth Circuit
705 F.2d 159 (1983) cert. denied, 464 U.S. 983, 104 S. Ct. 427 (1983)

KRUPANSKY, Circuit Judge.

This is a direct appeal, pursuant to 28 U.S.C. § 1293(b), from a judgment of the Bankruptcy Court for the Middle District of Tennessee declaring "invalid" Tennessee's "opt–out" statute, T.C.A. § 26–2–112. *Rhodes v. Stewart,* 14 B.R. 629 (Bkrtcy.M.D.Tenn. 1981). . . .

The pertinent substantive inquiry on appeal is the constitutionality of Tennessee's opt–out statute, T.C.A. § 26–2–112. The Bankruptcy Reform Act of 1978, 11 U.S.C. § 101 *et seq.,* created an express enumeration of exemptions from the bankruptcy estate. 11 U.S.C. § 522(d). Included within this federal exemption scheme is the following "homestead" exemption:

(1) The debtor's aggregate interest, not to exceed $7,500 in value, in real property or personal property that the debtor or a dependent of the debtor uses

as a residence, in a cooperative that owns property that the debtor or a dependent of the debtor uses as a residence, or in a burial plot for the debtor or a dependent of the debtor. (emphasis added) 11 U.S.C. § 522(d)(1). Congress, however, further vested in the states the authority to "opt out' of the federal exemption scheme and a significant number of other states, have rejected or opted–out of the federal exemption scheme embodied in 11 U.S.C. § 522(d):

§ 26–2–112. Exemptions for the purpose of bankruptcy The personal property exemptions as provided for in this part, and the other exemptions as provided in other sections of the Tennessee Code Annotated for the citizens of Tennessee, are hereby declared adequate and the citizens of Tennessee, pursuant to section 522(b)(1), Public Law 95–598 known as the Bankruptcy Reform Act of 1978, Title 11 USC, section 522(b)(1), are not authorized to claim as exempt the property described in the Bankruptcy Reform Act of 1978, 11 U.S.C. 522(d). T.C.A. § 26–2–112. At least a section of Tennessee's statutory exemption provisions are less beneficial to a debtor than those permitted in the federal exemption provision. In particular, T.C.A. § 26–2–301 establishes the following homestead exemption:

§ 26–2–301. *Basic Exemption*(a) An individual, regardless of whether he is head of a family, shall be entitled to a homestead exemption upon real property, which is owned by the individual and used by him, his spouse, or a dependent, as a *principal place of residence.* The aggregate value of such homestead exemption shall not exceed *five thousand dollars* ($5,000). (emphasis added)

Tennessee's homestead exemption is less beneficial to a debtor than its federal counterpart in terms of the value of the exemption ($5,000 versus $7,500) and in terms of restrictions; a Tennessee debtor may only exempt the homestead used "as a principal place of residence" whereas the debtor authorized to utilize the federal homestead exemption may exempt that used "as a residence."

Kenneth Rhodes (Rhodes) filed a voluntary Chapter 7 petition in bankruptcy and sought to rely upon the federal exemption scheme embodied in 11 U.S.C. § 522(d) to exempt all unencumbered real property including a 6/365 interval time–sharing ownership interest in a condominium located in Florida for which a purchase price of $3,800 had been paid. Since the condominium was not his principal place of residence, it was not exempted under Tennessee's homestead provision, T.C.A. § 26–2–301, although it would have been exempt were Rhodes permitted to apply the federal exemption. The trustee in bankruptcy petitioned the bankruptcy court to apply the more restrictive exemptions of Tennessee bankruptcy statutes since Tennessee had opted–out of the federal exemption scheme as permitted by 11 U.S.C. § 522(b)(1). The bankruptcy court declared Tennessee's opt–out statute ' invalid" and permitted Rhodes to utilize the federal exemption. This appeal ensued.

Congressional authority to enact uniform bankruptcy laws is derivative of Article 1, § 8, cl. 4 of the United States Constitution which gives to Congress power "To establish . . . uniform Laws on the subject of Bankruptcies throughout the United States" (Bankruptcy Clause). The Supreme Court has pronounced that the Bankruptcy Clause requires only geographical rather than personal uniformity. *Hanover National Bank v. Moyses,* 186 U.S. 181, 22 S.Ct. 857, 46 L.Ed. 1113 (1902). *See also: Stellwagen v. Clum,* 245 U.S. 605, 38 S.Ct. 215, 62 L.Ed. 507 (1918). This Court concludes that 11 U.S.C. § 552(b)(1), which authorizes states to opt–out of the federal exemption scheme allowing the states to elect differing exemption structures, is an exercise of the legislative prerogative to establish a "uniform law" and therefore falls within that scope of authority provided to Congress in the Bankruptcy Clause. Accord: *In re Sullivan,* 680 F.2d 1131 (7th Cir. 1982) (detailed and well–reasoned opinion): *In re Lausch,* 16 B.R. 162 (M.D.Fla. 1981); *In re Ambrose,* 4 B.R. 395 (Bkrtcy: M.D. Ohio 1980); *In re Curry,* 5 B.R. 282 (Bkrtcy. N.D. Ohio 1980). *See also: In re Morgan,* 689 F.2d 471 (4th Cir. 1982) (acknowledging validity of state exemption provisions without expressly addressing violation of Bankruptcy Clause). To the extent that the bankruptcy judgment in the action sub judice is predicated upon the proposition that T.C.A. § 26–2–112 is "invalid" as an impermissible delegation of Congressional legislative authority resulting in non–uniform state laws and therefore violative of the Bankruptcy Clause, such judgment must be reversed.

The bankruptcy court reasoned that "Congress clearly has preempted state law with regard to the exemption of property interests in bankruptcy cases" . 14 B.R. at 631. Contrasting the "lengthy and detailed" federal exemption scheme embodied in 11 U.S.C. § 522 with state exemption laws typified in the legislative history of the Act as "outmoded" , the bankruptcy court adjudged that "[f]or a state to effectively opt its citizens out of § 522(d) it must provide a scheme of exemptions which is consistent with this policy", to wit, not inconsistent with or more restrictive than the exemptions enumerated in § 522(d). 14 B.R. at 632, and 634 respectively. Having concluded that Congress had preempted the field of exemptions and that Tennessee's state homestead exemption conflicted with the federal homestead exemption Tennessee's opt–out statute was declared "invalid." 14 B.R. at 635.

It is fundamental that the state and federal legislatures share concurrent authority to promulgate bankruptcy laws, *Sturges v. Crowningshield,* 17 U.S. (4 Wheat) 119, 4 L.Ed. 529 (1819), and that the Supremacy Clause and the doctrine of preemption will serve to invalidate state promulgations to the extent that they are inconsistent with or contrary to federal laws. *Perez v. Campbell,* 402 U.S. 637, 91 S.Ct. 1704, 29 L.Ed.2d 233 (1971). It is equally axiomatic, however, that Congress has not preempted an area wherein it has legislated when it expressly and concurrently authorizes the state legislatures to disregard or opt–out of such federal legislative area. In such instance, rather than preempting the area, Congress expressly authorizes the states to "preempt" the *federal* legislation. Congress did not intend to preempt bankruptcy exemptions through promulgation of 11 U.S.C. § 522(d) since it vested in the states the ultimate authority to determine their own bankruptcy exemptions. 11 U.S.C. § 522(b)(1). Section 522(b)(1) encompasses no facial restrictions upon the states' authority to opt–out. The Fifth Circuit has recently adjudged that the states are empowered to create whatever exemptions they elect:

> The unambiguous language of section 522(b) implicitly indicates a state may exempt the same property included in the federal laundry list [§ 522(d)], more property than that included in the federal laundry list, or less property than that included in the federal laundry list. The states also may prescribe their own

requirements for exemptions, which may either circumscribe or enlarge the list of exempt property.

In re McManus, 681 F.2d 353, 355–56 (5th Cir. 1982) (footnote omitted). Similarly, the Seventh Circuit has rejected the contention that Illinois' less beneficial exemptions are preempted by § 522(d):

> In summary, however appropriate a preemption analysis might have been in *Cheeseman [v. Nachman*, 656 F.2d 60 (4th Cir. 1980)]*, we think that it is not relevant to the issue presented by the present case. To say that state exemption provisions providing less solace to debtors than the federal exemptions of section 522(d) are in "conflict" with either the language of the Code or expressions of Congressional intent underlying it is simply inaccurate. If Congress has the power to permit states to set their own exemption levels, the Illinois provisions are constitutional.

In re Sullivan, supra, 680 F.2d at 1137. The Fourth Circuit has adjudged that § 522(b)(1) affords each state the option to restrict its residents to the exemptions permitted by the laws of the particular state, and that residents of Virginia, which has exercised the option to opt–out, are not only restricted to state exemptions but must moreover comply with the state mechanisms for claiming those exemptions. *In re Morgan*, 689 F.2d 471 (4th Cir. 1982). *See also: In re Lausch*, 16 B.R. 162, 165 (M.D. Fla. 1981) ("§ 522(b)(1) is not an unconstitutional delegation of congressional legislative power but rather is merely a recognition of the concurrent legislative power of the state legislatures to enact laws governing bankruptcy exemptions."); *In re Curry*, 5 B.R. 282, 286 (Bkrtcy.N.D.Ohio 1980) ("[A] debtor domiciled in Ohio may only exempt from property of his estate property that is specified under Ohio Revised Code Section 2329.66."); *In re Ambrose*, 4 B.R. 395 (Bkrtcy.N.D.Ohio 1980).

> The Fifth Circuit has further observed that it
>
> is inescapable that Congress must have realized that the states may enact different exemptions which would possibly conflict with Congress' own exemption policy as it was reflected in § 522(d).

In re McManus, supra, 681 F.2d at 357, note 7. Indeed if Congress intended to foreclose the states from promulgating more restrictive exemptions it could simply have enacted the exemption scheme currently embodied in § 522(d) and not provided the states with an election to opt–out. The Supremacy Clause would have prevented the states from promulgating more restrictive and, therefore, inconsistent bankruptcy exemptions. When the bankruptcy court in the case at bar adjudged that Tennessee could not promulgate a homestead exemption less beneficial to debtors than that of its federal counterpart, said court effectively reduced § 522(b)(1) to an exercise in legislative futility.

As T.C.A. § 26–2–112 is constitutional as challenged, the judgment of the bankruptcy court is Reversed and this action is Remanded for further proceedings consistent with this opinion.

TAYLOR v. FREELAND & KRONZ

United States Supreme Court
503 U.S. —, 112 S.Ct. 1644, 26 C.B.C.2d 487 (1992)

THOMAS, J., delivered the opinion of the Court, in which REHNQUIST, C.J., and WHITE, BLACKMUN, O'CONNOR, SCALIA, KENNEDY, and SOUTER, JJ., joined. STEVENS, J., filed a dissenting opinion.

Section 522(l) of the Bankruptcy Code requires a debtor to file a list of the property that the debtor claims as statutorily exempt from distribution to creditors. Bankruptcy Rule 4003 affords creditors and the bankruptcy trustee 30 days to object to claimed exemptions. We must decide in this case whether the trustee may contest the validity of an exemption after the 30–day period if the debtor had no colorable basis for claiming the exemption.

I.

The debtor in this case, Emily Davis, declared bankruptcy while she was pursuing an employment discrimination claim in the state courts. The relevant proceedings began in 1978 when Davis filed a complaint with the Pittsburgh Commission on Human Relations. Davis alleged that her employer, Trans World Airlines (TWA), had denied her promotions on the basis of her race and sex. The Commission held for Davis as to liability but did not calculate the damages owed by TWA. The Pennsylvania Court of Common Pleas reversed the Commission, but the Pennsylvania Commonwealth Court reversed that court and reinstated the Commission's determination of liability. TWA next appealed to the Pennsylvania Supreme Court.

In October 1984, while that appeal was pending, Davis filed a Chapter 7 bankruptcy petition. Petitioner, Robert J. Taylor, became the trustee of Davis' bankruptcy estate. Respondents, Wendell G. Freeland, Richard F. Kronz, and their law firm, represented Davis in the discrimination suit. On a schedule filed with the Bankruptcy Court, Davis claimed as exempt property the money that she expected to win in her discrimination suit against TWA. She described this property as "Proceeds from lawsuit–[Davis] v. TWA" and "Claim for lost wages" and listed its value "as unknown." App. 18.

Performing his duty as a trustee, Taylor held the required initial meeting of creditors in January 1985. *See* 11 U.S.C. § 341; Bkrtcy. Rule 2003(a). At this meeting, respondents told Taylor that they estimated that Davis might win $90,000 in her suit against TWA. Several days after the meeting, Taylor wrote a letter to respondents telling them that he considered the potential proceeds of the lawsuit to be property of Davis' bankruptcy estate. He also asked respondents for more details about the suit. Respondents described the procedural posture of the case and expressed optimism that they might settle with TWA for $110,000.

Taylor decided not to object to the claimed exemption. The record reveals that Taylor doubted that the lawsuit had any value. Taylor at one point explained: "I have

had past experience in examining debtors. . . . [M]any of them . . . indicate they
have potential lawsuits. . . [M]any of them do not turn out to be advantageous and
. . . . many of them might wind up settling far within the exemption limitation."
App. 52. Taylor also said that he thought Davis' discrimination claim against TWA
might be a "nullity." *Id.,* at 58.

Taylor proved mistaken. In October 1986, the Pennsylvania Supreme Court
affirmed the Commonwealth Court's determination that TWA had discriminated
against Davis. In a subsequent settlement of the issue of damages, TWA agreed to
pay Davis a total of $110,000. TWA paid part of this amount by issuing a check
made to both Davis and respondents for $71,000. Davis apparently signed this check
over to respondents in payment of their fees. TWA paid the remainder of the
$110,000 by other means. Upon learning of the settlement, Taylor filed a complaint
against respondents in the Bankruptcy Court. He demanded that respondents turn
over the money that they had received from Davis because he considered it property
of Davis' bankruptcy estate. Respondents argued that they could keep the fees
because Davis had claimed the proceeds of the lawsuit as exempt.

The Bankruptcy Court sided with Taylor. It concluded that Davis had "no
statutory basis" for claiming the proceeds of the lawsuit as exempt and ordered
respondents to "return" approximately $23,000 to Taylor, a sum sufficient to pay
off all of Davis' unpaid creditors. *In re Davis,* 105 B.R. 288 (WD Pa. 1989). The
District Court affirmed, *In re Davis,* 118 B.R. 272 (WD Pa. 1990), but the Court
of Appeals for the Third Circuit reversed, 938 F.2d 420 [25 C.B.C.2d 167] (1991).
The Court of Appeals held that the Bankruptcy Court could not require respondents
to turn over the money because Davis had claimed it as exempt, and Taylor had
failed to object to the claimed exemption in a timely manner. We granted certiorari,
502 U.S. — (1991), and now affirm.

II.

When a debtor files a bankruptcy petition, all of his property becomes property
of a bankruptcy estate. *See* 11 U.S.C. § 541. The Code, however, allows the debtor
to prevent the distribution of certain property by claiming it as exempt. Section
522(b) allowed Davis to choose the exemptions afforded by state law or the federal
exemptions listed in § 522(d). Section 522(l) states the procedure for claiming
exemptions and objecting to claimed exemptions as follows:

> "The debtor shall file a list of property that the debtor claims as exempt under
> subsection (b) of this section. . . . Unless a party in interest objects, the property
> claimed as exempt on such list is exempt."

Although § 522(l) itself does not specify the time for objecting to a claimed
exemption, Bankruptcy Rule 4003(b) provides in part:

> "The trustee or any creditor may file objections to the list of property claimed
> as exempt within 30 days after the conclusion of the meeting of creditors held
> pursuant to Rule 2003(a) . . . unless, within such period, further time is granted
> by the court."

In this case, as noted, Davis claimed the proceeds from her employment
discrimination lawsuit as exempt by listing them in the schedule that she filed under

§ 522(l). The parties agree that Davis did not have a right to exempt more than a small portion of these proceeds either under state law or under the federal exemptions specified in § 522(d). Davis in fact claimed the full amount as exempt. Taylor, as a result, apparently could have made a valid objection under § 522(l) and Rule 4003 if he had acted promptly. We hold, however, that his failure to do so prevents him from challenging the validity of the exemption now.

A.

Taylor acknowledges that Rule 4003(b) establishes a 30–day period for objecting to exemptions and that § 522(l) states that "[u]nless a party in interest objects, the property claimed as exempt. . . is exempt." He argues, nonetheless, that his failure to object does not preclude him from challenging the exemption at this time. In Taylor's view, § 522(l) and Rule 4003(b) serve only to narrow judicial inquiry into the validity of an exemption after 30 days, not to preclude judicial inquiry altogether. In particular, he maintains that courts may invalidate a claimed exemption after expiration of the 30–day period if the debtor did not have a good–faith or reasonably disputable basis for claiming it. In this case, Taylor asserts, Davis did not have a colorable basis for claiming all of the lawsuit proceeds as exempt and thus lacked good faith.

Taylor justifies his interpretation of § 522(l) by arguing that requiring debtors to file claims in good faith will discourage them from claiming meritless exemptions merely in hopes that no one will object. Taylor does not stand alone in this reading of § 522(b). Several Courts of Appeals have adopted the same position upon similar reasoning. *See In re Peterson*, 920 F.2d 1389, 1393–1394 [24 C.B.C.2d 525] (CA8 1990); *In re Dembs*, 757 F.2d 777, 780 [12 C.B.C.2d 591] (CA6 1985); *In re Sherk*, 918 F.2d 1170, 1174 [24 C.B.C.2d 502] (CA5 1990).

We reject Taylor's argument. Davis claimed the lawsuit proceeds as exempt on a list filed with the Bankruptcy Court. Section 522(l), to repeat, says that "[u]nless a party in interest objects, the property claimed as exempt on such list is exempt." Rule 4003(b) gives the trustee and creditors 30 days from the initial creditors' meeting to object. By negative implication, the Rule indicates that creditors may not object after 30 days "unless, within such period, further time is granted by the court." The Bankruptcy Court did not extend the 30–day period. Section 522(l) therefore has made the property exempt. Taylor cannot contest the exemption at this time whether or not Davis had a colorable statutory basis for claiming it.

Deadlines may lead to unwelcome results, but they prompt parties to act and they produce finality. In this case, despite what respondents repeatedly told him, Taylor did not object to the claimed exemption. If Taylor did not know the value of the potential proceeds of the lawsuit, he could have sought a hearing on the issue, See Rule 4003(c), or he could have asked the Bankruptcy Court for an extension of time to object, See Rule 4003(b). Having done neither, Taylor cannot now seek to deprive Davis and respondents of the exemption.

Taylor suggests that our holding will create improper incentives. He asserts that it will lead debtors to claim property exempt on the chance that the trustee and creditors, for whatever reason, will fail to object to the claimed exemption on time.

He asserts that only a requirement of good faith can prevent what the Eighth Circuit has termed "exemption by declaration." *Peterson,* 920 F.2d at 1393. This concern, however, does not cause us to alter our interpretation of 522(l).

Debtors and their attorneys face penalties under various provisions for engaging in improper conduct in bankruptcy proceedings. *See, e.g.,* 11 U.S.C. § 727(a)(4)(B) (authorizing denial of discharge for presenting fraudulent claims); Rule 1008 (requiring filings to "be verified or contain an unsworn declaration" of truthfulness under penalty of perjury); Rule 9011 (authorizing sanctions for signing certain documents not "well grounded in fact and . . . warranted by existing law or a good faith argument for the extension, modification, or reversal of existing law"); 18 U.S.C. § 152 (imposing criminal penalties for fraud in bankruptcy cases). These provisions may limit bad–faith claims of exemptions by debtors. To the extent that they do not, Congress may enact comparable provisions to address the difficulties that Taylor predicts will follow our decision. We have no authority to limit the application of § 522(l) to exemptions claimed in good faith.

B.

Taylor also asserts that courts may consider the validity of the exemption under a different provision of the Bankruptcy Code, 11 U.S.C. § 105(a), despite his failure to object in a timely manner. That provision states:

> " The court may issue any order, process, or judgment that is necessary or appropriate to carry out the provisions of this title. *No provision of this title providing for the raising of an issue by a party in interest shall be construed to preclude the court from, sua sponte, taking any action* or making any determination necessary or appropriate to enforce or implement court orders or rules, or to prevent an abuse or process." § 105(a) (emphasis added).

Although Taylor stresses that he is not asserting that courts in bankruptcy have broad authorization to do equity in derogation of the code and rules, he maintains that § 105 permits courts to disallow exemptions not claimed in good faith. Several courts have accepted this position. *See, e.g., Ragsdale v. Genesco, Inc.,* 674 F.2d 277, 278 [6 C.B.C.2d 1170] (CA4 1982); *In re Staniforth,* 116 B.R. 127, 131 (WD Wis. 1990); *In re Budinsky,* No. 90–01099, 1991 WL 105640 (WD Pa. June 10, 1991).

We decline to consider § 105(a) in this case because Taylor raised the argument for the first time in his opening brief on the merits. Our Rule 14.1(a) makes clear that "[o]nly the questions set forth in the petition [for certiorari], or fairly included therein, will be considered by the Court," and our rule 24.1(a) states that a brief on the merits should not "raise additional questions or change the substance of the questions already presented" in the petition. *See Yee v. Escondido,* 503 U.S. (1992). In addition, we have said that "[o]rdinarily, this Court does not decide questions not raised or resolved in the lower court[s]." *Youakim v. Miller,* 425 U.S. 231, 234 (1976) *(per curiam).* These principles help to maintain the integrity of the process of certiorari. *Cf. Oklahoma City v. Tuttle,* 471 U.S. 808, 816 (1985). The Court decides which questions to consider through well–established procedures; allowing the able counsel who argue before us to alter these questions or to devise additional questions at the last minute would thwart this system. We see no "unusual circumstances" that warrant addressing Taylor's § 105(a) argument at this time. *Berkemer v. McCarty,* 468 U.S. 420, 433, n. 38 (1984).

The judgment of the Court of Appeals is

Affirmed.

[Dissenting opinion omitted.]

OWEN v. OWEN

Supreme Court of the United States
501 U.S. —, 111 S.Ct. 1833, 24 C.B.C.2d 850 (1991)

Justice SCALIA delivered the opinion of the Court:

The Bankruptcy Code allows the States to define what property a debtor may exempt from the bankruptcy estate that will be distributed among his creditors. 11 U.S.C. § 522(b). The Code also provides that judicial liens encumbering exempt property can be eliminated. 11 U.S.C. § 522(f). The question in this case is whether that elimination can operate when the State has defined the exempt property in such a way as specifically to exclude property encumbered by judicial liens.

I.

In 1975, Helen Owen, the respondent, obtained a judgment against petitioner Dwight Owen, her former husband, for approximately $160,000. The judgment was recorded in Sarasota County, Florida, in July 1976. Petitioner did not at that time own any property in Sarasota County, but under Florida law, the judgment would attach to any after–acquired property recorded in the county. *B.A. Lott, Inc. v. Padgett,* 153 Fla. 304, 14 So. 2d 667 (1943). In 1984, petitioner purchased a condominium in Sarasota County; upon acquisition of title, the property became subject to respondent's judgment lien. *Porter–Mallard Co. v. Dugger,* 117 Fla. 137, 157 So. 429 (1934).

One year later, Florida amended its homestead law so that petitioner's condominium, which previously had not qualified as a homestead, thereafter did. Under the Florida Constitution, homestead property is "exempt from forced sale . . . and no judgment, decree or execution [can] be a lien thereon . . . ," Fla. Const., Art. 10, § 4(a). The Florida courts have interpreted this provision, however, as being inapplicable to pre–existing liens, *i.e.,* liens that attached before the property acquired its homestead status. *Bessemer v. Gersten,* 381 So. 2d 1344, 1347, n. 1 (Fla. 1980); *Aetna Ins. Co. v. Lagasse,* 223 So. 2d 727, 728 (Fla. 1969); *Pasco v. Harley,* 73 Fla. 819, 824–825, 75 So. 30, 32–33 (1917); *Volpitta v. Fields,* 369 So. 2d 367, 369 (Fla. App. 1979); *Lyon v. Arnold,* 46 F.2d 451, 452 (CA5 1931). Pre–existing liens, then, are in effect an exception to the Florida homestead exemption.

In January 1986, petitioner filed for bankruptcy under chapter 7 of the Code, and claimed a homestead exemption in his Sarasota condominium. The condominium, valued at approximately $135,000, was his primary asset; his liabilities included approximately $350,000 owed to the respondent. The bankruptcy court discharged petitioner's personal liability for these debts, and sustained, over respondent's objections, his claimed exemption.

The condominium, however, remained subject to respondent's pre–existing lien, and after discharge, petitioner moved to reopen his case to avoid the lien pursuant to § 522(f)(1). The Bankruptcy Court refused to decree the avoidance; the District Court affirmed, finding that the lien had attached before the property qualified for the exemption, and that Florida law therefore did not exempt the lien encumbered property. 86 B.R. 691 (MD. Fla. 1988). The Court of Appeals for the Eleventh Circuit affirmed on the same ground. 877 F.2d 44 (1989). We granted certiorari. 495 U.S. (1990).

II.

An estate in bankruptcy consists of all the interests in property, legal and equitable, possessed by the debtor at the time of filing, as well as those interests recovered or recoverable through transfer and lien avoidance provisions. An exemption is an interest withdrawn from the estate (and hence from the creditors) for the benefit of the debtor. Section 522 determines what property a debtor may exempt. Under § 522(b), he must select between a list of federal exemptions (set forth in § 522(d)) and the exemptions provided by his State, "unless the State law that is applicable to the debtor . . . specifically does not so authorize," 11 U.S.C. § 522(b)(1)–that is, unless the State "opts out' of the federal list. If a State opts out, then its debtors are limited to the exemptions provided by state law. Nothing in subsection (b) (or elsewhere in the Code) limits a State's power to restrict the scope of its exemptions; indeed, it could theoretically accord no exemptions at all.

Property that is properly exempted under § 522 is (with some exceptions) immunized against liability for prebankruptcy debts. § 522(c). No property can be exempted (and thereby immunized), however, unless it first falls within the bankruptcy estate. Section 522(b) provides that the debtor may exempt certain property from property of the estate; obviously, then an interest that is not possessed by the estate cannot be exempted. Thus, if a debtor holds only bare legal title to his house–if, for example, the house is subject to a purchase–money mortgage for its full value–then only that legal interest passes to the estate; the equitable interest remains with the mortgage holder, 11 U.S.C. § 541(d). And since the equitable interest does not pass to the estate, neither can it pass to the debtor as an exempt interest in property. Legal title will pass, and can be the subject of an exemption; but the property will remain subject to the lien interest of the mortgage holder. This was the rule of Long v. Bullard, 117 U.S. 617 (1886), codified in § 522. Only where the Code empowers the court to avoid liens or transfers can an interest originally not within the estate be passed to the estate, and subsequently (through the claim of an exemption) to the debtor.

It is such an avoidance provision that is at issue here, to which we now turn. Section 522(f) reads as follows:

"(f) Notwithstanding any waiver of exemptions, the debtor may avoid the fixing of a lien on an interest of the debtor in property to the extent that such lien impairs an exemption to which the debtor would have been entitled under subsection (b) of this section, if such lien is–

"(1) a judicial lien; or

"(2) a nonpossessory, nonpurchase–money security interest. . . ."

The lien in the present case is a judicial lien, and we assume without deciding that it fixed "on an interest of the debtor in property." *See Farrey v. Sanderfoot,* U.S. (1991). The question presented by this case is whether it "impairs an exemption to which [petitioner] would have been entitled under subsection (b)." Since Florida has chosen to opt out of the listed federal exemptions, see Fla. Stat. § 222.20 (1989), the only subsection (b) exemption at issue is the Florida homestead exemption described above. Respondent suggests that, to resolve this case, we need only ask whether the judicial lien impairs that exemption. It obviously does not, since the Florida homestead exemption is not assertable against pre–existing judicial liens. To permit avoidance of the lien, respondent urges, would not *preserve* the exemption but would *expand* it.

At first blush, this seems entirely reasonable. Several Courts of Appeals in addition to the Eleventh Circuit here have reached this result with respect to built–in limitations on state exemptions, though others have rejected it. What must give us pause, however, is that this result has been widely and uniformly rejected with respect to built–in limitations on the federal exemptions. Most of the federally listed exemptions (set forth in § 522(d) are explicitly restricted to the "debtor's aggregate interest" or the "debtor's interest" up to a maximum amount. *See* § § 522(d)(1)–(6), (8). If respondent's approach to § 522(f) were applied, all of these exemptions (and perhaps others as well) would be limited by unavoided encumbering liens, see § 522(c). The federal homestead exemption, for example, allows the debtor to exempt from the property of the estate " the debtor's aggregate interest, not to exceed $7,500 in value, in . . . a residence." § 522(d)(1). If respondent's interpretation of § 522(f) were applied to this exemption, a debtor who owned a house worth § 10,000 that was subject to a judicial lien for $9,000 would not be entitled to the full homestead exemption of $7,500. The judicial lien would not be avoidable under § 522(f), since it does not "impair" the exemption, which is limited to the debtor's "aggregate interest" of $1,000. The uniform practice of bankruptcy courts, however, is to the contrary. To determine the application of § 522(f) they ask not whether the lien impairs an exemption to which the debtor is in fact entitled, but whether it impairs an exemption to which he would have been entitled but for the lien itself.

As the preceding italicized words suggest, this reading is more consonant with the text of § 522(f)–which establishes as the base line, against which impairment is to be measured, not an exemption to which the debtor "*is* entitled," but one to which he "*would have been entitled.*" The latter phrase denotes a state of affairs that is conceived or hypothetical, rather than actual, and requires the reader to disregard some element of reality. "Would have been" but for what? The answer given, with respect to the federal exemptions, has been but for the lien at issue, and that seems to us correct.

The only other conceivable possibility is but for a waiver–harking back to the beginning phrase of § 522(f), "Notwithstanding any waiver of exemptions. . . " The use of contrary–to–fact construction after a "notwithstanding" phrase is not, however, common usage, if even permissible. Moreover, though one might employ it when the "notwithstanding" phrase is the main point of the provision in question ("Notwithstanding any waiver, a debtor shall retain those exemptions to which he would have been entitled under subsection (b)"), it would be most strange to employ it where the "notwithstanding" phrase, as here, is an aside. The point of § 522(f) is not to exclude waivers (though that is done in passing, waivers are addressed directly in § 522(e)) but to provide that the debtor may avoid the fixing of a lien. In that context, for every instance in which "would have been entitled" may be accurate (because the incidentally mentioned waiver occurred) there will be thousands of instances in which "is entitled" should have been used. It seems to us that "would have been entitled" must refer to the generality, if not indeed the universality, of cases covered by the provision; and on that premise the only conceivable fact we are invited to disregard is the existence of the lien.

This reading must also be accepted, at least with respect to the federal exemptions, if § 522(f) is not to become an irrelevancy with respect to the most venerable, most common and most important exemptions. The federal exemptions for homestead (§ 522(d)(1)), for motor vehicles (§ 522(d)(2)), for household goods and wearing apparel (§ 522(d)(3)), and for tools of the trade (§ 22(d)(6)), are all defined by reference to the debtor's "interest" or "aggregate interest," so that if respondent's interpretation is accepted, no encumbrances of these could be avoided. Surely § 522(f) promises more than that–and surely it would be bizarre for the federal scheme to prevent the avoidance of liens on those items, but to permit it for the less crucial items (for example, an " unmatured life insurance contract owned by the debtor," § 522(d)(7)) that are not described in such fashion as unquestionably to exclude liens.

We have no doubt, then, that the lower courts' unanimously agreed–upon manner of applying § 522(f) to federal exemptions–ask first whether avoiding the lien would entitle the debtor to an exemption, and if it would, then avoid and recover the lienis correct.5 The question then becomes whether a different interpretation should be adopted for State exemptions. We do not see how that could be possible. Nothing in the text of § 522(f) remotely justifies treating the two categories of exemptions differently. The provision refers to the impairment of "exemptions to which the debtor would have been entitled under subsection (b)," and that includes federal exemptions and state exemptions alike. Nor is there any overwhelmingly clear policy impelling us, if we possessed the power, to create a distinction that the words of the statute do not contain. Respondent asserts that it is inconsistent with the Bankruptcy Code's "opt–out" policy, whereby the States may define their own exemptions, to refuse to take those exemptions with all their built–in limitations. That is plainly not true, however, since there is no doubt that a state exemption which purports to be available "unless waived" will be given full effect, even if it has been waived, for purposes of § 522(f)–the first phrase of which, as we have noted, recites that it applies "notwithstanding any waiver of exemptions." *See Dominion Bank of Cumberlands, NA v. Nuckolls,* 780 F.2d 408, 412 [13 C.B.C.2d 1249] (CA4 1985).

Just as it is not inconsistent with the policy of permitting state–defined exemptions to have another policy disfavoring waiver of exemptions, whether federal– or state–created; so also it is not inconsistent to have a policy disfavoring the impingement of certain types of liens upon exemptions, whether federal– or state–created. We have no basis for pronouncing the opt–out policy absolute, but must apply it along with whatever other competing or limiting policies the statute contains.

On the basis of the analysis we have set forth above with respect to federal exemptions, and in light of the equivalency of treatment accorded to federal and State exemptions by § 522(f), we conclude that Florida's exclusion of certain liens from the scope of its homestead protection does not achieve a similar exclusion from the Bankruptcy Code's lien avoidance provision.

III.

The foregoing conclusion does not necessarily resolve this case. Section 522(f) permits the avoidance of the "fixing of a lien on an interest of the debtor." Some courts have held it inapplicable to a lien that was already attached to property when the debtor acquired it, since in such a case there never was a "fixing of a lien" on the debtor's interest. *See In re McCormick,* 18 B.R. 911, 914 (Bkrtcy. Ct. W.D. Pa.), aff'd, 22 B.R. 997 (W.D. Pa. 1982); *In re Scott,* 12 B.R. 613, 615 (Bkrtcy. Ct. W.D. Okla. 1981). Under Florida law, the lien may have attached simultaneously with the acquisition of the property interest. If so, it could be argued that the lien did not fix "on an interest of the debtor." *See Farrey v. Sanderfoot,* U.S. (1991). The Court of Appeals did not pass on this issue, nor on the subsidiary question of whether the Florida statute extending the homestead exemption was a taking, *cf. United States v. Security Industrial Bank,* 459 U.S. 70 [7 C.B.C.2d 629] (1982). We express no opinion on these points, and leave them to be considered by the Court of Appeals on remand.

The judgment of the Court of Appeals is reversed, and the case remanded for proceedings consistent with this opinion.

It is so ordered.

Justice STEVENS, dissenting:

The Court's analysis puts the cart before the horse. As I read the statute at issue, it is not necessary to reach the issue the majority addresses. In construing the lien avoidance provisions of the Bankruptcy Code, it is important to recognize a distinction between two classes of cases: those in which the lien attached to the exempt property *before* the debtor had any right to claim an exemption, and those in which the lien attached *after* the debtor acquired that right. This case falls in the former category. As I shall explain, I believe it was correctly decided by the Bankruptcy Court, the District Court and the Court of Appeals, and that the judgment should be affirmed.

I.

The facts raise a straight forward issue: whether the lien avoidance provisions in § 522(f) of the Bankruptcy Code, 11 U.S.C. § 522(f) apply to a judicial lien that attached before the debtor had any claim to an exemption. It is undisputed that respondent's judicial lien attached to petitioner's Sarasota condominium when he acquired title to the property in November 1984. It is also undisputed that the petitioner was not entitled to a homestead exemption when he acquired title because he was single. At that time, the exemption was available only to a "head of a household" under Article 10, § 4 of the Florida Constitution. An amendment that became effective in 1985 broadened the exemption to extend to "a natural person." Fla. Const., Art. 10, § 4. On the effective date of this amendment petitioner became entitled to the homestead exemption at issue in this case.2 Thus, it is undisputed that the petitioner had an exemption on his condominium when he filed his bankruptcy petition in 1986, but did not have a right to that exemption in 1984 when respondent's judicial lien attached.

As I read the text of § 522(f), it does not authorize the avoidance of liens that were perfected at a time when the debtor could not claim an exemption in the secured property. The Bankruptcy Code deals with the subject of exemptions in two separate provisions that are relevant to this case. The first of these provisions, § 522(b), identifies property that is exempt from the claims of general creditors. Focusing on the legal interests in the property at the time of the bankruptcy, this section identifies property that is exempt from the bankrupt estate, and therefore cannot be sold by the trustee to satisfy the claims of general creditors. *See H. Rep.* No. 95–595, pp. 360–61 (1977); S. Rep. No. 95–989, pp.75–76 (1978). In this case, petitioner's condominium in Sarasota, Florida was entitled to a homestead exemption as a matter of Florida law when he filed for bankruptcy and therefore was properly excluded from the estate. *See* 877 F.2d 44, 45 (CA11 1989). The property was fully protected from the claims of general creditors by the operation of § 522(b).

The second provision that is relevant to this suit, § 522(f), is concerned with the priority of secured creditors not the claims of general creditors. Section 522(f) establishes a rule of priority between the debtor's legal interest and creditors' security interests in exempt property as opposed to the property of the estate. The statute establishes the priority by allowing the debtor to avoid the fixing of judicial liens and certain nonpossessory, nonpurchase–money security interests under the right circumstances to the extent that they encumber the exemption.

As it applies to judicial liens, § 522(f) raises two questions: (1) whether the exemption provides a basis for avoidance of the lien; and (2) if so, to what extent should the lien be avoided? The first question concerns the relative priority of conflicting claims on the same asset; on such issues, the timing of the claims is often decisive. The second question –I shall call it the " impairment question" –concerns the distribution of the proceeds of sale after the issue of priority has been resolved. This second question need not be reached unless the first question has been answered positively.

In determining whether the exemption provides a basis for avoiding the lien, § 522(f) turns our attention towards the exemption to which the debtor would have been entitled at the time the lien "fixed." *In United States v. Security Industrial Bank,* 459 U.S. 70 [7 C.B.C.2d 629] (1982), this Court was presented with the question whether applying § 522(f)(2) to avoid non possessory liens perfected before the enactment of the Bankruptcy Reform Act of 1978 would be a taking of property without compensation in violation of the Fifth Amendment of the Constitution. The Court avoided deciding that precise question by holding that § 522(f) did not apply retroactively to liens that had been perfected before the Bankruptcy Reform Act was enacted. Although there is no such constitutional question presented here, Security Industrial Bank, establishes that the critical date for determining whether a lien may be avoided under the statute is the date of the fixing of that lien.

The date of the fixing of the respondent's lien on petitioner's condominium is therefore controlling in this case. Because it is undisputed that petitioner was not entitled to an exemption when the lien attached, the subsequently acquired exemption does not provide a basis for avoidance of the respondent's lien. Thus, the priority question in this case was correctly decided by the Court of Appeals and its judgment should be affirmed.

II.

The Court frames the question it decides as whether the lien avoidance provisions in § 522(f) "can operate when the State has defined the exempt property in such a way as specifically to exclude property encumbered by judicial liens." *Ante,* at 1. That is an accurate description of the issue that has arisen in cases concerning the avoidability of nonpossessory, nonpurchase–money liens on household goods. *See* cases cited, *ante,* at 4, nn. 1. and 2.5 In each of those cases the state's definition of the exemption purported to exclude property interests that were subject to otherwise avoidable liens under § 522(f). Thus, the state's definition of the exemption itself defeated the purpose of the federal lien avoidance provisions by narrowing the category of exempt property.

The majority and dissenting opinions in *In re McManus,* 681 F.2d 353 (CA5 1982), adequately identify the issue to which the Court's opinion today is addressed. In that case a finance company (AVCO) held a promissory note secured by a nonpossessory, nonpurchase–money security interest in the form of a chattel mortgage on some of the debtor's household goods and furnishings. The debtors sought to avoid AVCO's lien under § 522(f) on the ground that their household goods and furniture were exempted under § 522(b). The Bankruptcy Court and the District Court refused to avoid the lien. The Court of Appeals, following the reasoning of the Bankruptcy Court, affirmed. Louisiana had established a homestead exemption for certain household goods and furniture. Yet, it had also explicitly established in a separate code provision that notwithstanding its definitions of homestead exemptions, any household goods or furniture encumbered by a mortgage are not exempt property. The majority of the Court of Appeals held that the liens were not avoidable because the State of Louisiana had utilized its authority under § 522(b) to define its exemptions to exclude household goods subject to mortgages; hence the liens did not impair an exemption to which the debtors would have been entitled under § 522(b).

Under my reading of § 522(f), the Court of Appeals erred because it focused its attention entirely on the situation at the time of the bankruptcy. If it had analyzed the case by noting that at the time AVCO's lien attached, the debtors were already entitled to an exemption, it should have concluded that the lien was avoidable. The dissenting judge came to that conclusion by correctly recognizing that the statutory text evidences an intent to consider the situation at the time of attachment. He wrote:

> " The opening phrase of § 522(f), notwithstanding any waiver of exemptions, indicates that the subsection's import is to return the situation to the status quo *ante, i.e.,* prior to any improvident waiver of any exemption by the debtor. When the debtors entered the creditors' office they enjoyed an exemption under Louisiana law from seizure and sale of their household goods; and when they left the office they could no longer claim an exemption for those goods solely because they had improvidently granted a security interest to the creditors covering such goods. I fail to see how this could be characterized as anything but a waiver of exemptions, subject to the avoiding power found in § 522(f)." *Id.,* at 358.

Although the Court's opinion today resolves the question that was presented in *McManus* by adopting the position of the dissent in *McManus,* I disagree with the Court's reasoning. The Court simply overlooks the fact that for purposes of determining whether a lien is avoidable–rather than for the purpose of determining the extent to which the lien should be avoided–the question whether the debtor "would have been entitled" to an exemption is addressed to the state of affairs that existed at the time the lien attached.

Finally, I must comment on the Court's conclusion "that Florida's exclusion of certain liens from the scope of its homestead protection does not achieve a similar exclusion from the Bankruptcy Code's lien avoidance provision." *Ante,* at 8. This statement treats Florida's refusal to apply its broadened homestead exemption retroactively as the equivalent of Louisiana's narrowing definition of its household goods exemption to exclude properties subject to a chattel mortgage. The conclusion is flawed. Petitioner would not have been entitled to a homestead exemption at the time respondent's judicial lien attached; for that reason the lien avoidance provisions in § 522(f) of the Bankruptcy Code are not applicable. I would therefore affirm the judgment of the Court of Appeals.

FARREY v. SANDERFOOT

Supreme Court of the United States
501 U.S. — , 111 S.Ct. 1825, 24 C.B.C.2d 84 (1991)

Justice WHITE delivered the opinion of the Court:

In this case we consider whether § 522(f) of the Bankruptcy Code allows a debtor to avoid the fixing of a lien on a homestead, where the lien is granted to the debtor's former spouse under a divorce decree that extinguishes all previous interest the parties had in the property, and in no event secures more than the value of the non–debtor spouse's former interest. We hold that it does not.

I.

Petitioner Jeanne Farrey and respondent Gerald Sanderfoot were married on August 12, 1966. The couple eventually built a home on 27 acres of land in Hortonville, Wisconsin, where they raised their three children. On September 12, 1986, the Wisconsin Court for Outagamie County entered a bench decision granting a judgment of divorce and property division that resolved all contested issues and terminated the marriage. *See* Wis. Stat. 767.37(3) (1989–1990). A written decree followed on February 5, 1987.

The decision awarded each party one–half of their $60,600.68 marital estate. This division reflected Wisconsin's statutory presumption that the marital estate "be divided equally between the parties." § –767.255. The decree granted Sanderfoot sole title to all the real estate and the family house, which was subject to a mortgage and which was valued at $104,000.00, and most of the personal property. For her share, Farrey received the remaining items of personal property and the proceeds from a court–ordered auction of the furniture from the home. The judgment also allocated the couple's liabilities. Under this preliminary calculation of assets and debts, Sanderfoot stood to receive a net award of $59,508.79, while Farrey's award would otherwise have been $1,091.90. To insure that the division of the estate was equal, the court ordered Sanderfoot to pay Farrey $29,208.44, half the difference in the value of their net assets. Sanderfoot was to pay this amount in two installments: half by January 10, 1987, and the remaining half by April 10, 1987. To secure this award, the decree provided that Farrey "shall have a lien against the real estate property of [Sanderfoot] for the total amount of money due her pursuant to this Order of the Court,*i.e.* $29,208.44, and the lien shall remain attached to the real estate property . . . until the total amount of money is paid in full." (App. to Pet. for Cert. 57a).

Sanderfoot never made the required payments nor compiled with any other order of the state court. Instead, on May 4, 1987, he voluntarily filed for Chapter 7 bankruptcy. Sanderfoot listed the marital home and real estate on the schedule of assets with his bankruptcy petition and listed it as exempt homestead property. Exercising his option to invoke the state rather than the federal homestead exemption, 11 U.S.C. § 522(b)(2)(A), Sanderfoot claimed the property as exempt "to the amount of $40,000" under Wis. Stat. § 815.20 (1989–1990). He also filed a motion to avoid Farrey's lien under the provision in dispute, 11 U.S.C. § 522(f)(1), claiming that Farrey possessed a judicial lien that impaired his homestead exemption. Farrey objected to the motion, claiming that § 522(f)(1) could not divest her of her interest in the marital home. The Bankruptcy Court denied Sanderfoot's motion, holding that the lien could not be avoided because it protected Farrey's pre–existing interest in the marital property. *In re Sanderfoot,* [18 C.B.C.2d 598] 83 B.R. 564 (E.D. Wis. 1988). The District Court reversed, concluding that the lien was avoidable because it "is fixed on an interest of the debtor in the property." *In re Sanderfoot,* 92 B.R. 802 (E.D. Wis. 1988).

A divided panel of the Court of Appeals affirmed. In re Sanderfoot, 899 F.2d 598 [22 C.B.C.2d 780] (CA7 1990). The court reasoned that the divorce proceeding dissolved any pre–existing interest Farrey had in the homestead and that her new interest, "created in the dissolution order and evidenced by her lien, attached to Mr. Sanderfoot's interest in the property." *Id.,* at 602. Noting that the issue had caused a split among the Courts of Appeals, the court expressly relied on those decisions that it termed more "faithful to the plain language of section 522(f)." *Ibid.* (citing *In re Pederson,* 875 F.2d 781 (CA9 1989); *Maus v. Maus,* 837 F.2d 935 [18 C.B.C.2d 188] (CA10 1988); *Boyd v. Robinson,* 741 F.2d 1112, 1115 (CA8 1984) (Ross, J., dissenting)).

Judge Posner, in dissent, argued that to avoid a lien under § 522(f), a debtor must have an interest in the property at the time the court places the lien on that interest. Judge Posner concluded that because the same decree that gave the entire property to Sanderfoot simultaneously created the lien in favor of Farrey, the lien did not attach to a pre–existing interest of the husband. The dissent's conclusion followed the result, though not the rationale, of *Boyd, supra, In re Borman,* 886 F.2d 273 (CA10 1989), and *In re Donahue,* 862 F.2d 259 (CA10 1988).

We granted certiorari to resolve the conflict of authority. 495 U.S. (1990). We now reverse the Court of Appeals' judgment and remand.

II.

Section 522(f)(1) provides in relevant part:

"Notwithstanding any waiver of exemptions, the debtor may avoid the fixing of a lien on an interest of the debtor in property to the extent that such lien impairs an exemption to which the debtor would have been entitled under subsection (b) of this section, if such lien is–

(1) a judicial lien. . . .

The provision establishes several conditions for a lien to be avoided, only one of which is at issue. *See In re Hart,* [13 C.B.C.2d 190] 50 B.R. 956, 960 (Bkrtcy. Ct. Nev. 1985). Farrey does not challenge the Court of Appeals' determination that her lien was a judicial lien, 899 F.2d, at 603–605, nor do we address that question here. The Court of Appeals also determined that Farrey had waived any challenge as to whether Sanderfoot was otherwise entitled to a homestead exemption under state law, *Id.,* at 603, and we agree. *See Owen v. Owen,*U.S. (1991). The sole question presented in this case is whether § 522(f)(1) permits Sanderfoot to avoid the fixing of Farrey's lien on the property interest that he obtained in the divorce decree.

The key portion of § 522(f) states that "the debtor may avoid the fixing of a lien on an interest in . . . property." Sanderfoot, following several Courts of Appeals, suggests that this phrase means that a lien may be avoided so long as it is currently fixed on a debtor's interest. Farrey, following Judge Posner's lead, reads the text as permitting the avoidance of a lien only where the lien attached to the debtor's interest at some point after the debtor obtained the interest.

We agree with Farrey. No one asserts that the two verbs underlying the provision possess anything other than their standard legal meaning: "avoid" meaning "annul" or "undo,' see Black's Law Dictionary 136 (6th ed. 1990); H.R. Rep. No. 95–595, pp. 126–127 (1977), and "fix" meaning to "fasten a liability upon," see Black's Law

Dictionary, *supra,* at 637. The statute does not say that the debtor may undo a lien on an interest in property. Rather, the statute expressly states that the debtor may avoid "the fixing" of a lien on the debtor's interest in property. The gerund "fixing" refers to a temporal event. That event–the fastening of a liability–presupposes an object onto which the liability can fasten. The statute defines this pre–existing object as "an interest of the debtor in property." Therefore, unless the debtor had the property interest to which the lien attached at some point before the lien attached to that interest, he or she cannot avoid the fixing of the lien under the terms of § 522(f)(1).

This reading fully comports with the provision's purpose and history. *See United States v. Ron Pair Enterprises, Inc.,* 489 U.S. 235, 242 (1989). Congress enacted § 522(f) with the broad purpose of protecting the debtor's exempt property. *See* S. Rep. No. 95–989, p. 77 (1978); H.R. Rep. No. 95–595, supra, at 126–127. Ordinarily, liens and other secured interests survive bankruptcy. In particular, it was well settled when § 522(f) was enacted that valid liens obtained before bankruptcy could be enforced on exempt property, *see Louisville Joint Stock Land Bank v. Radford,* 295 U.S. 555, 582–583 (1935), including otherwise exempt homestead property, Long v. Bullard, 117 U.S. 617, 620–621 (1886). Congress generally preserved this principle when it comprehensively revised bankruptcy law with the Bankruptcy Reform Act of 1978, Pub. L.. 95–598, 92 Stat. 2587, 11 U.S.C. § 522(c)(2)(A)(i). But Congress also revised the law to permit the debtor to avoid the fixing of some liens. *See, e.g.,* 11 U.S.C. § 545 (statutory liens).

Section 522(f)(1), by its terms, extends this protection to cases involving the fixing of judicial liens onto exempt property. What specific legislative history exists suggests that a principal reason Congress singled out judicial liens was because they are a device commonly used by creditors to defeat the protection bankruptcy law accords exempt property against debts. As the House Report stated:

> "The first right [§ 522(f)(1)] allows the debtor to undo the actions of creditors that bring legal action against the debtor shortly before bankruptcy. Bankruptcy exists to provide relief for an overburdened debtor. If a creditor beats the debtor into court, the debtor is nevertheless entitled to his exemptions." H.R. Rep. No. 595, *supra,* at 126–127.

One factor supporting the view that Congress intended § 522(f)(1) to thwart a rush to the courthouse is Congress' contemporaneous elimination of § 67 of the 1898 Bankruptcy Act, 30 Stat. 564. Prior to its repeal, § 67a invalidated any lien obtained on an exempt interest of an insolvent debtor within four months of the bankruptcy filing. The Bankruptcy Reform Act eliminated the insolvency and timing requirements. It is possible that Congress simply decided to leave exemptions exposed despite its longstanding policy against doing so. But given the legislative history's express concern over protecting exemptions, it follows instead that § 522(f)(1) was intended as a new device to handle the old provisions's job by "giv[ing] the debtor certain rights not available under current law with respect to exempt property." H.R. Rep. No. 95–595, *supra,* at 126–127.

Conversely, the text, history, and purpose of § 522(f)(1) also indicate what the provision is not concerned with. It cannot be concerned with liens that fixed on an interest before the debtor acquired that interest. Neither party contends otherwise. Section 522(f)(1) does not state that any fixing of a lien may be avoided; instead, it permits avoidance of the "fixing of a lien on an interest of the debtor." If the fixing took place before the debtor acquired that interest, the "fixing" by definition was not on the debtor's interest. Nor could the statute apply given its purpose of preventing a creditor from beating the debtor to the courthouse, since the debtor at no point possessed the interest without the judicial lien. There would be no fixing to avoid since the lien was already there. To permit lien avoidance in these circumstances, in fact, would be to allow judicial lienholders to be defrauded through the conveyance of an encumbered interest to a prospective debtor. *See In re McCormick,* 18 B.R. 911, 913–914 (Bkrtcy. Ct. WD Pa. 1982). For these reasons, it is settled that a debtor cannot use § –522(f)(1) to avoid a lien on an interest acquired after the lien attached. *See, e.g., In re McCormick, supra; In re Stephens,* 15 B.R. 485 (Bkrtcy. Ct. W.D. NC 1981); *In re Scott,* 12 B.R. 613 (Bkrtcy. Ct. W.D. Okla. 1981). As before, the critical inquiry remains whether the debtor ever possessed the interest to which the lien fixed, before it fixed. If he or she did not, § 522(f)(1) does not permit the debtor to avoid the fixing of the lien on that interest.

III.

We turn to the application of § 522(f)(1) to this case.

Whether Sanderfoot ever possessed an interest to which the lien fixed, before it fixed, is a question of state law. Farrey contends that prior to the divorce judgment, she and her husband held title to the real estate in joint tenancy, each possessing an undivided one–half interest. She further asserts that the divorce decree extinguished these previous interests. At the same time and in the same transaction, she concludes, the decree created new interests in place of the old: for Sanderfoot, ownership in fee simple of the house and real estate; for Farrey, various assets and a debt of $29,208.44 secured by a lien on the Sanderfoot's new fee simple interest. Both in his briefs and at oral argument, Sanderfoot agreed on each point. (Brief for Respondent 7–8; Tr. of Oral Arg. 39).

On the assumption that the parties characterize Wisconsin law correctly, Sanderfoot must lose. Under their view, the lien could not have fixed on Sanderfoot's pre–existing undivided half interest because the divorce decree extinguished it. Instead, the only interest that the lien encumbers is debtor's wholly new fee simple interest. The same decree that awarded Sanderfoot his fee simple interest simultaneously granted the lien to Farrey. As the judgment stated, he acquired the property "free and clear" of any claim "except as expressly provided in this [decree]." (App. to Pet. for Cert. 58a). Sanderfoot took the interest and the lien together, as if he had purchased an already encumbered estate from a third party. Since Sanderfoot never possessed his new fee simple interest before the lien fixed," § 522(f)(1) is not available to void the lien.

The same result follows even if the divorce decree did not extinguish the couple's pre–existing interests but instead merely reordered them. The parties' current position notwithstanding, it may be that under Wisconsin law the divorce decree augmented Sanderfoot's previous interest by adding to it Farrey's prior interest. If the court in exchange sought to protect Farrey's previous interest with a lien, § 522(f)(1) could be used to undo the encumbrance to the extent the lien fastened to any portion of Sanderfoot's previous surviving interest. This follows because Sanderfoot would have possessed the interest to which that part of the lien fixed, before it fixed. But in this case, the divorce court did not purport to encumber any part of Sanderfoot's previous interest even on the assumption that state law would deem that interest to have survived. The decree instead transferred Farrey's previous interest to Sanderfoot and, again simultaneously, granted a lien equal to that interest minus the small of amount of personal property she retained. Sanderfoot thus would still be unable to avoid the lien in this case since it fastened only to what had been Farrey's pre-existing interest, and this interest Sanderfoot would never have possessed without the lien already having fixed.

The result, on either theory, accords with the provision's main purpose. As noted, the legislative history suggests that Congress primarily intended § 522(f)(1) as a device to thwart creditors who, sensing an impending bankruptcy, rush to court to obtain a judgment to defeat the debtor's exemptions. That is not what occurs in a divorce proceeding such as this. Farrey obtained the lien not to defeat Sanderfoot's pre-existing interest in the homestead that was fully equal to that of her spouse. The divorce court awarded the lien to secure an obligation the court imposed on the husband in exchange for the court's simultaneous award of the wife's homestead interest to the husband. We agree with Judge Posner that to permit a debtor in these circumstances to use the Code to deprive a spouse of this protection would neither follow the language of the statute nor serve the main goal it was designed to address.

IV.

We hold that § 522(f)(1) of the Bankruptcy Code requires a debtor to have possessed an interest to which a lien attached, before it attached, to avoid the fixing of the lien on that interest. Accordingly, the judgment of the Court of Appeals is reversed, and the case is remanded for further proceedings consistent with this opinion.

It is so ordered.

[Concurring by Justice Kennedy, with whom Justice Souter joined, omitted]

TABLE OF CASES

[Principal cases appear in capital letters, with page references in italics. Other cases are those cited or discussed by the authors.]

[Principal cases appear in capital letters, with page references in italics. Other cases are those cited or discussed by the authors.]

[Principal cases appear in capital letters, with page references in italics. Other cases are those cited or discussed by the authors.]

[Principal cases appear in capital letters, with page references in italics. Other cases are those cited or discussed by the authors.]

[Principal cases appear in capital letters, with page references in italics. Other cases are those cited or discussed by the authors.]

[Principal cases appear in capital letters, with page references in italics. Other cases are those cited or discussed by the authors.]

[Principal cases appear in capital letters, with page references in italics. Other cases are those cited or discussed by the authors.]

[Principal cases appear in capital letters, with page references in italics. Other cases are those cited or discussed by the authors.]

INDEX

[References are to sections.]

[References are to sections.]

[References are to sections.]

C

[References are to sections.]

[References are to sections.]

[References are to sections.]

[References are to sections.]

[References are to sections.]

[References are to sections.]

GOVERNMENT—Cont.
Priority over other creditors—Cont.
    Solvent estate, nontax claims against . . .
    5.03
    Tax liens . . . 5.01
Public rights doctrine, claims brought by or against
    U.S. under . . . 12.02; 12.03[A]
Self-help repossession by government agency
    . . . 2.02[B]
Solvent estate, priority of nontax claims against
    . . . 5.03
Tax liens (See subhead: Federal tax liens)

H

HARASSMENT
Unreasonable tactics used by creditor to collect
    debt . . . 2.02[A]

HOMESTEAD EXEMPTION
Eligibility . . . 7.03; 17.06
Insurance policy proceeds, exemption of . . . .
    7.03
Lien, property subject to . . . 17.06
State provisions, examples . . . 7.03

HOUSEHOLD FURNISHINGS
Exemptions . . . 7.04
Necessary . . . 7.04

I

INCOME
Exemptions . . . 7.06
Family farmer with regular income; Chapter 12
    . . . 10.03[D]
Garnishment of wages (See GARNISHMENT OF
    WAGES)
Individual with regular income; Chapter 13 . . .
    10.03[E]

INCOME ASSETS
Exemptions . . . 7.06

**INDIVIDUAL'S DEBT ADJUSTMENT (CHAP-
TER 13)**
Generally . . . 10.03[E]
Allowance of claims . . . 16.02
Claims, allowance of . . . 16.02
Creditors, meeting of . . . 16.01
Debtor, discharge of . . . 17.01
Discharge of debtor . . . 17.01
Meeting of creditors . . . 16.01

INJUNCTIONS
Anti-Injunction Act, stay of proceedings under
    . . . 13.02

INJUNCTIONS—Cont.
Bankruptcy court, Section 105 Injunction by
    . . . 12.03[A]

INSIDERS
Preferential transfer by insolvent insider . . . .
    6.05[A]
Subordination of insider's claim . . . 16.04

INSOLVENCY
Generally . . . 1.09
Assignments for benefit of creditors . . . 9.02
Balance sheet test to determine . . . 6.02[B]
Calculation of debtor's liabilities . . . 6.05[B]
Chapter 7 (See LIQUIDATION (CHAPTER 7))
Debt adjustment defined . . . 9.03
Debt-pooling for consumer debtors as remedy
    . . . 9.03
Defined . . . 6.05[B]
Executed composition . . . 9.01
Fraudulent transfers . . . 6.02[B]
Insolvent defined . . . 1.09
Liquidation (See LIQUIDATION (CHAPTER 7))
Out-of-court settlements . . . 9.01
Receivership as remedy . . . 9.04
Remedies
    Assignments for benefit of creditors . . . .
    9.02
    Debt adjustment defined . . . 9.03
    Debt-pooling for consumer debtors . . . .
    9.03
    Out-of-court settlements . . . 9.01
    Receiverships . . . 9.04
Settlements, out-of-court . . . 9.01
Valuation of assets to determine . . . 6.05[B]

INSURANCE
Automobile insurance policy, attachment of . . .
    4.02[B]
Cash surrender value of, exemption of . . 7.05
Exemption of proceeds
    Homestead exemption . . . 7.03
    Life insurance . . . 7.05
Homestead, exemption of proceeds from insurance
    on . . . 7.03
Life insurance proceeds, exemption of . . 7.05
Seider-Roth doctrine . . . 4.02[B]

INTERLOCUTORY ORDERS
Appealability of . . . 12.03[B]

INTERNAL REVENUE CODE
Lien for taxes . . . 5.02[E]
Period of lien . . . 5.02[E]
Priority of lien against certain persons . . . . .
    5.02[E]

[References are to sections.]

[References are to sections.]

JURY TRIAL—Cont.
Fraudulent transfer action . . . 12.03[A]
Seventh Amendment requirement . . . 12.03[A]
Trustee's preference claim, creditor's right to trial on . . . 12.03[A]

K

KEOGH PLANS
Money judgments, protection of trusts under Keogh plans from . . . 7.06

L

LABOR UNIONS (See COLLECTIVE BAR-GAINING AGREEMENTS)

LANDLORD AND TENANT
Leases (See LEASES AND LEASING)
Lien, federal priority over landlord's . . . 5.01

LEASES AND LEASING
Adequate assurance . . . 14.02
Ipso facto clause . . . 14.07
Rejection of . . . 14.04
Trustee, lease of property by . . . 13.04[B]
Unexpired lease, assumption or rejection of . . . 14.04

LETTERS OF CREDIT
Attachment based on . . . 4.02[A]

LEVERAGED BUYOUTS
Fraudulent conveyances, as . . . 6.05[B]

LEVY
Defined . . . 1.02
Money judgments, enforcement of . . . . 3.10; 3.11[A]
Sheriff, by . . . 3.10; 3.11[A]
Tax liens, federal . . . 5.02[E]

LIENS
Generally . . . 1.07; 3.07
Artisan's lien . . . 1.07
Attachment, domestic (See ATTACHMENT)
Confirmation of plan, voided through . . 16.02
Consensual liens (See CONSENSUAL LIENS)
Defined . . . 1.07; 6.05[A]
Equitable lien . . . 1.07
Exemption of property subject to . . . 17.06
Extinguished by confirmation . . . 16.02
Federal tax liens (See FEDERAL TAX LIENS)
Innkeeper's lien . . . 1.07
Judgment liens
    Generally . . . 3.08
    Docket of judgment creating . . . 3.08

LIENS—Cont.
Judicial liens (See JUDICIAL LIENS)
Landlord's lien . . . 5.01
Levy and execution . . . 3.10; 3.11[A]
Lien creditor defined . . . 3.05
Mechanics' lien . . . 1.07
Mortgage lien . . . 5.01
Partition . . . 3.12[A]
Priority problems
    Generally . . . 16.03
    Enforcement of judgments . . . 3.12[A]
    Federal priority . . . 5.02[F]
    First-in-time-first-in-right rule . . . 5.01; 5.03
    First-in-time-first-in-right-rule . . . 5.02[F]
    Order of priority . . . 16.03
Prior lien, enforcement of money judgment on . . . 3.05
Redemption of property subject to . . . 17.04
Reorganization plan containing no provision on, effect of . . . 16.02
Sheriff, levy by . . . 3.10; 3.11[A]
Statutory liens (See STATUTORY LIENS)
Tax liens, federal (See FEDERAL TAX LIENS)
Title subject to, taking of . . . 3.10
Trustees as judicial lien creditor . . . 15.03[A]
Types of . . . 1.07
Vendors' lien . . . 1.07

LIFE INSURANCE
Exemption of proceeds . . . 7.05
New York Insurance Law on exemption of proceeds; Section 3212 . . . 7.05

LIQUIDATION (CHAPTER 7)
Generally . . . 1.10; 10.03[A]
Allowance of claims . . . 16.02
Automatic stay (See AUTOMATIC STAY)
Bankruptcy termination clauses, unenforceability of . . . 14.03
Discharge of debtor . . . 17.01
Federal priority over proceeds from . . . 5.01
Filing of claims . . . 16.02
Involuntary petitions . . . 11.04
Meeting of creditors . . . 16.01
Out-of-court settlements, preference for . . 9.01
Redemption of property subject to lien . . 17.04
Trustees (See TRUSTEES)
Valuation of claims . . . 16.02
Voluntary petitions . . . 11.03

LIS PENDENS
Attachment . . . 4.01[G]
Defined . . . 4.01[G]

[References are to sections.]

U